THE OXFORD HAN

BIBLICAL
NARRATIVE

THE OXFORD HANDBOOK OF

BIBLICAL NARRATIVE

Edited by

DANNA NOLAN FEWELL

OXFORD

UNIVERSITY PRESS

OXFORD
UNIVERSITY PRESS

Oxford University Press is a department of the University of Oxford. It furthers
the University's objective of excellence in research, scholarship, and education
by publishing worldwide.Oxford is a registered trade mark of Oxford University
Press in the UK and certain other countries.

Published in the United States of America by Oxford University Press
198 Madison Avenue, New York, NY 10016, United States of America.

Library of Congress Cataloging-in-Publication Data
The Oxford handbook of biblical narrative / edited by Danna Nolan Fewell.
pages cm
Includes bibliographical references and index.
ISBN 978-0-19-996772-8 (hardcover : alk. paper) — ISBN 978-0-19-091576-6 (paperback : alk. paper)
ISBN 978-0-19-996773-5 (e-book)
1. Bible—Criticism, Narrative.   2. Narration in the Bible.   I. Fewell, Danna Nolan, editor.
BS521.7.O94 2015
220.6′6—dc23
2015033360

CONTENTS

PART III THE BIBLE AND BODIES

PART IV THE NATURAL, SOCIAL, AND CONCEPTUAL LANDSCAPES OF BIBLICAL STORY WORLDS

PART V ON READING

Contributors

David L. Barr, Professor Emeritus of Religion, Wright State University

Bryan D. Bibb, Dorothy and B. H. Peace, Jr. Associate Professor of Hebrew Bible, Furman University

Keith Bodner, Professor of Religious Studies, Crandall University

Roland Boer, Professor of Literary Theory, Renmin University of China

Mark G. Brett, Professor of Hebrew Bible, Whitley College, University of Divinity

Brian M. Britt, Professor of Religion and Culture, Virginia Polytechnic Institute and State University

Austin Busch, Associate Professor of Early World Literature, The College at Brockport, State University of New York

Warren Carter, Professor of New Testament, Brite Divinity School, Texas Christian University

Ovidiu Creangă, Adjunct Professor of Hebrew Bible, Wesley Theological Seminary and Researcher, Center for Advanced Holocaust Studies, United States Holocaust Memorial Museum

Linda A. Dietch, Independent Scholar and Editor, Ambler, PA

Rubén René Dupertuis, Associate Professor of Religion, Trinity University

Kathleen Gallagher Elkins, Assistant Professor of Theology and Religious Studies, St. Norbert College

Scott S. Elliott, Associate Professor of Philosophy and Religion, Adrian College

Danna Nolan Fewell, John Fletcher Hurst Professor of Hebrew Bible, The Theological School at Drew University

Rachelle Gilmour, Lecturer in Biblical Studies, The University of Newcastle and The Broken Bay Institute

Deryn Guest, Senior Lecturer in Biblical Hermeneutics, University of Birmingham

David M. Gunn, A. A. Bradford Emeritus Professor of Religion, Texas Christian University

Norman C. Habel, Professorial Fellow, Flinders University

Martien A. Halvorson-Taylor, Associate Professor of Religious Studies, University of Virginia

Jione Havea, Senior Lecturer in Biblical Studies, United Theological College and School of Theology, Charles Sturt University

R. Christopher Heard, Associate Professor of Religion, Pepperdine University

Theodore W. Jennings, Jr., Professor of Biblical and Philosophical Theology, Chicago Theological Seminary

Melanie Johnson-DeBaufre, Professor of New Testament and Early Christianity and Associate Dean of Academic Affairs, The Theological School at Drew University

Amy Beth Jones, Director of External Relations and United Methodist Liaison, The Theological School at Drew University

Robert S. Kawashima, Associate Professor, the Center for Jewish Studies and the Department of Religion, University of Florida

Julie Kelso, Assistant Professor of Philosophy and Literature, Bond University

Dong Sung Kim, PhD Candidate, The Graduate Division of Religion, Drew University

Jennifer L. Koosed, Professor of Religious Studies, Albright College

Donna J. Laird, Adjunct Assistant Professor, Ashland Theological Seminary

Stuart Lasine, Professor of Religion, Wichita State University

Adriane Leveen, Senior Lecturer in Hebrew Bible, Hebrew Union College—Jewish Institute of Religion

Tat-siong Benny Liew, Class of 1956 Professor in New Testament Studies, College of the Holy Cross

Tod Linafelt, Professor of Biblical Literature, Georgetown University

Francisco Lozada, Jr., Charles Fischer Catholic Associate Professor of New Testament and Latina/o Church Studies, Brite Divinity School, Texas Christian University

Robert D. Maldonado, Professor of Philosophy, California State University, Fresno

Dora Rudo Mbuwayesango, Iris and George E. Battle Professor of Old Testament and Dean of Students, Hood Theological Seminary

Judith E. McKinlay, former Senior Lecturer in Biblical Studies, University of Otago

Monica Jyotsna Melanchthon, Associate Professor of Old Testament Studies, University of Divinity, Melbourne

Stephen D. Moore, Edmund S. Jaynes Professor of New Testament, The Theological School at Drew University

Carol A. Newsom, Charles Howard Candler Professor of Old Testament, Candler School of Theology, Emory University

Kenneth Ngwa, Associate Professor of Hebrew Bible, The Theological School at Drew University

Julie Faith Parker, Assistant Professor of Old Testament, Trinity Lutheran Seminary

Raymond F. Person, Jr., Professor of Religion, Ohio Northern University

Gary A. Phillips, Edgar H. Evans Professor of Religion, Wabash College

Stephanie Day Powell, Independent Scholar and Chaplain, Madison, NJ

Chesung Justin Ryu, Independent Scholar and Pastor, Campbell, CA

Jeremy Schipper, Associate Professor of Hebrew Bible, Temple University

Robert Paul Seesengood, Associate Professor of Religious Studies, Albright College

Abraham Smith, Professor of New Testament, Perkins School of Theology, Southern Methodist University

Terry Ann Smith, Director of Assessment and Academic Initiatives, Affiliate Assistant Professor of Biblical Studies, New Brunswick Theological Seminary

Daniel L. Smith-Christopher, Professor of Theological Studies, Loyola Marymount University

Ken Stone, Professor of Hebrew Bible, Culture, and Hermeneutics, Chicago Theological Seminary

Eric Thurman, Associate Professor of Religious Studies, Sewanee, The University of the South

Patricia K. Tull, A. B. Rhodes Professor Emerita of Old Testament, Louisville Presbyterian Seminary

Gerald West, Senior Professor, School of Religion, Philosophy, and Classics, University of Kwazulu-Natal

Anne-Mareike Wetter, Researcher and Editor at the Dutch Bible Society and Guest Researcher at Leiden University

PART I

OVERTURES

CHAPTER 1

THE WORK OF BIBLICAL NARRATIVE

DANNA NOLAN FEWELL

THE last five decades have witnessed the rise of a veritable academic industry addressing the relationships between knowledge and narrative. Narrative now claims a critical spotlight, not only in literary studies, but also in philosophy; linguistics; the arts, social sciences, and cognitive disciplines; systems theory; pedagogy; philosophy of science, medicine; law; theology; ethics; and even evolutionary theory (for a concise overview, see Meuter 2011). Reminding us constantly that narrative is "everywhere" (Currie [1998] 2011, 6) and not just the domain of the literary-minded or of certain storytelling cultures, this transdisciplinary enterprise is exposing how narrative is integral to self-perception and social orientation, indeed, is essential to our very survival. This often-labeled "narrative turn" attempts to rethink the results of structuralist and formalist narrative analyses—namely, the taxonomies of narrative components, discursive mechanics, and rhetorical strategies—and to reinscribe these "into a more comprehensive vision" of the roles narratives play in cognition, sociality, and identity formation (Margolin 1999). The field of biblical studies has in recent years also given much attention to narrative and is beginning to expand its understanding of the relationships between the poetics of biblical narrative and the kinds of cognitive, social, and identity-constructing work that biblical narratives do.

As Stephen Moore's chapter in this volume "Biblical Narrative Analysis from the New Criticism to the New Narratology," maps so eloquently, literary-critical engagement with the Bible's narratives has seen a number of shifts from the initial New Critical emphasis on the Bible's narrative "art" and "poetics." Final-form studies eager to reveal the Bible's narrative artistry, demonstrate its structural coherence, prove its ideological consistency and reliability, and protect its literary (and theological) integrity are giving way to poststructural and postclassical acknowledgment of textual instability and undecidability, opening biblical poetics to the realms of the personal and the sociopolitical. Biblical narrative critics now commonly reach across unexpected disciplinary lines for new analytical concepts to illuminate textual details. We witness biblical narratives shifting their points of gravity under the weight of different kinds of interpretive questions, exposing their innate historical, political, and social biases while simultaneously being strangely hospitable to other, often incongruent, political and social visions.

Consequently, some literary-critical inquiries are reuniting with historical interrogation to consider the social, political, and rhetorical dimensions of biblical narrative. Supplementing valuable ongoing investigations into the means of literary production and oral performance in the ancient world (e.g., Niditch 1996; Davies 1998; Carr 2005; Davies and Römer 2013; Horsley 2013), many of this volume's contributors have turned their attention to the communicative strategies biblical narratives employ,[1] the social impulses and political agendas that drive biblical storytelling,[2] and the ways in which biblical story worlds reflect the material realities[3] and social constructions[4] of the ancient world. At the heart of many of these contributions is the recognition of how biblical narratives work to construct communal identity in their generative contexts[5] and in their subsequent disseminations and versions.[6] Included here are explorations of how biblical narratives are rooted in the broader literary context of the ancient Near East and the Greco-Roman world,[7] yet continually branch out to generate new expressions of cultural identity.[8] These chapters ask: In what ways might we understand biblical narratives as historical artifacts? What work were they meant to do in their various socio-historical contexts? How well did they do that work? What was at stake in their successes and failures? How do we account socio-historically and narratologically for their multivocalities and ambiguities?

At the other end of the critical spectrum is the growing interest in how contemporary readers relate to biblical literature. The Bible's notorious and paradoxical reputation as a book that both liberates and kills (see Bal 1991, 14; Phillips and Fewell 1997, 1–10) keeps its stories foregrounded for many readers, even in an increasingly biblically illiterate society. As both weapon and wisdom, the Bible occupies a prominent place in political, social, theological, and ethical debates, often offering divergent, even incongruent, theological and moral visions that are put in service of every position imaginable. Several chapters in this volume attend to the Bible's perduring impact: What work do biblical narratives continue to do? How do readerly desires and concerns affect that work?[9] What happens to these stories as they cross cultural and temporal boundaries? Do they serve the functions for which they were originally co-opted, or do they gravitate toward expressing other cultural realities?[10] What are our responsibilities as historically and culturally distant readers, hearers, conveyors, and conversational partners to evaluate the "truths" that the Bible seems to offer?[11]

Consequently, as this volume exemplifies, "the art of biblical narrative" (Alter 1981) now makes room for "the work of biblical narrative," namely, what biblical stories accomplish cognitively, socially, and ethically, for good and ill, both as literary artifacts of the ancient world and as living literary specimens that continue to shape contemporary cultures and individual identities.

NARRATIVE IDENTITY, OR THE TRUTH ABOUT STORIES

The first observation generated by this transdisciplinary intellectual preoccupation with narrative is captured in the provocative refrain voiced by native North American novelist and essayist Thomas King (2005, 2, 32, 62, 92, 122, 153). "The truth about stories," he writes, "is that that's all we are." At first blush, this sounds like poetic overstatement, but similar sentiments have been voiced by a host of other significant thinkers of the past century: political theorist Hannah Arendt (1958), philosopher Jean-Paul Sartre (1964), hermeneutic phenomenologist Paul Ricoeur (1984), cognitive psychologist Jerome Bruner (1986, 1990, 1991, 2004), and post-Holocaust writer Elie Wiesel ([1964, 1966] 1982), to name a few. Namely, to be human is to tell and interpret stories, to conceive of ourselves as living out and living by stories, and to see our individual stories as components of, as contributions to larger family, social, institutional, or national stories. King's refrain points to a truth often taken for granted: whether as individuals or as collectives, we represent our identities with the language of narrative, because narrative, according to some (e.g., Bruner 1986, 1991, 2004; Polkinghorne 1988; Carr 1997; Crites 1997) is the best representational tool we have for capturing "the rich and messy domain of human interaction" (Bruner 1991, 4). Life as process requires a mode of temporally and spatially fluid representation. Moreover, we use narrative not just to represent reality, but to constitute it and construct it (Bruner 1991). We instinctively engage in retrospective representation and revision, bringing our past experiences to bear on our present and to frame further future discourse about who we are. Telling and retelling, interpreting and reinterpreting, listening to new and familiar stories are all crucial activities for ongoing identity formation.

Literary critic Frank Kermode (1981, 85) observes, "Stories as we know them begin as interpretations." Socio-narratologist Arthur Frank (2010, 81) puts the impetus for story in more visceral terms: "[S]tories compel because they express in narrative form what *begins in bodies*" (italics mine; cf. Fludernik 1996; Margolin 1999). Certain bodily experiences— fears, desires, striking impressions and encounters, moments of illumination, cognitive disruption, trauma—distinguish themselves from the arbitrary onslaught of lived reality, begging for narrative frames. Since, as recent neuroscientific studies show, the human brain "works through pattern recognition and metaphor, as opposed to logic" (Williams 2012, 24), we instinctively "chunk" (to use the educational term; see Herman 2003, 172–175) notable experiences into manageable narrative scenes and episodes that are circumscribed, classifiable, and recognizable. We give them Aristotelian beginnings, middles, and ends; we create islands of temporal and spatial determinacy against backdrops where time and space are, in actuality, infinite. Narratives provide frames, boundaries, even when telling something unfinished or without a foreseeable conclusion. Narratives come to an end, even when they do not provide closure—an especially useful characteristic when their plots concern personal or communal crisis. "[T]ellings," observes socio-narratologist David Herman (2003, 173–174), "mark even the most painful or disturbing experiences as endurable because finite. In such contexts, narrative is a tool for representing events not as over and done with, but as reaching a terminus that imposes a limit on the trauma-inducing (and cognition-disrupting) power of the events at issue." Our storytelling, in effect, protects us from existential overload; it carves us out from the rest of reality, distinguishing and yet contextualizing our identity-shaping experiences. In the words of narrative ethnographer Michael Jackson (2002, 23), storytelling "mediates our relation with worlds that extend beyond us," enabling us "to negotiate an existential balance between ourselves and such spheres of otherness."

Biblical narratives reflect "what begins in bodies" and "negotiate an existential balance" between self and other both in the ways they construct story worlds and in their storytelling performance. In biblical story worlds, individuals or communal groups are

typically distinguished from other such social spheres, foregrounded for narrative attention: Abraham is extricated geographically from Mesopotamia (Shinar, "Babel," and Ur),
genealogically from the line of Shem, and literarily from the rest of humanity as narrated in
the primeval history. Moses in Exodus and subsequently Jesus in Matthew are distinguished
from other children condemned to infanticide by oppressive regimes. Jesus in Mark's Gospel
is differentiated from all the others coming to John for baptism. Hannah in 1 Samuel, and
Elizabeth and Mary in Luke's Gospel are singled out from their respective familial connections and communal settings in order to give birth (literally!) to new stories. In each of these
cases and many others, the move to highlight an individual or group against a faceless backdrop launches a new story in which the fates of bodies and questions of identity and identity boundaries, both within the story world and in the social context of the story's telling,
become paramount for shaping communal identities for centuries to come.

And as we well know, other stories could have been—in fact were—told. Biblical narratives "negotiate an existential balance" between self and other in the very act of distinguishing themselves over against endless other narrative possibilities. As has long been observed,
the more myth-like accounts in Genesis emerge from a sea of ancient Near Eastern prototypes, retaining certain resemblances, yet telling unique stories. The Bible begins with a deity
establishing order out of chaos through speech rather than combat, reducing divine personalities to natural phenomena, and creating all humanity (as opposed to only monarchs) in
the divine image. Humanity is charged to subdue and have dominion over creation rather
than to be slaves to a divine pantheon. As a story speaking to a beleaguered community suffering the devastation, displacement, and aftermath of the Babylonian conquest, Genesis 1
counters the imperial master narrative of naturalized domination (see Lindemann Nelson
2001) with a story that restores self-worth and moral agency. It does so by offering a common vision that comforts the disoriented through its attention to divinely established order,
encourages a dwindling population with mandates to be fruitful and multiply, fosters self-
esteem with its language of *imago dei*, and even proposes, with its emphasis on Sabbath, hidden transcripts (see Scott 1990) for political and economic resistance in an imperial setting.

A New Testament corollary is Luke's Gospel, in which the writer makes explicit his aim
to write for a certain Theophilus an "orderly account of the events that have been fulfilled
among us," suggesting that other "orderly," even eyewitness, accounts are not as "orderly"
as they could be and have failed to reveal the whole "truth" of the early Christian movement. A story that competes with, and in some cases counters, other extant accounts, Luke's
Gospel foregrounds morally and socially relevant details about the Christian community
that underscore a group identity that is both worthy of respect and politically benign. Luke's
commanding version makes clear how the Christian movement's founder was innocent of
any legal infractions, invested in all humanity, not simply one group, and a teacher whose
instruction has practical applications for everyday life—even life under the shadow of the
Roman Empire. In subtle and not so subtle ways, Luke's Gospel signals its own worth, the
reasons its story should be told and heard, and suggests that members of the Christian movement should be accorded more respect and autonomy (on stories reclaiming moral agency,
see Lindemann Nelson 2001, 1–35).

As Luke's direct address makes explicit, storytelling involves, of course, not simply tellers,
but also listeners, readers, viewers, and responders. We have typically spoken of our connection to the narratives of others in terms of empathy and imagination (see, e.g., Booth 1961,
1988), but something more tangible may be taking place when we encounter new stories

(Currie [1998] 2011, 25–40; Frank 2010, 49) or hear old stories told differently. Co-opting an adaptation of Louis Althusser's (1971) concept of *interpellation*, which argues that narratives position their audiences ideologically, calling on them "to identify with, and therefore occupy, certain subject positions and social roles" (Currie [1998] 2011, 36), literary theorist Mark Currie explains how identities can be manufactured through the reading of fiction:

> Sympathy amounts to little more than a feeling of goodwill towards a character. Identification suggests self-recognition.... [S]ympathy will not profoundly change the world.... Identification, on the other hand, touches my own subjectivity in a more profound way, because I have seen myself in the fiction, projected my identity into it, rather than just made a new friend. This gives fiction the potential to confirm, form, or transform my sense of myself. (Currie [1998] 2011, 36)

Biblical narratives, too, inevitably hail their audiences, both ancient and modern, to position themselves as subjects in an ongoing story. Genesis 1, for example, calls on subjects to adopt, maintain, and promote a certain divinely ordained order; Luke's Gospel summons subjects to bear witness to and internalize an exceptional series of events. Such hailing and positioning are, of course, not without their dangers. A rigid adoption of Genesis 1's world of separations, distinctions, and hierarchies has been instrumental in distancing social groups, alienating human from nonhuman species, and bringing us to the brink of ecological disaster. Moreover, Luke's Gospel, in its efforts to accommodate Roman social standards and to be the only story Theophilus might need, routinely casts its female characters as supporting actors and social foils, denying women the moral agency accorded to men (see Schüssler Fiorenza 1983; D'Angelo 1990; Schaberg 1992; Phillips 1992; and Phillips, "The Commanding Faces of Biblical Stories," chapter 51 in this volume). Women are admonished to "choose the better part"—namely, to be silent, passive receivers of male wisdom (Reid 1996).

But whether we assume the position of compliant reader or find ourselves questioning or resisting aspects of what we are told, we nevertheless have a remarkable propensity to absorb the stories of others, a propensity that may have a basis in biochemistry, not simply in literary strategy or linguistic theory. Recent neurological studies (building on the study of mirror cells and canonical neurons by neuroscientists Giacomo Rizolatti [2008] and V. S. Ramachandran [2011]) have shown that exposures to new stories have physiological ramifications: our "brains on fiction" (Paul 2012) show levels and patterns of activity similar to those exhibited during our bodily experiences. Stories read, heard, or witnessed literally create mental pathways that become part of our physiological makeup. The more intense our emotional investment in the characters or events, the more lasting those neurological pathways become. And because, according to neuroscientist Antonio Damasio (1994, 260), we are "feeling machines that think, not thinking machines that feel," this physiological development is largely involuntary. In short, stories can "change our lives" by changing our very bodies. Inevitably, these neurological changes alter our thinking, expand our intellectual and emotional capacities, and affect our behaviors (see further Gottschall 2012; Williams 2012).

The physical absorption of story is indeed a concept intuited by the character Moses in the book of Deuteronomy, who, in providing the narrative context for the law, admonishes his listeners to "keep these words in your heart," to wear them like garments, to inscribe them in the architecture of home and community (Deut. 6). The story Moses tells and encourages his listeners to retell is intimately connected to the full fabric of their lives. Recounting the story of the wandering Aramean who becomes a great nation and is delivered from slavery expands the capacity for moral agency. To remember the story is to remember one's very identity (Deut. 26:1–11), which, in turn, becomes a matter of life and death (Deut. 30:15–20; see also Britt, "Remembering Narrative in Deuteronomy," chapter 12 in this volume; and cf. Barr's discussion of the affective work of Revelation in "Narrative Technique in the Book of Revelation," chapter 32 in this volume). Moreover, the way in which Deuteronomy "slips the frame" with its second person address, manifests Althusserian interpellation directly: all who listen to this recitation find themselves ensnared in the "you" who are beckoned "this day" to "choose life."

In a similar vein, when Luke hails "Theophilus" (Luke 1:1–4; Acts 1:1–2), he is not simply providing an informative report; rather, he is offering, in the words of Abraham Smith, a "witness for the defense," positioning his reader as judge and juror ("Witnesses for the Defense in the Gospel of Luke," chapter 27 in this volume); moreover, he is summoning him to become a more devout and informed "god lover" who can, through the reading of Luke's story, become part of a larger story. The third Gospel along with its second installment, the Acts of the Apostles, fashions a "document of effect," telling the story of a social movement that has resulted from a particular shaming and politically suspect incident, namely, the criminal execution of the leader in whom the community's political hopes had rested. Less concerned with depicting individual strategic actors meriting special attention, Luke's story instead plots a social movement that portrays even the major protagonists being swept up by forces beyond their personal control. Mary is "overshadowed" (*episkiasei*) by the power of the Most High (Luke 1:35); the disciples are "clothed" (*endysesthe*) with divine power after Jesus's ascension (Luke 24:49); characters, including Jesus, are constantly being seized by or filled with (*eplesthe, pleres*) the Holy Spirit, who impels them to do what they do; and crowds overcome *en masse* by fear and amazement are used to disseminate collateral stories about Jesus and his followers. Luke's story is not historical description *per se*—as is evident in its attempts to make events appear spontaneous and infectious—but is designed to continue to attract a following. By projecting a widespread, socially (and in this case, theologically) significant series of events, the story becomes a social magnet, pulling people who might otherwise have little in common, in this case Jews and Gentiles from diverse backgrounds and locales, into a mutual cause (on stories of social movements as "documents of effect," see further Polletta 2006; Frank 2010, 124–134). Theophilus, whether an individual or a generic reader, is being lured into adopting this story as his own and sharing it with others. And because Luke's carefully reframed and extended narrative replaces the elements of uncertainty, fear, and shame haunting the earlier Gospel of Mark with frequent expressions of joy and praise, the story is both inviting and shareable.

Both Deuteronomy and Luke's two-part tome attempt, in psychoanalytical terms, to effect a "narrative repair," functionally "untelling" other stories by offering counterstories that recast communal identity by expanding moral agency (see Lindemann Nelson 2001). By mimicking and rewriting a vassal treaty of Esarhaddon, Deuteronomy's covenantal genre turns a master narrative of imperial dominance into a gesture of political autonomy. Political allegiance is owed to YHWH alone, because YHWH, and not an Assyrian tyrant, is the ultimate scripter of the narrative past and future. By rewriting Mark's story and giving account of the Jesus movement, Luke makes a bid for social legitimacy, recasting Christian identity in a way that leverages social acceptance (on other gestures of rewriting in Luke-Acts, see Dupertuis, "The Acts of the Apostles: Narrative and History" chapter 28 in this volume).

But as Frank (2010, 2) remarks, "Stories make life good, but they also make life dangerous. They bring people together, and they keep them apart." In their efforts to present coherent reparative narratives, both Deuteronomy's gesture of political resistance and Luke's entreaty for accommodation also succumb to restricting representations. Deuteronomy creates a binary order in which obedience is valorized and suffering is connected to wrongdoing, leaving little room for moral agency or life experience that falls outside the realm of legalism. In addition to censoring women's voices and moral agency, Luke-Acts constructs its own binary marked by the belief in Jesus as the culmination of Jewish scripture. "Unbelieving" Jews are both condemned and portrayed as socially suspect (see Matthews 2013). The very stories that work to our benefit can also work to our detriment, limiting how we are able to see others or ourselves, "contracting," in the words of Lindemann Nelson (2001, xi), our "ability to exercise moral agency."

THE SOCIALITY OF NARRATIVE

Undergirding this discussion is the obvious but often overlooked insight that narrated experience is inevitably social. Stories, even supposedly individual and private ones, are inherently social and shared. As literary theorist Monika Fludernik (2007, 261) observes, "the self is projected in the first place in order to answer the glance of the other." We tell stories to meet others' demands to know who we are as well as our own demands for self-knowledge. In short, we tell stories to make sense of our lives, sense that is not always readily apparent. Moreover, as Fludernik continues, "Identities cannot be upheld without the co-operations of others" (261). If *stories*, by their very nature, situate particular human behaviors in the wider domain of human experience, story*telling* offers those behaviors to broader social contexts for interpretation and evaluation (Bruner 1991). This requires a certain amount of translation, as the linguistic anthropologist Elinor Ochs and the late developmental psychologist Lisa Capps have observed. While our personal experiences may be unique, our narratives of them "become socially forged . . . co-narrated according to local narrative formats, recognizable types of situations and people, and prevailing moral frameworks, which inevitably constrain representation and interpretation" (Ochs and Capps 2001, 55). Effective storytelling requires achieving a delicate balance between communicating the exceptional and the culturally recognizable and relatable. It is little wonder that Moses in Exodus bears uncanny resemblance to the Akkadian ruler Sargon, Jesus in the synoptic Gospels to heroic figures in Greco-Roman literature, Paul in Acts to classical philosophers (see, Busch, "New Testament Narrative and Greco-Roman Literature," chapter 4 in this volume) and divine cult figures (see Dupertuis, "The Acts of the Apostles: Narrative and History"), or Herod in Mark to the lampooned king Ahasuerus in the book of Esther.

Consequently, as we "answer the glance of the other" in different circumstances, our stories tend to mutate, reflecting our own evolution as selves and our ability to adapt to changing social contexts. We tailor form and content depending on our listeners or readers and the occasion for and the purpose of the telling. We customize in response to implicit and explicit questions: What makes this story worth telling or worth hearing in this particular location at this particular time by these particular people? How will this story's values and constructions of reality fit into larger domains of knowledge and experience represented in this particular group? As narrative anthropologist Linda Garro (2003, 21) observes, our narratives become "human dramas" in which "complex interactions with socially positioned agents . . . contribute to the unfolding understanding of 'lived experience' through legitimating, challenging, offering alternatives, or persuading shifts in the construal of life events." Shared narratives both facilitate and shape social engagement, thus affording "an optimal environment for social cognition" (Herman 2003, 164). Hence, our stories are never strictly our own, but are shaped by social interaction and inevitably imbued with cultural assumptions and expectations.

That in itself has ramifications for human survival. Evolutionary theorists, or evocritics, liken stories to play in that like play, stories focus our collective attention, fostering sociality and collaboration (Boyd 2009), which in turn enhances our chances for survival (Williams 2012, 107–109). The more we know about the thoughts and behaviors of others, the more likely we are to thrive. The hypothetical scenarios and the reconstructed pasts offered by narratives give us insights into the minds of others and provide critical tools for social problem-solving. They help us process the past (thereby assisting us in "answering the glance of the other") and prepare us for possible experiences yet to be encountered, permitting us opportunities to think through how we might respond. They show us what is good, what is dangerous, what is possible. They help us negotiate the known and the unknown, the desirable and the disruptive, providing a means of remodeling the self's or the community's sense of what is normal, acceptable, and sensible. They allow us, through comparison and contrast, to evaluate our current behaviors and circumstances and to see the world from multiple perspectives, not just in terms of its actualities, but also its possibilities (Shore 1996; Herman 2003; cf. Arendt 1958, 182–188).

The theme of survival, of course, raises the question, "survival for whom?" Evolutionary theory is hardly romantic about the role of competition in survival. The Bible's narratives bear the marks of enormous ecological, economic, political, and social competitions from various historical periods. From Genesis to Revelation, conflicts over natural resources, economic entitlements, social capital, political power, and theological worldviews abound. And while not every experience of oppression or marginalization finds narrative voice, actions of victors and fates of victims are regularly positioned "in the wider domain of human experience" and offered "to broader social contexts for interpretation and evaluation" (Bruner 1991), inviting analogy, critique, and self-reflection.

This brings us to some final observations about how stories contribute to human survival through both what they "say" and what they "do." Stories possess, to use the vocabulary of Michel de Certeau (1984, 115–130), "a spatial syntax" in which they plot the movements of bodies in space and time. In effect, stories are preoccupied with boundaries of various sorts: geographical, social, personal, emotional, ethical, and so forth. Plots commonly revolve around boundary-related issues: boundary establishment, boundary maintenance, boundary crossing, and the circumstances under which boundaries should be established, maintained, or crossed. Theorists have different ways of talking about this: de Certeau (1984) speaks of frontiers and bridges; Bruner (1991) thinks in terms of canonicity and breach; the Freudians imagine lacks in the status quo that must be filled (e.g., Brooks 1992). But whatever the terminology used, narrative theorists commonly maintain that navigations of boundaries, borders, limits, standards explicit or implicit, are critical to narrative communication.

Boundary establishment and maintenance are what stories themselves endeavor to accomplish as they carve coherence from the randomness of reality. The narrative gesture itself points to the importance and need for boundaries as a way of giving life shape and pattern. *Boundaries*, in Frank's (2010, 70) words, "humanize time and space." They make life meaningful, sensible, manageable, and livable. On the other hand, boundary *crossings* are what keep life in motion (69–70), show meaning to be malleable, truth to be multiple and excessive, possibilities to be endless. If the power of stories involves their ability to represent meaning in motion and in multiplicity, it is hardly surprising that the most moving stories are indeed about movement beyond prescribed limits. Perhaps only in moments of utmost insecurity do we incline toward stories in which everything remains the same. Even our "just so" stories and foundational cultural myths designed to explain and justify why things are the way they are, usually begin with some kind of transgression; consequently, the most "canonical" of stories, aimed at regulating thought and behavior, often also have the capacity to question or otherwise undercut those regulations by providing "delinquent" and "tactical" clues to how "established" social and ideological boundaries might be breached, evaded, or even abolished (de Certeau 1984, 129). One might, with Frank, wonder if stories in general— and, we might suggest, biblical stories in particular—are at their core preoccupied with how the fate of the world might depend on the balance between boundary maintenance and boundary crossing (Frank 2010, 70), or, at the very least, how identities are shaped, secured, or damaged by this balance.

The Bible's preoccupation with boundaries is inevitably tied to questions of survival. Many stories, especially those that include moral instruction (e.g., the Torah's Sinai narratives and Matthew's Sermon on the Mount), attempt to establish standards of communal behavior to "humanize time and space," though these same sorts of stories (e.g., Nehemiah and Ezra) can have the side effect of dehumanizing any who fall outside that time and space. Biblical narratives expose the fine lines between stability and stagnation, self-protection and social aggression, and self-identification and caricature.

Given the Bible's obsession with but ambivalence to boundaries, the prevalence of biblical tricksters is scarcely surprising. From Jacob to Jesus, biblical characters transgress conventions of all sorts, creating breaches in the social fabric, admitting a different kind of light, a different way of operating in the world. Even the divine character is not above trickery, nor is he above breaking his own commandments! In this light, we might consider how biblical narratives themselves both reflect and transgress their socio-historical constraints. As stories coming to literary expression in the shadows of master narratives of imperial dominance and as responses to various communal crises and challenges, biblical narratives inevitably tread a narrow, precarious trek between boundary maintenance and boundary transgression, because, indeed, in the ancient world, life always hangs in the balance. From Eden's garden gates to the walls of John's new Jerusalem, the Bible's stories probe the nature of human and divine limitations: Which boundaries humanize life and ensure survival? Which ones constrain and enslave? Which transgressions are necessary to give voice to human identity, to protect human integrity, to realize human (and divine) potential—in short, to move life forward? And which transgressions will cause more damage than good, and to whom?

TELLING TROUBLES

The relationship between stories, bodies, and boundaries brings us to consider "wounded storytellers" (Frank [1995] 2013). The political, social, and ecological traumas of the last century have inspired a renewed interest in the relation between trauma and memory. Revisiting the pioneering psychoanalytic studies of Pierre Janet (1859–1947) and Sigmund Freud (1856–1939), trauma and memory theorists continue to wrestle with the question of how memory, and its articulations in narrative form, conveys and fails to convey traumatic events. Trauma can manifest itself, on the one hand, as an event "engraved on the mind, never to be forgotten" and, on the other hand, as a memory that the mind suppresses as a means of self-protection (McNally 2003, 1). In either case, for recovery to be possible, traumatic memories "need to be integrated with existing mental schemes, and be transformed into narrative language" (van der Kolk and van der Hardt 1995, 176).

Traumatic events disrupt life stories, destabilize identities, and force identity re/construction. When we experience "shattered assumptions" (Janoff-Bulman 1992) or "narrative wreckage" (Frank [1995] 2013), we undergo cognitive disruption, sometimes so profound that the event defies integration into any coherent narrative. The inability to confront the extent of the pain results in memory failure, silence, narrative gaps, partial retellings, coded signifiers, or shape-shifting stories that attempt to address the trauma from different angles. Consequently, close readers and listeners are called to attend to what is not said, to what is said obliquely, to variant reiterations.

Alternatively, the event may be an insurmountable presence, demanding explanation and assimilation into our individual and communal stories, insisting that we scrutinize, redeploy, and integrate the existential rubble into a narrative framework that makes sense. The revised narrative must be credible; that is, it must speak the truth about the degree of damage incurred, and if possible, project a cogent way forward—whether or not that way forward accommodates us as the ongoing story's primary protagonists.

Crises are often the roots of cultural identity re/construction. Jackson contends that any "theory of culture requires a study of crisis—of those contexts and situations in which normative epistemes and customary routines are disrupted, suspended, contested, negotiated, and reshaped" (2002, 129; cf. 1989, 20). Crises, according to Jackson,

> transform the world from an apparently fixed and finite actuality into a bewilderingly open horizon of possibilities. At such times, people confront the world with which they identify as a world in which they are also alien. Crisis creates a consciousness of that which has been lost— "childhood" in the case of neophytes, "happiness" in the case of the bereaved, "home" in the case of refugees and exiles. But that which has been lost is also seen for the first time as a whole, like the earth seen from space, that excludes oneself, or exists independently of one's being part of it. It is for this reason that holistic concepts of human aggregates, such as "culture, " "tradition," and "identity" are, paradoxically, defined not *sui generis* from a position of belonging, but provisionally, from a position of exile and estrangement. Such concepts, arising out of ostracism, separation and loss, are pivotal to healing and reintegration. Their very detachedness makes them potential symbols of transcendence, or powerful means of realigning and revising identity. (Jackson 2002, 122n9)

Identity revision inevitably takes narrative form, and different narrative structures carry different existential ramifications. How does one narrate "chaos" and at the same time affirm a coherent self or communal identity? Can one recapture what has been lost with a credible story of "restitution"? That is, is it plausible that, after a crisis, life can resume its precrisis normality? If restitution proves to be impossible or undesirable, how might individual or cultural life be reconfigured as a "quest" for new understanding? (on chaos, restitution, and quest narratives, see further Frank [1995] 2013; Crossley 2000). Often, the impulse to provide order and coherence is offset by the desire to remain open to several narrative possibilities, especially in an ongoing crisis that forces continuing questions about priorities and future options. In such moments, multiple, even incongruent, narrative explanations and scenarios may be deemed relevant (Ochs and Capps 2001, 15), and even once the crisis is over, its significance may remain ambiguous and contested (Garro 2003, 21), continuing to generate different accountings.

The biblical corpus offers remarkable hospitality to different theodical rationales, even in the space of a single story. Our increased recognition of trauma's role in the Bible's literary production (in addition to works overviewed by Garber 2013, see Fewell 1996, 2010; Kelso 2007; Fewell and Phillips 2009; Janzen 2012; Koosed 2012; Carr 2014; Smith-Christopher, "Biblical Lamentations and Singing the Blues," chapter 48 in this volume) positions us as readers and analysts to better comprehend how, in their response to crisis, biblical narratives have contributed to the formation of cultural identities within the biblical world. In this regard, a different paradigm emerges with which to view the propensities of biblical narratives to shape-shift and rematerialize in ways that interrupt, supplement, or contest other narrative representations. Consider the Bible's "foundational narratives."

The narrative extending from Genesis through Kings is the Bible's most ambitious attempt to "answer the glance of the other." A prime example of "narrative accrual" (Bruner 1991, 18–20), the corpus gathers and arranges a multiplicity of stories and traditions, casting them as supporting actors in a comprehensive cultural narrative often categorized as a protracted etiology for the Babylonian conquest and exile. These various narrative representations both connect and compete with one another, constructing communal identity as a dense aggregate and recounting trauma in modes both palpably direct and evocatively furtive. The more domineering narrative expressions have led to the positing of a "Deuteronomistic History" (Deut. –2 Kings), with multiple editions responding to different socio-historical circumstances ranging from the Josianic reform to post-exilic Yehud. One set of narrative representations, dramatizing Roy Harris's dictum that narratives are never "unsponsored texts" (see Bruner 1991, 10), seems to justify Josiah's reforms, framing those political, religious, and social developments as a fulfillment of Deuteronomy's ideology. In its mimicry of Assyrian suzerainty treaties, Deuteronomy turns a genre of forced political submission into a gesture of political resistance and theological innovation. Parts of the ensuing narrative ventriloquize Deuteronomy, seemingly claiming legitimacy and "canonicity" (Bruner 1991) or the role of "master narrative" (Lindemann Nelson 2001). This deuteronomistic master narrative insists on a covenantal logic to history that characterizes YHWH as a deity primarily concerned with rewarding fidelity, punishing disloyalty, and responding positively to repentance.

One narrative strand casts Josiah as a new Joshua claiming promised territory and legislating an exclusive Yahwism. He is painted as a fortuitous intervener destined to save Judah from ruin. This triumphant storyline suffers "narrative wreckage," mirroring the social wreckage left in the wakes of Josiah's inopportune death and the ensuing destruction of Jerusalem. The wreckage exposes profound internal contradictions: Josiah's reforms emerge as a classic Derridean *pharmacon*, both "cure" and "poison"—a remedy for covenantal

neglect but inherently traumatic to the communities which must endure the resulting physical, economic, and religious damage (Carr 2014). Moreover, Josiah's repentance does nothing to deter the Babylonian invasion, YHWH's supposed retribution for covenantal betrayal
(Janzen 2012).

The social rupture brought about by military defeat and destruction is framed in terms of
cause and effect, with some causes more strident than others: theological failure, covenantal
infidelity, problems with monarchical leadership, failure to produce a homogenous popu-
lous. But twisted into these narrative strands are fibers of different colors and unwieldy tex-
tures that raise pronounced questions regarding YHWH's reliability and human culpability
(see Janzen 2012). These obstinate narrative threads thicken and snarl the narrative braid that
struggles to weave the devastating events into a coherent account, creating, in Bakhtinian
terms, a "hybrid construction" that combines within its single utterance multiple belief systems, social consciousnesses, and temporal realities (Bakhtin 1981, 305, 358–366). The story
frays into an unfinalized and unfinalizable end. The last of David's line is freed from prison,
but remains in exile, confined always to eat at the Babylonian king's table. The people—those
who were deported, those who remained, and those who fled—disappear from view. The
fates of all concerned are left in suspense.

An extension of the narrative's parameters, however, allows diverse interpretations to
emerge and different future possibilities to be entertained. With the Book of the Covenant
and the Holiness Code added to Deuteronomy's statutes for successful life in society, communal responsibility for internal justice is both complicated and implicated alongside
political leadership; priestly cultic laws suggest breaches of ritual correctness, not simply
theological exclusivism; Genesis narratives hint that YHWH has yet to discover smart weapons and is prone to indiscriminate violence (Gen. 6–9; 18–19); and the Exodus story suggests
that YHWH can be forgetful (Exod. 2:23–25), temperamental (Exod. 32; Num. 11), and more
concerned about his reputation than about justice for his people (Exod. 6:2–8; 7:3–5; 9:29–
30; 10:1–2; 14:1–4, 17–18, 30–31). When juxtaposed to the deuteronomistic master narrative,
these glimpses of YHWH's character suggest that, at the very least, the deity has yet to develop
"the capacity for 'normative self-disclosure'—the ability to reveal through his actions who
he is as a person" (Lindemann Nelson 2001, 25, discussing the work of Benson 1990 on free
agency; for further psychological understandings of the deity, see Lasine, "Characterizing
God in His/Our Own Image," chapter 40 in this volume).

The stories in Genesis and Exodus also reveal the multiple dimensions of the social crisis. As they reiterate incidences of migration forced (Gen. 3:22–24; 4:10–16; 11:1–9; 12:10–
20; 14:1–16; 16:9; 19:12–26, 30; 21:9–21; 26:1, 16–33; 37:25–28; Exod. 2:15–22) and otherwise
(Gen. 12:1–3; 13:1–13; 24; 28; 31; Exod. 4–15), they tangentially return to the source of trauma,
reframing exile and diaspora in different ways seemingly in an effort to come to terms with
a cultural rupture (Fewell and Phillips 2009) that appears to be ongoing. In gestures of *sideshadowing* rather than foreshadowing (see Bernstein 1994, 2–3; Morson 1994, 6–7; Ochs and
Capps 2001, 4–6), these episodes "restore the *presentness* of the past" and cultivate "a sense
that something else might have happened" (Morson 1994, 7). They suggest that what has
happened is not singular in its significance, nor is the outcome predetermined. And in a
substantial number of cases, they underscore human choice—about when to go, when to
stay, when to return, and how to live in new locales. Displacements are not all the same but
foster different kinds of pains and opportunities. They may breed fear, mistrust, hostility,
and exploitation as well as inspire hospitality, shelter, and commitment. They may occasion

divine protection, distance, or abandonment. Moreover, "return" is also shown to be displacement, making a simple "restitution story" impossible. But perhaps most importantly, these reiterations at the beginning show displacement to be something that has happened before, something endurable, and something that is but a chapter in a larger story.

This "return of the repressed" is a stammering attempt to bring trauma's truth, with all its variations, into the open. Moreover, these stories, along with others scattered throughout Genesis–Kings, provide resources for interpreting the open ending to this primary story. By drawing on prior episodes, the storytelling community is allowed a number of ways to thicken and complicate communal identity and, ultimately, to complete the story for themselves. The interrupted building of Babel, the call of Abraham, the journey of Rebekah, the homecoming of Jacob, the success of Joseph, the Exodus story, the admonitions of Moses in Deuteronomy, the numerous trickster stories in Genesis and Judges, Hannah's vision of power reversals, YHWH's own experience of displacement via the Ark of the Covenant, David's exiles and returns, the divine promises to David in 2 Samuel 7, David's confining hospitality to the last of Saul's line in 2 Samuel 9, and so on, each offers its own particular guidance in imaging the future (cf. Granowski 1992; Polzin 1993, 103–106; Schipper 2005; Harvey 2010; Chan 2013; and Bodner, "The Rule of Death and Signs of Life in the Book of Kings," chapter 16 in this volume). Moreover, if, as some have argued, this extended cultural narrative is imperially sponsored, it answers the glance of the empire in ambivalent ways. On the one hand, its narration of failure may justify imperial rule: a people who end in such political and social disarray surely need the oversight of Empire (see Berquist 2010). On the other hand, the extensive narrative accrual refuses an imperial halter. The divine promise of the land to the ancestors counters imperial jurisdiction. The foregrounding of monarchical failure broadly critiques any political sovereign claiming autonomy. The sideshadowing stories of migration (Abraham, Jacob, Joseph) hint at new beginnings—some even revolutionary in scope (Exodus). Other narrative sideshadows reporting and celebrating royal demises intimate politically subversive endings: what happens to one monarchical line can easily happen to another, even one of imperial stature.

Woven into this hybridized narrative tissue (on the "tissue of stories," see Lindemann Nelson 2001, 76) is the propensity for self-blame, a common strategy for responding to trauma that gives the suffering subject a means of control over future events. If certain behaviors are responsible for the traumatic event, then such behaviors can be adjusted. It is easier to take the blame and thus assert agency, than to confront the ideas of randomness or divine caprice, or to live with the shame of complete and inescapable vulnerability (see Terr 1990, 109–121; Janoff-Bulman 1992, 123–132). So, for example, if covenantal breach or ritual transgression is the primary reason for exile, then attending to these lapses can ensure that such a traumatic event does not repeat itself.

Self-blame, however, is not always a choice, but can evidence "infiltrated consciousness" (Lindemann Nelson 2001, 20–21), the internalization of guilt projected by others, in this case the deuteronomistic master narrative. This is a story where suffering is often presented as the result of failures to meet some set of responsibilities (cf. Garro's [2003] study of narratives of suffering in First Nation communities), a rationale that works only as long as the people are portrayed as a collective character. When, however, individual faces are allowed to emerge, the dichotomy of guilt and innocence begins to erode. The book of Judges is a case in point. While "the people" in deuteronomistic concert repeatedly do "the" often unclarified "bad thing" that warrants YHWH's punishment, spotlighted individuals dramatize a more complicated reality in which issues of economic autonomy (Judg. 3), family survival (Judg. 4:17–22), honor and shame (Judg. 9; 19), divine unreliability (Judg. 6:13), divine and communal silence in the face of domestic violence (Judg. 11), and divine ambivalence regarding sexual assault and civil strife (Judg. 19–21) are driving forces in human behavior. (For a sustained reading of altered subjectivity in Genesis–Kings, see Fewell and Gunn 1993; for a comprehensive treatment of trauma's "subversion" of deuteronomistic logic, see Janzen 2012.) There are glimpses of the blameless and the heroic as well as depictions of the deity with more on his mind than justice. Moreover, some faces remain forever ambiguous. As Fludernik (2007, 263) notes, "It is when a text gives expression to conflicting accounts of a protagonist's actions or motives, when speculations about his or her state of mind are encouraged, that the story becomes interesting and in the plenitude of life defeats the uniform banality of moralistic judgment." Such multiplicities and ambiguities give identity-constructing stories their "wide explanatory power" (Lindemann Nelson 2001, 90), allowing them to speak to a broad constituency. In sum, despite some narrative representations that attempt to settle the matter of conquest and deportation by positing a breach of covenant on the part of the people, others suggest that "the people" are multiple and diverse rather than an undifferentiated collective, that religious guidance is not infallible, that monarchical leadership is inconsistent, that God does not always meet covenantal obligations to reward the faithful and punish the guilty, and that displacements are not necessarily unqualified endings but possible moments of recalibration, reflection, and response. The excessive explanatory efforts of the narrative offer a picture of the community's identity and trauma "truer" than any one depiction, and create the occasion for open-ended existential reflection: Given all that has happened to us, who are we? And who should we now become? With the destiny of the Davidic line in question and YHWH's future actions uncertain, the people are left with the challenge of how to reassemble their communities after narrative wreckage.

The Chronicler's competing narration of communal selfhood does the work of narrative repair in a more directive fashion. Dispensing with complicating episodic sideshadowing and opting instead for lean, linear genealogies, Chronicles makes a documentary attempt, on the one hand, to justify post-exilic communal membership and land tenure and, on another, to streamline and underscore the albeit artificial notion (see Kelso, "The Patrilineal Narrative Machinery of Chronicles," chapter 24 in this volume) of continuity and connection. For Chronicles, with its preoccupation with the building of the YHWH's house and the organization of the cult, the Babylonian defeat and deportation is but a temporary disruption, allowing the land to make up for all its missed Sabbaths and to prepare itself ritually for a new start. Whatever narrative wreckage left by the Babylonians is quickly tidied up with Cyrus's edict declaring YHWH's personal patronage and mandating that deportees return to Jerusalem and rebuild the House of God. The Chronicler "saves face" by offering a narrative blueprint for the future: the shame of past political defeat is but a step toward a more worthy mission to rebuild the house of YHWH who has, in the meantime, been promoted to the "God of heaven" who now oversees world events and extends patronage to imperial movements. In contrast to the murky ending of Genesis–Kings, the Chronicler's denouement is crystalline: the Judaean monarchy's prospects are of no concern now that YHWH is the world's stage manager. Moreover, the people's future has already been decided: they are to return home and rebuild the house of God. The Chronicler offers a "remedy," a "restitution story," in which all can be as good as new (on the difference between the two constitutive stories, see further Fewell 2010).

A similar contrast manifests in the Gospel literature. Various characters throughout the synoptic Gospels give through their comments hints of an initial idealized story of messianic liberation. However, the public execution of Jesus and the subsequent destruction of Jerusalem in 70 CE produced successive chapters of narrative wreckage. The multiple Gospel accounts evidence attempts to come to terms with communal trauma. Mark's Gospel rewrites Jesus as one who both knows of and faces head-on his inexorable suffering (Carr 2014), reframing the catastrophe of Jesus's fate as an inevitable event courageously endured, but providing little instruction for the future except, perhaps, to confront portending suffering in the manner of Jesus. Other than its urging the women visiting the tomb to gather with other disciples in Galilee (an area known for its political unrest), the original ending of Mark (16:8) refuses closure and offers no concrete proposal for future action. The Gospel's flustered conclusion prompts not only a series of new endings but further editions of the Gospel story that, at least on their surface, rush to palliate and disavow Mark's political insinuations. Mark's earthly kingdom of God is replaced with Matthew's kingdom of heaven; hints of contemporary revolution are relegated to "the end of the age"; "carrying a cross" is transformed into Luke's metaphor for everyday ethics; current cultural tensions between church and synagogue rather than Roman discipline frame Jesus's demise and the fall of Jerusalem. In short, while the character Jesus continues to know the story he is in and what the story will require him to do, the social and political boundaries he transgresses are carefully redrawn to diminished effect. The apprehension and uncertainty voiced by the ending of Mark's Gospel is suppressed and replaced in Matthew and Luke with a prospective mission to "all nations" and the promise of Jesus's continuous presence. Mark's geographically and temporally constrained Gospel is opened up in Matthew and Luke to infinite spatial and temporal possibilities, becoming a mirror of Roman expansion. In short, Mark's chaotic ending is transformed into an unlimited quest, a pronounced narrative gesture of survival in a world gone awry.

The Fourth Gospel's response to trauma takes the form of a restitution narrative and further tamps down the political implications of the Jesus story by extending its spatial and temporal syntax beyond human history and the earthly world itself. In the only Gospel dramatizing "incarnation," the only Gospel whose story could have taken place anywhere or anytime, Jesus's self-knowledge intensifies, as he becomes not only the epitome of Greco-Roman ideals of masculine self-mastery (Conway 2003), but the very *logos* itself, the divine principle of reason and rationality who, from the beginning of time, has been woven into the fabric of the cosmos. Moreover, the person of Jesus is but a migrant (see Lozada, "The Narrative Identities of the Gospel of John," chapter 25 in this volume): having come "from the Father," he is a temporary worker who then returns "to the Father," bidding his disciples to follow his lead. John's Gospel, with its profoundly certain and temporally and spatially transcendent Jesus, lures Christians into a restitution story in which resurrection repairs trauma, and current crises are a messy, painful, but bearable, detour on the way to the ultimate destination: the Father's house.

THIS STORY WHICH IS NOT ONE

What these multiple versions of foundational stories indicate is that stories talk to one another. Every story is an "intertextual performance" (Currie [1998] 2011, 75–76) that inevitably exposes the presence of other stories lurking in the background conveying differently interpreted experiences. The multiple versions of stories in the Bible not only demonstrate that ancient communities, like modern ones, "think with" stories, but that they realize that "[o]ne story by itself is often not good at eliciting reflection on what that story has framed, and what it leaves out of that framing; what perspective it takes, and which perspectives it excludes" (Frank 2010, 151). No story is incomparable, and any "claim to incomparability carries privileges that are the beginning of danger," specifically, the dangers of individual or group entitlement (Frank 2010, 152), a danger that the Bible, when taken superficially as a monolithic, singular story, has perpetuated on numerous occasions.

The Bible's own composition, however, conveys the need to have multiple stories to think with—stories that complement, supplement, contradict, and undermine one another, stories that embed or use smaller stories as building blocks, and even multiscoped stories (see Turner 2003) that force the community to hold in their heads numerous stories simultaneously. For instance, Matthew's Gospel sends out various narrative tentacles into past tradition to co-opt building materials for its story of Jesus, a gesture that insists on continuity and at the same time suggests rivalry, ascendancy (see Phillips 1999; Fuller 2007), and inevitability. The book of Ruth with its frequent allusions to other stories of migration, ethnic differentiation, and trickery demands high levels of cultural and narrative competency (Bruner 1991) in order to appreciate the complex way it creates space for the social negotiation of communal boundaries (see Eskenazi and Frymer-Kensky 2011, xxi–xxvi; Fewell, forthcoming). As political, religious, and social satire, the book of Esther parodies the stories of Daniel, Moses, and Joseph, offering a rather different picture of what it might mean to collaborate with the enemy (see Maldonado, "Reading Others as the Subject(s) of Biblical Narrative," chapter 37, and Wetter, "Bodies, Boundaries, and Belonging in the Book of Esther," chapter 21, in this volume). Moreover, the scroll mocks all traditions sacred and secular that would insist that laws and statutes are "written in stone." Likewise, the story of Jonah subverts traditionally construed relationships between deity and prophet (see Ryu, "Divine Rhetoric and Prophetic Silence in the Book of Jonah," chapter 18 in this volume); but perhaps more daringly, the story lampoons the deuteronomistic valorizing of God's indiscriminate compassion toward the repentant (see further, Lasine, "Characterizing God in His/Our Own Image," chapter 40 in this volume) and exposes the problems inherent in explaining historical catastrophe with naïve theological categories. And to complicate the reading of Luke-Acts proffered earlier, Luke's double-scoped beginning, with its echoes of 1 Samuel, suggests a multicoded message that while on one level placating a seemingly gentilic Theophilus with a story that accommodates Roman values, also insinuates, to those with the appropriate narrative competence, a more politically subversive message. Elizabeth, Mary, and Anna together assume the part of 1 Samuel's Hannah, but they, like their male counterparts Zechariah and Simeon, are all passively acted upon by the Holy Spirit. In contrast, Hannah takes initiative in the midst of social corruption, moves YHWH to personal and political action, and ensures that her son is positioned to bring about change in the center of power (Jobling 1998; 131–150; Fewell 2003, 197–223). All these biblical intertextual performances are manifestations of dialogic storytelling, demonstrations of social conversation, debate, and negotiation.

The sociality of stories—the social context and construction of stories, stories as reflections of society, stories socializing with other stories—calls us to think beyond storytellers as autonomous individuals speaking to their audiences in unidirectional gestures of communication. Narratives are imaged instead as expressions of shared or "distributed intelligence"

(Brown, Collins, and Duguid 1989), of "cultural cognition" (Hutchins 1995), or, as Jackson (2002, 22) puts it, as "neither the pure creations of autonomous individuals nor the unalloyed expressions of subjective views, but rather a result of ongoing dialogue and redaction within fields of intersubjectivity." In other words, the deep entanglements of storytellers with their environments, stories as tapestries of individual and shared representations and perspectives, suggest that our efforts to distinguish neatly the tellers, their tales, their redactors, and their interpreters—whether we do this as an operation of historical criticism, reader-response criticism, narrative poetics, or ethical reflection—may be misguided. Notions of narrative authorship and authorization that are more dialogical and collaborative in nature may provide us with better models for understanding biblical narrativity. The work of Mikhail Bakhtin (1981, 1984a, 1984b, 1986, 1990), whose textual theories are making inroads into biblical studies (see Green 2000 and Boer 2007; Bakhtinian studies of individual biblical texts defy enumeration), is particularly important in this conceptualization, but other post-classical narratologists are also thinking along these lines. So, for example, Jackson, deeply influenced by the work of Arendt, claims,

> [T]he very purpose of storytelling is to invoke and counterpoint *various* points of view. . . . [S]tories cast doubt on the possibility of resolving ethical dilemmas according to any one principle, or on any *a priori* grounds . . . the actual performance of a story reinforces this relativity of perspectives, for in requiring the participation of both audience *and* storyteller in an interactive relationship of call and response, the storytelling event itself realizes *both socially and dialogically an ideal of tolerant solidarity in difference.* (Jackson 2002, 140–141)

Granted, Jackson is assuming dialogic, communally oriented storytelling, rather than the kind of monologic storytelling found in political propaganda, which seeks to exclude every perspective save one. As we have seen multiple times in the history of literacy, denying the existence of other perspectives in literature is the first step toward denying existence to other people (see Gottschall 2012, 139–155). Bodies and texts are always intimately connected. But even the least hospitable stories cannot completely silence all other perspectives, since, by their very telling, they expose their attempts to "untell" or overwrite other viable interpretations of experience. The more strident their demands to be "master narratives," the less obvious and compelling their versions are likely to be. Dialogic stories, on the other hand, because of both their social content and the social context of storytelling, dramatize the difficulties inherent in telling the truth and create an occasion, a discursive space, for multiple perspectives and representations, even multiple time frames, to converge in the same communicative plane.

This may seem obvious to those of us who work with composite texts and navigate the world of canonical diversity. Acutely aware that biblical narrative can be surprisingly congenial to multiple and sometimes incongruent representations, increasing numbers of studies are "reading the fractures," to co-opt David M. Carr's (1996) felicitous phrase, to better understand the dynamics of these richly divergent texts. These studies, for the most part, continue to be diachronic in nature, attempting to chart redactional history, plotting the variant textual voices as linear evolution, with the last contributing voice shouting down all others. But as Philip Davies states so incisively in relation to literary production and canonization, "[W]e do not have a single tradition or 'stream of tradition' here being gradually revised and rewritten, . . . but something more vigorous, varied and contested" (Davies 2013, 44). The complexities of biblical literary production, dissemination, and performance call for more fitting theories of textuality and narrativity to account for how these texts do their social, political, and theological work while realizing "an ideal of tolerant solidarity in difference." Rather than think about stories as unidirectional discourse conveyed through text from author to reader/audience (or even appealing to the more detailed reader-response models); rather than view composite narratives as linear, chronological deposits whose original meanings are redactionally massaged, co-opted, or distorted; rather than posit biblical narratives as bloodless texts whose words and meanings slip and slide in infinite, uncommitted play, we might better characterize biblical storytelling in Bakhtinian terms, as "a dialogue of social forces perceived not only in their static co-existence, but also as a dialogue of different times, epochs and days, a dialogue that is forever dying, living, being born: co-existence and becoming are here fused into an indissoluble concrete unity that is contradictory, multi-speeched and heterogeneous" (Bakhtin 1981, 365). In other words, biblical stories are transtemporal, fluid, and socially discursive spaces—Levinasian "living spaces" (Levinas 1989)—where multiple faces, voices, bodies, identities, experiences are textually incarnate and engaged in lively, sometimes testy, exchanges, and where attending guests are implicated in the pains, trials, and triumphs of the past and beckoned to collude in the text's ongoing intersubjective work.

Notes

1. David Barr, "Narrative Technique in the Book of Revelation"; Warren Carter, "Narrative Readings, Contextualized Readers, and Matthew's Gospel"; Scott Elliot, "Time and Focalization in the Gospel According to Mark"; Tod Linafelt, "Poetry and Biblical Narrative."

2. See Roland Boer, "The Economic Politics of Biblical Narrative"; Mark Brett, "Narrative Deliberations in Biblical Politics"; Linda Dietch, "The Social Worlds of Biblical Narrative"; Theodore Jennings and Tat-siong Benny Liew, "Narrativizing Empire in the Biblical World"; Donna Laird, "Political Strategy in the Narrative of Ezra-Nehemiah"; Abraham Smith, "Witnesses for the Defense in the Gospel of Luke"; and Terry Ann Smith, "Warring Words in the Book of Daniel."

3. See Bryan Bibb, "Blood, Death, and the Holy in the Leviticus Narrative"; Norman Habel, "Reading the Landscape in Biblical Narrative; Martien Halvorson-Taylor, "Displacement and Diaspora in Biblical Narrative"; Jennifer Koosed, "Sustenance and Survival in Biblical Narrative"; Dora Mbuwayesango, "Sex and Sexuality in Biblical Narrative"; Jeremy Schipper, "Plotting Bodies in Biblical Narrative"; and Ken Stone, "Animating the Bible's Animals."

4. See Kathleen Gallagher Elkins and Julie Faith Parker, "Children in Biblical Narrative and Childist Interpretation"; Deryn Guest, "Judging Yhwh in the Book of Judges"; Julie Kelso, "The Patrilineal Narrative Machinery of Chronicles; Robert Maldonado, "Reading Others as the Subject(s) of Biblical Narrative"; and Judith McKinlay, "Reading Biblical Women Matters."

5. See David Barr, "Narrative Technique in the Book of Revelation"; Danna Nolan Fewell and R. Christopher Heard, "The Genesis of Identity in the Biblical World"; Melanie Johnson-DeBaufre, "Narrative, Multiplicity, and the Letters of Paul"; Chesung Justin Ryu, "Divine Rhetoric and Prophetic Silence in the Book of Jonah"; Robert Seesengood, "Shifting Biblical Parables"; Abraham Smith, "Witnesses for the Defense in the Gospel of Luke";

Daniel Smith-Christopher, "Biblical Lamentations and Singing the Blues"; Patricia Tull, "Narrative Among the Latter Prophets"; and Anne-Mareike Wetter, "Bodies, Boundaries, and Belonging in the Book of Esther."

6. See David Gunn, "Telling and Retelling the Bible's First Story"; Carol Newsom, "Plural Versions and the Challenge of Coherence in the Book of Job"; and Eric Thurman, "Adam and the Making of Masculinity."

7. See Austin Busch, "New Testament Narrative and Greco-Roman Literature"; Rubén René Dupertuis, "The Acts of the Apostles, Narrative, and History"; Robert Kawashima, "Biblical Narrative and the Birth of Prose Literature"; and Tod Linafelt, "Poetry and Biblical Narrative."

8. See in this volume Keith Bodner, "The Rule of Death and Signs of Life in the Book of Kings"; Brian Britt, "Remembering Narrative in Deuteronomy"; Ovidiu Creangă, "The Conquest of Memory in the Book of Joshua"; Rubén René Dupertuis, "The Acts of the Apostles, Narrative, and History"; Rachelle Gilmour, "(Hi)story Telling in the Books of Samuel"; Adriane Leveen, "Becoming Israel in the Wilderness of Numbers"; Kenneth Ngwa, "The Story of Exodus and Its Literary Kinships"; and Raymond Person, "Biblical Historiography as Traditional History."

9. Stuart Lasine, "Characterizing God in His/Our Own Image"; Francisco Lozada, "The Narrative Identities of the Gospel of John"; Robert Maldonado, "Reading Others as the Subject(s) of Biblical Narrative"; Judith McKinlay, "Reading Biblical Women Matters"; and Stephanie Powell, Amy Beth Jones, and Dong Sung Kim, "Reading Ruth, Reading Desire."

10. Jione Havea and Monica Melanchthon, "Culture Tricks in Biblical Narrative"; Gerald West, "Global Thefts of Biblical Narrative."

11. Ovidiu Creangă, "The Conquest of Memory in the Book of Joshua"; Francisco Lozada, "The Narrative Identities of the Gospel of John"; Robert Maldonado, "Reading Others as the Subject(s) of Biblical Narrative"; Abraham Smith, "Witnesses for the Defense in the Gospel of Luke"; and Gary Phillips, "The Commanding Faces of Biblical Stories."

References

Alter, Robert. 1981. *The Art of Biblical Narrative*. New York: Basic Books.

Althusser, Louis. 1971. "Ideology and Ideological State Apparatuses (Notes towards an Investigation)." In *"Lenin and Philosophy" and Other Essays*, translated by Ben Brewster, 127–186. New York and London: Monthly Review Press. First published in *La Pensée*, 1970.

Arendt, Hannah. 1958. *The Human Condition*. Chicago: University of Chicago Press.

Bakhtin, Mikhail M. 1981. *The Dialogic Imagination*. Translated by Caryl Emerson and Michael Holquist. Austin: University of Texas Press.

Bakhtin, Mikhail M. 1984a. *Problems of Dostoevsky's Poetics*. Edited and translated by Caryl Emerson. Theory and History of Literature 8. Minneapolis: University of Minnesota Press.

Bakhtin, Mikhail M. 1984b. *Rabelais and His World*. Translated by Helene Iswolsky. Bloomington: University of Indiana Press.

Bakhtin, Mikhail M. 1986. *Speech Genres and Other Late Essays*. Translated by Vern W. McGee. Edited by Caryl Emerson and Michael Holquist. Austin: University of Texas Press.

Bakhtin, Mikhail M. 1990. *Art and Answerability: Early Philosophical Essays by M. M. Bakhtin*. Translated by Vadim Liapunov and Kenneth Brostrom. Edited by Michael Holquist and Vadim Liapunov. Austin: University of Texas Press.

Bal, Mieke. 1991. *On Story-Telling: Essays in Narratology*. Edited by David Jobling. Sonoma, CA: Polebridge.

Benson, Paul. 1990. "Feminist Second Thoughts about Free Agency." *Hypatia* 5(3): 47–64.

Bernstein, Michael André. 1994. *Foregone Conclusions: Against Apocalyptic History*. Berkeley: University of California Press.

Berquist, Jon L. 2010. "Identities and Empire: Historiographic Questions for the Deuteronomistic History in the Persian Period." In *Historiography and Identity (Re)formulation in Second Temple Historiographical Literature*, edited by Louis Jonker, 3–14. London: T&T Clark International.

Boer, Roland, ed. 2007. *Bakhtin and Genre Theory in Biblical Studies*. Semeia Studies 63. Atlanta, GA: Society of Biblical Literature.

Booth, Wayne C. 1961. *The Rhetoric of Fiction*. Chicago: University of Chicago Press.

Booth, Wayne C. 1988. *The Company We Keep: An Ethics of Fiction*. Berkeley: University of California Press.

Boyd, Brian. 2009. *On the Origins of Story: Evolution, Cognition, and Fiction*. Cambridge, MA: Harvard University Press.

Brooks, Peter. 1992. *Reading for the Plot: Design and Intention in Narrative*. Cambridge, MA: Harvard University Press.

Brown, John Seely, Allan Collins, and Paul Duguid. 1989. "Situated Cognition and the Culture of Learning." *Educational Researcher* 18: 32–42.

Bruner, Jerome. 1986. *Actual Minds, Possible Worlds*. Cambridge, MA: Harvard University Press.

Bruner, Jerome. 1990. *Acts of Meaning*, Cambridge, MA: Harvard University Press.

Bruner, Jerome. 1991. "The Narrative Construction of Reality." *Critical Inquiry* 18: 1–21.

Bruner, Jerome. 2004. "Life as Narrative." *Social Research* 71(3): 691–710.

Carr, David. 1997. "Narrative and the Real World: An Argument for Continuity." In *Memory, Identity, Community: The Idea of Narrative in the Human Sciences*, edited by Lewis P. Hinchman and Sandra K. Hinchman, 7–25. Albany: State University of New York Press.

Carr, David M. 1996. *Reading the Fractures of Genesis: Historical and Literary Approaches*. Louisville, KY: Westminster John Knox.

Carr, David M. 2005. *Writing on the Tablet of the Heart: Origins of Scripture and Literature*. Oxford University Press.

Carr, David M. 2014. *Holy Resilience: The Bible's Traumatic Origins*. New Haven, CT: Yale University Press.

Chan, Michael J. 2013. "Joseph and Jehoiachin: On the Edge of Exodus." *Zeitschrift für die alttestamentliche Wissenschaft* 125: 566–577.

Conway, Colleen M. 2003. "'Behold the Man!' Masculine Christology and the Fourth Gospel." In *New Testament Masculinities*, edited by Stephen D. Moore and Janice Capel Anderson, 163–180. Semeia Studies 45. Atlanta, GA: Society of Biblical Literature.

Crites, Stephen. 1997. "The Narrative Quality of Experience." In *Memory, Identity, Community: The Idea of Narrative in the Human Sciences*, edited by Lewis P. Hinchman and Sandra K. Hinchman, 26–50. Albany: State University of New York Press.

Crossley, Michele L. 2000. "Contemporary Ways of Making Meaning." In *Introducing Narrative Psychology: Self, Trauma, and the Construction of Meaning*, 159–178. Buckingham, UK, and Philadelphia: Open University Press.

Currie, Mark. (1998) 2011. *Postmodern Narrative Theory*. Transitions. New York: Palgrave Macmillan.

Damasio, Antonio. 1994. *DesCartes' Error: Emotion, Reason, and the Human Brain*. New York: G. P. Putnam's Sons.

D'Angelo, Mary Rose. 1990. "Women in Luke-Acts: A Redactional View." *Journal of Biblical Literature* 109(3): 441–461.

Davies, Philip R. 1998. *Scribes and Schools: The Canonization of the Hebrew Scriptures*. Louisville, KY: Westminster John Knox.

Davies, Philip R., and Thomas Römer, eds. 2013. *Writing the Bible: Scribes, Scribalism and Script*. Durham, NC: Acumen Publishing.

Davies, Philip R. 2013. "The Dissemination of Written Texts." In *Writing the Bible: Scribes, Scribalism and Script*, edited by Philip R. Davies and Thomas Römer, 35–46. Durham, NC: Acumen Publishing.

de Certeau, Michel. 1984. *The Practice of Everyday Life*. Translated by Steven F. Rendall. Berkeley and Los Angeles: University of California Press.

Eskenazi, Tamara Cohn, and Tikva Frymer-Kensky. 2011. *The JPS Bible Commentary: Ruth*. Philadelphia: Jewish Publication Society.

Fewell, Danna Nolan. 1996. "Imagination, Method, and Murder: Un/Framing the Face of Post-Exilic Israel." In *Reading Bibles, Writing Bodies: God, Identity, and the Book*, edited by Timothy K. Beal and David M. Gunn, 132–152. London and New York: Routledge.

Fewell, Danna Nolan. 2003. "Hannah's Song." In *The Children of Israel: Reading the Bible for the Sake of Our Children*, 197–223. Nashville, TN: Abingdon.

Fewell, Danna Nolan. 2010. "A Broken Hallelujah: Remembering David, Justice, and the Cost of the House." In *The Fate of King David: The Past and Present of a Biblical Icon*, edited by Timothy K. Beal, Claudia Camp, and Tod Linafelt, 111–133. Library of Hebrew Bible/Old Testament Studies 500. New York: T&T Clark/Continuum.

Fewell, Danna Nolan. Forthcoming. "The Ones Returning: Ruth, Naomi, and Social Negotiation in the Post-Exilic Period." In *Women and Exile: Conceptualizations of Gender during the Exilic Period*, edited by Katherine Southwood and Martien Halvorson-Taylor. London: T&T Clark.

Fewell, Danna Nolan, and David M. Gunn. 1993. *Gender, Power, and Promise: The Subject of the Bible's First Story*. Nashville, TN: Abingdon.

Fewell, Danna Nolan, and Gary A. Phillips. 2009. "From Bak to the Bible: Imagination, Interpretation, and *Tikkun Olam*." *ARTS* 21(1): 21–30.

Fludernik, Monica. 1996. *Towards a 'Natural' Narratology*. London and New York: Routledge.

Fludernik, Monica. 2007. "Identity/Alterity." In *The Cambridge Companion to Narrative*, edited by David Herman, 260–273. Cambridge, MA: Cambridge University Press.

Frank, Arthur W. (1995) 2013. *The Wounded Storyteller: Body, Illness, and Ethics*. 2nd ed. Chicago and London: University of Chicago Press.

Frank, Arthur W. 2010. *Letting Stories Breathe: A Socio-Narratology*. Chicago and London: University of Chicago Press.

Fuller, Christopher C. 2007. "Matthew's Genealogy as Eschatological Satire: Bakhtin Meets Form Criticism." In *Bakhtin and Genre Theory in Biblical Studies*, edited by Roland Boer, 119–132. Semeia Studies 63. Atlanta, GA: Society of Biblical Literature.

Garber, David. 2013. "Trauma Studies." In *Oxford Encyclopedia of Biblical Interpretation*, vol. 2, edited by Steven McKenzie, 421–428. New York: Oxford University Press.

Garro, Linda C. 2003. "Narrating Troubling Experiences." *Transcultural Psychiatry* 40(1): 5–43.

Gottschall, Jonathan. 2012. *The Storytelling Animal: How Stories Make Us Human*. Boston: Houghton Mifflin Harcourt.

Granowski, Jan Jaynes. 1992. "Jehoiachin at the King's Table: A Reading of the Ending of the Second Book of Kings." In *Reading Between Texts: Intertextuality and the Hebrew Bible*, edited by Danna Nolan Fewell, 173–188. Literary Currents in Biblical Interpretation. Louisville, KY: Westminster John Knox.

Green, Barbara. 2000. *Mikhail Bakhtin and Biblical Scholarship: An Introduction.* Semeia Studies 38. Atlanta, GA: Society of Biblical Literature.

Harvey, John E. 2010. "Jehoiachin and Joseph: Hope at the Close of the Deuteronomistic History." In *The Bible as a Human Witness to Divine Revelation: Hearing the Word of God through Historically Dissimilar Traditions*, edited by Randall Heskett and Brian Irwin, 51–61. Library of Hebrew Bible/Old Testament Studies 469. London: T&T Clark.

Herman, David. 2003. "Stories as a Tool for Thinking." In *Narrative Theory and the Cognitive Sciences*, edited by David Herman, 163–192. Stanford, CA: CSLI Publications.

Horsley, Richard. A. 2013. *Text and Tradition in Performance and Writing.* Eugene, OR: Cascade Books.

Hutchins, Edwin. 1995. *Cognition in the Wild.* Cambridge, MA: MIT Press.

Jackson, Michael. 1989. *Paths toward a Clearing: Radical Empiricism and Ethnographic Inquiry.* Bloomington: University of Indiana Press.

Jackson, Michael. 2002. *The Politics of Storytelling: Violence, Transgression and Intersubjectivity.* Copenhagen: Museum Tusculaum Press.

Janoff-Bulman, Ronnie. 1992. *Shattered Assumptions: Towards a New Psychology of Trauma.* New York and Toronto: Free Press/MacMillan.

Janzen, David. 2012. *The Violent Gift: Trauma's Subversion of the Deuteronomistic History's Narrative.* The Library of Hebrew Bible/Old Testament Studies. New York: T&T Clark.

Jobling, David. 1998. *1 Samuel.* Berit Olam. Collegeville, MN: Liturgical Press.

Kelso, Julie. 2007. *O Mother, Where Art Thou? An Irigarayan Reading of the Book of Chronicles.* London: Equinox.

Kermode, Frank. 1981. "Secrecy and Narrative Sequence." In *On Narrative*, edited by W. J. T. Mitchell, 83–101. Chicago: University of Chicago Press. Originally published in *Critical Inquiry* 7(1) in 1980.

King, Thomas. 2005. *The Truth about Stories: A Native Narrative.* Minneapolis: University of Minnesota Press.

Koosed, Jennifer L. 2012. "The Chronicler Buries Saul." In *Focusing Biblical Studies: The Crucial Nature of the Persian and Hellenistic Periods: Essays in Honor of Douglas A. Knight*, edited by Alice Hunt and Jon Berquist, 202–215. London and New York: Continuum.

Levinas, Emmanuel. 1989. "Revelation in Jewish Tradition." In *Beyond the Verse: Talmudic Readings and Lectures*, translated by Gary D. Mole, 129–150. Bloomington: Indiana University.

Lindemann Nelson, Hilde. 2001. *Damaged Identities, Narrative Repair.* Ithaca, NY: Cornell University Press.

Margolin, Uri. 1999. "Of What Is Past, Is Passing, or to Come: Temporality, Aspectuality, Modality, and the Nature of Literary Narrative." In *Narratologies: New Perspectives on Narrative Analysis*, edited by David Herman, 142–166. Columbus: Ohio State University Press.

Matthews, Shelly. 2013. *The Acts of the Apostles: Taming the Tongues of Fire.* Sheffield, Yorkshire: Phoenix.

McNally, Richard J. 2003. *Remembering Trauma.* Cambridge, MA: Harvard University Press.

Meuter, Norbert. 2011. "Narration in Various Disciplines." In *The Living Handbook of Narratology*, edited by Peter Hühn et al. and translated by Nina Stedman. Interdisciplinary Center for Narratology. University of Hamburg. http://wikis.sub.uni-hamburg.de/lhn/index.php/Narration_in_Various_Disciplines.

Morson, Gary Saul. 1994. *Narrative and Freedom: The Shadows of Time*. New Haven, CT: Yale University Press.

Niditch, Susan. 1996. *Oral World and Written Word: Ancient Israelite Literature*. Library of Ancient Israel. Louisville, KY: Westminster John Knox.

Ochs, Elinor, and Capps, Lisa. 2001. *Living Narrative: Creating Lives in Everyday Storytelling*. Cambridge, MA: Harvard University Press.

Paul, Anne Murphy. 2012. "Your Brain on Fiction." Sunday Review. *New York Times*, March 17.

Phillips, Gary A. 1992. "'What Is Written and How Do You Read?' The Gospel, Intertextuality, and Doing Lukewise." In *Society of Biblical Literature Seminar Papers*, edited by Gene Lovering, 266–301. Atlanta, GA: Scholars Press.

Phillips, Gary A. 1999. "The Killing Fields of Matthew's Gospel." In *The Labour of Reading: Desire, Alienation, and Biblical Interpretation*, edited by Fiona C. Black, Roland T. Boer, and Erin Runions, 249–266. Semeia Studies 36. Atlanta, GA: Society of Biblical Literature.

Phillips, Gary A., and Danna Nolan Fewell. 1997. "Ethics, Bible, Reading as If." In *Bible and Ethics of Reading*, edited by Danna Nolan Fewell and Gary A. Phillips. *Semeia* 77: 1–21.

Polkinghorne, D. E. 1988. *Narrative Knowing and the Human Sciences*. SUNY Series in the Philosophy of the Social Sciences. Albany: State University of New York Press.

Polletta, Francesca. 2006. *It Was like a Fever: Storytelling and Protest in Politics*. Chicago: University of Chicago Press.

Polzin, Robert. 1993. *David and the Deuteronomist: 2 Samuel*. Indiana Studies in Biblical Literature. Bloomington: University of Indiana Press.

Ramachandran, V. S. 2011. *The Tell-Tale Brain: A Neuroscientist's Quest for What Makes Us Human*. New York: W. W. Norton.

Reid, Barbara E. 1996. *Choosing the Better Part? Women in the Gospel of Luke*. Collegeville, MN: Liturgical Press.

Ricoeur, Paul. 1984. *Time and Narrative*. Vol. 2. Translated by Kathleen McLaughlin and David Pellauer. Chicago and London: University of Chicago Press.

Rizolatti, Giacomo, and Corrado Sinigaglia. 2008. *Mirrors in the Brain: How Our Minds Share Actions, Emotions, and Experiences*. Translated by Francis Anderson. Oxford: Oxford University Press.

Sartre, Jean-Paul. 1964. *The Words*. New York: Braziller.

Schaberg, Jane. 1992. "Luke." In *Women's Bible Commentary*, edited by Carol A. Newsom and Sharon H. Ringe, 275–292. Louisville, KY: Westminster John Knox.

Schipper, Jeremy. 2005. "Significant Resonances" with Mephibosheth in 2 Kings 25:27–30: A Response to Donald F. Murray." *Journal of Biblical Literature* 124: 521–529.

Schüssler Fiorenza, Elisabeth. 1983. *In Memory of Her: A Feminist Theological Reconstruction of Christian Origins*. New York: Crossroad.

Scott, James C. 1990. *Domination and the Arts of Resistance: Hidden Transcripts*. New Haven, CT: Yale University Press.

Shore, Brad. 1996. *Culture in Mind: Cognition, Culture, and the Problem of Meaning*. New York: Oxford University Press.

Terr, Lenore. 1990. *Too Scared to Cry: How Trauma Affects Children and Ultimately Us All*. New York: Basic Books.

Turner, Mark. 2003. "Double Scope Stories." In *Narrative Theory and the Cognitive Sciences*, edited by David Herman, 117–142. Stanford, CA: CSLI Publications.

van der Kolk, Bessel A., and Onno van der Hart. 1995. "The Intrusive Past: The Flexibility of Memory and the Engraving of Trauma." In *Trauma: Explorations in Memory*, edited by Cathy Caruth, 158–182. Baltimore: Johns Hopkins University Press.

Wiesel, Elie. 1982. *The Gates of the Forest*. Translated by Frances Frenaye. New York: Schocken Books. First published 1964 as *Les Portes de la Forêt*. Editions du Seuil. First English edition 1966. Holt: Rinehart and Winston.

Williams, David. 2012. *The Trickster Brain: Neuroscience, Evolution, and Narrative*. New York and London: Lexington Books.

CHAPTER 2

....

BIBLICAL NARRATIVE ANALYSIS FROM THE NEW CRITICISM TO THE NEW NARRATOLOGY

....

STEPHEN D. MOORE

WHAT is "narrative"? At its most basic, something so basic as to beggar definition—which, of course, has not prevented numerous narrative theorists from venturing definitions of it. James Phelan, for example, has proposed, perhaps too narrowly, that narrative is "the telling of a story by someone to someone on some occasion for some purpose" (1996, 8), while Mieke Bal has proposed, more abstractly, that narrative is "a series of logically and chronologically related events that are caused or experienced by actors" (Bal 1985, 5), and Gerald Prince has proposed, more bafflingly, that "for an entity to constitute a narrative, it must be analyzable as the representation of one (or more than one nonrandomly connected and noncontradictory) transformation of a state of affairs, one (or more than one) event of which does not logically presuppose that state and/or does not logically entails its transformation" (2005, 373).

Less formidable but nonetheless significant problems attend the definition of "biblical narrative." How far does "biblical narrative" extend? Does it respect the tidy borders implicit in the stock phrase, "the narrative books of the Bible"? That it does not is suggested by the fact that biblical narrative analysts have followed narrative's trail into books that are conventionally differentiated from the "narrative books," such as the Psalms (Wallace 2007, 2011) or the Pauline letters (Petersen 1985; Witherington 1994; Longenecker 2002). Narrative seeps and trickles throughout the entire Bible.

Still further problems of delimitation attend the expression "biblical narrative analysis." Assumedly, not every analysis of a biblical narrative—of whatever methodological stripe— qualifies as biblical narrative analysis. What does qualify, in the minds of most, is analysis that is attuned to plot, characterization, and other constitutive features of narrative—in a word (or two), *narrative criticism* (recent examples include Amit 2001; Merenlahti 2002; Rhoads 2004; Freedman 2005; Resseguie 2005, 2009; Roncace 2005; Vette 2005; Seybold

2006; Thatcher and Moore 2008; Yamada 2008; Andersson 2009; Malbon 2009a, 2009b; Walsh 2009; Farelly 2010; Elliott 2011; Iverson and Skinner 2011; Skinner 2012; Yamasaki 2012; Joseph 2012; Bennema 2014; and Paris 2014). As a term, narrative criticism's first conspicuous appearance was in a 1982 article by David Rhoads that limned a new literary methodology for analyzing the Gospel of Mark, one that had coalesced in the Markan Seminar of the Society of Biblical Literature during the 1970s. Analogous work was being done on Hebrew Bible narrative by then, as we shall see. Through the 1980s, however, the term *narrative criticism* connoted literary analysis of New Testament narrative, preeminently the gospels and Acts. Mark Allan Powell's *What Is Narrative Criticism?* from 1990 dealt only with this New Testament work. That same year, however, David Gunn affixed the title "Narrative Criticism" to an essay dealing almost exclusively with literary analysis of Hebrew Bible narrative. The term *narrative criticism* will denote a bi-testamental methodology in the remainder of the present chapter.

THE STORY OF NARRATIVE CRITICISM: FIRST TELLING

Around 1980, a quiet but decisive revolution in the analysis of biblical narrative that had been simmering for several years was coming to the boil. Robert Alter's *The Art of Biblical Narrative* (1981) would be its most influential product (more on which below). Alter's book had been preceded by the Hebrew version (1979) of Shimon Bar-Efrat's *Narrative Art in the Bible,* which would not appear in English for another decade (Bar-Efrat 1989). The main English-language precursor to Alter's book was *Narrative Art in Genesis* (1975) by the Dutch narrative critic J. P. Fokkelman. The first volume of Fokkelman's *Narrative Art and Poetry in the Books of Samuel* appeared in 1981 (see also Fokkelman 1986, 1992, 1993), and was succeeded by Adele Berlin's *Poetics and the Interpretation of Biblical Narrative* (1983), Peter Miscall's *The Workings of Old Testament Narrative* (1983), and Meir Sternberg's *The Poetics of Biblical Narrative* (1985). Meanwhile, the two most influential New Testament products of the narrative turn made their appearance, David Rhoads and Donald Michie's *Mark as Story* (1982) and Alan Culpepper's *Anatomy of the Fourth Gospel* (1983). Their most notable precursor was Norman Petersen's *Literary Criticism for New Testament Critics* (1978), and their successors included Jack Dean Kingsbury's *Matthew as Story* (1986) and the first volume of Robert Tannehill's *The Narrative Unity of Luke-Acts* (1986; see also Tannehill 1990).

Had this bi-testamental revolution had a slogan, it might have been this: biblical literature must be read *as* literature. But since most of the biblical literature being read literarily was narrative literature, the slogan instead might have been: biblical narrative literature must be read *as* narrative—that is, with due attention to plot, characters, and all the other constituent elements of narrative. "High" structuralism of the Lévi-Straussian variety was on the wane by 1980, but "low" structuralism in the form of structural narratology was not. Indeed, it was just cresting. Gérard Genette's elegant and elaborate theory of narrative had just been translated from French into English as *Narrative Discourse* (1980). Tzvetan Todorov's *Introduction to Poetics* (1981), also translated from French, appeared the same year as Alter's *The Art of Biblical Narrative.* Gerald Prince's *Narratology* (1982) was on the near horizon, and so were

Shlomith Rimmon-Kenan's narratological primer *Narrative Fiction* (1983); Franz Stanzel's *A Theory of Narrative* (1984), translated from the German; and Mieke Bal's *Narratology* (1985), translated from the Dutch. Most importantly, Seymour Chatman's *Story and Discourse* (1978) had already appeared. It was a skillful synthesis of French *narratologie* and Anglo-American narrative theory of the kind emblematized by Wayne Booth (see Booth 1961), and it would be a crucial enabling resource for New Testament narrative critics in particular, such as David Rhoads and Alan Culpepper.

As a term, *narrative criticism* originated within biblical studies. As a method, it typically appropriated narratology to analyze plot, characterization, point of view (or narrative perspective), narrative settings, temporal dynamics, and other stock features of biblical narrative, extending to the implied author, the narrator, and the implied reader (for brief introductions to narrative criticism, see Bowman 2007; Malbon 2008; and Tull 2013; for full-length introductions, see Powell 1990; Ska 1990; Tolmie 1999; Fokkelman 2000; and Resseguie 2005; and for a critical retrospective, see Anderson 2011). Narratology, for its part, was the theory (or, more accurately, competing theories) of narrative. With its roots in Russian formalism and French structuralism, it typically sought the underlying structures or general principles, enabling codes or conventions, or narrative "grammars" that served as the generative matrices for individual narratives (see further, Onega and Landa 1996; Prince 2003; Herman and Vervaeck 2005; Fludernik 2009; Schmid 2010). By now, narratology is more and other than it was, as we shall later see, and so, potentially, is biblical narrative criticism.

Case Study: A New New Critic

Narratology loomed so large in so many of the seminal works of narrative criticism that it was easy to lose sight of another presence looming equally large at the narrative critic's other elbow, a presence less likely to set academic pulses racing by the 1980s and so more likely to go unmentioned or unnoticed. This was the (once) New Criticism, a school of Anglo-American literary criticism that coalesced around 1940 (see Ransom 1941), gradually becoming so synonymous with US literary criticism in particular that it not only dominated published academic discourse on literature through the 1960s and into the 1970s, but was also formative for college and even high school curricula. What was new about New Criticism was its reconception of the literary work and the scholarly task. It reimagined the literary work as an autonomous, internally unified organism with an intrinsic meaning indissociable from the formal features of the work, while it reinvented the scholarly task as a method of "close reading" designed to elucidate the intricacies of the work's formal structure (see Davis 2008, an anthology of classic New Critical writings). The New Criticism did not emerge in a vacuum. Such notions as the autonomy and self-referentiality of the literary work of art, its untranslatable or unparaphrasable character, and the harmonious coherence of its parts as exquisitely balanced elements of an integrated whole had their roots in nineteenth-century German romanticism. Romantic aesthetics infiltrated academic literary theory in the twentieth century, reemerging as Russian formalism and, most notably, as Anglo-American New Criticism (see Brooks 1981, xxv–xxvi).

The quiet narrative-critical revolution gathering steam in biblical studies around 1980 was, to an extent seldom recognized at the time (for a notable exception, see Sternberg 1985, 7–8), a restaging of the New Critical revolution that had occurred in literary studies forty years earlier. New Critics and narrative critics were both rebelling against analogous modes of traditional scholarship. As the introduction to *Rereading the New Criticism* succinctly phrases it, the New Critics "saw themselves as counterposed against the 'historians,' . . . those in literary studies devoted primarily to historical scholarly research" (Hickman 2012, 7). Or as René Wellek and Austin Warren put it in their *Theory of Literature*, an enormously influential textbook responsible for the dissemination of New Critical ideas in the 1950s and 1960s:

> The natural and sensible starting-point for work in literary scholarship is the interpretation and analysis of the works of literature themselves . . . . But, curiously enough, literary history has been so preoccupied with the setting of a work of literature that its attempts at an analysis of the works themselves have been slight in comparison with the enormous efforts expended on the study of environment. (Wellek and Warren 1948, 139)

Distant echoes of New Critical protests such as these began to resound in biblical studies during the 1970s and early 1980s. They often had recourse to the trope of "excavation" to name the perceived deficiency in historical criticism that narrative criticism was designed to remedy. Robert Alter (1981), for example, alleges that the thrust of almost all biblical scholarship has been "excavative," undertaken, if not literally "with the archeologist's spade," then "with a variety of analytic tools" designed to unearth "the original meanings of biblical words, the life situations in which specific texts were used, the sundry sources from which longer texts were assembled" (13). Independently of Alter, Alan Culpepper (1983) begins his narrative-critical analysis of the Fourth Gospel by describing the text model traditionally used in Johannine studies as "a 'tell' in which archaeologists can unearth strata which derive from different historical periods" (3).

Having reflected elsewhere on Culpepper's *Anatomy of the Fourth Gospel* (Moore 1989, 45–55, 93–95; 1996, 50–62, 70; 2008) and Rhoads and Michie's *Mark as Story* (Moore 1989, 41–43; cf. 7–13; 2011), I will reflect here on Alter's *The Art of Biblical Narrative*. No work better illustrates the claims I have been making for the underremarked influence of the New Critical legacy on seminal narrative criticism. But there are, of course, other reasons for lingering on *The Art of Biblical Narrative*. Quite simply, it is the most widely celebrated example of biblical narrative analysis. It is best known for its skillful analyses of type-scenes, dialogue, repetition, and characterization in biblical narrative. But its full range is considerably broader. Alter offers the following précis of "the major techniques of biblical narrative" that he considers in his book:

> [T]he deployment of thematic key-words; the reiteration of motifs; the subtle definition of character, relations, and motives mainly through dialogue; the exploitation, especially in dialogue, of verbatim repetition with minute but significant changes introduced; the narrator's discriminating shifts from strategic and suggestive withholding of comment to the occasional flaunting of an omniscient overview; the use at points of a montage of sources to catch the multifaceted nature of the fictional subject. (Alter 1981, 176)

Interest in such matters is apparently widespread both within and beyond the biblical studies guild. A 2007 article on Alter's book cited its current sales figures as "an estimated 70,000 copies . . . an astounding number for an academic book." Toss in the number of favorable reviews it has received and the frequency with which it is cited, and "it is hard to imagine a more successful academic book" (Weitzman 2007, 196). In taking the measure of *The Art of*

Biblical Narrative, then, we will also be taking the measure of the particular brand of literary criticism that has exercised the broadest appeal in biblical studies.

For Alter (1981), most scholarly analysis of biblical literature has amounted to "nothing at all that any literary person would recognize as literary inquiry" (14). What kind of "literary person" are we to imagine here? Not biblical literary critics for the most part. Alter finds that literary criticism for most biblical scholars who have attempted to master it "remains . . . a foreign language laboriously learned"—not surprising, he acidly remarks, "after all those seminars in graduate school on Sumerian law and Ugaritic cult terms" (15). Alter himself speaks the language fluently, having internalized it as a student. An article in *The Jewish Daily Forward*, based on an interview with Alter, recounts that as an undergraduate at Columbia and subsequently as a graduate student at Harvard, "[he] studied under some of the most eminent literary critics of the day, including Lionel Trilling, F. W. Dupee and Reuben Brower," many of whom "were disciples of the New Criticism" (Weiss 2011). In the preface to the second edition of *The Art of Biblical Poetry*, the companion volume to *The Art of Biblical Narrative*, Alter himself lists "several elements in [his] own literary formation," the first of which was "[his] reading of the American New Critics as an undergraduate" (Alter [1985] 2011b, ix).

Alter's fundamental assumption about literature, including biblical literature, as reflected in *The Art of Biblical Narrative*, is indelibly formalist in the New Critical mode: literary form and literary meaning are an indissoluble unity, which means that literary meaning may be reliably established only through close attention to literary form. *The Art of Biblical Narrative* is studded with statements that channel New Critical values; for example, "it still seems to most scholars in the field much more urgent to inquire, say, how a particular psalm might have been used in a hypothetically reconstructed temple ritual than how it works *as an achieved piece of poetry*" (1981, 17; emphasis added). Also implicitly New Critical is Alter's critique of the celebrated first chapter of Erich Auerbach's *Mimesis* ([1946] 1953) contrasting the representational techniques of Genesis and the Odyssey: "Auerbach must be credited with showing more clearly than anyone before him how the cryptic conciseness of biblical narrative is a reflection of profound art, not primitiveness, but his insight is the result of *penetrating critical intuition unsupported by any real method* for dealing with the specific characteristics of biblical literary forms" (1981, 17; emphasis added). New Criticism constituted itself over against literary history, but it also constituted itself over against "literary appreciation," seen as an intuitive exercise that was insufficiently methodological. John Crowe Ransom, in his 1937 article, "Criticism, Inc.," which soon came to be seen as a New Critical manifesto, speaks disparagingly of literary appreciation, as "seem[ing] to stand for the kind of understanding that is had intuitively." Ransom contrasts "appreciation, which is private, and criticism, which is public and negotiable." Consummately New Critical, too, is Alter's statement from his concluding chapter: "I have tried to avoid interposing my explications between the reader and the text because I consider it a betrayal of trust to leave him with *critical discourse in place of a text*" (1981, 179; emphasis added). The name famously bestowed on such betrayal by the arch New Critic Cleanth Brooks was "the heresy of paraphrase" (1947, 192–214).

Nowhere in *The Art of Biblical Narrative* does Alter explicitly lay his New Critical cards on the table. But neither is Alter a doctrinaire New Critic. Specifically, he has not renounced "the intentional fallacy," the New Critical notion "that the design or intention of the author is neither available nor desirable as a standard for judging the success of a work of literary art" (Wimsatt and Beardsley 1946, 468). For Alter (1981), approximating the biblical authors' intentions is not only desirable but also attainable: "[W]e shall come much closer to the range of intended meanings—theological, psychological, moral, or whatever—of the biblical tale by understanding precisely how it is told" (179). Here Alter contrasts with David Robertson (1977, 2), who in *The Old Testament and the Literary Critic* (a book even more thoroughly suffused with New Critical values than *The Art of Biblical Narrative*) had urged students of "the Bible as literature" to set aside its "original context" and "original intentions." Had Alter renounced the quest for authorial intentions, however, his book would not, and could not, have been so warmly received by so many biblical scholars. Alter's own largely implicit orientation to the navigational star of authorial intentionality enables him to steer between the Scylla of structuralism, on the one hand, beginning to recede in his wake as he writes, and the Charybdis of poststructuralism, on the other hand, beginning to loom alarmingly on the immediate horizon. Moving our metaphors to dry land, we note that biblical literary criticism has, by and large and relative to the often radical options on offer from the extrabiblical field of literary studies, long been a moderate, middle-of-the-road enterprise (see Moore and Sherwood 2011, 107–115). Alter (1981, 178) presents his own project as a "more practical direction" taken between what he seems to see as two extremes: "the elaboration of formal systems of poetics," on the one hand, "that have only a hypothetical relation to any individual literary work" (read: structural narratology), and "virtuoso exercises of interpretation," on the other hand, "aimed . . . at undermining the very notion that the text might have any stable meanings" (read: deconstructive criticism).

The operative procedure of the deconstructive criticism beginning to take the US literary academy by storm as Alter was writing *The Art of Biblical Narrative* might be summed up in the following pronouncement of Paul de Man: "A deconstruction always has for its target to reveal the existence of hidden articulations and fragmentations within assumedly monadic totalities" (1979, 249). The fundamental axiom of Alter's (1981) narrative criticism, in contrast, is "that the [biblical narrative] text is an intricately interconnected unity" (11); or, as he phrases it later, the biblical narratives exhibit "a beautifully interwoven wholeness" (188). Alter finds this assumption of textual unity already present in the midrashic commentaries, from which, indeed, the "literary student of the Bible has more to learn" in certain respects "than from modern scholarship" with its assumption that the Bible "is a patchwork of frequently disparate documents" (11). "With their assumption of interconnectedness," claims Alter, "the makers of the Midrash were often as exquisitely attuned to small verbal signals of continuity and to significant lexical nuances as any 'close reader' of our own age" (11; see Berlin 1983, 17, for a parallel assertion). Yet even the midrashic commentators did not go far enough, Alter goes on to say, in recognizing the "literary integrity" of biblical literature (1981, 11). For that Alter doesn't say but implies, one needs to have recourse to one of the enabling assumptions of the inventors of literary "close reading," the New Critics—namely, that the successful literary work is an internally unified organism whose constituent parts combine to form an aesthetically harmonious whole. Even the "frequently composite nature" of the biblical text (19) does not impede Alter's view of it as an intricately interconnected unity. He manages to have his New Critical cake and eat it too, conceding that the narratives of the Torah, for example, are made up of antecedent sources, but dealing the trump card to the final redactor: "[E]ven if the text is really composite in origin, I think we have seen ample evidence of how brilliantly it has been woven into a complex artistic whole" (2).

The assumption that biblical narratives are artistically unified wholes is foundational, not just for Alter's *The Art of Biblical Narrative*, but also for Fokkelman's *Narrative Art in Genesis* and *Narrative Art and Poetry in the Books of Samuel*, Bar-Efrat's *Narrative Art in the Bible*, Rhoads and Michie's *Mark as Story*, Culpepper's *Anatomy of the Fourth Gospel*, Kingsbury's *Matthew as Story*, Tannehill's *The Narrative Unity of Luke-Acts*, and many other field-constituting works of biblical narrative criticism—so much so that narrative criticism was seen from its inception as an approach to biblical narratives that, above all, affirmed their literary unity in counterpoint to more traditional methods that focused on narrative disjunctions. So successful was narrative criticism, moreover, in terms of leavening the discipline, sensitizing thousands of scholars to such neglected staples of biblical narrative as plot, characters, implied author, implied reader—and narrative unity—that it came to function as a metonym for biblical literary criticism as such. Ironically, meanwhile, literary unity was the most beleaguered concept in extrabiblical literary studies due to the deconstructive deluge.

Not all seminal works of narrative criticism, however, wore their passion for unity on their sleeve. Berlin's *Poetics and the Interpretation of Biblical Narrative* is an interesting case in point. Unlike, say, Culpepper, Berlin does not lead off her narratological study with assertions about biblical narrative unity. But a deep concern for unity does eventually surface in Berlin's book. Essentially, her position matches that of Alter. She fully accepts that biblical narratives have complex prehistories and so have not "always existed in the form in which we now find [them]" (1983, 112). "What is the status of the present text[?]," she asks; "is it fundamentally a unity or is its unity artificial?" (117). She proceeds with caution, taking Genesis 37, the beginning of the Joseph story, as her case study, and eventually arrives at the following conclusion: "The poetic approach which I have applied to Gen 37 . . . points to the conclusion that the present text of those passages—and I speak here only of those passages—is a unified product, an integrated whole, not a composite of sources or layers of tradition" (128; cf. 81, 123–124). Berlin insisted at the outset of her investigation of Genesis 37 that "we must begin our reading without prior commitments to any theory. The text must speak for itself" (117). But what the text announces when it does speak is that it is an integrated literary whole, while Berlin had earlier described her method as "close textual reading, the basis for our poetics" (20)—all of which is to say that the ghost of New Criticism, with its romantic aesthetic of literary unity and its trademark method of close reading, haunts even *Poetics and the Interpretation of Biblical Narrative*, notwithstanding the fact that the book conjures up the ghost only once, and even then only to dismiss it (16; a reference to "the sin of New Criticism," that of "closing off the world of the text from the real world"). Among seminal works of narrative criticism, Sternberg's *The Poetics of Biblical Narrative* is the rule-proving exception that least affirms the literary unity of biblical narratives, although even Sternberg, having listed five of "the most basic assumptions shared by 'literary critics of the Bible,'" adds that he himself does not share any of them, "with the possible exception of the second"— which happens to be the tenet that "[t]he literary critic assumes unity in the text" (1985, 6–7).

Alter (1981, x, 15, 178) holds narratology at arm's length, while Berlin, Sternberg, and other seminal narrative critics embrace it. (Indeed, Sternberg more than embraced extrabiblical narratology; he helped shape the field. See Sternberg 1978; Sternberg and Perry 1986.) To begin to reflect on what Berlin, Culpepper, and company are doing with narratology, however, is to see the gap between them and Alter close. Narratology is about theory, while narrative criticism is about interpretation. Narratologists engage individual narratives to develop general narrative theories; while narrative critics appropriate those theories to explicate individual narratives.

Second, even when narratologists do treat individual narratives, their modes of engagement typically differ from those of narrative critics. Rather than engaging in sustained readings of individual narratives, narratologists read and run, multiplying brief examples culled from a nearly infinite spectrum of possible examples to illustrate specific narrative features (the embedded narrative, the unreliable narrator, the narrative focalizor, and so on). To put it another way, narrative critics engage in "close reading"; narratologists do not. (Or did not, at any rate. The narratology I have been generalizing about here, the kind available to the early narrative critics, has since undergone a metamorphosis, more on which later.) The term "close reading" is again significant; it is a practice of literary analysis indissociable from narrative criticism, whether as practiced by a narratology-wary Alter or a narratology-friendly Berlin. Yet close reading comes to narrative criticism from elsewhere than narratology. It comes to it from New Criticism, as a generally unacknowledged visitor, dragging much baggage in its wake.

Third, narrative critics are almost all much preoccupied with the assumed literary unity of the narratives they treat, as we have seen (for a notable exception, see Richter 2005; further exceptions will be considered later in the chapter), but narratologists are not. Typically, narratologists are concerned not with the unity of the individual narratives they are discussing but only with the unity of the narrative theories they are advancing. The preoccupation with literary unity, then, so characteristic of narrative criticism, also comes to it from elsewhere—the same elsewhere from which the method of close reading comes—again, the New Criticism, or, more precisely, its immensely diffuse and enormously influential legacy.

The Story of Narrative Criticism: Second Telling

What was narrative criticism, precisely, in its formative period? To understand what it was we must first understand what it was not. It was not the first encounter between narrative theory and biblical narrative. That inaugural encounter had occurred within French structuralism, and had been staged, moreover, by one of the leading structuralists. In 1969, Roland Barthes (1988a) produced a paper titled "The Structural Analysis of Narrative: Apropos of Acts 10–11" in response to an invitation from the French Catholic Association for the Study of the Bible. Emboldened by the experiment, Barthes (1988b) published a second structuralist analysis of a biblical text in 1972, "Wrestling with the Angel: Textual Analysis of Genesis 32:23–33," which, more even than the Acts essay, shows Barthes seesawing giddily between structuralism and what would later be termed poststructuralism as he "seeks to say, no longer where the text *comes from* (historical criticism), nor even *how* it is made (structural analysis), but how it is unmade, how it explodes, disseminates: according to what coded avenues it *goes*" (247). Other French structuralists were also grappling with biblical narrative (see the exegetical essays assembled in Johnson 1976, all of which date from 1971), which lit a fire in Anglo-American biblical studies (as did "Genesis as Myth" [1962], a Lévi-Straussian analysis of Genesis 1–4 by British anthropologist Edmund Leach).

Structuralism flashed brightly in biblical studies in the 1970s and early 1980s (see also Marin 1971; Calloud 1973; Via 1975; Patte 1976; Groupe d'Entrevernes 1977; Patte and Patte 1978; Polzin 1977; Jobling 1978) and quickly burned out, at least in North America. Yet structuralism's significance was considerable. Consider the fact that the first three biblical studies journals founded as forums for methodologies other than the historical-critical—*Linguistica Biblica* in Germany in 1970, *Semeia* in the United States in 1974, and *Sémiotique et Bible* in France in 1975—were devoted either principally or exclusively to biblical structuralism and its closest kin (semiotics, narratology, generative poetics, sociolinguistics, and the like). "High" structuralism, however, of, say, the Lévi-Straussian or Greimasian variety (for a survey of such work, see Bible and Culture Collective 1995, 76–83), floated free of the anchoring ballast of historical criticism—concern with original contexts of production, source and redaction, authorial intention—to a dizzying degree that has never been equaled since by any other methodology in biblical studies (even deconstruction), which is why structuralism soon drifted out of sight and out of mind for the majority of biblical scholars.

How did narrative criticism fit into the picture? Precisely as the mediating term between structuralism and historical criticism. Narrative criticism, particularly of the kind espoused by Bar-Efrat, Berlin, or Sternberg, on the one hand, or Rhoads/Michie, Culpepper, or Tannehill, on the other, had roots in structural narratology; but it also had roots in historical criticism to the extent that the narrative "artistry" with which narrative critics were centrally concerned implicitly evoked an "artist": an individual author (even if only a final redactor) who oversaw the interactions of the characters in the plot and all the other narrative elements, skillfully orchestrating them into a harmonious whole. Implicitly, the narrative critic was as committed to the quest for plausible authorial intentionality as any traditional interpreter of the Deuteronomistic History or the Lukan *Doppelwerk*. Implicitly too, therefore, the narrative critic's biblical author was as deeply rooted in the ancient historical context as that of any traditional biblical scholar, even if the narrative critic preferred to pull the blinds on that context much of the time. All of this was a far cry from Barthes's high-structuralist, anti-intentionalist announcement: "We know now that a text is not a line of words releasing a single 'theological' meaning (the 'message' of the Author-God), but a multidimensional space in which a variety of writings, none of them original, blend and clash" ([1968] 1977, 146). Barthes's "we" is a hyperstructuralist "we," those who "know" in the heady "now" of 1960s structuralist antihumanism that the literary text issues not from the genius or artistry of an individual author but from the impersonal and transpersonal systems of intelligibility that make the author, no less than the text, possible in the first place.

Narrative criticism, then, was structuralism adapted and assimilated to the field of biblical studies—hence, no longer structuralist. Such adaptation and assimilation had propelled narrative criticism fully into the mainstream of the discipline by the mid-1990s, at least in the Anglophone world (Joachim Vette 2010, 58n176, tells of resistance to narrative criticism in German biblical scholarship even "up to the present"), and most conspicuously in gospel studies. In 1997, for instance, another massive commentary on Luke made its appearance, authored by an established scholar, but one whose name was hardly synonymous with New Testament literary criticism. Joel Green's 1,000-page commentary combined throughout "concerns with first-century culture in the Roman world with [an] understanding [of] the text of Luke as a wholistic, historical narrative," as its jacket blurb attested, and "focus[ed] primarily on how each episode functions within Luke's narrative development" (Green 1997)—as good an index as any of the mainstreaming of narrative criticism in gospel studies. John Donahue and Daniel Harrington (2002), for their part, included in the introduction to their basically historical-critical commentary on Mark sections titled "The Literary Artistry of Mark" and "Narrative Criticism and the Gospel of Mark." "This present commentary," they write, "embodies certain aspects of the literary turn by focusing on Mark as Mark, as we call attention to a close reading of the text" (22). Many other such examples could be cited, and not only from gospel studies. The first textbook introduction to the New Testament with a narrative-critical basis had already appeared in 1987, David Barr's *New Testament Story: An Introduction.*

Generally speaking, New Testament narrative criticism had a frozen, fixed-in-amber quality by the 1990s. The literary studies discipline that mainstream New Testament scholars tended to engage—those who did—was essentially the same discipline, or the same slice of it, that Rhoads, Culpepper, and company had served up in the early 1980s. Most of these schol-ars did not identify primarily as narrative critics; they had simply added narrative criticism to their methodological repertoire. Perusal of a dedicated narrative-critical introduction from 2005, however, is instructive. The chapter titles of James Resseguie's (2005) *Narrative Criticism of the New Testament* (see also Resseguie 1998, 2001, 2009) are almost identical to those of Rhoads and Michie's *Mark as Story*—for example, "Rhetoric," "Setting," "Character," "Point of View," "Plot"—and the cast of narrative theorists conscripted to flesh out these top-ics are also largely identical to those who frequent the pages of *Mark as Story, Anatomy of the Fourth Gospel*, and other narrative-critical works of 1980s vintage.

But there were also attempts to break the formalist mold in which New Testament narra-tive criticism was encased. Among the earliest were Janice Capel Anderson's and Elizabeth Struthers Malbon's feminist narrative-critical studies of Matthew (Anderson 1983) and Mark (Malbon 1983). Fusions of narrative criticism and reader-response criticism also served to loosen the hold of the formalist mold (notable examples included Fowler 1981, 1991; Staley 1988; Powell 2001). Eventually, David Rhoads would attempt to extend his own narrative-critical model to engage with the social world of Mark, with issues of gender, and with the ethics of reading (Rhoads 2004; see also Rhoads and Syreeni 1999; Merenlahti 2002). Stephen Moore, meanwhile, had attempted to limn the contours of a poststructuralist nar-rative criticism, using Michel Foucault's study of panoptic surveillance to defamiliarize the narratological concepts of authorial omniscience and omnipresence (Moore 1992, 129–144; cf. Moore 1989, 52–55, 66–68).

Far and away the most decisive breaking of the standard narrative-critical mold, how-ever, was accomplished by Richard Horsley (2001) in *Hearing the Whole Story: The Politics of Plot in Mark's Gospel.* Horsley takes issue with certain classic narrative-critical readings of Mark (Tannehill 1977; Rhoads, Dewey, and Michie 1999) for allegedly assimilating the gospel to a modern, individual, Western model of discipleship: they assume Mark's plot is a story of failed discipleship, and they implicitly present Mark as a handbook of discipleship for the individual contemporary Christian (see especially Horsley 2001, 81–82). "When Mark is reduced to a religious story for individual modern Western readers," writes Horsley, "Jesus' sustained public campaign of preaching and healing in remote village communities and his execution by the Romans as a rebel leader becomes a mere backdrop for the devout indi-vidual disciple's struggle between guilt and repentance, between doubt/denial and recom-mitment" (30). Mark, for Horsley, is "a submerged people's history" (27–51) whose intensely political plot concerns a peasant renewal movement pitted against the Roman imperial order and its local representatives in the first-century Jewish homeland. Much of Warren Carter's work has also represented a notable politicization of New Testament narrative criti-cism. Carter has also extended narrative-critical analysis of the gospels into empire-critical analysis (e.g., 2004; 2006; 2008, 144–175), and has also taken issue with individualistic modes of gospel interpretation (e.g., 2008, 4–7).

Sketches for a Postclassical Narrative Criticism

Exceptions notwithstanding, narrative criticism of the New Testament has been a relatively monolithic enterprise. By the 1990s, narrative criticism of the Hebrew Bible was a far less tidy affair. As early as 1983, Peter Miscall had accorded the deconstructive concept of textual undecidability a prominent role in his account of *The Workings of Old Testament Narrative.* David Gunn's and Danna Nolan Fewell's (1993) *Narrative in the Hebrew Bible* also challenged the formalist model of narrative criticism by toppling it over into reader-response criticism, or, better, reader-responsibility criticism. They argued that the reader's ineluctable role in the creation of textual meaning undermines the concept of a "correct" method of interpretation. But this does not mean that all biblical interpretations are now equally viable. Rather, the untenability of objective meaning thrusts ethics to the forefront of the interpretive task by removing the mask of scholarly disinterestedness. Biblical interpreters must take full responsibility for the consequences of their readings urge Gunn and Fewell, and they must ensure that they are reading to liberate and not to enslave.

An especially challenging model that was set before Hebrew Bible narrative criticism in the late 1980s, enticing it to stray from the formalist path, was the work of Mieke Bal. A Dutch narratologist, Bal was best known for her internationally acclaimed *Narratology: Introduction to the Theory of Narrative* ([1978] 1985; see also Bal 1977). When Bal began to turn her energies to the Hebrew Bible, then, one might well have expected a book as tidy as her *Narratology,* on the one hand, or the books of Bar-Efrat, Berlin, Rhoads/Michie, or Culpepper, on the other hand, the chapter and section titles of *Narratology* serenely dictating the chapter and section titles of Bal's biblical narratological experiment: "The Narrator," "Levels of Narration," "Characters," "Space," "Focalization," and so on. That did not happen. To begin with, there was not one biblical Bal book but four (1986; 1987; 1988a; 1988b), the second a thorough revision of the first. And there was nothing tidy or clinical about any of them. The first book, *Femmes imaginaires,* was subtitled *L'Ancien Testament au risque d'une narratologie critique* (Bal 1986), a justifiable threat, since the brand of narratology being deployed was not the formalist, would-be scientific kind but a narratology that Bal was busily reinventing as feminist critique and ideology critique more broadly. The final book of the four, *Death and Dissymmetry: The Politics of Coherence in the Book of Judges* (Bal 1988b), is a narratological analysis of a biblical text that problematizes the classic biblical narratological preoccupation with textual unity, or textual *coherence,* as Bal prefers to call it. Yet she does not take the view that coherence can be easily dispensed with, or even dispensed with at all:

> The major point I wish to make in this study is that coherence is a readerly act, rather than a textual feature, but that the impulse to project coherence on a semiotic object in unavoidable. It is therefore not relevant to denounce coherent readings, but to specify the *kind* of coherence projected, and to analyze the interests that motivate those choices. In this respect, coherence is structurally similar to the concept of ideology. (Bal 1988b, 254n2)

Against the coherence normally posited for Judges, one centered on military-political chronology and history-as-theology, Bal argues a "countercoherence" centered on the murders of three nameless young women: Jephthah's daughter (Judg. 11:29–40), Samson's wife (15:1–6), and the Levite's concubine (19:22–30). Bal's primary concerns are feminist, and her methods, too, are feminist but also deconstructive to the extent that they entail a thoroughgoing dismantling of the hierarchical binary opposition of "center" versus "margin." She writes, "What is seen to be central will be marginalized, and what has been treated as marginal will become central" (1988b, 2).

In the 1980s, the apparently firm ground on which structural narratologists had erected their theoretical edifices began to quake and crumble. The path between the 1977 first edition of Bal's *Narratologie* and her 1986–1988 biblical quadrilogy leads through the ruins of structural narratology (although Bal herself does not say so). Ten years later still, the term "postclassical narratology" was coined by David Herman (1997; see further Alber and Fludernik 2010b) to identify the emerging new narratology and distinguish it from "classical" narratology—the scientistic, systematic, taxonomic, neologistic brand of narratology quintessentially (and internationally) represented by Greimas's *Sémantique structurale* (1966); Barthes's "Introduction à l'analyse structurale des récits" (1966); Todorov's *Grammaire du Décaméron* (1969), in which the term "narratologie" was first coined and tellingly defined as "la science du récit" (10); Genette's "Discours du récit" (1972); Bremond's *Logique du récit* (1973); Bal's *Narratologie* (1977) and *De theorie van vertellen en verhalen* (1978); Chatman's *Story and Discourse* (1978); Stanzel's *Theorie des Erzählens* (1979); Prince's *Narratology* (1982); and Rimmon-Kenan's *Narrative Fiction* (1983).

Bal's *Femmes imaginaires* (1986) was one of the earliest attempts to disturb the classical model; but so was Susan Lanser's (1986) "Toward a Feminist Narratology", which appeared the same year (see also Lanser 1988, 1992, 2010a; Homans 1994; Mezei 1996; Page 2006; Warhol 2012; Sasani 2013). But many other disturbances of the classical model were underway. By 1990, sometime narratologist Christine Brooke-Rose was inquiring plaintively, "Whatever happened to narratology?" and answering, "It got swallowed into story" (1990, 283). A more obvious answer is that it got swallowed into poststructuralism, which swept through US literary studies in particular during the 1980s, thoroughly reconfiguring the landscape. Narratology was a child of structuralism, but now embarrassingly out of vogue was the classic structuralist project of turning literary criticism into a science by constructing ultimate explanatory models that would lift the lid off literature once and for all and reveal the hidden mechanisms that made it tick. Bal found it necessary to revise the first English edition of her *Narratology* twelve years after its publication. Her list of reasons begins: "First of all, I was more and more uneasy about the tone of it, . . . all those remnants of the positivistic discourse of my training that inhere in structuralist thought" (Bal 1997, xiii). But Bal was still more sanguine about the narratological project than many of her narratological peers. Shlomith Rimmon-Kenan, for instance, in the afterword to the 2002 reprint of her narratological handbook *Narrative Fiction*, poignantly recalls that the poststructuralist deluge induced in her "a period of near-paralysis, caused by the destabilization of [her] 'certain certainties'" as a structurally inclined narrative theorist (2002, 143).

Narratology, however, although beleaguered and often befuddled, did not give up the ghost. Haltingly and unevenly, it went forward to meet poststructuralism—and gender studies and cultural studies and all the other theoretical and critical forces that were reshaping literary studies in the 1980s and 1990s—and passed through them and emerged on the other side. "Postmodern narratology" was born (see Gibson 1996; Currie 1998; Herman and Vervaeck 2005, 108–117; Richardson 2012), a movement "from discovery to invention, from coherence to complexity, and from poetics to politics," as one of its proponents characterized it (Currie 1998, 2). But other new narratologies also emerged. The first thing, indeed, to be said about the new narratology is that it is not one: chameleon-like, it has adapted to whatever critical environment it has found itself in (on which see Herman 1999; Nünning 2003; Fludernik 2005). It has morphed into feminist narratology, as we saw, but also into cultural studies narratology (or, more simply, cultural narratology: e.g., Bal 1999; Nünning 2000, 2004, 2009; Xu 2007; Russel 2009; Aldama 2011), postcolonial narratology (e.g., Fludernik 1999; Gymnich 2002; Prince 2005; Goebel and Schabio 2013; cf. Bhabha 1990), and queer narratology (e.g., Roof 1996; Farwell 1996; Lanser 1995, 1999, 2010b; Lanser and Warhol 2015), as well as poststructuralist narratology (e.g., O'Neill 1994; Gibson 1996; Currie 1998) and cognitive narratology (e.g., Fludernik 2003; Stockwell 2002; Herman 2003, 2010; Jahn 2005; Hogan 2011; Dancygier 2012), the latter a rapidly proliferating subfield concerned with mind-related aspects of narrative, similar in part to reader-response or reception theory, but far broader in scope.

The renunciation of narrative theory in the structuralist mold that is common to many works of postclassical narratology has also caused "narratological criticism" to crystallize fully as an end in itself (as opposed to a means to even bigger and better narrative theories), so that it now assumes a place on the spectrum of current narratological enterprises (see Nünning 2003, 243). This has the effect of closing one gap between secular narratology and biblical narrative criticism: the latter has, from its inception, really only ever been interested in interpretation, as we saw earlier, theory only ever being a means to that end. A second gap has closed as well. Another feature of postclassical narratology is that it is marked by a rediscovery of historical and sociocultural context, having broken with the formalist analysis of "intrinsic" literary properties that characterized classical narratology (see Shen 2005)—but biblical narrative critics have always had to be attentive to historical and sociocultural context, their discipline never allowing them to forget it for very long.

Yet it is not, of course, a simple case of secular narratology now finally catching up with biblical narrative criticism. For, while secular narratology is at present closer to narrative criticism than ever before, it is also simultaneously farther away from narrative criticism than ever before. Whereas narratology has, indeed, been reshaped by the "rediscovery" of historical context that has marked literary studies in general during the past quarter century or so (hence narratology's current closeness to narrative criticism), it has also been reshaped by the "poststructuralization" that has marked literary studies even more profoundly during this same period (hence narratology's current distance from narrative criticism). As a rough measure of the distance between postclassical narratology, in certain of its manifestations, and narrative criticism, in most of its manifestations, consider the following from Patrick O'Neill's *Fictions of Discourse*, one of the earliest examples of poststructuralist narratology:

> Narrative communication . . . involves both intratextual communication (between character and character, narrator and narratee, implied author and implied reader) and extratextual communication (between the real author and the real reader). Except that, as poststructuralist textology makes clear, reality is itself merely a fiction, and for extratextual we must read intertextual, which in turn emerges as only another way of saying intratextual. (O'Neill 1994, 129).

Even literary-leaning biblical scholars have generally been oblivious to the seismic shifts in narratology we have been chronicling (although see Andersson 2009, 62–68; Anderson 2011). The first sustained engagement with postclassical narratology on the part of a biblical scholar, so far as I am aware, was Leif Hongisto's (2010) *Experiencing the Apocalypse at the Limits of Alterity*. Specifically, Hongisto draws on cognitive narratology, particularly as developed by Monika Fludernik and David Herman, but not so much to reread the text of the Apocalypse as to reread the experience of the reader or hearer of the text of the Apocalypse. It is the pre-conceptual, elusive immediacy of the text-reader encounter that Hongisto's cognitive narratological model is attempting to capture:

> [M]y work rests on the assumption that an experiential encounter with an imagistically absorbing (oral) narrative experience precedes an analysis and the search for a symbolic interpretation. I describe that moment as awareness of a narrative experience when the reader is still short of material for conceptualization. It is the mental state of that experiential encounter with a textual or oral artefact, preceding analysis, that is most overlooked in scholarship, and which I find worth examining. (Hongisto 2010, 23)

In effect, then, Hongisto is attempting to shift biblical reader-response criticism from its customary adherence to formalist modes of analysis—typically, mappings of the author-regulated movements of the reader-in-the-text—and to begin to come to grips with the complexity, contingency, and sheer messiness of "real reading." Whether or to what extent Hongisto's analysis of the experience of reading or hearing the Apocalypse measures up to his methodological ambitions is an intriguing question, but one that will have to await separate discussion.

The only other sustained engagement with postclassical narratology on the part of a biblical scholar of which I am aware is Scott Elliott's (2011) *Reconfiguring Mark's Jesus: Narrative Criticism after Poststructuralism*. Elliott has recourse to poststructuralist narratology to attempt a thorough overhauling of the concept of "character" ordinarily employed in New Testament narrative criticism. David Rhoads and Kari Syreeni's (1999) edited collection *Characterization in the Gospels* had attempted something similar, but Elliott goes much farther. At base, Elliott sees the prevailing concept of character in narrative criticism as an unproblematized reflection of the post-Cartesian Western concept of individual interiorized human subjectivity. Indeed, argues Elliott, this naturalized, reified, undeconstructed concept of self predetermines not only narrative-critical construals of literary characters in the gospels and other ancient narratives, but also construals of the historical persons assumed to underlie these characters, not least the historical Jesus. Reading Mark in tandem with two ancient novels, *Leucippe and Clitophon* and the *Life of Aesop*, Elliott attempts to reread their literary characters without recourse to such concepts as "unity" or "coherence" (for Elliott, the poststructuralist challenge to the unity and coherence of the narrative text must be extended to its component elements, including characters); "flat" versus "round" characters (a distinction ultimately derived from E. M. Forster [1927] and still a staple of much narrative criticism); the "interiority" or "inner life" of characters; and the separation of the narrative content (the "story") from the narrative means of expression (the "discourse"). For Elliott,

> characters are completely bounded by and subjected to the narrative plots that present them. They are "paper people" absolutely unable to overcome, outlive, or outpace the stories of which they are a part. While it often appears that characters are what readers identify with . . . on the basis of personality traits and feelings of intimacy, it is in fact the experience of plot itself that

provides the basis of identification . . . . Human beings identify with characters most . . . in the way that their lives and experiences are mediated through narratives—discourses that are never complete, subjectivities that are perpetually under construction. (Elliott 2011, 23)

If for classic poststructuralism, "there is nothing outside the text," for Elliott's narratological inflection of poststructuralism, there is nothing outside the narrative, and narrative critics are themselves constructed narratively even as they analyze those other narrative constructions that are literary characters.

Other instantiations of postclassical narrative criticism are, of course, imaginable, and cognitive and poststructuralist narratology are only two variants of postclassical narratology. Some of the common threads that weave the different postclassical narratologies together have already been noted. One further thread should also be mentioned. Earlier we listed feminist, cultural, postcolonial, and queer narratologies as subsets of postclassical narratology. Jan Alber and Monika Fludernik, introducing the collection *Postclassical Narratology*, note what is at stake in these localized and politicized narratologies—these "contextual narratologies," as they are often called (see Nünning 2009). They introduce "variable emphases into the classical model [of narratology], whose core had consisted of invariable, that is, universal, categories" (Alber and Fludernik 2010a, 3).

Implicit or explicit appeal to universal categories has also been a feature of classical biblical narrative criticism. Consider once again, for example, Alter's *The Art of Biblical Narrative*. Alter himself is critical of what we are calling classical narratology. He is wary of "the vogue of Structuralism" (1981, 15) and skeptical of "the value of elaborate taxonomies" and "bristling neologisms" (x). Alter's approach differs from that of the structural narratologists "in [his] sense that it is important to move from the analysis of formal structures to a deeper understanding of the values, the moral vision embodied in a particular kind of narrative" (x). What values and what moral vision are these? Timeless values and a humanist moral vision is the answer implicit in Alter's book. He states, for instance, that "[t]he biblical tale . . . leads us again and again to ponder complexities of motive and ambiguities of character because these are essential aspects of its vision of man, created by God, enjoying or suffering all the consequences of human freedom" (22) and that "[f]iction fundamentally serves the biblical writers as an instrument of fine insight into [the] abiding perplexities of man's creaturely condition" (176), and that "by learning to enjoy the biblical stories more fully as stories, we shall come also to see more clearly what they mean to tell us about God, man, and the perilously momentous realm of history" (189). Hence, for Alter, the Bible merits the same "kind of disciplined attention" that other great works of literature merit, "for example, the poetry of Dante, the plays of Shakespeare, the novels of Tolstoy" (13). In the preface to the 2011 revised edition of his book, Alter writes revealingly,

> Other Bible scholars, in the supposed interest of literary understanding, have sought to apply to the Bible one or another fashionable academic ideology—postcolonialism, gender studies, radical feminism, deconstruction. My own position remains what it was thirty years ago— that the best way to get a handle on the Bible's literary vehicle is to avoid imposing on it a grid external to it but instead to patiently attend to its minute workings and through such attention inferentially build a picture of its distinctive conventions and techniques. (2011a, x–xi; see also Alter 1996, especially 3–5)

Of course, the combined contribution of the "academic ideologies" that Alter names has been that of showing the universal human(ist) subject—the subject implicit in Alter's statements about "man's creaturely condition" quoted earlier—to be a patriarchal subject, a colonizing subject, and a culturally constructed subject. These academic ideologies, fashionable or not, need to be folded into biblical narrative criticism along the lines modeled by certain important variants of postclassical narratology. Only thus can the ghost of the New Criticism, rattling its nineteenth-century romanticist, über-humanist chains, finally be exorcised from biblical narrative analysis.

REFERENCES

Alber, Jan, and Monika Fludernik. 2010a. Introduction to Alber and Fludernik 2010b, 1–31.

Alber, Jan, and Monika Fludernik, eds. 2010b. *Postclassical Narratology: Approaches and Analyses*. Theory and Interpretation of Narrative Series. Columbus: Ohio State University Press.

Aldama, Frederick Luis, ed. 2011. *Analyzing World Fiction: New Horizons in Narrative Theory*. Cognitive Approaches to Literature and Culture Series. Austin: University of Texas Press.

Alter, Robert. 1981. *The Art of Biblical Narrative*. New York: Basic Books.

Alter, Robert. 1996. *The Pleasures of Reading in an Ideological Age*. 2nd ed. New York: W. W. Norton.

Alter, Robert. 2011a. *The Art of Biblical Narrative*. 2nd ed. New York: Basic Books.

Alter, Robert. 2011b. *The Art of Biblical Poetry*. 2nd ed. New York: Basic Books.

Amit, Yairah. 2001. *Reading Biblical Narratives: Literary Criticism and the Hebrew Bible*. Translated by Yael Lotan. Minneapolis, MN: Fortress.

Anderson, Janice Capel. 1983. "Matthew: Gender and Reading." In *The Bible and Feminist Hermeneutics*, edited by Mary Ann Tolbert. *Semeia* 28: 3–28.

Anderson, Janice Capel. 2011. "Narratology: The Three Worlds of the Text and a Door to Engagement." In *Reading Ideologies: Essays on the Bible and Interpretation in Honor of Mary Ann Tolbert*, edited by Tat-siong Benny Liew, 138–159. Bible in the Modern World 40. Sheffield, Yorkshire: Sheffield Phoenix.

Andersson, Gregor. 2009. *Untamable Texts: Literary Studies and Narrative Theory in the Books of Samuel*. Library of Hebrew Bible/Old Testament Studies 514. New York: T&T Clark.

Auerbach, Erich. (1946) 1953. *Mimesis: The Representation of Reality in Western Literature*. Translated by Willard Trask. Princeton, NJ: Princeton University Press. First published in Germany.

Bal, Mieke. 1977. *Narratologie: Essais sur la signification narrative dans quatre romans modernes*. Paris: Klincksieck.

Bal, Mieke. 1978. *De theorie van vertellen en verhalen*. Muiderberg, Netherlands: Coutinho.

Bal, Mieke. (1968) 1985. *Narratology: Introduction to the Theory of Narrative*. Translated by Christine Van Boheemen. Toronto: University of Toronto Press.

Bal, Mieke. 1986. *Femmes imaginaires: L'Ancien Testament au risque d'une narratologie critique*. Utrecht: HES; Montreal: HMH; Paris: Nizet.

Bal, Mieke. 1987. *Lethal Love: Literary Feminist Readings of Biblical Love Stories*. Indiana Studies in Biblical Literature. Bloomington: Indiana University Press.

Bal, Mieke. 1988a. *Murder and Difference: Gender, Genre, and Scholarship on Sisera's Death*. Indiana Studies in Biblical Literature. Bloomington: Indiana University Press.

Bal, Mieke. 1988b. *Death and Dissymmetry: The Politics of Coherence in the Book of Judges*. Chicago Studies in the History of Judaism. Chicago: University of Chicago Press.

Bal, Mieke. 1997. "Preface to the Second Edition." In *Narratology: Introduction to the Theory of Narrative*. Translated by Christine Van Boheemen. 2nd ed. Toronto: University of Toronto Press, xiii–xvi.

Bal, Mieke. 1999. "Close Reading Today: From Narratology to Cultural Analysis." In *Grenzüb erschreitungen: Narratologie im Kontext/Transcending Boundaries: Narratology in Context*, edited by Walter Grünzweig and Andreas Solbach, 19–40. Tübingen: Gunter Narr.

Bar-Efrat, Shimon. 1989. *Narrative Art in the Bible*. Translated by Dorothea Shefer-Vanson. Bible and Literature Series 17. Sheffield, Yorkshire: Almond.

Barr, David L. 1987. *New Testament Story: An Introduction*. Belmont, CA: Wadsworth.

Barthes, Roland. 1966. "Introduction à l'analyse structurale des récits." *Communications 8*: 1–27.

Barthes, Roland. (1968) 1977. "The Death of the Author." In his *Image—Music—Text*. Edited and translated by Stephen Heath, 142–148. New York: Hill and Wang.

Barthes, Roland. 1988a. "The Structural Analysis of Narrative: Apropos of Acts 10–11." In his *The Semiotic Challenge*. Edited and translated by Richard Howard, 217–245. New York: Hill and Wang.

Barthes, Roland. 1988b. "Wrestling with the Angel: Textual Analysis of Genesis 32:23–33." In Barthes 1988a, 246–260.

Bennema, Cornelis. 2014. *A Theory of Character in New Testament Narrative*. Minneapolis, MN: Fortress.

Berlin, Adele. 1983. *Poetics and the Interpretation of Biblical Narrative*. Bible and Literature Series 9. Sheffield, Yorkshire: Almond.

Bhabha, Homi K., ed. 1990. *Nation and Narration*. New York: Routledge.

The Bible and Culture Collective. 1995. *The Postmodern Bible*. New Haven, CT: Yale University Press.

Booth, Wayne C. 1961. *The Rhetoric of Fiction*. Chicago: University of Chicago Press.

Bowman, Richard G. 2007. "Narrative Criticism: Human Purpose in Conflict with Divine Presence." In *Judges and Method: New Approaches in Biblical Studies*. 2nd ed, edited by Gale A. Yee, 19–45. Minneapolis, MN: Fortress.

Bremond, Claude. 1973. *Logique du récit*. Paris: Seuil.

Brooke-Rose, Christine. 1990. "Whatever Happened to Narratology?" *Poetics Today* 11: 283–293.

Brooks, Cleanth. 1947. *The Well Wrought Urn: Studies in the Structure of Poetry*. New York: Harcourt, Brace & World.

Brooks, Peter. 1981. "Introduction." In Tzvetan Todorov, *Introduction to Poetics*. Translated by Richard Howard, vii-xix. Theory and History of Literature 1. Minneapolis: University of Minnesota Press.

Calloud, Jean. 1973. *L'analyse structurale du récit. Elements de méthode. Tentations de Jésus au desert*. Lyons: Profac.

Carter, Warren. 2004. *Matthew: Storyteller, Interpreter, Evangelist*. 2nd ed. Peabody, MA: Hendrickson.

Carter, Warren. 2006. *John: Storyteller, Interpreter, Evangelist*. Peabody, MA: Hendrickson.

Carter, Warren. 2008. *John and Empire: Initial Explorations*. New York: T&T Clark International.

Chatman, Seymour. 1978. *Story and Discourse: Narrative Structure in Fiction and Film*. Ithaca, NY: Cornell University Press.

Culpepper, R. Alan. 1983. *Anatomy of the Fourth Gospel: A Study in Literary Design*. Philadelphia, PA: Fortress.

Currie, Mark. 1998. *Postmodern Narrative Theory*. Transitions. New York: St. Martin's Press.

Dancygier, Barbara. 2012. *The Language of Stories: A Cognitive Approach*. Cambridge: Cambridge University Press.

Davis, Garrick, ed. 2008. *Praising It New: The Best of the New Criticism*. Athens: Ohio University Press.

De Man, Paul. 1979. *Allegories of Reading: Figural Language in Rousseau, Nietzsche, Rilke, and Proust*. New Haven, CT: Yale University Press.

Donahue, John R., and Daniel J. Harrington. 2002. *The Gospel of Mark*. Sacra Pagina 2. Collegeville, MN: Liturgical.

Elliott, Scott S. 2011. *Reconfiguring Mark's Jesus: Narrative Criticism after Poststructuralism*. The Bible in the Modern World 41. Sheffield, Yorkshire: Sheffield Phoenix.

Farelly, Nicolas. 2010. *The Disciples in the Fourth Gospel: A Narrative Analysis of Their Faith and Understanding*. Wissenschaftliche Untersuchungen zum Neuen Testament 2.Reihe 290. Tübingen: Mohr Siebeck.

Farwell, Marilyn. 1996. *Heterosexual Plots and Lesbian Narrative*. New York: New York University Press.

Fludernik, Monika. 1999. "When the Self Is an Other: Vergleichende erzähltheoretische und postkoloniale Überlegungen zur Identitäts(de)konstruktion in der (exil)indischen Gegenwartsliteratur." *Anglia* 117: 71–96.

Fludernik, Monika. 2003. "Cognitive Narratology: Natural Narratology and Cognitive Parameters." In *Narrative Theory and the Cognitive Sciences*, edited by David Herman, 243–267. CSLI Lecture Notes 158. Stanford, CA: Center for the Study of Language and Information.

Fludernik, Monika. 2005. "Histories of Narrative Theory (II): From Structuralism to the Present." In *A Companion to Narrative Theory*, edited by James Phelan and Peter J. Rabinowitz, 36–59. Blackwell Companions to Literature and Culture 33. Malden, MA: Blackwell.

Fludernik, Monika. 2009. *An Introduction to Narratology*. New York: Routledge.

Fokkelman, J. P. 1975. *Narrative Art in Genesis: Specimens of Stylistic and Structural Analysis*. Assen, Netherlands: Van Gorcum.

Fokkelman, J. P. 1981. *Narrative Art and Poetry in the Books of Samuel*. Vol. 1, *King David (II Sam 9-20 and I Kings 1-2)*. Assen, Netherlands: Van Gorcum.

Fokkelman, J. P. 1986. *Narrative Art and Poetry in the Books of Samuel*, Vol. 2: *The Crossing Fates (I Sam 13-31 and II Sam 1)*. Assen, Netherlands: Van Gorcum.

Fokkelman, J. P. 1992. *Narrative Art and Poetry in the Books of Samuel*, Vol. 3: *Throne and City (II Sam 2-8 and 21-24)*. Assen, Netherlands: Van Gorcum.

Fokkelman, J. P. 1993. *Narrative Art and Poetry in the Books of Samuel*, Vol. 4: *Vow and Desire (I Sam 1-12)*. Assen, Netherlands: Van Gorcum.

Fokkelman, J. P. 2000. *Reading Biblical Narrative: An Introductory Guide*. Louisville, KY: Westminster John Knox.

Forster, E. M. 1927. *Aspects of the Novel*. London: Edward Arnold.

Fowler, Robert M. 1981. *Loaves and Fishes: The Function of the Feeding Stories in the Gospel of Mark*. Society of Biblical Literature Dissertation Series 54. Chico, CA: Scholars Press.

Fowler, Robert M. 1991. *Let the Reader Understand: Reader-Response Criticism and the Gospel of Mark*. Minneapolis, MN: Fortress.

Freedman, Amelia Devin. 2005. *God as an Absent Character in Biblical Hebrew Narrative: A Literary-Theoretical Study*. Studies in Biblical Literature 82. New York: Peter Lang.

Genette, Gérard. 1972. "Discours du récit." In his *Figures III*, 65–278. Paris: Seuil.

Genette, Gérard. 1980. *Narrative Discourse: An Essay in Method*. Translated by Jane E. Lewin. Ithaca, NY: Cornell University Press.

Gibson, Andrew. 1996. *Towards a Postmodern Theory of Narrative*. Hemel Hempstead, UK: Harvester Wheatsheaf.

Goebel, Walter, and Saskia Schabio. 2013. *Locating Postcolonial Narrative Genres*. Routledge Research in Postcolonial Literatures 43. New York: Routledge.

Green, Joel B. 1997. *The Gospel of Luke*. The New International Commentary on the New Testament. Grand Rapids, MI: Eerdmans.

Greimas, A. J. 1966. *Sémantique structurale: Recherche de méthode*. Paris: Larousse.

Groupe d'Entrevernes. 1977. *Signes et paraboles: Sémiotique et texte évangélique*. Paris: Seuil.

Gunn, David M. 1990. "Narrative Criticism." In *To Each Its Own Meaning: Biblical Criticisms and Their Applications*, edited by Steven L. McKenzie and Stephen R. Haynes, 172–178. Louisville, KY: Westminster John Knox.

Gunn, David M., and Danna Nolan Fewell. 1993. *Narrative in the Hebrew Bible*. Oxford Bible Series. Oxford: Oxford University Press.

Gymnich, Marion. 2002. "Linguistics and Narratology: The Relevance of Linguistic Criteria to Postcolonial Narratology." In *Literature and Linguistics: Approaches, Models, and Applications*, edited by Marion Gymnich, Ansgar Nünning, and Vera Nünning, 61–76. Trier: Wissenschaftlicher Verlag Trier.

Herman, David. 1997. "Scripts, Sequences, and Stories: Elements of a Postclassical Narratology." *PMLA: Proceedings of the Modern Language Association of America* 112: 1046–1059.

Herman, David, ed. 1999. *Narratologies: New Perspectives on Narrative Analysis*. Theory and Interpretation of Narrative Series. Columbus: Ohio State University Press.

Herman, David, ed. 2003. *Narrative Theory and the Cognitive Sciences*. CSLI Lecture Notes 158. Stanford, CA: Center for the Study of Language and Information.

Herman, David. 2010. "Directions in Cognitive Narratology: Triangulating Stories, Media, and the Mind." In *Postclassical Narratology: Approaches and Analyses*, edited by Jan Alber and Monika Fludernik, 137–162. Theory and Interpretation of Narrative Series. Columbus: Ohio State University Press.

Herman, Luc, and Bart Vervaeck. 2005. *Handbook of Narrative Analysis*. Lincoln: University of Nebraska Press.

Hickman, Miranda B. 2012. "Introduction: Rereading the New Criticism." In *Rereading the New Criticism*, edited by Miranda B. Hickman and John D. McIntyre, 1–21. Columbus: Ohio State University Press.

Hogan, Patrick Colm. 2011. *Affective Narratology: The Emotional Structure of Stories*. Frontiers of Narrative Series. Lincoln: University of Nebraska Press.

Homans, Margaret. 1994. "Feminist Fictions and Feminist Theories of Narrative." *Narrative* 2: 3–16.

Hongisto, Leif. 2010. *Experiencing the Apocalypse at the Limits of Alterity*. Biblical Interpretation Series 102. Leiden: Brill.

Horsley, Richard A. 2001. *Hearing the Whole Story: The Politics of Plot in Mark's Gospel*. Louisville, KY: Westminster John Knox.

Iverson, Kelly R., and Christopher W. Skinner, eds. 2011. *Mark as Story: Retrospect and Prospect*. Resources for Biblical Study 65. Atlanta, GA: Society of Biblical Literature.

Jahn, Manfred. 2005. "Cognitive Narratology." In *The Routledge Encyclopedia of Narrative Theory*, edited by David Herman, Manfred Jahn, and Marie-Laure Ryan, 67–71. New York: Routledge.

Jobling, David. 1978. *The Sense of Biblical Narrative: Three Structural Analyses in the Old Testament*. Sheffield, Yorkshire: JSOT Press.

Joseph, Abson Predestin. 2012. *A Narratological Reading of 1 Peter*. Library of New Testament Studies 440. New York: Bloomsbury T&T Clark.

Kingsbury, Jack Dean. 1986. *Matthew as Story*. Philadelphia, PA: Fortress.

Lanser, Susan S. 1986. "Toward a Feminist Narratology." *Style* 20: 341–363.

Lanser, Susan S. 1988. "Shifting the Paradigm: Feminism and Narratology." *Style* 22: 52–60.

Lanser, Susan S. 1992. *Fictions of Authority: Women Writers and Narrative Voice*. Ithaca, NY: Cornell University Press.

Lanser, Susan S. 1995. "Sexing the Narrative: Propriety, Desire, and the Engendering of Narratology." *Narrative* 3: 85–94.

Lanser, Susan S. 1999. "Sexing Narratology: Toward a Gendered Poetics of Narrative Voice." In *Grenzüberschreitungen: Narratologie im Kontext/Transcending Boundaries: Narratology in Context*, edited by Walter Grünzweig and Andreas Solbach, 167–184. Tübingen: Gunter Narr.

Lanser, Susan S. 2010a. "Are We There Yet? The Intersectional Future of Feminist Narratology." *Foreign Literature Studies* 32: 32–41.

Lanser, Susan S. 2010b. "Sapphic Dialogics: Historical Narratology and the Sexuality of Form." In *Postclassical Narratology: Approaches and Analyses*, edited by Jan Alber and Monika Fludernik, 186–205. Theory and Interpretation of Narrative Series. Columbus: Ohio State University Press.

Lanser, Susan S., and Robyn W. Warhol, eds. 2015. *Narrative Theory Unbound: Queer and Feminist Interventions*. Columbus, OH: Ohio State University Press.

Longenecker, Bruce W., ed. 2002. *Narrative Dynamics in Paul: A Critical Assessment*. Louisville, KY: Westminster John Knox.

Leach, Edmund. 1962. "Genesis as Myth." *Discovery* 23: 30–35. Reprinted in Edmund Leach, *Genesis as Myth and Other Essays*, 7–23. London: Jonathan Cape, 1969.

Malbon, Elizabeth Struthers. 1983. "Fallible Followers: Women and Men in the Gospel of Mark." In *The Bible and Feminist Hermeneutics*, edited by Mary Ann Tolbert. *Semeia* 28: 29–48.

Malbon, Elizabeth Struthers. 2008. "Narrative Criticism: How Does the Story Mean?" In *Mark and Method: New Approaches in Biblical Studies*, 2nd ed., edited by Janice Capel Anderson and Stephen D. Moore, 29–58. Minneapolis, MN: Fortress.

Malbon, Elizabeth Struthers. 2009a. *Mark's Jesus: Characterization as Narrative Christology*. Waco, TX: Baylor University Press.

Malbon, Elizabeth Struthers, ed. 2009b. *Between Author and Audience in Mark: Narration, Characterization, Interpretation*. New Testament Monographs 23. Sheffield, Yorkshire: Sheffield Phoenix.

Marin, Louis. 1971. *Sémiotique de la Passion. Topiques et figures*. Bibliothèque de sciences religieuses. Paris: Aubier, Cerf, Delachaux et Niestlé, and Desclée de Brouwer.

Merenlahti, Petri. 2002. *Poetics for the Gospels? Rethinking Narrative Criticism*. Studies of the New Testament and Its World. New York: T&T Clark.

Mezei, Kathy. 1996. *Ambiguous Discourse: Feminist Narratology and British Women Writers*. Chapel Hill: University of North Carolina Press.

Miscall, Peter D. 1983. *The Workings of Old Testament Narrative*. Semeia Studies 12. Chico, CA: Scholars Press.

Moore, Stephen D. 1989. *Literary Criticism and the Gospels: The Theoretical Challenge*. New Haven, CT: Yale University Press.

Moore, Stephen D. 1992. *Mark and Luke in Poststructuralist Perspectives: Jesus Begins to Write*. New Haven, CT: Yale University Press.

Moore, Stephen D. 1996. *God's Gym: Divine Male Bodies of the Bible*. New York: Routledge.

Moore, Stephen D. 2008. "Afterword: Things Not Written in This Book." In *Anatomies of Narrative Criticism: The Past, Present, and Futures of the Fourth Gospel as Literature*, edited by Tom Thatcher and Stephen D. Moore, 253–258. Resources for Biblical Study 55. Atlanta, GA: Society of Biblical Literature.

Moore, Stephen D. 2011. "Why There Are No Humans or Animals in the Gospel of Mark." In *Mark as Story: Retrospect and Prospect*, edited by Kelly R. Iverson and Christopher W. Skinner, 71–94. Resources for Biblical Study 65. Atlanta, GA: Society of Biblical Literature.

Moore, Stephen D., and Yvonne Sherwood. 2011. *The Invention of the Biblical Scholar: A Critical Manifesto*. Minneapolis, MN: Fortress.

Nünning, Ansgar. 2000. "Towards a Cultural and Historical Narratology: A Survey of Diachronic Approaches, Concepts, and Research Projects." In *Anglistentag 1999 Mainz: Proceedings*, edited by Bernhard Reitz and Sigrid Rieuwerts, 345–373. Trier: Wissenschaftlicher Verlag Trier.

Nünning, Ansgar. 2003. "Narratology or Narratologies? Taking Stock of Recent Developments, Critique and Modest Proposals for Future Usages of the Term." In *What Is Narratology? Questions and Answers Regarding the Status of a Theory*, edited by Tom Kindt and Hans-Harald Müller, 239–275. New York: De Gruyter.

Nünning, Ansgar. 2004. "Where Historiographic Metafiction and Narratology Meet: Towards an Applied Cultural Narratology." *Style* 38: 352–365.

Nünning, Ansgar. 2009. "Surveying Contextualist and Cultural Narratologies: Towards an Outline of Approaches, Concepts, and Potentials." In *Narratology in the Age of Cross-Disciplinary Narrative Research*, edited by Sandra Heinen and Roy Sommer, 48–70. Narratologia: Contributions to Narrative Theory. New York: De Gruyter.

Onega, Susana, and José Angel García Landa. 1996. *Narratology: An Introduction*. Longman Critical Readers. New York: Routledge.

O'Neill, Patrick. 1994. *Fictions of Discourse: Reading Narrative Theory*. Toronto: University of Toronto Press.

Page, Ruth E. 2006. *Literary and Linguistic Approaches to Feminist Narratology*. New York: Palgrave Macmillan.

Paris, Christopher T. 2014. *Narrative Obtrusion in the Hebrew Bible*. Emerging Scholars Series. Minneapolis, MN: Fortress.

Patte, Daniel. 1976. *What Is Structural Exegesis?* Guides to Biblical Scholarship. Philadelphia, PA: Fortress.

Patte, Daniel, and Aline Patte. 1978. *Structural Exegesis: From Theory to Practice. Exegesis of Mark 15 and 16: Hermeneutical Implications*. Philadelphia, PA: Fortress.

Petersen, Norman R. 1978. *Literary Criticism for New Testament Critics*. Guides to Biblical Scholarship. Philadelphia, PA: Fortress.

Petersen, Norman R. 1985. *Rediscovering Paul: Philemon and the Sociology of Paul's Narrative World*. Philadelphia, PA: Fortress.

Phelan, James. 1996. *Narrative as Rhetoric: Technique, Audiences, Ethics, Ideology*. The Theory and Interpretation of Narrative Series. Columbus: Ohio State University Press.

Polzin, Robert. 1977. *Biblical Structuralism: Method and Subjectivity in the Study of Ancient Texts*. Semeia Supplements 5. Philadelphia, PA: Fortress.

Powell, Mark Allan. 1990. *What Is Narrative Criticism?* Guides to Biblical Scholarship. Minneapolis, MN: Fortress.

Powell, Mark Allan. 2001. *Chasing the Eastern Star: Adventures in Biblical Reader-Response Criticism*. Louisville, KY: Westminster John Knox.

Prince, Gerald. 1982. *Narratology: The Form and Functioning of Narrative*. New York: Mouton.

Prince, Gerald. 2003. *A Dictionary of Narratology*. 2nd ed. Lincoln: University of Nebraska Press.

Prince, Gerald. 2005. "On a Postcolonial Narratology." In *A Companion to Narrative Theory*, edited by James Phelan and Peter J. Rabinowitz, 372–381. Blackwell Companions to Literature and Culture 33. Malden, MA: Blackwell.

Ransom, John Crowe. 1937. "Criticism, Inc." *Virginia Quarterly Review* 13: 586–602. http://www.vqronline.org/essay/criticism-inc-0.

Ransom, John Crowe. 1941. *The New Criticism*. Norfolk, CT: New Directions.

Resseguie, James L. 1998. *Revelation Unsealed: A Narrative Critical Approach to John's Apocalypse*. Biblical Interpretation Series 32. Leiden: Brill.

Resseguie, James L. 2001. *The Strange Gospel: Narrative Design and Point of View in John*. Biblical Interpretation Series 56. Leiden: Brill.

Resseguie, James L. 2005. *Narrative Criticism of the New Testament: An Introduction*. Grand Rapids, MI: Baker Academic.

Resseguie, James L. 2009. *The Revelation of John: A Narrative Commentary*. Grand Rapids, MI: Baker Academic.

Rhoads, David. 1982. "Narrative Criticism and the Gospel of Mark." *Journal of the American Academy of Religion* 50: 411–434. Reprinted in Rhoads 2004, 1–22.

Rhoads, David. 2004. *Reading Mark, Engaging the Gospel*. Minneapolis, MN: Fortress.

Rhoads, David, and Donald Michie. 1982. *Mark as Story: Introduction to the Narrative of a Gospel*. Philadelphia, PA: Fortress.

Rhoads, David, Joanna Dewey, and Donald Michie. 1999. *Mark as Story: Introduction to the Narrative of a Gospel*. 2nd ed. Minneapolis, MN: Fortress.

Rhoads, David, and Kari Syreeni, eds. 1999. *Characterization in the Gospels: Reconceiving Narrative Criticism*. Journal for the Study of the New Testament Supplement Series 184. Sheffield, Yorkshire: Sheffield Academic Press.

Richardson, Brian. 2012. "Antimimetic, Unnatural, and Postmodern Narrative Theory." In *Narrative Theory: Core Concepts and Critical Debates*, edited by David Herman, James Phelan, Peter J. Rabinowitz, Brian Richardson, and Robyn Warhol, 20–28. Theory and Interpretation of Narrative Series. Columbus: Ohio State University Press.

Richter, David H. 2005. "Genre, Repetition, Temporal Order: Some Aspects of Biblical Narratology." In *A Companion to Narrative Theory*, edited by James Phelan and Peter J. Rabinowitz, 285–298. Blackwell Companions to Literature and Culture 33. Malden, MA: Blackwell.

Rimmon-Kenan, Shlomith. 1983. *Narrative Fiction: Contemporary Poetics*. New York: Methuen.

Rimmon-Kenan, Shlomith. 2002. "Towards . . .: Afterthoughts, Almost Twenty Years Later." In *Narrative Fiction: Contemporary Poetics*. 2nd ed. New York: Methuen, 139–154.

Robertson, David. 1977. *The Old Testament and the Literary Critic*. Guides to Biblical Scholarship. Philadelphia, PA: Fortress.

Roncace, Mark. 2005. *Jeremiah, Zedekiah, and the Fall of Jerusalem: A Study of Prophetic Narrative*. Library of Hebrew Bible/Old Testament Studies 423. New York: T&T Clark International.

Roof, Judith. 1996. *Come as You Are: Sexuality and Narrative*. New York: Columbia University Press.

Russel, Heather. 2009. *Legba's Crossing: Narratology in the African Atlantic*. Athens: University of Georgia Press.

Sasani, Samira. 2013. *Feminist Narratology: George Eliot's Narrative Techniques in Adam Bede*. Saarbrücken, Germany: Lambert.

Schmid, Wolf. 2010. *Narratology: An Introduction*. New York: De Gruyter.

Seybold, Klaus. 2006. *Poetik der erzählenden Literatur im Alten Testament*. Poetologische Studien zum Alten Testament; Band 2. Stuttgart: Kohlhammer.

Shen, Dan. 2005. "Why Contextual and Formal Narratologies Need Each Other." *Journal of Narrative Theory* 35: 141–171.

Ska, Jean-Louis. 1990. *Our Fathers Have Told Us: Introduction to the Analysis of Hebrew Narrative*. Subsidia Biblica 13. Rome: Pontifical Biblical Institute.

Skinner, Christopher W., ed. 2012. *Characters and Characterization in the Gospel of John*. Library of New Testament Studies 461. New York: Bloomsbury and T&T Clark.

Staley, Jeffrey Lloyd. 1988. *The Print's First Kiss: A Rhetorical Investigation of the Implied Reader in the Fourth Gospel*. Society of Biblical Literature Dissertation Series 82. Atlanta, GA: Scholars Press.

Stanzel, Franz K. 1979. *Theorie des Erzählens*. Göttingen: Vandenhoeck und Ruprecht.

Stanzel, Franz K. 1984. *A Theory of Narrative*. Translated by Charlotte Goedsche. Cambridge: Cambridge University Press.

Sternberg, Meir. 1985. *The Poetics of Biblical Narrative: Ideological Literature and the Drama of Reading*. Indiana Studies in Biblical Literature. Bloomington: Indiana University Press.

Sternberg, Meir. 1978. *Expositional Modes and Temporal Ordering in Fiction*. Baltimore, MD: Johns Hopkins University Press.

Sternberg, Meir, and Menachem Perry. 1986. "The King through Ironic Eyes: Biblical Narrative and the Literary Reading Process." *Poetics Today* 7: 275–322. Rpt. Originally published in Hebrew in 1968

Stockwell, Peter. 2002. *Cognitive Poetics: An Introduction*. New York: Routledge.

Tannehill, Robert C. 1977. "The Disciples in Mark: The Function of a Narrative Role." *Journal of Religion* 57: 386–405.

Tannehill, Robert C. 1986. *The Narrative Unity of Luke Acts: A Literary Interpretation*, Vol. 1: *The Gospel According to Luke*. Philadelphia, PA: Fortress.

Tannehill, Robert C. 1990. *The Narrative Unity of Luke Acts: A Literary Interpretation*, Vol. 2: *The Acts of the Apostles*. Minneapolis, MN: Fortress.

Thatcher, Tom, and Stephen D. Moore, eds. 2008. *Anatomies of Narrative Criticism: The Past, Present, and Futures of the Fourth Gospel as Literature*. Resources for Biblical Study 55. Atlanta, GA: Society of Biblical Literature.

Todorov, Tzvetan. 1969. *Grammaire du Décaméron*. The Hague: Mouton.

Todorov, Tzvetan. 1981. *Introduction to Poetics*. Translated by Richard Howard. Theory and History of Literature 1. Minneapolis: University of Minnesota Press.

Tolmie, D. François. 1999. *Narratology and Biblical Narratives: A Practical Guide*. San Francisco: International Scholars. Rpt. Eugene, OR: Wipf & Stock, 2012.

Tull, Patricia K. 2013. "Narrative Criticism and Narrative Hermeneutics." In *The Oxford Encyclopedia of Biblical Interpretation*, vol. 2, edited by Steven L. McKenzie et al., 37–46. Oxford: Oxford University Press.

Vette, Joachim. 2005. *Samuel und Saul: Ein Beitrag zur narrativen Poetik des Samuelbuches.* Beiträge zum Verstehen der Bibel 13. Münster: LIT.

Vette, Joachim. 2010. "Narrative Poetics and Hebrew Narrative: A Survey." In *Literary Construction of Identity in the Ancient World: Proceedings of the Conference Literary Fiction and the Construction of Identity in Ancient Literatures*, edited by Hanna Liss and Manfred Oeming, 19–61. Winona Lake, IN: Eisenbrauns.

Via, Dan O., Jr. 1975. *Kerygma and Comedy in the New Testament: A Structuralist Approach to Hermeneutics*. Philadelphia, PA: Fortress.

Wallace, Robert E. 2007. *The Narrative Effect of Book IV of the Hebrew Psalter*. Studies in Biblical Literature 112. New York: Peter Lang.

Wallace, Robert E. 2011. "The Narrative Effect of Psalms 84-89." *Journal of Hebrew Scriptures* 11: 2–15.

Walsh, Jerome T. 2009. *Old Testament Narrative: A Guide to Interpretation*. Louisville, KY: Westminster John Knox.

Warhol, Robyn. 2012. "A Feminist Approach to Narrative." In *Narrative Theory: Core Concepts and Critical Debates*, edited by David Herman, James Phelan, Peter J. Rabinowitz, Brian Richardson, and Robyn Warhol, 9–13. Theory and the Interpretation of Narrative Series. Columbus: Ohio State University Press.

Weiss, Anthony. 2011. "An Alter-ed Perspective on the Bible: Scholar Robert Alter Has Issues with Translations of Holy Text." *Jewish Daily Forward* (December 2): http://forward.com/articles/146729/an-alter-ed-perspective-on-the-bible/?p=all.

Weitzman, Steven. 2007. "Before and after *The Art of Biblical Narrative*." *Prooftexts* 27: 191–210.

Wellek, René, and Austin Warren. 1948. *Theory of Literature*. New York: Harcourt, Brace and Company.

Wimsatt, William K., Jr., and Monroe C. Beardsley. 1946. "The Intentional Fallacy." *Sewanee Review* 54: 468–488.

Witherington, Ben, III. 1994. *Paul's Narrative Thought World: The Tapestry of Tragedy and Triumph*. Louisville, KY: Westminster John Knox.

Xu, Dejin. 2007. *Race and Form: Towards a Contextualized Narratology of African American Autobiography*. New York: Peter Lang.

Yamada, Frank M. 2008. *Configurations of Rape in the Hebrew Bible: A Literary Analysis of Three Rape Narratives*. Studies in Biblical Literature 109. New York: Peter Lang.

Yamasaki, Gary. 2012. *Perspective Criticism: Point of View and Evaluative Guidance in Biblical Narrative*. Eugene, OR: Cascade.

CHAPTER 3

....

BIBLICAL NARRATIVE AND THE BIRTH OF PROSE LITERATURE

....

ROBERT S. KAWASHIMA

INTRODUCTION

....

LANGUAGE, as the Russian literary critic and theorist Mikhail Bakhtin (1982) famously observed, is irreducibly "dialogic," which is to say, every single word uttered in our post-lapsarian universe of discourse necessarily encounters previous instances of speech: "Only the mythical Adam, who approached a virginal and as yet verbally unqualified world with the first word, could really have escaped from start to finish this dialogic inter-orientation with the alien word that occurs in the object. Concrete historical human discourse does not have this privilege" (279). Stories, by extension—at least those told ever since the very first campfires went out—necessarily build upon earlier stories as well. It follows that, in order to fully appreciate, understand, and interpret a given story, one must take into consideration its relationship to its literary milieu—oral and/or written.

The narratives of the Hebrew Bible are no different. As the vast array of documents from the surrounding cultures of the ancient Near East demonstrate (Hallo and Lawson 2003; Pritchard 2010), the biblical writers were products of their time. They freely and continuously borrowed—sometimes unconsciously, one should note—from the motifs, themes, conventions, and so forth, of their cultural milieu, their historical context. And how could it have been otherwise? Such an assertion differs little from the observation that Biblical Hebrew descends from Proto-Semitic—which is merely to say that biblical narrative, no less than Biblical Hebrew, was not created ex nihilo. At the same time, however, biblical narrative, as many readers can attest, constitutes a radical departure from storytelling as it generally existed in antiquity—a noteworthy event in the history of literature I would characterize as nothing less than the birth of prose literature. What is more, this literary development is one symptom of an underlying transformation in ancient thought or knowledge, in the conceptualization of reality—of the mortal, immortal, and natural realms. This discursive break—to invoke Michel Foucault's "archaeology of knowledge"—has been partially if inadequately recognized in the widespread idea of the "monotheistic revolution." The question is, then, what is the relationship of biblical narrative to its literary milieu? What light do the literatures of the surrounding cultures of the ancient Near East shed on the Bible? How should these inform the interpretation and analysis of biblical narrative? This calls for wisdom. One must simultaneously interpret biblical narrative in light of its clear historical connections to its literary milieu, while carefully analyzing the profound differences separating it from its milieu as well.

For the purposes of this brief chapter, I will limit my discussion to the prose narratives found in Genesis-Kings, less the book of Ruth, which does not follow Judges according to the Masoretic Text (MT) of Jewish tradition. While the dating of biblical texts is highly conjectural, one view places the composition of these stories in ancient Israel's monarchic period, 1000–586 BCE. They most likely grew out of oral traditions circulating in the culture(s) that would eventually become ancient Israel (Cross 1998, 22–52), which, according to one view, was coalescing as a distinct ethnic group around 1200–1000 BCE; conversely, they would only reach their final redacted form well into the post-exilic period. My point, however, is not to date these texts in absolute terms; it is, rather, to posit that, broadly speaking, this corpus of narratives belongs to the same literary culture. The literary milieu of this particular narrative corpus thus consists mainly of those documents produced by the numerous civilizations of the Fertile Crescent, stretching from Egypt up the Levant and down through Mesopotamia. The most relevant of these will be roughly contemporary with or older than biblical narrative, thus reflecting traditions available in principle to the biblical writers. However, one cannot rule out the possibility that a much later document might conserve older traditions related to biblical narrative—whence the occasional reference to Berossus, a Babylonian who wrote in Greek in the Hellenistic period (third century BCE).

At the broadest level, the Bible's cultural milieu comprises all the written documents and oral traditions that were available to the biblical writers and their oral-traditional precursors—something like the sum total of their "cultural knowledge" or "literacy." Since Israel's libraries, traditions, and so forth, are no longer available (save for the Bible itself, of course), a great deal of biblical scholarship has been devoted, in effect, to reconstructing this archive of knowledge on the basis of the culturally relevant documents that are still available. It is the defining task of philology, the scholarly project of understanding ancient languages and the texts they survive in, to reconstruct these ancient "archives." Biblicists have made particular use of various literary and bureaucratic texts, presumably written by a small, educated elite: myths and epics, political, legal, and administrative documents, and so on. But really, just about any fragment of writing might prove to be useful—an ostracon, a scrap of parchment, some graffiti scribbled onto a cave wall even—by shedding additional light on, say, an obscure word or a grammatical form or a cultural practice. Whence the significance of the Yavneh-Yam ostracon, which appears to be a scribal transcription of a complaint lodged by a worker against his supervisor regarding a confiscated garment (cf. Exod. 22:26–27; Deut. 24:12–13). The specifically *literary* milieu of biblical narrative refers more narrowly to those written and oral works of narrative art that the biblical writers drew on (consciously or not) in the process of their own literary creation. In this restricted sense, the Mesopotamian and Ugaritic myths and epics (dating to the mid to late second millennium BCE) provide us with the closest and most instructive parallels to biblical narrative, and so my discussion will focus on these.

The use of literary milieu to illuminate biblical narrative is premised on literary comparison (Kawashima 2007). For the very idea of this milieu is based on the relationship of a given verbal artifact to others created within the same historical context, more or less broadly defined. There are, however, two modes of literary comparison: what I would call historicist (or metonymic) comparison and formalist (or metaphoric) comparison. If historicist comparison relates literary works on the basis of geographical and chronological contiguity (metonymy), formalist comparison relates literary works on the basis of formal resemblance (metaphor). Since the latter does not depend on the operation of literary influence, it expands comparative analysis to include historically unrelated works. Biblical scholars have generally privileged the former, typically condemning the latter as comparison "on the grand scale." But in fact, the very categories of poetry and prose, which biblicists generally take for granted, are grounded in formal properties whose cross-cultural and transhistorical distribution cannot be explained by cultural interaction; they depend, rather, on the existence of linguistic and literary universals. Anyone who insists on rejecting such "grand" comparisons should, to be consistent, condemn all studies of biblical "poetry"—to take merely one noteworthy example—for the sin of "anachronism." But if, conversely, the widespread intuition that the psalms are poems is indeed correct, then biblical scholars must rethink the field's widespread commitment to narrowly historicist analysis. One should finally keep in mind that comparisons of both types involve differences as well as similarities. Thus, the broadly comparative category of prose narrative can only be properly understood in opposition to the equally broad category of verse forms. And the precise interpretation of a biblical passage might only come into focus after one has noted how it swerves, however subtly, from some literary parallel—whether the latter is to be found within the Bible or without.

I will organize this discussion around these issues. First, I describe the relationship of biblical narrative to its literary milieu as illuminated by historicist comparison. Second, in light of formalist comparison, I explicate the revolutionary literary development that biblical narrative constitutes in relation to its milieu—namely, the birth of prose literature out of oral-epic traditions. Finally, I briefly explore the implications of biblical narrative for the archaeology of knowledge as it pertains to the ancient Near East.

HISTORICIST COMPARISONS

At the level of historicist comparison, biblical narrative is by definition a product of the time and place of its composition. In a sense, historicist comparison deals with the content, rather than form, of narrative (and literature more generally)— that is, with specific instances of such general narrative devices as allusions, motifs, themes, type-scenes, and so forth. As a result, historicist comparison and the literary parallels it discovers are crucial to the interpretation of specific passages of biblical narrative. (Formalist comparison, as we will see, may have interpretive consequences, but it contributes only indirectly to the interpretation of a given passage.) Conversely, only interpretation can determine whether a given ostensible parallel is genuine and relevant. For it is not enough that some document excavated from one of the libraries of the ancient Near East resembles in various details some passage found in the Bible—the excesses of which impulse have been rightly condemned as "parallelomania" (Sandmel 1962). Rather, the similarities must be strong enough that the adduced parallel makes some nontrivial contribution to the interpretation of the biblical passage under consideration. If the cited parallel does not add significantly to the latter's interpretation, the similarity should rather be deemed a mere coincidence.

As a first example, let us consider the motif of "laughter" surrounding the annunciation and birth of Isaac to the aged couple, Abraham and Sarah. This cluster of narrative details is more fully understood when read in the light of—that is, in comparison with—the related set of motifs found in the Ugaritic narrative poems. Thus, both Danel and El are said to "laugh" in response to the annunciation of the birth (or rebirth) of the beloved son: "his brow relaxed and he laughed [*yṣḥq*] ... / he raised his voice and declared: / 'Now I can sit back and relax'" (*Aqhat* 1.2.10–14; *Baal* 6.3.16–18; Coogan and Smith 2012, 37, 149). That these quoted lines are identical in both passages betrays the conventionalized or stylized nature of the patriarchal response to the son's birth—more on which later. Danel's laughter is particularly instructive: it captures the joy and sheer relief inspired by the son of old age, who as a veritable *filius ex machina*, rescues the patriline from oblivion just in the nick of time. El's status as an "olden" god—a type of retired deity (Cross 1998, 73–83)—one should add, similarly strengthens his attachment to his son Baal, since in his elderly state, he is unlikely to sire another offspring. Let us reread Isaac's birth in this light. His very name, *yiṣḥaq* (he laughs), suggests that he began his literary existence as a plot function, a narrative hypostasis of the son of old age (see Gen. 21:7). At the same time, however, one should also carefully note how the biblical writers swerve from the underlying (oral) patriarchal tradition. In each and every instance, patriarchal joy and relief are reinterpreted in light of the cosmic joke that God has effectively played on the unsuspecting couple, who have had to endure decades of bitter disappointment and frustration before finally receiving their divinely promised son: Genesis 17:17; 18:12–15; 21:6f. It is the more or less direct historical relationship between Genesis and the Ugaritic narratives—whether the former "descends" from the latter, or from a common "ancestor"—that justifies drawing such interpretive inferences. Appealing to instances of laughter in, say, Shakespeare, one should note, would be irrelevant to the interpretation of Isaac's birth.

Even when an historical relationship can be reasonably posited, assessing the relevance of a given parallel for a given passage still requires a judicious appraisal of its interpretive significance. For this reason, an established parallel might be relevant for one passage but not for another. Take, for instance, the figure of the serpent, which plays various roles in numerous ancient Near Eastern narratives. As is well known, "Deep" (*tehom*) in Genesis 1:2 is etymologically related to Tiamat, the ur-goddess or cosmic dragon personifying the primordial ocean in the Mesopotamian creation myth, *Enuma Elish*: "When skies above were not yet named / Nor earth below pronounced by name, / Apsu, the first one, their begetter / And maker Tiamat, who bore them all, / Had mixed their waters together" (I.1–5; Dalley 2000, 233). Just as Marduk "sliced her in half like a fish for drying," putting "half of her ... up to roof the sky" (IV.137–38; Dalley 2000, 255), so, too, Elohim "made the firmament and separated the waters beneath the firmament from the waters above the firmament" (Gen. 1:7). If this connection sheds light on the Priestly (P) creation account in Genesis 1, helping us to discern within it faint traces of a cosmic battle between the creator god and the primal Sea, one must also carefully note how Deep here is a mere shadow of the mythic sea monster. Relatedly, the "great sea monsters [*tanninim*]" mentioned in Genesis 1:21 are no longer cosmic enemies of God, but merely one of the numerous kinds of beasts the deity creates in their proper time and place. P has effectively demythologized his source myth. Conversely, when Aaron's rod is transformed before Pharaoh into a *tannin* (Exod. 7:8–13)—which term, given its associations with the cosmic dragon as well as with the story's setting near the Nile, should be translated as "crocodile"—P is evoking this cosmic battle against Sea as an appropriately elevated historical stage upon which God will eventually "judge the gods of Egypt" (Exod. 12:12) and create the nation of Israel.

A serpent (*naḥaš*) also figures in the Garden of Eden (Gen. 2–3). Its presence there will tempt many readers to see it as an afterimage of the primordial sea monster. But sometimes a snake is just a snake. For one thing, this creation account, far from evoking a mythical sea, simply describes a barren field untouched as yet even by rain. It is not inconceivable that the spring/river rising up to water the earth (Gen. 2:6) subtly alludes to the Mesopotamian ur-god Apsu, the freshwater consort of Tiamat, or to River, the Ugaritic counterpart of Sea or Yamm. The question is: How does this proposed allusion contribute to the interpretation of Genesis 2–3? In fact, no convincing insight seems to be gained from such a parallel. (In the same way, when Moses's staff, in the middle of the desert this time, is transmogrified into a "snake" [*naḥaš*] in Exodus 4:3, no allusion to the cosmic dragon seems to be intended.) Rather, the garden's snake should be interpreted in light of two other literary topoi: the enmity that separates humans from beasts and the loss of immortality. On the one hand, in the Sumerian epic *Enmerkar and the Lord of Aratta*, dating from the early second millenium BCE, the "spell of Nudimmud" evokes a time when "there will be no snake, no scorpion, . . . / And thus there will be neither fear nor trembling, / For man will then have no enemy" (ll. 135–40; Vanstiphout 2003, 65). In other words, this version of the serpent (along with the scorpion) constitutes a synecdoche of the dangers of the natural world. Isaiah similarly envisions a utopian future in which even children will be able to play with venomous snakes unharmed (11:8). Over fifteen hundred years after the Sumerian epic was composed, the phrase "serpents and scorpions" could still be used to conjure up the enemies of humankind, albeit in a spiritualized form (Luke 10:18–19). *Gilgamesh* addresses the same theme in the transformation of Enkidu from a "primitive human" into a civilized man, as a result of which his erstwhile companions (gazelles, wild cattle, etc.) now run away from him in fear (I.iv; cf Gen. 9:2)—but not in connection to any serpent. It is only toward the end of the epic (XI.vi) that a snake will appear, where it will have no connection to the ontological rivalry alienating men from beasts. Rather, it steals the plant Gilgamesh has just named "[a]n old man grows into a young man" (Dalley 2000, 119) by virtue of which he hoped to achieve immortality. Gilgamesh must sink into the Apsu (the underground reservoir of fresh spring-water) in order to obtain this magical plant, and the serpent itself slithers through a pool of water when he steals it, and yet it still does not seem to allude to any notion of a primordial sea monster. The theft rather explains in etiological fashion why any garden-variety snake will shed its skin and thus apparently rejuvenate itself. To return to Eden, the Yahwist (J) seems to draw upon both of these topoi: the snake, by convincing Eve to eat the fruit of the tree knowledge, effectively robs the human race of the opportunity it would presumably have had to eat from the tree of life and thus live forever (Gen. 3:22–24). As a result, the snake not only is condemned to its lowly existence of slithering on its belly (no eternal youth for this serpent), but also becomes the ontological enemy of humanity (Gen. 3:15). There are, in other words, no interpretive shortcuts, for no mechanical application of an apparent literary parallel will do. Each appearance of the serpent must be carefully considered on its own terms.

I would note in passing that the biblical writers not only appropriated isolated motifs and themes, but small-scale narrative conventions as well (Parker 1989). The annunciation type-scene, for example—including that involving Isaac's birth and its attendant laughter—was bequeathed to the biblical writers from their literary milieu. Along the same lines, the ancient Near Eastern covenant form seems to have shaped the book of Deuteronomy and, to some extent, the account of the wilderness period stretching from Exodus through Numbers. However, broader attempts to analyze biblical narrative as such in terms of ancient Near Eastern genres are less convincing (Damrosch 1987). Once again, historicist comparison can only be justified on the basis of its interpretive consequences.

FORMALIST COMPARISONS

Formal literary features, as such, are not limited to dissemination via cultural contact. Consider that event I am calling the birth of prose literature—or the "birth of the scribe" (Kawashima 2004, 210–214). When Robert Alter (2011, 25–54) drew attention to the significance of the prose medium of biblical narrative, he was simultaneously contrasting biblical narrative to ancient Near Eastern myth and epic, on the one hand, and comparing biblical narrative with modern prose fiction, on the other: precisely the historical relationship constitutes a rupture. His thesis has been criticized for being "ahistorical," but in fact the wide distribution of prose and poetry across history and geography demonstrates that its dissemination is not limited to influence. What makes possible such transhistorical comparisons is the medium of language itself, as well as other abstract aesthetic principles—the use of form, pattern, repetition, symmetry, and so on.

The transition from oral tradition to literary prose brought about a radical shift in the narrative representation of reality. While Erich Auerbach does not address the distinction between oral poetry and written prose explicitly, what he accomplished in the celebrated opening chapter of *Mimesis* (1953, 3–23) was, in effect, to trace this shift in representation. Undertaking a formalist (non-historicist) comparison of the digression on Odysseus's scar in *Odyssey* 19 and the account of the binding of Isaac in Genesis 22, he noted how Homer's story takes place in a "perpetual foreground" (11), whereas that of Genesis is "fraught with background" (12). Thus, while the epithets Homer attaches to his heroes, for example, endow them with publicly observable virtues (6), no such epithets are to be found in biblical prose (9). What this means is that mythic/epic reality, in stark contrast to biblical reality, is "essentialized": its entities are endowed with unchanging qualities, fully externalized in a perpetual foreground (Kawashima 2011). Auerbach's point, then, was not to denigrate Homer's aesthetic achievement. It was, rather, to distinguish between two modes of narrative art: what I have called "traditional" and "post-traditional" art (Kawashima 2004, 161–189).

This same distinction accounts for the differences separating ancient Near Eastern narrative poetry—in which category I also include "archaic" biblical poems such as Exodus 15 and Judges 5—from biblical prose narrative. As a corollary, I would add that distinguishing between biblical narrative and ancient Near Eastern myth and epic does not amount to celebrating one at the expense of the other.

Let us return to Ugaritic. Here, too, one finds heroic epithets of the type Auerbach pointed to in Homer: El "the Bull," Danel "the man of Rapau," Kirta "the Noble." By extension, the significance of a son within this narrative world can be perfectly captured in terms of a set of publicly observable behaviors, as rehearsed here by Danel: "to set up a stela for my divine ancestor"; "to send my incense up from the earth"; "to shut the jaws of my abusers"; "to hold my hand when I am drunk"; "to eat my grain-offering in the temple of Baal"; "to patch my roof when it gets muddy" (*Aqhat* 1.2.17–23; Coogan and Smith 2012, 37). This litany of filial duties constitutes a type of extended epithet. It is not particular to Danel's personal point of view, but shared with the gods themselves—and thus with the entire cosmos—as is demonstrated by earlier iterations of this list recited by both El and (apparently) Baal (*Aqhat* 1.1.27–33; 1.2.1–7; Coogan and Smith 2012, 35–37). In other words, the birth of a son has a universally agreed-upon meaning—a type of narrative consensus in which "objective" fact perfectly coincides with "subjective" opinion (Kawashima 2008). In the same way, Danel's actual behavior perfectly conforms to the stereotype of a just ruler: "got up and sat at the entrance to the gate, / among the leaders on the threshing floor. / He judged the cases of widows, / presided over orphans' hearings" (*Aqhat* 1.5.5–9; 3.1.20–24; Coogan and Smith 2012, 39, 47), just as Pugat, Aqhat's sister, constitutes a paragon of feminine virtue: "You who carry water, / you who collect dew on your hair, / you who know the course of the stars" (*Aqhat* 3.2.1–3; 3.4.36–38; Coogan and Smith 2012, 48, 54). The world of Ugaritic myth and epic, no less than Homer's, is thus, to borrow another phrase of Auerbach's, "uniformly illuminated" (1953, 3). This closed world of idealized or stereotyped entities corresponds to what Walter Benjamin (1969) described as the traditional art of the storyteller; in Bakhtinian terms, it is "monologic," a term Bakhtin (1982) tellingly opposed to the "dialogic" realism of the modern novel.

Dialogism, however, is a feature not just of the modern novel but of literary prose in general, which is simply incapable of supporting the monologic world of oral epic poetry. As a result, the literary consensus of traditional narrative poetry breaks apart in biblical narrative. For example, the entities that populate biblical narrative are not graced with heroic epithets as are their epic counterparts, for as prosaic beings, they lack those essential qualities that would ground them (Auerbach 1953, 9). Not even Moses is capable of winning the universal approbation worthy of an epic hero: he is absolutely reviled by one (Pharaoh in Exod. 5–14), grudgingly revered by some (Pharaoh's servants in Exod. 9:20–21; 10:7; 11:3), bitterly resented by others (Korah et al. in Num. 16). What epithet could possibly suffice to capture the qualities of such a one in such a world? By extension, if the role of the son in Ugaritic tradition consists, as we have seen, of a universally accepted litany of publicly observable behaviors, the role of the son in biblical narrative, while undeniably crucial to the patriarchal lineage, is irreparably fragmented. Let us return to the birth of Isaac. God promised to make Abraham into a "great nation" as early as Genesis 12:2, and the providential design implied by such a promise would seem to ground the birth of his son and heir in some sort of bedrock of objective truth. For the human players involved in this unfolding drama, however, the divine plan is shrouded in obscurity—"fraught with background," to borrow Auerbach's formulation once again. It is arguably for this reason that Sarah comes to offer her servant Hagar to her husband as a second wife and surrogate mother (16:1–3): perhaps she will serve as the vehicle for God's promise, Sarah seems to think. Since the story nowhere specifies that Sarah is aware of this promise, however, it is just as plausible that she is merely seeking the material security provided by a son, albeit that of a surrogate (Fewell and Gunn 1993, 44–45). Such ambiguity is only to be expected, given biblical narrative's spare style. Needless to say, her plan backfires, ultimately resulting in the expulsion of the Egyptian slave and her unchosen son. The matriarch herself finally conceives and gives birth to a son, but God immediately proceeds to test her husband by commanding him to offer up Isaac as a whole burnt offering (Gen. 22). Given such twists and turns as these in the divine plan, one could easily imagine Sarah and Abraham exclaiming like Rebekah (the latter, in response to her difficult pregnancy): "If this is how it is to be, why do I live?" (Gen. 25:22). But the Bible's dialogic prose refuses to sustain this sort of uniform (monologic) response. Not even the laughter inspired by Isaac's celebrated birth is unalloyed with ambiguity. Rather, as I noted earlier, the joy occasioned by the birth of the son in Ugaritic is refracted in biblical narrative through the lens of irony, distorted by Abraham and Sarah's wry musings on the rather belated fulfillment of Yahweh's promise: Genesis 17:17; 18:12–15; 21:6f. By the time we get to the secondary echoes of "laughter" (ṣaḥaq) in Isaac's life in the form of "playing" (meṣaḥeq), we have entered the realm of self-conscious or reflexive literature (Gen. 21:9; 26:8). The motif of laughter has been, as Viktor Shklovsky would have said, "defamiliarized" (1965).

Conclusion

This shift in literary representation entails a corresponding shift in biblical narrative's representation of the divine. What has been inadequately interpreted as ancient Israel's "monotheistic revolution" actually constitutes a more profound transformation of the very concept of God. Whereas the distinction between monotheism and polytheism merely involves a distinction between singular and plural, the more important transformation involves a metaphysical reinterpretation of godhood.

Let us return to the contrast I drew earlier between *Enuma Elish* and Genesis 1. Tiamat, one recalls, personifies the primordial saltwater sea, while her consort Apsu personifies the freshwater source of rivers and springs. Everything that will ever exist within this cosmos descends "biologically" from their bodies: gods, humans, nature. The deities of Mesopotamian myth are thus "immanent" to the cosmos, which is also to say that the cosmos of myth constitutes a single whole, a monism—not unrelated to Bakhtin's notion of epic's monologic language. In the Priestly creation account in Genesis 1, everything has changed. Whereas Tiamat and Apsu together constitute the cosmos in its primitive state, Genesis 1 conceives of God precisely in opposition to the primordial "Deep": indeed, the description of the "wind [*ruaḥ*] of God" hovering over the "face of the waters" (Gen. 1:2) constitutes an hypostasis of what we now know as the dualism between spirit and matter (Kawashima 2006, 247–251). In other words, Elohim is external to the physical world, that is, transcends it.

In a sense, this transformation of the divine constitutes the subject matter of that veritable parody of "pagan" myth we find in Elijah's confrontation with the 450 prophets of Baal (1 Kings 18). In this well-known story, Elijah challenges his rivals to a contest, an empirical test of their respective deities' godhood. Both parties will set up a sacrifice, but without setting it on fire. They will then each call upon their god to accept their offering by sending down fire (i.e., lightning, portent of rain) from the skies to consume it: "And it will be, the god [*ha'elohim*] who answers with fire is God [*ha'elohim*]" (18:24). In order to correctly interpret what follows, one must call to mind the sorts of myth and ritual reflected in the *Baal* cycle. The very set-up of the biblical story evokes the cycle of life and death, fertility and famine, that is the Baal myth's subject. For it takes place in the third year of a drought (18:1) proclaimed by Elijah himself in the name of Yahweh (17:1). Drought according to *Baal* is a cosmic symptom of the death of Baal—this god being an immanent and embodied deity. In response to this grievous loss, El his father (*Baal* 5.6.17–22; Coogan and Smith 2012, 143–144) and later Anat his sister (6.1.2–5; Coogan and Smith 2012, 144) mourn his death by cutting their skin and "plowing" (*yḥrt / tḥrt*) their chests like a "garden" (*gn*), which ritual thus metaphorically connects the object of their grief to fertility and life. The dismissive "exoticizing" portrayal of the "primitive" rituals performed by Baal's prophets in 1 Kings 18—they "limped about" their altar (18:26) and "cried out in a great voice and cut themselves according to their custom . . . until the blood gushed forth" (18:28)—must be understood in this light. They are mourning Baal's apparent absence (death) in an attempt to reestablish his presence (rebirth) via sympathetic magic. Similarly, the taunts Elijah slings at Baal's representatives—perhaps he is lost in "contemplation" or "on a journey" or "asleep" (18:27)—effectively mock the mythic conceptualization of the gods, whose bodily life imposes various needs, desires, and other physical limitations upon them. In a revealing contrast to these prophets' impressive but ineffectual performance, Elijah successfully calls forth fire from Yahweh with a simple prayer (18:36–37)—not coincidentally, a prose prayer, the typical form of prayer in biblical prose narrative (Greenberg 1983). Once again, it is the literary milieu that brings biblical narrative into sharper focus.

REFERENCES

Alter, Robert. 2011. *The Art of Biblical Narrative*. 2nd ed. New York: Basic Books.

Auerbach, Erich. 1953. *Mimesis: The Representation of Reality in Western Literature*. Princeton, NJ: Princeton University Press.

Bakhtin, M. M. 1982. *The Dialogic Imagination: Four Essays*. Austin: University of Texas Press.

Benjamin, Walter. 1969. "The Storyteller: Reflections on the Works of Nikolai Leskov." In *Illuminations: Essays and Reflections*, 83–109. New York: Schocken Books.

Coogan, Michael, D., and Mark S. Smith. 2012. *Stories from Ancient Canaan*. 2nd ed. Louisville, KY: Westminster John Knox Press.

Cross, Frank Moore. 1998. *From Epic to Canon*. Baltimore, MD: Johns Hopkins University Press.

Dalley, Stephanie, ed. and trans. 2000. *Myths from Mesopotamia: Creation, the Flood, Gilgamesh, and Others*. Rev. ed. Oxford World Classics. Oxford: Oxford University Press.

Damrosch, David. 1987. *The Narrative Covenant: Transformations of Genre in the Growth of Biblical Literature*. San Francisco: Harper & Row.

Fewell, Danna Nolan, and David M. Gunn. 1993. *Gender, Power, and Promise: The Subject of the Bible's First Story*. Nashville, TN: Abingdon Press.

Greenberg, Moshe. 1983. *Biblical Prose Prayer: As a Window to the Popular Religion of Ancient Israel*. Berkeley: University of California Press.

Hallo, William W., and Lawson K. Younger, Jr., eds. 2003. *The Context of Scripture*. 3 vols. Leiden: Brill.

Kawashima, Robert S. 2004. *Biblical Narrative and the Death of the Rhapsode*. Bloomington: Indiana University Press.

Kawashima, Robert S. 2006. "The Priestly Tent of Meeting and the Problem of Divine Transcendence: An 'Archaeology' of the Sacred." *Journal of Religion* 86: 226–257.

Kawashima, Robert S. 2007. "Comparative Literature and Biblical Studies: The Case of Allusion." *Prooftexts* 27: 324–344.

Kawashima, Robert S. 2008. "What Is Narrative Perspective? A Non-Historicist Answer." In *Phantom Sentences: Essays in Linguistics and Literature Presented to Ann Banfield*, edited by Robert S. Kawashima, Gilles Philippe, and Thelma Sowley, 105–126. Bern: Peter Lang.

Kawashima, Robert S. 2011. "The Syntax of Narrative Forms." In *Narratives of Egypt and the Ancient Near East: Literary and Linguistic Approaches*, edited by F. Hagen, J. Johnston, W. Monkhouse, K. Piquette, J. Tait, and M. Worthington, 341–369. Leuven: Peeters.

Parker, Simon B. 1989. *The Pre-Biblical Narrative Tradition*. Atlanta, GA: Scholars Press.

Pritchard, James B. 2010. *The Ancient Near East: An Anthology of Texts and Pictures*. Princeton, NJ: Princeton University Press.

Sandmel, Samuel. 1962. "Parallelomania." *Journal of Biblical Literature* 81: 1–13.

Shklovsky, Viktor. 1965. "Art as Technique." In *Russian Formalist Criticism: Four Essays*, translated by Lee T. Lemon and Marion J. Reis, 3–24. Lincoln: University of Nebraska Press.

Vanstiphout, Herman L. J., trans. 2003. *Epics of Sumerian Kings: The Matter of Aratta*. Atlanta, GA: Society of Biblical Literature.

CHAPTER 4

··

NEW TESTAMENT NARRATIVE AND GRECO-ROMAN LITERATURE

··

AUSTIN BUSCH

THE Bible's status as a collection of authoritative religious writings encourages readers to search out and assign special hermeneutical significance to the invocations of earlier biblical works in later scriptural writings. This is appropriate, at least insofar as the writings the New Testament's authors identified as Scripture correspond to those anthologized in the Old Testament. New Testament writers treat Old Testament literature with extraordinary esteem. They constantly echo it and quote it approvingly, submitting to and drawing on its religious and rhetorical authority. Only rarely do they invoke an Old Testament text as an interlocutive voice with which to disagree, or point to one as a literary model to reject.

New Testament authors show much less deference toward classical Greek literature: their invocations of it are imaginatively suggestive, rather than hermeneutically decisive; they view it as useful rather than authoritative. The evangelists in particular implicate pagan Greek writings in complicated dialogues that at once acknowledge their value as touchstones of effective literary communication in the Greco-Roman world, while at the same time resisting their ideological, religious, and aesthetic exemplarity—unless, foregoing such a nuanced approach, they simply assimilate Hellenic literary others to their own compositional designs and theological purposes. According to either explanation, traces of Homer's *Odyssey* in Mark's gospel will appear faint when compared to more overt references to the Old Testament book of Daniel, for instance. But while allusions to Greco-Roman literature are qualitatively different from and often less obvious than invocations of prior biblical writings (including the related phenomenon of synoptic parallels), they surface frequently in the New Testament narratives, and scrutiny of them can generate significant interpretive insights.

This chapter explores some traces of pagan Greek literature's influence on Acts and the gospels. It begins by considering an explicit quotation of Aratus's *Phaenomena* in Acts, and then examines allusions to Euripides's *Bacchae* in the same work, before discussing a subtle echo of Homer's *Odyssey* in Mark. This survey does not uncover new points of contact between New Testament narratives and Greco-Roman literature. The first two literary relationships it considers have been studied thoroughly (e.g., Dibelius 1956; MacDonald 2013); the last, more cursorily (MacDonald 2000, 111–119; Louden 2011, 179–181).[1] It does, however, draw somewhat different and perhaps more nuanced interpretive conclusions than previous explorations. At the same time, the chapter locates these examples of intertextual engagement in their Greco-Roman rhetorical context, demonstrating that the kinds of literary relationships they exemplify conform to models of influence and techniques of literary adaptation discussed and employed by men of letters in the Roman imperial world.

ACTS AND ARATUS

While declaiming in front of the Athenian Areopagus (Acts 17:22–31), Luke's Paul quotes the *Phaenomena* of Aratus, a third-century poet closely associated with Athens. This is hardly surprising, for the *Phaenomena* was the most widely read poem in antiquity other than the *Iliad* and *Odyssey* (*OCD*[4], "Aratus [1]"), and allusions to it are ubiquitous (see Kidd 1961, 5–7; 1997, 36–48).[2] Paul begins his discourse by promising to proclaim the identity of the "unknown god" whose altar he had recently seen in the city (Acts 17:23). He identifies this god as the cosmic creator, who (paradoxically) does not live in man-made temples or require human service (17:24); on the contrary, the god gives and sustains human life: "In him we live and move and exist. As even some of the poets among you have said, 'for we too are his offspring'" (17:28, quoting *Phaen.* 5).[3] In light of the connection Paul draws between the Athenians' "unknown god" and Aratus's description of Zeus as humanity's nourishing progenitor, Acts's opening reference to the mysterious altar Paul observed while touring the city recalls a statement about Zeus that Aratus makes in the *Phaenomena* just before the quoted line: "full of Zeus are all the streets / and all the marketplaces of men" (2–3).

Luke's Paul both echoes the *Phaenomena* and implicitly questions some of its theological conclusions, which is to be expected insofar as he gestures toward a syncretistic association of the creator Zeus in Aratus's poem with Israel's God Yahweh (see Dibelius 1956, 48–53, for complementary analysis). For Paul, the differences between the correlated creators are no less (and probably much more) significant than their similarities. Thus, while Aratus, in the section of the *Phaenomena* from which Paul quotes, attributes to Zeus a scheme of cosmic organization that supports agricultural labor—divinely ordained astronomical signs tell human beings when to wake for work, when to plant, when to plow, and so on (ll. 6–13)—Paul proposes a universe designed by God to facilitate not physical toil but theological work. While affirming Aratus's fundamental conviction that an all-powerful divinity created and populated the world, Paul elaborates that basic idea with reference to Deuteronomy 32:8, explaining that God divided the world into discrete nations, each with its own boundaries, so that its human population might search for God efficiently: "He made . . . all nations of men to dwell on the entire face of the earth, marking out the times determined for them as well as the boundaries of their dwellings, in order that they might search for God, on the chance that they might grope for and even find him" (Acts 17:26–27). Luke's Paul thus draws a link between national identity and theological inquiry, which contextualizes his earlier compliment of the Athenians' capacious religious devotion (17:22), as well as the related ethnographic observation Luke makes about the city's insatiable appetite for innovative philosophical knowledge (17:21, cf. vv. 17–20). The Athenians fulfill the purposes of God's created cosmos by groping for and even happening upon God. Indeed, their persistent religious and theological explorations have borne significant fruit, as their altar to the unknown god and their poet Aratus's praise of the cosmic creator attest.

However, when Paul's declamation shifts to polemic against idolatry in Acts 17:29–31 (see also vv. 24–25), that modulation serves to underscore the limitations of the Athenians' theological discoveries, incriminating even their most productive religious impulses. Aratus claims in the section of the *Phaenomena* from which Paul quotes that humanity's appropriately grateful response for Zeus's ordering of the universe is divine propitiation: "therefore always, from first to last, do men propitiate (*hilaskontai*) him" (14). By implication, humans and the god are caught in a reciprocal cycle of mutually beneficial gratitude. Paul, however, insists that the creator Aratus's poem celebrates, whom he equates with the unknown god whose altar he had earlier discovered, "does not dwell in temples made by hands nor is he served by human hands, as if he needed anything" (17:24–25). The divine creator requires from people not cultic service but theological searching (17:27). Indeed, once they have happened upon him, he requires repentance exemplified in precisely the rejection of pagan religious rites (17:29–30), which distort the truth about God as much as they reveal it.

The Lukan Paul thus agrees with Aratus that God generates and sustains human life, but he rejects the poet's suggestion that God created humanity as a tautological entity, whose primary purpose is self-sustenance through efficient agricultural labor, and whose religious impulses originate in gratitude to God for its means of survival. On the contrary, God has conceived of humanity teleologically, as a confederation of political communities whose combined purpose is to discover their origins in him. By implication, human attention to divinity is not a grateful by-product of the cosmos's ordering, as Aratus would have it; it is its *raison d'être*. God wants nothing that human hands can offer (17:25); he rather wants groping human hands to find him, and he has ordered the cosmos so that they might do so efficiently (17:26–27). Luke leverages this idea to praise the Athenians for the successful theological explorations that issued in Aratus's hymn of praise to the creator, even while critiquing some of the theology and religious practices the *Phaenomena* advocates.

LUKE-ACTS AND EURIPIDES

An analogous approach to Greco-Roman literature underlies Luke's sustained engagement with Euripides's *Bacchae*.[4] In Acts 26, Paul reports that the risen Christ quoted Euripides when he appeared to him on the road to Damascus. In the *Bacchae*, Dionysus, disguised as a young man bringing the "new god's" rites to Greece (ll. 219, 256, etc.), had rebuked Pentheus for his obstinate resistance to the innovative religious movement focused on himself: "I would sacrifice to him rather than kick against the goads, / enraged, a mortal against a god" (*Bac.* 794–795). Paul's situation is analogous. Jesus appears to him in unrecognizable form (cf. Acts 26:15) and rebukes the ignorant persecutor for his futile resistance to the innovative religious movement focused on himself. He accuses Paul of "kick[ing] against the goads" (26:14), precisely the language with which Dionysus had warned Pentheus.[5] Of course, the stories of Pentheus and Paul play out differently. In response to Dionysus's intervention, Pentheus doubles down on his hostility to the new god's worshippers, vowing to slaughter the maenads during their sacred revelry and to offer them as the sacrifice the disguised Bacchus recommends (*Bac.* 796–797). This provokes the god's reversal of his words: Pentheus is slaughtered by deluded bacchantes during their celebration of the new god's rites. Luke's Paul, on the contrary, immediately halts his persecution of the new divinity's followers upon encountering the risen Christ and enlists himself as Jesus's envoy (Acts 26:19–20; cf. MacDonald 2013, 478, 480–482). The analogy the allusion to the *Bacchae* draws—not just between Pentheus and Paul, but between Dionysus, Greek god of nature's amoral vital forces, and Christ, who calls on men to repent from sin and behave accordingly (26:20)—is sufficiently jarring that Luke registers its strangeness in a peculiar linguistic note. Paul says that the risen Christ quoted the words of Euripides's Bacchus "in the Hebrew language" (26:14), a statement that calls attention to the boldness of Luke's literary transformation of Pentheus's encounter with Zeus's son Dionysus into Paul's encounter with Jesus, son of Yahweh.

Acts frequently draws on Euripides's *Bacchae* for ideologically resonant language, as well as for adaptable scenarios with which to describe the authorities' resistance to the new religious movement. Examples of both occur in the section that culminates in Luke's initial account of Paul's conversion (cf. MacDonald 2013, 476–479), in which the Pharisee Gamaliel warns his fellow council members to leave the apostles alone lest they become *theomachoi*, "god-fighters" (5:34–39). In the *Bacchae*, the verbal form of this Greek compound describes Pentheus's arrogant resistance to the new god's rites (ll. 45, 325, 1255; cf. 635–636, 789). In fact, in the material preceding Paul's conversion, Luke frequently describes his resistance to the religious movement he encounters in terms similar to Euripides's description of Pentheus. The god-fighter Paul participates in Stephen's stoning (7:58; 8:1)—the punishment Pentheus had planned for Bacchus in his guise as a young man (*Bac.* 355–357)—and he drags men and women of the church in Judea to prison (Acts 8:3), just as Pentheus had imprisoned the bacchantes (*Bac.* 226–227). Furthermore, Luke describes Paul as "breathing menace and murder against the disciples of the Lord" (9:1), a vivid elaboration of Euripides's more decorous descriptions of Pentheus as "breathing rage" (620) and "breathing mighty words" (640) against Bacchus and his followers (cf. MacDonald 2013, 478, who notes different correspondences).

Acts's numerous depictions of apostles' miraculous release from unjust imprisonment are likewise frequently modeled on the *Bacchae* (MacDonald 2013, 478–480, 484–487). The story of Peter's release in Acts 12:6–19 echoes Euripides's account of the maenads' divinely ordained deliverance in *Bacchae* 443–448: "of their own accord (*automata*) were the chains loosed (*dielythê*) from the women's feet / and the keys gave access to the doorway without a mortal's hand" (*Bac.* 447–448). Luke writes that "the chains (*halyseis*) fell away from his hands" and "the gate opened of its own accord (*automata*)" (12:7, 10; Dodds 1960, 132). The fact that Euripides's later account of the disguised Bacchus's supernatural escape incorporates a reference to the absconded prisoner's divinely deployed doppelganger, as does Luke's of Peter's escape in Acts 12, suggests a secondary connection between the two works (*Bac.* 630–631, cf. 618–621; Acts 12:15, cf. vv. 7–11).

Luke's reliance on the *Bacchae* is even more apparent in the account of Paul and Silas's release: "Suddenly an earthquake struck, so great that the foundations of the prison shook; all the doors were immediately opened and the chains of everybody were loosened" (Acts 16:26). Dionysus's miraculous escape from Pentheus likewise involved an earthquake, which destroyed the palace and provoked a panicked search for the missing prisoner (*Bac.* 576–637; MacDonald 2013, 484–485).[6] The parallels, like those between Paul and Pentheus discussed above, set the stage for Luke's sudden divergence from the Euripidean tragedy. Immediately after escaping, Bacchus travels straight to his previously freed maenads: "I have come to you, giving no thought to Pentheus" (*Bac.* 637). He vows to remain equanimous even when Pentheus pursues him (640–641) and repeatedly attempts to put Pentheus off (647, 656–659). After Pentheus vows to sacrifice the bacchantes to Bacchus (796–797, 809), however, Dionysus sets in motion the grisly revenge plot that culminates in the reversal of Pentheus's outrageous promise (ll. 810 until end). Paul, on the contrary, never deserts, let alone avenges himself on his hostile captors. He refuses to abandon his jailor to the suicidal panic that overtakes him when he finds the doors opened. Remaining within the jail even after it has been rendered incapable of holding him, Paul saves the warden's life and converts him to the new religion he promulgates (Acts 16:27–34)—precisely the opposite of the effect Euripides's liberated Bacchus has on his jailer Pentheus (cf. MacDonald 2013, 486). Euripides's play thus serves as a literary model allowing Luke to emphasize the futility of resistance to the "new god" his protagonists proclaim, but at the same time, strategic divergence from that model underscores the irenic strategy for overcoming adversaries that Christ and his emissaries adopt. Despite the awesome power their God wields, they win opponents over by showing compassion rather than vengefully defeating them.

Luke thematizes this divine restraint from violence most emphatically in the Annunciation, an episode rarely recognized as a Euripidean revision. At the beginning of the *Bacchae*, Euripides refers to the tradition according to which Dionysus is the product of an adulterous union of Zeus and Semele, who was destroyed with lightening when the divinity came to her in the form of the glorious god of the storm (ll. 6–9). Euripides's Bacchus is outraged that his mother's relatives claim Zeus destroyed her because she lied about her relationship with the god in order to cover up base fornication (26–42). Analogously, at the beginning of Luke's two-volume history, the evangelist recounts Jesus's origins in a union between Yahweh and Mary (cf. MacDonald 2013, 464), but one entirely chaste and remarkably tender. The angel Gabriel informs Mary that, though she is a virgin, she will nonetheless conceive God's son Jesus (Luke 1:31–34), and when she asks how, she is told that "the power of the most high will overshadow [*episkiasei*]" her (1:35). The Greek word *episkiazō* alludes to the Old Testament's depiction of Yahweh as God of the storm whose dangerous lightening (e.g., Ps. 18:7–15) is screened by clouds lest it destroy those who encounter it directly.[7] Thus, against Euripides's portrayal of Zeus, Luke underscores the gentleness of the biblical storm god Yahweh, who, metaphorically screening his lightning safely behind the cloud, gently overshadows his consort Mary. Indeed, he not only refrains from consuming her in his fiery embrace, but he manages to impregnate her while leaving her virginity intact!

THE GRECO-ROMAN RHETORICAL CONTEXT

No New Testament narrative announces its allusive relationship to classical Greek literature as clearly as Luke-Acts, which actually quotes Aratus and Euripides, and contains widely recognized allusions to Homer as well.[8] This will not surprise the careful reader. Luke's Greek is more sophisticated than the Greek of the other evangelists, a refinement complemented by occasional invocations of the Hellenic literary canon. Moreover, Luke's narrative, unlike that of the other evangelists, encompasses the church's expansion beyond Judea into the wider

Greco-Roman world, a larger canvas that benefits from the full palate of literary colors he employs, including quotations and echoes of classical Greek writings scattered throughout his two-volume history.

Yet, as my analysis of the use of the *Bacchae* in Luke-Acts implies, direct quotation and discrete verbal allusion are relatively minor elements of Luke's engagement with pagan Greek literature. By stressing literary imitation, emulation, and various forms of rewriting, Greco-Roman rhetorical training encouraged writers to foster radically revisionary relationships to earlier writings. Particularly relevant is rhetoricians' treatment of *paraphrasis*, a tactic of revision that involved the transformation of a literary text's form, but the maintenance of its fundamental sense (see, e.g., Theon, *Progymnasmata* 107–110 [citing Patillon 1997]; Quintilian, *Institutions* 10.5.4–11). *Paraphrasis* functioned as a complex mode of literary contention, with a later author at once following and improving an earlier model, acknowledging its exemplarity even as he underscored its flaws. A passage from Pliny articulates this tension:

> There is no harm, when you have read something to the point that you grasp its represented theme, to write, as it were, in rivalry (*quasi aemulum scribere*) and to compare what you have written with what you have read, and to consider assiduously what you and what the other writer more suitably accomplish. There is great satisfaction if you do something or other better, great shame if the other does all things better than you. (*Ep.* 7.9.3)

In practice, the revisionary improvements a later author might make were as likely to be ethical or theological as formal, even though ancient treatments of paraphrastic revision usually occur within discussions of rhetoric and are thus more attuned to style than to theme. Contentious thematic revision is ubiquitous in the Greco-Roman literary tradition, however. To cite but one instance, Virgil's *Aeneid* manages to retell Odysseus's encounter with the Cyclops Polyphemus so that the proto-Roman hero Aeneas saves and incorporates into his Trojan crew a sailor whom the Greek hero had abandoned on the Cyclopses' shore (*Aen.* 3.568–683; cf. *Od.* 9.105–566). Virgil's account of Aeneas at once imitates Homer's exemplary story of Odysseus's defeat of Polyphemus and, at the same time, draws attention to an ethical flaw in the Homeric hero, if not in the very concept of heroism that the *Odyssey* thematizes. Virgil's Aeneas is heroic precisely because he founds a new civilization for and with the Trojan remnant he saves, and this fundamentally political conception of heroism stands in tension with the individualized, domestic account Homer presents in his story of Odysseus, who is heroic insofar as he manages to return to his own family and set his own house aright, despite losing literally everyone who followed him to Troy. This crucial difference between the Homeric and Virgilian heroes is emblematized in the *Aeneid's* critical revision of the *Odyssey's* Cyclops episode, which concludes with Aeneas welcoming a crewman whom Odysseus had irresponsibly abandoned.

Ancient writers frequently advertised their contentious engagement with exemplary texts, through citation, quotation, or clear verbal allusion. The Virgilian example discussed above is a case in point. Writers were under no obligation to do this, however, for literary borrowing was ultimately an act of assimilative amalgamation rather than cataloging. As Seneca writes,

> We too ought to imitate these bees and separate whatever we have gathered from our diverse reading (for such things are better preserved if kept distinct) and then, by bringing to bear the

care and faculties of our own genius (*adhibita ingenii nostri cura et facultate*), we ought to conflate the various things we have extracted into a single flavor, so that it may still appear to be something other than its source, even if from where it was obtained will be apparent (*ut etiam si apparuerit unde sumptum sit, aliud tamen esse quam unde sumptum est appareat*). (*Ep.* 84.5)

As a result of the assimilative impulse, discrete cases of literary imitation may be extremely difficult to identify, as Seneca acknowledges (*Ep.* 84.8). Biblical scholars today rarely display the tolerance for allusive subtlety that Seneca's assessment of literary imitation would seem to call for, instead insisting on the presence of more-or-less extensive shared language as a requirement for acknowledging that a later writing engages with an earlier one (e.g., Sandes 2005; Winn 2010). For this reason, MacDonald's highly suggestive work on New Testament narrative's engagement with classical Greek literature has frequently been met with benign neglect by biblical scholars, if not with dismissive rejection (e.g., Hooker 2002; Mitchell 2003 offers a more sympathetic, but equally critical assessment). Many are simply not convinced that the kinds of parallels discussed earlier evince ancient literary influence rather than modern interpretive caprice, especially since the New Testament invokes the Old so much more overtly. Some biblical scholars interested in New Testament narrative's engagement with Greco-Roman literature avoid the problem of direct influence by comparing the gospels and Acts to classical writings generically. Richard A. Burridge's (2004) important argument that the gospels constitute Greco-Roman biographies of Jesus is an influential example of this approach, although many others might be cited (e.g., Robbins 2012, 47–113; Brant 2004; Bonz 2000; Tolbert 1989, which views Mark as a Greek novel; Via 1973).

Such approaches have great value. Moreover, MacDonald's detailed intertextual interpretations of specific New Testament narratives frequently fail to convince even scholars sympathetic to his maximalist approach to identifying allusions. Nonetheless, readers interested in the New Testament's engagement with classical Greek literature cannot legitimately avoid the kinds of problems MacDonald's work negotiates (admittedly, with mixed success) by refusing on methodological grounds to consider cases of intertextual engagement that are not explicitly flagged as such (e.g., by extensive shared language). Ancient authors, as Seneca makes clear, consciously collected discursive material from previous works in order to construct thematically and stylistically superior compositions possessing their own coherent shape (*Ep.* 84.5, quoted earlier), with the result that specific instances of literary engagement may be quite hard to discern (*Ep.* 84.8). But this difficulty, which only increases for contemporary readers largely unfamiliar with the corpus of extant Greco-Roman literature, does not relieve critical interpreters of their responsibility to produce historically informed readings of New Testament narratives. The New Testament's earliest audiences, we must presume, consisted in large part of pagan converts to Christianity whose literary canon would have included such authors as Homer, Aratus, and Euripides. Even if we concede that they would have come to assign the Law and the Prophets superior authority, we must also conclude that they would have been far more sensitive to subtle invocations of pagan Greek texts than most readers are today. If a plausible case can be made for even faint echoes of these writings in New Testament narratives, and if it can be demonstrated that their recognition deepens our understanding of the texts in which they appear, we ought to acknowledge that we have belatedly hit upon a semiotic complex that largely ceased to be recognized as the New Testament came to be read in a more and more exclusively Judeo-Christian context. In short, there are good reasons for embracing allusive subtlety, rather than demanding explicit citation or its equivalence in our examination of New Testament narrative's engagements with Greco-Roman literature.

MARK AND HOMER

This chapter has thus far focused on cases of explicit literary influence, insofar as the examples discussed involve quotation of the pagan Greek texts in question. I conclude by considering a more elusive case of literary revision, Mark's rewriting of the story of Eurycleia washing and anointing Odysseus (*Od.* 19.353–507) in his account of an anonymous woman anointing Jesus (Mark 14:3–9; cf. MacDonald 2000, 111–119; Louden 2011, 269–271). In Mark, a woman anoints the story's hero, as in Homer (*Od.* 19.505), where she bathes him as well.[9] In Mark, as in Homer, the woman breaks and/or spills a container while performing this service (Mark 14:3; cf. *Od.* 19.468–471; MacDonald 2000, 117). Finally, in Mark, as in Homer, the woman's service is linked to her unexpected recognition of the one she serves: in the course of bathing and anointing the disguised Odysseus, Eurycleia recognizes a scar on his thigh, which leads her, alone among Odysseus's servants, to realize that he is the master newly returned home (*Od.* 19.467–475); analogously, Jesus suggests that the anonymous woman's anointing of him signals her realization of his impending death (14:8)—a crucial feature of his identity in Mark (MacDonald 2000, 118).

These parallels become even more compelling when we take into account the context of the Markan scene, which immediately follows the parable of the Returning Master, the final section of Jesus's Olivet discourse (13:32–37). Jesus there compares the Son of Man to a householder who goes on a journey and leaves his slaves in charge of his home, warning them to do their work faithfully and guard the gate lest he return unexpectedly "in the evening, or at midnight, or at cockcrow, or at dawn," find them negligent, and presumably punish them (13:35). This is precisely the situation in which Odysseus finds himself in books 17–21 of the *Odyssey* (MacDonald 2000, 114). He has returned home to servants who have failed to guard his house. Not only have they allowed suitors of his wife to consume his resources in a neverending celebration, but in many cases, they have actually joined the party. This prompts Odysseus's brutal punishment of them.

In the context of Mark's subsequent Passion Narrative, the parable's slaves signify the disciples, who metaphorically and literally sleep as Jesus prepares to die—and at precisely the times when the parable indicates the servants ought to expect their master's return (originally, Lightfoot 1950, 48–59). At the Passover meal "in the evening" (14:17), Jesus warns his followers that one of them will betray (14:17–21), all will desert (14:26–28), and Peter will deny him (14:29–31), prompting from the disciples not self-reflection or mutual fortification, but rather one confusedly false refutation after another. In the middle of the night, Jesus twice orders Peter, James, and John to keep prayerful watch with him in Gethsemane, but they twice fall asleep (14:32–42). And it is of course at cockcrow that Peter denies knowing Jesus (14:66–72; esp. vv. 68 and 72), leaving his master totally forsaken (cf. 15:34) when "dawn" arrives (15:1) and he is handed over to Pilate for execution (15:1–15). Insofar as the faithlessness of the slaves in the parable of the Returning Master (13:35–36) corresponds to the faithlessness of Jesus's disciples in Mark's Passion Narrative, the master's return in that parable points not merely to the eschatological advent of the Danielic Son of Man, as an initial reading of Mark 13 leads us to expect (cf. 13:26), but also to Jesus's revelation as the rejected and crucified Son of Man, whose exposure is, after all, prophesied alongside that of the eschatologically vindicated Messiah elsewhere in Mark (e.g., 8:31, 38). Mark will later conflate these divergent conceptions of Jesus's messianic identity during the Passion Narrative by having the soldiers overseeing his crucifixion, alongside the chief priests and scribes, ironically mock him as "King of the Jews" (15:17–20, 26, 32) while he dies the death of a wretched thrall.

Juxtaposed as they are, Mark's parable of the Returning Master and account of the woman anointing Jesus for burial constitute an unsettling reversal of the *Odyssey*'s plot that serves to underscore the scandal of the Messiah's crucifixion. In Homer's epic, the Returning Master is disguised as a worthless beggar who suffers torment and abuse at the hands of his enemies. But he is recognized as the king of Ithaca by the faithful servant Eurycleia and soon thereafter reveals his true identity to all, punishes his adversaries and faithless slaves, and claims his rightful position. Mark initially holds before the reader the possibility that the anonymous woman recognizes Jesus as the rightful king, just as Eurycleia recognized Odysseus. Anointing, after all, symbolizes sovereignty in the Bible, and the people who observe her act note its extravagance: "the ointment could have been sold for more than three hundred denarii" (14:5). Her anointing of Jesus is clearly one fit for a king. But the evangelist in the end refuses this interpretive possibility by having Jesus insist that she preemptively anoints his body for burial—not to coronate him but to stave off the stench of decomposition (14:8). Like Eurycleia, then, the anonymous woman in Mark alone discerns the hero's hidden identity, but the content of her discovery must be formulated in terms that reverse the Odyssean servant's recognition. Mark's woman grasps not that Jesus appears humble and vulnerable, but is really the rightful king who, like Homer's Odysseus and the previous parable's Returning Master, has come to claim his authority and punish those who have not kept faith in his absence. She rather grasps that the anticipated messianic king—the master apparently come to possess his authority and his home—is in reality a vulnerable thrall who will be killed. Mark's sandwiching of her recognition within a brief report of Judas's agreement to betray Jesus (14:1–2, 10–11)—the most extreme form of discipular faithlessness—complements his reconfiguration of the Homeric plot, for the *Odyssey* likewise contrasts the faithful woman who recognizes her master to the faithless servants who betray him: after washing and anointing Odysseus, Eurycleia vows to help him punish the servants who have traitorously fraternized with Penelope's murderous suitors (*Od.* 19.48–95, 497–498). This points to a related reversal. Odysseus's servants are, in fact, brutally punished for their faithlessness and treachery when he regains his authority; Jesus's successfully flee when he is betrayed by one of them and arrested.

Mark 13:32–14:11 arguably constitutes a limit case for discerning New Testament narrative's allusions to Greco-Roman literature. Unlike Euripides's *Bacchae* with respect to Acts, Homer's *Odyssey* is not thematically congruent with Mark's gospel—at least not in any obvious way—and no specific verbal echoes link the two texts. One might suspect that we are comparing two otherwise unrelated writings, rather than uncovering an allusive matrix binding them together. In fact, MacDonald's original treatment of this scene has been criticized on precisely this score (Sandes 2005, 719–722, esp. n. 37). One could respond to this suspicion by noting that Mark seems to thematize the absence of allusive specificity when Jesus paradoxically insists that the Markan version of the Homeric servant will be remembered throughout the world, even as she remains anonymous (14:9). Homer's Eurycleia, whose name means "wide fame," is thus entirely subsumed within and solely identified by her narrative function in this gospel: to receive praise for recognizing the master (cf. MacDonald 2000, 119). The lack of a clearly identifiable allusive marker is thus the product of the evangelist's particular revisionary procedure, which involves reducing an individualized Homeric character into an instance of exemplary behavior, including the replacement of her name—the marker of her specificity—with a thematically related promise of reward for her archetypical Christian recognition that the anointed one (*Christos*) is really the one who is crucified. Mark adopts an analogous procedure when he reduces the complex story of the *Odyssey* to its basic plot in the parable of the Returning Master (13:34–36), presenting it as a generic warning to be prepared when the Son of Man comes, whether as the vindicated or the crucified one. Mark's strategy of revision is here one of schematization, with the result that readily identifiable textual details are all but entirely omitted. The extant evidence of revision is accordingly subtle, but faint traces remain for readers who look closely and are prepared to see something unexpected. Insofar as the anonymous woman's anointing of Jesus points to her recognition that the one who has just been identified as the Returning Master in the Odyssean parable is not, after all, the anointed king but rather the one who will die, this character is not only subject to but herself enacts the kind of intertextual reading this essay advocates. Mark's version of Homer's Eurycleia turns out to be exemplary in more ways than one.

NOTES

1. Dennis R. MacDonald's *The Gospels and Homer* and *Luke and Vergil* (Lanham, MD: Rowman and Littlefield, 2015) appeared too late to consult for this study.
2. The theory that Luke merely reproduces a quote he discovers in a popular philosophical text, rather than quoting directly from the *Phaenomena* (e.g., Edwards 1992), is unnecessary and unpersuasive, especially since Paul's discourse engages with the entire proem (ll. 1–18).
3. All translations are my own, unless otherwise noted.
4. MacDonald (2013) informs my analysis throughout this section, even when I arrive at interpretive conclusions different from his.
5. The phrase was proverbial in ancient Greek (cf. Pindar, *Pyth.* 2.94–95; Aesch., *Ag.* 1624; etc.), but the context of its employment in Acts so closely resembles that of Euripides's *Bacchae* that it seems indubitably drawn from the tragedy (against Hackett [1956], who rejects the great classicist E. R. Dodd's suggestions of this and other passages' influence on Acts in his commentary on the play [1960, 173; cf. 68, 132]).
6. Other details in the Lukan scene recall a related moment in the *Bacchae* when the new god's female followers find themselves miraculously liberated (ll. 447–448, quoted earlier).
7. Of particular conceptual relevance to Luke 1:35 are passages such as Exodus 16:9–10 and 40:33–35, in the latter of which God's glory is entirely shielded from sight by the walls of the newly erected tabernacle and the cloud that settles on top of it. The author informs us that only against the night's dark sky was Yahweh's fiery lightening capable of being seen within the safely screening cloud (40:38). Propp (1999, 595) offers an informative comment on Exodus 16:10's reference to God's clouded glory: "Yahweh's 'Glory' is the portion of his essence visible on the terrestrial plane . . . . [I]t appears as a fire (Exod. 24:17), most often shrouded in cloud . . . . Fire represents Yahweh's danger, purity and intangibility, as

well as his brightness. As first creation, light is of all things closest to God. The image of God as fire wrapped in cloud evokes … a thunderhead."

8. See MacDonald (1994, 1999).The most frequently cited such allusion would be the unusually poetic Greek phrase *epekeilan tên naun*, "they ran the ship aground" (Acts 27:41), which seems to be drawn from the *Odyssey* (cf. 9.146–150, 546–547; 10.511; 11.20; 12.5–6).

9. Bathing in the ancient Mediterranean world often involved anointing, and Luke, in his more famous version of the pericope, elaborates the anonymous woman's act into a foot washing that culminates in the application of oil (Luke 7:38, 44–46), perhaps bringing the passage even more closely into line with Homer (cf. *Od.* 19.356).

References

Bonz, Marianne Palmer. 2000. *The Past as Legacy: Luke-Acts and Ancient Epic*. Minneapolis, MN: Fortress.

Brant, Jo-Ann A. 2004. *Dialogue and Drama: Elements of Greek Tragedy in the Fourth Gospel*. Grand Rapids, MI: Baker.

Burridge, Richard A. 2004. *What Are the Gospels? A Comparison with Graeco-Roman Biography*. 2nd ed. Grand Rapids, MI: Eerdmans.

Dibelius, Martin. 1956. "Paul on the Areopagus." In *Studies in the Acts of the Apostles*, edited by Heinrich Greeven, translated by Mary Ling, 26–77. London: William Clowes and Sons.

Dodds, E. R., ed. 1960. *Euripides: Bacchae*. 2nd ed. Oxford: Oxford University Press.

Edwards, M. J. 1992. "Quoting Aratus: Acts 17, 28." *Zeitschrift für die neutestamentliche Wissenschaft* 83: 266–269.

Hackett, John. 1956. "Echoes of Euripides in Acts of the Apostles?" *Irish Theological Quarterly* 23: 219–227.

Hooker, Morna D. 2002. Review of *The Homeric Epics and the Gospel of Mark*, by Dennis R. MacDonald. *Journal of Theological Studies* 53: 196–198.

Kidd, D. A. 1961. "The Fame of Aratus." *Journal of the Australasian Universities Modern Language Association* 15: 5–18.

Kidd, D. A., ed. 1997. *Aratus: Phaenomena*. Cambridge Classical Texts and Commentaries. Cambridge: Cambridge University Press.

Lightfoot, R. H. 1950. *The Gospel Message of Saint Mark*. Oxford: Clarendon Press.

Louden, Bruce. 2011. *Homer's Odyssey and the Near East*. Cambridge University Press.

MacDonald, Dennis R. 1994. "Luke's Eutychus and Homer's Elpenor: Acts 20:7-12 and *Odyssey* 10-12." *Journal of Higher Criticism* 1: 5–24.

MacDonald, Dennis R. 1999. "The Shipwrecks of Odysseus and Paul." *New Testament Studies* 45: 88–107.

MacDonald, Dennis R. 2000. *The Homeric Epics and the Gospel of Mark*. New Haven, CT: Yale University Press.

MacDonald, Dennis R. 2003. *Does the New Testament Imitate Homer? Four Cases from the Acts of the Apostles*. New Haven, CT: Yale University Press.

MacDonald, Dennis R. 2013. "Classical Greek Poetry and the Acts of the Apostles: Imitations of Euripides' *Bacchae*." In *Christian Origins and Greco-Roman Culture: Social and Literary Contexts for the New Testament*, edited by Stanley E. Porter and Andrew W. Pitts, 463–496. Leiden: Brill.

Mitchell, Margaret. 2003. Review of Dennis R. MacDonald. The Homeric Epics and the Gospel of Mark. *Journal of Religion* 83: 244–260.

Patillon, Michel, ed. 1997. *Aelius Théon: Progymnasmata*. Collection Budé. Paris: Les Belles Lettres.

Propp, William H. C. 1999. *Exodus 1-18*. The Anchor Bible. New Haven, CT: Yale University Press.

Robbins, Vernon K. 2012. *Sea Voyages and Beyond: Emerging Strategies in Socio-Rhetorical Interpretation*. Emory Studies in Early Christianity 14. Dorset, UK: Deo.

Sandes, Karl Olav. 2005. "Imitatio Homeri? An Appraisal of Dennis R. MacDonald's 'Mimesis Criticism.'" *Journal of Biblical Literature* 124: 715–732.

Tolbert, Mary Ann. 1989. *Sowing the Gospel: Mark's World in Literary-Historical Perspective*. Minneapolis, MN: Fortress.

Via, Dan O. 1973. *Kerygma and Comedy in the New Testament: A Structuralist Approach to Hermeneutic*. Philadelphia, PA: Fortress.

Winn, Adam. 2010. *Mark and the Elijah-Elisha Narrative: Considering the Practice of Greco-Roman Imitation in the Search for Markan Source Material*. Eugene, OR: Wipf and Stock.

CHAPTER 5

··

BIBLICAL HISTORIOGRAPHY AS TRADITIONAL HISTORY

··

RAYMOND F. PERSON, JR.

MANY biblical scholars draw sharp distinctions between *epic* and *history*, identifying *epic* with oral poetry and *history* with written prose. They also do not take seriously enough the characteristic of textual plurality for the biblical texts, thereby clinging to the anachronistic notion that there is an authoritative "original" text. They also fail to accept that biblical texts were produced in a primarily oral culture, thereby requiring public reading as their primary way of distribution, as well as how this realization requires serious revision to older notions about composition and transmission.

Drawing from oral traditions, I challenge these assumptions in relationship to biblical historiography. Although generic distinctions existed, we too often overemphasize the distinction between *epic* and *history*, neglecting how they have similarities as interpretations of the past. I will demonstrate that ancient historiography was typically read aloud, thereby also existing in multiforms. In this way, biblical historiography (analogous to oral traditional epic) occurs in textual plurality and multiformity and, although this undermines its "historical" value from our modern perspective, we should value ancient historiography on its own terms before trying to mine it for historical data. Thus, biblical historiography is an example of what John Miles Foley (2010) calls "traditional history," which differs from "factual" history but nevertheless can be understood as a "true" interpretation of the past. I will briefly survey discussions concerning the supposed distinctions between *epic* and *history* and the portrayal of reading historiographical texts as oral performance in Greco-Roman culture and biblical texts, before applying Foley's notion of traditional history to Samuel-Kings// Chronicles as illustrated in a comparison of 2 Samuel 21:18–22//1 Chronicles 20:4–8.

"EPIC" AND "HISTORY" AS NARRATIVE GENRES IN ANCIENT LITERATURE

··

Older approaches tended to draw sharp distinctions between *epic* and *history*. For example, Frank Moore Cross (1973) argued that Genesis–2 Kings was a prose adaptation of earlier

Hebrew oral epic (analogous to Ugaritic epic), fragments of which nevertheless exist (for example, Exod. 15). In contrast, John Van Seters (1983) insisted that Genesis–2 Kings came from a prose literary tradition of historiography (analogous to Herodotus) that was little influenced by any purported oral epic as a source. Despite their antithetical conclusions, both Cross and Van Seters drew sharp dichotomies between oral epic (poetry) and written historiography (prose), and such distinctions continue to influence biblical studies (for a review, see Thompson 2013; Penner 2003).

Although different genres existed, comparative evidence requires us to moderate these sharp distinctions between *epic* and *history*. The distinction between epic as poetry and historiography as prose is problematic in that in some cultures epic is prose (Martin 2005, 9) and history is poetic (Levene and Nelis 2002; Miller and Woodman 2010). The distinction between epic as oral and historiography as written is also problematic, especially when we take into consideration the "interplay between the oral and the written in traditional cultures" (Niditch 1996, 4); that is, all ancient writing was composed and received within a primarily oral culture that necessitated public readings for any wide distribution of texts. Furthermore, comparative study strongly suggests that generic boundaries were easily traversed (Wiseman 2002; see also Foley 2003; Martin 2005). Therefore, it should not be surprising that Genesis–2 Kings, for example, contains various genres—including creation stories, genealogies, victory songs, folktales, prophetic stories, and historical narratives.

Even though some distinction existed between *epic* and *history*, both were ways in which the ancients interpreted their present and near future in terms of reflecting on their past. Moreover, since both genres as we have them are written texts that nevertheless existed (especially then, but even now) in a state of textual plurality—that is, the existence of an original text that was determinative for all preceding texts was extremely rare in the ancient and medieval world (see Person 2015)—epic and history as genres share some characteristics, most importantly multiformity.

As is evident in the study of oral traditions (Lord 1960; Foley 2005), no single performance of an oral epic is exactly the same as another. Nevertheless, every performance can be an accurate re-performance of the tradition. Therefore, a significant characteristic of oral traditions and texts with roots in oral traditions is multiformity—that is, a high degree of flexibility within a tradition so that any one performance or written text draws from "a flexible plan of themes, some of which are essential and some of which are not" (Lord 1960, 99), rather than, as most biblical scholars still imagine, from a fixed "original" text, which is either replicated exactly or deviated from on the basis of intentional changes or unintentional errors (Person 2010b). In the next section, I will argue that ancient historiography as a genre for public performance shares with epic this characteristic of multiformity.

ANCIENT HISTORIOGRAPHY AS PERFORMANCE

Even if we define history in such a way that requires writing as its medium, we must understand how writing functioned within ancient societies. Within elite circles, written documents such as letters would have been read aloud by scribes. Moreover, some texts—including "long-duration texts like the Bible, Gilgamesh, or Homer's works" (Carr 2005, 5)—would have functioned primarily as mnemonic aids with the primary locus for the texts being in the collective memory of the community (Carr 2008; Person 2011). In short, Niditch's conclusion that "Israelite writing is set in an oral context" (1996, 88) applies well to most (if not all) ancient literature. In what follows I will provide additional support for this contention as it relates to ancient Israelite historiography by reviewing some recent studies of later historiography, specifically Greco-Roman historiography, including Luke-Acts. I will then discuss the Deuteronomic History and the book of Chronicles as historiographies, both of which include portrayals of public readings of written documents by leading characters, thereby suggesting the oral/aural setting for their public distribution.

Rachel Zelnick-Abramovitz analyzed both Greek epigraphic evidence and classical literature and concluded that "historians, like *rhapsodoi*, logographers and sophists, were traveling performers" and that, "although historical works were written down and to a certain degree circulated as written texts from at least the fifth century BC, oral performance was still considered the best way to have one's work widely known and historians were praised and honored because of their readings" (Zelnick-Abramovitz 2014, 177, 183). That is, even during the time of Herodotus, the best way for a historian to distribute his written histories was through public performances.

Zelnick-Abramovitz provides numerous examples; however, here I will cite only two, one from a literary text and one from an honorary inscription. Lucian wrote the following about Herodotus:

> As soon as he had sailed for Greece from his home in Caria, he deliberated over the quickest and the least troublesome way of attaining fame and reputation for both himself and his works. He considered *reading (anagignōskein)* them while traveling around—now to Athens, now to Corinth or to Argos or Sparta by turns—a tedious and lengthy business that would waste much time . . . Waiting for the moment when the gathering (at Olympia) was at its fullest, one assembling the most eminent men from all Greece, he appeared in the temple hall, presenting himself not as a spectator but as a competitor in the Olympic games, *singing (aidōn)* his *Histories* and so bewitching his audience that his books were titled after the Muses, because they too were nine in number.(Lucian, *Herodotus or Aëtion* 1–3, quoted in Zelnick-Abramovitz 2014, 176–177)

Although Lucian was writing centuries after Herodotus, his testimony of ancient historians publicly performing their texts finds support in earlier literary texts and in earlier epigraphic evidence, such as the following inscription honoring the third century BCE historian Syriskos of Chersonesus: "Whereas Syriskos son of Herakleidas has diligently *recorded and read out (grapsas anegnō)* the epiphanies of Parthenos, has described in detail the (past acts of kindness) regarding the kings of Bosporos, and has given the People a fitting account of the past acts of kindness regarding the cities: so that he may receive the honor he deserves, the Council and the People have resolved to praise him on account of these things." (*IOSPE* I² 344, quoted in Zelnick-Abramovitz 2014, 179–180). Syriskos is honored for giving "the People a fitting account" through public recitation of his texts. Thus Zelnick-Abramovitz concluded that Greek historians' primary way of distributing their written works was through public readings and that "in Hellenistic and Roman times most people still preferred listening to the recitation of historical works to reading them with their eyes" (183), even if they were literate.

Zelnick-Abramovitz makes a convincing argument concerning the oral transmission of historical knowledge and texts by public reading. She distinguishes between "two types of traveling historians," (1) those like Herodotus, who wrote universal or regional histories and experienced widespread fame, and (2) local historians, whose works were more limited in scope and whose reputations were close to home (2014, 184). Nevertheless she concludes: "Local myths, stories and poems related to local cults, local historical traditions—all these served as the subject matter of works composed by these travelling historians" (185). Despite the difference between the Panhellenic culture represented by historians like Herodotus and the biblical historians, Zelnick-Abramovitz's conclusions provide insights into biblical historiography as well, especially if we think of the biblical historians as more analogous to local historians.

Although she devotes little space to a discussion of multiformity, Zelnick-Abramovitz nevertheless ends her essay as follows: "No text is conceived as authoritative while still performed orally" (2014, 193). She argues that the ancient local histories were dynamic, responding to various needs of the audiences in ways somewhat analogous to today's digital texts. Even if the historian used a written text for his performance, he may not have read every section of the text and may have paraphrased or elaborated extemporaneously; therefore, the presence of a physical text does not discount the characteristic of multiformity in oral performances.

Zelnick-Abramovitz's examples span the time prior to and during which the New Testament was written; therefore, we should not be surprised to find that Luke-Acts reflects the cultural tradition of local historians. The author's stated purpose is to "write an orderly account of the events that have been fulfilled among us" (Luke 1:1), drawing from eyewitness accounts and previously written accounts (Luke 1:1–3). Certainly, one of the written sources behind Luke-Acts is the Jewish scriptures. In six passages (Luke 4:16; 10:26; Acts 8:28–32; 13:27; 15:21; 17:11) the author portrays the reading of texts; in each case, a character is reading aloud from the scriptures within the community of faith. Furthermore, the reading of biblical narratives about the community's past is for the purpose of interpreting the present and near future. Jesus reads the Isaiah scroll in the synagogue and interprets it (Luke 4:16). When Jesus asks the lawyer what he "reads" in the law, the lawyer recites it (Luke 10:26–27). Philip overhears the Ethiopian eunuch reading Isaiah aloud, but the eunuch requires Philip's interpretation to understand it (Acts 8:27–35). The "residents of Jerusalem" did not recognize John the Baptist because they did not "understand the words of the prophets that are read every sabbath" (Acts 13:27). "Moses has had those who proclaim him, for he has been read aloud every sabbath in the synagogues" (Acts 15:21). The "Jews" in Beroea are more receptive to Paul and Silas's preaching than are those in Thessalonica, because they "examined the scriptures every day" (Acts 17:11). Thus, in Luke-Acts, the scriptures—including law and prophecy—are narratives about the past that continue to inform their present by their performance within the community, which includes not only their being read aloud, but also their interpretation (Weaver 2008).

Luke-Acts itself is this kind an interpretation of the past, as is clear in an analysis of the "we" passages (Acts 16:10–17; 20:5–15; 21:1–18, 27:1–29; 28:1–16; Byrskog 2003). Early Christian texts were written to be read aloud (Byrskog 2003; Shiner 2003; Shiell 2004). The "we" passages reflect this performative character of history. The "we" group is not clearly identified; nevertheless, the narrator/author is included in the "we" group as one of the "witnesses to Paul's words and deeds" (Byrskog 2003, 262); and in oral performance the narrator/

lector and the hearers would probably also understand themselves as members of the "we" group rather than mere spectators of someone else's story. That is, the "we" passages are a rhetorical device in Luke-Acts and the oral performance provided "a conceptual bridge between the *now* of the narrator and the *then* of Paul" (Byrskog 2003, 263).

Consistently in narratives of the Hebrew Bible the reading of the *torah* ("law," "teaching," "story," "history") is an oral performance that includes interpretation. Deuteronomy is imagined as Moses's farewell speech to the Israelites in the wilderness (1:1; 32:45), containing not only his recitation of the law (12–26) but also his recounting of their recent history and exhortations not to repeat their past disobedient ways (1–11; 27–32). Joshua begins with the LORD commanding Joshua that "this book of the *torah* shall not depart out of your mouth" (1:8), so that Joshua is now responsible for the oral performance and interpretation of the *torah* (8:30–35). When the *torah*-scroll is rediscovered, Josiah reads it aloud to the people and reforms the cult according to his interpretation of the *torah* (2 Kings 22–23; 2 Chron. 34–35). Ezra reads the *torah* aloud and interprets it for the people with the help of the Levites (Neh. 8). Although Moses, Joshua, Josiah, and Ezra are depicted as text brokers of the written *torah* to the people, they do so in a way that is based on oral performance with interpretation, thereby strongly suggesting multiformity as a characteristic of their performances. Their interpretations of the *torah* are based on their historical circumstances and what the people need to hear in order to be obedient to God. Thus, the portrayal of how the *torah* is read (as "story" and/or "history") within the historiographical works of both the Deuteronomic History and Chronicles-Ezra-Nehemiah suggests a model for how we should understand these competing historiographies (Person 2010a, 2010b), a model that explains not only the different sources behind Genesis–Deuteronomy but also the Temple Scroll and so-called Reworked Pentateuch of Qumran as Mosaic law (Crawford 2008).

BIBLICAL HISTORIOGRAPHY AS TRADITIONAL HISTORIOGRAPHY

From our modern perspective of factual history, biblical historiography often falls short. Those texts that underwent more than one redaction (for example, Samuel-Kings) are generally understood to have been updated and revised for theological reasons. Those texts that are understood to have been produced later based on a source text (for example, Chronicles after Samuel-Kings or Luke after Mark) are generally understood as theological reinterpretations that move the text further from factual history. That is, both oral epic and biblical historiography are, for similar reasons, typically denigrated as historical data for modern research. I have argued that we too often overemphasize the differences between *epic* and *history* and that these two genres share some characteristics, including multiformity. In this section I assert that, analogous to oral epic, biblical historiography is also a form of traditional history, despite their generic differences.

Based on his comparison of Greek and Latin epic poetry and historiography, T. P. Wiseman (2002) concludes: "It is difficult for moderns to imagine a world in which prophecy, poetry, history and moral exhortation were not always thought of as separate conceptual categories" (359). In "Traditional History in South Slavic Oral Epic," Foley (2010) helps us imagine that world. He notes that, because of our modern notions of factual history, "oral epic can only too easily fall victim to charges of inaccuracy, incompleteness, or even outright distortion" (347). Nevertheless, he insists that, when we set aside our much too positivistic notions of history, "oral epic can and does present a viable, functional view of history in its own right and on its own terms" (347)—that is, oral epic is a form of "traditionally constituted history and as cultural identity" (349) or, in short, "traditional history". He illustrates oral epic as traditional history by quoting the South Slavic *guslar* Ibro Bašić. When asked if the traditional oral epics were true, Bašić responds:

> It's all truth, I think, yes . . . but there were, by God, all these things, and there were heroes, and in earlier times there were enough of them—horses and heroes and sabers, and so many things there were. It wasn't then as it is today. (Foley 2010, 349)

If we take oral poets at their word, we must acknowledge that their understanding of the past differs from ours; nevertheless, it is their version of history.

> Within this historical model, tradition-bearers and -owners express long-standing beliefs and points of view in their own culture's terms and for this own culture's purposes. From the perspective of modern, textualized history . . . this brand of interpretation may seem false; it may appear to lack distance, to suffer from the interposition of a distorting lens, to fall victim to subjectivity. But on the positive side of the ledger, traditional history as encoded in oral epic boasts an immediacy, adaptability, and continuity that conventional history cannot match. Narrators and consumers of traditional history may often come into conflict with outsiders who claim a different truth, but for the purposes of the involved group that is a phenomenon as insignificant as it is inevitable. The role of traditional history is to serve as a charter for group identity, not to try to escape or explain away the built-in ideological blindspots from which, to one extent or another, all history suffers. (Foley 2010, 355–356)

In "Why Fiction May Be Twice as True as Fact," psychologist Keith Oatley (1999) distinguishes between three kinds of truth: "truth as empirical correspondence," "truth as coherence within complex structures," and "truth as personal relevance" (103). Noting that most psychology is only interested in the first kind of truth, "empirical correspondence," he criticizes the lack of the psychological study of fiction because "fiction can be twice as true as fact" (103)—that is, fiction contributes to "truth as coherence within complex structures" and "truth as personal relevance." When we apply Oatley's observation to Foley's discussion of traditional history, we can see how modern notions of history differ from traditional history. Our modern notions (at least in theory) evaluate historiography on the basis of the "truth as empirical correspondence" with what "actually" happened (as *we* reconstruct it); whereas traditional history promotes all three kinds of truth. So, for example, Bašić's notion of truth includes "horses and heroes and sabers" that at some level correspond with what "actually" happened during the Ottoman Empire, but these are presented in ways analogous to "fiction" so as to put forward a coherent interpretation of the past that provides for personal and communal identity in Bašić's present. In that sense, then, traditional history can be twice as true as modern history.

Interestingly, modern historiography includes a "new" method that moves modern history in the direction of traditional history—that is, the growing prominence of oral history as an approach by historians of the modern period. "Oral evidence, by transforming the 'objects' of study into 'subjects,' makes for a history which is not just richer, more vivid, and heart-rendering, but truer" (Thompson 2000, 117; see also Byrskop 2003, 275–279). Thus, Foley's "traditional history," Oatley's "fiction," and Thompson's "oral history" all share characteristics such as "immediacy, adaptability, and continuity" (Foley 2010, 356), which make the interpretations of reality in these narratives truer in that they more easily provide the "coherence within complex structures" that can further provide "personal [and communal] relevance" (Oatley 1999, 103). This relevance serves as "a charter for group identity" (Foley 2010, 356). Of course, this does not mean that we as modern historians should completely abandon seeking "truth as empirical correspondence"; but, as Thompson noted for the method of oral history, we must do so being more aware of how our "subjects" have interpreted their past in ways that may differ from our own notions of historiography, which, as Foley argued, includes our allowing them to define their own notions of history as part of our own historical data.

In his satirical *How Should One Write History*, the rhetorician Lucian wrote the following:

> The task of the historian is similar: to give a fine arrangement to events and illuminate them as vividly as possible. And when a man who has heard him thinks thereafter that he is actually seeing what is being described and then praises him—then it is that the work of our Phidias of history is perfect and has received its proper praise.(Loeb Classical Library translation; quoted in Zelnick-Abramovitz 2014, 182)

Thus, Lucian's notion of "history" is "traditional history" in which historical events are arranged in ways that will bring honor to the historian when he performs his history orally in ways that moves his audience emotionally and strengthens their group identity.

READING SAMUEL-KINGS AND CHRONICLES AS FAITHFUL PERFORMANCES OF TRADITIONAL HISTORY

Elsewhere (Person 2010a, 2011, 2015) I have argued that the Deuteronomic History and the Book of Chronicles were competing contemporary historiographies and that, when we take both the textual plurality in which they exist and the multiformity within and between these two works seriously, we can conclude that they are both faithful representations of the broader tradition, so that the ancients may not have understood them as containing much in the way of theological divergences. Our modern obsession with carefully comparing their differing minutiae leads us to reconstructing theological differences where none may have existed. Here I build on those arguments by insisting that, as examples of biblical historiography, both the Samuel-Kings and Chronicles are forms of traditional history and should be read as such, so that before we attempt any possible historical reconstruction that may draw from these ancient historiographies, we have a better understanding of how the ancient authors/lectors and readers/hearers understood these literary works on their own terms. I will illustrate this approach by discussing 2 Samuel 21:18–22//1 Chronicles 20:4–8, which I translate as follows:

MT–2 Sam. 21:18–22	MT–1 Chron. 20:4–8
[18]After this, war was still in Gob with the Philistines. Then Sibbecai smote Saph, who was of the offspring of Raphah.	[4]After this, war stood in Gezer with the Philistines. Then Sibbecai smote Sippai, who was from the offspring of the Raphaim and they were subdued.
[19]There was another war in Gob with the Philistines. Elhanan son of Jaare-oregim, the Bethlehemite, smote Goliath the Gittite, the shaft of whose spear was like a weaver's beam.	[5]There was another war with the Philistines. Elhanan son of Jair smote Lahmi the brother of Goliath the Gittite, the shaft of whose spear was like a weaver's beam.
[20]There was another war at Gath, where there was a man of strife, whose fingers of each hand and toes of each foot were six and six, twenty-four in number, who also was born to Raphah.	[6]There was another war at Gath, where there was a man of great size, whose fingers of each hand and toes of each foot were six and six, twenty-four in number, who also was born to Raphah.
[21]When he taunted Israel, Jonathan son of Shimei, the brother of David, smote him.	[7]When he taunted Israel, Jonathan son of Shimea, the brother of David, smote him.
[22]These four were born to Raphah in Gath and they fell by the hand of David and by the hand of his servants.	[8]These were born to Raphah in Gath and they fell by the hand of David and by the hand of his servants.

I should note that the above synopsis simplifies the complexity of relationship between these passages. For example, if I had included another column (for example, LXX 2 Sam. 21:18–21), the complexity would have increased. Nevertheless, a comparison of the two passages from the Masoretic Text (MT) should suffice for our present purposes.

The consensus model interprets Chronicles as a late rewriting of Samuel-Kings; therefore, changes made to Samuel-Kings in the text of Chronicles ("additions," "omissions," and "substitutions") reveal the Chronicler's theological themes, such as the idealization of David. This passage occurs within a section of Chronicles in which various "omissions"—for example, the rape of Tamar, Amnon's murder, and the civil war between David and Absalom (2 Sam. 13–20)—are explained as the Chronicler's minimizing the passages that question David's character (for example, Knoppers 2004, 737; Klein 2006, 410). Since I deal with the consensus model's general approach more fully elsewhere (Person 2010a), here I will focus on two discrepancies between 2 Samuel 21:18–22 and 1 Chronicles 20:4–8: (1) the difference between Gob (2 Sam. 21:18–19) and Gezer (1 Chron. 20:4–5) as the location of one of the battles, and (2) the difference between Elhanan killing Goliath (2 Sam. 21:19) or Lahmi, Goliath's brother (1 Chron. 20:5), and then look at how the consensus model's interpretation of these discrepancies tends to read them from our modern perspective of factual history, rather than as traditional history.

Despite their suspicion of using either Samuel-Kings or Chronicles as historically reliable sources (for example, in this passage the "epic-like" description of the opponents as giants), scholars within the consensus model still address these discrepancies from a perspective of factual history. Concerning the Chronicler's "substitution" of Gob with Gezer, Sara Japhet (1993) writes: "Chronicles locates this first combat at 'Gezer', a geographically plausible replacement for Gob, found only in II Sam. 21.18, 19. However, according to 1 Kings 9.16, Gezer was at the time a Canaanite, not a Philistine, city" (367). Given "truth as empirical correspondence," the replacement of "Gezer" for "Gob" is "geographically plausible" but historically implausible next to the purportedly earlier and more reliable account in 1 Kings 9:16. Therefore, Gezer should be rejected as historical data. When discussing the Chronicler's "substitution" of Goliath with Lahmi, Goliath's brother, commentators typically discuss these parallel passages in combination with 1 Samuel 17–18, the better-known story of David and Goliath. That is, even within Samuel, the story of the killing of Goliath occurs in multiforms, first in that MT 1 Samuel 17–18 is a conflation of two stories of David and Goliath (see Person 2010a, 74–78), in both of which David kills Goliath, and second, in 2 Samuel 21:19 in which Elhanan kills Goliath. The typical resolution of these inconsistencies assumes a linear model of textual production, which is more consistent with our modern notion of factual history based on empirical correspondence, and in which the original story of Elhanan the Bethlehemite killing the giant Goliath is transferred to the more famous Bethlehemite, David (McCarter 1984, 449–450; Japhet 1993, 367–369; Knoppers 2004, 736; Klein 2006, 412). The following quote from Japhet illustrates this approach well:

> The existence of two parallel traditions for such a crucial incident should not surprise us; a problem arises only when these traditions are pressed into service as historical sources for the reconstruction of the period. In this case, only one of them can be authentic, but a rejection of either tradition greatly weakens the reliability of the material in general. (Japhet 1993, 368)

Japhet then reviews the two typical approaches to overcome this historical problem. First, some ancient and modern commentators have argued that Elhanan and David are names/titles for the same person, thereby eliminating the inconsistency. Second, some "create maximum differentiation between the two traditions, emphasizing their independence" (Japhet 1993, 368), including the Chronicler, who changed the name of the giant Elhanan killed from Goliath to Lahmi, Goliath's brother. Interestingly, both options assume that "truth as empirical correspondence" is determinative so that both solutions solve the lack of correspondence, thereby making them more reliable.

Another possible solution would be to read these accounts in their multiformity as traditional history—that is, in such a way that does not emphasize "truth as empirical correspondence" over "truth as coherence within complex structures" and "truth as personal [and communal] relevance." Rather than determining one version as more plausible, we should try to understand how all of the versions were plausible to (at least some of) the ancients, even if this means setting aside the notion of factual history in order to understand the ancient notion of history. Does the exact location of the battle really matter in terms of providing an explanation of David's rise to power according to God's favor? Does it really matter exactly who killed what giant as long as they all are killed "by the hand of David and by the hand of his servants" (2 Sam. 21:22//1 Chron. 20:8)? If Elhanan is one of David's servants, then does David not gain some glory by the bravery of his servants in ways that it really does not matter exactly who did what in terms of providing for a communal identity connected to the past glory of David's reign? Even within Samuel itself we have multiforms in relationship to the battle with Goliath. Why, then, should we read Chronicles privileging Samuel as its theological and historical foundation based on some assumption of linear textual development that generally moves us further from the factual history behind an original text? It seems to me that if we truly want to read these ancient texts on their own terms, we must accept them as traditional history, taking seriously the textual plurality in which they exist and the multiformity found within them individually and between them collectively. Although this perspective may complicate our use of these texts as historical data for our own modern historiographies, it does not necessarily deny their use in these ways. In fact, understanding ancient texts on their own terms must be the first step toward putting them to other such uses.

References

Byrskog, Samuel. 2003. "History or Story in Acts—a Middle Way? The 'We' Passages, Historical Intertexture, and Oral History." In *Contextualizing Acts: Lukan Narrative and Greco-Roman Discourse*, edited by Todd Penner and Caroline Wander Stichele, 257–283. Symposium 20. Atlanta, GA: Society of Biblical Literature.

Carr, David M. 2005. *Writing on the Tablet of the Heart: Origins of Scripture and Literature*. Oxford: Oxford University Press.

Crawford, Sidnie White. 2008. *Rewriting Scripture in Second Temple Times*. Studies in the Dead Sea Scrolls and Related Literature. Grand Rapids, MI: William B. Eerdmans.

Cross, Frank Moore. 1973. *Canaanite Myth and Hebrew Epic: Essays in the History of the Religion of Israel*. Cambridge, MA: Harvard University Press.

Foley, John Miles. 2005. "Analogues: Modern Oral Epic." In *A Companion to Ancient Epic*, edited by John Miles Foley, 196–212. Oxford: Blackwell.

Foley, John Miles. 2003. "How Genres Leak in Traditional Verse." In *Unlocking the Wordhoard: Anglo-Saxon Studies in Memory of Edward B. Irving, Jr.*, edited by Mark C. Amodio and Katherine O'Brien O'Keefe, 76–108. Toronto: University of Toronto Press.

Foley, John Miles. 2010. "Traditional History in South Slavic Oral Epic." In *Epic and History*, edited by David Konstan and Kurt A. Raaflaub, 347–361. Chichester: Wiley-Blackwell.

Japhet, Sara. 1993. *I & II Chronicles*. Old Testament Library. Louisville, KY: Westminster/ John Knox.

Klein, Ralph W. 2006. *1 Chronicles*. Hermeneia. Minneapolis, MN: Fortress Press.

Knoppers, Gary N. 2004. *1 Chronicles 10–29*. Anchor Bible. New York: Doubleday.

Levene, D. S., and D. P. Nelis, eds. 2002. *Clio and the Poets: Augustan Poetry and the Traditions of Ancient Historiography*. Mnemosyne. Leiden: Brill.

Lord, Albert. 1960. *The Singer of Tales*. Harvard Studies in Comparative Literature. Cambridge: Harvard

Martin, Richard P. 2005. "Epic as Genre." In *A Companion to Ancient Epic*, edited by John Miles Foley, 9–19. Oxford: Blackwell.

McCarter, P. Kyle, Jr. 1984. *II Samuel*. Anchor Bible 9. New York: Doubleday.

Miller, John F., and A. J. Woodman, eds. 2010. *Latin Historiography and Poetry in the Early Empire: Generic Interactions*. Mnemosyne. Leiden: Brill.

Niditch, Susan. 1996. *Oral World and Written Word: Ancient Israelite Literature*. Louisville, KY: Westminster/John Knox Press.

Penner, Todd. 2003. "Contextualizing Acts." In *Contextualizing Acts: Lukan Narrative and Greco-Roman Discourse*, edited by Todd Penner and Caroline Wander Stichele, 1–21. Symposium 20. Atlanta, GA: Society of Biblical Literature.

Person, Raymond F., Jr. 2010a. *The Deuteronomic History and the Book of Chronicles: Scribal Works in an Oral World*. Atlanta, GA: Society of Biblical Literature.

Person, Raymond F., Jr. 2010b. "Identity (Re)formation as the Historical Circumstances Required." In *Historiography and Identity: (Re)formation in Second Temple Historiographic Literature*, edited by Louis Jonker, 113–121. London: T&T Clark.

Person, Raymond F., Jr. 2011. "The Role of Memory in the Tradition Represented by the Deuteronomic History and the Book of Chronicles." *Oral Tradition* 26: 537–550.

Person, Raymond F., Jr. 2015. "Text Criticism as a Lens for Understanding the Transmission of Ancient Texts in Their Oral Environments." In *Contextualizing Israel's Sacred Writings: Ancient Literacy, Orality, and Literary Production*, edited by Brian Schmidt, 197–215. Atlanta, GA: Society of Biblical Literature.

Shiell, William David. 2004. *Reading Acts: The Lector and the Early Christian Audience*. Biblical Interpretation 70. Boston: Brill.

Shiner, Whitney. 2003. *Proclaiming the Gospel: First-Century Performance of Mark*. Harrisburg, PA: Trinity Press International.

Thompson, Thomas L. 2013. "Why Talk about the Past? The Bible, Epic and Historiography." In *Biblical Narrative and Palestine's History: Changing Perspectives 2*, 147–161. Copenhagen International Seminar. Sheffield: Equinox.

Van Seters, John. 1983. *In Search of History: Historiography in the Ancient World and the Origins of Biblical History*. New Haven, CT: Yale University Press.

Weaver, John B. 2008. "Narratives of Reading in Luke-Acts." *Theological Librarianship* 1: 22–37.

Wiseman, T. P. 2002. "History, Poetry, and *Annales*." In *Clio and the Poets: Augustan Poetry and the Traditions of Ancient Historiography*, edited by D. S. Levene and D. P. Nelis, 331–362. Mnemosyne. Leiden: Brill.

Zelnick-Abramovitz, Rachel. 2014. "Look and Listen: History Performed and Inscribed." In *Between Orality and Literacy: Communication and Adaptation in Antiquity*, vol. 10, edited by Ruth Scodel, 175–196. Mnemosyne Supplements 367. Leiden: Brill.

CHAPTER 6

POETRY AND BIBLICAL NARRATIVE

TOD LINAFELT

NARRATIVES from the ancient world, especially long narratives, nearly all take the form of poetry. The ancient Mesopotamian creation and flood stories (the *Enuma Elish* and the *Tale of Atrahasis*, respectively), as well as the more famous *Epic of Gilgamesh*, are all in verse or poetic form. So, too, are the Greek epic narratives of Homer, the *Iliad* and the *Odyssey*. And those ancient narrative texts that are most closely related to the Bible, the Ugaritic poems (the *Epic of Kirta, Aqhat*, and *The Baal Cycle*), likewise take the form of poetry. Whether the poetic lines are determined by a fairly strict metrical pattern as in Homer or by the semantic and syntactical parallelism that we find in the Ugaritic texts (e.g., "She grabs Mot by the hem of his garment, / She seizes him by the edge of his cloak"), all these narratives proceed by way of the strong rhythmic regularity that characterizes poetry. It is somewhat surprising, then, to realize that the Bible contains virtually no verse narrative. To put it another way, extended narrative in the Bible always takes the form of prose, with verse reserved for nonnarrative genres, such as praise or lament (in the book of Psalms), love poetry (in the Song of Songs), social criticism (the prophets), or didactic rhetoric (Proverbs). It is true that one finds the occasional brief narrative run in the poetry (as in Judg. 5 or Ps. 114), or that biblical poetry sometimes makes use of narrative-like elements, in what we might think of as "pseudo-narrative" (as, for example, in the Song of Songs 3:1–5 and 5:2–8), but it is nevertheless clear that biblical literature exhibits a sort of division of labor, whereby narrative takes the form of prose, and verse is employed for these other, highly rhetorical genres. One might be given to expect, then, that any chapter on the topic of poetry and biblical narrative would be a very short piece indeed. But the fact is that, even though biblical narrative proper never takes the form of verse, verse nevertheless has an important role to play in biblical narrative.

EPIC POETRY IN ANCIENT ISRAEL?

Before considering the function of poetry in biblical narrative, it is worth asking whether extended verse narrative existed in ancient Israel or not. Is it simply the case that the Israelites never produced verse narrative, or is it rather that such narrative existed but did not make it into the canon of the Hebrew Scriptures and thus disappeared from the literary record? Scholars have long debated this question, often phrased as "did there exist a national biblical epic?", as the title of an important article by Shemaryahu Talmon (1981) puts it. The term "epic" is borrowed from the Greek (*epos*), and is generally understood to mean long narrative poems with roots in oral performance, often recounting the acts of Gods and of human heroes. Although Frank Moore Cross refers to the traditionally identified J and E sources as "epic" sources (Cross 1973: 6, 83, 124), nearly everyone agrees that we do not find genuine epic in the Bible, precisely because of the prose form that Hebrew narrative inevitably takes, whereas epic is by most accounts partly defined by its verse form. However, is it possible that ancient Hebrew epic poetry did indeed exist and perhaps, as Cross and others firmly believe, lies behind the long prose narratives as we now have them in the Pentateuch? Interest in the question was sparked most keenly by the archaeological discovery in 1929 of the decidedly epic poetry of Ugarit, a Canaanite city-state destroyed in the twelfth century BCE. Already in the mid-1930s Scandinavian scholars, such as Arvid Bruno (in *Das Hebräische Epos*) and Sigmund Mowinckel (in "Hat es ein israelitisches Nationalepos gegeben?"), were arguing strongly for the oral background to many of the biblical texts, and they were followed by Umberto Cassuto ("The Israelite Epic" [1943] 1975); and by Cross (*Canaanite Myth and Hebrew Epic* 1973). Writing in 1981, however, Cassuto's student Talmon answered his posed question in the negative, arguing that biblical prose narrative was a conscious, monotheistic repudiation of the polytheistic epic genre, rather than an outgrowth of it. And then, in 1991, Talmon's student Yair Zakovitch pushed the pendulum back with an article descriptively titled "Yes, There Was an Israelite Epic in the Biblical Period," and a rough consensus is now emerging to support Zakovitch's thesis (see the review by Dobbs-Allsopp, 2015).

While it seems entirely possible, and perhaps probable, that there existed some form of epic poetry in ancient Israel, this poetry remains unavailable to us. In order to say anything more about the relationship of poetry to biblical narrative, then, we must move in a different direction, asking what role the essentially nonnarrative poetry that we have might play in relation to biblical narrative. For, in fact, poetry shows up not infrequently within biblical narrative, even if it is not the primary formal mode (de Moor and Watson 1993; Watts 1992; Weitzman 1997). That is, within the bodies of prose narrative in the Bible one finds many places where the literature shifts into verse form, and it is worth asking what the various authors or editors achieve by bringing poetry into what is an overwhelmingly nonpoetic form.

POEMS AS MARKERS OF STRUCTURE

Perhaps the first thing that we might notice about the use of poetry in narrative contexts is that it often seems to mark a particularly prominent structural point in a developing plot, biblical book, or some other canonical unit. For example, two of the most prominent poems in the Torah are Jacob's deathbed blessing of his twelve sons in Genesis 49:2–27 and Moses's blessing of the twelve tribes of Israel in Deuteronomy 33:2–29. Both of these long poems of function as parade examples of a "testamentary blessing"—that is, a final blessing by an important character, usually a father or father figure, given before the character dies. It seems likely that these poems were preexisting compositions that an author or editor worked into their present narrative contexts. Whatever their prehistory, they function now to mark the end of the respective life stories of Jacob and Moses, two especially significant figures for Israel's sense of self-identity, even as the blessing genre, emphasizing as it does the waiting future, opens out to the next stage of the story. But the blessing poems of Jacob and Moses have a clear structural significance that goes beyond the immediate context of the life plots of their respective speakers, since they also mark the endings of the books of which they are a part. In each case there remains a chapter of prose narrative to come (Gen. 50 and Deut. 34, respectively), but the poems prepare for those prose endings by slowing the reader down and by adding a rhetorical gravitas to the proceedings. The book of Deuteronomy is the last book in the Torah, and perhaps because of that we find two poems near the end of the book, reinforcing not only the close of the book but also the close of the larger canonical unit. Thus, just before Moses's testamentary blessing in chapter 33, we find him uttering the long poem in 32:1–43, which is traditionally known as the *ha-azinu* (from its first Hebrew word, "listen") or as "the Song of Moses." This poem functions well to mark the ending of the Torah, focused as it is on the fraught relationship between God and Israel, rooted in the saving actions of God on Israel's behalf (vv. 4–14) but including also the predicted disobedience of Israel (vv. 15–18, 28–33) and abandonment on God's part (vv. 19–27).

This deliberate use of poems to mark noteworthy moments or important structural points in biblical narrative is not limited to endings, however. The justly famous poem in Exodus 15:1–18, for example, seems to function as a marker of Israel's transition from slavery to freedom, a major moment not only in the book of Exodus but in the larger biblical story. A similar, but somewhat more complicated structural employment of poetry can be found in 1 and 2 Samuel, which recount the rise of kingship in Israel, initially in the person of Saul and later, more successfully, with David. Whatever its editorial history, the story found in the books of Samuel represents a lengthy, artful, and coherent narrative. In many ways, the books of Samuel exemplify the very best of ancient Hebrew narrative technique, with complicated and conflicted characters who grow and change over the course of their lifetimes and who (unlike most ancient literary characters) are capable of surprising the reader; with plot twists and turns; with subtly deployed keywords and themes; and with the artful rendering of dialogue. Like all biblical narrative the books of Samuel are almost entirely in prose; though in about half a dozen places or so characters are presented as speaking (or singing) in verse form. There a few brief poetic insets, such as Samuel's classic prophetic criticism of Saul in 1 Samuel 15:22–23, the two lines of a victory song attributed to "the women" in 1 Samuel 18:7 (and repeated by the Philistine courtiers in 21:11), and David's brief dirge for Abner in 2 Samuel 3:34. But there are also three long poems, placed strategically at the beginning, middle, and end of the larger narrative. These three poems—the "Song of Hannah" in 1 Samuel 2:1–10, David's lament over Saul and Jonathan in 2 Samuel 1:19–27, and David's psalm of praise in 2 Samuel 22:2–51—not only bookend or frame the narrative but also divide it into two nearly equal sections. The Song of Hannah marks the beginning of the story by underscoring the birth of Samuel, the prophet who will anoint the first (and then second) king of Israel, and by offering a vision of Yahwistic justice that is to be embodied by the future king ("The LORD will judge the ends of the earth; / he will give strength to his king, / and exalt the power of his anointed" [1 Sam. 2:10]). One of the driving tensions of the plot of the books of Samuel is the fact that the first chosen and anointed king, Saul, is finally a failure and must be replaced by David. It is precisely this midnarrative tipping point moment—the moment Saul has died but David has yet to officially replace him—that is marked by David's dirge in 2 Samuel 1. The transitional function of the poem is exhibited by the way in which it begins by emphasizing the third-person "pastness" of Saul and Jonathan ("they were swifter than eagles, / they were stronger than lions"), before moving into the first-person present of David ("I am distressed for you, my brother Jonathan"; for a full exposition of the poem, see Linafelt 2008.) The third of the long poems prepares both David and the reader for the end of the story of Israel's first successful king. Though spoken in the first person, like the ending of his lament over Saul and Jonathan, David's own achievements are now also rendered in the past ("you exalted me above my enemies, / you delivered me from the violent" [22:49]). Moreover, this long poem (over one hundred lines) is paired with the shorter "last words of David," which begin immediately afterward in 23:1–7. Although there remains considerable debate about the origins and dating of all three of these poems, it seems likely that they were added to the narrative relatively late in order to, among other things, mark the beginning, middle, and end of the final form of the origin narrative of Israelite kingship.

POETRY AND GRAVITAS

Beyond serving to frame narratives or mark structurally important moments in them, we find inset poems functioning in a couple of other ways in narrative contexts. Although it appears to be the case that the third-person biblical narrator will never speak in poetry, there are quite a few poems, ranging from just two lines (biblical poetry rarely if ever appears in a narrative context in the form of a single line on its own) to a couple of dozen, attributed to various characters throughout the stories. In the garden of Eden story, for example, we encounter two verse sections: one brief (2:23) and one longer (3:14–19). In both of these—the first man's response to the creation of the first woman and God's response to the eating of the prohibited fruit, respectively—the poetry functions to add a certain gravitas or solemnity to the speech of the characters. Using the formal qualities of verse to add a formality of tone to the speech of characters is in fact one of the most common ways that poetry functions in biblical narrative. In the book of Genesis alone we find some twenty examples of poems functioning this way, from God's vow in 8:22 never to bring again a worldwide flood, to God's promise to Hagar (16:11–12), to God's response to Rebekah's inquiry about her difficult pregnancy (25:23). Blessings, both human and divine, are often rendered in verse, as in God's blessing of Abraham in 12:3 and Isaac's two blessings in chapter 27 (to Jacob in vv. 27–29 and to Esau in vv. 39–40); but so, too, are threats and curses, such as Lamech's cryptic threat of violence in 4:23, God's warning after the flood that "whoever sheds the blood of human, / by a human shall that person's blood be shed" (9:6), and Noah's curse of Canaan in 9:25–27. We have seen already the longer, deathbed blessings in the book of Genesis and beyond, and as one moves into other narrative books, this trend of using verse to convey authority, gravitas, or solemnity continues, as when God announces the divine name to Moses in Exodus 3:15 ("This is my name forever, / and this my title for all generations"), when Moses remonstrates with the Israelites in the desert when they demand water ("Why do you quarrel with me?/ Why do you test the LORD?" [Exod. 17:2]), when Joshua commands the sun and moon to stand still ("Sun, stand still at Gibeon, / and Moon, in the valley of Aijalon" [Josh. 10:12]), and when Solomon acknowledges the successful founding of the first temple ("I have built you an exalted house, / a place for you to dwell in forever" [1 Kings 8:12–13]).

FIGURATION AND THE EXPRESSION OF INTERIORITY

There are two other main ways that poetry functions in biblical narrative, ways that have to do with the specific literary resources of Hebrew verse over against Hebrew prose: the use of figurative language, on the one hand, and the expression of interiority on the other. Biblical narrative is famous for its economy of style, its essential terseness. It tends to avoid description in any form but even more so figurative language (metaphor, simile, personification, and the like). And with regard to characterization, the biblical narrator consistently, if not slavishly, refuses the reader access to the inner lives of the characters, so that their thoughts and feelings, and therefore what motivates their actions, are largely unavailable (Auerbach [1946] 1953, 8–14; Alter 1981, 12–19; Kawashima 2004, 77–123; Linafelt 2012, 18–32). These aspects of biblical prose narrative are part of what I take to be its nascent realism, where an objective third-person narrator is wont to present the world with neither commentary nor adornment and where literary characters, like those people we encounter in the physical world, are largely opaque to us. But biblical poetry has no such commitment to realism, and, in contrast with classical Hebrew narrative, it is rife with figurative language and imagery, and it fairly revels in the expression of thought and emotion, as any perusal of the poetic books (Psalms, Proverbs, Song of Songs, Job, much of the prophets) shows. In biblical narrative, then, verse functions to introduce both figurative language and the expression of thought and passion into a literary form where it is otherwise mostly absent. This use of verse in biblical narrative seems to be both calculated and subtle, and though it has been little noted by scholars, it is a significant literary technique that is worth exploring.

One sees the use of figurative language, albeit often fairly simple, throughout, for example, the snippets of verse attributed to characters in the book of Genesis: "he shall be a wild ass of a man" (16:12); "two nations are in your womb" (25:23); "may God give you of the dew of heaven, / and of the fatness of the earth" (27:28); "you shall break his yoke from your neck" (27:40); "the God who has been my shepherd" (48:15). And one sees it more fully in the long testamentary blessing of Jacob in chapter 49, where Reuben is called "unstable as water" (v. 3); Judah, a "lion's whelp" (v. 9) and one who "washes his garments in wine / and his robe in the blood of grapes; // his eyes are darker than wine, / and his teeth whiter than milk" (vv. 11–12); Issachar, a "strong donkey / lying down between sheepfolds" (v. 14); Dan, "a snake by the roadside, / a viper along the path, // that bites the horse's heels, / so that the rider falls backwards" (v. 17), and so on. These are just a few examples of the figurative language that fills Jacob's blessing of the tribes of Israel, and can be contrasted with the straightforward literalness with which the blessings are described or enacted in the surrounding prose narrative, as when Jacob describes to Joseph the respective blessings of Manasseh and Ephraim with the prosaic "I know my son, I know; he shall also become a people, and he shall also be great" (48:19), or when he tells Joseph (who is called a "fruitful bough" with branches running over the wall in the poem [49:22]) in very literal terms that "God will be with you and will bring you again to the land of your ancestors" (48:21). And we may notice how terse and nonfigurative is the narrator's comment on Jacob's long blessing: "All these are the twelve tribes of Israel, and this is what their father said to them when he blessed them, blessing each one of them with a suitable blessing" (49:28).

One might also compare in the book of Exodus the straightforward, prosaic description by the narrator in of the destruction of the Egyptians at the Red Sea with the pervasive use of metaphor, simile, and mythical language in the Song at the Sea. The narrator: "Moses stretched out his hand over the sea. The LORD drove the sea back by a strong east wind all night, and turned the sea into dry land" (14:21), and while the Israelites walked through on "dry ground" God "clogged the wheels" of the Egyptian chariots, which were caught when "the waters returned and covered the chariots and the chariot drivers," so that finally "Israel saw the Egyptians dead on the seashore" (14:30). Despite the presence of some form of divine intervention, the episode is rendered in a realistic manner, with nary a metaphor to be found. The poetic rendering of the episode in chapter 15, on the other hand, though not especially elaborate in its use of figuration, nonetheless makes good use of it. The whole poem is governed by the metaphor "the LORD is a man of war (*ish milḥamah*,15:3)," and God's martial acts against the Egyptians are themselves metaphorized, with "fury" imagined as a fire that "consumed them as stubble" (v. 7) and the wind that drove back the sea figured as "the blast of your nostrils" (v. 8). The poem also makes use of a key figure to anchor the three sections of the poem—that is, the image of an inert, weighty object: "they went down into the depths like a stone" (v. 5); "they sank like lead in the mighty waters" (v. 10); and, with reference to the inhabitants of Canaan who look on as the Lord leads the Israelites forward, "they became still as a stone" (v. 16). Although it is never made explicit, it is likely that lying behind the description of the panic manifested by the peoples of Philistia, Edom, Moab, and Canaan in verse 15 is the metaphor of a woman in labor, whose imagined "trembling," "pangs," and "dismay" become a standard trope in biblical poetry for the reaction to military threat (cf. Isa. 13:8 and 21: 3; Ps. 48:5–6; Jer. 6:24). And while obscured in English translations like the New Revised Standard Version (NRSV), the terms for "chiefs" of Edom and "leaders" of Moab (v. 15) are in fact the figurative "bulls" and "rams" in Hebrew. None of this imagery is to be found in the surrounding prose, and its presence here in the Song at the Sea adds vividness, metaphorical complexity, and emotional content to the narrative.

This latter aspect, emotional content, points toward the second major contribution of poetry to biblical narrative, namely its use in the expression or intensification of a character's emotional life, his or her thoughts, feelings, and commitments. We see this in several of the poems we have already looked at, including the Song at the Sea, where the expression of joy and thanksgiving at God's saving action is paramount. We see it too in the Song of Hannah, the first line of which is, after all, "my heart exults in the LORD" (1 Sam. 2:1). The matter-of-fact reporting of Hannah's conceiving of a child in 1 Samuel 1:19–21 ("In due time Hannah conceived and bore a son. She named him Samuel, for she said, 'I have asked him of the LORD.'") and the terse report on the passing of his early years in verses 23–24 ("So the woman remained and nursed her son, until she weaned him. When she had weaned him she took him up . . . to the house of the Lord at Shiloh, and the child was young") give little indication of the joy that Hannah must have felt at the conception, birth, and presence of this long-desired child. By allowing the reader insight into the exultation of Hannah's heart, the poem also, paradoxically, underscores the unstated pain that surely lies behind the narrator's prosaic note that after bringing young Samuel up to Shiloh "she left him there for the LORD" (1:28).

Perhaps an even more effective example of the meaningful integration of verse into plot and characterization can be found in the book of Ruth (Linafelt 2010). The book is in many ways a classic example of Hebrew narrative, with little access to the inner lives of its characters, despite the fact that their motivations are crucial for how one understands the unfolding of the plot. In two places, however, the narrative shifts into verse form: Ruth's speech in 1:16–17, and Naomi's speech in 1:20–21. I suggest that the author of the book shifts into the poetic mode here precisely to give the reader access to the inner lives of Ruth and Naomi, and to signal to the reader that he or she is doing so. Although for most of the book we are left to wonder what the characters are thinking, we are given to know, here at the beginning of the story, that Ruth's primary commitment and motivating factor for her actions is her allegiance to Naomi and, further, that Naomi specifically fails to understand that commitment. As a result, the two poetic speeches of chapter 1 set up our two protagonists as the bearers of the fundamental tensions of the plot. One of those tensions is personal: Ruth has expressed a nakedly emotional commitment to Naomi, while Naomi has ignored that commitment and deemed herself "empty" as she returns from Moab. Will Naomi recognize and accept Ruth's commitment to her? A second tension foregrounded by these speeches is theological: Ruth brings up God almost incidentally, as she includes a commitment to "your God" in her larger vow of solidarity with Naomi, but Naomi makes God the center of her speech, referring directly to God four times, and naming God as the primary agent in her life, an agent conceived of, moreover, in an entirely negative light. Will Naomi be confirmed in her dire judgment that God has inflicted calamity upon her and drained her life of meaning and relationship? And whose view of reality is correct here? Is Naomi right to attribute such agency to God, or is Ruth right to focus on human relationships, relegating divine action to the margins?

None of these tensions are finally resolved by the end of the narrative. We are still not sure of how Naomi views either Ruth or God. Recall that it is the women of the neighborhood who declare "blessed be the Lord" upon the birth of Obed [4:14] and who deem Ruth "better to you than seven sons" [4:15]). From Naomi, however, we hear not a word. Naomi does take the child to her bosom we are told (v. 16), and perhaps we are to imagine that she loves and hopes again after the tragedies that have defined her life to this point. Or, perhaps it is obligation or necessity that motivates Naomi to accept Obed into her life. Then, it may well be some combination of these that defines Naomi's inner life at the end of the book, since love and loss are hardly mutually exclusive.

And what of the theological tension between Ruth's and Naomi's views of reality? Here also much is left up to the reader. The book is in fact much less explicitly theological than is often claimed. Other than God "making Ruth conceive" (4:13; with of course the help of Boaz), all the action that gets done in the plot gets done by human characters enacting human agency in a world of recognizable human relationships, both personal and social. Indeed, it seems to me that Ruth's solidarity with Naomi is the central driving fact of the narrative, as Ruth first provides food to keep them alive and then provides the heir that Naomi needs to secure her legal rights in Judah. Still, it is certainly possible, as the many theological readings of the story demonstrate, to see God working behind the scenes of the narrative. In the end, this ambiguity, too, is characteristic of Hebrew narrative, which clearly prefers to hold together human and divine agency, affirming a certain amount of providential guidance in history while also admitting and encouraging human action and moral responsibility.

The book of Ruth, then, makes intentional use of the resources of poetry to add complicating tensions to the plot by providing rare insight into the interiority of its characters; but the opaqueness and ambiguity of the narrative mode remains paramount. Had the poems, with their revelation of inner lives, come near the end of the book, the tensions might be resolved more neatly and we might not be left wondering whether Naomi ever realizes the strength and depth of Ruth's commitment to her, or wondering whether Ruth ever comes to love Boaz, or wondering about the nature of reality and whether God might be said to have an explicit role in the shaping of human destiny. Verse is used strategically to set up the tensions of the plot, but not to solve them.

Conclusion

Ancient Hebrew prose and ancient Hebrew verse, as preserved in the Bible at least, were very different literary forms, with very different literary tools and resources, and they give rise to different literary genres. Biblical narrative's predominant form is prose, as we have noted, and in the service of its essentially realistic style biblical prose narrative tends to eschew figurative language and access to the interiority of its characters. The resulting stripped-down style of biblical narrative emphasizes ambiguity, complexity of motive, and the fundamentally unknowable nature of human existence. But when an author or an editor wants to break out of or supplement the conventions of prose narrative, he or she will very often do so by drawing on the resources of biblical poetry, which lend themselves to a formality of tone, to the generating of metaphor and other forms of figurative language, and to the expression or intensification of feeling. Sometimes the presence of verse seems little more than adornment, it must be admitted, but other times the poetry adds an irreplaceable element to the structuring or development of the plot or to the intricacies of characterization. Knowing the distinctive resources of biblical narrative and biblical poetry not only makes us better readers of each, but also helps us to negotiate the productive complications that arise when the two are used together.

References

Alter, Robert. 1981. *The Art of Biblical Narrative*. New York: Basic Books.

Auerbach, Erich. (1946) 1953. *Mimesis: The Representation of Reality in Western Literature*. Princeton, NJ: Princeton University Press.

Bruno, Arvid. 1935. *Das Hebräische Epos*. Uppsala: Almqvist.

Cassuto, Umberto. (1943) 1975. "The Israelite Epic," in *Biblical and Oriental Studies*, vol. 2. Jerusalem: Magnes.

Cross, Frank Moore. 1973. *Canaanite Myth and Hebrew Epic: Essays in the History of the Religion of Israel*. Cambridge, MA: Harvard University Press.

de Moor, Johannes C., and Wilfred G. E. Watson, eds. 1993. *Verse in Ancient Near Eastern Prose*. Kevelaer: Butzon and Bercker and Neukirchen-Vluyn: Neukirchener Verlag.

Dobbs-Allsopp, F. W. 2015. *On Biblical Poetry*. Oxford and New York: Oxford University Press.

Kawashima, Robert. 2004. *Biblical Narrative and the Death of the Rhapsode*. Bloomington: Indiana University Press.

Linafelt, Tod. 2008. "Private Poetry and Public Eloquence in 2 Samuel 1:17–27: Hearing and Overhearing David's Lament for Jonathan and Saul." *Journal of Religion* 88: 497–526.

Linafelt, Tod. 2010. "Narrative and Poetic Art in the Book of Ruth." *Interpretation* 64: 117–129.

Linafelt, Tod. 2012. "On Biblical Style." *St. John's Review* 54: 17–42.

Mowinckel, Sigmund. 1935. "Hat es ein israelitisches Nationalepos gegeben?" *Zeitschrift für die alttestamentliche Wissenschaft* 53: 130–154.

Talmon, Shemaryahu. 1981. "Did There Exist a Biblical National Epic?" in *Proceedings of the Seventh World Congress of Jewish Studies, Studies in the Bible and the Ancient Near East*. Jerusalem: World Union of Jewish Studies, 91-111.

Watts, James W. 1992. *Psalm and Story: Inset Hymns in Hebrew Narrative*. Journal for the Study of the Old Testament Supplment 139. Sheffield, Yorkshire: Sheffield Academic Press.

Weitzman, Steven. 1997. *Song and Story in Biblical Narrative: The History of a Literary Convention in Ancient Israel*. Bloomington: Indiana University Press.

Zakovitch, Yair. 1991. "Yes, There Was an Israelite Epic in the Biblical Period." *International Folklore Review* 8: 18–25.

PART II

BIBLICAL NARRATIVES

CHAPTER 7

TELLING AND RETELLING THE BIBLE'S FIRST STORY

DAVID M. GUNN

THE term "First Story" assumes a continuous narrative running from the beginning of Genesis to the end of 2 Kings. It is what others have called the Primary History or the Enneateuch (i.e., a nine-book work, counting Samuel and Kings as one book each and excluding Ruth, which in the Hebrew Bible belongs in the Writings). Curiously, however, it is a story not often told in modern scholarship. More often, the story of its composition is discussed. How have component parts derived from various authorial and editorial sources? When were these segments or strata combined or separated? The discussions are technical and dependent on a rich and long-standing body of such research concerning, especially, the Pentateuch (Genesis–Deuteronomy) and its relationship to a postulated Deuteronomistic History (Deuteronomy–2 Kings) and also involving hypotheses about the formation of a Tetrateuch (Genesis–Numbers) and Hexateuch (Genesis–Joshua).[1] But what a larger story of Genesis–2 Kings taken as a whole might mean to a reader is, in comparison, generally little developed.[2]

The concept of Genesis–2 Kings as a literary unit goes back at least to the seventeenth century. Benedict de Spinoza's argument against Mosaic authorship of the Pentateuch is well known. Perhaps less known is his further argument ([1670] 1891, 128–129 [chap. 8]) that the Pentateuch itself belonged to a larger work running from Genesis through 2 Kings, a work written and edited by a single historian—probably Ezra, Spinoza thought—who wished to relate the history of the Jews from the creation to the (first) destruction of Jerusalem. The evidence for a single work was clear, first, from explicit links between the books, such as "After the death of Moses" (Josh. 1:1–3), "After the death of Joshua" (Judg. 1:1), "After the death of Saul" (2 Sam. 1), and "After the death of Ahab" (2 Kings 1:1). Moreover, Spinoza contends, the narratives are put together in that order with a definite aim. The historian begins by relating the origins of the Hebrew nation, and then the events when Moses set out the law and made his predictions, after which the historian relates the invasion of the promised land in accordance with those predictions (Deut. 7). He then tells how the people turned against the laws after the land was taken and incurred misfortune (Deut. 31:16–17). He goes on to tell about how they wished for rulers and how they prospered or suffered depending on how those rulers observed the law (Deut. 28:36). Finally he tells how, as Moses foretold, the nation came to be destroyed. In short, everything in this corpus pertains to the aim of setting out the words and laws of Moses and showing how they were proven by subsequent events.

The demonstrable unity of subject throughout the books and the formal connections between them, taken together with Spinoza's preceding discussion of evidence that the books are compilations made generations after the events they relate, led Spinoza to conclude that they are a single historian's work. It should be added, however, that he seems to have viewed it as something of a work-in-progress, a compilation retaining features (e.g., inconsistencies, contradictions, and repetitions) that would not be expected were the work in final form ([1670] 1891, 133 [chap. 9]).

Three-and-a-half centuries later, Erhard Blum's (2011, 46) list of three main reasons for finding a "textual continuum" from Genesis to 2 Kings has obvious similarities with Spinoza's arguments. First, the books form "a continuous and consecutive narrative" that encompasses speeches, songs, and larger prescriptive texts, such as cultic and legal regulations. Second, within this larger narrative there is "a basic coherence of plot with regard to time, space, and characters: The timeline progresses to its end in a linear fashion, without breaks." A primeval beginning leads to a history of Israel's origins, of Israel in the land, and of Israel's loss of the land—an etiology of land possession and land loss. Blum's third reason (not one of Spinoza's) is that there are other compositional clues, such as chronological indicators, relating, for example, the exodus and the building of Solomon's temple; or correspondences, such as those between the making of the golden calf in Exodus 32 and the calves of Jeroboam I in I Kings 12. Such features are often taken as evidence of editorial processes, since for most current scholars the textual continuum represents what might be termed "a redactional unity," that is, the product of a complex editorial history.

The term most often used in English-language scholarship, Primary History, stems from David Noel Freedman (1963). In a more recent study, he and Sara Mandell (Mandell and Freedman 1993) write of the opening chapters of Genesis as prologue to a work framed by the expulsion from Babylon (Babel) in Genesis 11 and the return to Babylon at the History's end (2 Kings 24:12–17; 25:6–11). Israel's story, then, is a cyclical one in which "Babylon is the real place of beginnings and endings" (Mandell and Freedman 1993, 163). The hero is Israel, whose tragic flaw is its propensity to rebel against the divinity it has chosen to worship, although in the latter part of the History it is the leaders' sins that lead to the kingdom's division; and, eventually, it is their continuing errors in judgment and sins that lead to the two kingdoms' final collapse (152–153). While the hero is Israel, the deity is a *persona* who "plays so active a role that the text can be considered a limited, divine biography"—hence, the Primary History has sometimes been treated as an account of the mighty acts of God in history (158). The narrative's cyclic basis suggests that Babylon's victory over Judah at the History's end is not the end of the nation. Whereas the Babylonians saw victory over Judah as also victory over Judah's god, the surviving "Sons of Israel," former Judahites in exile, saw their defeat as their divinity's plan. Only with "the divestiture of nationality, a status predicated on possession, or at least the right to possession of the Land," was there potential for "a rebirth or a new birth from the surviving 'shoot,' but under a forgiving Yahweh" (168).[3]

Other "frames" for the Primary Story have received attention by various scholars. Bernard Gosse (2002), for example, details links between the loss of Eden and the fall of Jerusalem, arguing that they form an *inclusio* to Genesis–2 Kings. Cynthia Edenburg (2011) reads the Eden and Cain stories (Gen. 2–4) as together showing that failure to obey the deity's commandments and to maintain "essential social norms" leads inevitably to exile and alienation from him. The man, woman, and Cain are representatives not so much of humanity at large but of the relationship between Yahweh and Israel. These opening episodes thus establish a pattern of crime, punishment, and exile that will be replicated in the larger story: just as the humans are placed in the garden but banished for disobedience, Israel likewise is given the land but dispossessed for repeatedly breaking its treaty with Yahweh; and as Cain is banished for shedding his brother's blood, so Judah is cast out for Manasseh's sins and "the innocent blood which he shed" (2 Kings 24:3–4). Such studies, however, say less about the large stretches of text that lie within the frame.

Some recent challenges to conventional understandings of the relative dating of the various component blocks of what became Genesis–Kings do lead to significant interpretations of the whole corpus. Theodore Mullen (1997, esp. 283–331), building on John Van Seters's (1983, 1994) analyses, argues that instead of the Deuteronomistic History being a later addition to, or extension of, an earlier Tetrateuch or Pentateuch, it is in fact the prior work, centered on the question of the monarchy as pivotal to Israel's survival, to which a Tetrateuch has been added by priests and scribes under the auspices of the Persian king seeking to establish a "restored" ethnic community—in fact, a new ethnicity, "Israel"—centered instead around a "restored" cult. What changes, Mullen argues, is that the community's "history" becomes anchored in an account of communal ritual, sacred institutions, and priestly leadership, material constituting nearly one-fifth of the whole work (Exod. 19:1–Num. 10:28).

Striking, in that it is an account of "the story in its present form" and devoid of delvings into its putative compositional history, is an essay by David Clines (1988) who had written a pioneering book, *The Theme of the Pentateuch*, from a not dissimilar standpoint (Clines 1978). His reading of the Primary History (in which, like Spinoza, he includes Ruth) is both self-contained and part of a larger essay on the collection of books in the Christian canon, from Genesis through Esther. For Clines (1988), 1 Chronicles through Esther constitutes "the Secondary History," and he treats it as an alternative telling of the history of the Israelite people.

For Clines, the Primary History is a story "of fair beginnings and foul endings." In Genesis 12, Abraham is promised numerous descendants who will inhabit their own land, be divinely blessed, and be themselves a blessing to other nations. Yet by the end, despite signs of success along the way, the tribes are lost to Assyrian and then Babylonian captivity, cast out by God himself. As for other nations, "they have experienced from Israel no blessing but either military domination (when Israel ruled an empire) or else insubordination (when Israel formed part of the Assyrian or Babylonian empires)" (1988, 75).

It is also—and this is the crux of Clines's retelling—a story of failed leadership. "Every type of leader—warrior, judge, king, and prophet—though represented as Yahweh's gift to the nation, proves disastrous or at least ineffectual" (1988, 75). Clines traces this pattern of failure from Moses through Joshua and the judges raised up by God (moving from an unexceptionable Othniel to an ineffective Samson) to the monarchy. But kingship, too, soon proves its potential for disaster, starting with Saul, who is chosen but then rejected by Yahweh, and David, who is promised a dynasty that would rule "forever" (2 Sam. 7:13, 16) but who, because of his sin in the matter of Bathsheba and Uriah, is then promised a house riven with strife (2 Sam. 12:10). Even Solomon, who "loves" Yahweh (1 Kings 3:3) and builds him a temple (1 Kings 6–7), fails in the end to be wholly true to him (1 Kings 11:4), so that God sets in train the division of the kingdom. In the north, the narrator reports, the kings regularly followed in the steps of Jeroboam, who instituted unlicensed sanctuaries and provoked God to anger. In the south, while two kings—Hezekiah and Josiah—find Yahweh's approval, others earn but mixed praise, and the last seven do evil in Yahweh's sight (e.g., 2 Kings 21:2). As mediators between the divine and the human, the prophets hold out greater promise than other leaders, but in the end their influence on the national history is minimal. Clines traces them from Moses, Yahweh's mouthpiece, by way of various anonymous prophets, to the more prominent Samuel, Nathan, Elijah, and Elisha. Their words do little more than "announce a doom-laden future that is not open to adjustment" (1988, 77). Yahweh's prophet may successfully confront Baal's prophets, but it is King Jehu, not Elijah, who wipes out Baal from the nation as a whole (2 Kings 10:28). Prophets, argues Clines, may designate kings but they do not make them; that needs popular acclamation (1 Sam. 10:24–11:15) or a coup d'état (2 Kings 9:11–37).

Clines sees the falling hopes of the national history foreshadowed in the "primeval history" of Genesis 1–11: the first couple expelled, the first brother a murderer, increase in humankind accompanied by increase in wickedness, and cooperation at Babel become a permanent scattering. He finds it not surprising, then, that instead of the story of Abraham's family moving toward some undoing of the primeval tragedy, it becomes instead "but a long drawn out replay of it" (1988, 78). Nor can the final cameo of Jehoichin's release from prison in Babylon counteract the larger story's downward movement.

If Clines finds a focus on institutions, Thomas Thompson (1999) finds one in identity formation. The story's opening is a poem of God fashioning a world he understands to be good. The stories that follow, from the garden to Babel (Gen. 2–11), show rather a world in conflict with God, where people make a world *they* see as good, a world marked by alienation (89). The succeeding stories are in the business of creating self-identity or "self-understanding regarding closeness and distance among different groups" (91). Some are positive stories, recounting conflicts resolved (e.g., Gen. 26 or 33); others, with their rapes and massacres, are not (e.g., Gen. 34 or Judg. 19). Where there is conflict it is mostly not about ethnic hatred but religious belief. The Canaanites and Philistines play implacably hostile roles and come to represent false religious belief. From Exodus through 2 Kings, theological sectarianism constructs a polarity between Israel and others. When Israel abides by Yahweh's will he gives them land, governance, and security to walk a righteous path. But foreign wives corrupt Solomon and successive failures in both the north and the south, despite reforms by the pious Hezekiah and Josiah, lead to destruction like that of the Canaanites earlier. The people abandon their God and choose the way of evil; so God rejects the people he created and destroys Jerusalem, where his name had its home. "The story is a tragedy, not a piece of national propaganda" (Thompson 1999, 92).

For Mandell and Freedman, Clines, and Thompson, the story is about Israel. It is Israel's "history." Yet Mandell and Freedman suggest that it might also be considered a biography of the deity and Thompson's reading of a tragic ending in which Yahweh rejects his people and destroys his city opens up the question, whose is the tragedy, Israel's or God's? Another way of telling the First Story, therefore, is to tell it as a story about God.

Such a story is told by South African writer, novelist, and professor of English Dan Jacobson (1982) in the first part of his book *The Story of the Stories: The Chosen People and Its God*. Jacobson carries his story beyond the end of 2 Kings (see chap. 5, "The Rejection") and into the Prophets and Writings, but his account of Genesis–Kings is presented as a coherent story in its own right. Jacobson takes the story's God seriously as an imaginative creation, a single transcendent God with a determining relationship to one particular people upon whom he bestows a land. Jacobson's aim is to understand that relationship by following through the "plot" in which God and Israel are reciprocally engaged (1982, 1, 6).

The dynamics of reciprocity are central to Jacobson's retelling. He observes, for example, regarding the conquest of Canaan, the various injunctions on Israel to "devote to destruction" the inhabitants: "[A]t no point does one find an explicit expression of misgiving or compunction on the part of the writers about the fate of the Canaanites" (31). On the other hand, Jacobson detects distinct moral unease in passages that try to justify on God's behalf the violent treatment meted out (e.g., Deut. 9:4). And when, he notes, in Leviticus (18:24–26, 28) the people are told not to defile themselves as the inhabitants had done (and thus were punished), the threat is added: "lest the land vomit you out" as well. Jacobson discerns in reciprocal expulsion both "the real moral" of this story of God, Israelites, and Canaanites (1982, 32) and the larger tale's essential outline. God imposes on the Israelites an obligation to wipe out the Canaanites. In time, cruel invaders, agents of the same God, will inflict the same fate on the erstwhile conquerors (33).

The imposition of covenant law may likewise be viewed through reciprocity. Yahweh's deliverance of Israel from servitude in Egypt could be seen as simply deliverance into another servitude, this time to himself and his unquestionable will. Rather, says Jacobson, the centrality of covenant represents an attempt to put a restraining yoke on Yahweh: the people bind themselves to God, but God also binds himself to the people. Having seen God exercise his partiality in choosing them over others, the people now had to make "every effort . . . to ensure that henceforth his rule would be strictly 'according to the book'" (67). A tension—anxiety, perhaps—exists throughout the story (and its embedded law codes) between the willing acceptance of God's arbitrary favor and the desire that partiality not define the way Israelites conducted their lives and law (70).

In deconstructive vein, Jacobson stresses that an unfolding story or "dramatic myth" such as this one has an inherent quality of ambiguity, "a habit, as it were, of saying more than one thing at a time, and more than those who create it and those who attend to it actually want to hear" (36). In trying to "explain the past and control the future," it will disclose what it wants to suppress, and it will present possibilities alternative to what it strives to promote. Hence, the repeated harking back to the fate of the Canaanites—both as cause for gratitude and as a terrible warning—may be seen as the expression of deep-seated anxiety in the folk memory on which the writers draw, writers living beyond the story in, so to speak, a *post facto* (exilic) world. It is the reciprocity between the fate of Canaanites and Israelites/Judaeans that prevents the story of conquest from being read triumphally.

For Jacobson, God enjoys freedom except for one constraint: he cannot refrain from choosing (53–56). He chooses to bring the world into being, an action presented as an arbitrary exercise of will; and he chooses later to sustain the world he has created. He learns nothing from his first disastrous act of favoritism toward Abel. "I will be gracious to whom I will be gracious, and I will show mercy on whom I will show mercy," he goes on to say (Exod. 33:19–20). What follows, argues Jacobson (53), illustrates or elaborates this ambiguous utterance. Peoples, tribes, groups, lands, and places are chosen or rejected. The cult is marked by separations: God who separated Israel from other peoples insists that Israelites should therefore distinguish between the clean and the unclean beast (Lev. 20:24–25). And why is God such an inveterate chooser? Because he starts at creation from an "extraterritorial" position, just as his people start from outside the land, he must choose his world and then his people for himself (Jacobson 1982, 54–55; cf. 167–168).

In the context of choice and rejection, Jacobson asks, what does it mean that God is nothing if not jealous? He is like a jealous husband. It is this characteristic that he expresses in his utter intolerance of his people worshiping other gods, and it is essentially for that infraction that he finally rejects them. It means, Jacobson suggests, that we should think of God, like his people, as knowing from within what it is like to suffer the fear of being passed over, the dread of unrequited love, or, at the end, the solitude of the separation he has imposed on himself. Such understanding lends the story's ending with the destruction of Judah and Jerusalem a special poignancy.

> Israel was the solitary possession of this solitary God. On her he had to take a boundless revenge for any infidelity or wrongdoing. What was she without him? And he without her? (Jacobson 1982, 84)

Another retelling involves almost a genre shift. *God: A Biography* (1995) won its author Jack Miles—essayist, editor, and professor of religion—a Pulitzer Prize. Miles introduces his subject at the beginning, in Genesis 1, and relates God's story following the Hebrew Bible's traditional sequence of books. As with Jacobson, I stop at the end of Kings, where Miles finds a major break (1995, chap. 6, "Interlude: Does God Fail?").[4]

God, in this retelling, develops as a complex character (with competing names), a creator but also, because of the flood, a destroyer. God (Elohim), who creates the human in his own image, is "magisterially powerful" but also "splendidly generous"; but the Lord God (Yahweh Elohim), who labors to find the human a fitting helper, demands obedience to a deceptive command, violently curses the serpent (his creature), and punishes the human couple in "an almost wanton act," seems less powerful, less generous, and "far more vindictive" (35). In time, however, the differences meld into aspects of a more unitary but dynamic character, increasingly at a remove from direct human interaction but developing as a character through his interactions with and relationships to humans. Thus he becomes for Abraham and Jacob "friend of the family" (67–84) and later, for Moses, liberator, lawgiver, and liege.

God creates the world, Miles (1995, 28) suggests, because he wants humankind as an image through which he can learn more of himself, discover the depth and extent of his own personality. In effect, "the plot is, so to speak, trapped within the principal character" (401). It is only with the first murder committed that God knows he wishes to deny humankind the power to decide who may die; it is only when he sees humans multiplying that he learns he wishes to restrict human dominion over life (47). Thus, in promising to make Abraham a great nation, he rescinds a power that had earlier been in humankind's sole control. If Abraham's fertility depends on a special promise, then he lacks that power on his own. A jealous Lord takes back from humankind a significant part of the gift of life (48). Indeed, the covenant with Abraham is a compromise between God's creative and destructive impulses, his repentance of creation and then of total destruction. Within this covenant, "human fertility was implicitly restricted, divine destructiveness implicitly channeled and restrained" (187). The larger plot is thus driven in part by the upsurging of deep-seated traits and in part by the discovery of new possibilities in an emerging personality.

As the narrative unfolds, so God innovates. He speaks to Pharaoh using Moses as an intermediary. He directly manipulates Pharaoh's mind ("hardens his heart"). Later these will become customary actions, as he speaks through prophets and sends his spirit to rest upon friend and foe alike. But behind the innovation is God's insistence that the power to give life or destroy it, at will, is his. Thus the Israelites' departure from Egypt is not a victory for justice so much as a demonstration of God's power "to pursue fertility for his chosen people and wreck it for their enemy" (104). God at the exodus is the protagonist.

In a sense, the Israelites' cry to go back to Egypt (Exod. 14:11–12) is a plea to settle with the known, the mundane, even if that be servitude. Miles sees both Abraham and Jacob as initially resisting God's offer of a "reproductive covenant" but eventually accepting the promise. By the book of Joshua the issue is now the promise of land and whether Israel will meet the conditions God has imposed, a question that shadows the whole remaining narrative. God now becomes liege to his Israelite vassals. At first, when they are generally loyal, he leads them to success in battle, but by the end, their commitment abandoned, he abandons them to catastrophic defeat, as was predicted in Deuteronomy 28 (1995, 150–151).

In Deuteronomy, Miles sees God's character achieving a synthesis that is stable through the end of Kings, though with some elements of development. In Canaan, God confirms himself to be the conqueror who earlier promised (Exod. 23:27) to send his terror before the Israelites. There is a difference, however, between God in Egypt and God in Canaan. Whereas he ensures that the Pharaoh who has oppressed the Israelites knows his conqueror, God seems uninterested in the Canaanites' knowing who is really expelling and exterminating them, the Canaanites whose only fault (apart from inhabiting the land) is to be deemed a temptation to Israel to defect from the true (God's) religion. God and Israel are thus loyal to each other in the brutality of conquest; but the brutality spreads and by the end of Judges it is affecting relations among the Israelite tribes themselves (1995, 152). Hannah's prayer (1 Sam. 2:1–10) hints at development, as she identifies the conqueror God as also friend of the oppressed against the militarily powerful. God's announcement that he will adopt Solomon as his own son (2 Sam. 7) hints at a new relationship to Israel, as father. And in Kings he begins to see himself not only as Israel's liege but also "the arbiter of relations among all nations" (153), a role increasingly played out through Elijah and Elisha (178–186).

Miles's account of the plot from Deuteronomy to 2 Kings is the familiar one. Key passages are Joshua 24 and Judges 2, linking back to the blessing and curse of Deuteronomy 28. The people adamantly swear allegiance to God as Joshua warns that God will not tolerate their forsaking him; the angel of Judges 2 declares them already disobedient, so that the land's inhabitants will remain as a snare. A gradual downward spiral of "recurrent local apostasies" accumulates to "total, mass apostasy" and condemnation to catastrophe (157). Charismatic chieftains, a handful of prophets—"covenant loyalists" such as Elijah, Elisha, and Isaiah—and a few devout kings, notably Hezekiah and Josiah, stand against the foreign worship proliferating under Solomon and then spreading north and south. Reforms are attempted, the outcome merely postponed. The curse is finally inflicted: siege, conquest, and exile. Thus, the story prefaced by Deuteronomy is framed by genocide that Israel inflicts on its enemies at the start, and its enemies inflict on Israel at the end. "Both are the will and work of the Lord" (157).

Put another way, "a divine effort that, by the Bible's reckoning, has lasted for more than a millennium ends in wreckage, slaughter, and the ignominy of exile" (186). Miles, therefore, confronts the question, does God fail? "If the rupture of the covenant and the resulting genocide are only too obviously a catastrophe in the life of Israel, what are they in the life of God?" (187). If his only way of knowing himself seems to be through humankind as an image of himself, what can his next move be? To start again, going back to a time before the flood, "and resign himself to the consequences" (187)? Or, to judge that his failure with Israel meant a failure with humankind as a whole? "The story is over. The curtain comes down. But God cannot want the curtain to come down—on God" (192).

Miles takes what appears to be the eclipse of God at the end of Kings as a cue for a new story—in the Latter Prophets and Writings—in which God will "continue his contact with Israel, and thereby his own unfolding life, by making a change in himself" (192). Like many other interpreters, Miles sees the survival of a divine partnership with Israel prefigured in a speech by Moses toward the end of Deuteronomy. The words are weighted with irreversible judgment, yet they envision a future Israel listening in exile. Heed God's command, says Moses, and the Lord will take you back in love and bring you together again from those scattered places (Deut. 30:1–5, 11–14). Israel must base its behavior on the threat of inescapable punishment, but perhaps there would be room for hope one day in an unaccountable reversal, one of those "secret things [that] belong to God" (Deut. 29:29; Miles 1995, 193). The contradiction can allow the curtain to rise on a second act.

In *Gender, Power, and Promise: The Subject of the Bible's First Story*, Danna Nolan Fewell and I (1993) retell Genesis–Kings as a story of women and children. As presently constituted, the major subjectivity governing the story (including its embedded legal codes) is adult male; put another way, the interests these texts serve are primarily those of (usually propertied or privileged) adult males. We attempt to tell the story instead as if its Subject were female. In doing so, we also consider God as a character in the story and a powerful manifestation of the male Subject. Here, in the context of the focus on God by both Jacobson and Miles, I convey my own sense of how our joint retelling of the "First Story" might affect a retelling where God is the protagonist.

At the story's opening, as God divides up the world and is pleased by his efforts, we see a character who desires to create meaning through difference but also to replicate self through sameness, an impossible desire. Humankind, made in God's "image," emerges from that desire. We also see that with division comes a hierarchy: humans are to multiply while ruling—or, in the language of empire, subjugating—the rest of creation. A further experiment with a forbidden tree and a woman desiring food, beauty, and discernment turns out not so well. God encounters an intractable problem: be like me, but not too much like me! On the other hand, why are you so different, when I made you to be like me? (38). God, it appears, desires dominion. Dominion demands difference and too much likeness becomes a threat. His experiment gone awry, God expels his creatures the humans from their home. In the subsequent story, the dominant discourse naturalizes God's desire for dominion as simply the divine version of the (heterosexual) male's assumption of dominion in a gendered world. When the story is read, however, as a story of women and children, the way power is sought and dominion exercised by God as well as men, looks rather different.

To Abraham (for God plays favorites) God promises that he will be a blessing to "all the families of the earth" (Gen. 12:3). There follows an account of the man's manipulation of his wife, Sarah, and maidservant, Hagar, capped by his willingness (no questions here), at God's dictate and in Sarah's absence, to murder his son. When finally Isaac is spared, having gratified God's self-importance ("for now I know that you fear God" [Gen. 22:12]), Abraham's promise is renewed. His offspring are to "possess the gates of their enemies"; and through them, because Abraham obeyed God, all nations will be blessed (Gen. 22:15–18). Put another way, because Abraham willingly followed orders he will be a blessing to others, some of whose gates his descendants will occupy. An ostensibly benign blessing has become a bellicose one (55). Read from the end of the larger story, of course, the promise (as Jacobson would see it) is double-edged. If God can enable the descendents to occupy their enemies' gates, he can also do the reverse.

The Exodus, as Miles sees (also Gunn and Fewell 1993, 85–87), is not about God's heartfelt concern for his enslaved people (nowhere expressed) but his need to demonstrate his power and be recognized—hence, his hardening of Pharaoh's heart (cf. Exod. 5:2; 9:14–16; 10:1–2; 14:4, 18, 31). Delivered from slavery in Egypt, the people are offered a new future as a free nation in their own land, so long as they serve as vassals of their lord (so too Miles) under the law God stipulates through Moses. The law reveals a stratified society, involving men and women, husbands and wives, priests and elders—and slaves and free. One of the first laws in the "Book of the Covenant" (following the Decalogue) stipulates how a Hebrew master must treat a Hebrew male slave (Exod. 21:1–6). Despite providing a six-year limit to the servitude, the conditions under which he may take his family with him may amount to a choice between going free and abandoning his family or becoming permanently a slave along with his family. Clothed in rectitude, the law enshrines the master's dominion over men, women, and children and his interest in multiplying slaves (97). The divine master is replicated in the human master.

The covenant God, as both Jacobson and Miles stress, is a jealous god who forbids any relationship with another god (Exod. 20:3–6; Deut. 5:7–10). The root metaphor is drawn from marriage, its perspective the man's. God is a jealous husband, obsessed with fidelity, insisting throughout the story that wife Israel not commit adultery, not go "whoring" after other gods. Suspicious of future offence, he demands of the people a violent self-curse (Deut. 27:11–26; 28:15–19), just as is demanded of the woman accused of adultery in Numbers 5 (the Sotah). The ultimate threat in both cases is to their bodies and offspring (Deut. 28:21–27, 53–61; Miles 1995, 111). In the wilderness, frustrated at his people's rebellion, God afflicts them with plague (Num. 11). When Aaron and Miriam object to his favoritism toward Moses, God, unwilling to diffuse his power, finds fault with them both but takes out his anger on the woman's body, striking her with leprosy (Num. 12; 115–116). Jealous dominion begets violence throughout this story.

The story of Lot at Sodom is introduced, famously, by way of Abraham's debate with God, through binary categories of righteousness and wickedness (Gen. 18:16–33), and the city's destruction is generally read as its just desert. But if we stop to consider the body of Lot's wife, turned to salt (Gen. 19:26), as a *mis-en-abyme*,[5] and ask why she looked back, we might end up with a different view of Sodom, as the home of the innocent (*tsaddiq*), if not the righteous (*tsaddiq*), a place where Lot's daughters are not the only daughters, and where, as poet Kristine Batey (echoing Anna Akhmatova) puts it, "The Lord may kill the children tomorrow, but today they must be bathed and fed" (1988, lines 10–11). In the high-sounding talk of righteous and wicked, most of the inhabitants are invisible to both Abraham and God (67). So where, then, on a grid of innocent and evil, does God fit in light of Sodom's spectacular eclipse, not to speak of the deluge earlier, or later the killing of the firstborn of Egypt?

As the larger story unfolds, the question of God's dominion keeps reappearing in the disposition of women's bodies. The ten women, for example, whom David leaves behind at the onset of Absalom's rebellion suffer rape and lifelong imprisonment (2 Sam. 15:6; 16:20–23;

20:3) because God is displeased at David's taking of Bathsheba and proxy murder of Uriah (2 Sam. 12:11–12). As if the death of Bathsheba's baby (2 Sam. 12: 13–15) and the rape of David's daughter Tamar (2 Sam. 13) were not sufficient punishment of the innocent to appease God's displeasure at his favorite's behavior! By contrast, Jezebel, foreign queen, is accused of "countless harlotries" (2 Kings 9:22), that is, promoting foreign worship (cf. 2 Kings 18:3–5, 19; 19:1–2). She is thrown from a window and devoured by dogs (2 Kings 9:30–37), to become, as God ordained, dung on the ground (2 Kings 9:36–37; cf. 9:6–10). The narrative, too, makes her responsible for taking Naboth's vineyard and his judicial murder (1 Kings 21), a crime that compares strikingly with David's taking of Uriah's wife and his proxy killing. God ensures that King David's body is protected while that of the foreign queen, devotee of Baal and Asherah, is obscenely violated. In a larger story, where a paramount male divinity, demanding absolute fidelity, is the symbolic expression of, and justification for, men's control of women and their bodies, it is no accident that the account of an independent woman, polytheist Jezebel, comes to its climax in the disposal of her body.

The vehement denouncement of Manasseh marks the decisive turn in the plot toward Judah's destruction and brings back into view God's destruction of Sodom. Manasseh's cultic deviations provoke God to declare that he will bring evil upon Judah and "wipe Jerusalem clean as one wipes a dish, wiping it and turning it upside down" (2 Kings 21:11–15). Moreover, adds the narrator in a rare condemnation of bloodshed, "Manasseh shed very much innocent blood, until he had filled Jerusalem from one end to another" (2 Kings 21:16). But as the narrator's God turns the city upside down, who is to be dashed to the floor? Are we to suppose that Manasseh had already wiped the plate clean of innocents? Or were they there in Jerusalem, like Sodom's daughters, ignored by the narrator in his passion to justify a singular God's singular religion?

When Hazael of Syria asks Elisha why he weeps, the prophet answers in what could equally be an oracle concerning God and the final outcome of his jealous anger:

> Because I know what evil you will do to the people of Israel. You will set their fortresses on fire, you will put their young men to the sword, you will dash their little ones in pieces, and you will rip open their pregnant women. (2 Kings 8:12)

Our story began with a woman eating in a garden and hence, lest she and her man become too much like God, being driven into exile. It ends with erstwhile king Jehoiachin in exile, eating his royal captor's meal for the rest of his life (2 Kings 25:28–30). Our story, which began with hints of empire (subdue and subjugate), ends with Judah destroyed by God and its former monarch in thrall to God's agent-emperor. Yet God himself, in this story, proves to be in thrall to dominion. He desires a counterpart but cannot abide one who does not recognize his sole authority. He wants his image but not his image. In the end, it seems that he wants dominion above all other relationship, for he lacks the will to transcend his own power. As both Jacobson and Miles recognize, there is poignancy in his predicament. As he disgorges his chosen, he risks losing himself. After all, what is a god if he is not recognized?

Our reading of a singular God, jealous and given to violence, leads me to Regina Schwartz's (1997) *The Curse of Cain: The Violent Legacy of Monotheism*. Schwartz does not directly address the Primary History as her subject, but her study could easily be reconstrued as an analysis of this story and is germane to the retellings recounted here.[6] She is concerned with identity formation as the product of defining others negatively. Often in the narratives of the Hebrew Bible, she argues, such boundary setting is a line drawn in violence, violence emanating from an understanding of the world in terms of scarcity. "When everything is in short supply, it must be competed for—land, prosperity, power, favor, even identity itself" (1997: xi). She is keenly aware that these stories construct identity in various other ways and often point to internal critiques of authorized institutions and defining codes of conduct, and are occasionally premised on plenitude rather than scarcity. Nevertheless, her major argument shows how readily the material can be construed as a validation of violence in the interest of ethnic, national, and religious (among other) identities. Her book traces key themes in this story of forming identity: "inventing identity (covenants), owning identity (land), natural identity (kinship), dividing identities (nations), and inscribing identity (memory). From this analysis emerges an understanding of monotheism as the centerpiece of this network of violence. When there is only "the one" there are no legitimate "others." The claims of others count for nothing. This understanding resonates strongly with the retellings, above, of the jealous god. In short, she sees both the centrality and precariousness of religious fidelity as the defining criterion for the people's fate; she draws attention to the way women's bodies pay a special price in this story; and she shows why the legacy of the God who cannot tolerate others is bound to be violence. She challenges those who would retell the First Story as one worth the retelling to confront the problem at the story's core—namely, the singular God.

There are, of course, many other ways to tell this story. As Jacobson well observes, the narrative is fraught with ambiguity. It lends itself to being heard as multivoiced. We could retell it, following Robert Polzin (1980, 1989, 1993) and Mikhail Bakhtin (1973, 1981), with a voice of authority and another, contending, voice. We could retell it, following Claudia Camp (2000), as the story a post-exilic "priestly reader" might have read as he looked for affirmations of himself and his (male) priestly community and engagement with the issues that confronted them. What if the story were retold self-consciously as that of a cynical scribe in the employ of empire (a less co-opted Chronicler, perhaps), as novelist Stefan Heym (1973) might have retold it? Then again, Danna Fewell (2010) helps us to begin hearing a tale told by a "wounded storyteller," a survivor who mourns what has been lost in destruction and exile and attempts to make sense of the trauma. Beginning and ending with exile, it is a tale "rife with guilty rationalizations" about religious apostasy most prominently, but also cultic impurity, ethical lapses, societal violence, corrupt leadership, oblivious monarchy, and incompetent politics (106–107).[7] But the First Story is a stubborn narrative that keeps resisting tidy explanations, and as its telling of David's story epitomizes, the story presses its audience to attend to "the wounds, the silences, the incongruities, the compromises at its core" (122). David Janzen (2012) has offered an extended reading of the Deuteronomistic History in similar fashion, showing how trauma creeps into the master narrative, envisioning "suffering without explanation and punishment for no reason" (62). Thus it ambiguates and subverts the language of God and just punishment that is being used to explain and "ethicize" the exile to the point where the narrative ultimately collapses.

With a body of literature so extensive and variegated, retelling will inevitably depend, among other things, on the foregrounding and bracketing of constituent parts. Indeed, Mullen (1997) may be right to see, rather than a unified literary whole directed at those literate enough to read it as a whole, a body of text (a library, I suggest, organized according to a plot line) from which the ruling elite could draw appropriate segments to be read aloud and interpreted for the general populace on public and ritual occasions for the purposes of formulating ethnic and community identity around the Second Temple leadership. In support of this view, I might add, is the fact that the First Story has almost always, in its afterlife, been told in fragments.

NOTES

1. For a useful account of current research, see Dozeman et al., eds. (2011), especially the introduction by the editors and the chapters by Konrad Schmid, Thomas Römer, Erhard Blum, and Michael Konkel; cf. Römer and Schmid, eds. (2007). See earlier Kaiser's survey (2000).
2. See, for example, on the Enneateuch, in the volume by Kratz (2005, 216–221); or the extensive discussion of formative stages in the literature by Carr (2011, Part 2).
3. Elsewhere, Freedman (1993) has argued that Primary History's center is the covenant as presented in Deuteronomy, and the ten commandments of Exodus 20 and Deuteronomy 5. While broadly consonant with a story framed by Babylon in its particulars—each book in order, he argues, alludes to a commandment—this interpretation has not gained support.
4. So also Friedman (1995, 78). Friedman (1987) outlines the diminishing presence of God, which Miles traces from Genesis through Kings, and later further develops this theme (1995, 7–59). His account may be usefully read alongside that of Miles. See also Patrick (1981).
5. A figure or motif (a "mirror") in the text which refracts the whole while potentially exposing its artifice and destabilizing its apparent meaning.
6. See similarly, Römer's (2013) arguments in mitigation of the problematic God.
7. Thomas W. Mann (2011, 380–414) offers a discerning account of the criteria of judgment and unresolved tensions inherent in a Joshua–Kings narrative read as a theodicy, justifying God's destruction of Israel and Judah.

REFERENCES

Bakhtin, Mikhail. 1973. *Problems of Dostoevsky's Poetics*. Ann Arbor, MI: Ardis.

Bakhtin, Mikhail. 1981. *The Dialogic Imagination: Four Essays by M. M. Bakhtin*. Edited by Michael Holquist. Austin and London: University of Texas Press.

Batey, Kristine. 1988. "Lot's Wife." *Alive Now!* January/February: 27.

Blum, Erhard. 2011. "Pentateuch–Hexateuch–Enneateuch? Or: How Can One Recognize a Literary Work in the Hebrew Bible?" In *Pentateuch, Hexateuch, or Enneateuch? Identifying Literary Works in Genesis through Kings*, edited by Dozeman, Thomas B., Thomas Römer, and Konrad Schmid, 43–71. Atlanta, GA: Scholars Press.

Camp, Claudia V. 2000. *Wise, Strange, and Holy: The Strange Woman and the Making of the Bible*. Gender, Culture, Theory 9; Journal for the Study of the Old Testament Supplement 320. Sheffield, Yorkshire: Sheffield Academic Press.

Carr, David. 2011. *The Formation of the Hebrew Bible: A New Reconstruction*. New York: Oxford University Press.

Clines, David J. A. 1978. *The Theme of the Pentateuch*. Journal for the Study of the Old Testament Supplement 10. Sheffield, Yorkshire: JSOT Press.

Clines, David J. A. 1988. "Introduction to the Biblical Story: Genesis–Esther." In *Harper's Bible Commentary*, edited by James L. Mays, 74–84. San Francisco: Harper & Row.

Dozeman, Thomas B., Thomas Römer, and Konrad Schmid, eds. 2011. *Pentateuch, Hexateuch, or Enneateuch? Identifying Literary Works in Genesis through Kings*. Ancient Israel and Its Literature 8. Atlanta, GA: Scholars Press.

Edenburg, Cynthia. 2011. "From Eden to Babylon: Reading Genesis 2–4 as a Paradigmatic Narrative." In *Pentateuch, Hexateuch, or Enneateuch? Identifying Literary Works in Genesis through Kings*, edited by Dozeman, Thomas B., Thomas Römer, and Konrad Schmid, 155–167. Atlanta, GA: Scholars Press.

Fewell, Danna Nolan. 2010. "A Broken Hallelujah: Remembering David, Justice, and the Cost of the House." In *The Fate of King David: The Past and Present of a Biblical Icon*, edited by Tod Linafelt, Claudia V. Camp, and Timothy Beal, 101–122. Library of Hebrew Bible / Old Testament Studies 500. New York and London: T&T Clark.

Fewell, Danna Nolan, and David M. Gunn. 1993. *Gender, Power, and Promise: The Subject of the Bible's First Story*. Nashville, TN: Abingdon.

Freedman, David Noel. 1963. "The Law and the Prophets." In *Congress Volume: Bonn, 1962*, edited by G. W. Anderson, 250–265. Vetus Testamentum Supplement 9. Leiden: Brill.

Freedman, David Noel. 1993. *The Unity of the Hebrew Bible*. Ann Arbor: University of Michigan Press.

Friedman, Richard Elliott. 1987. "The Hiding of the Face." In *Judaic Perspectives on Ancient Israel*, edited by Jacob Neusner, Baruch A. Levine, and Ernest S. Frerichs, 207–222. Philadelphia, PA: Fortress.

Friedman, Richard Elliott. 1995. *The Disappearance of God: A Divine Mystery*. Boston and Toronto: Little, Brown.

Gosse, Bernard. 2002. "L'inclusion de l'ensemble Genèse–II Rois, entre la perte du jardin d'Eden et celle de Jérusalem." *Zeitschrift für die alttestamentliche Wissenschaft* 114: 189–211.

Gunn, David M., and Danna Nolan Fewell. 1993. *Narrative in the Hebrew Bible*. Oxford Bible Series. Oxford: Oxford University Press.

Heym, Stefan. 1973. *The King David Report*. London: Hodder & Stoughton.

Jacobson, Dan. 1982. *The Story of the Stories: The Chosen People and Its God*. London: Secker & Warburg.

Janzen, David. 2012. *The Violent Gift: Trauma's Subversion of the Deuteronomistic History's Narrative*. Library of the Hebrew Bible / Old Testament Studies 561; London and New York: T&T Clark.

Kaiser, O. 2000. "The Pentateuch and the Deuteronomistic History." In *Text in Context*, edited by A. D. H. Mayes, 289–322. Oxford: Oxford University Press.

Kratz, Reinhard G. 2005. *The Composition of the Narrative Books of the Old Testament*. Translated by John Bowden from the German edition (2000). London and New York: T&T Clark.

Mandell, Sara, and David Noel Freedman. 1993. *The Relationship between Herodotus' History and Primary History*. South Florida Studies in the History of Judaism 60. Atlanta, GA: Scholars Press.

Mann, Thomas W. 2011. *The Book of the Former Prophets*. Eugene, OR: Cascade Books.

Miles, Jack. 1995. *God: A Biography*. New York: Alfred Knopf.

Mullen, Theodore E., Jr. 1997. *Ethnic Myths and Pentateuchal Foundations: A New Approach to the Formation of the Pentateuch*. Semeia Studies. Atlanta, GA: Scholars Press.

Patrick, Dale. 1981. *The Rendering of God in the Old Testament*. Philadelphia, PA: Fortress.

Polzin, Robert. 1980. *Moses and the Deuteronomist: A Literary Study of the Deuteronomic History.* Part 1. New York: Seabury.

Polzin, Robert. 1989. *Samuel and the Deuteronomist: A Literary Study of the Deuteronomic History.* Part 2. San Francisco: Harper & Row.

Polzin, Robert. 1993. *David and the Deuteronomist. A Literary Study of the Deuteronomic History.* Part 3. Bloomington and Indianapolis: Indiana University Press.

Römer, Thomas. 2013. *Dark God: Cruelty, Sex, and Violence in the Old Testament.* Translated by Sean O'Neill from the French edition (2009). New York and Mahwah, NJ: Paulist.

Römer, Thomas, and Konrad Schmid, eds. 2007. *Les dernières rédactions du Pentateuque, de l'Hexateuque et de l'Ennéateuque.* BETL 203. Leuven: Leuven University Press and Peeters.

Schwartz, Regina M. 1997. *The Curse of Cain: The Violent Legacy of Monotheism.* Chicago and London: University of Chicago Press.

Spinoza, Benedict de. (1670) 1891. "A Theologico–Political Treatise" In *The Chief Works of Benedict de Spinoza*, vol. 1, translated by R. H. M. Elwes, 1–278. London: George Bell & Sons.

Thompson, Thomas L. 1999. *The Mythic Past: Biblical Archaeology and the Myth of Israel.* New York: Basic Books.

Van Seters, John. 1983. *In Search of History: Historiography in the Ancient World and the Origins of Biblical History.* New Haven, CT: Yale University Press.

Van Seters, John. 1994. *The Life of Moses: The Yahwist as Historian in Exodus–Numbers.* Louisville, KY: Westminster/John Knox.

....

CHAPTER 8

THE GENESIS OF IDENTITY
IN THE BIBLICAL WORLD

....

DANNA NOLAN FEWELL AND
R. CHRISTOPHER HEARD

GENESIS AS CONSTITUTIVE STORY

....

In the beginning of the Bible is the aptly named book *Bereshith*, "in the beginning of...," or in English parlance, Genesis. From its very first phrase, Genesis leans syntactically forward into its tale, pulling its readers and listeners into the first complicated installment of a story that stretches from creation to exile (see Gunn, "Telling and Retelling the Bible's First Story" [Chapter 7 in this volume]). The book's structure is typically described as falling into two parts: a mythologically inspired "primeval history" (Gen. 1–11) recounting the origins and dissemination of civilizations and a series of legendary family stories (Gen. 12–50) narrating the ancestry of the group that comes to be called Israel. The Babel story serves as narrative hinge, providing a funneling conduit for collective humanity to move and differentiate into particular groups and faces. From the universal, imperially constrained region of Babel (Fewell 2001; cf. van Wolde 1994) comes a certain Abraham and his family, doing their part to "fill the earth," bound (by YHWH) for a land of promise, an elusive possession dangling perpetually in the future.

But whether attending to humanity in general or Israel's precursors in particular, Genesis makes no secret of its identity-forming function. It poses, and gives multiple answers to, profoundly existential and ethnically specific questions: What does it mean to be human? What does it mean to be Israel? How are humans related to and distinguished from the rest of the material world and the divine realm? How is Israel to be related to and differentiated from other groups of people who claim connection and compete over resources? And how does what it means to be human inform what it means to be Israel?

Implicit in these questions is the idea of emplacement. From the beginning to the end of Genesis, place and space inform every narrative move. From the *ruach elohim* hovering homeless over the chaotic deep imagining and engineering an orderly system of habitats and a time and place of "rest" to Jacob's family displaced in Egypt and longing for Canaan, Genesis creates a world of itinerancy where its characters are constantly on the move, migrating freely or under coercion, finding themselves exiles, wanderers, sojourners, and strangers with tenuous conceptions of "home."

Stories, writes socio-narratologist Arthur Frank (2010, 81–82), begin with bodies. Body "troubles"—experiences, fears, desires—of individuals as well as groups, drive stories. Evolutionary critics, or evo-critics, inform us that storytelling is a problem-solving exercise and a necessary tool of survival. Not only do stories allow us to re-experience the past through memory and imagination, they give us the capability of reconfiguring the past in ways that speak to present dilemmas and project future possibilities (Boyd 2009, 157). The voices finding expression in Genesis are *anxious about survival*, the how of it, the where of it, the who of it. They seem to be struggling to find their place, to carve out a space in a world that threatens to absorb, disperse, and silence them. Their stories of the past speak to present quandaries, providing rationales for current situations and projecting possibilities for future endurance.

An increasing number of scholars consider Genesis, at least in its final form, to be the product of the post-exilic community of Yehud (e.g., Whitelam 1989, 1991; Fewell 1996; Brett 2000; Heard 2001; Blenkinsopp 2004; Knoppers and Levinson, 2007; but cf. the contrary arguments in Schniedewind 2004, 165–194; 2013, 126–163). This "community," however, is hardly monolithic. Comprising various social groups spanning several centuries and undergoing numerous social changes, post-exilic Yehud is better thought of in the temporal plural as well as in terms of fluid social heterogeneity. Consequently, we witness in Genesis's storytelling communit*ies* engaging in dialogue about their present circumstances and dealing with traumas of forced deportation and return, the challenges of immigration and colonization, the harsh economic and political realities of imperial oversight, and questions of ethnic identity and theological veracity. We should not then be surprised to find recurring plot motifs of expulsion and exile (Gen. 3; 4:9–16; 11:1–9; 13:5–13; 16; 21:14–21; 27:41–28:5; 37:18–36), of apprehensive visits to strange locales (Gen. 12; 19; 20; 26:1–22; 42–50), and of uneasy homecomings and reunions (Gen. 32–33; 43–50). Nor should we find strange repeated conflicts over natural and domestic resources (Gen. 1; 21:22–34; 26:12–33; 27; 30:25–31:55; 33; 34), speculations about ethnic origins and relationships (Gen. 9:20–27; 16; 19:30–38; 21; 25:1–6; 25:19–34; 31:43–55; 34), and rivalries over inheritance and favored status (Gen. 4:1–16; 21; 25:19–34; 37; 38:27–30; 48:8–20). Death and near-death experiences capture a sense of communal vulnerability (Gen. 21:14–21; 22:1–19; 23; 32:23–33; 35:16–21; 37:18–36); promises of future blessings promote communal persistence (Gen. 12:1–3; 13:14–18; 15; 17); and projected military victories subversively intimate political resistance (Gen. 22:17; 24:60; 49:8–10, 22–24, 27). Much is riding on this storytelling venue, for, as social philosopher David Carr notes, communities need such stories for their very existence:

> A community . . . exists by virtue of a story which is articulated and accepted, which typically concerns the group's *origins* and its *destiny*, and which interprets what is happening now in the light of these two temporal poles. Nor is the prospect of death irrelevant in such cases, since the group must deal not only with *possible external threats of destruction* but also with *its own centrifugal tendency to fragment*. (Carr 1997, 20; italics ours)

As a communally constitutive story, the dialogic narrative of Genesis is, in short, a matter of survival. As it struggles to establish and maintain internal group coherence, it also defends against external forces that press to permeate communal boundaries and absorb group identity—the sovereigns, both human and divine, who threaten to confiscate family members at will (Gen. 12:10–20; 20; 21:9–13; 22:1–19; 26:6–11; 34; 43–44), the patróns who deceive to secure labor (Gen. 29–31) or to protect their own interests (Gen. 38), the rulers who enslave entire countries for want of bread (Gen. 41–50). Some characters (Joseph) collude with such forces; others acquiesce (Abraham, Isaac, Jacob); a few are defiant (Tamar). There are brief shows of armed confrontation (Gen. 14; 34) and at least one instance of impassioned hand-to-hand combat (Gen. 32:23–33), but most resistance takes the form of trickery, the underdog's most reliable tactic (see, further, Niditch 1987; on gender and trickery, see the various essays in Exum and Bos 1988; Jackson 2012; on God as trickster, see Anderson 2011). Trickery wins the round, but rarely the entire match. Small victories bring about social change, but the effects come with a price. Some tricksters disappear from view (Rebekah, Tamar) once they have achieved their goal, leaving their personal futures in question. Some tricksters effect irreparable divisions between would-be allies (Abraham and Pharaoh; Abraham and Abimelek; Isaac and Abimelek; Jacob and Laban; Jacob and Esau; Jacob and the Shechemites). Some live only long enough to lament their unfortunate fates. We catch Rachel's final whisper, "son of my sorrow" (Gen. 35:16–21), and we overhear Jacob declare to Pharaoh, "Short and troubled have been the years of my life" (Gen. 47:9).

But no matter what the characters do, the stories themselves execute their own trickery (on stories as tricksters, see Frank 2010, 35–36, 45–70), offering resistance in their very telling. They are actors in and of themselves, producing people and events that call readers and listeners to identify, not simply to sympathize (see Currie [1998] 2011, 29–40), with their constructed world of hardship, fragility, and possibility. They gather the communities of Yehud into one narrative space, summoning them to take their respective places in the story and its telling, and urging them to find, create, vocalize a coherent identity while simultaneously acknowledging difference (see in this volume Fewell, "The Work of Biblical Narrative").

The stories of Genesis choreograph a subtle dance that marks group boundaries, sometimes maintaining them, sometimes stretching them, sometimes crossing them, but constantly debating the rules and conditions for boundary adjustments (cf. Frank 2010, 60–70). Genesis 1, with its desire for order, its insistence that all humanity (not just the royal elite) are created in the divine image and share responsibility for maintaining the created order, its encouragement to a dwindling colony to "be fruitful and multiply," and its implementation of the Sabbath as both a communal identity marker and a gesture of economic resistance against empire, sets the tone for what follows. The closing frame shows Israel in Egypt, carefully distinguished from the Egyptians in practice and residence (43:32; 46:28–46) and yet partially assimilated into the Egyptian political structure through Pharaoh's employment (47:5–6) and through Joseph's position, his marriage, and his children. The delicate balance of likeness and difference is merged with the larger questions: How will we survive? Where will we survive? Under what circumstances will we survive? And what boundaries will need to be maintained or transgressed in order to ensure our survival?

GENESIS IN LITERARY FOCUS

From the very beginning of its career as an object of interpretation, Genesis has been methodologically contested territory. Some early interpreters, such as Josephus (*Antiquities of the Jews*) and Basil of Caesarea (*Hexaemeron*, Homily IX.1), treated the book's storyline as straightforward historical reporting. Others, such as Philo (in multiple works, including *On the Creation of the World, On Abraham*, and *On Joseph*) and Origen (*On First Principles*) thought Genesis demanded allegorical interpretation. From late antiquity to the late Middle Ages, Christian clergy and theologians tended to take the allegorical path; Augustine tried three times before completing a "literal" commentary on Genesis that satisfied him, and even then he only carried the attempt through the end of Genesis 3. Early medieval Jewish commentators such as Saadiah Gaon continued to expound Genesis according to the principles of midrash. Eventually, Maimonides (*Guide for the Perplexed*) and Thomas Aquinas (*City of God*), above all others in their respective traditions, would turn their attention to blending their readings of Genesis with their interest in philosophy, with special emphasis on the creation stories in Genesis 1–3. Protestant interpretation of Genesis took a moralistic turn in the Reformation, with Martin Luther and other leading Reformers mining the book for life lessons applicable to the general Christian populace—or for ammunition in debates against selected Catholic practices (see Luther's *Lectures on Genesis* for numerous examples of both). In the eighteenth and nineteenth centuries, as biblical studies emerged as an academic discipline distinct from theology, such pioneers as Jean Astruc (1753) and magisterial synthesizers as Julius Wellhausen (1878) used Genesis primarily as a window onto its own literary prehistory and thence onto the historical development of Israelite and Judean religion. As a notable exception to this trend, Hermann Gunkel gave explicit attention to "the [literary] beauty of the legends in Genesis" (1997, xxiii), and his enduring contributions to the study of biblical literary genres is well known. Even Gunkel, though, felt it necessary to "examine Genesis, first, in the form it had in oral tradition" (1997, xxvii), and in his commentary on Genesis he treated the "flood legend in J" and the "flood legend in P" separately, rather than treat the composite form as a literary unity.

As late as the middle of the twentieth century, then, biblical scholarship had no strong tradition of reading biblical narrative *as such*, of studying the stories of Genesis *as stories*. Indeed, the very term "literary criticism" underwent a shift of meaning in latter decades of the twentieth century, from synonymity with "source criticism" to designating studies that primarily ask literary rather than historical questions. Literary criticism in the latter sense need not be hostile to historical-critical modes of research; for example, to avoid denying the potential of diachronic study to elucidate historical aspects of a text's origins, Robert Alter (1981) described the compositional process behind Genesis as "composite artistry" resulting in a text whose composite form could nevertheless be profitably studied as literature. Nowadays, the term "literary criticism" serves as an umbrella designation for a wide variety of approaches including formalism, rhetorical criticism, structuralism and poststructuralism (including deconstruction), reader-response criticism, psychoanalytic criticism, and certain forms of self-consciously ideological or perspectival criticism (including but not limited to feminist, womanist, queer, Marxist, and postcolonial criticisms; see Exum and Clines 1993, 15–20 for a similar catalog.) These diverse approaches all merit the term "literary" because of their programmatic synchronic attention to Genesis as a literary unity regardless of its origins as reconstructed by tradition, source, form, and redaction criticism.

Theorizing about narrative approaches to Genesis seems to have begun in earnest in the 1980s, although one can point to precursors. Many premodern writings reveal their authors' fine literary sensibilities (as documented briefly by Alter 2010, 13–14). J. G. Herder (1782) urged literary study of the Bible in late eighteenth century, but, for the most part, scholars tended to prioritize historical questions over literary ones throughout the nineteenth century. Erich Auerbach's (1953) justly famous *Mimesis*—source of the oft-quoted statement that biblical narrative is "fraught with background" (11–12)—partakes of both literary criticism and intertextual study of Genesis 22, though Auerbach apparently felt the need to justify such study by characterizing Genesis 22 as "a homogeneous narrative produced by the so-called Elohist" (8). Roland Barthes published a structuralist analysis of Genesis 32 in 1971, well before biblical scholars began to investigate structuralism's potential for exegesis (as in Miscall 1983; though we would hasten to add that both Barthes's and Miscall's brands of structuralism were already taking a deconstructionist turn). Meir Sternberg (1973) theorized about the "poetics" of biblical narrative, treating Genesis 34 in one such article; however, Sternberg's (1985) writings received little attention from biblical scholars until they were collected and published in English.

Alter's widely praised *Art of Biblical Narrative* (1981) introduced many English-speaking biblical scholars to the potential of literary study of biblical narrative. Despite his rhetorical nod to the diachronic study of textual origins, he nevertheless resolutely advocated synchronic studies, including a persuasive case study of the artful integration of Genesis 38 into the Joseph story, regardless of whether that chapter's core narrative had originated separately. The scrupulous care with which Alter explicated the biblical text lent weight to his assertion that

> [a]ttention to [literary] features leads not to a more 'imaginative' reading of biblical narrative but to a more precise one; and since all these features are linked to discernible details in the Hebrew text, the literary approach is actually a good deal *less* conjectural than the historical scholarship that asks of a verse whether it contains possible Akkadian loanwords, whether it reflects Sumerian kinship practices, whether it may have been corrupted by scribal error. (Alter 1981, 21)

Alter thus emphasized a key principle of all literary studies of Genesis, however diverse in tone or ideology: whatever else Genesis might be, and however it originated, readers now experience Genesis as a prose narrative, and as such it seems to invite the same kind of study that other prose narratives receive.

The earliest "properly literary" studies of Genesis to gain prominence focused especially on the style and internal structure of the stories examined, often approaching biblical literature in a formalist or new-critical manner (e.g., Fokkelman 1975; Fishbane 1979; Fox 1989; cf. the snippets collected in Preminger and Greenstein 1986). Scholars working in this mode emphasize such matters as wordplay, repetition, and phonological artistry through techniques like alliteration, assonance, onomatopoeia, and so forth (see Bar-Efrat 1979). As observed above, literary critics treat Genesis as a literary unity, and therefore seek to identify the internal structures evident in Genesis without regard to putative reconstructions of the Pentateuch's literary prehistory. The *toledoth* formula that recurs throughout Genesis provides an easily accepted example. Less overt structures have also been proposed, such as Fishbane's (1979) perception of a large-scale chiasm structuring the entire Jacob story.

However elegantly employed, phonological and structural artistry tends to remain opaque to readers who encounter Genesis in translation, although some translators—notably Fox (1983), Alter (1996), and Mitchell (1996)—have attempted to "translate" at least some of the book's stylistic artistry as well as its propositional content. Readers more often find themselves drawn to the book's plot (e.g., Culley 1976, 1992; Jobling 1986; Turner 1990) and, even more so, its exceedingly memorable characters. Indeed, for Alter (2010), "the persuasive weight of Auerbach's argument is that the seriousness expressed in [Abraham, Isaac, and Jacob] as representations of human life lies precisely in their being characters" (17). It surprises no one, therefore, that scholars have produced hundreds of studies of Genesis's characters (for books that emphasize character studies, see Fewell and Gunn 1993; Heard 2001; Jeansonne 1990; Schneider 2008, among others; individual articles and essays are too numerous to list even a representative sample).

For all the attention lavished on the book's human characters, though, the most ubiquitous character in Genesis—namely, God—still has received relatively little sustained attention as a literary character, and few studies take the characterization of God in Genesis as their main topic. Lee Humphreys (2001) offers a book-length treatment that remains the premiere study with this focus. This lacuna in scholarship may derive in part from apprehension that statements about God as a character in Genesis might be misconstrued as historical or theological claims, as Humphreys notes (4). The potential for such confusion is aptly demonstrated by Jack Miles's *God: A Biography* (1995). Miles disavows any attempt at history or theology and insists that "literary purposes" are "the only purposes of [his] book" about God (13; see 25–84 on Genesis), but the book's subtitle implies rather more than literary purposes. Similarly, Anderson (2011) offers a penetrating and persuasive literary account of God as a "divine trickster" in the Jacob stories, but also labels his study a "theology of deception." As exemplified by Stuart Lasine's "Characterizing God in His/Our Own Image" (Chapter 40 in this volume), psychological and psychoanalytical theory promises a new turn in the study of divine character that moves away from questions of history and theology to considerations of moral agency and the ethics of reading.

Storytelling is a communicative act, even when performed by a narrator who might not be identifiable with a specific author. Sternberg's (1973, 1985) attempts to rigorously delineate the "rules" governing biblical storytelling included two particularly provocative claims: that an inverse relationship obtains between ambiguity of fact and ambiguity of moral judgment in biblical narrative, and that the Bible exhibits "foolproof composition" such that "missing the point" is practically impossible. Sternberg attempted to illustrate these claims with an extended study of Genesis 34. According to Sternberg, the biblical narrator's rhetoric essentially constrains readers to consider Jacob's sons the heroes of the story, while Shechem is an incorrigible ne'er-do-well, Hamor and the other Hivites are crass materialists, Jacob is an ineffective and even derelict father, and Dinah is little more than a contested resource.

In a spirited response, however, Danna Nolan Fewell and David Gunn (1991) showed that Sternberg's account of the narrator's rhetoric and values is not the only account that makes good sense of the text. At a number of crucial points, Sternberg's reading turns out to depend heavily on factual inferences and value judgments that do not obviously emerge from the story itself. Neither the inverse relationship between factual and moral ambiguity nor the notion of foolproof composition really stand up under scrutiny. Indeed, readers' various perceptions of the (im)morality depicted in the story, and implicitly advocated by the narrator, have prompted a number of passionate and conflicting treatments (notably, Graetz 1993; Bechtel 1994; Scholz 1998, 1999; Camp 2000; Frymer-Kinsky 2002; Rashkow 2004; Yamada 2004; Fewell 2005; Penner and Cates 2007). The lively and varied attention that Genesis 34 has received testifies both to the degree to which readers' own ideologies affect their readings and to the scholarly turn toward self-consciously analyzing those effects.

Gunn and Fewell (1993) went on to offer their own guide to narrative-critical study, which opened with a survey of interpretations of Genesis 4 from Philo to Itumeleng Mosala. Along with many other studies, Gunn and Fewell's brief survey illustrates that "texts are multivalent and their meanings radically contextual, inescapably bound up with their interpreters" (9). This recognition that the narrator's words constrain interpretation, but not so tightly as to narrow the field to only one reasonable account, has been more widely accepted than Sternberg's more rigid approach.

Despite Sternberg's reference to biblical narrative as "ideological literature," biblical critics have focused more attention on readers' ideologies, moving rather quickly from formalism to rhetorical criticism to reader-response criticism and thence to various forms of advocacy. By the mid-nineties, Exum and Clines (1994, 17) considered formalism, rhetorical criticism, and structuralism to be "no longer new," and instead held up feminist criticism as "a paradigm for the new literary criticisms" because "its focus is not upon the texts in themselves but upon texts in relation to another intellectual or political issue."

Synchronic studies of Genesis from a feminist perspective were hardly "new" in the 1990s, though. Phyllis Trible was already practicing feminist rhetorical criticism in the early seventies to powerful effect. Trible (1982, 116, 118) later described three approaches that feminist biblical scholars might take, each of which has proved fruitful. In Trible's view, the first approach—"documenting the case against women" within the Bible—had already exposed the patriarchal bias behind many biblical passages by the early 1970s. Subsequent studies (including Bird 1989; Fuchs 1987, 1988, 1989), however, showed that there was more work yet to be done on this front. Trible's second approach involved "recovering traditions that challenge the culture" of patriarchy, opening up ways for feminist believers to remain engaged with the Bible without writing it off as "hopelessly misogynous" (for examples, see Trible 1973; Tamez 1987; Pardes 1992). Trible's (1984) third approach—"retell[ing] biblical stories of terror *in memoriam*, offering sympathetic readings of abused women"—has perhaps been the most frequently traveled course. Some who take this approach recast biblical stories as first-person narratives (so Ostriker 1997; Brenner 2005) or narratives that focalize female characters (so Fewell 1998), but more frequently use literary analysis to emphasize women's interests and points of view in specific biblical stories (so Brenner 1993; Bach 1993; Bledstein 1993; Exum 1993a, 1993b; Fewell and Gunn 1993; Fischer 2012; Jeansonne 1990; Schneider 2008).

As feminist studies of Genesis gained momentum, so, too, did studies concerned with ethnic dimensions of personal and social identity. Readings oriented toward African Americans' experiences have been particularly important in the United States, and reflect all three of Trible's strategies: identifying problematic passages and interpretations (Copher 1991, 146–153; Felder 1991, 128–135), identifying texts that resist racism or at least portray Africans positively (Copher 1991, 153–155, for Genesis), and reframing biblical narratives with an emphasis on African American experiences, often by analogy (Richards 2000). (By contrast, interpreters from the African continent have focused less on literary analysis and more on historical criticism and comparative studies.)

Womanist scholarship emerged partially in reaction to perceived blind spots in other forms of advocacy criticism, including the efforts of black men (Williams 2006, 171) and white feminists (Weems 1988, ix). As womanist interpretation gained a foothold in the discipline, scholars working at other intersections of "overlapping communities" (Kwok 1997) also articulated their own unique emphases. Womanism's most enduring contributions to the narrative study of Genesis have focused on Hagar and Ishmael. As a household servant or a slave in Abraham and Sarah's household, pressed into service as a surrogate mother of sorts and later ejected from the household, Hagar is a sympathetic figure whose experience resonates with the African American cultural memory of slavery and debilitating social stratification. African American biblical scholars, both women (Weems 1988, 1–21; Williams 2006) and men (Waters 1991, working in a historical-critical mode), have expressed a special feeling of kinship with Hagar, and have studied and retold her and Ishmael's story with special attention to ethnic and class dynamics.

The story of Hagar and Ishmael proves an enduring witness to the power the book of Genesis can exercise in the construction of identity, including both the identities of its characters and the identities of its interpreters. In Nicole Simopoulos's (2007) experience of reading Genesis 16 among Caucasian, Latina, and black South African women, she found that readers' initial and enduring impressions of Hagar as mistress, divorcée, exile, or exploited worker correlated significantly with those readers' self-understandings (cf. Mbuwayesango 1997). But this capacity to elicit identification is hardly new. As we will explore, Genesis may even have been "published," in part, to provide narrative reflections upon conflicts over group identity and family structures in Yehud.

FAMILY AND FOREIGN

The characters and situations of Genesis 16 and 21 continue to speak to contemporary readers in such a variety of cultural- and gender-specific ways in part owing to the narratives' dramatic focalization (on focalization, see Bal 1985, 100–118). What traditional critics have often considered to be blips on the screen of Abraham's story, narrative detours designed to build and sustain suspense, readers attentive to gender, class, and ethnicity have determined to be primary episodes of critical importance. Recalling Frank's observation that stories begin with bodies, we see most clearly how, against the backdrop of Abram's own aging body and his increasing anxiety regarding the possibility of an heir (Gen. 15), women's bodies frame the immediate narrative conflict. In Genesis 16 our focus is first shifted away from Abram to Sarai, who struggles with barrenness and its associated social and economic risks, and then to Hagar, who, initially at the bottom of the family hierarchy, enacts personal agency in a situation that tries to afford her none. As reading or listening participants in this story, we are summoned to consider the plights of women in the ancient world, their various and poignant vulnerabilities, the latitudes and constraints on their actions, and, for a brief moment, the possible ways they might have related to each other (see, e.g., Ostriker 1997). Each woman exhibits her own brand of desperation, dramatizing yet again a motif that appears with great frequency in Genesis—namely, desperate people doing desperate things to ensure their own survival.

The stories are also rife with tensions surrounding boundary crossings and maintenance. Sarai attempts to change her own status by changing Hagar's, but when she perceives that she has lost respect as a result of Hagar's pregnancy and attitude, she eagerly tries to shore up the boundaries that Hagar appears to be transgressing. With Abram's consent, Sarai "afflicts" Hagar, using corporal punishment to put her back in her original subservient place. As for Hagar, her challenge to hierarchical boundaries is paralleled by her transgression of geographical boundaries. She flees the family compound, and as readers and listeners, we are made to follow her footsteps, meet with her the messenger of Yhwh, and overhear both his instructions to return to her mistress as well as the strange pronouncement regarding her baby's future. Because Yhwh has heard her affliction, her son will be called Ishmael, "God/El hears." Her rejoinder, a seeming mixture of awe and audacity, has earned her among feminist critics the label of "theologian" (Trible 1984). She utters a garbled response about seeing and being seen by God; she gives Yhwh a new name, *El-Roi* ("El who sees"); and, like Abram's erection of altars, her experience is inscribed on geographical space (*Beer-lahai-roi*, "the well of a living one who sees me"), grounding (as it were) her identity in promised space.

In Genesis 21, Sarah, now mother of baby Isaac and the cause of laughter among all who hear of her post-menopausal motherhood, perceives Hagar's son, focalized without a name, to be transgressing yet another boundary in the family structure. She sees him "laughing"— or "playing"—and she insists that the "slave woman with her son" be cast out. Many efforts, ancient and modern, have been made to justify Sarah's callous demand (for an overview of interpretations of this scene, see Heard 2001, 82–86), but Ishmael's actions and Sarah's motives remain shrouded in ambiguity, raising all sorts of questions regarding Ishmael's culpability or innocence and Sarah's perceptions and possible fears. Is Ishmael's laughter meant to give offense? Does his laughter echo that of others around, making her and her son the brunt of a joke? Is he "mocking"? Is he "playing" in an inappropriate way "with Isaac" (as the LXX and the Vulgate suggest) or with himself? Is he, through his laughter (*mtsakheq*), somehow embodying, "playing Isaac" (*yitskhaq*)? The reason Sarah gives is economic: "The son of this slave woman shall not inherit with my son, with Isaac" (21:10). On the surface, it seems the inheritance does not bear sharing, but considering Abraham's oft-noted wealth, we might consider her response to be excessively greedy. The mention of "inheritance," however, carries with it unspoken, and potentially dangerous, realities. "Inheritance" envisions a scenario in which Abraham is no longer alive—no longer alive to keep the peace between the two women, no longer alive to protect the elderly Sarah from the younger, and no doubt stronger, Hagar, no longer alive to protect the youthful Isaac from a "wild ass" of a brother fifteen years his senior. That such fears haunt this scene is a testimony to the two women's painful history.

Sarah's demand is "exceedingly evil in Abraham's eyes on account of his son" (21:11), but God/Elohim encourages Abraham to heed Sarah's ultimatum, ameliorating the distasteful decision with promises to make nations of both sons. The next morning Abraham sends Hagar and Ishmael away with astonishingly meager provisions to sustain them. When the water is spent, Hagar casts her child under a bush and positions herself "a bowshot" away in order not to see him die. Although Hagar raises her voice in desperation, a messenger of God/Elohim hears the voice of the boy, and just in the nick of time, shouts from heaven a rather obtuse question: "What's the matter, Hagar?" Without waiting for a response, he speaks a message of consolation and promise, and reveals a water source. The story ends with the affirmation that "God/Elohim was with the boy" (21:20), that he grew up in the wilderness, and that his mother secured him a wife from her homeland Egypt.

Perhaps no other stories in the book of Genesis elicit as much empathy as do the stories in Genesis 16 and 21. Genesis 21 especially easily vies with Akedah (Genesis 22) and the crucifixion as the most illustrated biblical text in the history of Western art. Clearly, these stories have spoken powerfully to readers, listeners, and viewers in the history of popular reception. How might this communicative capacity have served the ancient community of Yehud, whose constituencies would have been struggling with numerous economic and social challenges, limited natural resources, and communal boundaries? How would these stories have spoken to a generation of immigrants who were "returning" to place they had never been before and finding their "home" to be occupied by others and otherwise ecologically inhospitable, who would have been keenly aware of their trifling numbers in the face of an ensconced indigenous population? How would these stories have functioned in a discursive context in which the theologically justified expulsion of foreign women and mixed children was high on the political docket (Ezra 9–10; Neh. 13)?

Scholars exploring this last question have not been blind to the stories' tensions and ambiguities, their narrative capacities for excessive signification and for emotional affect. Fewell, for example, has attempted to demonstrate how the stories can produce diametrically opposed meanings and affects (1993; 2002; 2003, 43–63). On the one hand, the focalization on Hagar pulls the audience into her plight, forcing identification and empathy, and reinforces the notion that God cares for the marginalized as well as the entitled. On the other hand, Hagar's story can communicate to a community anxious over the mandates of Ezra and Nehemiah that, though harsh, such measures are both necessary and divinely sanctioned. Abraham becomes a model for, albeit reluctant, obedience; and God's involvement in the futures of Hagar and Ishmael console any who might worry about the survival of the displaced women and children, letting the remaining community off the ethical hook as it were. The community, like Abraham, is permitted to be financially ungenerous and to disregard the suffering of these women and children because, after all, God will take care of them as he took care of Hagar and Ishmael.

Mark G. Brett (2000), reading through the lens of postcolonial theory and experience, has also understood the stories in Genesis to be addressing the community of Yehud in their deliberations over group membership. Recognizing that "as postcolonial theory would lead us to expect, stories of dissent can rarely be turned into tales of pure, egalitarian, rebel consciousness; more often than not, we have to deal with the ambiguities of solidarity and betrayal" (57), Brett finds in Genesis a complicated narrative that accommodates both social and economic exigencies as well as social critique. Working within a redactional framework, Brett distinguishes between the various narrators in Genesis and its editors, arguing that while some narrators of individual stories support an exclusive agenda that would have found purchase with the likes of Ezra and Nehemiah, the final editors undermine such sentiments by structuring the overarching narrative in ways that stretch "covenantal" parameters and highlight divine compassion and inclusivity. While he often blurs the distinction between characters' attitudes (e.g., Sarah's blatant self-interest, Abraham's indifference to Hagar's fate) and the narrator's agenda, he nevertheless sees the Genesis narrative tilting, in its final form, toward universal inclusion.

R. Christopher Heard (2001, 171), taking a "strongly literary-aesthetic approach to Genesis 12–36," meticulously teases out the numerous ambiguities of plot and character in both Genesis 16 and 21, demonstrating in each case how characters might be read positively, negatively, or neutrally. His conclusion is that, while character construction in Genesis leaves remarkable latitude for interpretation, in the end how one interprets the characters does not matter, since the narrator is simultaneously insisting on a particular family line that defines communal membership. Narrative treatment of "the Others" is not necessarily meant to be injurious and, indeed, leaves room for civil relations, but ultimately Genesis as a story of origins is firm about who the community is and who it is not.

The disparate conclusions reached by these studies can be instructive regarding the nature of biblical narrative textuality. One might say that we have succumbed to the text's own trickery. For, as Frank points out:

> As often as stories are conscripted to advance some cause, they do that work only for a while and then turn against those who conscripted them. They can always be told to a different effect. Stories readily take sides; they just refuse to stay on the same side, and stories conduct both tellers and listeners to take different sides. (Frank 2010, 36)

The narrative trickery of Genesis 16 and 21 is made possible at least in part by the multiple and conflicted subjectivities that crowd the narrative landscape, vying for communal attention and empathy: Abraham the chosen, the obedient, and the disenchanted transient immigrant; the barren, aging Sarah twice a pawn for her husband's security yet destined to become a figurative "princess" (*sarah*) and mother of nations; the enslaved Hagar, the quintessential "stranger" (*ha-ger*), whose body bears the brunt of her owners' fears and desires, who makes aborted bids for legitimacy and freedom, and who survives in spite of human cruelty and negligence; Ishmael who, while signifying divine heed and fierce freedom, is nevertheless taken blithely by God/Elohim to the brink of death; baby Isaac, who both embodies hope for the future and serves as a catalyst for family division and who will himself come, by divine fiat, within an inch of his life; and the bifurcated deity who, in his Yhwhistic persona, insists that Hagar and her son are to be part of Abraham's family, but who, in his generic Elohistic guise, sanctions their disinheritance and expulsion. We might well wonder if this two-faced deity personifies the theological conflicts of the community. On Yhwh (the local, personal god) is pinned the belief in a land allocated to an assembled heterogeneous community with promises to all, while "Elohim," palatably labeled for universal appeal, looks suspiciously like an imperial cipher who would have vested interests in undivided estates, where production could be streamlined and workers would have little autonomy (see Boer, "The Economic Politics of Biblical Narrative" [Chapter 46 in this volume]; and further Fewell forthcoming). Such a "god" would, no doubt, also be eager to develop a class of landless archers who could be tapped for military service and serve as a buffer between Persia and Egypt.

But however one identifies the texts' various sponsors or explains and assesses the text's multivalence, there is still no question that this multivalence is present and provides fertile ground for political and social debate over the genesis of Israelite identity. Brett's allowance for multiple conflicting narrative voices, Heard's exposure of relentless ambiguity, Fewell's demonstration of how the same text can elicit opposing emotional and ethical responses, as well as new speculations about the politics of theological representation point to a narrative that fails—or refuses—to produce a singular, unified, agreed-upon meaning. Rather, the narrative seems to have already invited a number of interlocutors and invested co-tellers into its rhetorically unstable sphere. Woven into the narrative fabric are a range of different questions, perspectives, and concerns, all intent on "probing moral dimensions of human experience" (Ochs and Capps 2001, 225) against a backdrop in which questions of identity and survival press with profound urgency. The answers that emerge are not clear-cut, consensual, final, or finalizable. In short, with all its displaced characters cognizant of death's eventual dominion and seemingly more than ready to exploit each other in their bids for social stability, and with its divine character(s) constituting a moral enigma, the story constructs a complicated world where "the plenitude of life defeats the uniform banality of moralistic judgment" (Fludernik 2007, 263). But therein lies its social viability as a constitutive story: identity, too, falls prey to this "plenitude of life," remaining fluid, multiple, elastic, contested.

References

Alter, Robert. 1981. *The Art of Biblical Narrative*. New York: Basic Books.

Alter, Robert. 1996. *Genesis: Translation and Commentary*. New York: Norton.

Alter, Robert. 2010. "Literature." In *Reading Genesis: Ten Methods*, edited by Ronald Hendel, 13–27. Cambridge: Cambridge University Press.

Anderson, John E. 2011. *Jacob and the Divine Trickster: A Theology of Deception and Yhwh's Fidelity to the Ancestral Promise in the Jacob Cycle*. Siphrut 5. Winona Lake, IN: Eisenbrauns.

Astruc, Jean. 1753. *Conjectures sur les mémoires originaux dont il paroit que Moyse s'est servi pour composer le Livre de la Genese*. Bruxelles: Fricx. Also available in a 1999 edition, edited by Pierre Gibert. Paris: Noêsis.

Auerbach, Erich. 1953. *Mimesis: The Representation of Reality in Western Literature*. Princeton, NJ: Princeton University Press.

Bach, Alice. 1993. "Breaking Free of the Biblical Frame-Up: Uncovering the Woman in Genesis 39." In *A Feminist Companion to Genesis*, edited by Athalya Brenner, 318–342. Sheffield, Yorkshire: Sheffield Academic Press.

Bal, Mieke. 1985. *Narratology: Introduction to the Theory of Narrative*. Translated by Christine van Boheemen. Toronto: University of Toronto Press.

Bar-Efrat, Shimeon. 1979. *Ha'itsuv ha'omanuti shel hassipur bammiqra*. Tel Aviv: Sifriyat Po'alim. Published in English in 1989 as *Narrative Art in the Bible*. Sheffield, Yorkshire: Almond Press.

Barthes, Roland. 1971. "La lutte avec l'ange: Analyse textuelle du Genèse 32.23–33." In *Image, Music, Text*, translated by Stephen Heath, 125–141. New York: Hill and Wang.

Bechtel, Lyn. 1994. "What if Dinah Is Not Raped? (Genesis 34)." *Journal for the Study of the Old Testament* 62: 19–36.

Bird, Phyllis A. 1989. "The Harlot as Heroine: Narrative Art and Social Presupposition in Three Old Testament Texts." In *Narrative Research on the Hebrew Bible*, edited by Miri Amihai, George W. Coats, and Anne M. Solomon. *Semeia* 46: 119–139.

Bledstein, Adrien Janis. 1993. "Binder, Trickster, Heel and Hairy-Man: Rereading Genesis 27 as a Trickster Tale Told by a Woman." In *A Feminist Companion to Genesis*, edited by Athalya Brenner, 282–295. Sheffield, Yorkshire: Sheffield Academic Press.

Blenkinsopp, Joseph. 2004. *Treasures Old and New: Essays in the Theology of the Pentateuch*. Grand Rapids. MI: Eerdmans.

Boyd, Brian. 2009. *On the Origin of Stories: Evolution, Cognition, and Fiction*. Cambridge, MA: Harvard University Press / Belknap Press.

Brenner, Athalya, ed. 1993. *A Feminist Companion to Genesis*. Sheffield, Yorkshire: Sheffield Academic Press.

Brenner, Athalya. 2005. *I Am—: Biblical Women Tell Their Own Stories*. Minneapolis, MN: Fortress.

Brett, Mark G. 2000. *Genesis: Procreation and the Politics of Identity*. Old Testament Readings. London and New York: Routledge.

Camp, Claudia. 2000. "The (E)Strange(d) Woman in the Land: Sojourning with Dinah." In *Wise, Strange, and Holy: The Strange Woman and the Making of the Bible*, 279–322. Sheffield, Yorkshire: Sheffield Academic Press.

Carr, David. 1997. "Narrative and the Real World: An Argument for Continuity." In *Memory, Identity, Community: The Idea of Narrative in the Human Sciences*, edited by Lewis P. Hinchman and Sandra K. Hinchman, 7–25. Albany: State University of New York Press.

Copher, Charles B. 1991. "The Black Presence in the Old Testament." In *Stony the Road We Trod: African American Biblical Interpretation*, edited by Cain Hope Felder, 146–164. Minneapolis, MN: Fortress.

Culley, Robert C. 1976. *Studies in the Structure of Hebrew Narrative*. Semeia Supplements. Philadelphia, PA: Fortress.

Culley, Robert C. 1992. *Themes and Variations: A Study of Action in Biblical Narrative*. Semeia Studies. Atlanta, GA: Scholars Press.

Currie, Mark. (1998) 2011. *Postmodern Narrative Theory*. Transitions. London: Palgrave Macmillan.

Exum, J. Cheryl. 1993a. "The (M)other's Place." In *Fragmented Women: Feminist (Sub)versions of Biblical Narrative*, 94–147. Valley Forge, PA: Trinity Press International.

Exum, J. Cheryl. 1993b. "Who's Afraid of the 'Endangered Ancestress'?" In *Fragmented Women: Feminist (Sub)versions of Biblical Narrative*, 148–169. Valley Forge, PA: Trinity Press International.

Exum, J. Cheryl, and Johanna W. H. Bos, eds. 1988. *Reasoning with the Foxes: Female Wit in a World of Male Power. Semeia* 42. Atlanta, GA: Scholars Press / Society of Biblical Literature.

Exum, J. Cheryl, and David J. A. Clines. 1993. *The New Literary Criticism and the Hebrew Bible*. Sheffield, Yorkshire: Sheffield Academic Press.

Felder, Cain Hope. 1991. "Race, Racism, and the Biblical Narratives." In *Stony the Road We Trod: African American Biblical Interpretation*, edited by Cain Hope Felder, 127–145. Minneapolis, MN: Fortress.

Fewell, Danna Nolan. 1993. "Changing the Subject: Retelling the Story of Hagar the Egyptian." In *Genesis: A Feminist Companion to the Bible*. Second Series, edited by Athalya Brenner, 182–194. Sheffield, Yorkshire: Sheffield Academic Press.

Fewell, Danna Nolan. 1996. "Imagination, Method, and Murder: Un/Framing the Face of Post-Exilic Israel." In *Reading Bibles, Writing Bodies: God, Identity, and the Book*, edited by Timothy K. Beal and David M. Gunn, 132–152. London and New York: Routledge.

Fewell, Danna Nolan. 2001. "Building Babel," In *Postmodern Interpretations of the Bible: A Reader*, edited by A. K. M. Adam, 1–15. St. Louis, MO: Chalice Press.

Fewell, Danna Nolan. 2002. "The Genesis of Israelite Identity: A Narrative Speculation on Postexilic Interpretation." In *Reading Communities Reading Scripture: Essays in Honor of Daniel Patte*, edited by Gary A Phillips and Nicole Wilkerson, 111–118. Valley Forege, PA: Trinity Press International. Reprinted in *The Global Bible*, edited by Daniel Patte.

Fewell, Danna Nolan. 2003. "The Other Woman and the Other Child (Genesis 16 and 21)" and "Other Women and Other Children Revisited (Ezra 9–10; Nehemiah 13:23–31; Genesis 12–34)." In *The Children of Israel: Reading the Bible for the Sake of Our Children*, 43–63. Nashville, TN: Abingdon.

Fewell, Danna Nolan. 2005. "Lecture Féministe: Viol, lecture et representation en Genèse 34." In *Guide des nouvelles de la Bible*, edited by André Lacocque, 97–114. Paris: Bayard Press.

Fewell, Danna Nolan. Forthcoming. 2017. "Facing the End of History: The Akedah under the Shadow of Empire." *Bible and Critical Theory*.

Fewell, Danna Nolan, and David M. Gunn. 1991. "Tipping the Balance: Sternberg's Reader and the Rape of Dinah." *Journal of Biblical Literature* 110: 194–211.

Fewell, Danna Nolan, and David M. Gunn. 1993. "The Way of Women (Genesis 24–Exodus 2)." In *Gender, Power, and Promise: The Subject of the Bible's First Story*, 68–93. Nashville, TN: Abingdon.

Fischer, Irmtraud. 2012. "Genesis 12–50: The Story of Israel's Origins as a Women's Story." In *Feminist Biblical Interpretation: A Compendium of Critical Commentary on the Books of the Bible and Related Literature*, edited by Louise Schottroff, Marie-Theres Wacker, and Martin Rumscheidt, 15–32. Grand Rapids, MI: Eerdmans.

Fishbane, Michael. 1979. *Text and Texture: Close Readings of Selected Biblical Texts.* New York: Schocken.

Fludernik, Monica. 2007. "Identity/Alterity." In *The Cambridge Companion to Narrative*, edited by David Herman, 260–273. Cambridge: Cambridge University Press.

Fokkelman, J. P. 1975. *Narrative Art in Genesis: Specimens of Stylistic and Structural Analysis.* Assen and Amsterdam: Van Gorcum.

Fox, Everett. 1983. *In the Beginning: A New English Rendition of the Book of Genesis.* New York: Schocken.

Fox, Everett. 1989. "Can Genesis Be Read as a Book?" In *Narrative Research on the Hebrew Bible*, edited by Miri Amihai, George W. Coats, and Anne M. Solomon. *Semeia* 46: 31–40.

Frank, Arthur W. 2010. *Letting Stories Breathe: A Socio-Narratology.* Chicago: University of Chicago Press.

Frymer-Kinsky, Tikva. 2002. "The Dinah Affair." In *Reading the Women of the Bible: A New Interpretation of Their Stories*, 179–198. New York: Schocken.

Fuchs, Esther. 1987. "Structure and Patriarchal Functions in the Biblical Betrothal Type-Scene: Some Preliminary Notes." *Journal of Feminist Studies in Religion* 3: 7–13.

Fuchs, Esther. 1988. "'For I Have the Way of Women': Deception, Gender, and Ideology in Biblical Narrative." In *Reasoning with the Foxes: Female Wit in a World of Male Power*, edited by J. Cheryl Exum and Johanna W. H. Bos. *Semeia* 42: 68–83.

Fuchs, Esther. 1989. "The Literary Characterization of Mothers and Sexual Politics in the Hebrew Bible." In *Narrative Research on the Hebrew Bible*, edited by Miri Amihai, George W. Coats, and Anne M. Solomon. *Semeia* 46: 151–166.

Graetz, Naomi. 1993. "Dinah the Daughter." In *A Feminist Companion to Genesis*, edited by Athalya Brenner, 306–317. Sheffield, Yorkshire: Sheffield Academic Press.

Gunkel, Hermann. 1997. *Genesis.* Translated by Mark E. Biddle. Macon, GA: Mercer University Press. German original published in 1901 by Vandenhoeck and Ruprecht, Göttingen.

Gunn, David M., and Danna Nolan Fewell. 1993. *Narrative in the Hebrew Bible.* Oxford Bible Series. Oxford: Oxford University Press.

Heard, R. Christopher. 2001. *The Dynamics of Diselection: Ambiguity in Genesis 12–36 and Ethnic Boundaries in Post-Exilic Judah.* Semeia Studies. Atlanta, GA: Society of Biblical Literature.

Herder, J. G. 1782. *Vom Geist der Ebräischen Poesie.* Dessau: [n.p.]. First translated into English by James Marsh as *The Spirit of Hebrew Poetry*. Burlington: Edward Smith, 1833.

Humphreys, W. Lee. 2001. *The Character of God in the Book of Genesis: A Narrative Appraisal.* Louisville, KY: Westminster John Knox.

Jackson, Melissa A. 2012. *Comedy and Feminist Interpretation of the Hebrew Bible.* Oxford Theological Monographs. Oxford: Oxford University Press.

Jeansonne, Sharon Pace. 1990. *The Women of Genesis.* Minneapolis, MN: Fortress.

Jobling, David. 1986. "Myth and Its Limits in Genesis 2.4b–3.24." In *The Sense of Biblical Narrative: Structural Analyses in the Hebrew Bible II*, 17–43. Sheffield, Yorkshire: JSOT Press / Sheffield Academic Press.

Knoppers, Gary N., and Bernard M. Levinson, eds. 2007. *The Pentateuch as Torah: New Models for Understanding Its Promulgation and Acceptance*. Winona Lake, IN: Eisenbrauns.

Kwok Pui-Lan. 1997. "Overlapping Communities and Multicultural Hermeneutics." In *A Feminist Companion to Reading the Bible: Approaches, Methods and Strategies*, edited by Athalya Brenner and Carole Fontaine, 203–215. Sheffield, Yorkshire: Sheffield Academic Press.

Mbuwayesango, Dora R. 1997. "Childlessness and Woman-to-Woman Relationships in Genesis and in African Patriarc[h]al Society: Sarah and Hagar from a Zimbabwean Woman's Perspective (Gen 16:1–16; 21:8–21)." In *Reading the Bible as Women: Perspectives from Africa, Asia, and Latin America*. edited by Phyllis A. Bird, Katharine Doob Sakenfeld, and Sharon H. Ringe. *Semeia* 78: 27–36.

Miles, Jack. 1995. *God: A Biography*. New York: Alfred A. Knopf.

Miscall, Peter D. 1983. *The Workings of Old Testament Narrative*. Philadelphia, PA, and Chico, CA: Fortress Press and Scholars Press.

Mitchell, Stephen. 1996. *Genesis: A New Translation of the Classic Biblical Stories*. New York: Harper Collins.

Niditch, Susan. 1987. *Underdogs and Tricksters: A Prelude to Biblical Folklore*. San Francisco: Harper & Row, 1987.

Ochs, Elinor, and Capps, Lisa. 2001. *Living Narrative: Creating Lives in Everyday Storytelling*. Cambridge, MA: Harvard University Press.

Ostriker, Alica Suskin. 1997. "Sarah, or Defiance" and "The Opinion of Hagar." In *The Nakedness of the Fathers: Biblical Visions and Revisions*, 67–80. New Brunswick, NJ: Rutgers University Press.

Pardes, Ilana. 1992. *Countertraditions in the Bible: A Feminist Approach*. Cambridge, MA: Harvard University Press.

Penner, Todd, and Lilian Cates. 2007. "Textually Violating Dinah: Literary Readings, Colonizing Interpretations, and the Pleasure of the Text." *Bible and Critical Theory* 3(3): 37.1–37.18.

Preminger, Alex, and Edward L. Greenstein, eds. 1986. *The Hebrew Bible in Literary Criticism*. New York: Ungar.

Rashkow, Ilona N. 2004. "The Rape(s) of Dinah (Gen. 34): False Religion and Excess in Revenge." In *The Destructive Power of Religion, vol. 3, Models and Cases of Violence in Religion*, edited by J. Harold Ellens, 53–80. Westport, CT: Praeger.

Richards, Phillip M. 2000. "The 'Joseph Story' as a Slave Narrative: On Genesis and Exodus as Prototypes for Early Black Anglophone Writing." In *African Americans and the Bible*, edited by Vincent L. Wimbush and Rosamond C. Rodman, 221–235. New York: Continuum.

Schneider, Tammi J. 2008. *Mothers of Promise: Women in the Book of Genesis*. Grand Rapids, MI: Baker.

Schniedewind, William M. 2004. *How the Bible Became a Book*. Cambridge: Cambridge University Press.

Schniedewind, William M. 2013. *The Social History of Hebrew: Its Origins through the Rabbinic Period*. New Haven, CT: Yale University Press.

Scholz, Suzanne. 1998. "Through Whose Eyes? A 'Right' Reading of Genesis 34." In *Genesis, A Feminist Companion to the Bible* (Second Series), edited by Athalya Brenner, 150–171. Sheffield, Yorkshire: Sheffield Academic Press.

Scholz, Suzanne. 1999. "Was It Really Rape in Genesis 34? Biblical Scholarship as a Reflection of Cultural Assumptions." In *Escaping Eden: New Feminist Perspectives on the Bible*, edited by Harold C. Washington, Susan Lochrie Graham, and Pamela Thimmes, 182–198. Sheffield, Yorkshire: Sheffield Academic Press.

Simopoulis, Nicole M. 2007. "Who Was Hagar? Mistress, Divorcée, Exile, or Exploited Worker: An Analysis of Contemporary Grassroots Readings of Genesis 16 by Caucasian, Latina, and Black South African Women." In *Reading Other-Wise: Socially Engaged Biblical Scholars Reading with Their Local Communities*, edited by Gerald O. West, 63–72. Atlanta, GA: Society of Biblical Literature.

Sternberg, Meir. 1973. "Delicate Balance in the Story of the Rape of Dinah: Biblical Narrative and the Rhetoric of the Narrative Text." *HaSifrut* 4: 193–231 (Hebrew). For an updated English version, see Sternberg 1985, 441–481.

Sternberg, Meir. 1985. *The Poetics of Biblical Narrative: Ideological Literature and the Drama of Reading*. Indiana Literary Biblical Series. Bloomington: Indiana University Press.

Tamez, Elsa. 1987. "The Woman Who Complicated the History of Salvation." In *New Eyes for Reading: Biblical and Theological Reflections by Women from the Third World*, edited by John S. Pobee and Barbel von Wartenberg-Potter, 5–17. Bloomington, IN: Meyer-Stone.

Trible, Phyllis. 1973. "Depatriarchalizing in Biblical Interpretation." *Journal of the American Academy of Religion* 41: 30–48.

Trible, Phyllis. 1984. *Texts of Terror: Literary-Feminist Readings of Biblical Narratives*. Overtures to Biblical Theology 13. Philadelphia, PA: Fortress.

Van Wolde, Ellen. 1994. *Words Become Worlds: Semantic Studies of Genesis 1–11*. Leiden: Brill.

Turner, Lawrence A. 1990. *Announcements of Plot in Genesis*. Library of Hebrew Bible/Old Testament Studies. Sheffield: Sheffield Academic Press.

Waters, John W. 1991. "Who Was Hagar?" In *Stony the Road We Trod: African American Biblical Interpretation*, edited by Cain Hope Felder, 187–205. Minneapolis, MN: Fortress.

Weems, Renita. 1988. *Just a Sister Away: A Womanist Vision of Women's Relationships in the Bible*. San Diego, CA: LuraMedia.

Wellhausen, Julius. 1878. *Geschichte Israels*. Berlin: G. Reimer. Later editions published as *Prolegomena zur Geschichte Israels*. First translated into English in 1885 as *Prolegomena to the History of Israel: With a Reprint of the Article "Israel" from the Encyclopaedia Britannica*. Translated by J. Sutherland Black and Allan Menzies. Edinburgh: A&C Black.

Whitelam, Keith. 1989. "Israel's Traditions of Origin: Reclaiming the Land." *Journal for the Study of the Old Testament* 44: 19–42.

Whitelam, Keith. 1991. "Between History and Literature: The Social Production of Israel's Traditions of Origin." *Scandinavian Journal of the Old Testament* 5(2): 60–74.

Williams, Delores. S. 2006. "Hagar in African American Biblical Appropriation." In *Hagar, Sarah, and Their Children: Jewish, Christian, and Muslim Perspectives*, edited by Phyllis Trible and Letty M. Russell, 171–184. Louisville, KY: Westminster John Knox.

Yamada, Frank M. 2004. "Dealing with Rape (in) Narrative (Genesis 34): Ethics of the Other and a Text in Conflict." In *The Meanings We Choose: Hermeneutical Ethics, Indeterminacy, and the Conflict of Interpretations*, edited by Charles H. Cosgrove, 149–165. London and New York: T&T Clark.

CHAPTER 9

....

THE STORY OF EXODUS AND
ITS LITERARY KINSHIPS

....

KENNETH NGWA

EXODUS AND ITS CRITICAL READERS

....

FROM Flavius Josephus's *Antiquities of the Jews* (1936) to Zora Neale Hurston's *Moses Man of the Mountain* ([1939] 1991), and from ancient rabbinic (Carasik 2005) to modern commentaries (Walzer 1985; Pixley 1987; Glaude 2000; Meyers 2005), interpreters have read Exodus (whole or in parts) as a *story* with several interrelated motifs: liberation and migration; theophany, covenant, and community identity; exile/diaspora and multiculturalism, and so on. With its different literary genres, narrative settings, mix of prose and poetry, and overlapping motifs, Exodus forces interpreters not only to make sense of narrative interruptions and gaps, literary units and transitions, and a range of characters and perspectives but also to develop reading strategies that highlight layers of meaning in the story (Olson 2010, 13–16; Langston 2006; Dozeman 2009).

Enlightenment criticism's self-conscious methodological separation of narrative from history and the reframing of hermeneutics around the historical verifiability of narrative "facts" in determining meaning (Frei 1974, 51–154) predictably influenced scholarship on Exodus (Frerichs and Lesko 1997; Vervenne 1996, 21–28). Rooted in the historical-critical method, discussions ignited now longstanding debates about Exodus's narrative kinships: its relations to Deuteronomy (Olson 2012, 82–92; Brenner and Yee 2012), to the patriarchal narratives in Genesis (Van Seters 2006, 1–16; Schmid 2010, 117–193), to the wilderness stories in Numbers (Buis 1978; Lawlor 2011), and indeed, to the entire Pentateuch (Noth 1962, 10–12). Such debates have left readers with irresolvable questions. Does/can Exodus stand alone, or does its itinerant fervor necessarily link the story to other literary corpuses, settings, and characters? Is Exodus an unsettled story, permanently deconstructing its narrative kinships in search of old *and* new ones?

A major shift in modern Exodus scholarship emerged in Brevard Childs's work. Before Childs produced his canonical commentary on Exodus, in 1974, he had published *Biblical Theology in Crisis* (1970), decrying the limits of the historical-critical method that failed to address the biblical text in its final form or its reception history. To illustrate his method,

Childs interpreted Exodus 2:11–15, noting its differences and similarities with Exodus 2:16–22 and concluding that both texts illustrate Moses's "active concern for justice" and show Moses to be "an exile who is forced to live apart from his people whom he has not succeeded in delivering." Accordingly, Childs noted that the New Testament writer of Hebrews (11:27), in depicting Moses as a fearless deliverer (contra Exod. 2:14), is "interpreting the content of the exodus story and does not feel bound to the text of Exodus" (Childs 1970, 173). The fuller exposition of the canonical method in *The Book of Exodus: A Critical, Theological Commentary* (Childs 1974) combined text-critical exegesis, literary and rhetorical analyses, and reception history.

Influenced by structuralism, semiotics, and reception history, the re-emergence of interest in narrative analyses of Exodus increased in the wake of Childs's commentary (Weitzman 2007, 192–199), crystallizing around diachronic and synchronic approaches that attend to the literary history/strata of texts as well as to their final-form narrative art. The study of Exodus 32–34 by R. W. L. Moberly was premised on the compatibility of final-form narrative analyses with the "complexity and disunity of its prehistory," from which "literary and theological exegesis" emerges and engages textual units and structure, thematic allusions (e.g., to covenant making; Exod. 19–24), and presuppositions about constructing a movable sanctuary in Sinai (Moberly 1983, 22–45). Similarly, for Jonathan Magonet, the repetitions and duplications in Exodus 6:2–8 are more than a reflection of different sources; they function as "narrative conventions and techniques for specific literary purposes" in a "concentric" story that links Exodus 6:2–3 to divine name revelation in 3:7–11 and thus facilitate the transition from a covenant with Abraham to a complex covenant with Israel (Magonet 1983, 56–67).

Gordon Davies's synchronic treatment of Exodus 1–2, anchored in rhetorical criticism, identifies "deep structures" that permeate the text, including "problem-attempted solution-result" and "danger-escape from danger" functions linking Genesis 50 and Exodus 1:1–7. Rhetorically, though, Exodus 1–2 does not have a single dominant structure, point of view, deep structure, or surface structure. Rather, it invites consideration of history, Israel's and Moses's sense of identity and place in the universe, and questions of justice that begin with liberation from oppression but move toward a vision of God's supremacy (Davies 1992, 28, 43, 179–181). Jopie Siebert-Hommes identifies a literary architecture in Exodus 1–2, with multiple narrative features, including an auditory element (e.g., the—*ot* sounding endings in the midwives' words in 1:19: *ha-mitsriyot ha-ivriyot ki ḥayot hena '*), interpretive gaps (in 2:25, the phrase "Elohim knew" has no object), word repetitions ("sons of Israel," "to see," "to know," etc.), narrative subunits, and a textual structure. Five sections (1:1–7, 8–22; 2:1–10, 11–22; 23–25) make up the literary corpus, with Moses's birth and adoption occupying a central position (Siebert-Hommes 1998, 17–29, 57–58). In one of the most thoroughgoing narrative studies of Exodus, that of Terence Fretheim, perception ("seeing," "hearing," "knowing," "remembering"), imagery (divine and human), and a confluence of themes (creation, law, ritual/worship, covenant) highlight the importance of point of view, irony, and openness, which continually construct and deconstruct narrative identity (Fretheim 1991, 12–49).

The intersection of rhetorical analyses with social and ideological interests and narrative ethics illumine ironic constructions and deconstructions of gender, ethnic/racial, and social binaries both in Exodus and in the uses of the exodus story in global politics and cultures (Said 1986; Gorospe 2007, 93–150). Scholars point out that, in overt and covert ways, women in the story transgress boundaries and undermine the death-dealing decrees of the male pharaoh, who ironically assumes that boys pose a greater threat than girls to his political structure (Lapsley 2005, 69–88). The sudden appearance of Moses's sister does not simply reflect the story's complex history of composition but also adds to its richness, irony, humor, and surprise, "giving the story a new direction" (Exum 1983, 75). Hebrew slaves overcome their Egyptian masters in the plague narratives, inviting reflection on the construction of social values by the powerful elite and on the way the powerless redefine reality (Weems 1992, 25–34). Moreover, ambiguity permeates Moses's narrative persona: he continuously self-identifies with the Hebrews but also has an enduring Egyptian identity (2:19). The motif of a heavy tongue (Exod. 4:10; 6:12, 30) allows Moses to circumvent questions about his identity, leaving such questions open, not just in relation to social identity (Junior and Schipper 2008, 428–441), but also in relation to political function: can Moses become a pharaoh? (Gunda 2009, 84–94).

Beyond institutional identity, the narrative map in Exodus also draws on geography, using the wilderness and the mountain area as narrative tropes and spaces in which the characters and the story itself forge new kinships. George Coats frames the discussion in terms of layered contrasts: although Egypt is defined by political oppression, the wilderness is concerned with God's aid and Israel's murmuring, Sinai revelation, and military conflicts—all woven into the current narrative (Coats 1972a, 288–295; 1972b, 135–152; 1979, 2–8). Moses's family reunion (ch. 18) in the wilderness functions as "literary catharsis, when tension is released and harmony returns" (Ber 2008, 147–170) following a risky trek that had been marred by violence. And "broadening of family conflict to include setting" in the wilderness holds promise for connecting Exodus to the stories of Hagar and family conflict in Genesis (Dozeman 1998, 23–43).

As with Egypt and the wilderness, the negotiation of space and meaning fuels the mountain area stories. Moses's trips to and from the mountaintop create a two-dimensional perspective on divine holiness and residence with humans; the Decalogue as direct or mediated divine law; and the symbolism and relation of mountains to the exodus story (Langston 2006, 186). Repeated attempts to provide material texture to the recurrent themes of divine residency, holiness, and law dominate the architectural imagery associated with tabernacle construction, the golden calf story, and, eventually, the tent of meeting (Dozeman 2009, 426–435, 577–583, 755–766). Fretheim rightly notes that about a third of the book is devoted to instructions for, and the production of, the tabernacle, dramatically slowing down the narrative pace and highlighting the contrast between the tabernacle and golden calf constructions in terms of (a) who initiates the construction, (b) the planning involved, (c) the duration of construction, and (d) the accessibility of the divine being (Fretheim 1991, 263–267). And yet, the language, rituals, and conversation (between Moses and Joshua [Exod. 32: 17–18]) about the calf suggest that it functions as a symbol of divine presence (and protection), a military emblem, in a precarious political circumstance (Janzen 1990, 597–607). The conflicting portrayals of the deity—as gracious and forgiving yet punishing—are perhaps reflective of the unresolved tensions that characterize narrative depictions (e.g., 24:1–12; 32:1–6) of the divine-human relationship, captured in notions of covenant, ritual practice, and responses to laws (McCann 1990, 277–281; Sparks 2010, 72–81).

William Propp asks why Exodus is so satisfying a story and argues that the reason is its narrative resonance with several traditional stories, particularly heroic tales in folklore (with Moses now a main hero); Canaanite mythology about the storm god, Balu, who conquered the mythical sea and established his abode in the mountains (here, Yahweh is the heroic character); and ancient rites of passage that transform the identity and social function of the initiated. Israel's journey through the wilderness brings them into a new relationship with Yahweh and into a new space. Overall, there is not one hero in Exodus but three: Moses, Yahweh, and Israel (Propp 1999, 32–36). Indeed, Exodus is a story with multiple motifs, plot-lines, settings, characters, and perspectives.

Over a century ago, William Edward Burghardt Du Bois ([1903] 1989) coined the expression "double consciousness" to describe an unresolved, perhaps unresolvable, sense of two-ness that defined the African American experience. Du Bois's theory can aptly be extended to Exodus, a story that produces multiple, layered consciousnesses regarding Israel's political, ethnic, religious, and geographical identity: Israel's political identity is a function of deliverance or expulsion from Egypt; an ethnic motif distinguishes Hebrews from other sub-groups; a religious motif straddles patriarchal traditions and Yahweh; and a geographical motif transitions liberated or refugee Israel (asylum-seeking Israel; Burnside 2010, 243–266) toward an extraterritorial land.

These consciousnesses constitute a cluster of markers that structure narrative pace, space, and memory; interlink narrative themes; and characterize the story's psychosocial and tran-sregional relevance. Egypt's military demise at the sea transitions Israel to the wilderness and to the mountain, where Egypt repeatedly re-emerges as a memory trope (16:6; 17:3; 20:2; 32:1, 4, 7, 11). Economic distress in the wilderness (16:1–36) is anticipated in the hard labor and plague narratives in Egypt (1–2; 12:14–20). Divine revelation, covenant discourse, and covenant making around the mountain (chs. 19–24, 32–33) expand on Moses's divine encounter in Midian and the wilderness (Exod. 3–4; 18). Through these layered consciousnesses, the narrative is broadly framed for its ongoing constructions, critiques, and reconstructions of communal values at the transitions *and* intersections of political, ethnic, religious, and regional identity markers.

KINSHIPS IN AND OUT OF EGYPT (EXODUS 1:1–15:21)

The story begins when the sons of Israel entered and flourished in Egypt (Exod. 1:1–6), and moves to describe the deterioration and eventual severing of the bonds between Israel and Egypt. Israel's exodus from Egypt (12:37–42) is a function of divine deliverance (*'ālāh*, "going up"; *yāṣā'*, "going out"; "brought out"; Exod. 12:38, 39, 41, 42) and of political expulsion (*gāraš* "driven out"; 12:39; cf. 6:1; 11:1) by Pharaoh. Both portrayals—exodus as deliverance and as expulsion—merge around an adoption motif. First, while under oppression, Israel is adopted and delivered as Yahweh's "son" (Exod. 4:23; cf. Hos. 11:1). Second, in the wake of conflicts around the Nile, Israel and a mixed multitude (12:38) are expulsed or flee into the wilderness (11:1; 14:3) en route to an extraterritorial land. Thus exposed, Israel is rescued and brought to a place of divine inheritance (14:10–31; 15:17). Yahweh is not just a political sovereign who adopts and *then* liberates oppressed Israel; he is also a wealthy benefactor who rescues and *then* adopts exposed Israel. The exilic allegory of Jerusalem's birth (Ezek. 16:1–5) depicts the rescuing and adopting personality (Yahweh) as a wealthy benefactor who showed compassion for[1] exposed and endangered Jerusalem.

Following Pharaoh's oppressive economic policies and attempted ethnic genocide in chapter 1, the adoption motif is introduced in Exodus 2, where it is constructed (2:1–10), deconstructed (2:11–15), and reconstructed (2:16–22). Its construction revolves around ethnic identity shaped by an encounter between an exposed Hebrew child and an Egyptian rescuer whom the storyteller views favorably (2:3–6); "ethnic nurturing" that reunites the rescued child with his biological kin (2:7–9); and ethnicity as malleable political identity by which the son of a Levite's daughter becomes the son of Pharaoh's daughter (2: 2, 10). Moses's adoption is the culmination of a cluster of economic, cultural, and political negotiations by members of his ethnic subgroup and the house of Pharaoh (Ngwa 2013, 164–168).

The perspective changes to counteradoption in Exodus 2:11–15, framed by two kinds of journeys. First, Moses "goes out" (*yāṣā'*) to his kin after he has "matured," echoing his adoption persona and his stature in Egypt (2:10–11; 11:3) and anticipating Israel's exodus from Egypt (12:38). Second, Moses "flees" as a political refugee (2:15; cf. 2:19) when Pharaoh seeks to kill him, anticipating Israel's expulsion or flight from Egypt (11:1; 14:3). The episode ends with Moses beside a well in Midian, away from the ethnic subgroup to which his adoption story assigns him and away from the adoption story's social and institutional setting.

In 2:16–22, the narrative texture and perspective changes, once again. Moses's identity and actions are marks of extraterritorial *alien*ation. Now an Egyptian refugee (2:19), Moses is adopted into Jethro's family, shifting the narrative's "institutional" framework from political to religious, and Moses's status from refugee to sojourner. Readoption occurs through Moses's social actions and exogamous marriage (Winslow 2005, 70; Leveen 2010, 399–402). This socio-genealogical formulation of kinship is signaled by the morphological rendering of Moses's act of driving away (*gršm*) the shepherds and by his son's name, Gershom (*gršm*).

The construction, deconstruction, and reconstruction of the adoption motif are part of the narrative use of memory as a cognitive framework for interpreting Israel's presence in and eventual departure from Egypt (12:14). Oppression is a consequence of political amnesia (1:8); transgenerational embodied identity—*sojourner*—redefines refugee Moses's stay in Midian; divine memory fuels liberation (2:24); Yahweh's multigenerational name engages ancestral traditions (3:15); and Moses eventually returns to his kinfolk in Egypt (4:18). This narrative mnemohistory—"reception theory applied to [narrative] history" (Assmann 1997, 9)—links individual, subgroup, regional, and national events. In words and themes reminiscent of the Egyptian princess's adoption of Moses, Yahweh "goes down," sees people crying in distress, identifies (3:9//2:6) and lays claim (3:7//2:7) to them, links their distress to the need for economic redress (3:8//2:9) through re-engagement with genealogical and cultural kin (3:6//2:7), and enlists the services of intermediaries to make claims on them (3:12//2:10). Irony, point of view, and fractured memories move the story toward an open future (Fretheim 1991, 36–49).

To signify his new adoption status and authorize his return—exodus in reverse—to his kinfolk, Moses becomes "like God" to Aaron (4:16–17) and later to Pharaoh (7:1). The message is twofold: first, Israel is "God's son" and deserves to be released from captivity (3:16–17; 4:22–23); second, ethnic Hebrews must go on a three-day pilgrimage into the wilderness (3:18). The first message promises deliverance as a function of adoption; the second promises a pilgrimage that anticipates readoption.

Portions of the ensuing narrative also convey counteradoption views. For example, Exodus 4:18–6:1 echoes 2:11–15 in interesting ways. Both begin with Moses's journey to his kin (4:18//2:11) and end with Israel and/or Moses forced out of the land (6:1//2:15). Just as Moses's post-adoption trips to his kinfolk provoked resistance (2:13) and forced exile (2:15), so, too, his return from Midian elicits threats against his life (4:24–26) and resistance from Pharaoh (5:2), creates sociopolitical anxiety for the Hebrews, and leads to Israel's expulsion from Egypt (5:15–6:1).[2] The overlap between liberation-exodus and exposure-exodus is conveyed in the prediction about Pharaoh's actions in 6:1: "By a mighty hand, he will let them go (*šlq*; cf. 4:23); by a mighty hand, he will drive them (*grš*) out of his land."

As the story unfolds, Yahweh's plan is to link ancestral and exodus traditions (6:3); and, recognizing the association of these traditions to distinct geographical spaces (6:4), to liberate and deliver Israel from servitude (6:6) before adopting Israel as his people and becoming Israel's god (6:7): "I will take you as my people, and I will be your God." The expression of Yahweh taking (*lqḥ*) Israel and becoming Israel's god (*hyh . . . l . . . lēlōhîm*) echoes the adoption language in 2:9–10 and its variant form in 19:6.[3] Israel's potential adoption infuses the plague narratives (7:1–11:3), which depict Moses's status "as God" to Pharaoh (7:1; cf. 4:16), repeatedly portray exodus as pilgrimage (7:16; 8:1, 20; 9:1, 13; 10:3, 24), and conclude with an exalted Moses (11:3).

Exodus 14:1–15:21 also exhibit counteradoption and readoption motifs. It opens with Israel camped beside the sea by way of the wilderness (13:18; 14:1–2) and ends with Israel acquired from the sea and firmly planted on Yahweh's mountain abode (15:18). The narrator places Israel in the wilderness and beside the sea, two locations associated with alienation, vulnerability, and potential adoption. From Pharaoh's perspective, Israel is a wandering and vulnerable people, exposed and enclosed. Indeed, Israel's actions and emotions echo Moses's counteradoption story: they flee (14:5 cf. 2:15) from Pharaoh and fear deadly action by Pharaoh (14:10cf. 2:14). Yet, the narrative also portrays Israel as a witness to divine action—through the mediations of an angel (14:19–20) and Moses (14:21–22)—that rescues Israel by transforming parts of the Sea into dry ground (14:22) and turning away or clogging Pharaoh's chariots (14:25; see LXX, Syriac, and Sam. Pentateuch). The seaside community is defined by specific forms of political, ethnic, religious, and regional markers that continuously construct, deconstruct, and reconstruct its relations to adopting personalities. Israel's song portrays Yahweh as a divine and political king, who adopts, liberates, and brings Israel into the divine abode, and as a wealthy king moved by steadfast love to rescue exposed and vulnerable Israel, and bring them to a place of inheritance (15:11–17).

KINSHIPS AND MEMORIES IN THE WILDERNESS (EXODUS 15:22–18:27)

The post–Red Sea community is repeatedly placed in three wilderness locations (15:22; 16:1; 17:1; 18:5). First, after trekking for three days, the people arrive at Marah and complain because of the bitter water. Moses cries to Yahweh (15:25). The last time someone had cried to Yahweh was when Israel faced Pharaoh's army (14:10); now, economic distress provokes a similar cry. Second, at Sin (16:1), the people's complaints about the lack of food contrast with memory of Egypt as a place of nourishment (16:3). Yahweh responds, providing manna and instructions for routine and Sabbath consumption (16:4–36). Interpreted as a test of loyalty to the deity, the law (16:4) is used to structure relations between a distressed people (16:7, 8, 9, 12) and their wealthy adopter-overlord who controls the elements of economic survival. Finally, while camping at Rephidim, the people argue with Moses and fear for their lives. Moses cries to Yahweh and is instructed to provide water that will flow from a rock (17:2–6).

Repetition reinforces the Exodus story's use of geography to grapple with nourishment in the wake of exposure. In contrast to the Nile, whose nearly every mention reflects its status as a sustained economic resource for Egypt's population and for Pharaoh (Exod. 2.3, 5; 4.9; 7.15, 17, 18, 20, 21, 24, 28; 8.5, 7; 17.5), the wilderness represents dangerous exposure for Israel (16:3; 17:3). Israel's trek echoes Hagar/Ishmael's exposure narratives. Partly as a result of expulsion (Exod. 6:1; 11:1; Gen. 21:10), Israel and Hagar/Ishmael are repeatedly placed in the wilderness (Exod. 15:22; 16:2; 17:1//Gen. 16:7; 21:15), a place of insufficient nourishment in contrast to a place of food security (Exod. 16:1–3; 17:3//Gen. 21:14, 15). When the exposed cry (Exod. 17:4//Gen. 21:16), a deity hears their voice/complaint (Exod. 16:7//Gen. 21:17) and responds with temporary nourishment, en route to settled life (Exod. 16:35//Gen. 21:21).

Stephen Geller identifies two traditions in the wilderness narrative in Exodus 16—covenantal and priestly—connected to Sabbath. This narrative link to Sabbath is evidenced by "leading words" with the Hebrew consonants *shin* and *bet*. These words include *šābat* (to stop, cease), *šabbatôn* (stoppage), *šabbāt* (stop), *yāšab* (sit, remain), *šĕbî'î* (seventh), and possibly *śōba'* (satiety, satisfaction). Echoes of the Genesis creation story with its focus on divine activity and rest provide narrative texture to the complex nature of Israel's covenantal relationship with her deity as creator and sustainer (Geller 2005, 5–16). In addition to the motif of being *rescued from water* (the Nile for Moses and the Red Sea for Israel), there is also a motif of being *rescued by water* that is appropriate for the wilderness. The two creation stories in Genesis depict deep waters and dry land as the simultaneously life-enhancing and life-challenging "stuff" of social and economic space. In this adoption scenario, unauthorized "going out" (*yāṣā'*, Exod. 16:27) in search of food is predictably unsuccessful, since divine patronage is normative, interpreted as evidence of deliverance (*yāṣā'*) from Egypt (16:32).

Alongside economic challenges, the wilderness narrative suggests a fragile political structure marked by constant conflict (17:8–14) and the need for a judicial system (ch. 18). Assisted by Aaron and Hur, Moses leads Israel to a hard-won victory over Amalek, and, counseled by Jethro, Moses establishes a judicial structure. Again, both events are interpreted as evidence of deliverance from Egypt (18:1, 10). The convergence of political and judicial motifs around Jethro's visit (18:5) recalls his role as a wealthy, adopting priest-become-father-in-law following Moses's forced exile from Egypt. The presence of Zipporah and her two sons confirms the symbolism of Moses's transformation through adoption. And just as Moses's integration into Jethro's family preceded his encounter with Yahweh at the burning bush (2:16–22), so, too, the festive family reunion, now expanded to include Israelite leaders (18:12), precedes Israel's encounter with Yahweh on Sinai. The chapter functions as a "concluding scene" to the narrative that began in chapter 2 (Childs 1974, 327), depicting journeys that take Moses and Israel to God's mountain/abode (Smith 1997, 192–195, 227–232). The chapter, however, also transitions Israel to the mountain narratives in Exodus and the wilderness narratives in Numbers, creating a narrative unit from Exodus 18 to Numbers 10 (Lawlor 2011). Will Israel undergo adoption, counteradoption, and readoption analogous to Moses's story?

KINSHIPS AT THE MOUNTAIN (EXODUS 19:1–40:38)

Yahweh guides Israel to an unnamed mountain linked with Sinai (19:2–3), a literary and symbolic representation of divine presence (Dozeman 1989, 30). Israel's association with this (divine) space is marked by arrival (*bā 'āh*) and by departure (*'ālāh*) for the land of Promise (19:1; 33:1), both movements echoing Israel's arrival (*bā 'āh*) and departure (*'ālāh*) from Egypt (1:1; 12:38). Arrival at Sinai initiates Yahweh's adoption of the people (ch. 19), followed by laws and statutes (chs. 20–24) that anchor the covenantal adoption, and a fracturing of the covenant relationship (ch. 32) prior to Israel's departure from the mountain. The departing community (ch. 33) bears the traumatizing effects of a fractured story but also begins to rec-reate its identity through multiple constructions: new stone tablets, a tabernacle, and coordi-nation of its travel itinerary with a mobile divine tent (chs. 34–40). Events at the mountains not only frame the beginning and end of Moses's narrative persona (Exod. 2–3; Deut. 34), but also address Israel's ongoing negotiation of her presence around the divine abode or resi-dence, ultimately using theophanic encounters as narrative tropes to shift divine presence/residence from the mountain to the tabernacle/tent, accentuating human activity in shaping the sacredness of the encounter (Olson 2012, 88–91; Hauge 2001, 21–96).

At the mountain (19:5–6), in language that foreshadows Yahweh's claiming of the Levites in Numbers 8:14, Israel becomes Yahweh's special possession (*hyh . . . l . . . sglh*) and a king-dom of priests (*hyh . . . l . . . mmlkt khnm*). The expression simultaneously describes and confers Israel's adoption status. Yahweh has not only affirmed Israel's adoption as the ratio-nale for liberation-exodus but has also conferred a new status on Israel as a function of wil-derness rescue (Davies 2004, 61–63). A visual, communal, and ritualistic depiction of this status-conferring encounter is the repeated symbolism of vertical motion (going up, going down) associated with the mountain. Moses "goes up" to God on the mountain (19:3, 20), "comes down" (19:21), and "goes" to Israel (19:7). Yahweh "comes down" on the mountain (19:11, 18, 20); the people's "going up" to the mountain is coordinated to trumpet call-sounds (19:12–13) but also forbidden (19:23). The trampoline-like imagery of the repeated vertical-spatial motion—reminiscent of Moses's raising and lowering of his arms and staff in the wilderness—is summed up in divine imperatives to Moses in 19:24: "Descend and ascend!" The cumulative effect is exhilarating and celebratory (24:9–11), legally empowering and binding (24:12), mysteriously dizzying (24:17), and, if left without structured boundaries, deadly (19:24, 25). Events around the mountain slow down the linear narrative pace as they forge a new sense of religious identity and of social belonging and boundaries (Dozeman 1989, 87–101; Olson 2010, 45–53; 2012, 89–92).

There is also a counteradoption strand in the mountain narrative, nowhere more evident than in the golden calf episode. Its perspective from the bottom of the mountain contrasts a top-down construction of identity associated with adoption, elsewhere illustrated in the construction of the tabernacle (Fretheim 1991, 266, 280–283). Moses delays coming down (32:1), creating a sense of abandonment. When the episode ends, Yahweh commands Israel to depart from Sinai, promising partial assistance (33:1–5) after sending a plague on the peo-ple (32:35). The counteradoption is variously depicted as a ritual act of self-stripping (32:2–3; 33:6), a political crisis of identity about whose people Israel is (Moses's [32:7] or Yahweh's [32:11]), as ethnic/tribal violence (32:12, 25–29), and as a legal breach of contract at the bottom of the mountain (32:19). Events mirror the counteradoption in 4:19–6:1: a festival celebration (5:1//32:5) threatens the authority of the overlord (5:3//32:5), is interpreted as inconsistent with the demands of the sovereign (5:6//32:8), and provokes a (potentially) deadly response (5:15–21//32:9–10). Moses's intercessions secure only a partial remedy (5:22–23//32:11–14). But here, ironically, it is *divine space* rather than Egypt that constitutes the defining place of departure/expulsion framing the counteradoption.

Yet, that departure introduces a new movement toward readoption, made possible by re-engaging ancestral traditions (32:13). Indeed, Moses ascends the mountain (32:30) to secure divine forgiveness and new tablets (34:1). The inability of Israel and Yahweh to share the same living space is ultimately reinterpreted and "resolved" by coordinating access to a mobile tent (40:34–38). Yahweh's readoption of Israel transforms the conception of the divine abode from permanent mountain to mobile residence, one that Israel can create and maintain (Dozeman 2009, 581–583). The Decalogue, covenant renewal (34:1–35:3), and elaborate tabernacle construction (35:4–40:38) structure this ongoing relationship that infuses Israel's sense of political, ethnic, religious, and regional identity.

CONCLUSION

Exodus is an identity-conferring story. Moses's encounter with an Egyptian princess results in his adoption and new, enduring identity. Yahweh's encounter with Moses on the burning bush fuels God's political and religious claim on Israel in Egypt. Through the adoption motif, the story presents Israel's political and ethnic identities both in relation to and distinct from Egypt's: Israel has become Yahweh's people, and Yahweh has become Israel's God. The story partially redefines exposure in the wilderness as a temporal sojourn, indeed, as a pilgrimage leading to adoption upon arrival at the mountain of God, symbolically, the divine abode.

And yet, as a story with several motifs, Exodus is unsettled and unsettling. Counteradoption permeates the story, severing Israel from Egypt, invoking memory of Egypt to challenge the rationing of economic resources in the wilderness, and using ritual ceremony around the golden calf to fracture identity conferred from above. Violence fractures Moses's relations with his ethnic subgroup and with his adopting institution, Egypt, causing his exile. Violence redefines the wilderness as a place of perpetual warfare against a transgenerational foe, Amalek. And violence at the mountainside breaks the symbols of the exodus story, its legal statutes, resulting in the deaths of thousands of Israelites. Forced exile or exposure continues to shape the story, leaving its imprint on geographical spaces and on community consciousness.

And Exodus as expulsion is unfinalized and unfinalizing. Extraterritorial sociology and genealogy converge to transform Moses's identity as refugee into one of voluntary sojourner under the tutelage of a local priest. The pilgrimage trek from Egypt into the wilderness anticipates readoption, enunciated during Yahweh's encounter with Israel on the fiery mountain. This post-wilderness mountaintop readoption creates a number of changes: the holiness of the mountain to which Israel is invited post Egypt (3:5, 12) extends to a holy people (19:6), as narrative geography and sociology converge. Yahweh's seeing the people's misery and his responsive action (3:7) becomes the people's witnessing of divine deliverance and their responsive action (19:4). Moses's fears of incredulity about divine claims (4:1) are reimagined, and the people commit to Moses's words (19:7–9). Uncertainty about divine revelation emanating from a distant place (4:1–5) is resolved by Yahweh speaking in the hearing of the people (19:9), combining the visual and auditory aspects of divine revelation on the mountain. Promises of divine presence to and the divine teaching of Moses (4:15) expand to include Joshua (24:12) and the entire community (cf. 20:1–17). And finally, the traumatized community that departs from the mountain of God re-engages ancestral traditions, appeals to divine mercy, re-creates the broken tablets, and builds a tent of meeting.

The story that begins with the sons of Israel in motion—entering Egypt—ends with the house of Israel coordinating her movements to divine movement around a tent. Read through the motifs of adoption, counteradoption, and readoption organized across different institutional and geographical spaces, the story develops a rich sense of multiple, layered consciousnesses. These consciousnesses reflect a range of feelings and perceptions, ranging from safety, belonging, and purpose to vulnerability, exposure, and alienation to reconstructions and reimaginations of shared, sometimes fractured, memories and spaces.

NOTES

1. The Hebrew idiom *ḥml... 'l* is used to describe the compassionate rescue of Moses and Jerusalem by the Egyptian princess and Yahwehin, respectively, Exodus 2:6 and Ezekiel 16:5.
2. Exodus 5 recalls the northerners' demands to hold separate festivals, away from Rehoboam's oppressive economic policy, following Jeroboam's return from Egypt (1 Kings 12).
3. A similar formula is used to describe Naomi's status as an adoptive mother to Obed in Ruth 4:15.

REFERENCES

Assmann, Jan. 1997. *Moses the Egyptian: The Memory of Egypt in Western Monotheism.* Cambridge, MA: Harvard University Press.

Ber, Viktor. 2008. "Moses and Jethro: Harmony and Conflict in the Interpretation of Exodus 18." *Communio Viatorum* 50(2): 147–170.

Brenner, Athalya, and Gale Yee, eds. 2012. *Exodus and Deuteronomy: Texts and Contexts.* Minneapolis, MN: Fortress Press.

Buis, Pierre. 1978. "Conflits entre Moïse et Israël dans Exode et Nombres." *Vetus Testamentum* 28(3): 257–270.

Burnside, Jonathan P. 2010. "Exodus and Asylum: Uncovering the Relationship between Biblical Law and Narrative." *Journal for the Study of the Old Testament* 34(3): 243–266.

Carasik, Michael. 2005. *The Commentator's Bible: The JPS Miqra'ot Gedolot: Exodus.* Philadelphia, PA: Jewish Publications Society.

Childs, Brevard S. 1970. *Biblical Theology in Crisis.* Philadelphia, PA: Westminster Press.

Childs, Brevard S. 1974. *The Book of Exodus: A Critical Theological Commentary.* Philadelphia, PA: Westminster Press.

Coats, George W. 1972a. "An Exposition for the Wilderness Traditions." *Vetus Testamentum* 22(3): 288–295.

Coats, George W. 1972b. "The Wilderness Itinerary." *Catholic Biblical Quarterly* 34(2): 135–152.

Coats, George W. 1979. "The Sea Tradition in the Wilderness Theme: A Review." *Journal for the Study of the Old Testament* 12: 2–8.

Davies, Gordon F. 1992. *Israel in Egypt: Reading Exodus 1-2.* Journal for the Study of the Old Testament Supplement Series 135; Sheffield, Yorkshire: Sheffield Academic Press.

Davies, John A. 2004. *A Royal Priesthood: Literary and Intertextual Perspectives on an Image of Israel in Exodus 19.6.* Journal for the Study of the Old Testament Supplement Series 395. London: T&T Clark International.

Dozeman, Thomas B. 1989. *God on the Mountain*. Archaeology and Biblical Studies 37. Atlanta, GA: Scholars Press.

Dozeman, Thomas B. 1998. "The Wilderness and Salvation History in the Hagar Story." *Journal of Biblical Literature* 117(1): 23–43.

Dozeman, Thomas B. 2009. *Exodus*. Eerdmans Critical Commentary. Grand Rapids, MI: W. B. Eerdmans.

Du Bois, William Edward Burghardt. (1903) 1989. *The Souls of Black Folk*. Repr. with an introduction by Henry Lewis Gates Jr. New York: Bantam Books.

Exum, Cheryl. 1983. "You Shall Let Every Daughter Live: A Study of Exodus 1:8–2:10." In *The Bible and Feminist Hermeneutics*, edited by Mary Ann Tolbert. *Semeia* 28: 63–82.

Frei, Hans W. 1974. *The Eclipse of Biblical Narrative: A Study in Eighteenth and Nineteenth Century Hermeneutics*. New Haven, CT: Yale University Press.

Frerichs, Ernest S., and Leonard H. Lesko, eds. 1997. *Exodus: The Egyptian Evidence*. Winona Lake, IN: Einsenbrauns.

Fretheim, Terence E. 1991. *Exodus*. Interpretation: A Bible Commentary for Teaching and Preaching. Louisville, KY: John Knox.; reprint 2010; Louisville, KY: Westminster John Knox

Geller, Stephen. 2005. "Manna and Sabbath: A Literary-Theological Reading of Exodus 16." *Interpretation* 59: 5–16.

Glaude, Eddie S. Jr., 2000. *Exodus! Religion, Race, and Nation in Early Nineteenth-Century Black America*. Chicago: University of Chicago Press.

Gorospe, Athena A. 2007. *Narrative and Identity: An Ethical Reading of Exodus 4*. Biblical Interpretation Series 86. Leiden: Brill.

Gunda, Masiiwa Raiges. 2009. "African Theology of Reconstruction: The Painful Realities and Practical Options!" *Exchange* 38: 84–102.

Hauge, Martin Ravndal. 2001. *The Descent from the Mountain: Narrative Patterns in Exodus 19-40*. Journal for the Study of the Old Testament Supplement Series 323. Sheffield, Yorkshire: Sheffield Academic Press.

Hurston, Zora Neale. (1939) 1991. *Moses, Man of the Mountain: A Novel*. New York: Harper Perennial.

Janzen, Gerald J. 1990. "The Character of the Calf and Its Cult in Exodus 32." *Catholic Biblical Quarterly* 52(4): 597–607.

Josephus, Flavius. 1936. *The Life and Works of Flavius Josephus*. Translated by William Whiston, A.M., with an introductory essay by Rev. H. Stebbing, DD. Philadelphia, PA: John C. Winston Company.

Junior, Nyasha, and Jeremy Schipper. 2008. "Mosaic Disability and Identity in Exodus 4:10; 6:12, 30." *Biblical Interpretation* 16(5): 428–441.

Langston, Scott M. 2006. *Exodus through the Centuries*. Blackwell Bible Commentaries. Malden, MA: Blackwell.

Lapsley, Jacqueline. 2005. *Whispering the Word: Hearing Women's Stories in the Old Testament*. Louisville, KY: Westminster John Knox Press.

Lawlor, John I. 2011. "The 'At-Sinai Narrative': Exodus 18–Numbers 10." *Bulletin for Biblical Research* 21(1): 23–42.

Leveen, Adriane. 2010. "Inside Out: Jethro, the Midianites and a Biblical Construction of the Outsider." *Journal for the Study of the Old Testament* 34(4): 395–417.

Magonet, Jonathan. 1983. "The Rhetoric of God: Exodus 6:2-8." *Journal for the Study of the Old Testament* 27: 56–67.

Meyers, Carol L. 2005. *Exodus*. New Cambridge Bible Commentary. Cambridge: Cambridge University Press.

Moberly, R. Walter L. 1983. *At the Mountain of God: Story and Theology in Exodus 32–34*. Journal for the Study of the Old Testament Supplement Series 22. Sheffield, Yorkshire: JSOT Press.

McCann, Clinton J. 1990. "Exodus 32:1–14." *Interpretation* 44(3): 277–281.

Ngwa, Kenneth. 2013. "Ethnicity, Adoption, and Exodus: A Socio-Rhetorical Reading of Exodus 2:1-10." *Journal for the Study of the Old Testament* 38(2): 163–187.

Noth, Martin. 1962. *Exodus: A Commentary*. Old Testament Library. London: SCM Press.

Olson, Dennis T. 2012. "From Horeb to Nebo: Exile, the Pentateuch, and the Promise of Home in Exodus 2:1–3:6 and Deuteronomy 34:1–12." In *By the Irrigation Canals of Babylon: Approaches to the Study of the Exile*, edited by John J. Ahn and Jill Middlemas, 82–92. New York: Bloomsbury T&T Clark.

Olson, Dennis T. 2010. "Literary and Rhetorical Criticism." In *Methods for Exodus*, edited by Thomas B. Dozeman, 13–54. Methods in Biblical Interpretation. Cambridge: Cambridge University Press.

Pixley, Jorge V. 1987. *On Exodus: A Liberation Perspective*. Translated by Robert R. Barr. Maryknoll, NY: Orbis Books.

Propp, William H. C. 1999. *Exodus 1–18: A New Translation with Introduction and Commentary*. Anchor Bible 2; New York: Doubleday.

Said, Edward W. 1986. "Michael Walzer's 'Exodus and Revolution': A Canaanite Reading." *Grand Street* 5(2): 86–106.

Schmid, Konrad. 2010. *Genesis and the Moses Story: Israel's Dual Origins in the Hebrew Bible*. Translated by James D. Nogalski. Winona Lake, IN: Eisenbrauns.

Siebert-Hommes, Jopie. 1998. *Let the Daughters Live! The Literary Architecture of Exodus 1–2 as a Key for Interpretation*. Biblical Interpretation Series, 37. Leiden: Brill.

Smith, Mark S., with Elizabeth M. Bloch-Smith. 1997. *The Pilgrimage Pattern in Exodus*. Journal for the Study of the Old Testament Supplement Series 239. Sheffield, Yorkshire: Sheffield Academic Press.

Sparks, Kenton L. "Genre Criticism." 2010. In *Methods for Exodus*. Methods in Biblical Interpretation, edited by Thomas B. Dozeman, 55–94. Cambridge: Cambridge University Press.

Van Seters, John. 2006. "The Report of the Yahwist's Demise Has Been Greatly Exaggerated!" In *A Farewell to the Yahwist? The Composition of the Pentateuch in Recent European Interpretation*, edited by Thomas B. Dozeman and Konrad Schmid, 143–157. Society of Biblical Literature Symposium Series 34. Leiden: Brill.

Vervenne, Marc. 1996. "Current Tendencies and Developments in the Study of the Book of Exodus." In *Studies in the Book of Exodus: Redaction, Reception, Interpretation*, edited by Marc Vervenne, 21–59. Bibliotheca Ephemeridum Theologicarum Lovaniensium CXXVI. Leuven: Leuven University Press.

Walzer, Michael. 1985. *Exodus and Revolution*. New York: Basic Books.

Weems, Renita J. 1992. "The Hebrew Women Are Not Like the Egyptian Women: The Ideology of Race, Gender, and Sexual Reproduction in Exodus 1." In *Ideological Criticism of Biblical Texts*, edited by David Jobling and Tina Pippin. *Semeia* 59: 25–34.

Weitzman, Steven. 2007. "Before and after the Art of Biblical Narrative." *Prooftexts* 27(2): 191–210.

Winslow, Karen Strand. 2005. *Early Jewish and Christian Memories of Moses' Wives: Exogamist Marriage and Ethnic Identity*. Lewiston, NY: Edwin Mellen Press.

CHAPTER 10

BLOOD, DEATH, AND THE HOLY IN THE LEVITICUS NARRATIVE

BRYAN D. BIBB

ATTENTION to Leviticus in its reception history has shown little concern for its narrative context. The book has been read primarily in an instrumental way—that is, as source for individual laws and instructions—or as evidence for the development of Israelite religion. Many of Rambam's 613 *mitzvot* in the Torah derive from Leviticus, and the book is most prominent in today's popular culture as a locus of debate over homosexuality. Scholars have mostly focused on source and redactional concerns, building upon and responding to the Documentary Hypothesis of Wellhausen (Nicholson 1998; Baden 2012). Interpreters have situated Leviticus within the "P" source, a complex of Priestly material centered in the Sinai pericope but extending throughout the Torah. Even within its boundaries, Leviticus has been dissected, with chapters 1–16 coming from the Priestly Torah (PT) and chapters 17–26 coming from the Holiness School (HS; Knohl 1995). This fragmenting of the book into sources has further obscured its literary and narrative quality.

And yet, Leviticus appears as a single scroll in the Torah, and it does display a significant degree of internal coherence (Bibb 2009, 18–33). The scribes who assembled the Torah put the book together in a particular way, and the text abides despite all efforts to use it for other purposes. Although Leviticus incorporates material of diverse origins, and although many of its passages have been dismantled to form decontextualized lists, the book itself resists these invasive reading strategies. To read within the literary flow and intention of the text is to encounter the book as *part of* a larger narrative, and thoroughly narrative in its own structure.

This chapter will survey the book of Leviticus as it stands within the tradition. After introducing Leviticus as narrative, we will consider three parts of the book in light of particular themes, as reflected in the titles of the chapter's main sections: "Blood Ritual and Mythic Drama," chapters 1–7 and 11–15; "Life, Death, and Ambiguity," chapters 8–10 and 16; and "Holiness and God's People," chapters 17–27.

LEVITICUS AS NARRATIVE

A narrative approach to Leviticus must begin with the complicated question of whether and in what way the "book" of Leviticus can be considered a literary work. This question has at least three components for literary interpreters. First, we may choose to read Leviticus as part of the Torah, as one chapter or episode within a single larger work. Second, we may choose to read Leviticus as a separate work with textual boundaries and its own internal literary coherence (Rendtorff 1996; Warning 1999). The choice between these is a matter of interpretive scope, and each approach is appropriate in its turn. A third possibility is to set the narrative frame of Leviticus in the context of its reception in Jewish and Christian tradition (Elliott 2012). In actual practice, these three frameworks may alternate and overlap. Schleiermacher's "hermeneutical circle" between *part* and *whole* is very important in this case. This chapter will focus on narrative questions within the book itself.

Moving beyond the instrumental breaking of Leviticus into list or source, we realize that, although the book contains ritual instruction of various types, it is a narrative. The book begins with a narrative statement, "The LORD summoned Moses and spoke to him from the tent of meeting" (Lev. 1:1), and proceeds to narrate this moment of divine speech to Moses within the hearing of Aaron and the assembled congregation. Israel's ritual laws are not time-less or abstract; they are rooted in a particular moment in the mythic past, and so must be interpreted within that narrative context. These instructions provide the bridge between the construction of the tabernacle in Exodus and the mustering of the congregation in Numbers, and so must be seen as an essential prerequisite for Israel's existence as a community and nation (Auld 1996).

The book alternates between moments of law-giving and moments of ritual and legal pro-cedure. Following the work of Christopher Smith, we may divide the chapters of the book into the following sections:

> 1–7, laws for sacrificial performance
> 8–10, narrative of the priests' first ordination
> 11–15, laws for ritual cleanness
> 16, narrative of Aaron's first atonement ritual
> 17–24:9, laws for holiness
> 24:10–23, narrative of Moses's first legal dispute
> 24–27, laws for redemption

The structure of the last half of the book (17–27) is difficult to determine and does not fit neatly the alternating pattern of law/narrative that we see clearly through chapter 16. However, the narrative of the blasphemer in chapter 24 does interject in order to provide a moment of reflection on how these laws might function in actual judicial practice. Andreas Ruwe (2003) divides the book into two sections, chapters 1–8 and 9–27, with chapters 17–26 being a "coherent, fairly independent complex" integrated into the larger narrative. The most imaginative proposal for the structure of Leviticus is Mary Douglas's comparison with the physical arrangement of the tabernacle in her book, *Leviticus as Literature* (1999). She argues that Leviticus is "a sacred text designed on the proportions of a temple" (58).

Whatever structure the book may have, it is clear that the final form is the result of the combination and alternation of different genres, law and narrative. Literary critic David Damrosch (1987) has emphasized this combination as the central literary genius of the book: "The mixing of law and narrative was not a crude blunder by incompetent editors.... [R]ather, it was the most important generic innovation of its age" (35). Damrosch argues that readers of ritual in Leviticus must perform a careful literary analysis of the surrounding story. He discusses the interaction of law and narrative with analogy to the Hebrew verbal system. Narrative, he says, is "perfective" while ritual is "imperfective;" their combination in Leviticus gives a timeless or imperfective aspect to the narrative while rooting the ritual within its historical moment (281–283).

James Watts (1999) has examined the generic interaction in Leviticus as a movement between "story" and "list," two of three ancient genres used by the writers of the Torah, the third being "divine sanction" of the blessings and curses (45). The laws and regulations "provide solutions to problems and issues detailed by narratives, which in turn demonstrate the necessity of law" (58–59). Drawing on both Damrosch and Watts, I have argued that Leviticus's alternating generic pattern creates a new kind of text at the intersection between ritual and narrative (Bibb 2009, 34–48). The Leviticus narrative is similar to Genesis 1 in that events happen in a mythical past whose purpose is to frame the conceptual world of the present. The narrative style of the text resonates more with liturgy than with history or folk narrative. Leviticus tells a story about things that God said to Moses, things that Moses said and did, and rituals that took place within this generative moment of law-giving. It is a "mythic tale of ritual founding" that includes both "ritualized narrative" and "narrativized ritual" (Bibb 2009, 35).

In Leviticus, *narrative* and *ritual* transform each other, working together to negotiate the tensions and ambiguities that are inherent in any interaction with the Holy. The narrative provides an authoritative, foundational context for the ritual laws. The ritual's repetition and precisions encourage confidence that Israel can successfully live in God's proximity. However, in repetition we perceive anxiety; this carefully constructed edifice of speech hides an absence. Alternation between ritual and narrative is not so much a conversation as it is a collaboration—or even a conspiracy—to create an ordered world in which priests lead worship competently, in which worshippers navigate the requirements of holiness safely, and in which the gathered congregation can flourish in its liminal wanderings in the wilderness and in the land for which it longs.

BLOOD RITUAL AND MYTHIC DRAMA

The first narrative theme that we will address concerns the mythopoetics of ritualized narrative. If we compare the most obviously "ritual" texts in Leviticus (chapters 1–7 and 11–15) with those of other ancient cultures, it is clear that the biblical text is doing something quite different on a literary level. Ritual texts from Ugarit, Egypt, and Mesopotamia express their imperative purpose either through the use of recitations or through language of direction and instruction. The daily ritual of the temple of Amun-Re at Karnak, for instance, uses a liturgical form with headings such as "Spell for putting incense on the flame" and "Words to be said" (Hallo and Younger 2003, 1:34). Some rituals are framed as speech from a leader who is providing the instruction, such as in Hittite scapegoat rituals that begin with "thus says" and proceed as quotation (Hallo and Younger 2003, 1:62–64). An Ugaritic "Liturgy against Venomous Reptiles" is framed as a mare's plea to the divine world for the healing of snake venom (Hallo and Younger 2003, 1:94). Each of these employs narrative techniques that place the liturgy or ritual within an idealized framework, either as authoritative words delivered across time to the hearer or using a spiritual analogy to the suffering of the worshiper. They do not, however, construct a comprehensive narrative framework. (For more on the relationship between ritual and narrative in Ugarit, see Wright 2000).

In the case of Leviticus, the congregation of Israel (standing in for later listeners) overhears God's instructions to Moses, telling him what to say to Israel with regard to sacrifices, other rituals, and the rules of purity. The text expresses its imperative purpose through the embedding of instruction within the mythic past. By constructing an authoritative voice that speaks into the present from the revered past, these ritual instructions are idealized and universalized. They are timeless because they are *embedded within* a narrative, not because they have been decontextualized. The rhetorical purpose of this ritualizing activity is evident when we remember that the texts themselves are the product of historical development over a long period of time. They reflect and encode controversies and disagreements about when, where, and how rituals should be performed. Rhetorically, the framing texts have attempted to close the debate and have erased any ambiguity through their embedding of ritual texts in a creation myth.

As we encounter chapters 1–7 and 11–15, therefore, we should attend to the literary form and setting of these ritual texts within the narrative of God's extended revelation to Moses at the foot of Mt. Sinai. Both the narrative and ritual elements of these texts bear the stamp of their "ritualization," rhetorical techniques that establish their timelessness within shifting historical realities and their correctness within a contested field. Catherine Bell (1997) has identified "ritualizing" strategies that are each evident within Leviticus. These include formality, traditionalism, rule-governance, sacral symbolism, and symbolic performance (139–160). These features establish the power and authority of those who control the text (authors and authorized interpreters). It is tempting for literary critics to underestimate the artistry of textual features such as repetition and formalism. Although we do not know as much as we would like about the historical context of the book's authorship, editing, and implementation, the text itself bears the marks of disagreement and the negotiation of power relations.

The ritual instructions in Leviticus 1–7 and 11–15 are mythological in the sense that they describe the direct engagement with and transformation of the human world by the divine. God is less of an anthropomorphic character here than in Genesis or Exodus. In the Leviticus theophany, God is experienced as an emotionless Voice rather than as the round character that we find in Exodus 20–34. God is the Holy One who has decided to abide in the midst of the community, and Leviticus establishes the conditions by which this is possible. Moses, Aaron, and the sons of Aaron (the priests) establish a safe perimeter around the Holy both spatially in the tabernacle as well as conceptually in the rules that govern sacrifice and purity. In the layered processes of speaking and acting, authority is transferred from the Holy—through Moses and Aaron—to the professional priesthood that maintains this holy perimeter. As a mythological narrative, therefore, Leviticus establishes the structure of the world/temple, the rules by which the world/temple will operate, and etiological explanations for human relationships within this world/temple.

As in Genesis 1, the myth extends into the world of the listener or reader, making claims about reality and giving structure to disordered existence. The conceptual heart of this mythological creation is blood ritual, the sacrifice of animals and manipulation of their blood to maintain the boundaries of creation (Gorman 1990). The high drama of animal slaughter has been domesticated through ritualized description. The text sounds dry and boring. However, for each dull repetition, a life is taken and blood is spilled. The violence at the heart of the sacrificial system speaks to a savage preoccupation with the elemental forces that make life possible and that make living difficult. "In the blood is the life" (Gen. 9:4; Lev. 17:11), and in the use of blood as sacred detergent, the priests preserve life and community. The fascination with blood and death is found as well in chapters 11–15, in the regulations for the eating of animals, the oozing of human blood, and the problem of creeping disease.

The narrative, therefore, does not describe a time that is past or bygone, but ever present. The priests who exercise the authority of Moses and Aaron in each generation embody this myth. Through their manipulation of blood and life, they do God's work of creation on behalf of a vulnerable world. By embedding ritual instructions within a mythical-narrative frame, the authors/editors of Leviticus have created a sacred world that is timeless and authoritative, and that resists challenge from dissent and doubt.

LIFE, DEATH, AND AMBIGUITY

And yet, dissent and doubt persist, even within the text. In repetition, there is anxiety. In formalism, there is uncertainty. In system, there is ambiguity. In the Holy, there is danger (Douglas 1966). The system of sacrificial offerings and rules about purity and holiness seeks closure. Narratives interspersed within these ritual texts expose ambiguities within the system and raise questions about the ability of the law to accomplish its purposes. How can God be circumscribed by human regulations? How can a sinful people live in close proximity to the Holy?

The mythic world described by the ritualized narrative is divided into zones or gradations of holiness (Jenson 1992). In the center is the Holy of Holies, surrounded in expanding circles by the tabernacle, the sacrificial courtyard, the camp, and the outside world. The closer people draw to the Holy, the greater the danger they face, and the more intense purity regulations they must follow. Leviticus 8–9 describes the initial consecration of the priests to serve within the holy precincts just beyond the Holy of Holies. This initial act of consecration marks them as the bearers of God's authority passed through Moses and Aaron. The cleansing, dressing, and waiting period enable the priests to negotiate the boundaries between holy and common and between the clean and unclean (Lev. 10:10). Thus, the ritual of consecration functions as a period of liminality in which the priests pass from common to holy. Once they are ordained to this duty, daily rituals of washing and dressing will preserve their ability to minister in God's presence. At last, the seven-day consecration ritual ends with an unmistakable mark of God's approval: "Fire came out from the LORD and consumed the burnt offering and the fat on the altar; and when all the people saw it, they shouted and fell on their faces" (Lev. 9:24). Chapter 9 is the dramatic and conceptual high-point of Leviticus, and if the book ended here it would be a story of priestly expertise and competence. However, the careful and detailed way in which the text describes the priestly ordination reveals an underlying anxiety about the possibility of ritual failure.

The beginning of chapter 10 deconstructs all that precedes it. In the next paragraph after the successful ordination of the priests, we read that two of Aaron's sons, Nadab and Abihu, perform an unauthorized, unorthodox, or incorrect incense offering, and fire comes forth from God and consumes them in the same manner as the animal sacrifice in chapter 9. It is a stunning narrative of ritual failure, and there has been much discussion of how and why they made such a fatal mistake (Kirschner 1983; Laughlin 1976; Milgrom 1991, 628–635). The story of Nadab and Abihu is the only text in Leviticus that has attracted a significant amount of literary-critical attention. In addition to the works mentioned already (Damrosch 1987; Smith 1996; Watts 1999), there have been insightful studies from Edward L. Greenstein (1989), Timothy Beal and Tod Linafelt (1995), and Deborah Sunoo (1999).

It may be that Nadab and Abihu were incompetent or that they made an intentional innovation or mistake in the way that they performed the offering. However, in light of the care and detail seen in the legislation so far, why would the priests suddenly start showing initiative or inattention? I have argued elsewhere (Bibb 2001) that rather than describing a willful violation, the narrative in Leviticus 10 exposes *gaps* and *ambiguities* in the ritual legislation. This moment of ritual failure motivates Moses to give several new rules for priests (Lev. 10:8–15) and to exercise more oversight over the priests' activities (Lev. 10:16–20). There is no indication in the text that the priests know that what they are doing is wrong. The story not only has gaps in its telling, but those gaps exist as well for the characters in the story.

When Nadab and Abihu transgress some unknown—or unknowable—boundary in their ritual performance, they step right into a gap and pay with their lives. Moses explains their deaths with the statement that "This is what the LORD meant when he said, 'Through those who are near me I will show myself holy, and before all the people I will be glorified.'" In bringing the offering near to God, the "near-ones" are destroyed, and in doing so, God has been sanctified. This dangerous sanctification is in fact a central emphasis of Leviticus. The people live in the presence of the Holy, and so they must develop a complex and careful system of ritual practice to keep them safe. However, there will always be anxiety and uncertainty in the people's negotiation of the boundaries between holy and common, and between clean and unclean. In the Priestly tradition (and in Ezekiel), the fear is that God will be repulsed by the transgressions of the community and *leave*. Within Leviticus, however, there is also an acute concern for the physical survival of those who minister in God's presence.

The personal risks taken by the priests come to a peak in Aaron's Day of Atonement ritual in Leviticus 16. If the "near-ones" of God risk a dangerous sanctification, then the High Priest faces the greatest danger of all in his annual trip into the Holy of Holies where the presence of God dwells, the very center of the ritual cosmos. The Talmud suggests that the High Priest had a rope tied around his waist so that if he died someone could pull him out. Leviticus 16:13 says that the High Priest must make sure that "that the cloud of the incense covers the mercy seat that is upon the covenant, or he will die." This is a dangerous process, made more uncertain by the episode of ritual failure in chapter 10.

Leviticus 16 frames the Day of Atonement with a future-tense narration of the first performance of this ritual by Aaron. In the narrative, the Day of Atonement is the first thing that happens after the tragedy of Nadab and Abihu (Lev. 16:1). Aaron's initial performance of the atonement ritual may even be an emergency measure. There is a tonal shift from Aaron's performance in Leviticus 16:2–28 to the general legislation for the annual Day of Atonement overseen not by Aaron but by "the priest who is anointed and consecrated as priest in his father's place" (Lev. 16:29–34). Aaron's ritual leadership becomes a model and guide for the unnamed priests who wield his authority in each generation.

Holiness and God's People

The conceptual world of Leviticus shifts after chapter 16. Although the community of Israel is addressed by the legislation in chapters 1–16, the people remain in the background, receiving the benefit of the ritual actions of the priests. In chapters 17–26(27), a section known generally as the "Holiness Code," God addresses the people directly with laws to govern their social relations and communal life. Leviticus 19:2 is a programmatic statement for this half of the book: "Speak to all the congregation of the Israelites and say to them, 'You are to be holy, because I, Yahweh your God, am holy.'" Rather than a strictly gradated and regulated ritual "holiness" emanating from the Holy of Holies, this statement presumes that holiness is a moral characteristic that can apply to the whole community as a default state (Kugler 1997). The command to "be Holy" (which can also mean "to become holy") places upon the community the burden of striving to live in the way that God requires. The ambiguity already shown with respect to priestly holiness, however, creates a certain anxiety about the attainability of this goal.

The differences between these two halves of the book are discussed most often as a source-critical matter (Knohl 1995). However, read in its final form, the expansion and reframing of "holiness" to apply to the whole community has a powerful transformative effect on the book as a whole. The gaps and ambiguities related to the ritual system break out into the broader communal context. Now the people must be careful to arrange their family and neighborly relationships in accordance with the requirements of God's holiness. The repetitive and detailed list of prohibited sexual relationships in Leviticus 18:6–23 and 20:10–21 imply anxiety about the ambiguous possibilities of sexual relationships. The danger if the people—even unknowingly—engage in "profane" sexual activity is that they will be "vomited out" of the land. These rules are cast as an expression of God's ownership over the people: "You shall be holy to me; for I the LORD am holy, and I have separated you from the other peoples to be mine" (Lev. 20:26). Ritual requirements of non-priestly people are also addressed through regulations about sacred times and seasons, including harvest festivals (Lev. 23) and Sabbath and Jubilee years (Lev. 25). The fact that the people *belong* to God transforms every aspect of their communal life. Their cosmos is ordered according to the requirements of holiness.

As a narrative theme, the command to "Be holy because I am holy" breaks the temporal boundary between the mythic past and the present. God is now present in the community through divine holiness, and not a remote deity perched on a mountain or hidden in a room, accessible only to priestly specialists. This is not an anti-priestly ideology, of course, but a recognition that priestly ritual is a cosmic reality that is broader and more transformative than what happens just in the Tabernacle.

As in Leviticus 10, ambiguity and anxiety about the requirements of holiness emerge in a narrative. The story of the blasphemer in 24:10–23 exposes a gap in the legislation laid down so far. Clearly the laws of holiness apply to Israelites, but what about residents of non-Israelite or mixed parentage, such as this man with an Israelite mother and an Egyptian father? He is observed fighting with an Israelite, during which he "blasphemed the Name in a curse." We are not informed about the nature of this blasphemy or curse, even though the narrative includes seemingly unimportant details about his mother (Leuchter 2011). Because of the insult to the Divine Name, the blasphemer is taken into custody "until the decision of the LORD should be made clear to them." The result is that Moses delivers new legislation that affirms that "aliens as well as citizens, when they blaspheme the Name, shall be put to death" (Lev. 24:16).

Contrary to those who see these chapters as more-or-less random, Leigh Trevaskis (2009) has argued that this brief narrative fits within Leviticus 24 as a whole, and within chapters 23–25 more broadly. He says that the temporal legislation for sabbatical rest in chapters 23 and 25 "seems to remind Israel of her covenant obligations as YHWH's new creation" (298). He suggests that the reference to the "lamp" in Leviticus 24:1–9 "is possibly intended to evoke the imagination of God's presence" (301), and so the legislation to keep the lamps burning is a reminder for Israel to follow the obligations imposed by living within that presence. Thus, the blasphemy that takes place *within the camp*, even though performed by a foreigner, is a serious threat to the integrity and safety of the community. Vroom (2012) shows that the Holiness authors have used this narrative to establish legal innovations in the verses that follow (24:15–22), the application of the "national *mišpāṭîm* corpus" to all people living in the land, not just Israelites.

In conclusion, a literary analysis of Leviticus 17–26 has two primary tasks, to explore the ambiguities of the narrative in 24:10–23, and to consider the overall movement of the book from a narrow ritual focus to a broader account of the community living in holiness in the presence of a Holy God. This conceptual shift encompasses such legal matters as sexual relations, festivals, blessings and curses, and the yearly calendar. Together, however, these rules establish a new cosmos, with Israel as the new creation of God set apart and structured according to God's plan and by God's direct intervention. The second half of Leviticus thus rounds out and completes the book's mythical account of Israel as God's people.

CONCLUSION

In conclusion, the book of Leviticus may not seem to be highly *literary* or *narrative* in nature, but it does merit analysis along these lines. The book contains ritual and legal texts but, rather than taking list form, these are embedded within the larger Torah narrative. Ritual instructions themselves are presented as the speech of God conveyed through Moses to the people, and the major rituals of ordination and atonement are presented as taking place during specific moments in the mythic past. In addition, we see that the alternation of narrative and law reveals a process of discovery and innovation in a context of ambiguity, anxiety, and danger.

There are many avenues for further research into Leviticus as narrative. One question that needs more research is the problem of "genre" in the book. There are no clear analogues with Leviticus anywhere in the ancient world, and the book is peculiar even within biblical literature. Mary Douglas (1999, 197) has gone so far to say that Leviticus *is* a genre. Given the advances in genre analysis in literary studies, what can we say about the kind of literature we find in Leviticus and how it functions? Related to this is the need to consider advances in text-critical and historical research. In spite of disagreements about the antiquity of P or the actual process of redaction, what can we know about the religious communities in which Leviticus took shape? How, for instance, did the practice of public reading shape the literary and narrative form of Leviticus?

Finally, there should be more work on the literary effect of the translation process, including attention to ancient translations (LXX) and adaptations (Targums) as well as contemporary translation projects. Should English translation of Leviticus render the text in a stilted "ritual" style or as a smooth literary narrative or rhetorical speech? How should translators render words and phrases with intertextual echo in other texts, including the New Testament? How are the narratives of animal sacrifice, ritual failure, and blasphemy read in global and post-colonial contexts? These questions get to the heart of what the narrative text of Leviticus *is* within particular reading communities, which is an essential part of understanding its literary significance and meaning.

REFERENCES

Auld, Graeme. 1996. "Leviticus at the Heart of the Pentateuch?" In *Reading Leviticus: A Conversation with Mary Douglas*, edited by John A. Sawyer, 140–151. Journal for the Study of the Old Testament Supplement Series 227. Sheffield, Yorkshire: Sheffield Academic Press.

Baden, Joel S. 2012. *The Composition of the Pentateuch: Renewing the Documentary Hypothesis.* New Haven, CT: Yale University Press.

Beal, Timothy K., and Tod Linafelt. 1995. "Sifting for Cinders: Strange Fires in Leviticus 10:1–5." In *Intertextuality and the Bible*, edited by George Aichele and Gary A. Phillips. *Semeia* 69–70: 19–32.

Bell, Catherine. 1997. *Ritual: Perspectives and Dimensions.* New York: Oxford University Press.

Bibb, Bryan. 2001. "Nadab and Abihu Attempt to Fill a Gap: Law and Narrative in Leviticus 10:1–7." *Journal for the Study of the Old Testament* 96: 83–99.

Bibb, Bryan. 2009. *Ritual Words and Narrative Worlds in the Book of Leviticus.* Library of the Hebrew Bible/Old Testament Studies 480. London: T&T Clark.

Damrosch, David. 1987. *The Narrative Covenant: Transformations of Genre in the Growth of Biblical Literature.* San Francisco: Harper & Row.

Douglas, Mary. 1966. *Purity and Danger: An Analysis of the Concepts of Pollution and Taboo.* London: Routledge and Keegan Paul.

Douglas, Mary. 1999. *Leviticus as Literature.* Oxford: Oxford University Press.

Elliott, Mark W. 2012. *Engaging Leviticus: Reading Leviticus Theologically with Its Past Interpreters.* Eugene, OR: Cascade.

Gorman, Frank H. 1990. *The Ideology of Ritual: Space, Time and Status in the Priestly Theology.* Sheffield, Yorkshire: Sheffield Academic Press.

Greenstein, Edward L. 1989. "Deconstruction and Biblical Narrative." *Prooftexts* 9: 43–71.

Hallo, William W., and K. Lawson Younger, Jr. eds. 2003. *The Context of Scripture.* 3 vols. Leiden: Brill.

Jenson, Peter. 1992. *Graded Holiness: A Key to the Priestly Conception of the World.* Journal for the Study of the Old Testament Supplement Series 106. Sheffield, Yorkshire: JSOT Press.

Kirschner, Robert. 1983. "Rabbinic and Philonic Exegesis of the Nadab and Abihu Incident (Lev. 10:1–6)." *Jewish Quarterly Review* 73: 375–393.

Knohl, Israel. 1995. *The Sanctuary of Silence: The Priestly Torah and the Holiness School.* Minneapolis, MN: Fortress.

Kugler, Robert A. 1997. "Holiness, Purity, the Body, and Society: The Evidence for Theological Conflict in Leviticus." *Journal for the Study of the Old Testament* 76: 3–27.

Laughlin, John C. 1976. "The 'Strange Fire' of Nadab and Abihu." *Journal of Biblical Literature* 95: 559–565.

Leuchter, Mark. 2011. "The Ambiguous Details in the Blasphemer Narrative: Sources and Redaction in Leviticus 24:10–23." *Journal of Biblical Literature* 130: 431–450.

Milgrom, Jacob. 1991. *Leviticus 1–16*. Anchor Bible 3. New York: Doubleday.

Nicholson, Ernest. 1998. *The Pentateuch in the Twentieth Century: The Legacy of Julius Wellhausen*. Oxford: Clarendon.

Rendtorff, Rolf. 1996. "Is It Possible to Read Leviticus as a Separate Book?" In *Reading Leviticus: A Conversation with Mary Douglas*, edited by John A. Sawyer, 22–39. Journal for the Study of the Old Testament Supplement Series 227. Sheffield, Yorkshire: Sheffield Academic Press.

Ruwe, Andreas. 2003. "The Structure of the Book of Leviticus in the Narrative Outline of the Priestly Sinai Story (Exod 19:1–Num 10:10)." In *The Book of Leviticus: Composition and Reception*, edited by Rolf Rendtorff and Robert A. Kugler, 55–78. Leiden: Brill.

Smith, Christopher R. 1996. "The Literary Structure of Leviticus." *Journal for the Study of the Old Testament* 70: 17–32.

Sunoo, Deborah. 1999. "God Bursts Forth: Unexpected Disruptions in the Narrative Landscape of the Hebrew Bible." PhD dissertation. Princeton Theological Seminary.

Trevaskis, Leigh. 2009. "The Purpose of Leviticus 24 within Its Literary Context." *Vetus Testamentum* 59: 295–312.

Vroom, Jonathan. 2012. "Recasting *Mišpāṭîm*: Legal Innovation in Leviticus 24:10–23." *Journal of Biblical Literature* 131: 27–44.

Warning, Wilfred. 1999. *Literary Artistry in Leviticus*. Leiden: Brill.

Watts, James W. 1999. *Reading Law: The Rhetorical Shape of the Pentateuch*. Biblical Seminar 59. Sheffield, Yorkshire: Sheffield Academic Press.

Wright, David P. 2000. *Ritual in Narrative: The Dynamics of Feasting, Mourning, and Retaliation Rites in the Ugaritic Tale of Aqhat*. Winona Lake, IN: Eisenbrauns.

CHAPTER 11

BECOMING ISRAEL IN THE WILDERNESS OF NUMBERS

ADRIANE LEVEEN

As the book of Numbers opens the children of Israel are camped in the wilderness of Sinai. Much has happened to them along the path from Egypt to Sinai. Celebration and hope exist in equal measure with persistent anxieties and fears. They have crossed the Reed Sea and witnessed God's revelation at Sinai. But the people are hungry and thirsty, and thus disgruntled and dissatisfied. They have journeyed for many wearying months. Despite these challenges, in the first chapters of Numbers all seems well in the camp of the Israelites. Yhwh covers the completed tabernacle with a cloud by day and a fire at night, providing a reassuring divine presence and reliable guidance through the desert (Num. 9). Yet only two chapters later, the people are so overcome by discontent that they weep, every family, in fact every person, at the opening of his and her tent, with the result that "Yhwh was greatly incensed and in the eyes of Moses it was displeasing" (Num. 11:10b; translation mine).

The narrative presented in the book of Numbers is a volatile and tumultuous one because it seeks to identify and depict both those experiences of the children of Israel that would shape them into a unified and flourishing collective and those that would threaten their very existence. The wilderness landscape provides the ideal setting for such an exploration, a blank screen on which to imagine the process through which a collective of recently freed slaves, or at least their children, become the People of Israel. Of course, Exodus and Leviticus also narrate the construction of a people out of a disparate group of slaves, but Numbers is unique in explicitly illustrating just how close the entire enterprise comes to collapse. It is perplexing that the national story of ancient Israel focuses so heavily on self-criticism and punishment. Yet, such a striking and extensive self-critique does produce a new generation, sobered but freed from the long shadow of Egypt and its influence. At journey's end, this new generation is on the verge of crossing over, intact and unified.

The Book of Numbers

A few preliminary matters include the dating, composition, and structure of the book. Numbers is considered an anthology of texts of great variety, containing prose tales, early poetry, itineraries, law, a calendar of festivals and the establishment of borders in the land. High drama, political tensions, and insubordination exist alongside a generous outpouring of gifts for the newly constructed tabernacle and visions of future celebrations in the land. These texts are not simply deposits in a random collection but are carefully edited together into a multitextured and coherent description of the journey through the wilderness.

Such an assortment of texts suggests a range of dates over several hundred years. There are priestly materials (P) from roughly the early seventh century through the exile and return, several non-priestly stories (designated by some scholars as J and E), and fragments of poems and tales that do not originate in either P or J/E. These materials were put together in stages or a late editor(s) might have edited together different sources, some from roughly the same time, others originating over time, in one sustained effort. Either way, a guiding consciousness can be discerned in how the materials have been ordered and juxtaposed to one another. Numbers likely reached its final form sometime in the years after the return from Babylon in 538 BCE. (For more extensive detail on these matters, see the indispensable commentaries of Milgrom [1990]; Levine [1993, 2000]).

Numbers is organized in three sections. Chapters 1–10 present an "eyewitness" account that is abruptly disrupted by memories of the recent past in chapters 11–25. That past must be put to rest (by killing off those with memories of Egypt) before a successful future in the promised land, as anticipated in chapters 26–36, can occur.

Chapters 1–10 focus on priestly materials, as evidenced in the use of formulaic language, a reliance on genealogy and lists (each a hallmark of priestly style), and a variety of ritual instructions. The camp is organized with the tabernacle at its center. The sons of Aaron are singled out and accorded the highest status in a hierarchy that divides them from the rest of the priestly class, the Levities. A subgroup of Levites, the Kohathites, may enter the holiest area of the tabernacle to transport its objects, but only after the sons of Aaron cover the holy implements. The identification of individuals who can, and of those who cannot, touch the holiest objects in the tabernacle engenders deep resentment.

The Levites are appointed as guards at the tabernacle's entrance, tasked with protecting it from anyone who might try to breach its boundaries. If a breach were to occur, the Levites, not the sons of Aaron or the people in general, would be killed. Thus do the Levites function in a dangerous situation. In fact, the Levites are labeled as a sacrifice—a wave offering or *tenufah* (Num. 8:15). The children of Israel even place their hands on the shoulders of the Levites as they might on an animal about to be sacrificed (Num. 8:10). Although they carry the burdens of the camp, the Levites do not reap the benefits of holiness, which are vouchsafed to the sons of Aaron. Jonathan Magonet (1982) traces the repercussions of this priestly conflict in later chapters of Numbers.

The sons of Aaron are responsible for various legislative and cultic duties (i.e., Sotah, Nazir, priestly blessing, consecration of the tabernacle). The culmination of these priestly chapters is the blowing of silver trumpets by the sons of Aaron, not only in the wilderness, but also for generations to come, once they are in the land. All appears to be well in the wilderness camp.

Without warning, chapter 11:1 shatters this vision of the people regulated and instructed by the priests. At last, we hear their voices: "and the people took to complaining bitterly in the ears of YHWH and YHWH heard and was incensed and a fire of YHWH burned against them and consumed the edges of the camp." The content of the complaint is yet to be communicated, but the image of a burning fire that threatens to spread rapidly within the camp captures the consequence of unstoppable complaint. Complaint appears in one form or another in at least seven of the next fourteen chapters, testifying to its pervasiveness.

The people's initial complaints have to do with the memory of Egyptian delicacies in Numbers 11:5. Their past in Egypt becomes an increasingly desired alternative to the journey toward the promised land. The desire to return to Egypt is explicitly stated in chapters 11, 14, and 16. After struggles over food (ch. 11 goes on to describe manna vs. quails), prophetic leadership (Miriam and Aaron bitterly protest that they, too, are confidants of YHWH), and a mission to scout out the land that misfires, the lowest point in the narrative arrives in chapter 14.

The chapter opens by drawing attention to the people as a whole—"all the assembly," "the people," and "all the children of Israel"—emphasizing that they speak in one voice. Convinced by ten of the twelve scouts, the people are ready to return to Egypt. God has had enough. Only Moses's immediate intercession results in a divine reprieve, but only for the generation under age twenty-one. Not so for their parents.

> Nevertheless, as I live and as the glory of YHWH fills all the land, none of those people who saw my glory and my signs that I did against Egypt and in the wilderness but tried Me these 10 times and did not listen to my voice, shall see the land that I swore to their ancestors; all of those who spurn Me will not see it . . . but your children who you said would be spoil, I shall bring them [to it] and they will know the land that you have rejected, but your carcasses shall fall in this wilderness. (Num. 14:21–23, 31–32)

God relies on the notion of measure for measure to formulate the divine punishment. Since the people listen to the scouts, who took forty days to explore the land, they will wander in the wilderness for forty years. Fearing for their lives, they will die in the wilderness. Because they refuse to go forward, they will retrace their steps along the very route that they have already traveled (Num. 21:4). The cruelty of God's condemnation of this generation lies especially in what it means for the next generation. Children must wait for, and watch, their parents die over the next forty years, as the wilderness turns into a land littered with corpses. Woe to those who reject the vision of God, the leadership of Moses, and the supervision of the priests.

But the complaints continue. Korah and his band rebel against Moses and Aaron in Numbers 16. Terrified by God's actions in putting down that rebellion, the people cry out for protection (Leveen 2013, 248–272). Miriam and Aaron die. Moses is told that he, too, will die. The themes of holiness and death become inextricably intertwined (see Mann 1987).

Chapter 26 introduces the third section, preparations for the future, after announcing the end of the wilderness generation:

> These are those counted by Moses and Eleazar the priest when they counted the children of Israel on the steppes of Moab at the Jordan near Jericho. And among these there was not one man from those counted by Moses and Aaron the priest when they counted the children of Israel in the wilderness of Sinai since YHWH said of them, "They shall surely die in the wilderness" and not one from them remained except for Caleb son of Jephunneh and Joshua son of Nun. (Num. 26:63–65)

This second census includes not only the generation that survives the deaths of their parents but also the generation that follows (Olson 1985, 66, 79). Israel has moved successfully beyond a preoccupation with an Egyptian past to the task of envisioning and preparing for the future. Chapters 27–36 do the job admirably.

Questions of inheritance (including that of daughters) and succession in leadership are clarified. A priestly calendar of weekly, monthly, and yearly sacrifices is established. An itinerary of the wilderness journey is juxtaposed with the allotment of tribal territories. Temporary stops in the wilderness will be replaced by stable settlements in the land.

Thus does Numbers imagine the formation of the people Israel. Their story begins in a harmonious present and ends in an equally satisfying and secure future, but only after they have navigated treacherous memories of an Egyptian past that nearly prevent the new generation from reaching the borders of the promised land.

NOTABLE NARRATIVE-CRITICAL WORKS ON THE BOOK OF NUMBERS

Christian Frevel identifies elements in Numbers that suggest a post-exilic date for its completion, especially hints of "a concrete social background . . . with questions of land ownership, land law, and inheritance laws, or with the organization of priesthood, its hierarchy, and succession" (Frevel 2013, 22). He also traces the way in which the term *Torah* evolves in Numbers, including references to a single instruction, a generalized term, and increasingly, a textual reality. Together these uses of the term "can be read as a signal of processes of the finalization of the *Torah*" (Frevel 2013, 24). Noting the significance of Numbers 36 as a supplement to the request of the daughters of Zelophehad in Numbers 27 leads Frevel to a final form which "integrate[s] not only legal supplements and amendments, but also their interpretation *as Torah* . . . . The modifying exegesis of the law, its amendments and pre-midrashic interpretation indicate completion that is close to closure" (Frevel 2013, 31). Frevel has reinforced and illustrated the crucial role of laws, and their expansion over time, in the book of Numbers in building a new or renewed (i.e., post-exilic) community in the promised land (cf. Römer 2007; Roskop 2011, who cite different evidence but concur with the post-exilic dating).

David Wright (2012, 208) analyzes "models and theories of ritual change." He notes that the rituals depicted in the wilderness "would need to be adapted to the current social and institutional conditions of the time. This no doubt would have been a task that the PH writers and their heirs would have gladly taken on" (201). Wright is referring to priestly texts and their revision by the later (possibly exilic or post-exilic) source, H, and the changes wrought by that source on priestly ritual that can be found in Numbers. He is well aware of the limits in studying rituals via texts rather than live performances. Wright therefore turns to literary analysis as a means of addressing this challenge. He describes his analytical process as looking "for intersections between theory and what is otherwise garnered through the study of a text's structure, Leitworter, gaps, tensions, contrasts, skewing of conventional ideas, plot development, description of characters, use of dialogue versus description, word choice, and so forth" (198). Numbers provides a rich source of material for the type of study Wright proposes, focused as it is on significant priestly conflict often dramatically expressed and even resolved in ritual performances.

Gendered readings continue to generate persuasive explanations of problematic aspects of biblical texts. For example, Claudia Camp suggests that Numbers 12—in which God inflicts only Miriam with leprosy even though Aaron also rebukes Moses—functions in part to substitute Miriam's disgrace for that of Aaron due to his role in the golden calf episode in Exodus 32. As Camp (2009, 125) argues, "The sister's estrangement leads to the full narrative acceptance of Aaron as the rightful priest: as the brother aligned with Moses against his other kin." Miriam pays the price. As Moses's first protector, Miriam is considered an "ideal sister" until she becomes a "dangerous one" when she "asserts her independence by speaking against Moses' choice of a Cushite wife" (Kalmanofsky 2014, 8–9).

These recent works place Numbers in its final form in a particular period in time, as well as consider the influence of legal developments, ritual, and gender on its content. Other literary approaches elevate the role of narrative in shaping national identity. Stories of competing memories and their role in destabilizing and restoring the wilderness camp provide a key to much of the drama (Leveen 2008). Pardes (2000, 56) captures the consequences of misplaced memories in the complaints they engender:

> The complaint scenes in the wilderness lay bare the violence and difficulties that are part and parcel of the shaping of ancient Israel. The character and future of the newborn nation are negotiated among the people, Moses and God through complaining (they all complain in one way or another) and testing.

Complaining elevates the role of speech, for both good and ill, in forming, maintaining, and disrupting a collective. Carol Newsom (2004, 2) argues that texts can be understood "as an action performed with words," while language "constitute[s] a world of meaning, a distinctive identity, a community of values and a structure of selfhood." So it is in Numbers. In Numbers 13:32, the scouts bring back a "word about the land" so negative that it extinguishes the people's will to advance. But the next generation manages to move beyond the conflicts of the parents to arrive at journey's end a unified people ready to fulfill God's plans. Even so, the power of Numbers lies in its preservation of a range of voices. Its discourse functions to preserve both dominant and subversive voices. As Newsom (19) notes, "Every particular discourse privileges the interests of some groups over others. The relatively disadvantaged know that by modifying the discourse or disrupting it and making it problematic they can secure attention, influence and other benefits."

In sum, an emphasis on narrative's power in shaping collective identity exposes a dynamic and chaotic process in Numbers fueled by intergroup conflicts: priests versus Levites; priests versus everyone else, including outsiders (Dozeman 2008); competing interests and desires; crisis; and even violence. However, language becomes a tool not only of rupture but also of resolution.

BECOMING ISRAEL IN THE WILDERNESS OF NUMBERS

Stephen Cornell's (2000) attention to the tales a people tells about itself influenced my emphasis on the juxtaposition of two ongoing stories of the wilderness journey as the key to reading Numbers. A community heads to the promised land, guided and ruled by the priests. Alternatively, that same people has lost its way by losing its heart. The latter, represented in the stories of complaint that dominate the middle chapters of Numbers, challenges the former—and must be resolved before the priestly agenda can be fulfilled.

The stories of complaint reveal a fledgling people who fail to achieve stability because they are overcome by desires for an Egyptian past they are not ready to leave behind and by doubts of their ability to conquer a land in which giants—the mighty sons of Anak—allegedly roam. Theirs is a story of fissures, peopled by riffraff and rebels who challenge the entire enterprise. In the end, God and Moses destroy the older generation to create the possibility of success. Those who held onto the past are now replaced by those who have a future secured only by leaving the wilderness and their parents behind. In what follows, I will trace the use of two key words—*eating* and *gathering*—that link the stories of complaint. I then consider the role played by strangers in moving the people Israel beyond complaint into a unified whole responsible for one another.

Stories of complaint begin in Numbers 11:1 in a generalized dissatisfaction that leads God to "eat" the edges of the camp. "Eating" becomes a trope, appearing a total of nine times in Numbers 11 alone. Eating triggers crisis (Num. 11:4–13), followed by lethal punishment (Num. 11:18–23, 31–34). In 11:4 the riffraff cry out for meat. The people echo them in verse 5 by crying for Egyptian foods that they sorely miss. They express a preference for those foods over God's manna. This first complaint leaves the people alienated from Moses and contributes to God's condemnation of the generation. In response to their discontent, Moses emphatically instructs them about "eating" in verses 18–23. Eating appears three times in verse 18: Moses informs the people that they shall "eat" since they desire to "eat," and so shall they "eat." But they shall not "eat" for one day only (v. 19). In verse 21 Moses challenges God to make sure that there will be enough quail for them to "eat" for a month. Indeed, God sends so much quail to the people that they cannot gather it quickly enough. The very sight of their chewing meat, even before they swallow it, so enrages God that God strikes them with a plague, killing off a significant number of the meat eaters. This one word, *eating*, traces how an entire collective can quickly fall apart. Ruptures between God, Moses, and the people fuel the tragedy. (On the editing of this key chapter, see Sommer 1999.)

Eating continues to subvert the maintenance of stability in Numbers 12:12 after Miriam and Aaron challenge Moses's unique relationship with YHWH. As a result of divine displeasure, Miriam is compared to a stillborn infant emerging from the womb with her flesh half "eaten." In Numbers 13:32 the spies report that the promised land "eats" its inhabitants, spreading terror and stopping the people in their tracks. After refusing to continue the journey, God's fire "eats" the rebels in 16:35 (mentioned again in the second census, 26:10). In a final act of transgressive eating (25:2), the wilderness generation "eats" the sacrifices offered by the Moabites, ensuring its destruction.[1] Desires for meat, memories of Egypt, dissent, jealousy, terror, idolatry and their consequences are illustrated by means of eating. The accumulation of such eating is catastrophic and explains why it is that the generation is so severely punished by God.

Yet, in this tale of two stories, "eating" takes on a radically different slant in the priestly tales. Certain foods are forbidden (grapes in 6:3–4) while others are commanded (matzo and bitter herbs in 9:11 and 28:17). A reassuring image of eating the bread of the land and sharing it in gratitude with God appears in 15:19. Rules for the priestly eating of sacrifices as a reward for loyal service are found in 18:10, 11, 13, and 31. The message is clear. Follow the priestly regulation of "eating" and the people of Israel will have reason to celebrate.

Gather works in similar fashion to *eating*. It links two separate stories within Numbers 11 together. The noun "riffraff" of 11:4, which appears only once in the entire Hebrew Bible, contains the three-letter root for *gather*. Remember that the riffraff trigger the desires for meat that wreak such damage in the camp as well as a crisis of confidence in Moses. Two different events—the provision of meat and a change in the leadership structure—are the response.

"Gathering" in its verbal form appears in 11:22 when Moses questions God's ability to provide so much meat for the people, and again in 11:32, where it is used to describe the people's rapid gathering of that meat. The other use of the word appears in a second episode that is related to the first. After hearing Moses bitterly complain about the terrible burdens of leadership, God out of compassion orders him in 11:16 to "gather" seventy elders with the requisite experience to share the burden. In 11:24 Moses implements God's suggestion, "gathering" seventy elders around the tent. In 11:30 Moses gathers them again. The crisis produced by the people's gathering of meat has been somewhat mitigated for Moses by the gathering of the elders. Thus, one word links the entire chapter and signals both the rupture and its possible resolution.

Gathering is also used to describe the joining of a person to his/her ancestors at the moment of death. It is used when Aaron dies in 20:24, 26 and in reference to the anticipated death of Moses in 27:13 and 31:2. This use of the term appears at a moment of transition in leadership made necessary by the delay in the journey toward the promised land. The wilderness generation, including Aaron and Moses, must die off in the wilderness. Poignantly, it is the gathering and eating of the quail that leads to that delay.

Thus, *eating* and *gathering* weave together stories of rupture and crisis and place a significant obstacle in the way of becoming a unified people Israel. Yet both words are also used to overcome the crisis and move toward the resolution (priestly regulation of "eating" and the "gathering" of an expanded leadership) found at the end of Numbers. In fact, rupture and resolution capture the conflict-ridden narrative of the wilderness journey. Cornell (2000, 45–46) describes how rupture may lead to resolution:

> The narrative process comes to the foreground in situations of rupture as groups try to make sense of new problems or opportunities, defend or assert claims, reframe identities, mobilize members for political action, or otherwise rethink who they or others are. The group's story is told or retold at such moments—in new or old forms—as this sense- and cause-making process goes forward, integrating new experiences or concerns with old understandings. (2000, 45–46)

Just such a "rethinking" of who they are must occur to the children of Israel as they make their way through the wilderness before they can cross over into the land.

Encounters with strangers also contribute to the story of becoming Israel in the wilderness. In fact, such encounters do nothing less than allow Israel to make sense of itself as a newly formed people. Brubaker's emphasis on ethnicity and nation brings into sharper focus the dynamic conflicts between Israel and the strangers that they meet along the way:

> [Such categories] are ways of understanding and identifying oneself, interpreting one's problems and predicaments, and identifying one's interests. They are ways—both institutionalized and informal—of recognizing, identifying and classifying other people, of construing sameness and difference and of "coding" and making sense of their actions. (2009, 34)

Such encounters create a state of ongoing flux and crisis that is productive in reinforcing the boundaries of the newly formed people Israel. Becoming Israel depends on who Israelites are not. I will briefly highlight two such significant interactions with strangers in the wilderness.

Moses sends messages to the king of Edom in Numbers 20:14 and uses the opportunity to describe his version of the journey. He calls his people "your brother Israel" in an attempt to create a sympathetic identification in the king for the "troubles" Israel has encountered. Moses describes the descent into Egypt, the oppression Israel experienced there, and God's intervention by means of a messenger (Moses) to free them. In so doing, Moses is hinting to the king of Edom that God is behind the messengers now standing in front of him. In telling the story to the king of Edom, Moses is also shaping the tale for a different audience, the people of Israel. Perhaps the story he tells can unify his people, still reeling from God's condemnation of the entire generation. Moses ends the story with a request—to move unmolested through the territory of Edom. The king of Edom is so unmoved that he not only refuses safe passage but also threatens Israel with an armed force. The encounter results both in the crafting of an official version of the journey and in unifying the people Israel out of necessity since they face a serious and shared threat. The story highlights Israelite powerlessness.

In the next encounter with a foreign king, the Canaanite from Arad (Num. 21:1–3), it is neither Moses nor his messengers who engage the king but the entire people Israel. They are ultimately successful, moving from a state of powerlessness to power. In response to the capture of some Israelites by the Canaanites, the people act in concert, vowing to YHWH that if granted victory, they will put all their opponents under a ban. The short tale communicates several things at once. Israel is beginning to see itself as a united entity, responsible for each member, since all of the people are distressed and feel compelled to act in response to the capture of some of them. All acknowledge YHWH as God. They are organized well enough to defeat their adversaries.[2] Finally, by putting their opponents under a ban, the Israelites have created a boundary that explicitly separates them from the Canaanites. Thus does this tale do its work of helping Israel unify itself in confrontation with strangers. Subsequent military victories against Sihon, king of the Amorites (21:21–25) and Og of Bashan (21:33–35) continue to consolidate a united Israel.

The territory obtained from Sihon and Og leads to another crisis. Its quick resolution in Numbers 32 illustrates that the obstacles to the formation of the people have been put to rest, at least temporarily. Two tribes—Reubenites and Gadites—ask Moses for the territory gained in the earlier battles. They have cattle and that land provides excellent pasture. Moses's panicked reaction suggests that something much larger is at stake. He fears that the two tribes will refuse to fight in the inevitable battle against the Canaanites once the people cross over. Worse, they might just infect the other tribes in their decision not to settle the promised land. So far Moses has offered them pragmatic reasons. Suddenly, he explodes,

> Thus did your fathers when I sent them from Kadesh-barnea to see the land. They went up to wadi Eshcol and saw the land and restrained the heart of the children of Israel from going to the land which YHWH had given them. And the wrath of YHWH flared in that day . . . and now you have risen up instead of your fathers—a great group of sinners—to add further to the wrath of YHWH against Israel. If you turn away from God and God again leaves them in the wilderness you will ruin all this people. (Num. 32:8–10, 14–15)

An old wound has been reopened. Moses instantly reverts to the terrible rebellions of the period of complaint, when all was nearly lost. Even after long years in the wilderness, he does not trust that the new generation has learned the terrible lesson from the ordeal of its parents.

The Reubenites and the Gadites reassure Moses. Not only will they cross over but will do so at the head of the troops. Only after the land has been settled will they return to the other side of the Jordan. The two tribes are willing to see their fate as intertwined with that of the entire collective. They make their allegiance to the people (rather than to the land) public and explicit. This tale elevates loyalty as a key ingredient in forming the people Israel.[3]

Many voices are present in Numbers. Neither a priestly voice nor a prophetic one controls the narrative. They are joined by voices of the people raised sometimes in despair, sometimes in celebration. Foreign kings and seers, God's voice and that of Miriam, not to mention that of Moses, are all heard in this work. Such a cacophony of voices is powerful indeed and conveys the tumultuous and difficult attempt to form a people. Obstacles to success include distorted memories of the past, gluttony and desire for the wrong sort of food, fear and doubt, and struggles over power so fierce that an entire generation must be left behind in the wilderness. The price paid is devastating and sobering. Yet the self-critique embedded in the tale of the journey though the wilderness is extraordinary. After all, such criticism leads a new generation to shake itself free of Egypt and replace dissatisfaction and dissent with a shared determination. A tale of struggles overcome gives the children of Israel, as well as subsequent generations, a chance to reach for a different future, imagined but not yet fulfilled.

NOTES

1. The list is not exhaustive. *Eating* appears elsewhere in Numbers in a poem on Sihon (21:28) and in Balaam's poetry (23:24; 24:8). *Gathering* has different shades of meaning in Numbers 10:25, 19:9, 10; and 21:16, 23.
2. Israel suffers a terrible defeat at Hormah (Num. 14:44–45) in the wake of God's condemnation of the wilderness generation. But the new generation is victorious at Hormah (Num. 21:3), signaling a positive shift in their fortunes.
3. In 32:33, half of the tribe of Manessah joins the two tribes in settling on the other side of the Jordan.

REFERENCES

Brubaker, Rogers. 2009. "Ethnicity, Race and Nationalism." *Annual Review of Sociology* 35: 21–42.

Camp, Claudia. 2009. "The Problem with Sisters: Anthropological Perspectives on Priestly Kinship Ideology in Numbers." In *Embroidered Garments. Priests and Gender in Biblical Israel,* edited by Deborah W. Rooke, 119–130. Sheffield, Yorkshire: Sheffield Phoenix Press.

Cornell, Stephen. 2000. "That's the Story of Our Life." In *We Are a People, Narrative and Multiplicity in Constructing Ethnic Identity,* edited by Paul Spickard and W. Jeffrey Burroughs, 41–53. Philadelphia, PA: Temple University Press.

Dozeman, Thomas B. 2008. "The Midianites in the Formation of the Book of Numbers." In *The Books of Leviticus and Numbers,* edited by Thomas Römer, 261–284. Leuven: Uitgeverij Peeters.

Frevel, Christian. 2013. "The Book of Numbers: Formation, Composition, and Interpretation of a Late Part of the Torah. Some Introductory Remarks." In *Torah and the Book of Numbers*, edited by Christian Frevel, Thomas Pola, and Aaron Schart, 1–37. Tubingen, Germany: Mohr Siebeck.

Kalmanofsky, Amy. 2014. *Dangerous Sisters of the Hebrew Bible*. Minneapolis, MN: Fortress Press.

Leveen, Adriane. 2008. *Memory and Tradition in the Book of Numbers*. Cambridge: Cambridge University Press.

Leveen, Adriane. 2013. " 'Lo We Perish': A Reading of Numbers 17:27-20:29." In *Torah and the Book of Numbers*, edited by Christian Frevel, Thomas Pola, and Aaron Schart, 248–272. Tubingen, Germany: Mohr Siebeck.

Levine, Baruch. 1993. *Numbers 1-20. A New Translation*. The Anchor Yale Bible Commentaries. New York: Doubleday.

Levine, Baruch. 2000. *Numbers 21-36. A New Translation*. The Anchor Yale Bible Commentaries. New York: Doubleday.

Magonet, Jonathan. 1982. "The Korah Rebellion." *Journal for the Study of the Old Testament* 24: 3–25.

Mann, Thomas W. 1987. "Holiness and Death in the Redaction of Numbers 16:1-20:13." In *Love and Death in the Ancient Near East: Essays in Honor of Marvin H. Pope*, edited by John H. Marks and Robert M. Good, 181–190. Guilford, CT: Four Quarters Publishing Company.

Milgrom, Jacob. 1990. *Numbers*. The JPS Torah Commentary. Philadelphia, PA: Jewish Publication Society.

Newsom, Carol A. 2004. *The Self as Symbolic Space. Constructing Identity and Community at Qumran*. Leiden: Brill.

Olson, Dennis. 1985. *The Death of the Old and the Birth of the New: The Framework of the Book of Numbers and the Pentateuch*. Chico, CA: Scholars Press.

Pardes, Ilana. 2000. *The Biography of Ancient Israel. National Narratives in the Bible*. Berkeley: University of California Press.

Römer, T. C. 2007. "Israel's Sojourn in the Wilderness and the Construction of the Book of Numbers." In *Reflection and Refraction: Studies in Biblical Historiography in Honour of A. Graeme Auld*, edited by Robert Rezetko, Timothy H. Lim, and W. Brain Aucker, 419–445. Leiden: Brill.

Roskop, Angela R. 2011. *The Wilderness Itineraries. Genre, Geography and the Growth of Torah*. Winona Lake, IN: Eisenbrauns.

Sommer, Benjamin D. 1999. "Reflecting on Moses: The Redaction of Numbers 11." *Journal of Biblical Literature* 118(4): 601–624.

Wright, David P. 2012. "Ritual Theory, Ritual Texts and the Priestly-Holiness Writings of the Pentateuch." In *Social Theory and the Study of Israelite Religion*, edited by Saul M. Olyan, 195–216. Atlanta, GA: Society of Biblical Literature.

CHAPTER 12

....

REMEMBERING NARRATIVE IN DEUTERONOMY

....

BRIAN M. BRITT

"THESE are the words that Moses spoke to all Israel beyond the Jordan" (Deut. 1:1). Thus Deuteronomy narrates the last words of Moses, a series of apodictic, narrative, and ritual discourses. The narrative of Deuteronomy contains Moses's "farewell speech," which in turn encompasses retrospective and prospective history, legal instruction, and covenant ritual. Past, present, and future merge within this narrative frame, which records and performs the divinely commanded acts of memory that give the book coherence. This chapter examines the narrative of Deuteronomy in relation to the book's coherence and complexity. Historical criticism, literary scholarship, sociopolitical approaches, and reception history all agree that Deuteronomy has a complex narrative structure and a fairly straightforward message. The questions that remain are whether and how such a complex text can yield a clear purpose.

Known for its repetition and emphasis on comprehensiveness, Deuteronomy would seem to be a clear case of narrative coherence, what Robert Polzin, utilizing the terminology of Mikhail Bakhtin, describes as monological narrative (Polzin 1980, 72). An even more forceful claim for the coherence of biblical narrative in general is Meir Sternberg's notion of *foolproof composition*: "By foolproof composition I mean that the Bible is difficult to read, easy to underread and overread and even misread, but virtually impossible to, so to speak, counterread" (Sternberg 1987, 50). But what kind of coherence is this? Deuteronomy lacks a singularity of message, logical consistency, and linear chronology, yet its purpose and meaning remain quite clear. My thesis is that narratives of divine action and human memory account for coherence in Deuteronomy.

I begin with a survey of modern scholarship on narrative in Deuteronomy. Historical-critical approaches, from Julius Wellhausen (1889) to Moshe Weinfeld (1992), clarified the position of Deuteronomy in the Pentateuch and biblical canon; but they also contributed to broader cultural debates about the Bible, history, Judaism, and Christianity in which narrative is central but often overlooked. The aesthetic attention paid by literary approaches, along with social, cultural, and political methods, arose within an increasingly diverse and contentious scholarly field. From all this emerged not only a wealth of insight into the meaning and effects of biblical narrative but also a broader awareness of the dynamics of biblical narrative in biblical scholarship. The chapter shifts from this survey to an overview and selected readings of Deuteronomy, with special emphasis on the place of memory as a source of coherence.

DEUTERONOMY AND BIBLICAL NARRATIVE

Since Deuteronomy is best understood as the "farewell speech" of Moses, a largely apodictic oration that resembles other valedictory testaments of ancient literature, the category of narrative plays a secondary role in many discussions of its genre and form (Weinfeld 1991, 4–6). Nevertheless, the book does contain a narrative frame and several narrative units. Like the modern novel, the narrative of Deuteronomy incorporates several other genres, including law, poetic texts, and ritual. The book's distinct sections—chapters. 1–4, 5–11, 12–26 (the Deuteronomic Code), 27–30 (the covenant ceremony), and 31–34 (the final words and acts and the death of Moses)—do not form a clear linear narrative, and there is still little agreement on how the book was written and edited (Lundbom 2013, 8–20).

In spite of its complexity, Deuteronomy seems straightforward and perhaps in need of little literary explication. It would be a travesty to complicate this apparent simplicity just for the sake of academic performance, but it would also be a mistake to take the book's apparent simplicity for granted. This chapter asks what the study of narrative can bring to impressions of the book's relative clarity. Despite considerable literary complexity, Deuteronomy achieves coherence through repetition, apodictic discourse, and a combined focus on divine sovereignty and human responsiveness, particularly in the form of narrative and memory.

Narrative operates in the dimensions of time and space. In the case of Deuteronomy, the space is fixed, and time elapses according to the long "farewell speech" of Moses. Yet in his speech Moses revisits the distant past and the places of Israel's memory and provides a detailed proleptic image of the future. The immediate future includes his own death and the Israelite conquest of the land across the Jordan River, while the distant future will stretch to the rise and fall of the Israelite kingdoms and return Israel to the status of a people without territory.

With its circumscribed setting in time and place, the narrative of Deuteronomy fulfills the book's Hellenistic name as a second law, a retrospective and prospective telling of the story from the privileged vantage point of a narrator and a prophet. The "plot" of Deuteronomy recapitulates the major covenant tradition of the Pentateuch, leading to the present time of Moses's valedictory address and covenant ceremony, and it anticipates the future conquest, settlement, monarchy, and exile from the land of Israel. The book thus juxtaposes the retrospective narrative standpoints of Moses and the later nameless Deuteronomist(s).

So unlike the modern literary concept of plot, in which uncertainty guides a suspenseful desire to discover what will happen, the outcome here is known. What, then, explains affective engagement with the narrative of Deuteronomy, since its plot is totally unsuspenseful? To answer this question requires a full reckoning with the differences between modern and ancient Israelite literature, beginning with what makes Deuteronomy distinctive. With its oratorical, apodictic, and ritualized nature, Deuteronomy combines ancient conventions of epic myth to create a new kind of narrative history designed to affirm and remember a particular set of traditions. The text's affective drive involves combining and contextualizing familiar narratives for contemporary ideological ends—namely, linking the monarchy and exilic periods of the late seventh and early sixth centuries to the tradition of Moses.

Identification of the Deuteronomic source goes back to an 1805 study by W. M. L. de Wette and had become widely accepted and more fully articulated by Wellhausen by the end of the century (de Wette 1805; Wellhausen 1889). Martin Noth's identification of Deuteronomy as the first in a series of seven books ending in 2 Kings led to major studies of Deuteronomy's meaning and significance, including Polzin's literary studies of the series (Noth 1943). Finally, Frank Moore Cross's proposal that there are at least two editions of the Deuteronomistic History, a pre-exilic Dtr1 and an exilic Dtr2, has further complicated the picture of narrative in Deuteronomy, raising the question whether a given passage was written with knowledge of the exile (Cross 1973, 274–289; Friedman 1987).

What do narrative studies of the Bible provide? As Hans Frei notes in *The Eclipse of Biblical Narrative*, the modern study of the Bible acknowledged the presence of narrative but failed to analyze it closely, often preferring to ask whether it was historically true (Frei 1974, 10–16). Narrative studies are thus relatively new to biblical scholarship, bringing attention to the contours and contexts of biblical texts in contrast to the tendencies toward abstraction in theology and toward fragmentation in historical research. What emerges is not only a wealth of insight into the meaning and effects of biblical narrative but also a broader awareness of the dynamics of biblical tradition.

At least three moments converge in the narrative of Deuteronomy: the time of the past events recounted by Moses, the time of Moses's recounting, and the later time(s) when all this is recorded in written form. Moses the prophet and lawgiver who serves as a prototype for King Josiah is thus also Moses the narrator in parallel to the nameless biblical narrator. The distance between the time of Moses and the seventh-century time of Deuteronomy can be approached from either point. In *The Death of Moses*, Dennis Olson argues that the final scenes in Deuteronomy form the basis for many later interpretive moves: "The death of Moses, the 'author' of Deuteronomy, freed the text and opened its horizons to a long and winding path of interpretation through generations upon generations of reading" (Olson 1994, 172). Gerhard von Rad, by contrast, takes the writing of the text as a moment of canon formation in which the past tradition of Moses is reactivated: "It is surely a very interesting fact that the Israel of the later period of the monarchy saw itself in the guise, which had become almost canonical, of the Israel of the Mosaic period . . . . The great cultic festivals had already taught Israel to realize that they were present at the redemptive events of the past" (von Rad 1966, 28; cf. Carmichael 1985:10). For von Rad, as for Michael Fishbane, biblical writing belongs to a hermeneutical tradition in which the past and present come together to shape the future (Fishbane 1985).

The double-framed narrative of Deuteronomy means that literary and historical analysis cannot be disentangled. For literary scholars, understanding the "art" of narrative requires some awareness of the historical standpoint of the "artists" writing before and after the Babylonian exile as they looked back to distant memories of Moses and the conquest. Likewise, historians interested in the world behind the text have no choice but to go through its narrative, noting elements of structure, language, and form.

The category of memory provides a key to the imbrication of narrative and history particular to Deuteronomy. Repeated injunctions to remember the words, narratives, and instruction (*torah*) of Deuteronomy link the past of the text to its present and future readings (Deut. 5:15; 7:18; 8:2, 18; 9:7, 27; 11:2; 15:15; 16:3, 12; 24:9, 18, 22; 25:17; 32:7). Just as spoken admonition frames narrative in Deuteronomy, so does memory, a set of practices that actualize the tradition, relating the past of Deuteronomy to the present and future. In this sense, Deuteronomy itself is what I have called a *textual memorial* (Britt 2000). Narrative is ritualized in Deuteronomy as events remembered by Moses, integrated with covenant ritual and retold from the perspective of later centuries. These layers of memory thus require the combination of literary and historical scholarship alike.

BIBLICAL HISTORY AND NARRATIVE

Modern conceptions of history as series of events that can be verified by evidence continue to challenge readings of the Bible that enshrine "fact" as the highest value. Neither Søren Kierkegaard, whose *Training in Christianity* (1850) brushed aside the historicist challenge of David Strauss's *The Life of Jesus* (1835), nor Friedrich Nietzsche (1887), whose sardonic attacks on Christianity conceded the robustness and complexity of biblical tradition, has ever generated enough popular reception to resolve the apparent crisis of biblical history. These nineteenth-century responses to biblical scholarship only underscored the modern divide between the scholarship and the religious communities that considered it a threat.

Nietzsche's apparent contempt for the Bible contains insights on the retrospective shaping of history in theological terms. "With unparalleled disdain of every tradition, every historical reality, they translated their own national past *into religious terms*, that is to say they made of it a stupid salvation-mechanism of guilt towards Yaweh and punishment, piety towards Yaweh and reward" (Nietzsche 1990, 149). Referring to the discovery of a "book of the law (*torah*)" in the time of Josiah (2 Kings 22:8) and its implications for the legitimacy of his (Deuteronomic) reforms, Nietzsche claims that for the priests a "literary forgery becomes necessary, a 'sacred book' is discovered—it is made public with all hieratic pomp, with days of repentance and with lamentation over the long years of 'sinfulness'" (Nietzsche 1990, 150). Though it contributes to an antireligious tirade, Nietzsche's account of the discovery of the book of the law that is now generally considered to comprise the core chapters of Deuteronomy accurately describes the combination of narrative, divine action, and ritual response that appears in Deuteronomy overall. What is more, Nietzsche's antireligious diatribes (in *Anti-Christ* and *Thus Spoke Zarathustra* especially) are paradoxically more biblical, by their imitations and observations of the Bible, than most biblical scholarship of the period (Britt 2011, 177–191).

Nietzsche's strikingly biblical attacks on biblical religion raise a question for current studies of narrative in Deuteronomy. What if, far from standing outside the Bible, scholarship on biblical narrative and history actually inherits and reflects biblical tradition? Conflicts over historical "fact" and religious "value," after all, are biblical. Deuteronomy and the Deuteronomistic History confront a theodicy in which history bafflingly undercuts covenant ideology. Attempts to correlate events with theology appear to collapse when Josiah, the greatest king of Judah, dies an untimely death that soon leads to the loss of homeland, temple, and king. Efforts to explain this disaster as the result of Josiah's wicked grandfather Manasseh (2 Kings 23:24–27) leave the reader to conclude that one bad king who lives a long and comfortable life can bring untimely death and unprecedented catastrophe to later kings, even a king whose goodness reflects that of Moses. The "biblical" nature of modern debates on biblical history challenge the division between a "sacred" Bible and a "secular" biblical scholarship. Peter Berger's suggestion that the Hebrew Bible represents an early phase of secularization, for instance, may in fact point to the collapse of the binary of sacred and secular. For the Bible, it turns out, is no more purely sacred or purely religious than Western modernity is purely secular (Berger 1969, 121; Britt 2011, 15–22).

Narrative Studies and the Book of Deuteronomy

Narrative literary studies and studies of biblical narrative stand far apart from each other. Literary studies reflect the history of novels and short stories written by single authors according to conventions of relative coherence and plot unity that have flourished since the eighteenth century (Herman et al. 2012). When fiction departs from these norms, critics characterize this work as innovative, avant-garde, postmodern, or antimimetic, while most fiction and criticism continue to follow conventions of genre, including linear narrative. It is a paradox that biblical narrative has more in common with postmodern, "nonmimetic" fiction than with its more conventional, monolithic counterparts (cf. Richardson 2012, 24).

Modern literary approaches to the Bible emphasize the "art" of biblical narrative, borrowing from research on modern literature to emphasize plot analysis, characterization, narrative, language, and structure in biblical texts. Robert Alter's *The Art of Biblical Narrative* is a landmark in the field, notable not only for its keen literary observations but also for its awareness of traditional rabbinic interpretations of the Bible (Alter 1981). For Alter and other literary scholars, such as Adele Berlin, the literary features of biblical texts challenged biblical scholarship that tended to fragment the text into numerous unrelated documentary parts (Berlin 1983; Alter 2007, 98). Yet modern literature and literary criticism emerged to a great extent outside or even against religious institutions. So even though the literary study of the Bible turned back to the text, its own assumptions about authorship, reading, and texts sometimes limited its impact.

In his groundbreaking *Moses and the Deuteronomist*, Polzin offers the first sustained engagement with narrative in Deuteronomy from the standpoint of literary theory. Placing Deuteronomy in the context of the Deuteronomistic History, Polzin argues that the narrator and Moses overlap to produce an ideologically monologic text, even though at the end of the book the narrator interrupts the flow of the narrative with many "frame-breaks" until the death of Moses, whereupon "the words of the narrator take center stage in the history" (Polzin 1980, 72). Like Sternberg, Polzin overstates the unity of the text, but his analysis does demonstrate the combination of literary complexity and coherence in Deuteronomy.

Olson offers a more dynamic model of the text. He characterizes Deuteronomy, with its focus on *torah*, as catechesis, a "process of education in faith from one generation to another based on a distillation of essential tradition" (Olson 1994, 11). An advantage of Olson's suggestion is that it explains the structure of Deuteronomy in terms of its obvious religious ideology. At the same time, the category of "faith" reflects a modern (especially Protestant Christian) contrast between "faith" and "action" that is not internal to Deuteronomy.

Literary studies of the Bible also engage in social and political critique. The feminist studies of Phyllis Trible, J. Cheryl Exum, Mieke Bal, and Renita Weems reflect a range of methods and approaches that include rhetorical criticism, close reading, and structuralist, narratological, and womanist perspectives. Tikva Frymer-Kensky's article on Deuteronomy for the *Women's Bible Commentary* understandably concentrates on how the book's legal instructions affect women but also notes the deeply patriarchal valences of divine jealousy and the book's emphasis on centralizing worship of one god at the expense of all others, especially female images (Frymer-Kensky 1992, 53). Concerned with uncovering and challenging the core assumptions and implications of biblical texts, feminist studies of biblical narrative make indispensible contributions to the understanding of biblical texts. Building on work by Exum, Bal, and Frymer-Kensky, one could read the relentlessly repetitive narrative of Deuteronomy as evidence of a discourse anxious, like a jealous husband (or god), to preserve patriarchal structures of power and privilege, from the exclusion of foreign gods and foreign wives to the centralization of power and worship in the Judahite monarchy.[1]

Narrative studies of the Bible recognize the dual roles of oral and written tradition. The reading of ancient Israel, like much religious reading, was typically oral recitation in a social and ritual setting. And while writing enjoyed a high level of prestige and religious value in biblical tradition, the transmission of texts was probably an elaborate combination of oral and written texts, particularly in the context of schools and academies (Carr 2005; van der Toorn 2007).[2] The idea of a Deuteronomic school, elaborated most fully in Weinfeld's work, suggests a process of scribal and compositional development for Deuteronomy, far from modern notions of single authorship, in which members of a "school" collected, assembled, edited, and wrote the book of Deuteronomy over several generations.

Yet the difference between biblical and modern ideas of authorship underscores a major limitation of literary scholarship on the Bible. When biblical scholars celebrate the originality, unity, and artistry of biblical texts, they risk anachronism. Biblical authors were self-effacing even when they were brilliant, and tradition-bound even when they were original. Authorial originality and its counterpart, readerly desire and enjoyment, are modern aesthetic constructs far removed from the biblical text. It is tempting to apply literary understandings of plot, such as that of Peter Brooks (1992), to biblical narrative, but it is difficult to imagine two more different literary worlds than that of modern fiction, in which individual reading reflects Freudian drives, and biblical narrative, in which community reading, guided not by suspense or desire but by traditional practices, predominates.

Poststructuralist approaches to literature, described in such terms as the *death of the author, radical polysemy,* and *textual fragmentation,* challenge modern ideas of textual unity and coherence that never fit the Bible in the first place. And though it is often couched in terms of radical novelty, poststructuralist analysis can suit the complexity of biblical texts better than some traditional literary approaches. Biblical narrative, one could argue, is more poststructuralist than contemporary fiction!

If a text like Deuteronomy, written and edited by many hands over many years to include many subgenres and loosely connected sections, nevertheless makes sense, then what kind of coherence is this? To answer this question, I suggest, would allow the Bible to expand the scope of narrative studies beyond their predominantly modern, secular orientation. The categories of divine sovereignty and memory, I argue, go far to explain the coherence of Deuteronomy, and the following discussion represents an initial effort in that direction.

A central insight of Fishbane's *Biblical Interpretation in Ancient Israel* is how closely hermeneutics *within* the Bible relate to hermeneutics *of* the Bible. Without minimizing differences of history and interpretation, this insight makes it possible to speak of biblical tradition(s) before and after the completion of the canon. The currently growing field of reception studies (or *Wirkungsgeschichte*), which investigates the many forms of commentary, retelling, and appropriation of biblical texts, thus becomes crucial to the enterprise of biblical studies, since reception is the living *traditio* acting in dynamic tension with the written text (*traditum*). Mutually constituted by writing and commentary, *traditum* and *traditio,* biblical texts thus conceived yield models of coherence quite different from the unities of time, place, and action derived from Aristotle's *Poetics* or the unities of plot, narrator, character, or author still expected of most narrative literature today.

Deuteronomy not only instantiates such a dynamic model of narrative text but also describes it. The reflexivity of the text(s), with its many self-references to written and spoken words, instruction, statutes and ordinances, and the Song of Moses, dramatizes and thematizes the process of text production. Yet when the narrator says "then Moses wrote down this law" (31:9) or when Moses admonishes Israel to "diligently observe all the words of this law" (32:46), it is not exactly clear what that law contains. Within an expanding canon, this ambiguity becomes a productive reminder of the intertextual links between the spoken, written, and narrated words within and beyond Deuteronomy. Readers are thus challenged to assign reference and meaning to the term *law* (*torah*) when they encounter it. Does it refer to the immediate chapter in which it appears, the entire Deuteronomic Code, or, even more expansively, Deuteronomy and other biblical books? Does "law" serve a mainly negative function as a "witness against" Israel for future wrongdoing (31:26) or the more positive role of their "very life" (32:47)? Open enough to reveal a complex compositional process and clear enough to enable its continuation, Deuteronomy provides a model of dynamic coherence constituted by writing, reading, and interpretation. Such a model fits surprisingly well with literary theories that regard narrative as performance and as a dynamic machine engaging new readers in new interpretations (Maclean 1988, 21).

Written and edited over many generations that precede and follow the Babylonian exile and making clear use of prebiblical written traditions, the narrative of Deuteronomy gains coherence from its many layers and disparate elements. This kind of coherence is far easier to perceive than the multiple documentary layers that appear to underlie the text. While debates continue on whether and how documentary sources flow into the final version of Deuteronomy (Yoo 2012), there can be little disagreement over the book's core message. The line of tradition does not begin with Deuteronomy, of course; it also extends back in time. Prebiblical farewell speeches have roots in ancient Near Eastern instructional testaments in which leaders transmit teachings to their successors. "Indeed, the book of Deuteronomy is a kind of manual for the future kings of Israel (cf. 17:14–23) written by scribes . . . just as were the instructions for the Egyptian and Mesopotamian kings" (Weinfeld 1991, 4; Berman 2013).

TIME AND MEMORY IN DEUTERONOMY

Since Deuteronomy is not a continuously linear narrative, many of its disparate sections or pericopes are held together by transitional phrases that repeat or echo an earlier phrase. This phenomenon, known as "resumptive repetition," can lend a sense of simultaneity rather than chronological flow to the text (Talmon 1993). Such may be the case in the phrases that begin Deuteronomy 4:1, 4:44, 12:1, 27:1, and 29:1, but as any reader of the text can tell, these phrases belong to the large set of stock Deuteronomic phrases that make the book seem repetitive (Weinfeld 1992, 320–365). As Weinfeld shows, the phrases and terms so emphatically repeated in Deuteronomy serve the ideological and pedagogical ends of the text. One illustration of the book's emphasis on comprehensiveness is the recurrence of the phrase "all the words," which appears nine times (9:10; 17:19; 27:3, 8; 28:58; 29:29; 31:12; 32:44, 46).

The concern for comprehensiveness reflects a general impulse toward control of time in Deuteronomy. The present of Moses's farewell speech seeks to unite the past and future, and the speech itself becomes even more stable as a past-framed later narration. For a book concerned with the fragility of covenant and its promise of land, securing the past, present, and future against historical contingency is paramount. The book's focus on the future can be seen in Moses's repeated statements about the territories Israel is about to enter (2:4; 3:21; 4:5, 14; 6:1; 7:1; 9:1; 11:10; 12:2, 29; 18:14; 23:20).

Narrative time, in fact, closely tracks divine sovereignty in Deuteronomy. Time never simply passes in the Deuteronomic narrative; like the people of Israel under the covenant, time is subordinate to divine will. Consider the following two commands regarding time:

> Beyond the Jordan in the land of Moab, Moses undertook to expound this law (*hatorah hazo't*) as follows: The LORD our God spoke to us at Horeb, saying, "You have stayed long enough (*rav-lakhem shevet*) at this mountain." (Deut. 1:5–6)
>
> So now (*ve'atah*), give heed to the statutes and ordinances that I am teaching you to observe, so that you may live to enter and occupy the land that the LORD, the God of your ancestors, is giving you." (Deut. 4:1)

In Deuteronomy 1:5, God "calls time" to Israel through Moses—they have stayed "long enough," and now it is time for them to move on, once Moses has delivered the law and died. In the second case (Deut. 4:1), Moses similarly announces that it is time for Israel to take action by following divine law in order to inherit the land. Time, and thus narrative, follows divine command.

In response to the divine sovereignty over time (and narrative), Deuteronomy structures acts of memory, from repeated injunctions to observe and remember divine commandments (e.g., chs. 4–6) to the ritual of the covenant ceremony (Deut. 27–30). Since the narrative presented by Moses and framed by the third-person narrator spans many centuries and took shape over many generations, it models a tradition of telling and retelling. It is tempting to apply what Jan Assmann calls "mnemohistory," the history of memory, to Deuteronomy, but this kind of memory, practiced according to the book's instructions, not only indicates the past, but is also designed to continue well into the future (Assmann 1997, 15–22). Yet these acts of memory, like narrative, are selective. No discussion of memory and narrative in Deuteronomy should overlook what is marginalized, forgotten, and expressly excluded. The most striking case of exclusion is the paradoxical injunction against Amalek, "Remember what Amalek did to you on your journey out of Egypt. . . . you shall blot out the remembrance of Amalek from under heaven; do not forget" (Deut. 25:17–19; cf. Exod. 17). As many critics of ideology have noted, acts of memory and history writing are also acts of erasure and forgetting (Benjamin 2003, 391–392).

How do the two elements of divine sovereignty and human memory fit together? For Paul Ricoeur, the combination of divine action and human retelling forms a basis for divine revelation. In a discussion of Deuteronomy 26:5b–10b, cited by von Rad as a kind of creed that affirms divine responsiveness to human action, Ricoeur notes how this text unites divine action—the deliverance from slavery in Egypt—with Israel's retelling of these actions. Marking the combined roles of the divine and human, the narrative also shifts from God, described in the third person, as rescuing and providing for Israel, to Israel's thankful offering of first fruits in response, addressing God in the second. In this condensed retelling of the exodus, the text, like Deuteronomy itself, combines divine with human, narrative with ritual. Ricoeur explains:

> What is essential in the case of narrative discourse is the emphasis on the founding event or events as the imprint, mark, or trace of God's act. Confession takes place through narration . . . God's mark is in history before being in speech. It is only secondarily in speech inasmuch as this history is brought to language in the speech-act of narration. . . . This subjective moment is no longer the narration insofar as the events recount themselves, but the event of narration insofar as it is presented by a narrator to a community. (1980, 79)

For Ricoeur, biblical narrative implies and requires community reception in the form of ritualized retelling.

Words from the root `ed (witness) appear frequently in Deuteronomy, often in reference to laws about teaching. Describing the law (torah) as a witness against Israel for future covenant violations (Deut. 31:26, 31:28, 32:46), Moses uses a term connoting temporal endurance and sometimes used to describe stone monuments (Josh 22:28) for the words of his text. On these grounds, I have proposed the notion of "textual memorial" as a heuristic model for the genre of the last chapters of Deuteronomy, and on the basis of the present discussion, I would venture to expand this claim to apply to the narrative of Deuteronomy as a whole (Britt 2000).

"I call heaven and earth to witness against you today." This statement appears early and late in Deuteronomy (4:26; 30:19) to form a striking *inclusio* for the entire book. There are no other cases of "I call" in the book. The first text anticipates the destruction of Israel, suggesting a post-exilic perspective (Cross's Dtr2): "I call heaven and earth to witness against you today that you will soon utterly perish from the land that you are crossing the Jordan to occupy; you will not live long on it, but will be utterly destroyed." The second, mirroring passage, near the conclusion of the covenant ceremony, leaves the matter open to Israel's choice:

> I call heaven and earth to witness against you today that I have set before you life and death, blessings and curses. Choose life so that you and your descendants may live, loving the LORD your God, obeying him, and holding fast to him; for that means life to you and length of days, so that you may live in the land that the LORD swore to give to your ancestors, to Abraham, to Isaac, and to Jacob. (Deut. 30:19–20 NRSV)

The appeal to choose life returns in 32:46–47, where Moses identifies the "words of this law" with the life of Israel. This union of text and life depends on the choice not only to follow divine commands but also to reactivate the past for the present and future. Like the ritual and legal prescriptions it contains, the narrative of Deuteronomy thus combines divine command with human memory in a dynamic process that yields a complex but coherent text.

Notes

1. See Fewell and Gunn (1993, 94–116), and the application of "repetition compulsion" to the wife-sister stories of Genesis in Exum (1993). Of course, repetition by itself is not clear evidence for repetition compulsion, but the emphatic repetitions in Deuteronomy certainly justify questions about why such persistent restatement is needed. On forms and uses of repetition in biblical narrative (*Leitwort*, motif, theme, sequence of actions, and type-scene), see Alter (1981, 95–96).
2. Robert W. Kawashima, for example, argues that "biblical narrative is the result of a specifically written verbal art" and that this "novelistic art" "results from decline of the epic arts in ancient Israel" (Kawashima 2004, 10; see also Kawashima in this volume).

References

Alter, Robert. 1981. *The Art of Biblical Narrative*. New York: Basic Books.

Alter, Robert. 2007. *The Book of Psalms: A Translation with Commentary*. New York: W. W. Norton.

Assmann, Jan. 1997. *Moses the Egyptian: The Memory of Egypt in Western Monotheism*. Cambridge, MA: Harvard University Press.

Benjamin, Walter. 2003. "On the Concept of History." In *Walter Benjamin: Selected Writings*, translated by Edmund Jephcott et al. Edited by Howard Eiland and Michael W. Jennings, vol. 4, 389–400. Cambridge, MA: Harvard University Press.

Berger, Peter. 1969. *The Sacred Canopy: Elements of a Sociological Theory of Religion*. New York: Doubleday.

Berlin, Adele. 1983. *Poetics and Interpretation of Biblical Narrative*. Sheffield, Yorkshire: Almond Press.

Berman, Joshua. 2013. "Histories Twice Told: Deuteronomy 1–3 and the Hittite Treaty Prologue Tradition." *Journal of Biblical Literature* 132: 229–250.

Britt, Brian. 2011. *Biblical Curses and the Displacement of Tradition*. Sheffield, Yorkshire: Sheffield Phoenix Press.

Britt, Brian. 2000. "Deuteronomy 31–32 as a Textual Memorial." *Biblical Interpretation* 8: 358–374.

Brooks, Peter. 1992. *Reading for the Plot: Design and Intention in Narrative*. Cambridge, MA: Harvard University Press.

Carmichael, Calum M. 1985. *Law and Narrative in the Bible: The Evidence of the Deuteronomic Laws and the Decalogue*. Ithaca, NY: Cornell University Press.

Carr, David. 2005. *Writing on the Tablet of the Heart: Origins of Scripture and Literature*. Oxford: Oxford University Press.

Cross, Frank Moore. 1973. *Canaanite Myth and Hebrew Epic: Essays in the History of the Religion of Israel*. Cambridge, MA: Harvard University Press.

Exum, J. Cheryl. 1993. "Who's Afraid of the Endangered Ancestress?" In *Fragmented Women: Feminist (Sub)versions of Biblical Narratives*. 148–169. Valley Forge: Trinity Press.

Fewell, Danna Nolan, and David M. Gunn. *Gender, Power, and Promise: The Subject of the Bible's First Story*. Nashville, TN: Abingdon Press, 1993.

Fishbane, Michael. 1985. *Biblical Interpretation in Ancient Israel*. Oxford: Oxford University Press.

Frei, Hans. 1974. *The Eclipse of Biblical Narrative*. New Haven, CT: Yale University Press.

Friedman, Richard Elliott. 1987. *Who Wrote the Bible?* New York: Harper and Row.

Frymer-Kensky, Tikva. 1992. "Deuteronomy." In *The Women's Bible Commentary*, edited by Carol A. Newsom and Sharon H. Ringe, 52–62. Louisville, KY: Westminster/John Knox.

Herman, David, James Phelan, Peter J. Rabinowitz, Brian Richardson, and Robyn Warhol. 2012. *Narrative Theory: Core Concepts and Critical Debates*. Columbus: Ohio State University Press.

Kawashima, Robert W. 2004. *Biblical Narrative and the Death of the Rhapsode*. Bloomington: Indiana University Press.

Lundbom, Jack. 2013. *Deuteronomy: A Commentary*. Grand Rapids, MI: Eerdmans.

Maclean, Marie. 1988. *Narrative as Performance: The Baudelairean Experiment*. London: Routledge.

Nietzsche, Friedrich. 1990. *The Anti-Christ*, in *Twilight of the Idols and the Anti-Christ*, translated by R. J. Hollingdale. New York: Penguin.

Noth, Martin. 1943. *Überlieferungsgeschichtliche Studien I*. Halle: Niemeyer.

Olson, Dennis T. 1994. *Deuteronomy and the Death of Moses*. Minneapolis, MN: Fortress.

Polzin, Robert. 1980. *Moses and the Deuteronomist: Deuteronomy, Joshua, Judges*. Bloomington, IN: Indiana University Press.

Rad, Gerhard von. 1966. *Deuteronomy*. Translated by Dorothea Barton. Philadelphia, PA: Westminster.

Richardson, Brian. 2012. "Antimimetic, Unnatural, and Postmodern Narrative Theory." In *Narrative Theory: Core Concepts and Critical Debates*, edited by Herman, David, James Phelan, Peter J. Rabinowitz, Brian Richardson, and Robyn Warhol, 20–25. Columbus: Ohio State University Press.

Ricoeur, Paul. 1980. "Toward a Hermeneutic of the Idea of Revelation." In *Essays on Biblical Interpretation*, 73–118. Philadelphia, PA: Fortress.

Sternberg, Meir. 1987. *The Poetics of Biblical Narrative: Ideological Literature and the Drama of Reading*. Bloomington: Indiana University Press.

Talmon, Shemaryahu. 1993. "The Presentation of Synchroneity and Simultaneity in Biblical Narrative." In *Literary Studies in the Hebrew Bible: Form and Content*, 112–133. Jerusalem: Magnes Press.

Toorn, Karen van der. 2007. *Scribal Culture and the Making of the Hebrew Bible*. Cambridge, MA: Harvard University Press.

Weinfeld, Moshe. 1991. *Deuteronomy 1-11: A New Translation With Introduction and Commentary*. The Anchor Yale Bible Commentaries. New York: Doubleday.

Weinfeld, Moshe. 1992. *Deuteronomy and the Deuteronomic School*. Winona Lake, IN: Eisenbrauns.

Wellhausen, Julius. 1889. *Die Composition des Hexateuchs und der historischen Bücher des alten Testaments*. Berlin: Reimer.

Wette, Wilhelm Martin Leberecht de. 1805. *Dissertatio critic-exegetica, qua Deuteronomium a prioribus Pentateuchi libris diversusm, alius cuisdam auctoris opus essay monstratur*. Jena: Literis Etzdorfii.

Yoo, Philip Y. 2012. "The Four Moses Death Accounts." *Journal of Biblical Literature* 131: 423–441.

CHAPTER 13

THE CONQUEST OF MEMORY IN THE BOOK OF JOSHUA

OVIDIU CREANGĂ

THE book of Joshua recounts Israel's entrance into and conquest and settlement of Canaan. The events it narrates mark the end of Israel's sojourn through the wilderness and the beginning of a period characterized by living in the land that God had promised to Israel's ancestors. Because the territory Joshua and the Israelites are about to occupy is understood to be God's promised and exclusive gift to them, the land of Canaan (hereafter the "Land") is declared sacred (Josh. 5:15), and its peoples are subject to a war of annihilation, known as the "ban" or *herem* (Josh. 6:16–18). The background to Joshua's conquest of the Land is the failure of the Exodus generation of Israelites to occupy it. The members of that generation had witnessed powerful acts of deliverance and provision during their journey to Canaan; yet when it came time to enter and conquer the Land, they lacked the courage (Num. 13). The book of Joshua is constructed as a series of similarities and contrasts between the two generations, showing that where the "old" generation had failed, the "new" generation has succeeded. The first part of this chapter summarizes the content of the book of Joshua, tracking the interlocking themes of "land," "identity," and "memory." The second part is an overview of the application of narrative approaches to the book. The final section proposes a spatial-critical reading of the conquest of the Land.

THE NARRATIVES OF THE BOOK OF JOSHUA

A cursory reading of Joshua quickly reveals the book's overarching structure: the conquest of the Land is narrated in chapters 1–12, while the parceling of the Land (on both sides of the Jordan River) is told in chapters 13–21. Short summaries bring the conquest and land-distribution narratives to their respective ends (11:16–23; 12; 21:43–45), whereas other reports bridge them (13:1–7). The dismissal of the two-and-a-half tribes that received their inheritance east of the Jordan River (the so-called Transjordan) in chapter 22 might seem to be a natural conclusion to the book, given Joshua's solicitation of their military help at the beginning of the conquest (1:12–15), but the book does not end there. Joshua's farewell speech in chapter 23 offers a further sense of ending; yet, still, the book marches on to recount a covenant-making scene at Shechem (24:1–27). The report concerning the deaths and burials of Joshua and Eleazar offers yet another likely conclusion, but again, the book presses forward to note the reburial of Joseph's bones at Shechem (24:28–32). This last report connects Joshua firmly to Genesis and Exodus, showing Israel's settlement in the Land to be the fulfillment of earlier promises (Gen. 50:25; Exod. 13:19).

The description of Joshua's conquest as a series of sweeping campaigns that quickly subdue the Land is challenged by other accounts that depict more modest gains and a longer struggle with the Canaanites. The prologue to Judges, in particular, indicates a piecemeal acquisition of the Land, as individual tribes fight for their own lands within it. According to Judges, Joshua's conquest was only the initial phase, and each tribe is responsible for finalizing the conquest (Judg. 2:6). Even more dramatic in Judges, however, is the estrangement from YHWH, the God of Israel, of the generations that come after Joshua (Judg. 1:1–2:10–15).

The events of the conquest narrative in Joshua (1–12) are artfully arranged along three geographical axes. Overlapping themes of the people's unity, obedience to the law of Moses, and divinely granted military success appear clearly in each axis. The foundational events for the nation's life occur along the first axis, which is a movement from east to west across the Jordan River. The people's miraculous crossing through the Jordan and encampment inside Canaan at Gilgal exhibit the defining features of the "new" Israel: (1) the leadership of God (represented by the leading Ark) and the people's dependence on him to overcome any obstacles, (2) the people's readiness to follow God/Joshua in battle, and (3) the commemoration of the past and present mighty deeds of YHWH (4:6–7, 20–24). The recall of God's former acts marks the people of Israel and draws a line of distinction between them and the Canaanites, who are not present in the camp and do not identify with those memories.

The Jericho stories (chs. 2, 6) and Ai (ch. 7) disrupt established lines of identity. A Canaanite prostitute named Rahab, the quintessential "other," recalls Israel's miraculous past and uses that knowledge to win her and her family a place in Israel. The quintessential "Israelite," Achan of Judah, on the other hand, disregards Joshua's instructions to destroy all property belonging to the Jerichonites. Achan's misdeed attracts YHWH's judgment upon himself and Israel. Jericho's ruins and Achan's burial site offer both a testimonial and a warning to those who oppose YHWH and his leader Joshua, be they Canaanites or Israelites. Geographical markers continue to proliferate. At the end of second battle against Ai (ch. 8), another pile of stones is erected over the king of Ai's lifeless body (8:28–29). The ceremony on Mount Ebal follows immediately after the conquest of Ai (in the Masoretic Text). While this is hardly explainable from a chronological or spatial point of view, thematically, it pinpoints the need to remember Moses's instructions (Deut. 27). The transcription and recitation of the law on Mt. Ebal are acts of memory that remake Israel's boundaries around the Torah and its hearers (8:30–35).

In Joshua 9 and 10, the conquest narrative moves along a southern geographical axis. Joshua and his men depart from Gilgal to aid Gibeon and continue south to engage in what turns out to be a military campaign of resounding success. The Gibeonites, a Hivite enclave at the foot of the central highlands, save themselves from destruction by pretending to be from far away. In their artful negotiation with Joshua's men, the Gibeonites at first obscure the most recent events in Israel's memory (namely, the miraculous crossing of the Jordan and the conquests of Jericho and Ai), recalling instead the Exodus and the conquests on the east side of the Jordan (9:9b–10). This calculated move immediately endears the Gibeonites to Israel (there sit before them a far-away people attracted by Yʜwʜ's fame, v. 9a) and, conveniently, depicts them to be innocently unaware of the latest events in the Land. Once the Gibeonites' true identity is discovered, however, the memory of the recent conquests at Jericho and Ai (9:3, 24) emerges in their negotiation. The Gibeonites clearly know about Moses's instruction concerning their destruction. They effectively recall those words amid supplications that they be accepted as servants and when addressing Joshua, who, although he is striving to fulfil Moses's commandment, appears to be more reasonable than the rest of the Israelites (cf. v. 26a). The Gibeonites' strategic use of Israel's memory seals the deal in their favor. Their survival contrasts with the fates of Adoni-Zedek, king of Jerusalem, and the four kings that join him against Gibeon. Joshua destroys the armies of the five kings with apparent ease, thanks to Yʜwʜ's involvement. The humiliation, execution, and burial of the five kings in the Makkedah cave reiterates Israel's adversarial relationship with the Canaanite rulers and demonstrates their desire to monumentalize the Canaanite failure to oppose them and Yʜwʜ (10:22–28). The description that follows the campaign in the south is formulaic. It stresses Israel's unity ("Joshua and all Israel with him"; see 10:29, 31, 34, 36, 38) in attacking one town after another (Makkedah, Libnah, Lachish, Eglon, Hebron, Debir). Because of Yʜwʜ's martial valor, the local rulers are unable to resist Joshua.

The battle against King Jabin of Hazor and his coalition army at the Waters of Merom (11:1–9) shifts the focus to the north. This story resembles the previous one, in that a decisive battle leads to a wider campaign in which Israel gains control of extensive territory. The disregard for Israel's past parallels Adoni-Zedek's story with a similar outcome. The campaign that ensues after the defeat of Jabin shows again the pitiful fate of those who oppose Yʜwʜ and his people. Desolate towns in the north speak to their inhabitants' demise before them (11:10–14).

After conquest summaries (11:16–23; 12), the allotment narrative (chs. 13–21) opens with an intriguing statement about Joshua's old age and the need to allocate areas that are still unconquered (13:1–7). The Israelite tribes, it appears, are unable to remove the indigenous populations from their allocated lands. Judah is not able to defeat the Jebusites in Jerusalem (15:63); the Ephraimites cannot remove the Canaanites from Gezer, one of the towns that they receive, and neither can the half tribe of Manasseh (16:10; 17:12–13); the Danites cannot get a handle on their portion and instead retreat to one city (19:47). The Israelites are forced—and eventually prefer—to coexist with the Canaanites, especially since material benefit can be obtained from the Canaanites' enslavement.

The stories of Achsah and the Zelophehad daughters (15:18–19; 17:3–6) are artfully integrated between and around the inheritance allocations of the tribes of Judah, Ephraim, and half-Manasseh, enlivening what otherwise are dry listings of place names. In these stories, Israelite women speak for the first time in the book. Their voices are subsumed under the narrator's concern with tribal allocations, but enough of their own particular needs and wants are retained to portray them as assertive women. They seek a fairer treatment of themselves and their families.

The next literary unit (chs. 18–20) concerns the inheritance of the seven remaining tribes. Joshua admonishes the tribes not to delay in taking possession of the Land, but his impatience seems unfair. How can they occupy their portions before knowing which are theirs? The account of tribal allocations is stylized, shifting from lists of territorial boundaries with requisite towns (Benjamin) to lists of inherited towns only (Simeon, Issachar, Dan) to lists of only territorial borders (Zebulun, Asher, Naphtali). Reserving the town of Timnath Serah (known also as Timnath Heres) for Joshua, the Israelites "finished dividing the land" (19:51). The job is not done, however, until towns of refuge (ch. 20) and towns for Levites (ch. 21) are chosen. The strategic naming and renaming of towns and regions, the listing and relisting of these sites in various inheritance reports, expresses Israel's ownership of the Land. This is a form of narrative *inscription*, a "writing-in" of Israel's identity into the literary surface of the Land. The tribes become contiguous with their allocations.

The tenuous unity of a divided nation living on both sides of the Jordan River surfaces in the crisis erupting with the building of an additional altar at Geliloth near the Jordan. The act sends Israel to the brink of civil war (ch. 22). This and Joshua's Deuteronomic warning in his farewell speech (23:13) that Israel will perish from the Land if it turns away from Yhwh show that not all is well with Israel. The suspicion persists in the following episode, the Shechem covenant, where Joshua both charges Israel to serve Yhwh (24:14–15) and spells their inability to do so: "You are not able to serve the Lord; He is a holy God" (24:14–15, 19). The people's repeated assurance that they will serve Yhwh and their ceremonial pledge (24:16, 21–27) are almost as inadequate as they are necessary.

Narrative Readings in the Book of Joshua

The first studies to read Joshua *as literature*, rather than as a complex literary document, were done in 1980s. This represented a shift in emphasis that came after a century of modern scholarship on Joshua that was fundamentally informed by the revolutionary ideas of Julius Wellhausen (1882), Hermann Gunkel (1906), and Martin Noth (1943) who sought to elucidate the documentary sources (J, E, D, P) and the literary genres (*Gattungen*) that characterize the book. Their influence on Joshua was—and still is—profound, as is clearly evidenced in the commentary tradition.

In his 1968 presidential address to the Society of Biblical Literature, James Muilenburg (1969) challenged the prevailing methodological status quo by asking biblical scholars to expand the scope of their inquiries and integrate an appreciation for the biblical text's final form. He named his proposed method "rhetorical criticism" (8). While his approach was eventually developed by others into the full-fledged method of biblical rhetorical criticism that we have today (Patrick and Scult 1990), Muilenburg's invitation to expound the text's poetic features encouraged the emergence of other methods that shared similar goals and assumptions (e.g., narrative criticism). It took another decade for the fruit of Muilenburg's approach to catch up with the scholars of Joshua. The first significant contribution to demonstrate an appreciation for the final text of Joshua was Robert Polzin's *Moses and the Deuteronomist* (1980). Polzin reads the narrative of Joshua (along with that of Deuteronomy and of Judges) as a dialogue between two opposing "voices" regarding the application of Moses's law in the account of Israel's settlement in the Land. Polzin's work was a nuanced application of a dialogic method inspired by the work of Mikhail Bakthin, but more than that, it was also a validation that the "new literary criticism" was capable of generating profound insights and lasting results. Following on Polzin's work was that of Lyle Eslinger (1989) who offers a synchronic reading of Joshua 1–9 that highlights the narrative's apparent contradictions concerning Israel's (and Yhwh's) achievements.

The "new" literary criticism found its expression within the framework of traditional ("old") literary or historical criticism.[1] Polzin's work, for example, placed Joshua firmly within the framework of the Deuteronomistic History. Subsequent studies in the 1990s embraced a somewhat similar approach, although the connection with historical criticism has become more and more tenuous, in part because of the great lack of consensus among historical literary critics. Gordon Mitchell (1993), for instance, examines the unresolved tensions between Israel's obedience and the remaining Canaanites, with an eye to a post-exilic setting in which the returnees must learn to live "together" with other peoples while wishing times had been more favorable to them. Lori L. Rowlett (1996) reads the conquest narrative's violence as a work commission by King Josiah to secure the support of his officials for reinstating the Yahwistic faith as sole religion and eliminating all other cults from the kingdom of Judah (including Samaria). The narrative's rhetoric of inclusion, exclusion, and marginality serves Josiah's program (prefigured by Joshua) by showing his opponents, whether ethnic Israelites (Achan) or non-Israelites ("Canaanites"), what awaits those who resist YHWH and his leader. Drawing on the resources of rhetorical and narrative approaches, my own reading (Creangă 2010a) positions Joshua 1–12's rhetoric of memory and commemoration in an exilic context, while Koert van Bekkum's (2011) granular reading of the conquest stories in Joshua 9–13 posits a composition period between the tenth and ninth centuries BCE.

Several book-length studies mark sharper departures from questions of the ancient historical context. L. Daniel Hawk (1991, 2000) has produced two significant studies, each exploring Joshua's internal dynamics. Both works expose, by means of narrative analysis, the assertion and contradiction of Israel's obedience to the law, possession of the Land, and ethnic purity, insisting that what really defines Israel is its choosing of YHWH. Elie Assis (1999, 2005) seeks the meaning of the conquest narrative in its literary structure. His analysis underscores a series of symmetries, or mirror-like structures, at the level of events and characters between the Pentateuch and Joshua, as well as God's departure from the expected leadership in war. Sarah Lebhar Hall's (2010) study on the characterization of Joshua examines a range of narrative techniques (epithet, dialogue, contrast, perspective, narrative pace, repetition, analogy, etc.,) that create Joshua's complex portrait. Two other books deserving of mention here are those of William T. Koopmans (1990) and Blažej Štrba (2008). Koopmans investigates in detail the poetic features of Joshua 24, while Štrba provides an in-depth literary analysis of Joshua 5:13–15 in order to demonstrate that Joshua enjoyed the same level of authority as Moses.

Alongside these lengthier studies, a plethora of shorter studies have appeared over the past three decades. These works, too, focus on the poetics of characterization (of story characters and events) and narrative artistry (Biddle 1998). To name a few, M. A. Beek (1994) examines Joshua's depiction as a "saving figure" bridging the gap between Deuteronomy and Judges; David Gunn (1987) points out thematic continuities and discontinuities between the Joshua and Judges narratives; Hawk (1992) reads Rahab's story intertextually with Lot's story; Assis (2004) attempts a similar act with Yael's and examines the repetitions and conflicts in the report of Israel's crossing of the Jordan River (Assis 2012); Robert Gordon (2003) examines the internal dynamics of the Gibeonites' story; and Hawk (1997), Rowlett (1992), Nancy Claissé-Walford (1998), and Robert Ellis (1998) have explored how the conquest narrative, through the use of ambiguous ethnic and theological markers, constructs Israel's identity in stable and unstable ways.

The analysis of gender in biblical literature has also enriched literary approaches to Joshua. Engaging the text closely, biblical feminist scholars have unmasked the androcentric features of the Joshua narrative and the patriarchal values that are inscribed in it (Creangă 2007). Feminist studies of Rahab (Bird 1989; Frymer-Kensky 1997; Brenner 2002; Sherwood 2006), Achsah (Fewell 1995), and the Zelophehad daughters (Sakenfeld 1998; Shemesh 2007) have exposed the men's concern with preserving their power and resources, as well as their insecurity around strong, confident women who resist being stereotyped. Creangă (2010a) underscores the sexist images conjured up by Deuteronomic laws of warfare against the inhabitants of Canaan (Deut. 20–22) in Joshua's conquest narrative. The current wave of biblical gender scholarship, drawing from masculinities and queer studies, interrogates Joshua's hitherto unexamined hegemonies or normativities (heterosexual, ethnic/racist, materialistic) that disadvantage men and women alike (Creangă 2010b; Carden 2006; Runions 2011).

Narrative artistry, of course, does little to diminish the thorny ethical questions arising from the book's colonial outlook (Warrior 1995). The deaths of Canaanites—men, women, and children—as victims of a war they did not start, coupled with the notion that God wills them to perish (Josh. 11:20), is distasteful to modern sensitivities. Israel's enrichment from the spoils of war (Josh. 6:24; 8:27; 11:14; 22:8) adds to the injustice. The legacy of these (and subsequent) acts of sanctified violence against a changing other has left a long trail of bloodstains on the canopy of premodern and modern Western civilization. Uncritical appropriations of the book's rhetoric of violence has fueled many of the colonial projects of the past. Close readings that uncover in the text of Joshua a critique of the dogmatic and authoritarian stance that characterizes much of the book can save us from repeating the mistakes of the past (see Hawk 2010).

NARRATIVE AND SPATIAL THEORY: THE LAND AS "THIRDSPACE" IN JOSHUA 1–12

The following short treatment of Joshua's conquest narrative joins the fruit of narrative analysis and postmodern spatial theory. Earlier attempts to uncover, through close readings, the ideologies of space underlying the book of Joshua have focused on geographical features, such as the River Jordan and the place of the Transjordan in Israel's imagination, or on the land map constructed in Joshua (Knight 2002; Jobling 1987; Havrelock 2007). Spatial theory claims that space is as much a cultural construct as a physical reality and that the production or rendition of space (be it in film, pictures, paintings, or texts) is often tied to identity and power struggles within the communities that produce representations of space. The approach proposed here follows this assumption as it applies to Joshua 1–12. Unlike other spatial studies in Joshua, the ensuing discussion not only uncovers binaries (as in structuralism) or official ideologies (as in symbolic geography), but also illustrates the agency of the spatially and socially marginalized Canaanites to reshape Israel's hegemonic outlook.

The concept of "Thirdspace" that informs my reading of the conquest narrative is associated with the geographer and urban specialist Edward W. Soja (1996). Drawing from the French Marxist philosopher, Henri Lefebvre (1974), Soja sees perceptions or epistemologies colliding and fertilizing over space and in response to it. The engagement with space, in Soja's view, gives rise to expressions of the hegemonies that are inherent in a particular society. These hegemonies–be they materialist, colonialist, sexist, or others—produce and reinforce rigid binaries through space. The notion of "Thirdspace" or, as Soja (1996, 60–61) calls it, "Thirding-as-Othering," expresses both the disruption of set binaries as well as their reconstruction as *trialectics*, that is to say, in dialogue and opening to radical otherness.

The starting point in deciphering the "Thirdspatial" nature of a place is the encounter and experience of the "Firstspace." This is the encounter with the perceived physical, objective reality of space. "Secondspace" is the conceived, ideational, artistic, and (we may add) theological representation of space. If Firstspace denotes the physical space and Secondspace the subjective interpretation/imagination of it, Thirdspace expresses the phenomenon of lived space, the experience of living in or occupying—or, neither living in nor occupying—a particular place. Thirdspace is a site of resistance in that those who are not inside a hegemonic spatial "center," whether because of their economic, racial, cultural, sexual, or religious differences, are not powerless entities but actors who fight their marginality by assaulting and potentially transforming the "center."

Joshua lends itself particularly well to a spatial analysis because it makes space (the Land) its central theme. Let us, therefore, begin by noticing the Land's Firstspatial features in the conquest narrative. The narrative opens with a spatial imperative: "[A]rise, go over the Jordan, you and all this people, into the land which I give them, to the sons of Israel" (1:2). In the next two verses, the designated territory is delineated. It encompasses the area between "the wilderness" (south) and the "great river" (the Euphrates, to the north), and between the "great sea" (the Mediterranean) in the west, and the "land of the Hittites" in the east. Nothing more is said at this point about the spatial features of the land enclosed between these geographical points, but over the course of the story, a multitude of relief features emerge: from the lowlands of the Jordan Valley to the high plateau of Mt. Ebal. Equally important in this description of the Land is the presence of urban, not only natural, space. Canaanite towns and settlements, from Gilgal to Jericho and Ai and to all other towns mentioned in the southern and northern parts of the country, dot the entire Land. A further dimension of the Land is its produce. Canaan is not a wild, unnourishing place. Its produce, consumed after the manna stops, affords Israel another means of knowing the space they have entered and are about to conquer (Josh. 5:12).

At the most basic level, Joshua's conquest of the Land is a Firstspatial endeavor. It occurs in a defined territory, over land, and concerns the acquisition of a place to settle in. In the process of conquest, the Israelites do not only traverse this natural and urban space, but they alter it. In some places they set up camp (Gilgal). Some towns they completely destroy (Jericho, Ai, Hazor), others only in part (Makkedah, Libnah, Lachish, Eglon, Hebron), while others not at all (Gibeon, Kephirah, Beeroth, Kiriath Jearim). In some sites, they erect shrines (Mt. Ebal); commemorative monuments come up in or near the Jordan (Josh. 4; 22); and tombstones mark the graves of those who disregarded or opposed YHWH for posterity (Josh. 7; 8; 10).

Relief features and localities mix with the narrator's rhetoric of conquest. In grand, sweeping generalizations, the narrator tells us that Joshua captured "all that land" (Josh. 10:40; 11:16, 23) and "all these cities" (Josh. 11:12) and "all these kings" (Josh 11:5, 12, 18). The report after the southern campaign recounts the captured land using such relief features as the hill country, the Negev, the western foothills, and the mountain slopes and such places as Kadesh Barnea, Gaza, and Gibeon (Josh. 10:40–41). Similarly, the concluding summary reviews the entire territory that the Israelites have conquered (Josh. 11:16–23). The report lists large blocks of land according to their relief features. Moving from south to north, the narrator's eye surveys the highland of Judah, all the Negev, the whole region of Goshen, the western foothills, the Arabah, and the mountains of Israel with their foothills (Josh. 11:16); taking a different look at the Land, he measures the Land from Mt. Halak to Baal Gad in the Lebanon Valley at the foot of Mt. Hermon (Josh. 11:17). This reporting largely focuses on geographical, rather than political space, with two noteworthy exceptions: this concluding summary does mention two contrasting entities, the Hivites from Gibeon who made peace with the Israelites (11:19) and the old and much-feared enemy, the Anakites, who are eliminated (only) from the central spine (the highlands) of the Land (11:21–22). The Land's former rulers do, however, become the subjects of the long victim list in the next chapter. The former centers of power in Canaan, the fallen indigenous rulers of the Canaanite nations, are counted one by one, along with their capital towns, in what looks like an arithmetic of death similar in style to other ancient Near Eastern war literatures (12:7–24).

When ideas and beliefs meet over a physical space, we are dealing with Secondspatiality. This aspect of Canaan's characterization manifests in the narrator's belief that it (and not any other territory) *is* the object of God's promise to Israel (1:6). Moving quickly from Firstspatiality (mapping the physical Land in 1:4) to Secondspatiality, the narrator describes the Land as Israel's "sworn inheritance" (1:6). In the allotment narrative, the noun "inheritance" denotes an allocated territory to be inhabited by a family, clan, or tribe (14:13; 16:4; 17:6). "Inheritance" in the conquest narrative, on the other hand, denotes a belief that that Land is the object of a binding contract between YHWH and Israel's ancestors and that Joshua (continuing the work of Moses) is to put Israel in possession of it. The word frames the conquest narrative appearing at the beginning and end (1:6; 11:23).

The stories's fusion of Israelite memory into concrete physical nature underscores the special connection of the Land to Israel. Gibeath Haaraloth—the hill of foreskins—receives its name from the second circumcision that occurs there; the memory of the pile of foreskins is now fixed in the place (5:2). The first Passover ceremony in the Land is observed at Gilgal, where, in addition, Egypt's shadow upon Israel is "rolled" away (5:9). On Mt. Ebal, Israel fulfills Moses's instruction to write and read the Torah, and the shrine that is built there confirms that it has happened. Stones from the River Jordan are used to erect a monument there to commemorate YHWH's miracles (4:5–7, 20–25); unchiseled stones form the sacrificial altar on Mt. Ebal; and other stones become the stele on which the words of the Torah are written on Mt. Ebal (8:30–32). The ruins of Jericho uphold Joshua's curse over the city (6:26). A pile of stones from Achor Valley cover Achan and his family (7:26), just as executed Canaanite kings lay buried under the rubble of their former habitat (8:28–29; 10:27). These are no longer ordinary places, the habitat no longer mere space. Such storied places are sites of Israel's memory and markers of Israelite identity.[2] They point to the law of YHWH and to the punishment that follows from breaking it.

Finally, a Thirdspatial analysis of this place of victory and struggle. The production of a spatial narrative such as the conquest of the Land betrays the narrator's interest in reconfiguring Israel's ties with the Land and with the Land's "other" inhabitants. One the one hand, the overall message of the conquest account expresses the power of YHWH/Israel over the Land. The victim list in Joshua 12 and the summary of the two military campaigns in the south and north (11:16–23; 12:7–8) convey the decentering of Canaanite hegemony. Secondspatial analysis indicates that the Land is Israel's "inheritance" and that Israel's bond to the Land runs deep into its ground. Although the map of the conquered territories resulting from the summary of all the conquests in 11:16–18 is smaller in size than the area described in Josh 1:4, the conquered Land is now Israel's, and Israel is "its" inhabitants. Canaan has become, as Joshua 11:22 puts it, "the land of the sons of Israel" (see also Josh. 1:2; 2:9, 18, 24; 5:6; 7:9; 9:24; 11:16, 23; 13:2; 21:43; 23:15; 24:3, 18).

On the other hand, even though the conquest account repositions the former Canaanite inhabitants at the margins of the Israelite hierarchy of power, the anxiety over the uncon-quered territories tells a different story. The Canaanite marginality is expressed spatially in a number of ways. Pacified Canaanites like Rahab and the Gibeonites live as insiders of sorts, incorporated but not fully absorbed into the Israelite community. The southwestern margin of the Land stretching along the Mediterranean coast, however, is an area that remains firmly in the hands of Anakim. The outer ring around the map of the conquered lands remains Canaanite at the end of Joshua's conquest. This territory runs from the border with Egypt (Shihor River) in the south to the coastal towns of Gaza, Gath, Ashdod, and Ashkelon, Ekron in the west, to Aphek, Dor in the north, and then moves northeastward to include the region of Lebanon, from Baal-Gad to Lebo Hamath at the foot of Mt. Hermon (11:22; 13:2–5). This "land that remains" unconquered is included in the promised Land but lies outside Israel's control at the end of Joshua's life.

This Canaanite margin—the outer space—not only interrogates the central claims of the conquest narrative (that Joshua took the entire promised Land, 11:23; 21:43), but also trans-forms the binaries (Israelites versus Canaanites) with which the narrative operates. The job of removing the unconquered inhabitants that remain in the Land at the end of Joshua's conquest is reassigned to YHWH alone: God takes it upon himself to finish off the surviving Canaanites (13:6). The departure from the typical approach, in which YHWH instructs Israel in how to defeat the Canaanites, is clearly shown in the ring that frames the book's center—chapter 12. In 11:21, the old binary is yet unchanged: Joshua eliminates the Anakim. In 11:22, where the survival of Anakim in the coastal towns is acknowledged, nothing is said about their future fate. But in 13:6, a change has been introduced: not Joshua, not Israel, but YHWH will deal with the remaining nations. Furthermore, note also in Joshua's farewell address the claim that YHWH, not Israel, will push out the remaining Canaanites from the Land, pro-vided Israel obeys the Lord (23:5). The narrator's charging of God to complete the job of con-quest is, in my view, a tacit recognition that Israel is not able to subdue those groups and that these groups challenge Israel's perception of itself; but, perhaps more importantly, it is a critique of the violence that has occurred before. YHWH no longer instructs Israel con-cerning the death of the survivors. And while the narrator commits YHWH to some level of violence necessary for removing the remaining Canaanites when (and if) he pleases, a lesser violence is to be enacted: YHWH will not "totally destroy" but only "drive out" or "push out" the remaining inhabitants (13:6; 23:5). The timing and manner of this divine action are not disclosed, and that is a good thing. It is now possible that YHWH will not do it. Thirdspatial insight, then, encourages a longer and deeper look into how the "periphery" causes the "cen-ter" to readjust. In this case, the strong Canaanite enclaves that remain after the conquest not only reject Israel's hegemony but create a better, more humane "center."

In conclusion, the narrative of Joshua continues to benefit from the marriage of new liter-ary criticism and historical criticism, on the one hand, and with deconstructive/poststructur-alist/postcolonial/cultural/gender studies, on the other. Disciplinary cross-fertilization and new analytical tools and insights continue to deepen our understanding of the biblical text.

My hope, however, is that close readings that illuminate the beauty and depth of the Joshua narrative will continue to do so with an eye to mitigating the social, political, economic disparity present in our nations. This is to imagine the exegetical task differently: the memories and impulses that cruelly and unnecessarily turn people into "others" must be conquered and replaced with life-giving visions of plenitude and care for each other that the Joshua narrative can also support.

Notes

1. The valuable work of scholars using a comparative literary approach (drawing comparisons with other conquest accounts from Greek, Egyptian, and Neo-Assyrian literatures of the ancient Near East) will not be discussed due to lack of space. For a useful summary of this and other directions of study in Joshua, see Hess (1995).
2. Elsewhere in the book of Joshua we find similar practices: erecting a stone memorial (24: 26–27), (re)naming (14:12–15) and tracing the pilgrimage of ancestors to this land (24:1–3). Such practices attribute special significance to the Land and turn it from "mere space" into a meaningful, if dangerous, "place" (Brueggemann 1977).

References

Assis, Eliyahu. 1999. "The Literary Structure of the Conquest Narrative in the Book of Joshua (chs. 1–11) and Its Meaning." Doctoral thesis. Bar-Ilan University.

Assis, Eliyahu. 2004. "The Choice to Serve God and Assist His People: Rahab and Yael." *Biblica* 85: 82–90.

Assis, Eliyahu. 2005. *From Moses to Joshua and from the Miraculous to the Ordinary: A Literary Analysis of the Conquest Narrative in the Book of Joshua*. Jerusalem: Magnes Press (Hebrew).

Assis, Eliyahu. 2012. "A Literary Approach to Complex Narratives: An Examination of Joshua 3–4." In *The Book of Joshua*, edited by E. Noort, 401–414. Leuven: Peeters.

Beek, M. A. 1994. "Joshua the Saviour." In *Voices from Amsterdam: A Modern Tradition of Reading Biblical Narrative*, edited by M. Kessler, 145–153. Semeia Studies. Atlanta, GA: Scholars Press.

Biddle, Mark E. 1998. "Literary Structures in the Book of Joshua." *Review and Expositor* 95(2): 189–201.

Bird, Phyllis A. 1989. "The Harlot as Heroine: Narrative Art and Social Presupposition in Three Old Testament Texts." In *Narrative Research on the Hebrew Bible*, edited by Miri Amihai, George W. Coats, and Anne M. Solomon. *Semeia* 46: 119–139.

Brenner, Athalya. 2002. "Wide Gaps, Narrow Escapes: I Am Known as Rahab, the Broad." In *First Person: Essays in Biblical Autobiography*, edited by Philip R. Davis, 47–58. Sheffield, Yorkshire: Sheffield Academic Press.

Brueggemann, Walter. 1977. *The Land: Place as Gift, Promise, and Challenge in Biblical Faith*. London: Society for Promoting Christian Knowledge.

Carden, Michael. 2006. "Joshua." In *The Queer Bible Commentary*, edited by Deryn Guest, Robert E. Goss, Mona West, Thomas Bohache, 144–166. London: SCM Press.

Creangă, Ovidiu. 2007. "The Silenced Songs of Victory: Power, Gender and Memory in the Conquest Narrative of Joshua (Josh 1–12)." In *A Question of Sex? Gender and Difference in the*

Hebrew Bible and Beyond, edited by Deborah W. Rooke, 106–123. Hebrew Bible Monograph Series 14. Sheffield, Yorkshire: Sheffield Phoenix Press.

Creangă, Ovidiu. 2010a. "The Conquest of Memory: Israel's Identity and the Commemoration of the Past in Joshua's Conquest Narrative (Josh 1–12)." Doctoral thesis. King's College London.

Creangă, Ovidiu. 2010b. "Variations on the Theme of Masculinity: Joshua's Gender In/stability in the Conquest Narrative (Josh 1–12)." In *Men and Masculinity in the Hebrew Bible and Beyond*, edited by Ovidiu Creangă, 83–109. The Bible in the Modern World 33. Sheffield, Yorkshire: Sheffield Phoenix Press.

de Claissé-Walford, Nancy L. 1998. "Covenant in the Book of Joshua." *Review and Expositor* 95: 227–234.

Ellis, Robert R. 1998. "The Theological Boundaries of Inclusion and Exclusion in the Book of Joshua." *Review and Expositor* 95: 235–250.

Eslinger, Lyle. 1989. *Into the Hands of the Living God*. Sheffield, Yorkshire: Sheffield Academic Press.

Fewell, Danna Nolan. 1995. "Deconstructive Criticism: Achsah and the (E)razed City of Writing." In *Judges and Method: New Approaches in Biblical Studies*, edited by Gale A. Yee, 119–145. Minneapolis: Fortress Press.

Frymer-Kensky, Tikva. 1997. "Reading Rahab." In *Tehillah le-Moshe. Biblical and Judaic Studies in Honor of Moshe Greenberg*, edited by Mordechai Cogan, Barry L. Eichler, Jeffrey H. Tigay, 57–67. Winona Lake, IN: Eisenbrauns.

Gordon, Robert. 2003. "Gibeonite Ruse and Israelite Curse in Joshua 9." In *Covenant as Context: Essays in Honour of E. W. Nicholson*, edited by A. D. H. Mayes and Robert B. Salters, 163–190. Oxford: Oxford University Press.

Gunkel, Hermann. 1906. "Die israelitische Literatur." In *Die Kultur der Gegenwart, I.7: Orientalische Literaturen*, edited by Paul Hinneberg, 53–112. Leipzig-Berlin: B. G. Teubner.

Gunn, David M. 1987. "Joshua and Judges." In *The Literary Guide to the Bible*, edited by Robert Alter and Frank Kermode, 102–121. Cambridge, MA: Belknap Press.

Hall, Sarah Lebhar. 2010. *Conquering Character: The Characterization of Joshua in Joshua 1–11*. New York and London: T&T Clark.

Havrelock, Rachel. 2007. "The Two Maps of Israel's Land." *Journal of Biblical Literature* 126(4): 469–667.

Hawk, L. Daniel. 1991. *Every Promise Fulfilled: Contesting Plots in Joshua*. Literary Currents in Biblical Interpretation. Louisville, KY: Westminster/John Knox Press.

Hawk, L. Daniel. 1992. "Strange Houseguests: Rahab, Lot and the Dynamics of Deliverance." In *Reading Between Texts: Intertextuality and the Hebrew Bible*, edited by Danna Nolan Fewell, 89–97. Louisville, KY: Westminster/John Knox Press.

Hawk, L. Daniel. 1997. "The Problem with Pagans." In *Reading Bibles, Writing Bodies: Identity and the Book*, edited by Timothy K. Beal and David M. Gunn, 153–163. London and New York: Routledge.

Hawk, L. Daniel. 2000. *Joshua*. Berit Olam Studies in the Hebrew Narrative and Poetry Series. Collegeville, MN: Liturgical Press.

Hawk, L. Daniel. 2010. *Joshua in 3-D. A Commentary on Biblical Conquest and Manifest Destiny*. Eugene, OR: Cascade Books.

Hess, Richard S. 1995. "Studies in the Book of Joshua." *Themelios* 20(3): 12–15.

Jobling, David. 1987. "The Jordan a Boundary: Transjordan in Israel's Ideological Geography." In *The Sense of Biblical Narrative: Structural Analyses in the Hebrew Bible*, vol. 2, 88–134. Journal for the Study of the Old Testament Supplement Series 39. Sheffield, Yorkshire: Sheffield Academic Press.

Knight, Douglas A. 2002. "Joshua 22 and the Ideology of Space." In *"Imagining" Biblical Worlds: Studies in Spatial, Social and Historical Constructs in Honor of James W. Flanagan*, edited by David M. Gunn and Paula McNutt, 51–63. Sheffield, Yorkshire: Sheffield Academic Press.

Koopmans, William T. 1990. *Joshua 24 as Poetic Narrative*. Journal for the Study of the Old Testament Supplement Series 93. Sheffield, Yorkshire: Sheffield Academic Press.

Lefebvre, Henri. 1974. *La production de l'espace*. Paris: Anthropos.

Mitchell, Gordon. 1993. *Together in the Land: A Reading of the Book of Joshua*. Journal for the Study of the Old Testament Supplement Series 134. Sheffield, Yorkshire: JSOT Press.

Muilenburg, James. 1969. "Form Criticism and Beyond." *Journal of Biblical Literature* 88(1): 1–18.

Noth, Martin. 1943. *Überlieferungsgeschichtliche Studien*. Halle: M. Niemeyer. English translation: 1981. *The Deuteronomistic History*, 2nd ed. Translated by J. Doull. Journal for the Study of the Old Testament Supplement Series 15. Sheffield, Yorkshire: JSOT Press.

Patrick, Dale, and Allen Scult. 1990. *Rhetoric and Biblical Interpretation*. Sheffield, Yorkshire: Sheffield Academic Press.

Polzin, Robert. 1980. *Moses and the Deuteronomist: A Literary Study of the Deuteronomistic History. Part 1: Deuteronomy, Joshua, Judges*. New York: Seabury Press.

Rowlett, Lori L. 1992. "Inclusion, Exclusion and Marginality in the Book of Joshua." *Journal for the Study of the Old Testament* 55: 15–23.

Rowlett, Lori L. 1996. *Joshua and the Rhetoric of Violence*. Journal for the Study of the Old Testament Supplement Series 226. Sheffield, Yorkshire: Sheffield Academic Press.

Runions, Erin. 2011. "From Disgust to Humor: Rahab's Queer Affect." In *Bible Trouble: Queer Reading at the Boundaries of Biblical Scholarship*, edited by Teresa J. Hornsby and Ken Stone, 45–74. Atlanta, GA: Society of Biblical Literature.

Sakenfeld, Katharine Doob. 1998. "Numbers." In *Women's Bible Commentary: Expanded Edition*, edited by Carol A. Newsom and S. H. Ringe, 49–56. Louisville, KY: Westminster/ John Knox Press.

Shemesh, Yael. 2007. "A Gender Perspective on the Daughters of Zelophehad: Bible, Talmudic Midrash, and Modern Feminist Midrash." *Biblical Interpretation* 15: 80–109.

Sherwood, Aaron. 2006. "A Leader's Misleading and a Prostitute's Profession: A Re-examination of Joshua 2." *Journal for the Study of the Old Testament* 31(1): 43–61.

Soja, Edward W. 1996. *Thirdspace: Journeys to Los Angeles and Other Real-and-Imagined Places*. Cambridge, MA: Blackwell Publishers.

Štrba, Blažej. 2008. *Take off Your Sandals from Your Feet! An Exegetical Study of Josh 5: 13–15*. Österreichische Biblische Studien. Frankfurt am Main: Peter Lang.

van Bekkum, Koert. 2011. *From Conquest to Coexistence: Ideology and Antiquarian Intent in the Historiography of Israel's Settlement in Canaan*. Leiden: Brill.

Warrior, Robert Allen. 1995. "Canaanites, Cowboys, and Indians: Deliverance, Conquest, and Liberation Theology." In *Voices from the Margins: Interpreting the Bible in the Third World*, edited by R. S. Sugirtharajah, 277–285. Maryknoll, NY: Orbis.

Wellhausen, Julius. 1882. *Prolegomena zur Geschichte Israel*, Berlin: Reimer. 1885. *Prolegomena to the History of Israel*. Translated by J. Southerland Black and Allan Menzies. Edinburg: Adam and Charles Black.

CHAPTER 14

JUDGING YHWH IN THE BOOK OF JUDGES

DERYN GUEST

JUDGES: the ancient Adventure Book for Boys. Heroic derring-do, improvised weaponry, spies, mutilations, escapades, life-or-death passwords, plus an undercurrent of eroticism and death for those who intuit the narratorial nods and winks; valiant and villainous activities are offset by moments of pathos and tragedy, and yet bawdy, comic humor prevails. An opening account of a partial conquest of Canaan locates us at the frontier, where Israel quickly forgets the deity who brought them there in favor of the indigenous deities. This prompts a twitchy deity to become increasingly exasperated with his recalcitrant people. Giving them over to the hands of oppressors, YHWH abandons his people until they protest sufficiently for him to raise up a Judge to defeat those enemies. The energy of the text drives readers rapidly through a series of Judges—Othniel, Ehud, Deborah, Gideon, Abimelech, Jephthah, Samson—ever worsening in moral fiber, to the unhappy culmination where Israelite tribes do battle with themselves rather than enemies, and, in an ironic debacle, far more women are abducted and raped than the one the tribes set out to avenge. Of course, it could be hailed as an Adventure Book for Girls, containing as it does the battle-rousing Song of the Woman of Flames, the tent-peg triumph of Wild Mountain Goat, and the erotic game-play of Delilah, whose name has become synonymous with the Femme Fatale. But such conquests cannot redeem the portrayal of a sacrificed daughter, a gang-raped woman, or the presentation of women as acceptable war booty. Women must read against their own interests if they are to enjoy the raucous romp of this text. However, this is a storyworld where men aren't always men, or women women, since the narrator playfully subverts categories of sex and gender, rendering them permeable and fragile (Guest 2011). And a Boy's Own reading is quickly compromised by the stupidity and fragile masculinity of certain male characters. It is hardly surprising, then, that such an intriguing text, rich with irony and literary artistry, has attracted narrative critics.

Historical-critical scholars noted the vividness, scathing humor, and sexual innuendo during their dissection of source material. They posited an earthy layer of folk tradition, characterized by coarseness, puns, pleasure taken in physical defects, and an unadulter-ated vivacious buoyant flavor; markedly different to the serious theological outlook of the

Deuteronomist. Various hypotheses emerged on how this earthy stratum was collated into a "Retterbuch," surrounded with insertions of material of various dates and provenance. Prioritizing interest in the transmission history of the text inevitably de-privileged overall coherence as Judges was subjected to an approach that tends to reduce biblical texts to "a mosaic of assorted literary scraps more or less cobbled together in a recognisable sequence" (Jasper 1987, 7).

The tide turned with a brief essay by J. P. U. Lilley (1967, 95) who called for a "fresh appraisal of Judges as a literary work, starting from the assumption of authorship rather than of redaction." Such an assumption was warranted by the evidence for "literary initiative and ability" of an author who "cast the book in its present mould, having conceived in his own mind the general idea and plan" (95). His argument, succinctly made, claims that the selection of material and its arrangement indicate an organizing hand across the entire text.

Further short studies followed, demonstrating this organizing hand in more detail. Gros Louis (1974) noted how Judges 1:1–2.5 could be seen as a deliberately contrived prologue with thematic connections to the central section, rather than a conglomeration of old traditions. Achsah thus constitutes a prototype of the qualities of opportunism, shrewdness, and mastery of the men subsequently exhibited by Deborah, Jael, Delilah, and the "certain woman" who throws the millstone on Abimelech's head. Likewise, the Bethel story introduces the motif of treachery, which will re-echo in the stories of Ehud, Jael, Abimelech, and Samson.

Gooding detected a symmetrical, concentric structure organizing the book. Samson thus connects and contrasts with Othniel, Jephthah with Ehud, and Abimelech with Deborah until we come to the Gideon, the hinge on which the structure pivots. Bookending this central section is a double introduction (1–2.5; 2.6–3.6) balanced by a double epilogue (chapters 17–18; 19–21) with shared but contrasting themes. Introduction I contains enquiry of the Lord, Othniel's winning of his wife, the failure of the Benjamites to drive out the Jebusites, and the weeping at Bochim. This is mirrored in Epilogue II, which opens with another enquiry of the Lord, the story of Benjamites getting wives, a Levite avoiding Jebus only to find horror in Gibeah and the people weeping again, this time at Bethel. Gooding (1982, 72) did not dispute that Judges might contain source material but believed there was strong evidence to justify that "the work of compiling them into their present form was the work of one unifying mind."

These pioneering papers were followed by a flurry of publications focused on the literary artistry of individual narratives. Examples include Globe (1974, 1990), Murray (1979), Exum (1980, 1981), Boogaart (1985), Revell (1985), Beem (1991), Satterthwaite (1992), and Vincent (2000). They paved the way for further articles (Exum 1990) and monographs that would investigate more fully the narrative coherence of the entire book of Judges. The studies of Webb (1987), Schneider (2000), and Wong (2006), have demonstrated how Judges is largely the work of a single controlling genius, using short- and long-range word/theme connections and a deep, rich intertextuality where one story informs another. In fact, Wong persuasively argues that we can only discern fully the principal message of the text (progressive deterioration from YHWH's kingly authority) when the central section is read as a deliberate adjunct of the prologue and epilogue. Meant to shock, the epilogue jolts the reader back to previous moments in the earlier stories and thereby "force[s] the reader to go back and re-evaluate the earlier narratives" (Wong 2006, 138). Wong's close analysis enables him to conclude that Judges is "an artful creation of a single author who, in spite of making use of diverse source materials, was nonetheless the one primarily responsible for shaping the entire book into its current form" (255).

The scathing humor of Judges, observed by the historical-critical commentators noted above, also features in narrative studies. Radday and Brenner (1990, 63) pick up on some of the comical names in Judges ("Superblack Double-Villain" for Cushan-rishathaim). Brenner (1994) reads Ehud's story with attention to the way humor satirizes the foreign ruler. Klein (1988) identifies elements of the comic in her treatment of irony in Judges. Davidson (2008, 93–106) finds in "carnivalesque-grotesque" a way to understand the ribald humor of Judges. The "carnivalesque-grotesque" contains several features, such as dismemberment, a topsy-turvy world, disguises and masks, parody, travesty, and burlesque. Such a reading reinforces the view that the primary genre of Judges is not history, but entertainment with a serious and didactic edge of the kind Gunn (1978, 61) mentions: "entertainment which demands the active engagement of those being entertained, which challenges their intellect, their emotions, their understanding of people, of society, and of themselves." The question of who can afford to share in these bawdy stories, however, merits critical attention.

Most concur that the chief rhetorical purpose of this single author is to advocate monarchy. It is not entirely desirable, argues Amit (1999), but is better than the instability and chaos that emerges from the Judges experiment, which has proved insufficient to keep Israel faithful. O'Connell (1996, 343) goes further, arguing that Judges endorses a certain kind of king: "a divinely appointed Judahite king who ... upholds such deuteronomic ideals as the need to expel foreigners from the land and the need to maintain intertribal loyalty to YHWH's cult and his regulations concerning social justice." For Schneider (2000, xiv), the focus is on mechanisms by which leaders arise, their relationship with the deity and the effects of that relationship on the wider community. Wong (2006: 252), contrarily, suggests that YHWH's kingship is advocated only because it may be able to halt the deterioration of the YHWH-Israel relationship. Jobling, however, reading Judges as a text that has its closure, structurally, in 1 Samuel 12, argues that the interest in leadership has no decisive argument in favor of one kind or another. The intervening periods between each judge could have been times when Israel experienced the direct rule of Yahweh, but that potential floundered because Israel always lapses into apostasy. Overall, Jobling argues that the editors had no easily definable opinion, nor were they trying to balance opposing viewpoints; rather they were talking aloud about a conundrum, a "contradiction that Israel should go on living *within*" (1986, 46).

A second rhetorical interest is the exaltation of YHWH. For Polzin (1980), it is YHWH's sovereign freedom that must be conveyed. Over and against Israel's preference for human insurance and their feeble attempts to guarantee divine insurance stands YHWH, who alone possesses knowledge, who is unpredictable, unknowable, therefore free of any human control. O'Connell's preferred phrase is YHWH's "glorification," seen in his involvement in battles that overwhelm supposedly strong foreign kings and their machinery of war, and in his manipulation of situations. Amit's emphasis on signs also fits within this rhetorical concern, since the signs demonstrate that history is not a random series of unrelated events but is subject to God's control.

A third rhetorical purpose, perhaps foundational for all others, concerns the relationship between YHWH and Israel. The book, as Schneider (2000, xv) states, is "fundamentally concerned with the relationship of Israel to its deity", and I will say more about this central issue.

Additional rhetorical interests include: tribal conflict and unity, social justice, the satirization of the foreigner, the denigration of the House of Saul. The latter interest is covered well by O'Connell (1996) and Brettler (1989), who note how the closing chapters of Judges cohere with narrative elements in Saul's story. The way in which the exile and the subsequent rebuilding of identity in the post-exilic period pervades Judges is also noted by Fewell (1997). The traumatic experience of exile, she argues, permeates the entire Hebrew Bible, and Judges can never be fully understood without appreciating the pervasive and unrelenting attempt to come to terms with the fall of Jerusalem and the dislocation of the people. Judges thus reruns Genesis in an attempt to rewrite its family (foreign) history, and explain why Israel ultimately lost the land, simultaneously dealing with the post-exilic need to construct a distinctive face of Israel.

While the multiplicity of conclusions regarding the central message of Judges may be problematic for some (e.g., Wong 2006), this phenomenon reminds us that readers will inevitably find rhetorical concerns in the text that, to some extent, mirror their own interests. Moreover, it is also possible to deconstruct that supposed coherence of the text in order to discern a countercoherence in Judges, where rhetorical interests are just as evidently at work but have been successfully hidden from view. In an astonishingly deft manner, Bal identifies repressed elements of the text to trouble the very notion of coherence and to look at what interests are at stake when commentators try to posit coherence. For Bal (1998, 16–17), Judges is actually just as much "about lineage, fatherhood, . . . virginity, mothers, and violence . . . sex, obedience and death. And . . . power—its dissymmetrical distribution, the conflicts and competition it generates, its consequences for those who have it and for those who lack it". Her work combines narrative criticism with tools drawn from feminist theory, psychological studies, artistic representations, and deconstructive techniques in order to bring to the center the themes and interests that have been marginalized. Uncomfortably insightful, her reading addresses the values of the author and of commentators who have situated women as pornographic victims of rape and murder, on whose backs the judges are supposedly taught valuable lessons by the deity.

Appearing before the critical study of masculinities had emerged, Bal examines the fragile masculinities on display in this text, where ownership of women is needed to shore up masculine identity, status, and honor. Using Freud, she analyzes how the purity of the women, the emphasis on their not having known a man, demonstrates how memories of a rival male cannot be tolerated. Men require monopoly over women's sexual experiences, and virginity offers this monopoly and "promise of attachment" (1988, 54). But once deflowered, the woman shifts from "an innocent and ignorant virgin" and becomes that "other" kind of woman—the "deadly, phallic woman" (1988, 55). Bal shifted the ground of commentary work, indicating how scholars need to unpack far more than the literary artistry of the text, how they need to stand at a critical distance from it and deconstruct its rhetoric, particularly when it comes to issues of gender. Feminist narrative critics have furthered the discussion, combining narrative criticism with their political commitments in order to analyze the effects of Judges (primarily) for women readers (e.g., Fewell and Gunn 1990, 1993; Fewell 1992; Brenner 1993, 1999; Exum 1995).

The extension of gender theory into the study of masculinities promises a new fruitful avenue of research. It enables us to investigate how the manipulation of gender norms and deliberate subversion of the sexed stability of characters contribute to themes of degeneration, or leadership; how Judges contributes to, and subverts, biblical hegemonic masculinity; how gender is manipulated to construct deviant sexualities. And YHWH should not escape scrutiny in such studies. He is the book's alpha male, and the effects of his interventions on the human males in the story world of Judges is worthy of critical investigation, as the remainder of this chapter will demonstrate.

Yhwh: Quite the Character

Character studies have been a staple of narrative approaches, but Yhwh rarely makes an appearance in them. Alter (1992, 23) argues that the invisible, supernatural force and inscrutability of the divine mean that "intellectual humility" is called for, together with the recognition that we are not dealing with "an antiquarian book" but with texts where humans are "confronted, challenged, confounded by a reality beyond human ken". There is little point in trying to understand Yhwh as a character because "the repeated point of the biblical writers is that we cannot make sense of God in human terms" (22–23). Yet Alter acknowledges that this inscrutable deity *is* the construct of the narrator, who "presumed to know, quite literally, what God knows, as on occasion he may remind us by reporting God's assessments and intentions, or even what He says to Himself" (1981, 157). Alter seems to require readers to be tacit in the game, granting the narrator knowledge that we know humans cannot possibly have.

Others are less at ease with such alignment. Bal is critical of any approaches that exonerate Yhwh by not evaluating him as a character among other characters. For her, it is "precisely this methodological rigour that allows a narratorial analysis to become truly critical" (1988, 34). Gunn and Fewell (1993, 81–89) include Yhwh in their chapter on characterization and it is worth noting why they distance themselves from the narrator's perspective. Using Absalom's rebellion as illustration, they note how the deity manipulates events to ensure that David is not betrayed to his death. David's women, however, do not experience divine support; they are disposable pawns, raped by Absalom and then left in David's house to see out their days as shamed widows. As Gunn and Fewell comment, the scales of this God are tilted. He "seems transfixed by his chosen 'son', oblivious to his chosen 'daughters'" (1993, 88).

If we turn to commentaries written with a believing audience in mind, we find that the character of God is well scrutinized. Arguing that Judges is entirely relevant to contemporary issues in society, McCann (2002, 2) states that "nothing will be right with our individual selves, our churches, or our world unless we, the people of God, manifest steadfast loyalty to God alone." Alienation from God, or worship of "something other than God" brings about "destructive and ultimately deadly" results (3). Here, then, we find acknowledgment of some of the deity's troublesome traits: the terrible wrath, vengeance, and the jealous demand for sole allegiance. However, whereas a narrative approach combined with insights from masculinity studies make this a starting point for a critical assessment of the book's main character, McCann encourages the reader to see these traits as necessary for instruction.

The central question posed by the narrator, for McCann, is, "Will Israel worship and serve God alone?" (2002, 15). The assumption is that this is a legitimate question for a theocratic author to be posing. And no doubt it is. But if one stands outside the community of faith, or if one has carved out a more critical, questioning position within it, then such a question could be indicative of the deity's obsessively megalomaniacal self-interest. A faithful reading resolves problems by reinforcing the narrator's "profound and fundamental theological claims that God alone is sovereign, and hence that the chief end of Israel is to honor, trust, and obey God alone" (24). But this naturalizes YHWH without evaluating his gendered performance. The following discussion considers what could be gained by looking at YHWH's character in ways informed by studies of masculinity, psychological, and queer theory. Bearing in mind Lasine's point that the book of Judges provides only its own textual outlook on the character of YHWH (see "Characterizing God in His/Our Own Image" in this volume), six character traits can be summarized as follows.

In Judges's opening verses YHWH is portrayed as the *earth's landlord*. Humans occupy territory only on a temporary and contingent basis. In 1:2 the tribes defer to him, asking who should begin the work of dispossessing the existing inhabitants, and he dictates that it will be given into the hand of Judah. Continued occupancy of the land depends on obedience to the tenancy agreement. YHWH sends messengers to remind the tribes of their terms and also sets up an experiment: leaving other nations present to test those who have no experience of war, and to find out whether Israel will be obedient to the laws he gave to Moses. The cosmic landlord, having set up a control mechanism, is also the panopticician who keeps underling males under scrutiny.

YHWH is also the *supreme military strategist and commander*, the proper object of all military inquiries. When inquiry is inadequate, disaster ensues. Eleven tribes thus end up massacring their own brothers in the final chapters as "YHWH, consulted only when the vital decisions have been made, plays out with ironic detachment his role as a god of convenience" (Gunn 1989, 119). He directs warfare strategies and intervenes to ensure the desired outcome. Sometimes an active part is given to the Israelites—in 1.4 they go and fight and capture foreign kings—but mostly YHWH accomplishes the rout himself, as in 4.15, 23. Judges 5 casts his military might in cosmic terms. His marching makes the earth tremble, the heavens cascade with water and mountains quake. And yet, there is a rather endearing, humanlike desire to be honored for such military maneuvers.

He is also the *grand manipulator of circumstances*, the master of the scene, putting individuals in each other's sights (Samson and the Philistine woman), sending Israel into victory, or into a disastrous cul-de-sac (the decimation of the Benjamites). Although humans do the actual "acting," YHWH is the ultimate game player, and humans follow through.

He is the *fertility fixer*. The theme of the barren woman, pervasive through the Primary History, recurs in Judges 13. "Barren," however, is rather a misnomer when it is YHWH's intervention that can close or open a women's womb. Her fertility is in *his* hands, not in the condition of her gynecological organs. He is the Gatekeeper of the Womb, and can enhance a woman's status by opening it and granting her sons, but with inevitable knock-on effects for the husband. Brenner (1997, 57) notes how motherhood "furnishes YHWH with a chance to interfere and prove his ability to change the situation." If we consider how colliding masculinities are caught up in this fertility scenario, that phrase "prove his ability" takes on fresh resonance for Judges 13, where one male is seriously sidelined by divine intervention. In their discussion of this text, Gunn and Fewell (1993, 64–68) note how Manoah, already unable to impregnate his wife, is further marginalized by being cut out of the dialogue between his wife and YHWH's messenger. His attempts to offer hospitality are maladroit, he fails to intuit the messenger's divine origins until the messenger ascends miraculously to heaven, and his wife names her son without consultation. Such an inept masculine performance is consistent with the rhetorical concern to exalt YHWH. Manoah rather understandably seeks the name of the man whose encounter with his wife will result in pregnancy, but the messenger points to the inscrutability of YHWH. So, focus on the glorification of YHWH who intervenes in history as fertility fixer comes at the expense of Manoah, who is sidestepped and emasculated, his sexual potency denied. He might be the child's putative father, but Yнwн has been here before him.

Human males, ultimately, are no real match for Yнwн. He is the *dominant* male to whom human males must submit, and Amit clearly recognizes how the deity's dominant masculinity has consequences for his servants. When God is "the one and exclusive source of deliverance and quiet, or of punishment," then "the saving hero, like the enslaving enemy, plays a merely secondary role—to assist in the accomplishment of the divine plan—and by the nature of things tends to lose his heroic charisma" (1999, 46; see also Sawyer [2002] for a wider analysis of this effect). Amit, here, writes more as a faithful interpreter than a gender theorist, but as is often the case, such interpreters discern the authority of the deity and its impact for other characters clearly. God is the main controller and principal actor; humans are secondary.

Nonetheless, Yнwн remains, a *jealous* deity who tolerates no divine rival for human males' loyalties. Successful continuation in the land depends on Israel abandoning all other deities and the destruction of their altars (6.25). The entire judges cycle is set in motion by his jealousy: selling Israel into the hands of enemies when they go astray. His indignation about their continued unfaithfulness comes to a head when Israel cries out to him yet again in chapter 10. Depending on one's perspective, Yнwн is moved to indignation by Israel's troubles, has an outburst of vehement anger or, in a rather camp display, a tantrum about their disloyalty, and abandons them in a huff.

Further features of Yнwн's characterization in Judges could be explored, but the foregoing provides sufficient material to see what happens when we relocate this analysis to a place where narrative criticism is also informed by queer theory, psychology, and the study of masculinities.

First, codes of honor and shame, culturally key for men in the ancient world, also relate to Yнwн. His acts of deliverance might be understood conventionally as indicators of his steadfast love, but they also point to an alpha male's need for honor. The supreme military commander wants to ensure that he gets the credit for Israel's victories. It is Yнwн, not Gideon, who will strike down every Midianite (6:16; 7:22), and he ensures that his recognition does not get redirected by instructing Gideon to cut the size of his army (7:2). There is vulnerability here. Despite his cosmic-sized interventions, it is all too plausible that the judges themselves will receive the plaudits or prove unable to resist self-aggrandizement (as when Gideon's apparent humility and resistance to kingship is undercut by his actions). Ensuring that humans do not take credit for these military achievements, the narrator, aligned with the deity, glorifies the sovereign God for the signs of his omnipotence and favor of Israel. The rhetoric of the text does not encourage us to consider how far the representation of Yнwн is caught up with the cultural dictates of honor and shame, whereby he needs human allegiance to give him recognition and status.

Second, the violence sanctioned or directed by Yнwн could be analyzed as part of a broader phenomenon. Whitehead (2002, 38) has suggested that some "dominant forms and codes of masculinity" have violence written into the script and that we need to examine the ways in which discourses reify what it is to be masculine. While Whitehead is talking to our current situation, Judges includes many of the acts he cites (sexual assault, mass violence, mass rape, random violence and torture). Yнwн does not escape from this association. In fact, one of his traits is a blazing anger (2:14; 3:7; 10:7). Disloyalty provokes this anger

(2:11, 14) and he responds by using the power of his "hand" to put Israel under the foreign oppressors. The foreigners are given this lease to oppress; they do not achieve it for themselves. YHWH's jealousy, his inability to tolerate rivals, is integrally related to violent outcomes. Feminists have long noted the problems associated with the (metaphorical) actions of an angry, violent deity, as have scholars such as Blumenthal (1993), Penchansky (1999), and Linafelt (1998). Analysis of how codes of ancient masculinity play into this characterization merits further investigation, building on the works assembled by Creangă (2010) and Creangă and Smit (2014).

Third, male vulnerability also informs the way YHWH is constructed. Israel may experience instructive punishment, but God is vulnerable to hurt and cannot let go. McCann (2002, 25) writes that God's steadfast love means that he "simply cannot and will not be unfaithful to an inveterately unfaithful people," Webb describes the theology of Judges as one "of conflict in which both parties suffer, and in which Israel survives only because Yahweh does not give up on her and simply walk away" (54). He notes God's unwavering commitment to the relationship: "Judges shows that not even Israel's apparently incurable unfaithfulness to God could thwart his determination that its history as a chosen nation would continue" (55). From a confessional perspective it is easy to see divine determination as a comforting trait, but psychoanalytically it could be seen as an assertion of power by the dominant party who will not let the other self-develop (for a wider discussion of this phenomenon, see Lasine, "Characterizing God in His/Our Own Image" in this volume).

Object relations theory provides a lens through which this can be fruitfully explored. Concerned with how infants develop in relation with their primary caregivers, attachment/dependency, and how maturation and individuation are facilitated, the work of British theorists, such as Winnicott (1965a, 1965b) or Bowlby (1969, 1973, 1980), is rarely applied to biblical texts. Indeed, as Gunn and Fewell (1993, 48) note, the dissuasion against doing this has been strong, given fears that one might be applying "modern psychological categories on texts entirely too ancient and different from contemporary experience.". However, using object relations theory is not "psychologizing" biblical characters so much as using psychological insights to understand the relational dynamics of the text. One of the instructive features of object relations theory is the notion of ego strength and the way in which a child must be permitted to develop this in order to grow into a healthy, mature adult. Arguably, the repeated acts of apostasy that the reader witnesses in Judges are opportunities for rebellious ego-strength development, to which God responds with "instructive" punishment and an overwhelming determination to stay in relationship with his people no matter what. But how far does that powerful determination undermine any genuine opportunity for Israel's self-development? If we step outside the rhetoric of the text and consider the character of God and his relationship with Israel from a position informed with insights from psychoanalysis, as did Bal, then we might look at this relationship from the perspective of attachment and codependency, ego strength, and individuation, and examine the stakes for both parties. Studies that are now discussing the psychological marks of trauma on the text, such as Kamionkowski (2003) and Janzen (2012), encourage such investigations.

Who, then, is this implied author and how are his interests served by being aligned so closely with this deity. If we are not to fall too easily into theological resolutions that suggest YHWH is inscrutable, then study of the implied author's motivations and context is required. Here, narrative approaches and historical-critical interest in the transmission of the text find a reconnection point. However, they alone cannot unlock the psychodynamics of what is going on in Judges. Approaches that have tools to deconstruct the power relations of a text and its repressed ideological assumptions are needed. So, while Rowlett's (2001) queer reading, informed by dynamics of sadomasochism, might initially appear an unlikely discourse to link with Judges, her work actually highlights the dominant-submissive relationship between YHWH-Israel. The cycle of YHWH's deliverance and abandonment is recast as YHWH alternating between "top" positions where he does intervene powerfully, and "bottom" positions where he relinquishes power. What this might mean is that YHWH's alternating positions met the needs of our narrator who, taking a "top" position himself, imposes a particular manifesto on his generation. His generation participates in religious diversity and has competing loyalties, but the narrator's agenda is one of zealously upheld monolatry. By describing repeated cyclical patterns of cultic fidelity and apostasy, where YHWH repeatedly resists the capitulating role and exerts power to bring the people back into submission, the narrator reiterates his message: religious diversity must repeatedly be put down. He has to exert his own agenda strongly and repeatedly in order to bring a recalcitrant generation to heel.

The work for future generations of Judges scholars is exciting. Narrative approaches have laid an excellent foundation for understanding Judges. Now is the time to further that work with gender theory and psychological insight that can evaluate critically the relationship dynamics of the text. Above all, it is time to recognize that the narrator is aligned to such an extent with YHWH that we are drawn to the inevitable conclusion that they are one and the same. YHWH's agenda is the narrator's agenda. The narrator/YHWH can evade scholarly critics no longer.

REFERENCES

Alter, Robert. 1981. *The Art of Biblical Narrative.* New York: Basic Books.

Alter, Robert. 1992. *The World of Biblical Literature.* London: SPCK.

Amit, Yairah. 1999. *The Book of Judges: The Art of Editing.* Translated from the Hebrew by Jonathan Chipman. Biblical Interpretation Series 38. London/Boston, Köln: Brill.

Bal, Mieke. 1988. *Death and Dissymmetry. The Politics of Coherence in the Book of Judges.* Chicago Studies in the History of Judaism. Chicago: University of Chicago Press.

Beem, Beverley. 1991. "The Minor Judges: A Literary Reading of Some Very Short Stories." In *The Bible Canon in Comparative Perspective*, edited by K. Lawson Younger, Jr., William W. Hallow, and Bernard F. Batt, 147–172. Scripture in Context 4. Lampeter: Edwin Mellen.

Blumenthal, David R. 1993. *Facing the Abusing God: A Theology of Protest.* Louisville, KY: Westminster/John Knox Press.

Boogaart, T. A. 1985. "Stone for Stone: Retribution in the Story of Abimelech and Shechem." *Journal for the Study of the Old Testament* 32: 45–56.

Bowlby, J. 1969. *Attachment.* Vol. 1 of *Attachment and Loss.* New York: Basic Books.

Bowlby, J. 1973. *Separation: Anxiety and Anger.* Vol. 2 of *Attachment and Loss.* New York: Basic Books.

Bowlby, J. 1980. *Loss, Sadness and Depression.* Vol. 3 of *Attachment and Loss.* New York: Basic Books.

Brenner, Athalya. 1994." Who's Afraid of Feminist Criticism?' Who's Afraid of Biblical Humour? The Case of the Obtuse Foreign Ruler in the Hebrew Bible." *Journal for the Study of the Old Testament* 63: 38–55.

Brenner, Athalya. 1997. *The Intercourse of Knowledge: On Gendering Desire and "Sexuality" in the Hebrew Bible*. Biblical Interpretation Series 26. Leiden: Brill.

Brenner Athalya, ed. 1993. *A Feminist Companion to Judges*. Feminist Companion to the Bible 4. Sheffield, Yorkshire: Sheffield Academic Press.

Brenner Athalya, ed. 1999. *Judges: A Feminist Companion to the Bible*. Feminist Companion to the Bible. Second series 4. Sheffield, Yorkshire: Sheffield Academic Press.

Brettler, Marc. 1989. "The Book of Judges: Literature as Politics." *Journal of Biblical Literature* 108(3): 395–418.

Creangă, Ovidiu, ed. 2010. *Men and Masculinity in the Hebrew Bible and Beyond*. The Bible in the Modern World 33. Sheffield, Yorkshire: Sheffield Phoenix Press.

Creangă, Ovidiu, and Peter-Ben Smit, ed. 2014. *Biblical Masculinities Foregrounded*. Hebrew Bible Monographs 62. Sheffield, Yorkshire: Sheffield Phoenix Press.

Davidson, E. T. A. 2008. *Intricacy, Design, and Cunning in the Book of Judges*. Philadelphia, PA: Xlibris.

Exum, J. Cheryl. 1980. "Promise and Fulfillment: Narrative Art in Judges 13." *Journal of Biblical Literature* 99: 43–59.

Exum, J. Cheryl. 1981. "Aspects of Symmetry and Balance in the Samson Saga." *Journal for the Study of the Old Testament* 19: 3–29.

Exum, J. Cheryl. 1990. "The Centre Cannot Hold: Thematic and Textual Instabilities in Judges." *Catholic Biblical Quarterly* 52: 410–431.

Exum, J. Cheryl. 1995. "Feminist Criticism: Whose Interests Are Being Served?" In *Judges and Method: New Approaches in Biblical Studies*, edited by Gale A. Yee, 65–90. Minneapolis, MN: Fortress Press.

Fewell, Danna Nolan. 1992. "Judges." In *The Women's Bible Commentary*, edited by Carol A. Newsom and Sharon Ringe, 56–77. Louisville, KY: Westminster John Knox.

Fewell, Danna Nolan. 1997. "Imagination, Method, and Murder: Un/Framing the Face of Post-Exilic Israel." In *Reading Bibles, Writing Bodies: Identity and the Book*, edited by Timothy K. Beal and David M. Gunn, 132–152. London: Routledge.

Fewell, Danna Nolan, and David M. Gunn. 1990. "Controlling Perspectives. Women, Men and the Authority of Violence in Judges 4 and 5." *Journal of the American Academy of Religion* 58(3): 389–411.

Fewell, Danna Nolan, and David M. Gunn. 1993. "Possessed and Dispossessed." In *Gender, Power, and Promise: The Subject of the Bible's First Story*, 117–140. Nashville, TN: Abingdon.

Globe, Alexander. 1974. "The Literary Structure and Unity of the Song of Deborah." *Journal of Biblical Literature* 83: 493–512.

Globe, Alexander. 1990. "'Enemies Round About': Disintegrative Structure in the Book of Judges." In *Mappings of the Biblical Terrain: The Bible as Text*, edited by Vincent L. Tollers and John Maier, 233–251. Lewisburg, PA: Bucknell University Review.

Gooding, D. W. 1982. "The Composition of the Book of Judges." *Eretz Israel* 16: 70–79.

Gros Louis, Kenneth R. R. 1974. "The Book of Judges." In *Literary Interpretations of Biblical Narratives*, edited by in Kenneth R. R. Gros Louis, James Stokes Ackerman and Thayer S. Warshaw, 141–162. Nashville, TN: Abingdon Press.

Gunn, David M. 1978. *The Story of King David: Genre and Interpretation*. Journal for the Study of the Old Testament Supplement Series 6. Sheffield, Yorkshire: JSOT Press.

Gunn, David M. 1989. "Joshua and Judges." In *The Literary Guide to the Bible*, edited by Robert Alter and Frank Kermode, 102–121. London: Fontana Press.

Guest, Deryn. 2011. "From Gender Reversal to Genderfuck: Reading Jael through a Lesbian Lens." In *Bible Trouble: Queer Reading at the Boundaries of Biblical Scholarship*, edited by Teresa J. Hornsby and Ken Stone, 9–43. Semeia Studies. Atlanta, GA: Society of Biblical Literature.

Gunn, David M., and Danna Nolan Fewell. 1993. *Narrative in the Hebrew Bible*. Oxford Bible Series. Oxford: Oxford University Press.

Janzen, David. 2012. *The Violent Gift: Trauma's Subversion of the Deuteronomistic History's Narrative*. Library of Hebrew Bible/Old Testament Studies 561. New York: T & T Clark International.

Jasper, David. 1987. *The New Testament and the Literary Imagination*. Basingstoke: Macmillan.

Jobling, David. 1986. "The Sense of Biblical Narrative. Structural Analyses in the Hebrew Bible II." Journal for the Study of the Old Testament Supplement Series 39. Sheffield, Yorkshire: Sheffield Academic Press.

Kamionkowski, S. Tamar. 2003. *Gender Reversal and Cosmic Chaos: A Study in the Book of Ezekiel*. Journal for the Study of the Old Testament Supplement Series, 368. Sheffield, Yorkshire: Sheffield Academic Press.

Klein, Lillian. 1988. *The Triumph of Irony in the Book of Judges*. Journal for the Study of the Old Testament Supplement Series 68. Sheffield, Yorkshire: Almond.

Lilley, J. P. U. 1967. "A Literary Appreciation of the Book of Judges." *Tyndale Bulletin* 18: 94–102.

Linafelt, Tod, and Timothy K. Beal, eds. 1998. *God in the Fray: A Tribute to Walter Brueggemann*. Minneapolis, MN: Fortress Press.

McCann, J. Clinton. 2002. *Judges*. Interpretation: A Bible Commentary for Teaching and Preaching. Louisville, KY: John Knox Press.

Murray, D. F. 1979. "Narrative Structure and Technique in the Deborah-Barak Story (Judges IV 4-22)." In *Studies in the Historical Books of the Old Testament 30*, edited by J. A. Emerton, 155–189. *Vetus Testamentum* Supplement 30 Leiden: Brill.

O'Connell, Robert H. 1996. *The Rhetoric of the Book of Judges*. Vetus Testamentum Supplement 63. Leiden: Brill.

Penchansky, David. 1999. *What Rough Beast? Images of God in the Hebrew Bible*. Louisville, KY: Westminster John Knox Press.

Polzin, Robert. 1980. *Moses and the Deuteronomist: A Literary Study of the Deuteronomistic History. Part One. Deuteronomy, Joshua, Judges*. Indiana Studies in Biblical Literature. New York: Seabury.

Radday, Yehuda T., and Athalya Brenner, eds. 1990. *On Humour and Comic in the Hebrew Bible*. Sheffield, Yorkshire: Almond.

Revell, E. J. 1985. "The Battle with Benjamin (Judges XX 29-48) and Hebrew Narrative Technique." *Vetus Testamentum* 35: 417–443.

Rowlett, Lori. 2001. "Violent Femmes and S/M: Queering Samson and Delilah." In *Queer Commentary and the Hebrew Bible*, edited by Ken Stone, 106–115. Journal for the Study of the Old Testament Supplement Series 334. London: Sheffield Academic Press.

Satterthwaite, Philip E. 1992. "Narrative Artistry in the Composition of Judges 20:29ff." *Vetus Testamentum* 42: 80–89.

Sawyer, Deborah F. 2002. *God, Gender and the Bible*. Biblical Limits. London and New York: Routledge.

Schneider, Tammi J. 2000. *Judges*. Berit Olam. Collegeville, MN: Liturgical Press.

Vincent, Mark A. 2000. "The Song of Deborah: A Structural and Literary Consideration." *Journal for the Study of the Old Testament* 91: 61–82.

Webb, Barry G. 1987. *The Book of Judges: An Integrated Reading*. Journal for the Study of the Old Testament Supplement Series 46. Sheffield, Yorkshire: Sheffield Academic Press.

Webb, Barry G. 2012. *The Book of Judges*. New International Commentary on the Old Testament. Grand Rapids, MI: W. B. Eerdmans.

Whitehead, Stephen M. 2002. *Men and Masculinities: Key Themes and New Directions*. Cambridge: Polity.

Winnicott, D. W. 1965a. *The Family and Individual Development*. London: Tavistock.

Winnicott, D. W. 1965b. *Maturational Processes and the Facilitating Environment: Studies in the Theory of Emotional Development*. London: Hogarth Press.

Wong, Gregory T. K. 2006. *Compositional Strategy of the Book of Judges: An Inductive, Rhetorical Study*. Vetus Testamentum Supplement 111. Leiden and Boston: Brill.

CHAPTER 15

(HI)STORY TELLING IN THE BOOKS OF SAMUEL

RACHELLE GILMOUR

THE books of Samuel recount an important period of Israel's history, describing the transition from a system of judges to kings, and the genesis of David's dynasty. While the subject matter is from the past and so suggests history, the mode of telling more closely resembles a modern idea of story. It integrates divine intervention, family drama, and personal struggles into its interpretation of Israel's political changes, military engagements, and national development. This chapter will introduce the books of Samuel from three angles. The first angle is an overview of its content and macro-structures, a necessary precursor to any other analysis. Second, we will shift our focus from the books themselves to the methods of reading them, tracing the development of narrative studies in Samuel. Finally, we will look more closely at the detail of 2 Samuel 20 and explore a new direction in narrative readings.

THE STORY OF THE BOOKS OF SAMUEL

It is a difficult undertaking to capture the detailed plot, rich characterizations, and complex themes of Samuel in a short summary. I will attempt this task by tracing the construction of two of its dominating concerns: the pattern of the rise and fall of leaders; and the election of David. Such a reading is the fruit of countless literary analyses, which I will survey shortly, and which have identified and explored these patterns, themes, and other narrative features in the book.

The rise and fall of Eli, Samuel, Saul, and then David as the leader of Israel form the core plot of the books of Samuel. Samuel, Saul, and David all gain leadership positions from humble beginnings, not by inheritance. Their rise is characterized by military and personal success aided by the Divine. This rise is disrupted by a great failure, and followed by a period, for Saul and David at least, of military and personal decline. The programmatic statement for this cycle of leaders is set in the opening of 1 Samuel by Hannah, herself raised up from the humility of barrenness, foreshadowing the rise of the books' leaders. She sings of the upheavals and reversals brought about by the Lord:

> "The LORD kills and brings to life;
> > he brings down to Sheol and raises up.
> The LORD makes poor and makes rich;
> > he brings low, he also exalts.
> He raises up the poor from the dust;
> > he lifts the needy from the ash heap,
> to make them sit with princes
> > and inherit a seat of honor.
> For the pillars of the earth are the LORD'S,
> > and on them he has set the world" (1 Sam. 2:6–8 NRSV)

This passage provides a theological lens through which the impressive rises and inevitable failures of the books' leaders can be understood: the LORD exalts them, so he also brings them low.

The first leader, Eli the priest, is introduced already in his decline. He struggles to interpret the barren Hannah's distressed plea for a child, seeing instead the corruption of strong drink. Conversely, he is blind to the corruption of his sons, a flaw mirrored by his physical blindness. The end of his priestly house and the death of his sons is foretold by a man of God and soon enacted, meaningfully interspersed with accounts of the rise of the young boy Samuel.

After the end of Eli, Samuel fills the leadership void, rescuing the ark from the Philistines and judging Israel. Already one of the patterns of leadership has emerged in 1 Samuel 8:1–3, when it is reported that Samuel, too, has corrupt sons. The problem of corrupt sons is a suggestive introduction to the request by the elders of Israel to make for them a king: an institution based around the transfer of leadership from father to son. Moreover, since the elders' request specifies a king "to judge us," the current judge Samuel must effectively anoint his own replacement, a task he is understandably reluctant to fulfill.

Although Samuel's decline is less marked by tragedy than the other three leaders, it is similarly interspersed with accounts of the rise of the next leader, Saul. Despite the shadows over Saul's rise (such as Samuel's hesitancy and parallels to the anarchy at the end of the book of Judges), Saul is unambiguously chosen by God to be king. However, Saul will soon also be rejected as leader, this time for his own sin, not the sin of his sons. Saul's dynasty is rejected in 1 Samuel 13 when he *makes a sacrifice* without waiting for Samuel. He himself is rejected as king in 1 Samuel 15 when he *omits to sacrifice* King Agag, as Samuel commanded him to do.

Immediately after the rejection of Saul, the young David is anointed by Samuel in secret, even though Saul will stay Israel's official king for many more years. David's rise is characterized by divinely wrought success and parallels the rise of Saul in many ways. They both have private anointings, accompanied by divine speech and the repetition of the root "to choose" (1 Sam. 9:2; 10:24; 12:13; 16:8, 9, 10; 17:8). They are young (1 Sam. 3:1; 16:11), good looking (1 Sam. 9:2; 16:12), and given a series of instructions before they are anointed (1 Sam. 3:9; 9:6, 19–20, 27; 16:11–12). Afterward the spirit rushes upon them (1 Sam. 10:10; 16:13), and they have an immediate military victory (11:1–11; 17:1–54).

On the one hand, these parallels highlight the book's theme that all leaders rise and fall in a similar way. On the other hand, it invites the question of what is ultimately special about David, if Saul and David were chosen in the same way. One way in which this question is explored in the text is through the juxtaposition of Saul's decline and David's rise, and the subsequent contrast between the two leaders. According to the pattern of leaders, Saul's son Jonathan and daughter Michal betray their father because they love David. Saul is constantly afraid and plagued by the Philistine threat whilst David thrives, killing Goliath and even exploiting the generosity of the Philistine King Achish.

Tension between Saul and David continues until the death of Saul and Jonathan in battle. The end of Saul's line is later completed with the defeat of his son Ishbosheth in a civil war between north and south.

Unlike the other leaders whose falls come quickly, David's rise is far more impressive than any before him. He finally overcomes Israel's enemies, including the Philistines, he captures Jerusalem as his capital and brings the ark there, and God promises him an eternal dynasty. These events consolidate his kingdom and confirm him as king.

However, eventually David's story also pivots on his sin, triggering a downward slope of bitter infighting in his family. After David's affair with Bathsheba and murder of her husband, the prophet Nathan announces punishments to David in 2 Samuel 12:1–14 that will be played out throughout the rest of the book: the sword shall not depart from his house; there will be evil from his own household; his wives will be taken in public; and his child will die. Following this, David's son Amnon rapes David's daughter Tamar, his son Absalom murders Amnon, and then Absalom begins a civil war against his father. Absalom even rapes David's concubines on the roof of the palace, fulfilling each of the punishments in Nathan's prophecy. Again, the sons of leaders are a problem. And again, David's decline contains many parallels to that of Saul, highlighting the pattern of leaders. The fall of each is marked by the visit of a prophet, and the sin of each is described as against God (1 Sam. 13:13; 15:11, 19; 23; 2 Sam. 12:9). They all struggle with problematic or rebellious children, conflict with a successor, and the absence of military success.

Nevertheless, there is one very important difference: David does not lose his dynasty or his kingship. This returns to our earlier question, why is Saul rejected but David promised an eternal dynasty? While it seems that Saul could have had an eternal kingdom (1 Sam. 13:13), it is never fully explained why Saul's sin excludes him so thoroughly and David's does not. Perhaps it is because David is promised an eternal dynasty in 2 Samuel 7 before his grossest sins take place in 2 Samuel 11. The promise is already made and so cannot be stripped away from him. However, this explanation is not entirely satisfactory, and others can be proffered: David's piety is greater, his repentance more sincere, his unconditional election arbitrarily more secure.

The optimism of David's eternal election, in contrast to Saul's rejection (2 Sam. 7:15), is reflected in the conclusion to Samuel in 2 Samuel 21–24, which offers a more positive picture than the civil war with Absalom and David's grief at losing such a rebellious son. Rather than the bleak picture of civil war and David's political impotence, the book concludes with a chiasm of positive Davidic propaganda: the outer stories demonstrate the end of the house of Saul (2 Sam. 21:1–13; 24); the next ring of lists show the bravery of his fighting men, suggesting David's own military success (2 Sam. 21:15–22; 23:8–38); and the core demonstrates David's piety and faithful dependence on God, regardless of how his other actions may have made him look (2 Sam.22; 23:1–7).

NARRATIVE READINGS OF THE BOOKS OF SAMUEL

Such a complex plot and cast of characters have a correspondingly complex history of narrative readings. I have chosen here to focus on the growth of narrative readings out of historical critical analyses. Narrative studies found their own identity and methodologies and were established as an independent branch within biblical studies, before returning to contribute and interact once again with more traditional investigations of the text. The reality is undoubtedly more complex than this, especially as we will overlook pre-twentieth-century interpretations, and many monographs that have been forgotten, despite their challenges to the prevailing fashions. Nevertheless, this will hopefully describe with some insight the development and maturation of modern narrative readings of Samuel.

Early suggestions that there were unified sections within the books of Samuel have encouraged narrative readings even when atomizing approaches to the text have dominated. Most notably, the "Succession Narrative" in 2 Samuel 13–20 has been admired for its sophisticated and sustained plot development. Although the term "Succession Narrative" was made prominent by Leonhard Rost (1926), who argued that it was a propaganda document for Solomon's succession, scholars had seen unity in this section many years before. Karl Budde (1890, 251) considered chapters 13–20 "an uninterrupted tragic course" containing only a few editorial glosses. Hugo Gressmann (1921) labeled the section "The Revolt of Absalom and Sheba," describing it as a long homogenous narrative. He recognized in his form critical analysis that "the most frequent change of situation, the great abundance of personalities and the constant changes of mood reveal a developed technique in high quality narrative art" (49). The influential work of Martin Noth (1943), translated into English as *The Deuteronomistic History,* also saw sections of relative unity in the books of Samuel when Noth identified only a few traces of Deuteronomistic editing.

Growing directly out of this perception of a sustained narrative in 2 Samuel 13–20, Charles Conroy (1978, 1) justified "an attempt to see how the literary excellence of the text is manifested in its techniques of narration and use of language." Taking this "relatively independent narrative identity" (6), he saw his task as building on Rost (1926) and Roger Whybray (1968), who each made useful remarks about the text's stylistic characterization even though it was not their main concern. Thus, working within the dominant paradigm of diachronic analysis of the text, a section of text substantial enough to sustain a close literary reading was found.

In the same year, David Gunn (1978) published a literary study of the story of the Succession Narrative, albeit with greater boundaries extending through 2 Samuel 2–4 and 9–20, and 1 Kings 1–2. Again, his study stayed within sources accepted by prevailing historical critical scholarship but offered an insightful narrative reading to argue for a genre of "serious entertainment." In 1980, Gunn published a second monograph, this time on Saul, which focused more specifically on a narrative reading. It was aimed at an audience beyond biblical studies: "To the reader who has been gripped by Sophocles' King Oedipus, Shakespeare's Macbeth, or Hardy's Tess of the d'Urbevilles, I suggest that the story of Saul might profitably be next on the reading programme" (Gunn 1980, 9). At the same time, there began to be more theoretical discussion on reading the Bible in its final form, largely influenced by the work of Brevard Childs (1979) and his method of canonical criticism.

Soon after, a number of studies arose that embraced a purely synchronic reading. They became more self-conscious in their methodological approach in terms of narrative theory, engaging with New Criticism and structuralism in varying degrees, and they defined a deliberate break from "critical" approaches to the book. In 1981, the first volume of Jan Fokkelman's massive opus appeared, claiming influence from structuralism but also resembling aspects of New Criticism in its close reading of minute details of language structure. In 1985, Lyle Eslinger engaged New Critical methods in a study of the Ark Narrative, looking at the structure of the work rather than the mind of its author or audience. He admitted that New

Criticism was to some degree superseded in literary theory, but demonstrated that it could nevertheless produce new insights into biblical narrative. Peter Quinn-Miscall (1986) also deliberately departed from historical critical methods, using a heterogeneous methodology that embraced New Criticism, structuralism, and deconstruction. Similarly, André Wénin (1988, 15) defined himself as "post-critical" in his work on the inauguration of the monarchy.

The general approach termed "poetics" by Robert Alter and Frank Kermode (1987), which engages less with literary theory but has much in common with structuralist and New Critical approaches, has also been exemplified in studies of Samuel. Moshe Garsiel (1985) offered a study of narrative analogies in 1 Samuel, which illuminated the dynamics of this feature in biblical narrative more generally at the same time that it offered a fresh reading of Samuel. A more recent work by Paul Borgen (2008) further builds on the literary structure of parallels, which has proved key to reading the books of Samuel, demonstrated in my own overview. There have been several commentaries and monographs that fall broadly within this category of offering a "literary" reading of the book, including those by Shimeon Bar-Efrat (2007), Keith Bodner (2005, 2008), and Walter Brueggemann (1990); in the latter case, combining many elements of a theological methodology. By contrast, David Jobling's narrative commentary (1998) deliberately broadens what he calls the "narrow narratology" of poetics and crosses a number of methodologies, such as structuralism, poststructuralism, feminism, deconstruction, and new historicism. Some of these methodologies take an audience-centered approach, marking a radical new direction but one that is skillfully kept in continuity with previous literary readings.

One final direction of narrative readings we will mention here was initiated by the final two volumes of a monumental work by Robert Polzin (1989, 1993) on the Deuteronomistic History. Alongside the types of analysis found in poetics, New Criticism, and structuralism, he also engaged with ideas from the Russian literary theorist Mikhail Bakhtin. In this way, Polzin produced a distinctive and insightful reading of the book and influenced later studies of Samuel that would engage with Bakhtin more deeply. A monograph by Barbara Green (2003) would prove to be just as much a handbook on the application of Bakhtinian concepts to the Bible as a reading of Samuel. *David Observed* by Bodner (2005) also offered a way of reading Samuel using Bakhtinian and other literary strategies. This work gives examples of the future direction in which fresh literary readings may head, beyond poetics, while remaining text, rather than audience-centered. The success of Bakhtin's theory for new readings of Samuel suggests the potential for other aspects of contemporary literary theory to push readings beyond a simplistic understanding of poetics.

Narrative readings of Samuel have established a separate branch of study in the last thirty years, as evinced by the absence of any narrative reading in the most authoritative historical critical commentaries on Samuel by P. Kyle McCarter (1980, 1984). By contrast, although Antony Campbell (2003, 2005) uses an explicitly form-critical methodology, he simultaneously incorporates an analysis sensitive to the literary features of the text.

However, there have also been narrative studies that have consciously integrated their techniques into diachronic and historical studies, and vice versa. Beginning as part of a historical investigation of Saulide Israel, Diana Edelman's literary study of Saul became a full-length monograph, *King Saul in the Historiography of Judah* (1991), which she described as "a necessary and integral step within the historical investigation of Saul's career" (11). The integration of literary and historical questions is given a number of different expressions in a collection of essays edited by A. Graeme Auld and Erik Eynikel (2010). V. Philips Long

(1989) uses literary study to argue for the unity of the Saul story. Herbert Klement (2000) also applies a narrative approach to argue for the coherence of the Samuel conclusion in 2 Samuel 21–24. Rather than the unity of the text, Auld (2011) and Robert Rezetko (2007) use insightful literary analyses in service of understanding the history of the text better. In diverse ways, Serge Frolov (2004) and a compilation of former essays and research by Walter Dietrich (2007) combine the diachronic and synchronic to give more holistic analyses of sections of Samuel. My own contribution (Gilmour 2011) uses literary analysis to examine the nature of ancient historiography in the books of Samuel.

In summary, narrative readings developed a conscious break from historical and critical studies. As the poetics of Samuel reach maturity, it is time to re-engage with the inquiries of more traditional research, such as historical and diachronic questions, and to use the sophisticated techniques and methodological awareness gained in narrative readings to contribute to these debates. Simultaneously, methodologies need to be developed that use the results of source and redaction histories to stimulate final form studies, rather than oppose them.

I will illustrate here an example of how this integration can take place, with the particular example of historical studies and narrative readings. In my monograph *Representing the Past: A Literary Approach to Narrative Historiography in the Book of Samuel* (2011), I demonstrate how characteristics of historiography, such as causation, meaning, evaluation, and coherence, are expressed using narrative techniques in the books of Samuel, in contrast to the methods of modern historiography. Historical theory can be used to inform a literary reading of the text, highlighting narrative strategies that are specific to historical writing about the past. In turn, an understanding of how the books of Samuel use narrative strategies to write historiography also reveals much about how we should be reading Samuel as an historical source. It is essential to understand how the book writes history if we are interested in learning about this period. Treating the book as historiography does not imply that the stories are history with a modern sense of historicity, but rather that the authors and editors were seeking to represent events and people belonging to their past, to find meaning in them and evaluate them.

(HI)STORY TELLING IN 2 SAMUEL 20

We will examine three characteristics of historiography, which we find in the books of Samuel, but which are not expressed in a way accustomed in modern historiography: causation, meaning, and evaluation. In the short space for analysis here, we will observe how these categories can enliven our literary reading of 2 Samuel 20, and, in turn, their use in 2 Samuel 20 can contribute to our understanding of how the books of Samuel functioned as historiography.

Causation is the study of the question "why" in history. In the narrative of Samuel these "why" questions are answered primarily through the plot. The causes for the resolution of the story are established through the intricacies of the plot leading to this point. Thus the study of causation begins with analysis of the plot, looking at its tensions and resolutions.

The primary tension established in 2 Samuel 20:1 is the revolt of Sheba, when he declares that Israel has no share in David. This tension is not a new one; it is rooted in the split of the kingdom between David and Ishbosheth, Saul's son, at the beginning of 2 Samuel. It arises again in 19:9–15 when Israel suggests returning David to the throne, but David sends word to Judah asking them why they do not also seek to return him when he is their flesh and blood. In 19:41–43, immediately juxtaposed with 2 Samuel 20, Judah and Israel engage in a conflict of words about who has the greater rights over David. Judah has kinship, Israel has numbers. Thus the problem is larger than Sheba alone; it is a long history of division between north and south, and David's management of unity between them.

However, there is a second tension in 20:4, which will also be resolved at the end of the story: David's promotion of Amasa ahead of Joab. Again, this tension was initiated in the previous story when David offered Amasa the post in exchange for the loyalty of Judah. From the beginning, the two tensions are interrelated. Second Samuel 19:5–6 sets the thematic context for these two chapters when Joab accuses David of rewarding loyalty with disloyalty. His words have immediate effect on David as he resumes his place as king at the city gate. However, David next responds to Joab's words by showing loyalty to the rebel Amasa over Joab, suggesting that David believed true loyalty was demonstrated by the preservation of his son, rather than the preservation of David's power. The theme is further explored when David repays or forgives those he has interacted with on his departure from Jerusalem (for more detail, see Gilmour 2011, 208–211). Now, 2 Samuel 20:4 increases the tension in that David places his trust in Amasa rather than Joab for the task of suppressing a new rebellion, only for this trust to prove to have been misplaced. The story concludes in 20:23 with Joab reinstated as commander of all Israel's army, "Now Joab was in command of all the army of Israel" (NRSV). This verse encapsulates the resolution to both tensions. Joab is again commander, and there is one unified army of Israel, signaling that the division between Judah and Israel is overcome.

The interconnection between the tensions and resolutions reflects the interconnection in their causation. It is demonstrated by the interweaving of the two plots in a crisscrossing, alternating pattern. David promotes Amasa, bringing loyalty from Judah. This causes division with Israel and Sheba's revolt. Sheba's revolt provides an opportunity for Amasa to neglect his duty, which in turn leads to Joab's assassination of him. Joab then resumes his post, independent of David's wishes, bringing an end to Sheba's rebellion through military action and negotiation. The nature of the negotiation, convincing the Israelite city to give up its rebel leader, brings unity again to Israel. The dual resolution is summarized by Joab's position at the head of the unified army. Thus, Joab's personal ambitions are integral to suppressing Sheba's rebellion, which would affect the whole nation and its future by bringing unity between north and south. This is a fascinating dimension to comprehending the past. Individuals serve the bigger political picture but can simultaneously have importance as character studies of ambition.

As we understand the significance of interwoven plots for understanding interwoven causation, our attention is drawn to a third subplot in the chapter, the imprisonment[1] of the concubines in verse 3, provoking the question of if/how it contributes to other causation in the chapter.[2] Although Shimei, Ziba, Amasa, and "all Israel" who fought with Absalom are allowed freedom, the ten concubines left to "look after [lit. guard] the house" are now placed "in a house under guard," the wordplay in the verse highlighting the reversal. Within the context of David's responses to loyalty in these chapters, David's treatment of the concubines is meaningfully sandwiched between reports of Sheba's rebellion and David entrusting an important task to Amasa. The symbolism of the number ten, in close proximity with 19:43, points to a parallel with the ten tribes of Israel. Just as David neglects to protect his concubines, so he neglects the ten tribes. And thus there is rebellion. Perhaps like the concubines, the ten tribes of Israel had no choice but to join Absalom. David left Israel to their fate with Absalom when he crossed the Jordan in the same way he left the concubines to Absalom in Jerusalem. Conversely, his treatment of the concubines demonstrates how he should have treated the disloyal Amasa. Instead, David gives Amasa responsibility and endangers his kingdom. The fate of the concubines contributes causation of a kind different to plot development, acting as *mise-en-abyme*, a scene within a scene. The fate of the ten concubines reflects in a short scene the larger story of the ten tribes and so illuminates the surrounding story.

A second important aspect of exploring the past and representing it in literary form is analysis of its meaning. Inevitably a study of causation will uncover meaning also, for example, the significance of the repayment of loyalty. We explore meaning in the past further by looking at elements of the story that fit into patterns established elsewhere in Samuel: assassination and the removal of the enemy's head.

As Polzin (1993, 199) has highlighted, this story draws many similarities to the story of Abner's defection and assassination, followed by the removal of Ishbaal's head, in 2 Samuel 2–4. Apart from these plot parallels, both stories are set at Gibeon (2:13; 20:8), passersby stand by the dead bodies (2:23; 20:12), the root *'ḥr* (after; to delay) is repeated throughout both stories, and the battles are ended by Joab blowing his trumpet (2:28; 20:23). David's enemies in both stories (Ishbaal, Sheba) lose their heads at the hands of their own people. Decapitation is a motif from the stories of Goliath in 1 Samuel 17, Saul in 1 Samuel 31:9, and the threat against Shimei in 2 Samuel 16:9, and bears similarity to Absalom's death after he is caught in the tree by his hair. Polzin (1993, 199) emphasizes the similarity of the "fratricidal pursuit of brethren" in the two stories. However, this points to the larger and deeper parallel of fratricidal conflict between north and south. The earlier conflict of deep divide within Israel has returned in an eerie repetition of its earlier incarnation. It may not be a battle between the house of Saul and the house of David, but it is drawn along the same lines of north versus south.

Again, this offers an insight into the books of Samuel's conception of history, suggesting that the past echoes itself, even within the lifetime of David. The meaning of the conflict lies in its repetitious connection to past events. The resolution reached in 2 Samuel 4 is successful in bringing a substantial period of unity and peace, and so the outlook in the second story is optimistic. On the other hand, the first period of unity came to an end with Absalom's civil war, and similarly, the second period will only extend until the end of David's son Solomon's reign.

Differences between these two stories also point to aspects of meaning. In 2 Samuel 2–4, David mourns Abner, places a curse upon Joab, and later punishes those who have decapitated his enemy Ishbosheth. In 2 Samuel 20, no reaction from David is reported at all. Perhaps David's reaction in the earlier story was calculated to clear him of crimes, but this propaganda is now no longer necessary. Perhaps it is because David now admits defeat before the maverick Joab, whose actions undeniably benefit David, even if they keep him tied to Joab's dominating presence. Another example of David's passivity is found in the difference in resolution in the two stories. Second Samuel 4 ends with David made king; 2 Samuel 20 ends with no mention of David and instead with Joab made head of all the army of Israel. Thus, both stories end with a leader bringing unity between the north and south. However, the first is David, and the second is Joab.

A final significant difference stems out of another parallel. In 2 Samuel 3:17–21, Abner transfers his allegiance to David and helps David by gaining the support of Israel for him. Similarly, David uses Amasa to gain the support of Judah. In both stories, Joab conveniently disposes of the defectors for his own private motivations. The difference is that now David must use the enemy to gain the support of his own kin, Judah. The fight for loyalty from Israel, then from Judah, and back to Israel, demonstrates the precarious nature of David's hold on power, even more so now that his grasp on Judah is gained by rewarding disloyalty.

At the culmination of the story in the books of Samuel, the meaning in 2 Samuel 20 is located in the context of the overall decline of David. He maintains a hold on his kingdom, but it is punctuated by his capitulation to his dominating general Joab, by divisions within his neglected kingdom, and by his own confused loyalty, clouded by blindness toward his son Absalom.

A third aspect of historical representation is the evaluation of the past, particularly its agents. This is primarily conveyed through aspects of their characterization and the characterization of the events in which they are actors. Sheba is given an explicit evaluation, a man of Belial (20:1), preparing the reader to evaluate his actions negatively. His rebellion is unlikely to be interpreted as a legitimate claim for independence because of David's neglect, but rather as opportunism, lifting arms to gain power. David's inaction throughout the story, with the exception of restraining his concubines, evaluates him as passive, leaving his kingly responsibilities to others. The description of Amasa as "delaying" (wy'ḥr) in v. 5 echoes Israel's withdrawal from "after" (m'ḥr) David in v. 2 by using the same root. This evaluates Amasa as one of the rebels, also withdrawing his support from David.

A more complex character in this story is Joab, who acts out of private ambitions but simultaneously advances the unity of David's kingdom. Joab is characterized as deceiving, yet his actions are characterized as achieving results. Joab's greeting to Amasa, "is there peace/are you well?" (hšlm) is ironic, not only because Joab is not really concerned with Amasa's health, but also because Joab knows there is no peace between them. The irony in his words and deceit is intensified by his gesture toward kissing him. Joab's response to the wise woman of Abel, "far be it from me, far be it, that I should swallow up and destroy," is similarly ironic considering his reputation as an army general and the murder he has just committed.

Alongside deceit, Joab is characterized by a combination of private ambition and loyalty to David. After the murder of Amasa, one of Joab's men asks in verse 11, "Whoever favors Joab, and whoever is for David, let him follow Joab." Loyalty to Joab comes before loyalty to David, suggesting that the assassination was about Joab regaining his position rather than taking revenge on Amasa for endangering David's position. Yet, despite David's having demoted Joab, it is unquestioned that Joab remains loyal to David and that following Joab is following David. Joab continually disobeys David, and yet his loyalty is never doubted. Furthermore, the result of Joab's deceit and violence is that he returns to Jerusalem with the head of Sheba. This is precisely what David had desired of Amasa. While Joab is evaluated as self-serving, violent, and disobedient, his actions are evaluated as serving a purpose for David.

Behind the success of Joab's actions is the wise woman of Abel of Beth-maacah. She, too, is given an explicit evaluation, "wise woman," although it is suggested that this is a profession rather than a description of an individual (Camp 1981). Nevertheless, her plan is also explicitly called "wise" in verse 22, demonstrating that, at the very least, she lived up to her profession's title. The meaning of the details in her speech is also debated, but its overall intention is clear: the people of Abel of Beth-maacah will transfer their allegiance to David and hand over Sheba. Her claim that they are a "mother in Israel"[3] perhaps points to the city's respected standing, and so, when this city gives its allegiance to David, it indicates that all Israel will now follow him. Parallel to Joab, the wise woman pursues her own self-interest, but simultaneously delivers the kingdom back to David.

The complexities of causation, meaning, and evaluation of past events are rarely described explicitly in the books of Samuel but are conveyed through narrative devices. This suggests a degree of literary shaping very different from modern historiographical methods. Furthermore, the attention to these features shared between modern and ancient historiography, albeit communicated in different ways, brings a fresh dimension to analysis of the story's poetics.

CONCLUSION

Possibly more than any other books of the Hebrew Bible, the books of Samuel have invited readings that pay close attention to its rich narrative and complex literary features. Drawing first on structuralism and New Criticism, and later on deconstruction and Bakhtin, narrative readings of Samuel have identified patterns, themes, aspects of characterization and plot, and other more complex narrative strategies and effects on audiences. With this firm foundation for reading the book with attention to its sophisticated storytelling, final form readings can be successfully integrated with other historical and source-critical questions of the book, each informing and developing the other. One example of this is our narrative reading of 2 Samuel 20 through the lens of its characteristics of historiography: causation, meaning, and evaluation. Attention to these categories deepens our literary reading, highlighting its values and conception of significance in the past.

NOTES

1. It is debated whether David is doing his duty or unfairly treating them as widows. Fokkelman (1981, 320) describes David's behavior as "a strange paradox of concern and abhorrence."
2. Another parallel in the story identified by Polzin (1993, 200), is that Joab finally besieges Sheba, and the same verbal root is used of the concubines' confinement. David besieges only his own concubines, whereas Joab successfully besieges the enemy, contributing to the characterization of David as passive and ineffective, and reliant on Joab to act.
3. See McCarter (1984, 430) on the interpretation of "mother" as a "mother city," presumably a tribal center. Also Fokkelman (1981, 334) interprets this as a reputation for wisdom.

REFERENCES

Alter, Robert, and Frank Kermode, eds. 1987. *The Literary Guide to the Bible*. Cambridge, MA: Belknap Press.

Auld, A. Graeme. 2011. *I & II Samuel: A Commentary*. Old Testament Commentary. Louisville, KY: Westminster John Knox.

Auld, A. Graeme, and Erik Eynikel, eds. 2010. *For and against David: Story and History in the Books of Samuel*. Bibliotheca Ephemeridum Theologicarum Lovaniensium 232. Leuven: Peeters.

Bar-Efrat, Shimeon. 2007. *Das erste Buch Samuel: Ein narratologisch-philogischer Kommentar*. Translated by Johannes Klein. Beiträge zur Wissenschaft vom Alten und Neuen Testament 176. Stuttgart: Kohlhammer.

Bodner, Keith. 2005. *David Observed: A King in the Eyes of His Court*. Sheffield, Yorkshire: Sheffield Phoenix Press.

Bodner, Keith. 2008. *1 Samuel: A Narrative Commentary*. Sheffield, Yorkshire: Sheffield Phoenix Press.

Borgen, Paul. 2008. *David, Saul, and God: Rediscovering an Ancient Story*. Oxford: Oxford University Press.

Brueggemann, Walter. 1990. *First and Second Samuel*. Interpretation. Louisville, KY: John Knox Press.

Budde, Karl. 1890. *Die Bücher Richter und Samuel, ihre Quellen und ihr Aufbau*. Giessen: Ricker.

Camp, Claudia V. 1981. "The Wise Women of 2 Samuel: A Role Model for Women in Early Israel." *Catholic Bible Quarterly* 43: 14-29.

Campbell, Antony F. 2003. *1 Samuel*. Forms of the Old Testament Literature 7. Grand Rapids, MI: Eerdmans.

Campbell, Antony F. 2005. *II Samuel*. The Forms of the Old Testament Literature 8. Grand Rapids, MI: Eerdmans.

Childs, Brevard S. 1979. *Introduction to the Old Testament as Scripture*. Philadelphia, PA: Fortress Press.

Conroy, Charles. 1978. *Absalom Absalom! Narrative and Language in 2 Sam. 13-20*. Rome: Biblical Institute Press.

Dietrich, Walter. 2007. *The Early Monarch in Israel: The Tenth Century B.C.E.* Translated by Joachim Vette. Biblical Encyclopedia 3. Atlanta, GA: Society of Biblical Literature.

Edelman, Diana. 1991. *King Saul in the Historiography of Judah*. Journal for the Study of the Old Testament Supplement Series 121. Sheffield, Yorkshire: JSOT Press.

Eslinger, Lyle M. 1985. *Kingship of God in Crisis: A Close Reading of 1 Samuel 1-12*. Bible and Literature 10. Sheffield, Yorkshire: Almond Press.

Fokkelman. Jan P. 1981. *King David*. Vol. I of *Narrative Art and Poetry in the Books of Samuel: A Full Interpretation Based on Stylistic and Structural Analyses*. Assen: Van Gorcum.

Frolov, Serge. 2004. *The Turn of the Cycle: 1 Samuel 1-8 in Synchronic and Diachronic Perspectives*. Berlin: Walter de Gruyter.

Garsiel, Moshe. 1985. *The First Book of Samuel: A Literary Study of Comparative Structures, Analogies and Parallels*. Ramat-Gan: Revivim.

Gilmour, Rachelle. 2011. *Representing the Past: A Literary Analysis of Narrative Historiography in the Book of Samuel*. Vetus Testamentum Supplement Series 143. Leiden: Brill.

Green, Barbara. 2003. *How Are the Mighty Fallen? A Dialogical Study of King Saul in 1 Samuel*. Journal for the Study of the Old Testament Supplement Series 365. Sheffield, Yorkshire: Sheffield Academic Press.

Gressmann, Hugo. 1921. *Die älteste Geschichtsschreibung und Prophetie Israels*. Die Schriften des Alten Testaments II.1. 2nd ed. Göttingen: Vandenhoeck & Ruprecht. 1991. *Narrative and Novella in Samuel: Studies by Hugo Gressmann and Other Scholars 1906–1923*. Edited by David M. Gunn. Translated by David E. Orton. Sheffield, Yorkshire: Almond Press.

Gunn, David M. 1978. *The Story of King David: Genre and Interpretation*. Journal for the Study of the Old Testament Supplement Series 6. Sheffield, Yorkshire: JSOT Press.

Gunn, David M. 1980. *The Fate of King Saul: An Interpretation of a Biblical Story*. Journal for the Study of the Old Testament Supplement Series 14. Sheffield, Yorkshire: JSOT Press.

Jobling, David. 1998. *1 Samuel*. Berit Olam. Collegeville, MN: Liturgical Press.

Klement, Herbert H. 2000. *II Samuel 21-24. Context, Structure and Meaning in the Samuel Conclusion*. Frankfurt am Main: Peter Lang.

Long, V. Philips. 1989. *The Reign and Rejection of King Saul: A Case for Literary and Theological Coherence*. Society of Biblical Literature Dissertation Series. Atlanta, GA: Scholars Press.

McCarter, P. Kyle, Jr. 1980. *I Samuel*. Anchor Bible 8. New York: Doubleday.

McCarter, P. Kyle, Jr. 1984. *II Samuel*. Anchor Bible 9. New York: Doubleday.

Noth, Martin. 1943. *Überlieferungsgeschichtliche Studien*. Halle: M. Niemeyer. 1981. *The Deuteronomistic History*. 2nd ed. Translated by J. Doull et al. Journal for the Study of the Old Testament Supplement Series 15. Sheffield, Yorkshire: JSOT Press.

Polzin, Robert. 1989. *Samuel and the Deuteronomist: A Literary Study of the Deuteronomic History Part Two. I Samuel*. San Francisco: Harper and Row.

Polzin, Robert. 1993. *David and the Deuteronomist: A Literary Study of the Deuteronomic History Part Three. II Samuel*. San Francisco: Harper and Row.

Quinn-Miscall, Peter D. 1986. *1 Samuel: A Literary Reading*. Indiana Studies in Biblical Literature. Bloomington: Indiana University Press.

Rezetko, Robert. 2007. *Source and Revision in the Narratives of David's Transfer of the Ark: Text, Language, and Story in 2 Samuel 6 and 1 Chronicles 13, 15–16*. Library of Hebrew Bible/Old Testament Studies 470. New York: T&T Clark.

Rost, Leonhard. 1926. *Die Überlieferung von der Thronnachfolge Davids*. Beiträge zur Wissenschaft vom Alten und Neuen Testament 42. Stuttgart: Kohlhammer. 1982. *The Succession to the Throne of David*. Translated by Michael D. Rutter and David M. Gunn. Sheffield, Yorkshire: Almond Press.

Wénin, André. 1988. *Samuel et l'instauration de la monarchie (1 S 1-12): Une Recherche littéraire sur le personnage*. Europäische Hochschulschriften, Reihe XXIII 342. Frankfurt am Main: Peter Lang.

Whybray, Roger N. 1968. *The Succession Narrative: A Study of II Samuel 9-20; I Kings 1 and 2*. Studies in Biblical Theology. London: SCM.

CHAPTER 16

....

THE RULE OF DEATH AND
SIGNS OF LIFE IN THE
BOOK OF KINGS

....

KEITH BODNER

THE epic account of Joshua-Kings begins with the people of Israel just on the other side of the Jordan river in Joshua 1 preparing to take possession of their land, and closes in 2 Kings 25 with the people on the other side of the river once again, but in Babylonian exile after their forfeiture of and dismissal from their ancestral inheritance. The expansive story between these bookends explores why such a displacement occurs, tracing Israel's tenuous experience in the land and ambivalent experiment with institutional monarchy. Scholars often refer to this collection of six books as the Deuteronomistic History because the theological challenge of Moses's last words to the Israelites—as they are camped in Moab after an eventful forty-year sojourn, poised to enter the land—echoes throughout the entire narrative. As the final installment of the Deuteronomistic History, 1 and 2 Kings continues and concludes the story of the monarchy formally set in motion in the book of 1 and 2 Samuel. Although kings and queens are lead actors in this narrative, a diverse cast of characters and an often unpredictable sequence of events greet the reader at every turn. This chapter begins with a short description of the major content of Kings, focusing on some key characters and larger plot movements and then moves to explore how, in the words of Danna Nolan Fewell and David M. Gunn (1993, 164), "death pervades the books of Kings." Indeed, the specter of death hovers over the book of Kings, in which an abnormal number of characters are violently killed, politically assassinated, painfully dismembered, or otherwise depart from the narrative in suspicious or ignominious ways. Yet for all the death and morbidity that pervade the storyline there are some exceptions along the way that will also occupy our attention. This reading for signs of life in the midst of the rule of death will showcase some recent trends in literary approaches to the Kings material.

KINGS CONFINED

....

The book of Kings begins with an image of confinement as the great King David—once virile and charismatic without equal—is old and seemingly approaching his death. The spatial setting for the opening scene is David's palace in Jerusalem, and from his residence the immobile king will never depart. David was given the divine promise of an enduring dynastic house in a startling promise in 2 Samuel 7, but 1 Kings 1 opens with a sense of uncertainty regarding the successor to his dynasty. Adonijah's plans are dashed by a clever machination choreographed by Nathan—who announces the enduring house back in 2 Samuel 7—and starring Bathsheba, the mother of Solomon. Not long after Solomon is crowned king, he embarks on a systematic purge of his central opponents, with Adonijah the first victim of Solomon's wisdom. The reader's initial impression is therefore a mixed one, as David's heir has undeniable talent but also a proclivity toward bloodshed, and, as he forges an alliance with Pharaoh king of Egypt in 1 Kings 3, intermarriage.

It should be noted that 2 Samuel 24 closes with the purchase of a threshing floor and the building of an altar at the eventual site of the temple in Jerusalem, the temple that is built ultimately not by David but by Solomon in 1 Kings 6–8. The construction of the temple dominates the middle section of Solomon's reign—with materials and workers supplied by Hiram of Tyre, the same king who earlier supplied materials for David's house—followed by an elaborate dedication ceremony and the divine presence that fills the new temple just like the tabernacle in the wilderness period of old. Yet amid the pomp and speeches there is a darker undercurrent in the narrative, as Solomon's habit of acquiring wives, horses, and gold is increasingly in tension with Deuteronomy 17, as is the king's evident ignoring of direct divine warnings (1 Kings 6:11–13; 9:2–9). By the time the reader arrives at the report of Solomon's apostasy in 1 Kings 11, it would appear that the gilded surface of the king's empire masks a corrupt undergirding.

The consequence for Solomon's divided heart is a divided kingdom, and the next phase of the story reports the schism of the nation and its fragmented aftermath (cf. Linville 2014, 203). In various phases of their careers, both David and Solomon can be accused of favoring the southern tribe of Judah, and such nepotism bears bitter fruit as the northern tribes secede in 1 Kings 12 and install Jeroboam, son of Nebat, as their inaugural monarch. Despite his great promise and apparent aptitude, the termination of Jeroboam's dynasty—owing to cultic violations and eschewing the sanctity of Jerusalem—is announced by the same prophet of his investiture, Ahijah of Shiloh in 1 Kings 14. The northern kingdom rarely enjoys any degree of stability: it experiences a series of short-lived dynasties and coups, and its leaders manifest a tendency to walk "in the sins of Jeroboam." In modest contrast, the southern kingdom of Judah at least has the same capital city of Jerusalem and a descendent of David on the throne, but like its northern counterpart, the south is also prone to idolatrous innovations and abject leadership.

In the midst of the long narrative of the divided kingdom, there arise some of the most intriguing figures in the Deuteronomistic History, the prophets Elijah and Elisha, and for a disproportionate stretch, attention is primarily focused on northern Israel, revolving around these prophets. They are foes of the powerful Omride dynasty operating in Samaria, and ample attention is devoted to them in 1 Kings 17–2 Kings 9, as first Elijah and then his successor Elisha consistently thwart the wayward kings and implore the people to return to covenant fidelity. Against the odds, the combined works of Elijah and Elisha eventually dismantle the regime, as Jehu son of Nimshi eradicates the Omride dynasty. Elisha even anoints a foreign king, Hazael of Damascus, expanding the prophetic jurisdiction beyond the borders of Israel. Despite the intensity of Elijah and his successor, the northern kingdom remains on course for disaster, and in 2 Kings 17 it is finally decimated by the Assyrian army that destroys Samaria and repopulates the region with a mixed multitude.

The southern kingdom of Judah miraculously survives the Assyrian invasion in 2 Kings 18–19, but the final stretch of the narrative leads inexorably to its demise, this time at the hands at the Babylonians. When Babylonian envoys visit Hezekiah in 2 Kings 20, the prophet Isaiah—who earlier predicted their rescue from Assyria in a stunning oracle—has searching words for the king's hospitality, forming an ominous cloud in the story as the Babylonians increasingly move to the forefront. Even the sweeping reforms of the famous Josiah are insufficient to offset the coming judgment, manifested in the invasion of Jerusalem in 2 Kings 25, which results in the burning of the city, razing of the temple, and exile of the citizenry (cf. Mobley 2009, 119–120). It takes several weighty chapters to describe the building of the temple, but only several short verses to demolish it: a foreign king supplies the material for its construction, and a foreign king ignites the fire for its destruction. So the final images of 2 Kings 25, like Foucault's panopticon (1975, 204–205), bring the reader full circle to a spatial setting that is hauntingly familiar: 1 Kings begins with the aged David confined to the royal palace of David, and 2 Kings ends with the last scion of his house incarcerated in the royal palace of Babylon.

ESCAPING KINGS

George Steiner's essay "A Death of Kings," discusses the affinity between death and the game of chess: "Allegoric associations of death with chess are perennial: in medieval woodcuts, in Renaissance frescoes, in the films of Cocteau and Bergman. Death wins the game, yet in so doing it submits, even if but momentarily, to rules wholly outside its dominion" (1984, 174). In a similar vein, our brief survey here suggests that associations of death pervade the book of Kings. Of course, it is true that David quietly "lays down with his ancestors" in 1 Kings 2:10, as does Solomon after him, and later, Jehoshaphat and a number of others. But for every monarch who has a peaceful burial, numerous other characters are shot by arrows, die of injuries sustained in battle, are overthrown in a popular uprising, or become victims of a conspiracy by an inner circle of advisers. Moral uprightness does not always have a bearing on the manner of a king's demise, as in the case of Manasseh, who is buried serenely in the garden of Uzza (Stavrakopoulou 2006), although even in these instances, there can be an ironic contrast with the next generation. So, Jeroboam may rest with his fathers in 1 Kings 14:20, but his (presumably) firstborn son dies prematurely of a serious illness, and his second son and dynastic heir is assassinated by Baasha after only two years, a far cry from the enduring house promised Jeroboam if he but walked in the statutes as outlined by Ahijah of Shiloh (Bodner 2012). Hezekiah is interred with his ancestors in 2 Kings 20:21 after a twenty-nine-year reign; but Isaiah the prophet had informed him that his offspring would undergo involuntary castration after being taken to Babylon—hardly an appealing destiny—and thus Hezekiah's survival of Assyria leaves him with only a sterile dynastic future.

Far from being uniform, there is a startling variety of fatalities in Kings. Consider, for instance, the stretch of text in the immediate aftermath of the schism, beginning with the moment Rehoboam unwisely sends out Adoniram—the superintendent of forced labor, surely a figure with few northern allies—to quell the mob in 1 Kings 12:18. Adoniram is promptly stoned by the crowd, and Rehoboam would doubtlessly have suffered the same fate had he not quickly mounted his chariot and fled from the riotous scene. One of the more abnormal deaths in a section filled with bereavements is the unnamed man of God in 1 Kings 13:24. After his corrugation of Jeroboam in Bethel, the man is hoodwinked by an old prophet and killed by a lion. Such a striking would be unique, except that it is matched in 1 Kings 20:36 when an unnamed prophetic figure is likewise attacked by a lion after refusing to hit his friend. The deadly illness of Jeroboam's son has already been mentioned, and the wayward king was also informed by Ahijah the prophet about the dismal prospects for his lineage: "Anyone belonging to Jeroboam who dies in the city, the dogs shall eat; and anyone who dies in the open country, the birds of the air shall eat" (14:11). Even in the southern kingdom of Judah the seemingly pleasant burial of Asa is obviated by his "diseased feet" in 15:23–24, a probable euphemism for genital dysfunction that Jeremy Schipper (2009) suggests is a private retribution for the king's apparent violation of Deuteronomy 24:5, a legal text stating that newly married males should be free from obligations for one year in order to *bring joy* to the brides. Later, in 1 Kings 16:9–10, the northern king Elah is assassinated by one of his commanders, Zimri, even as Elah is getting drunk. As for Zimri himself, he enjoys one of the strangest reigns ever, one that is abruptly terminated in 16:18 at his own hands: "When Zimri saw that the city was captured, he went into the stronghold of the royal palace, and then burned the palace on top of him with fire, and he died." Zimri thus occupies a unique place in the history of Israel's royal assassins, for he is guilty of killing two kings (including himself) within a single week.

After this short space of a few chapters, the death toll continues, and the reader duly encounters the stoning of Naboth, an arrow that pierces Ahab between the joints of his armor, Ahaziah's weird fall that precipitates his death without an heir, followed in due course by Athaliah's purge of her *own* offspring and Joash's murder by his conspiring servants. The fratricidal mania of Jehoram may not be recorded in Kings (cf. 2 Chron 21:4), but we still have the untimely death in battle of Josiah against Pharaoh Neco in 2 Kings 23:29 and numerous others. In terms of critical scholarship, the demise of Jezebel in 2 Kings 9 has attracted considerable attention in the past few decades, as issues of gender, power, and class all surface in different ways in the analysis of this multifaceted and ideologically charged character. So, Carey Ellen Walsh discusses the significance of her unmarked grave, as she is "denied a place in the land of Israel she sought to tamper with as queen. Jezebel was literally dismembered, not to be remembered, yet the Deuteronomistic History's gory spectacle in fact rendered her unforgettable" (2013, 328; cf. Fewell and Gunn 1993). Similarly, Janet Everhart explores the role of the "two or three" eunuchs who throw Jezebel out the window on Jehu's orders and raises an intriguing possibility: "Scholars rarely consider the possibility that the eunuchs' willingness to throw Jezebel into the street might represent a prearrangement between Jehu and court officials in Jezreel. Having *eunuchs* cast Jezebel to her death dramatizes the transition from one leader to another, since eunuchs are often involved in the rise and fall of monarchs and the shifting of boundaries" (2010, 698, citing Schulte 1994, 137–138). Everhart reminds us that in the *kethib* of the Masoretic Text, Jehu implores the eunuchs, "Throw *him* down," a further slippage in this royal dismemberment. As it stands, the eunuchs' role can be used as a segue to survival: death may pervade the book of Kings, but there are some fugitives along the way. In what remains of this chapter, I explore several characters who manage to escape the death of Kings.

DEATH WISH

Few figures in the book of Kings evoke interpretations as divergent as Elijah. His vague provenance and abrupt entry into the storyline, as Timothy Beal (2002, 174–175) has remarked, fuel speculation and endow his *character zone* with a certain ambiguity. Elijah's immediate opposition to Ahab—who in 1 Kings 16 marries Jezebel and erects a temple of Baal worship—sets the stage for Elijah's emergence as an agent of *anti-death*, punctuated with such events as feeding a Sidonian widow and healing her son, even as he announces a drought (on the struggle for life in this cycle, see Hauser 1990). The climax of the early confrontation with Ahab reaches its apex with an undeniable victory for Elijah, but as Frances Flannery (2008, 161) notes, the massacre of the Baal prophets after the pyrotechnics on Mount Carmel has garnered mixed reactions among recent interpreters: "Many commentators sidestep questions of morality raised by the incident of the slaying of the prophets of Baal in 1 Kings 18:40, deeming Elijah to be the hero who 'saved the Israelite faith'"(cf. Geller 2007). But arguably the most polarizing moment of Elijah's career is his complaint in 1 Kings 19:4, as he runs for his life toward Horeb after hearing Jezebel's threats: "Then he walked a day's journey into the desert. He came and sat underneath a solitary juniper shrub, and asked for his life to die, and said, 'Enough! Now, O Lord, take my life, for I am not better than my ancestors.'" The contrast between Elijah's confidence—rather against the numerical odds—in the contest with the Baal prophets and his apparent resignation here poses a challenge for the interpreter, as Robert Alter (2013, 707) comments: "The fear for his life inspired by Jezebel is, here, followed by despair. If, after his tremendous performance publicly demonstrating that YHWH is God, the royal couple still seek to kill him and remain unrepentant in the idolatrous ways they have fostered in Israel, his prophetic mission has been a failure, and there is no point in his going on." Nonetheless, if most scholars believe that Elijah has a quasi-suicidal urge here, Sigve Tonstad (2005, 255) compiles some harder questions that surface with the prophet's complaint:

> The account reveals a man in crisis (1 Kgs 19:4), but interpreters are at odds how to explain the debacle. Does Elijah flee from Jezebel because he panics and wishes to save his own skin? Does he set out for Horeb, as the narrative tells it, because he sees himself as another Moses, a man of equal stature to his illustrious predecessor? Should the foil for the subsequent lesson at Horeb be Elijah's own experience and thinking, setting the stage for a transformed view of God? Or, reflecting a very different path, is the entire narrative intended to show the contrast between Baal and Yahweh, continuing the lesson that was driven home at Carmel? Do we see the disconsolate prophet decommissioned and dismissed, or is he recommissioned and affirmed in the soon-to-come Horeb experience?

Of particular interest here is the contrast between the admission of defeat at Horeb and Elijah's dramatic departure from the later narrative in 2 Kings 2 as he is swept up by chariots and horses of fire. One can easily appreciate the wry reversal in the prophet's biography: he surrenders to fear and says "take my life," and God obliges in a manner that is scarcely expected, as though calling a bluff or creatively granting the prophet's wish, with a clever twist. "Elijah's ultimate destiny," says J. Edward Wright (2004, 124), "is no less mysterious than his origins." Recent interpreters usually affirm that Elijah makes great strides in opposing the house of Omri, but there are some variations that emerge from his story at Horeb. For instance, Stuart Lasine (2012, 122) raises a point about Elijah's claim to be the only one left in 1 Kings 19:10 and 14, a claim that appears problematic when the reader comes to 1 Kings 22 and the Micaiah episode. When Jehoshaphat asks Ahab if there are any *real* prophets around, Ahab answers in the affirmative, but then provides the name Micaiah (rather than Elijah, as the reader may have anticipated). As a result, Elijah now comes across as a much more intriguing figure than has been acknowledged by many commentators. When Elijah is finally taken in 2 Kings 2, Lasine wonders if God is rewarding the prophet or thwarting the earlier death wish (2012, 122). Furthermore, a strong case can be made that the divine character is portrayed in a more prismatic fashion than is often realized. As for Elijah, when he departs in the chariot, his successor Elisha, son of Shaphat, is left with his mantle, and the reader is left with an irony: the one character who *wants* to die does not, and the reader's only certainty is that Elijah survives the book of the Kings.

TOMB RAIDER

While Elijah was brooding at Horeb, God announced to him that his successor would, by all accounts, complete the task that he had started. After Elijah disembarks the book of Kings in fiery style, Elisha moves to a center position in the narrative. There may be a host of questions that still surround Elijah at Horeb and afterward (e.g., Lasine 2012, 130–131, "What kind of person would want to die so soon after a great victory, and immediately after he has fled precisely in order to *save* his life?"), but there is no question that upon departure he bequeaths Elisha with a double portion of his spirit. It can be argued Elisha, armed with his master's spirit and mantle, doubles the miracles of Elijah (see Cohn 2010, 119, for a tabular comparison) and so continues the task of dismantling the Omride dynasty. Similarly to and surpassing his forerunner, Elisha's career includes such hallmarks as feeding multitudes, thwarting both foreign and domestic kings, and enabling lepers to survive and skeptical officials to be trampled in the rush to purchase cheap food after the sudden end of famine. Elisha's encounter with the great woman of Shunem has garnered critical attention (e.g., Long 1991; Shields 1993; Siebert-Hommes 1996; Jobling 1999; Fewell 2000; Roncace 2000), as she is given the ostensible gift of a child through the prophet's mediation. Though some scholars debate whether this is a type-scene of the barren wife, it is highly significant that her nameless son is restored to life by Elisha since he is poised to inherit her land after a return from "exile" (see 2 Kings 8:5–6). Although there are numerous accounts of survival, near the outset of Elisha's career there is a memorable incident in 2 Kings 2:23–25 involving a bear attack on forty-two youths of Bethel. However, one should appreciate that this scene is immediately preceded by Elisha's healing the evil waters of Jericho that cause "bereavement" (Bodner 2013). Therefore the reader notices two different responses to the prophet: a supplication that brings healing and a taunt that elicits a curse, prompting the conclusion that rejecting the prophet is a risky proposition that could result in an early grave.

Elisha's own grave is the site of one of the most unusual occurrences in the book of Kings. He may not experience an incendiary departure like his master's, but his postmortem influence is considerable as he facilitates an escape from death that has no peer: "And Elisha died, and they buried him. Now raiding parties of Moab entered the land in the spring of every year. As they were burying a man, look!, they saw the raiding party, and threw the man in the grave of Elisha. The man went, touched the bones of Elisha, lived, and arose to his feet" (2 Kings 13:20–21). Instead of dismissing this episode as a redactional implant, recent interpreters have tended to analyze this short but lively scene within a broader context. For Lissa Wray Beal (2014, 411), the fear of the Israelites at the sight of foreign invaders is a crucial point: "The party's alarm at the approaching raiders provides an opportunity to show once more the life-giving prophetic power. Elisha's ministry has brought life to many through healed water (2:19–22), provision of food (4:1–7, 38–41, 42–44) and resurrection (4:32–35). Even though he is dead, Elisha's power remains." No doubt when the undertakers "cast" the corpse in fear, they are acting in self-preservation, but it should be noted that the same verb appears in the very next sequence, a description of how God refuses to "cast" Israel away on account of his covenant with Abraham, Isaac, and Jacob (v. 23). For Rachelle Gilmour, such placement is integral:

> In the story's current position, the miracle that a man comes to life becomes more prominent and stands alongside the theme of Elisha's reputation. This is primarily because of the juxtaposition with the Deuteronomic note in vv. 22–23. This note describes how the Lord had compassion on Israel in the time of Jehoahaz and, in particular, how he was not willing to destroy them or 'cast them out from his presence'—repeating the root *šlk* ('to throw') in *hšlykm* ('he cast them') from v. 21 where it is used in the *hiphil*. Thus a parallel is drawn: just as the man 'cast' into Elisha's tomb came alive, so also God will have compassion on the people of Israel. Elisha is dead but Israel may still be saved. (Gilmour 2014, 208)

Moreover, the reader may wonder if there is any significance in Moabite raiders creating this havoc. Near the beginning of Elisha's career, the king of Moab sacrifices his firstborn son and heir to his throne in 2 Kings 3:27, and now that Elisha is entombed, Moabites are threatening the sons of Israel. Throughout the story kings are surrounded by death, but in this vignette it is clear that even prophetic bones can breathe life and empower an escape from the grave.

PRISON BREAK

If there is a sense of confinement at the beginning of the book of Kings, then matters are much more claustrophobic as the story marches toward the end, with the city of Jerusalem under siege and poised for demolition at the hands of the Babylonians. Zedekiah is the last monarch to reign in Judah, having been earlier installed by the Babylonians before an ill-advised rebellion from under their yoke becomes a catalyst for the siege. Another unwise decision is made by Zedekiah when the siege is concluded: once the city wall is pierced in 2 Kings 25:4, he opts to flee with the rest of the army towards the Jordan Valley, only to be captured by the Babylonians and marched to Riblah for sentencing. Zedekiah is forced to watch his offspring executed before his eyes are gouged out; then he is led away as a blind captive in bronze fetters. Even with all the violent specificity of this scene in Riblah, the reader still might reflect that after much anticipation, the actual demolition of Jerusalem is reported in just a few lines: "The siege and its accompanying death, famine, destruction, and forced migration," says David Janzen (2012, 1), "is narrated in the most laconic of prose." Regardless of the exact reason for any paucity of description, the reader's attention turns to another actor in the drama, Jehoiachin, who is taken into captivity at an earlier point (24:15) but reappears for a striking cameo in the closing paragraph of the book. It could be said that Jehoiachin is the counterpart of the imprisoned Hoshea, the northern monarch who vanishes after his arrest and imprisonment by the Assyrians (Linville 1998, 262). Jehoiachin, on the contrary, does not disappear, and for him the destruction of Jerusalem does not mark the end of his story. Earlier in this essay it was noted that the book of Kings ends with a monarch in confinement, and this is strictly true but does need some qualification in light of the final events of the chapter:

> In the thirty-seventh year of the exile of King Jehoiachin of Judah, in the twelfth month, on the twenty-seventh day of the month, King Evil-merodach of Babylon, in the year that he began to reign, released [lit. *lifted up his head*] King Jehoiachin of Judah from prison; he spoke kindly to him, and gave him a seat above the other seats of the kings who were with him in Babylon. So Jehoiachin put aside his prison clothes. Every day of his life he dined regularly in the king's presence. For his allowance, a regular allowance was given him by the king, a portion every day, as long as he lived. (Kings 25:27–30 NRSV)

A vast amount of scholarly energy has been spent attempting to finalize this text. Arguments are mounted about the whether the narrative ends on an optimistic or a pessimistic note, or whether the author envisions (or advocates) a restoration of the Davidic monarchy or its dissolution. A current trend among researchers, however, inclines toward a more open-ended reading and includes attempts to identify intertextual echoes as Jehoiachin is granted parole by the king of Babylon. One creative effort, for instance, is to trace verbal links and connections between Mephibosheth at the table of David in 2 Samuel 9, an allusion that may infuse some tacit hope at the end of the story (Schipper 2005; MacDonald 2008, 175–179) or, alternatively, may be an ironic comment on the fact that the line of David ends in much the same way as the line of Saul (Jaynes Granowski 1992). The associations between the episode of Jehoiachin's release and the Joseph narrative in Genesis also offer provocative interpretive results. Starting with the phrase "lifting up the head" that occurs in both stories, John Harvey lists a number of striking parallels:

> As Joseph changed his clothes before meeting Pharaoh (Gen 41:14), and as Pharaoh gave Joseph a change of clothes (Gen 41:43), so upon being exalted by Evil-merodach Jehoiachin put aside his prison clothes (2 Kgs 25:29). Again, as Pharaoh provided Egypt with food through Joseph (Gen 41:55–57), so Jehoiachin was given food by Evil-merodach (2 Kgs 25:29). Finally, as Pharaoh then blessed Joseph with wealth (Gen 41:43), so Evil-merodach blessed Jehoiachin with an allowance (2 Kgs 25:30). (Harvey 2010, 54–55; cf. Jaynes Granowski 1992)

Building on this thesis, Michael Chan (2013, 568) further notes: "[T]he literary connection between Joseph and Jehoiachin has hermeneutical and theological implications. Just as Joseph's release from prison and his exaltation were a prelude to Israel's original exodus from Egypt, so Jehoiachin's own release and exaltation may be interpreted as a prelude to a new exodus—only this time, out of exile and back into Judah." At the beginning of the book of Kings, the aged founder of the dynasty is covered with clothes by his servants, and there is uncertainty about Israel's next king. At the end of the story, the last scion of the dynasty is given new clothes and released to eat at the table of Babylon's king, hinting that the promise of 2 Samuel 7 has not been abrogated and that there is a possibility of survival and prospects for the future, albeit with not the institutional monarchy of the Davidic house but a quite different leadership paradigm after the return from exile. So, the book of Kings ends with a survivor and an unlocked prison, and Jehoiachin is the one king of Judah whose death is not recorded.

Not so long ago, the book of Kings was primarily read for its historical content and to reconstruct the world described by the text, often employing comparative ancient Near Eastern data to venture behind the story. However, the past several decades have witnessed renewed interest in the literary contours of biblical narrative, and Kings has increasingly been appreciated for its poetics and structural design. Recent interpreters seem more comfortable with an unfinalized reading of this expansive text, with its ambiguities and puzzles, in which tyranny is often resisted and survivors emerge at strange times and when the pervasiveness of death is countered by unexpected signs of life that offer an implicit critique of Israel's unsuccessful experiment with institutional monarchy. The three escapees who are mentioned in this chapter—Elijah, the unnamed man who comes in contact with the bones of Elisha, and Jehoiachin, the last king—have something in common: a proximity to the prophetic word enables them to outlive the book of Kings and foreshadow new chapters in the story of Israel.

REFERENCES

Alter, Robert. 2013. *Ancient Israel: The Former Prophets: Joshua, Judges, Samuel, and Kings: A Translation with Commentary*. New York: W. W. Norton.

Beal, Timothy K. 2002. "Specters of Moses: Overtures to Biblical Hauntology." In *"Imagining" Biblical Worlds: Studies in Spatial, Social and Historical Constructs in Honor of James W. Flanagan*, edited by David M. Gunn and Paula M. McNutt, 171–187. Journal for the Study of the Old Testament Supplement 359. Sheffield, Yorkshire: Sheffield Academic Press.

Bodner, Keith. 2013. *Elisha's Profile in the Book of Kings: The Double Agent*. Oxford: Oxford University Press.

Bodner, Keith. 2012. *Jeroboam's Royal Drama*. Oxford: Oxford University Press.

Chan, Michael J. 2013. "Joseph and Jehoiachin: On the Edge of Exodus." *Zeitschrift für die alttestamentliche Wissenschaft* 125: 566–577.

Cohn, Robert L. 2010. "The Literary Structure of Kings." In *The Books of Kings: Sources, Composition, Historiography and Reception*, edited by Baruch Halpern and André Lemaire, with associate editor Matthew J. Adams, 107–122. Vetus Testamentum Supplement 129. Leiden: Brill.

Everhart, Janet S. 2010. "Jezebel: Framed by Eunuchs?" *Catholic Biblical Quarterly* 72: 688–698.

Fewell, Danna Nolan. 2000. "The Gift: World Alteration and Obligation in 2 Kings 4:8–37." In *A Wise and Discerning Mind: Essays in Honor of Burke O. Long*, edited by Saul M. Olyan and Robert C. Culley, 109–123. Providence, RI: Brown Judaic Studies.

Fewell, Danna Nolan, and David M. Gunn. 1993. "Until No Body Remains." In *Gender, Power, and Promise: The Subject of the Bible's First Story*, 164–186. Nashville, TN: Abingdon.

Flannery, Frances. 2008. "Go Back by the Way You Came": An Internal Textual Critique of Elijah's Violence in 1 Kings 18–19." In *Writing and Reading War: Rhetoric, Gender, and Ethics in Biblical and Modern Contexts*, edited by Brad E. Kelle and Frank Ritchel Ames, 161–173. Society of Biblical Literature Symposium Series 42. Atlanta, GA: Society of Biblical Literature.

Foucault, Michel. 1975. *Discipline and Punish: The Birth of the Prison*. New York: Random House.

Geller, Stephen A. 2007. "The Still, Small Voice: 1 Kings 19 and the Roots of Intolerance in Biblical Religion." In *Studies in Arabic and Hebrew Letters: In Honor of Raymond P. Scheindlin*, edited by Jonathan P. Decter and Michael Rand, 47–60. Piscataway, NJ: Gorgias Press.

Gilmour, Rachelle. 2014. *Juxtaposition and the Elisha Cycle*. Library of Hebrew Bible / Old Testament Studies 594. New York and London: T & T Clark.

Granowski, Jan Jaynes. 1992. "Jehoiachin at the King's Table: A Reading of the Ending of the Second Book of Kings." In *Reading between Texts: Intertextuality and the Hebrew Bible*, edited by Danna Nolan Fewell, 173–188. Literary Currents in Biblical Interpretation. Louisville, KY: Westminster John Knox.

Harvey, John E. 2010. "Jehoiachin and Joseph: Hope at the Close of the Deuteronomistic History." In *The Bible as a Human Witness to Divine Revelation: Hearing the Word of God through Historically Dissimilar Traditions*, edited by Randall Heskett and Brian Irwin, 51–61. Library of Hebrew Bible / Old Testament Studies 469. London: T & T Clark.

Hauser, Alan J. 1990. "Yahweh versus Death: The Real Struggle in Kings 17-19." In *From Carmel to Horeb: Elijah in Crisis*, edited by Russell Gregory and Alan J. Hauser, 11–89. Journal for the Study of the Old Testament Supplement 85. Sheffield, Yorkshire: Almond Press.

Janzen, David. 2012. *The Violent Gift: Trauma's Subversion of the Deuteronomistic History's Narrative*. Library of Hebrew Bible / Old Testament Studies 561. London: T & T Clark.

Jobling, David. 1999. "A Bettered Woman: Elisha and the Shunammite in the Deuteronomic Work." In *The Labour of Reading: Desire, Alienation and Biblical Interpretation*, edited by Fiona Black, Roland Boer, and Erin Runions, 177–192. Semeia Studies 36. Atlanta, GA: Scholars Press.

Lasine, Stuart. 2012. *Weighing Hearts: Character, Judgment, and the Ethics of Reading the Bible*. Library of Hebrew Bible / Old Testament Studies 568. New York and London: T & T Clark International.

Long, Burke O. 1991. "The Shunammite Woman: In the Shadow of the Prophet?" *Bible Review* 7 (1): 12–19, 42.

Linville, James R. 1998. *Israel in the Book of Kings: The Past as a Project of Social Identity*. Journal for the Study of the Old Testament Supplement 272. Sheffield, Yorkshire: Sheffield Academic Press.

Linville, James R. 2014. "On the Authority of Dead Kings." In *Deuteronomy–Kings as Emerging Authoritative Books: A Conversation*, edited by Diana V. Edelman, 203–222. Ancient Near East Monographs / Monografías sobre el Antiguo Cercano Oriente. Atlanta, GA: Society of Biblical Literature.

MacDonald, Nathan. 2008. *Not Bread Alone: The Uses of Food in the Old Testament*. Oxford: Oxford University Press.

Mobley, Gregory. 2009. "1 and 2 Kings." In *Theological Bible Commentary*, edited by Gail R. O'Day and David L. Petersen, 119–143. Louisville, KY: Westminster John Knox Press.

Roncace, Mark. 2000. "Elisha and the Woman of Shunem: 2 Kings 4.8-37 and 8.1-6 Read in Conjunction." *Journal for the Study of the Old Testament* 91: 109–127.

Schipper, Jeremy. 2005. "Significant Resonances" with Mephibosheth in 2 Kings 25.27-30: A Response to Donald F. Murray." *Journal of Biblical Literature* 124: 521–529.

Schipper, Jeremy. 2009. "Deuteronomy 24:5 and King Asa's Foot Disease in 1 Kings 15:23b." *Journal of Biblical Literature* 128: 643–648.

Schulte, Hannelis. 1994. "The End of the Omride Dynasty: Social-Ethical Observations on the Subject of Power and Violence." Translated by Carl S. Ehrlich. In *Ethics and Politics in the Hebrew Bible*, edited by Douglas A. Knight. *Semeia* 66: 133–148.

Shields, Mary E. 1993. "Subverting a Man of God, Elevating a Woman: Role and Power Reversals in 2 Kings 4." *Journal for the Study of the Old Testament* 58: 59–69.

Siebert-Hommes, Jopie. 1996. "The Widow of Zarephath and the Great Woman of Shunem: A Comparative Analysis of Two Stories." In *On Reading Prophetic Texts: Gender-Specific and Related Studies in Memory of Fokkelien van Dijk-Hemmes*, edited by B. Becking and M. Dijkstra, 231–250. Biblical Interpretation Series 18. Leiden: Brill.

Stavrakopoulou, Francesca. 2006. "Exploring the Garden of Uzza: Death, Burial and Ideologies of Kingship." *Biblica* 87: 1–21.

Steiner, George. 1984. "A Death of Kings." In *George Steiner, A Reader*, 171–178. New York: Oxford University Press.

Tonstad, Sigve. 2005. "The Limits of Power: Revisiting Elijah at Horeb." *Scandinavian Journal of the Old Testament* 19: 253–266.

Walsh, Carey. 2013. "Why Remember Jezebel?" In *Remembering Biblical Figures in the Late Persian & Early Hellenistic Periods: Social Memory and Imagination*, edited by Diana V. Edelman and Ehud Ben Zvi, 311–333. New York: Oxford University Press.

Wray Beal, Lissa. 2014. *1 & 2 Kings*. Appollos Old Testament Commentary. Downers Grove: InterVarsity Press.

Wright, J. Edward. 2004. "Whither Elijah? The Ascension of Elijah in Biblical and Extrabiblical Traditions." In *Things Revealed: Studies in Early Jewish and Christian Literature in Honor of Michael E. Stone*, edited by Esther G. Chazon, David Satran and Ruth A. Clements, 123–138. Supplements to the Journal for the Study of Judaism 89. Leiden: Brill.

CHAPTER 17

NARRATIVE AMONG THE LATTER PROPHETS

PATRICIA K. TULL

INTRODUCTION

FEW scholars writing on biblical narrative have dealt in depth with stories in the prophetic books Isaiah, Jeremiah, Ezekiel, and the Twelve. Yet narratives are employed in a variety of ways in several of these latter prophets. Reflecting on their features can enrich awareness of the kaleidoscope of literary genres contributing to these books.

Since even nonnarrative texts betray a narrative arc, I will first consider the prevailing storyline in the prophetic books overall, to which poetry, speeches, narratives, and other forms contribute. Narrativity can also be seen in individual passages of prophecy, and deserves more attention than this article can offer. But some examples will point in this direction.

Moving to passages that share features with classical biblical narrative, I will survey the occurrence of these narratives, pointing out atypical features in chapters of Isaiah and Jeremiah that also occur in 2 Kings; intermingling of first- and third-person narratives; and the truncated narrative settings of many prophetic oracles. Finally, I will comment on Jonah, which turns the prevailing prophetic story lines upside down.

THE NARRATIVE ARC OF THE PROPHETS

Biblical prophets and their books share certain narrative assumptions with biblical stories: that cause and effect link successive events; that humans, God, and the natural world are bound together in these links from the past to the future. Further, prophetic books assume that divine actions toward humans are ethically motivated, aimed to promote righteousness.

Tribulations during centuries of occupation by foreign empires, especially beginning in the eighth century BCE, were viewed by Judah's own theologians as divine attempts to call the nation to repentant reconciliation (see, e.g., Neh. 9:29–38). This could account for the inception of written prophetic books in the eighth century, even though stories of prophets precede these by many centuries (Nogalski 2011, 9–10). Judah's sin, resulting in successive disastrous destructions by foreign empires, and followed by Jerusalem's reconstruction while still enduring Persian rule, occupies the complex narrative arc seen especially in the books of Isaiah and the Twelve. To these multicentury accounts, Jeremiah and Ezekiel contribute testimonies concerning the critical years surrounding the Babylonian destruction.

Norman Gottwald (1984, 84–85) has discerned in the prophetic books, both individually and collectively, a narrative arc he describes as a U-shaped comedic plotline: "Without exception these books describe a declension into a present 'evil' situation. . . . Also without exception the prophetic books describe an ascension which will follow judgment and lead to political and natural restoration."

Subplots—sometimes U-shaped, sometimes inverted at least temporarily—likewise appear, carried through prophetic speech even where narrative forms are absent. Isaiah's first chapter, for instance, points out the present tragic relationship between God and Israel: "I reared children and brought them up, but they have rebelled against me. . . . Why do you seek further beatings?. . . . Daughter Zion is left like a booth in a vineyard, like a shelter in a cucumber field, like a besieged city" (vv. 2, 5, 8). A solution is proposed: "Wash yourselves; make yourselves clean; remove the evil of your doings from before my eyes" (v. 16). Visions of an improved future are articulated: "Zion shall be redeemed by justice, and those in her who repent, by righteousness" (v. 27). Happy endings are not inevitable, however. Some leaders will not enjoy the envisioned outcome: "Rebels and sinners shall be destroyed together. . . . The strong shall become like tinder, and their work like a spark" (vv. 28, 31). Such prophecy describes past, present, and days to come that will finally live up to original hopes (Tull 2010, 47–73).

Habakkuk similarly begins with complaints (1:2–4), this time conveyed not from God, but to God. A dramatic dialogue between prophet and deity follows. As the second chapter begins, Habakkuk soliloquizes, "I will stand at my watchpost. . . . I will keep watch to see what he will say to me" (v. 1), before reporting judgments that God communicates. The prophet takes a mediating role, standing with the people before God, speaking doom reluctantly, and finally offering a model of trust even though "the fig tree does not blossom, and no fruit is on the vines" (3:17).

Jeremiah similarly employs divine-human dialogue, representing the prophet as a lamenting mediator before God even while he is predicting unprecedented violence. This drama serves as a character witness for Jeremiah, defusing in advance his political foes' negative representations. The poetry enables Jeremiah to model a wide range of emotions and to offer others a vocabulary of lament.

In contrast, Isaiah 40–55, poised on the brink of Jerusalem's rebuilding, stresses the narrative arc's upswing, inviting the audience to recall God's deeds in the deep past (creation, exodus, befriending of Abraham) as models for present hopes. More recent tragedies are set firmly in the past. The prophet points toward political changes already on the horizon, interpreting them as God's redemption, planned long ago (Tull 1997).

Prophetic Narratives

Within this unfolding metanarrative, some portions of the prophetic books evince more obvious narrative features, such as dialogue between characters and narrated actions. Others are mere snippets, reports that "[t]he word of the Lord came to X" (perhaps including time or place), followed by the divine message (and sometimes the prophet's response), or reports that the prophet spoke or acted. Many accounts that begin dramatically disappear into prophetic sayings, leaving scene and players behind. Such curtailed reports hint that even where narratives do emerge, storytelling serves the purpose not of entertainment, nor of historical accounting, but of instruction. With those caveats in mind, we might catalog narrative segments in the latter prophets as consisting more or less of these:

1. Narratives Shared with 2 Kings
   - Isaiah 36–39 duplicates 2 Kings 18–20 (cf. Isa. 7:1/2 Kings 16:5).
   - Jeremiah 52 duplicates 2 Kings 24–25.
2. Narrative in Isaiah
   - Isaiah 6:1–13; 7:1–17; 8:1–8; 20:1–2 all disappear into divine messages, leaving the scene behind.
3. Narrative in Hosea and Amos
   - Stories in Hosea 1 and 3 are, like Isaiah's, truncated lead-ins to divine speech.
   - Amos 7:1–8:3, 9:1–4 describe Amos's encounters with God and with the priest Amaziah.
4. Narrative in Jeremiah
   - Dramatic first-person dialogues between the prophet and God characterize chapters 1–20.
   - First-person narratives in which Jeremiah reports hearing and acting on God's instructions are found in chapters 13, 18, 24, 25.
   - Third-person narratives begin in 19:14–15, continuing into chapter 20. They predominate beginning in chapter 26 (26:1–24; 28:5–17; 32:1–5; 34: 6–12; chs. 36–45). In this latter section, a third-person framework sometimes encloses Jeremiah's first-person narrative, in which divine speech prevails (as in 27:1–28:4; 32:1–25; 35:1–19). Jeremiah's narrative portions are not chronologically ordered: stories concerning King Jehoiachin (chs. 26, 36) intertwine with stories of King Zedekiah (chs. 21, 27–29, 32, 34, 37–39).
5. Narrative in Ezekiel and Zechariah
   - Except for a third-person superscription (1:2–3), Ezekiel's entire book is told in the first person. Divine speeches predominate, with very few dramas, or even dramatized dialogues. Interactions with other humans are minimal and lead to divine speeches.
   - Outside of the third-person superscriptions in Zechariah 1 and 7, the first eight chapters of Zechariah consist of first-person vision reports and oracles. An unnamed speaker in 11:4–17 describes God's instructions, his own symbolic actions, and God's interpretation.
6. Jonah as Narrative
   - Jonah 1–4 is a fully narrated third-person tale whose themes and story world differ from those of other prophetic books.

Among the stories in prophetic literature, certain norms prevail. Two scenes predominate: the prophet's interactions with God, who gives the prophet a message to deliver, and the prophet's interactions with human recipients of this message, including their various reactions and the ensuing struggles (Applegate 2000). Stories appear in both first and third person. Alternation between these two viewpoints can be abrupt, unexpected, and unexplained. And unlike many other biblical stories, including those concerning prophetic figures in the Pentateuch and Deuteronomistic narratives—with certain exceptions noted below—the prophetic stories lack supernatural features. What occurs beyond the plane of natural experience occurs as a vision report, generally but not always metaphorical, and often fanciful and extended.

NARRATIVES SHARED WITH 2 KINGS

The stories in category 1 above, generally viewed as originating with Kings, stand outside the norms of prophetic narratives as described above. Isaiah 36–39 relates a series of encounters between the prophet and King Hezekiah in which Isaiah conveys several divine messages. These stories are not naturalistic. Rather, like much of Kings, they include miraculous elements, from the sudden deaths of 185,000 Assyrians (37:36) to the sun's backward movement (38:8). Unlike typical prophetic narratives, these episodes focus not on the prophet's message, innocence, and troubles but on the mostly righteous reactions of King Hezekiah. They stand in some tension with portrayals of Hezekiah's administration in Isaiah 22 and 28–31 (see particularly 31:1–3; see Tull 2010, 418, 461–464, 523–559).

Aside from Jonah's cameo appearance in 2 Kings 14:25, Isaiah is the only latter prophet who appears in Kings. Given the Deuteronomic interest in promoting Hezekiah, the function of prophets as consultants in these narratives, and the fact that Isaiah alone of the eighth-century prophets lived in Jerusalem, his appearance in Kings is perhaps less surprising than the absence of Jeremiah, another pre-exilic Jerusalem figure who foretold its fate a century later.

These stories from Kings appear, slightly altered, in Isaiah 36–39 amid several chapters of non-Isaianic material. They add to the book, among other things, narrative accounting for the postponement of the judgments Isaiah foretold and a foretaste of the judgment readers know will occupy a later generation, a foreshadowing that appropriately leads to the often-predicted yet unrepresented moment of Jerusalem's destruction between 39:8 and 40:1.

Jeremiah 52, preceded by "thus far are the words of Jeremiah" (51:64), retells events already foretold by Jeremiah and depicted in his narratives, supplying details that do not involve the prophet, who had been removed to Egypt. Without mentioning Jeremiah, this chapter vindicates him. Whereas Isaiah's book moves on to Persian times, Jeremiah—having voiced higher hopes in chapters 30–31—concludes on the mildly consoling story of Jehoichin's release from prison, amnesty for the only recent king Jeremiah had not criticized.

NARRATIVE IN ISAIAH

Each of the four stories unique to Isaiah dissolves into divine speech, demonstrating that the episodes themselves, however vivid, are settings or even pretexts for prophetic instruction. Two appear in the first-person voice of the prophet, and two speak of Isaiah in third person.

Abrupt shifts between persons stand without transition or explanation. Like those in Amos, Jeremiah, and to some extent Ezekiel, Isaiah's stories exemplify the latter prophets' two prevailing narrative motifs: the prophet's encounter with and commissioning by God and the prophet's encounter with and rejection by the intended audience.

Isaiah 6:1–13 is the closest the book offers to a full narrative episode from the prophet's viewpoint (Tull 2010, 137–149). Isaiah recounts a vision of the temple as the divine throne room, where YHWH sits surrounded by attending seraphs. These seraphs, the prophet, and YHWH all speak, act, and interact. Even the room responds, filling with smoke while its thresholds shake. The story dissolves into divine words in verses 9–13, interrupted only by one two-word question.

Isaiah 7 offers a third-person account of the prophet's encounter (or encounters; see v. 10) with Hezekiah's father Ahaz. Although it follows immediately after chapter 6, the prophet does not here (or anywhere) offer the horrific message that God has just given him. What he offers instead is a salvation oracle followed by a sign.

This story, beginning with a verse that nearly repeats 2 Kings 16:5, goes out of its way to demonstrate parallels with Isaiah 36. In 36:1–2, an opening synopsis relates the Assyrian king Sennacherib's capture of all Judah's fortified cities, leading to a the dramatic scene in which the emperor's envoy stands "by the conduit of the upper pool on the highway to the fuller's field," verbally assaulting Hezekiah and his court. The parallel opening in 7:1–3 relates a failed attack by two kings combined, the terror of Ahaz and his household, and the directive to God's envoy Isaiah to meet Ahaz in the exact place where the Rabshakeh will later stand. Such extreme specificity demands that readers draw comparisons: Hezekiah, despite all discouragement, stands fast, while Ahaz, despite all encouragement, fails to do so. Whatever history may underlie Isaiah 7's evidently Deuteronomistic development, its final form offers not just a salvation oracle and sign but also a devastating rebuke that aligns thematically with other stories of prophetic encounters with civil leaders (Ackroyd 1984; Williamson 1998).

First-person narrative both precedes and follows this third-person story. As chapter 8 begins, Isaiah relates divine instructions to write on a tablet and have his words attested by witnesses. Isaiah then recounts the conception and birth of his own son, who is given the name written on the tablet. This is the chapter's only narrative snippet, brimming with unexplained intimations, but the self-referential voice continues through verse 18.

Isaiah 20 appears at first to present a brief but coherent third-person story of a prophetic sign-act highlighting the danger of seeking foreign military aid. But closer reading reveals a more tangled tale (Tull 2010, 324–327). Verse 1 offers a temporal note, but it remains unclear whether it announces the beginning context of the story (as in 36:1) or summarizes its outcome as well (as in 7:1). Both options are temporally problematic, rendering it impossible to determine whether Isaiah's walking naked and barefoot followed Ashdod's defeat or preceded it by three years, and at what point (and through whom) God comments on this action (see the difference between v. 2's verb tenses in NRSV and Tanakh, on the one hand, and in NIV and NJB on the other). These disruptions suggest that this story originated much later than Isaiah, based on inaccurately recollected events.

It is quite probable, in short, that both of these third-person narratives in Isaiah 7 and 20 were added considerably later than the first-person material, raising a question that becomes especially interesting in Jeremiah: In the prophetic books, does narrative viewpoint yield clues about authorial origins, as it seems to do in Nehemiah? May we suppose that first-person narratives authentically originated with the prophets themselves? Care to allow first-person narratives to stand, and to refrain from employing a fictitious first-person voice, could help explain the alternating viewpoints characterizing these books.

NARRATIVE IN HOSEA AND AMOS

Like Isaiah, Hosea, Amos, and Jeremiah flow back and forth, sometimes dizzyingly, between first- and third-person narration. Hosea's story of unhappy marriage begins in third person. God speaks four times, directing the prophet to dramatize within his own family God's failed relationship with Israel. Hosea never speaks, neither to respond to God nor to interpret God's directives.

The first-person speech in chapter 2 does not at first reveal its speaker, who could at first be Hosea. Not until verse 13 does an anchoring "says the Lord" occur. The speaker shifts abruptly in Hosea 3:1, where the "I" is no longer God but the prophet, reporting, "The Lord said to me again. . . ." This narrative is sustained for three verses before it issues in prophetic speeches that continue through the remainder of the book.

In Amos 7, the prophet relates visions accompanied by conversations: God shows judgments poised to commence; the prophet intercedes; and God, eager to show mercy, relents. Twice this pattern occurs, first with locusts (vv. 1–3), then with fire (vv. 4–6). The third instance begins the same way, but this time God asks Amos what he sees (a plumb line), and then elaborates its significance, threatening to destroy Israel's sanctuaries and to "rise against the house of Jeroboam with the sword" (v. 9).

Before Amos can intercede, a new story interrupts, making a cliffhanger of God's ominous words. This episode, told in the third person, begins not with God but with a new figure, Amaziah the priest of Bethel. Echoing God's message to Amos in the previous verse, Amaziah repeats the threat against Jeroboam. Yet in the priest's opinion the threat calls not for repentance but for expelling the prophet as a dangerous conspirator (God being the unrecognized co-conspirator). Telescoping the action, Amaziah speaks immediately to Amos, derisively warning him to leave the king's temple and go prophesy in Judah. Amos's reply is far longer and more caustic than the priest's: He is no prophet for profit. He was called by God, who will destroy Amaziah and his family.

Immediately the storyline reverts to first-person narration of one more encounter with God, patterned after the previous one, yielding yet again to divine speech, this time describing the coming human tragedy (8:1–3), one that now, thanks to Amaziah, seems inevitable. A new prophetic address follows, echoing the book's earlier themes. In 9:1–4 Amos offers a final vision report in which God stands beside the altar from which Amaziah had dismissed Amos, ordering its destruction on the heads of people who, though they flee, cannot evade God's pursuit.

On their own, the four previous first-person vision reports, with their divine-human dialogues, build to a climactic theophany. But the story that intrudes just as God stops relenting offers a third-party witness to the fairness of divine judgment, removing from the scene "the one person who had twice proven successful in intervening on Israel's behalf" (Nogalski 2011, 350).

Narratives in Isaiah, Hosea, and Amos demonstrate the complexity of prophetic stories intertwined with and buttressing prophetic messages. Interplay between the prophet's speeches and dramatic portrayals becomes a remarkably effective rhetorical tool in Jeremiah, which offers the lengthiest and most abundant narratives of all.

NARRATIVE IN JEREMIAH

This article cannot do justice to Jeremiah's stories, which have been discussed frequently by others. I offer only an overview with observations. The narrative arc of Jeremiah's life commences in chapter 1 where, following the superscription, Jeremiah himself recounts an inaugural dialogue with God, who like formidable figures of old speaks in poetic parallelism to the young prose-speaking prophet. After commissioning him, God begins showing Jeremiah visions similar to Amos's, asking "What do you see?" and affirming his interpretation with further words. Nowhere else in the prophets does such an elaborate divine-human dialogue unfold, approaching the complexity of divine exchanges with Abraham and Moses—but this one occurs in the first person, enhancing its intimacy.

From chapters 2 to 6, prophetic poetry reigns with few interruptions. Yet, conditioned by the opening, readers discern a narrative not only of national past, present, and future, but of Jeremiah's own developing responses (4:10; 5:3–5; see Henderson 2007). A major story arc slips in sideways when the prophet contextualizes personal threats within his interactions with God (vv. 19, 21).

Jeremiah is instructed in 13:1–11 to buy and then destroy a linen loincloth representing the nation. Similarly, in 18:1–11, Jeremiah is instructed to visit a potter, whose clay God compares with Israel. Verse 18 reports a conspiracy against Jeremiah, drawing rage he voices to God, who instructs the prophet to incite his enemies further with a public demonstration in the Hinnom Valley (Topheth), using a smashed jug as a visual aid (19:1–13). Jeremiah's actions are not related, but only implied by the first hint of a third-person narrator saying, "When Jeremiah came from Topheth . . . " (v. 14).

This snippet signals a shift that will occur over the course of transitional chapters. The narrator goes on to relate Jeremiah's overnight arrest and release by the priest Pashhur, and the prophet's boldly personal rebuke of the priest, reminiscent of Amos's words to Amaziah (20:1–6). This confrontation leads to Jeremiah's final, powerful lament (vv. 7–18).

From here on the third-person narrative voice increasingly takes control. After chapter 25, the few first-person accounts Jeremiah offers are introduced by and enclosed within the other narrative voice (see 27:1; 32:6; 35:1 [cf. vv. 12, 18]), until, with chapter 36, they disappear entirely. Thus the prophetic message is transmitted not only through Jeremiah's speeches, but through third-person testimonies to his suffering and vindication.

Up to Jeremiah 21, the royal family that will dominate the book's second half have hardly been mentioned. This all changes when an inquiry from Jerusalem's final king, Zedekiah, occasions a dire prediction of doom, followed by several other speeches in chapters 22–25, some of which involve Zedekiah's predecessor Jehoiakim. The prophet relates two visions (24:1–3; 25:16–17) that further convey divine intentions.

Although the narratives that follow demonstrate that Zedekiah's and Jehoiakim's reactions to Jeremiah differ dramatically, stories involving the two kings continue to interweave. Jehoiakim tales (Jer. 26; 36) lead into lengthier Zedekiah stories (Jer. 27–29; 37–39). While interactions with God are almost always narrated in first person, interactions with others are almost always told by a third party, allowing readers access Jeremiah does not have.

Jeremiah 26–28 ushers in the largely narrative portion of the book. Chapter 26, set in Jehoiakim's time, recaps in the third person Jeremiah's speech in the temple, already reported in chapter 7. Drama follows: Jeremiah is seized and his life threatened. In the ensuing trial he is accused of treason and defends himself. In an intertextual twist, some elders quote the prophet Micah, asserting that Hezekiah saved the city not by executing the prophet but by heeding his words. Their speech halts the proceedings but, underscoring Jeremiah's endangerment, Jehoiakim's pursuit and execution of another prophet is recounted.

Conflict narratives continue in Jeremiah 27–28, which jump to Zedekiah's reign. Jeremiah, introduced by the narrator, reports God's instructions to wear a yoke as an object lesson, warning envoys from surrounding nations that they too risk exile. He reports warning Zedekiah, the priests, and Jerusalem's people against other prophets' reassuring words. This lengthy speech prepares for chapter 28's drama, in which the prophet Hananiah confronts him. (By the time Jeremiah speaks in v. 5, the story has reverted to the third person.) Hananiah breaks Jeremiah's visual aid, offering further reassurances of speedy recovery from Babylon's "yoke." Jeremiah leaves, but later returns with a rejoinder, including news of Hananiah's impending death, which 28:17 announces.

Several chapters comprising various genres follow. Then, in the final, lengthy complex of Jeremiah 36–45, previous themes are reiterated at greater length. (For an analysis of parallel structure in Jer. 26–35; 36–45, in which chapters set in Jehoiakim's reign provide both framework and thematic cues; see Yates 2005.) The intervening chapters include letters to the exiles in Babylon (Jer. 29), anticipations of restoration (Jer. 30–31, 33), and, strikingly, a story told by Jeremiah in the siege's final days. This story of buying a field (32:6–15), with its clear expectation of restoration, suits its setting thematically. Yet it is framed by a third-person story containing details that will only emerge later—namely, King Zedekiah's visiting with Jeremiah in prison during Babylon's final siege and the prophet's explicit predictions of Zedekiah's fate (see 37:15–17; 38:14–28).

The accounts that follow further indict Jerusalem's leadership: a truncated story of injustice toward slaves (34:8–11) and Jeremiah's rebuke; Jeremiah's narrative of an incident during Jehoiakim's time in which the Rechabites' faithfulness underscores the previous chapter's injustice. The vivid portrayal in Jeremiah 36 of a contemptuous King Jehoiakim systematically burning the scroll Jeremiah sent to him contrasts sharply with King Zedekiah's tremulous consultations with the prophet in chapters 37–38. Both kings act at odds with those surrounding them: Jehoiakim's officials react in alarm, protecting Baruch and Jeremiah, but Zedekiah's officials arrest and beat the prophet and advise execution. These complex narratives and dialogues bring Zedekiah into high relief. He is not simply a steadfast God-seeker like Hezekiah or an adversary like Amaziah, Jehoiakim, or his own officials, but a frightened young man caught in a web of power dynamics far exceeding his capacity. (For illuminating analyses of these chapters see Callaway 1991; Willis 2000; Boyle 1999). The erratic treatment of Jeremiah mirrors the general chaos during the siege, which is as minutely told in Jeremiah as it is studiously silenced in Isaiah.

NARRATIVE IN EZEKIEL AND ZECHARIAH

As was stated earlier, both Ezekiel and Zechariah 1–8 are formulated in the first person. Very little action occurs outside the vision reports, which themselves offer vivid dramas. The prophets' primary interactions occur not with other humans but with God or, in Zechariah's case, God's messenger.

Ezekiel's visions and messages often come as he sits with others. He first locates himself among the exiles by the river Chebar (1:1), where God speaks to him, commissioning him to speak to Israel (2:3–4), and then returns him to the exiles. For seven days he cannot speak (3:14–15). His second vision comes as he sits with elders at home (8:1). The spirit transports him in a vision to Jerusalem, where God directs him to observe abominations occurring in the temple and a resultant divinely ordered slaughter, which the prophet protests in vain. He witnesses God's spirit leaving the temple before he himself is transported back to Chaldea and reports to the exiles what he has seen. The elders return to consult the prophet in 14:1, inspiring further divine reproaches. When they return in 20:1, Ezekiel is told to say to them, "I will not be consulted by you" (v. 3, cf. 14:3; 33:30–31). Thus, unlike the leaders in Jeremiah, these figures play little part in the story.

Even implied conversations with others are bounded by divine speech. After the prophet follows God's directions by acting out the king's escape from Jerusalem, it is God's speech to Ezekiel that discloses that others are asking about his actions and directs the prophet's response (12:9, cf. 12:22, 27; 13:2, 6, 10; 18:2, 19, 25; 21:7; 33:17, 24, 30; 37:11, 18). God also quotes the objectionable speech of surrounding nations (25:3; 26:2; 27:3, 32; 28:2, 9; 29:9 35:10, 12; 36:2, 13, 20, 35; 38:11). Exceptionally, at the end of the book's first portion, when Ezekiel's wife dies and he obeys God's instruction not to mourn, readers witness others inquiring directly, "Will you not tell us what these things mean for us, that you are acting this way?" (24:19), and when Jerusalem is destroyed, an escapee speaks to Ezekiel, saying, "The city has fallen" (33:21).

Even Ezekiel seldom speaks to God, silent until 4:14, where his protest against baking on human dung elicits mercy from God. Otherwise, his words rarely affect the story's outcome (9:8; 11:13; 20:49). Similarly, it is not clear how many of the symbolic actions God orders actually materialize, since Ezekiel's report is seldom offered. In Ezekiel 3 he reports eating the scroll and going to the valley in response to God's commands in verses 1 and 22. But subsequently God instructs him to portray Jerusalem's siege with a brick and other materials (4:1–3); to lie on his left and right side for extended periods (vv. 4–8); to cook over dung (vv. 9–13); and to shave his head and divide the hair (5:1–4). None of these actions is reported.

Ezekiel's narrative arc encompasses the difficult years preceding Jerusalem's final destruction, as seen from Babylon. Within God's speech, a much broader swath of history is reviewed, often metaphorically. Most of the book's significant narrative occurs within Ezekiel's visions, which describe imagined events such as the behavior of Jerusalemites and their slaughter (Ezek. 8–11), and within God's speeches, which sometimes rehearse ancient stories (Ezek. 20) or present bizarre allegorical narratives (Ezek. 16, 17, 23).

Zechariah 1–6 contains a series of visions. Following an opening oracle comparing the audience with their ancestors, in 1:8 the prophet begins to describe eight dreamlike visions, filled with baroque imagery, that are interpreted to him by an accompanying angel in terms of the immediate future. Chapter 7 narrates a consultation over fasting that leads to a divine response. Chapter 8 and following represent divine oracles concerning the future.

SUMMARY

Nearly all stories in the latter prophets involve obstacles for prophets conveying God's plans to humans, who generally resist or disbelieve. As such, two scenes are elaborated in multiple ways: the prophet's encounters with the divine, and the prophet's encounters with his message's intended recipients. Variations on the former run from straightforward reports of receiving God's word (with the message more or less elaborately reported) to lengthier, sometimes conflicted, accounts of dialogues with God. Variations on the latter run from straightforward reports of the prophet's delivering the message (also more or less elaborately reported) to dramatic and varied accounts of reactions to this message.

The stories adapted from Kings, as we have seen, do not follow this pattern, but instead feature the fate of rulers, shining favor on Hezekiah and, to a lesser degree, on Jehoiachin. There the prophet, if present, functions as a valued advisor. The Hezekiah stories turn on miraculous events—angelically instigated mass carnage, a dramatic healing, an astrophysical impossibility.

JONAH AS NARRATIVE

Like these, the book of Jonah falls outside the general parameters of prophetic narratives. Jonah's story, a fiction built on the nationalistic but otherwise unknown Israelite prophet Jonah ben Amittai (2 Kings 14:25; see West 1984), is told from a third-person perspective throughout. It turns on eye-poppingly supernatural events—a colossal sea storm, calmed by the prophet's ejection from the ship; a giant fish carrying Jonah landward; the dramatic conversion of the evil empire, from cattle to king; a plant that grows and dies in a day. Yet the prophet barely acknowledges these unearthly events. Although like other prophets he is sent to deliver a message to a straying community and its leaders, he evades, barely says anything, and spends himself on adamant vindictiveness.

Ironically, unlike all the other prophets, who despite valiant efforts fail to move most of their audience, Jonah succeeds so splendidly that he even inspires the sailors to whom God did not send him. This narrative turns the conventions of prophetic stories upside down: an uncompassionate prophet; a pliable king; a willing community; and a lesson turned not on the hearers but on Jonah himself, and upon all who too hastily identify with the righteousness of Israel's prophets.

REFERENCES

Ackroyd, Peter R. 1984. "The Biblical Interpretation of the Reigns of Ahaz and Hezekiah." In *In the Shelter of Elyon: Essays on Ancient Palestiian Life and Literature in Honor of G. W. Ahlström*, edited by W. Barrick and John R. Spencer, 247–259. Sheffield, Yorkshire: JSOT Press.

Applegate, John. 2000. "Narrative Patterns for the Communication of Commissioned Speech in the Prophets: A Three-Scene Model." In *Narrativity in Biblical and Related Texts*, edited by George J. Brooke and Jean-Daniel Kaestli, 69–88. Leuven: Leuven University Press.

Boyle, Brian. 1999. "Narrative as Ideology: Synchronic (Narrative Critical) and Diachronic Readings of Jeremiah 37-38." *Pacifica* 12: 293–312.

Callaway, Mary Chilton. 1991. "Telling the Truth and Telling Stories: An Analysis of Jeremiah 37-38." *Union Seminary Quarterly Review* 44: 253–265.

Gottwald, Norman K. 1984. "Tragedy and Comedy in the Latter Prophets." In *Tragedy and Comedy in the Bible*, edited by J. Cheryl Exum. *Semeia* 32: 83–96.

Henderson, Joseph M. 2007. "Jeremiah 2-10 as a Unified Literary Composition: Evidence of Dramatic Portrayal and Narrative Progression." In *Uprooting and Planting: Essays on Jeremiah for Leslie Allen*, edited by John Goldingay, 116–152. New York: T&T Clark.

Nogalski, James D. 2011. *The Book of the Twelve: Hosea–Jonah*. Smyth & Helwys Bible Commentary 18a. Macon, GA: Smyth & Helwys.

Tull, Patricia K. 2010. *Isaiah 1-39*. Smyth & Helwys Bible Commentary 14a. Macon, GA: Smyth & Helwys.

Tull, Patricia K. 1997. *Remember the Former Things: The Recollection of Previous Texts in Second Isaiah*. Society of Biblical Literature Dissertation Series 161. Atlanta, GA: Scholars Press.

West, Mona. 1984. "Irony in the Book of Jonah: Audience Identification with the Hero." *Perspectives in Religious Studies* 11: 233–242.

Williamson, H. G. M. 1998. "The Messianic Texts in Isaiah 1–39." In *King and Messiah in Israel and the Ancient Near East*, edited by John Day, 238–270. Sheffield, Yorkshire: Sheffield University Press.

Willis, Timothy M. 2000. "'They Did Not Listen to the Voice of the Lord': A Literary Analysis of Jeremiah 37-45." *Restoration Quarterly* 42: 65–84.

Yates, Gary E. 2005. "Narrative Parallelism and the 'Jehoiakim Frame': A Reading Strategy for Jeremiah 26-45." *Journal of the Evangelical Theological Society* 48: 263–281.

CHAPTER 18

DIVINE RHETORIC AND PROPHETIC SILENCE IN THE BOOK OF JONAH

CHESUNG JUSTIN RYU

THE story of Jonah is one of the best-known of biblical narratives, perhaps because of its "oversized" imagery: a big storm, a big fish, and the exaggerated repentance of a big, evil city. Its primary conflict, however, is a simple one, centering around the struggle between God and Jonah over the fate of Nineveh. God orders Jonah to go and preach against the great and wicked city of Nineveh, but Jonah runs away. Only later do we learn the reason—namely, that Jonah senses God's intention to forgive Nineveh. To curtail Jonah's flight, God hurls a great storm, and the sailors throw Jonah overboard to save their lives. God appoints a great fish to swallow Jonah and to vomit him out after three days. God gives a second order, and Jonah goes to Nineveh and preaches against it. The people of Nineveh repent, and God decides to forgive them. Jonah is angry, but God delegitimizes Jonah's anger using the *qiqayon* plant. God justifies the decision to save Nineveh by citing the great number of people in the city. Jonah does not respond to God, so the narrative ends with Jonah's silence.

LITERARY CRITICAL READINGS OF JONAH

The last four decades have witnessed many studies of the literary features of the book of Jonah. One result has been the growing consensus that the book should be read as a unified, integrated, and coherent whole. The works of Jonathan Magonet (1983), Jack Sasson (1990), Phyllis Trible (1994), and Kenneth Craig (1999) deserve specific attention because of their thorough and exhaustive studies of Jonah's literary features and devices. These studies have shown how the literary form and the meaning of the text are closely related. The repetition and parallels in the text draw a lot of attention. Some (Magonet 1983; Sasson 1990; Trible 1994; Simon and Schramm 1999) have found symmetrical or chiastic structures related to the repetition and parallelism between Jonah 1 and 3 or between the first scene (Jon. 1–2) and the second scene (Jon. 3–4), while other critics (Craig 1999) have focused on the reading process and the relationship between dialogue and narration demonstrated through reply, repetition, and parallels. These studies expose that the reading and meaning of the text is not just controlled by the author but rather occurs between the literary forms of the narrative and the active engagement of the readers to those literary forms and devices.

The role of the narrator and his/her ideological position has also been the subject of much study. By recognizing and analyzing the narrator's role of controlling information, some critics (Sasson 1990; Craig 1999) question if the narrator favors one position (such as God's) over others (such as Jonah's) while other critics (Levine 1984) distinguish the position of the author from that of the characters to emphasize that both God and Jonah are merely characters in the narrative.

Studies of the implied reader have extended our understanding of the text by including the historical, social, and cultural knowledge of the ancient audience. By considering the narrative competencies of implied readers, scholars (Cooper 1993; Person 1996; Kahn 2000; Muldoon 2010) have exposed the text's rhetorical strategies, including the use of intertextual allusions that would have been familiar to an ancient audience.

The fit and placement of the psalm in Jonah 2 has also garnered attention (Miles 1975; Sasson 1990; Gunn and Fewell 1993; Craig 1999), particularly the question of how the use of this psalm affects our understanding of Jonah's character and his theological outlook. Some critics (Miles 1975; Trible 1994) argue that the psalm helps to construct a comical and self-righteous portrait of Jonah, while others (Sasson 1990; Gunn and Fewell 1993) offer a more sympathetic reading that ties together human fidelity and divine justice.

Genre studies have also been popular in literary studies of Jonah. While historical critics have failed to agree on the book's historical context, stumbling over whether the book presents itself as history or prophecy, literary scholars have offered a number of genre alternatives: allegory (Ephros 1999), irony (Good 1981; Fewell and Gunn 1993), midrash (Trible 1963), parable (Allen 1976), parody (Miles 1975; Band 1990), satire (Ackerman 1981; Holbert 1981; Marcus 1995), and so on.

Although diverse methodologies have been applied to the interpretation of Jonah, traditional readings, which praise God's universal, inclusive mercy, emphasize themes of repentance and forgiveness and caricature Jonah as narrow-minded and xenophobic, still hold sway in popular religious culture. Moreover, despite the various theological, historical, and literary approaches, critical readings have yet to seriously consider the post-exilic context of the Jewish author and audience. How would a post-exilic Jewish author and audience have conceived of a book in which their oppressor is saved by their own God, a God they would have identified as a God of the oppressed? How would they have responded to a narrative rebuking their own nationalism or particularism, social stances essential for their survival and identity? How would they have reacted to a story blaming or mocking their revered prophet? It is unlikely that an oppressed or colonized people would have embraced such a book. This thematic incongruity could be the reason that modern critical scholars have failed to agree on the book's socio-historical setting, its genre, or its purpose.

Two recent developments in biblical narrative criticism are culturally contextual reading and the use of postcolonial theory. Both of these approaches allow for reading positions that question dominant political ideologies and theological constructions. In what follows, armed with my own postcolonial experience, I will conduct a postcolonial reading of the narrative to explore an understanding of the text that takes into consideration the oppressed and colonized Jewish audience in the post-exilic period.

A Postcolonial Reading of Jonah

Although it is brief, the book of Jonah is a rich narrative filled with dramatic, fantastic, strange, and mysterious episodes: the prophet's flight from God, the sudden storm, the casting of lots, the human sacrifice, the fish's swallowing and vomiting a man, the callous proclamation, the exaggerated repentance, Jonah's angry exchange with God, the growth of the gourd, the sabotage of the worm, the scorching sun and wind, and so on. Readers, however, are easily lost in the maze of these spectacular scenes and miss the main plot of the narrative, which is, in fact, very simple: It is about the struggle between two characters, God and Jonah, and the root of their struggle is God's decision to forgive Nineveh. From the beginning to the end of the narrative, the salvation of Nineveh is what God intends, plans, decides, and even justifies. It is the reason that Jonah runs away, grows angry, pouts, and argues against God. Therefore, the key question of the Jonah narrative is whose position regarding Nineveh is more justifiable or legitimate—God's or Jonah's. Given the struggles and the relationship of cause and effect in God and Jonah's interactions, the major plot of the narrative can be segmented as follows: (i) God's command and Jonah's refusal (1:1–1:3), (ii) God's enforcement and Jonah's submission (1:4–2:10), (iii) God's second command and Jonah's implementation (3:1–9), (iv) God's forgiveness and Jonah's anger (3:10–4:4), (v) God's justification and Jonah's silence (4:5–4:11).

God's Command and Jonah's Refusal (1:1–1:3)

Jonah narrative starts with God's order to Jonah. "Now the word of the LORD came to Jonah son of Amittai, saying, 'Go at once to Nineveh, that great city, and cry out against it; for their wickedness has come up before me'" (1:1–2 NRSV). The introduction is crucial for understanding the main issue of the story. Readers without historical knowledge may move quickly to the next verse about Jonah's running, but the implied readers[1] would have had many questions about this divine order, and might even have predicted Jonah's reaction. The implied readers would have known Jonah, the son of Amittai, as the patriotic prophet who foretold the territorial restoration of Israel during the reign of Jeroboam II (750 BCE; 2 Kings 14:25). To this Jonah, the Lord orders "go and preach against" the great city of Nineveh, the capital of Assyria, the destroyer and archenemy of Israel. This order stuns Jonah and its implied readers with perplexity and confusion. First of all, the commissioning of an Israelite prophet to preach in a foreign country is an anomaly in the Hebrew Bible (Bickerman 1967, 15–16). Even prophetic proclamations *about or against* foreign countries are typically addressed to Israelite audiences. While an order to *go to Israelites* and to *preach against nations* would not have been rare, a charge to *go abroad and preach to* or *against foreigners* would have been unimaginable. Second, when Jonah is ordered to go to and preach against Nineveh, Jonah knows immediately the possibility that Nineveh could be saved by his preaching (4:2). Given that a judgment proclamation often functioned as warning to induce repentance, and knowing that the repentance and salvation of Nineveh could ultimately lead to the fall of Israel, Jonah is stunned by this absurd order. How could the God of Israel send a prophet of Israel *to a foreign country for the benefit of Israel's enemy and at such a devastating cost to Israel*? Moreover, given his previous patriotic pronouncement regarding Israel's territorial restoration, Jonah is the last person who would agree to perform this order. Understandably, instead of obeying this order, Jonah flees from God and boards a ship heading in the opposite direction. Therefore, for the ancient audience, the logical question is not, why does Jonah run from God? but, why does God give such an incomprehensible order? Would God not know that Jonah would anticipate God's intention to forgive Nineveh? Would God not know that Jonah would resist any order that would save Nineveh and that could bring devastation upon Israel? If God knows this, why give such an order, especially to Jonah, the most unlikely prophet to implement it? What is God's true reason for ordering Jonah to go to and preach against this "great" and "wicked" city, Nineveh?

God's Enforcement and Jonah's Submission (1:4–2:10)

In the next scene, God sends a great storm to the ship that Jonah has boarded. However, what God prepares for Jonah is not just a great storm, but a series of miraculous occurrences. Through these miracles, God achieves many things. Through the great storm, God acquires the offerings, sacrifices, and solemn vows from the foreign sailors. Through the large fish, God receives Jonah's surrender and also Jonah's psalm. Moreover, we might imagine that, through these supernatural occurrences, God's reputation builds and spreads even as far as Nineveh. God gains all these advantages because of Jonah's flight. So, Jonah's flight is, in fact, strategic in communicating to the nations the name and power of God.

In a glance, Jonah seems to play an effective role maximizing the consequences of the miracles. He gives God chances to display these miracles. He proclaims the name of Yahweh among foreigners as "the God of heaven, who made the sea and the dry land" (1:9). Moreover, he finally becomes the right person to carry God's judgment proclamation to Nineveh, since everyone now surely knows of him and his mysterious, miraculous journey. However, Jonah is not just a passive divine instrument. In the midst of God's displays of power, Jonah also raises his own voice. When Jonah introduces himself to foreign sailors, he says that he is a Hebrew (*'bry*), who worships Yahweh (*YHWH*; 1:9). By mentioning Yahweh's name (*YHWH*) in contrast to the sailors who call each to his own god (*'lhm*: 1:5), Jonah emphasizes the special relationship between Yahweh and Israel (Limburg 1993, 45). The one Jonah worships is not a generic deity, or even a universal God who treats everyone equally, but the God who had come into a special covenantal relationship with the Israelites and who revealed to Israel this specific divine name. Jonah's self-identification as a "Hebrew" (*'bry*) also emphasizes this point, distinguishing Israel from foreigners (Sasson 1990, 116–17). Moreover, in his psalm in the fish's belly, Jonah purposefully calls out "holy temple" twice (2:4 and 2:7) without context. The mention of the holy temple is Jonah's veiled reminder to God that God's plan for Nineveh could threaten the holy temple of Israel. With its second mention Jonah attempts to reinforce the potentially harmful connection between the holy temple and Nineveh by adding references which imply the disposition of Nineveh: "Those who worship vain idols forsake their true loyalty" (2:8).

God's Second Command and Jonah's Implementation (3:1–9)

After the fish expels Jonah onto dry land, God again commands Jonah to go preach to Nineveh. This time Jonah goes to Nineveh, but "subjectively he does not really obey" (Trible 1963, 80): he half-heartedly and cryptically proclaims judgment, "Forty days more, and Nineveh shall be overthrown!" To Jonah's surprise, however, the Ninevites immediately respond to his proclamation with a big commotion. Perhaps the news of God's earlier miraculous works in the sea has preceded Jonah's entrance to Nineveh, creating sufficient reason for the Ninevites to take seriously the proclamation of this great prophet so miraculously delivered by a large fish (Freedman 1990, 30). All the Ninevites, including their king, don sackcloth and proclaim a fast. In their fear and effort to display their repentance clearly, they ludicrously even put sackcloth on their beasts! Their repentance, however, fails to target their brutal plunder of their weaker neighbors including Israel. There is no indication of restitution toward their victims. Furthermore, the implied readers would know that, historically, Nineveh never repented for its predatory activities against foreign countries. To Jonah and the implied readers, the repentance of Nineveh is *hypocritical* repentance, repentance only for a *domestic* matter, totally lacking the compensatory actions to the people they violated (Levine 1999, 201–17; Sasson 1990, 259). It is *temporary* repentance (Trible 1963, 98), perhaps even only for the sake of *deception* (Sherwood 2000, 197). To many Christian readers who stress forgiveness, overemphasize spiritual repentance, and overlook the absence of physical restitution, and to oppressors who emphasize the theme of immediate reconciliation and desire their predatory actions be forgotten by the public without appropriate compensation for their actions, the repentance of Nineveh might seem to make sense. However, to the oppressed whose lands had been plundered or exploited, who had experienced slavery or colonization, and who were still suffering from the long-lasting scars left by the actions of their oppressors, this type of repentance without any reference to restitution would have been considered insincere and totally unacceptable.

God's Forgiveness and Jonah's Anger (3:10–4:5)

Despite the fact that it is clear to Jonah and implied readers that Nineveh's repentance is not true repentance, God accepts their gesture and forgives them without punishment (3:10). This forgiveness is problematic for many reasons. First, such forgiveness without restitution is highly unusual in the Hebrew Bible. Forgiveness of sin does not occur without appropriate retribution as "ex post facto repentance" cannot alter "the significance of a deed" (Levine 1984, 242). Even the kings of Israel such as David and Ahab do not receive forgiveness without severe consequences. Although David's verbal repentance (2 Sam. 12:22) and Ahab's physical act of repentance (1 Kings 21:27) are significantly similar to those of Nineveh's king in Jonah 3:6 and 3:9 (see Ryu 2009, 208), the result for David is the death of his innocent child, and in Ahab's case, disaster is not averted but only delayed by a generation. Although Ahab was a notorious Israelite king, his deeds could not be considered worse than that of the Ninevites who had brutalized the Israelites. How could God, who punished David and Ahab despite their repentance, fail to punish Nineveh? How could God show more favor to the destroyer of Israel than to the Israelites, God's chosen people? This failure to punish Nineveh represents a serious violation of the covenantal relationship between the Israelites and God, effectively nullifying the distinction between Israelites and non-Israelites. By forgiving Nineveh without any "*quid pro quo*," God also effectively eliminates "the distinction between Good and Evil" by overlooking the injustices suffered by Israel at the hands of Nineveh (Levine 1984, 242). Levine writes, "To forgive the guilty is identical to punishing the innocent" (243). Under these circumstances, how can the God in Jonah continuously be called "the God of Israel" or even "the God of the oppressed"?

God's actions constitute a great injustice to Jonah, and he grows angry (4:1). In the midst of his anger, Jonah quotes the renowned "credo," "You are a compassionate and gracious God, slow to anger, abounding in kindness, repenting of evil" (4:2b–3). This credo, however, is unique when compared to the other credo passages in the Hebrew Bible. The credo in Jonah 4:3 is the only confession in which God's love *toward a foreign country* is referenced while in all the other passages (Num. 14:18; Deut. 7:8ff; Neh. 9:17; Joel 2:13; Ps. 85:5, 15; 103:8; 111:4; 145:8), God's love and mercy are praised *because Israel is the recipient of God's mercy*. God's attributes of compassion, mercy, slowness to anger, abundant kindness, and repentance from evil are meaningful to Israel when Israel is the beneficiary of these divine characteristics; they constitute Israel's credo because these characteristics are intended for Israel. Yet, here in Jonah Israel's core credo characterizes God's actions, not just toward a foreign country, but toward Nineveh, the destroyer of the northern kingdom of Israel. Thus, when Jonah invokes the credo, "God, slow to anger, abounding in kindness, repenting of evil," one rightly questions whether this recitation is intended as a sign of awe and respect or whether it is intended to convey sarcasm at the gross injustice of God's unprecedented forgiveness of the Ninevites.

When Jonah realizes that the God of Israel will spare Nineveh and that Jonah himself has been implicated in this decision, he is so aggrieved that he asks to die (4:3). To Jonah's agonizing plea for death, God answers simply, "Is it right for you to be angry?" (4:4). It is significant to note God does not refer to or inquire about *the reason for Jonah's anger* (as God does a few verses later in 4:9). For example, God does not ask Jonah directly "Is it right for you to be angry *at my sparing of Nineveh*?" If God had asked that, God and Jonah could have begun a dialogue about the justification of God's actions toward Nineveh. However, God chooses not to open this line of inquiry at this point, most likely because God would have had difficulty justifying his actions at that moment of the debate. Had God asked, "Are you that deeply angry at my sparing of Nineveh?" Jonah could have pointed out the negative implications for Israel in God's decision to save Nineveh. Jonah would also have been able to remind God of the special covenantal relationship between God and Israel. Moreover, Jonah could have brought up the issue of justice as the underlying reason for his anger. However, because God only inquires about the legitimacy of anger, and not the reason for it, Jonah, in his subordinate position, is not empowered to redirect the conversation and has no recourse but to leave the city in silence.

God's Justification and Jonah's Silence (4:6–4:11)

It seems that God is uncomfortable with Jonah's lack of response because Jonah's silence indicates that he is still angry (Trible 1963, 80). Furthermore, God has no effective arguments at this point to subdue Jonah's anger. Thus, in the next scene, God's actions can be interpreted as maneuvering to gain the advantage in his argument with Jonah. God "appoints" (*mnh*) the plant, "appoints" the worm, and "appoints" the east wind to kill the plant. In fact, throughout the book, the verb "appoints" (*mnh*) is an intentional term to explain what God does. After God, anticipating Jonah's disobedience, orders him to preach against Nineveh, God sends the storms and "appoints" the fish to swallow Jonah. God sets the stage to gain the advantage by sending and appointing the storms, the fish, the plant, the worm and the east wind. In the final scene staged by God's appointment (4:8), Jonah again desires to die after God kills the plant under which Jonah had found temporary respite. At this point, the ultimate purpose of God's orchestration becomes evident. In 4:9, God asks, "Is it right for you to be angry *about the plant*?" Jonah replies petulantly out of his frustration and anger, "Yes, angry enough to die." The critical point here is that God frames the reason for Jonah's anger as being "*about the plant*" unlike in 4:4 where God does not bring up the reason for Jonah's anger. However, is Jonah really angry enough to die *because of the plant*? Since his outrage at God's decision to forgive Nineveh in 4:1, Jonah's resentment has not subsided. All of Jonah's anger at God's apparent disregard for the serious implications for Israel is transferred to the plant. By reframing the focus of the dialogue from the larger issue of the legitimacy of God's plan to save Nineveh to the inconsequential issue of God's sovereignty over the plant, God distracts Jonah and deprives him of the opportunity to discuss the real reason for his anger. To uproot the voice of the oppressed from its proper historical context and to strip it of its historical relevance is an effective strategy employed by those in power to maintain their dominance over the weak and powerless. The perspective and the outrage of the oppressed can only be properly understood in the context of the painful events they endure through their history such as slavery or colonization. Their reactions in the present are an extension of their painful past. The dark shadows of those histories haunt the oppressed, and the scars that they carry into the present influence their perspective such that their actions and reactions may seem inappropriate for the current situation when historical context has been ripped from them by the dominant group. However, oppressors seek to erase their past acts of exploitation and oppression as soon as feasible and demand the oppressed deal only with current issues. They are quick to praise the value of forgiveness and reconciliation and even to elevate any opposition leader who supports these values, holding up the act of forgiveness as the proper moral norm that all the formerly oppressed people should follow. The weak have no options but to follow the recontextualizating rhetoric of the strong, not only because the powerless lack the social standing to set the ideological rhetorical norms for discourse (see Marx 1995, 64), but also because the weak have urgent and immediate survival needs that demand their attention and put them at a competitive disadvantage. In Jonah's case, the sun beats down on his head while he talks with God (4:8). Because of intense physical discomfort caused by a lack of resources, Jonah is in a weakened state and cannot help but answer impetuously. It is in precisely this kind of situation that the weak like Jonah become *trapped* in an unwinnable argument. In 4:4 Jonah could have legitimately poured out his anger at God's forgiveness of Nineveh, but the situation is now dramatically changed. In 4:9, Jonah's anger loses its legitimate basis because it is uprooted from its historical context and refocused to the current and inconsequential issue, *the plant*. At this strategic moment God gains the advantage in the conversation. In a dignified manner, God starts to give his reason for forgiving Nineveh:

> You cared about the plant, which you did not work for and which you did not grow, which appeared overnight and perished overnight. And should I not care about Nineveh, that great

city, in which there are more than twelve myriad persons who do not yet know their right hand from their left, and many beasts as well? (Bible verses 4:10–11 quoted from Simon and Schramm 1999, 44–46)

God's final statements form the climax of all of God's plans and preparation from the beginning of the narrative. In effect, God has appointed and set everything: God intention-ally gave the absurd order to the patriotic prophet Jonah expecting he would avoid the mis-sion. Because of Jonah's flight, God was able to display dazzling miracles that have likely caused Nineveh to listen to Jonah. (Who could ignore the words of this renowned prophet who serves the God of heaven and earth and who survived in the belly of the fish for three days?) Whether the repentance of Nineveh is genuine or not, God can justify the forgiveness of Nineveh with the pretext of their repentance. Moreover, by appointing a new setting and utilizing the rhetorical strategy of decontextualizaiton and dehistorization, God deprives Jonah of the legitimacy of his outrage and renders him silent. However, the critical point at the end of the Jonah narrative is not God's claim for universal mercy but God's description of Nineveh, which, in fact, parallels God's description of Nineveh in 1:1—"the great city which was wicked." The reason that God is concerned about Nineveh is because there are *a great number of people* there. Their wickedness, in fact, does not diminish despite their repenting action in chapter 3 because the people of Nineveh are still described as the people "who can-not discern between their right and left hands," that is, between "good and evil" (Magonet 1983, 46–47; Simon and Schramm 1999, 46–47). God says in the conclusion that Nineveh is wicked, but, still, it is a *great* (*gdl*) city (where there are more than 120 thousand people and great number of cattle). Throughout the book, the word echoes, "great" (*gdl*)—"great" city (1:2; 3:2; 4:11), "great" wind (1:4), "great" fear (1:10; 1:16), "great" storm (1:12), "great" fish (1:17). "Great" (*gdl*) is the only Hebrew word that is used in all four chapters (except a com-mon verb *'md* ["say"]—see Magonet 1983, 14), and, in fact, it is the justification that God uses for forgiving Nineveh. Therefore, from God's initial order to Jonah to God's culminat-ing rationale for saving Nineveh, *God's underlying intention is to forgive Nineveh because it is "great."* However, in the Hebrew Bible, *there is no precedent for God's judgment being swayed by the number of people potentially impacted. When and where has the number of the people ever been considered as the criteria of judgment? To God, have not justice and righteousness always claimed more importance than sheer numbers?* Were Sodom and Gomorrah not for-given because their populations were few? Were Samaria and the Northern Israel destroyed because there were not many lives there? Were there not thousands of Israelites not knowing their right hand from their left when destroyed by Nineveh? Moreover, is God not supposed to be the God of the underdog Israel, rather than the God of the many? When did God start loving the *great* city and the *great* number of people while ignoring justice and the fate of the weak? All these questions would have been boiling in the heart of Jonah, but he could not say a word because *he was trapped by the reframing rhetorical strategy of the strong, which neu-tralizes the recognition of the power difference between the strong and the weak, intentionally focusing on only the current situation through de-historization and de-contextualization.* His anger is now referenced only to the plant (instead of to God's forgiveness of Nineveh) and what is most unfortunate is that Jonah himself has confirmed it in an impetuous moment. Because Jonah is now trapped in a disadvantageous ideological rhetoric, suffering a pressing unmet physical need, a common situation of the weak, the only thing he can do is to remain silent. This silence has long been interpreted by traditional Christian readers as obedience to, or agreement with, God's universal love for all. However, the implied readers would have understood what the silence of Jonah meant; Jonah's silence is not a sign of agreement or obedience but is the only act of resistance that Jonah can display against this satirical authority. The book of Jonah, then, functions not to critique Jonah's exclusive attitude, but to critique a theology that elevates divine control over divine justice.

NOTE

1. A short definition of 'the implied reader" is "one who brings to the task of reading a knowledge of the cultural codes that the author presumed she or he shared with the readers" (Mitchell 2006, 627). I assume the implied reader of the Jonah narrative is the colonized Jewish audience during the post-exilic period (see Ryu 2009, 196).

REFERENCES

Ackerman, James S. 1981. "Satire and Symbolism in the Song of Jonah." In *Traditions in Transformation*. 213–246. Winona Lake, IN: Eisenbrauns.
Allen, Leslie C. 1976. *The Books of Joel, Obadiah, Jonah, and Micah*. Grand Rapids, MI: Eerdmans.
Band, Arnold J. 1990. "Swallowing Jonah: The Eclipse of Parody." *Prooftexts* 10: 177–195.
Bickerman, Elias J. 1967. *Four Strange Books of the Bible: Jonah, Daniel, Koheleth, Esther*. New York: Schocken Books.
Cooper, Alan. 1993. "In Praise of Divine Caprice: The Significance of the Book of Jonah." In *Among the Prophets*, edited by P. R. Davies and D. J. A. Clines, 144–163. Sheffield, Yorkshire: Sheffield Academic Press.
Craig, Kenneth M. 1999. *A Poetics of Jonah: Art in the Service of Ideology*. Macon, GA: Mercer University Press.
Ephros, Abraham Z. 1999. "The Book of Jonah as Allegory." *Jewish Bible Quarterly* 27(3): 135–151.
Freedman, David Noel. 1990. "Did God Play a Dirty Trick on Jonah at the End?" *Bible Review* 6(4): 26–31.
Good, E. M. 1981. *Irony in the Old Testament*. Sheffield, Yorkshire: Almond Press.
Gunn, David M., and Danna Nolan Fewell. 1993. *Narrative in the Hebrew Bible*. Oxford Bible Series. Oxford: Oxford University Press.
Holbert, John C. 1981. "'Deliverance Belongs to Yahweh!': Satire in the Book of Jonah." *Journal for the Study of the Old Testament* 21: 59–81.
Kahn, Pinchas. 2000. "The Epilogue to Jonah." *Jewish Bible Quarterly* 28(3): 146–155.
Levine, B. A. 1999. "The Place of Jonah in the History of Biblical Ideas." In *On the Way to Nineveh: Studies in Honor of George M. Landes*, edited by Stephen L. Cook and S. C. Winter, 201-217. Atlanta, GA: Scholars Press.
Levine, Etan. 1984. "Jonah as a Philosophical Book." *Zeitschrift für die alttestamentliche Wissenschaft* 96: 235–245.
Limburg, James. 1993. *Jonah: A Commentary*. Old Testament Library. Louisville, KY: Westminster/John Knox Press.

Magonet, Jonathan. 1983. *Form and Meaning: Studies in Literary Techniques in the Book of Jonah*. 2nd ed. Sheffield, Yorkshire: Almond Press.

Marcus, David. 1995. *From Balaam to Jonah: Anti-Prophetic Satire in the Hebrew Bible*. Brown Judaic Series 301. Atlanta, GA: Scholars Press.

Marx, Karl, and Friedrich Engels. 1995. *The German Ideology*. New York: International Publishers.

Miles, John A., Jr. 1975. "Laughing at the Bible: Jonah as Parody." *Jewish Quarterly Review* 65: 168–181.

Mitchell, Margaret M. 2006. "Rhetorical and New Literary Criticism." In *Oxford Handbook of Biblical Studies*, edited by J. W. Rogerson and Judith M. Lieu, 615–633. Oxford: Oxford University Press.

Muldoon, Catherine L. 2010. *In Defense of Divine Justice: An Intertextual Approach to the Book of Jonah*. Catholic Biblical Quarterly Monograph Series. Washington, DC: Catholic Biblical Association of America.

Person, Raymond F. 1996. *In Conversation with Jonah: Conversation Analysis, Literary Criticism, and the Book of Jonah*. Journal for the Study of the Old Testament Supplement Series. Sheffield, Yorkshire: Sheffield Academic Press.

Ryu, Chesung Justin. 2009. "Silence as Resistance: A Postcolonial Reading of the Silence of Jonah in Jonah 4.1-11." *Journal for the Study of the Old Testament* 34: 195–218.

Sasson, Jack M. 1990. *Jonah: A New Translation with Introduction, Commentary, and Interpretations*. Anchor Bible 24B. New York: Doubleday.

Sherwood, Yvonne. 2000. *A Biblical Text and Its Afterlives: The Survival of Jonah in Western Culture*. Cambridge: Cambridge University Press.

Simon, Uriel, and Lenn J. Schramm. 1999. *Jonah: The Traditional Hebrew Text with the New JPS Translation*. Jewish Publication Society Bible Commentary. Philadelphia: Jewish Publication Society.

Trible, Phyllis. 1963. "Studies in the Book of Jonah." PhD thesis. Columbia University. Ann Arbor, MI: University Microfilm.

Trible, Phyllis. 1994. *Rhetorical Criticism: Context, Method, and the Book of Jonah*. Guides to Biblical Scholarship, Old Testament Series. Minneapolis, MN: Fortress Press.

CHAPTER 19

··

PLURAL VERSIONS AND THE CHALLENGE OF NARRATIVE COHERENCE IN THE STORY OF JOB

··

CAROL A. NEWSOM

> It changes things quite a bit to see the canonical Job not as *the* source, the original impugned or misunderstood by later interpreters, but rather as one voice among others competing to define Job and the significance of his story.
>
> —Larrimore (2013, 40–41)

WHERE does a story reside? In a text- and author-focused culture one might tend to think in terms of a written document. But for a story that is traditional and has become part of a cultural heritage, the authorized written version is only one of its loci, and perhaps not the most important one. Such stories are carried in the memory of many people, in a variety of contexts, and in a number of versions. The story may be alluded to, retold, unconsciously or intentionally revised, or used as a template for another narrative. So it is with the story of Job.

In a culture formed significantly by Jewish or Christian tradition, many people will have some rough sense of the story of Job. Most will know Job primarily as a figure of extreme suffering, often as an innocent sufferer. Whether he is remembered as a figure of patient endurance or angry protest will vary. If called upon to tell the story, some could give an account of the most important characters and narrative actions—God and the accuser and the decision to test Job, Job's loss of his possessions and the death of his children, the tension between Job's response and the responses of his wife and friends, the confrontation between Job and God, and the restoration of Job at the end. And yet, those retelling the story might well find themselves telling a story somewhat at odds with what is preserved in the canonical version. This is partly because of the body of already existing variant versions of the Job story that compete with the canonical version in influencing cultural memory, but also partly because the story invites new adaptation to changing cultural and religious contexts.

This quality of the Job story as an "oft told tale" with a variety of permutations is not simply a feature of the oral precedents to the canonical book or its later reception history; it is also present in the canonical book itself, which appears to flaunt the notion that the story was never a single one, but rather a story that demands a variety of differing, even contradictory ways of telling the tale. One of the most important historical critical insights into the book is the recognition that the prose tale (1:1–2:13; 42:7–17) and the poetic sections (3:1–42:6) differ sharply from one another in generic features, style, characterization, and ideological perspective. Bruce Zuckerman expresses the puzzled reader's sense of the book's challenge to narrative coherency well: "Like oil and water, the Prose Frame Story and the Poem naturally tend to disengage from one another despite all efforts to homogenize them. The book of Job therefore appears to be at odds with itself; and however one may attempt to resolve its contradictory picture, the result never seems to be quite successful" (1991, 14; order of sentences reversed). The canonical book of Job is no product of clumsy editing, however. The segue between the prose and poetry is carefully developed (2:10–13; 42:7–8), and the narrative tension created by the accuser's prediction that Job will curse God to God's face (1:1–11; 2:5) only finds its climax in the encounter between Job and God at the end of the poetic section (40:1–5; 42:1–6). Thus the canonical book of Job creates something analogous to an optical puzzle. When looked at one way, it appears to be two sharply different ways of telling the story of Job, abruptly juxtaposed to one another; but when looked at another way, the story becomes a complex dramatic whole. Throughout the centuries readers have employed different strategies to address the challenges to narrative coherence posed by the book, as it brings together different approaches to the story of Job. In what follows, I will first briefly treat the evidence for a plurality of Job stories. Then I take up the ways in which the canonical book of Job simultaneously preserves and merges radically different ways of telling his story.

Job in Cultural Memory

That Job is not an Israelite but rather a resident of the land of Uz (1:1) itself suggests that the biblical version is an adaptation of an older ancient Near Eastern tale. Job's three friends, too, have non-Israelite names and places of origin (2:11). That stories were shared across national boundaries in the ancient world and adapted to new contexts is well attested, as one sees in the close relationships between the biblical flood story and the Mesopotamian versions in Atrahasis and in the Gilgamesh epic. Although no other versions of the Job tale are extant in ancient texts, a reference by the prophet Ezekiel strongly suggests the existence of a traditional tale about Job with currency among other peoples. In Ezekiel 14:14–20, the prophet insists that if a land is radically faithless to God, then even if "Noah, Danel, and Job" were resident in it, "they would save only their own lives by their righteousness" (v. 14). They would save "neither sons nor daughters" (v. 16).

What does the reference suggest about how the Job story was current among the sixth-century exiles of Judah? One may judge in part by the company in which Ezekiel places him. Noah, of course, is the hero of the Israelite version of the Mesopotamian flood story. Danel is a character known from a Ugaritic legend about a long-childless king, whose eventually granted son, Aqhat, is killed by the goddess Anat. Unfortunately, the text breaks off before the reader knows if Aqhat is restored or not. Ezekiel's characterization of these three figures both does and does not correspond to the written versions of the stories preserved about them. Noah and Job are known for righteousness in the biblical stories, but not so Danel.

Noah saves his children by his righteousness (Gen. 7:7), but neither Job nor Danel saves his children in the versions of their stories known to us. While it is possible that Ezekiel is playing fast and loose with the stories of these figures, his rhetorical point would be compromised if audiences did not recognize the stories to which he alludes. Thus, it is likely that Ezekiel knows versions of the stories of these three figures that did connect their extraordinary righteousness, not only with their own survival, but also with their ability to preserve their families from danger. If so, then Ezekiel's version of Job and the canonical version preserved in the prose tale would represents two variants.

Although scholars debate the date of the composition of the biblical book of Job, the majority opinion favors a date in the early post-exilic period (probably later than Ezekiel's reference; see, e.g., Seow 2013, 41–45). This ambitious literary work, which combines a version of the traditional tale with an exceptionally sophisticated poetic dialogue, would initially have circulated among a scribal elite. Moreover, in the largely oral cultures of antiquity, even a written text with cultural authority would have been complemented by a variety of oral versions, some derived from and some independent of the written version. This is clearly attested for Job. In the New Testament, the epistle of James reminds its recipients that "you have heard of the endurance of Job" (James 5:11), suggesting that they know the story from hearing rather than reading. Moreover, the allusion by James implies that the salient feature of the "heard and remembered" story was of Job as a steadfast sufferer. Job's vehement attacks against God in the canonical book are either not known or are suppressed in the cultural memory that James represents. Even more explicit is the testimony of Bishop Theodore of Mopsuestia (late fourth–early fifth century CE). Bishop Theodore denigrated the canonical book of Job as paraded learning by a show-off author, inferior to the oral tale popularly told both by Jews and others (Zaharopoulos 1989, 45–48).

Alongside the oral traditions about Job, there is evidence of one literary reworking of the Job story that is dependent on—but not particularly constrained by—the canonical Job in its Septuagint version. That is the Testament of Job. This text was probably composed in the first century BCE or CE in Alexandria, Egypt, by a Greek-speaking Jew (Spittler 1983, 830–833). Here, at the end of his long life, Job gives an account of his experiences to the sons and daughters born to him after his restoration. In this retrospective account, however, the narrative situation is cast in quite different terms from what is in the canonical book. In the Testament Job's trials arise because his opposition to idolatry has aroused the enmity of Satan. Moreover, God explains to Job in advance that Satan will attack him, but that if Job steadfastly endures these trials, he will be restored. Thus, the dramatic tension and the religious issues framed by the book of Job and the Testament are quite different. As in the book of James, this retelling is focused on the virtue of patient endurance (*hypomone*), and it is even possible that it is this narrative tradition rather than the prose tale of canonical Job to which James refers (Larrimore 2013, 41). Even though the Testament of Job was only rarely copied, certain persistent features of the iconography of Job are indicative of the persistence of the story as it was told in the Testament (Larrimore 2013, 48; Spittler 1983, 836).

The Christian interpretation and retellings of Job similarly suppress the anger and impiety found in the canonical book. Pope Gregory's *Moralia in Job* (late sixth century CE) employed a variety of interpretive approaches to present Job as an exemplary sufferer whose words must be understood according to their interior meaning (Seow 2013, 195). A different technique for reading with tradition and against the grain of the canonical book is reflected in the medieval French play *La pacience de Job*. The author displaces the angry and bitter words of Job onto other characters and so simplifies the narrative tension of the canonical book and leaves Job as the traditional model of patient endurance (Larrimore 2013, 140).

Perhaps in part because Job was esteemed as a righteous Gentile and even as a type of Christ in Christian interpretation, Rabbinic interpretation of Job displays more ambivalence. Thus some rabbinic traditions draw attention to the impiety of Job in the dialogues and cast him as "rebel, blasphemer, and heretic" (Seow 2013, 122). The medieval Jewish commentary tradition, however, though operating with high levels of philosophical sophistication, finds ways to diminish the dissonance within the book and give it a religiously and philosophically acceptable meaning (Seow 2013, 126–141).

The canons of cultural acceptability, of course, change with the times. The loosening of religious orthodoxy's dominance in Western culture and the horrific traumas of the two world wars in the twentieth century made the traditional version of Job seem inadequate, if not repulsive, to many. What had been suppressed in readings and appropriations of the canonical book suddenly stood out as the "real" Job. The repentant, reconciled, and restored Job of the prose ending became the intellectual scandal of the book (Wiesel 1964, 52). This hermeneutical shift is most strikingly displayed in literary retellings of the story, in particular by the handling of the God character and the ending of the story. Three post–World War II plays can illustrate. In Archibald MacLeish's *J.B.* (1958), both the frame story and the dialogues are clever cultural translations of the ancient story to a mid-century America. In the metaframe that introduces and punctuates the play, MacLeish casts the cynical but compassionate Nickles (i.e., "Old Nick," the Satan character) as more morally sympathetic than the pompous Zuss (i.e., "Zeus," the God character). Even though the divine speeches and J.B.'s reply are taken verbatim from the book of Job, MacLeish evades the apparent submission by Job by suggesting that J.B.'s response is simply a means of manipulating a deity in whom he no longer has faith. Moreover, the conclusion of the play is no restoration. Rather, J.B.'s wife locates what comfort there is to be found in a post-theistic humanism where the human heart is the only source of light and warmth.

In Wolfgang Borchert's *Draussen der Tor* (1947; translated as *The Man Outside*; see Borchert 1952) the prologue represents God ("the Old Man") as a grieving but utterly incompetent figure who identifies himself as "the God no one believes in now." At the end of the play Beckmann, the Job figure, a German soldier broken in body and spirit who has returned from the Russian front to a fire-bombed Hamburg, cries out, "Where is the old man who calls himself god? Why doesn't he speak? Answer! Why are you silent? Why? Will none of you answer? Will no one answer? Will no one, nobody answer me?" (127). With that cry the play ends. There is no answer from a whirlwind, because God is as impotent and defeated as Beckmann.

Finally, in Elie Wiesel's play *The Trial of God* (1986), which creatively combines elements from the biblical books of Job and Esther, the Job character Berish embodies the spirit of Job, as he is simultaneously alienated from and deeply entangled with God. As he and his household are again menaced by a gathering pogrom, Berish refuses the offer of the local Catholic priest to save himself by a sham conversion and insists rather on remaining in a stance of protest that can be the only expression of his paradoxical faith—one that echoes the opening words of Job 27. "I live as a Jew, and it is as Jew that I shall die—and it is as a Jew that with my last breath, I will shout my protest to God. And because the end is near, I shall shout louder! Because the end is near, I'll tell Him that He's more guilty than ever" (Wiesel 1986, 156). In contrast to the book of Job, however, where Job's protest eventually elicits a divine response, the last sound in Wiesel's play is "the deafening and murderous roar" of the pogrom (161).

In an inverse mirroring of the older retellings of the story of Job that suppressed the notes of anger and rebellion found in canonical Job, these twentieth-century recastings of the story repress the notes of abasement, repentance, reconciliation, and restoration that conclude the book. When placed in the context of oral traditions and reception history, both traditional and contemporary, the canonical book of Job truly does remain, as Larrimore describes it, as "one voice among others competing to define Job and the significance of his story" (148). Nevertheless, it is the central one.

Paradoxical Coherence and the Narrative Art of Canonical Job

The multiple ways in which the story of Job has been told point to the tendency of these other versions to tell a relatively simplified, monologic story. Turning to the canonical book after considering other versions underscores the astonishing manner in which the canonical work refuses such simplifications.

Modern scholarly discussion has generally agreed on the distinct literary elements in the book of Job, though no agreement exists as to how they came to be present in the book. Although one can never know how the present book of Job actually came together, what matters is the recognition of the different styles and genres and how they construct a distinctive way of presenting the story.

The prose tale is readily identified as the story that runs from 1:1 to 2:13 and then resumes in 42:7–17. It is a didactic narrative (Müller 1977, 77; Newsom 2003a, 41–51) including a beginning with two complete episodes (1:1–22; 2:1–10) and a conclusion (42:7–17). To many readers the middle seems to be missing, particularly the exchange between Job and his friends and the prose tale's version of God's appearance and reply to Job (2:11–13; *missing episode*; 42:7–10). Didactic tales characteristically feature predictable characters and plots, strong narratorial voices, and sufficient redundancy so that a reader is carefully guided through the story (Suleiman 1992). Thus it is not difficult to project, at least in a schematic fashion, what would have happened in the missing middle of the prose tale.

The first two episodes establish Job as a figure of exemplary righteousness (1:1, 8; 2:3). In keeping with the pattern of the Israelite wisdom didactic narratives, Job's virtues will be tested and reaffirmed (Newsom 2003a, 49–51). Thus the accuser's challenge that Job's righteousness is implicitly conditional upon his continuing to receive God's blessing (1:9–11; 2:4–5) sets up the narrative necessity of a test of Job's virtue, which follows in two episodes, as his possessions, children, and health are taken away (1:13–19; 2:7–8). Job's response to the calamity confirms his continuing unconditional righteousness (1:20–22; 2:10). Since traditional stories often test the hero through three trials, the appearance of Job's friends on the scene (2:10–13) intimates that they will be the means of his third trial. Indeed, the words of Job's wife in urging Job to "curse God" (2:9) suggests that the friends will play a similar role, prompting Job to rebuke and correct them, as he did his wife. With the three tests successfully completed, the story could then conclude with God's appearance and his rebuke of the friends and approbation of Job (42:7–10), and the restoration of the hero (42:11–17). My claim is not that such a missing episode actually existed and was cut out, but only that the expectations set up by the didactic tale make it easy for a reader to project what might have come next.

Whether or not this is precisely the version of the Job story that was known by James and Theodore of Mopsuestia, it fits with the traditional cultural memory of Job as an exemplary sufferer who steadfastly endures and who models a type of piety to be emulated. Though the story's stance has not been highly regarded in the disillusioned world of modern criticism, its moral imagination is worthy of serious engagement (Newsom 2003a, 51–65). Nevertheless, there are certain indications that the version of the prose tale in the canonical book of Job may also embody a certain ironic distance from its own project. It is almost too perfect a representation of the wisdom didactic tale not to be self-conscious about its own performance ("the briefest and most precise example"; Müller 1977, 77). Its highly repetitive style and symmetrical and balanced scenes have often been likened to naive folktale style but in fact are better characterized as faux-naive (Clines, 1985, "False Naivete").

More telling than the stylistic exaggerations, however, are the ethical discomforts that the tale provokes if one compares it with other wisdom didactic tales. Bad things happen to the heroes in those tales, of course. Joseph is imprisoned; Tobit is blinded; Shadrach, Meshach, and Abednego are thrown into a fiery furnace; and Daniel spends the night with hungry lions. Nevertheless, what happens to Job is excessive in comparison with all other tales of its type. In the other wisdom didactic tales, nobody close to the hero dies, as Job's children die. Other fates can be reversed and the characters made whole in the happy ending that concludes the wisdom didactic tale. But Job's dead children remain dead, even though ten more are born to him. Even in the case of the testing of Abraham, the test is arranged in such a manner that Isaac need not actually die (Gen. 22:12). Moreover, no hero in a wisdom didactic tale has to undergo a second endangerment in the way that Job does after demonstrating his virtue.

The second area of ethical discomfort arises from God's role. While the legitimacy of the divine testing of faithful followers is accepted as appropriate, as the case of Abraham demonstrates, the depiction of God verbally jousting with the accuser over their rival views of Job's motivations is disturbing. More pointedly, the vividness and relentlessness of Job's destruction, with God's explicit consent, has no parallel in other narratives, where those who endanger the heroes are humans with bad motivations (Gen. 37:28; 39:17–18; Dan. 3:15; 6:5) or accidents of fate (Tob. 2:10). God's role, by contrast, is in protecting the heroes (Dan. 3:28; 6:22; Tob. 3:16–17).

Even if some readers, ancient or modern, are disquieted by aspects of the prose story, the tale itself makes no place to explore the problematic aspects of the relationships it has set up among the characters. Indeed, it cannot. As a wisdom didactic story, it has a genius for modeling virtue tested and affirmed. But it lacks the capacity to self-reflexively examine the assumptions on which it is based. If one wishes to do that, then another way of telling the story is needed.

That, of course, is precisely what the author of the canonical book of Job did. The figure of the exemplary or emblematic sufferer was one that attracted considerable attention in the ancient Near East, most particularly in Mesopotamian literature. A variety of poetic genres represented such a sufferer, though most of the compositions more closely resemble biblical thanksgiving psalms than the book of Job (e.g., *Ludlul Bel Nemeqi,* the Sumerian "Man and

His God," and the Akkadian Dialogue between a Man and His God"; see Newsom 2003a, 73–79). The exception is the Babylonian Theodicy, a wisdom dialogue in which a sufferer and his friend take turns debating the causes and cures of the sufferer's misfortune and the issue of a moral world order. In both texts the sufferer's experience leads him to question divine justice and the moral order of the world. The friend's role is to reiterate the traditional advice for dealing with inexplicable suffering (i.e., to pray for mercy, to wait patiently for a reversal of fortune, and to admit that divine purposes are unknown and unknowable). The general similarities between Job 3–27 and the Babylonian Theodicy are striking enough, but even small details, such as the opening address to the other speaker with complimentary or deprecatory evaluations of his wisdom, strongly suggest that the two compositions are self-conscious instantiations of a genre with well-defined characteristics.

The Babylonian Theodicy and the other ancient Near Eastern examples of the wisdom dialogue are not narrative genres. Often, the characters are not even given names. No background to the encounter is supplied, and no real resolution occurs. Thus, the genius of the wisdom dialogue is of a very different order than that of the didactic wisdom tale. It serves not to provide a model to be emulated but a way of framing reality in terms of an argument that crystallizes points of contradiction. As Buccellati describes it, "[T]he dialog, pure and simple, emphasizes the unfolding of a thought process viewed dynamically in its becoming." It "reflect[s] the spirit of critical inquisitiveness" (1981, 39, 43).

The wisdom dialogue in Job does, however, have a dramatic momentum that differs from other examples of the genre. Both the nature of the interaction between Job and his friends and Job's own developing views show change across the three cycles of the dialogue. In the first set of exchanges the friends toss out a range of traditional theodicies and suggest actions that Job can take to induce God to change his situation (see Newsom 2003b). Job himself begins in such a state of traumatized despair that his only desire is for death (ch. 3). His mounting anger, however, begins to push him to a kind of angry play, as he parodies the friends' words and traditional hymns and prayers. Through his mockery of Eliphaz's words in 4:17 Job stumbles upon the notion of a trial with God (9:2–4), a mode of relating to God that offers a true alternative to the humble prayer that tradition recommended (13:13–27; 16:18–21; 19:23–27; 23:3–7).

Job's parodic attack in chapter 12 on the notion of a divinely directed world order appears to be the trigger for the friends' shift in the second cycle to a defense of the idea of the dire fate of the wicked (chs. 15, 18, 20). Job largely ignores them until his final speech in chapter 21, which shockingly depicts the triumph of the wicked, and thus the absence of moral order in the world. That speech provokes Eliphaz's violent denunciation of Job as being himself one of the wicked (22:1–20), initiating the third cycle. As commentators have long noted, the third cycle degenerates into disorder and incoherence. Rather than attempt to repair some imaginary scribal error, however, scholars should recognize that wisdom dialogues tend to end with irresolution and even paradox (cf. the Babylonian Theodicy and the Dialogue of Pessimism).

Recasting the Job story as a debate about the nature and origin of human suffering, the disposition of God, and the moral coherency of the world (or lack thereof) is a bold way of challenging the meaning and significance of the traditional tale of Job. The wisdom dialogue is by nature a skeptical genre that eschews any meaningful resolution. Its radical openness is the opposite of the closed world of the prose story. Truly, the wisdom dialogue and the wisdom didactic tale are oil and water, as Zuckerman (1991) describes them. But the author of canonical Job has not simply composed two different ways of telling the Job story on separate scrolls, as it were. He has inserted the one into the midst of the other. Thus he must create a bridge from the irresolution of the wisdom dialogue to the emphatic closure of the prose tale. He does this by adding other elements. The poem on wisdom in chapter 28 delivers a poetic judgment on the futility of the wisdom dialogue itself as a means for grasping the coherency that undergirds the cosmos. Thus it clears the way for the third major section of the book, the final speeches of Job and God. (Since I take the Elihu speeches to be a later addition to the composition by a frustrated reader, I will not deal with them here; see Newsom 2003a, 200–233).

Both Job's final speech and God's speech from the whirlwind are rhetorical masterpieces. Job's speech in chapters 29–31 is an extraordinary act of self-assertion. Job delineates the familiar moral world of ancient Near Eastern culture and defines his place in it. His act of self-clearance in chapter 31 not only persuasively justifies himself but also constructs a character for God (vv. 2–4, 6, 13–15, 23, 28, 35–37), who cannot but acknowledge Job's righteousness and the injustice of his treatment. Yet, as readers know, the shock of the divine speeches (chs. 38–41) is that they construct a God who is utterly alien to Job's image of God and a world whose vastness and strangeness seems to have little in common with Job's parochial village. It is a world of beauty and terror, order and violence—but not, it appears, a world based on principles of justice. The divine speeches differ as radically from the rationalism of the wisdom dialogue as they do from the narratively embodied virtues of the prose tale. Yet as a rhetoric of the sublime they provide release from the blockage that had threatened to leave the story stranded, suspended in mid-arc (Newsom 2003a, 252–256; Linafelt 2006). Job's enigmatic and grammatically ambiguous response in 42:2–6 clearly enacts some "subsidence" on his part, but it does not disclose just what he has now grasped through the seeing of his eyes (v. 5). Nevertheless, Job's response, when he does face God, is clearly not a cursing (1:11; 2:5), and so the prose story may resume its account of the end of Job's testing and his restoration.

Had the author of the canonical book of Job wished to write a seamlessly coherent literary version of the Job story, he undoubtedly could have done so. Instead, he has produced a work that requires the reader to negotiate both its intense centrifugal and centripetal forces in a manner that makes simple coherence not only impossible but undesirable. There is no doubt that in some sense the book is a coherent whole. One can, by emphasizing its centripetal forces read it as a profound deepening of the Job story that achieves its power through its complex characterization of Job. The bitter eruption from Job in chapter 3 at the end of seven days and nights of silence, so utterly different from his previous words, suggests an inner transformation that makes him into character of exceptional potential. Both the emotional scope of Job's words in the chapters that follow and his radical exploration of notions that were literally unthinkable apart from his furious engagement in the dialogue transform him from a traumatized figure into a dangerous one. After the dialogue exhausts itself, Job reinscribes himself in chapters 29–31 as a figure of dignified nobility. Although the reader is in some sense privy to Job's encounter with the transcendent sublimity of the divine that forms the climax of the book, Job's own appropriation of the divine words in an interior dialogue (42:2–6) intimates a character profoundly transformed by his encounter—yet in ways that remain just beyond the reader's grasp. In this manner one might read the canonical book of Job as one among many other ways of telling the Job story—a virtuoso version, perhaps, but still one version to be accepted or rejected, praised or condemned.

Yet if one emphasizes the centrifugal forces, then the book is not simply one among other ways of telling the story but rather a polyphonic composition that simultaneously enacts at least three utterly different ways of rendering the Job story, each one of which implicitly questions the others. Elsewhere, I have suggested how one might grasp the polyphonic unity of such a composition by imagining staging it as a piece of avant garde theater, with different casts of characters enacting the different parts of the book, yet all remaining visible to the audience throughout the play, even if the voices of the actors are sometimes muted so that their continuation of *their* version of the Job story is mimed and not heard (Newsom 2003a, 259–260). Reading the book of Job in this fashion, one recognizes both the author's genius and his humility. He cannot displace other versions of Job by composing his own. But he takes that fact seriously and makes it the central aesthetic trope of his composition. His own work, by presenting a plurality of Job stories, not only takes its place among others but becomes a continuing source for the generation of new ways of telling the Job story.

REFERENCES

Borchert, Wolfgang. 1952. *The Man Outside: Prose Works*. Translated by David Porter. London and New York: Hutchinson International Authors

Buccellati, Giorgio. 1981. "Wisdom and Not: The Case of Mesopotamia." *Journal of the American Oriental Society* 101: 35–47.

Clines, D. J. A. 1985. "False Naivete in the Prologue to Job." *Hebrew Annual Review* 9: 127–136.

Larrimore, Mark. 2013. *The Book of Job: A Biography*. Princeton, NJ: Princeton University Press.

Linafelt, Tod. 2006. "The Wizard of Uz: Job, Dorothy, and the Limits of the Sublime." *Biblical Interpretation* 14: 94–109.

MacLeish, Archibald. 1958. *J.B.: A Play in Verse*. Boston: Houghton Mifflin.

Müller, Hans-Peter. 1977. "Die weisheitliche Lehrerzählung im Alten Testament und seiner Umwelt." *Die Welt des Orients* 9: 77–98.

Newsom, Carol. 2003a. *The Book of Job: A Contest of Moral Imaginations*. New York: Oxford.

Newsom, Carol. 2003b. "The Consolations of God: Assessing Job's Friends across a Cultural Abyss." In *Reading from Right to Left: Essays on the Hebrew Bible in Honour of David J. A. Clines*, edited by J. Cheryl Exum and H. G. M. Williamson, 347–358. Sheffield, Yorkshire: Sheffield Academic Press.

Seow, C. L. 2013. *Job 1-21: Interpretation and Commentary*. Grand Rapids, MI, and Cambridge: Eerdmans.

Spittler, R. P. 1983. "Testament of Job." In *The Old Testament Pseudepigrapha*, edited by James Charlesworth, Vol 1, 829–868. Garden City, NY: Doubleday.

Suleiman, Susan Rubin. 1992. *Authoritarian Fiction: The Ideological Novel as a Literary Genre*. 2nd ed. New York: Columbia University Press.

Wiesel, Elie. 1964. *The Town beyond the Wall*. Translated by Stephen Becker. New York: Athenaeum.

Wiesel, Elie. 1986. *The Trial of God (as it was held on February 25, 1649, in Shamgorod): A Play in Three Acts*. Translated by Marion Wiesel. New York: Schocken.

Zaharopoulos, Dimitri. 1989. *Theodore of Mopsuestia on the Bible: A Study of Old Testament Exegesis*. New York: Paulist Press. 1989.

Zuckerman, Bruce. 1991. *Job the Silent: A Study in Historical Counterpoint*. New York: Oxford University Press.

CHAPTER 20

READING RUTH, READING DESIRE

STEPHANIE DAY POWELL, AMY BETH JONES, AND DONG SUNG KIM

THE book of Ruth: a story of desires evoked, desires hidden, desires realized, and desires displaced. A story in which the desires of storyteller and reader merge, collide, retract, and expand. A story that perpetually refuses to domesticate desire, despite the most resolute of efforts.

Ruth commences with the most fundamental of longings—a desire for bread. Bethlehem, the house of bread, has exhausted its supply. In the midst of this famine, an Israelite couple, Elimelech and Naomi, travels to the neighboring land of Moab. Moabites: a people thought by some to succumb to the basest of desires.

Bread is secured. But fullness begets emptiness, or so it seems. The giving of bread is followed by the taking of life as Naomi loses both husband and sons. All that remains are her two Moabite daughters-in-law, Ruth and Orpah.

Desires diverge. Ruth longs to return to Bethlehem with Naomi, while Orpah chooses to remain in Moab. And Naomi? She prefers to return to Bethlehem alone, but whether it is to spare her daughters-in-law more hardship or to unburden herself, it is not clear. In any case, Ruth resists. Like Adam to Eve, she cleaves to Naomi. *Do not press me to leave you. I want your land to be my land, your home to be my home, your god to be my god. I want to die where you die, never to be parted from you. My desire is resolute.*

The women arrive in Bethlehem at the beginning of the barley harvest. One is bitter, the other sweet. The longing for bread resumes. Ruth sets out to glean behind the reapers. As luck would have it, she finds herself in the field of Boaz, Naomi's kinsman. Boaz: a man of substance in whose eyes Ruth finds favor. *I have been told of all you did for your mother-in-law. May you be rewarded by Yahweh, under whose cloak you have sought protection.* Ruth returns home, her person weighed down with seed. Naomi's desires are rekindled.

A plan is devised. *You and I—I mean you—will go down to the threshing floor,* Naomi tells Ruth. *Boaz will take care of the rest.* But desire demands action. Under the shade of night, Ruth goes down and uncovers the feet of Boaz, rousing him from slumber. Desires at their most vulnerable. *Spread* your *cloak over me, Boaz, for* you *are a redeeming kinsman.* Earthly desires trump heavenly blessings. *It is true I am a near kinsman, but there is one more closely related than I. If he will act as redeemer, let him do it. If he is not willing, I am yours.*

Desires are nourished by delays. Boaz must best the rival redeemer in a public show of verbal prowess. *If you will redeem, redeem, but on the day you acquire the land, Ruth the Moabite will also be acquired so as to perpetuate the name of the dead.* Economies of desire collide. *Then I cannot redeem it, lest I impair my own estate.* Tensions are abated. Crises are averted. Pleasure is the absence of pain, or so it seems.

Boaz marries Ruth, and she bears a son, Obed, who becomes no less than the ancestor of the messianic king David. The elders and the people at the gate compare Ruth to other women of renown—Rachel, Leah, Tamar—who through their actions built up the house of Israel. The townswomen celebrate Ruth for her exceptional devotion to her mother-in-law. *She loves you as a bride loves her betrothed. She is better to you than seven sons.*

Naomi takes the child to her bosom and adopts him as her own. *A son is born to Naomi.* Desires satiated. And Ruth? A bittersweet ending. She is heralded, yet rendered silent by the narrator. Ruth: daughter, son, husband, wife, grandmother of kings. Purveyor of desires.

How does one *read* desire? With regard to the book of Ruth, as in many biblical narratives, characters are endowed with desires both rudimentary and complex; plots are fueled by longings spoken and unspoken; and readers respond out of yearnings conscious and unaware. The desires of the narrative world and the external desires of interpreters often come together in an elaborate dance characterized by movements of seduction and response. Writers, through strategies of exposition, transition, diversion and closure, *pattern* our desires and attempt to transform us into ideal kinds of desirers (Newsom 2003, 35). We, in turn, conform to or resist such seductions as the demands of our own questions and investments shape our reading.

In the move from formalist to structuralist and poststructuralist hermeneutics, narrative critics have increasingly shifted their focus from the internal elements of the text to the intersubjective relationship among stories, storytellers, and audiences. Since the late 1980s, methodologies such as deconstructionism, reader-response criticism, Bakhtinian hermeneutics, and other modalities coming under the umbrella of postmodernism (feminist, queer and postcolonial criticisms, for example) have had a growing impact on biblical studies. Due to the laconic nature of much Hebrew narrative, Hebrew Bible scholars have drawn on these approaches to interrogate the narrative gaps, linguistic ambiguities, and other indeterminate elements that constitute many texts. By raising awareness of the complex dynamics between narratives and readers in the production of meaning, biblical critics (particularly those who are weary of well-worn interpretations handed down over the centuries) are afforded fresh opportunities to wrest a reader's subjectivity from the straightjacket of expected outcomes.

One aspect of narrative dynamics that has received less explicit attention by biblical scholars is desire. The interdisciplinary inquiry into "narrative desire" brings together theoretical insights from narratology, psychoanalytic theory, philosophical studies, and queer theory. Broadly speaking, theorists of desire convene in their shared interest in the role of sexuality in shaping discourse. Steeped principally in the ideas of Sigmund Freud and Jacques Lacan, who themselves conceived of the workings of the unconscious in sexed and gendered terms, narrative desire seeks to bring to awareness the erotic interplay of narrative content, authorial/narrative intention,[1] textual indeterminacy, and readerly longing.

In this chapter, we seek to understand the desires shaping the book of Ruth. First, a brief history of narrative scholarship of Ruth illustrates how scholars' own methodological assumptions shape the history of the text's reception. Then, a critical examination of theories of narrative desire will help us to explore the libidinal economy at the heart of Ruth. While Ruth is ostensibly fueled by the desire for a fulfilling and resolute end, we complicate this assumption by considering an approach that lingers in the "dilatory" spaces of the narrative's middle (Barthes 1974, 75). Through a reexamination of the threshing floor scene of Ruth 3, we consider how such spaces can expose hidden desires and disrupt conventional readings of the narrative's climax.

READING RUTH

The book of Ruth has been categorized as romance, nursery tale, folktale, and comedy. Early studies on Ruth sought to define Ruth's genre in light of historical issues raised by the narrative, among them levirate marriage and land redemption, the origin of King David, and relations between Moabites and Israelites. Hermann Gunkel (1928, 20) classically identified Ruth as an "idyl," owing to the narrative's combination of eloquent poetics and moral stateliness with its focus on the simple affairs of ordinary individuals. The shift in emphasis from historical to literary analysis underscored the significance of Ruth's historical verisimilitude over its facticity; that is, Ruth's literary value lies less in its historical veracity than its ability to creatively dramatize and respond to the social pressures and communal crises facing its audience (Wojcik 1985, 147, 151–152).

It is difficult to overstate the influence of Gunkel's form-critical classification. Because the genre of idyll evokes images of the simple and the serene, interpreters have followed his instinct to read it as a narrative "intelligible at sight to our children," replete with noble adventures and happy endings (Gunkel 1928, 20). With its presupposition that God awards the moral and the pious, the genre of idyll also neatly underscores the theological assumption that a divine force guides the narrative's outcome (Wojcik 1985, 146). Subsequently, interpreters who read Ruth as an idyll have, to varying degrees, been prone to overlook the more ambiguous and troublesome aspects of the book, preferring instead to read it as a seamless work of art that neatly resolves all the dilemmas it raises.

Narrative-critical studies of Ruth initially focused on the story's design as a key to unlocking its themes and motifs. Barbara Green (1982, 55) argues Ruth's author carefully constructs a tightly wrought series of cause-and-effect relations leading up to a climax that, after it is realized, "the audience should be able to look back and see by what steps and with what hints the pathway was paved." Drawing on the work of Russian formalist Vladamir Propp, Jack Sasson identifies Ruth as "folkloristic" in genre and isolates the specific "functions" of characters in Ruth as defined by Propp. Significant to our discussion is Sasson's analysis of Ruth's structural elements alongside Erich Auerbach's well-known observation that Hebrew narrative is "fraught with background"—that is, stripped of "needless details" about each character's history, attitudes, and motives and focused primarily on the economical dialogue between them (Sasson 1979, 219). The marriage of Proppian syntax with the Spartan quality of Hebrew prose leaves "little opportunity for . . . [the] reader to relax attention," resulting in a remarkably suspenseful narrative (218). As such, Ruth is "completely satisfying":

> Once it is agreed that *Ruth* is modeled after a folktale pattern, it becomes possible to draw conclusions that are applicable to any literature of the same genre. . . . No complications are

introduced which are left unresolved; no character is given a role that remains ambiguous. *Heroes* find their mates, *villains* meet their fates, *dispatchers* find their ultimate reward, and *donors* fulfill their obligations. It is not surprising, therefore, that as a tale that hews closer to folktale patterns than most Biblical narratives, *Ruth* has constantly found favor in the eyes of a variegated audience. (Sasson 1979, 216; emphasis in the original)

In contrast to Sasson, other scholars draw on Auerbach's recognition of the Hebrew narrative's stylistic reticence to contemplate the *unsatisfying*, or at least deeply open-ended, nature of Ruth. Danna Nolan Fewell and David Miller Gunn (1990, 15) contend with former literary approaches, asserting that character and genre, and consequently, the meaning of a narrative are not fixed or mandated by the text. They argue for a reading that appreciates realistic characters, namely, people with "conflicting traits" who "are often different to different people" (16). Through a close reading of the play of perspectives between characters, they trouble the view that Naomi, Ruth, and Boaz act solely out of altruism and consider how their actions also reflect self-interests. In their reading, each character is "compromised" by his or her social reality; Naomi's reserve regarding her Moabite daughter-in-law cloaks her cultural prejudices (75), while Boaz cloaks his desire for Ruth the Moabite through his public show of honorable redemption (91–92). Between these two characters stands Ruth who "dances" between them for her survival (94). With mixed motives of loyalty, a desire for recognition, and the need to endure, Ruth paves her way into the Bethlehem community despite a precarious future (94–105).

With Fewell and Gunn's seminal influence, narrative scholars have continued to highlight Ruth's many narrative gaps and textual ambiguities. Some feminist scholars (e.g., van Wolde 1997; Brenner, 2005) have felt the need to rewrite the story from the vantage points of its central characters, using the text's indeterminacy as a vehicle to illuminate the issue of class, gender, and ethnicity only alluded to by the text. The degree of indeterminacy within Ruth led Tod Linafelt (1999, xiii) to devote his entire commentary to an examination of "that which is most unresolved and even perplexing about the narrative." Linafelt works from the premise that ambiguity underscores the role of the reader. By refusing to give the readers enough information to discern a character's motives, "the narrative forces the reader to formulate his or her own suppositions while never knowing for sure if they are correct" (xv–xvi).

Jennifer Koosed similarly underscores how indeterminacy is intrinsic to the very armature of the text. Drawing on the work of E. F. Campbell, Jr., she highlights a central narrative motif known as "doubling" (Koosed 2011, 2–3, 59–60; cf. Campbell 1975, 11–14, 24, 65). Doubling occurs on multiple levels, such as the couplet-structure of dialogues and the strategic placement of twice-repeated words (Koosed 2011, 2–3). Seven times (1:7 twice, 1:9, 1:11, 1:13, 1:19; 4:11), there is also a curious gender "doubling" in the Hebrew in which a masculine verb ending appears where the referent is two females (3, 59). Often doubling inscribes the centrality of relationships into the text (4), while paradoxically making the narrative ripe for deconstructive potential, particularly with regard to issues of gender. "As the narrative plays with masculine and feminine roles," Koosed writes,

> [T]he letters on the page play with the same binary oppositions. Identities and relationships can be read in multiple ways.
>
> Who loves whom? Who marries whom? Who acts as mother to whom; who acts as father? Naomi, Boaz, and Ruth circle around each other, changing positions, interchanging identities, destabilizing binaries and challenging our expectations as readers. (60)

The effect of doubling is to multiply the possibilities for interpretation, thereby provoking doubt in any singular reading of the text. "Such uncertainty does not obscure the meaning," Koosed concludes, "such uncertainty is the meaning" (63).

READING DESIRE

Uncertainty, however, is often deemed anathema to the aims of narrative and the desires of readers. In her influential 1984 essay "Desire in Narrative," Teresa De Lauretis identifies several key assumptions in mainstream narrative theory regarding the relationship between a narrative's structure and its intent/reception. Among them, theorists envisaged narrative movement to be inherently gendered as male and directed toward heterosexual climax— namely, a generative or (re)productive ending. Next, the fundamental purpose of reading is the pursuit of knowledge (the orthodox "pleasure of the text," Roland Barthes wrote, parallels the oedipal drive to unveil the truth). Finally, desire itself is typically assumed to be ahistorical, that is, a stable entity that spans all cultures and time periods (De Lauretis 1984, 103–133; cf. Barthes 1975, 10). In what follows, we turn to the work of Peter Brooks, whose influential theory of narrative desire embodies a representative view of these ideas.

In *Reading for the Plot: Design and Intention in Narrative,* Brooks (1992, 12) argues that most stories are shaped by a libidinal economy in which the outcome is "the realization of a blocked and resisted desire." Influenced by Freud's concept of the death drive, Brooks contends that most narratives are fueled by "male plots of ambition" (39). The logic of narrative is to move the (implicitly male) reader from the beginning through the pleasurable complications of the middle, to a fulfilling and total conclusion. Such pleasurable complications often center around women and other marginalized characters who, according to Brooks, constitute the "perverse middle" (37–61, 90–112).

For Brooks, irrespective of the particular desires that inspire a story or inform its reception, what motivates all storytellers and binds all readers together is the desire for a satisfying, climactic end. The temporal demands of any story are such that "the end writes the beginning and shapes the middle" (22). Readers long for coherence and closure, "a fully predicated, and readable, sentence" in which the story's original crisis is worked out and all threatening anomalies or deviations are suppressed or resolved (96). As we have observed, Ruth's tranquil setting and ostensibly good-natured characters often predispose a reader to an unspoiled reading in which ideological tensions are minimized and happy endings may be realized. It also appears in the case of Ruth that these idyllic features work in tandem with a male plot of ambition to produce a model reader—one who will conform to the values and outcomes envisaged by the storyteller.

It is particularly ironic that Ruth conforms to male emplotment given that it is typically heralded as a woman's story. While the plot is purportedly driven by the "brave and bold decision of women" (Trible 1978, 195), patriarchal desires and expectations nonetheless shape the narrative outcome. If we look closely at the narrative's exposition, we find that the calamity with which the story begins relates not just to Naomi's and Ruth's survival, but to the endurance of Elimelech's name. Moreover, though some scholars believe the genealogy (4:18–22) was a later addition, the narrative is arguably preoccupied with the Davidic lineage from chapter 1. Elimelech and his sons are said to be Ephrathites (1:2) and hence ancestors of Jesse, David's father (1 Sam. 17:12). In this light, their deaths portend nothing less than the tragedy of a kingdom unrealized.

Ruth's ultimate worth, therefore, is measured in terms of her ability to give Naomi an heir (4:13–15) and perpetuate the name of the deceased (4:5). To achieve these ends, she must enter the dangerous spaces of the grain field (2:22) and the threshing floor (3:14), where she risks being perceived as a selfish and sexually promiscuous Moabite (cf. Gen. 19:30–38; Deut. 23:3–5; Num. 25:1–3). Yet, like her literary ancestresses Rachel, Tamar, and Leah, Ruth's personal trials are secondary to her ability to build up the household of Israel (4:11–12). When Boaz prevails over his rival, he not only comes to the aid of Ruth and Naomi; he safeguards the national interest. He simultaneously ensures ongoing female dependence on men, thus handily straightening out the "perversities" of the middle. The "brave and bold decisions of women" are rendered mere plot devices, and the protagonist Ruth is made virtually invisible as the story that bears her name draws to a close.

REREADING DESIRE, REREADING RUTH

Is the book of Ruth captive to androcentric desires, or are there ways of reading beyond the male plot of ambition? If the implied reader is assumed to be a model patriarch, what does this mean for other readers, other desires? In this section, we turn to alternative theoretical models in order to consider ways of reading that can illuminate divergent, and even conflicting, desires within narrative. We then return to the story of Ruth and a brief exegetical exploration of chapter 3 in order to illustrate the proposed strategy of "reading for the middle."

While Lacan relied heavily on Freud to formulate his thinking on the subject of desire, a key difference in their theories lies in Lacan's *nonlinear* understanding of desire's movement. Generally speaking, Freud believed pleasure was the productive result of the forward movement of tension's intensification and release (MacKendrick 1999, 7); whereas Lacan imagined the realization of one's desire to be an elusive endeavor, involving a more circular process of continual displacement. According to Lacan's *stade du miroir*, in the course of human development, we find our identity in language. However, a loss occurs when we enter into the linguistic realm because language is only a *reflection* of the real. Our desires, originating in the unconscious, presignaficatory sphere, are inaccessible. The result is a psychic gap, what Lacan terms the "lost real." We attempt to access our original desire through speech and writing, but because our entry into language is predicated on an original loss, we are in a perpetual state of misrecognition in which the realization of desire is always postponed (López 2007, 9–11). As human beings, we only experience traces of our true desires through indirect expressions, such as dreams and slips of the tongue (Belsey 2002, 58). By analogy, narratives express the (often contradictory) desires contained within them through repetitions, gaps, polysemous language, and other textual anomalies.

How does one unlock the "lost" desires of a narrative? Post-formalist and poststructuralist narrative theorists have proposed disrupting the fixed structures of a narrative in order to discover its more variegated and even subversive elements. In *The Pleasure of the Text*, Barthes promoted "a process of profaning the oedipal sanctity of structure and control" (Roof 1996, xxiv) in order to uncover those interstices of "bliss," where unspoken narrative desires remain dormant (Barthes 1975, 6–7, 9–14). Whereas Barthes's proposal is more philosophy than methodology, later narrative critics have demonstrated various strategies for reading against the ideological grain of the text. We take our strategy of "reading for the middle" from those literary critics who argue for a resistance to teleological structures. Lloyd Pratt, for example, suggests an approach of reading "sideways" that focuses not on past or the future but rather the moment of "becoming" that constitutes the present (2011, 185–186). We illuminate these ideas in the following analysis of Ruth 3.

When we look more closely at the Ruth narrative, we find that chapter 3 significantly disrupts the teleological aims of the male plot of ambition at both the level of the narrative's content and at the level of reading. We first notice this disruption in the temporal setting of the chapter. Naomi tells Ruth to go down to the threshing floor where Boaz will be winnowing barley (3:2–3). However, this setting in time is illogical since we are told in the previous chapter that Ruth gleans in Boaz's field until the conclusion of the barley *and* the wheat harvest (2:23). Why would Boaz be winnowing barley at the end of the wheat harvest? While scholars have attempted to offer agricultural or linguistic explanations for this textual oddity (see, e.g., Campbell 117–119; Sakenfeld 52), arguably, the anomaly signals to the reader *time's arrest*. The manufactured causal relations that normally propel narratives forward are suspended, and all narrative possibilities are viable. The reader is invited to pause and consider the fullness of the present moment.

Chapter 3 is the only chapter in which all the principal characters intersect (perhaps, as we will see below, in an even more suggestive way than is at first apparent). Of course, the threshing floor scene is where many readers have lingered to discover what *really* happens between Ruth and Boaz, a question the text itself carefully obscures. The clandestine setting at midnight, the use of the terms "the man" and "the woman" (Campbell 1975, 130), and all the ambiguous cloaking and uncloaking between them[2] each adds to the erotic mystery of the scene. One of the persistent ironies of chapter 3 is the repetition of the verb "to know" (Heb. *yada*) (vv. 3, 4, 11, 14, 18; cf. v. 2), a term that often carries with it connotations of sexual activity. Knowledge, carnal or otherwise, becomes increasingly elusive as the scene progresses. If he knows she is in need, why has Boaz not sought out Ruth for marriage already? Is Naomi aware another redeemer could upset her plan? Why does not Naomi simply approach Boaz on Ruth's behalf?

Ruth herself slips and slides between the folds of other people's knowledge, even that of the narrator. Does she want to secure a home for herself? Does she want a child? Or does she enter the threshing floor with another agenda? Instead of following Naomi's instructions to allow Boaz to take the lead, Ruth takes the initiative. Later, Ruth tells Naomi that Boaz gave her the grain and said, "Do not go back to your mother-in-law empty-handed" (3:17 NRSV). She misrepresents his words to her, leaving "the narrative with a lie on her lips" (Koosed 2011, 93).

One additional mystery complicates matters further. In the Masoretic Text, there is a peculiar discrepancy found within Naomi's instructions to Ruth between what is read (*qere*) and what is written (*ketiv*) in 3:3–4. In the *qere*, Naomi instructs Ruth to go down to the threshing floor and lie down. In the *ketiv*, Naomi states *she herself* will do these things. The "perversities" of the middle are enacted quite literally as Naomi places herself between Boaz and Ruth. What might this signify from a Lacanian standpoint? What "lost" desires are seeking to come to light? Scholars suggest various explanations for Naomi's virtual presence. Perhaps it represents the narrator's attempt to play down the scene's sexual content by replacing Ruth with Naomi (Irwin 2008). Others argue Naomi's insertion links Naomi and Ruth sexually (Jennings 2005, 229) or, more broadly, that it is indicative of the ongoing subversion of sex and gender roles in the text (Exum 1996, 168–174; Koosed 2011, 59–60).

To these possibilities we add the observation that it is here, in the silhouetted figures of these three individuals, that past, present, and future come together. In her yearning for a child to replace the loss of her sons, Naomi embodies the nostalgia of the past. Boaz, conversely, represents the optimistic future driven by desires to secure both the land and the line of David.[3] Standing between them is Ruth, occupying the liminality of the present. To accentuate the immediacy of the encounter, the narrator draws attention to her presence at Boaz's feet with the Hebrew "*hinneh*" often translated as "Behold!" (3:8). Boaz, startled by her presence (3:8), exclaims, "Who are you?" (3:9), words Naomi will later echo with a similar sense of astonishment (3:16).

In what we might term a "dilated moment" (Pratt 2011, 185) Ruth (in her only words of dialogue on the threshing floor) asserts, "I am your handmaid (*'ămātekā*) Ruth. Spread your robe over your handmaid for you are a redeemer" (translation ours). On the surface, Ruth seems to be complying with Naomi's desires by offering herself as a wife to Boaz (cf. Ezek. 16:8). However, if we read her words with attention to the question of time, we find that Ruth speaks only to the present moment—"I [*am*] your handmaid" and "you [*are*] a redeemer." (The omission of the verb "to be" in the Hebrew accentuates the immediacy of her assertions). There are no references to past losses or future gains. In naming herself *'āmāh* Ruth declares herself on a par with Boaz,[4] an authority she subsequently demonstrates in assuming the power to name him a *gôel*.

In a story purportedly about Israelite history (being in time), Ruth occupies space (see Holland 2012, 10). She neither presses forward nor backward but calls "the now" into being. This is not to say the moment has no bearing on the future, only that Ruth resists the teleological pressures that would define her. Where Naomi and Boaz seek to order their worlds through the mastering of time, symbolized in the promises of procreation and land redemption, Ruth commandingly declares her presence in the now. Unencumbered by her foreignness, rival redeemers, or the possibility of future progeny, she calls upon Boaz to help her obtain a livable present.

"What happens," asks Sharon Patricia Holland (2012, 10), "when someone who exists in time meets someone who only occupies space?". For one "blissful" moment, Ruth disrupts the social and narrative order. She interrupts the male plot of ambition by upsetting the hierarchy of the narrative's end over the middle. She redirects our attention away from the (re) productive climax long enough to insist that we look her in the face. *Hinneh*! Even then, no ultimate truths are unveiled. Perhaps that is the point. The *irreducibility* of Ruth's desires reminds us that narrative desires are not univocal and that the possibilities for the story's end are not singular. If Ruth's desires cannot be named, they cannot be tamed or appropriated. The Moabite woman we think we know will not assimilate, despite the attempts of the writer and readers. We are consigned to perpetually gleaning. Desires deferred.

Nonetheless, as the quintessential purveyor of desires, Ruth's actions suggest something of the hidden longings of the story's post-exilic audience members. In the dark, Ruth conveys a series of conflicting yearnings—to be laid bare and yet to be covered, to exert her independence even as she seeks the good of others, and finally, to build up the patriarchal lineage while preserving the bonds between women. Such desires were likely shared by the returnees of Yehud, who sought to retain their exilic identity while pursuing a home within the folds of a new community. For women, the need to build this community stood at odds with desires to marry outside the clan, or even to forgo marriage and childbirth altogether. Naomi's "appearance" on the threshing floor suggests the conflicting loyalties set before Ruth, who seeks a life somewhere between the dream of female interdependence and the need for economic and social survival.

The book of Ruth's existence in the biblical canon itself reminds us that our protagonist stands at the crossroads of Israel's story. In a literary setting which looks backward and forward from the days of the judges to the monarchy, the book of Ruth portrays a people in-between. In the balance an unlikely candidate—a Moabite woman—ushers in a new future. As one who exceeds both the social and narrative world that contains her, Ruth "dilates the moment that is now . . . to such a degree that worlds unknown and impossible begin to seem undeniably real" (Pratt 2011, 185). By inviting us to transcend the border between the story world and lived experience, she makes a way forward for a seemingly unplottable future.

NOTES

1. Increasingly narrative scholars have ceased speaking of "authorial" intent. See Bal (2002) for a helpful distinction between authorial intention and an artistic work's "agency" or "narrativity."
2. Whereas most commentators assume Ruth uncovers Boaz's feet (a euphemism for his genitals), Kirsten Nielsen offers an alternative translation in which Ruth (in a risky proposal of marriage, according to Nielsen) uncovers herself at the place of his feet and calls on Boaz to cover her (1997, 68–71). Cf. the visual renditions of this scene by Marc Chagall.
3. While Ruth is concerned with legitimizing Davidic kingship, many scholars now date the text to the post-exilic period. A post-exilic dating allows us to consider what impact issues of land resettlement would have had on how the audience read/heard the book.
4. As Sasson notes, the use of the term ʿāmāh stands in contrast to Ruth's earlier self-designation as šipḥāh (2:13), "a female belonging to the lowest rung of the mišpaḥāh's social ladder" (1979, 80).

REFERENCES

Bal, Mieke. 2002. "Intention." In Traveling Concepts in the Humanities: A Rough Guide, 253–285. Toronto: University of Toronto Press.

Barthes, Roland. 1975. The Pleasure of the Text. Translated by Richard Miller. New York: Hill and Wang.

Barthes, Roland. 2002. S/Z: An Essay. Translated by Richard Miller. New York: Hill and Wang, 1974.

Belsey, Catherine. 2002. Poststructuralism: A Very Short Introduction. Oxford: Oxford University Press.

Brenner, Athalya. 2005. I Am: Biblical Women Tell Their Own Stories. Minneapolis: Fortress Press.

Brooks, Peter. 1992. Reading for the Plot: Design and Intention in Narrative. Cambridge, Mass: Harvard University Press.

Campbell, Edward F., Jr. 1975. *Ruth: A New Translation with Introduction, Notes, and Commentary*. Anchor Bible 7. Garden City, New York: Doubleday.

De Lauretis, Teresa. 1984. "Desire in Narrative." In *Alice Doesn't: Feminism, Semiotics, Cinema*, 103–157. Bloomington: Indiana University Press.

Exum, Cheryl J. 1996. *Plotted, Shot, and Painted: Cultural Representations of Biblical Women*. Sheffield, Yorkshire: Sheffield Academic Press.

Fewell, Danna Nolan, and David M. Gunn. 1990. *Compromising Redemption: Relating Characters in the Book of Ruth*. Literary Currents in Biblical Interpretation. Louisville, KY: Westminster/John Knox Press.

Green, Barbara. 1982. "The Plot of the Biblical Story of Ruth." *Journal for the Study of the Old Testament* 23: 55–68.

Gunkel, Hermann. 1928. *What Remains of the Old Testament and Other Essays*. Translated by A. K. Dallas. London: G. Allen & Unwin.

Holland, Sharon Patricia. 2012. *The Erotic Life of Racism*. Durham, NC: Duke University Press.

Irwin, Brian P. 2008. "Removing Ruth: Tiqqune Sopherim in Ruth 3.3-4?" *Journal for the Study of the Old Testament* 32(3) (March): 331–338.

Jennings, Theodore W., Jr. 2005. *Jacob's Wound: Homoerotic Narrative in the Literature of Ancient Israel*. New York: Continuum.

Koosed, Jennifer L. 2011. *Gleaning Ruth: A Biblical Heroine and Her Afterlives*. Studies on Personalities of the Old Testament. Columbia: University of South Carolina Press.

Linafelt, Tod, and Timothy K. Beal. 1999. *Ruth and Esther*. Berit Olam. Collegeville, MN: Liturgical Press.

López, Gemma. 2007. *Seductions in Narrative: Subjectivity and Desire in the Works of Angela Carter and Jeanette Winterson*. Youngstown, NY: Cambria Press.

MacKendrick, Karmen. 1999. *Counterpleasures*. Albany: State University of New York Press.

Newsom, Carol. 2003. *The Book of Job: A Contest of Moral Imaginations*. Oxford and New York: Oxford University Press.

Nielsen, Kirsten. 1997. *Ruth: A Commentary*. The Old Testament Library. Louisville, KY: Westminster/John Knox Press.

Pratt, Lloyd. 2011. "Close Reading the Present: Eudora Welty's Queer Politics." In *Queer Times, Queer Becomings*, edited by E. L. McCallum and Mikko Tuhkanen, 183–204. Albany: State University of New York Press.

Roof, Judith. 1996. *Come as You Are: Sexuality and Narrative*. New York: Columbia University Press.

Sakenfeld, Katharine Doob. 1999. *Ruth*. Interpretation. Louisville, KY: John Knox Press.

Sasson, Jack M. 1979. *Ruth: A New Translation with a Philological Commentary and a Formalist-Folklorist Interpretation*. Baltimore, MD: John Hopkins University Press.

Trible, Phyllis. 1978. "A Human Comedy." In *God and the Rhetoric of Sexuality*, 166–199. Philadelphia: Fortress Press.

Van Wolde, Ellen. 1997. *Ruth and Naomi: Two Aliens*. Translated by John Bowden. London: SCM Press.

Wojcik, Jan. 1985. "Improving Rules in the Book of Ruth." *Publications of the Modern Language Association* 100(2) (March): 145–153.

CHAPTER 21

BODIES, BOUNDARIES, AND BELONGING IN THE BOOK OF ESTHER

ANNE-MAREIKE WETTER

WITHIN the narrative corpus of the Hebrew Bible, the book of Esther seems somewhat of a misfit (cf. Koller 2014).[1] Set in Susa, the capital of the Persian Empire, it appears not at all concerned with the Promised Land. It owes its name and the resolution of its plot to a female main protagonist. And last but not least, it omits one central protagonist: God. However, although bewildering at first, these features serve to pervasively establish the narrative's function: to describe and partly resolve the struggle for physical and ideological survival experienced by a Jewish population in Diaspora surroundings.

PLOT SUMMARY

The first chapter is staged at the court of King Ahasuerus (often equated with Xerxes), who is portrayed as both immensely powerful and tragically dull-witted. When his queen Vashti refuses to be paraded before the drunken crowd attending him, the king is steered by his advisers to remove her from the court (1:19) and to pass a decree establishing each man's rule over his own household (1:22). Although apparently unconnected with the Jews, this chapter playfully sets the scene for what is to become a struggle of life and death for the Jewish population of the Persian Empire. All its ingredients—the vastness of the Empire, the erratic and manipulable character of its king, the arbitrary and simultaneously irrevocable nature of Persian Law, and finally, the removal of Vashti—are necessary for the main plot, whether as exemplars of later developments (e.g., the decree to extinguish the Jews), or as their direct conditions (i.e., Esther being taken to the royal court).

In chapter 2, the king has sobered up, and immediately regrets the removal of Vashti. Again, his servants suggest a solution: "Let fair virgins be sought for the king (2:2), and let the girl that pleases the king be queen instead of Vashti" (2:4). Enter—not Esther, but Mordecai,

Esther's guardian and Jew par excellence. This epitome of exiled Jewishness is introduced as an implied descendant of Saul, and directly connected with the first wave of exiles forced from Jerusalem in 598 BCE (2:5–6). His ward Esther finds herself at the margins of society— exiled, orphaned, and a woman. But she has potential—her beauty, the text implies, is comparable to that of Rachel, Joseph, and David (2:7; cf. Gen. 29:17; 39:6; 1 Sam. 16:18.). Indeed, once inside the palace, Esther beguiles everyone, including the king (2:15–17). Intriguingly, even as newly elected queen, she keeps her ethnic and religious identity hidden (2:20).

Some time after these events, and with no apparent connection to the main plot, Mordecai discovers a plot to assassinate king Ahasuerus. He informs Esther, who informs the king, and the would-be assassins are brought to justice (2:22–23).

Chapter 3 starts with the introduction of the chief villain: Haman, the son of Hammedatha, an Agagite. This new adviser to the king lives up to his name as a descendant of Israel's arch-enemy (cf. 1 Sam. 15; Exod. 17; Deut. 25:17–19). When Mordecai refuses to bow down before him, Haman immediately plots his revenge—a revenge that would be laughable in its disproportionality, were it not for the tragic reality it evokes, especially in a post-Shoah readership. Unwilling to punish only Mordecai, Haman resolves to destroy the entire Jewish people (3:6). He maligns them as "different," and promises Ahasuerus money for turning a blind eye to his murderous plans. As is to be expected, the king offers no resistance, and a law is passed ordering the annihilation of "all Jews, young and old, women and children, in one day, the thirteenth . . . of the month Adar" (3:13), a date that had previously been determined by casting lots (*purim*; 3:7).

Upon hearing the bad news, Mordecai and the rest of the Jews engage in conventional mourning rituals—wailing, sackcloth, and ashes—without, however, praying for deliverance (4:1–3). Instead, Mordecai begs Esther, via her eunuchs, to plead with the king (4:7–8). Esther hesitates—the king is notoriously fickle, and approaching him uninvited could equal a death sentence. However, after Mordecai's famous words that if Esther does not act, "relief and deliverance will arise for the Jews from another place (*mimakom acher*)" (4:14), she orders a communal fast and announces that she will go the king, come what may (4:16).

The king welcomes her favorably, and promises her "up to half his kingdom" (5:6). Esther's request is modest: "Would the king and Haman like to come to a dinner party?" (5:8). Of course they would! At the feast, Esther invites them for a second night.

On the night preceding this second feast, having trouble sleeping, the king orders the royal annals to be read to him. He discovers that Mordecai has yet to be rewarded for preventing the assassination plotted against him. Haman, come to talk to the king about hanging Mordecai from a gallows, is instead ordered to parade Mordecai around Susa, seated on the king's horse and wearing the royal robes. Unexpectedly, Haman's wife and friends warn him that since Mordecai is one of the Jews, his revenge will surely fail (6:13).

At the second feast, Esther finally discloses her real identity and the threat posed to her and her people by vicious Haman (7:6). At the suggestion of yet another eunuch, Haman is hung from the gallows he had prepared for Mordecai. Mordecai, on the other hand, is advanced to Haman's position of royal adviser.

Since the king's law about the annihilation of the Jews cannot be revoked, Ahasuerus grants the Jews the right to defend themselves. Their enemies are terrified into acting as Jews themselves—*mitjahadim* (8:17), a hapax legomenon probably denoting pretended rather than real conversion (Mason 2007).

In terms reminiscent of holy warfare as described in Deuteronomy, Joshua, and Judges, the Jews revenge themselves upon their enemies, killing more than 75,000. Mordecai and Esther order the spontaneous celebration of their victory to be turned into an annual feast—Purim—for all Jews (9:21–29). The narrative ends with some remarks on the splendor of "Mordecai the Jew," who was "great among the Jews . . . for he sought the welfare of his people and spoke peace to all his people" (10:3). Esther, on the other hand, silently fades out of the story.

NARRATIVE APPROACHES TO ESTHER

The book of Esther, although set in "real" historical surroundings and boasting a "real" king among its main protagonists, clearly does not relate "history." Rather, it expresses the perpetual and often well-grounded fear of persecution, even annihilation, experienced by the Jewish people since their inception. In Esther, this troubling motif and its equally troubling resolution come in a surprisingly appealing package: a narrative that not only reads as delightfully as an episode from the Arabian Nights, but whose "consummate artistry" (Day 2005, 3) also offers enough stylistic meat for a feast of literary scholarship—an appropriate metaphor for a book structured by a variety of lavish banquets (cf. Fox 2001, 157).

Studies of the book that foreground its narrative quality tend to focus on one or a combination of the following issues: the book's plot structure, characterized by a large number of doublures, opposites, reversals, and unlikely coincidences; the characterization of the main protagonists; the book's relationship to other texts, both biblical and extra-biblical; and related to all of the above, its genre and date. Lately, the comic (or farcical, or carnivalesque) nature of the narrative has received increasing consideration, as has the "hiddenness" of its meaning, already implied in the protagonist's name.[2]

Concerning the book's genre, various proposals have been made, and agreement does not seem to be at hand. Is the narrative based on the schema of Persian Chronicles (e.g., Gordis 1981), or does it borrow traits from Greek comedy (e.g., Berlin 2001, xxii)? Is it a novel or *novella* (e.g., Loader 1979; Humphreys 1985), perhaps even more specifically a *diaspora novella* (e.g., Meinhold 1976)? Or must the entire narrative be read as an elaborate etiology of Purim (e.g., Moore 1971, liii)? Is it a *farce* (Beal 1997)? As Day notes, "this very variety is in itself illustrative" (Day 2005, 11), and confirms the intuition that Esther is not easily caught in any one categorization. And perhaps a choice is neither necessary nor desirable. To read Esther as a specimen of one fixed genre would be in contradiction with its versatile character and its ability to relate to any number of biblical and extra-biblical sources.

Indeed, intertextuality—whether focusing on similarities in genre, plot, or vocabulary—constitutes one major focus of Esther scholarship. Within the biblical canon, the Exodus story, the Joseph cycle, Samuel's confrontation with Saul (1 Sam. 15), and various stories about female heroines have received the lion's share of attention as possible intertexts of the narrative. Gillis Gerleman, for example, reads Esther as a critical reframing of and emancipation from the Exodus tradition, in which the Diaspora community takes over YHWH's salvific function (Gerleman 1973). Quite to the contrary, Timothy Laniak assumes that the links between Esther and other biblical literature imbue the former with the religiosity that is so much more explicit in the latter (Laniak 2003, 86). Similarly, Berlin claims: "The Book of

Esther presents a tale of Persian Jewry, and by extension all exiled Jewry, as a continuation of the story of Israel, with the same type of enemies and heroes, and the same patterns of danger and deliverance" (Berlin 2001, xxxvi). Ultimately, as observed by, for example, Levenson (1997) and Day (2005), the reader has to make her own choice regarding the significance attributed to Esther's more traditionally religious intertexts.

The issue of divine involvement—or lack thereof—also figures into analyses of Esther's plot structure. Marked by an amassment of improbable coincidences, this structure is sometimes regarded as counteracting one of the unique and disturbing features of the narrative: the apparent absence of the divine character (e.g., Bush 1996, 323–326; Levenson 1997, 21). Esther's "theology," which paints God as much less "visible, audible, and dramatic" than other biblical texts (if at all), *can* be evaluated as "a profounder and more realistic stance of faith than that of most of biblical tradition" (Levenson 1997, 21) but also leaves room for agnosticism (Day 2005, 92).

Whether or not God is assumed to be the one pulling the strings, the way in which the narrative turns the world on its head can hardly be missed. In this line, Laniak approaches the narrative from the perspective of honor and shame (Laniak 1998 and similarly, Klein 1997). Exile, Laniak states, would have been experienced as a state of dishonor or shame in the socio-cultural context of the narrative, incompatible with Israel's status as Yнwн's chosen people. In Esther, as in a variety of other narratives (e.g., Moses, David, Joseph), the initially marginalized and "shamed" main protagonist "is honored by promotion, power, wealth and public respect" (Laniak 1998, 15), to the detriment of his or her adversary.

Other authors emphasize the ironic, at times outright comical effect achieved by the unexpected reversals in Esther (e.g., Goldman 1990). Reading Esther as a farce also helps to account for the excessive violence committed by the Jews against their enemies: "[L]ike Larry, Moe, Curly, and the Coyote, this violence is not *actual* violence—it is *story* violence. [. . .] Esther's violence offers escape, not a model for enactment" (Jackson 2012, 213).

Closely related are approaches that read Esther within a "carnivalesque" framework (e.g., Craig 1995; Fewell 2003; LaCoque 2008). A reading in terms of Bakhtin's concept of the *carnivalesque* (Bakhtin 1984), a temporary reversal of social realities whose function is primarily cathartic, indeed dovetails well with the carnival-like character of Purim and characteristics of the narrative itself (the emphasis on banquets and the consumption of wine, the dramatic reversals in status, the portrayal of Ahasuerus and Haman as fool and knave respectively, and the grotesque quality of various details of the text). Although there is no one-on-one match between Esther and the carnivalesque (e.g., the contrast between "folk" versus "elite" culture hardly fits the conflict between Haman and the Jews), Bakhtin's concept succeeds in pointing out and illuminating various textual features, not least among them the caricature-like depiction of Haman, the king, and indeed the entire Persian court.

Indeed, the characterization of Haman and the king must be counted among the comical highlights of biblical narrative. This is, perhaps, one reason why characterization in Esther has attracted much scholarly attention, despite Bush's assessment that in terms of genre the narrative "is a *short story that reveals the quality of a situation*" rather than focusing on "*developing* characters or a situation" (Bush 1996, 308–309; italics in original). The most profound study of this subject is undoubtedly Michael's V. Fox's *Character and Ideology in the Book of Esther* (Fox 1991, 2001). Arguing that "the central ideas are embodied in, rather than merely enunciated by, the persons in the text" (Fox 2001, 2), Fox reads Esther and Mordecai as exemplars for Jews in a diaspora setting.[3] He vindicates both from the accusations of shrewdness, opportunism, and lack of feminist assertiveness sometimes voiced against them (e.g., Wyler 1995; Davies 2001) by pointing out "the severity of the crisis that stands at the story's heart: the mortal danger to the Jewish people" (Fox 2001, 208).

Whereas Fox emphasizes the straightforward (though by no means simple) message of Esther, others have read the narrative as a literary game of hide-and-seek (e.g., Loader 1979). The basic assumption of these readings is that "at various junctures Esther conveys mixed messages: one is a surface message, but another, often conflicting message lies beneath the surface" (Grossman 2011, 239). Perhaps the most cutting-edge analysis of this kind is Beal's *Book of Hiding* (1997). Employing contemporary theory on gender, (ethnic) identity formation, and othering, Beal discovers in Esther a "palimpsest," in which traces of the "exscribed" woman Vashti reappear in Esther and Mordecai. This perspective leads him to read the book "as a literary farce that highlights the impossibilities of locating and fixing the not-self, or other (specifically the woman as other and the Jew as other) over against 'us'" (Beal 1997, ix). With somewhat less attention for contemporary theory, but all the more for details of the Hebrew text, Grossman (2011) discovers a wealth of intra- and intertextual allusions, multivalent expressions, and ironical statements. All of these, he argues, add up to a "hidden reading," which is less positive about Diaspora and Diaspora Jews like Mordecai, but more positive about God's involvement than the surface meaning suggests. Similarly, according to Korpel (2003), the author criticizes the Diaspora community by scattering subtle hints about their alienation from Israel, her God and her traditions.

Analyses presupposing a "hidden meaning" in Esther always run the risk of discovering more than is warranted by the text. Their strength lies in raising awareness of the unique character of the book, which, in its intricate, multilayered, and ambivalent composition, "places great faith in its readers" (Grossman 2011, 245).

BRINGING THE MARGINS TO THE CENTER

Narrative-critical scholarship has done much to elucidate the literary quality of the book of Esther. Still, its "message" or "meaning" remains subject to debate. Is exile embraced or rejected? Is the Diaspora community applauded or condemned? Is the slaughter of the enemies of the Jews a tragedy or part of the "comical" plot of the book? Is the border between "self" and "other" upheld or destabilized? And last but not least, is God absent or present, punisher or deliverer?

My own assessment of the narrative's emphasis on plot reversals, irony, and hidden meanings, its extensive yet subtle appropriation of older texts, as well as its genre, which seems to borrow from a variety of biblical and nonbiblical texts, leads me to read it as self-assertion of a Jewish community in Diaspora. My analysis is centered on the assumption that the community described in the book positions itself not just within and against the Persian Empire, but also within and partly against Judaism. This assumption has far-reaching consequences, not just in terms of genre (even if one assumes the existence of the "diaspora novella" as a separate genre), but also in terms of methods and concepts suited for its interpretation.

Construing the book of Esther as a minority group's struggle to maintain their religious and ethnic identity suggests post-colonial theory as an appropriate tool of analysis. This basic conceptual framework, uniquely suited to uncover the subtle play of power and subversion in a text, can fruitfully be supplemented by concepts from religious studies and ethnology in order to grasp hints of religious and ethnic identity. Within religious studies, the concept of ritualization deserves special attention, as it helps to uncover processes of identity formation by pointing out how details of the plot mimic and simultaneously contrast Persian *and* more orthodox Jewish practices and characteristics. Finally, reading the narrative through the combined lenses of postcolonial studies and gender studies points to processes of representation that involve not just Esther and Mordecai as embodiments of Israel in exile, but also Ahasuerus, Haman, and the various eunuchs paraded throughout the book.

Admittedly, none of these concepts and methods is intrinsically literary or narratological; nevertheless, each of them can be adapted in order to make sense of specific features of the book of Esther. I briefly set out two lines of investigation, linking both to the struggle for religious and ethnic identity: the tendency to "compare and contrast" the Jews with their Persian surroundings, and the mechanisms of representation involving various male and female protagonists (see further Wetter 2013 and 2015).

Ritualizing Esther

Despite some proposals to the opposite (recently, e.g., Haag 2003), the unity and careful construction of the book of Esther are well established. Nonetheless, its plot is characterized by a number of obvious gaps, which, to an uninformed reader, render it almost nonsensical. Why would Mordecai forbid Esther to reveal her ethnic identity to a king who appears tolerant toward ethnic minorities (2:20; 1:3)? Why does he refuse to pay homage to Haman, and why does Haman react with such exorbitant plans for revenge? Apparently, the book of Esther is not intended to stand by itself—the reader is required to supply additional information in order to make the plot "work." The source of this information is not entirely arbitrary: the reader is subtly steered toward other texts of the Hebrew Bible, particularly the so-called Deuteronomistic History. The traditions about Amalek (1 Sam. 15:2; Exod. 17:16; Deut. 25:18) are an especially eloquent example of hidden intertexts the reader must activate to fill a gap in the plot. The text thus creates an in-group of informed readers who alone are able to fill the gaps in the plot with meaning. In addition, it firmly establishes the Diaspora community's place within "Israel."

A similar function is fulfilled by repeated occurrence of literary instances of ritualization, i.e., of taking an ordinary event, time, concept, and the like, and placing it within a sacred context:

> Viewed as practice, ritualization involves the very drawing, in and through the activity itself, of a privileged distinction between ways of acting, specifically between those acts being performed and those being contrasted, mimed, or implicated somehow. [. . .] Ritualization gives rise to (or creates) the sacred as such by virtue of its sheer differentiation from the profane. (Bell 1992, 90–91)

Admittedly, the concept of ritualization is rooted in the analysis of lived rituals and practices. Nevertheless, it offers a useful tool for grasping processes in the text that might otherwise go unnoticed. Specifically, it points to the drawing of lines between "sacred" and "profane," and by implication, between "us" and "them."

The book of Esther is in constant dialogue both with details within the book itself and with texts from other books of the Hebrew Bible. This twofold intertextuality results in a twofold movement: by associating (though not necessarily identifying) the "Jews" in the book of Esther with the Israelites of other biblical narratives, the author distances the former from their Persian surroundings. The Jews' actions are literally "sanctioned," while those of the Persians are "profaned."

This literary technique can be demonstrated with the example of *mishte* "feasting" and *simḥah*, "joy." The book of Esther presents itself as the book of feasting from the outset. It starts with a six-month royal drinking bout (*mishte*) to which the entire Persian Empire is invited (1:1–5). Having resolved that the Jews must be eliminated, "the king and Haman sat down to drink" (3:15). And Esther, knowing that dinner parties are the Persian equivalent of an afternoon on the golf course, organizes two feasts in order to implore the king to save her people. For the Persians in the book of Esther, feasting is a way of life, and getting drunk a matter of law abidance: "Drinking was according to this edict: there are no restrictions" (1:8).

In this context, the fast of the Jews fulfills the function of a carnivalistic countermovement. The Jews' behavior forms a stark contrast to the casual glass of wine Haman and the king enjoy at the same time. Here, the carnivalesque critique of the status quo and, even more importantly, of the abuse of power is not accomplished by a Bakhtinian "banquet for all the world" (Bakhtin 1984, 19), but by its opposite: a fast and rites of mourning that express not just individual horror, but a silent condemnation of the "brimming-over abundance" (Bakhtin 1984, 19) that characterizes the lifestyle of the elite. The fast, unaccompanied by prayer, fails to meet the standard of a conventional "Jewish" ritual. And yet, by setting the Jews apart from their environment, it fulfills the most basic function of religious rituals in general.

The first part of the book shows feasting Persians and fasting Jews. However, from chapter 8 onward, the tables are turned. In response to the edict allowing the Jews to defend themselves, "there was celebration and gladness for the Jews, feasting (*mishte*) and a good day" (8:17). In terms of vocabulary, there is no difference between Jewish and Persian feasting: *mishte* is used for the Persian festivities in chapters 1 and 2 as well as for the banquet Esther organizes for the king and Haman. This seems to affirm the conclusion that the book must be read as a critique of Diaspora Judaism, which has become indistinguishable from its Persian surroundings (cf. Korpel 2003; Grossman 2011). And yet, a distinction *is* possible. Precisely by employing the same term for both the Jewish and Persian feasts, the author can point out the convergences, but also the differences between the two groups and their respective *mishte*. Subtle though the differences may be, reading them within the framework of ritualization suggests that their significance cannot be overestimated.

At the Persian feasts described in the narrative, wine is consumed in abundance. The association of *mishte* with drinking is not surprising (cf, Ezra 3:7, where it is used next to and in contrast with *maʾakhal*, "food"), but in the book of Esther, this connotation is emphasized by explicitly stating that wine was consumed as a matter of course during each Persian *mishte* (Esther 1:7, 10; 5:6; 7:2, 7–8). How different are the Jewish instances of *mishte* in Esther 8:17; 9:17, 18, 19 and 22! There is no mention of wine; instead, one word resurfaces time and again: *simḥah*, "joy." And not just any joy—in the rest of the Hebrew Bible, *simḥah* is regularly associated with joy in Yʜᴡʜ or in a holy festival (Num. 10:10; Deut. 12:7; 14:26; 16:11; 26:11; 27:7; Isa. 30:29; Jer. 15:16; Ezra 6:22; 2 Chron. 20:27; 30:21). In the terminology of ritualization, the use of the word *mishte* thus "mimes" or "implicates" the Persian feasts. At the same time, the lack of drinking or other kinds of excesses and the association with *simḥah*, (holy) joy, creates an unmistakable contrast—unmistakable, at any rate, for a reader who is sufficiently rooted in the traditions of the Hebrew Bible. Several effects are achieved. The first is, again, the creation of an in-group of readers who are able to take a hint. Second, the joy of the Jews in the book of Esther is literally sanctioned by construing it as belonging to the same category as, for example, David's joy about the Ark (1 Sam. 16:8) or the people's joy about YHWH's blessings (Isa. 29:19). Finally, the Persians' feasts are mocked as both excessive and meaningless.

GENDER AND THE POLITICS OF REPRESENTATION

The Persian feasts are just one example of a general tendency of the book of Esther: the Judeo-centered perspective of the author leads to an "orientalizing" depiction of anything that is not Jewish. At the same time, the reader is made painfully aware of the situation of the Jews as the de facto subordinate party within the power matrix of the Empire. Gendered processes of characterization and representation are uniquely suited to communicate this complexity.

Many scholars have construed either Esther or Mordecai or both as personifications of Israel in Diaspora (e.g., Crawford 1988). Especially, Esther's gender is deemed significant in this regard: as a woman, she is naturally associated with the subordinate, "shamed" position of a people in exile. However, the construction and deconstruction of Mordecai's, Haman's, and Ahasuerus's gender may turn out to be equally meaningful.

According to LaCocque "It is befitting the traditional distribution of functions between genders to have male aggressiveness adopted by Mordecai the Jew, and a female secretiveness assumed by Queen Esther" (LaCoque 1990, 67). He also claims that "it becomes clear that Mordecai has been in control from the beginning" (LaCoque 1990, 50). I find it difficult, however, to find much "male aggressiveness" in Mordecai. And contrary to LaCocque's second statement, it seems to be precisely the *lack* of control felt by Mordecai and the Diaspora community that constitutes their most basic experience.

Construed negatively, one could claim that the text has Mordecai prowling on the fringes of the center of power (2:11, 19–22), biding his time, vying with Haman for the King's favor. Like Daniel, who is "appalled" by the dream foretelling the king's downfall (Dan. 4:16), Mordecai hurries to inform his king of a plot against the latter's life (Esther 2:19–22). He has internalized what Ezekiel struggled so hard to accept (cf. Lemos 2012): conventional male values such as self-assertion, military strength, and even control over his own household are no longer available to him. Resistance must be attempted from within the system, "female-like," if at all.

If Mordecai has, to some degree, internalized a "female" (or deficient masculine)[4] role, it seems logical to assume that Haman and the king occupy the place of "real" men. However, this is not the case, either. The king, lord over a vast empire, basking in the "riches of the glory of his kingdom and the splendor of the beauty of his greatness" (1:4), is unable to control his own wife (1:10–12) or make an autonomous decision (1:13; 2:2–3; 3:7–11). Lounging in his palace like a virgin in the harem, he embodies the opposite of male initiative and involvement with the outside world. The author employs the same metaphorical field as Jeremiah 51:30: "Babylon's warriors have ceased fighting, they have returned to their strongholds.

Their strength has dried up—they have become like women." Mordecai may not be in a position to access conventional instruments of male power, but Ahasuerus's loss of masculinity is worse because it is self-elected.

Then there is Haman, mortal enemy of the Jews and, particularly, of Mordecai. Interestingly, the social roles filled by him and Mordecai are very similar: Diplomacy, not vigor in battle is their strong suit. Neither man is cast in a fully male role: their autonomy is curtailed by the all-encompassing power of the king, however feminized the latter may be, and they are reduced to the use of "female" wiles, directly or by proxy.

Does this affirm Davies's construal of Mordecai as acting with the premeditated viciousness usually ascribed to Haman (Davies 2001)? No, ultimately, it is the result of their actions that count. Haman plots murder, while Mordecai prevents the death of both the king and the Jewish people. Consequently, the last chapter of the book sees Mordecai's masculinity restored, albeit still as second in command to the king. The farce-like character of the narrative reminds the reader that this restoration is counterfactual ("*kontra-präsentisch*"; cf Assmann 1999)—a dream, no more and no less. Still, the subtle but pervasive links with Israel's grand narrative suggest that a day may come when the tables are turned in the waking world as well. On that day, perhaps, God will be mentioned again with more confidence. Until that time, "Jewishness" goes underground, hiding (*str*) in a narrative world habitable only for those who possess the key: knowledge of Israel's literary traditions.

Notes

1. This article focuses on the Hebrew text of Esther (MT Esther). For the Greek versions (Alpha Text and LXX, sometimes referred to as Greek A and B), the literary development and interdependence of the different texts or comparisons between them, see, e.g., Clines 1984. One general tendency that can be observed in the Greek texts is the presence of material that is more clearly "religious" (prayers, overt references to God's involvement, etc.).
2. Esther's Hebrew name, *Ester* is likely derived from *str*, "to hide."
3. Characterization appears to be a theme particularly well suited for comparative analysis. In *Three Faces of a Queen* (1995), Linda Day compares the figure of Esther as she appears in the Masoretic text and two Greek versions, focusing on categories such as "authority," "religion," "connection with the Jews," and "sexuality." In her conclusions, Day pleads for a more balanced appraisal of the canonical and the two non-canonical versions, arguing: "The very variety of the forms of the story, as well as their variant portrayals of its heroine, suggests the plurality of diaspora culture" (Day 1995, 235).

   A. Kay Fountain's *Literary and Empirical Readings of the Books of Esther* (2002) presents another comparative study of all three versions of the text, focusing on the characterization of all main protagonists. It is guided by one central question: "What effect does each text have in terms of developing ethical judgment in the reader?" (Fountain 2002, 5). The perspective of the reader is brought to the fore in the empirical part of the study, in which different groups of readers (male/female, churched/unchurched) respond to selected parts of the texts.
4. Needless to say, I do not mean to reinforce the Freudian notion that women are "deficient men." However, in the sociocultural setting in which most, if not all, of the biblical books were written, stereotypical and hierarchical notions of gender not only determined the interaction between men and women, but also supplied a great store of metaphorical images.

References

Assmann, Jan. 1999. *Das kulturelle Gedächtnis. Schrift, Erinnerung und Identität in frühen Hochkulturen*. München: Beck.

Bakhtin, Mikhail. 1984. *Rabelais and His World*. Translated by Helene Iswolsky. Bloomington: Indiana University Press.

Beal, Timothy Kandler. 1997. *The Book of Hiding: Gender, Ethnicity, Annihilation, and Esther*. Biblical Limits. London: Routledge.

Bell, Catherine. 1992. *Ritual Theory, Ritual Practice*. New York: Oxford University Press.

Berlin, Adele. 2001. *Esther: The Traditional Hebrew Text with the New JPS Translation*. Jewish Publication Society Bible Commentary. Philadelphia, PA: Jewish Publication Society.

Bush, Frederic W. 1996. *Ruth, Esther*. World Biblical Commentary. Dallas, TX: Word Books.

Clines, David J. A. 1984. *The Esther Scroll. The Story of the Story*. Journal for the Study of the Old Testament Supplement Series 30. Sheffield, Yorkshire: JSOT Press.

Craig, Kenneth M. 1995. *Reading Esther: A Case for the Literary Carnivalesque*. Literary Currents in Biblical Interpretation. Louisville, KY: Westminster/John Knox.

Crawford, Sidnie White. 1988. "Esther: A Feminine Model for Jewish Diaspora." In *Gender and Difference in Ancient Israel*, edited by Peggy L. Day, 161–177. Minneapolis, MN: Fortress Press.

Davies, Philip R. 2001. "Haman the Victim." In *First Person. Essays in Biblical Autobiography*, edited by Philip R. Davies, 137–154. London and New York: Sheffield Academic Press.

Day, Linda. 1995. *Three Faces of a Queen. Characterization in the Book of Esther*. Journal for the Study of the Old Testament Supplement Series 186. Sheffield, Yorkshire: Sheffield Academic Press.

Day, Linda. 2005. *Esther*. Abingdon. Old Testament Commentaries. Nashville, TN: Abingdon.

Fewell, Danna Nolan, ed. 2003. "Nice Girls Do (the Book of Esther)." In *The Children of Israel. Reading the Bible for the Sake of Our Children*, 133–194. Nashville, TN: Abingdon.

Fountain, A. Kay. 2002. *Literary and Empirical Readings of the Book of Esther*. Studies in Biblical Literature 43. New York: Peter Lang.

Fox, Michael J. 1991. *Character and Ideology in the Book of Esther*. Studies on Personalities of the Old Testament. Columbia: University of South Carolina Press.

Fox, Michael J. 2001. *Character and Ideology in the Book of Esther*. 2nd, revised edition. Grand Rapids, MI: Eerdmans.

Gerleman, Gillis. 1973. *Esther*. Biblischer Kommentar: Altes Testament 21. Neukirchen Vluyn: Neukirchener Verlag.

Goldman, Stan. 1990. "Narrative and Ethical Ironies in Esther." *Journal for the Study of the Old Testament* 47: 15–31.

Gordis, Robert. 1981. "Religion, Wisdom and History in the Book of Esther: A New Solution to an Ancient Crux." *Journal of Biblical Literature* 100: 359–388.

Grossman, Jonathan. 2011. *Esther. The Outer Narrative and the Hidden Reading*. Siphrut 6. Winona Lake, IN: Eisenbrauns.

Haag, Ernst. 2003. "Das Estherbuch und die Tradition von Jahwes Krieg gegen Amalek." *Trierer Theologische Zeitschrift* 112: 19–41.

Humphreys, W. Lee. 1985. "The Story of Esther and Mordechai: An Early Jewish Novella." In *Saga, Legend, Tale, Novella, Fable: Narrative Forms in Old Testament Literature*, edited by G. W. Coates, 97–113. Journal for the Study of the Old Testament Supplement 35. Sheffield, Yorkshire: JSOT Press.

Jackson, Melissa A. 2012. *Comedy and Feminist Interpretation of the Hebrew Bible*. Oxford Theological Monographs. Oxford: Oxford University Press.

Klein, Lillian R. 1997. "Honor and Shame in Esther." In *A Feminist Companion to Esther, Judith and Susanna*, edited by Athalya Brenner, 149–175. London: T&T Clark.

Koller, Aaron. 2014. *Esther in Ancient Jewish Thought*. Cambridge: Cambridge University Press.

Korpel, Marjo. 2003. "Theodicy in the Book of Esther." In *Theodicy in the World of the Bible*, edited by A. Laato and Johannes C. de Moor, 334–350. Leiden: Brill.

LaCoque, André. 1990. *The Feminine Unconventional: Four Subversive Figures in Israel's Tradition*. Minneapolis, MN: Fortress Press.

LaCoque, André. 2008. *Esther Regina: A Bakthinian Reading*. Rethinking Theory. Evanston, IL: Northwestern University Press.

Laniak, Timothy S. 1998. *Shame and Honor in the Book of Esther*. Society of Biblical Literature Dissertation Series 165. Atlanta, GA: Scholars Press.

Laniak, Timothy S. 2003. "Esther's *Volkcentrism* and the Reframing of Post-Exilic Judaism." In *The Book of Esther in Modern Research*, edited by Sidnie White Crawford and Leonard J. Greenspoon, 77–90. London: T&T Clark.

Lemos, Tracy M. 2012. "'They Have Become Women': Judean Diaspora and Postcolonial Theories of Gender and Migration.' In *Social Theory and the Study of Israelite Religion. Essays in Retrospect and Prospect*, edited by Saul M. Olyan, 81–109. Society of Biblical Literature Resources for Biblical Study 71. Atlanta, GA: Society of Biblical Literature.

Levenson, Jon Douglas. 1997. *Esther: A Commentary*. Old Testament Library. Louisville; KY: Westminster/John Knox.

Loader, James A. 1979. "Esther as a Novel with Different Levels of Meaning." *Zeitschrift für die alttestamentliche Wissenschaft* 90: 417–421.

Mason, Steve. 2007. "Jews, Judaeans, Judaizing, Judaism: Problems of Categorization in Ancient History." *Journal for the Study of Judaism* 38: 457–512.

Meinhold, Arndt. 1976. "Diasporanovelle, I, II." *Zeitschrift für die alttestamentliche Wissenschaft* 88: 79–93.

Moore, Carey A. 1971. *Esther*. Anchor Bible Commentary. New York: Doubleday.

Wetter, Anne-Mareike. 2013. "Speaking from the Gaps: The Eloquent Silence of God in Esther." In *Reflections on the Silence of God: A Discussion with Marjo Korpel and Johannes de Moor*, edited by Bob Becking, 153–167. Leiden: Brill.

Wetter, Anne-Mareike. 2015. "On Her Account. Reconfiguring Israel in Ruth, Esther, and Judith. LHBOTS 623. London: Bloomsbury T&T Clark.

Wyler, Bea. 1995. "Esther: The Incomplete Emancipation of a Queen." In *A Feminist Companion to Esther, Judith and Susanna*, edited by Athalya Brenner, 111–135. London: T&T Clark.

CHAPTER 22

WARRING WORDS IN THE BOOK OF DANIEL

TERRY ANN SMITH

FOR religiously committed readers, the book of Daniel has traditionally been seen as a beacon of unwavering faith and inspiration. It is a book in which God appears as both immanent and transcendent, serving as a source of hope for the suffering faithful in times of national and international crisis. Written in both Aramaic and Hebrew, the book captivates with its tales of villainous kings and Jewish heroes set amid the backdrop of rulers and the ruled, victors and the vanquished. As readers, we become spectators, peering into an ancient world where mythical figures and bizarre images collide, where empires rise and fall, and where the Ancient of Days pronounces the final word of judgment on earthly realms. Herein the unsuspecting reader will find metaphorical symbolism attending dreams and dream interpretation that becomes the means to invert power relations, not only between empire and the story's protagonist, but also between the protagonist and other ethnic groups. All too obvious are the laborious efforts of Daniel and his compatriots to assert, reassert, and legitimate their identity while competing with other royal courtiers for coveted positions of authority and control. In this scripted world of resistance, constructions of privilege, power, control, and subversive indirection converge to reveal the tumultuous relation between the powerful and the powerless, the elite and the socially disadvantaged. Given the subversive undertones of the text, the Daniel narrative wages its own form of combat, which, at times, appears no less violent than the campaigns that accompany real life warfare.

CRITICAL VENTURES INTO THE BOOK OF DANIEL

In general, critical ventures into the book of Daniel have explored a wide range of topics and issues. Biblical scholars continue to examine the book's composition and reception, focusing on matters of genre, language, textual history, and theology. In recent years, more attention has been given to literary, sociological, and ideological concerns. Like many other books in the Hebrew Bible, the complicated and lengthy compositional history of the book of Daniel has left numerous traces: chapters 1–2:4a and 8–12 are written in ancient Hebrew, while chapters 2:4b–7:28 are written almost exclusively in the more commonly used language of the times, Aramaic. The book falls into two major generic units, with hero stories comprising Daniel 1–6 and mystic visions making up Daniel 7–12. Most scholars concur that the book reached its final form around 167–164 BCE making it most likely the last book of the Hebrew Bible to be written. The discoveries of additional nonbiblical writings, such as the Mari tablets of ancient Mesopotamia, the Ras Shamra texts of Ugarit, and the Dead Sea Scrolls of the Qumran community, have also shed light on the book's compositional structure. Many scholars now speculate that the traditions in the book of Daniel were not the exclusive property or product of a single group (Collins and Flint 2001; Flint 2001; Knibb 2001; Paul 2001).

Scholars intrigued by the mythical, cosmic, and eschatological imagery found in Daniel (and the book of Revelation) argue for a novel type of literary genre, *apocalypse*, which focuses symbolically on otherworldly and salvific elements that purport to divulge divine mysteries (John Collins 1979; Adela Collins 1979). The ambiguous nature of the term, *apocalypse*, has increased over the years, as critical discourse has tended to interweave apocalyptic with such words as eschatology, millennialism, and messianism. Daniel 1–6 has also been the focus of genre considerations where the designations of folklore and court tale continue to hold sway (Humphreys 1973; Niditch and Doran 1977), though now nuanced by arguments for political satire (Fewell 1991; Valeta 2002, 2008). Scholars have long recognized that the book, as a particular form of Jewish writings, presupposes a context of *struggle* and have sought to ascertain the nature of the struggle—against what, by whom, and why. For example, historical-critical analyses have convincingly argued that the book reflects a collision between secular and religious forces (Wilson 1980; Collins 1993; Hanson 1989, 2002).

Recent inspections of the book as apocalyptic literature presume, among other things, its propagandistic nature and expose the ways in which the book attempts to sway an audience toward the predisposed posture of its author(s). For example, Paul Redditt (1998, 2008) views the book's literary form and social *Sitz-im-Leben* as a portrait of an elite class of educated scribes. For Redditt, the book's ideology works to affirm participation, loyalty, and accommodation toward foreign rule. Philip Davies (1985, 1991), however, contrasts the Jewish ambivalence toward empire in Daniel with the antagonistic and highly politicized noneschatological attitude of the Hasidim found in the books of Maccabees. Still others like Danna Nolan Fewell (1991, 2003) and Daniel Smith-Christopher (1996, 2002) emphasize the thematic links between the book's portraits of imperial power and the oppositional strategies of the disempowered. Both of these scholars draw our attention to textual constructions that subversively undermine and resist imperial hegemony. In particular, Fewell's examinations of the court tales in Daniel 1–6 (1991) has exposed how the narratives "plot" political resistance; her subsequent analysis of Daniel 1 (2003) focuses specifically on the dilemma of Jewish children forced into imperial service, who overcome adversity and survive an oppressive system. Smith-Christopher's sociological and political analysis of the book's dreams and visions (2002) yields a reading that reveals the longings of the marginalized and dispossessed. Provocatively, these scholarly examinations hold in tension authorial concerns with religious fidelity, identity formation, political resistance, and imperial assimilation.

The innovative analyses of Amy Merrill Willis (2010) and Anathea Portier-Young (2011) with their emphases on theoretical issues of cognitive dissonance, structures of dominance, and state-sponsored terrorism provide fresh insights into the book's theologies of resistance. The complex issue of the book's theodicy is taken up in the interpretative analysis of Walter

Brueggemann (2008), who suggests that the book's rhetoric, specifically, its language about God, should be understood in tandem with neighboring nations and their gods. For Willis, Portier-Young, and Brueggemann, the subversive nature of words, couched in the book's theological message of divine sovereignty, is a powerful rhetorical tool that undermines imperial claims to power and knowledge. Here, too, the works of David Valeta (2002, 2008), Athalaya Brenner (2002), and Edwin Good (1984) are also instructive. Valeta's analysis of the court tales from the perspective of Menippean satire and rhetoric suggests a deliberate challenge to Jewish orthodoxy. His assessment of Daniel as *apocalyptic satire*, although understood as resistance literature, rejects scholarly assessments that view the work as the product of Jewish scribes. Both Brenner and Good argue for the subversive nature of satire and comedy. While for Good Daniel is an "escape fiction" a "what if?" world that never existed, functioning similar to Greek tragedies, for Brenner the book's satire functions primarily to ridicule foreigner rulers. In teasing out the book's subtle and subversive discourses, all of these critical efforts deepen our understanding of the context and the possible rhetorical functions of the book of Daniel.

Altogether, recent scholarly treatments of the book of Daniel provide valuable insight into the various kinds of social and political exploitation associated with imperial domination and uncover some of the practical ways in which oppressed groups during this timeframe could successfully vent their frustration in the face of their own powerlessness. Moreover, the use of theoretical models that address matters of terror, trauma, and recovery experienced by crisis-stricken individuals and communities prove to be fruitful avenues of pursuit for further studies on the book of Daniel and the resistance strategies and theologies of the marginalized and oppressed. Complementing these studies would be approaches that consider the ways in which the Daniel narrative constructs a critique of its own community. Such assessments would further aid our understanding of the power relations (and brokering) attending Jewish subordination to imperial rule and the resulting fractions created within and among Jewish sectarian groups. When understood in this fashion, the message of Daniel survives as one that not only subverts imperial authority, but one that also speaks truth to the ideological and religious authorities of its day, including those among its own constituency. With this internal critique in mind, I now turn to the text of Daniel 7 as a case study for a closer look at how words become the weapons of the disempowered.

ONTO THE COSMIC BATTLEFIELD

Ber Fox says ""Dis is my time, I'm hungry dis mornin.' I'm goin' ketch you."—"O Ber Fox! Leave me off dis mornin'? I will sen' you to a man house where he got a penful of pretty little pig, an' you will get yer brakefus' fill. Ef you don' believe me, you can tie me here, an' you can go down to de house, an' I'll stay here until you come back." So Ber Fox tie him. When he wen' down to de house, de man had about fifty head of houn'-dawg. An' de man tu'n de houn'-dawg loose on him. An' de fox made de long run right by Ber Rabbit. Ber Fox say, "O Ber Rabbit? Dose is no brakefus', dose is a pile of houn'-dawg."—Yes, you was goin' to eat me, but dey will eat you for your brakefus' and supper to-night." An' so dey did. Dey cut (caught) de fox. An' Ber Rabbit give to de dawgs, "Gawd bless yer soul! dat what enemy get for meddlin'

Gawd's people when dey goin' to church." Said, "I was goin' to school all my life an'
learn every letter in de book but d, an' D was death, an' death was de en' of Ber Fox."

—Willie Lee Nichols Rose

The trickster tales of Ber Rabbit (Rose 1999, 518) represent a repository of African, African American, and Native American Indian folklore pressed into service to address systemic oppression and abuse. In these tales, the implication is clear. Those that prey on the weak are subject to become prey themselves. We are increasingly aware that stories of this sort inspired hope with their messages of an inverted world and retributions. As a form of subversive discourse, the preponderance of such tales reflects an inability of subjugated groups to confront their oppressors openly. Rhetorically, these tales, and others like them, become the tactical place where resistance, suppression, and subversion take place. For the same reason they also serve as the place where power and control is asserted, thwarted, and redistributed. Comparatively, we find a similar subversive strategy at work in Daniel 7. Somewhat symptomatic of those suffering from post-traumatic stress disorder (PTSD), Daniel's vision of kingdoms, disruptive turbulence, and frightening creatures reads much like the paralyzing night terrors one might experience following a traumatic, life-threatening episode.

> In the first year of King Belshazzar of Babylon, Daniel had a dream and visions of his head as he lay in bed. Then he wrote down the dream. I, Daniel, saw in my vision by night the four winds of heaven stirring up the great sea, and four great beasts came up out of the sea, different from one another. (Dan. 7:1–3)[1]

In Daniel 7:1–3, the narrator juxtaposes the seemingly known with the unknown thereby drawing attention to the threatening nature of both. Whereas the book's first half began by recalling the offensive exploits of the infamous Babylonian king Nebuchadnezzar, chapter 7, cast in the realm of mystic symbolism, opens recounting the reign of Belshazzar. For the most part, history records Belshazzar as the son of Nabonidus rather than Nebuchadnezzar. Here, the reference to Belshazzar maintains the fictive linkage previously established in Daniel 5:2. Given this, we could speculate that the writer intends for an audience to link these kings with another pair of regents more contemporary to his own era—namely, Antiochus and Antiochus IV. Perceptively, the battle lines have been drawn and the opponents indirectly named. Heretofore, the story has scripted dreams and visions from the perspective and dictates of imperial rulers. In each case, the dream or vision conveys circumstances in which the ruler was portrayed as excessively unreasonable, violent, or bewildered (Dan. 2:1, 5; 4:5–6; 5:5–7). Rhetorically, the authorial assassination of imperial decorum and rigidity in these accounts displays a subversive ingenuity that is surpassed only by the concomitant satire that humorously whisks away portraits of perceived power. Yet, in a bizarre narrative twist, Daniel in chapter 7 becomes the recipient rather than interpreter of dreams. In this new role, his first person report of disturbing nightmares supplants the king's speech to become the authoritative voice in the text. The imagined implication of this grammatical shift is unmistakable as we witness the moment at which power and control, like that in the Ber Rabbit tales, is not only thwarted but also redistributed. This bit of narrative indirection ingeniously renders the rhetorical situation innocuous by eliminating any explicit references to the Seleucid reign, and thus, mitigating any recourse and confrontation from potential pro-Seleucid sympathizers, Jewish or otherwise. This guise is extremely beneficial since the excluded audience may apprehend the substitution, and yet fail to comprehend its subversive significance as the language mirrors imaginative constructions common to literary motifs of the period.

The symbolism continues in Daniel 7:4–8 with a graphic and intriguing portrait of the rapacious activity of a lion, a bear, a leopard, and a beast too terrifying to name:

> The first was like a lion and had eagles' wings. Then as I watched, its wings were plucked off, and it was lifted up from the ground and made to stand on two feet like a human being; and a human mind was given to it. Another beast appeared, a second one, that looked like a bear. It was raised up on one side . . . and was told "Arise, devour many bodies! After this, as I watched another appeared, like a leopard . . . and dominion was given to it. After this I saw . . . a fourth beast, terrifying and dreadful and exceedingly strong . . . devouring, breaking in pieces, and stamping what was left with its feet. It was different from all the beasts that preceded it, and it had ten horns. I was considering the horns when another horn appeared, a little one. . . . there were eyes like human eyes in this horn, and a mouth speaking arrogantly. (Dan. 7:4–8)

These animalistic metaphors, historically symbolic of the Assyrian, Babylonian, Persian and Greek empires, respectively, line up with the four-kingdom schema referenced in Daniel 2:36–44, and are consistent with the topos of the rise and fall of empires. Since the topos is typically presented in an *vaticinium ex eventu* format (prophecy after the event) and is prevalent throughout the literary products of various cultures in the ancient Near East, primarily as a means of political propaganda, we could venture that, among other things, its appearance here and elsewhere in the book functions polemically as a political commentary on the predatory practices of empires and their leaders. Categorically, lions, leopards, and bears (and possibly a beast too terrifying to name) are all creatures that devour others and potentially each other. Thus, the ravenous and insatiable appetite of these voracious animals masks an understanding of empire as aggressive, indifferent, and wholly destructive to cultures subsumed under imperial rule. According to Daniel 7:8, this catastrophic destructiveness is specifically observable in the beleaguered actions of one ruler, the *little horn*, the one with "*human eyes*" who speaks "*arrogantly.*" First Maccabees's description of Antiochus IV's persecution of Jews in second-century BCE states, "*He shed much blood, and spoke with great arrogance*" (1 Macc. 1:24).[2] The description of the little horn in 7:8 leaves little doubt that the writer had in mind this Hellenistic king and perceived his activities as far more egregious than the kings who preceded him. In this cacophony of words and symbols, the animalistic portrait of beasts *devouring, breaking,* and *treading* expresses the inexpressible horrors of war for those caught in its wake. The sheer brutality of imperial conquest and all it entails is memorialized in the symbolism as one envisions the broken bodies of slaughtered humans lying trampled underfoot by the invading armies that swept through the land. Vividly, the cultural memory of a conquered past and the reality of a dominated present collide, cloaked in the metaphoric symbolism of the frightfully bizarre, a stark reminder to an ancient audience of the atrocities committed under the current régime.

Having characterized foreign kings in inhuman terms, the text counters this animalistic portrait with the introduction of the sagacious Ancient One and his court in 7:9–10.

> As I watched, thrones were set in place, and an Ancient One took his throne, his clothing was white as snow, and the hair of his head like pure wool; his throne was fiery flames, and its wheels were burning fire. A stream of fire issued and flowed out from his presence. A thousand thousands served him, and ten thousand times ten thousand stood attending him. The court sat in judgment, and the books were opened.

The passage, indeed the entire chapter, shares close affinities with portions of 1 Enoch, where we also encounter references to the Ancient One, holy ones, the opening of the book, and the vindication of the slain. It is apparent that the otherworldly kingdom of Daniel 7:9–10 is meant to be contrasted with the animal-like kingdoms in Daniel 7:4–8. As the mythic council convenes with the Ancient One as its overseer, we are told that "the court sat in judgment, and the books were opened." Framed like a judicial proceeding, the account suggests the accountability and temporality of imperial rule. Daniel 7:11–12 records the court's decision, and for the second time, the narrative mentions the violent end of a foreign king (cf. Dan. 5:30). Just as the story replaces one king as the authoritative voice in Daniel 7:1–3, another king is obliterated in Daniel 7:11–12 following a royal court martial that sentences the regent to an execution-style demise. Nor, is it enough to destroy the king (i.e., beast), but all traces of him must be purged from existence. Mercilessly, there are no opportunities for retreat or surrender. Thus, in retaliatory fashion, the dream envisions the same fiery end to this ruler as had been planned for Daniel's compatriots in chapter 3. Moreover, the narrator seems only minimally concerned with the fate of the other three kingdoms and its rulers stating simply that "their dominion was taken away," and they lived "for a season and a time" (Dan. 7:12). Theologically, the end to imperial rule comes about through divine intervention where God becomes the destroyer of imperial hubris and self-exaltation. In this case, religion vouches as the authorizing agent for invoking imagery, and language that, under different circumstances, might be construed as seditious or, in the words of Pierre Bourdieu (1991, 128), "subversively heretical." Overall, the entire scene disrupts the imperial discourse of power and control with its discourse of religious authority, intimating with the regent's death that even the most powerful kings may find themselves objects of divine retribution.

This disruption continues as the portrait of condemnation and judgment leads to the selection of another king in Daniel 7:13–14. The account mimics earlier scenes in which Daniel appears before the king prior to assuming a position of authority in the regent's court. Here, the Ancient One confers upon the unnamed humanlike being (whose humanity is juxtaposed to the monsterlike predators), the position and power of kingship, thus keeping with previous narrative assertions that the deity "deposes kings and sets up kings" (Dan. 2:21; 4:25). Suspiciously, Daniel 7:14 applies language to this new leader (i.e., dominion, glory, sovereignty) that had been previously reserved for the deity (Dan. 2:44; 4:3; 6:26). Where exactly does this new rule take place? The text is not specific to either earthy geography or divine locality. Furthermore, the reimaging of a new social order, accomplished by reproducing the hegemonic discourse of subordination, provides ample cause to be circumspect regarding the motivations driving this imagery. For example, when Daniel 7:14 subjects "all people, nations and language" to the authority of the humanlike being, it exploits and re-inscribes the language of domination, formerly attributed to the king and empire, to this new leader. Thus, the text merely exchanges one dominating faction for another one, prompting an inquiry into who or what group benefits from this new social arrangement. Therefore, despite the lack of geographical specificity, what can be ascertained with certainty is that "dominion" refers to temporal control over humans. When read alongside the words of Daniel 2:44, "And in the days of those kings the God of heaven will set up a kingdom that shall never be destroyed," it appears the overall rhetorical thrust of the symbolism points once more to political circumstances occurring within an earthly realm.

Shifting events to the earthly realm gives way to the dream's interpretation in Daniel 7:15–28 and reiterates the problem and solution already put forth in Daniel 7:1–14. In Daniel

7:15–16, Daniel expresses his extreme distress concerning the dream, thus emulating the king's response in Daniel 2:1–2 and 4:5. Nevertheless, Daniel 7:17–27 exposes the inherent bias of this concern with its repetitive emphasis on the "holy ones of the Most High" (all italics are mine):

> But the *holy ones of the Most High* shall receive the kingdom and possess the kingdom forever—forever and ever. (7:18)
> As I looked, this horn made war with *the holy ones* and was prevailing over them, until the Ancient One came; then judgment was given for *the holy ones of the Most High*, and the time arrived when *the holy ones* gained possession of the kingdom. (7:21–22)
> He shall speak words against the Most High, shall wear out *the holy ones of the Most High*, and shall attempt to change the sacred seasons and the law; and they shall be given into his power for a time, two times, and half a time. (7:25)
> The kingship and dominion and the greatness of the kingdoms under the whole heaven shall be given to the people of *the holy ones of the Most High*; their kingdom shall be an everlasting kingdom, and all dominions shall serve and obey them." (7:27)

Who are these holy ones? Celestial beings? Faithful Jews? Scholars seem to be divided. It is just as likely that the sustained and repeated emphasis points to one particular group of devout individuals who are attempting to legitimate and authenticate themselves as inheritors of the Jewish faith and sole representatives of the Most High. The warring words, once externally focused on foreign rulers, are redirected to internal matters of identity and religious authority. Prompted by competing claims of sectarian groups, Daniel's vision of holy war imagines the defeat of the opposition in favor of a devout group who believe they have been divinely chosen as the preferred replacement. The insistent claims of exclusivity compel a closer inspection of the meaning and intent of "*kingdom*" as it applies to the textual construction of ruling authorities. Throughout Daniel, we find several morphological forms of "*mlk*" (reign, royalty) employed interchangeably to denote both personal power and authority (Dan. 2:37, 42, 44; 3:33; 5:18, 20; 6:1; 8:23; 11:21) and a designated region of control (Dan. 5:26–8; 9:1; 10:13; 11:2–4). Contextually, the latter, geographical, usage seems appropriate to Daniel 7:18–27, and thus, easily reads politically and theologically as a desire by this group to *gain possession* of a specific place/location—namely, Jerusalem and its temple.

Still, on the surface, the re-imaging of the world to the advantage of a select few appears a bit disingenuous since it merely reverses the hegemonic order. Yet, for those living and suffering under the life-threatening conditions of an oppressive regime because they belong to a group ostracized within a religious system that purports a "right-to-rule" in the public domain, hearing words and symbols that disrupt the hegemonic majority may be a necessary strategic line of defense. Therefore, when taken as a whole, the depiction of cosmic conflict, the futuristic end of world empires, and the vindication of the just rejects and replaces the dominant script with an alternate script that is liberating, life affirming, and empowering. The chapter closes with Daniel's "terrified" and ailing reaction to the vision, which satirically parodies the royal reactions in Daniel 4:4 and 5:9. "I Daniel, was deeply troubled by my thoughts, and my face turned pale, but I kept the matter to myself" (7:28). Could Daniel's aggrieved state reflect an authorial awareness of the violence and mayhem that erupts when contestations to power emerge? Josephus's *Antiquities* and the books of Maccabees effectively capture the conflictual relationships among the Jewish elite and priestly factions, confirming the fragility of Jewish inner social structures. Undergirding these sociopolitical dynamics are the imperial relations instigating and supporting them. Antiochus IV's persecution of certain portions of the Jewish populace obviously made association with these groups perilous. Retrospectively, Daniel's reticence lends a sense of poignancy to these circumstances and those ensnared within them. Victory, even confidently foretold, is not without cost and consequences. War is, after all, a "nasty business," taking its toll on those involved and those who become collateral damage in its aftermath.

In sum, taken together, the hero stories and apocalyptic imagery of Daniel, cast in the shadows of imperial hegemony, are ripe with the stuff that makes for intriguing storytelling and theological reflection. Hence, biblical scholars continue to examine the disparate ways in which the book of Daniel, as literature of the marginalized and oppressed, nuances the dichotomous relationship between empire and the Jews subjugated under imperial rule. When read as a critique of cultural and ideological hegemony, the book places in full view the social and historical conditions of oppression as it manipulates characters, plots, and story construction to expose social inequities. Yet, attending conditions of domination are the hierarchical structures created among the dominated. Could the book's depiction of religious intolerance and persecution, its construction of an ethnocentric and nationalistic protagonist Daniel, as well as its subtle chastisement of temple leadership (Dan. 1, 9, 11), function not only to critique the external forces of Empire, but also to articulate dissension among individuals and subgroups within the Jewish religious community? Daniel 7 is a craftily constructed narrative that polemically undermines imperial hubris by appropriating and reinterpreting the language of dominance, but one could also ask whether this acquisition of language and image subverts the status quo with its symbolic portrait of an inverted world, or merely manipulates it, and thus, perpetuates elitist paradigms of power and privilege. Perhaps, what the writer wanted an audience to contemplate was this: as long as the need to struggle persists, his group would engage in the struggle, daily or otherwise, using whatever means—or words—necessary.

NOTES

1. All scripture references are based on the New Revised Standard Version.
2. Here, we may contrast between the Hebrew adjective *rabrab* (great: figuratively of power) in Daniel 7:8 and the Greek *uperêthanian* (arrogance, pride) in 1 Macc. 1:24. Although both terms have been translated in English versions as "arrogant" and "arrogance" respectively, it is clear that the Hebrew emphasizes the power inherent in the king's speech, while the Greek usages appear directed toward the character of the king as egotistical and grandiose.

REFERENCES

Bourdieu, Pierre. 1991. *Language and Symbolic Power*. Edited by John B. Thompson Translated by Gino Raymond and Matthew Adamson. Cambridge, MA: Harvard University Press.

Brenner, Athalya, ed. 2002. *A Feminist Companion to Prophets and Daniel*. New York: T&T Clark.

Brueggemann, Walter. 2008. "Faith in the Empire." In *In the Shadow of Empire: Reclaiming the Bible as a History of Faithful Resistance*, edited by Richard A. Horsley, 25–40. Louisville, KY: Westminster John Knox Press.

Collins, Adela Yarbro. 1979. "The Early Christian Apocalypses. In *Apocalypse: The Morphology of a Genre*, edited by John J. Collins. *Semeia* 14: 60–121.

Collins, John J. 1979. "Introduction: Towards the Morphology of A Genre." In *Apocalypse: The Morphology of a Genre*, edited by John J. Collins. *Semeia* 14: 1–19.

Collins, John J. 1993. *Daniel: A Commentary on the Book of Daniel*. Hermeneia: A Critical and Historical Commentary on the Bible. Minneapolis, MN: Fortress Press.

Collins, John J., and Peter Flint, eds. 2001. *The Book of Daniel: Composition and Reception*. Leiden, Brill.

Davies, Philip R. 1985. *Daniel*. Sheffield, Yorkshire: Sheffield Academic Press.

Davies, Philip R. 1991. "Daniel in the Lions' Den." In *Images of Empire*, edited by Loveday Alexander, 160–178. Sheffield, Yorkshire: JSOT Press.

Fewell, Danna Nolan. 1991. *Circle of Sovereignty: Plotting Politics in the Book of Daniel*. Nashville, TN: Abingdon Press.

Fewell, Danna Nolan. 2003. "Resisting Daniel." In *The Children of Israel: Reading the Bible for the Sake of Our Children*, 117–130. Nashville, TN: Abingdon Press.

Flint, Peter W. 2001. "The Daniel Tradition at Qumran." In *The Book of Daniel: Composition and Reception*. Vol. 2, edited by John J. Collins and Peter W. Flint, 329–367. Leiden and Boston: Brill.

Good, Edwin. 1984. "Apocalyptic as Comedy." In *Tragedy and Comedy in the Bible*, edited by J. Cheryl Exum. *Semeia* 32: 41–70.

Hanson, Paul D. 2002. "Prophetic and Apocalyptic Politics." In *The Last Things: Biblical and Theological Perspectives on Eschatology*, edited by Carl E. Braaten and Robert W. Jensen, 43–66. Grand Rapids, MI: Eerdmans.

Hanson, Paul D. 1989. *The Dawn of the Apocalyptic: The Historical and Sociological Roots of Jewish Apocalyptic Eschatology*. Philadelphia, PA: Fortress Press.

Humphreys, W. Lee. 1973. "A Life-Style for Diaspora: A Study of the Tales of Esther and Daniel." *Journal of Biblical Literature* 92: 211–223.

Josephus, Flavius. 1999. *The New Complete Works of Josephus*. Translated by William Winston. Edited by Paul L. Maier. Grand Rapids, MI: Kregel.

Knibb, Michael A. 2001. "The Book of Daniel in Its Context." In *The Book of Daniel: Composition and Reception*. Vol. 2, edited by John J. Collins and Peter W. Flint, 16–35. Boston: Brill.

Niditch, Susan, and Robert Doran. 1977. "The Success of the Wise Courtier: A Formal Approach." *Journal of Biblical Literature* 96(2): 179–193.

Paul, Shalom. 2001. "The Mesopotamian Babylonian Background of Daniel 1–6." In *The Book of Daniel: Composition and Reception*. Vol. 2, edited by John J. Collins and Peter W. Flint, 55–68. Boston: Brill.

Portier-Young, Anathea. 2011. *Apocalypse against Empire: Theologies of Resistance in Early Judaism*. Grand Rapids, MI: William B. Eerdmans.

Redditt, Paul L. 1998. "Daniel 11 and the Sociohistorical Setting of the Book of Daniel." *Catholic Biblical Quarterly* 60(3): 463–474.

Redditt, Paul L. 2008. *Introduction to the Prophets*. Grand Rapids, MI: William B. Eerdmans.

Rose, Willie Lee Nichols. 1999. *A Documentary History of Slavery in North America*. Athens: University of Georgia Press.

Smith-Christopher, Daniel L. 1996. "The Book of Daniel." In *New Interpreter's Bible: Introduction to Apocalyptic Literature, Daniel, The Twelve Prophets*, 17–156. Nashville, TN: Abingdon Press.

Smith-Christopher, Daniel L. 2002. "Prayers and Dreams: Power and Diaspora Identities in the Social Setting of the Daniel Tales." In *The Book of Daniel: Composition and Reception*, edited by John J. Collins and Peter W. Flint, 266–290. Boston: Brill Academic.

Valeta, David M. 2002. "The Satirical Nature of the Book of Daniel." In *Apocalyptic in History and Tradition*, edited by Christopher Rowland and John Barton, 81–93. Journal for the Study of the Old Testament Supplement Series 43. Sheffield, Yorkshire: Sheffield Academic Press.

Valeta, David M. 2008. *Lions and Ovens and Visions: A Satirical Reading of Daniel 1-6*. Hebrew Bible Monographs. Sheffield, Yorkshire: Sheffield Phoenix Press.

Willis, Amy C. Merrill. 2010. *Dissonance and the Drama of Divine Sovereignty in the Book of Daniel*. New York: T&T Clark.

Wilson, Robert R. 1980. *Prophecy and Society in Ancient Israel*. Philadelphia, PA: Fortress Press.

CHAPTER 23

POLITICAL STRATEGY IN THE NARRATIVE OF EZRA-NEHEMIAH

DONNA J. LAIRD

THE TEXTURED MOSAIC OF EZRA-NEHEMIAH'S NARRATIVE

Two seemingly contradictory features distinguish the narrative style of Ezra-Nehemiah. On the one hand, a variety of literary forms and shifting narrative perspectives communicate the storyline (Eskenazi 1988, 131). Stitched together are first- and third-person narratives, letters and edicts written in Hebrew and Aramaic, penitential prayers, and various lists of families, materials, and priestly genealogies. The account is schematic, skipping multiple decades while treating in detail events covering a few months (Neh. 1–7) or a single year (Ezra 7–10). Additionally, later editors added material (e.g., much of Neh. 9–12) and shifted Ezra's ceremonial reading of Torah from Ezra's mission (Ezra 7–10) to Nehemiah 8 (Williamson 1985, 127). On the other hand, these diverse materials are woven together into a sharply focused argument targeting unwanted people (Hays 2008, 60). Each episode constructs and celebrates temple, Torah, or Jerusalem's wall—gestures both suggesting that the importance and roles of these entities are heavily contested at the time of writing and drawing bold lines between outsiders and the community (Clines 1984, 25, 62). Dissenting voices are refuted or silenced so thoroughly that a trusting reader is unlikely to grant validity to any other perspective.

Much critical work has been done on the composition of these books (Wright 2004; Pakkala 2004; Boda and Redditt 2008) and other excellent works discuss their historical context and/or theological concerns (Williamson 1985; Blenkinsopp 1988; Weinberg 1992; Hoglund 1992; Berquist, 1995; Carter, 1999; Fried 2004; Edelman 2005; Lipschits and Oeming 2006; Lipschits, Knoppers, and Albertz 2007; Southwood 2012). Many studies consider the rhetorical purposes of the texts to some degree (e.g., Torrey 1910; Smith, 1971; Davies 1999). However, Tamara Eskenazi's superb study *In an Age of Prose* remains the consummate narrative analysis of Ezra-Nehemiah. In the use of the various literary forms Eskenazi (1988,

37) detects innovative artistry and identifies an overarching structure for the entire work: *potentiality* (Ezra 1:1–4), *process of actualization* (Ezra 1:5–Neh. 7:72), and *success* (Neh. 8:1–13:3), with Nehemiah 13:4–31 providing a coda. The "house of God" is actualized in three successive movements each with its own potential, process, and success (Eskenazi 1988, 39): the building of the temple (Ezra 1–6), the community (Ezra 7–10), and the wall (Neh. 1–7:72). Chronological succession and similar plot structures link these movements: exiles journey to Jerusalem bringing goods and personnel necessary for their divinely mandated tasks and overcome obstacles (associated with people labeled as foreign) that threaten the completion of each mission. Throughout these books, Eskenazi also traces three interlaced themes: the centrality of the community, the house of God (expanded to include the city and community), and the primacy of the written text (49). Thus the divine decree that the community build is conveyed through written imperial edicts (encapsulated in Ezra 6:14b); the community certifies its decisions in written documents (Ezra 10; Neh. 10); and the numerous lists of people (Ezra 2; 10:19–44; Neh. 3; 7; 10; 11; 12) express structurally and thematically the importance of written documentation and of the community (40–41).

In Ezra 1–6 restoration begins with the reconstruction of the Jerusalem Temple. The narrative incorporates modified elements of ancient Near East temple-building reports (e.g., the community, instead of a monarch, carries out the project; see Hurowitz 1992). As is typical in such accounts, an obstacle to construction arises; in this case activity halts when the king receives an accusatory letter sent by "adversaries" (Ezra 4:8). (At this point, the narrative shifts into Aramaic until the temple's completion in Ezra 6:19.) An ensuing archival search of Jerusalem's history substantiates the accusation. Only after a second archival investigation unearths Cyrus's edict is the project successfully concluded. Darius issues his own supportive decree (Ezra 6:8–12); the temple is completed and dedicated, and the community celebrates Passover (Eskenazi 1988, 47). In these chapters documents function in multiple ways: letters and written edicts convey the plot of the narrative, are central to the conflict with adversaries, and, ultimately, validate the temple's right to exist (Eskenazi 1988, 58). Their instrumental role underscores the political value of documents (and of the scribes who write them).

Ezra's memoir (Ezra 7–10) picks up a half-century later (sometime during the reign of Artaxerxes I, 465–425 BCE) with a simple, "After these things" (Williamson 1985, 91). Ezra, skilled in the law of Moses, appears on stage carrying lineage, titles, and a written royal mandate to teach the law of his God, to provide for the temple, and to enforce the law of God and king (Ezra 7:12–26). As the journey to Jerusalem begins, Ezra takes over as first-person narrator (Ezra 7:27), although lists, a royal decree, and further third-person narrative intermittently disrupt his voice. Concern for proper rituals permeates chapters 7 and 8. Ezra gathers Levites from Casiphia; the travelers fast; and priests transport the temple donations. Upon their arrival the gifts are weighed out into the hands of other priests and the travelers offer large numbers of animals for burnt offerings. The mood shifts abruptly in Ezra 9, as concerned local officials inform Ezra of marriages to foreign women (Ezra 9:1) that all agree are a transgression of the law. The "law" is likely an allusion to Ezra's reading of the Law in Nehemiah 8, which, in the original sequence, preceded Ezra 9 and provided motivation for the divorce measures. The migration of the law reading, however, now frames the marriages as knowing and willful transgressions. After a prayer of repentance (Ezra 9:6–15), the people assemble (Ezra 10:7–9) and are ordered to "send away" these women. Implementation is difficult, so leaders are appointed to "investigate the matter" (Ezra 10:13–16). Those who "dwelt with" foreign women are documented, and the list of offenders concludes the account. The legal status of the women is ambiguous and a garbled final verse in the Masoretic Text leaves the outcome uncertain. This leads many translators to incorporate the corresponding conclusion from 1 Esdras 9:36, "All these had married foreign women, and they put them away together with their children" (Ezra 10:44 NRSV). Others, however, choose to reconstruct the conclusion as, "All these had married foreign women, among whom were some women who had borne children." (*JPS Tanakh*).

Eskenazi argues that Ezra's delegation of responsibility to community leaders communicates the importance of the community and creates a deliberate critique of Nehemiah's more autocratic methods (Eskenazi 1988, 138, 144). However, the collaboration results in the ethically troubling divorce and removal of foreign wives with their children. Perhaps the account is meant to commend sacrifices made for the purity of the community, but economic sanctions are threatened against those who resist (Ezra 10:8), and Christopher Hays (2008, 68) observes that, narratively, the women are represented as nameless, voiceless objects: "we see neither their reaction nor their departure." The one-sided perspective and insistent tone of the narrative that couches the measures in language of holiness, covenant, and obedience to God suggest that this action was highly contested (Hays 2008, 71).

Written in the first person, the Nehemiah memoir (Neh. 1:1–7:5; 13) borrows from the collective mythology of folktales, such as we find in Daniel or Esther. Nehemiah, governor of Yehud (c. 445–433) under Artaxerxes I (Neh. 5:14; 12:26; see Blenkinsopp 1988, 140) and a confidant of the king, triumphs over adversaries on behalf of his vulnerable community. At the outset Nehemiah learns of Judeans in disgrace because Jerusalem has no wall. Nehemiah alone seems able to rebuild Jerusalem's walls in the face of intrigue, threats, and accusations by opponents. His opponents, Sanballat and Tobiah, are reduced to ineffective anger and fear when their repeated efforts to stymie Nehemiah fail (Neh. 6:16). Holy war motifs add urgency to the construction of the boundary with the outside world. Set squarely in the midst of this tense external conflict is a tense internal confrontation over economic disparity (Neh. 5). Nehemiah resolves the issue in his usual authoritative manner, but the account suggests imperial demands underlie this tension as the chapter concludes with a defense of Nehemiah's economic practices.

Upon completion of the wall, attention turns to enrolling the people by genealogy (Neh. 7:5). The narrative continues via a later insertion (Neh. 7:6–13:3) that exhibits a concern for textual authority (Polaski 2012, 51). The list that follows (Neh. 7:6–73 replicates Ezra 2) links membership with exilic heritage. Ezra's solemn reading of the law, followed by a celebrative Festival of Booths then binds the community together (Neh. 8). A more somber second assembly follows which includes a lengthy penitential prayer (Neh. 9:6–37) that portrays servitude in the land as a consequence of religious disobedience. The prayer concludes with a list of signatories who agree to keep the law of Yhwh: to maintain ethnic purity, keep the Sabbath, and support the temple (Neh. 10). The people then cast lots to populate Jerusalem, and lists of clans, priests, and Levites follow (Neh. 11:4–12:25). Jerusalem's walls are then dedicated (Neh. 12:27–46). In the final chapter Nehemiah rectifies failures on all the agreements. His actions affirm the community's commitments, but the placement gives final credit to the lay leader, Nehemiah, for the enforcement of cultic reform and warns the audience to remain vigilant in their religious obligations (Clines 1989, 207; Williamson 1985, 169–170).

Historical reality and the need for coherence and meaning give shape to these accounts (Eskenazi 1988, 7); but so do the authors' rhetorical goals. Each literary form buttresses a favored vision of the community. Persian edicts support the divine purpose to return exiles who will rebuild the temple and city. Lists of families, signatories on edicts, and narrative depictions of a united community validate the actions taken and commend similar policies for the future community. As leaders and people overcome setbacks, opponents, and threats, they embolden readers to persevere against similar challenges. Penitential prayers (Ezra 9; Neh. 1:5–11a; 9:6–37) express shame over past or current guilt and underscore the dangers of faithlessness (Boda 2006, 185; Werline 2006, 188). Failure to keep Torah courts divine wrath and another, more permanent, loss of the land. Together they create a powerful argument that shapes and defines the community.

The Rise of Jerusalem and the Fall of Jericho: Nehemiah's Rhetorical Strategy

The composite nature of Ezra-Nehemiah testifies to the fact that texts are *intertextual*; they are in dialogue with a host of other voices (Fewell 1992, 12). Texts call on "pre-existing forms, conventions, genres and codes" of literary language and intersect with a community's cultural codes (Allen 2003, 15). For example, Nehemiah's account of the construction of Jerusalem's walls and the fall of Jericho's walls in Joshua are infused with the language and images of holy war. Such mythology transforms "cultural values into a universal and natural value" (Allen 2003, 37). Holy War's resonance with community beliefs facilitates Nehemiah's representation of reality as unavoidable and natural (Allen 2011, 87; cf. Barthes 1974, 206). Comparing its usage in these two texts can refine our understanding of its rhetorical purpose in Nehemiah.

Texts find their full meaning within a social context. Used in struggles to impose the definition of the social world best suited to a group's interests, a text's form and content is intertwined with the writer's interests and social location—as well as how those interests are being contested (Bourdieu 1991, 167; see also Rowland 2008). An examination of the social operation of symbolic language and the competition of agents within a social field provide a framework to posit the kind of situation and social struggle that would generate such a text.

Holy war builds on an underlying paradigm of a divine warrior reducing primeval chaos to order (Jones 1989, 299). An inspired charismatic war leader delivers the oppressed and gains control of the land. Such narratives generally begin in a situation of oppression and distress. A leader arises who calls followers, and they engage in battle that culminates with total victory over the enemies (von Rad 1991, 42). Joseph Blenkinsopp (1994, 205) and Hugh Williamson (1985, 224) have identified many of these features in Nehemiah 4:1–15, but the ideology permeates the memoir.

In response to misfortune, the call to arms is normally preceded by repentance and mourning, and an oracle confirming the divine decision is always required (von Rad 1991, 41). Once assured of divine help, the leader can proclaim that God has given the enemy into their hands (von Rad 1991, 42). Upon crossing the Jordan, Joshua will learn Yhwh's will directly (Josh. 6:1–5). Nehemiah will first mourn and repent over news of the burned city gates (Neh. 1:4). After seeking God's aid (Neh. 1:11), Nehemiah perceives divine support when he gains royal approval for his request, "And the king granted me what I asked, for the gracious hand of my God was upon me" (Neh. 2:8). On this basis, Nehemiah musters the people: "I told them that the hand of my God had been gracious upon me, and also the words that the king had spoken to me. Then they said, 'Let us start building!'" (Neh. 2:18). The divine will is made manifest through the actions of the human king.

Central to holy war is a two-part assurance: first, that Yhwh will lead the people in their cause and, second, that God will hand the enemy over to his people, striking the enemy with confusion and fear (Fleming 1999, 220). Nehemiah expresses this assurance in his response to Sanballat's and Tobiah's mockery of the efforts to rebuild the wall, "Then I replied to them, *'The God of heaven is the one who will give us success,* and we his servants are going to start building'" (Neh. 2:20; cf. Neh. 4:20). Yet his opponents are not given into Israel's hand as enemies are in Joshua (cf. Josh. 2:24; 6:2; 8:1; 8:18, 10:30, 32); instead, the completion of Jerusalem's wall provides evidence of divine aid and signals the enemy's defeat. "And *when all our enemies heard of it, all the nations around us were afraid* and fell greatly in their own esteem; *for they perceived that this work had been accomplished with the help of our God"* (Neh. 6:16; cf. Josh. 2:9–11; 5:1; 10:10). Often, divine victory requires little from the Israelite army, thus diminishing the importance of Israel's contribution (von Rad 1991, 50). Jericho's walls, for example, fall before the Israelites ever lift a sword (cf. Exod. 14:13). In Nehemiah, the sustained account of the community's labor on the wall (including a list of laborers in Neh. 3) affirms the importance of the community's participation to accomplish the divine will.

City walls in Nehemiah and the story of Jericho form mirror images. Jerusalem's walls are rebuilt in steps that echo the destruction of Jericho's walls. Jericho's walls are initially solid (Josh. 6:1, 24); whereas Nehemiah hears of Jerusalem's broken walls and burned gates (Neh. 1:3). Mentioned four times (Neh. 1:3; 2:3, 13, 17), the broken walls and burned gates are interpreted as a great disgrace (Neh. 1:3; 2:17; 3:34, 36 MT; 4:2, 4 CEB). Both accounts include secret nighttime inspections of the cities. A scouting party spies out Jericho (Josh. 2:1), and Rahab is warned not to tell their business (Josh. 2:14). Similarly, Nehemiah, in concert with the common holy war motif of nocturnal espionage (cf. Judg. 7:10–15), goes at night to investigate the condition of Jerusalem's walls, and he pointedly tells no one his plans (Neh. 2:12). In both narratives, standing walls are ritually circumnavigated, and their final condition marks the climax of each narrative.

In Nehemiah the status of Jerusalem's wall becomes a recurring refrain (Neh. 4:1, 6, 7, 11; 6:1, 15). By the end of the account, the wall with "no gap left in it" (Neh. 6:1) with gates in place (Neh. 7:1) now has guards (gatekeepers, singers, and Levites!) and Nehemiah orders the gates "not to be opened until the sun is hot" (Neh. 7:3). Following acts of purification, the walls are dedicated as the congregation circles them, giving thanks and offering sacrifices (Neh. 12:30–43). When, in both Nehemiah and Joshua, the people carry out the will of Yhwh, it culminates in the city as a space dedicated to God—by *herem* in Joshua and by restoration and purification in Nehemiah. Each city contains only what is purified and dedicated to the Lord.

The focus on purity dovetails with concerns over community membership. In Joshua 5, lines are drawn when the Canaanite and Amorite kings' hearts melt after Israel crosses the Jordan (Josh. 5:1). The ritual of circumcision that follows signals the end of the stigma of Egyptian slavery (Josh. 5:9), and Passover further demarcates boundaries by marking only Israel as Yhwh's people (Josh. 5:10). Nehemiah's first words to Sanballat and Tobiah deny them any claim on Jerusalem (Neh. 2:20), and he asks God to "give them over as plunder in a land of captivity" (Neh. 3:36 MT; 4:4 NRSV)—conditions he hopes to reverse for his own people. He encourages the nobles to fight "for your brothers, your sons, your daughters, your wives, and your homes"—all couched in familial language (Neh. 4:8 MT; 4:14 NRSV) that excludes anyone outside that boundary. Confirmed by later rituals, this rhetoric marks inclusion and exclusion as surely as circumcision and Passover define membership in Joshua.

In Joshua, the recurring refrain "there were none *who were left*" (Josh. 8:17, 22; 10:28, 30, 37, 39, 40) describes defeated enemies. Furthermore, the terms *escapees* and *those left* describe the unfortunate condition of Ai's population following that city's defeat; "no one *was left* who survived or *escaped*" (Josh. 8:22). At the beginning of Nehemiah, the Judeans, *escapees* and *those left* from the captivity (Neh. 1:2), are in great distress and *reproach* (*kherpah*, cf. Neh. 1:3), which is narratively linked to the broken walls and burned gates. In both accounts, "reproach" has ties to captivity or military defeat. In Joshua, circumcision removes the "reproach of Egypt" (Josh. 5:9), while in Nehemiah, the construction of the walls and purification remove reproach (Neh. 2:17; 12:30). In both books. purifying ritual acts remove the reproach of captivity and foreign power. The final state of the city wall and the ceremonial acts confirm the claims that the shame of captivity and foreign influence has ended— although in Nehemiah this is limited to local foreign influence.

The high point and conclusion of holy war is *herem*, the consecration of the booty to YHWH (von Rad 1991, 49). Susan Niditch (1993, 29) states that *herem* can be understood as sacrifice, giving God his due (Lev. 27:21, 28–29), or as justice. As sacrifice it is the "means of rooting out . . . the impure, sinful forces damaging to the pure relationship between Israel and God" (1993, 56). *Herem* as justice emphasizes purity through demands for separation from foreigners; it draws "a sharp line . . . between us and them, between clean and unclean, between those worthy of salvation and those deserving elimination" (77). This reasoning provides logic and motivation for war "in order to purify the body politic of one's own group, to eradicate evil in the world beyond one's group, and to actualize divine judgment" (77). It is this understanding of *herem* that informs and justifies the actions in Nehemiah and Joshua and sends a striking message in Ezra 10:8, where the term's only usage in Ezra-Nehemiah denotes the penalty for failing to attend the assembly called to address mixed marriages.

In Joshua, objects of *herem* burned with fire include the cities of Jericho (6:24), Ai (8:8, 19), and Hazor (Josh. 11:11), and the family of Achan (7:15, 25). Once Jericho's walls fall, everything *inside* Jericho (once Rahab and her family are removed) becomes *herem*, or devoted to the Lord. When Achan smuggles devoted items into camp, it is described as an act of deceit and a transgression of the covenant of the Lord (Josh. 7:15). Their presence marks the entire community as *herem*, and YHWH threatens to abandon Israel unless they "destroy the devoted things from among you" (Josh. 7:12; cf. 7:13). The slippage in these verses, over what constitutes an object of *herem*—Israel, stolen items, or Achan and his family—displays anxiety about the integrity of the community. Repair of the damage requires rituals of purification (*qadosh*) for the community (Josh. 7:13) and the *herem* of Achan and his family.

In Nehemiah no one, and nothing, is devoted to physical destruction; instead, *herem* is reconfigured as a construction project that protects the purity of the Jerusalem community from "all those of foreign descent" (Neh. 13:3; Janzen 2004, 194). Sources of contamination are removed, beginning with Tobiah and his possessions (Neh. 13:7). The high priest Eliashib, like Achan a man of standing within Judah, is accused of abetting the infiltration of this dangerous "foreign" entity who threatens the community's status as a holy people. Temple chambers are cleansed, as are Levites (Neh. 13:9) so that they can guard the gates to keep the Sabbath day holy (Neh. 13:22). The newly rebuilt wall with its gates and guards now controls entrance to the site of worship and denies merchants entrance on days of religious observance (Neh. 13:13–22). The city's past trouble, a sign of God's wrath, becomes motivation for the nobles to be vigilant and to ban Tyrians from the city on the Sabbath (Neh. 13:16–18). Only Israel may sacrifice, and outsiders are problematic (Janzen 2004, 187). Marriage with foreign women is identified as a source of sin (13:25–26), and Nehemiah chases away the grandson of Eliashib, who had married the daughter of Sanballat the Horonite (13:28). Nehemiah summarizes these actions with the claim that he cleansed the priests and Levites "from everything foreign" (13:30). This purification culminates in the last two "remember" clauses. The priests are to be remembered for their impurity (Neh. 13:29), and Nehemiah for good because of his cleansing efforts (Neh. 13:30–31). A bounded and purified community attests to successful holy war. Purity is now defined in exclusionary terms (Neh. 13:7–9) as an act of religious obedience and loyalty to Yhwh.

As a rhetorical production the Nehemiah memoir gains traction with its audience by combining multiple familiar strands of ideology and social anxieties. It fuses a shared belief in a warring patron deity, traditions regarding covenant loyalty, and religious conceptions of purity. All this appears self-evident to those who share the same social environment (Bourdieu 1980, 58). Now, however, the maintenance of ritual purity and covenant loyalty are equated with proven genealogies of exilic families. The reasoning links anxiety about chaos with worries about communal boundaries, while devotional failure is tied to fears of foreign conquest. Failure to live within the (narrowly defined) covenant threatens war and subjugation (Hansen 1984, 349). Holy war imagery now lends support to the sectarian and insular social order advocated in the text. The rhetoric defines righteousness in terms that excludes all rivals and reserves compassion for a carefully defined and exclusive community (Hansen 1984, 360).

To gain control over the community, Nehemiah denounces collaboration and compromise, which might strengthen the group but threaten his influence (Bourdieu 1991, 189). Waging a purist, ideological war is the most viable option if one lacks sufficient economic or coercive force to defeat competitors. Economically or culturally powerful opponents are symbolically demolished through the compelling and fear-laden language of holy war. Sanballat and Tobiah become purveyors of chaos through their efforts to halt the rebuilding of a wall that would remove the community's shame and protect its sanctity. Nehemiah casts suspicion on Eliashib, the high priest, noting his failure to maintain the purity of the temple (Neh. 13:7) or his lineage (Neh. 13:28), and marks him also as a font of dangerous impurity. Nehemiah establishes himself as a hero, holding chaos at bay and bringing order and purity to a community in need. His stature grows further as he rectifies economic injustice (Neh. 5) and rejects kingship (Neh. 6). His account depicts the wall and his leadership as essential for the safety and good of the community.

The call for purity is fed, in part, by competition with opponents. Because of the duality of the fields of reference (the reading audience and Nehemiah's competitors), the rhetoric must address both internal and external struggles (Bourdieu 1991, 183). To advance his own position with the readership, Nehemiah disqualifies his political peers by countering benefits the community might gain through ties with them. Thus, Nehemiah promotes purity, solidarity, and the symbolic profits derived from association with "a rare, prestigious group" (Bourdieu 1985, 249). Yet Nehemiah must step carefully so as not to threaten imperial interests. Violence against local competitors could damage the wider economy and jeopardize the goodwill of the satrap or monarch. Accordingly, Nehemiah's triumph is achieved without bloodshed, but he leaves a trail of suspicion regarding his opponents' motives.

The forceful rhetoric promoting walls, purity, and limited citizenship suggests community membership is a matter of contention. (Others have positive relations with Tobiah and Sanballat [Neh. 6:17–19; 13:4, 28].) Nehemiah resists compromise and collaboration, so useful for economic power, because entrenched alliances with regional powers weakens his own position. Instead he lays out a call to purity. The highly charged language of holy war paints local competitors as opponents of the good of the community, turning collaboration with them into threats to religous integrity. Nehemiah's strategy creates a more cohesive communal identity while securing his dominance within a smaller, but well-defined, community.

In a classic struggle to control the social field, how it is defined and who defines it (Bourdieu and Wacquant 1992, 97), Nehemiah must navigate between Persian rule and the local population and the influence of nobles, priests, and regional polities. These demands influence his memoir and his self-portrait. Lacking the religious legitimacy of ordained priests, he instead draws on the Joshua tradition and his imperial appointment to legitimate his efforts to rebuild and define the Jerusalem community. His account uses the language of holy war to mark all outside influence as dangerous, and the priests, who hold significant cultural influence, as careless in their religious duties. He presents himself as an imperial appointee who is friend to the Judeans. His call to religious fidelity garners the assent of the reader to embrace a small, cohesive, carefully policed community with Nehemiah clearly in command.

References

Allen, Graham. 2003. *Roland Barthes*. Routledge Critical Thinkers. New York: Routledge.

Allen, Graham. 2011. *Intertextuality*. 2nd ed. The New Critical Idiom. New York: Routledge.

Barthes, Roland. 1974. *S/Z An Essay*. Translated by Richard Miller. New York: Hill and Wang.

Berquist, Jon. 1995. *Judaism in Persia's Shadow: A Social and Historical Approach*. Minneapolis, MN: Fortress Press.

Blenkinsopp, Joseph. 1988. *Ezra-Nehemiah*. The Old Testament Library. Philadelphia, PA: Westminster Press.

Blenkinsopp, Joseph. 1994. "The Nehemiah Autobiographical Memoir." In *Language, Theology, and the Bible: Essays in Honor of James Barr*, edited by Samuel E. Balentine, John Barton and James Barr, 199–212. Oxford: Clarendon Press.

Boda, Mark J. 2006. "Form Criticism in Transition: Penitential Prayer and Lament, Sitz im Leben and Form." In *Seeking the Favor of God: Volume 1: The Origins of Penitential Prayer in Second Temple Judaism*, edited by Mark J. Boda, Daniel J. Falk, and Rodney A. Werline, 181–192. Atlanta, GA: Society of Biblical Literature.

Boda, Mark J., and Paul L. Redditt, eds. 2008. *Unity and Disunity in Ezra-Nehemiah: Redaction, Rhetoric and Reader*. Sheffield, Yorkshire: Sheffield Phoenix Press.

Bourdieu, Pierre. 1980. *The Logic of Practice*. Translated by Richard Nice. Redwood City, CA: Stanford University Press.

Bourdieu, Pierre. 1985. "The Social Space and the Genesis of Groups." *Theory and Society* 14(6): 723–744.

Bourdieu, Pierre. 1991. *Language and Symbolic Power*. Edited by John B. Thompson. Translated by Gino Raymond and Matthew Adamson. Cambridge, MA: Harvard University Press.

Bourdieu, Pierre, and Loic J. D. Wacquant. 1992. *An Invitation to Reflexive Sociology*. Chicago: University of Chicago Press.

Carter, Charles E. 1999. *The Emergence of Yehud in the Persian Period*. Sheffield, Yorkshire: Sheffield Academic Press.

Clines, David J. 1984. *Ezra, Nehemiah, Esther*. New Century Bible. Grand Rapids, MI: Eerdmans.

Clines, David J. 1989. "The Force of the Text: A Response to Tamara C. Eskenazi's 'Ezra–Nehemiah: From Text to Actuality.'" In *Signs and Wonders: Biblical Texts in Literary Focus*, edited by Cheryl J. Exum, 199–215. Atlanta, GA: Society of Biblical Literature.

Davies, Gordon. 1999. *Ezra and Nehemiah*. Berit Olam. Collegeville, MN: Liturgical Press.

Edelman, Diana. 2005. *The Origins of the "Second" Temple: Persian Imperial Policy and the Rebuilding of Jerusalem*. Oakville, CT: Equinox.

Eskenazi, Tamara C. 1988. *In an Age of Prose: A Literary Approach to Ezra-Nehemiah*. Atlanta, GA: Scholars Press.

Fewell, Danna Nolan, ed. 1992. *Reading between Texts: Intertextuality and the Hebrew Bible*. Literary Currents in Biblical Interpretation. Louisville, KY: John Knox Press.

Fleming, Daniel E. 1999. "The Seven-Day Siege of Jericho in Holy War." In *ki Baruch Hu: Ancient Near Eastern, Biblical and Judaic Studies in Honor of Baruch A. Levine*, edited by Robert Chazan, William H. Hallo, and Lawrence H. Schiffman, 211–228. Winona Lake, IN: Eisenbrauns.

Fried, Lisbeth S. 2004. *The Priest and the Great King: Temple-Palace Relations in the Persian Empire*. Winona Lake, IN: Eisenbrauns.

Hansen, Paul D. 1984. "War and Peace in the Hebrew Bible," *Interpretation* 38(4): 341–362.

Hays, Christopher B. 2008. "The Silence of the Wives: Bakhtin's Monologism and Ezra 7-10." *Journal for the Study of the Old Testament* 33: 59–80.

Hoglund, Kenneth G. 1992. *Achaemenid Imperial Administration in Syria-Palestine and the Missions of Ezra and Nehemiah*. Atlanta, GA: Scholars Press.

Hurowitz, Victor. 1992. *I Have Built You an Exalted House: Temple Building in the Bible in the Light of Mesopotamina and Northwest Semitic Writings*. Sheffield, Yorkshire: JSOT Press.

Janzen, David. 2004. *The Social Meanings of Sacrifice in the Hebrew Bible*. New York: Walter de Gruyter.

Jones, Gwilym H. 1989. "The Concept of Holy War." In *the World of Ancient Israel: Sociological, Anthropological and Political Perspectives*, edited by Robert E. Clements, 299–321. Cambridge: Cambridge University Press.

Lipschits, Oded, Gary N. Knoppers, and Rainer Albertz, eds. 2007. *Judah and the Judeans in the Fourth Century BCE*. Winona Lake, IN: Eisenbrauns.

Lipschits, Oded, and Manfred Oeming, eds. 2006. *Judah and the Judeans in the Persian Period*, Winona Lake, IN: Eisenbrauns.

Niditch, Susan. 1993. *War in the Hebrew Bible: A Study in the Ethics of Violence*. New York: Oxford University Press.

Pakkala, Juha. 2004. *Ezra the Scribe: The Development of Ezra 7-10 and Nehemiah 8*. New York: Walter de Gruyter.

Polaski, Don. 2012. "Nehemiah: Subject of the Empire, Subject of Writing." In *New Perspectives on Ezra-Nehemiah*, edited by Isaac Kalimi, 37–59. Winona Lake, IN: Eisenbrauns.

Rad, Gerhard von. 1991. *Holy War in Ancient Israel*. Edited and translated by Marva J. Dawn. Grand Rapids, MI: William B. Eerdmans. Translated from the third edition of *Der Helige Kreig im alien Israel*, 1958.

Rowland, Christopher. 2008. "Social, Political, and Ideological Criticism." In *The Oxford Handbook of Biblical Studies*, edited by Judith M. Lieu and John William Rogerson, *Oxford Handbooks online*. doi:10.1093/oxfordhb/9780199237777.003.0037.

Smith, Morton. 1971. *Palestinian Parties and the Politics That Shaped the Old Testament*. New York: Columbia University Press.

Southwood, Katherine. 2012. *Ethnicity and Mixed Marriages in Ezra 9-10: An Anthropological Approach*. Oxford: Oxford University Press.

Torrey, Charles C. 1910. *Ezra Studies*. Chicago: Chicago University Press.

Weinberg, Joel. 1992. *The Citizen-Temple Community*. Translated by Daniel L. Smith-Christopher. Sheffield, Yorkshire: Sheffield Academic Press.

Werline, Rodney A. 2006. "Defining Penitential Prayer." In *Seeking the Favor of God: Volume 1: The Origins of Penitential Prayer in Second Temple Judaism*, edited by Mark J. Boda, Daniel J. Falk, and Rodney A. Werline, xiii–xvii. Atlanta, GA: Society of Biblical Literature.

Williamson, Hugh G. M. 1985. *Ezra, Nehemiah*. Nashville, TN: Thomas Nelson.

Wright, Jacob. 2004. *Rebuilding Identity: The Nehemiah Memoir and Its Earliest Readers*. New York: Walter de Gruyter.

CHAPTER 24

THE PATRILINEAL NARRATIVE MACHINERY OF CHRONICLES

JULIE KELSO

The whole of what is called world history is nothing but the creation of man by human labor, and the emergence of nature for man; *he therefore has the evident and irrefutable proof of his self-creation, of his own origins.*

(Marx 1975, 357; my emphasis)

Underlying the doctrine that man makes history is the undiscussed reality of why he must.

(O'Brien 1981, 53)

(T)he son is unable to accept the debt of life, body, nourishment and social existence he owes the mother. An entire history of Western thought is intent on substituting for this debt an image of the self-made, self-created man.

(Grosz 1989, 120–121)

THE TEXT AND ITS READERS

THE book of Chronicles is understood to be a history of the people of Israel, from Adam up to the declaration of the Persian king Cyrus who orders the return to the land of those who are among the people of Yahweh (2 Chron. 36:23). The idea that the book of Chronicles is to be read as a type of historiography is attested since ancient times, notably through the titles given to the originally untitled book (see Japhet 1993, 1–2; Knoppers 2003, 47–51). Of course, it cannot be claimed that Chronicles is an example of history as we have come to understand the term. Nevertheless, as Japhet, following Noth (1943) states: "A consideration of the work's relevant features, such as aim, plan, form, and method, must lead to the conclusion that Chronicles is a history, an idiosyncratic expression of biblical historiography" (Japhet 1993, 32).

The book is formally divided into two basic literary sections: genealogy (1 Chron. 1–9) and narrative (1 Chron. 10–2 Chron. 36; including speeches, sermons, and poetic prayer). The former constitutes nine long and, for many readers, tedious chapters of genealogical lists, military notes, land and cultic divisions, and so forth, while the latter is fundamentally a retelling of a story that is more or less familiar to us from the alternative, so-called Deuteronomistic, history: the monarchic history of Israel, with a focus on the Davidic line of the Judahite kings and the temple cultus. These two features of Chronicles—its opening nine chapters that can test the sturdiest of scholarly attentions or even the patience of the most devout Bible-reading believers, along with its seemingly overall lack of substantial innovation regarding narrative—have led to Chronicles's reputation as the poor cousin of the Deuteronomistic history.

Of course, it is not true that Chronicles is a simple, derivative rehashing of Israel's past; the originality of Chronicles as a literary product has been recognized since the beginnings of modern critical biblical scholarship and is now well established. Chronicles' narrative emphasis is on the Southern Kingdom of Judah, specifically on Jerusalem and its religious cult, comparatively ignoring the Northern Kingdom and passing over the history of the rival city of Samaria (see, e.g., Ewald 1867, 174; Noth 1987; Torrey (1909) 1970, 209; Wellhausen 1973, 187–188). Furthermore, many have noted that Chronicles does not acknowledge the exodus and conquest traditions in its version of history, and displays little interest in presenting the law-giving Moses as a crucial founding figure (see, e.g., Japhet 1979, 1997, 363–368; Wright 1997, 157–158). The relationship between the God of Israel, the people of Israel (understood far more inclusively with respect to other peoples in the land than it is in Ezra and Nehemiah), and the land itself is eternally given. Chronicles presents Israelite identity in terms of both an eternal (because tied directly to Adam, the first man) and a *natural* entity, one which emerges "*autochthonously* in the land of Israel" (Dyck 1998, 122; Japhet 1979, 218). In other words, from the beginning the land thus belongs to the Israelites because of their status as first inhabitants. From Adam, it seems, Israel simply emerges as a natural entity. There are no real debts to forefathers such as Abraham, Moses, or Joshua, who, according to the so-called Deuteronomist's version of the past, had to fight for the land their god bestowed upon them to enable Israel as a people to emerge and become strong in that land. Chronicles is thus, in general terms, the story of how a particular people, who worship a particular God within a particular land, came to be, how they managed to remain in that land for generations, how they came to lose that land, and how they came to return to it. Of course, who "they" are is a cloudy issue, but it seems that the main character of this story, Israel, here is constituted by the elites: the Davidic-Judahite monarchy and the Jerusalem cultus.

In terms of interpretive methods, unlike critical work on other biblical books, such as Genesis, Judges, Samuel, and Kings especially, Chronicles scholarship seems to have been slow to introduce the newer, indeed more political literary-critical modes of interpreting narratives. Of course, the diverse range of literary-theoretical practices that scrutinize the workings of the various literary forms (narrative, drama, poetry, etc.) emerge out of the developments made in nineteenth-century European scholarship, notably the "higher criticism" of German scholars of the Bible. However, it seems that contemporary Chronicles scholarship is still enamored with these methodological roots; in this, the scholarship is not unlike the book of Chronicles itself, a text that demonstrates a fascination with origins. Since the beginning of the nineteenth century, Chronicles scholarship has been monopolized by historical criticism, with its various methodologies including text criticism, form criticism, redaction criticism, rhetorical criticism, source criticism, etc. Chronicles scholars have been, and largely still are, concerned about whether the "Chronicler" authored Chronicles and Ezra-Nehemiah, or whether Ezra was the sole author; whether there are two distinct authors, despite the similarities between the two texts;[1] whether Chronicles is the work of one author or many (the unity/compositional history of Chronicles); whether the genealogical chapters of 1 Chronicles (1–9) were a later addition or part of the original text; and, in general, the questions of textual boundaries, dating, sources (earlier biblical and extrabiblical), historical credibility, genre, and overall purpose, the Chronicler's theology, and so forth (see Duke 2009). In other words, studies of Chronicles as a work of literature have largely been driven by the more traditional historical-critical methods and theological questions than by an engagement with the literary and narrative theories that emerged in (especially the latter half of) the twentieth century. For example, very little feminist work has been done on Chronicles, despite decades of feminist contributions to all other biblical books (except Ezra-Nehemiah, which likewise remains underread by feminist biblical scholars; Kelso 2013).

Marxist, feminist, gender-critical, queer, poststructuralist, psychoanalytic, and postcolonial theories and methods, long standard in nonbiblical literary studies, (although with varying degrees of continued influence; see Bible and Culture Collective 1995; Brewton n.d.; Eagleton 1996; Culler 1997) are only now finding their way into Chronicles research. There is currently strong critical interest in Chronicles and Ezra-Nehemiah, both long underread by the majority of biblical scholars. Now viewed as important documents of post-exilic life in Israel, these books aid our understanding of the construction of Jewish identities, in relation to nascent Judaism(s). They are also now of great interest with respect to the rest of the Hebrew Bible itself, more of which is understood to have been redacted, if not even entirely conceived, during this period. As a part of this renaissance, there have been recent engagements with Chronicles by scholars who are interested in the newer modes of literary and narrative analysis. Christine Mitchell (2002) introduces intertextuality, and the Bahktinian concepts of dialogism and heteroglossia (Mitchell 1999) to the interpretive field of Chronicles scholarship, while Roland Boer (1997) and Steven Schweitzer (2007) have both produced fascinating and original readings of Chronicles based on Marxist utopian literary theories. James Trotter (1999) utilizes an historicized, reader-oriented interpretive practice to explore the possible reasons for the use of Saul's death as narrative origin, while John W. Wright (1999) brings narratology to the study of the genealogies in Chronicles. My own approach is to analyze the genealogies and narratives of Chronicles through the double lens of feminism and psychoanalysis (Kelso 2007a, 2007b).

The Monosexual, Masculinist Production of the Past in Chronicles

I maintain that when we read Chronicles symptomatically, paying attention to the uniqueness of this discourse, at both the macro and micro levels, we can discern that the overall absence and silence of women, relative to the alternative "story" of Israel's past (Genesis– 2 Kings), is a symptom of more complex modes of silencing at work in the text. That the dearth of women is one of the defining features of Chronicles at the macro level has largely remained invisible to scholars, including feminist scholars who prefer to overemphasize the meager presence of women in the text (e.g., Laffey 1992; Wacker 2012). To date, when the relative absence of women is noted, it is typically dismissed as a mere by-product of the Chronicler's focus on the Jerusalem cult and the monarchy of Judah. This, however, begs the pressing question: *why* is the absence and relative silence of women seemingly so necessary to this particular version of the past? Comparatively speaking, Chronicles is almost entirely about men and their social, political, and religious endeavours. All in all, the political, religious, and social past depicted in Chronicles—as what constitutes the "post-exilic" past of "Israel"—is almost exclusively a male affair. Indeed, when we consider the alternative pasts of Israel constructed within the other books of the Hebrew Bible, the relative absence and silence of women in Chronicles needs to be read as one of its *constitutive* features.

Whether one believes that the plot does or does not develop an overall story line, there is an obvious temporal logic in Chronicles common to both the genealogical section and the narrative that follows: patrilineality. There is undoubtedly a complexity in relation to the fabula (the overall story told in chronological order) and the chronology presented in the text (see Wright 1997), but the logic of both is the same: both narrative and story time progress through the production of sons, and it is a production overwhelmingly attributed to fathers alone.

Biblical genealogies usually consist of a series of male generations, both vertical (constituted by a series of names in ascending or descending order, going back or forward through generations and time), and horizontal (across a generation). With descending vertical lists the literary-temporal movement is often constituted by the verbal act "to beget." The form of this "begetting" is usually A begat B, and B begat C, and C begat D, and so on, and both the subject and object of the verb are masculine. The English word *begat* (past tense of *beget*) is a translation of a number of masculine forms of the Hebrew verb *yalad* (third masculine singular of "to bear, bring forth, issue out of"). When feminine forms of this verb appear, the verb is translated as "she bore." Importantly, while the masculine forms of the verb *yalad* (all translated as "begat") appear ninety-one times in 1 Chronicles 1–9, there are only seventeen instances of an active, feminine form of the verb *yalad*. The act of generation, here in Chronicles, is depicted as predominantly a masculine act, and it is this masculine generation that pushes us through time as we read.

Given this dominant association between masculinity and generation, despite the fact that in reality it is women who give birth, it is interesting that, when female figures do appear in the genealogies as maternal figures, there is more often than not a breakdown in genealogical meaning and sense (see further Kelso 2007b, 36.2–36.11). These problematic moments in the genealogies concerning maternal figures reveal the dominant phantasy underwriting Chronicles: monosexual, masculine production; a literary-imaginary world where men produce men, without the need for women. For such a phantasy to be sustained, the reality that women's maternal bodies are the actual origin of all needs to be silenced. With the genealogical chapters of Chronicles, this silencing takes place through a *disavowal* of maternal origins ("I know I am born of woman, but all the same . . ."). There are women named as maternal figures in this discourse, though relatively few. At the same time, the genealogies mainly construct time unfolding largely according to masculine monosexual production, from father to son, only rarely mentioning the mother. Tellingly, maternal genealogical figures have the ability to shatter the continuity of this discourse; they disrupt the flow. The grammatical problems that emerge around these maternal figures suggest that this language cannot cope when "she" and "it" (the specter of her maternal body) appear. Because the maternal body is disavowed here in the genealogical construction of the past, an acknowledgement of the factual reality, and perhaps even power, of the maternal body ends up threatening this masculine order of representation because the productive maternal body contradicts what constitutes the "reality" of this masculine discourse: a world of (self-producing) men.

When it comes to the narrative chapters that follow, the temporal logic of the Chronicles narrative, like the genealogies, is patrilineal. The implicit logic here is what I call the *patrilineal narrative machinery* of Chronicles in which the temporal movement of Chronicles, the "motor" or "drive" to use Peter Brooks's psychoanalytic-inspired terms (Brooks 1984), operates upon the logic of succession from father to son, not from mother to son or father to daughter or mother to daughter. This narrative movement or plotting from the father to the son, *what pushes the story forward*, has become so naturalized in Western patriarchal cultures that it is almost invisible, not even worthy of comment. And yet, this particular narrative logic is utterly ideological: it props up the sense that history is indeed the purview of those born men. Such a narrative logic is complicit in writing women out of the picture. The gendered machinery of narrative begs for analysis to ascertain exactly how this takes place.

Time and story move forward through the production of and subsequent succession of sons and their stories. Indeed, the consistency of this version of Israel's monarchic history depends on this logic. For the order of meaning to be maintained, another complex means of silencing the maternal-feminine is required: repression. However, through a careful reading informed by a feminist, psychoanalytic mode of interpretive practice, the silenced (repressed) maternal body becomes audible at certain points in the narrative. As a case in point, I turn to the strange story that functions as narrative origin in this version of Israel's past: the murder of Saul and his sons (1 Chron. 10). In Chronicles, the logic of the production of meaning depends upon the logic of patrilineal succession for its consistency. Close analysis of 1 Chron. 10 exposes how this narrative logic depends on the silencing of the maternal body for its consistency. The murder of Saul and his sons (1 Chron. 10) may be read symptomatically as a narrative of the originary repression of the maternal body, a repression necessary to sustain the phantasy of monosexual production that underwrites this masculinist history.

THE DEATH OF SAUL AS NARRATIVE IGNITION; OR, THE "MURDER" OF THE MOTHER

And so with this dominant patrilineal logic as the machinery of narrative temporality in mind, I turn now to the question of how such a narrative machinery gets itself started. I am not interested in proffering an argument regarding authorial intention—that is, in providing a purposive motivation by the author for choosing to begin the story this way. Given their preference for such traditional matters, scholars have long debated the Chronicler's reason for using Saul's death as narrative beginning, generally favoring the idea that the choice communicates the author's preference for the Davidic ideal (see Zalewski 1989, 449–451). However, when we consider a number of curious features in this story that are not present in the other version (1 Sam. 31), we may read them symptomatically as revealing what is supposed to remain silent: the necessary "murder" or repression of the mother, the silencing of the maternal, required to initiate and sustain the phantasy of monosexual masculine production.

The story begins with a battle between the Philistines and Israel. The "men of Israel" flee from the Philistines, and, we are told, "they fell slain on Mount Gilboa." The Philistines then pursue Saul and his sons, and after they strike down Jonathan, Abinadab, and Malchishua (10:2), the Philistines find and wound Saul (10:3). Saul asks his armor bearer to pierce him with his sword, to protect him from whatever deeds the uncircumcized might have in mind for him. His armor bearer refuses, however, so Saul has to do the job himself, falling on the sword (10:4b). When his armor bearer realizes that Saul is dead, he too falls on his sword and dies (10:5). In verse 6 we are given a statement about the deaths of Saul, his three sons, and "his whole household." When the men of Israel in the cities in the valley hear of their deaths, they flee, and the Philistines move in (10:7). The next day, the Philistines find the corpses (lit. "the pierced" or "the slain"; 10:8) of Saul and his sons. They strip Saul, take his head and his armor, and send it about the land as a celebratory message for their idols and their people (10:9). They hang up his armor in the house of their gods and gruesomely fasten his head to the house of Dagon (10:10). The valiant men of Jabeth-Gilead collect the headless body (gufath) of Saul and the bodies (gufoth) of his sons, and bury what are now "the bones" of these fast decaying bodies (10:11–12). In verses 13 and 14, we are given the reasons for Saul's death: he did not keep the word of the Lord (10:13a), and also he "inquired by necromancy" (lish'ol ba'ov; 10:13b). Because of this second transgression, the Lord slew Saul and turned the kingdom over to David (10:14).

In this version of Saul's death, functioning as narrative beginning in Chronicles, Saul's body is a site of ambiguity. First of all, in verse 3 it is unclear what the Philistines do to Saul: "The battle weighed heavily upon Saul, and the archers found him with the bow and he was wounded/he became frightened of the archers (wayyahel min-hayyorim)" (1 Chron. 10:3).

The final clause of 1 Chronicles 10:3 (wayyahel min-hayyorim) is difficult to translate with certainty. Depending upon how one construes the verbal root and form, it is possible to translate the clause as "and he was wounded by the archers" or "he became frightened of the archers" or "he writhed in fear from the archers." In other words, we cannot be certain as to whether Saul has been wounded yet, penetrated by the enemy at this early point, or whether he is simply fearful of what is to come. In fact, in verse 4 Saul declares that he is worried lest those with a different male body or, rather, a different phallus, the uncircumcized (ha'arelim), get to his own presumably circumcized body and do something (wehith'allelu) that is also ambiguous. The meaning of the verb 'alal can range, depending upon its form, from "to act arbitrarily," "to deal wantonly," "to humiliate," or "to insert or to thrust in." Thus, given both the context (the phallic focus) and the semantic range of 'alal, we can legitimately sense that Saul fears that the Philistines will humiliate him by raping him.

Alongside Saul's fear of penetration is the refusal of his armor bearer to put the sword through him. In verse 5 it is unclear whether the armor bearer falls on his own sword or Saul's, or whether there is one sword or two ("he also fell upon the sword"). However, what is clear is that the problems concerning the body of Saul involve the issue of penetration. Saul might have been penetrated by the Philistines' arrow in verse 3, and penetration is most likely what Saul fears in verse 4, the humiliation of rape by the uncircumcized. His armor bearer refuses to penetrate his body with the sword because he is too afraid. In the end, Saul has to penetrate himself, although this too is made ambiguous by verse 14, where it is the Lord who is given credit for the fatal penetration of the body of Saul. This divine slaying of Saul instigates the installation of the Davidic kingdom, and indeed the Davidic story. All in all, the issue of penetration concerning Saul's body is both thoroughly ambiguous and over-determined.

But this "body" of Saul and the "bodies" of his sons are remarkable for another reason. The Hebrew word used In 1 Chronicles 10:12 is not the usual *gewiyyah*, which is used in the parallel text of 1 Samuel 31:12, but the highly unusual, and feminine, construct form *gufah*. *Gufah* is a strange word found nowhere else in the canon, and its semantic range includes "hollowness" and "closed-ness" (*guf*). The image conjured by this word is of bodies that are empty, contained vessels. Such a word represses any sense of corporeal organs or fluids, imaging, rather, the male body as an enclosed, empty space, an exterior shell encasing an empty space. This is all rather clean when one considers the mess that bodies and corpses can make. Actually, the choice of this word over the far more common *gewiyyah* seems consistent with the fact that, by verse 12, these bodies have rather rapidly decomposed. The diegetic tempo at this point has either jumped forward in time, or these strange bodies have somehow quickly been reduced to bones without any external interference into the process of decay (in contrast to, for example, the burning of the bodies in 1 Sam. 31:12).

And what of Saul's principal crime? Unlike the book of Samuel, Chronicles gives reasons why Saul is killed. We are told that his death is punishment for his faithless acts against Yahweh: for not observing the word/command of Yahweh (10:13), for consulting a "medium" or "necromancer" for guidance (10:13), and for not seeking out Yahweh (10:14). Saul, it seems, is guilty of going to a *different* source of knowledge. In 1 Samuel 28:7, the text is explicit about the gender of this source that Saul prefers over Yahweh, given Yahweh's silence: he inquires of the "witch" of Ein Dor. In Samuel, Saul goes to a woman who has access to the underworld, to Sheol (*she'ol*). In Chronicles, however, and consistent with the relative exclusion of women from this text in comparison to the alternative accounts, we are informed that Saul consults a male who has access to the world of spirits (*'ov* is a masculine singular noun meaning "necromancer"). Nevertheless, Saul is seeking out guidance from the underworld, not from Yahweh. Indeed, this nether world Sheol (*she'ol*) is a feminine noun that has the same consonantal spelling as Saul (*sha'ul*) and is related to the verb root *sha'al* meaning "to ask or inquire." These wordplays construct the reasons why Saul and his sons must be killed and the kingdom handed over to David and his line: this story of origins is a story about the removal of the one who inquires of the feminine realm, not of Yahweh (the "god of the fathers"), whose murder by the god leads to the properly ideal patrilineal, patriarchal line. What functions, then, as narrative "origin" of this past, this history, is the removal of the man who inquires of the feminine, who seeks a response from the feminized place of the dead. There is something of a contradiction here, for while Chronicles cannot seem to admit the female *character* into the scene (the witch of Ein Dor),[2] the feminine must still, for some reason, be constitutive of Saul's punishment, his inadequacy for the role of ideal king.

Saul himself is heavily associated with the feminine. Indeed, he and his sons are feminized, but more specifically maternalized. The body, in *this* genealogy of father and sons, is imagined as pure exterior enveloping nothing but space, an empty vessel waiting to be filled, a feminine body ripe for maternity as men might imagine it. Furthermore, the problem concerning Saul's body is one of penetration, and it is a problem that is thoroughly overdetermined in this representation of monarchic origins. Thus, what instigates the story of Israel's monarchic and cultic past, what functions as narrative "origin," is the murder of this feminized and maternalized body of Saul, along with the feminized, maternalized bodies of his sons. There are no women in this first story about men. This is not a mythological account of the murder of the mother, such as we get in *Enuma Elish*, for example. Already, women have been silenced from the scene and their silence on a simple or general level is readable through their absence. However, when we pay attention to those strange features unique to this story—the overdetermined nature of Saul's body, the images of penetration, the unusual word choices, the feminine constructions of Saul's principal crime—we begin to realize that the silence of women in the Chronicles narrative takes place on a more complex level. Reading the death of Saul symptomatically enables the silence of women to become audible and readable here at the beginning of the narrative: the murder/silencing of the maternal-feminine constitutes the generative origin of this narrative history; it ignites and fuels the narrative. This story functions, then, as a narrative account of the primary *repression* required to sustain this particular masculine identity in relation to narrative history: the repression of the maternal body and the mother-daughter genealogy institutes the *properly masculine* subject of history, along with the genealogical logic proper to its telling. Such a repression ensures that this masculine subject, embodied first in the figure of David, is without debt to maternal matter, specifically, and without debt to nature, in general. Thus, the masculine subject may see himself as the sole, productive agent and focus of history: the phantasized, narrativized epitome of the "self-made man."

NOTES

1. There is a degree of consensus that Chronicles and Ezra-Nehemiah were originally separate works, largely due to the influence of Japhet (1968, 1991, 1993) and Williamson (1977). See also Throntveit (1982). However, Blenkinsopp (1988) argues for the unity of authorship.
2. A similar excision happens in 1 Chronicles 10:10, where the Philistines install Saul's armor "in the temple of their gods, and displayed his skull in the temple of Dagon". In 1 Samuel 31:10, Saul's armor is hung in the "house of Ashtaroth." Ashtaroth is the plural of Ashtoreth, a goddess associated with war.

REFERENCES

Bible and Culture Collective. 1995. *The Postmodern Bible*. New Haven, CT: Yale University Press.

Blenkinsopp, Joseph. 1988. *Ezra-Nehemiah: A Commentary*. The Old Testament Library. Philadelphia, PA: Westminster Press.

Boer, Roland. 1997. *Novel Histories: The Fiction of Biblical Criticism*. Sheffield, Yorkshire: Sheffield Academic Press.

Brewton, Vince. "Literary Theory." *Internet Encyclopedia of Philosophy*. http://www.iep.utm.edu/literary/.

Brooks, Peter. 1984. *Reading for the Plot: Design and Intention in Narrative*. Oxford: Clarendon.

Culler, Jonathan. 1997. *Literary Theory: A Very Short Introduction*. Oxford: Oxford University Press.

Duke, Rodney K. 2009. "Recent Research in Chronicles." *Currents in Biblical Research 8(1)*: 10–50.

Dyck, Jonathan E. 1998. *The Theocratic Ideology of the Chronicler*. Leiden, Boston, Köln: Brill.

Eagleton, Terry. 1996. *Literary Theory*. Minneapolis: University of Minnesota Press.

Ewald, Heinrich. 1867. *History of Israel*. Translated by R. Martineau. London: Longmans and Green.

Grosz, Elizabeth. 1989. *Sexual Subversions: Three French Feminists*. St Leonards: Allen & Unwin.

Japhet, Sarah. 1968. "The Supposed Common Authorship of Chronicles and Ezra-Nehemiah." *Vetus Testamentum* 18: 330–371.

Japhet, Sarah. 1979. "Conquest and Settlement in Chronicles." *Journal of Biblical Literature* 98: 205–218.

Japhet, Sarah. 1991. "The Relationship between Chronicles and Ezra-Nehemiah." In *Congress Volume: Leuven, 1989*, edited by John A. Emerton, 298–313. Vetus Testamentum Supplement 43; Leiden: E. J. Brill.

Japhet, Sarah. 1993. *I and II Chronicles: A Commentary*. The Old Testament Library. Louisville, KY: Westminster/John Knox Press.

Japhet, Sarah. 1997. *The Ideology of the Book of Chronicles and its Place in Biblical Thought*. Beiträge zur Erforschung des Alten Testaments und des Antiken Judentums 9. Bern: Peter Lang.

Kelso, Julie. 2007a. *O Mother Where Art Thou? An Irigarayan Reading of the Book of Chronicles*. London: Equinox.

Kelso, Julie. 2007b. "The Transgression of Maacah in 2 Chronicles 15:16: A Simple Case of Idolatry or the Threatening Poesis of Maternal 'Speech'?" *Bible and Critical Theory* 3(3): 36.1–36.18.

Kelso, Julie. 2013. "Reading Silence: The Books of Chronicles and Ezra-Nehemiah, and the Relative Absence of a Feminist Interpretive History." In *Feminist Interpretation of the Hebrew Bible in Retrospect. I. Biblical Books*, edited by Suzanne Scholz, 268–289. Sheffield, Yorkshire: Sheffield Phoenix Press.

Knoppers, Gary N. 2003. *I Chronicles 1-9: A New Translation with Introduction and Commentary*. Anchor Bible 12. New York: Doubleday.

Laffey, Alice L. 1992. "I and II Chronicles." In *The Women's Bible Commentary*, edited by. Carol A. Newsom and Sharon H. Ringe, 110–115. London: SPCK.

Marx, Karl. 1975. "Economic and Philosophical Manuscripts." In *Early Writings*. Translated by Rodney Livingston and Gregor Benton, 279–400. New York: Vintage Books.

Mitchell, Christine. 1999. "The Dialogism of Chronicles." In *The Chronicler as Author: Studies in Text and Texture*, edited by M. Patrick Graham and Steven L. McKenzie, 311–326. Journal for the Study of the Old Testament Supplement 263. Sheffield, Yorkshire: Sheffield Academic Press.

Mitchell, Christine. 2002. "Transformations of Meaning: The Accession of Solomon in Chronicles." *Journal of Hebrew Scriptures* 4: article 3. http://www.jhsonline.org/.

Noth, Martin. (1943) 1987. *The Chronicler's History*. Translated by H. G. M. Williamson. Journal for the Study of the Old Testament Supplement 50. Sheffield, Yorkshire: Sheffield Academic Press.

O'Brien, Mary. 1981. *The Politics of Reproduction*. London: Routledge and Kegan Paul.

Schweitzer, Steven. 2007. *Reading Utopia in Chronicles*. Library of Hebrew Bible/Old Testament Studies 442. London: T&T Clark International.

Throntveit, M. A. 1982. "Linguistic Analysis and the Question of Authorship in Chronicles, Ezra and Nehemiah." *Vetus Testamentum* 32: 201–216.

Torrey, C. C. (1909) 1970. "The Chronicler as Editor and Independent Narrator." In *Ezra Studies*, 208–251. New York: Ktav.

Trotter, James M. 1999. "Reading, Readers and Reading Readers Reading the Account of Saul's Death in 1 Chronicles 10." In *The Chronicler as Author: Studies in Text and Texture*, edited by M. Patrick Graham and Steven L. McKenzie, 294–310. Sheffield, Yorkshire: Sheffield Academic Press.

Wacker, Marie-Therese. 2012. "Book of Chronicles: In the Vestibule of Women." In *Feminist Biblical Interpretation: A Compendium of Critical Commentary on the Books of the Bible and Related Literature*, edited by Luise Schottroff and Marie-Theres Wacker, 178–191. Grand Rapids, MI: Eerdmans.

Wellhausen, Julius. 1973. *Prolegomena to the History of Israel*. Translated by W. Robertson Smith. Gloucester, MA: Peter Smith.

Wright, John W. 1997. "The Fight for Peace: Narrative and History in the Battle Accounts of Chronicles." In *The Chronicler as Historian*, edited by M. Patrick Graham, Kenneth G. Hoglund and Steven L. McKenzie, 150–177. Journal for the Study of the Old Testament Supplement 238. Sheffield, Yorkshire: Sheffield Academic Press.

Wright, John W. 1999. "The Fabula of the Book of Chronicles." In *The Chronicler as Author: Studies in Text and Texture*, edited by M. Patrick Graham and Steven L. McKenzie, 136–155. Sheffield, Yorkshire: Sheffield Academic Press.

Williamson, H. G. M. 1977. *Israel in the Books of Chronicles*. Cambridge: Cambridge University Press.

Zalewski, Saul. 1989. "The Purpose of the Story of the Death of Saul in 1 Chronicles X." *Vetus Testamentum* 39(4): 449–467.

CHAPTER 25

TIME AND FOCALIZATION IN THE GOSPEL ACCORDING TO MARK

SCOTT S. ELLIOTT

NARRATIVE ASPECTS IN THE GOSPEL ACCORDING TO MARK

UNLIKE Matthew and Luke with their genealogies and birth stories, and unlike John with his poetic overture depicting the preexistent Word, Mark begins, despite its reference to "the beginning," *in media res*. References to "the gospel," the words of prophecy, and the proclamation of John the Baptist in the wilderness, signal a new Exodus. Jesus appears, is baptized, and then is driven into the wilderness by the Spirit. Forty days later, he returns heralding "the gospel of God" which is nothing short of the arrival of God's kingdom. For the next eight chapters, Jesus teaches with authority, performs spectacular deeds of power, and attracts a crowd of enamored, if fickle, followers, as well as enemies. Amid the excitement, he repeatedly tells others to be silent about him, wanders off alone, and claims that he teaches in parables so "those outside" will *not* understand (4:10–12). Ironically, it is not clear who the insiders and outsiders are. In chapter 8, the plot thickens, with ominous overtones: Jesus begins to speak of impending betrayal, arrest, mistreatment, suffering, and death. This leads only to increased misunderstanding, confusion, tension, and conflict. As Jesus's passion begins to unfold, he is portrayed as one struggling against the circumstances that engulf him. His only words from the cross speak of abandonment. The temple curtain is torn, and a centurion reacts to Jesus's final breath by calling him, in a stroke of exquisite ambiguity, "God's son"—the only human in the narrative to refer to him thus. The story ends as enigmatically as it began: with an open tomb, a "young man, dressed in a white robe," and three women in silence, "for they were afraid."

Naturally, attempts to summarize Mark's story will always fall short. Ultimately, it is Mark's discourse that captures the narrative critic's fascination. Kermode (1979, ix) found in it "extremely difficult and interesting problems of interpretation." To begin, Mark's narrator is a masterful storyteller. He[1] relies more heavily on mimesis than on extradiegetic statements;

i.e., he is more inclined to show than to tell. He has an eye for detail, some of which is rather curious (e.g., the "other boats" of 4:36b; the "green grass" of 6:39). Using clever rhetorical devices, he weaves together the various strands of his gospel to create an intricate narrative tapestry. A good example of this is his use of intercalation, whereby he "sandwiches" one episode within another in order to create a dialogue between them (e.g., 5:21–43; 6:7–30; 11:12–21; see Edwards 1989).

There is a sense of mystery and wonder in Mark's gospel, which is related closely to aspects of characterization and to the identity and location of the implied reader. Using the so-called "Messianic secret" or "commands to silence" motif, the narrator depicts Jesus repeatedly attempting to keep his identity quiet and referring constantly to the "son of man," which may or may not be an indirect self-identification (see, e.g., Aichele 1996: 106–109; cf. Malbon 2009). The reticence and inscrutability of Jesus (ironically juxtaposed, as it is, with his frank speech; see, e.g., 8:32a) intersects with the provocative and sometimes troubling play between insiders and outsiders. Throughout the gospel, those who presumably should understand— whether because they are Jesus's close associates or religious leaders and experts—only mis-understand time and again. Meanwhile, characters whose identities or lots in life suggest they would lack understanding often seem to grasp something important (see, e.g., the clever retort of the Syrophoenician woman at 7:28, or the centurion's ironic comment at 15:39). Add to this the narrator's tendency to pull the rug out from under the reader's own sense of cer-tainty. Consider Peter's confession (8:27–33): the reader may applaud Peter's pronouncement of Jesus as the Christ, but she is then forced to distance herself from Peter when he is rebuked for protesting Jesus's prediction of suffering. Or consider the words of the young man in white at Jesus's tomb (16:6–7): he instructs the women to tell the disciples that Jesus will meet them in Galilee. But earlier (13:21), Jesus had warned his followers about those who would claim to know where the messiah was.

Mark's gospel is demanding. To whatever extent it is about discipleship (see Malbon 1983, 1986; Shiner 1995; Tannehill 1977; cf. Horsley 2001, 79–86), it is a notion of discipleship char-acterized by suffering and an austere sense of faith. Unlike John's Gospel, Mark does not present faith as the result of miracles but rather as something one must possess before mir-acles can take place. Jesus's own power can be either activated by faith (5:24b–34) or limited by its absence (6:5). Moreover, unlike the other canonical gospels, Mark offers no proofs of Jesus's resurrection. There is only an empty tomb, and the reader is left to decide whether she will believe "he has risen" (16:6; see further Fowler 1989).

Throughout Mark, Jesus speaks in parables. But the gospel itself also borders on being a parable of sorts (Tolbert 1989). Hence, the demanding nature of Mark's gospel is not limited to its story or its particular theological message; the discourse itself is demanding. Drawing on the work of Barthes, Aichele (1996, 127) describes the text as an unreadable and thus "writerly" text of bliss that "resists decidable coherence" and eludes control. Indeed, the ris-ing action of conflict within Mark's story (e.g., with religious leaders [2:13–3:6], Jesus's fam-ily [3:31–35], his community [6:1–6a], and even the disciples; see Kingsbury 1989) refracts a tension between the reader and the text, wherein the reader actively engages the text, con-stantly wrestling meaning and significance from her experiences with it, lest she be num-bered among those who naively imagine themselves to be "inside," only to be found looking but not perceiving (4:12).

The narrator's interest in written words adds depth and dimension to the characteristics described above. It appears at the outset in relation to Mark's somewhat cryptic prologue (see Boring 1991; cf. Matera 1988) with its ambiguous designation of "the beginning," and its composite quotation attributed to "the prophet Isaiah" (1:2–3). It surfaces again with the unusual transposition of "Elijah and Moses" at the Transfiguration (9:4), and with the invitation to the reader to understand (13:14). Then it culminates at the passion where Jesus on the cross becomes a text, a psalter of sorts (see, esp., 15:24, 31, 34), published beneath an epigraph (15:26). Amid these and other Hebrew Bible citations and allusions, Jesus states, "the Son of man goes as it is written of him, but woe to that man by whom the Son of man is betrayed" (14:21 RSV; cf. 9:12). The referent for such writing is ambiguous and unlocatable, unless one reads it as a self-referential commentary on the narrative discourse that occasions the character's speech. This fits well with a fundamental plot motif woven throughout Mark's narrative: Jesus is repeatedly manhandled (e.g., driven into the wilderness to be tempted, destined to be betrayed, doomed to die), not only within the story but also by it. He is thus subject to a plot and a discourse that is beyond his control. Barthes (1974, 15) describes "the work of commentary" as "*manhandling* the text, *interrupting* it" (author's emphasis). Mark's narrative regularly manhandles and interrupts the texts it reads—both real and figurative. Making no assertion of totality, it leaves itself open, even inviting its readers to act likewise, signing off with an abrupt interruption of silence in the narrative's final sentence (16:8). As a function of his narrative role, the narrator of Mark is at once a commentator (Kermode 1979), a betrayer (see Aichele 1996, 19–24, 106–109), and an escape artist who is not about to let any of this be pinned firmly on himself (see 14:51–52; 16:5; Moore, 1992, 30–38).

READING MARK'S STORY

Mark's gospel was the proving ground for New Testament narrative criticism, and the story of Mark's story largely parallels that of New Testament narrative criticism generally. Like all methods, narrative criticism was born out of a desire to make better sense of some of the aforementioned features of Mark by approaching them from a different angle. Rhoads's programmatic essay, "Narrative Criticism and the Gospel of Mark" (1982/1999), laid the foundation for analyzing the narrative elements of Mark. Rhoads began by calling for a shift in focus from fragmentation to unity,—that is, from treating the work as a patchwork compilation of preexisting material (à la source criticism, etc.) to considering it holistically in its final form. Next, he argued for a reorientation from history to fiction, that is, from treating the work as an artifact to be analyzed and interpreted solely in relation to its various contexts (e.g., social, cultural, political, religious) to recognizing the narrative as a literary creation crafted by an author, a "world-in-itself" to be read on its own terms. Finally, drawing on Booth (1961) and Chatman (1978), Rhoads distinguished elements of Mark's "story" (i.e., the content or "what" of a narrative, e.g., events, characters, and settings) from aspects of Mark's "discourse" (i.e., the articulation or "how" of a narrative, e.g., the narrator, point of view, standards of judgment, implied author, readers, style, and rhetoric).

Rhoads's essay spawned a rich variety of narrative-critical studies of Mark. The most notable is the book he wrote in collaboration with Mitchie, *Mark as Story: An Introduction to the Narrative of a Gospel* (1982).[2] The book offers a fuller, more detailed narrative-critical interpretation of Mark that builds upon Rhoads's earlier article, and serves as a more concrete and practical introduction to the method (cf. Malbon 2008). Kingsbury analyzed both Mark's Christology (1983) and the conflict central to Mark's plot (1989). Malbon (1986) examined Mark's use of space in the construction of narrative meaning. Tolbert (1989) published a narrative-critical reading of the parable of the sower (Mark 4:3–8) in relation to various characters' responses to Jesus throughout the gospel. Shiner (1995) demonstrated how Mark's portrayals of the disciples function in relation to the gospel's narrative rhetoric. And Moloney (2004) attempted to better understand the author of Mark through an investigation of his storytelling and interpretive techniques. In addition to these studies of isolated aspects in Mark's narrative, Moloney (2002) published a full-fledged narrative critical commentary, while Smith (1996), drawing more broadly on "secular" narratology and benefiting from two decades of narrative criticism on Mark, published what amounts to his own revised and expanded version of *Mark as Story*. More than two decades after *Mark as Story*, Resseguie (2005, 17) would describe narrative criticism as an uninvited "interloper" crashing the party and upsetting the status quo "with vexing indecorum," staging "unsettling interpretive acts that infuse originality and excitement." Indeed, narrative-critical work on Mark seemed to be a rogue methodological approach, intended, if not destined, to overturn and unravel dominant historical-critical approaches.

The most extensive narrative critical work on Mark has centered on characterization, with Malbon clearly leading the way (see Malbon 2000, 2009b).[3] Malbon's *Mark's Jesus: Characterization as Narrative Christology* (2009a) pushes narrative critical analysis of Mark beyond the frameworks established by Rhoads, attending more closely to the discursive figuration of Jesus as a character. "Remembering the experience of the character Peter," she writes, "a narrative christology of Mark looks for something more than coming up with the correct title" (2009a, 16). Her focus on Mark's narrative discourse and on some of the more subtle aspects of narrative theory results in a complex appreciation of the theological dimension of Markan literature and language.

Malbon (2009a, 17) argues that, like any other literary figure, Jesus is constructed through four channels: what the character says and does, and what other characters say and do "to, about, or in relation to" that character. These channels are tempered, qualified, and articulated in five different ways: enactment, projection, deflection, refraction, and reflection (18). What is most intriguing about *Mark's Jesus* is that Malbon explicitly calls into question the prevailing assumptions that the character of Jesus and the narrator of Mark share the same point of view, and that the narrator of Mark and the implied author of Mark are one in the same. For her, "the distinction between the narrator and the implied author [are] essential to perceiving and expressing Markan narrative christology" because "the Markan Jesus and the Markan narrator do not speak with the same voice" (233–234). The implied author lies behind both, giving expression to each point of view, thereby creating the tension between the two that runs throughout the narrative (243).

Malbon draws on the work of Stanzel (1984) and Yamasaki (2007) to suggest that this tension between character and narrator be understood, in part, as the result of a situation in which "events are filtered through the consciousness of a character ('reflector') who exists in the story world … though the narration is given in the third person" (2009a, 241). For Malbon, the authorial narrative situation (that of the Markan narrator) and the figural narrative situation (that of Mark's Jesus) are presented side by side as "polyphony" (242). She sees Mark's narrative as representing a point of view on the figure of Jesus, who in turn presents a self-reflective point of view on himself in relation to God (242). The result is that "Mark's Gospel subverts its own narrator's manifest sense of what it means for Jesus to be the Christ, the Son of God, by its protagonist's manifest sense of what it means for God to be God" (256).

On the whole, narrative-critical studies of Mark share a common interest in explicating the work. "Secular" narrative theory has provided these interpreters with useful tools for deciphering the mechanics of Mark's gospel. In their view, the author of Mark, whomever he may have been, sought to convey a particular meaning that can only be properly accessed by identifying and understanding the various constituent elements (always in relation to the narrative as a whole) that create and transfer this meaning to the ideal reader. Narrator, narration, plot, characters, characterization, settings, point of view, audience, and so on, are regarded as rhetorical devices wielded by an author to communicate his message. In sum, narrative critics of Mark have maintained a threefold emphasis on (1) taking the finished work both as a whole and as a "world-in-itself," (2) making a clear distinction between story and discourse, and (3) attempting to occupy the position of the ideal reader.

This leaves them susceptible to a number of criticisms. On one hand, despite employing the concepts of "secular" narratology, narrative critics of Mark actually do something very different (see Moore 1989, 4–55). Whereas secular critics typically use individual narratives to theorize narrativity (e.g., Kermode 1979; Genette 1980), biblical critics use narrative theory as a method to study and better understand Mark's gospel. Moreover, Moore (1989, 60) rightly questions the fundamental distinction between story and discourse upon which their operating assumption rests: "If story is to be understood strictly as the 'what' of the narrative, and rhetoric as 'how' that story is told, then everything in the narrative (which is all a 'telling,' after all) is rhetorical." On the other hand, for as much as narrative criticism took shape in reaction against standard assumptions and orientations of historical criticism, narrative analyses of Mark regularly take recourse to matters of historical context in their interpretations. Admittedly, narrative critics working on Mark do so more subtly and with different orientations and goals than historical-critical exegetes. Nevertheless, they seem no less intent on laying hold of what they perceive to be a clear and specific textual referent— that is, an historical actuality behind the narrative, whether it be an essentialized character or an author's intended message.

Time and Focalization in Mark 6:7–30

Narrative theory has changed drastically since New Testament scholars first began using it to interpret Mark. Narratology has moved "from discovery to invention, from coherence to complexity, and from poetics to politics" (Currie 1998, 2; cf. Cobley 2001, 171–200; Elliott 2011, 59–73). In other words, narrative theorists have become increasingly concerned with the fundamentally unstable, intertextual, and unbounded characteristics of narrative discourse.

Due to the persistent notion in much of New Testament criticism that the story Mark tells is something independent of, and existing prior to, its narration, narrative criticism on Mark has become relatively at home among more traditional historical-critical methodologies. Room remains for more venturesome work premised on fundamentally different understandings of narrativity. Recent publications by Rhoads (2004), Malbon (2009b), and Iverson and Skinner (2011), and especially Moore (1992), Wilson (2007), and Aichele

(2006; 2011), reflect promising developments. These studies, to varying degrees, have moved away from viewing narrative discourse as a vehicle through which an author delivers a stable message that precedes its articulation. Driven more by theory than by method, much of this work treats narrative discourse as a highly complex semiotic mechanism that always threatens to unravel the very story it seems to tell (see e.g., Elliott 2011, 163–196).

Two narrative aspects of Mark warrant further attention: time and focalization. Smith (1996) devotes half of a chapter to the aspect of time in his analysis of Mark. He rightly points out the complexity of this aspect, noting differences between story time and plotted time, between mundane or historical time and monumental or cosmic time, and between chronological and typological time; the subdivisions of plotted time (beginning, middle, and end); and the narrator's management of time by way of arrangement, duration, and frequency. To these he adds the extent to which perspectives on time depend on whether the question concerns characters, narrator, author, or readers (125). Smith demonstrates a variety of instances in Mark where time is exploited by the narrator and plays a key role in the effect and meaning of the narrative.

Focalization refers to the relationship between the controlling or determining vision from which a narrative is presented and the narrative element that is "seen" or perceived. (Recall, for example, Malbon's analysis of Mark's narrative christology.) Focalization differs from the more familiar aspect of point of view insofar as it distinguishes between "the vision through which the elements are presented" and "the identity of the voice verbalizing that vision" (Bal 1997, 142–143; cf. Yamasaki 2012). Narrative focalization has both a subject (i.e., the "focalizer"), which is the agent whose perception orients the presentation, and an object (i.e., the "focalized"), which is what the focalizer perceives (O'Neill 1994, 87; Rimmon-Kenan 2002, 75). However, it is often best to think of the focalizer as "a chosen *point* . . . from which the narrative is perceived as being presented at any given moment" (O'Neill 1994, 86).

Focalization, like time, is a complicated aspect of narrative discourse. Narratives may be focalized from an omniscient, unrestricted narrating position (i.e., a vantage point capable of seeing across time and space and inside the minds of characters), externally from a position entirely outside of the story, or internally through a particular character within the story. Internal focalization may be fixed in relation to a single character, variable (i.e., various story elements seen through the perspectives of various characters), or multiple (i.e., a single story element seen through multiple perspectives). Finally, focalization can operate at multiple levels (O'Neill 1994, 89–95), and types of focalization can vary throughout a narrative.

All narratives, to varying degrees, disguise the originating point of their discourse through a variety of means, a characteristic of narrative discourse that O'Neill (1994, 58, 76–82) labels the "ventriloquism effect." When one encounters a shift in focalization it marks an instance of embedded focalization. Character focalization, embedded within a narrative, is compound focalization: a focalizer (the focalizing subject) is at the same time the focalized (object of focalization). One effect this has is to relativize various perspectives reflected in the narrative. The ambiguity and indeterminacy that characterizes this sort of focalization unsettles the certainty and reliability of the story being narrated. By extension, it obscures the boundary between inside and outside the story, and threatens to undermine the reader's confidence by pointing to the fact that, while *every* narrative is told from somewhere, that location is at once both outside the narrative and everywhere within it, and accessible only through it.

Compound focalization involving more than one focalizer (e.g., when a character-focalizer's vision is embedded within an external focalizer's enveloping perspective), especially when further complicated by a narrator's manipulation of time, presents interesting interpretive problems. Ambiguous and indeterminate in nature, it presents at once too much and too little information to allow one to firmly locate the vision governing the narrative episode. Hence, segments of Mark's narrative wherein the narrator embeds one episode within another provide excellent case studies.

For example, consider Mark 6:7–30. Here, the narrator inserts, by way of flashback, the story of John the Baptist's death (vv. 14–29) into the story of Jesus sending out "the twelve" (vv. 7–13) and their subsequent return (v. 30). The embedded story, especially when read together with the framing story, is a particularly interesting moment in which characterization, the themes of suffering and discipleship, and the boundary between insiders and outsiders all hinge upon actual and metaphorical acts of seeing. In Mark, the act of seeing is a fundamental trope, intimately related to the state of knowing. Sight is a principle criterion whereby the identities of insiders and outsiders are determined (see Aichele 2011, 141–163), and upon which competing interpretations in and of the narrative hinge.

Edwards (1989, 204–205) and Smith (1996, 138–139) consider Mark 6:7–30 in relation to Markan interpolation and to time, respectively. Edwards, in support of his overarching argument that Mark uses the technique of interpolation in service to "an intentional and discernible theological purpose," contends that 6:7–30 primarily aims to illustrate the "relationship between missionaries and martyrdom, discipleship and death." However, the distinct literary characteristics of 6:14–29 noted by Edwards (viz., the fact that it is the only episode in Mark that is not about Jesus, and its language and style) are better interpreted, from a narrative-critical perspective, as a decision on the part of the narrator to shift focalization. Smith, meanwhile, describes the episode as "an internal, completing analepsis" and argues that the narrator's rationale for portraying the event of John's death here and in this manner is because (a) depicting it earlier (e.g., following 1:14) would have detracted from the purposes of Mark's prologue, and (b) its present location serves narrative and theological interests by presenting "the illusion of the passing of time" and by illustrating the consequences of incorrectly identifying Jesus. But why is an illusion of the passing of time necessary here, and how does either the illusion or the passing of time itself relate to the theological implications, whether they be the consequences of misidentification or the risks of discipleship?

The length of this episode, relative to the rest of the narrative as a whole and to other individual scenes throughout, highlights its importance (Glancy 1994). Contrast the terseness that characterizes the account of the twelve's missionary excursion, and especially the generic summary of their report upon their return. Whereas the disciples are focalized externally in 6:12–13 and 30, focalization is quite different in 6:14–29. In the embedded episode, Herod serves as both a focalizer and an object of focalization: "we watch Herod and his guests watch the girl dance" (Glancy 1994, 40). Of course, the reader is not seeing these events through Herod's eyes as they unfold, but rather as he recollects them. Moreover, this is not an actual recollection of that notorious evening, but the narrator's portrayal of a particular character's remembrance. "The framework invites readers to share Herod's *memories* of the execution" (Glancy 1994, 38; my emphasis). But it is not on the execution where the camera, as it were, lingers (note how swiftly and matter-of-factly the beheading is recounted in 6:27b). Rather, it is the camera itself, quickly piling up shifts in time and focalization, that the narrative considers, demonstrating the limitations of locating narrative meaning with any specific actant or event at the expense of the discourse itself.

The interplay of time and focalization is a key narrative device in the film *La jetée* (1962), which offers an illustrative intertext for thinking about these aspects in Mark's narrative. Set in a postapocalyptic, dystopian future, the film tells the story of a man, haunted by a memory from his youth, prior to the war. The memory involves a woman and a disturbing incident he witnessed on the observation deck of an airport. This man is one of many that scientists use to experiment with time travel in order to seek help from the worlds of the past and future to rescue their present. The scientists eventually succeed in their efforts, and the man is able to remain for a period in the past. While there, he develops a relationship with the woman from his memory. He is later transported to the future and receives a device that will restore his world. The people of the future also offer to bring him to their world, but he opts instead for the more distant past where he can be with the woman of his memory. Upon returning there and finding her on the airport jetty, he notices, as he runs toward her, one of the scientists responsible for the time travel experiments, and in that moment realizes that the disturbing incident inscribed upon his memory was in fact his own death.

One of the most fascinating aspects of the film is that the narrative is presented almost entirely through still shots, unevenly paced, with a voice-over narrator speaking in place of dialogue. There is one key segment in which the pace quickens. The viewer is drawn closer and closer to the woman's face until, for one fleeting moment, we see her breathe in real time. Of course, the entire setup of the film forces the viewer to immediately question that perception.

Like *La jetée*, Mark's narrative is presented largely through episodic vignettes focalized mainly from an omniscient, unrestricted narrating position. Furthermore, like *La jetée*, Mark's narrative frequently looks backward and forward. Both the narrative and the reader are actively engaged in the production and reproduction, the interpretation and reinterpretation, of memory. But in 6:14–29, the narrator delves into the processes of such production and revision, in real time as it were, exploring them in and through characters inside a particular event and, by juxtaposition, in and through characters only tangentially related to the event but connected discursively. Setting one alongside the other, or embedding one within the other, the narrator is not only exploring but experimenting with the fabrication of meaning, thereby making manifest certain defining characteristics of narrative discourse: selection, causation, and emplotment.

Mark 6:7–30 oscillates between acceleration and delay. As flashback and interpolation, the portrayal of Herod's party and John's beheading is an interruption, but one that is not entirely necessary (e.g., to create suspense or provide the illusion of time's passing) insofar as verse 30 actually provides less information than what was already offered in verses 12–13. The pace alternately slows and quickens in conjunction with shifts in focalization, increasingly compounded, as the episode shuttles from one character to another, from one history to another, from one reading to another. The instability and questionable reliability of character-focalizers makes the episode one of desperation and frustration in the search for meaning. The narrator reaches further and further backward, framing and reframing the seemingly serendipitous (a narrative illusion) "opportunity" (v. 21), which then unfolds slowly until Herodias's daughter comes "immediately with haste" to convey her mother's request for John's head as if it were her own wish. But it is all a chimera. The agency of characters is limited and their fates are not subject to their control. Desires and decisions are predicated on what others say and do. The substance of what Herod heard (v. 14) is not perfectly clear. It may be exigencies of narrative discourse and commentary that draw the narrator aside, but it is rumors and competing interpretations that trigger Herod's recollection. Is Herod, then, an object or a subject? To what extent, if any, does he possess agency? Is it his position as a king or his superstitious and weak-kneed character that makes him the epitome of power and collusion? Does he embody the system, or is he a product of it? Furthermore, which cause are we to regard as primary to account for the circumstances and events the narrator portrays in this episode? Who or what is ultimately responsible for the revolting request and gruesome death? And where, when all is said and done, do we locate the point of origin or source of the discursive voice? With each shift in time and each change in point of view, focalization becomes increasingly ambiguous, offering the reader greater interpretive freedom, even while raising the stakes and demanding more of her in order to make proper sense of the narrative. But that is just the sort of risk Mark's narrative compels the reader to take.

NOTES

1. The author of Mark is unknown, and the narrator's gender is nowhere explicitly identified. I follow convention in referring to the author as "Mark" and using the male third-person pronoun. While it is probably safe to assume that the author was male, Hedrick (1987, 253–254) suggests that the "rather prominent and generally affirmative role given to women by the narrator, in contrast to the rather negative description of the twelve male disciples, suggests that the narrator has a positive view of women and raises the intriguing possibility that the narrator might even be intentionally cast as a 'female' voice."

2. Dewey joined the team for the second edition (1982/1999). A third edition appeared in 2012, attesting to the continuing significance and influence of both book and method. Skinner provides an excellent analysis of this book's impact in Iverson and Skinner (2011, 1–16).

3. Danove has produced a considerable body of work on characterization in Mark also (see, esp., Danove 2005); however, he makes no claim to be doing narrative criticism, per se, and his approach, concerned primarily with linguistic style, rhetorical forms and mechanics, and semantics, differs considerably from traditional New Testament narrative criticism. cf. Funk (1988).

REFERENCES

Aichele, George. 1996. *Jesus Framed*. Biblical Limits. London: Routledge.
Aichele, George. 2006. *The Phantom Messiah: Postmodern Fantasy and the Gospel of Mark*. London: T&T Clark International.
Aichele, George. 2011. *Simulating Jesus: Reality Effects in the Gospels*. Bible World. London: Equinox.
Bal, Mieke. 1997. *Narratology: Introduction to the Theory of Narrative*. 2nd ed. Toronto: University of Toronto Press.
Barthes, Roland. 1974. *S/Z An Essay*. Translated by Richard Miller. New York: Hill & Wang.
Booth, Wayne C. 1961. *The Rhetoric of Fiction*. Chicago: University of Chicago Press.
Boring, M. Eugene. 1991. "Mark 1:1-15 and the Beginning of the Gospel." In *How Gospels Began*, edited by Dennis E. Smith. *Semeia* 52: 43–81.

Chatman, Seymour. 1978. *Story and Discourse: Narrative Structure in Fiction and Film*. Ithaca, NY: Cornell University Press.

Cobley, Paul. 2001. *Narrative*. New Critical Idiom. London: Routledge.

Currie, Mark. 1998. *Postmodern Narrative Theory*. Transitions. Basingstoke: Palgrave.

Danove, Paul L. 2005. *The Rhetoric of the Characterization of God, Jesus, and Jesus' Disciples in the Gospel of Mark*. Journal for the Study of New Testament Supplement Series 290. New York: T&T Clark.

Edwards, James R. 1989. "Markan Sandwiches: The Significance of Interpolations in Markan Narratives." *Novum Testamentum* 31: 193–216.

Elliott, Scott S. 2011. *Reconfiguring Mark's Jesus: Narrative Criticism after Poststructuralism*. The Bible in the Modern World 41. Sheffield, Yorkshire: Sheffield Phoenix Press.

Fowler, Robert M. 1989. "The Rhetoric of Direction and Indirection in the Gospel of Mark." In *Reader Perspectives on the New Testament*, edited by Edgar V. McKnight. *Semeia* 48: 115–34.

Funk, Robert W. 1988. *The Poetics of Biblical Narrative*. Foundations and Facets: Literary Facets. Sonoma, CA: Polebridge Press.

Genette, Gérard. 1980. *Narrative Discourse: An Essay in Method*. Translated by J. E. Lewin. Ithaca, NY: Cornell University Press.

Glancy, Jennifer. 1994. "Unveiling Masculinity: The Construction of Gender in Mark 6: 17–29." *Biblical Interpretation* 2: 34–50.

Hedrick, Charles W. 1987. "Narrator and Story in the Gospel of Mark: Hermeneia and Paradosis." *Perspectives in Religious Studies* 14: 239–258.

Horsley, Richard A. 2001. *Hearing the Whole Story: The Politics of Plot in Mark's Gospel*. Louisville, KY: Westminster John Knox.

Iverson, Kelly R., and Christopher W. Skinner, eds. 2011. *Mark as Story: Retrospect and Prospect*. Resources for Biblical Study Series. Atlanta, GA: Society of Biblical Literature.

Kermode, Frank. 1979. *The Genesis of Secrecy: On the Interpretation of Narrative*. Cambridge, MA: Harvard University Press.

Kingsbury, Jack Dean. 1983. *The Christology of Mark's Gospel*. Philadelphia, PA: Fortress Press.

Kingsbury, Jack Dean. 1989. *Conflict in Mark: Jesus, Authorities, Disciples*. Minneapolis, MN: Fortress Press.

Marker, Chris, dir. 1962. *La jetée*. Neuilly-sur-Seine, France: Argos Films.

Malbon, Elizabeth Struthers. 1986. *Narrative Space and Mythic Meaning in Mark*. New Voices in Biblical Studies. San Francisco: Harper & Row.

Malbon, Elizabeth Struthers. 2008. "Narrative Criticism: How Does the Story Mean?" In *Mark and Method: New Approaches in Biblical Studies*, 2nd ed, edited by Janice Capel Anderson and Stephen D. Moore, 29–57. Minneapolis, MN: Fortress Press.

Malbon, Elizabeth Struthers. 2000. *In the Company of Jesus: Characters in Mark's Gospel*. Louisville, KY: Westminster John Knox.

Malbon, Elizabeth Struthers. 2009a. *Mark's Jesus: Characterization as Narrative Christology*. Waco, TX: Baylor University Press.

Malbon, Elizabeth Struthers, ed. 2009b. *Between Author and Audience in Mark: Narration, Characterization, Interpretation*. Sheffield, Yorkshire: Sheffield Phoenix Press.

Matera, Frank J. 1988. "The Prologue as the Interpretive Key to Mark's Gospel." *Journal for the Study of the New Testament* 34: 3–20.

Moloney, Francis J. 2002. *The Gospel of Mark: A Commentary*. Peabody, MA: Hendrickson Publishers.

Moloney, Francis J. 2004. *Mark: Storyteller, Interpreter, Evangelist*. Peabody, MA: Hendrickson Publishers.

Moore, Stephen D. 1989. *Literary Criticism and the Gospels: The Theoretical Challenge.* New Haven, CT: Yale University Press.

Moore, Stephen D. 1992. *Mark and Luke in Poststructuralist Perspectives: Jesus Begins to Write.* New Haven, CT: Yale University Press.

O'Neill, Patrick. 1994. *Fictions of Discourse: Reading Narrative Theory.* Toronto: University of Toronto Press.

Resseguie, James L. 2005. *Narrative Criticism of the New Testament: An Introduction.* Grand Rapids: Baker Academic.

Rhoads, David. 1982. "Narrative Criticism and the Gospel of Mark." *Journal of the American Academy of Religion* 50: 411–434.

Rhoads, David. 2004. *Reading Mark: Engaging the Gospel.* Minneapolis, MN: Fortress Press.

Rhoads, David, Joanna Dewey, and Donald Michie. 1982/1999. *Mark as Story: An Introduction to the Narrative of a Gospel.* 2nd ed. Minneapolis, MN: Fortress Press.

Rimmon-Kenan, Shlomith. 2002. *Narrative Fiction.* 2nd ed. New Accents. London: Routledge.

Shiner, Whitney Taylor. 1995. *Follow Me! Disciples in Markan Narrative.* Society of Biblical Literature Dissertation Series 145. Atlanta, GA: Scholars Press.

Smith, Stephen H. 1996. *A Lion with Wings: A Narrative-Critical Approach to Mark's Gospel.* Biblical Seminar 38. Sheffield, Yorkshire: Sheffield Academic Press.

Stanzel, Franz K. 1984. *A Theory of Narrative.* Translated by Charlotte Goedsche. Cambridge: Cambridge University Press.

Tannehill, Robert C. 1977. "The Disciples in Mark: The Function of a Narrative Role." *Journal of Religion* 57: 386–405.

Tolbert, Mary Ann. 1989. *Sowing the Gospel: Mark's World in Literary-Historical Perspective.* Minneapolis, MN: Fortress Press.

Wilson, Andrew P. 2007. *Transfigured: A Derridean Rereading of the Markan Transfiguration.* Library of New Testament Studies 319. Playing the Texts 13. London: T.&T. Clark.

Yamasaki, Gary. 2007. *Watching a Biblical Narrative: Point of View in Biblical Exegesis.* London: T.&T. Clark.

Yamasaki, Gary. 2012. *Perspective Criticism: Point of View and Evaluative Guidance in Biblical Narrative.* Eugene, OR: Cascade Books.

CHAPTER 26

NARRATIVE READINGS, CONTEXTUALIZED READERS, AND MATTHEW'S GOSPEL

WARREN CARTER

NEW Testament narrative criticism emerged in the 1970s and early 1980s (Moore 1989, 2011; Powell 2011). David Rhoads is credited with the first use of the term *narrative criticism* in the title of a 1982 article, "Narrative Criticism and the Gospel of Mark." He defined narrative criticism as "an approach" that investigates "the formal features of narrative in the texts of the Gospels, features which include aspects of the story-world of the narrative and the rhetorical techniques employed to tell the story" (Rhoads 1982, 411–412). As his coauthored book-length study of Mark employing narrative criticism shows (Rhoads and Michie 1982), these formal features include setting, plot, characters, points of view, and rhetoric. Christopher Skinner (2011, 1) describes this book as "one of the significant contributions to New Testament studies in the latter half of the twentieth century."

While the earliest narrative work concerned itself with the Gospels of Mark (Rhoads and Michie) and John (Culpepper), narrative discussions of Matthew's Gospel soon followed, with book-length studies from Edwards and Kingsbury. Edwards (1985, 9–10) describes his narrative approach as following "the development of the plot or the flow of the narrative," reading it as a reader who "begins at the beginning" and being attentive to "the progress of the story" and the "cumulative process" of reading. The plot, characterization, and point of view are of special concern. Further, Edwards explains that his reader is the implied reader, "the person posited *by the text* as the reader" (emphasis in the original), and that he, Edwards, is concerned with the Gospel's "effect . . . on the implied reader."

Kingsbury (1986) spends the first chapter outlining his "literary-critical approach" method informed by secular narrative theorists, such as Seymour Chatman, Boris Uspensky, and M. H. Abrams, as well as by Rhoads's work on Mark. Kingsbury approaches Matthew as a unified narrative comprising the "story" of Jesus (involving plot, characters, and setting). Also important is its "discourse," or how the story is told, including its point of view and implied reader, an "imaginary person" who responds "to the text at every point with whatever emotion, understanding, or knowledge the text ideally calls for . . . in whom the intention of the text is to be thought of as always reaching its fulfillment" (1986, 36). Thereafter, three chapters follow on Matthew's plot (1:1–4:16; 4:17–16:20; 16:21–28:20), two on characters (Jesus, the disciples), and a final chapter on Matthew's community, the "real readers of Matthew" for whom the implied reader is "an index, even if only approximate" (120).

Evident in these two pioneering book-length narrative studies are five key features of narrative-critical work on Matthew.

UNIFIED COHERENT NARRATIVES

First, these studies emphasize an approach to Matthew that not only assumes but indeed values the unity of the flow and finished form of the Gospel. Kingsbury (1986) sets this commitment to the finished form of the narrative in contrastive relation to composition or redaction criticism concerned with the authorial editing or redacting of sources identified through comparative readings of the Gospel and its sources (Mark; Q; "M" material). In a subsequent study on Matthew's narrative portrait of disciples, Edwards (1997, 4–11) engages similar contrasts. In his 1990 discussion of narrative criticism, Powell distinguishes narrative criticism's focus on the current or finished form of the text from source, form, and redaction criticisms' interests in the process by which the text came into being (1990, 7). Similarly, in his narratively shaped study of Matthew, Carter (1996, 273–281) includes an appendix that set narrative approaches in contrastive relationship to redaction work.

LINEAR READING EXPERIENCE

Second, both Edwards and Kingsbury emphasize the linear reading experience that engages Matthew's Gospel through the sequence of its plot. Both Edwards and Kingsbury spend considerable space narrating this sequential reading experience through the Gospel from its beginning to its end. This emphasis on the sequential nature of the reading experience also contrasts with redaction criticism and its doubly awkward reading strategy. Redaction criticism required the reader to progress across a text by jumping from one textual change to another, ignoring the unchanged material in-between. And, second, it required the reader simultaneously to read horizontally and comparatively across the columns in a Gospel synopsis.

DIMENSIONS OF NARRATIVE

Third, both Edwards and Kingsbury focus attention on the formal dimensions of the narrative—its plot, characters, points of view, settings, and rhetoric—as the primary areas of attention for narrative-critical work. Subsequent discussions of narrative work have continued to emphasize the same features. Rhoads (1999, 265) draws these features together as comprising "the storyworld of the narrative," the analysis of which is the first task of narrative criticism. Book-length works on narrative criticism—that of Powell (1990) and Resseguie (2005)—and narrative analyses of Matthew (Anderson 1994; Carter 1996, 2004; Carter and Heil 1998; Powell 2009)—have continued to attend to these features, often structuring their discussions around chapter-length investigations of these dimensions. Studies have focused on rhetoric and point of view (Howell 1990, 161–203; Anderson 1994, 46–77; Black 2002; Carter 2004, 92–131), plot (Bauer 1988; Matera 1987; Howell 1990, 93–160; Carter 1992; Powell 1992; Anderson 1994, 133–191; Branden 2006), text segments (Bauer 1996), and characterizations (Anderson 1994, 78–132; Powell 1996; Weaver 1996; Edwards 1997; Yamasaki 1998; Brown 2002; Carter 2004, 167–227).

IMPLIED READERS

Fourth, narrative criticism has often employed a distinctive understanding of the gospel reader, notably that of the "implied reader." Powell argues that this notion of the implied reader is in fact the central feature of the "reading strategy" called narrative criticism. Powell (2011, 22–23) says, "The principles and procedures of narrative criticism are designed to answer one important question: How is the implied reader expected to respond to the text?" Significantly, Powell's question styles the implied reader as acted on by the text (rather than acting on the text) and as passively receptive to it.

Kingsbury (1986, 36–38) similarly defines his implied reader as one who denotes "no flesh-and-blood person of any century but an imaginary person who is to be envisaged . . . as responding to the text at every point with whatever emotion, understanding, or knowledge the text ideally calls for" (36). This textually constituted reader fulfills the intention of the text and comprehends the whole story. Kingsbury also emphasizes the effect of the text on this passively receptive, imaginary reader. So the author arranges the events of the plot and constructs characterization "so as to elicit from the reader some desired response" (2, cf. 9, 16–17, 33).

Edwards similarly distinguishes the real reader from an implied reader and chooses to read from the perspective of the latter as "the person posited *by the text* as the reader" (1985, 10; italics in the original). Edwards likewise posits a receptive, passive, nonactive implied reader on whom Matthew's Gospel has an "effect." This implied reader follows the sequence of the narrative, is impressed by the narrative, and "accepts the reliability of the narration." In a subsequent study, Edwards argues that "narrative criticism tries to answer the question, How has the hypothetical *implied reader* been informed, guided, or influenced by the story being told?" When the question is answered, the "intention of the implied author" can be "carefully uncovered" (Edwards 1997, 5). Edwards identifies this "implied reader" as the "text-connoted reader." While real readers might utilize data from outside the story to comprehend the narrative, the implied or text-connoted reader is influenced or informed only by data from the text's narrative world.

The identity of "the reader" in narrative criticism has developed somewhat in subsequent narrative work. In his survey, Powell (2011, 26–42) argues that narrative criticism has operated with three notions of the reader. One option seeks to read the text in relation to a reconstructed first-century reader or audience. Powell (26–32) claims that such reading is a means of discerning authorial intention. It should be said, however, that it is mistaken to claim that all concern with an "authorial audience" is an attempt to discern authorial intention. For some users, the term "authorial audience" (Carter 1994), is used to designate and locate an audience in a particular historical moment and cultural setting, in this case in the circumstances of the origin of the Gospels, the circumstances and time period an audience shares to a significant degree with the author. The term in this use has nothing to do with authorial intent but situates an audience as the context for the reconstructed reading. By contrast, one might choose a (reconstructed) sixth- or tenth- or sixteenth-century audience and investigate its reading of a Gospel.

Powell's second option is a text-oriented reader that continues the emphasis on the textually constructed implied reader evident in the approaches of Edwards and Kingsbury. A third option is reader-oriented narrative criticism. Powell claims that, in his own use of this approach, this reading strategy begins by establishing "expected" readings—essentially, it seems, using the text-oriented "implied reader" approach of the second option. Then attention is given to actual readings, and an attempt is made to account for the disparity between the actual and the "expected" readings of implied readers. We will return to Powell's approach later.

NARRATIVE AND HISTORICAL CRITICISMS

And fifth, narrative criticism has raised the issue of the relationship, if any, between narrative and historical criticisms. Edwards draws a strict line in attending only to the Gospel story and its narrative world. The implied reader, his "text-connoted" reader, does not pay any attention to "the historical background" or *Sitz im Leben* of the text (1997, 4–11). Edwards's approach is to see the Gospel text as an end in itself that creates its own autonomous narrative world. He does not attempt to look through, behind, or beyond the text of Matthew's Gospel to external historical knowledge or circumstances.

Edwards's approach that emphasizes Matthew's Gospel creating autonomous narrative worlds has perhaps been typical of how narrative approaches have addressed—or, more accurately, skirted—historical questions (Rhoads 1982, 413). But other exponents of narrative criticism have sought to connect narrative and historical approaches. Kingsbury, for example, begins in a place similar to that of Edwards with attention, as we noted earlier, to reading as the text-constructed, implied reader who fulfills perfectly whatever the text requires. But Kingsbury goes further, arguing that this implied reader and Matthew's narrative world function "as an index ... of the real readers" (1986, 120). This indexing happens by inferring from Matthew's narrative "the kind of things ... the events or circumstances" the implied reader "is expected to know." On this basis, Kingsbury (120–133) draws conclusions about Matthew's community or the original real readers of the Gospel: its constituency (Greek-speaking Jewish and Gentile Jesus followers c. 85–90 CE living in an urban context, such as Antioch of Syria); social standing (well-to-do in an urban area), social climate (intense conflict), and organization (a community or "brotherhood," with prophets and teachers but a strong communal ethos). While some of these conclusions raise the very debatable question of the Gospel's transparency and referentiality (do references to cities and high-value currency necessarily indicate a wealthy, urban audience?), the point here is to note Kingsbury's move to view the implied reader as an "index" of the real (original) readers.

Another attempt to draw narrative and historical approaches to Matthew together has used the notion of an "authorial audience" (Rabinowitz 1987; Carter 1994, 2004). This approach does not employ the notion of an implied reader. Rather, it recognizes the active role of an actual reader in interpreting the text and constructing historical and cultural contexts. This approach employs narrative categories in engaging the text—plot, characters, setting, points of view, rhetoric—but it recognizes the role of real readers or audiences in, for example, determining plots and building characters. It also employs historical criticism in recognizing in various ways that Matthew's Gospel came into being in particular historical-cultural circumstances that are assumed by, and relevant for understanding, the text. The notion of an "authorial audience" recognizes, not authorial intention, but the historical-cultural knowledge and experience that an audience located in the time, place, and circumstances of the Gospel's origin might be assumed to possess and supply in engaging the text. This approach posits that the audience's active supplying of appropriate knowledge is crucial to the reading experience, and that this knowledge is not only textual, as Edwards posits, but is also socio-historical, including the experience of hearing the text in oral-aural environment (Yamasaki 1998, 37–41). In this approach, interpreting Matthew's Gospel involves attempts to construct something of the assumed sociocultural knowledge that impacts the reading-hearing experience such as communal worship (Carter 1995), cultural codes (Carter 1994), previous traditions about Jesus (Carter 2004, 47–65), social conflicts (Carter 2004, 66–91), and daily life in negotiating the Roman empire (Carter 2000, 2001). This approach also recognizes that real interpreters/readers construct such knowledge and experience.

Evaluations

Subsequent discussions have raised questions about various aspects of these five features of narrative criticism (Rhoads 1999, 266–270). For example, Stephen Moore (1989, 53), influenced by narratology and deconstruction, has raised questions about the quest for narrative "wholeness and internal consistency" in the face of textual fragmentation, gaps, anomalies, surplus of meaning, and the uncontrollable nature of the act of interpretation. Matthew's narrative is not, he argues, so readily corralled into order and conformity; it is more diverse, unstable, multivalent, open-ended, and plural. This is not to say that readers do not seek or claim coherent readings, but it is to recognize the elusiveness of that unity and coherence and that readings claiming unity and coherency selectively set aside much that belies the claim. David Rhoads (1999, 268) remarks judiciously and modestly, "Narrative critics may show where they find the narrative to be coherent and at the same time be open to its lack of coherence *as a narrative*" (italics in the original).

Another aspect of Matthean narrative criticism that has raised considerable discussion concerns the role of history and historical criticism (Rhoads 1999, 268). Initial forays into narrative criticism caused considerable ripples throughout the academic guild. Some historical critics frequently dismissed Matthean narrative readings that did not engage historical matters as unworthy or even illegitimate, insisting that Matthew is a historically shaped Gospel that is to be examined only with form, source, or redaction criticisms. Others felt the sting of a narrative method and its exponents that seemed to have little regard for the conventional matters of history and that moved the focus of inquiry to the Gospel story and its settings, plots, points of view, characters, and rhetoric. Frequently, narrative criticism's textual focus was—and still is by some—understood to leave no place for any historical inquiry. Narrative critics who claim that Matthew creates an autonomous narrative world reinforce such views.

Yet others are able to reconcile historical and narrative criticisms by recognizing the historically conditioned and contextualized nature of the Gospel narrative. As an historical artifact, Matthew emerged from particular circumstances. It assumes of its readers/audiences' particular knowledge of cultural practices, societal structures, and historical events which historical investigation can elaborate or construct—to some extent—for readers/audiences of another historical era. Rhoads (1999, 268) observes, "More than ever, interpretations of the Gospel narratives are drawing upon our knowledge of the history, society and cultures of the first-century Mediterranean world *as a means to help us understand the story better.*"

Involved in these concerns with the unity and coherence of Matthew and of the relationship between narrative and historical approaches is a more fundamental issue— namely, the problematic notion of the implied reader with which some narrative criticism has operated. We noted above Powell's threefold categorizing of author-oriented, text-oriented, and reader-oriented narrative criticisms. At the heart of these classifications is, according to Powell, the central focus of narrative criticism on how the implied reader responds in an ideal manner to what Matthew's Gospel requires. This notion of the implied reader, I suggest, is problematic.

This implied reader, according to Powell (2011, 24), "receives the narrative in the manner that [this implied readership] would be expected to receive it, (2) knows everything that the reader of this story would be expected to know—but nothing else, and (3) believes everything the reader of this story is expected to believe—but nothing more." For Powell, this implied reader produces the expected readings invited by signals in the text. He does recognize a range of expected responses—some "polyvalence within these perimeters" (2011, 24)—but the recognition seems to play a minimal role. Powell in fact seems worried about both the possibility and actuality of multiple readings. His use of the implied reader has the merit, apparently, of economy in limiting the number of possible readings. "Otherwise, discussion about how readers respond to narratives would have to account for an infinite number of factors" (23).

Powell describes his reader-response narrative criticism of Matthew in a four-stage process. The first step involves identifying actual responses to the Gospel. The second involves establishing the expected response of the implied reader and comparing the responses of actual readers. The third step endeavors to account for the disparity between the actual responses and the expected responses. The fourth step concerns evaluating the expected and unexpected readings of actual readers. Powell describes this fourfold scheme as "basically a template for the use of narrative criticism" (2011, 40).

What is the point of such readings that attempt to discern "the expected response of the implied reader?" Powell offers two justifications. One is that "discerning the expected responses of the implied reader helps me to identify the factors that produce divergent readings." The second is that "I personally regard the New Testament Gospels as authoritative scripture, so I have theological reasons for wanting to know how readers are expected to respond to them" (40–41). Powell is confident that he can establish the reading expected of the implied reader and that he can align his reading with it, knowing that "the rhetoric is working as intended: I respond to the narrative as I do because I am following the text's signals" (41).

I will suggest, however, that these claims for narrative-critical work involving Matthew are most problematic. They assert and assume something that is not at all self-evident. Does an expected reading of Matthew's Gospel actually exist? Is the responding role of the implied reader so obvious and so monolithic? If so, who "expects" the expected reading? If Powell is creating the expected reading, then no wonder his own reading aligns with it as he "follows" (read, interprets) the text's signals. I suggest that the extensive and prolonged interpretive debates about Matthew's Gospel that have spanned the last two millennia indicate the falsity of claims that an "expected reading" exists. Such claims, in fact, mask the continuing and active interpretive work of real readers and actual interpreters.

Take, for example, the matter of Matthew's plot. Frank Matera (1987) proposed an analysis of Matthew's plot that employed Seymour Chatman's notion of kernels and satellites. Chatman argues that in any narrative all events are not created equal, that in the hierarchy of events there are significant events that are branching or turning points or events that move the action forward (which he calls "kernels"), and minor or lesser events (satellites) that elaborate or fill in the action. Matera identified six kernels: 2:1a, the birth of Jesus; 4:12–17, the beginning of Jesus's ministry; 11:2–6, the question of John the Baptist; 16:23–28 Jesus's conversation at Caesarea Philippi; 21:1–17, the cleansing of the temple; and 28:16–20, the great commission.

In a 1992 article, Carter (1992) evaluated Matera's proposal. He argued that it is Jesus's conception and commission (1:18–25), rather than his birth (a consequence and therefore a satellite), that is the action that gets the plot underway and so constitutes the first kernel. He also modified Matera's second kernel (4:12–17) agreeing that the commencement of Jesus's public ministry provides the second kernel but saying that the actual scene is 4:17–25. Carter agreed with Matera's third kernel (11:2–6) but disputed his fourth (16:13–28), arguing that it is not Peter's confession that moves the action forward but Jesus's announcement that he must go to Jerusalem and die (16:21–28). Carter extended Matera's fifth kernel from 21:1–17 to 21:1–27 on the basis that the inclusion of verses 23–27 makes explicit the section's concern not primarily with the temple but with Jesus's authority to act and teach as he does. He replaced Matera's sixth kernel (28:16–20) with 28:1–10, arguing that the resurrection moves the plot forward with 28:16–20, a satellite elaborating implications of the resurrection.

In the same year, Powell (1992) published his own analysis of Matthew's plot. Powell's approach does not draw on the "kernels-satellites" model used by Matera and Carter. Rather, he foregrounds the notion of conflict. He posits that Jesus is in conflict with the religious leaders who reject Jesus's authority, and with the disciples who reject his teaching of suffering and servanthood. These conflicts actually constitute the gospel's subplots with the plot comprising conflict between God, whose plan is to save people from their sins, and Satan.

Powell's analysis—which significantly resembles Rhoads and Michie's (1982) analysis of Mark—is by no means convincing. Is it accurate, for example, to claim a "conflict" between Jesus and the disciples or is it more accurate to observe a process of unlearning and learning as Jesus offers teaching that contests cultural practices? Likewise, the accuracy of naming "God vs. Satan" as the main conflict of the plot seems dubious given the lack of appearances and scenes involving both characters, let alone directly challenging one another. It seems more realistic to identify the oppositional positioning of God and Satan as one involving conflicting points of view. The crucial point, though, is that we have here three readings of Matthew's plot (Matera, Carter, Powell) that differ in approaches and analyses. How are we to determine the expected reading with which Powell is so concerned? Any of Matera, Carter, or Powell might claim that his is the expected reading but on what basis other than that it is his reading? How are we to know that the implied reader is receiving the narrative, to use Powell's words, in the expected manner? Does this formulation make much sense of interpretive activity and diversity?

The same questions arise around matters of character. Powell identifies one of his sub-plots as a conflict between Jesus and "the religious leaders." Presumably, Powell would claim this nomenclature as consonant with the implied reader's expected reading of the Gospel. Of course, the Gospel does not use this language, so it is immediately evident that its use by an interpreter signifies the construction of an interpretation. Carter's reading utilizes a quite different understanding informed by Josephus (*Ant* 20.249–51) and other studies (Saldarini) that the Jerusalem-based authorities in the Gospel—chief priests, Sadducees, scribes, Pharisees, Herodians—do not fit into an exclusively "religious" category akin to twenty-first century clergy. Such a division of "religious" and "political" is anachronistic to the first-century world from which the Gospel emerged. Rather, these groups are societal leaders who in the first-century context of a province under the control of the Roman empire exercise power in alliance—albeit contestive and tensive—with the Roman governor. They are societal leaders or authorities. An interpreter/reader can only maintain a "religious" reading of these figures as the "expected" reading of the apolitical "implied reader" if the interpreter/reader chooses to ignore the imperial realities of the world from which the text emerges and which it encodes. So what is an expected reading? Who determines it? Who decides the implied reader's reception?

Another example emerges around Matthew's scene involving Pilate and Jesus (27:11–26). What is the expected reading of this scene? Is it a matter of the Jewish "religious leaders" forcing the nice Pilate, against his will, into crucifying someone he thinks is innocent? Or is it a matter of elite ruling groups (Jerusalem leaders and the Roman governor) struggling with one another in tensive power relationships to assert their own advantage while simultaneously allying together to resist and destroy a non-elite figure who poses some challenge to their self-benefitting status quo? (Carter 2003). Of course, scholars have long ignored any imperial realities in their "expected readings" of the "religious" Gospel, so much so that Helen Bond can, incredibly, declare that Pilate retains his political "neutrality" in Matthew's scene—even while he exercises ultimate political power in enforcing the death penalty! (Bond, 133) What is the expected reading? Who decides the implied reader's reception of the text?

These examples—and they could be multiplied by appealing to interpretive debates about any aspect of Matthew's Gospel—are sufficient to highlight the limitations and arbitrary nature of claims of producing a reading in which the implied reader supposedly responds to the text in "expected" ways. None of these readings can live up to the postulated theoretical model of an expected reading of ideal implied readers. These examples show that claims of an expected reading fail to persuade. Perhaps such claims reflect a desire for an objectively verifiable reading of the Gospel against which other readings can be measured. Such claims may also be motivated—as they appear to be for Powell—by the desire to maintain the theological authority of the Gospels. But the long history of interpretive discussions about the Gospel point to another reality. Readings result from and reflect the constructive, interpretive work of interpreters. Maintaining the impression that somehow a narrative reading attentive to the plot, setting, characters, points of view, and rhetoric of a Gospel produces the expected reading of an ideal implied reader is an illusion that is best abandoned.

A Way Ahead: Real Readers Reading

Redaction criticism claimed that, by attending to redactional activity, it could produce definitive interpretations of authorial intent and audience circumstances. Multiple and conflicting interpretations of redactional activity and multiple claims about the situations supposedly being addressed showed that the method could not deliver what some promised. Similarly, narrative critical discussions have shown that claims to produce definitive readings of Matthew's Gospel—the expected readings of the ideal implied reader—are not tenable.

Is there a way ahead for narrative critical work on Matthew's Gospel?

One way ahead involves, first, the separation of the notion of "reading as the implied reader impacted by the text" from attention to narrative elements of Matthew's Gospel such as plot, characters, settings, rhetoric, and so on. The above discussion has shown that the first of these notions (implied reader) should be abandoned. Rhoads (1999, 269) remarks that "when narrative critics are constructing the reading experience of a hypothetical 'ideal reader' or ... possible ancient audiences, it is of course, the narrative critics themselves as readers who are constructing these imaginary reading experiences." Given that this is so, there is no need to maintain the facade of a supposedly objective "expected" reading behind which interpreters hide instead of claiming responsibility for their readings of the Gospel.

Second, a way ahead involves continued attention to the conventional narrative matters of Matthew's plot, characters, settings, points of view, rhetoric, and so on. Narrative criticism has helpfully highlighted these narrative features and drawn attention (with the assistance of reader-response work) to the reading experience. The key difference, though, is the recognition that real readers and actual interpreters, in dialogue with the text, construct readings of the plot, build characters, determine the significance of settings, identify points of view.

Third, freed from the distraction of "implied readers" and impossibly imagined ideal or "expected" readings, narrative criticism of Matthew's Gospel provides space for the interpretive activity and reading experience of diverse real readers and actual interpreters. Segovia (1995, 2000) identifies this space and approach as cultural or ideological criticism. Such readers do not merely respond passively to the Gospel and readily assume supposedly assigned roles. They are not merely acted on by the text as supposed "implied readers" are. Rather, real readers construct meanings as they interact with the Gospel text. They might be, for example, variously puzzled, inquisitive, accepting, resisting, bored, repelled or intrigued by it. They might form unities, and notice and fill gaps, or they might concern themselves with only an isolated section. Having social locations and agenda, they bring their own experiences, locations, investments, and questions to the Gospel. Not surprisingly, they produce diverse and creative, not monolithic, readings, constituting a situation of "radical plurality" as Segovia (1995, 4) names it. This foregrounding of real readers and their contexts and commitments welcomes rather than seeks to limit multiple voices from multiple locations, sexual and gender orientations, social level, and religious perspectives (Segovia 1995, 7–15).

Such a turn to real readers and alliance with ideological or cultural criticisms have exposed unacceptable and prejudiced anti-Jewish readings of Matthew (Levine 1996) as well as produced insightful readings of the Gospel employing postcolonial (Dube 2000, 127–195; Carter 2007; Segovia 2009), queer (Bohache), feminist (Levine 2001; Wainwright 2009), intertextual (Carter, 2001), and ecological perspectives (Wainwright 2010), among others. This work portends further insightful and exciting readings of Matthew from real readers.

References

Anderson, Janice Capel. 1994. *Matthew's Narrative Web: Over, and Over, and Over Again.* Journal for the Study of the New Testament Supplement Series 91. Sheffield, Yorkshire: JSOT Press.

Bauer, David R. 1988. *The Structure of Matthew's Gospel: A Study in Literary Design.* Journal for the Study of the New Testament Supplement Series 31. Sheffield, Yorkshire: Almond.

Bauer, David R. 1996. "The Literary and Theological Function of the Genealogy in Matthew's Gospel." In *Treasures New and Old: Contributions to Matthean Studies,* edited by David R. Bauer and Mark Allan Powell, 129–159. Society of Biblical Literature Symposium Series 1. Atlanta, GA: Scholars Press.

Black, Stephanie. 2002. *Sentence Conjunction in the Gospel of Matthew: kai, de, tote, gar, oun and Asyndeton in Narrative Discourse.* Journal for the Study of the New Testament Supplement Series 216. Sheffield, Yorkshire: Sheffield Academic Press.

Bohache, Thomas. 2000. "Matthew." In *The Queer Bible Commentary,* edited by Deryn Guest, 487–516. London: SCM Press.

Bond, Helen. 1998. *Pontius Pilate in History and Interpretation.* Cambridge: Cambridge University Press.

Branden, Robert Charles. 2006. *Satanic Conflict and the Plot of Matthew.* New York: Peter Lang.

Brown, Jeannine K. 2002. *The Disciples in Narrative Perspective: The Portrayal and Function of the Matthean Disciples.* Atlanta, GA: Society of Biblical Literature.

Carter, Warren. 1992. "Kernels and Narrative Blocks: The Structure of Matthew's Gospel." *Catholic Biblical Quarterly* 54: 463–481.

Carter, Warren. 1994. *Discipleship and Households: A Study of Matthew 19-20.* Journal for the Study of the New Testament Supplement Series 103. Sheffield, Yorkshire: JSOT Press.

Carter, Warren. 1995. "Recalling the Lord's Prayer: The Authorial Audience and Matthew's Prayer as Familiar Liturgical Experience." *Catholic Biblical Quarterly* 59: 514–530.

Carter, Warren. 1996. *Matthew: Storyteller, Interpreter, Evangelist.* 1st. ed. Peabody MA: Hendrickson.

Carter, Warren. 2000. *Matthew and the Margins: A Religious and Socio-Political Reading.* Maryknoll: Orbis Books.

Carter, Warren. 2001. *Matthew and Empire: Initial Explorations.* Harrisburg: Trinity Press International.

Carter, Warren. 2003. *Pontius Pilate: Portraits of a Roman Governor.* Interfaces. Collegeville, MN: Liturgical Press.

Carter, Warren. 2004. *Matthew: Storyteller, Interpreter, Evangelist.* 2nd ed. Peabody MA: Hendrickson.

Carter, Warren. 2007. "The Gospel of Matthew." In *A Postcolonial Commentary on the New Testament,* edited by Fernando Segovia and R. Sugirtharajah, 69–104. Louisville, KY: Westminster John Knox.

Carter, Warren, and John Paul Heil. 1998. *Matthew's Parables: Audience-Oriented Perspectives.* Catholic Biblical Quarterly Monograph Series 30. Washington DC: Catholic Biblical Association.

Culpepper, R. Alan. 1983. *Anatomy of the Fourth Gospel: A Study in Literary Design.* Philadelphia, PA: Fortress.

Dube, Musa W. 2000. *Postcolonial Feminist Interpretation of the Bible.* St. Louis, MO: Chalice.

Edwards, Richard A. 1985. *Matthew's Story of Jesus.* Philadelphia, PA: Fortress.

Edwards, Richard A. 1997. *Matthew's Narrative Portrait of Disciples: How the Text-Connoted Reader Is Informed.* Harrisburg: Trinity Press International.

Howell, David. 1990. *Matthew's Inclusive Story: A Study in the Narrative Rhetoric of the First Gospel.* Journal for the Study of the New Testament Supplement Series 42. Sheffield, Yorkshire: JSOT Press.

Kingsbury, Jack Dean. 1986. *Matthew as Story.* Philadelphia, PA: Fortress.

Levine, Amy-Jill. 1996. "Discharging Responsibility: Matthean Jesus, Biblical Law, and Hemorrhaging Woman." In *Treasures New and Old: Contributions to Matthean Studies,* edited by David R. Bauer and Mark Allan Powell, 379–397. Society of Biblical Literature Symposium Series 1: Atlanta, GA: Scholars Press.

Levine, Amy-Jill, ed. 2001. *A Feminist Companion to Matthew.* Sheffield, Yorkshire: Sheffield Academic Press.

Matera, Frank. 1987. "The Plot of Matthew's Gospel." *Catholic Biblical Quarterly* 49: 233–253.

Moore, Stephen. 1989. *Literary Criticism and the Gospels: The Theoretical Challenge.* New Haven, CT: Yale University Press.

Moore, Stephen. 2011. "Why There Are No Humans or Animals in the Gospel of Mark." In *Mark as Story: Retrospect and Prospect,* edited by Kelly R. Iverson and Christopher Skinner, 71–93. Atlanta, GA: Society of Biblical Literature.

Powell, Mark Allan. 1990. *What Is Narrative Criticism?* Minneapolis, MN: Fortress.

Powell, Mark Allan. 1992. "The Plot and Subplots of Matthew's Gospel." *New Testament Studies* 38: 187–204.

Powell, Mark Allan. 1996. "Characterization on the Phraseological Plane in the Gospel of Matthew." In *Treasures New and Old: Contributions to Matthean Studies,* edited by David R. Bauer and Mark Allan Powell, 161–177. Society of Biblical Literature Symposium Series 1: Atlanta, GA: Scholars Press.

Powell, Mark Allan. 2009. "Literary Approaches and the Gospel of Matthew." In *Methods for Matthew,* edited by Mark Allan Powell, 44–82. Cambridge: Cambridge University Press.

Powell, Mark Allan. 2011. "Narrative Criticism: The Emergence of a Prominent Reading Strategy." In *Mark as Story: Retrospect and Prospect,* edited by Kelly R. Iverson and Christopher Skinner, 19–43. Atlanta, GA: Society of Biblical Literature.

Rabinowitz, Peter J. 1987. *Before Reading: Narrative Conventions and the Politics of Interpretation.* Amherst: University of Massachusetts Press.

Resseguie, James. 2005. *Narrative Criticism of the New Testament: An Introduction.* Grand Rapids, MI: Baker Academic.

Rhoads, David. 1982. "Narrative Criticism and the Gospel of Mark." *Journal of the American Academy of Religion* 50: 411–426.

Rhoads, David. 1999. "Narrative Criticism: Practices and Prospects." In *Characterization in the Gospels: Reconceiving Narrative Criticism,* edited by David Rhoads and Kari Syreeni, 264–285. Journal for the Study of the New Testament Supplement Series 184. Sheffield, Yorkshire: Sheffield Academic Press.

Rhoads, David, and Donald Michie. 1982. *Mark as Story: An Introduction to the Narrative of a Gospel*. Philadelphia, PA: Fortress.

Saldarini, Anthony J. 2001. *Pharisees, Scribes and Sadducees in Palestinian Society: A Sociological Approach*. Grand Rapids, MI: Eerdmans.

Segovia, Fernando F. 1995. "Cultural Studies and Contemporary Biblical Criticism: Ideological Criticism as Mode of Discourse." In *Reading from This Place*, vol. 2 of *Social Location and Biblical Interpretation in Global Perspective*, edited by Fernando F. Segovia and Mary Ann Tolbert, 1–32. Minneapolis, MN: Fortress.

Segovia, Fernando F. 2000. *Decolonizing Biblical Studies: A View from the Margins*. Maryknoll, NY: Orbis Books.

Segovia, Fernando F. 2009. "Postcolonial Criticism and the Gospel of Matthew." In *Methods for Matthew*, edited by Mark Allan Powell, 194–237. Cambridge: Cambridge University Press.

Skinner, Christopher. 2011. "Telling the Story: The Appearance and Impact of *Mark as Story*." In *Mark as Story: Retrospect and Prospect*, edited by Kelly R. Iverson and Christopher Skinner, 1–16. Atlanta, GA: Society of Biblical Literature.

Wainwright, Elaine M. 2009. "Feminist Criticism and the Gospel of Matthew." In *Methods for Matthew*, edited by Mark Allan Powell, 83–117. Cambridge: Cambridge University Press.

Wainwright, Elaine M. 2010. "Place, Power and Potentiality: Reading Matthew 2:1-12 Ecologically." *Expository Times* 121: 159–167.

Weaver, Dorothy J. 1996. "Power and Powerlessness: Matthew's Use of Irony in the Portrayal of Political Leaders." In *Treasures New and Old: Contributions to Matthean Studies*, edited by David R. Bauer and Mark Allan Powell, 129–159. Society of Biblical Literature Symposium Series 1: Atlanta, GA: Scholars Press.

Yamasaki, Gary. 1998. *John the Baptist in Life and Death: Audience-Oriented Criticism of Matthew's Narrative*. Journal for the Study of the New Testament Supplement Series 167. Sheffield, Yorkshire: Sheffield Academic Press.

CHAPTER 27

WITNESSES FOR THE DEFENSE IN THE GOSPEL OF LUKE

ABRAHAM SMITH

INTRODUCTION

WHETHER the Gospel of Luke and the book of Acts should be read sequentially as a two-volume work (a la Luke-Acts) or simply as two individual works written by the same author (a la the Gospel of Luke and the book of Acts) is a debated matter (Parsons and Pervo 1993; Gregory and Rowe 2010). What seems clearer, though, is that both works deploy "witness" terminology (e.g., witness [*martus*], testify [*martureō*], testimony [*marturia*], eyewitness [*autoptai*]), as if witnessing is a critical theme. In Acts, not only are the "apostles" described as witnesses (Acts 1:8; 1:22; 2:32; 3:15; 5:32; 10:39, 41; 13:31; cf. 4:33), but other characters in the story, such as Saul/Paul (22:15; cf. 20:26; 22:18; 23:11; 26:16, 22) and Stephen (22:20), also bear this description (cf. Trites 1974). Even the Holy Spirit, which is given to obeying believers, is described as a witness (5:32). All such witnesses are so described because they have seen or heard something about the basic truth of the prophetic movement of which they are a part from its beginnings and beyond (cf. Acts 1:22; 4:19, 20; 22:15).

In the Gospel of Luke, the story's preface or opening (1:1–4) mentions those who from the beginning were "eyewitnesses (*autoptai*) and ministers of the word." The Lukan author (whose identity also remains debated) deems such "eyewitnesses and ministers of the word" as important for passing on "the things [presumably about Christ or his prophetic movement] that have been fulfilled" (1:2).[1] Furthermore, in words apparently directed to the post-narrative historical circumstances of the Gospel's earliest auditors, the Lukan Jesus foretells a time when his followers will have an opportunity to give a testimony (*marturion*) before kings and governors, Rome's imperial representatives (21:12–19; cf. 12:11). In his closing statements in the Gospel of Luke, moreover, Jesus also predicts that his followers will be witnesses (*martures*) of everything that happened to him (24:48). Presumably, then, witnessing entails (1) speaking what has been seen or heard of God's continuing story of salvation as demonstrated through John, Jesus, and the latter's prophetic movement; and (2) speaking either in the context of duress, such as at a trial before Rome's representatives, or as a part of a larger goal of open proclamation to all the nations (24:47). Given that the Gospel of Luke and the book of Acts precisely seek to relate what has happened to John, Jesus, or to the latter's larger prophetic movement, both works are themselves, then, documentations of the larger witnessing process that the two works attempt to explain. Those who hear the Gospel of Luke and the book of Acts thus have an opportunity to be shaped or formed as witnesses themselves. As John A. Darr (1994, 87) has stated, "[T]he primary purpose of Luke-Acts is to form its readers [or auditors] into ideal witnesses of and to sacred history."

Yet, what does the Gospel seek to defend? The Gospel of Luke seeks to argue with *certainty* (*asphaleian*; 1:4) that the heroic figure Jesus, though humiliated through crucifixion, is yet the primary agent of Israel's restoration and of the deity's universal plan of salvation. In an imperial world in which the earliest auditors may have been influenced by a "politics of respectability" (Higginbotham 1993, 185–229), moreover, the Gospel offers certainty that Jesus's movement has not ended in shame and failure. Although the Gospel repeatedly speaks of scenes of shame and humiliation—from the perceived shame and humiliated distress of Elizabeth and Mary (1:25, 52), respectively, to the reproach that the disciples could expect as Jesus's followers (6:22; cf. 21:12) to the assorted rituals of humiliation that attend Jesus's crucifixion (23:16, 33, 35; cf.18:32)—the Gospel argues that Jesus's prophetic movement is ultimately *not* one of failure. His movement goes on both because God vindicated him through resurrection and his followers are ready to be witnesses to all the nations in accordance with scripture (24:45–48).

Five "Looks" at the Lukan Author

Today's interpreters are not furnished with backflap blurbs that summarize the Gospel's content or explain its impact on Luke's earliest auditors. We, therefore, have to learn how to hear the Gospel and its defense in its imperial setting. The approach taken here is to offer a plausible audience-oriented narrative critical reading of the Gospel's defense. For some perspective, a few initial words are in order about the methodological prisms or "looks" through which critical biblical scholars have understood the role of the Lukan author. So, while some scholars have read the Lukan author largely as a historian or as a theologian, this essay appreciates that author as a literary artist negotiating respectability in imperial times. Then, the essay offers a reading of the whole of the Third Gospel as an insiders' document. That document, cast in a biographical format, repeatedly seeks to rehabilitate the image of Jesus and his prophetic movement.

Since the dawn of biblical criticism in the modern period, interpreters have taken at least five "looks" at the Lukan author. Most scholars of the nineteenth century and, roughly, the first half of the twentieth century understood the Lukan author to be a historian (van Unnik 1980, 19). Within this period, only a few scholars (for example, B.H. Streeter 1925, 548; Henry Cadbury 1920; 1927) gave a nod to Luke's literary features. Thus, until the "new look" that came with redaction criticism in the 1950s, most Lukan scholars examined Luke atomistically for historical information either on the historical Jesus or on the precompositional oral transmission period as developed by form critics (van Unnik 1980, 16). The "new look" or the view of the Lukan author as a "theologian" was a part of a great post–WW II "storm center" in Lukan studies (van Unnik 1980, 16; Talbert 1981, 197). While redaction criticism's interest in compositional criticism focused on narrative features of the Third Gospel, this "new look" could not give full attention to Luke's artistry because redaction criticism's prism also had the goal of determining the historical contours of a so-called Lukan community. That is, the "new look" presupposed that Luke's redaction of earlier sources revealed a theological agenda addressed to a specific, local community (Conzelmann 1961).

A third "look" and a fourth "look" would follow the "new look" as Lukan scholars viewed the Lukan author, respectively, as a *literary artist* and as a *reflector* of the social conventions of the first-century CE world. Thus, the "third look," introduced with a literary critical prism, at first demonstrated independently the formal aesthetics of the Third Gospel (Petersen 1978; Tannehill 1986; Dawsey 1986; Brawley 1990), and, later, the ways in which Lukan aesthetics likely affected its earliest audiences (Darr 1990; Roth 1997; Spencer 2007). Some works deployed this prism creatively with redaction criticism and with "gender as an analytic category" (Seim 1994, 10; Corley 1993). The "fourth look," introduced with a sociocultural critical prism, featured the Lukan author's appropriation or critique presumably of a variety of ancient social conventions, such as prevailing notions of prestige or esteem in the eyes of one's peers, the infrastructure of slavery, expectations of reciprocity in the patron-client system of relations, and the hospitality customs that governed how people dined and with whom they ate (Danker 1982; Esler 1987; Neyrey 1991; Braun 1995; Smith 2007).

The fifth "look" is sometimes donned as an "empire-critical" prism because it seeks explicitly to assess how the Lukan author responded to its imperial times. In a recent "empire-critical" work, for example, Yong-Sung Ahn (2006, 74) critiques a brand of Lukan scholarship that both advocates a "religion–politics" divide in the first-century CE world and simplistically asserts—as did Hans Conzelmann—that the Lukan author accommodated to the Roman Empire. At the same time, Ahn (2006, 74) questions whether it is possible to say that Luke in every instance was "anti-Roman." This type of scholarship, then, particularly when informed by postcolonial criticism's examination of the historical and discursive effects of colonization, seeks to read the Third Gospel as a strategic response to the power complexes of the Lukan author's time. The expression "empire-critical," then, need not refer to the Third Gospel as either a pro-imperial or anti-imperial document. The *critical* dimension is simply an informed and often interdisciplinary optic for understanding the power complexes of an imperial society (Edwards 1996).

Given these five "looks," or prisms, the proposed audience-oriented narrative critical reading of the Third Gospel's defense seeks to offer a plausible yet provisional thesis on how Luke's earliest auditors likely understood the Gospel's defense as a story that could have brought respectability to Jesus's prophetic movement. The interpretive model developed here, moreover, benefits greatly from audience-oriented theories: H. R. Jauss's emphasis on given readers' "horizon of expectation"; Wolfgang Iser's phenomenological reading theory on a given text's repertoires; and Peter Rabinowitz's concept of an "authorial audience."

According to Jauss's theory, today's interpreters may be able to imaginatively yet plausibly reconstruct the "horizon of expectation" (a.k.a. *Erwartungshorizont*) that given readers or hearers had when they first read or heard a given text, especially through a reconstruction of the literary environment "which the author could expect his contemporary public to know either explicitly or implicitly" (Jauss 1982, 18–19). The concept of an "horizon of expectation" is thus critical because, at least theoretically, it helps interpreters to establish some distance between their own time and a much earlier period of time, such as the time when Luke's earliest auditors would likely have heard the Third Gospel. While interpreters today may have substantial information at their disposal or the luxury of processing meaning, we cannot possibly project all of what we know upon Luke's earliest auditors. At the same time, if we are truly interested in the horizon of expectation of such auditors and readers, we cannot read these texts as if they were politically innocuous. Certainly, in the case of the Third Gospel, too much is said about Rome's representatives—from emperors to Rome's "friendly" rulers to provincial governors—to read the Gospel of Luke as if its auditors would not have reflected on their circumstances relative to the power complexes of their imperial society.

Iser's (1980, 178) theory argues that gaps in the reading or the hearing of a narrative must be filled in, with varying degrees of flexibility, in order to actualize a story and to create a mental image of characters or character groups. Guiding such textual actualization in Iser's theory if not always in his practice, moreover, is a text's repertoires or those "familiar literary patterns and recurrent literary themes, together with allusions to familiar social and historical contexts" (Iser 1974, 288). Repertoires then may be intratextual (based on the progressive constellation of previous textual information, such as Luke's patterns of repetition), intertextual (based on a set of literary expectations shared between an author and an audience, such as Luke's use of topoi from the biographical genre), or extratextual (based on a given text's allusions to external stocks of knowledge, such as Luke's assumptions about how respectability is gained). With respect to respectability, for example, the Gospel appears to assume from an extratextual repertoire that respectability is typically enhanced through a venerable ancestral past, virtuous (and divinely authorized) practices, and a valiant and consistent posture in the face of suffering and death. These and any other repertoires, though, are not static directions for reading or hearing texts. Rather, in every instance, they are constructed by interpreters and subject to scrutiny based on varying degrees of open, public, and accessible notions of interpretive plausibility.

Finally, Rabinowitz (1977, 126) provides the concept of an "authorial audience," a hypothetical construct of the audience that an author was likely to have had in mind when composing a work. Thus, the term "authorial audience" offers a heuristic construct for the effort to apprise oneself of the horizon of expectation of Luke's earliest auditors. In the reading of the Gospel that follows, then, we will seek to join such an audience to hear more carefully the whole of the Third Gospel's defense.

HEARING THE WHOLE GOSPEL'S DEFENSE IN AN IMPERIAL CONTEXT

To hear the Third Gospel's defense, we must first acknowledge to whom the defense would have been directed in the "horizon of expectations" of Luke's earliest auditors. Luke's theme of witnessing should not make interpreters think that the Gospel's defense is for an external party. Neither the Gospel of Luke nor the book of Acts is a defense *for Rome* as some early modern interpreters once argued (Maddox 1982; Walasky 1983). Nor do these two works establish a defense for Paul or for the church *to Rome*. Rome and its representatives are not consistently portrayed in positive ways. Paul is not the subject of the Gospel of Luke, nor is he the key protagonist in the first twelve chapters of Acts. Furthermore, the church does not offer an apology to Rome or a case for the political innocence of Jesus or of his followers as if Roman officials would be interested in hearing a reading of either work to find the remnants of an apology (on Lukan apologetics, see, further, Neagoe 2002). The rhetoric of both works, moreover, is directed to insiders who would have known the Septuagint (LXX) well enough to appreciate the Third Gospel's multiple citations and allusions to the LXX (particularly to Isaiah; cf. Mallen 2008).

Even so, the Gospel also is not written to settle an apologetic for an intragroup debate (Tiede 1972). Rather, both works appear to be written against the perception of failure. A perennial problem for early Christianity was that of social criticism and ostracization. While Celsus, Lucian and other writers traded barbs against Christianity in the second century CE, others had likely charged the movement with such polemics in the first century CE. Some of the charges, which often had more hyperbole than truth, castigated Christianity as "a lower class movement . . . as uneducated and socially insignificant, if not downright irresponsible or dangerous" (Malherbe 1985, 196). Worst of all perhaps was the problem for Christians of explaining the ignominious death of their founder, Jesus. In a world where the perception of others is always foremost (Lendon 1997, 37), how could the early Christians explain the horrendous death of Jesus, that is, death by crucifixion? The quandary then was one of respectability. How could Christians explain the slave-like death of their kingly leader? How could the early Christians talk about the greatness of their movement and its leader vis-à-vis other complexes of power, including the larger sphere of Judaism (of which early Christianity was a subset) and even the larger world dominated by Rome? How could the early Christians respond to social criticism with any sense of confidence and assurance? Accordingly, both the Gospel of Luke and Acts were written to provide a basic story or foundational narrative for those who would have been instructed (or catechized, [katēchēthēs]) so that they might know the certainty of the things that they were taught (Luke 1:4; cf. Neagoe 2002, 16). Thus, the defense is not for *outsiders*; as a defense of the Christian christological proclamation and of Jesus's prophetic movement, the Gospel is a defense for *insiders* as symbolically represented by Theophilus, the Lukan addressee (1:3; Acts 1:1; cf. Johnson 1991, 9).

Furthermore, to hear the Third Gospel's defense, we must also hear some of the repertoires or conventions that Luke's earliest audience would likely have heard. At least two conventions would have assisted Luke's auditors. *First*, the audience would likely have heard the Gospel as a *full* biography with a *popular* style and Socratic themes. If one presupposes Markan priority (that Mark was written first and that Luke and Matthew drew on Mark), Luke's Gospel, to use the terms of Tomas Hägg (2012, ix), reconfigures Mark's *professional* biography (a biography that features the adult or professional life of a legendary or historical hero) into a *full* biography (a biography that traces the life of a legendary or historical hero from ancestry and formative years to the end of life).

Yet, Luke—like the other canonical gospels—does not match the refined aesthetics of the prototypical biographical works written by Suetonius (late first century CE) and Plutarch (early second century CE). Instead, in its style, Luke is a *popular* biography.[2] So, while its formal preface (1:1–4) displays a Greek that exploits nicely balanced clauses, Luke's Greek in 1:5–2:52 is more similar to the Greek of the LXX, while its Greek in 3:1–24:53 is largely a common (*koiné*) or marketplace Greek.

As a popular work, moreover, the Gospel of Luke seems to cohere with intertextual popular traditions or themes that defended valiant Socrates as "the prototypical philosophic-hero" (Spencer 2008, 50). Those popular traditions included, for example: "[Socrates's] divine call ([through a] Delphic oracle), teaching mission, and a series of unjust trials leading to imprisonment and martyrdom" (Spencer 2008, 50; Alexander 1993, 31–64). Such a schema is remarkably close to Luke's presentation of Jesus in the Gospel of Luke. So, even while Luke presents Jesus as a prophet, the Third Gospel also presents him as a philosopher type on the order of Socrates. Like Socrates (cf. *Crito*, 43b, 43d, 44a), for example, Jesus repeatedly uses the impersonal verb *dei* (it is necessary) to refer to the presence of a divine imperative throughout his life (2:49; 4:43; 9:22; 13:33; 17:25; 19:5; 22:37; 24:7, 44). Furthermore, as Greg Sterling (2001, 395–400) has argued, it is possible to read the death of Jesus in Luke in light of the *mors philosophi* (the death of a philosopher), particularly when one notes similarities between Socratic traditions and the Jewish proto-martyrological traditions, on the one hand, and Luke's construction of Jesus as a calm, innocent, and paradigmatic figure in the face of death on the other. Those early Lukan auditors seeking to make sense of the ignominious way in which Jesus died, then, could take solace in the depiction of Jesus as an innocent/ righteous hero, as a man who—like Socrates—faced unjust suffering and death in a dauntless, resolute, and calm manner (cf. Plato, *Apology* 28b, 38d–e; *Phaedo* 68c–d, 117c; Luke 23). Far from being a failure, moreover, his movement—as with Socrates's successors—continues to make an impact on society. Through his witnessing successors, Jesus's prophetic message potentially will go to all the nations (24:47–48).

Second, Luke's earliest auditors would likely have heard the acoustical arrangement or sequential and cumulative development of Luke's Gospel. That is, a case could be made that the appearance of parallels or synkrises (comparison or contrasts) in the initial collection of anecdotes in 1:5–2:52 would have served as an intratextual repertoire for the subsequent anecdotes in the rest of the Gospel as well. So, if one joins Luke's authorial audience and hears the multiple parallels in Luke's description of John and Jesus in 1:5–2:52, a door is opened for reading or hearing the whole of 3:1–24:53 as yet another synkrisis (Edwards 1981, 17; Fitzmyer 1981, 313–315; Kodell 1987, 417; Brown 1993, 250).

Accordingly, the whole of the Gospel of Luke could be read as a formal preface (1:1–4) and three synkrises (1:5–56; 1:57–2:52; 3:1–24:53). In the first synkrisis between John and Jesus (1:5–56), Luke features the announcement of heroic (prophetic) births and subsequent conceptions and statements of praise. Similarly, in the second synkrisis (1:57–2:52), Luke charts the birth and early life of both heroes (prophets). As a part of Luke's full biography, moreover, the first two synkrises strategically link Jesus's prophetic movement to antiquity, one of the well-known means through which ancient groups enhanced their respectability (Edwards 1996, 28–48; Macmullen 1981, 2–4; Bowie 1974, 166–209). So, for example, while some interpreters may read Luke's account of the census (Luke 2:1–5) as a sign of political innocence or obedience to the Roman imperial order, Luke's own marked emphasis on the census's first occurrence is narrated in a context in which Luke mentions Bethlehem as the venerable city of David. In its Septuagint style and its typological portraits of John and Jesus as Septuagint prophets, moreover, Luke 1:5–2:52 repeatedly connects John and Jesus solidly to an ancient prophetic past. Such a contrast between the relatively recent power of Rome and the venerable lineage of Joseph could have been heard subversively then, especially in a narrative context in which Luke also speaks about the promises of God made long ago to Abraham (1:55, 73).

In the third synkrisis (3:1–24:53), Luke shifts to the adult ministries of the two prophets, with details about the beginning, the growth, and the ending stages of those ministries. Each heroic figure begins his ministry in association with Isaianic declarations of the deity's universal salvation. While describing the opening of John's prophetic ministry of proclamation (3:1–6), for example, the narrator cites Isaiah 40:3–5, including the lines "all flesh shall see the salvation of God." In the opening of Jesus's prophetic ministry (3:23–4:44), Jesus's identity is confirmed as the Son of God through a genealogy (3:23–38) and a debate with the devil (4:1–13). Center stage is given, though, to what many scholars view as a programmatic statement on Jesus's ministry (4:16–30). That programmatic statement, which was also based on Isaianic texts (Isa. 61:1–2; 58:6), informs the authorial audience of the continuing role of the Spirit in Jesus's life and of the virtuous practices of beneficence (such as offering good news to the poor, sight to the blind, or "release" [aphesin] to captives) for which Jesus was sent. Furthermore, Jesus himself interprets those texts in an inclusive way (see, further, Garrett 1989).

In the middle part of John's ministry (3:7–17), auditors hear about John's teaching mission. That is, John speaks to variegated groups on practices of social justice toward others, including society's disenfranchised. Similarly, in the middle part of Jesus's ministry (5:18–30), auditors hear about Jesus's teaching mission, particularly as he calls, catechizes (or trains), and commissions disciples to follow his prophetic ideals of open commensality and unguarded hospitality toward all, including society's disenfranchised. Many of his parables in this part of the Gospel reveal, moreover, the deity's favorable regard for those otherwise marginalized by polite society: those who could not participate in elitist gift-exchanges (14:12–24); those who—though penitent—were often swallowed up in distancing polemical labels, such as the word "sinners" (15:3–32); those who were destitute like Lazarus (16:19–31); those who were vulnerable like some widows (18:2–5); and those who—like toll collectors—were ostracized because their occupations supported Rome's colonial bureaucracy (18:10–13).

The ending of John's ministry (3:18–22) is consistent with its beginning, for John continues his role as a proclaimer (3:18; cf. 3:3), though he is ultimately opposed by Herod Antipas, one of Rome's representatives. Even with the opposition, though, John's ministry is vindicated through a prophetic succession motif. That is, John is followed by the rise of another prophet—namely, Jesus. By noting the eclipse of John at the Jordan and the presence of the Spirit descending on Jesus (3:22), the narrator marks Jesus, in the tradition of Elijah and Elisha (2 Kings 2), as John's successor. Likewise, the ending of Jesus's ministry (18:31–24:53) is consistent with the way it begins. He continues to offer sight (18:35–43) and good news (20:1). As demonstrated through the parable of the tenants, moreover, he remains God's son (20:9–15). Now, though, he is not rejected at Nazareth but by many in Jerusalem, especially the Sanhedrin and two of Rome's representatives, Pilate and Herod. Yet, he remains valiant and as true to his convictions as did Socrates. As with John, moreover, Jesus's vindication is revealed through a prophetic succession motif. That is, the ending of Luke's gospel depicts Jesus's departure or assumption into heaven after the impartation of a blessing—again within the Elijah-Elisha tradition—to his own successors (24:50–53; cf. Talbert 1975). That Jesus is both raised by God and ascends, moreover, suggests God's vindication of Jesus despite the injustice of his trial and the shame of his crucifixion (cf. 24:26, 46–47).

The upshot of the third synkrisis, then, is that John and Jesus are presented as Septuagint-like prophets who offered the deity's beneficence in word or deed to all despite horrific and shameful results—arrests and ultimately dysphoric deaths. The depiction of the two prophets offering the deity's *universal* salvation also had rhetorical caché in ancient society. In its propaganda treatises, for example, Rome prided itself as being "an empire without end" (*Aeneid* 1.333–334) extending salvation (or liberation and beneficence) to all. Virgil depicts its first emperor, Augustus, moreover, as the long-expected restorer of peace (*Aeneid* 1.342–355; Livy, *Ab Urbe Condita* 1.1–2.6; cf. Squires 1993, 41). By contrast, the Lukan author lauds Jerusalem as a "powerful geographical symbol" from which Jesus's prophetic movement will go out to reach the *oikumene* (Luke 24:47 and all of Acts; cf. Edwards 1996, 72). Furthermore, for Luke, only Jesus is Savior (2:11), God's salvation "prepared for all persons" (2:30), and "a light for the revelation of the nations and glory for [God's] people, Israel" (2:32).

ASSESSING THE DEFENSE TODAY

If this chapter's hearing of the Gospel's defense is plausible, then, joining Luke's authorial audience presents a challenge for readers today. On the one hand, as a sample of subversive literature from the ancient world, Luke's Gospel models how communities can re-create, through narrative, their self-images and reimagine their futures. If, as is argued here, Luke's earliest auditors were a minoritized group, then such a group needed certainty. It faced the serious public relations problem of a crucified Messiah as the leader of a prophetic movement. Luke's story therefore negotiated a politics of respectability for a minoritized movement within the various "webs of power" that intertwined at the "local, regional, imperial, and cosmic" levels of the ancient world (Edwards 1996, 72). In so doing, Luke thus mimicked "empire" (cf. Bhabha 1994, 86). Luke appealed to conventions that could rehabilitate the image of Jesus and his prophetic successors. As the chapter has shown, moreover, a key element of the image makeover was a presentation of Jesus's prophetic movement in the form of benefactors offering a universal salvation. Furthermore, Luke's emphasis on cosmopolitan beneficence could be construed as a claim in competition with the Roman Empire's own claims of worldwide benefaction, voicing, as it were, an alternative and subtly subversive world vision.

On the other hand, when removed from the minoritized context, Luke's claim carries certain dangers. Constructed on a dichotomy that asymmetrically pits one group deemed as superior against another group deemed as inferior, Luke's narrative "witness for the defense" provides the basic scaffolding for subsequent colonizers informed by this gospel to construct themselves as superior to those they colonize. Such colonizers can easily understand themselves to be appointed by the deity to bring "light" to benighted "others," others who—in the colonizers' estimation—are "sitting in darkness" (1:79).[3] Furthermore, if Jesus's status is gained through a venerable past that features an agnatic (male) line of descent, as in the genealogy of 3:23–38), a second danger of Luke's story is that its description of Jesus's status endorses an androcentric model of ancestry (on such a model, see Bernstein 2003, 354; cf. Kelso on Chronicles in this volume). Here, though, the Lukan aside "as it was supposed" (3:23) attenuates the typical androcentric force of heroic genealogies. So, given the narrative's earlier emphasis on Mary as a virgin (1:26–27), today's interpreters may be able to see competing gender ideologies in the narrative. Finally, if today's interpreters are ethically informed by (dis)ability studies, we would likely also find Luke's premium on "seeing" and "hearing" problematic. While the excessive use of these two sensory metaphors likely helped the early Christians to show the public and open character of their movement and thus avoid the stigma associated with clandestine movements of that day, such a premium is built on an "ideology of normalcy" (Betcher 2004, 82). Luke's witness for the defense, then, has remarkable capacities both to galvanize and to splinter the very audience it summons to render judgment.

NOTES

1. Throughout the essay, I use "Luke" as a shorthand for the writer of the Third Gospel, but not to suggest that a "Luke" was the real author or to suggest that we may recover the real author's intentions.
2. Another example of a popular yet full biography is the pseudo-Herodotean biography of Homer. Among the professional lives, the *Life of Aesop* was also written at this popular level. Many of these popular works deployed *koiné* (common, marketplace) Greek, a simple vocabulary, and a paratactic style (literally meaning a side-by-side ordering of episodes), with a relative preference for coordinating conjunctions, such as *kai* (and), as opposed to the subordinating conjunctions that characterized the more refined prose of the day (Tolbert 1996, 68).
3. On asymmetrical dichotomies, such as light and darkness imagery, see Elbarbary (1993, 113–128); Brantlinger (1985, 166–203).

REFERENCES

Ahn, Yong-Sung. 2006. *The Reign of God and Rome in Luke's Passion Narrative: An East Asian Global Perspective*. London: Brill Press.

Alexander, Loveday. 1993. "Acts and Ancient Intellectual Biography." In *The Book of Acts in Its Ancient Literary Setting*, edited by Bruce W. Winter and Andrew D. Clarke, 31–64. Grand Rapids, MI: Eerdmans.

Bernstein, Neil W. 2003. "Ancestors, Status, and Self-Presentation in Statius' *Thebaid*." *Transactions of the American Philological Association* 133: 353–379.

Betcher, Sharon. 2004. "Monstrosities, Miracles, and Mission: Religion and the Politics of Disablement." In *Postcolonial Theologies: Divinity and Empire*, edited by Catherine Keller, Michael Nausner, and Mayra Rivera, 79–99. St. Louis, MO: Chalice Press.

Bhabha, Homi.1994. *Location of Cultures*. New York: Routledge.

Bowie, E. L. 1974. "Greeks and Their Past in the Second Sophistic." In *Studies in Ancient Society*, edited by M. J. Finley, 166–209. Boston: Routledge and Kegan Paul.

Brantlinger, Patrick. 1985. "Victorians and Africans: The Genealogy of the Myth of the Dark Continent." *Critical Inquiry* 12: 166–203.

Braun, Willi. 1995. *Feasting and Social Rhetoric in Luke 14*. Society for New Testament Studies Monograph Series 85. Cambridge: Cambridge University Press.

Brawley, Robert L. 1990. *Centering on God: Method and Message in Luke-Acts*. Louisville, KY: Westminster/John Knox Press.

Brown, Raymond. 1993. *The Birth of the Messiah*. Updated ed. New York: Doubleday.

Cadbury, Henry J. 1920. *The Style and Literary Method of Luke*. Cambridge, MA: Harvard University Press.

Cadbury, Henry J. 1927. *The Making of Luke-Acts*. London: Macmillan.

Conzelmann, Hans. 1961. *The Theology of St. Luke*. Translated by G. Buswell. New York: Harper and Row.

Corley, Kathleen E. 1993. *Private Women, Public Meals: Social Conflict in the Synoptic Tradition.* Peabody, MA: Hendrickson.

Danker, Frederick W. 1982. *Benefactor: Epigraphic Study of a Greco-Roman and New Testament Semantic Field.* St. Louis, MO: Clayton.

Darr, John A. 1990. *On Character Building: The Reader and the Rhetoric of Characterization in Luke-Acts.* Louisville, KY: Westminster/John Knox Press.

Darr, John A. 1994. " 'Watch How You Listen' (Luke 8:18): Jesus and the Rhetoric of Perception in Luke-Acts." In *The New Literary Criticism and the New Testament*, edited by Edgar V. McKnight and Elizabeth Struthers Malbon, 87–107. Valley Forge, PA: Trinity Press International.

Dawsey, James M. 1986. *The Lukan Voice: Confusion and Irony in the Gospel.* Macon, GA: Mercer University Press.

Edwards, Douglas R. 1996. *Religion and Power: Pagans, Jews, and Christians in the Greek East.* New York: Oxford University Press.

Edwards, O. C., Jr. 1981. *Luke's Story of Jesus.* Philadelphia, PA: Fortress Press.

Elbarbary, Samir. 1993. "*Heart of Darkness* and Late-Victorian Fascination with the Primitive and the Double." *Twentieth Century Literature* 39:113–128.

Esler, Philip Francis. 1987. *Community and Gospel in Luke-Acts: The Social and Political Motivations of Lucan Theology.* Cambridge: Cambridge University Press.

Fitzmyer, Joseph. 1981. *The Gospel According to Luke I-IX: Introduction, Translation and Notes.* Garden City, NY: Doubleday.

Garrett, Susan R. 1989. *Demise of the Devil: Magic and the Demonic in Luke's Writings.* Minneapolis, MN: Augsburg/Fortress Press.

Gregory, Andrew F., and C. Kavin Rowe, eds. 2010. *Rethinking the Unity and Reception of Luke and Acts.* Columbia: University of South Carolina Press.

Hägg, Tomas. 2012. *The Art of Biography in Antiquity.* New York: Cambridge University Press.

Higginbotham, Evelyn Brooks. 1993. *Righteous Discontent: The Women's Movement in the Black Baptist Church, 1880–1920.* Cambridge, MA: Harvard University Press.

Iser, Wolfgang. 1974. *The Implied Reader.* Baltimore, MD: Johns Hopkins University Press.

Iser, Wolfgang. 1980. *The Act of Reading: A Theory of Aesthetic Response.* Baltimore, MD: Johns Hopkins University Press.

Jauss, Hans. 1982. "Literary History as a Challenge to Literary Theory." In *Toward an Aesthetics of Reception*, translated by Timothy Bahti, 3–45. Theory and History of Literature 2. Minneapolis: University of Minnesota Press.

Johnson, Luke Timothy. 1991. *The Gospel of Luke.* Sacra Pagina. Collegeville, MD: Liturgical Press.

Kodell, Jerome. 1987. "Luke and the Children: The Beginning and End of the Great Interpolation (Luke 9:46-56; 18:9-23)." *Catholic Biblical Quarterly* 49: 415–430.

Lendon, J. E. 1997. *Empire of Honour.* New York: Oxford University Press.

Macmullen, Ramsay. 1981. *Paganism in the Roman Empire.* New Haven, CT: Yale University Press.

Maddox, Robert. 1982. *The Purpose of Luke-Acts.* Edinburgh: T&T Clark.

Malherbe, Abraham. 1985. " 'Not in a Corner': Early Christian Apologetic in Acts 26:26." *Second Century* 5: 193–210.

Mallen, Peter. 2008. *The Reading and Transformation of Isaiah in Luke-Acts.* Library of New Testament Studies. New York: T&T Clark International.

Neagoe, Alexandru. 2002. *The Trial of the Gospel: An Apologetic Reading of Luke's Trial Narratives.* Cambridge: Cambridge University Press.

Neyrey, Jerome, ed. 1991. *The Social World of Luke-Acts: Models for Interpretation*. Peabody, MA: Hendrickson.

Parsons, Mikeal, and Richard Pervo. 1993. *Rethinking the Unity of Luke and Acts*. Minneapolis, MN: Fortress Press.

Petersen, N. R. 1978. *Literary Criticism for New Testament Critics*. Guides to Biblical Scholarship. Philadelphia, PA: Fortress.

Rabinowitz, Peter. 1977. "Truth in Fiction: A Reexamination of Audience." *Critical Inquiry* 4: 121–141.

Roth, John S. 1997. *The Blind, the Lame, and the Poor: Character Types in Luke-Acts*. Journal for the Study of the New Testament Supplement 144. Sheffield, Yorkshire: Sheffield Academic Press.

Seim, Turid Karlsen. 1994. *The Double Message: Patterns of Gender in Luke and Acts*. Nashville, TN: Abingdon.

Smith, Mitzi J. 2007. "Slavery in the Early Church." In *True to Our Native Land: An African American Commentary on the New Testament*, edited by Brian K. Blount, Clarice Martin, Cain Felder, and Emerson Powery, 11–22. Minneapolis, MN: Fortress Press.

Spencer, Patrick E. 2007. *Rhetorical Texture and Narrative Trajectories of the Lukan Galilean Ministry Speeches: Hermeneutical Appropriation by Authorial Readers of Luke-Acts*. Library of New Testament Studies. New York: T&T Clark.

Spencer, F. Scott. 2008. *The Gospel of Luke and Acts of the Apostles*. Nashville, TN: Abingdon.

Squires, John T. 1993. *The Plan of God in Luke-Acts*. Cambridge: Cambridge University Press.

Sterling, Greg. 2001. "Mors philosophi: The Death of Jesus in Luke." *Harvard Theological Review* 94: 383–402.

Streeter, B. H. 1925. *The Four Gospels: A Study of Origins*. New York: Macmillan & Co.

Talbert, Charles H. 1975. "The Concept of Immortals in Mediterranean Antiquity." *Journal of Biblical Literature* 94: 419–436.

Talbert, Charles H. 1981. "Shifting Sands: The Recent Study of the Gospel of Luke." In *Interpreting the Gospels*, edited by James Luther May, 197–213. Philadelphia, PA: Fortress Press.

Tannehill, Robert. 1986. *The Narrative Unity of Luke-Acts*. Vol. 1. Philadelphia, PA: Fortress Press.

Tiede, David. 1972. *Prophecy and History in Luke-Acts*. Philadelphia, PA: Fortress Press.

Tolbert, Mary Ann. 1996. *Sowing the Gospel: Mark's World in Literary-Historical Perspective* Minneapolis, MN: Fortress Press.

Trites, A. A. 1974. "The Importance of Legal Scenes and Language in the Book of Acts." *Novum Testamentum* 15: 278–284.

van Unnik, W. C. 1980. "Luke-Acts, a Storm Center in Contemporary Scholarship." In *Studies in Luke-Acts: Essays Presented in Honor of Paul Schubert*, edited by Leander E. Keck and J. Louis Martin, 15–32. 2nd ed. Philadelphia, PA: Fortress Press.

Walasky, Paul. 1983. *"And So We Came to Rome": The Political Perspective of St. Luke*. Cambridge: Cambridge University Press.

CHAPTER 28

THE ACTS OF
THE APOSTLES,
NARRATIVE, AND HISTORY

RUBÉN RENÉ DUPERTUIS

ACTS begins with a prologue that establishes the narrative as a continuation of a previous account to Theophilus (1:1; cf. Luke 1:1–5). Whatever the precise relationship of the Gospel of Luke and the book of Acts (for a summary of recent discussion, see Spencer 2007), the second volume to Theophilus presents itself as a continuation of the first volume, providing a narrative of the post-Easter Christian movement that begins in Jerusalem moments before Jesus's ascension and its spread throughout the Mediterranean through the activities of some of Jesus's followers.

BRIEF OUTLINE OF ACTS

The emphases in the book of Acts on major characters and on the map help us to see the organization of the whole. Continuing the Gospel of Luke's focus on Jerusalem, Acts begins in that city with the activity of Jesus's apostles, but with a clear focus on Peter and John (1:1–8:3). Immediately following Jesus's ascension (also narrated in the final verses of Luke) and the replacement of Judas, we encounter a pivotal scene depicting the outpouring of the Holy Spirit on the gathered apostles, which leads to a miraculous and public manifestation of the Spirit's power because the apostles can suddenly be understood in some of the many languages spoken throughout the Roman Empire. Once empowered by the Spirit, the apostles perform miracles and begin preaching publicly. Although they are well received by many, their activities meet with resistance from Jewish authorities and lead to arrests and trials, inaugurating a theme that recurs throughout the narrative. In Acts, as Richard Pervo (2009, 11) notes, "Luke uses persecution as the engine that drives his plot."

Acts then highlights the activity of the apostles and other missionaries beyond Jerusalem in a section (8:4–12:25) that functions as a transition away from Jerusalem and into activity around the Aegean in the second half of the narrative, and from a focus primarily on

Peter in the early chapters to one on Paul from Acts 13 to the end. Fulfilling Jesus's words in Acts 1:8, the message travels beyond the boundaries of Jerusalem through Philip's activity in Samaria and his encounter with an Ethiopian Eunuch; the newly converted Saul's preaching in Damascus; and Peter's visit to Lydda, Joppa, and eventually, Caesarea. Two episodes of this section are worth highlighting. The first is the gradual introduction of Paul: initially as Saul, an approving observer of the stoning of Stephen, then through a dramatic encounter with the risen Jesus while on his way to do violence to believers, and then as a witness who, like Peter, speaks boldly and meets with resistance and opposition. The second is the conversion of Cornelius, a lengthy episode that makes it clear that God engineers the inclusion of Gentiles in the movement, as both Peter and Cornelius receive divine messages. Acts' use of repetition to underscore important themes is also in evidence here: Peter's vision of unclean animals God has declared clean is experienced twice by the reader, once in a third-person narration and a second time in a first-person narration as Peter recounts the vision to Jerusalem's leaders.

After a brief return to Jerusalem, in episodes that highlight resistance, principally Jewish, to the gospel (Acts 12), Saul, who from this point on is referred to as Paul, takes center stage in Acts 13 and remains the focus of the narrative until its conclusion. Paul's Gentile mission in the Mediterranean world (13:1–20:38) has him traveling through Syria, Cilicia, Asia Minor, and Greece in a series of excursions based upon Antioch. In the final leg of Paul's travels, he visits major Aegean cities, including Philippi, Thessalonica, Athens, and Corinth—all told with significantly more detail and local color than is the case in the first half of the narrative—before returning to Jerusalem.

The free movement of Paul in the previous sections is curtailed significantly when Paul is accused of inflammatory teaching and defiling the Temple by Jewish authorities and placed under arrest. This final section (21:1–28:31) follows Paul when he is in Roman custody as he works his way through and up the Roman judicial system. Paul's legal troubles provide opportunities for trials and defense speeches that both vindicate him and mirror the trials of Jesus in Luke. Paul then survives a dramatic shipwreck en route to an expected confrontation with the emperor. Paul's remarkable survival serves, like the successive trials in this section, to vindicate him. The anticipated audience with the emperor never occurs; instead, readers encounter a less than successful meeting with Jewish leaders in Rome and what to some has felt like an abrupt conclusion to the narrative with Paul, still under arrest and awaiting a hearing before the emperor but preaching the gospel "boldly and unhindered" (28:31).

APPROACHING ACTS AS A NARRATIVE

The book of Acts has long played a significant role in shaping the way the history of early Christianity is reconstructed, both in the early years, by such Christian leaders as Eusebius (Cameron 1994), and in recent scholarship (Penner 2004b). The increased attention given to the literary and narrative features of Luke and Acts in the last few decades has shown that Acts is, in many ways, much more and much less than a straightforward history, if we measure history by modern standards. Indeed, Acts is a highly selective and very carefully constructed narrative of the early spread of the Jesus movement. Despite the traditional title by which the work comes to be known, *praxeis apostolōn*, or "the Acts of the Apostles," the narrative focus is on particular witnesses—primarily Peter in the first half (chaps. 1–12) and Paul, who in Acts is not actually granted the title of apostle, in the second (chaps. 13–28). But even this is an oversimplification, for as significant as these named figures are, Acts makes it clear that they act at the direction of and under the guidance of God and the Spirit, who emerge in the narrative as characters with speaking parts. If, in its focus on key figures, the narrative fails to correspond to its traditional title, it is also selective in its geographical scope. Despite Jesus's clear charge to the apostles to be witnesses in Jerusalem, Judea, Samaria, and, eventually, at the ends of the earth (Acts 1:8), the narrative's actual geographical focus drives ever westward, from Jerusalem to the coast and into Syria, Asia Minor, and Rome, creating a narrative arc from Jerusalem to Rome. Any narrative, including one that purports to be historical, makes choices about what events to highlight and in what order (Marguerat 2002, 5–6). What, then, does one make of Acts? How do we understand the choices made, the places covered, and the particular ways in which the spread of the movement is described?

Sustained narrative-critical or narratological approaches to Acts began in earnest in the 1970s but did not come out of nowhere. Attention to the literary features of Acts can be seen in the work of historical critics, perhaps especially in that of Henry Cadbury (1920, 1927), who argued for reading Luke and Acts as a two-volume work on the strength of their similar language, themes, and style. Martin Dibelius's (1956) important essay on the style criticism of Acts highlighted its narrative differences from the Luke narrative, which then require different approaches and methods for understanding what the second volume to Theophilus does. Literary features are also central in the work of redaction critics, such as Hans Conzelmann (1961) and Ernst Haenchen (1966). But in the end, the literary features of particular gospels facilitated the search for the communities behind the texts. Attention then shifted to tracing themes, motifs, and patterns in Luke and Acts (Goulder 1964; Minear 1976; Talbert 1974). Drawing on emerging literary theory, readings of Acts soon began to bracket historical concerns (and questions of historicity explicitly) emphasizing the value of focusing on the narrative itself and on the text. As Norman Petersen (1978, 20) put it, "[T]he text itself must be comprehended in its own terms before we can ask of what it is evidence whether in relation to the time of writing or in relation to the events referred to in it." Petersen went on to focus on the repetition of the pattern of Paul's preaching to Gentiles after being rejected by Jewish audiences, identifying it as a plot device inextricable from the narrative world created by Luke.

The next two decades saw a number of works drawing on narrative-critical approaches that typically emphasized the ways in which the theology and the purpose of Acts are carried through the narrative features of both Luke and Acts (Parsons 1987; Tannehill 1990; Brawley 1990; Kurz 1993). While some of the early narrative-critical studies focused almost exclusively on the text itself, a number of scholars began to turn to contextualization and comparison to understand the ways in which the narrative of Acts would have been read or heard in a Greco-Roman context. David Gowler (1991), for example, examines the characterization of the Pharisees in Acts using modern narratological tools but also gives attention to the scripts and narrative conventions available at the time by situating Acts among a broad set of contemporary narratives. Other studies of characterization in Acts also rely heavily on comparison to understand the kinds of meaning or meanings the narrative would have evoked in its Mediterranean setting (Darr 1990; Roth 1997; Penner and Vander Stichele 2003; Marguerat 2002; Alexander 2005). A number of scholars expanded the scope of comparison beyond textual and literary materials to include the social world (Danker 1982; Esler 1987; Neyrey 1991).

It as also worth highlighting the studies focused on the question of the genre of Acts. While Acts does not fit neatly into any genre category, it evokes historiographical expectations (Phillips 2006; Penner 2004a; Witherington 1996), or, in the preface at least, the expectations one finds in technical writing (Alexander 1993), novels (Pervo 1987), and epics (Bonz 2000; MacDonald 2003). Some of these studies might not necessarily be classified as "narrative critical"; however, they were significant in providing models for how Acts might or might not have been read or heard in the early Roman Empire.

Careful attention to the world constructed by the book of Acts, the particular discourses—linguistic and cultural codes—invoked, and the ways in which the particulars of the narrative would have been understood in an early Roman context are now, for the most part, the norm in Acts studies. The reading of Acts that I develop in what follows pays particular attention to the ways in which the narrative draws on conventions and patterns that readers would have expected to encounter in the telling of the story of the expansion of the Christian movement.

READING ACTS IN AN ANCIENT MEDITERRANEAN SETTING

The prologue addressed to Theophilus (Luke 1:1–4), which the secondary preface in Acts recalls (Acts 1:1–2), provides a kind of reading contract for the reader that can help us to see the aims of the work (Marguerat 2002, 23). Two aspects are worth highlighting here. The first is that the narrator, in the repeated use of "us" (*hēmeis*; Acts 1, 2), inscribes himself into the community for which the ensuing narrative is relevant, suggesting that Acts' ideal reader is imagined as a part of a community of believers. The second is what I take to be the narrator's statement of purpose for the work: to provide his readers with "surety" or "certainty" (*asphaleia*; 1:4). The author goes about providing this surety through a narrative (*diēgesis*; 1:1) that in the second volume takes up the events that occur after Jesus's ascension. One of the striking features of Acts is the use of several narrative voices: the preface in Luke (1:1–4) has an extradiegetic narrator; a third-person omniscient narrator appears throughout the book of Acts; and a first-person plural narrator—also omniscient—appears intermittently in the second half of the narrative (16:10–17; 20:5–15; 21:1–18; 27:1–28:16). Long seen as evidence for the author's written sources, these multiple narrative voices are probably best seen as attempts to construct a reliable identity for the narrator that draws on the credibility of both an authoritative observer and an eyewitness (Eisen 2010, 227–228). Although a clear genre identification has proven elusive, this story of beginnings can be fairly understood as a foundational narrative, whose "truth lies in the interpretation it gives to the past and the possibility it offers to a community to understand itself in the present" (Marguerat 2002, 8). Acts provided readers in the late first century, or, more likely, the early second century (Pervo 2006; Tyson 2006) with a means of constructing a Christian identity and providing the movement with legitimacy (Marguerat 2002, 30–34; Esler 1987, 16–23).

The particular discourses, or linguistic and cultural codes, on which Acts draws suggest a world view steeped in an understanding of the Hebrew Bible (likely the Septuagint version) and "presumes that history is the unfolding of a divine plan for the salvation of God's chosen people and that great men, of humble origins, are called by God to be instruments in the execution of that plan" (Matthews 2013, 8–9). Divine intervention often appears at key moments—empowering the apostles (Acts 2), converting the first clearly identified Gentile (Acts 10–11), and commissioning Paul at the start of his travels (Acts 13), for example.

In addition, Acts draws on the larger literary, narrative, and cultural patterns available in the Greco-Roman world. In so doing, the author of Acts reflects compositional practices of his time that are sometimes difficult to appreciate from our modern vantage point. Whereas we privilege originality and innovation, in the early Roman Empire imitation of classical models was highly valued and reinforced in the Greek educational system, which emphasized the imitation of Greek classical models. Through repeated imitation at each stage of their education, students would develop a familiarity with a core group of classical texts—Homer, Euripides, and Plato, among others—and develop a compositional ethos that was highly allusive as well as indebted to a relatively small set of literary models (Dupertuis 2007). Perhaps the most significant implication for the study of the literature of the period, including Christian literature, is that we should expect to find writings conforming to the principles of composition instilled throughout the various stages of education, including attention to the classical models that were the typical targets of imitation. The use of models, as well as the *topoi* and type-scenes that develop from them over time, would have also been expected by an audience of the early era. Attention to the ways in which Acts drew on these models and type-scenes from the available cultural repertoire in a narrative aimed at providing surety or certainty to Christian readers is central for understanding Acts in its context.

Reading Christian Expansion

The book of Acts is a spatially oriented narrative perhaps best read with the aid of a map.

The centrality of geography and of movement in the narrative is signaled in Jesus's charge to the disciples in Acts 1:8, which is often read as a programmatic statement for the narrative. It is also evident in the fact that the narrator's preferred term for the movement is "the Way" (9:2; 18:25; 19:9, 23; 22:4; 24:14, 22), as well as the significant travel of the movement's emissaries and the numerous references to place names. The scope of Acts is both "universalizing" and "translocal" (Burrus 2007, 133). As Robert Maddox (1982, 11) puts it, "[T]he story of Jesus and of the Church is a story full of purposeful movement."

Actual travel in Acts follows a typical there-and-back structure: Peter ventures into Samaria, then returns to Jerusalem (8:14–25); Paul repeatedly returns to Jerusalem throughout Acts; and his missionary travel (Acts 13–19) is structured as a series of trips, with Antioch as a base. That said, the overall progression of the narrative is clearly from Jerusalem, the focal point at the beginning, toward the Aegean, and eventually, to Rome. In this movement, Acts can be read as a narrative of expansion and, though the imagery is not necessarily military, perhaps even as a narrative of conquest of the Roman world.

In the light of the steady westward expansion of the movement throughout the narrative, it is worth noting the repeated use of patterns, codes, type-scenes, and language associated with the founding of a city, institution, or colony. The pivotal events of the outpouring of the Spirit on the disciples and the subsequent language miracle in Acts 2 evoke language that is typical of the foundation of an institution or city (Balch 2003; Penner 2003; Weaver 2004). Similar language appears in the account of the conversion of Cornelius, which sets the stage for Paul's Gentile mission (Wilson 2001). Paul's visit to Philippi (Acts 16:11–40), which I will look at in more detail later, also draws on imagery of the foundation of a movement, as does Paul's arrival in Rome (Acts 28:16–31), the center of imperial power (Marguerat 2002, 249). These "foundation" narratives mark key moments in the advance of a mission that in Acts is presented geographically, with the clear movement of Christianity's center from Jerusalem to Rome. Luke Timothy Johnson (1992) notes that the author's skill is such that the degree to which an investment in a Gentile mission drives the geographic sense and movement of Acts is often overlooked. He goes on to state, "[The author] has wonderfully joined a spatial progression to a demographic phenomenon (conversion of Gentiles more than Jews), and has joined this to a cultural transformation (ever-increasing sense of the 'Greek World' as the story progresses)" (11). I might go a bit further and suggest the geographical movement described in Acts has a double function. On the one hand, it quite fairly and plausibly represents historical facts—there was a demographic shift in early Christianity, and at one point the Christian movement expanded westward. On the other hand, geography in Acts also functions symbolically. Through the use of civic and cult foundation imagery as the gospel moves into new territories, Acts also serves to legitimate the presence of Christianity in the Roman world.

We can now take a more detailed look at one of the stories of the expansion of the movement into new territory. The story of Paul's missionary activity in the Aegean (16–19) begins in Philippi (16:11–40). After being prevented by the Spirit from carrying out their planned itinerary, Paul and Silas receive a vision in which a Macedonian man asks them for help (16:6–10). With divine sanction for the new destination clearly established, the narrator (now using the first-person plural for the first of the four "we-passages" in Acts) reports brief stops at Troas, Samothrace, and Neapolis before finally arriving in Philippi, which is identified as a leading city of the district of Macedonia and a Roman colony. The usual visit to the local synagogue is replaced here by an encounter with women at a place of prayer (*proseuchē*) outside the city. There Lydia, identified as dealer in purple cloth, accepts the message given by Paul, is baptized along with her household, and offers the missionaries hospitality. On the way to the place of prayer, the missionaries encounter a slave girl with a prophetic spirit, an ability the girl's owners benefit from financially. The girl publicly identifies Paul and his associates as servants of the Most High God, proclaiming the way of salvation. After many days of this activity, Paul becomes annoyed and demands that the spirit leave her. This upsets the girl's owners, who bring charges against the missionaries with the local authorities. The men are beaten and thrown in jail without a trial. But the walls of the prison do not hold them long, as an earthquake tears at the foundations and springs the doors open. The distraught jailer is prevented from committing suicide by Paul and Silas, who do not take the opportunity to escape. The jailer is subsequently converted, along with his household. Ordered released, Paul reveals that he and Silas are Roman citizens and have been unjustly treated given their status. They receive an apology, and after visiting Lydia, they depart.

Internally, this episode reflects a pattern of mission, arrest, trial (or at least a trial-like situation), and vindication through release (Acts 2–5; 16–19; Pervo 1987, 12–57; Tannehill 1990, 201–203). It also parallels two earlier miraculous jailbreak scenes featuring Peter (Acts 5, 12). But as is often the case in Acts, and in keeping with the expectations of an ancient audience, Acts modifies the type-scene to mark the significance of the arrival of the movement on Greek soil. To do so, Acts invokes cult foundation narratives, specifically the arrival of the worship of Dionysus on Greek soil as told in Euripides's *Bacchae*.

In Acts 16, as in the *Bacchae*, an emissary of a new god arrives on the Greek mainland for the first time. In both, the god is primarily accepted by women associated with Lydia, a region in Asia Minor. The *Bacchae* suggests that Lydia is the birthplace of Dionysus; whereas the use of the name Lydia in Acts, as well as linking her to Thyatira, a city in Lydia, appears to evoke Dionysian traditions. Whereas Dionysus drives the women of Thebes mad, Paul rids a slave girl of a spirit of divination. Both actions lead to accusations by city officials, who feel threatened by the new god's power, and result in the incarceration of the god's emissary. In both the *Bacchae* and Acts, the imprisonments are short-lived, because earthquakes destroy the prisons and the captors rush in with swords drawn. Whether the result of direct dependence (MacDonald 2004) or the use of a topos or type-scene (Matthews 2001, 72–78; Pervo 2009, 409–411), it is clear that Acts draws on and evokes narrative patterns associated with the founding of a cult to mark the arrival of the gospel in Greece.

It is worth noting that the sense that the gospel is expanding into new territory is heightened by the fact that the "mental map" assumed in Acts up to this point is centered around Jerusalem, leaving places like Philippi and other Greek cities off the field of view entirely. To the Jerusalem-centered world of Acts 2, with its well-known list of nations (2:9–11), the Aegean is "unknown territory, and its penetration by the emissaries of the gospel is a geographical achievement worthy of celebration" (Alexander 2005, 79–80).

But the story in Acts marks more than simply the arrival of the gospel into a new territory. Philippi was, indeed, an important city, having been the capital of Alexander the Great. While Paul's arrival in Philippi is like Dionysus's arrival in Thebes—both represent entry onto the Greek mainland—Acts emphasizes the Roman identity of Philippi by calling it the "first city of the district of Macedonia, and a Roman colony" (Acts 16:12). The Christian movement's presence in Philippi is thus not merely an advance into Greek territory, although it is that; it is also an incursion into the sphere of Roman imperial authority. This impression is also supported by the fact that Philippi is the only place in Acts where the resistance or opposition Christian emissaries encounter does not include a representative of Judaism (Skinner 2010, 123). The opposition comes from the Philippian owners of a slave girl and the Philippian authorities.

The brief encounter with the prophesying slave girl (16:16–18) adds a defeat of pagan religion to the geographical expansion of the movement into Greek (and Roman) territory. The slave girl, who follows Paul and Silas for days proclaiming them servants of the Most High God thanks to a "spirit of divination" (*pneuma pythona*), is linked to the god Apollo, who defeated the Python at Delphi to acquire divinatory powers. Despite the fact that what the slave girl says is right, the narrator disapproves of the source of her powers, and, accordingly, Paul exorcises the spirit. The slave girl, who might otherwise be a victim, functions in the narrative as the "bad-girl" in contrast to Lydia's "good-girl" (Staley 1999, 126–128) and serves as a vehicle to showcase the defeat of pagan religious practices. That she disappears from the narrative suggests that she has served her purpose (Gaventa 2003, 238).

Paul's actions enrage the girl's owners, who drag him and Silas before the local magistrates. The reader is privy to the real motivation for the charges—the loss of income (16:19)—whereas in the public charges, Paul and Silas are accused of disturbing the city and advocating customs that were illegal for Romans (16:21). The trial devolves into a mob scene, showing the first part of the charge to be false. That the magistrates are the ones carrying out the beating on Paul and Silas is a challenge to credibility, but it makes a point: Paul and Silas are certainly not the agitators in this scene. The second part of the charge will become ironic by the end of the episode, as the categories of "insider" and "outsider" become increasingly blurry.

The third of the miraculous prison-break scenes in Acts (16:25–31) differs from the previous two in a number of ways, but most prominent among them is that it does not feature an escape at all. Robert Tannehill (1990, 198–199) notes that "in Philippi Paul is twice presented with opportunities for freedom (vv. 26, 35–36) and twice refuses them. These developments focus attention not on the fact of miraculous release, but on Paul's reasons for rejecting these opportunities, which involve the jailer on the one hand and the city officials, on the other." The actions of Paul and Silas certainly lead to the jailer's conversion and the confrontation with city authorities, but Acts adds an additional layer of meaning by narrating the non-escape in language and imagery that evoke philosophers generally, and Socrates in particular. According to tradition, Socrates, who had by the early Roman Empire become the model of philosophic virtue, composed a hymn while in prison and refused to take advantage of an opportunity to escape (Pervo 2009, 410–412). While the earthquake vindicates Paul and Silas in language and imagery that are strikingly Dionysian, their behavior and its aftermath take a turn to the Socratic, revealing them to be genuine philosophers.

The tendency in this section to highlight the Roman aspects of Philippi's identity comes into play in the final confrontation with the Philippian officials. Why the magistrates order Paul and Silas released (Acts 16:35) is unclear. The omission of motive—a narrative "blank" because it is deemed not essential by the narrator (Tannehill 1990, 199)—serves to highlight what the narrator does deem important, and in this scene it appears to be a confrontation with the magistrates over the issue of identity. Paul's stunning revelation that both he and Silas are Roman citizens, and the magistrates' desire to make their blunder disappear, is a trope used here to create the space to restore Paul's honor. Indeed, Paul's refusal to let the shameful (and from the narrator's standpoint) illegal public beating be handled quietly and privately would have been heard in terms of the ancient competition for honor (Johnson 1992, 303). Paul's citizenship provides a surprising twist on the earlier accusation of behavior that is not Roman. "The question of who in fact reflects the ideal of Roman citizenship here receives an ironic answer" (Gaventa 2003, 241). The arrival of Christianity in Philippi through Paul is both a conquest, celebrated and justified in the language and imagery of the arrival of a foreign cult, and a return home, since the movement is, like Paul, legitimately and legally at home in the Roman world.

CONCLUSION

While the journey is central in both Luke and Acts, the theme is developed differently in the two volumes addressed to Theophilus. In Luke, the extended journey from Galilee to Jerusalem becomes a frame on which to hang Jesus's teaching. In Acts, however, the journey takes the form of a series of adventures in which the reader follows the expansion of the movement. In Acts, the characters and their carefully plotted and represented geographical movements become means of relating the passing of the message from the provincial outskirts to the center of the Greco-Roman world. In earlier scholarship this was often read as an apology for empire, but empire is a given in the world in which Acts was first heard. Acts provides its Christian readers in need of surety a narrative of the past that allows them to see a legitimate space for themselves in a world dominated by Rome. The narrative does this, in part, through a telling of past events that stresses the divine initiative and sanction of the Gentile mission. It also relies on cultural codes that would have been familiar to first readers. It is a testament to the skill of the author of Acts that it is difficult to see the constructed nature of the narrative. Attention to how Acts would have been read in its own time allows us to see the ways in which Acts draws on and challenges expectations in the story of first days of the church.

References

Alexander, Loveday. 1993. *The Preface to Luke's Gospel*. Society for New Testament Studies Monograph Series 79. Cambridge: Cambridge University Press.

Alexander, Loveday. 2005. *Acts in Its Ancient Literary Context: A Classicist Looks at the Acts of the Apostles*. Library of New Testament Studies 289. New York: T&T Clark.

Balch, David L. 2003. "METABOLH POLITEIWN—Jesus as Founder of the Church in Luke-Acts: Form and Function." In *Contextualizing Acts: Lukan Narrative and Greco-Roman Discourse*, edited by Todd C. Penner and Vander Stichele, 139–188. Society of Biblical Literature Symposium Series 20. Atlanta, GA: Society of Biblical Literature.

Bonz, Marianne Palmer. 2000. *The Past as Legacy: Luke–Acts and Ancient Epic*. Minneapolis, MN: Fortress Press.

Brawley Robert L. 1990. *Centering on God: Method and Message in Luke-Acts*. Literary Currents in Biblical Interpretation. Louisville, KY: Westminster John Knox Press.

Burrus, Virginia. 2007. "The Gospel of Luke and the Acts of the Apostles." In *A Postcolonial Commentary on the New Testament Writings*, edited by Fernando F. Segovia and R. S. Sugirtharajah, 133–155. The Bible and Postcolonialism 13. London and New York: T&T Clark.

Cadbury, Henry J. 1920. *The Style and Literary Method of Luke*. Cambridge, MA: Harvard University Press.

Cadbury, Henry J. 1927. *The Making of Luke-Acts*. London: Macmillan Press.

Cameron, Ron. 1994. "Alternate Beginnings—Different Ends: Eusebius, Thomas, and the Construction of Christian Origins." In *Religious Propaganda and Missionary Competition in the New Testament World*, edited by L. Bormann, K. Del Tredici, and A. Standhartinger, 501–525. Leiden: Brill.

Conzelmann, Hans. 1961. *The Theology of St. Luke*. Translated by G. Buswell. New York: Harper and Row Press.

Danker, Frederick W. 1982. *Benefactor: Epigraphic Study of a Greco-Roman and New Testament Semantic Field*. St. Louis, MO: Clayton Press.

Darr, John A. 1990. *On Character Building: The Reader and the Rhetoric of Characterization in Luke-Acts*. Literary Currents in Biblical Interpretation. Louisville, KY: Westminster/John Knox Press.

Dibelius, Martin. 1956. "Style Criticism of the Book of Acts." In *Studies in the Acts of the Apostles*, translated by Mary Ling, 1–13. London: SCM Press.

Dupertuis, Rubén R. 2007. "Writing and Imitation: Greek Education in the Greco-Roman World." *Forum* (3rd series) 1: 3–29.

Eisen, Ute E. 2010. "Fiction and Imagination in Early Christian Literature: The Acts of the Apostles as a Test Case." In *Literary Construction of Identity in the Ancient World: Proceedings of the Conference Literary Fiction and the Construction of Identity in*

Ancient Literatures: Options and Limits of Modern Literary Approaches in the Exegesis of Ancient Texts, Heidelberg, July 10–13, 2006, edited by Hanna Liss and Manfred Oeming, 215–233. Winona Lake, IN: Eisenbrauns.

Esler, Philip E. 1987. *Community and Gospel in Luke-Acts: The Social and Political Movitations of Lucan Theology.* Cambridge: Cambridge University Press.

Gaventa, Beverly Roberts. 2003. *Acts.* Abingdon New Testament Commentaries. Nashville, TN: Abingdon Press.

Goulder, Michael D. 1964. *Type and History in Acts.* London: S.P.C.K.

Gowler, D. B. 1991. *Host, Guest, Enemy, and Friend: Portraits of the Pharisees in Luke and Acts.* Emory Studies in Early Christianity. New York: Peter Lang.

Haenchen, Ernst. 1966/1980. "The Book of Acts as Source Material for the History of Early Christianity." In *Studies in Luke-Acts Essays Presented in Honor of Paul Schubert*, edited by Leander E. Keck and J. Louis Martyn, 258–278. Philadelphia: Fortress Press.

Johnson, Luke Timothy. 1992. *The Acts of the Apostles.* Sacra Pagina 5. Collegeville, MN: Liturgical Press.

Kurz, William S. 1993. *Reading Luke-Acts: Dynamics of Biblical Narrative.* Louisville, KY: Westminster John Knox Press.

MacDonald, Dennis R. 2003. *Does the New Testament Imitate Homer? Four Cases from the Acts of the Apostles.* New Haven, CT: Yale University Press.

MacDonald, Dennis R. 2004. "Lydia and Her Sisters as Lukan Fictions." In *A Feminist Companion to the Acts of the Apostles*, edited by Amy-Jill Levine with Marianne Blickenstaff, 105–110. Cleveland, OH: Pilgrim Press.

Maddox, Robert. 1982. *The Purpose of Luke-Acts.* Göttingen: Vadenhoeck & Ruprecht.

Marguerat, Daniel. 2002. *The First Christian Historian: Writing the "Acts of the Apostles."* Society for New Testament Studies Monograph Series 121. Cambridge: Cambridge University Press.

Matthews, Shelly. 2001. *First Converts: Rich Pagan Women and the Rhetoric of Mission in Early Judaism and Christianity.* Contraversions. Redwood City, CA: Stanford University Press.

Matthews, Shelly. 2013. *The Acts of the Apostles: Taming the Tongues of Fire.* Phoenix Guides to the New Testament. Sheffield, Yorkshire: Sheffield Phoenix Press.

Minear, Paul. 1976. *To Heal and Reveal: The Prophetic Vocation according to Luke.* New York: Seabury.

Neyrey, Jerome, ed. 1991. *The Social World of Luke-Acts: Models for Interpretation.* Peabody, MA: Hendrickson Press.

Parsons, Mikael C. 1987. *The Departure of Jesus in Luke-Acts: The Ascension Narratives in Context.* Journal for the Study of the New Testament Supplement 21. Sheffield, Yorkshire: Sheffield Academic Press.

Penner, Todd C. 2003. "Civilizing Discourse: Acts, Declamation and the Rhetoric of the Polis." In *Contextualizing Acts: Lukan Narrative and Greco-Roman Discourse*, edited by Todd C. Penner and Caroline Vander Stichele, 65–104. Society of Biblical Literature Symposium Series 20. Atlanta, GA: Society of Biblical Literature.

Penner, Todd C. 2004a. *In Praise of Christian Origins: Stephen and the Hellenists in Lukan Apologetic Historiography.* New York: T&T Clark.

Penner, Todd C. 2004b. "Madness in the Method? The Acts of the Apostles in Current Study." *Currents in Biblical Research* 2: 223–293.

Penner, Todd C., and Caroline Vander Stichele, eds. 2003. *Contextualizing Acts: Lukan Narrative and Greco-Roman Discourse.* Society of Biblical Literature Symposium Series 20. Atlanta, GA: Society of Biblical Literature.

Pervo, Richard. I. 1987. *Profit with Delight: The Literary Genre of the Acts of the Apostles.* Philadelphia: Fortress Press.

Pervo, Richard. I. 2006. *Dating Acts: Between the Evangelists and the Apologists.* Santa Rosa, CA: Polebridge Press.

Pervo, Richard. I. 2009. *Acts: A Commentary.* Hermeneia. Minneapolis, MN: Fortress.

Petersen, Norman R. 1978. *Literary Criticism for New Testament Critics.* Guides to Biblical Scholarship. Philadelphia: Fortress Press.

Phillips, Thomas E. 2006. "The Genre of Acts: Moving toward a Consensus." *Currents in Biblical Research* 4: 365–396.

Roth, John S. 1997. *The Blind, the Lame, and the Poor: Character Types in Luke-Acts.* Journal for the Study of the New Testament Supplement 144; Sheffield, Yorkshire: Sheffield Academic Press.

Skinner, Matthew L. 2010. *The Trial Narratives: Conflict, Power, and Identity in the New Testament.* Louisville, KY: Westminster John Knox Press.

Spencer, Patrick E. 2007. "The Unity of Luke-Acts: A Four-Bolted Hermeneutical Hinge." *Currents in Biblical Research* 5: 341–366.

Staley, Jeffrey, L. 1999. "Changing Woman: Postcolonial Reflections on Acts 16.6-40." *Journal for the Study of the New Testament* 73: 113–135.

Talbert, Charles H. 1974. *Literary Patterns, Theological Themes, and the Genre of Luke-Acts.* Missoula, MT: Scholars Press.

Tannehill, Robert C. 1990. *The Narrative Unity of Luke-Acts: A Literary Interpretation.* Vol. 2: *The Acts of the Apostles.* Minneapolis, MN: Fortress Press.

Tyson, Joseph B. 2006. *Marcion and Luke-Acts: A Defining Struggle.* Columbia: University of South Carolina Press.

Weaver, John B. 2004. *Plots of Epiphany: Prison-Escape in Acts of the Apostles.* Berlin and New York: Walter de Gruyter.

Wilson, Walter T. 2001 "Urban Legends: Acts 10:1–11:18 and the Strategies of Greco-Roman Foundation Narratives." *Journal of Biblical Literature* 120: 77–99.

Witherington, Ben, ed. 1996. *History, Literature, and Society in the Book of Acts.* Cambridge: Cambridge University Press.

CHAPTER 29

THE NARRATIVE IDENTITIES OF THE GOSPEL OF JOHN

FRANCISCO LOZADA, JR.

THE Gospel of John is a journey narrative. Jesus, the logos, departs from the world above at the beginning of the plot, travels throughout the world below, and returns to the world above at the end of the narrative. Some, like myself, might even call it a migration journey. Jesus, an outsider, is not of this world but of another world—the world above. He crosses all sorts of borders, encounters various characters—some friendly and some not so welcoming—experiences death, and is vindicated at the end with a new sense of home through the community of disciples. This is a basic sequencing of the narrative of John: a narrative of unsettlement (1:1–18), a narrative of journey (1:19–17:26), and a narrative of return (18:1–21:25).

The narrative of John begins with a moment of unsettlement. This is best viewed in the prologue (1:1–18), where the reason to come to the world below is so that all believe in his identity as the Word. The narrative of journey (1:19–17:26) consists of stories of Jesus and the various attitudes he encountered in this world: attitudes of suspicion, as with the story of Nicodemus, Jewish authorities, and Thomas; stories of hospitality, as with the story of the Wedding at Cana, the Samaritan woman, and miraculous feeding of people, and the washing of the disciples' feet at a dinner; and an attitude of outright opposition, as with the story of Jesus's death, exploiting Jesus as a local cultural, political, and economic problem. For Jesus, this is a temporary journey. He does return home in the narrative of return, but leaves an indelible footprint behind through the gift of the spirit (18:1–21:25). This is one narrative identity of John: an identity constructed through the plot development of the Gospel.

Drawing on the contributions of narrative criticism in the field of Johannine studies has allowed the study of various literary elements in the story world of John, such as the role of plots as they unfold the sequence of events in the story, the settings as they provide context where events occur and characters act, and the point of view (e.g., ideological, temporal, spatial) from which a story is narrated. All of this is possible with Johannine scholars suspending questions regarding compositional history to focus on questions of how the narrative constructs meaning in its final form. This chapter will first provide an overview of Johannine narrative studies and their methodological strategies and significance; second, it offers a macro look at John 13:1–11 as an exploration in a new direction in narrative readings; and third, it will impart some concluding remarks on the benefits of such a direction to Johannine narrative studies.

The Narrative Identities of John

Literary or narrative critical scholars of John have paved the way in exploring the narrative identity and features of the Fourth Gospel. They have done so from a variety of pointed expressions in relation to the text of John. There are those studies that are text-centered in that they read John as a text—namely, a literary and a rhetorical product. Some examples, from North America, include Culpepper (1983), Kysar (1984), O'Day (1986), Segovia (1991), Segovia and Culpepper (1991), and Resseguie (2001). The text is a message between the sender and the receiver within the story world along various levels of narration. John's artistic and rhetorical qualities attracted studies of its structure by scholars on questions of its formal features, characterization, and point of view. This first expression of literary interest in John became a springboard to analyze John from the perspective of social analysis on identity, as Segovia (1998), Conway (1999), and Hylen (2009) have done more recently—identity located in the world of the text and with the characters of the text. These studies combined areas of study outside literary criticism or turned away from traditional ways of studying John with a fresh evaluation of the narrative or a feature of the story. At the same time, Johannine narrative critics continued this turn toward other studies to examine John's narrative world. In a sense, the cutting-edge studies by Staley (1988, 1995) and Segovia (1996) took a sharp turn toward cultural studies. Their work both attended to the role of the real reader in constructing this Johannine narrative world but also respected the narrative identity of John brought forth in previous studies. This third direction, with its focus on the role of the real reader, engaged John not just as a rhetorical product but also as an ideological one, bringing to bear questions of reading experience and power to the narrative of John. All of these directions, intersecting one another at times, contributed to constructing a narrative identity of John—a move away from John as history and toward John as story.

Johannine narrative studies owe much to Culpepper's (1983) *Anatomy of the Fourth Gospel*. This is one of the earliest and most influential studies done from a literary perspective and is a representation of the text-centered approach. In a way, it marks the beginning of Johannine narrative criticism proper, for it is a study that concentrates on the text's narrative world: the literary integrity of the text as a whole and its narrative features, such as narrator and point of view, narrative time, plot, characters, implicit commentary, and the implied reader. Such study incorporates modern narratology, as well as reader-response criticism of the sort that focuses on the reader who is inscribed in the narrative text. It sparked a flurry of publications in the field, including commentaries by Moloney (1993, 1996, 1998), Talbert (1992), Stibbe (1993), and, eventually, Culpepper (1998) himself.

Following this significant study, O'Day's (1986) *Revelation in the Fourth Gospel*, though informed by the narrative principles Culpepper established, turns from focusing on the anatomy of the Fourth Gospel in general toward looking at one narrative rhetorical technique—namely, the use of irony. Drawing on Culpepper's (1983) work on irony, as well as studies on irony by Wead (1970) and Duke (1985), O'Day's work is significant because it invites readers to focus not so much on what irony is but on how irony works, particularly how the implied author persuades, via the use of irony, the implied reader to believe that the narrative is the revelatory experience. More specifically, the implied author invites the readers not only to understand the use of irony, but also to participate in it as a way to extend the story to others. At the same time, O'Day, like others reading John from a text-centered approach, pays no attention (consciously or unconsciously) to the identity of the real reader. Her reader is inscribed in the text. Yet O'Day's and other text-centered studies provide valuable information of certain ancient narrative conventions of another time and culture.

Soon after this text-centered impulse, an exciting turn occurred in Johannine narrative studies. Narrative studies for the most part remained focused on certain elements of the narrative, but several began to integrate social analysis as well. This integration, though it is limited in scope, was reflected in a collection of essays edited by Segovia (1998), but then received a more thorough expression in studies of John's treatment of gender. Fehribach (1998) and Schneiders (1999) combine a literary approach with a diachronic look at women from a feminist point of view, with a focus on showing how female characters are equal to male characters. In contrast, a study by Conway (1999) shows how female characters are constructed in relation to male characters. Some years later, Hylen (2009), drawing from the flurry of character studies, took another look at the characters in John. Rather than looking at whether they are presented in a positive or negative light, as "believer" or "unbeliever," Hylen, based on direct and indirect modes of characterization, sees these characters as ambiguous in their responses to Jesus. Hylen prefers not to fall into a dualistic characterization categorization (believer/unbeliever) but rather to be open to characters who do not fit neatly into such a system. Like the text-centered studies, these studies see the reader in the text, yet they give attention to the reading process and the formation of identity.

Other studies exploring notions of ambiguity, identity, and power include Staley's (1991) character analysis of the lame man and the blind man; Moore (1994), who is the first to put the Fourth Gospel in direct conversation with poststructuralist theory; Dube and Staley (2002), combining postcolonial theory and Johannine studies; and later, Liew (2009), who, informed by queer theory, investigates the masculinity of Jesus. These studies opened the door for other postmodern and postcolonial approaches to John. Two studies that showcase the ethnic, religious, ideological, and geopolitical identities of individual readers are works by Reinhartz (2002) and Segovia (2007). Interested in the question of her relationship with John, Reinhartz uses the metaphor of John as friend to engage the Gospel's implied author. For Segovia, John is a postcolonial textual challenge of absolute power at the cosmic (between God and Satan), global (between the Word of God and imperial Rome), and local (between Jesus and the colonial elite of Judea) levels. The Fourth Gospel's prologue proposes a postcolonial alternative in that the Word of God, who dispenses power to those who are followers or children of God, transmits such power to the world. Finally, the plot proposes a postcolonial program in that all those who do not believe in the Word of God are condemned, and all those who believe are victorious. At the end, God wins the battle and Satan is defeated. Segovia's postcolonial reading of the Fourth Gospel is not possible without his narrative examination of its plot and the various journeys Jesus takes in his encounter with opposition. Segovia's studies compliment those of other scholars (e.g. Carter 2008) interested in the imperial identity of the text, and spark a variety of studies that bring to bear the personal, the cultural, and the global worlds on other texts of the New Testament (e.g., Lozada and Carey 2012).

My own work attempts to draw from this latter analytical impulse to comprehend the narrative identity of John from this angle (Lozada 2000, 2011). In what follows, I provide a reading of John 13:1–11 from the perspective of postcolonial hospitality. Reading from this position does not mean that the compositional history and reception history of this particular text are not important, but rather a literary look at the text from a narrative perspective sheds light on a different element of John's identity.

JOHANNINE HOSPITALITY: THE MIGRANT AS GUEST/HOST

In migration studies (e.g., Luibhéid and Cantú 2005; Portes and Rumbaut 2006; Castles and Miller 2009), a number of questions drive critics: What is the role of hospitality between migrants and hosts when such encounter arises? How do migrants respond to the loss of home and the shift to a new culture? Is going home possible? What happens to the migrant's identity when he or she returns home? How do they deal with double or triple identities? How are such identities created and maintained? How do these identities change over time, and why? How are migrants expressed in a variety of mediums, films, newspapers, and literary texts, and how do scholars make use of such sources? In this brief reading of John 13:1–11, the footwashing scene, I explore the category of hospitality that is typically associated with migration to new places. As noted earlier, I read John as a migrant journey—one in which Jesus, the migrant, travels to a new place (this world) and engages in various encounters with his hosts. As described in 13:1–11, the conventions of hospitality in such encounters are explored from the perspective of point of view—the perspective from which the story is narrated.

How is hospitality played out in 13:1–11? I work from the understanding that hospitality is not simply the benevolent (or colonial) welcoming of the guest (or stranger) by a host; rather, it is the encounter between the guest (or stranger) and the host in which the continuum of roles of guest/host is constantly in motion (Rosello 2001). On the one hand, Johannine hospitality challenges the notion that the guest is always the recipient of benevolence and the host is always the provider of benevolence. On the other hand, the Johannine point of view also maintains this fixed relationship (guest as guest and host as host) and, at times, lacks moments of hospitality. When the fixed roles of guest and host are reversed, a re-envisioning of hospitality is experienced. This moment is experienced when the guest, in the home of the host, can become the host and welcome others as guests, while the host resigns him- or herself to this act of hospitality. It is when the guest remains guest and the host remains host that the guest will be perceived, as many migrants are today and have been throughout history, as unwelcome guests and the hosts perceived as meanspirited. In what follows, a narrative reading of John 13:1–11, the footwashing scene, will explore how hospitality is constructed in the scene through the literary element of point of view.

John 13:1–11 appears in the narrative of journey division (1:19–17:26)—a division of the plot with various encounters in which the relationships on the guest/host continuum are negotiated: for example, 2:1–12 (the wedding at Cana), 4:1–42 (Jesus's encounter with the Samaritan woman), 6:1–14 (the feeding the multitude), and 12:1–8 (the anointing at Bethany). In these narratives, the guest, Jesus, reverses his role and plays host, thus destabilizing fixed roles of guests and hosts. This role reversal is also illustrated in 13:1–11, a text that is marked as the beginning of a long farewell narrative unit (13:1–17:26) during a dinner and over the course of Jesus's last journey to Jerusalem. From a temporal point of view, the pace of the plot slows down in John 13, thus directing attention to what is to follow. The use of the deictic "now" at the beginning of 13:1 slows down the pace, thus privileging the narrator's point of view, as Resseguie (2001, 110) suggests, to command the attention of the reader. The footwashing scene is an instance of hospitality in which Jesus gestures through this act that it is time to leave and return home—to the world above.

The literary structure and development of John 13:1–11 can be divided into two subsections: 13:1–5, entering the dinner, and 13:6–11, the conversation between the host and his guests. In the first subsection the narrator introduces not only the footwashing scene but also the beginning of the remainder of the narrative of journey. The narrator reports the general temporal context of the footwashing scene—prior to the feast of the Passover (1:1a)—as well as specific theological context—the hour had arrived for his return to the world above (1:1b). Jesus, the one who has entered this world as a guest from the world above, recognizes (knows) that his time to leave the world below (this world) has arrived, thus heightening the upcoming narrative of death (18:1–21:25; Resseguie 2001, 62). The narrator, in a sense, gestures (1:1b) that it is now Jesus's time to return to the world above. This inside view demonstrates that Jesus is surely in command of his situation. Jesus, from the beginning of the scene, switches from guest to host. This instability of the guest/host continuum opens the door for an act of hospitality to occur, for Jesus plays host and the disciples play guests. Such a break in the continuum can only result from an unselfish act. Jesus does so out of an act of love (1:1c), and not simply a temporary love, but a love to the end (1:1d). Hospitality is about resigning oneself to the needs of others (Rosello 2001, 171), as Jesus does in this scene.

Such hospitality takes place during a meal/supper (*deipnou*; 13:2). Thus, both the host and the guests take the risk of sitting down, so to speak, and abiding by the politeness and respect of the cultural rules of meals. This kind of risk is part of hospitality. For when a host invites a guest, the host must be willing to accept the unrestrained behavior of a guest if it happens. In fact, the narrator reports such a potential risk. Judas Iscariot, who is present at the supper, not only possesses the devil in himself, but is out to betray Jesus (13:2). The guest is contrasted with the host, who is willing to endure violence by the guest and against other guests. Hospitality is occurring. The continuum is functioning and it experiences friction (inhospitality). The narrator establishes two opposing points of view in this scene: those who will follow Jesus and those who will betray him. Through the use of this friction, the host unconditionally accepts the risks and the threats created by the presence of a guest (Rosello 2001, 172). If the host chooses not to accept this risk, hospitality cannot endure.

The first subsection of this scene continues when it is reported that Jesus, knowing that Judas is going to betray him, prepares to wash the feet of the disciples (13:4). But prior to this, the narrator reports two things that Jesus knows about himself. Jesus knows (1) that the Father has given him all things and that Jesus is in control of his hour (13:4a), and (2) where he is from and where he is going (13:4b). Such information from the narrator surely highlights Jesus's omniscient character. He knows his role or mission and he knows his identity. But such inside information leads to the thought that maybe Jesus is not really ready to resign himself to the guests at the supper, or, maybe he is ready to acknowledge his power. For Jesus to resign himself to another, he must acknowledge his own identity and power. In

13:3, the continuum of guest/host is swinging. Hospitality is in progress. Knowing who he is, Jesus does not pretend the guests are the host and the host is the guest. He knows who he is and he knows his role as host. The narrator once again is setting the stage for the gesture of hospitality proper by forwarding the point of view that Jesus, having all the control and power in the situation, is the host and the followers are the guests.

As the host, Jesus resigns himself to his guests (13:4) by rising up from supper, putting aside his clothes, and fixing a towel around himself. All three actions (rising, putting aside, fixing) expressed through the narrator signify that Jesus, the host, is preparing to resign himself as a guest. Jesus is willing to be changed by his guests. Hospitality is working. Jesus, from the beginning of the subsection, prepares for his role as host. He acknowledges his identity and authority as the host of the supper, but he is also preparing himself to be a guest. He welcomes all who are present at the supper, even those who are there with the intent to betray him later. As indicated by his rising, disrobing, and fixing a towel around himself, he is preparing to be challenged and changed through his intended actions. All three actions, actions that point to the role of a servant rather than a master, are confirmed through the inside information that Jesus knows his hour, his mission, and his identity, and still resigns himself to these guests.

It is in this context, Jesus begins to wash the feet of the disciples (13:5). The narrator again reports that Jesus first pours water into a basin (13:5a), begins to wash the disciples' feet (13:5b), and then finishes by drying their feet with a towel (13:5c). The act of washing the disciples' feet illustrates Jesus's inclusion of his guests as hosts. Jesus, the one who entered into this world (Johannine world) has reciprocated a gesture of hospitality toward his hosts (disciples) by becoming one of them, and the disciples reciprocate by becoming one with Jesus through their belief. Such gestures portray Jesus, the migrant traveler, as one who could become host. In other words, the narrator's point of view is forwarded once again: Jesus can vacillate between the roles of guest and host, always keeping hospitality open for those who are present.

What follows in the next subsection (13:6–11) is an explanation, given mainly through direct discourse, of the gesture of hospitality through the washing of Simon Peter's feet.

The subsection begins with Jesus approaching Peter, preparing to wash his feet (13:6). Before Jesus begins, Peter asks him whether he intends to wash his feet, thus suggesting it is not common for a guest—as Peter sees him—to wash the feet of a host. The narrator introduces Peter through his new name, Simon Peter (1:40), thus underscoring his precedence (Resseguie 2001, 150–151). Peter will be the only disciple singled out in this scene. Peter, unlike Jesus who knows all things, is confused by or unsure of Jesus's acts of hospitality. There is surely some ambiguity between the two. However, hospitality is rarely free of uncomfortableness or tension. Apparently, the hosts (disciples) and the guest (Jesus) do not share the same assumptions about hospitality. The protocol of hospitality (from Peter's point of view) has been broken. But before Peter can try to stop Jesus from washing his feet, Jesus tells him that although it appears that the etiquette of hospitality will be broken, Peter will understand such breach after the act of hospitality (washing his feet) is completed (13:7). The temporal point of view expressed through the character of Jesus highlights Peter's confusion or misunderstanding (Resseguie 2001, 152). Again, the narrator portrays Jesus as all-knowing and in command of his hour, and still, Jesus is willing to break the cultural laws of hospitality in order for Peter to get to know Jesus, and for Jesus to get to know him.

Peter is characterized as misunderstanding Jesus's statement about not knowing at the present time (story time) but knowing in the future why he has done these things (plot time). This is confirmed when Peter, in the future (negative) tense, tells Jesus that he will never wash his feet (13:8a). Again, Peter is unwilling to concede to breaking any cultural laws of hospitality. His point of view is reinforced through his continual characterization as one who understands hospitality to have fixed roles. A guest does not wash the feet of a host. His misunderstanding of Jesus's true identity is revealed, while Jesus's true identity is being made known through his actions. Jesus's response, framed under a conditional clause, lets Peter know that if he (Jesus) does not wash his feet, Peter cannot be a part of him. Hospitality is not an object to be known; rather, it is an experience that brings host and guest together to explore an unknown experience that pushes their identities together—so close together that one identity cannot be named (host or guest) unless the other identity already exists. In other words, one can only identify as a host if a guest exists, and vice versa. It is through this encounter that the ritualized practice of hospitality continues being negotiated, as between Jesus and Peter. The point of view is forwarded that an act of hospitality is occurring unbeknownst to Peter.

Peter's response is one of belief and misunderstanding. He addresses Jesus as "Lord" (*kurios*; 13:9b), thus separating Jesus from others, but he interprets Jesus's request to wash (*niptein*) his feet to mean his entire body (13:9c). Peter wants to experience the act of hospitality throughout his entire body in order to resign himself to Jesus, the guest. Peter's words are an instance of hospitable inflation. Resseguie (2001:152) calls it an instance of overeagerness. Peter causes an imbalance on the guest/host continuum that keeps the guest as guest and the host as host. But Jesus keeps hospitality alive by explaining to Peter what he means. Jesus tells Peter that the one who is bathed (*louein*) does not need to wash (*niptein*) more than the feet. This explanation restores some balance to the continuum and keeps hospitality alive. Jesus corrects Peter's expectation as well as his understanding of what it means to be washed. Jesus's hospitable gesture is a call for Peter to be a guest and thus to give something of himself so that the other can be understood. This something is the washing of the feet and the understanding that hospitality is acceptance of what is to come from such a relationship. Those who accept it will be clean, and those who refuse it will not be clean. Jesus further explains to Peter and the disciples (*humeis*) that hospitality is not a given. It is either provided or not. Hospitality is not without friction (Rosello 2001, 173). And in this case, the friction is expressed when Jesus tells the disciples that not all will be clean (13:10f). Not all will be clean or one with Jesus. The narrator confirms Jesus's words by once again providing inside information that Jesus knows who will betray him. The narrator even quotes Jesus's words, "You are not all clean" (13:11c), and thus brings even the (modern) reader into this gesture of hospitality and thus challenges the reader to accept such gestures of hospitality or reject them.

John 13:1–11 is an example of hospitality. It is not a hospitality centered on benevolence or charity, but rather a hospitality in which both the guest and the host must switch places (physically and mentally) and be willing to resign oneself to the other in order for hospitality to function. This is the overall point of view of the scene. Jesus, the guest in this world, ventures into an unknown space (dinner) and takes the role of the host in order to experience the hosts now turned guests (disciples). Peter, representing the believers, reciprocates by playing the role of guest, and thus giving up a part of himself to experience Jesus. The characters must allow some vulnerability and discomfort to exist for hospitality to be activated.

This reading of John 13:1–11 is a small glimpse of an alternative reality—one that exhibits genuine hospitality. However, when John 13:1–11 is seen in relation to the entire Gospel, the story runs against the dominant ideological point of view of the Gospel's plot. The Gospel's overall point of view is couched within a binary/colonial program, one that leaves the disciples to espouse the message that those who do not believe in Jesus as the Son of God are excluded from the community and those who do believe are children of God. Such a dualistic program does not point toward hospitality but to usurpation of the world (much like colonizers) in which guests are guests and hosts are hosts. As a result, the implied author's overarching ideological point of view presents a failed gesture of hospitality. Such reality only leads to racialization, violence, residential segregation, and unjust labor practices if the program is adopted and practiced. It is only in such moments as the footwashing scene that glimpses of a genuine form of hospitality (some might say a postcolonial form) are expressed.

CONCLUSION

Bringing the postcolonial notion of hospitality to bear on a narrative reading through the use of point of view is an act of self-reflexivity of both the reader and the reader's world. It is not only a way of seeing the narrative identity of the text as many literary studies of John have done; it is also, and perhaps most importantly, a way of seeing the reader, the self, and the reader's world in narrative terms. In an era of a heightened sense of migration due to the rapid effects of globalization, how do communities grapple with the new forms of community brought forth by migration? What does migration do to the range of the everyday cross-cultural practices and settings, such as hospitality? This move toward seeing narrative as being central to ideological conceptions of the self is much needed in Johannine studies. Narrative studies, unlike historical studies, are the best place to stage this examination. Narrative studies can bring other stories of hospitality home to the flesh-and-blood readers and help them conceptualize other practices of hospitality that might be helpful in this rapidly changing world.

REFERENCES

Carter, Warren. 2008. *John and Empire: Initial Explorations*. London and New York: T&T Clark.

Castles, Stephen, and Mark J. Miller. 2009. *The Age of Migration: International Population Movements in the Modern World*. 4th ed. New York: Guilford Press.

Conway, Colleen M. 1999. *Men and Women in the Fourth Gospel: Gender and Johannine Characterization*. Society of Biblical Literature Dissertation Series 167. Atlanta, GA: Society of Biblical Literature.

Culpepper, R. Alan. 1983. *Anatomy of the Fourth Gospel: A Study in Literary Design*. Philadelphia, PA: Fortress Press.

Culpepper, R. Alan. 1998. *The Gospel and Letters of John*. Nashville, TN: Abingdon.

Culpepper, R. Alan, and Fernando F. Segovia, eds. 1991. *The Fourth Gospel from a Literary Perspective*. *Semeia* 53. Atlanta, GA: Society of Biblical Literature.

Dube, Musa W., and Jeffrey L. Staley. 2002, eds. *John and Postcolonialism: Travel, Space and Power*. The Bible and Postcolonialism 7. London and New York: Sheffield Academic Press.

Duke, Paul. 1985. *Irony in the Fourth Gospel*. Atlanta, GA: John Knox Press.

Fehribach, Adeline. 1998. *The Women in the Life of the Bridegroom: A Feminist Historical-Literary Analysis of the Female Characters in the Fourth Gospel*. Collegeville, MN: Liturgical Press.

Hylen, Susan E. 2009. *Imperfect Believers: Ambiguous Characters in the Gospel of John*. Louisville, KY: Westminster John Knox Press.

Kysar, Robert. 1984. *John's Story of Jesus*. Philadelphia, PA: Fortress Press.

Liew, Tat-siong Benny. 2009. "Queering Closets and Perverting Desires: Cross-Examining John's Engendering and Transgendering Word across Different Worlds." In *They Were All Together in One Place? Toward Minority Biblical Criticism*, edited by Randall C. Bailey, Tat-siong Benny Liew, and Fernando F. Segovia, 251–288. Semeia Studies 57. Atlanta, GA: Society of Biblical Literature.

Lozada, Francisco, Jr. 2000. *A Literary Reading of John 5: Text as Construction*. Studies in Biblical Literature 20. New York: Peter Lang.

Lozada, Francisco, Jr. 2011. "Journey and the Fourth Gospel: A Latino/a Exploration." *Interpretation* 65(3): 264–278.

Lozada, Francisco, Jr., and Greg Carey, eds. 2012. *Soundings in Cultural Criticism: Perspectives and Methods in Culture, Power, and Identity in the New Testament*. Minneapolis, MN: Fortress Press.

Luibhéid, Eithne, and Lionel Cantú, eds. 2005. *Queer Migrations: Sexuality: U.S. Citizenship, and Border Crossings*. Minneapolis: University of Minnesota Press.

Moloney, Francis J. 1993. *Belief in the Word: Reading John 1–4*. Minneapolis, MN: Fortress Press.

Moloney, Francis J. 1996. *Signs and Shadows: Reading John 5–12*. Minneapolis, MN: Fortress Press.

Moloney, Francis J. 1998. *Glory not Dishonor: Reading John 13–21*. Minneapolis, MN: Fortress Press.

Moore, Stephen D. 1994. *Poststructuralism and the New Testament: Derrida and Foucault at the Foot of the Cross*. Minneapolis, MN: Fortress Press.

O'Day, Gail R. 1986. *Revelation in the Fourth Gospel: Narrative Mode and Theological Claim*. Philadelphia, PA: Fortress Press.

Portes, Alejandro, and Ruben Rumbaut. 2006. *Immigrant America: A Portrait*. 3rd ed. Berkeley: University of California Press.

Reinhartz, Adele. 2002. *Befriending the Beloved Disciple: A Jewish Reading of the Gospel of John*. New York: Continuum.

Resseguie, James L. 2001. *The Strange Gospel: Narrative Design and Point of View in John*. Biblical Interpretation Series 56. Leiden: Brill.

Rosello, Mireille. 2001. *Postcolonial Hospitality: The Immigrant as Guest*. Redwood City, CA: Stanford University Press.

Schneiders, Sandra M. 1999. *Written That You May Believe: Encountering Jesus in the Fourth Gospel*. New York: Herder & Herder.

Segovia, Fernando F. 1991. *The Farewell of the Word: The Johannine Call to Abide*. Minneapolis, MN: Fortress Press.

Segovia, Fernando F., ed. 1996. *"What Is John?" Readers and Readings of the Fourth Gospel*. Society of Biblical Literature Symposium Series 3. Atlanta, GA: Scholars Press.

Segovia, Fernando F., ed. 1998. *"What Is John?" Vol. 2 of Literary and Social Readings of the Fourth Gospel*. Society of Biblical Literature Symposium Series 7. Atlanta, GA: Scholars Press.

Segovia, Fernando F. 2007. "The Gospel of John." In *A Postcolonial Commentary on the New Testament Writings*, edited by Fernando F. Segovia and R. S. Sugirtharajah, 156–193. The Bible and Postcolonialism 13. London and New York: T&T Clark.

Staley, Jeffrey L. 1988. *The Print's First Kiss: A Rhetorical Investigation of the Implied Reader in the Fourth Gospel.* Society of Biblical Literature Dissertation Series 82. Atlanta, GA: Scholars Press.

Staley, Jeffrey L. 1991. "Stumbling in the Dark, Reaching for the Light: Reading Character in John 5 and 9." In *The Fourth Gospel from a Literary Perspective*, edited by R. Alan Culpepper and Fernando F. Segovia. *Semeia* 53: 55–80.

Staley, Jeffrey L. 1995. *Reading with a Passion: Rhetoric, Autobiography, and the American West in the Gospel of John.* New York: Continuum.

Stibbe, Mark W. G. 1993. *John.* Readings: A New Biblical Commentary. Sheffield, Yorkshire: JSOT Press.

Talbert, Charles H. 1992. *Reading John: A Literary and Theological Commentary on the Fourth Gospel and the Johannine Epistles.* New York: Crossroad.

Wead, David. 1970. *The Literary Devices in John's Gospel.* Basel: Friedrich Reinhardt Kommissionverglag.

CHAPTER 30

SHIFTING BIBLICAL PARABLES

ROBERT PAUL SEESENGOOD

THE PROBLEM WITH PARABLES

AND the Sunday school teacher taught them saying, "A parable is an earthly story with a heavenly meaning." A parable of sorts itself, this definition is traditional, pithy, analogical, aphoristic, and mysterious in origin. It seems to "mean" but evades precision; it inspires more questions than it resolves; it provokes nostalgia more than discovery. Ironically, this traditional definition has many of the characteristics of biblical parables. Parables are deceptively complex narratives, and reading biblical parables involves a creative engagement with their complexity. Sifting through the questions and problems raised by biblical parables, and shifting interpretive assumptions and interests as a result, creates awareness of an array of what parables might "mean." In the end, the meaning of a parable lies in the process of interpretation itself and transcends simple articulation.

Hebrew Bible parables are found most frequently in the *Navi'im*, with a notable cluster in Ezekiel and the former prophets. In the New Testament synoptic gospels, Jesus frequently teaches in parables. (There are no uncontested examples of parables in John's Gospel.) The Greek word *parabolē* means "to cast or lay alongside." In the Septuagint, *parabolē* is the normal translation of the Hebrew *mashal* (pl. *meshalim*). Parables are found in Jewish wisdom literature from the centuries prior to our common era and among the Dead Sea Scrolls (e.g., 1QpHab 12.2–10). Parables appear in the Mishnah, indicating their presence in proto-Rabbinic teaching, including traditions prior to the destruction of the Jerusalem Temple in 70 CE (Evans 2000, 63–72). Within contemporary Greco-Roman literature, parables were also common. Consequently, scholarship concurs that parabolic teaching was commonplace in ancient Judaism and a hallmark of the historical Jesus (Funk, Scott, and Butts 1988, 14–17; Jeremias 1956, 11).

What actually constitutes a *mashal* and how a *mashal* reflects or relates to its surrounding literary context remains unclear (Evans 2000, 54–61; Schipper 2009, 5–12). In some cases we find a fairly complex story (e.g., Ezek. 17:2–10; 20:44–49; 24:3–5; Isa. 5:1–7). Yet *mashal* can also indicate a simple analogy (e.g., Ps. 28:1), a taunt (Isa. 14:4; Hab. 2:6; Mic. 2:4), or a generic aphorism or proverb (e.g., Prov. 1:1, 6, etc.; 1 Sam. 10:12; 14:13–14). Moreover, parabolic narratives appearing in Hebrew Bible are not always labeled as such (e.g., 2 Sam. 12:1–7 or Ezek. 16:1–54; 17:2–24; 19:2–9, 10–14; 23:1–49; 24:3–14). All but two of the fifty uses of *parabolē* in the New Testament—Hebrews 9:9 and 11:19—appear in the synoptics. The synoptics use *parabolē* to describe brief stories (e.g., Luke 13:6–9) but also to identify proverbs or analogies (Matt. 13:33; Luke 18:1–8), aphorisms (Luke 4:23), and riddles (Mark 3:23). The New Testament also contains parabolic narratives that are not explicitly identified (e.g., John 10:1–5; 3:29; 8:35; 11:9–10; 12:24) What a parable is, indeed, even how many parables there are and where they are located, is contested territory.

Ancient Near Eastern, Jewish, and Greco-Roman sapiental traditions used parables as pedagogic or illustrative devices. However, the definition of a nonbiblical Greek *parabolē* is contested. Greeks used multiple words (e.g., *mythos*) for what we would call narrative parables, and used *parabolē* for what we would call fable or folktale (Snodgrass 2008, 46–50). While there is consensus that the Rabbinic and proto-Rabbinic Jewish teachers used *meshalim*, there is no agreement about exactly when and where. Our principle witness to Second Temple Judaism, the Mishnah, was compiled sometime around 200 CE; while it clearly provides examples of Jewish teachers using parables, these examples are collected, edited, and anthologized long (sometimes centuries) after the lives of the rabbis and proto-rabbis whose teachings it records (Evans 2000, 53–60; Stern 1991; cf. Feldman 1924; Wailes 1987). Scholars agree that parables are integral to biblical narrative, and that they were part and parcel of the literary and cultural world around the Bible. They disagree, however, about what a parable is, where parables can be found in biblical text, and what (if any) aspects of the extrabiblical context are relevant for understanding the genre of the biblical parable.

Parables and Their Interpretation

With so much disagreement on description and genre, parable study is best initiated with a review of the critical literature (see, e.g., Bailey 1976; Blomberg 1990; Hultgren 2000; Snodgrass 2000, 2008; Spencer 2012; Stein 2000; Tolbert 1979). For most of the history of Christian biblical interpretation, parables were taken as allegories (see Snodgrass 2000, 4–5). Each element of a parable's narrative—character, setting, plot—became a symbol for a deeper spiritual truth or theology. Such a view was consistent with patristic confidence in multiple—often fourfold—levels of meaning inherent in all biblical texts. Allegorical readings of parables also take cues from the biblical text; Jesus interprets his parables via allegory (e.g., Mark 4:1–20 and its parallels).

In the late eighteenth century, Adolph Jülicher (1888, 1899) condemned allegorical readings of the parables, arguing that allegory was too prone to eisegesis and an inferior mode of literature. The parables, he insisted, were best regarded as simple, self-interpreting, narrative analogies with one—exactly one—self-evident point. Jesus, Jülicher argued, eschewed allegory, and any allegory in the gospels was later interpolation. Though his position, particularly his views on synoptic interpolations, was challenged in its details, Jülicher's anti-allegorical agenda was widely accepted by nineteenth-century scholarship.

The twentieth century saw an expansion of parable interpretation. Accepting Jülicher's dismissal of allegory and, to an extent, his assertion that parables were about precisely one point, C. H. Dodd and Joachim Jeremias argued that the parables' main arguments lie in systematic analysis of Jesus's teaching as a whole and Jesus's historical context. Dodd (1936, 34) insisted that the primary point of all of Jesus's parables was the kingdom of God. He produced what is perhaps the most widely cited definition of New Testament parables: A "parable is a metaphor or simile drawn from nature or common life, arresting the hearer by its vividness or strangeness, and leaving the mind in sufficient doubt about its precise application to tease it into active thought" (11). Jeremias (1956, 125-128) argued that this kingdom language must be read vis-à-vis eschatology, the real focus. Middle and later twentieth-century interpreters continued the campaign against allegory via structuralism and socio-historical critiques. For example, Fuchs (1964) argued, using proto-semiotic tools, that the parables were best understood as performative language events in themselves. Crossan (1973, 1974) and Funk (1966) examined the traditional nature of parables and their use by the historical Jesus (with particular attention to the formal similarities among prebiblical, biblical, and Rabbinic parables); they used structuralist methodologies to explore how parables paralleled oral folk literature. Other significant critical inquiries include renewed attention to the relationships among Jesus's parables, Rabbinic parables, and Hebrew Bible parabolic traditions (Young 1989) and questions of genre classification (see, e.g., Hultgren 2000; Kissinger 1979). Though increasingly precise about the context, origins, developmental history, formal structure and subcategories of parables, many such studies leave readers still wondering what any particular parable might "mean."

Attempts to address this quandary appear in studies devoted to the ethical (or "theological") content and significance of parables, with results equally as sweeping and confident. Mary Ann Tolbert (1979, 68-71) argues that parables have no fixed meaning; they are polyvocal, and their "interpretation is a creative act" in which scholar and text play together. Opposition to what is taken by some as Tolbert's nihilism arises from a wide spectrum. For example, Kyle Snodgrass (2000), while granting that a given parable can teach more than one lesson or have more than one point, argues aggressively that the meaning of parables must be confined to what Jesus himself would have intended. This intention is discovered exclusively by reconstructing the first-century and gospel context of Jesus; scholars who do not do so "have ceased being hearers of the parables and have become tellers of the parables instead" (21); they are "no longer interpreting the parables of Jesus Christ" (22). For Snodgrass, polyvocality is a de facto (if not de jure) allegory. William Herzog (1994) has argued that the parables as a whole have an overarching, single frame for meaning: the (colonial) control and domination by the Romans and Jesus's (largely peasant) opposition to systems of oppression and power. Herzog's perspective has influenced liberationist and postcolonial readings of parables that range from intentional support of the poor and oppressed to a general critique of dominating powers (e.g., Beavis 1992, 2012).

Combining socio-critical historiography and structuralist reading strategies, John Dominic Crossan (2012) has returned to parabolic literature to argue that biblical and Rabbinic parables reflect a unique and creative blend of Hebrew Bible *meshalim* and Greco-Roman fable and folk traditions. This blend results in three basic categories of parable: aphorism / proverbial saying, limited brief narrative, and extended narrative. As Crossan notes, what distinguishes a parable from other prose fiction, is that the story is fundamentally metaphoric. Parables are unique forms of narrative in that they are explicitly metaphoric and didactic; their intent and function, more than their form or context, set them apart.

> An *ordinary story* . . . wants you to focus *internally* on itself, to follow the development of character and plot, to wonder what will happen next and how it will end. It wants you to get *into* the story and not *out* of it. . . . On the other hand, a parable, that is, a *metaphorical story*, always points *externally* beyond itself, points to some different and much wider referent. Whatever its actual content is, a parable is never about *that* content. Whatever its internal subject, a parable always points you toward and wants you to go to some external referent. (Crossan 2012, 9)

For Crossan, the sine qua non of parable is effect (or, perhaps, though he does not use the term, "affect"). He also argues that parables are not only integral for understanding the historical Jesus, but that the synoptic gospels are, themselves, parables (Crossan 2012, 3–5).

S(h)ifting (for) Meanings in Parables

Shifting from scholarship attempting to theorize parables to scholarship actually interpreting parables reveals that a parable's "meaning" depends on how an interpreter resolves the various formal and contextual questions posed by parabolic literature. While this is a commonplace observation about narrative in general, parables in particular seem to invite such shifts. Shifting attention to different textual details or assumptions regarding the parable's narrative context results in notable shifts in what one thinks a parable "means."

For example, how one interprets Luke's parable of the prodigal son (Luke 15:11–32) depends upon how one constructs the broader context of Luke 15 and understands the parable's three main characters. The prodigal son arises at the climax of a discourse by Jesus responding to Pharisaic disapproval of Jesus's attention to "tax collectors and sinners" (15:1–2). It is preceded by two parables about loss, obsessive search, and discovery: the parables of the lost sheep (15:3–7) and the lost coin (15:8–10).

Yet the prodigal son story differs from its narrative companions. Longer and more developed, it lacks any search for the lost. The character one might expect to search, the father, remains at home the entire time the prodigal is away. The parable shifts its focalization to the point of view of the missing. The prodigal "comes to himself" (15:17), realizes how far he has sunk, and returns to a gracious father. That the "older brother," most often taken as representing "the Jews," does not welcome the prodigal is taken by many as a sign of the elder brother's legalism and selfishness, and he is rebuked for lack of love by the loving father. Traditional reading of the prodigal son, shaped by its strategic position in this triptych of parables about loss, focuses on the preciousness of the returning sinner, the exuberance of the father, and usually includes a side note on the grumpy legalism of the older brother (cf. Snodgrass 2008, 126–141).

Yet, as Donald Juel (1997, 12) observes, the prodigal's inner "transformation" does not result from moral reflection but from hunger. His epiphany (15:17–19) is not that he has betrayed his father's love and familial obligation, but that his father has significant wealth and is (overly?) generous. While the prodigal, a "classic manipulator" (Juel 1997, 10), scripts an apologetic speech to ease his father's anger, his motivation remains physical comfort. The motivation of the prodigal before and after "coming to himself" is constant, suggesting his transformation is cognitive, not ethical.

In a move suggested by Tolbert's psychoanalytical reading of the parable, which stresses family dynamics (Tolbert 1979, 74, 93–114), Juel shifts focus to the characters of the older brother and father, renaming the parable "the Lament of a Responsible Child" (Juel 1997:11). The elder brother who has faithfully worked the family farm returns home dirty and tired to find his wastrel brother, again, getting his father's indulgence and refuses to join the celebration. Juel does not, however, condemn the older brother. His is an understandable, even justified, grudge, familiar to more than a few families with a struggling child. In this parable, the father is an enabling, overindulgent parent (Juel 1997, 12). Having shifted attention from the father-prodigal binary to the entire family unit, Juel argues that the parable's focus is not upon repentance, per se, but upon familial tension in response to loss and estrangement. It adds nuance to, but does not replicate, the other two parables about the grief of loss and joy of reunion.

Shifting assumptions about the broader, extrabiblical socio-historical context of a parable also results in shifts in meaning. Reconstructing ancient context can, indeed, provide an interpretive frame—perhaps control—for parables, yet precisely how one reconstructs the "context" has significant outcome; the reconstruction of context itself is often contested. Consider the parable of the good Samaritan (Luke 10:25–37). Interpreters have rightly noted that, in the gospels' narrative contexts, Jesus uses the parable to argue that one must do good to all without regard to racial or religious difference (e.g., Ambrose 2010; Hultgren 2000, 93–100). Amy-Jill Levine (2007, 144) counters, however, that many readings interject modern notions of "race" and have often relied on reconstructions of ancient Judaism that do not, actually, comply with any extant evidence of ancient Jewish norms. For many, the parable juxtaposes the unprejudiced Jesus to deeply prejudiced Jews adding a dash of religious supercessionism. The focus in the parable must not become "Jews behaving badly" (Levine 2007, 144–149), and interpreters should reconstruct Jesus's "Judaism" in ways that guard against anti-Semitic readings.

A second example is the parable of the laborers in Matthew 20:1–16. For many, this parable is, again, a commentary on Jewish and Christian relations, with the landowner understood to be God, the first workers Jews, and later workers Gentiles. At the "day's end" (i.e., the eschaton), all receive the same wages, prompting the Jew to grumble (cf. Snodgrass 2008, 370–379). More contemporary readings, particularly those influenced by Herzog (1994, 79–97), see a commentary on economic ethics and social injustice. For some, Jesus is promoting egalitarianism, perhaps even endorsing a Marxist/socialist economic structure.

Amy-Jill Levine and Myrick C. Shinall Jr. reexamine many of these interpretive decisions, noting that many are superimposed on the parable (Levine and Shinall 2013). To describe the Jesus movement as egalitarian fails to incorporate the full narrative of the gospels. The kingdom of God has a clear hierarchy, and Jesus does not advocate democracy. While Jesus in the synoptics is a relentless advocate for the rights and needs of the poor, he does not oppose wealth per se, but rather the improper use of wealth (Levine and Shinall 2013, 98–99). In fact, his followers include wealthy people who financially support and enable his work. Levine and Shinall argue that some readings overlay an entire economic narrative, particularly a Marxist-influenced one of class rivalry and the condemnation of economic disparity, and rename the parable "the Contentious Householder" (Levine and Shinall 2013, 96–98). Levine and Shinall survey and critique an array of assumptions and interpolations by interpreters—many arising from a desire to protect or impugn the character of the landowner (2013,

100–111). There is no narrative need, they argue, to make assumptions regarding "Jewish" ideas about the relationship between wealth, God's blessings, and social ethics. There is no narrative need to assume that the landowner is trying to be minimalist in his daily hiring needs. There is no narrative need to assume that workers hired later were among the less employable, the infirm, or the lazy. In fact, "the parable makes no mention of the *need* for more labor" at all (Levine and Shinall 2013, 107); the landowner hires workers, in part, for the simple sake of hiring more workers, to employ as many people as possible. Traditional interpretation has taken the landowner as cipher for God. Levine and Shinall, however, argue that this, too, is an assumption, one which has placed undue limits on the parable's interpretation. They counter, "The parable opens up the view that the householder—that is, the well-off disciple—should continue to go to the market, should continue to invite others in" (107).

The structure of the parable, particularly its final scene, is dramatic. Narrative tension is enhanced by the revelation of the inner thoughts of the earliest workers and by their surprise at the identical payments. This structure also belies arguments that the parable's central point is justice or fairness. The surprise—and then the clarifying commentary, the "point" or "hook" of this parable—depends upon the presumption that the equal pay distributed is fundamentally *unfair*. The parable is a *challenge to* the priority of "fairness." "Fairness" is not the landowner's priority; instead, it is his right to distribute his property as he likes (Levine and Shinall 2013, 110–111). The parable suggests that the use of wealth should be motivated by inclusion rather than efficiency and maximum return on investment or "fairness." Far from being a rebuke of Judaism, this thesis is resonant with an extraordinarily similar parable found among rabbinic literature (Levine and Shinall 2013, 109–110; Snodgrass 2008, 364–365). Levine and Shinall conclude that the parable makes the following points: In God's kingdom, all should (and will) get enough. Householders are encouraged to support laborers. "Jesus is neither Marxist or capitalist. Rather he is both idealist and pragmatist. His focus is not only 'good news to the poor'; it is also on 'responsibility to the rich.' Jesus follows Deut. 15:11" (114). Finally, Jesus assumes an interdependence between worker and employer in mutual responsibility. Their reading moves away from either debating who gets into Heaven (and whether that is fair) or celebrating socialist values; the parable focuses, instead, upon "who gets a day's wage" and offers a challenge to economic complacency or any sense of economic entitlement, among both rich and poor (Levine and Shinall 2013, 115).

Shifting assumptions about the parabolic genre shifts the meaning one finds in a parable. Jeremy Schipper (2009, 5, 7–10, 12–16), after an admirably brief but thorough survey of scholarly understanding of *mashal/meshalim*, advocates a shift from a structural to a functional description of the genre *meshalim*. He notes that narrative parables frequently appear with prophetic oracles in which a character (or prophet) is also articulating a rebuke that is dependent upon comparison. For Schipper, narrative *meshalim* have a collaborative intent; parables spoken by one character (normally God's representative) draw in other characters in the narrative, and by extension the reader, making rebuked characters self-indicting participants in the condemnation (18). Narrative Hebrew Bible parables are devices designed to shift perspectives and provoke empathy. A paradigmatic example is 2 Samuel 12:1–7 (which Schipper 2009, 41–56, treats in detail, cf. Altpeter 1982; Kruschwitz 2012; Simon 1967; Vorster 1985). Here, Nathan's parable both articulates the rationale for God's curse and establishes its convicting power. Parables most often arise, Schipper (2009, 17–19) argues, when the indictment addresses kinship obligation, suggesting that the point of the parable is to (re)establish empathy and (re)iterate emotively the degree of the violation. On Schipper's analysis, parables in the Hebrew Bible function not to bring about self-actualization or change, but to sharpen curse language (122–123). Narrative *meshalim* do not teach so much as they convict.

In Judges 9:7–15, Jotham integrates his "parable of the bramble" into a rebuke of Abimelech. Abimelech and Jotham are two of seventy-one sons of Gideon sharing governance after their famous father's death. Abimelech forges an alliance with the Shechemites and, arguing that diffuse power is less in everyone's interests than a single ruler, captures and executes all his brothers save Jotham. On hearing that Abimelech has been made king, Jotham comes out of hiding, stands before the people, and offers a parable and a rebuke.

Schipper contends that this story (which he, to be strict, identifies as a "fable" that is "applied parabolically"; Schipper 2009, 25; cf. Cathcart 1995, 214–218; Coates 1981; Rofé 1974; does not have reformative purpose but is, instead, partnered with Jotham's curse. Jotham follows his parable about unwise coronation with his specific charge (Judg. 9:16–19) that the people have forgotten their loyalty to Gideon and acted dishonorably by appointing the fratricidal Abimelech king. To demonstrate the truth of his indictment, Jotham calls for fire (a motif from the parable) to issue mutually from Abimelech and his supporters consuming them all as confirmation of Jotham's rebuke (9:19–20). There is, Schipper notes, no offer of repentance in 9:19–20, only a call to reflection. Jotham is not offering a discourse on proper government or Godly submission (his anger is about failed reciprocity and kinship obligation). He is not outlining effective political theory in narrative form (e.g., Bartelmus 1985; Lindars 1973; Maly 1960; Ogden 1995; Waard 1989). He is instead using his parable as a means to provoke discovery and establish empathy in order to reinforce (frankly, to actualize) condemnation and curse (Schipper 2009, 37–38).

Finally, shifting attention from ancient literary and cultural contexts to modern geopolitics also results in shifts of parabolic meaning. For example, Jotham's parable has also been invoked in discussions of how formerly colonized peoples should respond to the West and to their own emerging political contexts. Oscar Suarez (2005) reads the parable as an indictment of the passivity of the colonized. He notes how Christianity within Asia has tended to be shaped by largely Western ideas and structures. With a shift in narrative interest from the bramble to the other trees, he observes how the trees capable of producing useful goods fall victim to the "messianic savior" promises of the bramble, who promises comfort in exchange for submission (141–142). The cost, however, is lost autonomy and neglect of indigenous resources (143). Edwardneil Benavidez and Doreen Benavidez (2010) shift their attention to the character of Jotham, noting that his commitment to integrity and truth prompt him to speak out against Abimelech. "[Jotham's] speech on this mountain has one basic purpose, to condemn and to pronounce judgment upon the abandonment of 'truth and integrity' by Abimelech and the Schechemites" (131). Benavidez and Benavidez go on to reflect on their contemporary Pilipino context, taking particular notice of how others have articulated opposition to oppressive governments via "music, drama, comedy, comics and in many other ways" (142). Shifting their focus to identify with Jotham, they see his parable as potential paradigm for an oppressed people speaking truth to oppressors through folkart (cf. Okyere 2012).

Meaning-*full*, Meaning-less Parables

There is little scholarly consensus on the genre, origins, or techniques for interpretation of parable, current or historic. The "meaning" of a parable shifts depending upon how one defines "parable," which character is considered central, the proposed socio-political-historical context, the location and information of the reader/hearer, and more. As Tolbert (1979) has noted, parables are dynamic moments of meaning-making via engagement and shared storytelling. Parables as didactic tools invite reflection and participation in unique ways. It is in this invitation, this shifting process of interpretation and engagement, that, I would argue, the "meaning" of a parable is best located.

In the synoptic gospels themselves, Jesus indicates that he uses parables not to make his insights more or more broadly accessible, but to effect the precise opposite, to obscure the didactic content of his teaching and to invite (allegorizing) reflection and community identification (Mark 4:11–12 paralleled in Luke 8 and Matt. 13; see Herzog 2012; Juel 2002). Whether one approaches biblical parables in search of theological truth or to explore narrative structure and function, one must be brought short by the fact that the one time in the biblical text when a character who uses parables explains his intent, he invites allegory and clearly indicates that he intends to *evade*—in Mark and Luke, to *prevent*—simple, facile, didactic, or *logical* interpretation. In the Hebrew Bible, as Schipper noted, we are confronted again and again with *meshalim* whose purpose is to draw the listener into participating in the construction of the parabolic meaning (a move common to both 2 Sam. 12 and, say, Luke 11:36–37). Parables occlude simple, singular meaning in order to foster reflection and empathy. Parables in biblical text are not simplifications of complex or spiritual ideas in order to make them accessible to the masses. They are, by intention, reserved for the more intimate and initiated whom they invite into the interpretive process. They are shifty, most rewarding to serious—indeed, creative—collaborative engagement. The interpretation of a parable requires a series of decisions and shifts by the interpreter, none of which are value neutral. The "problem" with parables is that meanings shift as interpreters sift through their own assumptions and options.

More accurately, the "problem" with parables may well be that, as narratives, they do not do what interpreters often want them to do. They are not rational or exclusive. Readers choose, deliberately or passively, how to enter a parable, how to construct context, and where to focus narrative attention. Parables are so fraught with potential background (as per Auerbach) that they alternate between being wildly meaning-*full* and strictly (at least singularly) *meaning*-less; they persistently elude any single, final reading even as they beg for and reward deeper reading and reflection. They "work" on a level that transcends or precedes rational engagement and logic. To risk being a bit formalist: one can not articulate a single, indicative meaning behind a parable exactly because parables are narratives. As with metaphor, to articulate a single, indicative, didactic meaning in a parable "breaks" or reduces the central comparison itself. Parables, instead, compel reflection, collaboration, and emotional engagement. The essential problem presented by parables is the problem of narrative in general: a parable does not precisely "mean" anything; meaning shifts, and the emotive connection (and process of analysis and discovery) is, itself, a major part of the "meaning" inherent in the form. Observing the spectrum of parable interpretation(s), Juel (2002, 273) notes,

> This century has witnessed such significant development in the interpretation of parables that a student might wonder if interpreters are reading the same texts. The differences between Jülicher and Jeremias, on one hand, and Funk and Wilder, on the other, are striking. One group is more interested in the intent of the author, the other in the power of the story to work on its hearers .... It is a different matter to ask what a parable "means"—to study in order to

know how the story will play in the present . . . . Meaning must furthermore be understood to include affect.

In discussions of hermeneutics and narrative in the ten years since Juel wrote these words, "affect" has taken on significant, pregnant, meaning (Koosed and Moore 2014). In psychology and psychobiology, "affect studies" describes the exploration of pre- (or supra)rational cognition. Affect in literary criticism explores the way narrative engages, awakens, or uses emotion and how such emotion is an inseparable aspect of narrative "meaning." For critics influenced by Eve Sedgwick, Sara Ahmed, and others, this shift in attention disrupts the tendency in structuralist and formalist approaches to reduce meaning to a simple (or binary) didactic "point," and also dissolves the tendency in poststructuralism to reify, despite an explicit temerity toward binary thinking, analysis and engagement (Ahmed 2010; Gregg 2010; Sedgwick 2003). Affect readings attempt to recognize (exactly, to re-cognize) that simple critique of the dominance of linear rationality is not sufficient; rationality *itself*, is decentered by an acknowledgment of the affectual. The affectual is the exact union of the two interests among parable interpreters—between the "intent" and the power of the parable.

In parable criticism (and, by extension, narrative criticism, of which the parabolic is a type), an affectual turn would recognize that parables are fundamentally *relational* stories. They are, as is often observed, metaphors. Metaphors, at their most basic, construct meaning via nonrational relationships, forced marriages between dissimilar partners that reveal a new insight or truth, often a truth with an emotive force that eludes simple or rational expression (Booth 1978). Parables foster relationship and empathy and, in this function, "mean" affectually. In any relationship, "meaning" and "significance" are never static.

Attending to the affectual in biblical parables attunes us to the conflicted family dynamic of the prodigal son, the self-risk of the good Samaritan as he attends to the wounded, the issues surrounding a hunger for "fairness" in the parable of the laborers, the shock of recognition in the parables of Nathan and Jotham. Affectual reading of parables sees these emotive responses and actions themselves as central to the meaning. How these parables make us feel *is* what they mean. The "purpose" or intent of a parable lies within its form; it is the inculcation of empathy, the sparking of creativity, and the collaborative co-creation of "truth," the affect of the parabolic narrative upon both characters and readers.

References

Ahmed, Sara. 2010. *The Promise of Happiness*. Durham, NC: Duke University Press.

Altpeter, G. 1982. "II Sam. 12, 1–15a: Eine struckturalistische Analyse." *Theologische Zeitschrift* 38: 46–52.

Ambrose, Colin M. 2010. "Desiring to Be Justified: An Examination of the Parable of the Good Samaritan in Luke 10:25-37." *Sewanee Theological Review* 54(1): 17–28.

Bailey, Kenneth. 1976. *Poet and Peasant: A Literary Cultural Approach to the Parables in Luke*. Grand Rapids, MI: Eerdmans.

Bartelmus, R. 1985. "Die sogenannte Jothamfabel—eine politisch-religiöse Parabeldichtung: Anmerkungen zu einem Teilaspekt der vordeutero-nomischen israelitischen Literaturgeschichte." *Theologische Zeitschrift* 41: 97–120.

Beavis, Mary Ann. 1992. "Ancient Slavery as an Interpretative Context for the New Testament Servant Parables with Special Reference to the Unjust Steward (Luke 16:1-8)." *Journal of Biblical Literature* 111(1): 37–54.

Beavis, Mary Ann. 2012. "'Like Yeast That a Woman Took': Feminist Interpretations of the Parables." *Review and Expositor* 109: 219–230.

Benavidez, Edwardneil, and Doreen Benavidez. 2010. "Truth and Integrity: Considering the Issue of Standard (Judges 9:7-21)." *Asian Journal of Pentecostal Studies* 13(1): 125–142.

Blomberg, Craig L. 1990. *Interpreting the Parables*. Downers Grove, IL: InterVarsity.

Booth, Wayne C. 1978. "Metaphor as Rhetoric: The Problem of Evaluation." *Critical Inquiry* 5(1): 49–72.

Cathcart, Kevin James 1995. "The Trees, the Beasts and the Birds: Fables, Parables and Allegories in the Old Testament." In *Wisdom in Ancient Israel*, edited by John Day, Robert P. Gordan, and H. G. M. Williamson, 212–221. Cambridge: Cambridge University Press.

Coates, George W. 1981. "Parable, Fable and Anecdote: Storytelling in the Succession Narrative." *Interpretation* 35: 368–382.

Crossan, John Dominic. 1973. *In Parables: The Challenge of the Historical Jesus*. New York: Harper.

Crossan, John Dominic. 2012. *The Power of Parable: How Fiction by Jesus Became Fiction about Jesus*. New York: HaperCollins.

Crossan, John Dominic. 1974. "Structuralist Analysis and the Parables of Jesus." In *A Structuralist Approach to the Parables*, edited by Robert W. Funk. *Semeia* 1: 192–221.

Dodd, Charles Harold. 1936. *The Parables of the Kingdom*. London: Nisbet.

Evans, Craig A. 2000. "Parables in Early Judiasm." In *The Challenges of Jesus' Parables*, edited by Richard N. Longnecker, 51–78. McMaster New Testament Guides. Grand Rapids, MI: Eerdmans.

Feldman, Asher. 1924. *The Parables and Similes of the Rabbis*. Cambridge: Cambridge University Press.

Fuchs, Ernst. 1964. *Studies of the Historical Jesus*. Naperville, IL: Allenson. 1964.

Funk, Robert W. 1966. *Language, Hermeneutic, and the Word of God*. New York: Harper and Row.

Funk, Robert W., Bernard Brandon Scott, and James R. Butts. 1988. *The Parables of Jesus: A Report of the Jesus Seminar*. Sonoma, CA: Polebridge Press.

Gregg, Melissa, and Gregory J. Seigworth eds. 2010. *The Affect Theory Reader*. Durham, NC: Duke University Press.

Herzog, William R. II. 1994. *Parables as Subversive Speech*. Louisville, KY: Westminster/John Knox Press.

Herzog, William R. II. 2012. "Sowing Discord: The Parable of the Sower (Mark 4:1-9)." *Review and Expositor* 109: 187–198.

Hultgren, Arland J. 2000. *The Parables of Jesus: A Commentary*. Grand Rapids, MI: Eerdmans.

Jeremias, Joachim. 1956. *The Parables of Jesus*. New York: Charles Scribner's Sons.

Juel, Donald H. 1997. "The Strange Silence of the Bible." *Interpretation* 51(1): 5–19.

Juel, Donald H. 2002. "Encountering the Sower Mark 4:1-20." *Interpretation* 56(3): 273–283.

Jülicher, Adolf. 1888/1899. *Die Gleichnisreden Jesu*. 2 vols. Freiburg: Akademische Verlagsbuchhandlung von J. C. B. Mohr.

Kissinger, Warren S. 1979. *The Parables of Jesus: A History of Interpretation and Bibliography*. American Theological Library Association. Metuchen, NJ: Scarecrow Press.

Koosed, Jennifer L., and Stephen D. Moore, eds. 2014. *Affect Theory and the Bible*. Special issue of *Biblical Interpretation* 22.

Kruschwitz, Jonathan A. 2012. "2 Samuel 12:1-15: How (Not) to Read a Parable." *Review and Expositor* 109: 253–258.

Levine, Amy-Jill. 2007. *A Misunderstood Jew*. San Francisco: HarperSanFrancisco.

Levine, Amy-Jill, and Myrick C. Shinall, Jr. 2013. "Standard and Poor." In *The Message of Jesus*, edited by Robert B. Stewart, 95–116. Minneapolis, MN: Fortress Press.

Lindars, Barnabus. 1973. "Jotham's Fable: A New Form-Critical Analysis." *Journal of Theological Studies* 24(2): 355–366.

Maly, Eugene H. 1960. "The Jotham Fable: Anti-Monarchical?" *Catholic Biblical Quarterly* 22: 299–305.

Ogden, Graham S. 1995. "Jotham's Fable: Its Structures and Functions in Judges 9." *Bible Translator* 45: 301–308.

Okyere, Kojo. 2012. "Culture of Politico-Religious Intrigues (Judges 9:1-21): Implications for Africa." *Ogbomoso Journal of Theology* 17(3): 57–75.

Rofé, A. 1974. "Classes in the Prophetical Stories: Didactic Legenda and Parable." Vetus Testamentum Supplement 26: 143–164.

Sedgwick, Eve Kosofsky. 2003. *Touching Feelings: Affect, Pedagogy, Performativity*. Durham, NC: Duke University Press.

Schipper, Jeremy. 2009. *Parables and Conflict in the Hebrew Bible*. Cambridge: Cambridge University Press.

Simon, U. 1967. "The Poor Man's Ewe-Lamb: An Example of a Juridical Parable." *Biblica* 48: 207–242.

Snodgrass, Klyne R. 2008. *Stories with Intent: A Comprehensive Guide to the Parables of Jesus*. Grand Rapids, MI: Eerdmans.

Snodgrass, Klyne R. 2000. "From Allegorizing to Allegorizing: A History of the Interpretation of Parables of Jesus." In *The Challenge of Jesus' Parables*, edited by Richard N. Longnecker, 3–29. McMaster New Testament Guides. Grand Rapids, MI: Eerdmans.

Spencer, F. Scott. 2012. "Speaking in Parables: Methods, Meanings, and Media." *Review and Expositor* 109: 161–164.

Stein, Robert H. 2000. "The Genre of Parables." In *The Challenge of Jesus' Parables*, edited by Richard N. Longnecker, 30–50. McMaster New Testament Guides. Grand Rapids, MI: Eerdmans.

Stern, David. 1991. *Parable in Midrash: Narrative and Exegesis in Rabbinic Literature*. Cambridge, MA: Harvard University Press.

Suarez, Oscar S. 2005. "Building Communities of Peace." *Ecumenical Review* 57(2): 136–146.

Tolbert, Mary Ann. 1979. *Perspectives on the Parables*. Philadelphia, PA: Fortress.

Vorster, Willem S. 1985. "Reader-Response, Redescription, and Reference: 'You Are the Man' (2 Sam 12:7)." In *Text and Reality. Aspects of Reference in Biblical Texts*, edited by B. C. Lategan and W. S. Vorster, 95–112. Atlanta, GA: Scholar's Press.

Waard, J. de. 1989. "Jotham's Fable: An Exercise in Clearing Away the Unclear." In *Wissenschaft und Kirche*, edited by K. Aland and S. Meurer, 362–370. Texten und Arbeiten zur Bibel, 4. Bielefeld: Luther.

Wailes, Stephen L. 1987. *Medieval Allegories of Jesus' Parables*. Berkeley: University of California Press.

Young, Brad H. 1989. *Jesus and His Jewish Parables: Rediscovering the Roots of Jesus' Teaching*. New York: Paulist.

CHAPTER 31

NARRATIVE, MULTIPLICITY, AND THE LETTERS OF PAUL

MELANIE JOHNSON-DEBAUFRE

Paul is a man of the proposition,
the argument and the dialogue,
not a man of the parable or story.

—J. Christiaan Beker

PAUL and his coworkers wrote letters addressed to several urban Christ assemblies of the ancient Mediterranean.[1] Letters are not narratives. Letters feature argument and persuasion, not character and plot. While most of the Pauline letters flag a particular geographic setting at the outset—be it Corinth, Thessalonikē, Philippi, or Rome—they do not tell a story within that setting. Instead, they address the audience directly, refer obliquely to events outside the world of the letter, and meditate on abstractions like justice, freedom, and wisdom. Reading a letter as a narrative flouts literary convention.

Nevertheless, and contrary to Beker's insistence that Paul is a man of proposition, Paul is also a man of story in at least two respects. First, Paul is a central, even paradigmatic, character in both popular and scholarly versions of Christian origins, creating the illusion that there is a singular, coherent story of Paul that can be reconstructed from the seven letters widely accepted as Pauline, the six additional letters attributed to him, and the canonical and apocryphal acts in which Paul is a primary character. However, this range of sources has not produced a singular Paul. The history of interpretation suggests the opposite: Pauls abound (Pervo 2010; Seesengood 2010). Acknowledging this malleability, this chapter builds on the feminist critique of Paul-centered interpretation in order to claim the historical, ethical, and theological value of the many characters and stories within and around the Pauline letters (Schüssler Fiorenza 2007; Johnson-DeBaufre and Nasrallah 2011). Thinking with the multiplicity of Pauls and the stories entangled with his also insists that the representation of his subjectivity be conceptualized as located, changing, and in relation (see, differently, Lopez 2008; Boer 2011; Ehrensberger 2015; Charles 2014).

Second, certain methodological trends in Pauline studies have also established Paul as a man of story, but not as a character so much as a mind. The rise of narratology in literary studies and the popularity of narrative theology have revived this traditional construction of Paul beginning in the 1980s with two influential publications by Richard Hays ([1983] 2001, 1989). Drawing on structuralist theory, Hays argues that Paul's thought is deeply formed in and through theological narratives about God's relationship to creation and to Israel. Paul's "storied perception of reality" makes possible the identification and reconstruction of a "narrative substructure" in his letters that undergirds his argumentation and ethics. In this frame, Paul is not a storyteller; the letters are "reflective discourse" on story rather than narratives themselves. This effectively bypasses the genre mismatch and brings narrative into the historical and theological explication of the New Testament letters (see Witherington 1994; Longnecker 2002a and b; Grieb 2002; Wright 2013).

This approach expands the dimensions of Paul's story beyond the texts of the letters and the first-century CE contexts, temporally to include the storied past and future and spatially to encompass stories of the peoples of the world and the entire cosmos. It thereby departs from structuralist narratology insofar as these stories are not in the text but are narrated by scholars, thus enlarging the textualization of "Paul's thought" beyond the few extant sources. It makes eminent sense to consider that Paul, his coworkers, and his audiences had storied views of their worlds. The study of narrative in general has similarly gone well beyond the forms and structures of particular narrations of setting, plot, and characters on a page or in performance and into a multidisciplinary exploration of human cognition, individual and collective memory and identity formation, and the construction of social worlds (see the introduction to this volume by Danna Nolan Fewell). Stories make worlds. They order and reorder human experience. The story of interest for the predominant narrative approach to Paul is nothing less than the Christian metanarrative of God and the world. What is striking is its attempt to balance this large scale with its singular focus: the mind or "mindset" of Paul. This chapter takes up this interest in large-scale Pauline theology, but in a way that presupposes and values irreducible multiplicity, both locally and translocally.

A Multitude of Stories Small and Large

The narrative approach to Paul composes his worldview about God, peoples, and the world. This search for a comprehensive vision mirrors recent nontheist interest in Paul as a political philosopher. While the first strongly historicizes, and the latter notably does not, the result of each is large-scale and trans-temporal. For N. T. Wright (2013, xv), Paul "actually *invents* something we may call 'Christian theology,' in this particular way (Jewish beliefs about God, reworked around Messiah and spirit), for this particular purpose (maintaining the new messianic people in good order)." For Alain Badiou, once one understands the texts as local interventions in the same problematic of disjoining truth from law, there is "not one maxim ... that cannot be appropriated for our situation and our philosophical tasks" (2003, 15). Although Wright and Badiou differ about Paul's thinking and its meanings, both have found a particular theopolitical system in Paul's letters—worked out by one thinker—usable across time and space.

These theological and philosophical readers of Paul emphasize a large, coherent vision that runs against the grain of most liberationist and postmodern thinking. There is much at stake. For biblical theologians, there is a desire to defragment biblical interpretation and to unify Christian identity under one narrative umbrella. For philosophers, global capitalism's totalizing grip demands a politics that does not fracture into commoditized difference. Both approaches contrast with ideologically-minded interpreters who are suspicious of metanarratives and universalisms. Lyotard famously generalized postmodernism as a suspicion of all grand narratives, or "any idea or system purporting to be an overarching explanation or organizing system" (Seesengood 2010, 185). Both a comprehensive story of the world and a theory of the universal require a God's eye view, or a view from nowhere and everywhere. Stories are always situated, although grand narratives often mystify this fact by masking "the contradictions and instabilities that are inherent in any social organization and practice" (Johnson et al. 2012, 4). These contradictions and instabilities become apparent when one attends to pluralities. The ideological-critical response to the problem of grand narratives has been to emphasize localized stories, micro logics, and a politics of difference.

The historical-critical insistence on reading Paul's letters separately as occasional letters has also contested and disassembled metanarratives of biblical theology and resisted the universalizing tendencies in Paul's thought. Christian biblical theology—already shaped by the ordering and particular content of the Christian canon—tells the story of the progress of civilizations and the triumph of God, beginning at creation and ending with the redemption of the world via the second coming of God's Christ, to bring justice to the righteous and unrighteous. Paul's key role as the Jew who saw the Christian light is cast in the early Christian origin story of the Acts of the Apostles, and his letters provide his incomparable voice. Historical scholarship has dismantled both the historicity of Acts and any clear connection to the letters (see Pervo 2010). The voice or mind of Paul has also been dis-integrated when his theological thinking is recognized as highly contextual, and his rhetorical self-fashioning as constructed to persuade. Situating each letter in its own local story has played a role in biblical theology's loss of credibility in Pauline studies, as well as in the emergence of "Paul" as a site for exploring the concept of subjectivity and self-representation in complex locations and relations (Seesengood 2010, 195–213).

And yet, it is important to acknowledge that, like those who attempt to reconstruct Paul's mind or worldview, Paul was also in the business of thinking big stories about God, justice, peoples, and salvation. Those gathering to listen to him and to interpret his texts likely would have been—and certainly still are—interested in thinking big stories as well. While ideological and some historical resistances to universalizing theological and philosophical readings of Paul focus on the crucial values of particularity and locality, it seems, as Namsoon Kang has argued, that this binary approach to grand versus small "makes one incapable of dealing with the complex reality of human life in this contemporary world." The question is not "*whether* a theory is grand or small, or whether it is universal/global or particular/local, but *what function* a theory plays and *whose* interest it serves" (2013, 2). The universal, the abstract, and the theological are problematic because they purport to address ALL without attention to the endless particularities of ALL. When the universal is countered with the particular, particularity often becomes the site of multiplicity and embodiment. How might thinking the multiplicity of stories around Paul connect and infuse particularities *within* the universal and translocal rather than opposing them?

For narrative critics of Paul, the variety and plasticity of stories is often taken as more of a problem than an interpretive opportunity. Biblical theology seeks to answer "[t]he Problem of Diverse Voices in Scripture" and to articulate its unity across its historical, theological, and literary plurality (Hays 2008). Likewise, Pauline theology addressed cultural diversity insofar as it "was necessary if the church, otherwise adrift in a world of a thousand cultural pressures, was to stay unified and holy" (Wright 2013, xvi). Although more politically akin to biblical scholars working with an ideological, ethical, or emancipatory framework, political philosophers seek a way beyond the problem of fracturing difference in the context of globalization. Many feminist, cultural, and empire critics have understood that Paul is the in the business of thinking the world through theology or ideology. However, a persistent central focus on Paul himself injects a certain purity and singularity into this theologizing that does not account for the fact and value of multiplicity and its attendant contestation and complexity (Johnson-DeBaufre and Nasrallah 2011). How can thinking in narrative multiplicities around Paul's letters also inspire plurality in theories and theologies that imagine a world of justice, peace, and planetary thriving? With this question in mind, we turn to the characters, plots, and memories in and around the letters of Paul.

How Many Characters Is Paul?

The only stories that Paul narrates with any detail are autobiographical stories (e.g., Gal. 1–2; 2 Cor. 12; 1 Thess. 2; Philem.). He is, arguably, the only named author in the Christian scriptures if an author is someone who claims the authority to write one's own life and whose "mind" is constructed beyond the texts in which his or her "I" is inscribed. Five out of seven of Paul's letters indicate co-senders with Paul; yet because he tells his own story and frequently speaks with "I," only Paul is inscribed and remembered as an author (Kittredge 2003). Because of this status, Paul's authority transfers to readers—religious or academic— who identify with him and ventriloquize through him (for the problem of identification, see Schüssler Fiorenza 2007, 86–89). There are many other named, but silent, figures in the letters attributed to Paul, such as Chloe, Andronicus, Junia, Tertius, Prisca, Sosthenes, to name just a few.[2] What might we learn from these people if we knew their stories? What stories did they know of God, of Israel, of Christ, of the world?

There are few opportunities to identify with or explore characters other than Paul in the letters. The letter to Philemon provides one case, with its underlying autobiographical story—although with torturously minimal narration—of Paul's becoming and acting the father to Onesimus by sending his son and his advice concerning him to Paul's friend Philemon. What is Onesimus's story? According to the letter's scant details, Onesimus has traveled, been transformed by the gospel, learned with and been under the judgment of group leaders. Chances are good that he, too, has worked with his hands and has suffered pain and humiliation. Despite these similarities to Paul's autobiography, Onesimus is not an author or a subject but the object of deliberation and action. Interpreters of this letter commonly draw on slaveholder tropes and scant textual details to weave his story as one of a fugitive and thieving slave who is now repentant and thus deserves acceptance and debt release from his master.

Other stories can be and have been told. Ordained minister and nineteenth-century abolitionist John Gregg Fee and contemporary biblical scholar Allen D. Callahan both utilize the historical-critical approaches of their times to argue that Onesimus was actually Philemon's younger brother (see Williams 2012, 24–26). In 1991, womanist biblical scholar Renita Weems enacted an alternative identification process, giving the benefit of the doubt to Onesimus and suggesting that he may have fled because of his Christian master's harshness (Weems 1991; for a different angle on Onesimus's suffering, see Marchal 2011). The possibility that Onesimus was Philemon's brother or a mistreated slave changes the underlying theological story from one about the redemption of even the least deserving ("ransom for many") to one of human reconciliation ("love your neighbor"). The one in need of redemption is no longer the depraved slave but the unreconciled older brother or brutal master. Brotherhood in Christ can redeem *even the most powerful of these* ("nothing is impossible with God").

Stories play a fundamental role in collective identity formation. Questions about identification and perspective thus relate to ethical questions about how readers are being formed and to what effect. For example, stories school privileged people in how to understand and behave toward the dis-privileged, and vice versa. Martin Luther, for example, saw Onesimus as a person misled by the idea of freedom and Paul as a proponent of property rights (Williams 2012, 18). As Paul's story is often the authoritative story, he must somehow be the hero of the story. This Paul's story often resembles hagiography. His humility is demonstrated and extolled. As he intervenes in a situation of social disparity, he acts without disdain or arrogance. But at what cost is the silencing of Onesimus and even Philemon? Are free readers taught to expect nothing but gratitude from the unfree when they attempt to act justly? Will Philemon "effectively make the past disappear by saying to Onesimus, 'I'm sorry I enslaved you'"? "If [Onesimus] cannot articulate the anger and pain he endured in the past," is he not "being silenced in the present"? (Johnson et al. 2012, 8) Still, reaching for Onesimus's voice sometimes brings forth not action or words but "groans and sighs too deep for words" (Johnson et al. 2012, 7). Still suspended in anticipation of freedom, enslaved ghosts rattle Christian self-assuredness.

Identifying with Paul and calling all to a Christ-like solidarity with the least of these is not the whole or only possible story. But neither is identifying only with Onesimus. Thomas Aquinas said, "We are all [Christ's] Onesimi if we believe it" (Williams, 2012, 17). This kind of universalizing is attractive theologically, but it masks the considerable differences between the lives of the free and the unfree, both in Paul's day and in ours. And who identifies with Philemon? Who is identified with Philemon? After a visit of African American scholars to South Korea, a pastor sent a letter of thanks saying, "All over the world, Onesimus is still with us. Philemon is still with us, too. Most people in the Third World suffer from a common enemy of humankind, such as exploitative capitalism and neo-liberalism, with the rich getting richer and the poor getting poorer. The demonic power which threatens the peace and brings disorder to the cosmos should be defeated by the solidarity of Onesimus (*Minjung*)" (Johnson et al. 2012, 6). How does each side figure Paul in this story? Are these Pauls the same, or do they differ?

Constructing universal theologies and large-scale political solidarities out of processes of identification with scriptural characters fixes categories with which people make sense of the world. There are Onesimuses and there are Philemons. There are those striving to be Paul even as he strove to be Christ. In this way, the space of a character connects the particularity of one person's story and the big story of the world as it is or might be. That connection between specificity and abstraction gives stories legs to traverse time and space and to signify in different worlds, while also being able to speak to and about individuals and their contexts perhaps compelling motion or at least constituting self-understanding. However, even autobiographical stories include the stories of others, whether articulated or not.

The presence of multiple characters in commonly held stories creates spaces from which fixed categories that organize the world can also be challenged and changed. This dimensionality of stories has been crucial for marginalized readers. Whether in historical narrations or bibliodrama, characters such as Pheobe and Junia have been spaces where women have interrupted and altered the stories told about the Pauline assemblies and the modern church. So also has been Onesimus for the currently or historically unfree. But not all Onesimi are the same. James Noel uses the figure of Nat Turner to read Onesimus as a nightmare character in white fears, while Demetrius Williams explores the fluid spaces of racial identity in enslaved contexts by thinking with James Grimké, the son of a white father and a slave mother whose white brother re-enslaved him (Johnson et al. 2012, 78–82, 45). Even within a character (or a subject position), there is multiplicity that enables different ways of thinking about the self, the other, and the world. This is why it is important not to overstress the "auto" in Paul's autobiography. The self that is narrated is never an autonomously constituted self but one produced in relation, in the spaces between the self and others. All the characters in Paul's story—whether they are narrated or not—are a part of Paul's own story. Whether he knew it or not, Onesimus's story shaped his own. Whether we like it or not, Paul's self-narration does not preclude the malleability and multiplicity of the author named "Paul."

ENTERING CHRIST'S PLOT AT THE MIDDLE

Many have discerned ways that Paul's autobiographical narration repeats a pattern of Christ's voluntary self-sacrifice on the cross (e.g., Gal. 2:20). Collapsing Paul's "I" with Christ, Paul's story becomes "paradigmatic, not in the particulars of individual life journey, nor in his achievements, but in the sense—and to the degree—that his encounter with Christ crucified has refashioned his existence" (Barclay 2002, 144). The Christ event—which for Paul is central to the story of God's salvation of the world—serves as a narrative pattern through which to discern the meaning of and reconfigure all other stories, such as the story of Israel or the story of the communities Paul is addressing.

This Christological paradigm thus informs Paul's ethical mandate to bear each other's burdens, precisely to *be Christ* to one another (Gal. 6:2; Rom. 15:1–6). Michael Gorman identifies this pattern of self-emptying, encapsulated in Philippians 2:5–11 as "although [x], not [y], but [z]," where x is Christ's status in the form of God, y is Christ's disposition toward that status, and z, the action taken. So goes this counterintuitive story of Christ's "downward mobility": "the Messiah Jesus . . . who possessed equality with God ([x]), did not exploit it for selfish advantage ([y]), but, like a slave, emptied himself . . .([z]) such that the result was death—death on a cross" (2009, 16, 25). Numerous encapsulated personal stories throughout Paul's letters show signs of this pattern. In 1 Thessalonians 2:6–8 and 1 Corinthians 9:1–23, for example, Paul presents his own apostleship: *although* having acquired a status with certain privileges, he did *not* selfishly exploit them, *but* took a position of service and sacrifice. For

Hays, the "faithfulness of Christ" (*pistou Christou*), so central to the argument of Romans, functions as a synecdoche for this Christological story of self-sacrifice on behalf of others. For Gorman (2009, 10), "Paul's master story is (in part) about the counterintuitive character, essentially kenotic—or cruciform—character of God."

This Christological narrative has considerable explanatory power for reading Paul's arguments across the letters. For those so interested, it also makes for powerful theology. However, taking the reality of multiple stories seriously can raise a different or, at least, broader range of historical and theological insights. Antoinette Wire's work provides a classic example. She critically reimagines how the Corinthian women prophets might have responded to Paul's instructions based on the syncing of his own story with the self-negating Christ story. For the basic story pattern of although [x], not [y], but [z] to work, the protagonist must have an elevated status to ensure the valence of the "although." In other words, in order to be able to perform the negation ("not") that leads to the action that defies expectation ("but"), the character must have some status to negate. Being "in the form of God" secures Christ's status (Phil. 2:5); being an apostle secures Paul's. For Wire, the stories of their lives as women who experience considerable physical and social hardship would shape how they hear and where they enter the story. Do they enter in a position of status [x] or at an already lowly position [z]? Wire emphasizes that Christ's self-negation results in being lifted up, that is, vindication and glorification (see Phil. 2:9-11). Entering, then, at the middle of the story of Christ-Paul may explain the apparent differences in theology between Paul and the women prophets: "People once immobilized in humiliation and self-abnegation . . . experienced salvation in Christ not as Paul did in relinquishing special privilege and learning the way of the cross but in gaining a new identity. Greek slave women risen in Christ were drawing the whole world into God's image. This was their experience of the risen Christ, their participation in God's glory. They would not lightly set down this life because someone else's experience of Christ had been different" (Wire 2000, 48; see also Wire 1990).

But women's stories are not homogeneous. Perhaps Paul indeed recognizes their status as prophets, as he seems to in 1 Corinthians 11:2, and they share his relatively higher social privilege as free or educated. The research on women in antiquity gives us reason to imagine that (at least some of) the women prophets of Corinth may have numbered among the free/d householders of the assembly rather than among the enslaved or the most poor. If so, then perhaps Paul confirms their status and presses them to bring their theology and practice in line with his own story, and that of Christ, and to model their understanding of wisdom, freedom, and self-control on his own paradigms of wisdom-in-foolishness, freedom in mutual enslavement, and individual self-control for the sake of the whole body. With this framing, both Paul and the women prophets are in the positions of relative status (their stories begin at the "although"), and those without such status are positioned as the beneficiaries of Christ/Paul/prophet's self-lowering. For this reconstruction of the Corinthian women prophets, the beneficiaries of their practices of self-lowering would be those who cannot practice sexual self-control (ch. 7), those who are distressed by unclear boundaries (chs. 8, 10), those coming late to the common meal (ch. 11), those least honored or valued in the body (ch. 12), and those confused or distracted by ecstatic speech in the assembly (ch. 14).

However, even if we imagine that Paul addresses the Corinthian women as peers, he also frames their self-subordination in terms of human hierarchies naturalized by Genesis 2 (1 Cor. 11:2–16) and in terms of a hierarchy of gifts in the assembly (chs. 12, 14). A story in which the already subordinate renew their subordination does not parallel the kind of self-emptying or other-regard valorized in Christ's story. Nor does it easily match the other story of humanity that runs through the letters—that is, of broad commonalities and equality before God. Distinctions of race, status, and gender are negated in Galatians 3:28, and in Romans all flesh is enslaved to sin, and God—as a judge—shows no partiality. This tension between the particularities of structurally unequal characters-in-relation and a universalized plot of God's impartiality may be a reason there are so many exceptions, compromises, and qualifications in the argumentation in 1 Corinthians: women still pray and prophesy (11:6); slaves should take advantage of freedom if they can get it (7:21); the unmarried and widows should not marry (7:8). This ambivalence in the Pauline letters marks a tension among stories of God and Christ in the assemblies, but also becomes a place where new characterizations of Paul and his disciples—whether Timothy or Thecla—contend over which Paul should speak authoritatively in the later Christian communities (see MacDonald 1983; see also Pervo 2010). Underscoring the multiplicity of stories, the assemblies of Christ emerge not as faulty realizations of Paul's ideals, but as the very social spaces in which the memories and values that make up collective identity are formed through the collision and contention of a variety of personal and abstract stories (for an exploration of the Corinthian story via local discourses of ethnicity, see Concannon 2014; for reconstructing the Philippian assembly, see Marchal 2008, 35–36, 91–110).

An exercise in historical reconstruction that privileges multiple persons and perspectives positions readers in a more complicated relationship with canon, presupposing that the letters point to the meeting of stories of God, not *a* story of God or *the* story of God. Presupposing, even valuing, multiple stories demands more of both the historical and the theological reader: listening for unheard voices, watching for unreported experiences, pondering social and theological tensions rather than resolving or dissolving them (for the idea that Paul's audience likely misunderstood him because of cultural difference, see Smith 2011). Taking up Paul's ethical narrative of Christ's self-sacrifice, retelling it in particular contexts, with different characters, calls for recognition of the complexities of stories and a discernment and adjudication of their effects on the variety of people who live with and through them.

PAST AND PRESENT WORLDING

Stories of the past figure prominently in the ways communities construct and revise identity in the present. Unsurprisingly, then, narratives from the Hebrew Bible make a regular appearance in the Pauline letters: Sarah and Hagar in Galatians 4; Sarah's surprising pregnancy without mention of Hagar in Romans 4; Adam without Eve in Romans 5; and, of course, God's promise to Abraham and his descendants in Galatians 3 and Romans 4. Hebrew tribes wander in the desert with Moses in 1 Corinthians 10 and 2 Corinthians 3. Paul does not retell these narratives. He interprets them and puts them to work in his arguments, most often negotiating markers and borders of racial-ethnic-religious identity—both Jewish and non-Jewish (e.g., in relation to Gentile circumcision, Jewish eating practices, Gentile eating practices, and Jewish and Gentile assessments of Paul's Messiah).

In the process of building a particular (if also hybrid) communal identity via these stories, Paul's letters make claims about God and the whole world, and thereby articulate a vision of the world as it should be or will be, perhaps most potently in Romans as the story of God's justice for all. In this sense, the letters enact the theorizing practice of "worlding the world," which is always, also a provincial practice rooted in the vernacular of particular contexts (Kang 2013, 3–6). Throughout Romans, the particular promise to Abraham of a multitude of descendants anchors Jewish identity as the children of God and *also* provides a foundation story for a cosmos-wide family made up of Jews (figured as the natural offspring) and non-Jews (the adoptive, or grafted offspring) who share faithfulness to God as a response to God's gracious justice. This genealogical work is not mere metaphor indicating the transcending of local identities. The in-Christ-assembly is a rather queer ethnic space where there is no longer Judean, nor Greek, but both are the seed (*sperma*) of Abraham, and heirs of the promise (Gal. 3:28–29). There is no longer ethnically parsed difference, and yet they are the seed and heirs of Abraham in particular. The invocation of Abraham's story as the founding story of the Gentiles-in-Christ does not strip the story of its power to constitute a particular people; rather, it precisely draws on that power in order to render the ethnic borders porous enough to bring in all the Gentiles without losing the specificity of the enduring (even fixed) promise to Abraham (see Johnson Hodge 2007; for the challenges of reading ethnic/racial and religious identity around Paul's letters, see Buell 2014).

Origin stories often provide their fixity through naturalizing arguments, built on family genealogies and the links of seed, blood, or resemblances. These produce a sense of stable and essential identity across time and place, and thus inform the logic of both cultural heritage and of racism. Communal belonging and social profiling hover together as potent alternatives, depending on who is telling the origin story. Paul's Jewish Messianic story of God's justice and salvation for all can be and has been turned into a story of western humanity's progress from Judaism to Christianity, undergirding millennia of ethno-religious racism and violence. Efforts to (re)assert the fundamental particularity of Paul's Jewish "worlding" not only make better sense of texts such as Romans, they also participate in multiplying the stories that readers might wrestle with as they engage in theorizing and theologizing about the world and its peoples using Paul's letters (compare, for example, the Jewish texts used by Stowers 1997 and Grieb 2002).

This worlding-from-particularity can be productively examined from a variety of storied angles. For example, there are at least three narratives that contend to be the story behind the story in Paul's caricature of those who "did not honor God as God" in Romans 1:18–32, and each has implications for thinking about ancient and contemporary identities. Narrative biblical theologians posit the Jewish story of creation in Genesis 1–3—albeit with a particularly Christian interpretation—as the primary intertext for Romans 1–3, conveying "the story of a world gone wrong" (Grieb 2002, 25–31). In this context, the sinfulness of all of humanity is being caricatured in gender relations that contradict the heteronormative order of creation (male/female, Adam/Eve). Awkwardly, all Jews are both ontologically part of sinful humanity (via the creation story), while ancient Jews provide the framework that link sexual sin and gentile idolatry (via Wisdom of Solomon). To bridge these universal and particular stories, one has to add Exodus 32 (or Pss. 105:20 LXX) as a secondary intertext in order to account for Paul's characterization of (presumably all of) confused humanity as making and worshipping idols (Rom. 1:23). In this approach, the Christian story of ontologically sinful humanity is preserved. However, the visceral judgment of homoeroticism is attributed to Paul's Jewishness and the only theological recourse for Christians seeking to ameliorate the impact of this text on same-gender loving people is to utilize Paul against Paul by confirming that sinful humans cannot presume to judge other sinful humans (Rom. 2).

Another possibility emerges with a different intertext. Stanley Stowers (1997, 85) locates Romans 1:18–32 as one among many ancient stories that "looked to humanity's distant past or beginnings in order to explain the present state of society." Using Genesis to explain human sin was alien to the Jewish scriptural interpretation of Paul's time; however, stories of social decline were common, and Romans represents Paul's narrative of the decline of Gentile culture (not of humanity in general) into confusion and impiety. According to Stowers, Paul's particular Jewish caricature of gender errors reflects the cultural milieu of *both* Jews and Gentiles, in which all cultures represented "outsiders as less pure and less self-controlled than themselves" (94). In this frame, Paul's condemnation of homoeroticism cannot be chalked up to ancient Jewish particularity or to specific Gentile practices. If Christian readers consider this intertext, they are confronted with broad cultural tendencies that narrate communal identity in a way that vilifies outsiders as unnatural, sexually excessive, or confused.[3] Here, the notion that no law/culture/people is capable of producing justice, a notion more akin to recent philosophical readings of Romans 1–3, invites Christians, through their Scriptures, to practice "worlding" that does not presume that one culture (or religion) can ever fully or purely embody or articulate Justice/Truth/Good for all.

This philosophical reading draws on a third intertext for Romans 1:18–32. Here, the story is the social chaos of the time of the Julio-Claudian emperors. Even Roman historians will come to describe the reigns of Tiberius, Caligula, Claudius, and Nero as an era of social madness and injustice, "a time of the rule of paranoid gangsters who sought to destroy any and all rivals" (Jennings 2013, 36; see Elliot 2008). In this context, Paul indicts dominant Roman/Gentile society by calling attention to the obscenity of prominent men and women who claim to know the truth and to be the guarantors of justice, but who embody error, antisocial behavior, and injustice. In this frame, Paul's story of unnatural women and men targets not types of sexual practices, but the social and political excesses of imperial women and men, particularly in the time of Caligula. This theopolitical reading of Romans ratchets the scale of the story up from personal sexual practices or identities to a broad anticultural script, in which injustice and hypocrisy figure as unnatural excess. This tableaux is akin to a voracious Uncle Sam raping Mother Earth or depicting the world's wealthy one percent as promiscuously in bed with each other. Because this reading figures God as Justice to Come, there is a trans-contextual and, therefore, "improvisational" quality to God's justice, which promises that a theory or theology of justice can never be claimed by one culture or community or people, including Christianity (Jennings 2013, 182–186). While this does not, in fact, remedy the everyday reality that the predominant reading of Romans 1 marks some bodies as unnatural, it seeks to interrupt the presupposition that this text is a story about any bodies in particular. Recognizing this tension cultivates an awareness that all large-scale stories think with and from the embodied and the local, and thus can, even must, also be interrupted and rethought with and from these spaces.

Paul is in the business of constructing communal identity and thinking about the whole world and its peoples through both naturalizing and universalizing stories. The ongoing place of scripture in shaping Jewish and Christian identity as well as in theological and philosophical "worlding" means that the considerable twin dangers of essentializing/naturalizing particular identities and claiming to transcend any particularity always lay close by. Theorizing Paul's letters as places where different cultural and personal stories collide, challenge, and shape each other—both in the past and across times—may best serve a process of worlding the world in a way that can both ground particularity while being ever in motion, ever self-undoing, on behalf All.

Multivoiced and Multivalent

People experience the world and their own lives as stories. Narratives of origins, traumatic events, and life-giving renewal play a fundamental role in the constitution and negotiation of communal identity and authority. Generations of people who somehow value the Pauline letters have built and rebuilt storied worlds in which the letters have meaning. Thus, parsing Paul's worldview and world narration alone is not sufficient to explore the impact, value, and valence of the letters addressed to diverse Christ assemblies across the Mediterranean. Thinking about them as a space where storied worlds—from small to large—meet, interact, mingle, and contest comes closer to the way texts and contexts together produce and revise meaning. It opens the Pauline assembly, as well as the communities of readers of Paul, as productive spaces where a multiplicity of people gather and deliberate over communal ideals and ways of life—not always with equal power or voice, but with equally storied worlds.

Multiplicity is not the end of the story. It is the beginning. This is true for theology, where, "blossoming at the edges of tradition and at the margins of power," some theologies do not seek to overcome multiplicity, open-endedness, and relationality, but instead see them as constitutive of the very matrix of Divine revelation (Keller and Schneider 2011, 1; see, differently, Schneider 2008; Rieger and Kwok 2013). And it is true for feminist biblical scholars who reject the politics of othering so frequent in the Pauline letters and scholarship and place the most marginalized wo/men at the center of political-theological theory and practice (see Schüssler Fiorenza 1999, 2013). And even when conceptualizing the Bible itself, multiplicity is a starting point. David Carr suggests that the multivoiced and multivalent nature of the biblical text is precisely what ensures continued sacred value to its communities of readers. Given the complexity and changing nature of human communities, the Bible must be changeable too. If it were not multivalent, Carr (2000, 348–349, 358) says, readers would make it so. The Pauline tradition, with its iterations, corrections, and divergent meanings demonstrates just such contention and creativity. A multivoiced and multivalent Bible does not confine the story of God to any text or even to the canon. Valuing multiplicity and relationality in local and translocal terms challenges the sufficiency of any "great" or normative story or storyteller to narrate or theorize world, God, or All. The ideals of justice, equality, and mutuality do not stand apart from the complexity of multiplicity, but are continually signified and energized by new embodiments and ethical-theological improvisations. Even Paul would not be the theopolitical thinker he is without a multitude of others.

Notes

1. Neither "church" nor "Christian" accurately describe Paul's first addressees. Paul's term *ekklēsia*, evoking a civic assembly, and the frequent reference to their shared loyalty to Jesus as *Christos* are the basis for describing them as Christ assemblies.

2. It is also reasonable to assume that there were hundreds of other unnamed people who knew Paul or a Christ disciple and who shared with them various practices, beliefs, and stories.

3. Stowers writes for an academic audience. The question of whether and how scholarship participates in contemporary discourses of identity formation and negotiation is relevant to the topic of narrative approaches to the Bible, but beyond the scope of this essay.

REFERENCES

Badiou, Alain. 2003. *St. Paul: The Foundation of Universalism*. Redwood City, CA: Stanford University Press.

Barclay, John M. G. 2002. "Paul's Story: Theology as Testimony." In *Narrative Dynamics in Paul: A Critical Assessment*, edited by Bruce W. Longnecker, 133–156. Louisville, KY, and London: Westminster John Knox Press.

Boer, Roland. 2011. "Paul's Uncertain Transitions." *The Bible and Critical Theory* 7: 27–43.

Buell, Denise Kimber. 2014. "Challenges and Strategies for Speaking about Ethnicity in the New Testament and New Testament Studies." *Svensk Exegetisk Årsbok* 49: 33–51.

Carr, David. 2000. "Untamable Text of an Untamable God: Genesis and Rethinking the Character of Scripture." *Interpretation* 54: 347–362.

Charles, Ronald. 2014. *Paul and the Politics of Diaspora*. Minneapolis, MN: Fortress Press.

Concannon, Cavan W. 2014. *"When You Were Gentiles": Specters of Ethnicity in Roman Corinth and Paul's Corinthian Correspondence*. New Haven, CT: Yale University Press.

Ehrensberger, Kathy. 2015. *Paul at the Crossroads of Cultures: Theologizing in the Space Between*. London: Bloomsbury T. & T. Clark.

Elliot, Neil. 2008. *The Arrogance of Nations: Reading Romans in the Shadow of Empire*. Minneapolis, MN: Fortress Press.

Gorman, Michael. 2009. *Inhabiting the Cruciform God: Kenosis, Justification, and Theosis in Paul's Narrative Soteriology*. Grand Rapids, MI: Eerdmans.

Grieb, Katherine. 2002. *The Story of Romans*. Louisville, KY: Westminster/John Knox.

Hays, Richard B. (1983) 2001. *The Faith of Jesus Christ: An Investigation of the Narrative Substructure of Galatians 3:1–4:11*. Chico, CA: Scholars Press. Reprint, Grand Rapids, MI: Eerdmans.

Hays, Richard B. 1989. *Echoes of Scripture in the Letters of Paul*. New Haven, CT: Yale University Press.

Hays, Richard B. 2008. "Can Narrative Criticism Recover the Theological Unity of Scripture?" *Journal of Theological Interpretation* 2(2): 193–211.

Jennings, Theodore. 2013. *Outlaw Justice: The Messianic Politics of Paul*. Redwood City, CA: Stanford University Press.

Johnson, Matthew V. et al. 2012. "Introduction: Paul's Relevance Today." In *Onesimus Our Brother: Reading Religion, Race, and Culture in Philemon*, edited by Matthew V. Johnson, James A Noel, and Demetrius Williams. Minneapolis, MN: Fortress Press.

Johnson-DeBaufre, Melanie, and Laura S. Nasrallah, 2011. "Beyond the Heroic Paul: Toward a Feminist and Decolonizing Approach to the Letters of Paul." In *The Colonized Apostle: Paul in Postcolonial Eyes*, edited by Christopher Stanley, 161–174. Minneapolis, MN: Fortress Press.

Johnson Hodge, Caroline. 2007. *If Sons, Then Heirs: A Study of Kinship and Ethnicity in the Letters of Paul*. Oxford and New York: Oxford University Press.

Kang, Namsoon. 2013. *Cosmopolitan Theology: Reconstituting Planetary Hospitality, Neighbor-Love, and Solidarity in an Uneven World.* St. Louis, MO: Chalice Press.

Keller, Catherine, and Laurel Schneider. 2011. *Polydoxy: Theology of Multiplicity and Relation.* New York: Routledge.

Kittredge, Cynthia Briggs. 2003. "Rethinking Authorship in the Letters of Paul: Elisabeth Schüssler Fiorenza's Model of Pauline Theology." In *Walk in the Ways of Wisdom: Essays in Honor of Elisabeth Schüssler Fiorenza,* edited by Shelly Matthews, Cynthia Briggs Kittredge, and Melanie Johnson-DeBaufre, 318–333. Harrisburg, PA: Trinity Press International.

Longnecker, Bruce W. 2002a. "The Narrative Approach to Paul: An Early Retrospective." *Currents in Biblical Research* 1(1): 88–111.

Longnecker, Bruce W., ed. 2002b. *Narrative Dynamics in Paul: A Critical Assessment.* Louisville, KY, and London: Westminster John Knox Press.

Lopez, Davina. 2008. *Apostle to the Conquered: Reimagining Paul's Mission.* Minneapolis, MN: Fortress Press.

MacDonald, Dennis Ronald. 1983. *The Legend and the Apostle: The Battle for Paul in Story and Legend.* Philadelphia: Westminster John Knox.

Marchal, Joseph A. 2011. "The Usefulness of an Onesimus: The Sexual Use of Slaves and Paul's Letter to Philemon." *Journal of Biblical Literature* 130(December): 749–770.

Marchal, Joseph A. 2008. *The Politics of Heaven: Women, Gender, and Empire in the Study of Paul.* Minneapolis, MN: Fortress Press.

Pervo, Richard I. 2010. *The Making of Paul: The Construction of the Apostle in Early Christianity.* Minneapolis, MN: Fortress Press.

Rieger, Joerg, and Pui-lan Kwok. 2013. *Occupy Religion: Theology of the Multitude.* New York: Rowman & Littlefield.

Schneider, Laurel. 2008. *Beyond Monotheism: A Theology of Multiplicity.* Abingdon and New York: Routledge.

Schüssler Fiorenza, Elisabeth. 1999. *Rhetoric and Ethic: The Politics of Biblical Studies.* Minneapolis, MN: Fortress Press.

Schüssler Fiorenza, Elisabeth. 2007. *The Power of the Word: Scripture and the Rhetoric of Empire.* Minneapolis, MN: Augsburg Fortress.

Schüssler Fiorenza, Elisabeth. 2013. "Critical Feminist The*logy of Liberation: A Decolonizing Political The*logy." In *Political Theology: Contemporary Challenges and Future Directions,* edited by Francis Schüssler Fiorenza, Klaus Tanner, and Michael Welker. Louisville, KY: Westminster John Knox Press.

Seesengood, Robert Paul. 2010. *Paul: A Brief History.* Gloucestershire, United Kingdom: Wiley-Blackwell.

Smith, J. Z. 2011. "Re: Corinthians." In *Redescribing Paul and the Corinthians,* edited by Ron Cameron and Merrill P. Miller, 17–34. Atlanta, GA: Society of Biblical Literature.

Stowers, Stanley. 1997. *A Rereading Romans: Justice, Jews, and Gentiles.* New Haven, CT: Yale University Press.

Weems, Renita J. 1991. "Reading *Her Way* through the Struggle: African American Women and the Bible." In *Stony the Road We Trod: African American Biblical Interpretation,* edited by Cain Hope Felder, 57–80. Minneapolis, MN: Fortress Press.

Williams, Demetrius. 2012. "'No longer a Slave': Reading the Interpretation History of Paul's Epistle to Philemon." In *Onesimus Our Brother: Reading Religion, Race, and Culture in Philemon,* edited by Matthew V. Johnson, James A Noel, and Demetrius Williams, 11–46. Minneapolis, MN: Fortress Press.

Wire, Antoinette. 1990. *The Corinthian Women Prophets: A Reconstruction through Paul's Rhetoric*. Minneapolis, MN: Fortress Press.

Wire, Antoinette. 2000. "Women Prophets in the Corinthian Church," In *Conflict and Community in the Corinthian Church*, edited by J. Shannon Clarkson, 35–52. Nashville, TN: United Methodist Church.

Witherington, Ben III. 1994. *Paul's Narrative Thought World: The Tapestry of Tragedy and Triumph*. Louisville, KY: Westminster John Knox.

Wright, N. T. 2013. *Paul and the Faithfulness of God*. Books I and II. Minneapolis, MN: Fortress Press.

CHAPTER 32

NARRATIVE TECHNIQUE IN THE BOOK OF REVELATION

DAVID L. BARR

Too often, the book of Revelation has been read as an allegory wherein various elements of the story are taken to refer to other, external events, especially events of the interpreter's time. Most often these interpreters claim to be taking the story of Revelation literally, but that is clearly not the case. The story itself says nothing about the modern world, America, the second coming, or the end of the world. It is, rather, a narrative of what happened to John—what he saw and heard—a story, not a puzzle or an essay on the end times. Even scholars have tended to interpret Revelation as an allegory of ideas rather than as a narrative, and so they speak of John's ecclesiology or his eschatology (Wainwright 1993, 125–158). But the book of Revelation is neither a guide to the end of the world nor a handbook of theology. It is a narrative.

In this narrative John recounts what happened to him on Patmos, describes what he saw and heard when he ascended into the sky/heaven, and recounts the cosmic conflict between the forces of good and evil—a definitive Holy War. It is thus a complicated narrative, recounting both John's actions (what happened to him) and the actions he recounts in the stories he tells (what he saw and heard). He functions as both the narrator and as a character in the story. This chapter explores the various techniques used to tell the story, focusing on its genre, structure and plot, temporal and spatial distortions, performance, and rhetorical effect.

NARRATIVE GENRE

The book of Revelation belongs to a genre modern scholars have named *apocalypses*, minimally described as autobiographical narratives recounting the reception of revelations. These represent a subset of a larger category we can label *vision reports*. The genre includes a diverse literary corpus, exhibiting different ideologies, addressing different social situations, and employing different narrative strategies. The modern effort to define the genre began in the nineteenth century (Lücke 1852), and was carried forward in significant ways by Russell (1964), Hanson (1979), and Hellholm (1989). Their insights have been analyzed, refined, and advanced in the work of the Society of Biblical Literature's Genre Project, especially as articulated in the writings of John Collins (1979). What is now the standard definition runs as follows:

> "Apocalypse" is a genre of revelatory literature with a narrative framework, in which a revelation is mediated by an otherworldly being to a human recipient, disclosing a transcendent reality which is both temporal, insofar as it envisages eschatological salvation, and spatial insofar as it involves another, supernatural world. (Collins 1979, 9)

In the first instance, every apocalypse is an account of an experience (real or imagined) of some prophetic figure (real or imagined). They typically begin with such statements as "after this I saw another dream and I will show it all to you" (1 *Enoch* 85:1); "the fourth vision which I saw, brethren, 20 days after the former vision . . . I was going into the country on the via Campania" (*Shepherd of Hermas* 1:1); and "I saw in my sleep what I now show to you with the tongue of flesh and with my breath" (1 *Enoch* 14:2). John, too, begins autobiographically: he is telling what he heard and saw in the spirit when he was on the island called Patmos (Rev. 1: 9–12).

In this way, an apocalypse is a narrative re-presentation of a revelation experience so that the audience can imaginatively share that experience (Aune 1986). These narratives recount the experience of the seer in another (sacred) time or another (sacred) place. While all apocalypses concern both sacred space and sacred time, an individual apocalypse will focus on one or the other. Those that focus on sacred space usually include an otherworldly journey in which the seer visits the heavens (and later, also the underworld). Those that focus on sacred time usually include the device of historical review, also called *ex eventu* prophecy, a symbolic portrayal of historical events up to the time of the audience (Barr 2013).

Both types intend to interpret the present situation of the audience. Indeed, those who enter into these stories will find the present situation changed by the experience. Now, this is not something magical or even religious. It is what stories do.

> A story on the page is like a printed circuit
> For our lives to flow through,
> A story told invokes our dim capacity
> To be alive in bodies not our own. (Doctorow 2000, 181)

In the same way, John pronounces a blessing on those who hear and retain his story (Rev. 1:3). The effectiveness of an apocalypse does not depend on whether it corresponds to history or successfully predicts the future. It depends on whether the story captures the audience. Again, this is what stories do.

> "There is nothing better than imagining other worlds," he said, "to forget the painful one we live in. At least I thought so then. I hadn't yet realized that, imagining other worlds, you end up changing this one." (Eco 2002, 99)

Stories can change the world, because one of the primary ways we understand the world is by telling stories about it. In John's world the dominant story was that of Rome and Caesar: the

Pax Romana. Caesar had slain the monster of chaos with its civil wars and economic turmoil. John retells the story from the opposite perspective: the chaos monster is the Caesar (Wengst 1987; van Henten 2006). And this is not just some general story about a primordial time or a faraway place, for John includes himself and his audience in the story. It is the audience that must keep its hands unsullied and its forehead unmarked by the beast (Rev. 13:16–17; 20:4).

It is the experience of the story of the Apocalypse, with its reconfiguration of the world in which they lived, that allowed the audience to achieve a new understanding of life (Schüssler Fiorenza 1998a, 181–203). The Apocalypse is both a story and a performance in which the story is orally presented to the audience. John was not so much predicting the coming of a new age as making it a reality in the lives of his audience when they experienced the story of his revelation—"happy are those who hear" (Rev. 1:3; Barr 2006).

In this story the hero is Jesus. In fact, the story announces itself as "the Revelation of Jesus Christ" (1:1). But we should not let our familiarity with the gospel versions of that story control our reading of John's narrative. The story is not told in chronological order, does not follow a consistent action from beginning to end, and contains a high degree of repetition.

NARRATIVE ORDER

There is no agreement on the proper outline or structure of the book of Revelation. It is often said that there are as many outlines as there are interpreters (Smith 1994). There are several reasons for this diversity. While some of the material is consciously numbered into a series of seven items (churches, seals, trumpets, and bowls), it is not clear how the rest of the material relates to the numbered sequences. There are also interruptions within the numbered sequences—the series of seals is interrupted after seal six with the story of the sealing of God's servants; the series of trumpets is interrupted after trumpet six with several small stories. The complexity of the traditions recounted is an additional factor; these traditions seem to come from basically different spheres and to be about different things. Some take this as evidence of different sources being combined together. In addition, certain elements of the narrative are repeated again and again. Finally, some of the material seems to be wildly out of place chronologically (for example, the beast is introduced in chapter 13 but has appeared already in the story in chapter 11).

The difficulty in finding an outline for Revelation stems in part from asking the wrong question—the question of how to divide the material. We should rather be asking how the author took such diverse material and wove it into a narrative unity (Thompson 1989). If we take the implied setting seriously, that it was composed for an oral performance before an audience (1:3), our attention shifts to how this diverse material is unified (Barr 1986). The author's hand can be traced in the themes, characterizations, and story plot.

All interpreters agree that chapters 1 through 3 form a discrete unit, the theme of which is a written communication from an otherworldly being. In this unit Jesus is presented as a magnificent heavenly, humanlike figure. The only action of this unit is the instruction to John to write specific letters to the messengers of specific churches. Having completed this task, John is whisked away to heaven, where he witnesses the eternal liturgy of all creation gathered around the throne of God. In this scene Jesus is presented as the slain but living lamb who is worthy to share the throne of God. The action of this unit centers on a scroll which the Lamb opens, moving from the chaos of war, famine, and death (6:1-8) to the declaration that the kingdoms of this world have become the kingdom of God (11:15). After this, John peers into the heavenly Temple and sees astrological and mythological signs of the final battle between good and evil. In this unit Jesus is (or should be) presented as the ultimate heavenly warrior (19:11–16), but in large measure the characterization of the second unit (the slain but living lamb) persists. Still, the theme of holy war permeates all the action of the section, culminating one thousand years of peace, the creation of a new heaven and a new earth, and the manifestation of a new city of God.

We have, then, three broad thematic units having to do with letter writing (1–3), heavenly worship (4–11), and holy war (12–22). Each of these contains some dissimilar materials, and none of them makes conscious reference to the others. John forces the audience to make sense of them by placing them in a common narrative framework of his experience.

John appears in each of the thematic units just described, but with different functions. In the first unit he is a secretary for the heavenly figure; in the second unit he is a heavenly traveler; and in the third unit he is a prophetic seer.

NARRATIVE SPACE

While John's actions include the ordinary space of the audience—real places like Ephesus, Smyrna, and Pergamum—the action occurs in other places. The first action occurs on Patmos, an island off the coast of Asia Minor. It is a real and easily imagined place but as an island is not contiguous with ordinary space. It is in some ways Other. Having secured the readers' imagination of this other place, John now sees a door in the sky and ascends though it into the throne room in heaven—a sacred space radically distinct from ordinary space— and yet, connected to the audience by the portrayal of a worship service, almost certainly analogous to theirs. As the worship service culminates John sees into the heavenly Temple and experiences a further vision. The narrative complexity here is marvelous: the audience sees John on Patmos, having a vision of himself in which he ascends into heaven, where he has a vision of himself having a further vision of the dragon's coming attack.

Spatial location of this third section is not easy to determine. John sees a vision of omens in the sky (12:1), which would imply that he is back on earth, looking up. This would seem to be confirmed by the account of the war in heaven, at the end of which Satan is cast down to earth (12:12). And the Lamb gathers his army on Mount Zion, an earthly place projecting into the sky above (14:1). Mt. Zion is also a symbolic way of referring to Jerusalem, a place that is both historic and mythic; another battle has the armies gathering at Armageddon—an entirely mythic place not found on any map, despite the ingenuity of many interpreters. And one can hardly imagine where John is standing when he sees the creation of a new heaven and a new earth—the old having fled the scene (21:1).

Still, there is a logic and symmetry to John's use of space. The story begins and ends with the author on stage as a character in the drama, directly addressing the audience (1:9; 22:8). The opening action occurs on an island in the midst of the sea, and the action ends in a world in which there is no more sea (21:1). And the central action pivots around the throne of God. Thus, the actions reported in these three units occur in identifiable, if ever more remote, locations: on Patmos, in the heavenly throne room, and in the space of conflict located between heaven and earth. Yet the temporal sequence of the action is anything but straightforward.

NARRATIVE TIME

The narrative strategy of the book of Revelation distorts the audience's sense of time in several ways: telling events out of order, describing some actions in great detail while passing quickly over others, and by frequent repetitions with variations. There is little agreement on the meaning of these distortions. At a minimum, we can conclude that there is not one unfolding story in the Apocalypse. At a minimum, we must conclude that events are not told in a chronological order.

Order

The birth of the Messiah is narrated in highly symbolic form in chapter 12; but he has already appeared in the story as the slaughtered, yet living, lamb whose conquest has made him worthy to open the scroll in chapter 5. Chapter 11 culminates in the announcement that the kingdom of God has come and taken control of the kingdoms of this world; yet chapters 13 narrates the emergence of two world beasts whose rule is antithetical to that of God's. The primeval battle between Michael and Satan, which results in Satan's expulsion from heaven, is narrated as if it occurs after the death of Jesus (12:7–12). In addition, there are several story fragments inserted into otherwise connected narratives, breaking up the flow. For example, presentation of the seven seals is broken off after the sixth seal by the lengthy recounting of the sealing of the elect for their protection. The series of seven trumpets is broken off after trumpet six with the recounting of three short stories, unconnected to the trumpets. In both instances the story shifts abruptly back to the seventh item in the series. The order in which events are narrated in John's story is not necessarily related to the order in which he understood them to happen in that story.

Duration

All narratives radically compress the time of the story, but within this compression we can recognize three different temporal shifts: summary (when events are narrated briefly), scenic (when events are narrated in detail), and slow motion (when the events narrated are elaborated by descriptions, explanations, or other nonnarrative material). Good examples of the latter include the elaborate description of Jesus in chapter 1, the detailing of the heavenly throne room chapter 4, and the descriptions of Babylon as prostitute and of the new Jerusalem as bride in chapters 17 and 21. In each case, the progress of the narrative is brought to a virtual standstill while the audience contemplates the meaning of the setting.

At the other extreme, some material is passed over in such rapid summary as to be almost invisible. For example, battle scenes are never actually portrayed; the narrative passes directly from the announcement of battle to announcement of its completion (see 19:19–20).

Instead of focusing on the battle, the narrative focuses on the one who wins the battle, with an elaborate slow-motion description (19:11–16). By manipulating the duration of his narration, John directs the audience's attention to the aspects of the story he deems important.

Frequency

Numerous elements of John story are repeated, usually with variation. It is not always clear whether he is narrating the same event in different words or different events in similar words. Some instances seem to be simple repetitions. There are two scenes of the twenty-four elders worshiping before the heavenly throne (4:10; 11:6), two portrayals of the censer full of the prayers of the faithful (5:8; 8:3), two openings of the heavenly temple (11:19; 15:5), two instances of John offering worship to the heavenly messenger (19:10; 22:8), and several joltings of the great earthquake (6:12; 8:5; 11:13; 11:19).

More important are the repetitions with variation. For example, the seven bowls of judgment echo almost exactly the seven trumpets (compare 8:7–11:15 with 16:2–17). And while it is common to speak of the final battle in the book of Revelation, there are in fact five such battles (16:14; 17:14; 19:11, 19:19; 20:8). In a similar way, the fall of Babylon—that great enemy of God—is noted six times: as burned (14:8–11), destroyed by an earthquake (16:18–21), as consumed by the kings of the earth (17:16–18), as abandoned (18:2–4), as burned (18:8–20), and as being thrown into the sea (18:21–24). It seems impossible to take these as any kind of a chronological sequence.

John's narrative technique thus involves deliberate temporal distortions of order, duration, and frequency. It operates under different time schemes in different parts. And even the characters that persist throughout the narrative (John and Jesus) are characterized differently in different actions. Is it possible, then, to speak of the plot of John's narrative?

NARRATIVE PLOT

Some see the work as a continuously unfolding plot (a linear sequence; Resseguie 2009, 44–47); others see it as is lacking a plot altogether—preferring to speak of its "dramatic structure" (Bowman 1955) or mythic unity (Thompson 1969). Still others see it as a collection of stories within an overarching narrative structure (more circular or spiral than straight line; Barr 2003).

These different perspectives derive in part from different understandings of plot. Some regard plot as the arrangement of the incidents of the story so that they achieve a particular impression on the reader. Such critics usually look for broad categories of action, such as the setting, the problem, the crisis, the resolution, and the new setting (for example, Jang 2003). At this very broad level of generalization one can argue that chapters 1–3 provide the setting of the story, a story that begins in heavenly unity (4–5) but then descends into chaos with the emergence of the Dragon into beasts (12–13); this chaos is overcome in the war between the Lamb and the Dragon (14–19), resulting in a new state of ideal unity (20–22). This might rightly be called a comic plot and is a useful way to view the story of the Apocalypse (Resseguie 2009).

Others, going back to Aristotle, define plot not as the incidents of the story but as the relationship between the incidents, the causality, the logic of the arrangement of the incidents— the probability or necessity that one thing should follow another (Aristotle 1953, 1450a, 51). This is what Aristotle meant when he said every story should have a beginning, middle, and end; the initial incident starts the ball rolling; middle incidents receive their impetus from the preceding incidents and pass it on to the next; the final incident brings the movement to a stop. Of course, Aristotle was talking about the relatively tightly plotted genre of Greek tragedy. Actual plots vary over a broad continuum from the very tightly plotted (such as a tragedy) to the very loosely plotted (such as an epic).

Using this definition, it is impossible to draw a straight line through the apocalypse wherein each incident is related to that which goes before and after. There are just too many incidents, too many different kinds of incidents, too many loose ends. A prime example is the opening section in which John is directed to write letters to the seven churches; the audience sees the dictation of the letters, but they are never delivered. We never get to see what Jezebel says when she reads what John says of her! In fact the letters are never referred to again. Instead, John plays on the reference to the heavenly throne in the seventh letter and then proceeds to describe a vision of the throne of God with all creation gathered round—an entirely new action.

The throne scene centers on opening another scroll, one sealed with seven seals. Its opening culminates in silence, the blowing of seven trumpets, and the announcement that God's kingdom has come: "the kingdom of this world has become the kingdom of our Lord and of his Messiah and he shall reign forever and ever" (11:15). Heavenly worship resumes. On one level, this represents the end of the story. What could possibly happen after this?

But instead of stopping, the story continues with an essentially new cast of characters: a heavenly woman crowned with the sun and a great red dragon, who now initiates a war on God's people. The Dragon conjures two other new characters: the primordial beasts from land and sea. Then something surprising happens. In characterizing the forces that will oppose this evil triumvirate, John reaches back to the throne scene, transforming the 144,000 marked for protection into the holy Army led, not by a new hero, but by the slaughtered-standing lamb. By (re)using these characters, John ties this new action to the previous one even though there is no logical connection to the action.

There are, then, three separate thematic and dramatic units in the narrative that John has constructed: a heavenly figure commands John to write letters to the seven churches, dictating the messages. John journeys in the spirit to the heavenly throne room, where he witnesses the heavenly liturgy. John peers into the heavenly Temple and witnesses the holy war between good and evil. Nevertheless, John has used these three stories to create a unified narrative.

The narrative strategy of the book of Revelation entails incorporating these three separate stories within a common narrative framework of John's revelatory experience. He begins his narrative with the declaration, "I John was on the island called Patmos . . . and I heard . . . and turned to see . . ." (1:9–12) And after telling us his stories he reasserts, "I John am the one who heard and saw these things" (22:8). This corresponds exactly to what the opening narrator declares "the revelation of Jesus Christ, which God gave him to show his servants what must soon take place; he made it known by sending his angel to his servant John, who testified to the word of God and to the testimony of Jesus Christ, even to all that he saw" (1:1–2). And the scene of the angel presenting the revelation to John is dramatized near the midpoint of the narrative (10:1–10).

The motif that holds all this together is the need to conquer evil (Bauckham 1988). In the letters, each of the seven churches is promised a reward to the one who conquers (2:7, 11, 17, 26–28; 3:5, 12, 21), and each promise is eventually fulfilled in the final scenes of the story (see the chart in Barr 2012, 92–93). And the means of this conquest are revealed in the second story, where the only one worthy to open the divine scroll is the slaughtered Lamb "who has conquered" (5:1–10). While other early writers explained Jesus's conquest in historical terms (the Gospels), John has chosen a thoroughly mythic form. The third scene portrays the actual conquest of the Lamb over the Dragon, using the metaphor of holy war. This war is not something that happens after the heavenly liturgy, not some future struggle; it is something that happens in the liturgy and in the prior events, showing how the Lamb conquered.

NARRATIVE CLOSURE

Stories should come to a satisfying conclusion, a final scene or narrator's summary in which the conflict is resolved and there is no need for any further action—an end: closure. Sometimes this closure is complete, all the loose ends wrapped up, but most often the closure is only partial. But whether partial or complete, the ending of the story enables the audience to understand story in a new way. We now know how it comes out. Looking back, we can now see what was important and what was not. The ending offers the audience the final clue to the story's meaning; now the audience must exercise its imagination.

The end of John's story has been a long time coming (Barr 2001). And when it does come it is not what we expect. It can be read in at least three ways, considering the story of the narrator, of the characters in the story, and of the implied audience.

From the viewpoint of the narrator, nothing has changed. Our circling plot eventually comes back to where it began, with John directly addressing the audience in his own voice, "I, John, am the one who heard and saw these things" (22:8; cf. 1:9). In this way, nothing has changed. The anticipated time is still near (22:10; cf. 1:3), and Jesus is still coming soon (22:12; cf. 1:1). The dogs are still outside (22:15).

But from the viewpoint of the characters in the story, everything has changed. The city of God has descended from heaven, bringing the tree of life to all (22:2), and "there shall be no curse anymore" (22:3). The failure of Eden has been undone by the one who conquers. The world has changed. To the degree that the audience identifies with these characters, their world, too, may be changed. For closure is not complete; there is more, more to the story, for at the very end of the story something is happening. The audience is invited to come and drink of the water of life; and Jesus promises to come to them. Some further action is contemplated. We do not know what it is, for it happens outside the story—we do not even know if those gathered to hear the story (the narratee) will come. But we do know there is more to the story. The end is not necessarily the end.

NARRATIVE RHETORIC

Things heard, things seen, things told. The overarching story of Revelation is the narrative of how John experienced three increasingly fantastic stories, located in increasingly fantastic places. What John sees and hears in these places is meant to persuade those in his community to live appropriately in their present political and social situation. Just what that situation was is not entirely clear. What is clear is that we must not mistake the narrative setting for the actual setting. Narratives present the world as the author wishes us to see it, not simply the world as it is (Krieger 1964; Petersen 1978).

The narrative world of the Apocalypse is a dangerous place, full of beasts and dragons. For a long time interpreters assumed that this was also true of John's historical world, assumed that John lived in a time of Roman persecution of Christians. But careful historical research has shown that this is not likely. Late first-century Roman Asia minor was a time and place of increasing prosperity (Thompson 1990).

On the other hand, for rhetoric to be effective, the audience must discern some true connection between elements of the story and their own life experience. The experience must be such that the story is seen as a "fitting response" to their world (Schüssler Fiorenza 1986, 1987, 1998b). Disentangling the narrative world, the rhetorical world, and the actual historical world is an exceedingly complicated task.

For example, in John's narrative world there is a notorious woman prophet named Jezebel living at Thyatira (2:20), and there is a "synagogue of Satan" at Smyrna (2:9)—neither of these existed in the actual historical world. Yet there must have been some prophet whose opposition to John was well enough known that the audience could say "you know who he is talking about, don't you?" And there must have been a synagogue of some sort whose vision of the world was so opposite of John's that he regarded it as Satanic. The point is, John refracts the life world of the audience in such a way as to persuade his audience that they ought to live in a certain way (Barr 2011).

Serious analysis of the narrative rhetoric of John's Apocalypse has only just begun (DeSilva 2009). John was determined to persuade his audience that Rome was evil, including its manifestations in culture and commerce. They would not have needed such persuasion if Rome had been actively persecuting them; it would have been obvious. The problem seems to be the opposite: Roman culture was all too attractive to John's audience. The rhetoric of John's narrative demonstrates the folly of such thinking.

The book of Revelation is not an allegory of supposed future events, nor is it a symbolic portrayal of theological ideas. It is, instead, an autobiographical narrative of John's experience of a revelation while "in the Spirit" on the island Patmos. As he tells the tale, he encounters Jesus as a majestic human figure with messages to the seven assemblies of Asia Minor, then as a slaughtered, standing lamb worthy to open a sealed scroll, and, finally, as a heavenly warrior victorious over the forces of evil.

It is a tale artfully told in the genre of a vision report, distorting the audiences' sense of time and place, engaging them in both the oral presentation of the story and in some subsequent ritual action. By sharing John's story, the audience shares his revelation. They become those happy folk who hear and keep John's words (1:3).

References

Aristotle. *Poetics.* 1953. Loeb. Translated by W. H. Fyfe. Cambridge, MA: Harvard University Press.

Aune, David E. 1986. "The Apocalypse of John and the Problem of Genre." In *Early Christian Apocalypticism: Genre and Social Setting,* edited by Adela Yarbro Collins. *Semeia* 36: 65–96.

Barr, David L. 1986. "The Apocalypse of John as Oral Enactment." *Interpretation* 40: 243–256.

Barr, David L. 2001. "Waiting for the End That Never Comes: The Narrative Logic of Johns Story." In *Studies in the Book of Revelation*, edited by Steve Moyise, 101–112. Edinburgh: T&T Clark.

Barr, David L. 2003. "The Story John Told: Reading Revelation for Its Plot." In *Reading the Book of Revelation: A Resource for Students*, edited by David L. Barr, 11–23. Atlanta, GA: Society of Biblical Literature.

Barr, David L. 2006. "Beyond Genre: The Expectations of Apocalypse." In *The Reality of Apocalypse: Rhetoric and Politics in the Book of Revelation*, edited by David L. Barr, 71–89. Atlanta, GA: Society of Biblical Literature.

Barr, David L. 2011. "Idol Meat and Satanic Synagogues: From Imagery to History in John's Apocalypse." In *Imagery in the Book of Revelation*, edited by Michael Labahn and Outi Lehtipu, 1–10. Leuven: Peeters.

Barr, David L. 2012. *Tales of the End: A Narrative Commentary on the Book of Revelation*. 2nd ed. Salem, OR: Polebridge Press.

Barr, David L. 2013. "John Is Not Daniel: The Ahistorical Apocalypticism of the Apocalypse." *Perspectives in Religious Studies* 40(1): 49–63.

Bauckham, Richard J. 1988. "The Book of Revelation as a Christian War Scroll." *Neotestamentica* 22: 17–40.

Bowman, John Wick. 1955. "The Revelation to John: Its Dramatic Structure and Message." *Interpretation: A Journal of Bible and Theology* 9: 436–453.

Collins, John J., ed. 1979. "Apocalypse: The Morphology of a Genre." *Semeia: An Experimental Journal for Biblical Criticism* 14: 5-8.

DeSilva, David Arthur. 2009. *Seeing Things John's Way: The Rhetoric of the Book of Revelation*. Louisville, KY: Westminster/John Knox Press.

Doctorow, E. L. 2000. *City of God: A Novel*. New York: Random House.

Eco, Umberto. 2002. *Baudolino*. Translated by William Weaver. New York: Harcourt.

Hanson, Paul D. 1979. *The Dawn of Apocalyptic: The Historical and Sociological Roots of Jewish Apocalyptic Eschatology*. Rev. ed. Philadelphia, PA: Fortress.

Hellholm, David. 1989. *Apocalypticism in the Mediterranean World and Near East: Proceedings of the International Colloquium on Apocalypticism*. Uppsala. August 12-17, 1979. 2nd ed. Tübingen: Mohr-Siebeck. Original edition, 1983.

Jang, Young. 2003. "Narrative Plot of the Apocalypse." *Scriptura: International Journal of Bible, Religion, and Theology in Southern Africa* 84: 381–390.

Krieger, Murray. 1964. *A Window to Criticism: Shakespeare's Sonnets and Modern Poetics*. Princeton, NJ: Princeton University Press.

Lücke, Friedrich. 1852. *Versuch Einer Vollständigen Einleitung in Die Offenbarung Des Johannes Und in Die Apokalyptische Litteratur*. Bonn: E. Weber.

Petersen, Norman R. 1978. *Literary Criticism for New Testament Critics*. Guides to Biblical Scholarship. Philadelphia, PA: Fortress.

Resseguie, James L. 2009. *The Revelation of John: A Narrative Commentary*. Grand Rapids, MI: Baker Academic.

Russell, D. S. 1964. *The Method and Message of Jewish Apocalyptic: 200 B.C.–100 A.D.* Old Testament Library. Philadelphia, PA: Westminster Press.

Schüssler Fiorenza, Elisabeth. 1986. "The Followers of the Lamb: Visionary Rhetoric and Socio-Political Situation." In *Early Christian Apocalypticism: Genre and Social Setting*, edited by Adela Yarbro Collins. *Semeia* 36: 123–146.

Schüssler Fiorenza, Elisabeth. 1987. "Rhetorical Situation and Historical Reconstruction in I Corinthians." *New Testament Studies* 33: 386–403.

Schüssler Fiorenza, Elisabeth. 1998a. *The Book of Revelation: Justice and Judgment*. 2nd ed. Minneapolis, MN: Fortress.

Schüssler Fiorenza, Elisabeth. 1998b. "Visionary Rhetoric and Socio-Political Situation." In *The Book of Revelation: Justice and Judgment*, 133–156. Minneapolis, MN: Fortress.

Smith, Christopher R. 1994. "The Structure of the Book of Revelation in Light of Apocalyptic Literary Conventions." *Novum Testamentum* 36: 373–393.

Thompson, Leonard L. 1969. "Cult and Eschatology in the Apocalypse of John." *Journal of Religion* 49: 330–350.

Thompson, Leonard L. 1989. "The Literary Unity of the Book of Revelation." *Bucknell Review* 33: 347–363.

Thompson, Leonard L. 1990. *The Book of Revelation: Apocalypse and Empire*. Oxford: Oxford University Press.

van Henten, Jan Willem. 2006. "Dragon Myth and Imperial Ideology in Revelation 12-13." In *The Reality of Apocalypse: Rhetoric and Politics in the Book of Revelation*, edited by David L. Barr, 181–203. Atlanta, GA: Scholars Press.

Wainwright, Arthur. 1993. *Mysterious Apocalypse: Interpreting the Book of Revelation*. Nashville, TN: Abingdon Press. Reprinted by Wipf and Stock, 2001.

Wengst, Klaus, ed. 1987. *Pax Romana and the Peace of Jesus Christ*. Philadelphia, PA: Fortress.

PART III

....

THE BIBLE
AND BODIES

....

CHAPTER 33

PLOTTING BODIES IN BIBLICAL NARRATIVE

JEREMY SCHIPPER

NARRATIVES in the Hebrew Bible tend to describe the physical traits of characters in only very general terms, such as hairy, fat, tall, lame, blind, beautiful, or handsome, among others. These descriptions, however, lack sufficient detail to assist the reader in imagining a biblical character's appearance with any precision. Although biblical narrative contains physical descriptions of its characters, the descriptions rarely indicate for the reader what its characters look like. As Adele Berlin notes, "What is lacking in the Bible is the kind of detailed physical or physiological descriptions of characters that creates a visual image for the reader. We know that Bathsheba was beautiful but we have no idea what she looked like. The text does not help us visualize characters concretely" (Berlin 1983, 34). If one tries to imagine these characters based on the physical descriptions provided in biblical narrative, one might conclude that the characters are "underdescribed."

That biblical narratives tend to describe characters using general terms does not mean that the biblical authors were incapable of more detailed physical description, as is evidenced by their descriptions of certain locations or objects. Biblical narratives include ample descriptions of the Garden of Eden (Gen. 2:5–14), Noah's ark (Gen. 6:14–16), Solomon's Temple (1 Kings 6:2–7:51), and Ezekiel's chariot ([Ezek. 1:4–28]; Berlin, 1983, 34). As Berlin observes, "It is not [detailed] physical description that is lacking, but [detailed] *physical description of human beings*" (Berlin, 1983, 34; emphasis in the original). For example, in 1 Samuel 17:4–7, the narrative provides much more detail about Goliath's armor than it does about his physical features:

> And there came out from the camp of the Philistines a champion named Goliath, of Gath, whose height was six cubits and a span. He had a helmet of bronze on his head, and he was armed with a coat of mail; the weight of the coat was five thousand shekels of bronze. He had greaves of bronze on his legs and a javelin of bronze slung between his shoulders. The shaft of his spear was like a weaver's beam, and his spear's head weighed six hundred shekels of iron; and his shield-bearer went before him.[1]

Similarly, Exodus 28:2–40 describes the priestly vestments worn during altar service in detail. Yet, priestly literature never provides physical descriptions of any of the priests who serve at the altar. Rather, it only lists physical features that would disqualify a priest from altar service (Lev. 21:16–24). This list does not describe what the priest serving at the altar looks like. It only describes what he should not look like. Aside from his vestments, his physical appearance is simply nondescript.

If the unspecific descriptions of humans do not reflect the limited descriptive ability of a biblical author but the style of narrative in which an author writes, we may analyze these sparse descriptions as a means of better understanding the typical narrative style of biblical prose. As Berlin and others have argued, physical description in this style of narration is used primarily to convey important information for understanding the plot, rather than to present a clear visual image of the character for the reader. The present chapter will examine some of the implications of this argument for the critical study of disability and nondisability imagery in biblical narrative.

The two most frequent types of physical descriptions in biblical narrative, attractiveness and disability, operate according to the same narrative logic as physical description in general. As with other physical features or conditions throughout the Hebrew Bible, they are not necessarily included to indicate an extraordinary or unusual physical feature. Instead, they are described to help explain the plot of the story, regardless of how unusual or commonplace the feature or condition was in ancient Israelite cultures. This calls into question reading strategies that assume that disability is presented as abnormal in biblical narrative. These reading strategies reinforce the normativity of nondisability through historically privileged interpretive assumptions, rather than clear biblical or historical evidence.

PHYSICAL DESCRIPTION AND PLOT DEVELOPMENT

Over the last several decades, scholarship on narrative in the Hebrew Bible has maintained the position that, whatever else these descriptions accomplish, they make an important contribution to the development of the plot. For example, in his seminal study of biblical narrative published in 1981, Robert Alter noted that,

> Rachel's beauty is not mentioned when she first appears [in Gen. 29:6] but only just before we are told of Jacob's love for her [in vv. 17–18; cf. v. 30].. . . [David's] good looks are not mentioned until the moment Goliath lays eyes on him in the middle of the battlefield [in 1 Sam. 17:42].. . . [In Goliath's eyes, David is a] mere boy, and an egregiously redheaded, pretty boy at that. (81)

According to Alter, the narrator does not engage in physical description of the characters until the description becomes important for the plot. Berlin (1983), while acknowledging the importance of physical descriptions for characterization in biblical narrative, makes a similar point:

> When we are given some detail about a character's appearance or dress, it is usually because this information is needed for the plot. The mention of Tamar's royal tunic is not a gratuitous description but one that more dramatically conveys the degradation felt by the princess; and it is not for nothing that we are told that Bathsheba was beautiful, or Esau hairy, or Eglon fat.. . . the reader knows that Mephibosheth was lame, that Eli was old and his sight was failing, that

Saul was tall and David ruddy. These features become part of the reader's reconstruction of the character, even though the information may have been intended to explain the plot or the circumstances surrounding it. (34)

In a study published ten years later, in 1993, David M. Gunn and Danna Nolan Fewell write,

Physical description [of humans] is sparse in biblical narrative, but occasionally a very general description of a character's appearance or a particular physical characteristic is mentioned ... As far as Rebekah, Rachel, Joseph, Bathsheba, and David's daughter Tamar are concerned, the information [about their physical attractiveness] usually communicates their sexual desirability in stories of courtship, seduction, or rape. (57)

This implies that the reader's awareness of these characters' sexual desirability is important for understanding the events that unfold in the subsequent verses. In an article published in 2009, Tod Linafelt characterizes biblical narrative as "rarely describing either objects or characters and including very little in the way of specifics not strictly necessary to the plot" (Linafelt 2009, B6–B9).

Even if a character is central to the plot, as Adam and Eve are in Genesis 2–3, she or he is not described physically unless it helps the plot to develop in some way or another. When the LORD performs surgery on Adam to create Eve, the narrator mentions Adam's body but does not describe what it looks like, since the plot does not require a detailed description beyond what is necessary to depict the divine surgery (2:21). When the LORD brings Eve to Adam, Adam sees what Eve looks like, but the narrator does describe what he sees (vv. 22–23). Although the narrator states that Adam and Eve are "naked" in verse 25, this description does not reveal what their individual bodies look like. Instead, it explains why the LORD clothes them later in the story (3:21).

DESCRIPTIONS OF UNUSUAL AND COMMONPLACE PHYSICAL FEATURES

Physical description in biblical narrative is not reserved for unique or anomalous physical features but for those features that contribute to the plot. Thus, the use of a physical description in biblical narrative does not indicate whether the described feature was considered unusual within ancient Israelite cultures. For example, Esau's hairy appearance, noted in Genesis 27:11 (cf. 25:25), creates the need for Rebekah to disguise Jacob in animal skins (vv. 16, 20). Yet, the text does not necessarily present Esau's hairiness as an abnormal physical feature.

In fact, even if a described feature can be considered abnormal, it may have been included in the narrative because of its relevance for the plot, rather than the fact that it was abnormal. For example, the description of an unnamed Philistine from Gath as "a man of great size, who had six fingers on each hand, and six toes on each foot, twenty-four in number" (2 Sam. 21:20 [= 1 Chron. 20:6]) occurs in the context of David and his warriors' triumph over four descendants of Philistine giants who "fell by the hands of David and his servants" (2 Sam. 21:22 [= 1 Chron. 20:8]). As with Goliath of Gath in 1 Samuel 17, the physical description of this Philistine reinforces the impressive nature of this Israelite victory over such a formidable opponent. Similarly, the description of Eglon as "a very fat man" (Judg. 3:17) helps to explain how Ehud kills this king later in the narrative (vv. 21–22). As scholars have often noted, Elgon's name creates a pun with the Hebrew word for a slaughtered "fatted calf" (ʿēgel; e.g., Lev. 9:2; 1 Sam. 28:24; Amos 6:4). It provides no indication, however, of how rare or common obesity was among Moabite royalty.

A physical feature was described if it was necessary for the story regardless of whether it would be considered unusual, like a giant warrior with twenty-four digits, or not all that unusual, like a man with an abundance of body hair. Features that might be considered ordinary could develop the plot just as easily as those that might be considered extraordinary. A described physical trait did not have to be considered unusual to serve the interests of the plot. This claim can be further demonstrated with the features of attractiveness and disability in biblical narrative.

DESCRIPTIONS OF PHYSICAL ATTRACTIVENESS AND PHYSICAL DISABILITY

Physically attractive characters and characters with disabilities are the most frequently described characters in biblical narrative. Although the exact descriptions of attractiveness in Hebrew may vary—for example, "beautiful of appearance" (Gen. 12:11); "very beautiful" (12:14); "very good of appearance" (24:16); "beautiful of form" (29:17; Esther 2:7); "good of form" (1 Kings 1:6); and so on (my translations)—they all indicate that a character is beautiful or handsome. Likewise, although the exact descriptions of disability in Hebrew may vary—for example, "dimmed [eyes]" (Gen. 27:1; 1 Sam. 3:2); "heavy [eyes]" (Gen. 48:10); "heavy of mouth" (Exod. 4:10); "mute," "deaf," "blind" (4:11); "set [eyes]" (1 Sam. 4:15); "lame in both feet" (2 Sam. 9:13), and so on (my translations)—they all describe characters with physical disabilities (for a detailed discussion of disability as a category of difference, consult Schipper 2006, 64–73; 2011, 14).

The use of these general physical descriptions of certain characters, however, does not imply that we should only imagine a character as physically attractive or as having a disability if the text provides explicit confirmation of their appearance. Biblical narrators do not usually present physical attractiveness or disability as unusual traits. While not everyone is considered attractive or disabled, neither trait is necessarily uncommon. If physical description was usually included in biblical narrative only when required by the plot, there is no reason to assume that an undescribed character is not attractive or does not have a disability. A character's physical appearance or ability may simply remain unmentioned because it is not germane to the development of the plot. Even if one does not assume a character's attractiveness or disability unless informed otherwise (and there is no reason one must), the descriptions of several characters' attractiveness or disabilities in biblical narrative does not necessarily limit these traits to only these characters.

Although one may be noticed for one's beauty (e.g., Gen. 12:14–15), a character can also simply be one of an unspecified number of beautiful people in the story (e.g., Esther 2:7; Dan. 1:4). Biblical narrators do not necessarily reserve descriptions of beauty for only the most physically attractive characters in the Bible. A number of characters in biblical narrative are described as physically attractive, including Sarai (Gen. 12:11, 14), Rebekah (24:16; 26:7), possibly Leah (29:17a), Rachel (29:17b), Joseph (39:6), possibly Moses (Exod. 2:2), David (1 Sam. 16:12; 17:42), Abigail (25:3), Bathsheba (2 Sam. 11:2), David's daughter Tamar (13:1), Absalom's daughter Tamar (14:27), Abishag (1 Kings 1:4), Adonijah (1:6), Esther along with an unspecified number of women in the Persian empire (2:7), and an unspecified number of men from the Judean royal court (Dan. 1:4). Yet, these descriptions of physical attractiveness are not detailed enough to confirm anything more than the conventional beauty of a character. At most, some of these characters are described as "very beautiful." Also, in each of these cases, the disclosure of the character's physical attractiveness helps to explain some aspect of the plot without claiming that their appearance was extraordinary.

In a few texts, the narrator indicates a character's extraordinary or abnormal beauty through an explicit contrast with what might be considered a normal but undescribed appearance. For example, in 1 Samuel 9:2, the narrator creates a physical contrast between Saul and other Israelites: "There was not a man among the people of Israel more handsome than he; he stood head and shoulders above everyone else." This verse depicts Saul as unusually handsome and tall. Along similar lines, 10:23 reads, "When [Saul] took his stand among the people, he was head and shoulders taller than any of them." When describing Absalom, the narrator notes, "Now in all Israel there was no one to be praised so much for his beauty as Absalom; from the sole of his foot to the crown of his head there was no blemish in him" (2 Sam. 14:25). These explicit contrasts, however, suggest that Saul's or Absalom's appearance should not be taken as representative of characters whose physical appearance are left to the reader's imagination.

In Genesis 29:17, Rachel's beauty seems to contrast with her sister Leah's appearance, although it is unclear whether the verse describes Leah's eyes as beautiful or her eyesight as impaired when the narrator refers to her eyes as "delicate" or "soft." Either term could indicate that her eyes were "weak" (JPS; NIV) or that her eyes are "lovely" (NRSV). If one interprets the verse as describing Leah as attractive, this could imply that she is not as attractive as Rachel. We might say that Leah is conventionally beautiful but not extraordinarily beautiful. Also, unlike with Saul or Absalom, the narrator does not imply that Rachel is the most beautiful person among her peers, but only that she is more attractive than her sister. Likewise, Daniel 1:15 does not describe Daniel's and his friends' appearance as extraordinarily attractive, but only more attractive than "all the young men who had been eating the royal rations."

Typically, however, physical descriptions do not compare or contrast the character's appearance with the appearance of others. Biblical narrators do not often depict physical attractiveness or disability in relative terms. Even in 2 Samuel 14:25, the narrator does not indicate that no one except Absalom was beautiful. Rather, the narrator indicates that no one else's beauty was praised as much as Absalom's. This implies that there were others within the general population who were considered beautiful. This verse may also depict physical impairments as commonplace (e.g., Lev. 24:19). Blemishes could include certain visual and mobility impairments (e.g., Lev. 21:18; Deut. 15:21) and 2 Samuel 14:25 seems to depict Absalom's complete lack of blemishes as extraordinary. As with beauty, disabilities are often described in general terms with no indication that they were considered abnormal. At most, some legal texts seem to indicate that some blemishes were considered more severe than other blemishes. For example, Deuteronomy 15:21 refers to visual and mobility impairments as "severe blemishes" (my translation). In fact, since descriptions of physical disabilities never include a contrast with the physical capabilities of the general population, the notion that disabilities represent an anomaly in biblical narrative is a product of the reader's imagination rather than of the textual evidence.

As with descriptions of attractiveness, descriptions of disabilities help to develop the plot rather than mark the character as abnormal. For example, in Genesis 27:1, the narrator states, "Isaac was old and his eyes were dim so that he could not see." In the following verses, Rebekah and Jacob take advantage of Isaac's dimmed eyesight to pass Jacob off as his brother Esau (vv. 15–29). As with Esau's hairiness, the description of Isaac's eyes as "dim" is necessary for the plot. There is no reason to assume that Isaac's eyesight is mentioned because it was unusual or unexpected in ancient Israelite cultures for an elderly person's eyesight to diminish. Isaac is not the only character whose impaired vision is associated with old age. Others include his son Israel (Gen. 48:10; also called Jacob), the priest Eli (1 Sam. 4:15) and the prophet Ahijah (1 Kings 14:4).

Other texts in the Hebrew Bible associate physical impairments with advanced age. For example, Zechariah 8:4 describes Zion's utopian future as including elderly residents with impaired mobility: "Old men and old women shall again sit in the streets of Jerusalem, each with staff in hand because of their great age." (In prophetic literature, Zion's utopian future frequently includes residents with various disabilities, although the ages of the characters with disabilities are usually not mentioned; e.g., Isa. 43:5–8; Jer. 31:6–8; Mic. 4:6–7; Zeph. 3:16–20.) The fact that the eyesight of Moses did not dim when he died at age 120 marks him as extraordinary (Deut. 34:7). He is said to be a prophet without parallel in the history of Israel (34:10–12). The descriptions of Isaac, Israel, Eli, and Ahijah could be representative of standard expectations for advanced age in ancient Israelite cultures. It is quite possible that visual impairments among the elderly were an expected element of the aging process that usually went unmentioned unless it helped the plot to develop.

As with Isaac in Genesis 27, the disclosures of Israel, Eli, and Ahijah's visual impairments are necessary for the plot. Israel's impaired eyesight may explain why Joseph has to bring Ephraim and Manasseh near, so his father Israel can tell them apart, and why Joseph assumes that his father blessed the wrong grandson (Gen. 48:8–14). In 1 Samuel 3:2, Eli's impaired eyesight plays off the previous line that "visions were rare" (3:1), and it helps to explain why the LORD not only speaks but also appears to Samuel rather than to Eli (3:10). Ahijah's impaired eyesight makes it necessary for the LORD to inform the prophet of the identity of Jeroboam's wife despite her disguise and then to provide him with the subsequent oracle regarding Jeroboam's household (1 Kings 14:1–18).

These disclosures of impaired eyesight fit with the conventional use of physical description in biblical narrative: it is related to plot requirements and unrelated to how common or uncommon the described feature may have been in ancient Israelite cultures. In the foregoing examples of impaired eyesight, the narrator could simply be using a commonplace physical condition for plot development. There is no reason to assume that, aside from these four characters, all the other characters in the Hebrew Bible had unimpaired, Moses-like vision until they died.

The fact that biblical narrators rarely describe the characters as physically attractive or disabled does not mean that we should imagine that biblical characters are rarely attractive or disabled or that people were rarely considered physically attractive or disabled in ancient Israelite cultures. Rather, it suggests that indicating physical attractiveness or disability is only occasionally necessary for the plot to develop. The infrequent descriptions of physical beauty or disability in biblical narrative do not confirm that beauty or disability was considered abnormal in biblical literature or in ancient Israel.

INTERPRETATIVE DOUBLE STANDARDS

As discussed earlier, physical attractiveness and disability, the most frequently described physical characteristics in biblical narrative, usually have a similar function: they indicate information that is important for the plot rather than that a character had an extraordinary or abnormal appearance. Yet, although their use operates according to a similar narrative logic, they are often interpreted according to very different standards. Biblical narratives are often read as if attractiveness can be assumed but disabilities are anomalous. The characters are nondisabled unless the text explicitly states otherwise. This reading strategy might unreflectively map nondisability onto biblical characters instead of pausing to ask what in the narrative indicates that a given character is nondisabled.

The book of Ruth provides an instructive example of the double standard at work. Ruth's narrator does not provide any physical descriptions of the characters in the book. Nonetheless, the title character is often assumed to be physically attractive in academic writings as well as in popular culture (for a few of the many examples, consult Exum 1996, 129–73; Fewell and Gunn 1990, 115–16n32). Interpreters have noted striking similarities between Ruth and the matriarchs Sarai, Rebekah, and Rachel in the book of Genesis. In fact, in 4:11, Ruth is explicitly compared to Rachel. In Genesis, all three matriarchs are described as physically attractive (Gen. 12:11, 14; 24:16; 29:17b, respectively). Moreover, the narrator in Genesis notes Jacob's attraction to Rachel immediately after mentioning her beauty (29:18a). This could potentially explain Boaz's initial interest in Ruth (2:5) and therefore contribute to the development of the plot. If Ruth is interpreted against the backdrop of these matriarchal traditions, some interpreters may simply assume her attractiveness as a stock feature of these matriarchal traditions.

Yet, another stock feature of these matriarchal traditions is infertility. Sarai, Rebekah, and Rachel are each described as infertile in Genesis (*ʿăpārâ*; Gen. 11:30; 25:21; 29:31, respectively) prior to a divine intervention (21:1–2; 25:21; 30:22, respectively). If one assumes Ruth's beauty on the basis of comparisons with the descriptions of the matriarchs in Genesis, one could on the same basis also assume her infertility prior to a divine intervention (Ruth 4:13). Moreover, the absence of the word *ʿăpārâ* in Ruth does not necessarily mean that one should assume the characters are fertile by default. Several texts indicate short-term or long-term infertility without using this word (Gen. 16:2; 20:17–18; 1 Sam. 1:5–6; Isa. 66:9; and possibly 2 Sam. 6:23; 2 Kings 4:14).

In Ruth 4:11, the comparison to Rachel, Leah, and Tamar occurs in the context of an appeal for fertility. According to Ruth 1:4, both Orpah and Ruth were married for "about ten years" without any indication that they had children. Some scholars compare these ten-year marriages to the statement in Genesis 16:3 that after "ten years" Sarai gave Hagar to Abram because she claims "the LORD has prevented me from bearing children" (Gen. 16:2; Hubbard 1988, 95; Sasson 1989, 21). A rabbinic legal tradition discusses re-marriage if the couple does not produce children after ten years (*m. Yeb.* 6.6). In Genesis 24:60, Rebekah's mother and brother bless her with a prayer that she will have thousands of descendants. The following chapter attributes her conception to a divine intervention after Isaac prays for her (25:21). Similarly, Ruth only has a child after an explicit divine intervention following the townspeople's appeal to God (4:11–12). According to a rabbinic tradition, Ruth did not have a uterus until the LORD granted her conception (*Ruth Rab.* 7:14). Interpreting Ruth or her two husbands as infertile could explain certain aspects of the plot (including the lack of children after ten years of marriage) in the book's first chapter or the blessing and divine intervention in its last chapter.

This does not prove that Ruth was infertile prior to 4:13, but shows that the fertility of Ruth (or Boaz) remains inconclusive prior to 4:13. There is no reason to assume her fertility by default. As with Ruth's alleged beauty, mapping fertility onto her character is a historically privileged interpretative strategy that nonetheless must be justified with the same standard for textual evidence that is often demanded of those who map infertility onto one or more of the characters in Ruth. That one can assume Ruth's beauty but not her infertility is an exegetical double standard reflecting nondisabled privilege that assumes the normality of beauty and the abnormality of disability without clear textual evidence.

In general, textual evidence of nondisability is not held to the same standard to which disability is held in interpretations of biblical narrative. Even when characters experience serious but nonfatal injuries, interpreters often assume that they recover fully rather than acquire a chronic disability. In Genesis 32, Jacob sustains a hip injury in a wrestling match that causes him to limp (vv. 25, 31). Yet, the description of Jacob's injury does not convey the severity, or lack thereof, of his limp or indicate whether his injury was only temporary or resulted in a permanent disability (v. 31). Nevertheless, as Kerry Wynn documents, scholars often assume Jacob's limp was temporary without citing evidence from the text to support the assumption (Wynn 2007, 99).

It is possible that scholars may assume Jacob's limp was temporary because the narrator never mentions in the subsequent chapters that he walks with a limp. This silence, however, does not necessarily indicate that he recovered, but only that the nature of his gait was immaterial for the development of plot lines involving his character after Genesis 32. In the current form of this chapter, the narrator connects the relevance of his injury to a unique dietary practice (v. 33). Yet this practice is mentioned nowhere else in the Hebrew Bible, including the remaining chapters of Genesis that narrate Jacob's life.

Other biblical texts associate leg injuries resulting in a limp with lifelong disabilities rather than temporary conditions (Schipper 2011, 24–25). For example, Mephibosheth's limp, resulting from a childhood injury (2 Sam. 4:4), is noted repeatedly in stories of his adulthood (9:3, 13; 19:26). This does not indicate the uniqueness of his mobility impairment but the fact that the nature of his gait is relevant to the plot lines involving his character after his initial injury. Physical disabilities resulting from injuries could have been considered commonplace in ancient Israelite cultures but were only noted in biblical narratives when they were relevant to the plot.

CONCLUSIONS AND IMPLICATIONS

This chapter has not tried to prove that undescribed characters in biblical narrative had disabilities. A close study of the physical descriptions in biblical narrative, however, gives us no reason to assume that the described bodies, including those described as attractive or disabled, could not be commonplace in ancient Israelite cultures. Biblical narrators describe characters physically not because the characters have unusual or abnormal bodies but because such descriptions are necessary for plot development.

Yet, when it comes to disability, readers often assume that characters must be nondisabled unless the narrator explicitly states otherwise. The assumption of nondisability reflects what a reader might imagine as normative by default more than by what the biblical text indicates. Nevertheless, nondisability is not the same as normality even though, as a dominant cultural form of identity, it often masquerades as normality. As with any historically responsible biblical scholarship, the critical study of physical disability (and nondisability) in biblical narrative requires readings that can be supported with textual evidence rather than ones that are dependent on mapping ahistorical, and possibly anachronistic, assumptions about physical normality onto the biblical narrative and its characters.

NOTE

1. All translations are from the NRSV and follow its versification unless otherwise indicated.

REFERENCES

Alter, Robert. 1981. *The Art of Biblical Narrative*. New York: Basic Books.

Berlin, Adele. 1983. *Poetics and Interpretation of Biblical Narrative*. Sheffield, Yorkshire: Almond.

Exum, J. Cheryl. 1996. *Plotted, Shot, and Painted: Cultural Representations of Biblical Women*. Journal for the Study of the Old Testament Supplement Series 215. Sheffield, Yorkshire: Sheffield Academic Press.

Fewell, Danna Nolan, and David M. Gunn. 1990. *Compromising Redemption: Relating Characters in the Book of Ruth*. Literary Currents in Biblical Interpretation. Louisville, KY: Westminster John Knox.

Fewell, Danna Nolan, and David M. Gunn. 1993. *Narrative in the Hebrew Bible*. Oxford Bible Series. Oxford: Oxford University Press.

Hubbard, Robert L. 1988. *The Book of Ruth*. New International Commentary on the Old Testament. Grand Rapids, MI: Eerdmans.

Linafelt, Tod. 2009. "The Bible's Literary Merits." *Chronicle of Higher Education* 55(31): B6–B9.

Sasson, Jack M. 1989. *Ruth: A New Translation with a Philological Commentary and a Formalist-Folklorist Interpretation*. 2nd ed. The Biblical Seminar 10. Sheffield, Yorkshire: JSOT Press.

Schipper, Jeremy. 2006. *Disability Studies and the Hebrew Bible: Figuring Mephibosheth in the David Story*. Library of Hebrew Bible/Old Testament Studies 441. New York: T&T Clark.

Schipper, Jeremy. 2011. *Disability and Isaiah's Suffering Servant*. Oxford: Oxford University Press.

Wynn, Kerry. 2007. "The Normate Hermeneutic and Interpretations of Disability in Yahwistic Narratives." In *This Abled Body: Rethinking Disability and Biblical Studies*, edited by Hector Avalos, Sarah Melcher, and Jeremy Schipper, 91–101. Semeia Studies 55. Atlanta, GA: Society of Biblical Literature.

CHAPTER 34

READING BIBLICAL WOMEN MATTERS

JUDITH E. McKINLAY

THERE surely is no argument: biblical women matter. The question is how do they matter. Here, indeed, there are critical matters to be asked and debated. The plural "women" is significant, countering any sense of one essentialist category. This is no surprise, as they appear in many guises, and are the product of a long line of scribal writers and editors, sitting at their desks, putting pens to scrolls and codices over a vast range of time, space and context, many re-presenting characters long known in narratives treasured by their traditions. In tales told in early Iron Age villages to those written and read in large Roman and Hellenistic cities, biblical women appear in their differing roles and subject positions. The more one looks, the more one sees. Would there have been an Exodus without the midwives, or an enterprising sister or Pharaoh's daughter? Who has not heard of Eve, Sarah and Hagar, Deborah and Jael, Jezebel, Mary and Martha, Mary Magdalene? The list is long, some named, others not. But who could forget the persistent Shunammite in 2 Kings 4, or the woman anointing Jesus with the costly ointment in Mark 14? Nameless they may be, but their "personalities and stories (are) vital, vibrant, and vivid" (Reinhartz 1998, 3). Over the centuries stories of biblical women have been retold, dramatized, painted on stained glass windows and canvases and, in recent years, watched on film.

While for these writers, dramatists, painters and filmmakers there has been no question that reading biblical women matters, how they have been understood, interpreted, and represented has varied considerably. Open Genesis and one is confronted with Eve. A woman "born" of a man, or is she split from an androgynous earth creature? Is she the woman decried for bringing sin into the world or revered for gaining the gift of ethical discernment? She is a passive victim for Paul in 2 Cor. 11:3, yet in 1 Tim. 2:14 she is an active transgressor. What is clear is that for both writers, Eve proved a useful tool for their particular theses, and so she has been employed over the centuries, her taking the fruit mostly seen and used as a symbol of whatever sin or decried act has been the subject of concern, much less often as the purveyor of wisdom. While the needs and the readings differ, what is not in doubt is that reading Eve, and her female biblical companions, matters.

THE IMPACT OF LITERARY CRITICISM

The turn to literary analysis in the 1970s and 1980s brought a fresh appreciation of how women are used as literary characters, fitting the plot lines, acting with agency, or relegated to the textual margins. Rhetorical critics, such as Phyllis Trible, both in *God and the Rhetoric of Sexuality* (1978) and her later works, drew attention to the significance of form, even in its minutiae. Reading Sarah's speech in Genesis 16:2–6 with its verbal imperative, she noted how "dialogic order and verb construction match content to present this woman as the commanding figure" (1984, 10). The role of character and characterization was highlighted in the poetics employed in Adele Berlin's readings of David's wives (1983). In a scanning of literary patterns, Jopie Siebert-Hommes's chiastic analysis of Exodus 1:2–1:10 found Pharaoh's daughter occupying the pivot, surrounding the child as she herself is surrounded concentrically by the child's sister and mother (1994, 71). Mieke Bal's semiotic analysis pointed to links between the honor/shame opposition and the sexes in Judges 4, with Deborah fatefully predicting Sisera's fall "into the hand of a woman" (v. 9), and Jael carrying out the deed. Yet this same analysis revealed the complication: "the discourse [Deborah] pronounces is embedded in that of the narrator whom we have supposed to be a man" (1988a, 116–117). The hand of a woman may deliver the deed, but the tale comes from the hand of a man, leading to the question, who, then, is responsible for this concept of man's shame? Seduction in bedroom skirmishes was recognized as a literary motif, employed repeatedly, as in the Samson/Delilah and Judith/Holofernes narratives, and, more poignantly, in the Tamar/Amnon rape scene of 2 Samuel 13. Gender indeed matters here, and matters even when women are not the subject of any speech or action, as Bal notes of the women taken and given as wives in Judges 3:6. Even though they are "objects of action" rather than subjects, it is their abduction that "narratologically . . . triggers the following episode," so that "their relevance as elements in the story has to be assessed." Unnamed and passive, they are yet a significant part of this literary narrative (1988b, 33).

THE MEETING WITH FEMINIST THEORY

The 1970s and 1980s were also the years when literary criticism met feminist theory, as seen in the subtitle of Trible's *Texts of Terror: Feminist-Literary Readings of Biblical Narrative* (1984). While Cady Stanton's *The Woman's Bible* (1898), in its own provocative way, had highlighted the roles of biblical women, and works such as Edith Deen's, *All the Women of the Bible* (1955), had directed attention to biblical women, second-wave feminism led to a renewed interest, initially with a move to retrieve women from the margins of texts, and the margins of biblical scholarship. Trible's 1989 study "Bringing Miriam Out of the Shadows" is a classic example. There was, however, the accompanying recognition that while figures such as Miriam appeared in full view, albeit in fragments of the Moses story, the quest for biblical women also involved "reading between the lines of alien texts, looking for invisible women, listening for muted voices" (Fewell 1993, 238–239). Ellen van Wolde wrote of "a stream of headscarves" going "through history" (1997, 1), yet some figures were so well hidden and engulfed in shadows that even their headscarves could not be seen. They might be included in references to "all Israel," "the congregation," or "the people," but this could not be assumed.

A feature of the retrieval was the variety of methodological analyses employed. While Trible applied a literary rhetorical critical methodology, both to retrieve the women and "de-patriarchalize" the texts, Carol Meyers's search for the pre-monarchic Israelite woman in *Discovering Eve: Ancient Israelite Women in Context* (1988) combined textual readings with socio-historical reconstruction. In the field of New Testament, 1983 saw the publication of *In Memory of Her: A Feminist Theological Reconstruction of Christian Origins* by Elisabeth Schüssler Fiorenza, injecting a hermeneutics of suspicion into her historical reconstruction. Ross Shepard Kraemer (1983, 1992) included the matter of gender in early Christianity in her studies of women's religious lives in the Greco-Roman world (see also Kraemer and D'Angelo 1989). Whether the women following Jesus were considered disciples, and, if so, how to explain their silence at the end of Mark's Gospel, were questions that occupied many New Testament scholars. Were they "fallible followers," as Elizabeth Struthers Malbon's (1983) study suggested? Her narrative-critical study provoked considerable response (Dewey 1994; Mitchell 2001). Schüssler Fiorenza's "dance of interpretation," including a "hermeneutics of creative imagination," offered scholars an ever-wider choice of critical tools (1992, 73–75). Jennie Ebeling's fictitious "Orah's Story," heading each chapter of her study of Iron Age *Women's Lives in Biblical Times* (2010) is effectively imaginative. So, too, the interest in biblical women's afterlives concerns the question: how have gaps in the narrative been filled by later writers, musicians, artists and film makers (Clanton 2009; Hawkins and Stahlberg 2009)? How have women been *"plotted, shot and painted"* (Exum 1996)? Representations of Salome and her deathly dance provide answers indeed (Anderson 1992; Joynes 2007; Apostolos-Cappadona 2009; Nutu 2009; Stocker 2009; Vander Stichele 2009).

THE ROLES OF WOMEN OR THE MALE VIEW OF WOMEN'S ROLES

Feminist theory brought an awareness that communities and societies set the boundaries for gender role performance, that what it means to be a woman depends on agreed or regulated social arrangements, within inevitable power politics. Feminist biblical criticism recognized that the biblical texts themselves were the product of those who maintained and perpetuated such gender constructions, so that readers are, for the most part, confronted by a male view of women's roles. Not surprisingly, throughout much of the Hebrew Bible women appear as wives, mothers and daughters (Brenner 1985; Fuchs 2000; Stiebert 2013). This is particularly true of Genesis, with women concentrated in family narratives. Wives, however, need to be mothers. Woe to the barren woman, especially if the co-wife is fertile and already a mother of sons: hence the repeated motif of sons of the promise born to "barren" women, through divine intervention. Yet mothers also are dispensable, rarely appearing in biblical narratives where daughters are at risk or abused (Fuchs 1989). Where are the mothers of Dinah (Gen. 34), Jephthah's daughter (Judg. 11), and Tamar (2 Sam. 13)? And where is Sarah at the binding of Isaac in Genesis 22 (Trible 1999)? Moreover, when women *are* present, they are frequently alongside their men, much more rarely speaking or interacting among themselves, the small book of Ruth being a notable exception. Moses's mother and sister, Pharaoh's daughter and her female attendants may all be involved in the rescue and survival of Moses in Exodus 2, talking and acting together in defiance of the powerful Egyptian Pharaoh, but they owe their roles to their part in the Moses narrative. What seems to be exceptional turns out not to be the case: "The role the women play in the birth of the nation is comparable to the role usually played by mothers in the Bible: they yield their power, and their stories, to their husbands and sons" (Exum 1994, 82–83).

It is no surprise to find women in the Hebrew Bible's historical narratives mostly related to, or involved with, Israel's leaders and kings, David's wives being a prime example (Fewell and Gunn 1993, 141–163). While, as Malbon notes in another context, "a character cannot be understood alone but only in relationship" (2011, 61), what is striking here is that each wife appears separately. As Alice Bach (1994, 113) notes, "There is no interdependence . . . although in their actual lives there might well have been . . . seen through the stereotyping lens of male authority, each of these women typifies a particular aspect of *wife*; Michal is the dissatisfied daughter/wife of divided loyalties; Abigail is consistently the good-sense mother-provider, and Bathsheba the sexual partner." Even Ruth and Naomi, who appear to plot their own destinies, are, in the closing genealogy, finally tied into kingly matters. Women who have a part in the New Testament gospel accounts, even the most strong-willed and prominent, owe their appearances to their supporting roles in the Jesus narrative. Perhaps it is Judith, in the deutero-canonical collection, who stands most firmly alone, with Holofernes's head so graphically in her grasp, before retiring to live in accepted widow mode.

Yet—there is always that yet. As Susan Ackerman's title, *Warrior, Dancer, Seductress, Queen* (1998) indicates, there are always the exceptions. Some women do act very much on their own, and some dangerously, from the writers' perspective. As Bach notes, "If you are a Philistine, then Delilah is a war hero (1999, xxi. see also Bach 1997; Frolov 2013). Proverbs (2:16–19; 7:5,10–27) notably warns of "strange" seductive women (Camp 2000). Joseph is ill equipped to deal with Potiphar's wife, who skilfully manipulates the truth with wily words (Gen. 39). Yet, following folklore, not all tricksters are villains (Niditch 1987; Jackson 2012): Tamar, denied the husband owed her by Levirate law, returns trick for trick, justifiably seducing her father-in-law, Judah, to gain the prize of sons (Gen. 38). Ruth, using trickery on the threshing floor, wins a husband and a son and becomes an ancestor of David and Jesus (Matt. 1:5). Sexual trickery is, however, deathly for John the Baptist, at the connivance of Herod's wife and daughter (Matt. 14:2–12; Mark 6:14–28). But who is wielding the pen?

In the cult, Miriam, whom tradition sets as sister to Aaron and Moses, appears, in her own right, as prophet and leader in the ritual celebration of Israel's deliverance (Exod. 15:20). Nor is there any apology or special explanation regarding the prophetic roles of Deborah (Judg. 4–5), Huldah (2 Kings 22; 2 Chron. 34:22–28) and Anna (Luke 2:36). Then there are the glimpses in the Hebrew Bible of women performing religious roles that are not entirely understood, such as serving at YHWH's tent of meeting (Exod. 38:8; 1 Sam. 2:22), and weaving vestments for the female Asherah figure (2 Kings 23:7). Jeremiah 7:18 and 44:17–19 refer to women making offerings and libations to the Queen of Heaven, seemingly with their husbands' agreement. In 1 Kings 15:13 Ma'acah is removed from her queen mother role because of the *abominable image* she had had made for Asherah, indicating not only a royal role for kings' mothers, but the prescribed response to such devotion. That women are apparently engaging in religious rites not approved by the scribal tradition, and even considered abominations, is a reminder that the Bible is not a clear mirror to the past, and that there are facets of women's lives only hinted at in these narrative texts.

FURTHER COMPLICATIONS IN THE VIEWINGS

The 1990s brought further complications, as feminist theory called for greater attention to diversity, pointing to the interlocking of the inequalities of class, race, ethnicity, and sexuality. Renita Weems's (1992, 30) subtitle in "The Hebrew Women Are Not like the Egyptian Women: The Ideology of Race, Gender and Sexual Reproduction in Exodus 1" illustrates the move, as Weems notes that "the entire narrative pivots on the axis of difference." Ideology was now firmly on the agenda. Gale Yee (1995, 107), considering the treatment of the butchered concubine in Judges 19, set her eye on the writer's ideological strategy: "As the Levite literally mutilates the body of his wife, the Deuteronomist narratively dis-members the 'body' of the tribes". The woman is not only the pawn of the Levite but of the Deuteronomist. Yee's later *Poor Banished Children of Eve* (2003) is notable for combining close textual readings with a feminist materialist approach that takes specific account of class, ethnicity and colonial status. Silences, however, also convey ideological messages, so "the interpreter must step back from the ideology of the biblical texts and raise questions not simply about what a text says about women but also about what it does not say" (Exum 1998, 208–209). What is Sarah's view of Abram's ploy to pass her off as his sister in Genesis 12 and 20? Abram's fear is expressed, but from Sarah there is not a word. She, too, is a pawn of the plot.

Womanist readings, such as Weems's *Just a Sister Away* ([1988] 2005) had already presented different perspectives. Recognizing that contexts matter, scholars of different ethnicities, based not only in the United States but in South America, Asia, Africa, and, indeed, from all parts of the globe, began challenging accepted ways of interpretation. Laura Donaldson, writing "as a person of Cherokee descent," reads Ruth's choice "involv[ing] the relinquishing of her ethnic and cultural identity" as a negative, with Orpah's (1999, 144) "choosing of the indigenous mother's house over that of the alien Israelite Father" the positive. That changes the story. Kyung Sook Lee (2011) employs neo-Confucian ideology in her interpretation of Ruth, moving "toward a cross-checking hermeneutics." Seong Hee Kim (2010) applies a Korean *Salim* hermeneutic, alongside her feminist and postcolonial readings, in a study of four "woman" passages in Mark (12:41–44; 14:1–11; 15:40–41,47; 16:1–8), "making things come alive" by drawing on the reader's imagination. Contextual difference is now a hermeneutical key.

While literary studies dominate the field, these continue to be complemented by historical and social-scientific studies. Richard Bauckham's *Gospel Women: Studies of the Named Women in the Gospels* (2002) combines both, asking "what happened" and "how the text constructs its literary version of what happened" (xviii). Philip Esler and Ronald Piper (2006) apply social-scientific approaches to a reading of Lazarus, Mary and Martha in John's gospel. In a major revision of her 1988 work, Meyers describes *Rediscovering Eve: Ancient Israelite Women in Context* (2012) as "a project of sociocultural anthropology … which draws heavily on data supplied by ethnography" although her focus is on the "ordinary Israelite women apart from the Hebrew Bible, which tells us so little about them" (14). The women in Mercedes Bachmann's (2013, 15) socio-historical *Women at Work in the Deuteronomistic History* are textually visible, but only just, being the largely anonymous female laborers who, in serving household needs, have mostly "gone unrecognized in [the Deuteronomistic

History] and in modern scholarship." Avaren Ipsen not only applies a materialist hermeneu-tic, drawing on Marxist and feminist standpoint theory, as she considers the conditions of prostitutes in her study of "Solomon and the Two Prostitutes," and later of three others, but reads the text with representatives of a prostitutes' rights group (2008, 2009).

FURTHER INTERPRETIVE CHALLENGES

While the task of identifying ideological agendas requires locating texts in their socio-historical contexts, what often results are possibilities rather than conclusions. Different dat-ings imply different interpretations. For example, is the prophet Huldah in 2 Kings 22 really working under orders of King Josiah, and playing her part in his political maneuvrings, or for an Ezra in a Yehud-based script, where Torah-based identity is crucial for a people under Persian rule? That would see Huldah employed in quite a different role.

Amy-Jill Levine begins her introduction to a collection of essays on Luke by pointing to difficulties in the textual discourse itself. While her first paragraph begins, "The Gospel of Luke celebrates women's discipleship, self-determination, and leadership," the second states, "the Gospel of Luke threatens any attempt made by women, the poor, or the disenfranchised to find a voice in either society or church. The narrative consistently depicts women in ancil-lary capacities" (Levine 2002, 1). As Levine acknowledges, both paragraphs present extreme views, but both find a basis in the texts. They simply interpret it differently.

The brief tale of Mary and Martha's welcoming Jesus into their home in Luke 10:38–42 poses the challenge of how to understand the women's roles, and, indeed, Jesus's response. On both, as Levine (2002, 15) writes, "no consensus has been, or likely will be, reached." Here the complication is textual: different Greek manuscripts have different versions of what Jesus says to Martha in verses 41–42. Is he rebuking her for the role she has chosen (the shorter reading), or simply suggesting she reorder her priorities (the longer reading)? Is the scene one of friends sharing a meal, with Martha serving, or is the passage written as a teaching tool about ministry? A narratological analysis that asks, "who speaks?" highlights Mary's silence. Is sitting silently listening to Jesus the role of a faithful disciple? If so, how does one interpret the body language? Is Jesus affirming women as hearers of the Word, with Mary presented as a model disciple at his feet? This interpretation has long been held and valued. What then for Martha's role? The challenge posed by Schüssler Fiorenza's socio-historical reconstruction sees this passage reflecting a Lukan community struggle over women's roles, with an interest in silencing women leaders of house churches. So "it is not the *Kyrios* but the writer of Luke 10:38–42 who promotes such patriarchal restrictions" (1992, 68). Read in its larger literary context, however, the sense of the encounter can change again. John Darr, reading it in line with Luke's "discourse on anxiety" (12:22–26), suggests it is anxious disci-pleship that is not the good thing (Darr 2011). In the end, one imagines the three, Jesus, Mary, and Martha waiting, pawns of the interpreter, to hear their encounter played back to them, knowing that it will change according to the times, concerns, and contexts of the readers.

Scholars have long noted that "the fourth evangelist is doing something distinct with the pre-sentation of women characters" (Conway 2003, 80; 1999; Brown 1975; Reinhartz 2003). Here are to be found the Samaritan woman, theologically engaging with Jesus, perhaps even founding a Christian community: Martha, whose confession appears the very expression of Johannine faith; Mary of Bethany, prophetically anointing, and Mary Magdalene, the primary witness of the resurrection. Women certainly seem to matter in this gospel. Yet, if Exum's (1998, 208–209) dictum is followed, that "the interpreter must . . . raise questions about (a text's) underlying assumptions about sex and gender roles and the gender expectations it presents as natural (and thus normative)," this prominence of women may be viewed a little differently. While these women have highly significant roles on the earthly level, "they are celebrated for their recognition of and devotion to the ultimate male figures in the narrative—the Father and the Son," so that, "the customary relationship between male and female is reinscribed in the spiritual realm" (Conway 2003, 102). As Conway's title suggests, there are indeed "Gender Matters in John."

Two Case Studies

Rahab

There is yet more to be considered. Female characters frequently appear as ciphers or symbols. Musa Dube's postcolonial analysis highlights the way in which Rahab, the Canaanite prostitute of Joshua 2, not only "reflects the colonizer's desire to enter and domesticate the land of Canaan," but she, herself, "represents a land to be colonized." Her description as a prostitute (*zona*) is telling: she is open to be entered. In short, she is "a literary phantom of imperialism's 'cultural time bomb'" (Dube 2000, 77, 80).[1] As always, others see her differently. Indeed, as the key character in the prelude to the taking of Jericho, this quick-witted trickster, who bends the truth for godly purposes, has been scrutinized from so many angles that viewing her is like looking through a kaleidoscope. As a Jericho prostitute, she is not only Israel's Other, but Israel's sexualized Other. Indeed, she is "the quintessential outsider in the whole book of Joshua . . . as Canaanite as they get!" (Spina 2005, 54), so that, as Carolyn Sharp writes, "underneath its seductive surface, this story throbs with the terror of ideological nightmare. . . . [T]he spies spending the night with Rahab portrays the ultimate risk: that the vanguard of the Israelite invasion might be corrupted by the enticements of an actual Canaanite" (Sharp 2009, 98). And one who indeed is capable of delivering an authentically Israelite Deuteronomistic testimony. Horror indeed! But for whom? Does Rahab's narrative belong to an Israel entering to possess Canaan, or is the entire narrative a reminder to post-exilic returnees from Babylon that "true Israel" does not include the people of the land? Turn the kaleidoscope a little more sharply, however, and, the ideological shaping appears different again. For while Michael Carden acknowledges that "Rahab might be the absolute Other," he suggests that "as a type of Israel she places Otherness at the heart of what it means to be Israelite," that "as the walls of Jericho collapse bringing together inside and outside, Rahab, the woman of the walls, collapses the distinction between Israelite and Canaanite." The result? She has "begun expanding the boundaries of who is included in Israel" and this, for Carden, is seen as positive (2006, 158, 160). Another postcolonial twist sees Rahab already the hybrid, who, living in her liminal space in the city wall, not only knows the ways of her own Canaanite world but those of the Israelites and their god. Yet, a further turn views her, now saved and accepted by Israel, left "outside the camp" (Josh. 6:23). "Racialized, minoritized, and sexualized," standing in the ruins of the "old" order at the turn of the hybridized "new," she may be "a model minority" but located in this "outside" space, she is the "perpetual foreigner." Kah-Jin Jeffrey Kuan and Mai-Anh Le Tran (2009, 39, 41) do, however, add the rider "she can be what you make of her," closing with the question "but for better or for worse?". A queer turn of the kaleidoscope finds this sexualized Rahab, with her borderline identity, the subject both of disgust and humour (Althaus-Reid 2007; Runions 2011). That the matter of disgust is introduced comes as no surprise, for Israelite tradition decreed those who followed Canaanite ways were to be vomited out of the land (Lev. 18:28). Yet in the narrative itself, Rahab is not treated with disgust but, on the contrary, appears as the heroine, having outsmarted both the king of Jericho and the Israelite spies. How to explain the contradiction? In Erin Runions's (2011, 65–66) analysis, there is more than one layer to the story: in the first "the signifying operations that stick disgust to the Canaanites are reversed. They lose their stickiness." The audience laughs: disgust has turned to humor. The Deuteronomistic layer then changes the response, bringing "a kind of static," for a transgressive trickster blurring the boundaries causes ideological discomfort, unsettling accepted Deuteronomistic norms. In the final form, however, the humor of the narrative overturns this discomfort allowing the audience to relax into laughter "with others and at ourselves" (70). This is, indeed, a kaleidoscopic Rahab, a literary sign put to use according to writers' or communities' agendas and read differently according to readers' interpretive choices. There is nothing new in this. Early in her literary afterlife, Rahab was cited as a model of Christian faith by the writer of Hebrews (11:31) and noted in the Talmud as one of "the four women of surpassing beauty in the world" (b. Meg 15a), becoming a Jewish proselyte and wife to Joshua, a prize indeed.

The Syrophoenician or Canaanite Woman

If Rahab is a cipher, so, too, is the unnamed Syrophoenician woman, whose encounter with Jesus, pleading with him to heal her demon-stricken daughter, is a tale told twice, with variations, in Mark 7:24–30 and Matthew 15:21–28. Matthew's version identifies her as Canaanite, a troubling ideological marker, positioning her as ethnically Other, a Rahab *rediviva*. In Dube's postcolonial analysis, she, too, represents both the land itself and its people, and so "must be invaded, conquered, annihilated." Or, if a survivor, she then represents the colonized, one who "must parrot the superiority of her subjugators" (Dube 2000, 147). Mark's version differs in describing her as Greek, of Syrophoenician origin, inviting analysis of the particularities of social and cultural difference. Much depends on which facet of the woman's representation is key. Is it her gender, her identity as a mother risking rebuff and shame for the sake of her stricken daughter, or her ethnicity, privileged if Greek, "other" and vulnerable if Canaanite? Here, too, body language speaks as she falls or kneels before Jesus, another woman at Jesus's feet (Glancy 2010). This is a worrisome narrative in gospel terms in that it pivots on Jesus's harsh responses to her cry for help. Is this Jesus "caught with his compassion down" (Ringe 1984, 69)? Jesus the healer! But who is the main character? Apply a literary analysis to the Matthean version and the insistent and demanding "Canaanite" is revealed as the protagonist, holding center stage. If a suggested chiasm is accepted, her quick-witted retort can even be seen at the scene's focal point (Ringe 2001, 82). Intertextual analysis finds connections with the Hebrew Bible's lament psalms, bringing the added irony that here it is a "Canaanite" crying out for help in line with ancient Jewish tradition, and "cling[ing] to the faithfulness of the [divine] promise" (O'Day 2001, 116–118, 124). Eventually, she gains that help. But is she merely the receiver or, as Ellen Davis suggests, is she an agent in that "Jesus hands her a line that makes him sound like an 'authoritative dogmatist' with respect to Jewish-Gentile relations (Matt. 15:26; Mark 7:27) . . . (and) she exposes the inadequacy of that position (Matt. 15:27; Mark 7:28)." The result? Jesus reinterprets the notion of holiness, blurring the boundary between Jew and Gentile (Davis 2003, 176)? Or is this "mutual ministry"? She gives Jesus "the power to recognize his ministry to the Gentile people," and he, in turn, gives her "the power of life by healing her daughter" (Rebera 2001, 108). Initially set among the dogs by Jesus, she leaves commended for her faith. Difference in understanding this woman has a long history. In the early centuries of her afterlife, in sermons, commentaries, and devotional texts, she tended to be used either as a figure of Otherness, even an "anathema," or as a universal "exemplum" of faith (Klancher 2013, 1). Difference continues. While interpretive efforts to keep her within closed viewing boundaries may have failed, what cannot be denied is the impact of her role in the Jesus narrative, however that is to be understood.

CONCLUSION

Interpretive matters are complex. As Nancy Klancher (2013, 283) writes in the epilogue to her reception-history study of the Syrophoenician/Canaanite woman, "Texts are less *things* and more *cultural negotiations* or even transactional *events*." Scribal and gospel writers bequeath the narratives, the tales, and reported memories entrusted to them, without commentary, as scriptural gifts. How they are accepted, perused, and used in turn is left to the readers. This is a challenge indeed. For interpretation is not only a matter of asking and scrutinizing how these ancient authors presented and represented the women seen moving in and through their texts. It is also a matter of readers asking themselves what they, as readers and interpreters, are doing as they read. Whose view of the women is to be accepted? What *cultural negotiations* are required? Will it be a matter of recuperation (Bellis 1994) or critique and resistance (Fuchs 2008, 211)? For the critical and hermeneutical choices that readers make have consequences. While literary analyses have highlighted the intricacies and subtleties of plots and characters, the more recent feminist, postcolonial, and queer approaches have highlighted the significance of agenda, ideology, and the inequalities of power, of both authors and interpreters. As Fuchs urges (2008, 221), readers and interpreters must constantly ask "*cui bono?*" Who benefits? For whose good is this interpretation? For reading biblical women does matter, even as the matters of interpretation are complex and a continuing challenge.

NOTE

1. A term Dube quotes from Ngugi wa Thiongo. 1986. *Decolonizing the Mind: The Politics of Language in African Literature.* London: James Curry, 3.

REFERENCES

Ackerman, Susan. 1998. *Warrior, Dancer, Seductress, Queen: Women in Judges and Biblical Israel.* New York: Doubleday.

Althaus-Reid, Marcella. 2007. "Searching for a Queer Sophia-Wisdom: The Postcolonial Rahab." In *Patriarchs, Prophets and Other Villains*, edited by Lisa Isherwood, 128–140. London: Equinox Press.

Anderson, Janice Capel. 1992. "Feminist Criticism: The Dancing Daughter." In *Mark & Method: New Approaches in Biblical Studies*, edited by Janice Capel Anderson and Stephen D. Moore, 103–134. Minneapolis, MN: Fortress Press.

Apostolos-Cappadona, Diane. 2009. "Imagining Salome, or How *La Sauterelle* Became *La Femme Fatale*." In *From the Margins 2: Women of the New Testament and their Afterlives*, edited by Christine E. Joynes and Christopher C. Rowland, 190–209. Sheffield, Yorkshire: Sheffield Phoenix Press.

Bach, Alice. 1994. "The Pleasure of her Text." In *A Feminist Companion to Samuel and Kings*, edited by Athalya Brenner, 106–128. Sheffield, Yorkshire: Sheffield Academic Press.

Bach, Alice. 1997. *Women, Seduction, and Betrayal in Biblical Narrative*. Cambridge: Cambridge University Press.

Bach, Alice. 1999. "Introduction: Man's World, Women's Place: Sexual Politics in the Hebrew Bible." In *Women in the Hebrew Bible: A Reader*, edited by Alice Bach, xiii–xxvi. New York: Routledge.

Bachmann, Mercedes L. García. 2013. *Women at Work in the Deuteronomistic History*. International Voices in Biblical Studies 4. Atlanta, GA: Society of Biblical Literature.

Bal, Mieke. 1988a. *Murder and Difference: Gender, Genre, and Scholarship on Sisera's Death*. Translated by Matthew Gumpert. Bloomington: Indiana University Press.

Bal, Mieke. 1988b. *Death and Dissymmetry: The Politics of Coherence in the Book of Judges*. Chicago: University of Chicago Press.

Bauckham, Richard. 2002. *Gospel Women: Studies of the Named Women in the Gospels*. Grand Rapids, MI: Eerdmans.

Bellis, Alice Ogden. 1994. *Helpmates, Harlots, and Heroes: Women's Stories in the Hebrew Bible*. Louisville, KY: Westminster John Knox Press.

Berlin, Adele. 1983. *Poetics and Interpretation of Biblical Narrative*. Sheffield, Yorkshire: Almond Press.

Brenner, Athalya. 1985. *The Israelite Woman: Social Role and Literary Type in Biblical Narrative*. Sheffield, Yorkshire: JSOT Press.

Brown, Raymond E. 1975. "Roles of Women in the Fourth Gospel." *Theological Studies* 36: 688–699.

Camp, Claudia V. 2000. *Wise, Strange and Holy: The Strange Woman and the Making of the Bible*. Sheffield, Yorkshire: Sheffield Academic Press.

Carden, Michael. 2006. "Joshua." In *The Queer Bible Commentary*, edited by Deryn Guest, Robert E. Goss, Mona West, Thomas Bohache, 144–166. London: SCM Press.

Clanton, Dan W. 2009. *Daring, Disreputable, and Devout: Interpreting the Bible's Women in the Arts and Music*. New York: T&T Clark International.

Conway, Colleen M. 1999. *Men and Women in the Fourth Gospel: Gender and Johannine Characterization*. Atlanta, GA: Society of Biblical Literature.

Conway, Colleen M. 2003. "Gender Matters in John." In *A Feminist Companion to John*, vol. 2, edited by Amy-Jill Levine, 79–103. London: Sheffield Academic Press.

Davis, Ellen F. 2003. "Critical Traditioning: Seeking an Inner Biblical Hermeneutic." In *The Art of Reading Scripture*, edited by Ellen F. Davis and Richard B. Hayes, 163–180. Grand Rapids, MI: Eerdmans.

Darr, John A. 2011. "'Be Not Anxious': Reading Martha and Mary (Lk. 10.38-42) Within Luke's Overall Discourse on Anxiety." In *Reading Ideologies: Essays on the Bible and Interpretation in Honor of Mary Ann Tolbert*, edited by Tat-siong Benny Liew, 76–92. The Bible in the Modern World 40. Sheffield, Yorkshire: Sheffield Phoenix Press.

Deen, Edith. 1955. *All the Women of the Bible*. New York: Harper and Row.

Dewey, Joanna. 1994. "The Gospel of Mark." In *Searching the Scriptures, vol. 2: A Feminist Commentary*, edited by Elisabeth Schüssler Fiorenza, 470–509. New York: Crossroad.

Donaldson, Laura E. 1999. "The Sign of Orpah: Reading Ruth through Native Eyes." In *Ruth and Esther: A Feminist Companion to the Bible (Second Series)*, edited by Athalya Brenner, 130–144. Sheffield, Yorkshire: Sheffield Academic Press.

Dube, Musa W. 2000. *Postcolonial Feminist Interpretation of the Bible*. St. Louis, MO: Chalice Press.

Ebeling, Jennie R. 2010. *Women's Lives in Biblical Times*. New York: T&T Clark International.

Esler, Philip E., and Ronald Piper. 2006. *Lazarus, Mary and Martha: Social Scientific Approaches to the Gospel of John*. Minneapolis, MN: Fortress Press.

Exum, J. Cheryl. 1994. "Second Thoughts about Secondary Characters: Women in Exodus 1.8-2.10." In *A Feminist Companion to Exodus-Deuteronomy*, edited by Athalya Brenner, 75–87. Sheffield, Yorkshire: Sheffield Academic Press.

Exum, J. Cheryl. 1996. *Plotted, Shot, and Painted: Cultural Representations of Biblical Women*. Sheffield, Yorkshire: Sheffield Academic Press.

Exum, J. Cheryl. 1998. "Developing Strategies of Feminist Criticism/Developing Strategies for Commentating The Song of Songs." In *Auguries: The Jubilee Volume of the Sheffield Department of Biblical Studies*, edited by David J. A. Clines and Stephen D. Moore, 206–249. Sheffield, Yorkshire: Sheffield Academic Press.

Fewell, Danna Nolan. 1993. "Reading the Bible Ideologically: Feminist Criticism." In *To Each Its Own Meaning: An Introduction to Biblical Criticisms and Their Application*, edited by Steven L. McKenzie and Stephen R. Haynes, 237–251. Louisville, KY: Westminster/John Knox Press.

Fewell, Danna Nolan, and David M. Gunn. 1993. *Gender, Power, and Promise: The Subject of the Bible's First Story*. Nashville, TN: Abingdon Press.

Frolov, Serge. 2013. "Sleeping with the Enemy: Recent Scholarship on Sexuality in the Book of Judges." *Currents in Biblical Research* 11(3):308–327.

Fuchs, Esther. 1989. "The Literary Characterization of Mothers and Sexual Politics in the Hebrew Bible." In *Narrative Research on the Hebrew Bible*, edited by Miri Amihai, George W. Coats, and Anne M. Solomon. *Semeia* 46:151–166.

Fuchs, Esther. 2000. *Sexual Politics in the Biblical Narrative: Reading the Hebrew Bible as a Woman*. Journal for the Study of the Old Testament Supplement Series 310. Sheffield, Yorkshire: Sheffield Academic Press.

Fuchs, Esther. 2008. "Biblical Feminisms: Knowledge, Theory and Politics in the Study of Women in the Hebrew Bible." *Biblical Interpretation* 16:205–226.

Glancy, Jennifer A. 2010. "Jesus, the Syrophoenician Woman, and Other First-Century Bodies." *Biblical Interpretation* 18:342–363.

Hawkins, Peter S. and Lesleigh Cushing Stahlberg, eds. 2009. *From the Margins 1: Women of the Hebrew Bible and their Afterlives*. Sheffield, Yorkshire: Sheffield Phoenix Press.

Ipsen, Avaren E. 2008. "Solomon and the Two Prostitutes." In *Marxist Feminist Criticism of the Bible*, edited by Roland Boer and Jorunn Økland, 134–150. Sheffield, Yorkshire: Sheffield Phoenix Press.

Ipsen, Avaren E. 2009. *Sex Working and the Bible*. Durham, NC: Acumen Publishing.

Jackson, Melissa. 2012. *Comedy and Feminist Interpretation of the Hebrew Bible: A Subversive Collaboration*. Oxford: Oxford University Press.

Joynes, Christine E. 2007. "Visualizing Salome's Dance of Death: The Contribution of Art to Biblical Exegesis." In *Between the Text and the Canvas: The Bible and Art in Dialogue*, edited by J. Cheryl Exum and Ela Nutu, 145–163. Sheffield, Yorkshire: Sheffield Phoenix Press.

Kim, Seong Hee. 2010. *Mark, Women and Empire: A Korean Postcolonial Perspective*. Sheffield, Yorkshire: Sheffield Phoenix Press.

Klancher, Nancy. 2013. *The Taming of the Canaanite Woman: Construction of Christian Identity in the Afterlife of Matthew 15:21-28*. Berlin: de Gruyter.

Kraemer, Ross Shepard. 1983. "Women in the Religions of the Graeco-Roman World." *Religious Studies Review* 9:127–139.

Kraemer, Ross Shepard. 1992. *Her Share of the Blessings: Women's Religions among Pagans, Jews, and Christians in the Greco-Roman World*. Oxford: Oxford University Press.

Kraemer, Ross Shepard, and Mary Rose D'Angelo, eds. 1989. *Women and Christian Origins*. Oxford: Oxford University Press.

Kuan, Kah-Jin Jeffrey, and Mai-Anh Le Tran. 2009. "Reading Race Reading Rahab: A 'Broad' Asian American Reading of a 'Broad' Other." In *Postcolonial Interventions: Essays in Honor of R. S. Sugirtharajah*, edited by Tat-siong Benny Liew, 27–44. Sheffield, Yorkshire: Sheffield Phoenix Press.

Lee, Kyung Sook. 2011. "Neo-Confucian Ideology in the Interpretation of the Book of Ruth: Toward a Cross-Checking Hermeneutics." In *Korean Feminists in Conversation with the Bible, Church and Society*, edited by Kyung Sook Lee and Kyung Mi Park. 1-13. Sheffield, Yorkshire: Sheffield Phoenix Press.

Levine, Amy-Jill. 2002. Introduction to *A Feminist Companion to Luke*, edited by Amy-Jill Levine, 1–22. London: Sheffield Academic Press.

Malbon, Elizabeth Struthers. 1983. "Fallible Followers: Women in the Gospel of Mark," In *The Bible and Feminist Hermeneutics*, edited by Mary Ann Tolbert. *Semeia* 28:29–48.

Malbon, Elizabeth Struthers. 2011. "Characters in Mark's Story: Changing Perspectives on the Narrative Process." In *Mark as Story: Retrospect and Prospect*, edited by Kelly R. Iverson and Christopher W. Skinner, 45–69. Atlanta, GA: Society of Biblical Literature.

Meyers, Carol L. 1988. *Discovering Eve: Ancient Israelite Women in Context*. New York: Oxford University Press.

Meyers, Carol. 2012. *Re-discovering Eve: Ancient Israelite Women in Context*. New York: Oxford University Press.

Mitchell, Joan L. 2001. *Beyond Fear and Silence: A Feminist Literary Reading of Mark*. New York: Continuum.

Niditch, Susan. 1987. *Underdogs and Tricksters: A Prelude to Biblical Folklore*. San Francisco: Harper & Row.

Nutu, Ela. 2009. "Reading Salome: Caravaggio and the Gospel Narratives." In *From the Margins 2: Women of the New Testament and Their Afterlives*, edited by Christine E. Joynes and Christopher C. Rowland, 210–225. Sheffield, Yorkshire: Sheffield Phoenix Press.

O'Day, Gail R. 2001. "Surprised by Faith: Jesus and the Canaanite Woman." In *A Feminist Companion to Matthew*, edited by Amy-Jill Levine, 114–125. Sheffield, Yorkshire: Sheffield Academic Press.

Rebera, Ranjiri Wickramaratne. 2001. "The Syrophoenician Woman: A South Asian Feminist Perspective." In *A Feminist Companion to Mark*, edited by Amy-Jill Levine, 101–110. Sheffield, Yorkshire: Sheffield Academic Press.

Reinhartz, Adele. 1998. *"Why Ask My Name?" Anonymity and Identity in Biblical Narrative*. New York: Oxford University Press,

Reinhartz, Adele. 2003. "Women in the Johannine Community: An Exercise in Historical Imagination." In *A Feminist Companion to John*, vol. 2, edited by Amy-Jill Levine, 14–33. Sheffield, Yorkshire: Sheffield Academic Press.

Ringe, Sharon H. 1984. "A Gentile Woman's Story." In *Feminist Interpretation of the Bible*, edited by Letty Russell, 65–72. Philadelphia, PA: Westminster Press.

Ringe, Sharon H. 2001. "A Gentile Woman's Story, Revisited: Rereading Mark 7.24-31a." In *A Feminist Companion to Mark*, edited by Amy-Jill Levine, 79–100. Sheffield, Yorkshire: Sheffield Academic Press.

Runions, Erin. 2011. "From Disgust to Humor: Rahab's Queer Affect." In *Bible Trouble: Queer Reading at the Boundaries of Biblical Scholarship*, edited by Teresa J. Hornsby and Ken Stone, 45–74. Atlanta, GA: Society of Biblical Literature Press.

Schüssler Fiorenza, Elisabeth. 1983. *In Memory of Her: A Feminist Theological Reconstruction of Christian Origins*. New York: Crossroad.

Schüssler Fiorenza, Elisabeth. 1992. *But She Said: Feminist Practices of Biblical Interpretation*. Boston: Beacon Press.

Sharp, Carolyn J. 2009. *Irony and Meaning in the Hebrew Bible*. Bloomington: Indiana University Press.

Siebert-Hommes, Jopie. 1994. "But if She Be a Daughter ... She May Live!: 'Daughters' and 'Sons' in Exodus 1.8-2.10." In *A Feminist Companion to Exodus to Deuteronomy*, edited by Athalya Brenner, 62–74. Sheffield, Yorkshire: Sheffield Academic Press.

Spina, Frank Anthony. 2005. *The Faith of the Outsider: Exclusion and Inclusion in the Biblical Story*. Grand Rapids, MI: Eerdmans.

Stiebert, Johanna. 2013. *Fathers and Daughters in the Hebrew Bible*. Oxford: Oxford University Press.

Stocker, Margarita. 2009. "Short Story, Maximal Imbroglio: Salome Ancient and Modern." In *From the Margins 2: Women of the New Testament and Their Afterlives*, edited by Christine E. Joynes and Christopher C. Rowland, 176–189. Sheffield, Yorkshire: Sheffield Phoenix Press.

Trible, Phyllis. 1978. *God and the Rhetoric of Sexuality*. Philadelphia, PA: Fortress Press.

Trible, Phyllis. 1984. *Texts of Terror: Literary-Feminist Readings of Biblical Narratives*. Philadelphia, PA: Fortress Press.

Trible, Phyllis. 1989. "Bringing Miriam out of the Shadows." *Bible Review* 5(1):120–190. Repr. 1994 in *A Feminist Companion to Exodus to Deuteronomy*, edited by Athalya Brenner, 166–186. Sheffield, Yorkshire: Sheffield Academic Press.

Trible, Phyllis. 1999. "Genesis 22: The Sacrifice of Sarah." In *Women in the Hebrew Bible: A Reader*, edited by Alice Bach, 271–289. New York: Routledge.

Weems, Renita J. 1992. "The Hebrew Women Are Not like the Egyptian Women: The Ideology of Race, Gender and Sexual Reproduction in Exodus 1." In *Ideological Criticism of Biblical Texts*, edited by David Jobling and Tina Pippin. *Semeia* 59:29–34.

Weems, Renita J. 1988. *Just a Sister Away: A Womanist Vision of Women's Relationships in the Bible*. San Diego, CA: LuraMedia.

Weems, Renita J. 2005. *Just a Sister Away: Understanding the Timeless Connection between Women of Today and Women in the Bible*. New York: Warner Books.

Vander Stichele, Caroline. 2009. "Herodias Goes Headhunting," In *From the Margins 2: Women of the New Testament and Their Afterlives*, edited by Christine E. Joynes and Christopher C. Rowland, 164–175. Sheffield, Yorkshire: Sheffield Phoenix Press.

Wolde, Ellen van. 1997. *Ruth and Naomi: Two Aliens*. Translated by John Bowden. London: SCM Press.

Yee, Gale A. 1995. "Ideological Criticism: Judges 17-21 and the Dismembered Body." In *Judges and Method: New Approaches in Biblical Studies*, edited by Gale A. Yee, 146–170. Minneapolis, MN: Fortress Press.

Yee, Gale A. 2003. *Poor Banished Children of Eve: Woman as Evil in the Hebrew Bible*. Minneapolis, MN: Fortress Press.

CHAPTER 35

ADAM AND THE MAKING OF MASCULINITY

ERIC THURMAN

MASCULINITY studies is a multidisciplinary field of inquiry into the social construction of what it means to be a "man" (Kimmel and Bridges 2011). Perhaps the most obvious goal of such study is to "make masculinity an explicit and visible object of analysis" (Reeser 2010, 4). As the field has developed to date, it primarily aims "to highlight both the collective privileges from which men as a group benefit as well as the disadvantages that certain groups of men face." Consequently, scholars "often refer to masculinities in the plural to highlight the diversity of meanings, roles, and behaviors" of men from various social locations and cultural contexts and historical periods (Kimmel 2011). Masculinity studies thus might be best understood as a belated reply to the arch observation of Simone de Beauvoir ([1949] 2010, 5), the intellectual founder of modern feminism: "It would never occur to a man to write a book on the singular situation of males in humanity."

Historical reviews of the field, in fact, routinely point out that the interrogation of "masculinity" as a distinct gender formation was enabled by insights first developed in women's and gay and lesbian studies, areas of inquiry that in turn had grown out of the feminist and gay liberation movements of the 1960s and the critique of social inequalities based on gender and sexuality. The "conflicted dependency" of masculinity studies on feminist theory, especially in its beginning, notes Judith Gardiner (2002, 2), reflects a "relationship between masculinity, masculinity studies, feminism, and feminist theories" that is "asymmetrical, interactive, and changing." Those changes are marked in part by shifts in the self-descriptions of the field, from the initial label of "men's studies" to the more encompassing "masculinity studies" and, more recently, to "critical studies of men and masculinities" (Brod 2011, 19).

Looking at the present state of masculinity studies, Harry Brod (2011, 24), one of the early architects of the field, takes these changes as evidence that the "initial intellectual trajectory has indeed reached some sort of completion, and it therefore stands on the brink of a critical turning point." This turning point is perhaps best reflected in a consensus the field seems to have reached on a number of fundamental issues (though perhaps not much further; see Adams and Savran 2002, 2; Edwards 2006). Number one on the list is the "insight that masculinity, too, is a gender and therefore that men as well as women have undergone historical and cultural processes of gender formation that distribute power and privilege unevenly" (Gardiner 2002, 11). That point reflects, and is enabled by, a second, the adoption of social constructionist theories as the guiding methodological perspective on the study of gender.

These two points of agreement lead in turn to a third, that "masculinity" is not a universal given of human experience, but is "changeable and is constantly changing, variously institutionalized, and recreated through media representations and individual and collective performances." That reports of "masculinity in crisis" are typically pearl-clutching reactions to broader historical changes, rather than symptoms of actual male decline, is a corollary to this point. Last, but certainly not least, is the recognition that both men and woman can contribute to the study of masculinity, and of gender more broadly, a point of some contention in the mid-eighties when the question of men's involvement in feminism and feminist scholarship was a live one. Men, it now seems agreed, can indeed be feminists (Gardiner 2002, 11–12).

The extent to which these insights seem familiar, if not downright banal, is precisely the extent to which critical work on masculinities over the last three decades has been smoothly incorporated into scholarship in academic fields ranging from anthropology to Classics and from religious studies to sociology. Work produced in these and other disciplines also addresses new issues and perspectives that help set the agenda for the future of the study of masculinities, assuming, correctly it seems, it has such a future. Key among these concerns, perhaps, is the importance of better understanding the ways masculinity intersects with, and is in part constituted by, other axes of social identity, encompassing not only race, class, and sexual orientation, but also age, ableness, nationality, ethnicity, and religious affiliation (Brod 2011, 29; Gardiner 2002, 12–15).

Biblical Studies and/as Masculinity Studies

"Defining 'masculinity' and the field of 'biblical masculinities' is more difficult than it seems," observes Ovidiu Creangă (2014, 4), "but very simply put, biblical masculinities is the study of the representation/s of the male gender (what 'mans' a man or a woman, including what 'mans' God) in biblical and related literature." The study of masculinity arrived on the steps of the discipline in the mid-nineties with the publications of Howard Eilberg-Schwartz's *God's Phallus* and Jennifer Glancy's "Unveiling Masculinity: The Construction of Gender in Mark 6:17–29," both appearing in 1994 and both drawing primarily on psychoanalytic approaches that brought the anxieties and instabilities of male biblical subjects into the critical spotlight. These were followed by a few additional studies, including some on the predominant males of the Bible, such as David (Clines 1995), Jesus (Clines 1998; Moore 1996), and Yhwh himself (Moore 1996; cf. Guest, "Judging Yhwh in the Book of Judges" in this volume), which also aimed to expose, if not always provide a feminist critique of, the distinctively gendered characterization of biblical figures.

Small of stature at first, the study of masculinity grew up slowly on a diet of studies produced outside the discipline, especially from the data-rich field of Classics, producing such pivotal contributions by Stephen D. Moore and Janice Capel Anderson as their *Journal of Biblical Literature* essay "Taking It like a Man: Masculinity in 4 Maccabees" (1998) and their edited collection *New Testament Masculinities* (2003), as well as Colleen Conway's landmark monograph *Behold the Man: Jesus and Greco-Roman Masculinity* (2008). With the more recent publication of additional monographs on texts in both the Hebrew Bible (Haddox 2011) and the New Testament (Flessen 2011), and not one but two edited collections, *Men and Masculinity in the Hebrew Bible and Beyond* (Creangă 2010) and *Biblical Masculinities Foregrounded* (Creangă and Smit 2014), the study of masculinity in the Bible has, as David Clines (2010, 234), one of the subfield's "founding fathers," puts it, "come of age." Indeed, with two dictionary entries (Stone 2006; Moore 2014), a (forthcoming) themed issue of the *Journal of the Bible and Its Reception*, and an International Society of Biblical Literature program unit, "Biblical Masculinities," also to its name, the subfield has not only come of age but has found its voice.

Perhaps the most discussed issue within biblical masculinity studies is the question of what agenda(s) will guide future work. In posing his own version of the question, Clines (2010) also offers one of the most direct, and ambitious, answers: the problem, as he sees it, is that biblical masculinity studies "seem strangely lacking in passion" in light of the high stakes involved—namely, the "injustice, damaging to women and men alike," of the Bible's "assumption" of "normative masculinity" (238). The solution he imagines is nothing less than a "masculinity movement" that aims "to assess, critique and roll back from the kinds of unthinking masculinity that are spread all over the Hebrew Bible" and, presumably, the New Testament as well. According to Clines's (2010, 239) mini-manifesto, the threefold agenda of this movement involves (1) "consciousness raising" and (2) providing a justification or "apology" for studying biblical masculinities that includes (3) "constantly refin[ing] what it is about masculinity that is objectionable." The answer to this last concern, already implied in Clines's comments, is surely that "masculinity" is a strategy for maintaining male power and privilege as well as other forms of social inequality, as postcolonial and queer theory have taught us.

In any case, the call for a more ethically engaged and politically focused approach to the study of biblical masculinities is not an outlier, and similar calls have been made, repeatedly, in reflections on the state of the subfield. Where, for example, Moore (2003, 20–22) opens the pioneering *New Testament Masculinities* with a warning to biblical scholars about the risk of eliding the queer and feminist politics that animated early work on masculinity in the field of Classics, Jeffrey Staley (2003, 334) closes the collection with an ethical challenge of his own: "We, as biblical interpreters and scholars, need to be thinking hermeneutically, asking whether there is a hermeneutical framework or interpretive angle to these canonical texts that can lead to fresh visions of manhood." Likewise, Creangă (2014, 5) introduces the more recent *Biblical Masculinities Foregrounded* by saying that the "critical study of biblical masculinities works to interrogate and subvert an arranging of the world that 'naturalizes' a particular hierarchy of masculinity"; while Björn Krondorfer (2014, 294) concludes the book with a forthright call to activism: "Scholarship on masculinity, may then, have to conceive of itself as an agent of change."

If this is the future of biblical masculinity studies, as it seems to be, then the area is perhaps best described as a species of ideological criticism. More specifically, biblical masculinity studies is a form of what Brod (2011, 30) has dubbed "superordinate studies." These are "fields that use categories such as race, class, gender, and sexual orientation to study dominant groups" and, crucially, the often-unexamined privileges held by those groups. Like Marxist studies, whiteness studies, and some forms of postcolonial studies, all examples of superordinate studies, biblical masculinity studies in this mode would "insistently put the unmasking and overthrowing of the workings of privilege at the heart of their enterprise (Brod 2002, 174; cf. Moore 2010, 244).

In this way, the objectives of biblical masculinity studies would be similar to, but not identical with, those of feminist biblical studies. Creangă ably points this out, addressing the relationship between the two areas more directly than most. "The hegemony of the 'first sex,'" he observes, "is an issue for feminist and masculinity scholars alike." Whereas for "feminist scholars, the major problem is the Bible's patriarchy and androcentrism," the problem for masculinity scholars "is the hegemony of certain expressions of masculinity that discriminate not only against women but also against other men who do not fit, or like, those images" (2014, 6).

None of this is to ignore or downplay the potential risks involved in making a dominant formation like "masculinity" an academic preoccupation. Indeed, as Moore (2010, 244) notes, the very rationale of biblical masculinity studies inherently involves such a risk, that of re-instituting the concerns of a group that, historically, always has been the center of intellectual attention (cf. Adams and Savran 2002, 7). It is to say, however, that at the current moment, the question is not whether but how biblical masculinity studies will contribute to feminist projects. And among the projects still waiting to be undertaken in earnest is the exploration of the ways biblical texts are being used in the construction of masculinities in the present. Numerous scholars have stressed the importance of this task, but none as forcefully as Krondorfer.

Like Clines, Krondorfer (2014) observes that a sense of "urgency" has yet to attend the study of biblical masculinities. He therefore calls scholars to redirect their focus outside the halls of the academy to where the real interpretive action happens: the world of popular piety and politics. In fact, he says, "biblical scholars may have a mandate to contribute to public discourse," in this case by countering "simplified understandings of biblical masculinity that float around in the public arena" (287). Those simplified understandings are, by and large, the product of "evangelical and fundamentalist interpretations of biblical masculinities," given the outsized influence those groups have on "determining the kind of gender issues debated in the public."

"In spite of the many differences that exist within fundamentalist [and evangelical] movements," Krondorfer continues, "they widely agree on gender issues, especially when it comes to pushing women out of public life and reclaiming a more militant and assertive masculinity" (293). It is thus imperative that biblical scholars speak out effectively against the uncritical promotion of "biblical" patriarchal gender norms. To do so, he insists, scholars need to address a broader, more general audience. More to the point, they need to offer an alternative moral perspective on the "ideals of masculinities as they are distilled and derived from a critical study of the biblical Scriptures" (294).

In the interest of further developing such critical work, the rest of this chapter will sketch a cultural-historical approach to biblical masculinity. With its focus on the ideological discourses that, both consciously and unconsciously, shape the production and reception of "biblical" phenomena of all sorts, cultural-historical interpretation on its face offers a challenge to recent defenses of a divinely ordained and fixed gender order. Of equal importance, a cultural-historical approach can examine competing productions of "biblical masculinity" and explore how they either reproduce or challenge relationships of power between differently gendered subjects. When explicitly informed by feminist and queer theory and politics, a cultural-historical approach can thus help scholars speak in a more public voice about contemporary forms of "biblical masculinity" and the broader ideological entanglements of gender, culture, and religion they represent (cf. Moore 2014, 545–546; Guest 2012).

Toward a Cultural History
of Biblical Masculinity

In a series of recent publications, Timothy Beal (2011a, 2011b, 2013) has given reception history, the precursor to a cultural-historical approach, a critical twist, with some radical implications for the study of biblical masculinity. The difference between the two approaches, he says, is that "whereas reception history focuses on the impact or influence of biblical texts, the cultural history of Bible focuses more sharply on the cultural meanings of them, as well as of 'the biblical' and 'the Bible' itself, insofar as those too are cultural constructs whose meaning and value are culturally contextual." Indeed, he stresses, the Bible itself "is not a singular thing or a self-evident object of our analysis; it is not eternal; it has never been fixed or unchangeable; its form, content, and meaning change within different cultural networks of knowledge and power" (2013, 4).

"The cultural history of Bible," as Beal (2013, 4) thus describes it, "explores the ways the meanings of biblical texts, images, and 'the Bible' itself take form within culture" through "spoken or written words" as well as "through popular media, material objects, and embodied actions." In other words, form and content cannot be separated in the process of interpretation and analysis. "The cultural historian of Bible, therefore, treats these data as meaning-bearing signs, 'symptoms' of biblical culture." And this is where a cultural-historical approach differs the most from other types of biblical interpretation: "[I]t is less about interpreting the Bible via culture than it is about interpreting culture via Bible" (2013, 6). Or, in the present case, it is about interpreting masculinity via the Bible.

What follows, then, is a small gesture toward what a cultural history of biblical masculinity might look like. The exegetical example sketched below focuses on a biblical character that to date has received scant attention from scholars of biblical masculinity—Adam. Like Eve, Adam is a ubiquitous character in contemporary culture, and the appropriation of Genesis 1–3 to be discussed turns to the biblical creation myth(s) in a self-conscious and explicit effort to make sense of masculinity in twenty-first century America. As its title makes clear, *A Guide to Biblical Manhood: How to Serve Your Wife; How to Mold Men through Baseball; How to Make Men in Church and More*, by Southern Baptist ministers Randy Stinson and Dan Dumas (2011), is a devotional self-help book that embraces "manly" ideals believed to be promoted by the Bible.

Unsurprisingly, those ideals are framed, both explicitly and implicitly, to exclude feminist and gay and lesbian voices, hence the importance of interpreting this discourse from an ideological-critical perspective. As a representative example of evangelical Christian discourse on gender, the *Guide* provides a good test case for a cultural-history approach to the study of biblical masculinity. In line with that approach, the exposition that follows aims to elucidate the particular hermeneutical rules and ideological interests that govern the meaning of Adam as an exemplar of biblical masculinity. Used in this way, the cultural history of the biblical Adam becomes a tool for understanding the complex process by which forms of biblical masculinity are produced, contested, and become dominant in particular historical contexts. Perhaps more importantly, it undermines the assumption that "biblical masculinity" is a singular thing or self-evident object at all.

ALL-AMERICAN ADAM

A Guide to Biblical Manhood presents the same kind of essentialist discourse on gender that can be found in countless evangelical Christian books, magazine articles, radio programs, blog posts, sermons, and conferences produced over the past forty years by a network of loosely affiliated church and parachurch organizations, such as Focus on the Family. Key to this essentialist discourse is the idea of gender "complementarity": the notion that "women are considered ontologically equal in being, but not equal in responsibility, function, and authority" to men (Nording 2010, 503). John Piper (1991, 43), a prominent evangelical theologian, puts it this way in the introductory chapter to *Recovering Biblical Manhood and Womanhood*, a nearly 500-page apologia for biblical complementarity: "This is the way God meant it to be before there was any sin in the world: sinless man, full of love, in his tender, strong leadership in relation to woman; and sinless woman, full of love, in her joyful, responsive support for man's leadership. No belittling from the man, no groveling from the woman. Two intelligent, humble, God-entranced beings living out, in beautiful harmony, their unique and different responsibilities."

Viewed in the longer sweep of American history, the discourse of gender complementarianism championed by the *Guide*'s publisher, the Council of Biblical Manhood and Womanhood, and other evangelical groups represents what Seth Dowland calls a "new kind of patriarchy." What was "new" about "the new patriarchy" was the visible effort required to make white male authority appear natural in the face of a growing chorus of critics in the 1960s and 1970s who questioned the historical rationales for gender and racial inequality. No longer able to take the social superiority of white males for granted, conservative evangelicals instead "sanctioned masculine privilege through explicit reference to scripture" and "placed adherence to biblical gender norms at the heart of theological orthodoxy" (Dowland 2009, 247). Yet, as Dowland and other scholars also acknowledge, "this new kind of patriarchy" is at the same time a reiteration of older gender ideologies. Indeed, the ideals of the Christian household as imagined by complementarians bear more than a passing resemblance to both Puritan domestic ideals rooted in Reformed theology and the Victorian-era ideology of "separate spheres" of work for men and women that was particularly promoted by the evangelicalism of the First and Second Great Awakenings (DeBerg 1990; Gallagher 2003; Pope-Levison 2012).

With this bit of history in mind, the hermeneutical rules that govern the *Guide*'s depiction of Adam as an exemplar of "biblical manhood" become more legible. The authors use at least two historically distinct discourses of masculinity to fill in the gendered traits and roles of the first human, who is sketched only in bare outline in the biblical narrative itself. Since both discourses were produced primarily (though not exclusively) by white, heterosexual, Protestant men of the middle class, they are inextricably bound up with developing ideologies of religion, race, sexuality, and class, as American historians have pointed out (Rotundo 1993; Bedderman 1995, Lippy 2005; Kimmel 2011). On the one hand, there are traces of the colonial-era Puritan discourse of what Tom Rotundo (1993, 2–3) calls "communal manhood," which emphasized a man's civic responsibility and domestic authority more than his individual abilities and achievements. This model of manhood was epitomized by the figure of the "dutiful patriarch," who, according to Charles Lippy (2005, 24), worked "to maintain order within the household, the order that reflected the work of God the Father in creating and sustaining the universe."

On the other hand, the *Guide* also contains traces of the Victorian-era discourse of "self-made manhood," a model rooted in "separate spheres" discourse that stressed that "a man took his identity and social-status from his own achievements, not from the accident of his birth" and that "a man's work role, not his place at the head of the household, formed the essence of his identity" (Rotundo 1993, 3). This model was embodied by "the gentle entrepreneur, the man whose life exemplified honesty, integrity, hard work, trustworthiness and a host of other values that would ensure success in the mercantile world" and that could even be fired up by evangelical revivalism to address social ills beyond that world (Lippy 2005, 68). Although one should not assume a neat chronological or ideological break between these two discourses, they do reflect changes in the ways many white middle-class men experienced and thought about their relationships to their "private" and "public" lives, especially their families and their work in the late nineteenth century. And though the *Guide*'s authors claim that "the origins of manhood" can be found by consulting "the Maker," these discourses are what ultimately breathe life into the construction of Adam as the ideal "leader, provider, and protector" (Stinson and Dumas 2011, 7–9).

Like the *Guide*'s cover image, the illustration for the chapter on Adam depicts in summary form how the authors see the object of their discussion, in this case Adam (8). He is clearly imagined as a breadwinner, a man whose authority in the world and at home is tightly linked to his initiative and success at work, an idea reinforced in the biblical text that serves as a caption: "The Lord God took the man and put him in the garden of Eden to work it and keep it" (Gen. 2:15). Presented in three-quarter profile, this Adam is young, light skinned, clean-shaven, shirtless, and carrying a thick sheaf of wheat in muscled arms, and no postlapsarian signs of toil or sweat mar the image of productive labor. His focused but confident gaze is fixed on a horizon outside the frame. Perhaps he looks at Eve and the home that his effort supports. Perhaps he looks at the harvest field, proud of a job well done. Perhaps he looks farther in the distance at new land as yet untamed by his hand. In any case, Adam appears alone, as does each man in the other chapters' illustrations, which sets him apart as an individual and exemplar—the first leader.

Throughout the chapter on Adam, the authors describe in practical terms where and how men should lead based on Adam's example. Tellingly, his areas of leadership can be broken down into two overarching spheres, home and work, presented in distinctly gendered terms. Homes and families, for example, are established by men, the authors say, because "God set a pattern with Adam of men taking the lead in forming new families," especially according to Genesis 2:24 ("Therefore a man shall leave his father and his mother and hold fast to his wife and they shall become one flesh"), which they read as a virtual command to men to enter a heterosexual marriage. "You should not wait on the sidelines for women to take the risks of approaching you," they insist. "You should consider who in His sovereignty God has put around you and take the risk of pursuing a suitable partner" (13).

Like Adam, despite his infamous lapse, each man also bears "a distinct responsibility as the spiritual leader," both as a husband and father and as a member of the local church (10). Oddly though, the authors give more attention to the spiritual virtues men are to cultivate as leaders, such as "self-mastery" and "good stewardship," than to any specific spiritual practices they might enjoin on others (10). Once a man's home is established, the authors also warn, he must "lead in fighting the curse" of Adam and Eve in Genesis 3:16, which on their reading entails "increased challenges" for the married couple and, especially, "conflict over these roles—who's leading and who's following" (13–14). If women are tempted to usurp male authority, they aver, men are tempted to "be either passive or domineering" in response, a temptation men must overcome lest the divinely established domestic order be overturned (15).

Working outside the home is also primarily a man's role. Although the authors point out that men and women "each have a role in production, procreation and provision" in light of Genesis 1, their roles are distinct and fulfilled in separate arenas (12). "Women," they claim, "have a significant role in procreation—as the bearers of life" (12). Little to nothing is said about what other work women might do. Instead, the authors insist that "[m]en bear the responsibility of providing—of knowing where the house payment, the groceries and other provisions are going to come from" (12). Like Adam, each man "has a leadership role to bear in production and provision" in light of Genesis 2:15: "The Lord God took the man and put him in the garden of Eden to work it and keep it" (12). "You may not have land to cultivate" as Adam did, the authors inform the reader, "but God has given you a domain somewhere. All of your leadership should demonstrate some aspect of taking dominion as you bring order and structure" (10).

The impulse to organize and bring order to one's environment comes naturally to all men, according to the authors, but it is also a habit that needs to be cultivated to ensure efficient and productive labor, as their advice suggests. If "God gives you opportunities to take dominion by giving you some area of domain—anywhere from a locker to a whole company," they observe, then even your "home, dorm room, garage, office and car should bear the mark of your masculinity as you subdue it and keep it in order" (11). In light of Adam's curse at Genesis 3:24, self-discipline and a strong work ethic are needed all the more. "Expect thorns and thistles," the authors advise. "But keep working. Embrace the work God gives you without excuses. Don't grumble or complain" (15). Adam's leadership amounts to taking initiative in both economic production and social reproduction and receiving deference from Eve as the guide to how that work should be done. "And," the authors insist, "that hasn't changed. If you're a man, it's not optional to be a leader. It's your God-given assignment and identity" (10).

As Adam emerges from the *Guide*'s pages, he appears to be made in the image of the ideal American man as much as in the image of the biblical deity. Like the dutiful patriarch, he is authoritative and responsible, especially for the order and lives of his wife and the members of his household, upon which his reputation as a true man and faithful citizen greatly depend. Like the gentlemen entrepreneur, he is self-disciplined and hardworking outside the home, where his initiative and integrity among other working men is rewarded with trust and lucrative gain. In fact, in light of the authors' focus on Adam's prelapsarian life as an active, pragmatic leader ready to subdue the new land before him, he easily recalls the literary archetype that also bears his name, the "American Adam." Traces of this mythical figure are found throughout nineteenth- and twentieth-century American arts and letters, particularly in the novel, where, according to R. W. B. Lewis (1959, 5), he represents "a radically new personality, the hero of new adventure: an individual emancipated from history, happily bereft of ancestry, untouched and undefiled by the usual inheritances of family and race; an individual standing alone, self-reliant and self-propelling, ready to confront whatever awaited him with the aid of his own unique and inherent resources."

To be sure, the *Guide*'s authors would balk at such a close association between "biblical" and "American" manhood. Perhaps, sensing the similarities, they are even compelled at the one point to remind the reader that they are not, in fact, prescribing "a self-reliant vision of masculinity." "As a man," they recall, "you are called to act, to lead and work hard and at the same time, you are ultimately dependent on God" (7). In the authors' vision, it seems, dependence on God precludes celebrating the autonomous self that is central to middle-class American culture. Ironically, however, it is the *Guide*'s insistence on the divine origins of manhood that, nevertheless, helps to legitimize the discourse of white middle-class American masculinity, not least by disavowing that discourse's historical particularity and construction by human agents.

CONCLUSION

In *The Second Sex*, Beauvoir offers a brief but trenchant critique of the narrative of Adam and Eve as an incalculably influential myth of male primacy and superiority.

> Eve was not formed at the same time as man; she was not made either from a different substance or from the same clay that Adam was modeled from: she was drawn from the first male's flank. Even her birth was not autonomous; God did not spontaneously choose to create her for herself and to be directly worshipped in turn: he destined her for man; he gave her to Adam to save him from loneliness, her spouse is her origin and her finality; she is his complement in the inessential mode (Beauvoir [1949] 2010, 159–160; cf. Pardes 1993, 17–19).

What a cultural-historical approach might offer to the feminist critique of the narrative of Adam and Eve, this chapter has tried to show, is a focus on how "biblical masculinity" is produced through a network of ideological discourses situated in a specific cultural moment. Yet that focus is perhaps more radical than it first appears. For, as Beal (2013, 5) points out, the "proper focus of cultural-historical criticism in biblical studies is not *the* Bible, but Bible. We omit the definite article because 'Bible' is, from the perspective of cultural history, indefinite." In fact, he says, "there is no singular, fixed, original 'the Bible' or 'the biblical' to be received across history" at all (5). Hence, as the cultural historian of Bible might say, there is no singular, fixed, original "biblical masculinity" either, and that might be the most important point biblical scholars can make.

REFERENCES

Adams, Rachel, and David Savran. 2002. *The Masculinity Studies Reader*. Malden, MA: Wiley-Blackwell.

Beal, Timothy. 2011a. "Reception History and Beyond: Toward the Cultural History of Scriptures." *Biblical Interpretation* 19: 357–372.

Beal, Timothy. 2011b. *The Rise and Fall of the Bible: The Unexpected History of An Accidental Book*. New York: Houghton Mifflin Harcourt.

Beal, Timothy. 2013. "Cultural-Historical Criticism of the Bible." In *New Meanings for Ancient Texts: Recent Approaches to Biblical Criticisms and Their Applications*, edited by Steven L. McKenzie and Joseph Kaltner, 1–20. Louisville, KY: Westminster John Knox Press.

Beauvoir, Simone de. (1949) 2010. *The Second Sex*. Translated by Constance Borde and Sheila Malovany-Chevallier. New York: Alfred A. Knopf.

Bedderman, Gail. *Manliness and Civilization: A Cultural History of Gender and Race in the United States, 1880-1917*. Chicago: University of Chicago Press, 1995.

Brod, Harry. 2002. "Studying Masculinities as Superordinate Studies." In *Masculinity Studies and Feminist Theory*, edited by Judith Kegan Gardiner, 161–175. New York: Columbia University Press.

Brod, Harry. 2011. "The Construction of the Construction of Masculinities." In *Constructions of Masculinity in British Literature from the Middle Ages to the Present*, edited by Stephen Horlacher, 19–32. New York: Palgrave MacMillan.

Conway, Colleen. 2008. *Behold the Man: Jesus and Greco-Roman Masculinity*. Oxford: Oxford University Press.

Clines, David. 1995. "David the Man: The Construction of Masculinity in the Hebrew Bible." In *Interested Parties: The Ideology of Writers and Readers of the Hebrew Bible*, 212–241. Sheffield, Yorkshire: Sheffield Academic Press.

Clines, David. 1998. "Ecce Vir, or, Gendering the Son of Man." In *Biblical Studies/Cultural Studies: The Third Sheffield Colloquium*, edited by J. Cheryl Exum and Stephen D. Moore, 352–375. Sheffield, Yorkshire: Sheffield Academic Press.

Clines, David. 2010. "Final Reflections on Men and Masculinity." In *Men and Masculinity in the Hebrew Bible and Beyond*, edited by Ovidiu Creangà, 234–239. Sheffield, Yorkshire: Sheffield Phoenix Press.

Creangà, Ovidiu, ed. 2010. *Men and Masculinity in the Hebrew Bible and Beyond*. Sheffield, Yorkshire: Sheffield Phoenix Press.

Creangà, Ovidiu. 2014. Introduction to *Biblical Masculinities Foregrounded*, edited by Creangà, Ovidiu and Peter-Ben Smit, 3–16. Sheffield, Yorkshire: Sheffield Phoenix Press.

Creangà, Ovidiu, and Peter-Ben Smit, eds. 2014. *Biblical Masculinities Foregrounded*. Sheffield, Yorkshire: Sheffield Phoenix Press.

DeBerg, Betty A. 1990. *Ungodly Women: Gender and the First Wave of Fundamentalism*. Minneapolis, MN: Fortress Press.

Dowland, Seth. 2009. "A New Kind of Patriarchy: Inerrancy and Masculinity in the Southern Baptist Convention." In *Southern Masculinities: Perspectives on Manhood in the South since Reconstruction*, edited by Craig Thompson Friend, 246–268. Athens: University of Georgia Press.

Edwards, Tim. 2006. *Cultures of Masculinity*. New York: Routledge.

Eilberg-Schwartz, Howard. 1994. *God's Phallus: And Other Problems for Men and Monotheism*. Boston, MA: Beacon Press.

Flessen, Bonnie. 2011. *An Exemplary Man: Cornelius and Characterization in Acts 10*. Eugene, OR: Wipf and Stock.

Gallagher, Sally. 2003. *Evangelical Identity and Gendered Family Life*. New Brunswick, NJ: Rutgers University Press.

Gardiner, Judith Keagan. 2002. Introduction to *Masculinity Studies and Feminist Theory*, 1–30. New York: Columbia University Press.

Glancy, Jennifer. 1994. "Unveiling Masculinity: The Construction of Gender in Mark 6:17–29." *Biblical Interpretation* 11: 34–50.

Guest, Deryn. 2012. *Beyond Feminist Biblical Studies*. Sheffield, Yorkshire: Sheffield Phoenix Press.

Haddox, Susan. 2011. *Metaphor and Masculinity in Hosea*. New York: Peter Lang.

Kimmel, Michael. 2011. *Manhood in America: A Cultural History*. 3rd ed. New York: Oxford University Press.

Kimmel, Michael, and Tristan Bridges. 2011. "Masculinity." *Oxford Bibliographies Online: Sociology*. http://www.oxfordbibliographies.com/view/document/obo-9780199756384/obo-9780199756384-0033.xml

Krondorfer, Björn. 2014. "Biblical Masculinity Matters." In *Biblical Masculinities Foregrounded*, edited by Ovidiu Creangă and Peter-Ben Smit, 286–296. Sheffield, Yorkshire: Sheffield Phoenix Press.

Lewis, R. W. B. 1959. *The American Adam*. Chicago: University of Chicago Press.

Lippy, Charles. 2005. *Do Real Men Pray? Images of the Christian Man and Male Spirituality in White Protestant America*. Knoxville: University of Tennessee Press.

Moore, Stephen D. 1996. *God's Gym: Divine Male Bodies of the Bible*. New York: Routledge.

Moore, Stephen D. 2003. "'O Man, Who Art Thou . . .?': Masculinity Studies and New Testament Studies." In *New Testament Masculinities*, edited by Stephen D. Moore and Janice Capel Anderson, 1–22. Atlanta, GA: Society of Biblical Literature.

Moore, Stephen D. 2010. "Final Reflections on Biblical Masculinity." In *Men and Masculinity in the Hebrew Bible and Beyond*, edited by Ovidiu Creangà, 240–255. Sheffield, Yorkshire: Sheffield Phoenix Press.

Moore, Stephen D. 2014. "Masculinity Studies." In *The Encyclopedia of the Bible and Gender Studies*, edited by Julia O'Brien, 540–547. Oxford: Oxford University Press.

Moore, Stephen D., and Janice Capel Anderson. 1998 "Take It like a Man: Masculinity in 4 Maccabees." *Journal of Biblical Literature* 117: 249–273.

Moore, Stephen D., and Janice Capel Anderson, eds. 2003. *New Testament Masculinities*. Atlanta, GA: Society of Biblical Literature.

Nording, Cherith Fee. 2010. "Gender." In *The Oxford Handbook of Evangelical Theology*, edited by Gerald McDermott, 497–512. Oxford: Oxford University Press.

Pardes, Ilana. 1993. *Countertraditions in the Bible: A Feminist Approach*. Cambridge, MA: Harvard University Press.

Piper, John. "Manhood and Womanhood Defined by the Bible." In *Recovering Biblical Manhood and Womanhood: A Response to Evangelical Feminism*, edited by John Piper and Wayne Grudem, 25–55. Wheaton, IL: Crossway Books, 1991.

Pope-Levison, Priscilla. 2012. "Separate Spheres and Complementarianism in American Christianity." In *Sex, Gender, and Christianity*, edited by Priscilla Pope-Levison and John R. Levison, 58–79. Eugene, OR: Wipf and Stock.

Reeser, Todd. 2010. *Masculinities in Theory: An Introduction*. Malden, MA: Wiley-Blackwell.

Rotundo, Anthony. 1993. *American Manhood: Transformations in Masculinity from the Revolution to the Modern Era*. New York: Basic Books.

Staley, Jeffrey. 2003. "Manhood and New Testament Studies after 9/11." In *New Testament Masculinities*, edited by Stephen D. Moore and Janice Capel Anderson, 329–336. Atlanta, GA: Society of Biblical Literature.

Stinson, Randy, and Dan Dumas. 2011. *A Guide to Biblical Manhood*. Louisville, KY: Southern Baptist Theological Seminary Press.

Stone, Ken. 2006. "Masculinity Studies." In *The New Interpreter's Bible Dictionary*, vol. 3, edited by Katherine Doob Sakenfeld. Nashville, 829–830. TN: Abingdon Press.

CHAPTER 36

CHILDREN IN BIBLICAL NARRATIVE AND CHILDIST INTERPRETATION

KATHLEEN GALLAGHER ELKINS AND JULIE FAITH PARKER

CHILDREN in the Bible are far more prevalent than most readers realize. Although children have been largely overlooked in biblical scholarship, they are essential to biblical narratives and to the culture that produced them. In this chapter, we discuss the burgeoning field of childist interpretation. First, we provide an overview of emerging issues. To identify the presence of children in the Bible, we then touch on terms that designate young people in both the Hebrew Bible and the New Testament. Finally, we offer and demonstrate a six-step methodology for childist interpretation by analyzing the stories of the Israelite slave girl (2 Kings 5:1–14) and the daughter of Herodias (Mark 6:17–29). Our goal is to convince scholars and readers of the Bible that noticing and appreciating child characters in biblical narratives has significant implications for understanding the text. Childist interpretation also summons readers to counter a culture of indifference toward children, in the text and beyond, and to appreciate their agency and contributions to the worlds (biblical or modern) in which they reside.

ISSUES IN BIBLICAL SCHOLARSHIP RELATED TO CHILDREN

One of the key issues in Hebrew Bible scholarship is discovering how the ancient Israelites perceived their children. This issue raises a debate in childhood studies, stemming from the seminal work of the French demographer Philippe Ariès. In his landmark book *Centuries of Childhood* (1960; translated into English; see Ariès 1962), Ariès proposed that children were perceived as mini-adults until the fifteenth century, when the concept of childhood started to emerge. Only at this time, Ariès suggests, did adults begin to value and cherish children, while noticing their distinct needs and capabilities. Ariès's theory has been seriously questioned and largely debunked, especially by medieval scholars, who have summoned significant evidence showing parental devotion to children in this period (see Classen 2005). Nonetheless, some biblical scholars have adopted Ariès's underlying theory without thorough examination or understanding of its history (Blenkinsopp 1997; Dearman 1998; King and Stager 2002).

This raises the question of whether or not childhood existed in the minds of biblical writers. Western societies commonly view children as innocent, cute, and carefree. These romantic ethnocentric understandings of children are inaccurate and anachronistic when applied to the biblical world. Some scholars suggest that, because children and adults lived largely integrated lives, discussions of childhood are irrelevant to biblical understanding (Michel 2004; Kunz-Lübcke and Lux 2006). However, while the biblical text does not share modern concepts of children, it reveals its own understandings of childhood as distinct from adulthood (Koepf-Taylor 2013; Parker 2013).

Prior to the twenty-first century, much of the work on children in the Hebrew Bible was an ancillary part of large projects that looked at biblical narratives from feminist, historical, archeological, or religious perspectives. Biblical scholars now examine young characters in the text through a number of different critical lenses. Some seek to contribute to larger movements that advocate for children (Fewell 2003; Akoto 2006). Others focus on children in the ancient world and archaeology (Garroway 2014; more broadly, see Baxter 2005), exploring their places in economics (Koepf-Taylor 2013), legal texts (Fleishman 1999), and family relations (Balla 2003; Gallagher Elkins 2013). Related work reviews biblical texts from child-centered perspectives (Bunge 2008; Fischer 2002; Dieckmann and Erbele-Küster 2006; Gies 2009; Gundry-Volf 2001; Michel 2003, 2004) and explores children's lives in the ancient world (Aasgaard 2006, 2009; Bakke 2005; Kunz-Lübcke 2007; Horn and Martens 2009).

Historiographical issues are key sites of debate for scholars of ancient childhood. For example, in Greco-Roman antiquity, exposure (Latin: *expositio*; Greek: *ekthesis*; see Boswell 1988, 24–26), or the abandonment of a newborn, was practiced as a method of population control. For a variety of reasons, the family or the *paterfamilias* alone may have decided not to rear a newborn. There were both practical/economic reasons and medical reasons: there may have been a concern for other children (in terms of material survival or inheritance), or the newborn may have been malformed or thought to be unhealthy. While modern audiences often find the idea of exposure horrifying, it was apparently viewed as a kind of family planning. In addition, exposure should be distinguished from infanticide, since exposure may or may not have resulted in the child's death; often the child would have been reared by another family (whether as a slave or a free person).

New Testament scholars are often eager to discuss how and whether the early Christians and Jews treated their children differently (that is, better) than did other inhabitants of the Greco-Roman world. Many ancient Jewish texts condemn exposure, infanticide, and abortion; the Roman historian Tacitus famously notes that the Jews raise all of the children born to them (*Histories* 5.5). These practices are not mentioned in the New Testament, though they are discussed in other early Christian texts (e.g. *Didache* 2.2; *Epistle to Diognetus* 5.6). As with many historical topics, the question is often posed as, did Christianity make a difference? Some scholars argue that Christianity did make a positive difference in the lives of children, pointing to the baptism of infants as one example. For others, this question is too limiting and fraught with definitional problems to have any meaningful answer.

As with any burgeoning field, interdisciplinary work has proved essential. Scholars of childhood studies, by necessity, build on work done in a variety of academic fields, such as psychology, sociology, and anthropology. New Testament scholars focusing on children attend to the important work being done by Greco-Roman historians (Wiedemann 1989; Dixon 2001; Rawson 2003). The study of the ancient family is a flourishing subfield within the fields of both biblical studies (Osiek and Balch 1997; Moxnes 1997; Perdue et al. 1997; Henten and Brenner 2000; Hellerman 2001; Balch and Osiek 2003; Francis 2006; in Jewish studies, see Cohen 1993; Cooper 1996; in late-ancient studies, see Nathan 2000; Horn and Phenix 2009; in Christian theology, see Bunge 2001) and classics (Rawson 1986; Bradley 1991; Evans 1991; Dixon 1992; Martin 1996; Rawson and Weaver 1997; Gardner 1998; George 2005). Although this development is still relatively recent, studies are emerging on ancient slavery (Wiedemann 1981; Bradley 1994; Murnaghan and Joshel 1998), marriage (Rawson 1991; Treggiari 1991; in Jewish studies, see Satlow 2001), and mothers (Dixon 1988; Demand 1994; López 2009; Petersen and Salzman-Mitchell 2012). Children are heavily represented in Roman memorial epigraphs, so an acquaintance with material remains (and related theoretical issues) is crucial. Contextualizing texts in the canon with reference to material remains and contemporaneous texts gives a richer sense of the discursive world in which the early Christians and Jews lived.

CONSTRUCTING CHILDREN THROUGH VOCABULARY

Narratives usually signal the presence of child characters through vocabulary. Various terms for childhood show that the biblical writers recognized children as separate from adults, signifying successive stages of a person's life.[1] Hebrew and Greek terms that explicitly indicate children and youth are common throughout the Bible.

Within the Hebrew Bible, relational words may indicate a young person, such as *ben* (son), *bat* (daughter), and *'ach* (brother) *'achot* (sister), *bekor* (firstborn), *bekira* (older sister), *qaton* (little one), *tsair* (young/-er one), and *yatom* (orphan). Further terms for children and youth can be grouped in successive stages of growth and development, such as *bachur* (young man), *betulah* (young woman), *na'ar* (boy, youth, or servant), *na'arah* (girl, youth, or servant), *'elem* (older boy/teenager), *'almah* (older girl/teenager), *yeled* (child or boy), *yaldah* (girl). Words suggesting infancy include *taf* (dependents or little ones), *gamul* (weaned, safe, small child), *'awil* (small child), *yoneq* (nursing baby or small child), and *'olel* (baby or small child in danger). The subtle implications of the various words can be discerned by the context. Words that designate children and youth in the Hebrew Bible frequently reflect attention to kinship, birth order, gender, development, and safety (see, further, Eng 2011, 58–94).

In the New Testament, common terms for children and youth include *huios* (son); *thugater* (daughter); and more general words, such as *teknon* (child), *nepios* (baby), *brephos* (young child or infant), and *paidion* (child), a diminutive of *pais*. *Pais, paidion*, and other similar words are related to the Greek words for education (*paideia* means "discipline" or "instruction"). *Pais* can indicate either a young person (see Matt. 2:16) or a slave (see Luke 7:1–10, where *doulos* is used interchangeably with *pais*); for this reason, texts containing *pais* are sometimes ambiguous in meaning. Moreover, this semantic overlap indicates the shared low status of children and slaves in antiquity.

While readers can identify the presence of young characters through vocabulary, we also need to recognize that children are integral to the text's *Umwelt*. They were vital participants in household economies, religious communities, and tribal organizations in the ancient world. Settings that involve collectives—for example, families, crowds, congregations, clans, assemblies, nations, and foreign peoples—would contain many children within these general groups. While children in the Bible are rarely the explicit object of attention, they are implicitly present in much, if not most, of the biblical world.

CHILDIST INTERPRETATION OF BIBLICAL NARRATIVES

The word *childist*, while still unfamiliar to many, has been in the academy for decades. Psychoanalyst and political theorist Elisabeth Young-Bruehl uses the term *childism* to name a harmful prejudice that discriminates against children. She argues that anti-child policies and attitudes have become so engrained in American society that they are rarely challenged (Young-Bruehl 2012). Ethicist John Wall agrees that children face prejudices that marginalize and dehumanize them, yet he sees *childism* as a positive term. Wall defines childism as "the effort to respond to the experiences of children by transforming understanding and practices for all" (2010, 3). Wall suggests that, like feminism, womanism, or humanism, childism questions assumptions about certain people's roles and rights. Childism also recognizes children as a distinctive social group with its own perspectives and experiences that often go unnoticed or unappreciated by adults. Following Wall, we use the term *childist* to describe interpretation that focuses on the agency and action of children and youth in the biblical text, instead of seeing them primarily as passive, victimized, or marginalized. Along with feminist and womanist approaches to the text, childist interpretation examines the construction and function of certain kinds of biblical characters while challenging traditional hegemonic assumptions.

The first step of childist interpretation is simply to read against the grain of the text to notice child characters. Since life for children is rarely the concern of the biblical writers, children's appearances in the text are often brief, making it easy to gloss over their presence. To explore these characters, we draw on narrative critical methods and place the child(ren) at the center of attention. Applying a six-step process, the childist interpreter systematically focuses on specific areas as a guideline for interpretation. These steps enable the reader to gain a fuller understanding of young characters who are frequently overlooked both in the text and commentaries. The interpreter begins with concentrated attention to the (1) **setting**, (2) **characters**, and (3) **plot** in a given passage. After gleaning information related to the child character(s), the interpreter then offers (4) **interpretation** based on narrative information related to the child(ren), (5) cultural or historical **insights**, and (6) **connections** with other texts involving children. By examining the setting of the story world, the interpreter foregrounds how the spatial and temporal context permits and constrains character behavior. A focus on the characters ensures that the children are noticed for their relationships with others. The interpreter then reviews the plot with the child(ren) as the center of attention and, paying close attention to literary analysis, offers her or his childist interpretation. This leads to social insights about being a child in the text and perhaps the ancient world. Finally, the interpreter makes connections between the child in the passage and other children in the Bible to shed further light on other stories with child characters.

As mentioned earlier, we offer text studies of two narratives that include girls: the Israelite slave girl (2 Kings 5:1–14) and the daughter of Herodias (Mark 6:17–29). Although traditional commentaries tend to afford these figures little attention, both girls exhibit notable agency as they speak, take action, and influence the outcome of their stories.

A Childist Interpretation of 2 Kings 5:1–14

As part of the Elisha cycle, 2 Kings 5:1–14 extols the wondrous workings of Yhwh's prophet. This story features a leprous commander, Naaman, who has an anonymous slave girl. She has been snatched from her home in Israel by raiders who brought her to serve Naaman. The girl mentions to Naaman's wife that there is a prophet in Samaria (i.e., Elisha) who can cure Naaman. Naaman goes to the king of Aram, who writes a letter to the king of Israel about Naaman's mission. To prepare for the trip, Naaman gathers silver, gold, and garments, presumably as payment for prophetic services. The king of Israel reads the letter from the king of Aram and declares that he cannot cure Naaman. Elisha hears of this and sends for the commander, who arrives at the door of Elisha's house. Via a messenger, the prophet instructs Naaman to dip himself in the Jordan River seven times. At first Naaman is furiously insulted at getting the instructions from a lackey, but his servants reason with him to try the cure. Naaman does, and is healed. Commentaries tend to focus on Naaman's miraculous restoration; few seem to notice that the entire scene is predicated on a few words uttered by an unknown Israelite slave girl.

This short story transpires in international, national, and domestic settings. The text reports that raiders from Aram have snatched a girl from Israel who serves Naaman's wife (2 Kings 5:1). Hearing the girl's suggestion, Naaman and his entourage proceed to Samaria, where Elisha resides, then on to the Jordan River, where Naaman is healed. The narrative arc starts with Israel, the girl's place of origin (v. 1), and ends in Israel (vv. 8, 14), as the healing comes from the child's homeland.

The narrative begins by introducing Naaman, who appears to have the perfect life. He is respected, rich, powerful, and victorious—but he has a horrible skin disease, *metsorah* (usually translated as "leprosy"). *Na'aman* means "pleasant," though this character is a man of war. The commander does not act sickly but gives orders throughout the story. The raiders who capture the girl serve to explain how the girl came to Naaman's household and to highlight her defenselessness. As a young, foreign, female slave, she epitomizes vulnerability. She serves Namaan's wife, who speaks the child's words to the commander. The contrast between the girl and Naaman is stark: she is the small, female, captive, Israelite slave who serves; he is the great, male, powerful, Aramean commander who conquers. This girl is described as "little" (Heb.: *qetannah*), so we can infer that she has not reached puberty; yet the other characters take her suggestion very seriously. She speaks only ten words in the entire Hebrew Bible: "If-only my-master would-go-before the-prophet who is-in-Samaria then he-would-cure him of-his-leprosy" (2 Kings 5:3). Nonetheless, these words set the plot in motion.

Having witnessed the clear conviction of Israelite slave girl, the reader sees the kings of Aram and Israel as confused. These rulers almost appear as buffoons as they jostle against one another vying for position, in contrast to the weak servants who are rational and helpful. The prophet Elisha is the character who acts royally. When Naaman arrives at his house, Elisha sends a messenger to utter the necessary instructions, showing disdain that befits a monarch. Naaman is enraged and rants about the menial instructions to bathe in the Jordan. His servants calm him down (v. 13), addressing him as "my father" (Heb.: ʿavi). Like the Israelite slave girl, they speak hopeful and helpful words.

The Israelite slave girl features most prominently in the first part of the narrative (vv. 1–4), and her words are the catalyst for the ensuing action. She begins her wish with a volitive appeal, "would that" (Heb.: ʿachale), couching her suggestion as a hope (v. 3). Naaman gives the child credit for this idea, describing her as "*the* girl from the land of Israel," not "*a* girl from Israel" (emphasis added). Readers get the impression that she is unique in the area because of her age and nationality. Kings and commanders proceed to follow her advice.

Naaman needs to become like the slave girl in humility and knowledge, becoming subject to others and learning about Elisha's power. The narrator reinforces the association between Naaman and the slave girl with a paronomastic connection that is usually lost in translation. The girl is described as a *naʿarah qetannah* (little girl) in verse 2, and in verse 14, the commander's restored skin is like that of a *naʿar qaton* (little boy). The contrast between the great Aramean and the poor Israelite diminishes as he becomes like her in outward appearance and inner awareness.

This story raises issues about children and slavery, which was an assumed and accepted institution in the ancient world. People who were slaves often had been captured as prisoners of war or sold as debt slaves. Children offered benefits as slaves: they were easy to train and cost less to feed. Many slaves worked in household settings, performing simple domestic tasks that could be handled by children. If placed in her social-historical context, a foreign girl serving as a domestic slave is a window into the lives of many children in the ancient world.

The Israelite slave girl calls attention to other girls in the Hebrew Bible. Like Rebekah, she is kind to an older man (Gen. 24:17–20). Like Dinah, she is among foreigners (Gen. 34:1). Most notably, the Israelite slave girl's story recalls that of Moses's sister in Exodus 2:4–9 (presumably Miriam, though not here named) as she approaches Pharaoh's daughter. The Israelite slave girl and Moses's sister are both young Israelite female slaves. Each extends herself across lines of nationality and class to help a male figure who is part of her household. In both scenarios, the girls speak, take action, and achieve the desired results: the commander is cured, and the baby lives. In both stories, males benefit from females' actions. These girls then serve two masters: those who rule over them and a patriarchal Weltanschauung. However, they also act as quiet mavericks, pushing the limits of their expected roles to shape the outcome of their stories.

A CHILDIST INTERPRETATION OF MARK 6:17–29

The child in Mark 6:17–29 is the daughter of Herodias; she dances for King Herod and his guests at a celebration for Herod's birthday. When he offers her anything she wants, "even half of [his] kingdom" (6:23), she confers with her mother and asks for the head of John the Baptist on a platter. Interpreters often focus on the adults in this narrative: John the Baptist, Herod, and Herodias. But this story of John the Baptist's death hinges on the actions of a little girl (*korasion*; 6:22, 6:28), Herodias's daughter (*thugater*; 6:22). Although the daughter and her mother are often blamed for John's death in subsequent interpretations, viewing this brief story from a childist perspective allows for seeing the daughter as both an active agent and a pawn in a political game.

The ostensible focus of the narrative is John's death, although he is not himself present and alive for much of it. As is typical of Mark's style, the narrative is set up in reverse: in 6:14, we are told that King Herod, hearing that Jesus and the twelve were healing people and exorcising demons, feared that "John, whom I beheaded, has been raised" (6:16). In this flashback, John has been telling Herod that his marriage to Herodias is not lawful because she was first the wife of his brother, Philip; but the narrative focuses more on the actions of the Herodians than on John. His presence is most striking at the end of this pericope, when his head is brought in on a platter and given to the girl, who gives it to her mother.

During Herod's birthday celebration, the girl dances for her father (or stepfather? uncle? It is unclear how Herod and the girl are related) and his clients. One of the key interpretive questions for critical scholars of Mark concerns the relationship between Herod and the dancing girl: there are ancient witnesses to both "his daughter Herodias" and "the daughter of Herodias herself." Moreover, the brother of Herod named "Philip" is not attested in any other ancient account of the Herodian family. Josephus discusses the death of John the Baptist and likewise attributes it to Herod, but does not blame Herodias or her daughter (*Antiquities* 18.116–19; elsewhere, Josephus calls Herodias's daughter "Salome," but she is unnamed in Mark).

The mother of this girl is often portrayed in purely negative terms: she is unlawfully married to Herod; she has a grudge against John the Baptist and seeks his death; she suggests the execution to her daughter; and then she receives his head on a platter. In the Markan version of John's death, Herodias has wanted to kill John for some time (indicated by the imperfect verbs in verse 19, suggesting continuous action) but was unable to do so until her daughter asks her, "What should I ask for?" (6:24). While Herod himself orders the execution, prompted by the daughter's request, the narrator at least partially absolves them both by blaming Herodias.

The girl's parents do most of the speaking and acting in this narrative, but her dance and request are what facilitate the execution of John. She is only mentioned in verses 22–26 and 28, but her dance is the hinge on which this narrative turns. With her brief question to her mother ("What should I ask for?" is even briefer in Greek: *ti aitesomai*) and then her request to Herod ("I want you to give me at once the head of John the Baptist on a platter"), she ensures John's death. When she danced, "she pleased Herod and his guests," leading to Herod's rash oath. In the artistic and cinematic versions of this scene, she dances seductively, and Herod is incestuously attracted to his daughter (or stepdaughter). Although this interpretation may seem warranted, and it certainly enhances the audience's sense that the Herodians are unlawful and lascivious, the vocabulary used in Mark 6 does not necessitate such an interpretation.

Minor characters play key roles in the narrative. Herod's guests, like Herod himself, are pleased with the girl's dancing, and Herod agrees to her request "out of regard for his oaths and for the guests" (6:26). Their presence backs Herod into a corner, ensuring that he will order John's execution. Likewise, the soldier of the guard is instrumental to the plot: he beheads John and brings the head to the daughter. The soldier and the daughter are the only characters who move in and out of the dining space; all the other characters remain either inside or outside the banquet.

While John had attempted to put distance between Herod and Herodias, the girl brings them together: by moving between her parents, she is able to unite her mother's murderous intentions (but inability to kill) with her father's ability (but reluctance) to kill (6:20, 26), mediating a classic instance of differentiated power and authority. Although she is often seen as doing her mother's bidding, she is not merely a parrot for Mommie Dearest. When she asks her mother's advice, her mother tells her to ask for the head of John the Baptist. The daughter "immediately rushed back to the king" (6:25) and adds both a sense of immediacy ("at once") and a detail that her mother did not mention ("on a platter"). Why she adds these things to her request is not discussed, but the changes make clear that she has and voices thoughts of her own.

With the daughter at the center of the narrative, readers are led to ask different questions and have different concerns. While many interpreters have focused on the gendered division of space in this scene, childist interpreters may foreground the presence of a young girl at a banquet and her role in John the Baptist's death. This little girl is more powerful than the compelling prophet and, in the end, overpowers even the king's wishes: he was "deeply grieved" at her request, but "did not want to refuse her" (6:26). Yet, even with her power, she remains a minor character in a brief narrative in Mark's Gospel; we do not hear from her again.

Although this daughter is by no means the only child in Mark's Gospel, or the only daughter, she is one of the most compelling figures simply because she is so ambiguous: are we to see her as a bloodthirsty daughter of her murderous mother or as a helpless victim in a horrible family? Is her dance innocent or seductive? Is she to blame for John's death, or is it really the fault of her parents? Fitting uneasily in any of these binary categories, this daughter is an example of a girl exercising agency in a situation of limited influence, and she indicates the surprising power that children have over their parents.

Various other biblical texts are referenced, either explicitly or implicitly, in this narrative about John's death. The parallels to Esther's story seem to be the clearest, even in the language: *korasion* for Esther (in the LXX) and the dancing girl; "half my kingdom" being offered by the king. Some interpreters have also argued that this narrative invokes Ahab and Jezebel conspiring to kill Elijah. The stories of Judith and Jael similarly have a murderous woman, a food/banquet scene, and a dead male leader. Jephthah makes a rash oath that results in someone's death (though, in this case, it is his daughter who dies as a result, not a political enemy) and the narrative features a young girl dancing. While many of the biblical parallels to the scene in Mark 6 also have a young girl/woman in a heroic (Esther, Judith) or pitiful role (Jephthah's daughter), this child and her mother are figured as enemies of the godly prophet. Herodias, especially, is portrayed as murderous and resentful; her daughter is portrayed, at minimum, as caught up in an evil family, if not bloodthirsty herself.

The daughter invites modern readers to ask questions about our own ideas of childhood: are all children innocent? Do we assume too easily that children are merely products of their parents? When are children to blame (or accountable) for their actions and when are they not yet able to understand consequences? Why are young girls sexualized so pervasively?

Conclusion

As in many fields that have been informed by advocacy concerns and poststructuralist theories, we hope that childist interpretation will be a vehicle both for social transformation and for new insights into the biblical text, the nature of language, and historical matters. For example, interpreters might find that ancient notions of childhood contrast so strongly with modern ones that we must interrogate which characters are children, what is meant by "child" and "childhood," and how to identify other child characters. Or, interpreters might extend the work of other, advocacy-based fields to apply to texts about children; for instance, interpreters focused on gender and slavery have critiqued the power structures enshrined in the New Testament Household Codes (Col. 3:18–4:1, Eph. 5:22–6:9, 1 Pet. 2:13–3:7). If "Wives, submit to your husbands" and "Slaves, submit to your masters" have been contextualized, analyzed, and ultimately seen as harmful, perhaps "Children, submit to your parents" might similarly be examined for the ways it promotes unhealthy relationships and family structures. Similarly, the injunction for parents to discipline children corporally (Prov. 13:24) should not be held up as the "biblical view" on raising children. Proverbs is itself a varied collection that reflects a dualistic outlook. Understanding children as good/disciplined or bad/undisciplined is particular to this book that eschews character complexities.

Attention to child characters sheds new light on biblical texts, whether those texts are well-known or more obscure. Readers are invited to ask questions about their perceptions of children and childhood in biblical narratives, the ancient world, their own lives, and modern sociopolitical discourses. Just as feminist interpretation calls interpreters, not just to notice female characters in the Bible, but also to interrogate larger structures of domination related to gender, sex, and sexuality, childist interpretation has the potential to herald significant shifts in biblical studies as a field. Childist interpretation of biblical narratives enables readers to notice something small but far from insignificant, by questioning dominant interpretations and offering unexpected discoveries. As the field grows and develops, we hope that childist interpretation will expand readers' approaches to the biblical text, in addition to making the world more hospitable for children themselves.

Notes

1. The terms for "young childhood" *tsirah* (Gen. 43:33), "older childhood" *'elumim* (Isa 54:4; Ps. 89:46 [Eng. 89:45]; Job 201:11; 33:25), and "late teenage years" *bechurim* (Num. 11:28; Eccles. 11:9; 12:1) are not prevalent in the Bible; nonetheless, they show awareness of children's development through progressive stages of youth. The most common word for childhood or youth is *ne'urim*, occurring forty-six times. Attestations of this word show children as workers (Gen. 46:34; Isa. 47:12; Zech. 13:50), living with parents (Lev. 22:13; Num. 30:4 [Eng. 30:3], 17 [Eng. 30:16]), and gaining belief (1 Kings 18:12; Ps. 71:17). Another general word for childhood, *yaldut*, appears in later writings (Eccles. 11:9; 12:1; Ps. 110:3) and may reflect an understanding that this period is less encumbered than adulthood.

References

Aasgaard, Reidar. 2006. "Children in Antiquity and Early Christianity: Research History and Central Issues." *Familia* 33: 23–46.

Aasgaard, Reidar. 2009. *The Childhood of Jesus: Decoding the Apocryphal Infancy Gospel of Thomas*. Eugene, OR: Cascade Books.

Akoto, Dorothy B. E. A. 2006. "Women and Health in Ghana and the *Trokosi* Practice: An Issue of Women's and Children's Rights in 2 Kings 4:1-7." In *African Women, Religion, and Health: Essays in Honor of Mercy Amba Ewudziwa Oduyoye*, edited by Isabel Apawo Phiri and Sarojini Nadar, 96–110. Maryknoll, NY: Orbis.

Ariès, Philippe. 1962. *Centuries of Childhood: A Social History of Family Life*. Translated by Robert Baldick. New York: Knopf.

Bakke, O. M. 2005. *When Children Became People: The Birth of Childhood in Early Christianity*. Translated by Brian McNeil. Minneapolis, MN: Augsburg Fortress.

Balch, David, and Carolyn Osiek, eds. 2003. *Early Christian Families in Context: An Interdisciplinary Dialogue*. Grand Rapids, MI: Eerdmans.

Balla, Peter. 2003. *The Child-Parent Relationship in the New Testament and Its Environment*. Tübingen: Mohr Siebeck.

Baxter, Jane Eva. 2005. *The Archaeology of Childhood: Children, Gender, and Material Culture*. Walnut Creek, CA: AltaMira.

Blenkinsopp, Joseph. 1997. "The Family in First Temple Israel." In *Families in Ancient Israel*, edited by Leo G. Perdue, Joseph Blenkinsopp, John J. Collins, and Carol Meyers, 48–103. Louisville, KY: Westminster John Knox.

Boswell, John. 1988. *The Kindness of Strangers: The Abandonment of Children in Western Europe from Late Antiquity to the Renaissance*. New York: Pantheon Books.

Bradley, Keith R. 1991. *Discovering the Roman Family: Studies in Roman Social History*. New York: Oxford University Press.

Bradley, Keith R. 1994. *Slavery and Society at Rome*. New York: Cambridge University Press.

Bunge, Marcia J., ed. 2001. *The Child in Christian Thought*. Grand Rapids, MI: Eerdmans.

Bunge, Marcia J., Terence E. Fretheim, and Beverly Roberts Gaventa, eds. 2008. *The Child in the Bible*. Grand Rapids, MI: Eerdmans.

Classen, Albrect. 2005. "Philippe Ariès and the Consequences: History of Childhood, Family Relations, and Personal Emotions: Where Do We Stand Today?" In *Childhood in the Middle Ages and the Renaissance: The Results of a Paradigm Shift in the History of Mentality*, edited by Albrecht Classen, 1–65. Berlin: de Gruyter.

Cohen, Shaye J. D., ed. 1993. *The Jewish Family in Antiquity*. Atlanta, GA: Scholars Press.

Cooper, John. 1996. *The Child in Jewish History*. Northvale, NJ: Jason Aronson.

Dearman, J. Andrew. 1998. "The Family in the Old Testament." *Interpretation* 52(2): 117–129.

Demand, Nancy. 1994. *Birth, Death, and Motherhood in Classical Greece*. Baltimore, MD: Johns Hopkins University Press.

Dieckmann, Detlef, and Dorothea Erbele-Küster, eds. 2006. *"Du hast mich aus meiner Mutter Leib gezogen" Beiträge zur Geburt im Alten Testament*. Neukirchen-Vluyn: Neukirchener.

Dixon, Suzanne. 1988. *The Roman Mother*. Norman: University of Oklahoma Press.

Dixon, Suzanne. 1992. *The Roman Family*. Baltimore, MD: Johns Hopkins University Press.

Dixon, Suzanne, ed. 2001. *Childhood, Class, and Kin in the Roman World*. New York: Routledge.

Elkins, Kathleen Gallagher. 2013. "Mother, Martyr: Reading Self-Sacrifice and Family in Early Christianity." PhD diss. Drew University.

Eng, Milton. 2011. *The Days of Our Years: A Lexical Semantic Study of the Life Cycle in Biblical Hebrew*. New York: T&T Clark.

Evans, John K. 1991. *War, Women, and Children in Ancient Rome*. New York: Routledge.

Fewell, Danna Nolan. 2003. *The Children of Israel: Reading the Bible for the Sake of Our Children*. Nashville, TN: Abingdon.

Fischer, Irmtraud. 2002. "Über Lust und Last, Kinder zu haben: Soziale, genealogische und theologische Aspekte in der Literatur Alt-Israels." *Jahrbuch für Biblische Theologie* 17: 56–82.

Fleishman, Joseph. 1999. *Parent and Child in Ancient Near East and the Bible*. Jerusalem: Magnes.

Francis, James M. M. 2006. *Adults as Children: Images of Childhood in the Ancient World and the New Testament*. Bern, Switzerland: Peter Lang.

Gardner, Jane F. 1998. *Family and Familia in Roman Law and Life*. New York: Oxford University Press.

Garroway, Kristine. 2014. *Children in the Ancient Near Eastern Household*. Winona Lake, IN: Eisenbrauns.

George, Michele, ed. 2005. *The Roman Family in the Empire: Rome, Italy, and Beyond*. New York: Oxford University Press.

Gies, Kathrin. 2009. *Geburt—ein Übergang: rituelle Vollzüge, Rollenträger und Geschlechterverhältnisse*. Arbeiten zu Text und Sprache im Alten Testament 88. St. Ottilien: Erzabtei St. Ottilien.

Gundry-Volf, Judith M. 2001. "The Least and the Greatest: Children in the New Testament." In *The Child in Christian Thought*, edited by Marcia Bunge, 29–60. Grand Rapids, MI: Eerdmans.

Hellerman, Joseph H. 2001. *The Ancient Church as Family*. Minneapolis, MN: Fortress Press.

Henten, Jan Willem van, and Athalya Brenner, eds. 2000. *Families and Family Relations as Represented in Early Judaisms and Early Christianities: Texts and Fictions*. Studies in Theology and Religion 2. Leiden: Deo.

Horn, Cornelia B., and John W. Martens. 2009. *"Let the Little Children Come to Me": Childhood and Children in Early Christianity*. Washington, DC: Catholic University of America Press.

Horn, Cornelia, and Robert Phenix, eds. 2009. *Children in Late Ancient Christianity*. Tübingen: Mohr Siebeck.

King, Philip J., and Lawrence E. Stager. 2002. *Life in Biblical Israel*. Louisville, KY: Westminster John Knox.

Koepf-Taylor, Laurel W. 2013. *"Give Me Children or I Shall Die": Children and Communal Survival in Biblical Literature*. Minneapolis, MN: Fortress.

Kunz-Lübcke, Andreas. 2007. *Das Kind in den antiken Kulturen des Mittelmeers*. Newkirchen-Vluyn: Neukirchener.

Kunz-Lübcke, Andreas, and Rüdiger Lux, eds. 2006. *"Schaffe Mir Kinder . . .": Beiträge zur Kindheit im alten Israel und in seinen Nachbarkulturen*. Arbeiten zur Bibel und ihrer Geschichte 21. Leipzig: Evangelische Verlagsanstalt.

López, Rosa María Cid, ed. 2009. *Madres y Maternidades: Construcciones Culturales en la Civilización Clásica*. Oviedo: KRK Ediciones.

Martin, Dale B. 1996. "The Construction of the Ancient Family: Methodological Considerations." *Journal of Roman Studies* 86 (January): 40–60.

Michel, Andreas. 2003. *Gott und Gewalt gegen Kinder im Alten Testament*. Forschungen zum Alten Testament 37. Tübingen: Mohr Siebeck.

Michel, Andreas. 2004. "Sexual Violence against Children in the Bible." In *The Structural Betrayal of Trust*, translated by John Bowden and edited by Regina Ammicht-Quinn, Hille Haker, and Maureen Junker-Kenny, 51–60. Concilium. London: SCM.

Moxnes, Halvor, ed. 1997. *Constructing Early Christian Families: Family as Social Reality and Metaphor*. London: Routledge.

Murnaghan, Sheila, and Sandra R. Joshel, eds. 1998. *Women and Slaves in Greco-Roman Culture: Differential Equations*. New York: Routledge.

Nathan, Geoffrey S. 2000. *The Family in Late Antiquity: The Rise of Christianity and the Endurance of Tradition*. New York: Routledge.

Osiek, Carolyn, and David Balch. 1997. *Families in the New Testament World: Households and House Churches*. Louisville, KY: Westminster John Knox Press.

Parker, Julie Faith. 2013. *Valuable and Vulnerable: Children in the Hebrew Bible, Especially the Elisha Cycle*. Brown Judaic Study Series 355. Providence, RI: Brown University.

Perdue, Leo G., Joseph Blenkinsopp, John J. Collins, and Carol Meyers. 1997. *Families in Ancient Israel*. Louisville, KY: Westminster John Knox.

Petersen, Lauren Hackworth, and Patricia Salzman-Mitchell, eds. 2012. *Mothering and Motherhood in Ancient Greece and Rome*. Austin: University of Texas Press.

Rawson, Beryl. 2003. *Children and Childhood in Roman Italy*. Oxford: Oxford University Press.

Rawson, Beryl, ed. 1986. *The Family in Ancient Rome: New Perspectives*. Ithaca, NY: Cornell University Press.

Rawson, Beryl, ed. 1991. *Marriage, Divorce, and Children in Ancient Rome*. New York: Oxford University Press.

Rawson, Beryl, and P. R. C. Weaver, eds. 1997. *The Roman Family in Italy: Status, Sentiment, Space*. New York: Oxford University Press.

Satlow, Michael L. 2001. *Jewish Marriage in Antiquity*. Princeton, NJ: Princeton University Press.

Treggiari, Susan. 1991. *Roman Marriage: Iusti Coniuges from the Time of Cicero to the Time of Ulpian*. New York: Oxford University Press.

Wall, John. 2010. *Ethics in Light of Childhood*. Washington, DC: Georgetown University Press.

Wiedemann, Thomas E. J. 1981. *Greek and Roman Slavery*. Baltimore, MD: Johns Hopkins University Press.

Wiedemann, Thomas E. J. 1989. *Adults and Children in the Roman Empire*. New Haven, CT: Yale University Press.

Young-Bruehl, Elisabeth. 2012. *Childism: Confronting Prejudice against Children*. New Haven, CT: Yale University Press.

CHAPTER 37

···

READING OTHERS AS THE SUBJECT(S) OF BIBLICAL NARRATIVE

···

ROBERT D. MALDONADO

A FORAY INTO ANCIENT OTHERING

···

HUMAN beings have long constructed identity, individual and group, human and nonhuman, by rendering certain members Other to a more primary Subject. These constructions have been embedded in the various traditions that have survived to the present day. Thus, otherness has existed within human perspective and discourse for millennia prior to the category itself being theorized. These constructions have also contributed to the institutions that support the communities that preserved the traditions over the same period of time. The various communities and their institutions, however, are not monolithic, and what has emerged are complex dynamics of hermeneutics and social-political practices. It is precisely because of these complexities that particular constructions, institutions, and communities can arise, change, and recede in history.

Otherness thus is about power, the power of identity constructions that get embedded in social-political institutions and, in dialectic fashion, shape and are shaped by the discourses that emerge from them. Obviously, when the question of Otherness is foregrounded in interpretation, the location of ostensible Others is immediately raised. There are three primary locations for Others in the face of this inquiry. First is within the textual tradition itself. This is primarily reflected in how characters or groups are constructed and interact within the text(s). These would be the Others as they were viewed, consciously or unconsciously, in ancient times. The second location is in the community of the contemporary interpretation. This does not require the Others (former or current) to be the interpreters; Otherness itself is present, again consciously or unconsciously, explicitly or implicitly, in the act of interpretation. Its presence is consequential to Otherness being a category of the historical construction of identity. The third location is in the tradition history. Essentially, this consists of the historical layers of past contemporary interpreters, that is, the tradition history of otherness. With biblical (and classic) texts and traditions, the historical canonical dynamics have contributed to the preservation and reception of the tradition. For communities of faith, as well as for communities of a particular cultural religious heritage, these dynamics have constituted the interpretive community itself, at least in part.

As a hermeneutical category Otherness can therefore be embedded in the text under interpretation. Additionally, it can be heuristically present (or not) within the contemporary interpretive construal. This is not simply because it may or may not be a lens or a value of the contemporary interpretive community. It is also because many texts, and especially biblical texts, have had an ongoing historical/tradition-historical component. Thus there is a canonical economy that has contributed to the situatedness of the contemporary community itself, a kind of normative inertia.

As an example of these dynamics, let us first consider an extrabiblical text, Homer's *The Odyssey*. In book 5, we find Odysseus being held captive by Calypso. Zeus sends Hermes to Calypso to convince her to release Odysseus so that he might return home to save his house. Calypso gives an ideologically telling response: she complains bitterly that the gods get to have their dalliances with mortal women, but when goddesses do the same thing, their interests get subordinated to those of men. "You are hard-hearted, you gods, and jealous beyond all creatures besides, when you are resentful toward the goddesses for sleeping openly with such men as each has made her true husband" (Lattimore 1975, 5.117–120). This speech would have made no sense to Homer's audiences unless they were aware of a double standard and of women complaining about it. Our contemporary awareness of this dynamic complicates our interpretation as we assess the significance and evaluation of the double standard. The important point is that the text provides evidence of women being othered as well as offering resistance. If they were embedded in ancient discourse, these dynamics presumably existed in the ancient audience as well.

We can demonstrate the complication of interpretation by a previous scene. Athena is sent to encourage Telemachos to be a man and to go find his father, saying, "You should not go on clinging to your childhood. You are no longer of an age to do that" (1.296–297). His act following the "be a man" speech is to publicly humiliate his mother in front of the suitors. He tells her, "Go therefore back in the house, and take up your own work, the loom and the distaff, and see to it that your handmaidens ply their work also; but the men must see to discussion, all men, but I most of all. For mine is the power in this household" (1.356–359). Void of explicit explanation or commentary, the scene offers little interpretive guidance. It could be that Telemachos's behavior simply reflects a conventional expression of male identity that would have seemed unremarkable to the ancient audience. Or, his speech could be construed as ironic. Given the articulation of the double standard in the Calypso scene, we might be inclined toward the latter. Homer's intention, however, does not ultimately matter. The values of the contemporary interpretive community will shape the reading. If we value the othering of women or do not care either way, we might not even notice the scene as having much significance except perhaps as a plot point. If we disvalue the othering of women, we might side with the critical reading. While we cannot determine either Homer's thoughts or those of the audience, we have reason to think that the ancient audience was also debating the issues. Homer's contemporary community was not unlike our own; neither is monolithic.

ON THE HISTORY OF OTHERNESS AS A CRITICAL CATEGORY

Otherness began to be theorized as a critical category in the twentieth century. Although it is impossible to do justice in the brief space of this chapter to this category's complex development, it has its roots in various trajectories from Descartes (1993) to Hegel (1977) and onward. Initially, the focus was on the Self in relation to the Other, the privilege of the Subject. The subjectivity of the self was primary; the Other was instrumental. As Otherness and othering developed as a critical category, those who had mostly been silenced by the power of the Subjects over them began to speak and to speak back to power. This happened in three interrelated domains: gender, ethnicity/race, and empire. Freedom movements around the world responded not just politically and economically, but also in terms of identity and voice. Not to diminish significant roots in the nineteenth century, notably abolition movements regarding African chattel slavery and the enfranchisement of women, the mid-twentieth century was a remarkable time of these confluences. From Simone de Beauvoir applying notions of sexual reciprocity in the definition of self to Gandhi responding to British Empire to the civil rights movement in the United States and various freedom and independence movements in Africa, Asia, and Latin America, there was a veritable explosion of critical Otherness perspectives in the late twentieth century.

What all these perspectives have in common is a critical analysis of the self as Object of another's Subject. This work is political, re-situating relationships between the previous subjects and objects. Beauvoir (1953), Fanon (1963, 1967), Foucault (1965), Lévinas (1969, 1987), Said (1979), Anzaldúa (1987), Trinh (1989), Spivak (1999), and Bhabha (1994) have been some of the more influential theoretical resources in this explosion in religious and biblical studies, informing the pivotal works of Sugirtharajah (1995), Segovia and Tolbert (1995a, 1995b), Dube (2000), Segovia (2000), Kwok (2005), and Bailey et al. (2009), among others (for an overview of expressly feminist work, see McKinlay in this volume). What particularly characterizes Otherness within biblical studies is the explicit engagement of the canonical economy of the Bible, especially as its use has contributed to the othering of others.

As a critical category, Otherness changes the constellation of the hermeneutical framework. Reading is now done with explicit Others (Wit and West 2008; West 2001, 2007). To the extent that the othered have voice, and they do, even ignoring them does not undo the changed constellation. It is also the case that the othered are not a monolithic Subject. The dominant groups do not have monolithic agreement among themselves. To expect it of Others is to continue their othering. What matters is that we who have been considered Other are Subjects within public discourse.

Of course, the ethics of Otherness is controversial and fraught because of the very dynamics of the nonmonolithic identities of Otherness. Whether Otherness is seen as something to be resisted and subverted or endorsed is a separate, but related, issue. While some disagreement over what constitutes Othering is inevitable, and while at some level, rendering others as object to one's subjectivity may be a necessary component of human identity; nevertheless, a totalizing project of othering in which groups or individuals are cast in a more or less permanent position cannot be ethically sustained. It is these ethical commitments that orient the hermeneutical approach to the world, including tradition. In this matrix, the Bible becomes a conversation partner in an ethical project. It, too, is fraught because the canonical and hermeneutical economies are complex. The Bible, its interpretation, and its interpreters all have contributed and continue to contribute to the othering of Others, while simultaneously inspiring counter-trajectories. Thus, the goal of reading for the Other is not to find the answer in the Bible, like some kind of rabbit pulled out of a hat, but rather to enter into an ethical discourse in which a variety of voices emerge and transform the hermeneutical landscape, and we contemporary interpreters exercise our critical judgment (see Phillips in this volume).

As an example, let me reflect on the conversation among myself (Maldonado 1995), Laura Donaldson (1999), and Francisco García-Treto (2001) on the function of *mestizaje* (mixture) within the book of Ruth. Donaldson focuses on the genocidal implications of past politics of mixing and rejects Ruth in favor of Orpah. I find the book and, especially, the character of Ruth profoundly ambiguous with respect to the nature and value of her identity. This ambiguity, for me, casts the ethics back into our contemporary world and readings; it does not let us off the hook, then or now. García-Treto brings both of our interpretations into reflection with his own experiences. He, too, sees mixed messages in Ruth. On the one hand, he, unlike Donaldson, does not identify *mestizaje* with assimilation (García-Treto 2001, 55) but acknowledges the problem of mixing as a final solution (Donaldson 1999, 137). García-Treto and I are more in agreement with each other than Donaldson is with us. The point here is that we each foreground the problematic of Otherness and *mestizaje* from our particular perspectives.

To be sure, some arguments are more compelling than others, but reasonable people can disagree. Again, the important point is not that we agree in the end, but that we are having the conversation and that Otherness is an heuristic lens through which we can evaluate the text and the identities within it and reading it. Otherness is not a mere lens, instrument, or means to something else, as if yet another chapter in the othering of Others. Rather, to the extent that the ethics of identity is foregrounded in the contemporary world, claims are made on all of us to remake the world, its discourses, and institutions in the light of the values that emerge. The focus on the ethics of identity in the contemporary world and the variety of voices in the conversation keeps the use of Otherness as an heuristic lens from itself making Otherness and Others an instrument for privileged Subjects.

READING OTHERS IN THE FIRST TESTAMENT: THE BOOK OF ESTHER

I approach Esther as I approach most things, as a light-skinned, first-generation, fairly assimilated Mexican American. Inevitably, the politics of passing comes to the foreground. In part, that is related to my identity and experience, but is also a significant dynamic of the text. In this light, Esther poses a number of questions. If this is a tale of the Diaspora, what should the original audience have gleaned from it? Is it an instruction to pass as a non-Jew on the off chance that we find ourselves in a position where we might be of benefit to our people? Given the reality of passing, a reality in which the individual loses much, we may pass out of our own community so that when that off chance occurs, we are not interested in saving our people. Of course, there is in this story the added plot complication of massacre, threatened and actualized, that raises the stakes of passing.

Esther provides an interesting contrast to, say, Daniel (as Ezra/Nehemiah might be to Ruth). Daniel does not pass, quite the opposite, and is rewarded with health and miraculous deliverances. Esther passes and is rewarded, but with the god(less) miracle of 75,810 foes massacred with no other losses.

Imperial power, manifested through various edicts and executions, extravagant parties and taxation, collaboration and resistance are all clearly present in the text of Esther. Given the difficulty of discerning the genre, it is difficult to assess the stance of the text/author vis-à-vis empire. The ethical perspective of the contemporary interpretive community in large part constitutes the interest in reading. Within this context of imperial power, passing and nonpassing are presented as dynamics for negotiating imperial power. Esther passes; Mordecai does not. Again, given the dynamics of the story, it is difficult to discern any particular recommendation either way.

Reading Others and Others reading might provide a way through the conundrum of the genre of Esther. These have ranged from relatively straight readings, reacted to with either approval or horror, through farce, satire, and parody. Of course, if the text is farcical, satirical, or a parody, the question remains: A parody of what? Whose story is it? What purpose does it serve? For an audience sensitive to the problematics of passing (then or now), especially under the dominance of imperial power, how should they/we read?

Violence is generalized throughout the text both as an implicit power and in actualized or dramatized instances. For example, the enforced liberality of the festivities at the beginning protests too much. The very command to have fun and to drink excessively and freely betrays fear and anxiety, not only within the narrative, but also reflected in the audience. It is noteworthy that while the Jews are remarkably (miraculously?) spared combative violence during the massacre, they are nevertheless general recipients of imperial violence that goes beyond the threat instigated by Haman.

While there are numerous recipients of the specific acts of violence, it might be useful to note some of them here: Vashti, of course, as the former fancy of the King; Esther, as the newly taken woman of the king; the various eunuchs, from the more generalized violence of crushed testicles to the particular plots and executions of court intrigue; Haman and his ten sons; and the 75,810 victims of the massacre.

These specific acts of violence do not occur spontaneously; there are perpetrators as well. These perpetrators are caught within the webs of imperial power. At the top, dimwitted though he might be, is Ahasuerus. His edicts authorize the threat against the Jews and their response to their foes. Within this dynamic, Mordecai participates in the violence against eunuchs, Haman and his sons, and the foes of the Jews. Esther, too, participates through her intercession for her people, her nonintercession for Haman, and her letter writing.

The harem in Esther offers a provocative intertextual comparison and contrast with the Joseph story. Vashti refuses the king's request for display. Joseph refuses Potiphar's wife. Joseph's refusal leads to his immediate downfall, which, of course, sets up his ultimate ascension. Vashti's refusal leads to her ultimate downfall, which sets up Esther's success. As Joseph becomes second-in-command in Egypt, so Haman is a type of Joseph, and Mordecai (through one woman's refusal and another's compliance) becomes the new Joseph.

What is significant here is that both stories, the Joseph story and the alternate Joseph story, result in second-in-command status for an exemplary Jew. The result of Joseph's elevation, is, of course, the ownership of all by Pharoah, and collaboration with empire results in the enslavement of the formerly favored. The result of Mordecai's ascension is not just the massacre of foes, but also taxation/tribute/corvée on the land and coast (10:1). From the perspective of the subjugated Other, this does not seem to be a desirable consequence.

This returns us to the problem of passing, in particular, with Esther's identification as a Gentile (2:10–20) being chiastically linked with Gentiles identifying as Jews (8:17; Levenson 1997, 8). This latter passage is particularly troubling. There are significant losses associated with passing (for all the presumed gains). That the peoples of the land would be placed in the position of doing what the Jews have had to do is more than ironic. It is critical. The Septuagint goes even further than the Masoretic Text by declaring "many of the Gentiles were circumcised, and became Jews" (8:17). Given the massacre, echoes of Dinah's story resound (Gen. 34). How could an audience (then or now), sensitive to the problematics of passing, not be troubled even by foes being pressured to pass? We know that the fear of imperial power results in passing, co-optation, and assimilation. Collaboration with imperial power results in the same for our foes. This is not victory.

With so many oblique and not so oblique oddities, misidentifications, ironies, and intertextual associations and allusions, it is hard to imagine that Esther was not meant to be taken as code, but the question remains, code for what?

The dynamics of living under imperial power (in all its ranges) result in intracommunal tension. Daniel Boyarin's suggestion that the *Yehudim/Ioudaioi* are yet another subset of second temple Judaism who clashed culturally and religiously with the "people of the land" (Boyarin 2002, 224–225), prompts the question: What if the *Yehudim* of Esther are not the Jews in general but a sect within Judaism? The postcolonial *malinchista* in me asks even further: What if Haman himself represents a Jew but not a *Yehudi*? The politics of othering complicates internal dynamics of the othered community. The characters Haman and Mordecai would then reflect an intracommunal competition for the place of Joseph (second-in-command) under Pharaoh (Ahasuerus). The book of Esther would then be not unlike the strife presented in Maccabees between the more and less pure/passing/assimilating/collaborating segments of Judaisms.

This might provide a clue to the direction of the parody/satire/farce. There are at least three choices. The book could (1) reflect the perspective of the *Yehudim*, critical of the accommodations of the Hamans of this world and presenting Esther and Mordecai as flip sides of the *Yehudim* (passing and public) playing the intrigue against Haman and reaping the appropriate reward; (2) offer the perspective of the non-*Yehudim*, presenting a ridiculous godless story critiquing those who presume to be more godly; and (3) convey the perspective of an audience itself cognizant of the problems of living under imperial domination and the consequences for identity and intracommunal life. The farce/satire/parody/carnival then lampoons all pretensions from all perspectives, showing that the ambitions of both sides (ruling in second place by assimilated collaboration or maintaining purity) is itself a mistaken goal that can only lead to more imperial exploitation.

It seems unnecessary to decide which of these might be a more likely reading. Each possibility foregrounds important issues about identities struggling to survive under the oppressions of dominant imperial powers. All the readings can be held up, maintained in tension with each other, with the text, and with other critiques of power. Much like in the modern world, there are similar struggles for identity and intracommunal conflicts. We can therefore imagine that the author of Esther knew of some of these kinds of dynamics and their consequences for community. This portrait of life under empire, whatever the author's particular views, is a worthy conversation partner as we pass through our own negotiations of sex, violence, and identity.

READING OTHERS IN THE SECOND TESTAMENT: THE GOSPEL ACCORDING TO MARK

As mentioned earlier, Otherness is particularly about power. This has included a type of exclusionary "power over." In my second example, from Mark's Gospel, I would contrast "power over" with "power with." These are hardly the only two conceptual possibilities or the only important ones. "Power within" and "power for" are also critical, as are other construals. However, "power over," as vertically coercive power, has been the most dominant for Otherness. It is the hallmark of patriarchy and empire. "Power with" is less familiar perhaps. Power with is the power of solidarity, or collaboration, of egalitarian or communitarian ethics.

Reflecting on power over and power with in the light of the history of civil rights movements or women's movements is revealing. Much of the history of dominant groups' responses to the liberation struggles of the oppressed exposes a fear of power over. Power over is practically the only kind of power empire and oppressors know. Thus, they cannot understand the oppressed's claims to power as anything other than the oppressed trying to exert power over them, switching places, as it were, in a vertically coercive power relationship. It seems reasonable, given the way that power shapes the imagination, to expect that sometimes this is the case. But it is not the only way for the oppressed to express power. They can also express power with.

Power with is collaborative. It is not coercive. It is attractive. It attracts the other to join into a project together. My thesis is that Mark's community constructs the gospel narrative to promote a Christianity that is antihierarchical, and in particular in opposition to other Christian communities who are incorporating the Greco-Roman household codes as appropriate models for the Church and Christian discipleship. Mark does this throughout the gospel, especially in the construction of the characters of Jesus and the disciples, but also structurally in the second half of the Gospel in the thrice-iterated pattern of passion prediction, negative reaction by some disciples, and a teaching of Jesus (Mark 8:31–35; 9:31–35; 10:33–45). In these sections, Mark consistently rejects the top halves of the household codes (especially fathers and master, but also husbands) and endorses only the bottom halves of the codes as appropriate epithets for followers of Jesus: women, slaves, and children. The characters of the disciples, cast in a particularly negative light, represent those hierarchical Christians Mark is familiar with and opposes.

Mark is apparently familiar with the experience of being othered by those Christians "down the street" who have adopted the household codes as blueprints for the Church. For Mark, rejecting this othering rejects the shape and shaping of the vertical coercion that constitutes the household codes. This situates Mark as anti–Greco-Roman and anti-patriarchal Christianity. Thus, Mark is situated between the proverbial rock and a hard place: patriarchalizing Christianity and patriarchalized paganism. But with the gesture to resist othering goes the corollary admission that otherness sets a substantial portion of the agenda and still proffers the beguiling allure of power over. It is too easy, especially for reforming elites, to fall back into old patterns of domination. This is the trap Mark simultaneously resists and falls into. He does this primarily in terms of his presentation of the character of Jesus.

Mark's Gospel exhibits different examples of silence and voice. Some characters silence others; some ask questions to elicit a response from the silent; some choose to remain silent in response to probing questions; some simply have little to say. Jesus appears to talk the most; yet the truly dominant voice is often unnoticed. Jesus is allowed less than three-eighths of the words in the Gospel, and in total, all the other characters combined get less than one-eighth. Thus, over half the Gospel is literally in the voice of the narrator, Mark, and in an important sense, all of the words—even those he cites—are his, for it is he who has selected which quotes to include or exclude, which voices to privilege or to silence. So, Mark's voice is the often unacknowledged exercising of power.

In the narrative, and especially with Jesus, Mark uses two different verbs for silencing depending on the object. When Jesus silences demons, he "rebukes" (*epitimaō*) them (1:25; 3:12; 4:39; 9:25). When he silences humans, he "orders" (*diastellomai*) them (5:43; 7:36; 9:9). Silencing demons tends to succeed; silencing humans does not. The one time Jesus rebukes a human it is Peter, and each tries to silence the other (8:30, 32–33), one of only two places where humans are the subject of "rebuking" other humans (see also 10:13, 48). Jesus's rebuke of Peter (as though he were a demon) suggests that success in controlling demons and failure at controlling humans results in Jesus's attempting to control humans as if they were demons. This seemingly desperate resort to "power over" serves as poor modeling for the disciples.

Thus, while demons are apparently fair game when it comes to coercion, Jesus is presented as flawed in his attempt to exercise coercive power over another human. It is remarkable the number of times that Jesus attempts to control and fails. Why present Jesus this way? Why have him succeed in controlling demons, but not in controlling humans?

Many have noted the absence of "Father" as an epithet for God in Mark's gospel. Less noted is the ambivalence around other titles of privilege. For example, nearly every character addressing Jesus as "Teacher" is on the brink of a misstep in relation to Jesus. As a teacher myself, I find this pattern disturbing. Why would Mark present this title on the lips of those interacters with Jesus who expose their lack of insight or who are about to misbehave? Could it be a concern for the way that vertical relationships affect the dynamics between humans? Power over excludes power with?

So, for example, "teacher" occurs twelve times in the gospel. The disciples address Jesus thus in the stilling of the storm episode (4:38). The daughter of Jairus has died and some folks do not want the Teacher bothered (4:35). The father of the boy in the synagogue addresses Jesus as Teacher, and Jesus rages at the failure of the disciples and the father (9:17). John addresses Jesus thus in the strange exorcist story (9:38). The rich young man calls Jesus the Good Teacher (10:17) and then Teacher (10:20), obviously concluding that Jesus is not good in the same manner as God but is nevertheless still addressable as Teacher, but then fails to follow him. James and John want Jesus the Teacher to do whatever they ask (10:35). The Pharisees and some Herodians try to trap the Teacher on taxes (12:14). The Sadducees follow suit with the Teacher on divorce/remarriage and afterlife (12:19). The disciples marvel with the Teacher on the magnificence of the Temple (13:1). Jesus himself uses the title in seeking provision for the Passover (14:14). The only case that might be positive is the scribe who approves of Jesus's citing of the obligations of Torah, which stress interpersonal relationship as consequential to evidencing love of God (12:32). This is *not* power over but power with one's neighbor. The scribe is not far from the reign of God. But everyone else is silent as a consequence of this interaction and scribal voice. Maybe this scribe, like the Syrophoenician woman of chapter 7, functions to qualify Jesus's own pretensions to power.

In spite of the power of the cross to confound empire, Mark does not present anti-imperial, antipatriarchal discipleship as a singular or easy route. Growing up in institutions of power over shapes the imaginative landscape, desires, and expectations of followers. Perhaps this is why Mark's Jesus fails in his efforts and gets confused, mixing up his own role as benefactor, and why the term Teacher is so deeply fraught, even, or especially, with Jesus or God. Mark could very well be speaking to patriarchalizing Christians in his rejection of power over. Nonetheless, power over is like foot binding. The bindings may be removed, but the feet are still deformed. Maybe religion in general is like that. Even Jesus cannot escape the confounding of power over. Mark's Gospel suggests that impulses and expectations of privilege and being served thrive in Christianity's own ranks and carry a particular danger because of the veneer of godliness. Complacency, however, is not an option. Reminiscent of the reformation slogan "reformed, ever reforming," Mark envisions a moment when followers no longer simply react to coercive and demonic power over; that is, no longer allow empire to set the agenda, but, like Bartimeaus, set off on their own with openness to the needs of others.

CONCLUSION

When we read for Others, with Others, or read Others reading Others, we open the text to join in a broad historical and ethical discourse about identity, about the institutions of oppression and liberation. Voices in this project bring their own subjectivity and resist the constraints of being objectified by the powerful. The goal is not to make the texts' answers (or questions even) ours, but to widen that discourse to value their struggles for identity as much as our own. In that project, answers emerge that join the contemporary hermeneutical communities with the othered of the past and present.

REFERENCES

Anzaldúa, Gloria. 1987. *Borderland/La Frontera: The New Mestiza*. San Francisco: Spinsters/ Aunt Lute.

Bailey, Randall C., Tat-Siong Benny Liew, and Fernando F. Segovia. 2009. *They Were All Together in One Place?: Toward Minority Biblical Criticism*. Atlanta, GA: Society of Biblical Literature.

Beauvoir, Simone de. 1953. *The Second Sex*. New York: Knopf.

Bhabha, Homi K. 1994. *The Location of Culture*. London: Routledge.

Boyarin, Daniel. 2002. "The *Ioudaioi* in John and the Prehistory of Judaism." *Pauline Conversations in Context: Essays in Honor of Calvin J. Roetzel*, edited by Janice Capel Anderson, Philip Harl Sellew, and Claudia Setzer, 216–239. London: Bloomsbury/T & T Clark.

Descartes, René. 1993. *Meditations on First Philosophy: In Which the Existence of God and the Distinction of the Soul from the Body Are Demonstrated*. Indianapolis, IN: Hackett.

Donaldson, Laura E. 1999. "The Sign of Orpah: Reading Ruth through Native Eyes." *Ruth and Esther: A Feminist Companion to the Bible*, edited by Athalya Brenner, 130–144. Sheffield, Yorkshire: Sheffield Academic Press.

Dube, Musa W. 2000. *Postcolonial Feminist Interpretation of the Bible*. St. Louis, MO: Chalice.

Fanon, Frantz. 1963. *The Wretched of the Earth*. Translated by Richard Philcox. New York: Grove.

Fanon, Frantz. 1967. *Black Skin, White Masks*. Translated by Richard Philcox. New York: Grove.

Foucault, Michel. 1965. *Madness and Civilization: A History of Insanity in the Age of Reason*. New York: Pantheon.

García-Treto, Francisco O. 2001. "Mixed Messages: Encountering Mestizaje in the Old Testament." *Princeton Seminary Bulletin* 22(2): 150–171.

Hegel, Georg Wilhelm Friedrich. 1977. *Phenomenology of Spirit*. Translated by A. V. Miller. Oxford: Clarendon.

Homer. 1975. *The Odyssey of Homer*. Translated by Richard Lattimore. New York: Harper Perennial.

Kwok, Pui-lan. 2005. *Postcolonial Imagination and Feminist Theology*. Louisville, KY: Westminster John Knox.

Levenson, Jon Douglas. 1997. *Esther: A Commentary*. Louisville, KY: Westminster John Knox.

Lévinas, Emmanuel. 1969. *Totality and Infinity: An Essay on Exteriority*. Translated by Alphonso Lingis. Pittsburgh, PA: Duquesne University Press.

Lévinas, Emmanuel. 1987. *Time and the Other and Additional Essays*. Translated by Richard A. Cohen. Pittsburgh, PA: Duquesne University Press.

Maldonado, Robert D. 1995. "Reading Malinche Reading Ruth: Toward a Hermeneutics of Betrayal." *Semeia* 72: 91–109.

Said, Edward W. 1979. *Orientalism*. New York: Vintage.

Segovia, Fernando F. 2000. *Decolonizing Biblical Studies: A View from the Margins*. Maryknoll, NY: Orbis.

Segovia, Fernando F., and Mary Ann Tolbert. 1995a. *Reading from This Place. Vol 1, Social Location and Biblical Interpretation in the United States*. Minneapolis, MN: Fortress.

Segovia, Fernando F., and Mary Ann Tolbert. 1995b. *Reading from This Place. Vol. 2, Social Location and Biblical Interpretation in Global Perspective*. Minneapolis, MN: Fortress.

Spivak, Gayatri Chakravorty. 1999. *A Critique of Postcolonial Reason: Toward a History of the Vanishing Present*. Cambridge, MA: Harvard University Press.

Sugirtharajah, R. S. 1995. *Voices from the Margin: Interpreting the Bible in the Third World*. Maryknoll, NY: Orbis/SPCK.

Trinh, T. Minh-Ha. 1989. *Woman, Native, Other: Writing Postcoloniality and Feminism*. Bloomington: Indiana University Press.

West, Gerald. 2001. "A Real Presence, Subsumed by Others: The Bible in Colonial and Postcolonial Context." In *A Vanishing Mediator? The Presence/Absence of the Bible in Postcolonialism*, edited by Roland Boer and Gerald West, 199–212. Atlanta, GA: Society of Biblical Literature.

West, Gerald O. 2007. *Reading Other-Wise: Socially Engaged Biblical Scholars Reading with Their Local Communities*. Atlanta, GA: Society of Biblical Literature.

Wit, Hans De, and Gerald O. West. 2008. *African and European Readers of the Bible in Dialogue: In Quest of a Shared Meaning*. Leiden: Brill.

CHAPTER 38

....

ANIMATING THE BIBLE'S
ANIMALS

....

KEN STONE

ANIMALS wander in and out of biblical literature from beginning to end. In the opening chapter of Genesis, diverse categories of animals are created across two days, recognized as good by God, blessed, and commanded to reproduce and multiply throughout their habitats. At the other end of the Christian Bible, in the closing chapter of Revelation, a lamb sits on a throne in a city populated by God's servants, while dogs are excluded from the city together with several species of evildoers. The books between Genesis and Revelation are variously populated with different types of animals, who appear, disappear, and reappear in numerous passages and multiple genres. Few readers of the Bible who are watching for animals will fail to spot them.

Given the frequency with which animals turn up in biblical literature, one might assume that biblical scholars would study them closely. Certainly, some scholars have noticed how often they appear. As long ago as 1917, Hermann Gunkel made the prevalence of animals central to his argument that "folktale motifs" were incorporated into biblical literature (Gunkel [1917] 1987, 51–60). Although many of Gunkel's methodological assumptions are now outdated, he did take the presence of animals, plants, and other features of the natural world in biblical literature seriously. By contrast, for much of the twentieth century, scholarship on the Hebrew Bible assumed a sharp distinction between nature and history, and it associated biblical literature more closely with history than nature (Hiebert [1996] 2008, 3–22). Within this framework, the Bible's animals attracted little attention. Indeed, it is striking that an anthropologist rather than a biblical scholar wrote what was arguably the most influential discussion of biblical animals published during the twentieth century: a chapter on food laws and unclean animals in Mary Douglas's (1966) *Purity and Danger*. Biblical scholars themselves acknowledged animals mostly in passing as evidence for the social niche inhabited by certain Israelites (said to be "pastoralists" and "small cattle farmers"), or as minor props in a story focused on humans and God. Even commentaries sometimes ignored the appearance of animals in specific verses.

More recently, however, the Bible's animals have started to creep more regularly into the literature of biblical studies. This re-emergence has taken several forms. Following the path opened by Douglas, some scholars use the distinction between clean and unclean animals to interpret biblical religion (e.g., Houston 1993). Other scholars, cognizant of new developments in archaeology, such as zooarchaeology, give animals a more prominent place in reconstructions of the history and material world of ancient Israel (e.g., Borowski 1998; King and Stager 2001, 112–122). Howard Eilberg-Schwartz suggested more than twenty years ago that greater attention needed to be given to the use of animal symbols in Israel's understanding of itself and God (Eilberg-Schwartz 1990, 115–140), and there now exist several monographs that examine such symbolism by focusing on either a specific species (e.g., Strawn 2005; Way 2011) or a particular book (e.g., Forti 2008). Animals are getting closer attention in studies of sacrifice (e.g., Klawans 2006). The growing literature on ecological hermeneutics includes animals within its purview as well (e.g., Tucker 1997, 2000).

Alongside these approaches, a few scholars have called attention to the potential relevance for biblical interpretation of a growing body of interdisciplinary animal studies emerging outside of biblical scholarship (e.g., Koosed 2014; cf. McKay 2002), reflecting insights that exceed zoological, ethological, and associated disciplines. While those fields continue to expand our knowledge of animals in significant ways, questions about animals are increasingly raised in literary and cultural studies, philosophy, history, sociology, and anthropology as part of what is sometimes called an "animal turn" in the humanities and social sciences (e.g., Weil 2012, 3–24; see also Kalof and Fitzgerald 2007; DeMello 2012; Gross and Vallely 2012; Waldau 2013). This heterogeneous body of writing is already having an impact on the attention given to animals in nonbiblical religious studies (e.g., Patton 2000; Waldau 2002; Waldau and Patton 2006; Deane-Drummond and Clough 2009).

If scholars from multiple disciplines have made us aware of the importance of "making animal meaning" (Kalof and Montgomery 2011), then biblical scholars, too, may wish to reanimate the Bible's animals and reconsider the meanings associated with them. Numerous biblical texts might be reinterpreted from the perspective of what Aaron Gross, in his introduction to a collection of interdisciplinary animal studies, calls a "multifaceted, critical 'animal hermeneutics.'" As explicated by Gross, such a hermeneutics underscores a "basic observation that *across time and across cultures humans imagine themselves through animal others*" (Gross 2012, 5; emphasis original). To be sure, distinctions between humans and other animals are constructed in many different ways, and animal studies usually emphasize the fact that "even within a given time and place, multiple understandings of the human/animal operate in relation to and competition with one another" (11). Yet the human tendency to conceptualize identity and otherness in relation to nonhuman animals is extremely widespread and goes far back in history.

It is therefore time for biblical scholars to take more seriously the roles that animals play in both the texts that we study and those texts' representations of both humans and God. Toward that end, I reconsider here a well-known biblical story from the perspective, to borrow Gross's (2012, 5) phrase, of a "multifaceted, critical 'animal hermeneutics.'" The particular story chosen for my point of departure has been selected in part because of its usefulness for engaging several different themes or emphases that have emerged in contemporary animal studies. Nevertheless, such themes or emphases could also be brought to bear on many other biblical texts.

ANIMALS IN THE JACOB STORY

In his discussion of animal hermeneutics, Gross (2012, 8) argues that animals "invariably play a decisive role in human self-conception." If we wish to explore the role of animals in the "self-conception" of the writers of the Hebrew Bible, it is useful to consider the Jacob narratives in Genesis. After all, Jacob is given a new name, "Israel," in Genesis 32:28 and 35:10, making him the legendary eponymous ancestor of the Israelites. His sons are understood as ancestors of the tribes who collectively constitute Israel as a people, and the story in Genesis 30 of the births of those sons to four women has long been read as a narrative representation of imagined relations among those tribes. The stories about Jacob and his family thus offer opportunities to interpret the relationship between biblical literature and the self-conception of those who wrote it.

Early in Jacob's story, his elder brother, Esau, is said to be "red" from birth, "all of him like a hairy mantle" (Gen. 25:25). He is characterized by excessive hairiness. As Susan Niditch (2008) has shown, male hairiness has connotations in biblical literature that are often positive in context. These connotations include an association between hairiness and manhood. Such hairiness might also associate Esau with animals, however, or in any case mammals, who generally have more hair than the hairiest of men. Esau's hairiness is sometimes used to place him in the folk tradition of "wild men," who, like Enkidu in the Gilgamesh story, are closely associated with animals (Mobley 1997). This association with animals could be strengthened by Esau's characterization as "a man who knows hunting, a man of the field" (25:27), although "wild men" such as Enkidu also protect animals from hunters. Esau is located where animals are, and he knows how to find them. Jacob, by contrast, is found among the tents (25:27); and in chapter 27, Jacob explicitly refers to himself as "a smooth man" in distinction from Esau, described as "a hairy man" (27:11).

In chapter 27, however, after Esau goes to the field to hunt game for his father in order to receive Isaac's blessing, Rebekah instructs Jacob, "Go to the flock, and get me from there two young goats" (27:9). From the goats she makes food for Isaac. Because Jacob is "smooth," while his brother is "hairy," Rebekah takes another step. After dressing Jacob in Esau's clothing, "she put the skins of the young goats on his hands and on the smooth parts of his neck" (27:16). Jacob then takes the goat dish to his blind father, claims to be Esau, and asks for a blessing. Isaac hesitates initially, since the voice he hears sounds like Jacob's. But when he feels the hair on his son's hands, eats the goat dish, drinks wine, and smells the clothes on his son, Isaac blesses Jacob instead of Esau. The blessing explicitly states that various peoples, including those descended from his brothers, will bow down to Jacob (27:29). It thus confirms God's message to Rebekah in 25:23 that her elder son will serve the younger. Only after Esau arrives with game does Isaac realize that he has been tricked into blessing Jacob (27:30–37). Both Jacob and Rebekah play active roles in tricking Isaac. But the trick's success depends, crucially, on the bodies of young goats. Without the goat parts that his mother cooks for food, or the goat skins and hair that are attached to his body, Jacob would not receive Isaac's blessing.

The presence of animals thus structures Jacob's story, and hence the story of Israel's origins and identity, from the beginning. And animals recur throughout Jacob's story. In chapter 29, his first encounter with Rachel involves the watering of flocks of sheep. We learn in 30:29 that the work Jacob does to acquire Laban's daughters includes tending Laban's livestock, which flourish under Jacob's care. Jacob continues working for his uncle as part of a deal that allows Jacob to keep "all the sheep that are speckled or spotted and all the sheep that are black among the lambs and all the spotted or speckled among the goats" (30:32). Though Laban attempts to hide such animals, the text describes in detail how Jacob, through a kind of magic, manipulates the breeding of goats and sheep to increase the number of animals received as wages. By the end of the chapter, Jacob has not only amassed "great flocks" of sheep and goats, but also "female slaves and male slaves and camels and donkeys" (30:43).

In chapter 31, Jacob calls Rachel and Leah to join him among the flock. There he notes how God increased his livestock by causing speckled animals to be born when Laban pays in speckled animals, and striped animals to be born when Laban pays in striped animals. He then recounts a dream about male goats mounting other goats. God's messenger in the dream implies that God caused only striped, speckled, and spotted male goats to breed, to Jacob's benefit. After Jacob departs for Canaan, Laban chides him for sneaking away with Laban's daughters and accuses him of stealing Laban's household gods, which are hidden in Rachel's camel saddle. When the gods are not found, Jacob gives a speech about the twenty years he spent tending Laban's flocks and assuming the costs when sheep or goats were taken by wild animals. As Jacob notes, "I served you fourteen years for your two daughters and six years for your flock" (31:41). In the next chapter, Jacob attempts to defuse Esau's anger with a gift of "two hundred female goats and twenty male goats, two hundred ewes and twenty rams, thirty nursing camels and their offspring, forty cows and ten bulls, twenty she-asses and ten he-asses" (32:14–15). If animals played a role in the original schism between Jacob and Esau, now Jacob hopes that animals can resolve the conflict. The chapter concludes with a wrestling match between Jacob and a figure who initially appears to be a man but actually is nonhuman. When this figure cannot win the match, he blesses Jacob and names him "Israel" (32:28). The narrator notes, however, that because Jacob has been struck on the thigh, "the sons of Israel" will not eat certain sinew meats from the thighs of their animals (32:32).

Other animals appear in the story of Jacob and, later, in the stories of his sons. But even this brief summary of a few chapters should indicate how common animals are in the story of Israel's origins. Israel's emergence is inextricably intertwined with domesticated animals in particular, especially goats and sheep.

Rereading with an Animal Hermeneutics

Biblical scholars usually integrate these animals into the conventional reading strategies of biblical studies. One can find discussions, for example, of the historical role of small-cattle herding in both commentaries (e.g., von Rad 1972) and studies of Israel's social world (e.g., Matthews and Benjamin 1993, 52–66). I suggest, however, that our interpretation of Jacob's story may be enriched if we re-examine it from the perspective of an animal hermeneutics as well. More specifically, I note three emphases that have emerged from contemporary animal studies: (1) the constitutive importance of companion species, (2) the instability of the human/animal binary, and (3) the ubiquitous association between species difference and differences among humans, particularly, in this case, gender and ethnic differences. Though the emphases are interrelated, I take each in turn, summarizing a few points made in animal studies while returning to Jacob's story and other texts throughout to indicate the potential relevance for biblical interpretation.

Companion Species

The phrase "companion species" is associated with feminist cultural theorist and biologist Donna Haraway. As explicated by Haraway, "companion species" include, but are not identical to, "companion animals," those individual animals (such as pets) with whom many humans live. The notion of companion species is used in a more comprehensive sense to analyze what Haraway (2008, 73) calls "co-constitutive human relationships with other critters" (cf. Haraway 2003). Human nature and human cultures do not preexist such relationships. Individually and collectively, humans always "become who they are" with other living and nonliving entities in particular "situated histories, situated naturecultures" (2008, 25). As the neologism "naturecultures" indicates, Haraway's understanding of companion species calls into question dichotomizing oppositions between "culture" and "nature," as well as associated oppositions between "human" and "animal," "living" and "non-living," or, to cite again that opposition beloved by biblical scholarship, "history" and "nature." Against tendencies to understand human existence independently of other beings and circumstances, Haraway argues that we are always "entangled" with other "critters" in specific "contact zones." Haraway takes the phrase "contact zone" from canine agility training, but she notes that it occurs also in postcolonial studies, acknowledging thereby that power relations and complex histories structure companion species contact zones.

Although engaged with critical theory, Haraway's analyses of companion species relationships are usually developed around concrete cases. Starting from specific examples of species interaction (this training dog with this woman, these herding dogs with these sheep, these sheep with this scientist) in particular contact zones, she explores these interactions in ways that make animals active participants, worthy of attention, rather than simply objects or background. While Haraway is especially interested in interactions between humans and dogs, she also gives attention to other companion species, including other domesticated animals, such as sheep, and to the histories of labor, economy, technology, geography, migration, colonialism, ethnic relations, gender relations, and so forth, that shape the contact zones in which humans and our companion species coevolve. Significantly for my purposes, Haraway includes novels, photographs, and other forms of symbolic representation among the sites that are useful for analyzing companion species relations.

Now, it is not difficult to recognize that the goats and sheep populating Jacob's story and other biblical texts could be considered examples of "companion species" in Haraway's sense. Their presence testifies to the origin of biblical literature in the "situated naturecultures" of the ancient Levant, where, as histories of domestication and archaeological evidence have shown, the herding of goats and sheep (often referred to collectively, in biblical terminology, as a "flock") was crucial for human livelihood long before the emergence of Israelites (Clutton-Brock 1987, 52–61; 2007; 2012, 47–69; Borowski 1998, 39–71). By associating goats and sheep with Jacob's blessing and the growth of Jacob's household, Genesis can be read as encouraging us to understand these animals as an integral part of Israel's "becoming who they are," to borrow Haraway's language. Indeed, the struggle between Leah and Rachel that results in the proliferation of Jacob's sons is narratively tied to the proliferation of Jacob's goats and sheep. Both Jacob and Laban link Jacob's acquisition of daughters to Jacob's acquisition of livestock (Gen. 31:41–43). If these daughters are subsequently understood to have "built up the house of Israel," in the words of Ruth 4:11, so, too, the reproduction of Jacob's animals in the same story represents Israel's expansion. The blessing of Israel is signified narratively by the propagation of both Israel's children and Israel's companion species. In Genesis 33:13, Jacob, in a single verse, expresses concern for both his children and his nursing animals.

Given how inextricably intertwined the narrated lives of the Israelite ancestors are with their animals, it is unsurprising that biblical writers found in relationships with goats and sheep a rich resource of political and religious imagery. Like other ancient texts, biblical literature utilizes the language of shepherding and flocks to refer to both human leaders and to God, on the one hand, and the people they lead, on the other hand. This imagery is sufficiently common that many readers of the Bible are unlikely to ponder it (e.g., Num. 27:17; 2 Sam. 5:2; 7:7–8; 1 Kings 22:17; Pss. 23:1–4; 44:12, 23; 74:1; Isa. 56:9–12; Jer. 3:15; 6:3; 10:21; 12:3, 10; 13:20; 23:1–8; 25:34–38; Ezek. 34; Zech. 11:4–17). Yet the consequent impact of very specific species of animals—flocks of sheep and goats—on Western literary and religious thought is considerable. We only have to imagine how differently Judaism and Christianity might have looked if the cross-species relationships used to represent relationships between humans and God involved elephants and mahouts, for example, rather than flocks and shepherds. Goats and sheep are "co-constitutive" partners in the creation of Israelite religion. Indeed, as genetic analyses of Qumran parchments have shown, biblical and related literatures were literally preserved on the skins of animals, especially goats (Kahila Bar-Gal et al., 2001). Without goat skins, neither Israel's story nor the Bible might have existed.

Destabilizing the Human/Animal Binary

When the Bible uses shepherd images to represent political leaders or God, the logic of its symbolism puts human beings in the positions of sheep and goats. Rather than simply place animals alongside Israel as companion species, it also represents the Israelites as animals. Indeed, the animals of the Israelites are sometimes included among the people, as, for example, when they are spared by God in Egypt, while Egyptian animals and offspring are killed (Exod. 11:4–7; 12:12, 29–32). The Israelites are distinguished from Egyptians in that narrative, even as the line between human and animal is blurred within Israel and within Egypt.

What does such symbolism do to the very distinction between human and animal? Many scholars associated with animal studies, including Haraway, raise critical questions about this distinction. Another influential example is Jacques Derrida, who, in several works, analyzes the ways in which Western philosophical and literary traditions attempt to draw a dogmatic line between "man" and "animal" to define the properly human (e.g., 1995, 2004, 2008, 2009). Derrida's critique of this attempt does not entail the elimination of differences between humans and other animals. He emphasizes instead the multiple differences that exist among humans themselves, and the multiple differences that exist among diverse types of animals that are both similar and dissimilar to humans in many different ways. Yet Derrida (2009) also calls attention to the recurring use of animal imagery to characterize certain types of humans, including, for example, the comparison of some human rulers to wolves and other beasts.

Derrida's work, like Haraway's, engages ethical questions about violence carried out against other animals as well as other humans (see Calarco 2008, 103–149). The attempt to establish a clear boundary between humans and animals provides a foundation for the human exceptionalism (which some writers refer to as "speciesism," e.g., Waldau 2002) that fuels such violence. Thus, rather than focus solely on politics and activism to address violence against other living creatures, Derrida's work encourages us to look for places in which our traditions assume human exceptionalism—for example, by permitting the non-criminal killing of animals—and yet destabilize the grounds for that exceptionalism by blurring the lines between humans and other animals.

The trick that Rebekah and Jacob play on Isaac combines these dynamics. Both Isaac's request to Esau for game and Rebekah's request to Jacob for goats assume, as numerous biblical texts do, that animals can be slaughtered for meat. Such an assumption partly reinforces the boundary between humans and animals. Yet this boundary is also disturbed by the storyline. Isaac, having lost his sight, relies in part on the sense more closely associated with other mammals than with humans: the sense of smell, which he uses to identify the clothes of Esau that Jacob wears. He is also tricked by the hairy goat skins that Rebekah places on Jacob's hands and neck. Jacob wears the skins of dead animals, yet Rebekah's trick is effective only because the hairy skins feel sufficiently like the skin of Esau. Human and animal are, for carnivorous Isaac, impossible to distinguish.

The Hermeneutics of Carnophallogocentrism

The boundary between human and animal is also used to distinguish those humans thought to fall closer to, and those humans thought to fall further from, an assumed norm for the properly human. Some humans are associated with animals more often than others, frequently in ways that stigmatize the humans in question. Since violence against the other-than-human is sanctioned by, for example, our killing of animals for food, then, in the words of Cary Wolfe (2003, 8), the "discourse of species will always be available for use by some humans against other humans as well, to countenance violence against the social other of *whatever* species—or gender, or race, or class, or sexual difference" (emphasis original). If animals can be killed, and if humans can be animalized, then a careful analysis of the ways in which animal difference is construed is crucial for grappling with the ethical implications of differences among humans. Derrida's (1990, 953; 1995, 280) neologism "carnophallogocentrism" was coined partly to suggest that the exclusion of animals from ethical consideration cannot be separated from the exclusion of other humans from subjectivity and ethics, including women (note the way in which "carnophallogocentrim" builds on the better-known term "phallogocentrism"), feminized men (Derrida [1995, 281] makes an explicit reference to homosexuality in this context), and other men deemed less than human on the basis of, for example, race, ethnicity, nation, class, or religion. Although Derrida's comments on carnophallogocentrism are especially focused on modernity, his engagement with biblical literature in his animal writings indicates that biblical scholars, too, may find it useful to ask how women and some men are associated with animals in biblical literature. Indeed, it is partly on the basis of Derrida's reading of the Garden of Eden story that philosopher Kelly Oliver (2009, 143) asserts, "In the Judeo-Christian tradition, animal difference and sexual difference are intimately associated from the beginning of time."

How are animal difference and sexual difference associated in Jacob's story? At the beginning of the story, Esau is closely associated with signifiers of masculinity, especially body hair, hunting, and his father's favor. Jacob, the favorite of his mother, is associated with tents and smoothness. He is, arguably, the more "effeminate" man (Niditch 2008, 115), who masquerades as his manly brother by wearing animal skins and clothes that smell like a field. Here, animalization appears to be linked to manhood. Yet two forms of animalized manhood actually appear in Jacob's story. If Esau is associated with masculinity and wild animals, Jacob is associated with women and domesticated animals. Indeed, Niditch proposes "domesticated man" as one possible translation for the description of Jacob (*ish tam*) that contrasts with Esau in 25:27. The contrast reminds us of the distinction between wild and domesticated that structures Israel's conceptualization of animals elsewhere in the Hebrew Bible (Tucker 1997, 2000).

As Jacob's story progresses, however, an association between animals and women also becomes apparent. Rachel, whose name means "ewe," first appears "coming with the flock" (Gen. 29:6). Though the meanings of the names Leah and Rebekah are more obscure, "cow" is sometimes given as a possibility for each (Meyers 2000, 108, 143). As we have seen, a parallel is created between Jacob's work for Leah and Rachel, who bear his children (together with their slave women), and his work for the goats and sheep who become his animals or produce animals for him. In Jacob's words, "I served you fourteen years for your two daughters and six years for your flock" (31:41).

The association between women and animals as objects acquired by men appears in other texts as well. Exodus 20:17, for example, uses masculine linguistic forms to warn a male audience that "you will not covet the house of your neighbor. You will not covet the woman of your neighbor, or his male slave, or his female slave, or his ox, or his donkey, or anything that belongs to your neighbor." This prohibition lists things belonging to one male Israelite that another male Israelite might be tempted to desire, including women, slaves, and animals. Danna Nolan Fewell and David Gunn note, on the basis of this and other legal texts, that "well-to-do male heads of households . . . are the Subject the law is constructing. Everyone else is presented as Other" (1993, 94). Because Fewell and Gunn are writing about gender, they focus on the exclusion of women from this construction of the Subject of biblical law. But the appearance of animals alongside women and slaves in this passage could be taken as a biblical illustration of the argument made by Derrida as well as by certain ecofeminist writers (e.g., Adams 1995) that exclusions of gender *and species* are constitutive of Western subjectivity and culture. Women and animals are already placed together in a shared category of biblical objects.

Similarly, in 2 Samuel 12, Nathan represents Bathsheba (*bat-sheva*) as a small female lamb who is loved like a daughter (*bat*) by the poor man who owns her. The poor man's lamb is said to "lie on his bosom" (12:3), language that can have either maternal or sexual connotations in other texts. Yet, a rich man, not wishing to use his own flocks and herds to feed a traveler, steals the poor man's lamb and feeds it to a guest. As Nathan makes clear, this rich man represents David, who has stolen another man's woman rather than being content with the women God gave him. Thus the lamb beloved like a daughter (*bat*) who is taken and served as food represents *bat-sheva*, the woman taken by David for sex. In *Practicing Safer Texts* (2005), I emphasize the conjunction in this story between sex and food, a conjunction that appears multiple times in the Bible. But rather than focus on food in a general sense, I want to stress here that Bathsheba is symbolized by an edible *animal*. Thus Nathan's parable, and the story in which it is embedded, put on display a biblical example of what Derrida not only calls "carnophallogocentrism" but also "carnivorous virility," where a man's authority to consume a woman sexually and a man's authority to slaughter an animal for meat form background assumptions against which the behavior of Israel's king is evaluated. (And here, it is worth noting that Derrida's [1995, 281] discussion of carnophallogocentrism is explicitly articulated with reflection on the type of man who can be a head of state, and the unlikelihood that this man would be a vegetarian or a homosexual. We want our leaders to consume meat and women.)

The fate of Bathsheba is perhaps less troubling than those of other women who are animalized in biblical narrative, including the daughter of Jephthah, whose sacrifice in Judges 11 puts her in the position of an animal, or the young woman in Judges 19, whose dismembered body is used to send a message that parallels a message sent by Saul with the butchered bodies of cattle (1 Sam. 11:5–7). But, together with all these texts, the story of Jacob's labor for women and flocks underscores the presence in the Bible of what Oliver (2009, 145) calls the "intimate association between animal difference and sexual difference." We should not forget how often care for domestic animals is referred to, both inside and outside biblical studies, as "animal husbandry."

Yet biblical literature also articulates animal difference and gender difference with ethnic difference (Stone 2014). The story of Jacob, who represents Israel, and Esau, who represents Edom, is one of several Genesis narratives that appear to use family tales to navigate relationships between the Israelites and their ethnic neighbors in the Persian period (cf. Brett 2000; Heard 2001). The gendered animalization involved in the distinction between a more manly but wild Esau, and a less manly but clever and domesticated Jacob, may benefit from further analysis from that perspective.

Conclusion

Although I have necessarily simplified insights from animal studies, I hope to have shown that the study of biblical literature can benefit from interdisciplinary engagement with "the animal turn." Numerous biblical texts can be re-examined by asking about the roles animals play in the self-conception of the Bible's writers and characters, and in their conceptions of other peoples, of other species, and of God. Biblical scholars now routinely acknowledge that biblical studies needs to pay greater attention to the ways in which biblical texts both represent and obscure a range of human others—women, children, non-Israelites, insufficiently orthodox Israelites, Israelites with bodies deemed disabled or impure, and so on. If we begin to give animals comparable attention, we may not only animate the Bible's animals. We may also discover that animals animate the Bible itself.

References

Adams, Carol J. 1995. *Neither Man nor Beast: Feminism and the Defense of Animals.* New York: Continuum.

Borowski, Oded. 1998. *Every Living Thing: Daily Use of Animals in Ancient Israel.* Walnut Creek and London: AltaMira Press.

Brett, Mark G. 2000. *Genesis: Procreation and the Politics of Identity.* New York: Routledge.

Calarco, Matthew. 2008. *Zoographies: The Question of the Animal from Heidegger to Derrida.* New York: Columbia University Press.

Clutton-Brock, Juliet. 1987. *A Natural History of Domesticated Animals*. Austin: University of Texas Press.

Clutton-Brock, Juliet. 2007. "How Domestic Animals Have Shaped the Development of Human Societies." In *A Cultural History of Animals in Antiquity*, edited by Linda Kalof, 71–96. New York: Berg.

Clutton-Brock, Juliet. 2012. *Animals as Domesticates: A World View through History*. East Lansing: Michigan State University Press.

Deane-Drummond, Celia, and David Clough, eds. 2009. *Creaturely Theology: On Gods, Humans and Other Animals*. London: SCM Press.

DeMello, Margo. 2012. *Animals and Society: An Introduction to Human-Animal Studies*. New York: Columbia University Press.

Derrida, Jacques. 1990. "Force of Law: The 'Mystical Foundation of Authority.'" *Cardozo Law Review* 11: 921–1045.

Derrida, Jacques. 1995. "'Eating Well,' or the Calculation of the Subject." In *Points...: Interviews, 1974–1994*, edited by Elizabeth Weber and translated by Peggy Kamuf et al., 255–287. Redwood City, CA: Stanford University Press.

Derrida, Jacques. 2004. "Violence against Animals." In Jacques Derrida and Elisabeth Roudinesco, *For What Tomorrow ...: A Dialogue*, translated by Jeff Fort, 62–76. Redwood City, CA: Stanford University Press.

Derrida, Jacques. 2008. *The Animal That Therefore I Am*. Edited by Marie-Louise Mallet. Translated by David Wills. New York: Fordham University Press.

Derrida, Jacques. 2009. *The Beast and the Sovereign*. Vol I. Edited by Michel Lisse, Marie-Louise Mallet, and Ginette Michaud. Translated by Geoffrey Bennington. Chicago: University of Chicago Press.

Douglas, Mary. 1966. *Purity and Danger: An Analysis of the Concepts of Pollution and Taboo*. London: Routledge and Kegan Paul.

Eilberg-Schwartz, Howard. 1990. *The Savage in Judaism: An Anthropology of Israelite Religion and Ancient Judaism*. Bloomington: Indiana University Press.

Fewell, Danna Nolan, and David M. Gunn. 1993. *Gender, Power, and Promise: The Subject of the Bible's First Story*. Nashville, TN: Abingdon Press.

Forti, Tova L. 2008. *Animal Imagery in the Book of Proverbs*. Leiden: Brill.

Gross, Aaron S. 2012. "Introduction and Overview: Animal Others and Animal Studies." In *Animals and the Human Imagination: A Companion to Animal Studies*, edited by Aaron S. Gross and Anne Vallely, 1–23. New York: Columbia University Press.,

Gross, Aaron S., and Anne Vallely, eds. 2012. *Animals and the Human Imagination: A Companion to Animal Studies*. New York: Columbia University Press.

Gunkel, Hermann. (1917) 1987. *The Folktale in the Old Testament*. Translated by Michael D. Rutter. Sheffield, Yorkshire: Almond Press.

Haraway, Donna. 2003. *The Companion Species Manifesto: Dogs, People, and Significant Otherness*. Chicago: Prickly Paradigm Press.

Haraway, Donna. 2008. *When Species Meet*. Minneapolis: University of Minnesota Press.

Heard, R. Christopher. 2001. *Dynamics of Diselection: Ambiguity in Genesis 12–36 and Ethnic Boundaries in Post-Exilic Judah*. Semeia Studies. Atlanta, GA: Society of Biblical Literature.

Hiebert, Theodore. (1996) 2008. *The Yahwist's Landscape: Nature and Religion in Early Israel*. Minneapolis, MN: Fortress Press.

Houston, Walter. 1993. *Purity and Monotheism: Clean and Unclean Animals in Biblical Law*. Sheffield, Yorkshire: Sheffield Academic Press.

Kahila Bar-Gal, Gila, Charles Greenblatt, Scott R. Woodward, Magen Broshi, and Patricia Smith 2001. "The Genetic Signature of the Dead Sea Scrolls." In *Historical Perspectives: From the Hasmoneans to Bar Kokhba in Light of the Dead Sea Scrolls*, edited by David Goodblatt, Avital Pinnick, and Daniel R. Schwartz, 165–171. Leiden and New York: Brill.

Kalof, Linda, and Amy Fitzgerald, eds. 2007. *The Animals Reader: The Essential Classic and Contemporary Writings*. New York: Berg.

Kalof, Linda, and Georgina M. Montgomery, eds. 2011. *Making Animal Meaning*. East Lansing: Michigan State University Press.

King, Philip J., and Lawrence E. Stager. 2001. *Life in Biblical Israel*. Louisville, KY: Westminster John Knox.

Koosed, Jennifer L., ed. 2014. *The Bible and Posthumanism*. Atlanta, GA: Society of Biblical Literature.

Matthews, Victor H., and Don C. Benjamin. 1993. *Social World of Ancient Israel 1250–1587 BCE*. Peabody, MA: Hendrickson.

McKay, Heather A. 2002. "Through the Eyes of Horses: Representation of the Horse Family in the Hebrew Bible." In *Sense and Sensitivity: Essays on Reading the Bible in Memory of Robert Carroll*, edited by Alastair G. Hunter and Philip R. Davies, 127–141. London and New York: Sheffield Academic Press.

Meyers, Carol, Toni Craven, and Ross S. Kraemer ed. 2000. *Women in Scripture: A Dictionary of Named and Unnamed Women in the Hebrew Bible, the Apocryphal/Deuterocanonical Books, and the New Testament*. Boston: Houghton Mifflin.

Mobley, Gregory. 1997. "The Wild Man in the Bible and the Ancient Near East." *Journal of Biblical Literature* 116(2): 217–233.

Niditch, Susan. 2008. *"My Brother Esau Is a Hairy Man": Hair and Identity in Ancient Israel*. New York: Oxford University Press.

Oliver, Kelly. 2009. *Animal Lessons: How They Teach Us to Be Human*. New York: Columbia University Press.

Patton, Kimberley C. 2000. "'He Who Sits in the Heavens Laughs': Recovering Animal Theology in the Abrahamic Traditions." *Harvard Theological Review* 93(4): 401–434.

Rad, Gerhard von. 1972. *Genesis: A Commentary*. Rev. ed. Philadelphia: Westminster.

Stone, Ken. 2005. *Practicing Safer Texts: Food, Sex and Bible in Queer Perspective*. London and New York: T&T Clark.

Stone, Ken. 2014. "Wittgenstein's Lion and Balaam's Ass: Talking with Others in Numbers 22–25." In *The Bible and Posthumanism*, edited by Jennifer L. Koosed, 75–102. Atlanta, GA: Society of Biblical Literature.

Strawn, Brent A. 2005. *What Is Stronger Than a Lion? Leonine Image and Metaphor in the Hebrew Bible and the Ancient Near East*. Fribourg: Academic Press Fribourg.

Tucker, Gene M. 1997. "Rain on a Land Where No One Lives: The Hebrew Bible on the Environment." *Journal of Biblical Literature* 116(1): 3–17.

Tucker, Gene M. 2000. "The Peaceable Kingdom and a Covenant with the Wild Animals." In *God Who Creates: Essays in Honor of W. Sibley Towner*, edited by William P. Brown and S. Dean McBride, Jr., 215–225. Grand Rapids, MI: Eerdmans.

Waldau, Paul. 2002. *The Specter of Speciesism: Buddhist and Christian Views of Animals*. New York: Oxford University Press.

Waldau, Paul. 2013. *Animal Studies: An Introduction*. New York: Oxford University Press.

Waldau, Paul, and Kimberley Patton, eds. 2006. *A Communion of Subjects: Animals in Religion, Science, and Ethics*. New York: Columbia University Press.

Way, Kenneth C. 2011. *Donkeys in the Biblical World: Ceremony and Symbol*. Winona Lake, IN: Eisenbrauns.

Weil, Kari. 2012. *Thinking Animals: Why Animal Studies Now?* New York: Columbia University Press.

Wolfe, Cary. 2003. *Animal Rites: American Culture, the Discourse of Species, and Posthumanist Theory*. Chicago: University of Chicago Press.

CHAPTER 39

SEX AND SEXUALITY IN BIBLICAL NARRATIVE

DORA RUDO MBUWAYESANGO

BIBLICAL CONSTRUCTIONS OF HUMAN SEX AND SEXUALITY

THE Hebrew Bible presents sex and sexuality in a very limited way. Two intricately linked ideologies—patriarchy and imperialism—provide the context in which limited aspects of sexuality are featured. The Hebrew Bible presents and promotes a heteronormative view of sexuality (on heteronormativity, see Warmer 1999; Schilt and Westbrook 2009). The central idea behind the notion of heteronormativity is that heterosexuality is the norm and that any other form of sexual desire, expression, or relationship is abnormal and wrong. According to the sociologist and feminist Diane Richardson (1996, 2; 2000, 20), "Heterosexuality is institutionalized as a particular form of practice and relationships, of family structure, and identity. It is constructed as a coherent natural, fixed and stable category; as universal and monolithic." There are ways in which heterosexuality is made to appear natural and normative in societies; and in the Hebrew Bible it is made to look natural through a focus on procreation and the recognition of only two biological sexes with two corresponding genders—male and female / man and woman— in biblical narratives. The dichotomous notions of understanding sex and gender have been challenged successfully in social theory (see West and Zimmerman 1987; Butler 1990, 1993; Delphy 1993). Patriarchal culture and imperial interests influenced how sex and sexuality are used in plot and character development in biblical narratives. There is a range of sexual representation framed by two extremes—invisibility and demonization—and sexuality linked to reproduction falls somewhere in the middle. There is a significant focus on female sexuality as it is narrowly linked to reproduction.

The support of the normativity of heterosexuality in the Hebrew Bible is reflected from the very beginning of the canon in the conception of humanity in binary categories of male and female and heterosexuality's connection to procreation. The main purpose of sexuality is sustaining the species, which include the human race. In the creation narratives (especially Genesis 1), the concern is the sustainability of creation. Thus vegetation and trees are created with the ability to reproduce "according to their own kind." They are said to be created with seed as integral to their essence. The animals are also created with the ability to create, but that ability is situated in sexual dimorphism; that is, they are created male and female. Genesis 1 does not talk about human or animal seed but is nevertheless focused on connecting sexuality to reproduction: animals and humanity are created in two biological sexes so that they can multiply.

In patriarchy, sexuality is organized around male pleasure. Woman is created for the sexual pleasure of man. A man has sexual autonomy; whereas female sexuality is possessed and controlled by the male. Male sexual desire for the female is represented as natural and enjoyable, while female desire is represented as unnatural and painful (Gen. 2–3). The roles of man and woman are presented in ways that inscribe male superiority and female subordination. The seed, the essence of life necessary for procreation, is understood as contained in the male, and the perpetuation of family is the perpetuation of the man. As Esther Fuchs (2000, 55) states, "With Abraham we learn that sons belong to their fathers." But the assumption that children belong to their fathers is underscored in the genealogies prior to Abraham. The idea that the woman's womb is merely a vessel for incubating male seed is demonstrated resoundingly by the genealogies, especially in Genesis 1–11 and 1 Chronicles 1–9 (see Kelso in this volume). The genealogies present men producing male offspring without the mention of the mothers, underscoring the idea that the man is the seed bearer and the woman is simply an instrument. This, in turn, justifies male ownership of the children and the woman's body.

Another strategy the Bible uses to construct paternity is through the narrative motif of female barrenness. Stories of female barrenness suggest that the father's potency is guaranteed; whereas female sexual potency is presented as unreliable. So, for example, mothers suddenly appear in Genesis 11, just before the narratives of Abraham, to point out that Abram was heirless because his wife was barren. Male fertility is secure; what is unreliable is the woman, and, as Fuchs (2000, 65) states, "The rights of fathers over their female counterparts as well as over their offspring are ensured by emphasizing the contingency of women's procreativity. Hence the repeated presentation of prospective mothers as naturally barren women." Although procreation is the technique used to justify the claim that sexuality should be between a male and female, it is also used to construct and justify male domination of women. While barrenness is used to justify male domination of women, the rigid binary distinction of gender serves to suppress all the other genders that might not fit into this system of gender categorization.

In the patriarchal context, men relate to women's bodies as objects of male possession purely for male satisfaction. Although some feminist scholars, such as Phyllis Trible (1978, 72–99), have seen mutuality in the depiction of the male and female relationship in Genesis 2, it is quite clear that the man, Adam, is claiming ownership of the female body for his pleasure. That the woman, Eve, is depicted as the object and the male as the subject is demonstrated well, as the male says of the female, "This at last is bone of my bones and flesh of my flesh; this one shall be called Woman, for out of Man this one was taken" (Gen. 2:23). Athalya Brenner (1997) looks at the terminology of love, desire, and sexual activity in the Hebrew Bible and concludes that males are presented as the agents and subjects of love, as loving more frequently and more positively than females, and as permitted to engage in illicit sexual relationships. In sexual intercourse, men are the active partners, and women are the passive recipients. As Brenner states, "[I]t is men who 'know' women, and women who are 'known'; it is men who are the active agents of love and desire, and it is women who are the passive recipients of such agency. In short, it is men alone who possess sexuality (understood as the 'autonomous potential for socio-sexual behaviors motivated by desire')" (178).

Literary and linguistic representations of masculinity and femininity are always male centered. Men are often portrayed as strong and dominating. Masculinity is linked to strength and femininity to fragility. This phenomenon seems to be reflected in the depiction of the nature of the consequences of the disobedience of Adam and Eve. Man will fight with thistles and thorns to make the cursed ground produce food—an engagement that requires strength and perseverance (Gen. 3:17–19). Woman will experience multiple childbirth pains but will nevertheless continue to have desire for man—woman is vulnerable to sexual pain and male aggression (Gen. 3:16). There is an assumption in patriarchal societies that women are and should be sexually passive (see Reiss 1986; Caplan 1987). Sexually passive woman is depicted as the ideal, while sexually aggressive male is the ideal. Sex is presented as something done by man to woman. Language assigns the subject position to man, and woman becomes the object. When sex is defined and categorized from the male point of view, it does not just become unilateral, monolithic, and biased against women, it hides or condemns other forms of sexual expression in heterosexuality and non-heterosexuality.

The normativity of heterosexuality in the Hebrew Bible results in the denial of any expressions of genders other than masculine and feminine. The denial of the existence of other sexual identities and the connection of sex (especially female) to procreation makes heterosexuality the only normal way to express sexuality. Also, the linking of heterosexuality to reproduction denies the existence of other forms of sexual expression. This phenomenon of denial is reflected in the nature of the visibility and nonvisibility of sexuality in the Hebrew Bible narratives. The understanding of heterosexuality as a tool of reproduction involving penile-vaginal penetration is reflected in how sexuality is used in characterization and plot development: the presentation of sexuality in biblical narratives is mostly limited to reproduction and sexual violence.

Reproductive Sexuality in the Biblical Narratives

Although sexuality is the fuel that propels the plots in many biblical narratives, it is not often developed. Few narratives depict sexual acts. In many cases, as in stories employing the barren-mother motif, the conception of the woman is not connected directly to a sex act with a man. Rather, an action of Yahweh, not sex with the concerned husband, brings about conception. Although concentrated in the book of Genesis (Sarah, 21:1–2; Rebekah, 25:21; Rachel, 30:22–23), these narratives are also found in other parts of the Hebrew Bible (Hannah, 2 Sam. 1–3; Samson's mother, Judg. 13; the Shunamite woman, 2 Kings 4) and the New Testament (Elizabeth, Luke 1). The reason that Sarah conceives is depicted as a result of YHWH's activities, which are characterized in terms that hide sexual activity—"YHWH dealt with Sarah as he had said, and YHWH did to Sarah as he had promised. Sarah conceived and bore Abraham a son in his old age, at the time of which God had spoken to him" (Gen. 21:1–2). Isaac's connection to his wife's conception is his prayer to YHWH because his wife was barren, "and YHWH granted his prayer, and his wife Rebekah conceived" (Gen. 25:21). In the case of Rachel, God "remembered" her, and "heeded her and opened her womb" (30:22). In the case of Hannah, there is a link between the husband's activities and Yʜwʜ's activities. In the case of the Shunamite woman, Yʜwʜ is not directly involved with the conception, but it happens as Elisha, Yʜwʜ's prophet, had declared. The only reference that comes close to connecting a barren woman's conception to sexual activities is in the case of Hannah and Elkanah, but even then it is depicted in a euphemistic way that hides the act and that suggests that Yʜwʜ is involved (1 Sam. 1:19).

Barren mothers are often paired with fertile mothers. In most cases the fertile mother's immediate conception, unlike that of the barren wife, is directly tied to a sexual act—penile-vaginal penetration—especially of the woman the husband is given by his wife. Sarah gives Hagar to Abraham and "he went into her and she conceived" (16:4). In a similar way, the barren Rachel gives Bilhah to Jacob, who "went into her. Then Bilhah conceived and bore Jacob a son" (30:3–5). In the narrative, there is a female-male-female heterosexuality triangle. What makes the arrangement viable is the need for male children. The importance of bearing children is now expressed as a female need. In that regard, a particular kind of female agency is introduced. Sarah, Rachel, and Leah act as sexual agents by giving other women to their husbands. There is a gap in the narratives in that the women given by other women to men for sex are not given voices, and the relationship between the women is not presented in a way that reveals its nature. Interpreters just assume the relationship between *shifhah* (generally translated "maid") and *giburah* (generally translated "mistress") is a mistress-servant/slave relationship. So, according to Susanne Scholz, the sex between the husbands and these women should be categorized as rape because, as slaves, they were not capable of consenting or not consenting. But then, according to this logic, women (wives) given to men by their fathers would also fall into this category, since it is not known that wives had a choice to consent to having sex with their husbands.

More significantly, however, the narratives involving multiple women hide the possibility of female-female sexual relations. Female sexuality is focused exclusively on reproduction. The cause of friction between the women in a female-male-female triangle is not sexual tension but the need for children. This need is sometimes depicted with dire urgency, as in Rachel's plea to Jacob, "Give me children or I will die!" (Gen. 30:1). Since, in the biblical world, sexual activity is conceived in terms of penile-vaginal penetration, any activity of sexual nature taking place between the women is totally obscured. Consequently, in the narrative world of the Bible, Sarai, Rachel, and Leah do not look to these other women for their own sexual desires but to satisfy male desires that they have failed to fulfill.

Narratives that depict a male-female-male triangle suppress both female-female sexuality and male-male desire. In the trio of "wife-sister tales" in Genesis (Gen. 12:10–20; 20:1–18; 26:1–35) and in David's notorious scandal involving Bathsheba and Uriah (2 Sam. 11:1–27), a woman is put in a position of having sex with two men. These narratives are categorized by Fuchs (2000, 116–176) as adultery-type scenes employing a masculine contest motif, and by Scholz (2010, 85–92) as rape scenes that play out a male neurosis in which a man envisions that his wife is with another, more powerful man, fantasies seeking to protect a man's sexual dominance over his wife (see also Exum 1993, 148–169). In both the Genesis narratives and in 2 Samuel 11, the husband is depicted as less powerful than the other man. In the case of Abraham, who relinquishes his wife on two occasions (Gen. 12:10–20; 20:1–18), there are differences in the identities of the two kings: the first is Egyptian, the second Philistine. There is ambiguity in what happens to Sarai when she is taken into the house of Pharaoh. Some scholars argue that Pharaoh has no sexual intercourse with Sarai, while others interpret that Pharaoh has sex with her because he says he took her as wife (Gen. 12:19). Sarai, however, does not conceive after her encounter with Pharaoh because she is barren (Gen. 11:30). Abraham's virility is not in question because he is able to impregnate Hagar, the Egyptian woman (Gen. 16: 3–4). In the case of Abimelek, there is no ambiguity. Because Abimelek is warned in a dream about Sarah's real status, he never has sex with Sarah. Moreover, the narrator stresses that all the wombs of the women in his household had been divinely closed fast (Gen. 20:18). It is significant to note that the virility of men, including foreign men, is never questioned, even though the pressing concern in these narratives seems to be the purity of the paternity of the heir to the promise. The possibility that Sarah's child might not be Abraham's is completely ruled out. It is the same case with Isaac in Genesis 26. The encounter with Abimelek comes after Isaac already has heirs, but even then, Rebekah is not taken into the foreign king's household. In the case of David, the child, who is the product of his sexual encounter with Bathsheba before the murder of Uriah, is killed. His death is presented in the narrative as punishment for David's sin of committing adultery and murder. But more significantly, it points out that the heir to the throne, Solomon, is neither an illegitimate son of David nor a son of Uriah, the Hittite (2 Sam. 12:14). Thus, the patriarchal desire for Israel's ethnic purity continues beyond the stories of origin in the Torah. These narratives seem to allay the fear that the Israelites are not ethnically pure, while at the same time dismissing fears about the real paternity of heirs. In these patriarchal narratives, males are assured that the children produced by their wives are their own issue (Gen. 15) and that male surrogacy only happens after their death (through the custom of levirate marriage).

SEXUAL VIOLENCE IN BIBLICAL NARRATIVES

Sexual violence, in the form of rape, is another aspect of sexuality featured in biblical narratives (on theories on the definition of rape, see Brownmiller 1975; MacKinnon 1979; Rich 1980; Cahill 2000). Rape is depicted as either resulting in killings or a demonstration of wickedness. There are two general types of rape as determined by the respective gender identity of the perceived perpetrator and perceived victim. The first type is heterosexual violence in which the aggressor is one gender and the victim is the other gender. There are two narratives in which the aggressor is male and the victim is female (Gen. 34; 2 Sam. 13) and one in which the aggressor is female and the victim is male (Gen. 39). In the second type of sexual violence depicted in biblical narratives (Gen. 19; Judg. 19), heterosexual and same-gender violence are juxtaposed. The initial violence targets men, but women are offered as substitutes, and in the case of Judges 19, the woman is violated as an extension of her man. The characters, acts, and consequences are determined by what the agenda is—whether internal political and social issues (Judg. 19; I Sam. 13), external imperial interests (Gen. 19; 34; 39), or both. Elements of heterosexuality in a heteronormative society are highlighted and manipulated depending on the specific function of the sexual violence in the narrative and the broad ideology of the Hebrew Bible in general. Characterization and development of plot are determined by the specific function of the narrative in the broad imperial-patriarchal context, characterized by social, political, and cultural interests.

Genesis 34 fits very well into the patriarchal and imperial construction of sexuality. It should be looked at within the larger context of the Jacob cycle that plots the development of the promise of land and descendants. Genesis 34 is one of the narratives in the cycle depicting the third generation (Dinah, chap. 34; Judah, chap. 38; and Joseph, chap. 39).[1] Dinah is being contrasted to her two brothers in different ways. She is contrasted to Judah, who both marries a Canaanite woman and subsequently has sex with Tamar, his Canaanite daughter-in-law, and to Joseph, who is able to resist being raped by a woman. Judah's story exhibits the properties of a type-scene that depicts the measures taken by a woman to overcome child-lessness because of the absence of a suitable mate. Fuchs (2000, 65–82) shows how these acts are valorized. Judah's line continues through the manipulation of the line of descent. Instead of perpetuating seed through his son, Judah gets access to his son's wife. Tamar is depicted as taking the initiative to preserve Judah's line by manipulating him into having sex with her. In contrast to Tamar, Dinah is passive and becomes virtually invisible through most of her story. And in contrast to Judah, whose lineage is salvaged through the resourcefulness of a Canaanite woman, Dinah is denied a Canaanite partner and left without children.

Joseph's resistance of a powerful foreign woman in Genesis 39 is juxtaposed to Dinah's vulnerability to a powerful foreigner in Genesis 34. The larger imperial context of the Genesis 34 narrative plays a major role in character and plot development. The depiction of what happened to Dinah is deliberately ambiguous. The identity of Shechem as a Hivite—that is, a Canaanite—is enough to cast suspicion on him as a rapist. And because of the ethnic difference and the androcentric code of honor and shame, Dinah does not need to speak for the encounter to be categorized as rape.[2] Dinah's "defilement" leads to the killing of all Hivite men and the capture of their children and wives. The narratives forecast the later demand for the annihilation of the Hivites (Canaanites) in the book of Deuteronomy. Though Israel can capture Canaanite women in war, the Israelites will not intermarry with them—the exchange of wives indicates mutuality. And as Danna Nolan Fewell (2005, 107) suggests, Genesis 34 serves larger social ends: "[P]erhaps the story voices the fears and/or the fantasies of a vulnerable community desperately attempting to shore up the boundaries of its identity."

The second rape scene in 2 Samuel 13 should be read in the larger context of the Succession narrative—the elimination of Solomon's competition and the legitimation of his claim to the throne. The narrative serves to show the disharmony in David's family and David's ineffectiveness as a father. The rape of Tamar by her half-brother, Amnon, results in the revenge by her full brother, Absalom. Absalom's killing of Amnon is not directly connected to Solomon's accession to power; thus the story makes the revenge seem natural. There are no narratives in which women are able to escape rape on their own. This, according to Fuchs (2000, 201–224), serves patriarchal ideology by justifying fathers'/brothers' control and domination of daughters/sisters.

Two narratives—Genesis 19 and Judges 19—that juxtapose heterosexual rape and same-gender rape show more clearly how the heteronormativity of heterosexuality hides other gender identities and suppresses or demonizes other sexualities and other forms of sexual expressions in heterosexuality. The broad setting of the narratives is different. Genesis 19 is part of the narrative tracing Lot's line of descent to the Moabites and the Ammonites, Israel's neighbors. The Judges 19 narrative and its aftermath conclude the book of Judges with a civil war. Both narratives presents a case of violent assault directed against males by other males and fathers offering daughters (and a wife in the case of Judges 19) as substitutes. Lot offers his two virgin daughters (Gen. 19:8), who are spared from rape; and the Ephraimite offers his virgin daughter, who is spared, and the Levite's wife (concubine), who is gang raped and cut into pieces (Judg. 19:22–30). The demonization of same-gender sex is accomplished through the characterization of it as something that is not done by an individual but a group of perverse men. That the men in both narratives are spared from same-gender sexual violation communicates that men are never truly under such threat. At the same time, the gang rape of the Levite's wife communicates that women are vulnerable and powerless in sexual assaults (see Fuchs 2000, 208–211). The characterization of the threatening men is different in the two narratives. In the Genesis context, it says, "[T]he men of Sodom, both young and old, all the people of Sodom, surrounded the house" (v. 4), indicating the utter corruption of the city of Sodom. In the case of Judges, the men are identified as "a perverse group," not all the men of the city (v. 22). The whole city of Sodom deserves complete annihilation; whereas the Benjaminites deserve to remain part of Israel. The story of the near rape of Lot's male guests and his daughters will conclude with a story that depicts him fathering his daughters to produce the Moabites and Ammonites; the sequel to the gang rape story in Judges leads to war and concludes in the capture of women to revive the tribe of Benjamin (Judg. 20–21).

Sexual violence in biblical narratives is depicted as something that happens to women and results in war and as a result of war. Men are never depicted as plausible victims of sexual violence, whether by other men or women. The biblical narratives present women as helpless victims of male sexual aggression. Women need men to protect them from threats of rape and to avenge them when they are raped. Women are not real sexual agents but are more often objects. The only case in which a man is presented facing sexual violence is somewhat comical: Potiphar's wife is left holding Joseph's clothes while he escapes.

SEXUALITY AS AN ANTI-CONQUEST STRATEGY

Sexuality is also used as anti-conquest strategy in the biblical narratives. Anti-conquest ideology manifests itself in "literary strategies that allow 'colonizers' to claim foreign lands while securing their innocence" (Dube 2000, 60; on anti-conquest ideology in postcolonial theory, see Pratt 1992). The Torah, in particular, is an imperial text that justifies Israel's possession of a land that is initially identified as occupied by other peoples—the Canaanites (Gen. 12:6; on Genesis as an anti-conquest narrative, see Mbuwayesango 2008). Through an analysis of the narratives of the wife-sister motif (Gen. 12:11–20; 20:1–18; 26: 1–11), Lot and his daughters (Gen. 19:29–38) and Noah and Ham (Gen. 9:18–28), Randall Bailey (1994) demonstrates how the depictions of the breaking of sexual taboos in narratives are used to ridicule the foreign nations surrounding Israel and Judah "and thus, sanctioning, or sanctifying, Israelite hatred and oppression of these people" (123–124). But more importantly, another anti-conquest strategy is the use of women, especially their sexuality, in the acquisition of property. Thus both Abraham and Isaac acquire wealth through the abuse of their wives' sexuality.

Finally, sexuality is used as an anti-conquest strategy to justify and foreshadow the annihilation of the Canaanites. For example, this phenomenon is reflected in the Dinah and Shechem narrative (Gen. 34). The Hivites are listed as one of the Canaanite peoples with whom Israel must not intermarry. To guarantee that never happens, Deuteronomy (7:2;

20:16–17) insists they be annihilated, and the book of Joshua (7:21; 8:24–26) reports the deed done.

Conclusion

The Hebrew Bible does not provide a definition of sexuality. Its construction of sex and sexuality is influenced by imperial and patriarchal concerns. Heterosexuality, with its emphasis on reproduction and the sexual dimorphism required for procreation, is depicted as the natural expression of sexuality. At the same time, patriarchal ideology constructs a hierarchical structure to dominate women. Sexuality is used to rationalize the male domination and control of women. Focus on reproduction and male powers makes women vulnerable to male control and aggression. Although the Hebrew Bible has a very narrow perspective of sexuality, sexuality is a major strategy in plot and character development in biblical narratives, often functioning to build suspense, serve political agendas, and make social statements. Its pervading presence in biblical narrative renders it a critical subject of narrative analysis. Moreover, pressing issues of sexual identity, sexual expression, and sexual violence in the world today underscore that any interpretation of the Bible cannot exclude this important aspect.

Notes

1. The categorizing of these narratives into type-scenes separates them from their immediate context, but the immediate context should not be overlooked because it shows the interlock of imperialism and patriarchy and its effect on the marginalized and suppressed segments in biblical narratives.
2. Whether or not Dinah was raped is a controversial matter. For example, see Scholz 2000; Camp 2000; Gunn & Fewell 1993; Frymer-Kensky 1988, 200; Bechtel 1994; Keefe 1993.

References

Bailey, Randall C. 1994. "They're Nothing but Incestuous Bastards: The Polemical Use of Sex and Sexuality in Hebrew Canon Narratives." In *Reading from This Place: Social Location and Biblical Interpretation in the United States*, Vol. 1, edited by Fernando Segovia and Mary Ann Tolbert, 121–138. Minneapolis, MN: Fortress Press.

Bechtel, Lynn M. 1994. "What if Dinah Is Not Raped? (Genesis 34)." *Journal for the Study of the Old Testament* 62: 19–36.

Brenner, Athalya. 1997. *The Intercourse of Knowledge: On Gendering Desire and "Sexuality" in the Hebrew Bible*. Leiden: E.J. Brill.

Brownmiller, Susan. 1975. *Against Our Will: Men, Women and Rape*. New York: Simon and Schuster.

Butler, Judith. 1990. *Gender Trouble: Feminism and the Subversion of Identity*. New York: Routledge.

Butler, Judith. 1993. *Bodies That Matter: On the Discursive Limits of Sex.* New York: Routledge.

Cahill, Ann J. 2000. "Foucault, Rape, and the Construction of the Feminine Body." *Hypatia* 15 (1): 43–63.

Camp, Claudia. 2000. *Wise, Strange and Holy: The Strange Woman and the Making of the Bible.* Journal for the Study of the Old Testament Supplement Series 320. Gender, Culture, Theory 9. Sheffield, Yorkshire: Sheffield Academic Press.

Caplan, Pat. 1987. *The Cultural Construction of Sexuality.* London and New York: Routledge.

Delphy, Christine. 1993. "Rethinking Sex and Gender." *Journal of Women's International Forum* 16 (1): 1–19.

Dube, Musa W. 2000. *Postcolonial Feminist Interpretation of the Bible.* St. Louis. MO: Chalice Press.

Exum, J. Cheryl. 1993. *Fragmented Women: Feminist (Sub)versions of Biblical Narratives.* Valley Forge, PA: Trinity Press International.

Fewell, Danna Nolan. 2005. "Lecture Féministe: Viol, lecture et representation en Genèse 34." In *Guide des nouvelles de la Bible*, edited by André Lacocque, 97–114. Paris: Bayard Press.

Frymer-Kensky, Tikva. 1988. "Law and Philosophy: The Case of Sex in the Bible." In *Thinking Biblical Law*, edited by Dale Patrick. *Semeia* 45: 89–102.

Fuchs, Esther. 2000. *Sexual Politics in the Biblical Narratives: Reading the Hebrew Bible as a Woman.* London and New York: Continuum.

Gunn, David M., and Danna Nolan Fewell. 1993. *Narrative in the Hebrew Bible.* Oxford Bible Series. Oxford: Oxford University Press.

Keefe, Alice A. 1993. "Rapes of Women/Wars of Men." In *Women, War, and Metaphor*, edited by Claudia Camp and Carol Fontaine. *Semeia* 61: 79–97.

MacKinnon Catherine. 1979. *Sexual Harassment of Working Women: A Case Study of Sexual Discrimination.* New Haven, CT: Yale University Press.

Mbuwayesango, Dora Rudo. 2008. "'The Canaanites Were in the Land': The Book of Genesis as an Anti-Conquest Narrative." *Journal of Commonwealth and Postcolonial Studies* 15 (1): 84–93.

Pratt, Mary Louise. 1992. *Imperial Eyes, Travel Writing and Transculturation.* New York: Routledge.

Reiss, Ira L. 1986. *Journey into Sexuality: An Exploratory Voyage.* Englewood Cliffs, NJ: Prentice-Hall.

Rich, Adrienne. 1980. "Compulsory Heterosexuality and Lesbian Existence." *Signs* 5 (4): 631–660.

Richardson, Diane. 1996. "Heterosexuality and Social Theory." In *Theorising Heterosexuality: Telling It Straight*, edited by Diane Richardson. London: Open University Press.

Richardson, Diane. 2000. *Rethinking Heterosexuality.* London: SAGE Publications.

Schilt, Kristen, and Laurel Westbrook. 2009. "Doing Gender, Doing Heteronormativity: 'Gender Normals,' Transgender People, and the Social Maintenance of Heterosexuality." *Gender and Society* 23 (4): 440–464.

Scholz, Susanne. 2000. *Rape Plots: A Feminist Cultural Study of Genesis.* New York: Peter Lang.

Scholz, Susanne. 2010. *Sacred Witness: Rape in the Hebrew Bible.* Minneapolis, MN: Fortress Press.

Trible Phyllis. 1978. *God and the Rhetoric of Sexuality.* Philadelphia: Fortress Press.

Warmer, Michael. 1999. *The Trouble with Normal: Sex, Politics and the Ethics of Queer Theory.* New York: The Free Press.

West Candace and Don H. Zimmerman. 1987, "Doing Gender." *Gender and Society and Society* 1 (2): 125–151.

CHAPTER 40

....

CHARACTERIZING GOD IN HIS/OUR OWN IMAGE

....

STUART LASINE

> Coming to some understanding of the character of Yahweh is one of the great
> challenges of the Hebrew Bible.
>
> —Gunn and Fewell 1993, 89

PERHAPS the greatest challenge in evaluating Yahweh's character is the fact that his "multi-faceted" personality includes a "dark side" (Barton 2010; Clines 1998, 503; cf. Gunn and Fewell 1993, 88). Because this anthropomorphic deity is often described as a parent, husband, king, or warrior, we must therefore ask, what *kind* of father is Yahweh shown to be, what *kind* of husband and king? At times, God plays more than one of these roles in the same passage, inviting readers to ponder what the common elements of his behavior in these roles tell us about his character.

The way in which the deity is presented also depends on who is doing the presenting. We must therefore paraphrase the questions Jesus puts to his disciples in Mark 8:27, 29 and ask, Who does Yahweh say that he is? Who do other characters say he is? Who do the narrators show him to be? And, who do (and should) *we* say that Yahweh is? Clearly, theological issues cannot be separated from literary analysis when one examines the presentation of God's character. This includes taking account of the ways in which readers understand and evaluate characters in narrative, exposing their own values and expectations—that is, their own character—in the process.

I begin with an analysis of the way God is presented when he discusses the fate of Sodom with Abraham in Genesis 18, and then sketch the ways in which Yahweh's character changes after Genesis. The next section focuses on passages such as Exodus 34:6–7 in which Yahweh characterizes himself. This is followed by a survey of cases in which other characters, and biblical narrators, give their views of God's character, or apply God's self-descriptions to their own situation. The chapter concludes by asking whether the various portrayals of Yahweh constitute a coherent representation of a "round" character, and why this character has so many problematic features.

JUDGING GOD'S JUDGMENT IN GENESIS
AND LATER BOOKS

In Genesis 18:17–33, readers are allowed to overhear a private conversation between God and Abraham. First, we are given access to Yahweh's thoughts when he decides to share "what he is doing" with Abraham because he had promised nationhood to Abraham's descendants. We also learn that Yahweh defines his own "way" as involving the practice of justice, and that he has "known" Abraham in order that he and his family might do the same (v. 19). Readers who are used to viewing God as a father figure might hear God being paternal here, deciding that it's time for his son to start interning in dad's law firm.

God's thoughts now turn to a practical example of keeping the way of justice: what to do about Sodom, whose cry is great and whose sin is very heavy (vv. 20–21). What God "says" in these verses had apparently been audible to Abraham, because in verse 23, he draws near before Yahweh and says, "Will you indeed sweep away the righteous with the wicked?" God certainly did not have to wait long for Abraham to start "practicing law"!

Commentators disagree about which party has a better grasp of justice, and who is "teaching" whom, in the ensuing conversation. Abraham's opening question reveals his assumption that God has already decided to destroy all the inhabitants of Sodom, even though no such decision has been reported and Abraham apparently heard Yahweh say that he plans to investigate before doing anything (v. 21; cf. Deut. 13:13–16). Before God can respond, Abraham posits a hypothetical number of fifty righteous in Sodom who might die if the entire city were destroyed, adding, "far be it from you[1] to kill the righteous with the wicked" (v. 25). In effect, Abraham is claiming that he knows God's true nature, and that it is against his nature to kill innocent people (which God has *not* said he planned to do!). Abraham then goes further, asking "shall not the judge of all the earth do justice?" as though he knows what "doing justice" means, and knows it better than God does. In effect, Abraham charges the world's judge with planning to commit an injustice, according to Abraham's notion of justice.

Commentators who accept Abraham's assumption that God had already decided to destroy Sodom tend to conclude that God is learning a lesson about justice from the "teacher" Abraham (e.g., Brueggemann 1982, 109, 168–176; Whybray 1996, 102–103). The fact that God does not attempt to counter Abraham's criticisms may seem to support this view. Instead of rebutting, rebuking, or becoming angry at Abraham, God patiently agrees to each of the patriarch's proposals to spare the city if an ever-smaller minimal number of righteous people are present. After agreeing to withhold punishment for the sake of ten righteous, Yahweh simply leaves (v. 33).

The inadequacy of Abraham's solution only becomes manifest when we read about the actions of the two investigating divine emissaries in chapter 19. If Abraham argued that destroying the entire city meant treating "the righteous as the wicked," his own method means treating the wicked as the righteous, letting them off the hook so that they don't have to be accountable for their sins. God's actual method—which he does not attempt to "teach" to Abraham during their conversation—turns out to be removal of the relatively "righteous" from the city before it is overthrown.

Although Abraham twice implores God not to be angry at him for his persistence concerning justice to Sodom, there is no hint from either the narrator or God's quoted words that Yahweh is, or might become, angry. On the contrary, God shows himself to be extremely patient and forbearing with Abraham during this exchange, as a supportive parent or teacher might be. In point of fact, God is never said to be angry *anywhere* in Genesis (see Lasine 2010, 48–49). Even when God decides to flood the world, he is said to be pained at heart and regretful, not angry (although the LXX later replaces the regret and pain with anger in Gen. 6:7).

While the Sodom story does not illustrate all the ways in which God appears and acts in Genesis, the issue of God's justice remains crucial throughout scripture. The absence of divine anger is not the only way in which Genesis presents God differently from later books. Yahweh displays new character traits after he takes on his new role as Israel's divine king in Exodus (Exod. 15:18). These include wrathfulness, jealousy, holiness, covenantal loyalty (*hesed*), and mercy. His relations with Israel are soon expressed not only on the model of a suzerain and his vassal but also on that of a parent to his or her children and a husband to his wife. In general, the divinely executed punishments of death reported in Genesis are also qualitatively different from the deaths caused by God after we encounter holiness in Exodus 3. For example, in the case of the Egyptian plagues (Exod. 7–12), the issues of human violence, immorality, and incivility highlighted in Genesis 6–8 and 18–19 are less salient than lack of respect for Yahweh's dignity, the power of his holiness and his ultimate authority, as well as the dignity of his "son" Israel.

At first glance, "holiness" might not seem to qualify as a character trait. However, it has led many commentators to describe Yahweh as "demonic" and "amoral." According to Jenson (2003, 104–105), considering holiness to be an essential component of Yahweh's character "helpfully corrects approaches to holiness which suggest that it is an impersonal force or power." And because character is indicated above all "by how a person acts in a story," we must understand holiness "in relation to the actions and purposes of the holy God." Similarly, Rogerson (2003, 21) believes that holiness in the Old Testament is "ultimately grounded in the moral character" of Israel's God, whose chief attributes he takes to be "unfailing love, mercy and forgiveness." However, if Yahweh's holiness is grounded in his moral character, we must assess his character in terms of his actions and purposes as a moral agent, *including* his responses to perceived disrespect for his defining trait of holiness. We are then forced to ask whether actions such as destroying vast numbers of people in Beth Shemesh for looking at or into the ark (1 Sam. 6:6) expresses the character traits of "unfailing love, mercy and forgiveness" or immoral grandiosity and rage. Since Yahweh is not a representation of natural forces, expressions of his holiness also express his personality. Thus, the death of a character such as Uzzah (2 Sam. 6:8) is not the impersonal effect of a natural force like electricity, which is indifferent to human intentions and divine moral considerations. It is an expression of the wrathful *person* Yahweh being indifferent to human intentions and to the morality of Uzzah's actions (see Lasine 2010, 41n31).

DIVINE SELF-CHARACTERIZATION: WHO DOES GOD SAY THAT HE IS?

> Yahweh, Yahweh, God, compassionate and gracious, long to anger and abundant in covenantal loyalty and truth;... Yahweh, his name is Jealous, he is a jealous God.
>
> —Exodus 34:6, 14

Yahweh's list of his own personality traits in Exodus 34:6–7 has been called a "timeless expression of the character of YHWH" (Barton 2001, 81) and "a kind of 'canon'" defining Israel's God

(Fretheim 2010, 302). Crenshaw interprets these descriptors in terms of Yahweh's roles as Israel's ruler and parent, "Together they characterize YHWH as a superior who looks with favor on an inferior within a prescribed relationship," and "one who turns toward another with solicitous concern akin to that of parents." When Yahweh "repents from the evil" (Exod. 32:12, 14), he is reconsidering "intended punishment when circumstances warrant" (Crenshaw 1995, 136), thereby curbing his anger. Fretheim (2010, 302) goes further, asserting that Yahweh's wrath is "not a continuous aspect of the nature of God but a particular response to a historical situation." These scholars take Yahweh's wrath and intended punishments to be a function of the people's situation and attitude toward him, rather than as an indicator of God's own character.

In contrast, Yahweh assigns himself the trait of being "long to anger" ('erek 'appayîm), acknowledging that he can become angry under certain conditions and implying that his anger is under his control, and manifests itself only when he is pushed to the limit of his patience. As God says later in the Mekilta, "I am ruler of my jealous anger" (Mek., Bahodesh 6). Does this mean that Yahweh would never have the kind of angry knee-jerk response that Moses exhibits when he breaks the tablets in anger in Exodus 32:19? Earlier in Exodus 32, Yahweh had told Moses to leave him alone so that his anger will get hot against them and consume them (v. 10). In the following chapter, Yahweh seems unsure that he can rule his anger at the Israelites because, in effect, they push his buttons. He tells Moses that he cannot continue to go among his people for even "one moment" lest he destroy them when they begin acting according to their "stiff-necked" nature (Exod. 33:3, 5).

Yahweh's self-description in Exodus 34:6–7 is part of an ongoing debate with Moses about covenantal fidelity to a guilty people. After Yahweh agrees to remain with, and work wonders for, his covenanted people (v. 10), he warns the people against making covenants with the inhabitants of the promised land and bowing down to their gods. In fact, they must destroy the cult objects of these gods, for "Yahweh, his name is Jealous, he is a jealous God" (v. 14; cf. Exod. 20:4), who demands exclusive devotion from his people/children.

Later in the wilderness wandering narrative, Yahweh shows how he understands his jealousy in a specific situation. After Yahweh's wife Israel "yokes" herself to Baal, Aaron's grandson Phineas acts as a jealous husband might when he catches his wife in bed with another man: he kills both the unfaithful spouse (in this case, the Israelite male Zimri) and the "lover" (the Midianite woman Cozbi). In response, Yahweh lauds and rewards Phineas, because the priest was "jealous with my jealousy among them" (Num. 25:11). In other words, Yahweh identifies with what he perceives to be Phineas's identification with his divine emotions, even though Phineas acted without being ordered to do so by Yahweh.

The prophet Elijah and Jehu the king of Israel are the only other characters called "jealous for Yahweh" in the Hebrew Bible (1 Kings 19:10; 2 Kings 10:16). Because they describe themselves as jealous for Yahweh, their subsequent actions reveal their understanding of divine jealousy. Like the priest Phineas, Elijah and Jehu kill on Yahweh's behalf without being ordered to do so (1 Kings 18:40; 2 Kings 10:18–28). In all three cases, jealousy for Yahweh includes identification with the divine emotion of outrage against his unfaithful spouse Israel and Yahweh's tendency to kill humans when jealousy drives him to do so (e.g., Deut. 29:19; 32:16, 21; Ezek. 16:38).

Yahweh also reveals his self-understanding by using the expression "far be it from ..." in reference to himself. Using an anonymous man of God as his messenger, Yahweh tells the priest Eli, "I did indeed say that your house,... would walk before me forever; but now

Yahweh says: far be it from me; for them that honor me I will honor, and they who despise me will be dishonored (or "disdained" [yēqāllû]; 1 Sam. 2:30). In the next chapter Yahweh directs the child Samuel to tell Eli that he is about to punish his house forever (1 Sam. 3:11–15). He also informs Samuel that he will judge Eli's house "forever," because they acted blasphemously and Eli "did not rebuke/weaken them" (kihâ bām).

In these verses, Yahweh declares first that it is far from his character to honor those who despise him, even if "lightly esteeming" them means canceling his earlier assurance that Eli's house would walk before him "forever" and replacing it with a curse on that house "forever." In addition, the narrator makes it clear that Eli himself is being cursed not for his own behavior but for that of his sons. Moreover, the narrator prevents readers from accepting Yahweh's charge that Eli had not rebuked his son by reporting earlier that Eli *did* rebuke them (1 Sam. 2:23–25) and that the reason they did not heed their father's warning was that Yahweh "took pleasure to kill them" (v. 25). The last statement clashes with the prophet Ezekiel's insistence that Yahweh feels no pleasure at the death of the wicked or anyone else (Ezek. 18:23, 32).

According to Jeremiah 9:23, the things in which Yahweh takes pleasure are practicing *hesed* together with "justice and righteousness in the earth." If readers wish to cite 1 Samuel 2:25–3:15 as proof of this assertion, they must demonstrate how the eternal punishment of Eli and his descendants exemplifies true justice and divine *hesed*. Or perhaps they merely need to appeal to Yahweh's executive privilege. After all, Yahweh had earlier told Moses, "I shall favor whom I favor, and show compassion to whom I show compassion" (Exod. 33:19). This tautology may also be a way for God to assert his unaccountability, a feature of his preeminent position acknowledged by Job when he asks the formulaic question, "Who can say to him, 'What are you doing?'" (Job 9:12; see Lasine 2001, 177–179).

YAHWEH THROUGH HUMAN EYES

Who do people say that I am?

—Mark 8:27

Only rarely does the narrator directly "say who Yahweh is." He does so by describing God's actions as an illustration of his compassionate, loyal or gracious character (Gen. 19:16; 39:21; 2 Kings 13:23; cf. 2 Chron. 7:6). More commonly, prophets describe Yahweh's traits in their own voices, as well as by quoting Yahweh's self-descriptions. For example, in Deuteronomy 32, Moses sketches God's character and deeds in verses 3–6, 10–16, 30–32, while Yahweh speaks about himself in verses 20–27, 34–42. For Moses, God is the father who created Israel and the adoptive caretaker who discovered Israel in a howling desert wasteland and then encompassed and cared for him as "the little man in his eye," like an eagle in the nest protecting its young (32:6, 10–11). God is also the mother who has given birth to, and gone through labor for, Israel (v. 18; see Lasine 2001, 208–211).

Moses emphasizes that Yahweh is Israel's only true "rock," the rock of its salvation (Deut. 32:4, 15, 18, 30–31; cf. Ps. 89:27), who made Israel suck oil from the flinty rock (v. 13). In Isaiah 44:8 Yahweh himself asks, "Is there a God beside me? There is no rock; I know not any." The "rock" is a powerful symbol of divine reliability, permanence, and protection (Nielsen 2005, 264–273). Early in the poem, Moses lists the traits and actions of Yahweh the rock: "his work has integrity (*tāmîm*), for all his ways are justice, a God of faithfulness and without iniquity; righteous and upright is he" (Deut. 32:4). These traits are also attributed to humans, such as Job. Apart from fidelity, the divine traits listed by Yahweh in Exodus 34:6–7 are not highlighted here. Moses's purpose is to contrast God's sterling qualities with the corruption and folly of his children (Deut. 32:5–6). In verses 10–11 he stresses the forlorn and dangerously exposed condition of the foundling Israel when it was discovered by Yahweh, which emphasizes the ingratitude of Israel when it forgets the rock of its salvation after becoming fat with prosperity.

Moses does not raise the question whether it was the divine pampering itself which contributed to the foundling's becoming spoiled and disloyal to God, even though he had warned his listeners of this danger earlier, in Deuteronomy (8:11–20), a danger illustrated by the behavior of the kings Yahweh later takes as his "sons," David and Solomon. Instead, Moses describes how Israel's ingratitude has roused Yahweh to jealousy (v. 16) and quotes Yahweh's statement that they have roused him to jealousy with their non-gods (v. 21). Yahweh then expresses his violent anger and the ways in which he will vindicate himself by making these ungrateful adoptees suffer in various horrible ways (vv. 22–27; cf. Ezek. 16).

The image of God as a parental bird encircling Israel is reminiscent of God offering protection within the "hidden shelter of his wings" in Psalms 61:5, and "hedging in" Job with blessings and prosperity (*śûk*; Job 1:10). Yet divine enclosure can also feel like oppressive imprisonment in pain, as Job discovers (*sûk*; Job 3:23). To one used to being protected by a divine mothering bird, being abandoned can transform one's perception of that mother bird into one of the uncaring ostrich who abandons her eggs on the road, where they might be trampled, because she is hardened against her young as though they were not hers (Job 39:13–16). In Isaiah 49:15 and 54:7–8, Yahweh is made to claim that he will never forget his womb-like maternal compassion for Israel, and then to admit that he *did* momentarily abandon them in his anger. And most poignantly, Job describes naked victims clinging to or embracing (*ḥibqû*) the rock for shelter in the storm (Job 24:8), which forms a stark contrast to the expected image of Yahweh being a rock and a refuge to those in distress. The image expresses disillusionment over the fact that Yahweh isn't reliably all that he—and others—say he is and fails in that respect when it matters most. Job no longer shares Abraham's assumption that it is against God's character to "sweep away the righteous with the guilty" (see Job 9:22; 12:16–25; 21:1–26).

In Psalm 89, God's self-presentation is challenged by the juxtaposition of his voice and that of another speaker. Ethan the Ezrahite, the "wise" man of 1 Kings 5:11, praises Yahweh's *ḥesed*, faithfulness, justice, righteousness, truth, and incomparability. He quotes Yahweh declaring that his covenant with his "first-born" David and his seed will stand fast and endure "forever" (vv. 4–5, 29–30, 36). Even when he mentions the conditional aspect of the promise to David's heirs (vv. 31–33), Yahweh declares that while he will punish them for their transgression, his *ḥesed* will not "break off" from them (v. 34).

However, in Psalm 89:39, Ethan begins a lament directly addressed to Yahweh as "you," accusing him of having despised and rejected the descendants of David, weakening them while strengthening their adversaries and covering them in shame. He asks God how long he will continue to express his wrath, and what happened to his promised *ḥesed* and faithfulness. Ethan believes that the degree and duration of the punishment for unnamed sins does not justify the continued absence of the merciful divine traits that were promised "forever." In effect, Yahweh has broken his word. His *ḥesed* really wasn't *ḥesed* in the first place, because it was not as permanent and reliable as a "rock."

The formation of an eternal bond between Yahweh and the house of David is first reported in 2 Samuel 7, although it is not described as a "covenant." Yahweh speaks (through the prophet Nathan) of David's son becoming God's adoptive son, rather than David himself being in that role ("I will be to him for a father, and he shall be to me for a son"; v. 14). He then tells David that he will punish David's son if he commits iniquity, but "my *ḥesed* will not depart from him, as I made it depart from Saul, whom I made to depart from before you" (v. 15; cf. 1 Sam. 16:14, 23; 1 Sam. 18:12–13). Steussy (2000, 146) rightly observes that "there is something quite unnerving about a promise never to withdraw 'steadfast love' that in its very enunciation mentions that God has a track record of withdrawing such loyalty."

Then 2 Samuel 11–12 go on to recount how David violates three of Yahweh's ten commandments and receives punishment for these sins. After Nathan uses a parable to trap David into unknowingly condemning himself to death, the prophet delivers Yahweh's condemnation in the deity's own words (12:7–8). This speech communicates Yahweh's perception of (if not shock at) David's monumental ingratitude. He uses the most emphatic form of the pronoun "I" to express all that he has done for David—and all he would have done in addition—and contrasts that with David having despised his "word" by doing what Yahweh considers to be evil (12:9; cf. 11:27). As Fewell (2010, 120n46) puts it, Yahweh's indictment of David is "framed as a personal affront."

While Yahweh's reaction might remind readers of an indulgent father who is chagrined when his spoiled son goes bad (especially after Yahweh had earlier used the adoption formula in reference to David's son), the father-son metaphor is not employed here. Basically, Yahweh is speaking as a benefactor or patron lamenting that the man he benefited has become so ungrateful. In addition to failing to appreciate the gifts that were bestowed upon him, he violated the gift giver's most basic rules. Yahweh's condemnation does not acknowledge the possibility that it was *his* gifts to the king that led David to violate his specific commandments against coveting, adultery, and murder. Given the warnings concerning satiety in Deuteronomy (e.g., 8:7–14; 17:17; 32:13–15) and other biblical texts, it should hardly have come as a surprise that the leader who had been given his master's wives would go on to "take" more women who belonged to another (2 Sam. 12:9–10; cf. 1 Sam. 8:11–19).

Finally, Jonah "says who God is" by interpreting his own situation through the lens of Yahweh's self-characterization in Exodus 34:6–7. Praying angrily to God about the sparing of Nineveh, he claims that he fled to Tarshish because he "knew that you are a gracious God, and compassionate, long to anger, and abundant in mercy, who repents of the evil." He then implores Yahweh to take his life from him, because it was better for him to die than to live (Jon. 4:2–3). In effect, he explains his desire to die in terms of Yahweh's character, rather than his own. In fact, one reason that Jonah sees his situation as both unbearable and unchangeable is his assumption that Yahweh's character traits are robust and unchanging.

Readers are not told what Yahweh specifically wants Jonah to proclaim against Nineveh. Our only hint is his statement that Nineveh's evil has come up to him (Jon. 1:2), and the narrator's later report that Yahweh did not do "what *he* said he would do" to the Ninevites (3:10). In stark contrast to the furious and jealous Yahweh of Nahum, who will "by no means clear the guilty" (Nah. 1:2–3; cf. Exod. 34:7), in Jonah we are not told that God was angry at, or roused to jealousy against, the Ninevites, even though the Ninevites them-selves later assume that God is experiencing "burning anger" (Jon. 3:9). It is only Jonah himself who is said to feel anger in the book (4:1, 4, 9). The fact that Yahweh is professedly "long to anger" is for Jonah a cause for complaint; God doesn't get angry quickly enough when anger is called for. If Jonah is in fact speaking Yahweh's words when he pronounces the oracle in 3:1, his grievance seems to be that God had committed himself to destroying Nineveh—with no possibility of remission of punishment—and then remitted punish-ment anyway, allowing his merciful personality to trump the destructive anger called for by the situation.

According to Cooper (1993, 153–154), Jonah is asserting "that God is *unreliable*" when he reformulates one of the divine attributes listed in Exodus 34:6: instead of "being 'reliable' (*ᵉmet*), Jonah's God 'renounces evil' (*niḥām ʿal-hārāʾâ*)." In other words, Yahweh's reliable mercy makes him unreliable in enforcing justice. Does God reliably repent from evil in the Hebrew Bible? After Joel lists Yahweh's merciful attributes, he, too, declares that Yahweh "repents of the evil," but then weakens this claim by asking "who knows whether he will . . . repent" (2:13–14). In Exodus 32:14, the narrator states that Yahweh repented from the evil which he said he would do to his people (cf. 1 Sam. 15:11, 29, 35). This implies that Yahweh came close to *not* doing so, and needed the intervention of Moses to prevent him from being unreliable in this sense.

CONCLUSION: WHO DO YOU SAY THAT I AM?

> For God's dark ways no one has yet invented a lantern.
>
> —Sigmund Freud, letter of 8/6/1873

> One day, a priest, it is said, gave inadvertently, instead of the sacrament, a counter, which had by accident fallen among the holy wafers. The communicant waited patiently for some time, expecting it would dissolve on his tongue: But finding that it still remained entire, he took it off. I wish, cried he to the priest, you have not committed some mistake: I wish you have not given me God the Father: He is so hard and tough there is no swallowing him.
>
> —Hume 2007, 67

Having surveyed the many complexities in the presentation of God's character in the Hebrew Bible, is it possible to "say who he is" without underplaying an essential dimension of his character? This task is made more challenging by the fact that we tend to evaluate character in a reductive manner. As Hochman (1985, 46) puts it, our perception of people is typological in life as well as in literature, even with characters who are presented as radically individual. That is, our perception of *other* people tends to be typological. Social psychologists call this the *actor-observer effect*. In daily life, we *need* to categorize others by their supposed dispo-sition in order to efficiently navigate our way through potential dangers (see Lasine 2012, 12–19, 219–228).

Are our judgmental tendencies any different when it comes to evaluating God's character in the Hebrew Bible? While scholars have increasingly called attention to God's "dark side," to reduce Yahweh to a "demonic," "capricious," or "amoral" deity is to flatten the complex manner of his presentation in biblical narrative (and poetry). As we have seen, God acts in a number of different ways in scripture, and displays different traits in different situations. In addition, readers may differ in their evaluation of God's behavior in a specific case if they differ in their assumptions, expectations, and values.

The fact that Yahweh's personality is occasionally dark has been explained in a wide variety of ways. For Volz (1924, 27–32), the need to make Yahweh a truly monotheistic, universal deity led to the "Yahwehization of the demonic." Speaking more generally, Hume (2007, 78–84) also stresses that there is an inverse relationship between a god's power and his goodness. When the god's power has become universal, humans cannot risk complaining about his "hard and tough" qualities; in fact, they must submissively abandon their reason and praise qualities which in humans would be condemnable.

With biblical books such as Job, this approach helps explains the focus is on the "fear of God" rather than love of this deity, whose defining traits (in this book) include his infinite power, his vulnerability to manipulation by haśśatan, and his unaccountability for even the most shocking actions. According to Noll, "no sane reader would have worshiped" even the God of Samuel.[2] If so, how much more "insane" would a believer have to be to worship the God who torments Job and kills his children and workers, precisely because Job has been incomparably obedient and loyal to him—and then justify himself to the victim solely by trumpeting his immeasurable power (see Lasine 2001, 177–239)? If this is how God behaves, one could argue that it would be "insane" to deny that reality, pretending that God's traits are limited to those listed in Exodus 34:6–7. Even Job seems to accept that the God with whom he must deal is "hard and tough," if his recantation in 42:6 is understood as a recognition that it is pointless to demand justice and accountability from the kind of God who has just revealed himself from the whirlwind.

The origin of the "hard" divine traits, for Hume, is the tendency to imagine a humanlike deity whose nature would explain all the disasters and capriciousness that permeate human life. This means projecting onto God "human passions and infirmities" as well as "superior power and authority" (Hume 2007, 41). Freud also believes that humans tame the terror of nature by humanizing it—in a specific way. By giving the forces of nature "the character of a father," we can feel ourselves "at home in the uncanny" (Freud 1928, 24–26). Once God was envisioned as a single individual, people's relations to him could "recover the intimacy and intensity of the child's relationship" with his father (29). While the child has reason to fear his parents, and "especially one's father," the child was also "sure of his protection against the dangers he knew," prompting him to "align the two situations with one another" (25).

Freud (1950, 217) shows the kind of "father" he has in mind when he claims that all the traits of "the great man" are traits of the father: "decisiveness of thought, strength of will, the vehemence of his deeds, . . . but above all, self-reliance and independence," as well as "godly unconcern which may increase to the point of ruthlessness." The great man/father "must be admired, he may be trusted, but one cannot help being also afraid of him" (217).

If we agreed that all fathers have the character Freud assigns to them, and the biblical God always displayed these Vaterzüge, we could easily conclude that Yahweh's character is simply a reflection of the reality of father-child relations. Theologians like Blumenthal make the less universal claim that the way we envision God is necessarily shaped by the way we have viewed our own parents and experienced childhood (1993, 13; cf. O'Brien 2008, 99). Recent social-psychological studies support this assumption (e.g., Morewedge and Clear 2008, 183).

For many readers of the Hebrew Bible, Yahweh certainly does represent an "a protective and caring parent who is always reliable and always available" when needed (Kaufman 1981, 67). And it is not only infants who, in Bowlby's (1982, 303) metaphor, yearn for "a haven of safety" when they are frightened; a number of biblical speakers describe Yahweh in the same way. Even adults who were abused in childhood may need to imagine the abusive parent as being an all-good and merciful god-figure in order to cope with their life-situation (Lasine 2002, 39–40).

There are certainly enough references to Yahweh as a haven of safety and nurturance in scripture to allow readers to configure his *gestalt* totally in terms of this image, relegating the "hard and tough" aspects of his personality to the background. It is more difficult to determine whether *all* Yahweh's traits and actions in his various roles can be understood in terms of one coherent personality.[3]

By describing God in terms of the patriarchal parent, husband, *and* king metaphors, the biblical narrators underscore the fact that in each case the humans' role is to be totally obedient to the power and control of the divine partner. If that condition is met, the child/wife/subject can expect to receive care and protection from the dominant father, husband, or king. If not, the outcome will be the opposite. In this version of the master/slave dialectic, the reward for submissiveness is caring, but at the cost of autonomy. As Benjamin (1988, 35–36; cf. 39, 70–71) points out, a human parent may be unable to tolerate their child's independence, let alone surrender to it. When this occurs, the child will either feel that the price of freedom is aloneness or that freedom is not possible. If the child does not want to do without approval, she must give up her will.

It is in his relations with his "special treasure" Israel (Exod. 19:5) and favorites like Job that Yahweh shows signs of being a father and husband with a specifically narcissistic personality (see Lasine 2001, 177–263). While the concept of narcissism has been understood and used in a wide variety of ways, it is consistently associated with some type of mirroring (Lasine 2002, 36–37). In the case of parents, this includes looking adoringly at the "the little man in the eye" (Deut. 32:10), the mirror supplied by their child. The little man (or woman; see Lam. 2:18; Ps. 17:8) is the image of oneself visible in another person's pupil when viewed from up close (Lasine 2002, 36–37nn2–4). If Yahweh's human children were allowed to get close enough to their divine parent to see themselves in his eyes, the texts we discussed earlier imply that they could not rely upon Yahweh to return their gaze with the smiling face of an adoring parent.

As King Yahweh's children, the Israelites are members of the "royal family." This creates the possibility that Yahweh might treat his children with the ambivalence, suspicion, and rivalry which characterize the attitude of a human monarch when he views members of the royal family as competing to succeed—or overthrow—him. It may also mean that the divine father may support *and* undermine special favorites like Job. In some cases, the double attitude manifests itself in support for kings such as David, who mirror him by being "after his own heart" and by undermining ones such as Saul, the flawed mirrors whom he eventually humiliates or smashes. A narcissistic royal father may seek the loyalty and submission he needs from his children by breaking (or removing) their spirit, by burdening them with feelings of guilt and inadequacy, or by keeping them cravenly dependent upon him. Whatever else being created "in the image and likeness" of this God may imply, it means that the divine father can view his children's bad behavior as reflecting negatively on himself. From the children's point of view, this kind of fathering can indeed be "hard to swallow."

Yahweh's children are consistently given reason to expect that if they succeed at mirroring their holy divine parent, they can rely upon Yahweh to treat his children/wife/subjects with *ḥesed* and compassion. If that expectation is disappointed, they can call upon Yahweh to "awake" and help them, for the sake of his *ḥesed* (Ps. 44:24, 27; cf. Ps. 35:23). What if that call is *not* answered? Should one keep calling or resign oneself to receiving no answer? For Freud, an acceptance of "Ananke," reality with all *its* "hard to swallow" aspects, requires both resignation and the surrender of father religion and childhood narcissism (1956, 98). Freud misses the fact that the Bible itself exposes the necessary harshness of reality for mortals whose divine father can act like an unreliable parent. Far from requiring a denial of Yahweh's existence, coping with this reality requires dealing with the fact that Yahweh is *all* that he is said and shown to be in the Bible. The young Freud once told a friend that no one has yet invented a lantern to illuminate God's "dark ways." During his long life, it never occurred to Freud that his ancestors' Bible might itself be that lantern.

NOTES

1. In effect, characters who utter the self-imprecation "*ḥālîlāh lî/lᵉkā*" (far be it from me/ you) stake their life on the accuracy of their self-knowledge or, as in the present case, their knowledge of another (Lasine 2012, 201–203).
2. Noll (1999, 34, 36–39) assumes that "sane" readers in Iron Age Palestine would have expected Yahweh to behave like a typical "dynastic patron deity."
3. Miles's (1996) well-known "biography" of God precludes the possibility of such coherence. Miles begins with the historical assumption that Yahweh's character is the "fusion" of several "ancient Semitic divinities" that "nomadic" Israel "met in its wanderings" (13, 20, 72, 327, 401). Because this fusion "is inherently unstable," at various points God has to engage in "a life-or-struggle to hold himself together in fusion" (197; cf. 21). As a result, God's character "is trapped within its contradictions," and clarity for readers disappears "beneath the welter of personalities and functions that are gathered together in him" (401, 408).

REFERENCES

Barton, John. 2001. *Joel and Obadiah: A Commentary*. Old Testament Library. Louisville, KY: Westminster John Knox.

Barton, John. 2010. "The Dark Side of God in the Old Testament." In *Ethical and Unethical in the Old Testament: God and Humans in Dialogue*, edited by K. J. Dell, 122–134. Library of Hebrew Bible/Old Testament Studies, 528. New York: T&T Clark.

Benjamin, Jessica. 1988. *The Bonds of Love: Psychoanalysis, Feminism, and the Problem of Domination*. New York: Pantheon.

Blumenthal, David R. 1993. *Facing the Abusing God: A Theology of Protest*. Louisville, KY: Westminster John Knox.

Bowlby, John. 1982. *Attachment*. 2nd ed. New York: Basic Books.

Brueggemann, Walter. 1982. *Genesis*. Interpretation: A Bible Commentary for Teaching and Preaching. Louisville, KY: John Knox.

Clines, David J. A. 1998. "Yahweh and the God of Christian Theology." In *On the Way to the Postmodern: Old Testament Essays 1967-1998*, vol. 2, 498–507. Sheffield, Yorkshire: Continuum.

Cooper, Alan J. 1993. "In Praise of Divine Caprice: The Significance of the Book of Jonah." In *Among the Prophets: Language, Image and Structure in the Prophetic Writings*, edited by P. R. Davies and D. J. A. Clines, 144–163. Journal for the Study of the Old Testament Supplement Series 144. Sheffield, Yorkshire: JSOT Press.

Crenshaw, James L. 1995. *Joel: A New Translation with Introduction and Commentary*. Anchor Bible 24C. New York: Doubleday.

Fewell, Danna Nolan. 2010. "A Broken Hallelujah: Remembering David, Justice, and the Cost of the House." In *The Fate of King David: The Past and Present of a Biblical Icon*, edited by Tod Linafelt, Timothy Beal, and Claudia V. Camp, 101–122. London: T&T Clark.

Fretheim, Terence E. 2010. *Exodus*. Interpretation: A Bible Commentary for Teaching and Preaching. Louisville, KY: Westminster John Knox.

Freud, Sigmund. 1928. *Die Zukunft einer Illusion*. 2nd ed. Leipzig: Internationaler Psychoanalytischer Verlag.

Freud, Sigmund. 1950. *Der Mann Moses und die monotheistische Religion*. In *Gesammelte Werke*, vol. 15, edited by Anna Freud, 103–246. London: Imago.

Freud, Sigmund. 1956. *Totem und Tabu: Einige Übereinstimmungen im Seelenleben der Wilden und der Neurotiker*. Frankfurt: Fischer Taschenbuch.

Freud, Sigmund. 1989. *Jugendbriefe an Eduard Silberstein, 1871-1881*. Edited by Walter Boehlich. Frankfurt: Fischer.

Gunn, David M., and Danna Nolan Fewell. 1993. *Narrative in the Hebrew Bible*. Oxford Bible Series. New York: Oxford University Press.

Hochman, Baruch. 1985. *Character in Literature*. Ithaca, NY: Cornell University Press

Hume, David. 2007. *A Dissertation on the Passions and the Natural History of Religion: A Critical Edition*. Edited by Tom L. Beauchamp. Oxford: Clarendon.

Jenson, Philip P. 2003. "Holiness in the Priestly Writings of the Old Testament." In *Holiness Past and Present*, edited by S. C. Barton, 93–121. London: T&T Clark.

Kaufman, Gordon D. 1981. *The Theological Imagination: Constructing the Concept of God*. Philadelphia, PA: John Knox.

Lasine, Stuart. 2001. *Knowing Kings: Knowledge, Power and Narcissism in the Hebrew Bible*. Semeia Studies 40. Atlanta, GA: Society of Bible Literature Press.

Lasine, Stuart. 2002. "Divine Narcissism and Yahweh's Parenting Style." *Biblical Interpretation* 10: 36–56.

Lasine, Stuart. 2010. "'Everything Belongs to Me': Holiness, Danger, and Divine Kingship in the Post-Genesis World." *Journal for the Study of the Old Testament* 35: 31–62.

Lasine, Stuart. 2012. *Weighing Hearts: Character, Judgment and the Ethics of Reading the Bible*. Library of Hebrew Bible/Old Testament Studies 568. New York: T&T Clark.

Miles, Jack. 1996. *God: A Biography*. New York: Vintage.

Morewedge, Carey K., and Michael E. Clear. 2008. "Anthropomorphic God Concepts Engender Moral Judgment." *Social Cognition* 26: 182–189.

Nielsen, Kirsten. 2005. "Metaphors and Biblical Theology." In *Metaphor in the Hebrew Bible*, edited by P. van Hecke, 263–273. Leuven: Peeters.

Noll, K. L. 1999. "Is There a Text in This Tradition? Readers' Response and the Taming of Samuel's God." *Journal for the Study of the Old Testament* 83: 31–51.

O'Brien, Julia M. 2008. *Challenging Prophetic Metaphor: Theology and Ideology in the Prophets*. Louisville, KY: Westminster John Knox.

Rogerson, John. 2003. "What Is Holiness?" In *Holiness Past and Present*, edited by S. C. Barton, 3–21. London: T&T Clark.

Steussy, Marti J. 2000. "The Problematic God of Samuel." In *Shall Not the Judge of All the Earth Do What Is Right?*, edited by D. Penchansky and P. L. Redditt, 127–161. Winona Lake, IN: Eisenbrauns.

Volz, Paul. 1924. *Das Dämonische in Jahwe*. Tübingen: Mohr (Paul Siebeck).

Whybray, Norman W. 1996. "The Immorality of God: Reflections on Some Passages in Genesis, Job, Exodus and Numbers." *Journal for the Study of the Old Testament* 72: 89–120.

PART IV

THE NATURAL, SOCIAL, AND CONCEPTUAL LANDSCAPES OF BIBLICAL STORY WORLDS

CHAPTER 41

....

READING THE LANDSCAPE
IN BIBLICAL NARRATIVE

....

NORMAN C. HABEL

I have deliberately entitled this study "Reading the Landscape." Over the years I have had a number of Australian Aboriginal elders as my mentors. They have no written texts comparable to the Bible. They do have, however, a remarkable capacity that has evolved over thousands of years, a capacity to "read" the landscape. This skill has enabled them to survive and celebrate life in many diverse environments, including the red desert in the center of Australia.

Reading the landscape has many dimensions—including place, presence, and person/ story. As these elders journeyed from season to season across the landscape in regions the respective communities called "country"; they read and remembered "places" where they could find water, native foods, and shelter. These were their "homes" on the journey through their landscape. Just as important were places where they could read a "Dreaming story" embedded in the shapes of the hills, in the rocks of a waterhole, or in a cluster of trees. Those stories linked them with the life (or lives) of the landscape, whether those lives were kangaroo, emu, or eucalypts. The stories also reflected the specific beliefs associated with a given location—or, in modern terms, their ideology of nature. A third level of reading in the landscape was that of "presence." Throughout the landscape they discerned the presence of life forces at sacred sites, locations where rites and secret business took place. The landscape was alive and children from an early age were taught to read the text of nature, enjoying rites of initiation at key moments as their reading skills developed.

Another important consideration in this exploration of the landscape is the emerging field of environmental hermeneutics, a field that claims to be somewhat different from the field of ecological hermeneutics with which I have been associated (Habel and Trudinger 2008). Environmental hermeneutics is concerned with "interpreting nature" or reading "the Book of Nature," employing a range of disciplines and hermeneutical approaches. Environmental hermeneutics addresses "questions of how environments are mediated in our intellectual, moral, and perceptual experience" (Clingerman et al. 2013, introduction). Elements of this approach will be reflected in the ensuing analysis of how the narrator interprets the environment and the perspective from which he reads the landscape in the narrative.

It is now generally recognized in narrative analysis that "the narrator controls the story's presentation" including the plot, the characters and the point of view (Gunn and Fewell 1993, 53; cf. Fokkelman 2000). Relatively few narrative analyses, however, pay close attention to how the narrator "controls" the environment by selecting, describing and characterizing the locations where the plot takes place. In an analysis of Genesis 11–22, for example, David Gunn and Danna Nolan Fewell (1993, chap. 4) refer to some of the locations in the plot, but the role the environment plays in the hands of the narrator tends to be ignored. Similarly, in Jan Fokkelman's (1991) *Narrative Art of Genesis*, the focus seems to be on the structure of the narrative plots, rather than on the "place" where the plot is constructed. In my analysis, I seek to complement these works by exploring how the narrator controls the environment, using the Abraham narratives as a point of departure and related narratives from Exodus and Numbers to illustrate the narrator's role.

EMPLACEMENT

Our understanding of place is vital to any reading of the environment. Forrest Clingerman (2010, 223) defines *emplacement* as "the mediation between the abstract concept of 'place,' the individual experiences we experience, and the interaction of our place in place." In my analysis, I approach the text with a question: How does the narrator read a given place? This necessarily involves asking whether the narrator seems to identify with a given place, names that place as an integral part of the environment, and interprets the significance of that place for the plot of the narrative. Or, as a correlative, does the narrator have the characters of the plot identify with a given place and interpret its significance for them as part of the environment?

"Emplacement" reflects an awareness of how we experience "place" in the specific places we have encountered. Our memories of places with which we connect reach back into our childhood, when we experienced place as the home to which we belonged and other "places" that evoke memory. I recall, as a boy, that place on the farm to which I and my family all belonged, including dogs, sheep, cows, roosters, and the kookaburra, who woke us each morning. Just as important were the numerous trees we climbed, living extensions of our "place" called home. "Place" is the locus where I belong within the total environment of my world. Emplacement is my reflection on, and connection with, that place.

It is useful to recognize that in biblical wisdom literature the word "place" (*maqom*) is a technical term for the locus of a phenomenon in the environment or nature. Dawn and darkness, for example, both have their "places" in the cosmos (Job 38:12, 19), as do all the phenomena that Job visits as the divine Sage takes him on a tour of the cosmos (Job 38–39). In Job 28 the question is asked whether wisdom, too, has a "place" in the cosmos. God, by reading the landscape of Earth, comes to know the "place" of wisdom (Job 28:23). "Place" is the locus, where a given element belongs in the design of nature (Habel 2003).

I begin my reflection on how the biblical narrator controls and interprets place with an analysis of the Abraham narrative of Genesis 12–14. The narrator relates how Abraham leaves Ur of the Chaldeans, lives for some time in Haran, and finally travels to Canaan at the instigation of YHWH. We notice at the outset that the locations outside Canaan are not presented as meaningful "places" that Abraham remembers. There is no description of or connection with these "places." A moment of displacement rather than emplacement is reflected in the narrator's allusion to these locations.

When Abraham arrives in Canaan, the narrator reports how Abraham travels through the land with his family and livestock to a specific location, the "place of Shechem" (Gen. 12:6). Abraham's emplacement at this place is linked to an oak tree, "the oak of Moreh." His belonging to that place is also expressed by his building an altar to Yʜwʜ, who promises Abraham that this land will one day belong to his offspring. This "place" will be their future "place," their home. This location is the first Abraham "place"!

The narrator then outlines how Abraham travels to several other locations in the land of Canaan, which is to be the future "place" for his progeny. In this way, the narrator connects Abraham to a range of locations that are linked to the destiny of his children. When Abraham and his family travel to Egypt to escape a famine, no place is named in Egypt, no description is given, and no link to the land is made. Abraham is displaced in Egypt, but when the household of Pharaoh is afflicted with plagues, Abraham returns to his home in the Negeb.

Abraham and Lot are described as prosperous in the land, moving from place to place and building an altar where appropriate. When strife arises between the herders of Abraham's stock and the herders of Lot's stock, Abraham mediates a settlement whereby Lot is free to select the area of the land he prefers for his place. The narrator has Lot read the landscape of the plain of Jordan and gets excited. He states that Lot saw the landscape as "well watered everywhere, like the garden of God, like the land of Egypt" (Gen. 13:10). The narrator suggests that Lot saw his "place" as a beautiful and fertile location to which he would soon belong. That this location, associated with Sodom, did not prove to be paradise does not negate the emplacement Lot is said to have experienced at this point in the plot. The reference to Egypt as fertile seems to be ironic, given the absence of any such description when Abraham lived in Egypt.

If we move ahead to a sequence in the Sodom narrative, we have the narrator portraying Abraham as an intercessor seeking to save Sodom (Gen 18:22–33). We note here that the narrator hears the response of Yʜwʜ to Abraham's plea as follows: "If I find at Sodom fifty righteous in the city, I will forgive the whole place for their sake" (Gen. 18:26). The focus is not ultimately on the people of Sodom, but the "whole place," the people and the environment. When Abraham departs at the end of his intercession he is said to return to "his place," that location where he belongs in the land of Canaan.

In another event of the Sodom cycle, Abraham, living in his place among the oaks of Mamre, is ready to take the 318 men of his household to rout the alien forces that had invaded Canaan (Gen. 14:13–16). When he returns, Abraham is narrated as having met with the king of Sodom in the valley of Shaveh, which is interpreted as "the king's valley," clearly a place of significance. Just as significant is Abraham's connection with Salem and his celebrations with Melchizedek, the priest-king of Salem, who blesses Abraham in the name of El Elyon, maker of heaven and Earth. Here, Abraham is portrayed as recognizing El, the God of Canaan, by offering tithes to that deity (Gen. 14:17–20). Abraham not only recognizees Canaan as the domain of his place, but also El as the traditional deity of that place.

In the preceding chapters, several references have been made to the fact that the Canaanites were then in the land. The Canaanites are not depicted here as enemies, but as neighbors, and in Genesis 14, as partners in defense of the land and in recognition of its deity. Some years ago, in my book *The Land Is Mine*, I highlighted how the narrator depicts Canaan as a host country:

> Significantly, the land seems open to migrants; there is no mention of any barriers set up by the inhabitants. Abraham migrates, it would seem, to a friendly and inviting land. Canaan is depicted as a peaceful place to live, a welcome host country for immigrants and settlers. Abraham moves without restraint through the length and breadth of the land. (Habel 1995, 118)

The narrator of the initial Abraham stories commences with the hero of the narrative coming to a land of peace to find a place where he belongs. In this narrative Abraham is happily "emplaced" in the "place" which is to become his home and that of his descendants.

DISPLACEMENT

The Exodus narrative reflects a very different relationship with the environment, including descriptions that might be designated as displacement. From the beginning of the narrative, the people of God are displaced, far from the place where they are destined to belong, the "place" of the patriarchs and matriarchs. The language of displacement throughout this cycle varies from one situation to another, from alienation and desolation to bold intervention.

After Israel's initial prosperity in Egypt, the people are subjected to hard labor. Their place is described in terms of "mortar and bricks," and "work in the field." In frustration the Pharaoh commands that every male child born be thrown into the Nile. The Nile, a symbol of rich life in Egypt, is the symbol of death for God's people.

The opening episode of the Moses's cycle illustrates how the process of dis-placement and alienation is reflected in the narrator's description of the environment. The first place where the infant Moses lives is described as "a basket made of bulrushes and daubed with bitumen and pitch." The child is then placed "among the reeds at the river's bank" (Exod. 2.3). After being discovered and adopted by Pharaoh's daughter, the child is given a name that identifies him with his initial environment. He is named "Moses," which is interpreted to mean "out of the water" (Exod. 2:10).

No description is given of Moses's life in the palace of the Pharaoh, a place far from his own people. After identifying with, and being challenged by, his own people, he flees to a place that is even more distant from his people and the land of his people. He is located by a well in the land of Midian, a well used by the daughters of the priest of Midian. The priest rewards Moses for defending his daughters and gives one of them, Zipporah, to Moses to be his wife. Again, Gershom, their name for the child, reflects Moses's alien relationship with the environment: "I have become a sojourner (ger) in a foreign land" (Exod. 2:22).

In this alien environment, totally displaced from his own people and place, the narrator has Moses discover a new dimension of the environment: presence in place. The narrator describes the location of this experience as "the west side of the wilderness" and "Horeb, the mountain of God" (Exod. 3:1). While tending his flocks at this location, Moses reads the landscape; he sees a burning bush that is not consumed by flames. The narrator explains the nature of this burning bush as the "angel of YHWH" appearing in the flame (Exod. 3:2). While interpreters may wish to focus on the famous words of God emanating from the bush, this text points to an environmental phenomenon that is found several times in such biblical narratives. "Place" or "components of place" can be more than location. They can be revelations of "presence" in a wide variety of modes.

Here "presence" finds its environmental place in a bush out in the wilderness near a mountain. Moses also discovers that "the place on which you are standing is holy ground" (Exod. 3.5). The focus is not only on God's presence, but also on the immediate environment. Even if God's people or representative are displaced, God, it seems, may reveal a "presence" among them in the wilderness, even in specific "places."

Upon returning to Egypt, Moses announces the promise of God to the people of God: "I will bring you to the land which I swore to give to Abraham, to Isaac and to Jacob" (Exod. 6:8). The narrative cycle of the ten plagues outlines the way God is portrayed as affecting this promise. The narrator has no problem in describing this action of God in all its gory detail—abuse of the environment time after time. The "place" of bondage is apparently not to be described in terms of its beauty or bounty. No empathy or identification with the environment happens in the place of displacement.

Some scholars suggest that the plagues in Egypt actually reflect natural environmental disasters. Greta Hort (1957, 1958), for example, espoused a theory based on

> the infrequent occurrence of an unusually heavy rainfall in the Highlands of Ethiopia! The annual rise of the river that starts in July and reaches its peak in mid-September is said, on rare occasions, to result in catastrophe rather than fertility. The soil in the basin of the Blue Nile and its tributary, the Atbara, is tropical red earth. This red sediment emerges along the Nile when floods from the Highlands pour downstream and discolour the waters so that they look much like blood. (summary from Habel 2009, 17)

The narrator, however, emphasizes that the abuse of the environment was a deliberate act of God. Neither the narrator nor the characters in the plot shows any empathy for the environment in the place of displacement. As I have written elsewhere,

> The waters of the Nile are a life-giving force, a massive eco-system that sustains both humans and non-humans along the length of the Nile. The waters of the Nile are the life-blood of several countries. The waters of the Nile flow for some 3,500 miles with a watershed that is estimated to be about a million acres. God, however, informs Moses that God will "strike the water of the Nile," an act designed to impart a curse (cf. 7.25). The symbol of that curse is blood. The life-blood of the land is turned into blood that is shed, the symbol of death. The waters of life can no longer sustain life. Instead of water, there is blood "throughout all the land of Egypt." The land is like a bleeding corpse. (Habel 2009, 17)

The narrator in this section of the Exodus narrative views the environment of Egypt as one of total alienation. There is no positive presence of God, only destruction of the landscape called Egypt. The orientation of the promise to return God's people to their place in Canaan seems to justify as valid the narrator's description of a plagued environment in Egypt.

The dramatic crossing of the Reed Sea represents a climactic departure from the land of displacement. Once again, God is portrayed as manipulating the environment to achieve specific ends. The location of the experience is said to be "by the sea." The response of the Pharaoh was expected to be that "they are entangled in the land; the wilderness has shut them in" (Exod. 14.3). The crossing is presented as escaping from one wilderness into another. When the army of Pharaoh appears, the people of God read the landscape, see the Egyptian army, and attack Moses: "Are there no graves in Egypt that you have take us away to die in the wilderness" (Exod. 14.). The land of displacement is apparently more desirable than the wilderness, a dimension of the plot that is to be tested in the journeys ahead.

As they travel, God is depicted as controlling unnatural phenomena in the environment to protect the people: a pillar of cloud that moves between the people and the Egyptians. The actual crossing is described by the narrator as the result of a strong east wind from God that blows all night, making the sea dry land and dividing the waters. Once again, the environment is manipulated for the benefit of God's people. The outcome is that the "people of Israel walked on dry land through the sea, the waters being a wall to them on their right hand and on their left." The natural order of things in the environment is reversed. Sea becomes dry land. Waters that flow stand like the walls of a hallway. The crossing from a land of displacement to a wilderness that promises re-placement is presented by the narrator as evidence of a divine control of the environment that is other than natural.

RE-PLACEMENT

From the beginning of the people of Israel's journey home to their place, a journey anticipating re-placement, the story is one of repeated frustration. The wilderness in which the people of God travel is not described as a place of wonder and majesty. Yet amid the wilderness they discover places like Elim, where there are "twelve springs of water and seventy palm trees" (Exod. 15:27). As they journey, the refrain is repeated: the land of Egypt was a better place than "this wilderness" (Exod. 16:3). Bread from heaven, however, does not really cause the people to feel at home in the wilderness. Negativity toward the wilderness in the biblical record is a perspective that scholars have often recognized (Leal 2005), yet the narrator identifies this negativity as an unacceptable attitude of people supposedly on their way home.

A potentially new relationship between the people and their environment takes place when, at the instigation of Aaron, they read the landscape. As they look toward the wilderness, they behold the *kabod YHWH*, the vibrant fire presence of God, enveloped in a cloud (Exod. 16:10). There are several striking features of this unique environmental surprise. First, it is represented as a visible moving cloud that envelops a divine presence. Second, this presence does not appear as a dramatic revelation from the heavens, but emerges from the wilderness. Third, this cloud presence seems to surprise no one, even though this is the beginning of the cloud's long and dramatic journey with God's people through the wilderness and beyond. The presence is an integral part of the wilderness even though it may later be linked to a specific "place" in Canaan. Presence may emerge from the landscape, an experience to which my Aboriginal mentors would happily testify.

A pivotal moment in the wilderness narrative happens on the third new moon after the people of Israel have left the land of Egypt. "They came into the wilderness of Sinai; where they camped before the mountain" (Exod. 19:1–2). The journey home to re-placement was portrayed as camping in one wilderness after another. In this wilderness, however, there is a mountain, and, as the people read the landscape, they behold thunder, lightning, and a thick cloud over the mountain along with a trumpet blast that makes the people tremble with fear. Then Moses takes the people of God to the foot of the thundering, quaking mountain that is wrapped in smoke (Exod. 19:16–17).

On that mountain, the "presence" that previously had emerged from the desert, now erupts with fire within the cloud covering the mountain. Once again, the wilderness environment is the medium of divine revelation en route to the re-placement of the people of God, but in this case the experience is much more dramatic and overwhelming. Nevertheless, Moses merges with the landscape as he enters the cloud of divine presence on the mountain, where he receives the two tablets of stone and hears again the promise of emplacement in Canaan (Exod. 23:23–33). This narrator, however, unlike the narrator of the Abraham narratives, views the re-placement of God's people as a violent eviction of the Canaanites who had once befriended Abraham. The Canaanites "shall not dwell in the land" because they are now viewed as a snare, not as a neighbor (Exod. 23.33).

When Moses again climbs the mountain, the *kabod YHWH*, the vibrant presence in the landscape, is described as a fire cloud, a "devouring fire" enveloped in cloud. The mountain is a specific "place" in the environment where the presence "settles." Yet that same presence fills the tabernacle and leads the people through the wilderness (Exod. 40:34). It is perhaps significant that the dream of re-placement of those journeying through the wilderness is denied. The narrator has God declaring that "none of those who have seen my presence *(kabod)* shall see the land I swore to give to their ancestors" (Num. 14:22–23).

Prior to this divine declaration, this narrator has the people camped in the wilderness of Paran, at which point God tells Moses to send spies into the land of Canaan. After the spies have read the landscape of Canaan during their forty day visit, they announce that the land "flows with milk and honey, and this is its fruit" (Num 14.27). Most of their report, however, is about the people living in the land. A second report by a second group among the spies exaggerates the nature of the people of the land and describes them as giants, beside whom the spies felt like grasshoppers (Num. 14:33). Perhaps the most damning language employed by the narrator is found in the second report of the spies: Canaan is "a land that devours its inhabitants" (Num. 14:32). The promised land has been transformed in the mind of the people, according to the narrator, into a land that is just the opposite of a land "flowing with milk and honey."

Once again the people long for Egypt (Num. 14:4) even though Moses and Aaron encourage them to enter the promised land and enjoy the promised emplacement. Once again the presence of the *kabod YHWH* appears and threatens a disobedient people at the very border of the promised land (Num. 14:10–11). God eventually forgives the people, but none of them will enjoy the land. Displacement will be their fate until they die, and the men who gave the unfavorable report will die from a plague. Finally, all the many "places" in the wilderness are named as a testimony to their rebellious times on the way to re-placement (Num. 33).

Another narrator adds a postscript to the time of anticipated re-placement. Moses climbs to the top of Mt. Nebo, where God allows Moses to read the landscape of Canaan and see the places where the people will find re-placement in the promised land—from Gilead as far as Zoar, including the city of palms (Deut. 34:1–3). In his dying moments Moses is finally "placed" in his home—albeit at a distance—and Joshua is given the task of re-placing the next generation of God's people. By reading the landscape of Canaan Moses returns home!

CONCLUSION

While my analyses of biblical narrative is necessarily selective, I believe they demonstrate how a series of narrators have read the landscape of Canaan, Egypt, and the wilderness in relation to the land promised as the "place" for the people of God. What is remarkable, it seems to me, is how editors (supernarrators?) have incorporated this diverse array of narratives, each with its own control of the environment, and united them in the grand narrative of the Pentateuch, which traces the "places" of God's people from emplacement in Canaan, through displacement in Egypt along journeys toward re-placement, journeys in which most of the Pentateuch is said to have been revealed. The "places" of God's revelations are located primarily outside the promised land; yet the promise Canaan as the chosen "place" is an essential structuring theme of the overarching narrative of the Pentateuch.

References

Clingerman, Forrest. 2010. "Wilderness as the Place between Philosophy and Theology: Questioning Martin Drenthen on the Otherness of Nature." *Environmental Values* 19(2): 211–232.

Clingerman, Forrest, Brian Treanor, Martin Drenthen, and David Utsler, eds. 2013. *Interpreting Nature: The Emerging Field of Environmental Hermeneutics*. New York: Fordham University Press.

Fokkelman, J. P. 1991. *Narrative Art in Genesis*. 2nd ed. Sheffield, Yorkshire: JSOT Press.

Fokkelman, J. P. 2000. *Reading Biblical Narrative. An Introductory Guide*. Philadelphia, PA: Westminster John Knox.

Gunn, David, and Danna Nolan Fewell. 1993. *Narrative in the Hebrew Bible*. Oxford: Oxford University Press.

Hort, Greta. 1957 "The Plagues of Egypt." *Zeitschrift for alttestamentliche Wissenschaft* 69: 85–103.

Hort, Greta. 1958 "The Plagues of Egypt." *Zeitschrift for alttestamentliche Wissenschaft* 70: 48–59.

Habel, Norman. 1995. *The Land Is Mine: Six Biblical Land Ideologies*. Minneapolis, MN: Fortress Press.

Habel, Norman C. 2003. "The Implications of God Discovering Wisdom in Earth." In *Job 28: Cognition in Context*, edited by Ellen van Wolde, 281–298. Leiden: Brill.

Habel, Norman. 2009. *An Inconvenient Text: Is a Green Reading of the Bible Possible*. Adelaide, AUS: ATM Press.

Habel, Norman, and Peter Trudinger, eds. 2008. *Exploring Ecological Hermeneutics*. Atlanta, GA: Society of Biblical Literature.

Leal, Robert Barry. 2005. "Negativity towards the Wilderness in the Biblical Record." *Ecotheology* 10: 382–399.

CHAPTER 42

....

SUSTENANCE AND SURVIVAL IN BIBLICAL NARRATIVE

....

JENNIFER L. KOOSED

EVERYBODY eats, every day, often several times a day. Obtaining and preparing food establishes the primary rhythms of daily life. This is true today, but the centrality of food was even greater in times and places without our modern food industry, mechanized production, and complex distribution systems. In ancient Israel and early Judaism, food production and preparation structured lives, and what one did in the process was determined by gender and class status and sometimes even marked by ethnic and religious identity. Food has never just been something one eats; rather, it is a comprehensive social and cultural code. Consequently, food also serves to structure narrative, shape characterization, and add layers of symbolic signification to story. In the Bible, the drama of the first few chapters revolves around proper versus improper eating, and the final book portrays God as a lamb sacrificed for the Passover meal. Between picking and tasting the forbidden fruit and slaughtering and eating God, a whole host of food-related plots, characters, and images proliferate. Food is, indeed, a central element of biblical narrative.

To read stories of sustenance and survival, it is necessary to take a multidisciplinary approach that draws on the natural sciences, the social sciences, history, literary methods of reading, material criticism, and archaeology. Attention to the ways biblical societies turned plants and animals into food is an aspect of social-scientific criticism. Social-scientific criticism attends to the assumptions about cultural practices that lie behind every narrative. To give examples from English literature, how often does a Victorian writer stop to explain the elaborate choreography of dinner time, when age, gender, and class are all performed with painstaking precision? There may be sufficient clues in the story itself to indicate these cultural realities to a careful reader, or additional research on eating practices in Victorian England may be necessary. Understanding the cultural language of food is particularly important when the food is used as a symbol or to further plot or characterization. For ancient Israel, early Judaism, and early Christianity, sometimes the Bible itself gives sufficient information, but understanding is often enhanced through archaeological and anthropological research on early Middle Eastern food practices. Studies of human, floral and faunal remains, climate and soil, and even new DNA research can illuminate the eating habits of biblical peoples.

Social-scientific criticism focuses on questions common to sociologists and anthropologists and attempts to understand biblical cultures using archaeology and cross-cultural comparisons. The first serious and systematic studies of foodways emerged in anthropology because anthropologists immediately recognized that understanding food is essential to understanding culture (Counihan and van Esterik 1997, 1–2). Attention to the environment (location, physical geography, climate, native plants and animals, and soil composition and quality) is also important. The way a people eats is shaped by the environmental opportunities and constraints determined by where the people live. The environment also contributes to a society's general culture and worldview. As Daniel Hillel, an environmental scientist who has researched the biblical world writes,

> The environment is not merely a passive and static stage on which cultural evolution takes place, but, indeed, a set of dynamic processes inducing that evolution. At the outset, the environment conditions the material life of a society. Reciprocally, a society's responses to the opportunities, challenges, constraints, and hazards presented by the environment tend to modify the environment. Thus a society's interaction with the environment inevitably affects its values and attitudes—indeed, its entire worldview. (Hillel 2006, 11)

The foodways of any culture are affected by, and in turn affect, the environment. Environment and culture, in all of their aspects, are inextricably intertwined.

Emerging in anthropology and grounded in understandings of the environment, the interest in and study of food soon overtook other fields, such as history, literature, philosophy, and religious studies. However, food studies have intersected with biblical studies only rarely and at first such interventions were actually performed by anthropologists (Douglas 1966, on Leviticus; Feeley-Harnik 1981, on the Last Supper). The first volume by biblical scholars devoted to food in the Bible was published in 1999, *Food and Drink in the Biblical Worlds*, edited by Athalya Brenner and Jan Willem van Henten. And yet, almost a decade later, Nathan MacDonald's two volumes on food in the Hebrew Bible (both published in 2008) note that little more had been done in the intervening years. As MacDonald states, "There is scarcely a page in the Old Testament where food is not mentioned" (MacDonald 2008a, 2); yet there have been only a few comprehensive approaches—archaeological, anthropological, or even literary—to the food in the Hebrew Bible. The same can be said of the New Testament.

It may be evident why food studies is important for understanding the cultures of ancient Israel, early Judaism, and early Christianity and thus a proper object of archaeological and historical investigation. But food studies is also important to literary readings of the scriptures. Reading is an act of imagination and empathy in which we travel into the world of the story. Without assuming a direct and transparent relationship between the text and the peoples that created it, the story world is constructed out of the materials available to the author(s). The author in fact assumes that the reader shares a certain cultural background and knowledge. Yet, without adequate knowledge of the cultural backgrounds, multiple layers of meaning may be completely lost on the contemporary reader.

The primary context for biblical writers was agrarian. The vast majority of the population of Israel, from the Iron Age to the Greco-Roman era, was involved in food production (King and Stager 2001, 8). Through much of its history, Israel was a subsistence economy. Much of an individual's time and energy was spent producing and preparing food, and this preoccupation is reflected in biblical texts. In the Hebrew Bible, *akhal* ("to eat") is the thirteenth most frequently used verb (appearing 806 times). In the New Testament, *esthein* is also a common verb. Even though a large period of time exists between the writing of the first and the last biblical stories, from the earliest songs of the Hebrew Bible to the last of the epistles in the New Testament (dating biblical texts is always speculative and sometimes contentious, but the span of biblical literature is at least one thousand years), little changed in terms of diet or food production technologies.[1] Recently, through archaeology, attention to everyday life and material culture, scholars have been able to recover much of what biblical authors assumed about how people lived and how they filled their time, time which was largely spent producing, preparing, and consuming food. And the primary food was bread.

Cereal products made up between 53 percent and 75 percent of a person's daily caloric intake (MacDonald 2008b, 19). "Bread" (in Hebrew, *lehem*; in Greek, *artos*) is a frequently used noun in the Hebrew Bible (296 times) and the New Testament. In Hebrew and in Greek, "bread" is also synonymous with "food." The phrase "to eat bread" in Hebrew also means "to eat food," and it is used so frequently—fifty-three times—that Brenner and van Henten argue that "it merits the status of a primary term" (Brenner and van Henten 1999, xii). Today, bread is so simple and plentiful that we overlook it in the literature and barely think twice about it in our own lives. Yet each one of the basic ingredients of bread—flour, yeast, salt— represents a revolution in the human understanding and manipulation of nature:

> Bread is the most everyday and familiar of foods, the sturdy staff of life on which hundreds of generations have leaned for sustenance. It also represents a truly remarkable discovery, a lively pole on which the young human imagination may well have vaulted forward in insight and inspiration. For our prehistoric ancestors it would have been a startling sign of the natural world's hidden potential for being transformed, and their own ability to shape natural materials to human desires. (McGee 2004, 516)

How did anyone discover that the seed of certain wild grasses could be harvested, ground, combined with water and other ingredients, and then baked or fried? The transformation of grain to bread must have seemed like a minor miracle to the earliest people.

CREATION AND THE CURSE

The centrality of food and food production with an emphasis on bread is evident from the beginning, in the creation narratives that open the book of Genesis. In Genesis 1, creation climaxes with the making of male and female human beings (1:26–27). The people are then commanded to be "fruitful and multiply" and given "dominion" over all other creatures (1:28). As the final ordering act of God, all living creatures are given plants to eat (1:29). Instructions for eating constitute the denouement of the drama, the last of God's spoken words. Bread has not yet entered the picture, nor has meat (even for the other animals), but these food stuffs soon follow as the harmony envisioned in this first story is broken in the next.

In Genesis 2–3, how one eats establishes the boundaries between nature and culture and between human and animal, as well as between human and the divine. In Genesis 2, the man and the woman presumably eat in ways indistinguishable from the other animals—they are all given the fruits of the field. They are forbidden two fruit trees, however, and these trees represent that which is in the purview of God: knowledge and immortality (2:16–17). Hence, there is a relationship between divinity and certain kinds of eating. When the man and woman disobey the commandment to not eat of the fruit of the tree of knowledge of good and evil, they immediately move out of the realm of the other animals, for they alone realize that they are "naked," and they are ashamed (Gen. 3:7). The man and the woman have moved from animals toward the divine, but the transformation is not complete. Before they have a chance to eat the other forbidden fruit and gain immortality, they are cursed and exiled from the garden. These actions by God prevent the man and woman from attaining divine status and thus permanently entrap them between animality and divinity.

Food mediates the boundaries between human, animal, and God. Proper eating maintains these categories, and forbidden eating transgresses the boundaries and confuses the categories. Food is the symbol of the confounding of these basic categories because food is the way we actually do cross the boundaries, a transgression in which we participate daily. Eating is the process by which we take in the other and digestion is the process by which we transform the other into the self. Categories are transgressed and then erased. Our very lives are dependent upon this transgression and transformation. In the creation stories, order is established and confounded, life is given and taken, through eating. This perpetual process is at the core of the human condition.

The curses further establish the new relationships between the environment, plants, animals, God, the man and the woman, and define their new material conditions. All the curses entail new ways of eating. The snake eats the dust of the earth (Gen. 3:14) and is forever locked in mutual enmity with human beings (3:15). The woman will suffer to bring others into the world and will still labor alongside her husband in the fields; she will be unable to avoid this situation because her own body will betray her through its sexual desire (following Meyers's translation of 3:16; Meyers 1988, 95–121; see also Stone 2005, 42–43). The ground itself is cursed—no longer easily and abundantly fruitful, it must be worked in order to produce a meager harvest. In this final curse, agriculture is born: "cursed is the ground because of you; in toil you shall eat of it all the days of your life; thorns and thistles it shall bring forth for you; and you shall eat the plants of the field. By the sweat of your face you shall eat bread." (Gen. 3:17b–19a NRSV). The curse, which is foundational to human history and culture, is the curse of bread production.

The curses not only establish new foodways, but also the commensurate changes to gender roles. Contemporary readers are in danger of projecting their own understanding of traditional gender roles and power dynamics onto these curses, especially since there are contemporary faith communities that still use the curses to justify their own ideal hierarchical gender relations. However, attention to bread can help us avoid some of the pitfalls of projection. Not only do bread and other cereal products make up far less of the daily caloric intake of industrial societies (and most of today's Jewish and Christian communities are in industrial societies), but women rarely make the bread for the family. At most, an occasional loaf is baked, but this requires only a fraction of the labor involved in the bread production of early agricultural societies. Today, how one gets one's bread plays almost no role in establishing identity and relationship. In the biblical world, it was one of the primary markers of both and was particularly instrumental in the power dynamics of the family.

Even before the curses, women's pivotal role in ancient Israel's foodways is reflected in the narrative: in Genesis 3, the woman hands the fruit to the man. In the ancient Israelite household, women made and distributed the food. As opposed to our current idea of the family "breadwinner" (a role that did not exist in Israel because it was largely a subsistence economy, with cottage industries that operated out of the home), the "bread producer" played a key role.

And once the seeds were separated from the chaff, women took over bread production (Meyers 2003, 39–40). First, women ground the grain into flour between two basalt stones, a very time-consuming activity. Next, they transformed the flour into food by baking, frying, boiling—there were a number of different types of preparation for making the family's daily bread. Finally, women distributed the bread to the members of the family. As Carol Meyers writes,

> Thinking about power usually means examining formal institutions, but in traditional societies informal power is the concomitant of the control of economic activities and is often just as important, if not more important, than formal relations of power. That is, issues of household power in pre-modern agrarian societies are typically resource based and involve labor output, expertise in technologies, and control of foodstuffs. (Meyers 2003, 42)

The women in the households of Israel wielded considerable informal power through their control of bread production and distribution.[2]

The expulsion from Eden is an ambivalent event. On the one hand, it is certainly portrayed as punishment by the deity. The life described or prescribed by the curses is a life of brokenness—the Edenic harmony between human, animal, earth, and God no longer obtains. On the other hand, life as we know it begins with this expulsion. Human history—the good and the bad—would not exist if we were all still running around a garden ignorant and naked in a state of arrested development. The agricultural revolution is also an ambivalent event. Beginning some twelve thousand years ago, our Neolithic ancestors first discovered the power of seeds and their ability to control them. The first seeds to be domesticated were the cereal grains, alongside some legumes. Changing food ways, from hunting and gathering to growing and harvesting, also necessitated profound changes in social organization and intellectual knowledge:

> The need arose for planning the sowing and the distribution of the harvests, for anticipating seasonal changes before they occurred, for organizing the work, and for keeping records. Some of the earliest known writing and arithmetical systems, dating from at least 5,000 years ago, are devoted to the accounting of grain and livestock. So the culture of the fields encouraged the culture of the mind. (McGee 2004, 452)

The agricultural revolution is credited with the development of settled communities, population expansion (more children are needed in agricultural contexts than in nomadic ones because their labor is necessary and their vulnerabilities are less of a liability), the beginnings of scientific observation and categorization, and writing. And yet, the agricultural revolution came at a price. Although less predictable and reliable, hunter-gatherer societies eat a richer and more varied diet and thus are healthier. Hunter-gather societies also have simpler and therefore more egalitarian social organizations; agricultural communities develop more social stratification and economic disparity. Bread is indeed blessing and curse.

RUTH AND A CRISIS

The obtaining of grain is a complicated, labor-intensive process that requires the coordination and cooperation of a whole society, men and women, young and old, rich and poor.

Both societal structures and agricultural technologies must reach a critical level of sophistication in order for bread to be widely available. Because bread production takes a village, one's status in society dictated one's role. In the Bible, such roles and responsibilities are most evident in the book of Ruth, a story set in the "House of Bread" (Bethlehem), a narrative structured by the harvests, with a plot driven by the hunger for fertility, both human and agricultural. What Ruth and Naomi do in order to obtain their food is dictated by their economic and gender status, and their final reintegration into Bethlehem's kinship structures is also an integration into the village's foodways. The backstory of Ruth may be famine, but the crisis of food that compels the plot is a crisis of bread production (see, further, Koosed 2011). Alone, Ruth and Naomi could not produce their own bread.

Ruth and Naomi arrive in Bethlehem at the beginning of the barley harvest (Ruth 1:22). This is not an incidental detail; it contributes to both characterization and plot. In terms of the former, the character of barley reflects the characterization of the two widows. Barley does not need rich soil and a moderate climate to grow; rather, it is more salt resistant than other grains and requires less water. It can grow where and when other grains cannot, which means it is less expensive to produce. It is also not the most desirable grain for breadmaking. Barley produces coarse flour that lacks sufficient gluten to make a high-rising dough. Consequently, it was the grain of the poor across the ancient Near East. It was also frequently used as food for animals (King and Stager 2001, 94; MacDonald 2008b, 20–21). Ruth and Naomi enact their class status in the fields. The first grain mentioned in their story, and the first grain they will eat, is the grain of the poor.

The women's arrival at the beginning of the barley harvest also contributes to the plot. To grow grain, one must own sufficient land and have access to sufficient resources (both human and material capital) to plant, tend, and harvest. Unlike vegetables, grains must be processed before they are edible, and this also requires labor and capital. Naomi may own land (as is revealed toward the end of the book, in Ruth 4:3), but she lacks the money to buy seed and the labor necessary to produce grain. Even if Naomi had had seed and labor, the two women have arrived at the wrong time—at the beginning of the harvest. Their poverty, lack of capital, and arrival out of season create a scenario that leaves only one option for obtaining the grains necessary to produce bread: gleaning.

Ruth goes to the fields to glean (2:2). Those with wealth enough to own their own fields were required by Israelite law to allow the poor of the community to follow behind the harvesters and pick up what they left behind. Harvesters were also required to leave the corners of the fields unharvested, also to give to the poor, the "alien," widows, and orphans (Lev. 19:9; 23:22; Deut. 24:19). Gleaning marks Ruth as one of the poor, an alien, and a widow. Although women did participate in the harvest (harvesting could require all available able-bodied workers in a community), women in the field were also subject to harassment, possibly even rape. A paid woman working in a group was not as vulnerable as a poor woman working alone. Boaz leaves instructions that Ruth may glean and that she is to stay with his female workers to avoid any harassment (2:8–9). Gleaning exposes Ruth as a poor and vulnerable woman in her community, in need of protection that is both wealthy and male. Boaz performs his gender and class when he permits her to glean in his fields, gives her extra food and privileges (2:14–16), and orders others not to molest her. He provides the grain so that she can make the bread.

The narrative moves from the barley harvest to the end of the wheat harvest (2:23). While the harvests are in progress, gleaning is a viable option for the two indigent widows. Once the wheat harvest ends, they must live only on what they were able to save from Ruth's gleaning.

Naomi determines that Ruth's future is not secure enough and schemes to provide more for her daughter-in-law and, by extension, herself. Again, the rhythms of the harvest establish the rhythms of the plot: Naomi sends Ruth to the threshing room floor (3:1–3).

Threshing and winnowing the harvested grasses was one of the most difficult labors of grain processing. The bound sheaves would be gathered up and taken to the threshing floor. There, the threshing was aided by both tools and animal labor: studs made of basalt or flint were fitted into wooden boards, and these threshing sledges were dragged over the grasses by oxen or donkeys. After the grasses had been broken up by the threshing, they were thrown up into the air so that the wind could separate the grain from the chaff (King and Stager 2001, 89). The labor of threshing and winnowing was performed primarily by the men of the community. And, if the evidence from Ruth is any indication, the hard work was often accompanied by a celebratory (or maybe compensatory) party.

The time of threshing certainly provides the opportunity for Ruth to approach Boaz, but the setting also is rich in symbolic import as well. Ancient cultures, including Israel, regarded agriculture as a divine gift. For polytheistic religions, the deities associated with agriculture were also associated with fertility in general: the intermingling of seed, rain, and soil produced the crops, and such intermingling was often conceived in erotic terms (Plate 2014, 163). Even in biblical literature, Yahweh is a powerful fertility God—over and over God's beneficence is conceived as God's giving of rain and food (for just a few examples, see Lev. 26:4; Deut. 8:7–10; 32:13–14; Job 5:10; Zech. 10:1). God bestows fertility to both land and women throughout the Bible; in Ruth, in fact, these are the only two actions attributed directly to the deity (1:6; 4:13). In Ruth, the plot reaches its climax on the threshing-room floor, a space charged with erotic tension, where God's blessings are invoked. Ruth leaves at the break of dawn, her skirts full of Boaz's seed (3:17). The denouement comes when Boaz barters fields with Mr. So-and-So to secure the right to marry Ruth; they marry, and she conceives their son. Agricultural fertility and human fertility come together. Ruth is fully integrated into Israelite foodways, and her crisis of bread production comes to an end.

JESUS AND THE END

Ruth returns to the biblical story in the Gospel of Matthew when her name is listed in Jesus's genealogy (Matt. 1:5). According to Matthew, Jesus is a descendent of Ruth's and was also born in Bethlehem (Matt. 2:1; Luke does not explicitly name Ruth in his genealogy, but he also has Jesus as born in Bethlehem and a descendent of Ruth [Luke 2:4–6; 4:32]). For some first-century Jesus followers, it was essential that the Christ be born in Bethlehem because of the village's association with David. Attention to bread indicates that the desire to link Jesus to Ruth and Bethlehem may have other facets as well. Jesus is not seen growing, harvesting, winnowing, grinding, or baking bread. Jesus has no role in the production of bread; rather, Jesus *is* the bread. He is the one who nourishes and provides sustenance to the people, signaled by his birth in this most evocative of towns.

In addition to being the only Gospels that place Jesus's birth in Bethlehem, Matthew and Luke are also the only Gospels that claim Jesus was conceived when Mary was still a virgin (Matt. 1:18; Luke 1:31–35). Virginal conception and birth in the House of Bread evoke an intricate web of associations that would have been particularly resonant with people (whether

Gentile or Jew) living in polytheistic religious contexts. The stories of the conception of Jesus may be stripped of any explicitly erotic material, but they otherwise follow the pattern of any number of stories of divine-human intercourse from the polytheistic traditions, particularly prominent in Greco-Roman traditions. The divine-man Jesus, then, functions like any number of dying-and-rising gods and goddesses (examples include Tammuz, Adonis, and Persephone)—again, all associated with agricultural fertility. The dying-and-rising deity provides ways to think about the cycles of the natural world, the cycle of the seasons, as well as the cycle of a seed that is seemingly dead but that once buried in the soil will rise again as life-giving food. In the case of Jesus, he dies and then rises as the Bread of Life.

As God's consort and virgin mother of a dying-and-rising God, Mary also participates in the divinity of fertility. Early depictions of Mary borrow from the iconography of several goddesses, including Ceres, goddess of agriculture (Plate 2014, 164), and at least one early Christian sect, later condemned as a heresy, honored her by offering bread sacrifices. As Stephen Benko writes about this tradition in his study of Mary, "In the sacred mystery of bread, every woman could view herself as possessing a portion of the creative power of the gods, for in every act of intercourse, conception and birth, the sowing of the seed, the miracle of death and life, is repeated" (quoted in Plate 2014, 164–165). God provides the seed and Mary bakes the bread. Jesus, the bread, is then broken and distributed to the whole world (symbolized by his own actions during the Last Supper and enacted during the ritual of Eucharist). As biblical history begins with the curse of bread production, as the scriptures continue through various crises in bread production, they end with the elimination of bread production. In the messianic age, the bread that was once the product of great labor now walks among us, abundantly and eternally present.

Carole Counihan and Penny van Esterik (1997, 1) open their edited volume *Food and Culture* by declaring, "Food touches everything. Food is the foundation of every economy. It is a central pawn in political strategies of states and households. Food marks social differences, boundaries, bonds, and contradictions. Eating is an endlessly evolving enactment of gender, family, and community relationships .... Food-sharing creates solidarity, and ... food scarcity damages the human community and the human spirit." What Counihan and van Esterik fail to note is that because food is the site of our deepest anxieties and our highest hopes, it is also at the heart of our theologies and scriptures. Religion is more than what is thought and believed, more than a spiritual practice; rather, religion is also what is done, eaten, smelled, touched. Religion is embedded in material conditions and experienced through the body. The Bible's stories about food are more than just chronicles of sustenance and survival. The sacred is what we talk about, when we talk about bread.

NOTES

1. The one major technological innovation in bread production was the development of continuous grinding processes, which allowed animals to aid in the work of milling flour. By the first century in Israel, mills and bakeries had developed as a result of these new grinding technologies, increased urbanization, and cross-cultural exchange. A city-dweller could buy flour and even a variety of breads. Many women, however, especially in rural households, still ground their grain by hand and baked the family's daily bread. The image of women grinding together is even employed in one of Jesus's sayings about the end times (Luke 17:35).

2. Women continued to be the primary producers of the family's food through the periods of early Judaism and early Christianity. In fact, as kosher practices increasingly became important for marking ethnic and religious identity in Second Temple Judaism, food preparation took on spiritual import as well, thus bestowing even more honor to the women of the household (Levine 1994, 23–26).

REFERENCES

Brenner, Athalya, and Jan Willem van Henten, eds. 1999. *Food and Drink in the Biblical Worlds*. Semeia Studies 86. Atlanta, GA: Society of Biblical Literature.

Counihan, Carole, and Penny van Esterik, eds. 1997. *Food and Culture: A Reader*. New York: Routledge.

Douglas, Mary. 1966. *Purity and Danger: An Analysis of Concepts of Pollution and Taboo*. New York: Routledge.

Feeley-Harnik, Gillian. 1981. *The Lord's Table: The Meaning of Food in Early Judaism and Christianity*. Symbol and Culture Series. Philadelphia: University of Pennsylvania Press.

Hillel, Daniel. 2006. *The Natural History of the Bible: An Environmental Exploration of the Hebrew Scriptures*. New York: Columbia University Press.

King, Philip J., and Lawrence E. Stager. 2001. *Life in Biblical Israel*. Louisville, KY: Westminster John Knox Press.

Koosed, Jennifer L. 2011. *Gleaning Ruth: A Biblical Heroine and Her Afterlives*. Studies on Personalities of the Old Testament. Columbia: University of South Carolina Press.

Levine, Amy-Jill. 1994. "Second Temple Judaism, Jesus, and Women: Yeast of Eden." *Biblical Interpretation* 2: 8–33.

MacDonald, Nathan. 2008a. *Not Bread Alone: The Uses of Food in the Old Testament*. New York: Oxford.

MacDonald, Nathan. 2008b. *What Did the Ancient Israelites Eat? Diet in Biblical Times*. Grand Rapids, MI: Eerdmans.

McGee, Harold. 2004. *On Food and Cooking: The Science and Lore of the Kitchen*. New York: Scribner.

Meyers, Carol. 1988. *Discovering Eve: Ancient Israelite Women in Context*. New York: Oxford University Press.

Meyers, Carol. 2003. "Where the Girls Are: Archaeology and Women's Lives in Ancient Israel." In *Between Text and Artifact: Integrating Archaeology in Biblical Studies*, edited by Milton C. Moreland, 31–52. Boston: Brill.

Plate, S. Brent. 2014. *A History of Religion in 5½ Objects: Bringing the Spiritual to Its Senses*. Boston: Beacon Press.

Stone, Ken. 2005. *Practicing Safer Texts: Food, Sex and Bible in Queer Perspective*. New York: T&T Clark.

CHAPTER 43

DISPLACEMENT AND DIASPORA IN BIBLICAL NARRATIVE

MARTIEN A. HALVORSON-TAYLOR

DEPORTATION and migration, which were formative for ancient Judaism, were also seminal for its literature: the experiences of living outside the land contributed to both the emergence and also the thematic shaping of the Hebrew Bible. Dislocation features in historiographical accounts about exile for Israel in the eighth century BCE and Judah in the sixth century BCE, and provides the premise of literature about Jews living in a foreign land, such as Daniel, Esther, and Tobit. The narratives of Israel's beginnings and indeed the wider Pentateuch are reshaped in light of thinking about dislocation: the migration of Abram, the escape of Jacob, the servitude of Joseph, the death of Moses on the verge of crossing the Jordan. Just these few examples reveal some of the variety of forms that dislocation took, each differently valenced, in Israel and Judah's collective memory—from forced displacement, resulting in exile and diaspora, to migration, essential and desirable in the origin accounts of Israel.

Much of the Hebrew Bible is judged to be a response to dislocation by those who experienced the forced migrations of the sixth century BCE or by their descendants. It is not surprising, then, that dislocation, whether it is conceived of as forced or voluntary, influenced Israel's recollection of her more distant past. Early pre-exilic narratives were redacted during and in response to these dislocations, so that, for example, earlier Abram and Joseph traditions were reshaped drawing on the realities of exile and diaspora; these reworked traditions, in turn, informed narratives, such as Esther and Daniel, that took exile and diaspora as their explicit subject. In other words, the stories of Israel's origins and its accounts of post-exilic and diasporic existence exerted a reciprocal influence on each other; and thus Israelite history came to be narrated as a series of exiles and returns in which current dislocations were understood in terms of primeval patterns, and ancestral stories were revised in light of current dislocations. Indeed, given the fragmentary history that the Bible provides of the exilic period and of the Assyrian and Babylonian exiles, it is perhaps easier to speak of the *conceptualization* of dislocation within its literature; regardless of the historical realities of the experience, dislocation is an essential feature of biblical poetics that reverberates throughout the biblical canon (e.g., see Carroll 1998).

The biblical literature that deals with dislocation includes more straightforward reportage about the fall of Samaria and of Jerusalem and the ensuing deportations, as well as texts that deal with the "end" of the Babylonian exile and the efforts of returnees to restore a community in Judah, as in the books of Ezra and Nehemiah. Although these "historical" accounts are valuable for their theological framing of dislocation, there is another category of narrative that is particularly useful for thinking about the relationship between dislocation and the development of biblical literature, particularly in the Second Temple period. These are works that meditate on the theme of dislocation by narrating stories about Israelites or Jews in a foreign land. Among these, we have a group of somewhat fanciful narratives produced after the sixth century BCE about Jews living in the East. These historical fictions are sometimes grouped under the heading "diaspora literature" or "diaspora novels" and figure such characters as Daniel, Esther, and Tobit. Literature about displaced Jews has a counterpart in accounts about venerable ancestors of Israel—such as Abraham and Sarah, Joseph, and Moses—who sojourn in a foreign land before the exodus; these accounts, we will see, were reworked in light of the exilic experience and in response, perhaps, to the rise of the diaspora histories. Accounts of diaspora life and legends of Israel's origins thus come to resemble one another through the powerful pull of the poetics of dislocation.

Esther and Fictional Histories of Diaspora

Both the Hebrew and the Greek canons contain a number of fictional histories, written during the Second Temple period, that center around a Jewish protagonist living outside the land who rises to a privileged position, often within a foreign court. Each has distinctive features, but, in many of these narratives, the endangered protagonist acts in some remarkable fashion to save her- or himself (or even the Jews as a whole) and often without direct intervention or even clear direction from the deity; the people are delivered and their enemies sometimes dispatched through a coincidence that implies or is attributed to divine orchestration. Prime examples of these narratives are the story of Joseph (Gen. 37–50), the book of Esther, and Daniel 1–6.[1] These share the view that it is possible and even desirable to live successful lives among foreigners—a diasporic perspective that evokes the reality of large numbers of Jews who remained settled in Egypt and Babylonia.

Within this group, the book of Esther is perhaps the most diasporic of diasporic literature. Esther has been regarded as anomalous because God is not mentioned once in the course of the narrative and because it does not include a number of normative Jewish pieties. Alongside these, the book should also be reckoned with for its notions of space, in which the scattering is without apparent reference to a center; the book has a comparatively more extreme poetics of dislocation, one that further distinguishes it within the wider canon. There is but one lone reference to Jerusalem, and that in the genealogy of Mordecai (2:6), which is difficult if not impossible to square with plausibility;[2] the city's prime function appears to be to give Mordecai the pedigree of the first generation of exiles, but otherwise the homeland has receded from view.[3] In the book of Daniel, by contrast, Jerusalem is ever before the protagonist and the reader, from start to finish. The spatial orientation is evident when Daniel retreats to his house, "which had windows in its upper room facing toward Jerusalem"; there he would "get down on his knees three times a day to pray to his God and praise him, just as he had done previously" (Dan. 6:11 [Eng. 6:10]).

Daniel presents diasporic living as living apart while living abroad, but Esther gives no indication that she conducts herself differently from those in the palace before, during, and even after her intercession for her people. The book of Esther not only lacks an interest in Jerusalem, but it appears not to have the book of Daniel's interest in prayer, keeping kosher, and other basic Jewish pieties. Daniel keeps Jewish dietary laws in the foreign court (with outstanding results, 1:5–20) and prays to his God despite the nefarious Babylonian edict prohibiting him from doing so (6:10). Judith refuses to partake in the fare at the Assyrian general Holofernes's table in order to keep kosher (Judg. 12:1–2, 19) and secures leave to pray (vv. 6–9). Their radical adherence to traditional Jewish pieties both threatens and subsequently assures their survival. Bringing the Esther tradition into more standard biblical if not diasporic form, the Greek Esther includes substantial additions that refer to prayer, keeping kosher, and God (Clines 1984). Still, even with these additions, the LXX maintains the Esther tradition's silence about the land.

While the book does not have the pull to the land that characterizes diasporic if not more overtly exilic literature, Esther evokes the Jewish people at the periphery in a different but no less significant way. Haman's description of "a certain people scattered and separated among the peoples in all the provinces of [the] kingdom" (Esther 3:8), presumably the Jews, underscores the peoples' decentered status; the logistics of this come to the fore in the complicated date notices for Purim, which account for the Jews of Susa and the rest of the provinces separately (Esther 8:1–19).

Esther's startling poetics of dislocation emerge further by way of comparison to another body of literature that has not yet been so well rehearsed, the wife-sister stories, which also explore life among foreigners. This narrative tradition presumably would have been known to the redactors of Esther—though perhaps not in the form that we now have it—since it appears three times within Genesis, in 12:10–20; 20:1–16; and 26:1–33. As the wife-sister stories now stand in Genesis, they function to anticipate the exodus. And yet, if we consider them alongside Esther, they reveal a key facet of Esther's poetics of dislocation—namely, the assumption of no return.

There are a number of other comparisons to be made between Esther and the wife-sister motif in Genesis. In both Esther and Genesis 12, for example, male figures obscure their true relationship to their female relation when in a foreign land: Sarah is Abraham's wife, whom he will pass off as his sister (Gen. 12:13), and Esther is Mordecai's cousin and ward in the Hebrew and his future wife in the Greek (Esther 2:7), whom he asks twice to conceal her kin (Esther 2:10, 20; Halvorson-Taylor 2013). Both women are then taken (*lqh*; Esther 2:8; Gen. 12:15) into the foreign king's palace (cf. Gen. 20) and thus the wife is passed off as a sister, the foster daughter (Hebrew), or betrothed (Greek) as a stranger, an outsider. In both cases this obscuring is leveraged to the male figures' advantage. In Genesis 12, Abraham instructs Sarah, "Say that you are my sister, so that it may go well with me because of you, and that my life may be spared on your account" (v. 13). Abraham will go away rich from the encounter, with livestock and servants (v. 16). And when the edict against the Jews is issued, Mordecai asks Esther to intervene to preserve the lives of him and his people (Esther 4:8).

The similarities between Genesis 12 and Esther highlight several features of how setting is construed in both the narratives. First, the male protagonists are presented as willing to compromise kinship relatedness to ensure survival. This may be a sobering statement about the precariousness of living among foreigners, or it may suggest an undue sense of vulnerability. In any case, both texts are rather sanguine about the ethics of the compromise; they present it as a problem but also acknowledge that it creates prospects: Mordecai will rise to prominence (Esther 10); Abraham goes away wealthy (Gen. 12:16, 20). Taken together, these similarities suggest that both narratives reflect on questions of Jewish identity in diaspora: the narratives acknowledge the wide scope of human agency, both its potential and its dangerous pitfalls in a particularly diasporic context. The male protagonist's actions may be morally compromised despite the eventual successes that they yield, which may be an allusion to the complex theology, as Joseph told his brothers, that "even though you intended to do harm to me, YHWH intended it for good" (Gen. 50:20; cf. 45:5–8).

The resemblances between the two traditions serve to highlight what, in the end, is remarkable about the final outcome in the book of Esther: in Gen. 12:20, Abraham and Sarah are sent on their way (and 13:1 reports that they travel to the Negeb), but in Esther there is no return and no apparent concern with return. Esther remains within the palace, without even the hope of restoration, while in Genesis, Sarah returns to Abraham. But this is part, too, of the artistry of the book and its theological depth: Esther posits the ambiguities of Jewish identity in Susa and holds out the possibility of survival and even prestige in a protracted diaspora. Return and even the recollection of the homeland are nowhere in view. Instead, Susa is the center and the enduring reality.

Joseph and Israelites in a Foreign Land

The narrative of Joseph and his family's sojourn in Egypt provides another vantage point onto the complex poetics of dislocation: An earlier narrative, not originally caught up in the issues of living outside the land, was redacted in light of the events of the sixth century BCE to resemble diaspora literature like Esther and Daniel. Although literary scholars view the Joseph narrative as an early iteration of the genre of diaspora novels, and thus term it "diasporic," we might just as easily term it "exilic literature" based on its redaction; in its current form, particularly with the addition of the divine promise to return (Gen. 46:1–5a), the Joseph narrative reflects the imposition of an exile-return framework on an earlier tradition about Israel's origins.

Genesis 37–50 as it now stands is widely regarded as the early forerunner to the diaspora narrative, because of its similarities to comparable literature and its hopeful attitude toward success in the foreign land (Rosenthal 1895; Meinhold 1975, 1976; Niditch, 2000). In an earlier version of the narrative, however, Israel's sojourn in Egypt was not envisioned as a protracted stay. And, indeed, the time in Egypt was not, in this earlier form, regarded as geographically off-center, as often characterizes literature about diaspora; even in the final form of Genesis 37–50, Joseph does not evince a sustained longing for homeland, the spatial orientation that we see in, for example, Daniel and Ezra-Nehemiah. Joseph's dislocation in Genesis 37 was, first and foremost the dislocation from family, a fratricidal rift, with Egypt as the backdrop for the establishment of his dominance over his brothers.

As an early narrative tradition was reconceived in the wake of Israel's dispersion, what was a temporary and somewhat felicitous sojourn was lengthened, tinged, and reshaped into a prelude for exodus; this redaction, which comes in the wake of the Babylonian exile, positions the narrative to prefigure the enslavement of the Moses generation and thus makes the period in Egypt typologically significant. The overlay of the "promises to the patriarchs," including the assurances that YHWH will bring the people back to Canaan (Gen. 46:1–5a in the Joseph story), were essential to this transformation. The Joseph narrative as it now stands thus reckons with the place of dislocation in Israel's larger history, according it the prestige of association with early Israel. And a familial story that focused on Joseph's ascendancy over his brothers became the story of Joseph's ascendancy over Egypt, much as Mordecai ascends within Susa (Esther 8:15).

Genesis 37–50 grew out of a complex (and contested) redactional process of long duration, accumulating a host of smaller notices, including Genesis 37:1–2a and 46:1–5a, along with several key chapters; the latter include, for example, Genesis 38, the encounter between Tamar and Judah; Genesis 48, the blessing of Manasseh and Ephraim; and Genesis 49, Jacob's blessing.[4] So, too, an older independent account of an encounter between Potiphar's wife and Joseph, now Genesis 39, was folded into the Joseph complex (Albertz 2003; Schmid 2010, 2012; Carr 2011). Thus, while the original scope of a comprehensive Joseph narrative extended from Genesis 37 through 50 and was further supplemented to become an early example of a diaspora novella, it began largely as a story of fraternal conflict. This original Joseph story was distinctive for presenting a comparatively positive view of living outside the land, with little anxiety about return; Egypt is the place where the family will be fed and preserved, and there is no indication that the sojourn will extend beyond the remaining years of famine (45:4–11). The brothers request formal permission to stay, under no apparent duress (47:4). In earliest form, the narrative may not have been diasporic in orientation at all, since the dislocation lacks the intimation of permanence.

Several additions give the narrative of familial rift the ring of diaspora. After Joseph presents the possibilities for his family in Egypt in Genesis 45 and before Pharaoh grants the brothers' request to stay, Jacob, identified as "Israel," encounters God at Beersheva. Genesis 46:1–5a, which is unusual for presenting the only encounter with the deity in the Joseph novel, is also unusual for asserting that Joseph and his family will remain in the land; this is framed as divine permission with the promise of divine presence (see also 48:21b, which with vv.13–15 is also, like 46:1–5a, a later exilic addition; Albertz 2003; Wöhrle 2013). The deity's assurance is tied to the promise to the patriarchs that YHWH will bring the people back to Canaan. This is essential for transforming the family sojourn in Egypt, which was for the purposes of being fed, into an "Egyptian exile" narrative. With the additions, there is a new emphasis on eventual return, and Israel is now also situated in Egypt, in need of the deliverance that will come through exodus.

Already these additions begin to assimilate the Joseph chapters to literature about dislocation; so, too, the addition of Genesis 39 develops the theme of Joseph the Hebrew's vulnerability and the dangers of existence outside of the land. It is not simply the false accusation by Potiphar's wife, but the manner in which she deploys a pejorative reference to Joseph's ethnicity (vv. 14, 17)—this in a larger narrative that has been more concerned with relations within the family than with how the family, Israel, is regarded by others. In its present placement, the inauspicious ending of Genesis 39 (in which Joseph lands in prison) puts Joseph in the right position, however lowly, to be raised up, eventually, by the Egyptian Pharaoh by virtue of his encounter with the royal cupbearer (41:9–12). The chapter as a whole now contributes to a pattern of reversals of fortune, the lowlights and highlights of existence as a foreigner. A rare mention of YHWH's presence in 39:2–5 suggests that these vicissitudes are under divine control. By featuring these upheavals, YHWH's oversight of Israel's fate, and ethnic terms for Joseph, the chapter reflects on aspects of diasporic existence in a more focused fashion than the rest of the narrative.

In its earlier form, the narrative described how Joseph and his brothers came to inhabit another land largely without typological significance, since exile had not yet exerted its influence in the canon. The original composition was already amenable to these exilic-minded expansions: it had a positive depiction of Pharaoh as a wise ruler[5] and a sanguine attitude toward Joseph's marriage to an Egyptian woman, which makes him the son-in-law of an Egyptian priest. Even the focus on familial relationships, as much as Joseph's success in court, becomes an opportunity for a new emphasis in diasporic living. Whether or not Joseph's brothers actually sell him into slavery (cf. 37:26–27 vs. v. 28), they in effect cause his forced migration, his exile. (Although, again, to interpret their action in this way is to sense the exilic overlay on the family narrative.) Although the Joseph narrative has a theology congenial to diasporic novels—namely, that the deity works even through human malevolence to preserve a people—it is distinctive in that the human malevolence is not foreign, but familial.

Even in the final form, Joseph's experience can be measured less in his successful encounter with the Egyptians, and more as an estrangement from his brothers—and the disappointment of a father who perhaps too willingly gives him up for dead, both by sending him along to his fratricidal brothers (39:13) and then jumping to a precipitous conclusion when presented by circumstantial evidence (vv. 32–35). It is this familial estrangement that presents both the ominous undertones of the story, in the name of Manasseh (41:15; "God has made me forget all my hardship and all my father's house"), and in the narrative's emotional climax: Joseph, who by now has become the master of self-restraint in his dealing with the sexual advances of his master's wife (39:8–10, 12) and in contending with his own ambitions before the Pharaoh (41:16, 25, 28, 33–36), cannot contain his emotions before his brothers (45:1–3). The Egyptian court becomes a place of opportunity, but for Joseph it is, most of all, the opportunity to feed his family (45:5–7). Indeed, the narrative is framed by the notice, however belatedly redactional in origin, that "this is the story of the family Jacob" (37:2), which enfolds the court genre up into genealogy. The story of Joseph is as much about separation from and reunion with family; and, indeed, the separation and dislocation were instigated by family. This familial dysfunction is portable, as is the nation itself; as Jacob's deathbed speech makes clear, the rivalries between brothers will endure (Gen. 49).

The Joseph narrative is comparable to other Pentateuchal narratives about the common, and indeed most venerable, ancestors of Israel, for whom dislocation was an essential aspect of their identity: Abraham is exiled from his homeland to the land "that YHWH will show [him]" and almost immediately after he reaches the Promised Land, descends to Egypt, in a prefiguring of the people of Israel's descent at the end of Genesis (12:1, 10); if Genesis 20:13 is a later comment on these instructions, then Abraham appears to be called to a life of perpetual dislocation (Albertz 2003). Jacob is renamed Israel, eponymous ancestor of the nation, only after his maturing sojourn with his greedy uncle Laban, also the result of sibling rivalry (Gen. 32). Moses is raised in the Egyptian Pharaoh's palace by Pharaoh's daughter, who knows from her first encounter with her foundling that he is "one of the Hebrews' children" (Exod. 2:6). Over and over again, the memory of these figures is invoked in the biblical and midrashic tradition as identity-conferring for Israel.

The identity of these major figures of Israel's collective memory is, moreover, complicated. Moses's years in Egypt, for example, mark him not only a stranger in a strange land, but as estranged from his own people. While the text is at pains to identify Moses as an Israelite by genealogy (2:1), the Israelites themselves resent his intrusions into their affairs (2:14). Indeed, when God designates him to lead the Israelites, Moses audaciously asks for assurances—which come in the form of names, signs, and symbols—that he will have authority within the Israelite community (3:13; 4:1). Based on his past, Moses assumes that he will be regarded as an outsider (Exod. 3:13).

Further, although many later biblical texts depict heroes like Daniel and Tobit clearly identifying as Jewish and maintaining the basic practices of Judaism despite the challenges of being in exile, the texts within this group are comparable in demonstrating a surprising playfulness toward identity outside the land, which is made possible because Israel has not yet entered into the land; these narratives indicate a certain fascination with the Israelite protagonist "passing" in a foreign place—with Moses, for example, being mistaken for an Egyptian (2:19) and with Joseph marrying into an important Egyptian family (Gen. 41:45). This may, indeed, be at work in the Esther narrative, in which she passes as a Gentile for a significant portion of the book.

Conclusion

The impact of the exile and diaspora on biblical narrative gave rise to new narratives that reflected on the ambiguities of Jewish existence outside the land. But dislocation also affected the shaping of Israel's collective memory of her past; pre-exilic Pentateuchal materials were redacted in light of the experience of exile, transforming the narratives of Israel's origins into narratives about dislocation. "Exile" thus becomes a theme that recurs throughout the Hebrew Bible (Scott 1997) and serves as an important literary device to disclose narrative artistry, a narrative's concerns, and developing notions of collective memory.

Biblical narratives not only refer to Israel and Judah's historical experience of forced migration and exile, but also to a number of other dispersions as well. These begin with the banishment of Adam and Eve from Eden (Gen. 2:24) and include the dislocations (and relocations) of such figures as Abraham and Sarah, Jacob, Rachel and Leah, Joseph, Moses, Jephthah, David, Daniel, and Mordecai and Esther. A number of major characters in the Hebrew Bible are described as having experienced living outside the land (in some cases, repeatedly) and, as such, dislocation is a formative experience in the cultural memory of the nation and emerging concepts of Jewish identity.

Dislocation functions as a vehicle for exploring wider questions of Jewish identity apart from the land. These include basic existential questions; in a number of biblical narratives, exile expresses not simply geographic displacement, but a variety of other alienations as well, including political disenfranchisement, socioeconomic marginalization, and the spiritual condition of feeling estranged from Yhwh (Halvorson-Taylor 2011). In still other narratives, for example, the books of Esther, Daniel, Judith and Tobit, exile has been transformed into "diaspora;" these narratives hold out the possibility of finding a home and thriving even in the face of dislocation, social vulnerability, and political disenfranchisement. Diaspora literature explores how a minority people could and did successfully negotiate to survive, even at personal cost. As such, these narratives have had lasting appeal and relevance.

NOTES

1. Humphreys 1973, 1988; Wills 1995; Fewell 2003. The books of Tobit and Judith also share a number of similar features—but there are notable differences: Tobit is part of the Assyrian diaspora, and in Judith the action takes place within the land, a powerful statement about the author's understanding that a Jew in a land dominated by foreigners can be vulnerable in similar ways to a diasporic Jew. This group might also include the tale of the three youths in 1 Esdras, in which Zerubbabel figures as a diaspora hero in the vein of Joseph or Daniel.

   Some of these fictions bear similarities to literature about the non-Jewish figure Ahiqar, who is attested among the literary remains of the Elephantine community of Egyptian diasporic Jews. The resemblances suggest that these biblical diasporic fictions participated in a popular genre with wide appeal. On the book of Esther as diaspora literature, see Levenson 1997 and Fox 2001, and on the artistry of Esther's fictionality in its imitation of the writing of history, see Berlin 2001.

2. Even this reference may be a later gloss since it does not appear in certain Greek manuscripts (for the Alpha-text) of the book of Esther that may intimate an earlier iteration of the Esther tradition (Halvorson-Taylor 2013).

3. In the MT, Mordecai is introduced in Esther 2:5–6 as "son of Jair son of Shimei son of Kish, a Benjaminite, who has been carried away from Jerusalem among the captives carried away with King Jeconiah of Judah whom King Nebuchadnezzar of Babylon had carried away." The "who" would most literally refer to Mordecai, in which case, because the book is thought to be set at a date significantly after the Babylonian exile of the sixth century, Mordecai is unfathomably old. Translators, in an effort to make the dating more feasible, therefore often take the "who" that was exiled to refer instead to Kish, Mordecai's great-grandfather.

4. Its early northern pre-exilic traces are evident in its focus on Joseph as the ancestor of the two major northern tribes of Ephraim and Manasseh and on the brothers' slow dawning recognition that Joseph is destined to rule.

5. Joseph does evoke a pejorative view of Egypt in the name of Ephraim, "For God has made me fruitful in the land of my misfortunes," but the misfortunes may well refer to the family rift that landed him there; indeed, this latter phrase, "the land of my misfortunes," finds no correlation in the name Ephraim (41:52).

REFERENCES

Albertz, Rainer. 2003. *Israel in Exile: The History and Literature of the Sixth Century B.C.E.* Translated by David Green. Studies in Biblical Literature 3. Atlanta, GA: Society of Biblical Literature.

Berlin, Adele. 2001. "The Book of Esther and Ancient Story Telling." *Journal of Biblical Literature* 120: 3–14.

Carr, David M. 2011. *The Formation of the Hebrew Bible: A New Reconstruction.* Oxford: Oxford University Press.

Carroll, Robert P. 1998. "Exile! What Exile? Deportation and the Discourses of Diaspora." In *Leading Captivity Captive: "The Exile" as History and Ideology*, ed. Lester Grabbe, 62–79. Journal for the Study of the Old Testament Supplement Series 278. Sheffield, Yorkshire: Sheffield Academic Press.

Clines, David J. A. 1984. *Esther Scroll: The Story of the Story*. Journal for the Study of the Old Testament Supplement 30. JSOT Press: Sheffield.

Fewell, Danna Nolan. 2003. "Resisting Daniel." In *The Children of Israel: Reading the Bible for the Sake of Our Children*, 117–131. Nashville, TN: Abingdon Press.

Fox, Michael V. 2001. *Character and Ideology in the Book of Esther*. 2nd ed. Grand Rapids, MI: Eerdmans.

Halvorson-Taylor, Martien A. 2011. *Enduring Exile: The Metaphorization of Exile in the Hebrew Bible*. Vetus Testamentum Supplement 141. Brill: Leiden.

Halvorson-Taylor, Martien A. 2013. "Secrets and Lies: Secrecy Notices (Esth 2:10, 20) and Diasporic Identity in the Books of Esther." *Journal of Biblical Literature* 131: 467–485.

Humphreys, W. Lee. 1973. "A Life-Style for Diaspora: A Study of the Tales of Esther and Daniel." *Journal of Biblical Literature* 92: 211–223.

Humphreys, W. Lee. 1988. *Joseph and His Family: A Literary Study*. Studies on Personalities of the Old Testament. Columbia, SC: University of South Carolina Press.

Levenson, Jon D. 1997. *Esther: A Commentary*. Old Testament Library. Louisville, KY: Westminster John Knox.

Meinhold, Arndt. 1975 "Die Gattung der Josephsgeschichte und des Estherbuches: Diasporanovelle I". *Zeitschrift for alttestamentliche Wissenschaft* 87: 306–324.

Meinhold, Arndt. 1976 "Die Gattung der Josephsgeschichte und des Estherbuches: Diasporanovelle II". *Zeitschrift for alttestamentliche Wissenschaft* 88: 72–93

Niditch, Susan. 2000. *A Prelude to Biblical Folklore: Underdogs and Tricksters*. Urbana: University of Illinois Press.

Rosenthal, Ludwig A. 1895. "Die Josephsgeschichte, mit den Büchern Ester und Daniel verglichen." *Zeitschrift for alttestamentliche Wissenschaft* 15: 278–284.

Schmid, Konrad. 2010. *Genesis and the Moses Story: Israel's Dual Origins in the Hebrew Bible*. Siphrut 3. Winona Lake, IN: Eisenbrauns.

Schmid, Konrad. 2012. *The Old Testament: A Literary History*. Minneapolis, MN: Fortress Press.

Scott, James M., ed. 1997. *Exile: Old Testament, Jewish and Christian Conceptions*. Brill: Leiden.

Wills, Lawrence M. 1995. *The Jewish Novel in the Ancient World*. Myth and Poetics. Ithaca, NY: Cornell University Press.

Wöhrle, Jakob. 2013. "Joseph in Egypt: Living under Foreign Rule according to the Joseph Story and Its Early Intra- and Extra-Biblical Reception." In *Between Cooperation and Hostility: Multiple Identities in Ancient Judaism and the Interaction with Foreign Powers*, edited by Rainer Albertz and Jakob Wöhrle, 53–72. Journal of Ancient Judaism: Supplements 11. Göttingen: Vandenhoeck & Ruprecht.

CHAPTER 44

NARRATIVIZING EMPIRE IN THE BIBLICAL WORLD

THEODORE W. JENNINGS, JR. AND
TAT-SIONG BENNY LIEW

In what way is empire a subject of narrative in the Hebrew Bible and early Christian Scriptures? In this chapter we will attend to the marked ambivalence toward empire to be found in biblical narratives. These narratives are found not only in large-scale narrative texts but also—and perhaps more importantly—in micronarratives: in prophetic oracles, hymn-like psalms, and parables. We can only make a rather suggestive sampling of such materials in order to gain a sense of the deep ambivalence that may ultimately come to expression as a tale of two (kinds of) empires.

AMBIVALENCE TOWARD EMPIRE IN THE HEBREW BIBLE

In the Torah the predominant narratives of empire concern Egypt. The Egyptian empire appears both as a place of refuge and as the land of unjust oppression. As we shall see, this ambivalence about empire will characterize both the Hebrew Bible and the earliest Christian writings.

Already, at the beginning of the saga of Abram, we find this ambivalence foreshadowed. Abram enters the territory of Egypt on account of a famine (Gen. 12:10). But while there, even though Abram is well treated, his wife/sister Sarai is taken into Pharaoh's "house" (harem?), occasioning the displeasure of Yhwh, who sends plagues as punishment (Gen. 12:17).

This brief vignette anticipates the larger narrative in which Egypt will play an important role. In the sagas concerning Joseph (Gen. 37–50), Egypt is depicted as a land of refuge. It is there that Jacob finds an escape from the fratricidal intentions of his brothers. It is there also that Joseph rises to a position of great importance (anticipating other stories, such as those of Esther and Daniel) and is thus in a position to offer refuge to his father and brothers when once again famine makes the Egyptian empire an attractive place of abundance for the putative ancestors of the Hebrew people. It is precisely this narrativizing of the Egyptian empire as a place of refuge that will come into play in the Gospel of Matthew, when another Joseph will flee persecution in the land of Israel to find safety in Egypt (Matt. 2:14–15).

On the other hand, the Egyptian empire will be depicted as the site of injustice and oppression in the narrative of Exodus. Those who had found safety and prosperity in Egypt's welcoming imperial embrace now find it a place of implacable hostility and exploitation. The rationale for Egyptian oppression is said to be the multiplication of the people of Israel (Exod. 1:9). "Therefore they set taskmasters over them to afflict them with heavy burdens" (Exod. 1:11a Revised Standard Version). The response of YHWH is, "I have seen the affliction of my people who are in Egypt, and have heard their cry because of their taskmasters; I know their sufferings, and I have come down to deliver them out of the hand of the Egyptians" (Exod. 3:7–8a RSV). Thus is set in motion the narrative of the escape from Egypt, an escape which turns from a mere respite of three days into a journey whose beginning is forever memorialized in the celebration of Passover. Indeed, it is the prominence of this cultural memory of Egypt that often obscures the rather different light in which Egypt is narrated as a place of refuge. In any case "Egypt" and "exodus" will serve as ways to think though Israel's experiences of destruction, collaboration, and subjugation in relation to later empires.

This negative narration of empire is foreshadowed in the much earlier story of the tower of Babel (Gen. 11:1–9), which in turn is a hyperbolization of the attribution of the founding of the first city by the fratricidal Cain (Gen. 4:17). The tower of Babel, which may be a fabulation of the Babylonian empire, is a story that combines (1) the wonder at what humans can accomplish in the togetherness that empire affords, and (2) a repudiation of global imperial ambition.

We may even detect a similar ambivalence in the stories of the cities of the plain, which appear first in alliance with Abram and then as sites of violence perpetrated against traveling strangers. In subsequent recollections of the sin of Sodom, what is in view is the arrogance and violence associated with affluence and power. Sodom is told, "Behold, this was the sin of your sister Sodom: she and her daughters had pride, surfeit of food, and prosperous ease, but did not aid the poor and needy" (Ezek. 16:49 RSV). This becomes a kind of biblical trope that will reappear whenever empire is cast in a negative light.

This ambivalence is carried forward into the various narrations of what we may call the Davidic or Solomonic empire. Israel's own imperial ambitions are foreshadowed in the promise of YHWH not only to deliver Israel from Egyptian bondage and oppression but also to deliver to Israel the land and the peoples of "the Canaanites, the Hittites, the Amorites, the Perizzites, the Hivites, and the Jebusites" (Exod. 3:8, 17 RSV). Much of the narrative material that follows from Joshua and Judges through Samuel, Kings, and Chronicles is concerned with the ways that Israel configures itself as a new empire. Of course, much of this may well be an empire of the imagination, since historical evidence of this Davidic empire is, to say the least, slim. But imagination, too, has its consequences. From the time of the king Josiah down to the present day yearning for control of the whole "land of Israel"—the Davidic empire together with its rule over the inhabitants of that land—has geopolitical consequences.

The character of that empire is perhaps best captured in the narratives concerning David's heir in 2 Chronicles, which exclaim, "Thus King Solomon excelled all the kings of the earth in riches and wisdom" (2 Chron. 9:22 RSV).

However, even in the narratives regarding the constitution of such an Israelite empire we read elements of a counternarrative. From the very beginning, we hear of YHWH's great reluctance to allow the selection of a king (1 Sam. 8). Saul's ordination as king of Israel is represented as a reluctant concession to the will of a recalcitrant people. Again, only with great reluctance does YHWH seem to permit the erection of a state temple that will serve as the sacralization of these imperial ambitions (1 Chron. 17:6).

That even the beloved David can be seen as YHWH's opponent precisely in terms of imperial ambition is narrated in the stories of YHWH's ire when David introduces the trappings of imperial rule: a standing army, a census, a system of taxation (2 Sam. 24). Thus YHWH is granted a sort of plausible deniability with respect to Israel's own imperial ambitions.

In spite of these negative portrayals of imperial ambition and accomplishment, the dream of a Davidic empire that will extend its rule throughout the world will surface again and again, becoming the focal point of messianic longing.

Much of the subsequent narration of the history of Israel is a story of Israel being caught between the imperial ambitions of its neighbors to the south and the north. To the south there is always Egypt, which ultimately puts an end to Josiah's attempt to (re)establish a Davidic empire (see Kim 2005). To the north there will come a succession of empires: Assyria, Babylon, Persia, the Hellenistic empire, and, ultimately, the Roman empire (these last two will finally succeed in incorporating the empire to the south and so encompass Israel as well).

The first mortal threat to Israel comes from Assyria. After that empire had overwhelmed the Israelite kingdom it seemed possible to face down this threat. Perhaps foolishly, King Hezekiah seeks rescue through alliance with Egypt (Isa. 30; 36:6), but the prophet Isaiah counsels simple reliance upon divine rescue, which seems to come in the form of a plague (Isa. 37:36). This, it would seem, has been YHWH's favored means of intervention since the time of Egypt, from Abram to Moses. Deliverance from imperial aggression is short-lived. The destruction of Israel and the ongoing threat from the north will be rationalized as a result of Israel's faithlessness to the covenant with YHWH, a faithlessness that is expressed by Amos as a failure to embody justice for the poor. Thus the sin of Israel, which brings upon itself utter destruction, is the way Israel mimics the arrogance and injustice that characterize empire in its most negative aspects—hence the parallelism of divine judgment against Damascus, Tyre, Edom, Moab and that threatened against Israel and Judea (Amos 1–3).

The fall of Assyria to Babylon provides a very brief respite in which Josiah tries his hand at establishing the Davidic empire. This is a short-lived experiment. Once Babylon has digested Syria it turns its attention to Judah. Despite the warnings of Jeremiah about the need to practice justice, Judah, too, will fall victim to the imperial appetite of the superpower to the north (see Davidson 2011).

The prophets are concerned with the question of how to explain the abandonment of Israel and Judah to the clutches of the imperial powers to the north. One way of doing so is to emphasize the injustice of God's people, the very sorts of injustice that make them easy prey to their more powerful, though scarcely more just, neighbors. Another, however, is to point to Israel's infatuation with these very empires as itself a desertion from loyalty to YHWH. Thus Jeremiah compares Judah to a camel in heat, seeking intimate alliance wherever it may be found (3:1–5). And Ezekiel will detail promiscuous Israel's lusting after Egyptian, Babylonian, and Chaldean lovers (Ezek. 16:26–29; 23:5–49). The rather ribald (homo)eroticism of these mini-narratives of flirtation with empire serves to emphasize the allure of empire as well as YHWH's displeasure with those who embrace the temptations afforded by imperial alliance.

Even in prophetic literature of the sixth century, however, the empires are not regarded as unambiguously negative. Those who are taken away to Babylon are counseled to become good citizens of the empire in which they are held. Second Isaiah will even go so far as to cast the leader of the Persian empire, which swallows the Babylonian empire, as not only an instrument of divine justice and mercy but also perhaps the first foreign, post-Davidic figure to be deemed "messiah." It is Persian rule that will restore to Israel, now reduced to the provincial colony of Yehud, a certain limited measure of autonomy through its collaborators, Nehemiah and Ezra. Thus the relatively enlightened imperial policies of Persia will make it seem plausible that empires can be benign as well as despotic (see Berquist 2003).

We might also briefly note the ambivalence with respect to the Hellenistic empire that succeeded the Persian. The story of the imperial overreach of Antiochus IV Epiphanes and the militant resistance to his policies is well known from the accounts of Maccabees. What may not be noticed is that this overreach seems to have been endorsed by those of the leadership elites under Jason who invited the hellenization of Judea, including the establishment of a gymnasium adjacent to the (second) temple in Jerusalem itself (2 Macc. 4:7–12). As we shall see, the book of Daniel both critiques empire and yet also dreams of a different sort of empire (see Portier-Young 2011).

CHRISTIANITY AND EMPIRE

The first literary evidence we have for the emergence of "Christianity" comes from the letters of Paul. How is Paul to be understood in relation to the ambivalent narration of empire that we have seen in the Hebrew Bible? In Romans, Paul does adopt the view held by some of the prophets that the empires are the (ultimately) disposable instruments of divine justice (9:22).

But Paul may also be read as the implacable foe of the Roman Empire. This is a reading proposed by Nietzsche (1997, 71) who writes: "[T]he crucified Jew as symbol of salvation was the profoundest mockery of the splendidly arrayed provincial governors, for they now appeared as symbols of ill-fortune and of 'world' ripe for destruction."

More recently we have the assertion by Jacob Taubes (2004, 16) that Paul's writings entail a veritable declaration of war on Caesar. That one who was executed by the Roman imperial state—"the rulers of this age" (1 Cor. 2:8 NRSV)—is the chosen messiah of divine justice may be seen as judgment on the Roman imperial order, an order that sustained itself through the regular employment of crucifixion as one of its favorite instruments of terror.

This view of Paul's resistance to imperial ideology has been the subject of much discussion, which is best accessed in the volumes of essays edited by Richard Horsley (1997; 2000; 2004). Brigette Kahl (2010) has also interpreted Paul's letter to the Galatians as an identification with the oppressed Gallic peoples of Galatia (see also Lopez 2010).

This stands in considerable contrast to the way Paul has been read—since Constantine based on a few verses from Romans 13—as proposing cooperation or even collaboration with the Roman imperial project. The newer scholarship serves at least as a counterbalance to the ways Paul (and not only Paul) has been conscripted as apologist, not only for Rome, but also, more crucially, for all succeeding (Christian) imperial projects.

On the other hand, the Apocalypse of John has long been regarded as an explicit (if coded) critique of the Roman Empire. Indeed Friedrich Engels (1964) regarded it as an index of early Christianity as a revolutionary movement. However, Stephen Moore (2014) has given us a more complicated picture by showing how Revelation might be appropriating some of the worst forms of imperial ideology in the service of Christian aims. Certainly, the acclamation of the lamb slain from the foundation of the earth as king of kings and lord of lords exhibits both a critique of the existing empire and an appropriation of its ideology; an appropriation that will have dire consequences in Christian history.

The reading of New Testament texts as containing an anti-imperial message has not been restricted to the reading of the letters of Paul. Warren Carter's (2000) commentary on the Gospel of Matthew, for example, has attempted a rather thoroughgoing reading of that text from this perspective.

An image that is quite basic to the rhetoric of the Synoptic Gospels, although playing some role in Paul and in the Fourth Gospel, is that of the kingdom or empire of God. On the one hand, this term seems to embrace a certain version of the imperial dream, albeit now as the empire of justice, an empire in which the poor, the despised, the sick, and the suffering have a very prominent role. Yet it may also be read as an implicit or even explicit critique of the actually existing empire of its time.

METAPHORIZING EMPIRE

One way of seeing the comparison and contrast between the actual empire and the anticipated divine empire is by pursuing clues embedded in a sort of micronarrative:

> What is the reign of God like and what could we compare it to? It is like a grain of mustard which when it is sown on the earth, being smaller than all the seeds of the earth but when it is sown it comes up and becomes greater than all the herbs and makes large branches so that the birds of the air are able to dwell in its shade. (Mark 4:30–32)

The parable has to do with the mission of announcing and enacting the reign of God, a mission already launched by Jesus and to be carried on by his followers. As Jesus says, "If you have ears, open them" (Mark 4:9).

The meaning of the parable is concentrated in a line that is really a kind of chorus or tag line that Jesus's hearers and Mark's and Matthew's readers are expected to know. The line is "[t]he birds of the air make nests in its branches." It is a refrain that we know from a number of Hebrew Bible texts, and a review of the way that image functions may helpfully bring into focus the ambivalence toward empire that we have followed in biblical texts.

These texts begin with an image found in many cultures of a great tree at the center of the earth. This image had been used by Babylon to refer to itself: to the imperial design of uniting the disparate nations and peoples of the earth into a single great empire where peace and prosperity would reign.

The prophet Ezekiel was among the first to use this image for empire: the great tree in which the birds of the air found rest, to speak of world political events from the point of view of Israel's faith. In Ezekiel 31 he addresses to the other great superpower of his time, Egypt. For Egypt was growing great and arrogant. And so he reminds Egypt of another superpower of old, the Assyrian empire that had now fallen into decay. He does this to warn Egypt of a similar fate awaiting its own imperial and colonial designs. He writes:

> Who are you like in your greatness? Consider Assyria, a cedar of Lebanon with fair branches and forest shade and of great height, its top among the clouds . . . .
> **All the birds of the air make their nests in its boughs.** Under its branches all the animals of the field gave birth to their young; and in its shade all great nations lived. (Ezek 31:2b–3, 6 NRSV)

The great tree is the mighty empire. And the birds that find shelter in its branches are the nations that find refuge, protection, and prosperity within the bounds of the empire. Here it is the empire of Assyria, which in its pride was cast down:

> On the mountains and in all the valleys its branches have fallen and its boughs lie broken in all the water courses of the land; and all the peoples of the earth went away from its shade and left it. (Ezek 31:12b NRSV)

And so, the prophet warns, will it also be of the great Egyptian empire.

> Now you shall be brought down with the trees of Eden to the world below; you shall lie among the uncircumcised, with those who are killed by the sword. This is Pharaoh and all his horde, says the LORD GOD. (Ezek 31:18 NRSV)

This image of the great tree whose branches shelter the birds of the air, of the great empire within whose bounds the nations of the earth find refuge, is found again in the book of Daniel. Here, we find it in the dream of the great king of Babylon, the emperor Nebuchadnezzar.

> Upon my bed this is what I saw; there was a tree at the center of the earth, and its height was great. The tree grew great and strong, its top reached to heaven, and it was visible to the ends of the whole earth. Its foliage was beautiful, its fruit abundant, and it provided food for all. The animals of the field found shade under it, **the birds of the air nested in its branches**, and from it all living beings were fed. (Dan. 4:10–12 NRSV)

When Daniel is summoned to interpret the dream, we discover that the great tree whose branches shelter the birds of the air is Nebuchadnezzar, and his great empire that stretches "to the ends of the earth." And we also learn that this great tree will be chopped down and the birds of the air will flee its branches; for in its arrogance, the great empire had forgotten that it is the "Most High" to whom true sovereignty belongs over the earth and its nations. Thus the emperor is warned to "break off your sins by doing justice, and your iniquities by showing mercy to the oppressed" (Dan. 4:27 NRSV). The prophets' constant message to the empires is: Do justice, show mercy to the oppressed. Only in this way can the empire survive the judgment of God.

In both Ezekiel and Daniel we find the judgment on the great empires of Assyria, Egypt, Babylon, the great trees in whose branches for a time the nations of the earth found shelter. But there is not only judgment here but also admiration for the security and prosperity that these great empires provide, if only for a time. The problem is that the great empires do not truly know God. And so they are avaricious and violent and arrogant, and they oppress the poor and destroy the weak. Therefore the great trees of empire must be cut down.

It need not always be so. For the prophets also dream of an empire in which violence, avarice, and arrogance will not rule, but peace, justice, and generosity.

So Ezekiel can also dream of the coming of such an empire. Thus in Ezekiel 17 the prophet speaks:

> Thus says the LORD GOD: I myself will take a sprig from the lofty top of a cedar; I will set it out. I will break off a tender one from the topmost of its young twigs; I myself will plant it on a high and lofty mountain.
> On the mountain height of Israel I will plant it, in order that it may produce boughs and bear fruit, and become a noble cedar. **Under it every kind of bird will live; in the shade of its branches will nest winged creatures of every kind.**
> All the trees of the field shall know that I am the LORD. I bring low the high tree; I make high the low tree; I dry up the green tree and make the dry tree flourish. I the LORD have spoken it, I will accomplish it. (Ezek. 17:22–24 NRSV)

In Ezekiel's vision, the great empire will come. But this empire reverses the values of worldly empire; the lowly are raised up and the proud brought low—a "transvaluation of values" expressed in Hannah's song in 1 Samuel 2:1–10 (which offers an ironic commentary on the Davidic dynasty) and echoed in Mary's Magnificat in Luke 1:46–55.) Thus, true justice prevails and the nations of the earth nest in peace.

Ezekiel is not alone in this dream. For in the Psalms we encounter this image again in the great hymn to creation in Psalm 104. It begins:

> Bless the LORD, O my soul. O LORD my God, you are very great. You are clothed with honor and majesty, wrapped in light as with a garment. (Ps. 104:1–2a NRSV)

Then it speaks of the wonders of the created world:

> You set the earth on its foundations, so that it will never be shaken. You cover it with the deep as with a garment; the waters stood above the mountains. At your rebuke they flee; . . .
> You make springs gush forth in the valleys; they flow between the hills, giving drink to every wild animal; . . .
> The trees of the LORD are watered abundantly, the cedars of Lebanon that he planted. **In them the birds build their nests;** . . .
> O LORD how manifold are your works! In wisdom you have made them all; . . .
> May the glory of the LORD endure forever. (Pss. 104:5–7a, 10–11a, 16–17a, 24a–b, 31a NRSV)

This long and beautiful hymn of praise will conclude with "Bless the LORD, oh my soul" (Ps. 104:35c NRSV). But immediately preceding that we hear:

> Let sinners be consumed from the earth, and let the wicked be no more. (Ps. 104: 35a–b NRSV)

Why this odd and discordant note? Is it to help us to realize that the earth described by the psalmist is the creation already cleansed of evil? It is creation restored and renewed, set free from the stain of avarice and violence. It is in this creation that the great trees put forth their branches and the birds of the air build their nests in them. It is in this renewed creation that the peoples of the earth at last find justice and joy. It is the new creation in which the violent stain of empire has been eradicated by the judgment of God upon all injustice and arrogance.

The image of the great tree in which the birds of the air find shelter brings to expression one of humanity's greatest hopes. It is the hope for the empire in which violence and avarice and arrogance will be expelled, the empire in which justice for the poor and vulnerable will reign, in which the peace of peoples living in harmony with one another and with nature itself will prevail. This dream may be the secret hope that drives the course of human history. As 2 Peter says, it is the hope "for new heavens and a new earth in which justice is at home" (3:13).

This is the messianic hope crystallized in the image of the great shrub, herb, or, weed in which the birds of the air find shelter. For this is the reign of God. That is why in his introduction to the image Jesus appears to underscore it so strongly: "What is God's reign like; to what shall we compare it?" (Mark 4:30).

And it is this empire of unrestricted justice—which Paul had maintained has love at its root (Romans 13:8–10)—that grows from the tiniest of seeds, from the announcement and enactment of the good news of God's favor.

But it is important to notice that it is no longer a tree, it is an herb, a weed; it is not a tree-like structure but more like crabgrass. In this the messianic vision is radically different from the great trees of empire—even to its root structure. It is the empire of the lowly, or as we like to say, of the grass roots. It is a rule of justice and mercy in which the sick and despised, the poor and oppressed find welcome and dignity.

EMPIRE AND CONTEMPORARY DISCOURSE

There are many ways in which what may be termed a biblical ambivalence toward empire comes to be theorized in contemporary discourse. Today the question of empire is less that of the rule of one people over many others than it is the question of the development of a truly global order (or disorder) that embraces the entire planet and all its peoples. Rome was always aware, however dimly, of an outside to itself, which it attempted, vainly as it turned out, to keep at bay. But today, the depiction of Rome that we can read in Nietzsche (1997, 71)—"the circle was closed the whole future seemed to be fixed"—seems all too apt: there is no outside; all is being progressively incorporated into one vast "civilization," sometimes called capitalism, sometimes democracy, and sometimes globalization portending "the end of history."

A certain ambivalence concerning global capitalism goes back to Karl Marx, who is often portrayed as an implacable foe of capitalism. However, Marx understood, as did Lenin, that capitalism was, relative to feudalism, an emancipatory project that was the necessary prelude to democratic socialism—hence his rather regrettable essay on India (1978, 653–664) in which he argues that British colonialism was necessary to bring India into the orbit of a capitalist economy as a prelude to world-wide socialism.

More recent theorists, however, have tended to abandon a simple apocalyptic periodization of capital and social life by seeking to discern within and alongside the expansion of the empire of globalization another and contravening dynamic, which at least some hope may herald a new possibility for human flourishing within and beyond global capitalist empire.

One such model is proposed by Gilles Deleuze and Felix Guatari (1987, 3–25) who distinguish between arboreal and rhizomatic structures. *Arboreal* in this case would refer to the fabled cedars of Lebanon, towering institutions of impressive power and success. *Rhizomatic* would refer to what might be termed grass-roots movements, communities, and networks that eschew the arboreal heights in favor of small-scale but loosely interconnected associations of those who develop and inhabit alternative forms of life. In a way, both could be regarded as having a kind of imperial or global ambition. But the rhizomatic systems would presumably not be characterized by the violence, avarice, and arrogance of the arboreal structures.

Some such distinction seems to be at work in the triology by Michael Hardt and Antonio Negri, of which the first, *Empire* (Hardt and Negri 2000), identifies the interlocking structures of the global political economy as a new "Empire," while the second and the third (Hardt and Negri 2004; 2009) explain how the multitude works to constitute a "Commonwealth" by developing modes of sharing life and labor that subvert the laws of Empire.

In addition, there are others with perhaps less sweeping visions (or narratives) who seek to bring to expression a critique of the imperial global order as we know it and to offer with that order the working out of an equally "global" but significantly more just and humane sociality. Thus, for example, Jacques Derrida (2002, 371–386) makes the conceptual distinction between what he calls "globalatinization" (what is usually called globalization) and cosmopolitanism characterized by hospitality and the sharing in the vision and work of democratization. In a somewhat similar vein, Jean Luc Nancy (a close friend of Derrida's) writes of the globalization as the destruction of the shared world and calls instead for the mutual ongoing creation of the world (Nancy 2007). Neither Derrida nor Nancy engages in developing a grand narrative about the overcoming of injustice and the emergence finally of a just social order. Instead, what they propose is a model of thought that may guide action on a global or cosmopolitical scale that persistently resists the violence of empire in its modern guise.

This all-too-brief review of certain ways of thinking of empire in our contemporary time and space may suggest that the ambivalence about empire that we have traced in biblical literature continues to have relevance for thinking about the world in which we are living now. For ours, too, is a world in which the arrogance, avarice, and violence of empire are on full display, in which people alternately embrace and denounce imperial schemes, and in which we may be torn between the grandeur of the peace and prosperity promised (and betrayed) by imperial projects and the tyranny—cultural, political, and economic—of the all-embracing and increasingly anonymous empire. It is a world, now as then, in which many long for a very different sort of empire in which all are valued, all find security, and all find one another as neighbors.

References

Berquist, Jon. 2003. *Judaism in Persia's Shadow: A Social and Historical Approach.* Eugene, OR: Wipf and Stock.

Carter, Warren. 2000. *Matthew and the Margins: A Religious and Socio-Political Reading.* Maryknoll, NY: Orbis Books.

Davidson, Steed. 2011. *Empire and Exile: Postcolonial Readings of the Book of Jeremiah.* New York: T&T Clark.

Deleuze, Gilles, and Felix Guatari. 1987. *A Thousand Plateaus: Capitalism and Schizophrenia.* Translated by Brian Massumi. Minneapolis: University of Minnesota Press.

Derrida, Jacques. 2002. *Negotiations: Interventions and Interviews, 1971-2001.* Edited and translated by Elizabeth Rottenberg. Cultural Memory in the Present. Redwood City, CA: Stanford University Press.

Engels, Friedrich. 1964. *On the History of Early Christianity.* In *Karl Marx and Friedrich Engels on Religion.* New York: Schocken.

Hardt, Michael, and Antonio Negri. 2000. *Empire.* Cambridge, MA: Harvard University Press.

Hardt, Michael, and Antonio Negri. 2004. *Multitude: War and Democracy in the Age of Empire.* New York: Penguin.

Hardt, Michael, and Antonio Negri. 2009. *Commonwealth.* Cambridge, MA: Harvard University Press.

Horsley, Richard A., ed. 1997. *Paul and Empire: Religion and Power in Roman Imperial Society.* Harrisburg, PA: Trinity Press International.

Horsley, Richard A., ed. 2000. *Paul and Politics: Ekklesia, Israel, Imperium, Interpretation.* Harrisburg, PA: Trinity Press International.

Horsley, Richard A., ed. 2004. *Paul and the Roman Imperial Order.* Harrisburg, PA: Trinity Press International.

Kahl, Brigette. 2010. *Galatians Re-Imagined: Reading with the Eyes of the Vanquished.* Minneapolis MN: Fortress.

Kim, Uriah. 2005. *Decolonizing Josiah: Toward a Postcolonial Reading of the Deuteronomistic History.* Sheffield, Yorkshire: Sheffield Phoenix Press.

Lopez, Davina. 2010. *The Apostle to the Conquered: Reimagining Paul's Mission.* Minneapolis, MN: Fortress.

Marx, Karl. 1978. *On Imperialism in India.* In *The Marx-Engels Reader,* edited by Robert C. Tucker. New York: W. W. Norton.

Moore, Stephen D. 2014. *Untold Tales from the Book of Revelation: Sex and Gender, Empire and Ecology.* Atlanta, GA: Society of Biblical Literature.

Nancy, Jean Luc. 2007. *The Creation of the World or Globalization.* Translated by Francois Raffoul and David Pettigrew. SUNY Series in Contemporary French Thought. Albany: State University of New York Press.

Nietzsche, Friedrich. 1997. *Daybreak: Thoughts on the Prejudices of Morality.* Translated by R. J. Hollingdale. Cambridge Texts in the History of Philosophy. Cambridge: Cambridge University Press.

Portier-Young, Anathea. 2011. *Apocalypse against Empire: Theologies of Resistance in Early Judaism.* Grand Rapids, MI: Eerdmans.

Taubes, Jacob. 2004. *The Political Theology of Paul.* Redwood City, CA: Stanford University Press.

CHAPTER 45

THE SOCIAL WORLDS OF BIBLICAL NARRATIVE

LINDA A. DIETCH

BIBLICAL narrative is a medium in an almost metaphysical sense: it serves as an intermediary between the thoughts and imaginations of people long since deceased and the modern individuals and communities that find its tales intriguing, important, or instructive. Contrary to popular understanding, the exchange between past and present is not simple or straightforward. Given that there is a distinction between the ancient world and the world created in biblical narrative—between the actual events and peoples of the past and a story focused on select characters, events, and settings—we must ask, to what degree might the social dimensions of the worlds created in the narrative mimic the social conditions of the writers or editors, reproduce their social values or ideologies, or accurately reflect the social dynamics of an earlier time? Assuming there exists some level of homology between the ancient and biblical worlds, then a logical follow-up question would be, how might a modern reader go about teasing out these social values, systems, and relations?[1]

Many resources describe social customs, religious practices, and historical developments within the ancient Near East and Mediterranean to help readers make sense of the strange worlds they encounter in the Bible—to help explain, for example, everything from ancient midwifery to mourning rituals. This chapter is not concerned with these helpful works but with studies that explicitly use social-scientific models and theories to describe and explain how social forces, institutions, and practices impacted the origin and development of biblical religions, biblical texts, and the peoples and communities behind both. Social-scientific analysis—which draws from sociology, anthropology, psychology, economics, and political science—is often conducted in concert with other methods of biblical interpretation, such as literary criticism, or integrates data from other disciplines, such as archaeology.

OPENING WINDOWS ONTO ANCIENT SOCIAL WORLDS

Social-scientific criticism is not a single method but an expanding subfield that uses the fruits of social-scientific study to analyze ancient cultural and material artifacts. It provides a fresh perspective on older problems and challenges prevailing assumptions and long-held opinions regarding the origins, developments, institutions, and aspects of ancient social worlds. Since the breadth of the social sciences permits various avenues of study, the shape the discussion takes depends on the theorist or the approach being used, the focus of one's analysis, and the text and its nature. Amid this diversity, approaches can be generally categorized as inductive or deductive—that is, as moving from particulars or a collection of data to general conclusions (inductive) or from a broad principle to specific hypotheses that can be tested (deductive). The social sciences expect consistencies in human behavior and use theories developed in the study of ancient and modern cultures. Some degree of homology or analogy between different societies is accepted, and comparative data from ancient and modern societies is utilized to plausibly explain social phenomena, shed light on group and individual social behaviors, and identify patterns or systems of behaviors and thought.

Although the glimpses the Bible provides into ancient lives are partial and fragmentary, the text remains encoded with social values and relations that can be mined with the help of the social sciences. The approach has been utilized to answer questions related to (1) the origin and growth of biblical sects, states, and religion; (2) social institutions, such as kinship and family, households and hospitality, and ancient economies; (3) cultural values, such as honor and shame, group versus individual identity, purity and pollution, gender and sexuality, health and healing, landscape and spatiality, and collective memory; and (4) genres and cultural scripts (i.e., how texts function within and are shaped by social settings and conventions). Social-scientific analysis can help generate a fuller description of the complex social processes whereby discrete oral and written compositions were remembered, associated, inscribed, arranged, and passed on. It can open windows on the social worlds behind biblical narratives as well as those constructed by the narratives.

THE EMERGENCE AND WAVES
OF SOCIAL-SCIENTIFIC CRITICISM

Modern biblical scholarship and social science both emerged in Europe during the Enlightenment and subsequently developed during a climate of sweeping social and economic change (see Wilson 1984). Given the state of intellectual ferment, which breached disciplinary boundaries, it is perhaps unsurprising that the earliest methods of biblical scholarship are protosociological in the sense that the text was often approached as a means to learn about the religious, political, and social settings and institutions behind it. This is perhaps most obvious with older form criticism, given its aim to connect speech form and genre to a *Sitz im Leben*. Even during these early days, however, there were modest attempts to consciously apply social-scientific ideas to biblical texts and religions.

Of special note during the "first wave" of social-scientific criticism (1880–1960) are William Robertson Smith's (1889) lectures on the religion of early Semites; Max Weber's (1952) study of ancient Judaism; Ernst Troeltsch's (1912) work on the social teaching of Christian churches; Louis Wallis's (1912) evolutionary study of Christendom, along with the works of his Chicago School colleagues Shailer Mathews, Shirley Jackson Case, and Donald Riddle; Johannes Pedersen's (1920) study of covenant and Israelite institutions; Karl

Kautsky's (1925) Marxist analysis of the foundations of Christianity; and Antonin Causse's (1937) work on the origins of ancient Israel. Much of the work of this period centered on the origins and development of biblical religions vis-à-vis their social worlds and relied on comparative data and an evolutionary view of culture. Though pioneering, it has been criticized for its inattention to cultural differences and to sociological method and theory. As biblical scholarship grew alongside the emerging fields of sociology, anthropology, and psychology, many excellent questions were raised but not adequately resolved. Combined with a scholarly climate that was largely nonconducive to social-scientific inquiry owing to its conditioning by traditional European scholarship, neoorthodoxy, and the Biblical Theology movement, it failed to stimulate a broader program within the discipline (Cook and Simkins 1999, 2).

During the 1960s, renewed interest in social world studies is noted in Edwin A. Judge's (1960) study of the social characteristics of Roman-era Christianity; George Mendenhall's (1962) peasant revolt model for understanding Israel's establishment in Palestine; Roland de Vaux's (1965) work on ancient Israelite social institutions; Mary Douglas's (1966) study of pollution and taboo in Levitical dietary and sacrificial regulations; and Martin Hengel's (1969) analysis of early Judaism in a Hellenistic context. Spanning both testaments, early Judaism, and early Christianity, these works anticipate the "second wave" of social world studies, which begins with the 1970s and continues to the present. Much of the earliest work of this phase exhibits similar historical interests as the first wave but begins to remedy the first wave's faults with analyses that attempt a more sophisticated engagement with ethnographic data and select theorists (especially Karl Marx, Max Weber, and Émile Durkheim). For the sake of clarity and space, developments during the second wave will be discussed very briefly and according to testament.

Norman Gottwald's *The Tribes of Yahweh* (1979) is a major contribution to the sea change in Hebrew Bible scholarship. Building upon Mendenhall's peasant revolt model while breaking free of the biblical historian's spell in terms of religious determinism, he hypothesizes the emergence of ancient Israel as an internal development within Palestine, in which Yahwism is not the sole impetus for social cohesiveness or change but is rather a function of material realities and one of many factors that contribute to state formation and development (Carter 1996, 19). The tome is among the first to exhibit a systematic application of sociological insights to the premonarchic period and, as such, becomes a resource scholars must reckon with as they (and Gottwald) revise, extend, and add to the study of ancient Israelite origins by considering, for example, patterns and trends in population, agricultural production, and social stratification (Frick 1985; Coote and Whitelam 1986; Gottwald 1993; Boer 2002). In addition to pursuing largely historical interests, research has delved into an ever-expanding and often overlapping array of topics such as socioeconomics, class (Sneed 1999), kinship and marriage (Steinberg 1993), the role of women in the domestic sphere and cultus (Bird 1987; Meyers 1988), spatiality (Flanagan 1999; Berquist and Camp 2007), ideology vis-à-vis propaganda (Berlinerblau 1999), and prophecy (Chaney 1993).

Within New Testament scholarship, Gerd Theissen energizes use of the social sciences with a thesis and method that was groundbreaking in its day (Elliott 1993). Practicing a sociology of literature, which considers how social and cultural conditions contribute to the shape and content of texts, Theissen (1973) insists the radical content of Jesus's sayings must be understood in relation to the material and social conditions of the transmitters of these sayings. Although it was typical for scholars to understand Jesus's teaching on renouncing family, home, and wealth as an unachievable ideal, Theissen maintains instead that it reflects the praxis of Jesus's followers (Elliott 1993). Besides subsequent contributions from Judge and Hengel, other significant works of this decade include Fernando Belo's (1974) materialist analysis of the social setting, narrative, and ideology of Mark and John Gager's (1975) study of the social forces that shaped Christianity and fostered its rapid growth (Elliott 1993). John Elliott (2008) observes New Testament social world studies develop along two trajectories: social history and social-scientific analysis. With the founding contributions of Elliott (1981), Bruce Malina (1981), and others, the latter course produces The Context Group, a prolific group of international biblical scholars. During this phase, methodological rigor intensifies as approaches and interests expand in similar ways as first testament studies, yielding many discrete sociological, anthropological, and ethnographic studies on a wide variety of social institutions, cultural values, and cultural scripts.

Presenting key works and select scholars can give the false impression that breakthroughs occur in a vacuum. They should be understood, of course, as part of the fabric and tensions of the discipline and its social worlds. Casting a sociological gaze upon the discipline alerts us to the vast network of agents, institutions, and social processes shaped by various ideologies, theologies, economies, and so on, complicit in the emergence and growth of a subfield. One conviction that emerged from the epistemological questions raised by the modern-postmodern debate, which is in full force during the second wave, is that context is as significant a factor in the lives of the ancient producers of the biblical text as it is for those of any time or location who seek to interpret it. Scholars are increasingly recognizing the effect of their own and others' culturally informed presuppositions on the task of interpretation, as well as the social, political, and ethical implications and world-constructing power of various readings of biblical narratives. This state of affairs forbids methodological naïveté that fails to consider the motives behind and the social consequences of different modes of interpretation.

Biblical scholars' lack of training in the social sciences, the isolation of academic disciplines, or fear of reductionism might explain the unevenness and slowness of acceptance of social-scientific methods (Elliott 1993, 18), but these challenges are to be expected as biblical scholars study outside their disciplines and a new brand of research emerges (Carter 1996, 25). As with any method of interpretation, there is potential for misuse, such as allowing particulars to be universalized or wrenching social data out of one setting and applying them to another, and limitations, such as finding an appropriate fit between a particular theory and text or subject. In order to avoid the pitfalls of reading modern assumptions into the text or allowing a model to determine outcomes, Charles Carter (1996, 25–28) advocates that the use of the social sciences should be regarded as a necessity among biblical scholars and recommends the following safeguards: interdisciplinary cooperation, wider use of ethnographic data to dispel evolutionary or elitist notions about ancient and modern societies, increased sensitivity to the complexity of social processes, and adopting methods that are rigorous and self-critical.

Bearing these thoughts in mind, it will be helpful to demonstrate what might be gleaned by applying early and more recent sociological theory to Judges 3:12–30: classical sociologist Émile Durkheim's conceptions of sacred and profane and of the function of religious ritual and modern sociologist Pierre Bourdieu's conceptions of field, habitus, and *doxa*. Ehud's judgeship presents a comic and crude tale of an unlikely assassin who frees the Israelites from the eighteen-year domination of King Eglon of Moab. Although largely absent, YHWH plays a critical role by both initiating this political and economic oppression in response to Israel's bad behavior and by raising up a deliverer in the person of Ehud in response to Israel's outcry. Within a monolatrous framework, the story focuses on Israel's relationship with a near neighbor, a people who lay just south and east of the territory of Benjamin.

Judging Ehud's Judgeship with Durkheim

Durkheim (1995, 44) defines religion as "a unified system of beliefs and practices relative to sacred things, that is to say, things set apart and forbidden—beliefs and practices which unite into one single moral community called a Church, all those who adhere to them." Although beliefs and practices unite the religious community, Durkheim considers religious beliefs to be dichotomous at their core: "they presuppose a classification of the real or ideal things that men conceive of into two classes—two opposite genera—that are widely designated by two distinct terms, which the words profane and sacred translate fairly well" (Durkheim 1995, 34). He focuses on the power of religion to create cohesion, but he does so by positing sacred and profane as two necessary and distinct categories of religious belief that are hostile to one another and derive from different sources, collective versus individual (37). The sacred spring from collective representations of a society, from "common traditions and emotions, feelings which have a relationship to objects of general interest"; whereas profane things are constructions from "personal sense data and experience" (Durkheim 1994, 95).

Evaluating Ehud's judgeship through this framework highlights the social role religion plays to unite the community. The Israelites' social and religious identities are essentially one according to the narrative. Their oppression is cast as divine retribution for corporate error, and is reversed through collective outcry to YHWH. This vocalization conveys the anomie created by a combination of religious crisis, economic exploitation, and sociopolitical infringement. Like some of the other judgeships, Ehud's actions resolidify Israel's commitment to YHWH, at least temporarily. The non-Israelite (i.e., native) presence tests Israel's communal solidarity as the "clean" ostensibly mingle with the "unclean." Durkheim suggests that "religious and profane life cannot coexist in the same space. If religious life is to develop, a special place must be prepared for it, one from which profane life is excluded" (Durkheim 1995, 312). Although he is speaking of the institution of sacred spaces, such as temples or sanctuaries, the notion can perhaps be extended to YHWH's land gift to the Israelites. According to the introduction to the book of Judges, Israel fails to conquer the land's inhabitants, which creates a syncretistic environment.

The introduction associates Israel's errant religious practice and belief, which is sacrilegious in terms of monotheistic faith, as the cause for divine reprisal in the form of sociopolitical oppression. During the deliverance phase of (most of) the major judgeships, the sacred exhibits the value that has been ascribed to it as deliverance is achieved through a sacred object or person(s). This ascription is explicit in the case of Ehud's dagger, rather than his person. Although its description is veiled in ambiguous terms, it can be understood as a secret thing and a message from the god(s). The homicide is framed by references to the carved stones in Gilgal (Judg. 3:19, 26), a detail that sets the profane idols in sharp contrast to Ehud's sacred mission and YHWH's superiority.

Durkheim's thoughts on religious ritual can add another dimension to the relation of sacred and profane. He states that rites are above all the "means by which the social group reaffirms itself periodically" (Durkheim 1995, 390). The act of sacrifice is both a form of renunciation and communion for the worshipper, as "some part of his substance or his goods" is relinquished (Durkheim 1995, 346–347). The cult's purpose "is not only to bring the profane into communion with sacred beings but also to keep the sacred beings alive, to remake and regenerate them perpetually. To be sure, the material offerings do not produce this remaking through their own virtues but through mental states that reawaken and accompany these doings, which are empty in themselves" (Durkheim 1995, 350). For Durkheim, it is the thought the worshiper gives to her or his god that renews both. This collective experience of communion as pursued through a religious rite is the means of rekindling belief. It resuscitates both community and deity by invoking thoughts of the god through physical sensations. Religious rites also induce the masses to act: "its effect is to bring individuals together, to put the masses into motion, and thus induce a state of effervescence—sometimes even delirium—which is not without kinship to the religious state" (Durkheim 1995, 386–387).

With this understanding of ritual in mind, sacrificial allusions in the discourse may be noted. Three specific aspects of the narrative suggest the killing of the Moabite king may metaphorically represent a sacrifice. As many have noted, the name Eglon is a play on the word calf ('egel); the term used to describe his stoutness (bry') is typically used for cattle (Barré 1991, 27n24); and the term used to describe Ehud's presentation of tribute, which is unusual for this activity, appears frequently in contexts of animal sacrifice (Brettler 1991, 294–295). Coupled with the description of the dagger as a secret and sacred thing/word, the application of Durkheim's concepts would suggest that the homicide represents Israel's enactment of a religious rite to reorient Israel's faith toward YHWH. Like a male calf fattened from the produce and possessions of Israel, which signals Eglon's power and excess (see Boer's "The Economic Politics of Biblical Narrative" in this volume), Ehud offers Eglon to YHWH with a sacred dagger.

The one who formerly received offerings from Israel becomes the offering for Israel. The Israelites relinquish part of their substance and goods through the killing of Eglon, which re-establishes and safeguards the sacred. Following this event, the people of Israel are set in motion by the rite of sacrifice and unite with their god in battle against the Moabites. Understood in this manner, the act reawakens and renews Israel's devotion and moral obligations as the community, in solidarity, turns from its dependence on the idols to dependence on YHWH. At the same time, this event of sacrifice enlivens YHWH to the community, as the deity becomes the source for the assurance of victory.

Applying Durkheim's thoughts on religion and ritual to the narrative highlights certain aspects that open a window on the social world of the ancient community. The analysis underscores the decisive role religious practice plays in communal cohesion, economic prosperity, and sociopolitical endurance in the worldview of the story's creators. Select concepts of Bourdieu will now be utilized to explore whose interests the story reflects and how these interests are consciously and unconsciously communicated.

JUDGING EHUD'S JUDGESHIP WITH BOURDIEU

Bourdieu conceives of the social world as a multidimensional space "constructed on the basis of principles of differentiation or distribution constituted by the set of properties active in the social universe under consideration, that is, able to confer force or power on their possessor in that universe" (Bourdieu 1991, 229). Agents are defined by their relative positions in a social universe or field, which is a site of ongoing struggle for power and profit (as these are defined in the specific field). They develop a type of practical sense suited to their particular field that Bourdieu (1977, 82–83) terms *habitus*, "a system of lasting, trans- posable dispositions which, integrating past experiences, functions at every moment as a matrix of perceptions, appreciations and actions and makes possible the achievement of infinitely diversified tasks." Field and habitus shape each other, and their pairing attempts to reconcile understandings of culture that overemphasize either objective phenomena or subjective experience.

The principles that structure the social world also shape perceptions of the social world, yet, since they remain largely hidden, "incline agents to accept the social world as it is, to take it for granted, rather than to rebel against it, to put forward opposed and even antag- onistic possibilities" (Bourdieu 1991, 235). Consequently, agents recognize their places within a social universe as given, and distinction between positions—that is, the sense of one's place—tends to curb certain social behaviors. The principle underlying this process is termed *doxa*, the silent comprehension of "the way things are" that remains outside the reach of discourse. *Doxa* reflects a dominant view of the social world that is unreflectively absorbed by all who inhabit it. To Bourdieu what a society regards as sacred or profane is not determined by its source in collective *or* in individual interests as Durkheim hypothesizes, but by social processes and structures that collectively and individually reproduce the inter- ests of the dominant.

The concept of *doxa* helps readers distinguish between what the biblical writers unwittingly communicated about their social world and what they wanted their audi- ence to know or believe—between unconscious (doxic) assumptions and propaganda (Berlinerblau 1999). Undisclosed, and often unchallenged, assumptions about the shape of and relations within the social world underlie texts that intentionally advance a par- ticular view or theology. For example, the book of Judges describes Israel's worship of "foreign" gods alongside or in place of Yhwh as idolatry in order to affirm the theologi- cal stance that Yhwh is the only deity worthy of Israelite worship. This agenda is clearly expressed and appears to be combating views and practices to the contrary. On the other hand, that punishment for "foreign" worship is meted out collectively via "foreign" oppres- sion rests on doxic assumptions about identity (e.g., corporate vs. individual, Israelite vs. Canaanite).

The propagandistic function of the Ehud story is recognized in its thorough disparage- ment of the Moabites. Ehud smuggles a deadly weapon into the Moabite king's presence not once but twice (Judg. 3:17, 19). Commentators who desire to make this detail seem plausible suggest the dagger evades notice because Ehud attaches it to his right thigh, and the guards would be more apt to check his left thigh since this side would be suitable for a right-hand draw (Halpern 1988, 43). Even so, this hardly mitigates their incompetence. King Eglon is caricaturized as a "little calf" (Soggin 1981, 49), is quickly duped into thinking he is about to receive a secret message (or a homosexual encounter; see Miller 1996), and naively dis- misses his staff. That he is objectified and feminized in the assassination seems assured by the combination of semantically broad terms and the sexual connotations of their private meeting: Ehud reaches under his cloak, pulls out his secret thing from his thigh/loins, and thrusts it into Eglon's belly/womb (Alter 1981, 39; Niditch 1993, 117–118). The force of the blow causes the release of Ehud's excrement, which may hint at an association between Chemosh, Moab's god, and "filth" (1 Kings 11:7). Eglon's attendants, who return to find a locked door and presumably a pungent odor, wait to the point of embarrassment to enter, only to find their king dead from no apparent cause as the dagger is engulfed in Eglon's fat. Their delay gives Ehud time to flee and spontaneously rally troops that make easy work of ten thousand sturdy Moabite warriors (Judg. 3:24–27). The narrator concludes the tale by stating Moab "humbled itself" under Israel's hand (3:30).

As propaganda the story cultivates in-group cohesion by fostering a negative attitude toward Moab, thereby reinforcing the boundary between "Israel" and "Moab," and by under-scoring the importance of the link between YHWH and Israel. The triumph-of-the-underdog theme—where human deliverers are ill-matched to their adversaries on account of social position, gender, age, and so on, yet succeed—affirms that loyalty to Israel's cause and god is more important than human political or social power. This conscious message depends upon many assumptions about social order and hierarchy.

In its original context, the portrayal of Eglon as a sacrificial animal and sexual object would be especially debasing to the king, yet why this is so depends largely on *doxa*—upon deep-seated assumptions about a king's authority vis-à-vis the place and function of women and livestock in a patriarchal society that lives close to the earth. Men and gods could be positively associated with animal or female attributes, as the biblical text sufficiently dem-onstrates, so the humiliation does not derive from the mere correlation but from the objec-tification. In ancient society it was customary for men to treat women as sexual objects and animals as sacrificial objects, and for a king to oppress his vassals. However, in the Ehud story this "natural" order is inverted: a vassal dominates a sovereign, and the king's shame correlates to the difference in their social and economic capital and to the manner of the objectification.

In a book in which foreign rulers bear comical names (see Guest's "Judging YHWH in the Book of Judges" in this volume), calling the Moabite king a "little calf" blatantly renders him an animal ripe for sacrifice. Yet the motivation to imagine him in this particular way could suggest something about the interests of the story's creator(s). It is possible that some of the details that support the sacrificial calf imagery were less than intentional. For example, using a term associated with sacrifice to describe the presentation of the tribute could reflect a linguistic habit rather than a deliberate decision. That the passage depends on sacrificial imagery to describe the overthrow of a tribute-devouring king might reflect a priestly field and habitus, especially when one considers that the conditions the story describes would severely limit the Israelites' ability to support a priestly body that depends on offerings from the land and its people.

The story functions as propaganda on another front. Although Ehud is YHWH's answer to Israel's outcry and successfully subdues the enemy, his characterization is complicated by his contact with bodily filth and the innuendos noted above. Ehud is a Benjaminite ("son of the right") who has an "impeded" right hand, though it is unclear whether he is left-handed by birth, injury, or design.[2] Whether or not there is contact between Eglon's feces and Ehud's left hand, most commentators understand Ehud's path of escape to be down and through the toilet. Given the deviant and questionable nature of Ehud's engagements with Eglon, the Benjaminite appears to be an object of some derision. Even YHWH is distanced from the vic-tory: absent from the story is the rushing of YHWH's spirit or a statement that he subdued the enemy on that day. Ehud's portrayal suggests the narrative functions as a prolepsis to the anti-Saulide polemic contained in the book's final chapters (cf. Brettler 1989). Beneath this agenda, readers can detect hints of doxic assumptions about tribal identity, handedness, and YHWH's role in politics that could be tested and developed through further analysis of the book of Judges and beyond.

SYNTHESIS

Like a palimpsest that shows traces of earlier writing, the narrative portions of the Hebrew Bible and New Testament are understood to have developed through a complex and often extended process that involves communities from various social, geographical, and temporal settings. Biblical scholars have long sought windows onto the social contexts behind these stories, a task that is complicated, especially in relation to the Hebrew Bible, by a dearth of textual artifacts from the times the narratives describe or from which they derive. Regardless of testament, however, there remains the challenge of extrapolating social values, systems, and relations from a mere slice of an ancient culture's textual and material production. This state of affairs recommends the careful use of the social sciences to help bridge the gaps between the modern interpreter and the ancient sources and between the ancient narratives and the societies that created them.

The results of the readings here of the Ehud discourse, though not definitive or entirely novel, reinforce and add breadth and detail to previous scholarship on a passage that has seldom been the object of sociological examination. To those who resist the notion that Judges 3:12–30 demonstrates clear sacrificial overtones (see Stone 2009), the analysis offers a rebuttal that supports the intuitions of the many commentators who note these qualities. Conducting a functional analysis using Durkheim's concepts highlights the story's cultic interests, allowing it to be understood as a metaphorical religious rite that underscores the interdependence of the deity and the collective.

By consulting Bourdieu's understanding of social worlds, we can begin to hypothesize the effect of social field and habitus on ancient producers and parse between their explicit views and doxic assumptions. Although this brief foray into a sociology of literature would benefit from more extensive analysis, it tentatively suggests the resort to a metaphorical sacrifice of a Moabite king demonstrates a strong priestly influence, while the combination of tension between Israel and Moab and between the Benjaminites and the unmentioned Judahites implies the *doxa* that undergirds the ethnic and communal/tribal identities of the text's producers has been sufficiently exposed and challenged to prompt reinforcement.

Although social-scientific criticism can and often does point to a historical context, whether or not the Ehud narrative is historically based makes little difference to the approaches taken here. Evaluating how the characters and events of biblical narrative relate to the fabric and tensions of ancient social worlds can move the discussion beyond the question of historicity or actual events to analogous social forces and structures in modern contexts, which permits a more sophisticated and critical interchange between ancient and modern worlds.

Notes

1. I would like to thank David Chalcraft for his help in developing an abstract for this chapter, which was to be our joint effort.
2. Halpern (1988, 40–41) argues there was likely a military benefit to fostering left-handedness, which could be achieved through binding the right hand from youth.

References

Alter, Robert. 1981. *The Art of Biblical Narrative*. New York: Basic.

Barré, Michael L. 1991. "The Meaning of Pršdn in Judges 3:22." *Vetus Testamentum* 41(1): 1–11.

Belo, Fernando. 1974. *Lecture matérialiste de l'évangile de Marc: Récit, pratique, idéologie*. Paris, Éditions du Cerf.

Berlinerblau, Jacques. 1999. "Ideology, Pierre Bourdieu's *doxa*, and the Hebrew Bible." In *The Social World of the Hebrew Bible*, edited by Ronald Simkins and Stephen L. Cook. *Semeia* 87: 193–214.

Berquist, Jon L., and Claudia V. Camp, eds. 2007. *The Constructions of Space I: Theory, Geography, and Narrative*. Library of Hebrew Bible/Old Testament Studies 481. New York: Clark.

Bird, Phyllis. 1987. "The Place of Women in the Israelite Cultus." In *Ancient Israelite Religion: Essays in Honor of Frank Moore Cross, Jr.*, edited by Paul D. Hanson, S. Dean McBride, and Patrick D. Miller, 397–419. Philadelphia, PA: Fortress.

Boer, Roland, ed. 2002. *Tracking "The Tribes of Yahweh": On the Trail of a Classic*. Journal for the Study of the Old Testament Supplement Series 351. London and New York: Sheffield Academic Press.

Bourdieu, Pierre. 1977. *Outline of a Theory of Practice*. Translated by Richard Nice. Cambridge Studies in Social and Cultural Anthropology. Cambridge: Cambridge University Press.

Bourdieu, Pierre. 1991. *Language and Symbolic Power*. Edited by John B. Thompson. Translated by Gino Raymond and Matthew Adamson. Cambridge, MA: Harvard University Press.

Brettler, Marc. 1989. "The Book of Judges: Literature as Politics." *Journal of Biblical Literature* 108(3): 395–418.

Brettler, Marc. 1991. "Never the Twain Shall Meet? The Ehud Story as History and Literature." *Hebrew Union College Annual* 62: 285–304.

Carter, Charles E. 1996. "A Discipline in Transition: The Contributions of the Social Sciences to the Study of the Hebrew Bible." In *Community, Identity, and Ideology: Social Science Approaches to the Hebrew Bible,* edited by Charles E. Carter and Carol L. Meyers, 3–36. Sources for Biblical and Theological Study 6. Winona Lake, IN: Eisenbrauns.

Causse, Antonin. 1937. *Du groupe ethnique à la communauté religieuse: Le problème sociologique de la religion d'Israël*. Études d'histoire et de philosophie religieuses 33. Paris: Alcan.

Chaney, Marvin. 1993. "Bitter Bounty: The Dynamics of Political Economy Critiqued by the Eighth-Century Prophets." In *The Bible and Liberation: Political and Social Hermeneutics*, edited by Norman K. Gottwald and Richard A. Horsley, 250–263. Maryknoll, NY: Orbis.

Cook, Stephen L., and Ronald A. Simkins. 2001. "Introduction: Case Studies from the Second Wave of Research in the Social World of the Hebrew Bible." In *The Social World of the Hebrew Bible*, edited by Ronald Simkins and Stephen L. Cook. *Semeia* 87: 1–14.

Coote, Robert, and Keith Whitelam. 1986. "The Emergence of Israel: Social Transformation and State Formation Following the Decline in Late Bronze Age Trade." In *Social-Scientific Criticism of the Hebrew Bible and Its Social World: The Israelite Monarchy*, edited by Norman K. Gottwald. *Semeia* 37: 109–147.

de Vaux, Roland. 1965. *Ancient Israel: Social Institutions. Religious Institutions*. New York: McGraw-Hill.

Douglas, Mary. 1966. *Purity and Danger: An Analysis of the Concepts of Pollution and Taboo*. London: Routledge and Kegan Paul.

Durkheim, Émile. 1994. *Durkheim on Religion*. Edited by W. S. F. Pickering. American Academy of Religion Texts and Translations Series 6. Atlanta, GA: Scholars Press.

Durkheim, Émile. 1995. *The Elementary Forms of Religious Life*. Translated by Karen E. Fields. New York: The Free Press. Original French version: Paris: F. Alcan, 1912.

Elliott, John H. 1981. *A Home for the Homeless: A Sociological Exegesis of 1 Peter, Its Situation and Strategy*. Philadelphia, PA: Fortress Press.

Elliott, John H. 1993. *What Is Social-Scientific Criticism?* Minneapolis, MN: Fortress Press.

Elliott, John H. 2008. "From Social Description to Social-Scientific Criticism: The History of a Society of Biblical Literature Section 1973–2005." *Biblical Theology Bulletin* 38: 26–36.

Flanagan, James W. 1999. "Ancient Perceptions of Space/Perceptions of Ancient Space." In *The Social World of the Hebrew Bible*, edited by Ronald Simkins and Stephen L. Cook. *Semeia* 87: 15–43.

Frick, Frank S. 1985. *The Formation of the State in Ancient Israel*. Edited by J. W. Flanagan. Social World of Biblical Antiquity Series 4. Sheffield, Yorkshire: Almond Press.

Gager, John G. 1975. *Kingdom and Community: The Social World of Early Christianity*. Englewood Cliffs, NJ: Prentice-Hall.

Gottwald, Norman K. 1979. *The Tribes of Yahweh: A Sociology of the Religion of Liberated Israel, 1250–1050 B.C.E.* Maryknoll, NY: Orbis.

Gottwald, Norman K. 1993. *The Hebrew Bible in Its Social World and in Ours*. Atlanta, GA: Scholars Press.

Halpern, Baruch. 1988. *The First Historians: The Hebrew Bible and History*. San Francisco: Harper & Row.

Hengel, Martin. 1969. *Judentum und Hellenismus: Studien zu ihrer Begegnung unter besonderer Berücksichtigung Palästinas bis zur Mitte des 2. Jh.s v.Chr.* Wissenschaftliche Untersuchungen zum Neuen Testament 10. Tübingen: Mohr.

Judge, Edwin A. 1960. *The Social Pattern of Christian Groups in the First Century*. London: Tyndale Press.

Kautsky, Karl. 1925. *Foundations of Christianity: A Study of Christian Origins*. New York: International.

Malina, Bruce J. 1981. *The New Testament World: Insights from Cultural Anthropology*. Atlanta, GA: John Knox Press.

Mendenhall, George. 1962. "The Hebrew Conquest of Palestine." *Biblical Archaeologist* 25: 66–87.

Meyers, Carol. 1988. *Discovering Eve: Ancient Israelite Women in Context*. New York: Oxford University Press.

Miller, Geoffrey P. 1996. "Verbal Feud in the Hebrew Bible: Judges 3:12–30 and 19–21." *Journal of Near Eastern Studies* 55(2): 105–117.

Niditch, Susan. 1993. *War in the Hebrew Bible: A Study in the Ethics of Violence*. New York: Oxford University Press.

Pedersen, Johannes. 1920. *Israel: Its Life and Culture, I–IV*. London: Oxford University Press.

Robertson Smith, William. 1889. *Lectures on the Religion of the Semites. Fundamental Institutions. First Series*. London: Adam & Charles Black.

Sneed, Mark, ed. 1999. *Concepts of Class in Ancient Israel*. South Florida Studies in Religion 201. Atlanta, GA: Scholars Press.

Soggin, J. Alberto. 1981. *Judges*. Old Testament Library. Philadelphia, PA: Westminster Press.

Steinberg, Naomi. 1993. *Kinship and Marriage in Genesis: A Household Economics Perspective*. Minneapolis, MN: Fortress.

Stone, Lawson G. 2009. "Eglon's Belly and Ehud's Blade: A Reconsideration." *Journal of Biblical Literature* 128(4): 649–663.

Theissen, Gerd. 1973. "Wanderradikalismus: Literatursoziologische Aspekte der Überlieferung von Worten Jesu im Urchristentum." *Zeitschrift für Theologie und Kirche* 70: 245–270.

Troeltsch, Ernst. 1912. *Die Soziallehren der christlichen Kirchen und Gruppen*. Tübingen: J. C. B. Mohr (Paul Siebeck).

Wallis, Louis. 1912. *Sociological Study of the Bible*. Chicago: University of Chicago Press.

Weber, Max. 1952. *Ancient Judaism*. Edited and translated by Hans H. Gerth and Don Martindale. Glencoe, IL: Free Press. Originally published in German as part of *Gesammelte Aufsatze zur Religionssoziologie*. Tübingen: J. C. B. Mohr (Paul Siebeck), 1920–1921.

Wilson, Robert R. 1984. *Sociological Approaches to the Old Testament*. Philadelphia, PA: Fortress Press.

CHAPTER 46

....

THE ECONOMIC POLITICS
OF BIBLICAL NARRATIVE

....

ROLAND BOER

POLITICS is ultimately determined by the socioeconomic situation. That situation generates divisions in labor and thereby class, and from there politics arises. So I begin by focusing on the socioeconomic tensions as the basis of politics. The key tension is between a system of palatine estates and the subsistence survival agriculture of village communities, a tension that characterized the marginal economic zone of the southern Levant in which Israel sparked briefly before becoming an imperial province. But how do texts respond to this situation? I suggest that they do so in mediated and unexpected ways, attempting to resolve the socioeconomic tension in the production of their stories, poetry, myths, and song. Neither windows onto reality nor expressions of the ideologies of the various groups that purportedly produced them, texts have indirect and contradictory connections with the socioeconomic context to which they respond. In order to show how, I deal with Genesis 1–3, the narrative of Joseph and Moses in Genesis 41–Exodus 15, Job, Proverbs, and 1 Samuel 8.

ESTATES VERSUS VILLAGE COMMUNITIES

....

I propose that the constitutive economic contradiction in the southern Levant of the first millennium was one between palatine estates and the agricultural labor of village communities (Diakonoff 1982; 1999, 21–55). Estates were initially a feature of temples (as in fourth-millennium Sumer with its *en*, or supreme priest), which formed the focus of activities in more powerful towns or "little kingdoms," as they called such places themselves (Diakonoff 1991b, 37; Liverani 1982, 250; 2005, 7). Soon enough, the estates were subsumed under the power of the palace. The basic purpose of the estates was the supply of "goods for a minority" (Diakonoff 1999, 36), that is, to supply those who were not gainfully employed—priests, monarchs, and their perpetual dinner guests—with food, alcohol, and textiles. After all, they needed to live in the way to which they had become accustomed. Estates were therefore established in the vicinity of temples and then ruling centers, administered either directly by functionaries or by tenure to landlords. Those who labored on them were indentured permanently or temporarily (corvée, conquest, and debt-labor). Given the perpetual labor shortage, the estates constantly sought to draw more laborers from the village communities, with little concern for the continued viability of the latter.

Why not simply tax the village communities instead of establishing estates? Two reasons are relevant. First, the power of the petty despots tended to be intermittent and uncertain. They might make grandiloquent claims concerning the vastness of their lands (1 Kings 4:21), but the reality was quite different, for without elaborate administrative apparatuses, clear borders, and the ability to police the territory claimed, the real power exercised was quite weak. For this reason, the ability to tax villages regularly was not within their power. The farther away a collection of villages was from the capital, the weaker was the power. If villages found the burdens of corvée labor or taxation too onerous, they would simply move out of harm's way—to a distant place or even into the mountains to join the ever-present Habiru. Second, villages were taxed at 10 percent, while estates supplied between one-half and two-thirds of the produce going to the temple or the palace. Estates were clearly the better economic option, for they enabled higher yields and could be policed reasonably consistently.

As for the village-communes themselves, the diverse and versatile mechanisms of animal husbandry (with 2:1 ratios of sheep and goats) and crop growing (Sasson 2010; Hald 2008, 44–121; Hole 1991) are of less interest on this occasion than the social determination of economic life. That life was centered on what Soviet-era Russian scholars called the extended-family household commune or a village-commune (Diakonoff 1974; 1975; 1982, 35; 1991a, 88; 1991b, 34–35; Jankowska 1969; 1991, 253; Vasilʹev and Stuchevskii 1967, 28–32; Bartlett 1990), and what Western scholars have dubbed *musha'* farming (Wilkinson 2003, 2010; Guillaume 2012, 28–42). It designates a strikingly persistent approach to subsistence agriculture, largely because it has been tried and tested. Typically, farmers lived in a village cluster, with a population of 75 to 150 and coterminous with the clan, although smaller settlements often had less than seventy-five (Knight 2011, 122–123). From here, farmers would go out to the fields to work, as archaeological investigation of such settlements and their pathways indicates (Wilkinson 2010, 56–57; 1994; 2003; Casana 2007). But those fields were not held in perpetual possession by the farmers. Instead, noncontiguous strips of land were allocated to each household for cultivation. In the Bible, this is the *ḥelĕqat haśadeh* of Genesis 33:19–20; Ruth 4:3; 2 Samuel 14:30–31; 2 Kings 9:21, 25; Jeremiah 12:10; Amos 4:7 (see also Josh. 14:2; 18:2–10; Kitz 2000). These were social units of measurements rather than clear demarcations of land for the purpose of ownership. They would usually be of considerable length (up to one kilometer, or along the twisting path of a terrace in areas such as the Judean highlands), but with a width of a few furrows. At set times, usually annually or biannually, those strips were reallocated on the basis of need, fertility, labor power, and so on. The means of such reallocation varied, whether by lot, by all the adult males, a council of elders, or perhaps a village headman. Needless to say, the process involved all manner of unwritten rules and much argument, but the outcome was that the strips were reallocated.

Collective activity was inescapable within the village and between villages that were two to four kilometers apart, for the individual was helpless in the face of natural and social disaster, needing cooperation and reciprocal aid to survive (Diakonoff 1976, 66; Hopkins 1985, 256). Thus, kinship, both highly flexible and embodied in the patriarchal household, was crucial. A further factor was the advantage of combined labor, whether with plough teams, sowing, or harvesting. Finally, the close-knit village-commune, with its headman and council of elders, was also advantageous for protection and defense against raiders. We may, following Roberts, describe these three factors as the communality of assent, of economizing, and of enforcement (Roberts 1996, 35–37).

THE ESTATE OF EDEN

With this proposed reconstruction in mind, let me turn to a number of biblical texts that respond to this situation. That they do so in a number of unexpected and mediated ways will become clear as the analysis unfolds. I begin with the two myths of Genesis 1–3, in which the underlying pattern is the ordering of domesticated agricultural space.[1] Thus, the deity "planted a garden in Eden, in the east" (Gen. 2:8), in which he puts the being—Adam—just created. The specific task of this being is to till the garden and keep it (Gen 2:18). Genesis 1 reinforces this image, with mention of "plants yielding seed, and fruit trees of every kind on earth that bear fruit with the seed in it" (Gen. 1:11–12; see also Gen. 2:9, 16). Of course, this agricultural landscape is extended somewhat to include the whole of nature, more so with the animals than the plants. While the animals include "cattle" (*hēmah*) as a generic marker for domesticated types, they also include creeping things, animals of the field, wild animals, birds of the air, sea creatures, indeed every kind of living creature (Gen. 1:20–22, 24–25; 2:19–20). These are all under the dominion of human beings, a dominion that is marked by the act of naming (Gen 2:19–20). The created world is ideally an agricultural one; domestication is the norm. At this level, the domesticated agricultural space is ultimately the deity's own creation, a divine ordering of the world for the sake of human flourishing. That act of domestication turns uncultivated land—which is formless and void—into what is cultivated. Here we may detect a trace of that perpetual problem in ancient Southwest Asia of vast stretches of uncultivated land. Given the smallness of the population and the continual shortage of able hands, the issue was not the shortage of land but the ability to cultivate that land.

The question remains as to whether the agricultural space in question applies to the village communities or the estates. Generically, it would seem to be both. Yet, other signals in the text lean toward estates rather than village communities. The tasks of keeping and tilling the land are mere tokens of labor, for the deity is the one actually responsible for making the plants grow and the animals flourish (Gen 1:11–12, 24–25, 29; 2:8–9; see also Gen 9:3). Everything seems to grow of its own accord, so that all the first human beings need do is avail themselves of the abundant produce. Here we find metaphorical traces of a ruling-class perspective on estates. From this perspective, estates do seem to produce of their own accord. The actual labor is effaced, for the productiveness of estates is attributed not to human labor but to divine abundance. Sitting in palaces and temples and towns, estates may well appear as such. Food, textiles, and luxury items seem to gush forth from the estates, mediated perhaps by landlords. But in classic style, the labor involved in their production somehow disappears—as if there were no labor in estates. For this reason, the differentiated man and woman (out of the undifferentiated "Adam") appear very much like royalty (Brueggemann 1972). They are the apex of creation (Gen.1:26–28), needing only to avail themselves of the abundant produce that simply hangs from trees or from the stalks of seed-bearing plants. For these reasons, I suggest that *gan*, which is usually translated as "garden," should actually be translated as "estate."

Now tensions begin to appear in the myth, of which two are important for my argument. The first is that despite the effort to universalize the agricultural estates, a distinction still applies between the domesticated and the wild. Apart from the differentiation between domesticated "cattle" and other animals, the one who causes trouble in the garden is specifically designated as a "wild animal" (Gen. 3:1). The very unpredictability of such animals was a source not only of omens but also of potential danger (Foster 2002, 274; Scurlock 2002, 364–367; Albertz 2008, 101). Further, the garden in question does have an outside, marked by the burly cherubim with the flaming sword (Gen. 3:24). This distinction is also marked by the need for discipline and obedience within the estate (Gen. 2:17). Obedience ensures the continued existence of the estate, or at least the continued presence of the man and woman within the estate, while disobedience signals what lies outside. This theme of disobedience brings me to the second tension, which is between the ruling-class nature of the man and woman within the garden and their peasant status outside. As a result of following the crafty advice of the serpent, the man is cursed to till ground full of thorns and thistles. Any food produced will now be the result of hard labor, by the sweat of his brow as the older translations would have it (Gen. 3:17–19). Ruling-class status has suddenly become peasant life.

This transition may be read as simple propaganda in favor of estate labor. In the perpetual drive to draw more labor into the estates from the village communities, the text of Genesis 3 may be seen as an advertisement for the easy life of estate labor in contrast to the backbreaking work of the village communities. However, I suggest that the text's tensions give voice to the deeper ideology of palatine estates. The village communities become the hard lot of peasants, who are despised, while the estates are zones of ease and plenty. Little is to be gained from village life, while estates are clearly the better option—if you happen to be one of the functionaries of the palace and the temple. The catch is that Genesis 3 also unwittingly expresses a fear of the precariousness of such an easy life. It takes little to turn even the most comfortable ruling-class life into one of hard labor, pain, and death. After all, one is subject to a capricious deity.

Between Joseph and Moses

The second exhibit of a textual mediation of socioeconomic contradictions is the struggle between Joseph and Moses (Gen. 41–Exod. 15). Why Joseph? Is not the fight to the death between Pharaoh and Moses? The text does indeed attempt to switch the protagonists, pointing out that the new pharaoh did not know Joseph and therefore began to oppress the Israelites (Exod. 1:8). Rather than claim that the text deviously attempts to redirect the reader's gaze, I prefer to see this as one of the many mediations of the basic conflict in the text. To draw out that conflict, I focus on four features: the estate-subsistence opposition itself; the insertion of distance between the opposition, now in terms of Egypt and Canaan; the pattern of traversing that distance; and the depth of rupture required to break the stranglehold of the estates.

First, Joseph clearly establishes a hyper-estate system once he achieves recognition and then power in Egypt. Genesis 41 tells the fabulous story in which Joseph is first called from prison to interpret the pharaoh's double dream. Indeed, the fat cows of the dream (Gen. 41:1–8) already signal the tone of the narrative. Overfattened cows, to the point where they could hardly walk, were a distinct marker of relative affluence and power, and one can well imagine the idle rich dreaming about them. By contrast, the small number of bovines in rural villages were normally used for traction; they consumed vast amounts of water and fodder and were not normally used for consumption (Brewer 2002, 434–438).[2] Having successfully interpreted the dream, Joseph is promptly appointed as the overseer of not one estate among many, but of a hyper-estate that is the land of Egypt itself (Gen. 41:33–45; see Skinner 1910, 501–502). Apart from the sheer embellishment of such an image, it also assumes the fiction of sweeping royal power that is found throughout ancient Southwest Asia. Petty despots routinely liked to claim they had more power than they could possible manage (see 1 Kings 4:21). Now Joseph does what any estate manager would do if given free rein: he gathers up all the grain, so much of it that the people have nothing left for themselves and have to come to him for sustenance (Gen. 41:46–49, 53–57). Forget the requisition of one-third or perhaps one-half of the estate produce; Joseph wants it all. Yet produce is only half of the story, for the key lies with labor, and the best estate labor is indentured labor. So later in the story (Gen. 47:13–26), Joseph manipulates the situation so that people are forced to sell their bodies into slavery in order to eat.

The text says less concerning the other side of the opposition (Gen. 46:8–27), although I suggest that the clan of Jacob may be seen as the moment of the village community. The clan of "keepers of livestock" numbers seventy persons. Although this is an ideal number (marking fullness), that does not equate with the genealogical list (Gen. 46:8–27), I would suggest that it also marks—if we include women and children—the normal range of a village-commune. Clan and village-commune were usually coterminous, as suggested by Judges 6:24; 8:32; 2 Samuel 14:7; and Jeremiah 3:14 (Jankowska 1969, 239–253; Schloen 2001, 155–165; Liverani 2005, 21–22). It may be objected that the depiction is of a semi-nomadic group rather than a settled village community. However, the opposition between the "desert and the sown" is far from clear, for village communities were highly mobile (seasonally or when under pressure from a despot) and nomadic groups would periodically settle (Schloen 2001, 155). In this light, both pastoral nomadism and sedentary agriculture were variations, with many overlaps, on the resilient economic form of subsistence survival.

The tale has already provided one instance of exacerbation (Joseph's mega-estate), but another follows. Instead of the tension between estates and subsistence agriculture taking place in close proximity, that tension is stretched out, as it were, with each end pushed as far apart as possible. Rather than being in the same agricultural space, they are now placed far apart, among other peoples and in other places. So Canaan stands for the village-commune, while Egypt is the locus of estates. That distance is emphasized by two features of the narrative: the physical amount of text that concerns this spatial separation (Gen. 41–50) and the constant travel between the two places. Such travel requires significant effort, whether the loading up of animals with provisions for the journey (the brothers seeking provisions), or the elaborate task of transporting a whole clan from one place to the other, or, indeed, the escape from the later bondage in Egypt. Narrative distance, then, emphasises the economic gulf between estates and village communities.

The issue of traversing distance leads to the third point—namely, the co-option of labor for the estates. At its most obvious level, the story concerns clan squabbles and a grand reconciliation, but through that narrative we find the metaphorical mediation of the securing of labor. This co-option begins with hostage-taking (Gen. 42:18–25), and then includes the "surety" of other family members (43:8–10), the fear that all the brothers will become slaves (43:18) and whatever trick it takes—the golden cup—to secure their labor (44:10–13, 18–34). Here it is worth noting that from the perspective of the village community, when someone was indentured for estate labor, that person was "no more" (Gen. 42:6). They might as well be dead. Yet, this is only the beginning, for eventually Joseph manages to indenture his whole family into the estate system—a possibility already foreshadowed in Genesis 44:16–17. Thus, the call goes out for the clan to settle in Egypt, and it turns out that none other than God approves of such a move (Gen. 45:4–14; 46:1–4).[3] What do they do when they arrive in Egypt? They become indentured laborers, keepers of the landlord's livestock (Gen. 47:1–6). In the same way that Joseph secured the labor of all the Egyptians as his slaves, so also does he indenture the labor of his own clan. It is not the new pharaoh of the early chapters of Exodus who enslaves the Israelites, but Joseph himself. Indeed, the text hints that Joseph and the oppressive pharaoh become one, for the name of the territory where Jacob's clan is settled is Rameses (47:11), the same name connected with slave labor and storage facilities in Exodus 1:11 (Brodie 2001, 397).

While the various metaphorical items of the story—golden cups, foreign places, hostages, and then enslavement—indicate the convoluted strategies used to co-opt labor for the estates, they also suggest the constituent resistance of village communities to such co-option. Despotic power and its system of estates are not at the center of the narrative; rather, that power must constantly adapt to find new ways to commandeer the labor so desperately needed for the estates. This brings me to the final point of the narrative: the depth of the rupture required to break the hold of the estate system. Exodus 1–15 may be read as a massive story of breaking with the estates and their indentured labor.[4] It is worth noting that the story attempts to shift the blame not only onto a cruel pharaoh (as I indicated earlier) but also onto the increasingly oppressive conditions of labor (Exod. 1:8–22; 2:23–25; 5:10–21). As if the indentured labor secured by Joseph is any different! Of course, it is easier to blame a foreigner for oppression. But the key is the amount of effort required to break away from the estate system. In this legendary tale, that effort takes the form not so much of sporadic violence (Exod 2:11–15) as of the drawn-out account of the divinely ordained plagues (Exod. 5:1–12:36). It becomes even tougher since God hardens Pharaoh's heart time and again. Then we have the violence, not only of the first born of the Egyptians, but also of the drowning of Pharaoh's chariots in the sea (Exod. 13:17–15:21). This violence marks not merely the rupture, but also the sheer eagerness with which people would seek the destruction of despots and their centers and symbols of power.

These twenty-five chapters that cover the transition between Genesis and Exodus may then be seen as tale in which the struggle between estates and village communities leaves its traces on one of the most significant accounts in the Hebrew Bible. As one would expect with such a tale, these traces have been mediated and metaphorized in terms of clan struggles, exotic places, foreign depots, and miraculous escapes. But let me close this section with another signal of the depth of the tension I have been tracing. When Jacob hears that Joseph is alive and powerful in Egypt, the text reads, "He was stunned; he could not believe them" (Gen. 45:26). I suggest that Jacob expresses surprise not that Joseph is alive, but that the bastard is running a mega-estate.

FORMAL AND ETHICAL CODES: JOB AND PROVERBS

The story of the violent break from the exoticized estate system in Egypt gains, as may be expected, other levels of complexity with the wilderness wanderings. Here Moses the liberator becomes also a tyrant against whom the people constantly murmur and rebel, so much so that the people clamor precisely for the Egyptians' leeks, lentils, and fleshpots (see, further, Boer 2014; Langston 2006, 4–8). But my interest is specifically in the way the socioeconomic tensions of the estates and subsistence agriculture are mediated through the texts. In this section, I consider a number of other texts in which these tensions leave their traces.

To begin with, I suggest that the much debated contradictions within and between the prologue-epilogue and poetry of Job may be seen also from the angle I have been pursuing. Obviously, the prologue depicts what may be called an uber-landlord, with his thousands of sheep, camels(!), oxen, and donkeys. More importantly, he has a multitude of slaves, indentured laborers to manage the flocks and deal with the crops. Even the life of leisure and partying of his sons and daughters betrays the ostentatious wastage of the unemployed ruling class (Job 1:4). However, more intriguing is the mark in the narrative of an all-too-familiar pattern: the periodic destruction of the power of the ruling class (Job 2:13–19). The explanations are pure legend—Sabaean and Chaldean raiders, fire from heaven, and a wind from the desert—but the destruction of landlord estates and power at the hands of peasants, estate laborers, and bands of Habiru were common enough. Given the opportunity, they would eagerly hasten the demise of yet another hated landlord or, indeed, despot (Kozyreva 1991, 99; Yee 2007, 13–15). Indeed, the mythical accounts of the Tower of Babel (Gen.11) and of Sodom and Gomorrah (Gen. 18–19) embody such a perspective in their own way, as do the warnings of 1 Samuel 8, the parable of the bramble in Judges 9:8–15, the long account of the failings of the kings of Israel and Judah and the eventual punishment in 1–2 Kings, and the account of the resistance by the "people of the land" and myriad other groups in Ezra-Nehemiah to the imposition of an imperial regime of plunder with the return of the exiles. As far as Job is concerned, the epilogue then also marks the effort once again to re-establish the estates, in the ever-repeated cycle that is part of the struggle between subsistence survival and the palatine estate system (Job 42:10–17).

Questions remain as to how we may read the relations between the prologue-epilogue and the much larger poetic text of Job. At one level, the trenchant criticisms, the laments, the demolition of the arguments of his "friends," and, above all, the challenge to Yahweh, who allows such suffering (and who is actually forced by Job to answer) may be read as a devastating undermining of all that justifies an estate system, as indeed of the later (first millennium BCE) tribute-exchange system that came to displace the estate system elsewhere in ancient Southwest Asia. If we see the excesses described in prologue and epilogue as implicit criticisms of the life Job leads, then those criticisms may enhance what is found in the poetic texts. However, another level also appears in this long section of Job: it may also be seen as the lament of a landlord who feels that the life to which he has become accustomed has been unjustly stripped away from him. That world is one in which all made way for him with deference and the poor were grateful for his assistance (Job 29). In this light, he is, of course, "blameless"—the persistent theme of the book (Fokkelman 2012, 199, 242–243). Job 42 offers a good example of this perspective, with its alienated clan members, the abhorrence of his wife, the despising by children, and his bones clinging to his skin and flesh. Above all, I am struck by Job 42:15–16:

> My female slaves count me as a stranger;
> I have become an alien in their eyes.
> I call to my slave, but he gives me no answer;
> I must myself plead with him.

Truly, suffering must be real if even the indentured laborers treat one with disrespect and ignore what one commands! No wonder he feels as though the "hand of God" has touched him (Job 42:21; see also Job 30).[5]

Whereas Job reveals tensions at the level of textual structure, Proverbs does so on a different register again. Here it is clearly ideological, manifesting itself in what may be called ethical oppositions. Proverbs is built on a series of contrasts, between wise and foolish, prudent and simple, humble and proud, righteous and wicked, industrious and lazy, sound and rotten, truth and lies, and, of course, between rich and poor.[6] None of these terms is ideologically innocent; indeed, none are innocent of class consciousness. While we may initially feel that the criticisms of the proud, the wicked, and the lying are directed at the idle rich, it soon becomes apparent the positive virtues attach to the ruling class. They are the ones who are wise, righteous, industrious, and therefore, rich. All of these are signs that they have been blessed by God. It requires little imagination to see here the ethics and class consciousness of landlords and of the perpetual dinner guests at the monarch's table. Of course, the despised are precisely those who work the estates or the village communities. They are wicked, simple, lazy, rotten, and therefore, poor. At the same time, Proverbs reveals the subtlety of this ruling-class consciousness, especially with the occasional mild warnings against riches (Prov. 11:4, 28; 15:16–17; 16:8; 17:1, 5; 18:23). Are these perhaps relics of village wisdom? If so, they have been co-opted into the subtle assertion that one should always attain to the higher calling of humility, wisdom, and righteousness. These are signposts on the way to real and moral wealth; earthly gain is therefore a secondary concern, which should not distract one from the higher virtues. Of course, the studied disdain of filthy lucre is possible only for those who have more than enough, so that they need not worry themselves about the needs of daily life. This is a far cry from the subsistence survival of the village communes.

Conclusion

By now it should be obvious that the ways texts respond, politically and ideologically, to socioeconomic tensions are as varied as the texts themselves. Those attempts may involve narrative ambivalences (Gen. 1–3), narrative structures (Gen. 41–Exod. 15), textual form (Job) and ideological oppositions (Proverbs). Mediated and unexpected are these responses, but they boil down to the fact that texts often attempt ideological and narrative resolutions to socioeconomic contradictions. And the determinative contradiction is one between palatine estates and the subsistence survival economy of village-communes, a contradiction that was both constitutive and limiting.

However, I close on a slightly different note, which is actually a case of Freud's observation that sometimes a cigar is just a cigar. In 1 Samuel 8:11–18, we find a pure vignette of what may be the expression of the village communities' attitude to the palatine estate system. The king, warns Samuel, will take your sons to "plough his ground and reap his harvest"; he will force your daughters to be "perfumers and cooks and bakers." Even this pattern of drawing away more and more clan members to labor on estates is not enough, for the despot will also seize the "best of your fields and vineyards and olive orchards and give them to his functionaries." He will also tax the grain and animals of the village communities at 10 percent. The result: "you shall be his slaves." So it was with the palatine estate system.

NOTES

1. Out of the myriad interpretations of Genesis 1–3 (and I have consulted many), surprisingly few deal with socioeconomic matters (Kennedy 1990; Steinberg 1993; Simkins 1999; Yee 1999).
2. The "fatted calf" and "fatted cattle" in biblical texts thereby become signals of power and excess (1 Sam. 28:24; 1 Kings 1:9, 19, 25; 15:17; Jer. 46:21; Amos 5:22).
3. This assertion of divine will, as well as the theme that Joseph prospered under divine protection, is one among many signals of biblical ambivalence over palatine estates and subsistence agriculture. Many are seduced by the divine approval of Joseph (e.g., Kim 2010), but others note the negative tone (e.g., Stone 2012).
4. For a useful recent overview of Exodus studies, see Dozeman's *Methods for Exodus* (Dozeman 2010).
5. Surprisingly, of the multitude of studies on Job, very few focus on economic and class features (Newsom 2003, 48, 66–67; Pelham 2012, 170–183). Of those that do, only Dawson's (2013) does so to any extent.
6. Ste. Croix shows a comparable situation in Greek ethics, which borrowed heavily from ancient Southwest Asia (Ste. Croix 2006, 338–339; 1972, 371–376).

REFERENCES

Albertz, Rainer. 2008. "Family Religion in Ancient Israel and Its Surroundings." In *Household and Family Religion in Antiquity: Contextual and Comparative Perspectives*, edited by John Bodel and Saul M. Olyan, 89–112. Malden, MA: Blackwell.

Bartlett, Roger P., ed. 1990. *Land Commune and Peasant Community in Russia: Communal Forms in Imperial and Early Soviet Society*. London: Palgrave Macmillan.

Boer, Roland. 2014. *Marxist Criticism of the Hebrew Bible*. London: Bloomsbury.

Brewer, Douglas. 2002. "Hunting, Animal Husbandry and Diet in Ancient Egypt." In *A History of the Animal World in the Ancient Near East*, edited by Billie Jean Collins, 427–456. Leiden: Brill.

Brodie, Thomas L. 2001. *Genesis as Dialogue: A Literary, Historical, and Theological Commentary*. Oxford: Oxford University Press.

Brueggemann, Walter. 1972. "From Dust to Kingship." *Zeitschift für alttestamentlische Wissenschaft* 84:1–18.

Casana, Jesse J. 2007. "Structural Transformations in Settlement Systems of the Northern Levant." *American Journal of Archaeology* 112: 195–222.

Dawson, Kirsten. 2013. "'Did Not He Who Made Me in the Belly Make Him, and the Same One Fashion Us in the Womb?' (Job 31:15): Violence, Slavery, and the Book of Job." *Biblical Interpretation* 21: 435–468.

Diakonoff, Igor M. 1974. "The Commune in the Ancient East as Treated in the Works of Soviet Researchers." In *Introduction to Soviet Ethnography*, vol. 2, edited by Stephen P. Dunn and Ethel Dunn, 519–548. Berkeley: Highgate Road Social Science Research Station.

Diakonoff, Igor M. 1975. "The Rural Community in the Ancient Near East." *Journal of the Economic and Social History of the Orient* 18(2): 121–133.

Diakonoff, Igor M. 1976. "Slaves, Helots and Serfs in Early Antiquity." In *Wirtschaft und Gesellschaft im alten Vorderasien*, edited by János Harmatta and Geörgy Komoróczy, 45–78. Budapest: Akadémiai Kiadó.

Diakonoff, Igor M. 1982. "The Structure of Near Eastern Society before the Middle of the Second Millennium B.C." *Oikumene* 3:7–100.

Diakonoff, Igor M. 1991a. "Early Despotisms in Mesopotamia." In *Early Antiquity*, edited by Igor M. Diakonoff and Philip L. Kohl, 84–97. Chicago: University of Chicago Press.

Diakonoff, Igor M. 1991b. "General Outline of the First Period of the History of the Ancient World and the Problem of the Ways of Development." In *Early Antiquity*, edited by Igor M. Diakonoff and Philip L. Kohl, 27–66. Chicago: University of Chicago Press.

Diakonoff, Igor M. 1999. *The Paths of History.* Cambridge: Cambridge University Press.

Dozeman, Thomas B., ed. 2010. *Methods for Exodus.* Cambridge: Cambridge University Press.

Fokkelman, Jan. 2012. *The Book of Job in Form: A Literary Translation with Commentary.* Leiden: Brill.

Foster, Benjamin R. 2002. "Animals in Mesopotamian Literature." In *A History of the Animal World in the Ancient Near East*, edited by Billie Jean Collins, 271–288. Leiden: Brill.

Guillaume, Philippe. 2012. *Land, Credit and Crisis: Agrarian Finance in the Hebrew Bible.* Sheffield, Yorkshire: Equinox.

Hald, Mette Marie. 2008. *A Thousand Years of Farming: Late Chalcolithic Agriultural Practices at Tell Brak in Northern Mesopotamia.* Oxford: Archaeopress.

Hole, Frank. 1991. "Middle Khabur Settlement and Agriculture in the Ninevite 5 Period." *Bulletin of the Canadian Society for Mesopotamian Studies* 21: 17–29.

Hopkins, David C. 1985. *The Highlands of Canaan: Agricultural Life in the Early Highlands.* Sheffield, Yorkshire: Almond.

Jankowska, Ninel B. 1969. "Communal Self-Government and the King of the State of Arrapha." *Journal of the Economic and Social History of the Orient* 12: 233–282.

Jankowska, Ninel B. 1991. "Asshur, Mitanni, and Arrapkhe." In *Early Antiquity*, edited by Igor M. Diakonoff and Philip L. Kohl, 228–260. Chicago: University of Chicago Press.

Kennedy, James M. 1990. "Peasants in Revolt: Political Allegory in Genesis 2-3." *Journal for the Study of the Old Testament* 47: 3–14.

Kim, Hyun Chul Paul. 2010. "Reading the Joseph Story (Genesis 37-50) as a Diapora Narrative." *Catholic Biblical Quarterly* 75: 219–238.

Kitz, Anne M. 2000. "Undivided Inheritance and Lot Casting in the Book of Joshua." *Journal of Biblical Literature* 119: 601–618.

Knight, Douglas A. 2011. *Law, Power, and Justice in Ancient Israel, Library of Ancient Israel.* Louisville, KY: Westminster John Knox.

Kozyreva, Nelly V. 1991. "The Old Babylonian Period of Mesopotamian History." In *Early Antiquity*, edited by Igor M. Diakonoff and Philip L. Kohl, 98–123. Chicago: University of Chicago Press.

Langston, Scott M. 2006. *Exodus through the Centuries.* Oxford: Blackwell.

Liverani, Mario. 1982. "Ville et campagne dans Ie royaume d'Ugarit: Essai d'analyse economique." In *Societes and Languages of the Ancient Near East: Studies in Honour of I. M. D'iakonoff*, edited by Muhammad A. Dandamaev, J. Nicholas Postgate, and Mogens Trolle Larsen, 250–258. Warminster, PA: Aris and Phillips.

Liverani, Mario. 2005. *Israel's History and the History of Israel*. Translated by Chiara Peri and Philip Davies. London: Equinox.

Newsom, Carol A. 2003. *The Book of Job: A Contest of Moral Imaginations*. New York: Oxford University Press.

Pelham, Abigail. 2012. *Contested Creations in the Book of Job: The-World-as-It-Ought-and-Ought-Not-to-Be*. Leiden: Brill.

Roberts, Brian. 1996. *Landscapes of Settlement: Prehistory to the Present*. London: Routledge.

Sasson, Aharon. 2010. *Animal Husbandry in Ancient Israel: A Zooarchaeological Perspective on Livestock Exploitation, Herd Management and Economic Strategies*. London: Equinox.

Schloen, J. David. 2001. *The House of the Father as Fact and Symbol: Patrimonialism in Ugarit and the Ancient Near East*. Winona Lake, IN: Eisenbrauns.

Scurlock, JoAnn. 2002. "Animals in Ancient Mesopotamian Religion." In *A History of the Animal World in the Ancient Near East*, edited by Billie Jean Collins, 361–388. Leiden: Brill.

Simkins, Ronald. 1999. "Patronage and the Political Economy of Ancient Israel." In *The Social World of the Hebrew Bible*, edited by Ronald Simkins and Stephen L. Cook. *Semeia* 87: 123–144.

Skinner, John. 1910. *A Critical and Exegetical Commentary on Genesis, The International Critical Commentary*. Edinburgh: T&T Clark.

Ste. Croix, Geoffrey E. M. de. 1972. *The Origins of the Peloponnesian War*. London: Duckworth.

Ste. Croix, Geoffrey E. M. de. 2006. *Christian Persecution, Martyrdom, and Orthodoxy*. Edited by Michael Whitby and Joseph Streeter. Oxford: Oxford University Press.

Steinberg, Naomi. 1993. *Kinship and Marriage in Genesis: A Household Economics Perspective*. Minneapolis, MN: Fortress.

Stone, Timothy J. 2012. "Joseph in the Likeness of Adam: Narrative Echoes of the Fall." In *Genesis and Christian Theology*, edited by Nathan MacDonald, Mark W. Elliott, and Grant Macaskill, 62–73. Grand Rapids, MI: Eerdmans.

Vasil'ev, Leonid S., and Iosif A. Stuchevskii. 1967. "Three Models for the Origin and Evolution of Precapitalist Societies." *Soviet Review* 8(3): 26–39.

Wilkinson, Tony. 1994. "The Structure and Dynamics of Dry Farming States in Upper Mesopotamia." *Current Anthropology* 35(1): 483–520.

Wilkinson, Tony. 2003. *Archaeological Landscapes of the Near East*. Tucson: University of Arizona Press.

Wilkinson, Tony. 2010. "The Tell: Social Archaeology and Territorial Space." In *Development of Pre-State Communities in the Ancient Near East*, edited by Dianne Bolger and Louise C. Maguire, 55–62. Oxford: Oxbow.

Yee, Gale A. 1999. "Gender, Class, and the Social-Scientific Study of Genesis 2-3." In *The Social World of the Hebrew Bible*, edited by Ronald Simkins and Stephen L. Cook. *Semeia* 87: 177–192.

Yee, Gale A. 2007. "Recovering Marginalized Groups in Ancient Israel: Methodological Considerations." In *To Break Every Yoke: Essays in Honor of Marvin L. Chaney*, edited by Robert B. Coote and Norman K. Gottwald, 10–27. Sheffield, Yorkshire: Sheffield Phoenix.

CHAPTER 47

NARRATIVE DELIBERATION IN BIBLICAL POLITICS

MARK G. BRETT

THIS chapter will describe some of the textual evidence for inner-biblical deliberation, especially as it is manifested in debates concerning political governance and social identity in ancient Israel. The methodology will take a middle path between the kind of historical criticism that is overly confident in reconstructing literary sources and editorial layers in the history of a text's composition and, at the other extreme, the formalistic narratology that is largely indifferent to such developments. Taking a cue from social identity theory (e.g., Hogg 2001), I will focus on the theme of leadership and examine Israel's shifting social imagination in the transition from tribalism to monarchy, as well as in the necessary reconstruction of biblical politics in post-monarchic times.

A number of social theorists have recently expressed doubts about the very possibility of political deliberation in ancient Israel on the grounds that divine initiative in biblical narrative ultimately tends to overwhelm merely human action. In Charles Taylor's work, such doubts have even been extrapolated to cover the entire ancient world, where populations characteristically saw themselves as so deeply embedded in primordial social ties that their agency was severely limited, particularly in the sense that their choices were enabled or policed by gods and spirits (Taylor 2007; Brett 2010). Many studies have suggested ways in which the thorough transformation of social identities was explicitly promoted in the theological visions of the New Testament writings (e.g., Žižek 2000; Badiou 2003; Baker 2012), but here our biblical examples will focus on material that might appear to be less promising, the so-called Deuteronomistic History (Deuteronomy through 2 Kings).

It is often supposed that the sacred social norms established in Deuteronomy's law reappear frequently throughout this narrative material, but, on close investigation, the issues are more complicated. The speeches of leading characters, and even the narrator's evaluations of events, have fewer intertextual links with Mosaic law than might be expected. As we shall see, the insight that Israel's complex political history should be evaluated according to Deuteronomy's norms is something that was hard won, only through bitter experience and discernment on the part of later editors.

Monarchs and Social Identities

The historic kings of Israel and Judah are repeatedly tried and found wanting by the biblical narrators, but whatever their flaws, these monarchs are often the key agents in the forming and contesting of social imagination. Interestingly, the kings are measured against standards that seem to vary from context to context (Schmid 2012). It is remarkable how infrequently the law of Moses is actually mentioned in Samuel–Kings. More often, kings are criticized for failing to follow in the ways of their father David, or for allowing multiple cultic sites to exist outside of Jerusalem. The cultic reform of King Josiah is the exception that proves the rule, as we shall see. Overwhelmingly, it is the sins of the monarchy that explain the fall of Judah, most notably, the sins of Manasseh, and Yhwh ordains the loss of political sovereignty.

To illustrate these issues in more detail, let us turn now to the narratives in the books of Samuel that describe the invention of kingship in Israel. These stories provide a more promising window on the phenomenon of "politics," if, as Michael Walzer (2012) has argued, we should think of politics as necessarily including public deliberation, disagreement, negotiation, and compromise (73–75; 210–211). With this definition in hand, Walzer suggests that debates among tribal elders might provide evidence of political deliberation in his required sense, but it is precisely the absence of such debate in biblical narrative that leads him to think that elders came to have a "secular and non-covenantal character" in the eyes of biblical narrators. The elders were no doubt prominent members of ancient Israelite society, and therefore they were not expunged from the historical record. Indeed, they were useful participants or witnesses at decisive covenantal ceremonies, Walzer suggests; but apart from that, their social functions were of no great interest to the authors of the canonical literature (197).

In light of Walzer's argument, the role of the elders in the rise of kingship is simply remarkable. I would even flirt with some anachronism in order to suggest that 1 Samuel 8 and 10 carry the residue of a political notion that might today be seen as "social contract theory." To make this hypothesis workable, one would no doubt need to neglect the details of this theory as expounded by Hobbes, Locke, and Rousseau and begin instead with a single generalization that may be derived from this tradition: societies are formed when citizens surrender some of their freedoms to a sovereign authority in exchange for certain protections. The key feature of my hypothesis is that the arrival of kingship in Israel was negotiated with the participation of elders, rather than derived from the absolute religious obligations of the Mosaic Torah. The law of kingship in Deuteronomy arose, as we shall see, from later reflection on the careers of actual kings.

Social contract theory has often been seen as a uniquely modern construct in Western tradition, and as a departure from medieval convictions about the divine right of kings. On this overly simple account, popular resistance to tyranny might appear to require a modern theory of human rights, configured as the residual freedoms that were not surrendered in the virtual social contract—or in more practical terms, not surrendered in the invention of modern nation-states. This secular version of history founders on the inconvenient truth that the makings of social contract theory can already be found in the writings of Catholic lawyers at the beginning of the seventeenth century (Skinner 1978, 148–178). And it is no coincidence that Oliver Cromwell's parliamentarians were well versed in the details of Deuteronomy.

Bernard Levinson (2006) and Eric Nelson (2010), among others, have drawn our attention to the oddly modern appearance of Deuteronomy when it is considered as a contribution to constitutionalism in the West, with its separation of civil, religious, and judicial powers. Our analysis of Israel's political sovereignty begins, however, not with the peculiarities of Deuteronomy, but with narrative fragments in Samuel that are noticeably lacking in allusions to Deuteronomy—precisely when such allusions might be thought self-evidently relevant. Beginning from these observations about the making of kingship in Israel and Judah, we may then explore much larger questions about the formation and contestation of ethnic identity in the Hebrew Bible.

Rousseau briefly suggested in *The Social Contract* (bk 3, ch. 6, sec. 5) that Samuel's warning to Israel in 1 Samuel 8 may be compared to Machiavelli's *The Prince*. While political historians have long recognized that Machiavelli's work presents a subtle engagement with the "mirror for princes" genre in previous centuries, interestingly, Jonathan Kaplan has recently suggested that 1 Samuel 8:11–18 can indeed be understood as part of the *Fürstenspiegel* discourse that was found already in Assyrian and Babylonian texts of the eighth and seventh centuries BCE. Expressed through a number of different genres, this literature seems to have been designed as a warning against monarchic abuses, suggesting, for example, that the gods would requite a king for improper jurisprudence or the excessive imposition of forced labor. In light of Kaplan's argument, our discussion will review some of the evidence in Samuel–Kings that points to Israelite attempts to constrain the power of kings, and in the first instance, we will be looking at evidence of legal mechanisms that were not derived from the law of kingship in Deuteronomy 17.

In 1 Samuel 10:25, for example, we find that Samuel is quite willing to write a "*mišpāt* of the monarchy" rather than defer to the authority of Moses: "And Samuel proclaimed to the people the justice of the monarchy, and he wrote it in a document and deposited it before YHWH." It stretches credulity to suggest, as Ralph Klein does (2008, 100, 76), that "the redactor may have had Deut 17:14–22 in mind." Unlike the previous narrative, in 1 Samuel 9:1–10:16, in which Saul is anointed privately, here in 10:17–27, there is a public ceremony and a document is formalized "before YHWH," presumably in a sanctuary. The narrative context cries out for a reference to Deuteronomy's law of kingship, but the redactor does not provide it. The later Deuteronomistic editors apparently refrained from filling in the blanks, in clear contrast with 1 Kings 2:3, where David's parting advice to Solomon refers explicitly to a king's obligation to follow the "statutes, commandments, judgments and decrees as written in the Torah of Moses." The manifest difference between 1 Kings 2:3 and 1 Samuel 10:25 points to the likelihood that the Deuteronomists have inherited some older material in 1 Samuel 8–10, and while they have added their own contributions at various points, they have not created these chapters entirely in their own image.

The "*mišpāt* of the monarchy" in 1 Samuel 10:25 is a solemn agreement between king and people, not just a declaration of the rights and duties of the king himself (Dietrich 2010, 471–472). This is the kind of thing that social contract theory would lead us to expect. The text is ambiguous enough to allow the possibility that Samuel creates the legal rights of the king without negotiating consent. But following in the footsteps of some earlier research, Dietrich rightly insists that 1 Samuel 10:25 fits within a much larger body of evidence for popular participation in northern Israelite politics. Quite independently of Dietrich's work, Daniel Fleming (2012) has recently argued that the peculiarities of the north are better described in terms of collaborative politics, rather than even ethnic solidarity. For our present purposes, there is enough value in the combined efforts of Dietrich and Fleming to provoke us to look for popular political participation in the north, at least on the part of senior landholders.

In 2 Samuel 5:3, for example, we find that David needs to secure a covenant with the "elders of Israel" before they anoint him: "And all the elders of Israel came to the king at Hebron; and King David cut a covenant (*bĕrît*) with them at Hebron before Yʜwʜ, and they anointed David king over Israel." Strikingly, it is precisely the *elders* who anoint him in this narrative, rather than Samuel. This seems appropriate given the overtures from Abner in 2 Samuel 3:12 and 21, where Saul's uncle seeks a *bĕrît* with David that will allow him to rule over the northern tribes. In executing this plan, Abner first exhorts the "elders of Israel," in 2 Samuel 13:17, to participate. By contrast, in 2 Samuel 2:4, we learn that the "men of Judah" anoint David without any reference to a prior covenant. Accordingly, Dietrich (2010, 471–472) is more willing to speak of a "primitive democratic element" in the case of the northern tradition.

Parenthetically, if we were provoked by social contract theory to look for evidence that senior males retain some rights and freedoms, even after their agreement to create monarchic sovereignty, then the northern secession narrative in 1 Kings 12 fits well with this picture. According to this chapter, Jeroboam led a rebellion against Solomon's son Rehoboam, mainly because the southern king reiterated his threat to impose a harsh regime of forced labor. Instead of acknowledging an enduring covenant with David established through the prophet Nathan (as in 2 Sam. 7), the narrative in 1 Kings 12 seems to construct a revolutionary interpretation of the exodus, configuring Jeroboam as a new Moses—a Moses who apparently provided no law of cultic centralization in Jerusalem. The northerners retreat to their own cult of Yʜwʜ in the north, and establish the boundaries of Israelite nationhood (Bodner 2012). We might conclude, then, that 1 Kings 12 provides evidence of the power of kings to shape solidarity between tribal groups, whether in synthesizing ethnic "fusion" in the case of David, or "fission" in the case of Jeroboam (for this contrast, see Eriksen 1993, 67–69).

The "elders of Israel" play an explicit role, as we have noted, in securing a covenant with David in 2 Samuel 5:3, and it is worth reflecting on the use of this same phrase in 1 Samuel 8:4–5 to designate the leaders who bring the request to Samuel for a king. The fact that this group is subsequently referred to simply as "the people" (vv. 7, 10, 19, 21) might point to multiple layers of authorship in 1 Samuel 8, but this does not seem to be as significant as the overall representation of a popular will. It may well be that these references to elders represent a residue of the older forms of authority within kinship networks, which were largely supplanted by the centralized judicial organization imagined in Deuteronomy (Rofé 2001).

Some scholars detect another parallel between 1 Samuel 8 and 2 Samuel 5:3 in the uses of formal terminology derived from the vassal treaty tradition: Samuel is instructed in 1 Samuel 8:9 "to warn" and "to declare" to the people the justice of the king. The wording here is different from the more explicit term "covenant" or "treaty" (*bĕrît*) that appears in 2 Samuel 5:3, but according to a well-established line of interpretation, 1 Samuel 8:9 uses Hebrew terminology equivalent to what we find in Assyrian treaties (Weinfeld 1972, 65, 85–86; Klein 2008, 76). Given the host of parallels between Deuteronomy and Assyrian material that have been found, the apparent adoption of this particular terminology in 1 Samuel 8:9 only serves to heighten the problem here: Deuteronomy mimics and contests the Assyrian treaty imagination, and by implication, so does 1 Samuel 8, but without mentioning the law of Moses.

The elders of Israel in 1 Samuel 8:5 ask for a king "like all the nations," and the choice of words here matches the same phrase in Deuteronomy 17:14, yet there is no invocation of a preexisting Mosaic covenant, even at this moment when Israelite identity is clearly at issue: if Israel assimilates the foreign institution of kingship, how could they retain a distinctively Israelite social order? What Samuel declares at this point is almost a satire on the kind of justice that this king would enact, highlighting only the onerous obligations that will fall on the people, rather than the benefits that they might receive in exchange. Nevertheless, the people persist with their request for a king "like all the nations," repeating the same phrase in 8:20. In response, the divine instruction to Samuel is that, regretfully, he should listen to the "voice of the people" (8:7, 22). Given that there is evidence of covenant-treaty discourse in 1 Samuel 8:9, along with this repeated use of a phrase that corresponds to one found in Deuteronomy 17:14, the lack of an explicit reference in 8:11–17 to Deuteronomy's law of the king is extraordinary.

Mark Leuchter (2005) has also drawn attention to some peculiarly Assyrian parallels for the idea in 1 Samuel 8:13 that a king might force women and girls to become perfumers, cooks, and bakers—a claim that is elsewhere never made about Israel's own kings. Similarly, he argues that the claim in 8:12 that a king would draft cavalry units with a thousand riders, in addition to chariot conscription, points to Assyrian rather than Israelite practice. Such comparisons suggest, at the very least, that the generalizing description of 1 Samuel 8 as "anti-monarchic" is far too blunt an instrument for investigating this narrative. Instead, Leuchter suggests that the antipathy in 1 Samuel 8:11–17 is directed toward imperial Assyrian kings. His argument runs into difficulties, however, when he proposes that the underlying purpose of 1 Samuel 8:11–17 is to contrast the oppressive excesses of imperial kings with the native Israelite monarchs. Israel's native kings are quite capable of social abuses, and their distinctiveness would have been much better established in 1 Samuel 8 by referring explicitly to the norms established by the Torah of Moses. There would seem to be no better way to assert the superiority of native Israelite ideals.

Instead of being straightforwardly anti-monarchic or looking to Mosaic law to constrain their monarchs, the northern tribes sought a covenantal relationship with their kings. And in line with social contract theory, it seems that within this covenantal relationship the sovereign might extract a justifiable measure of resources from the landowners, as long as he provided the protections that served society as a whole. According to 1 Kings 12, as noted above, Solomon's program of forced labor did significant damage to this balanced conception of the common good, and in 12:3, Jeroboam acts in concert with the "assembly of Israel" to put their case to Solomon's successor. When Rehoboam does not "listen to the people" in 1 Kings 12:15, the northern tribes withdraw themselves from his jurisdiction. The terminology describing ethnic fission here relates specifically to land allocations: Israel's "portion" and "inheritance" no longer belong to the house of David:

> What portion do we have in David?
> We have no inheritance in the son of Jesse.
> To your tents, O Israel!
> Look now to your own house, O David. (1 Kings 12:16)

We can be sure that no Deuteronomist could have let this northern invention of sovereignty pass without comment, and accordingly, we might consider 1 Samuel 8:18 to be a southern response expressed in prophetic mode: "[a]nd you will cry out in that day on account of your king, whom you have chosen for yourselves, but Yhwh will not answer you in that day."

This verse seems out of place in the narrative context because in the very next chapter Saul is divinely chosen, and anointed by Samuel, precisely because the cry of the people has been heard (9:16–17; 10:1, 24). Nor does the description of oppressive kingship in 1 Samuel 8 relate to Saul's tenure. In short, 1 Samuel 8:18 makes little sense as a comment on Saul's kingship, but it makes good sense as a Deuteronomistic commentary on the disastrous consequences of the "social contract" tradition of the northern kingdom as a whole (cf. the reference to the king "you have chosen" in 1 Sam. 12:13, as opposed to the one "whom YHWH will choose" in Deut. 17:15). We might even be tempted to cite Maimonides in support of this proposal, since he suggested that only the royal house of David was subject to Torah, not the northern kings of Israel (*Hilkhot Sandherin* 2:5; see Flatto 2008, 71).

However, before we conclude that the consensus between Maimonides and the Deuteronomists has resolved all the puzzles in 1 Samuel 8 and 10, we might need to question whether there is any evidence of popular agency in the south. Perhaps the most relevant comparisons would be with the references to the Judean "people of the land" who figure in a number of royal succession narratives. In her description of the social profile of this group, Lisbeth Fried draws attention particularly to Jeremiah 34:19, which provides a list of the Judeans who participated in Jeremiah's covenant, all of whom undertook in this episode to release their slaves: officials, eunuchs, priests and "people of the land." The implication seems to be that the people of the land are certainly free men who hold land and slaves, but they can be distinguished from officials within the highest social strata. Fried makes a good case for thinking that, in pre-exilic texts, "people of the land" are the "landowning full citizens of an area" (Fried 2006).

Fried also claims that the people of the land "are found participating in the revolt against Athaliah" in 2 Kings 11, but on closer inspection of the narrative, it would be more accurate to conclude that the plot against Athaliah is orchestrated by the high priest Jehoiada, and the agency of the people of the land is largely restricted in 2 Kings 11:14 to celebrating the outcome of Jehoiada's clandestine actions. The details of this episode are of some interest to the Chronicler, who did not let this narrative pass without emendation. The narrative in 2 Kings 11:12 says that Jehoiada "brought out the king's son, put the crown on him, and gave him the insignia," but then it shifts to a plural verb form: "they proclaimed him king, and anointed him; they clapped their hands and shouted, 'Long live the king!'" The Chronicler may have been concerned with the implication at this point that the people of the land participated in the anointing, so apparently by way of clarification, 2 Chronicles 23:11 reads instead "*Jehoiada and his sons* anointed him; and they shouted 'Long live the king!'" In other words, it may be that the Chronicler was perturbed by the suggestion of popular agency in the anointing of a southern king, even if the resistance to Athaliah was led by a high priest.

The participation of the "people of the land" in the accession of both Josiah and his son Jehoahaz is reported only briefly: 2 Kings 21:24 notes tersely that "the people of the land killed all those who had conspired against King Amon, and the people of the land made his son Josiah king in place of him." Similarly, following the death of Josiah, 2 Kings 23:30 claims that "the people of the land took Jehoahaz son of Josiah, anointed him, and made him king in place of his father." In these cases, the Chronicler does not provide any alternative renderings of significance (see 2 Chron. 33:25; 36:1). Perhaps these brief reports were considered simply summaries that were conveyed with the assumption that the actual anointing was done by the appropriate priestly authority, with the consent of the landholders (cf. 2 Kings 14:21).

Even if this is so, it is still striking that in the case of Jehoahaz there is no account of the king's accession being conditional upon observance of the laws of Moses. We need not perhaps expect a reference to Torah in the accession of Josiah, since it is only during the course of Josiah's reign that a lost law book is discovered in the temple. But if Josiah's law book included some version of Deuteronomy 17:14–20, then surely there should have been some reference to Mosaic Torah in the accession of Josiah's son.

Against expectations, then, we might need to acknowledge not only the evidence for a social contract tradition in the north, but at least some element of popular participation also in the south. While the textual evidence regarding the Judean "people of the land" is meager, it is at least consistent with Shemaryahu Talmon's (1967) argument that this group was consistently loyal to the house of David. Interestingly, they are represented as more interested in the politics of royal succession than in the constitutional provisions of Deuteronomy. Even in the accession of Josiah's son to the throne, the narrative mentions only popular agency and places no emphasis on the Torah of Moses. In the case of Josiah himself, his reforms appear to be focused on cultic matters, rather than eliminating the social exploitation that is the focus of 1 Samuel 8:11–17, or implementing the social, economic, and legal vision of Deuteronomy, let alone its remarkable division of powers. The content of Josiah's law book remains something of a puzzle.

IMPLICATIONS

Proverbs 14:28 offers the potentially subversive observation that "[t]he glory of a king is a multitude of people; without people a prince is ruined." If the power of a king derives from his numbers of supporters, rather than from his patron divinity, then the metaphysical roots of royalty lie exposed here to the skepticism of the wisdom tradition. The Deuteronomistic historians did not go this far, but they did at least envisage a range of conditions under which a population might offer or withdraw their consent to the making of human sovereignties. This is perhaps more explicit in the narratives concerning the northern kingdom than in those concerning the south, but we may be justified in concluding that something like a "social contract" tradition has left its residue in 1 Samuel 8 and 10.

However, the diversity of ways in which kings are evaluated by the Deuteronomistic historians provokes another set of questions about how the legitimacy of Judah's monarchy was viewed in different periods. For the earlier authors of the books of Kings, there was apparently a time when a king's religious "infidelity was not enough to cancel the divine grant to David" (Levenson 1975, 227). This is illustrated in the case of Joram:

> He walked in the way of the kings of Israel, as the house of Ahab had done, for the daughter of Ahab was his wife. He did what was evil in the sight of Yhwh.
> Yet Yhwh would not destroy Judah, for the sake of his servant David, since he had promised to give a lamp to him and to his descendants forever. (2 Kings 8:18–19)

The confidence that had been placed by these earlier narrators on the Davidic covenant was later put into question, and whether "the people of the land" should be regarded as consistently loyal followers of the house of David turns out not to be the key issue in the long run. The more significant question was: what kind of covenant can endure an exile?

The Deuteronomistic historians must have flinched as they read in their sources that Samuel wrote his own law of kingship rather than referring to Mosaic law. Yet they did not move to undo the heresy in 1 Samuel 10:25. Perhaps instead they added the prophetic warning of 1 Samuel 8:18 that "you will cry out in that day on account of your king, whom you have chosen for yourselves, but YHWH will not answer you in that day." They would surely have known that in the very next chapter YHWH chooses Saul, precisely because the cry of the people has been heard (9:16–17; 10:1, 24), but any need for narrative consistency was apparently overwhelmed by more weighty matters.

The last Deuteronomistic historians of the Persian period knew that the great experiment with kingship in Judah was necessarily a joint venture in divine and human agency, and that even the most distinguished kings could not save it. The security provided by the Davidic covenant was exhausted, and new grounds for hope were needed. Experience eventually taught these historians that the Torah of Moses would outlive the experiment in Judean sovereignty, and indeed, they apparently came to the conclusion not just that the northern kingdom had taken a wrong turn, but that the entire story of kingship was better understood as fundamentally a matter of human choice—an optional rather than essential feature of government. As the elders had long before suggested in their secular wisdom, there was indeed some room for choice. Their message seems to have been translated into a permissive divine command and inserted into Deuteronomy 17:

> When you have come into the land that Yhwh your God is giving you, and have taken possession of it and settled in it, and you say, "I will establish a king over me, like all the nations that are around me," you may indeed establish a king over you whom Yhwh your God will choose. (Deut. 17:14–15)

On the other hand, the figure of Samuel was left in 1 Samuel 10:25 to author a primitive social contract, destined for tragedy.

The Deuteronomists were, of course, not the only biblical historians. In Persian times, the Chronicler undertook a thorough revision of the entire national story, reflecting particularly on the memory of past kings precisely in order to shape the social imagination for post-monarchic times. We may be justified here in using the singular "story" to describe this complex narrative work, because it seems that Chronicles has reinterpreted the division of the kingdoms in order to provide a vision of unity for Yehud and Samaria—what amounts to a renewed vision of ethnic "fusion." In stark contrast with the proposals in Ezra–Nehemiah, which sought a narrowly Judean reformation of social identity (Southwood 2012), Chronicles provides a way of seeing both the northern and southern polities as belonging in some sense to a single story of "Israel." Whether this construal of Chronicler's purposes needs to be framed in terms of a particular school of social identity theory is a matter for further debate (Jonker 2007; cf. Baker 2012). Theory aside, careful comparison of the reforms of Josiah as described in Kings and Chronicles illustrates the renewed possibilities for "all Israel" in the later text—both for northerners who are offered new avenues of repentance, and also for southerners, who are freed from burdens of intergenerational guilt as it was described in the books of Kings. In particular, the sins of Manasseh no longer form a viable explanation for the fall of Jerusalem (Japhet 2004).

If, as Gary Knoppers (2003) suggests, "Chronicles was composed not necessarily as a replacement of, but as an alternative to the primary history" (133–134), we have returned to the fundamental issues with which this chapter began. The biblical literature does not explicitly theorize a pluralist doctrine of revelation, but the canonical narratives of scripture supply a plurality nonetheless (Walzer 2012, 33). If there was a metaphysical restraint placed on the political deliberations of Israel, perhaps it is also revealed in the evident reluctance to replace or erase the contributions of many of the earlier authors who played a part in the composition of these narratives. Instead, the canonizers have bequeathed to later readers the necessity of continuing processes of deliberation.

References

Badiou, Alain. 2003. *Saint Paul: The Foundation of Universalism.* Redwood City, CA: Stanford University Press.

Baker, Coleman A. 2012. "Social Identity Theory and Biblical Interpretation." *Biblical Theology Bulletin* 42: 129–138.

Bodner, Keith. 2012. *Jeroboam's Royal Drama.* Oxford: Oxford University Press.

Brett, Mark G. 2010. "National Identity as Commentary and as Metacommentary." In *Historiography and Identity: (Re)formulation in Second Temple Literature*, edited by Louis Jonker, 29–40. London: Continuum.

Dietrich, Walter. 2010. *Samuel: 1 Sam 1–12.* Biblischer Kommentar Altes Testament VIII/1. Neukirchen-Vluyn: Neukirchener.

Eriksen, Thomas. 1993. *Ethnicity and Nationalism: Anthropological Perspectives.* London: Pluto.

Flatto, David C. 2008. "The King and I: The Separation of Powers in Early Hebraic Political Theory." *Yale Journal of Law and the Humanities* 20: 61–110.

Fleming, Daniel E. 2012. *The Legacy of Israel in Judah's Bible: History, Politics, and the Reinscribing of Tradition.* Cambridge: Cambridge University Press.

Fried, Lisbeth S. 2006. "The 'am ha'aretz in Ezra 4.4 and Persian Imperial Administration." In *Judah and the Judeans in the Persian Period*, edited by O. Lipschits and M. Oeming, 123–145. Winona Lake, IN: Eisenbrauns.

Hogg, Michael A. 2001. "Social Identification, Group Prototypicality, and Emergent Leadership." In *Social Identity Processes in Organizational Contexts*, edited by M. A. Hogg and D. J. Terry, 197–212. Philadelphia, PA: Psychology Press.

Japhet, Sara. 2004. "Theodicy in Ezra-Nehemiah and Chronicles." In *Theodicy in the World of the Bible*, edited by A. Laato and J. C. de Moor, 429–469. Leiden: Brill.

Jonker, Louis C. 2007. "Reforming History: The Hermeneutical Significance of the Books of Chronicles." *Vetus Testamentum* 57: 21–44.

Kaplan, Jonathan. 2012. "1 Samuel 8:11-18 as 'A Mirror for Princes.'" *Journal of Biblical Literature* 131: 625–642.

Klein, Ralph. 2008. *1 Samuel.* 2nd ed. Word Biblical Commentary 10. Nashville, TN: Thomas Nelson.

Knoppers, Gary N. 2003. *I Chronicles 1–9.* Anchor Bible 12. New York: Doubleday.

Leuchter, Mark. 2005. "A King like all the Nations: The Composition of 1 Samuel 8:11-18." *Zeitschrift für die alttestamentliche Wissenschaft* 117: 543–558.

Levenson, Jon D. 1975. "Who Inserted the Book of the Torah?" *Harvard Theological Review* 68: 203–233.

Levinson, Bernard M. 2006. "The First Constitution." *Cardozo Law Review* 27: 1853–1888.

Nelson, Eric. 2010. *The Hebrew Republic: Jewish Sources and the Transformation of European Political Thought*. Cambridge MA: Harvard University Press.

Rofé, Alexander. 2001. "The Organization of the Judiciary in Deuteronomy." In *The World of the Aramaeans: Festschrift P.E. Dion,* edited by P. M. M. Daviau, J. W. Wevers, and M. Weigl, 92–112. Sheffield, Yorkshire: Sheffield Academic Press.

Schmid, Konrad. 2012. "Deuteronomy within the 'Deuteronomistic Histories' in Genesis-2 Kings." In *Deuteronomy in the Pentateuch, Hexateuch, and the Deuteronomistic History,* edited by R. F. Person and K. Schmid, 8–30. Forschungen zum Alten Testament II 56. Tübingen: Mohr Siebeck.

Skinner, Quentin. 1978. *The Foundations of Modern Political Thought*. Vol. 2. Cambridge: Cambridge University Press.

Southwood, Katherine. 2012. *Ethnicity and the Mixed Marriage Crisis in Ezra 9–10: An Anthropological Approach*. Oxford: Oxford University Press.

Talmon, Shemaryahu. 1967. "The Judean 'am ha'aretz in Historical Perspective." *Fourth World Congress of Jewish Studies* 1: 71–76.

Taylor, Charles. 2007. *A Secular Age*. Cambridge, MA: Belknap Press.

Walzer, Michael. 2012. *In God's Shadow: Politics in the Hebrew Bible*. New Haven, CT: Yale University Press.

Weinfeld, Moshe. 1972. *Deuteronomy and the Deuteronomic School*. Oxford: Clarendon.

Žižek, Slavoj. 2000. *The Fragile Absolute; or, Why Is the Christian Legacy Worth Fighting For?* London: Verso.

CHAPTER 48

BIBLICAL LAMENTATIONS AND SINGING THE BLUES

DANIEL L. SMITH-CHRISTOPHER

I cried, I moaned
I cried, I moaned
I asked how long, how long?
I asked my captain for the time of day
Say he throwed his watch away.
If I listened at my mother, in a farther day
I never would-a been here today
If I ever get back home, oh baby, to stay
I never be treated this-a-way
How long, how long
How long, how long
How long, oh how can I go on?
I rise with the blues
And I wake with the blues, Nothing I can't get but bad news.

"Chain Gang Trouble," byCharlie Lincoln
(Sackheim 2003, 314–215)

Narrating Trauma

Scholars who defend the central importance of stories to human self-understanding have sometimes asserted that this is so central to the human condition that we ought to replace our self-designation of homo "sapiens" (wise) with homo "narrans" (storytelling; see Niemeyer 2006, 69). The human need to tell stories to make sense of life is also emerging as a significant method of analysis within the growing field of trauma studies.

Trauma studies describes a field of inquiry that involves a dialogue across a number of disciplinary fields, including psychology, sociology, human geography, and history. But what is particularly significant in the context of this chapter is the fact that scholars of literature (Caruth 1996; Tal 1996), including biblical studies (Janzen 2012; Carr 2014), are now fully engaged. The first international gathering on the topic, a conference titled "Trauma and Traumatization in and beyond Biblical Literature," was held in 2012 at the University of Aarhus in Denmark, and a section of the Society of Biblical Literature dedicated entirely to trauma studies and scripture commenced its first sessions in 2013.

Given the complexity of the trauma studies field, however, it is important to briefly locate the narrative approach, which is especially prominent among theorists working on human recovery strategies. The most prominent example of this approach is the theoretical and clinical work done by Richard Tedeschi and Lawrence Calhoun (Tedeschi and Calhoun 1995; Calhoun and Tadeschi 2006) on posttraumatic growth (PTG), which they propose as an alternative to the otherwise rather exclusive focus in trauma studies on the negative impact and symptomology of posttraumatic stress disorder (PTSD). For those interested in narrative, a great deal of work has followed in the path of a research agenda proposed by Ronnie Janoff-Bulman's (1992) work *Shattered Assumptions*. Janoff-Bulman speaks of an "assumptive world" that all humans operate with, which allows them to function on a day-to-day basis. Briefly stated, Janoff-Bulman's (1992, 6) "three fundamental assumptions" are (1) the world is benevolent; (2) the world is meaningful; (3) the self is worthy. Trauma occurs when individuals are forced by the impact of events to question any or all of these assumptions. Janoff-Bulman (and many others who continue to work with these ideas) often draws explicitly on religious teachers and texts in history (Maimonides, Calvin, Buber, the book of Job; see Janoff- Bulman 1992, 6) as examples whose influence has tended to buttress Western cultural narratives that build these "fundamental assumptions." One need not agree with the precise formulations of Janoff-Bulman's proposals, however, to understand the significance of challenges to one's prevailing sense of the world in the context of traumatic events.

The work of Robert Niemeyer (2006), provocatively entitled "Re-Storying Loss: Fostering Growth in the Posttraumatic Narrative," is especially suggestive for those interested in the intersection of trauma studies, narrative studies, and biblical studies. Niemeyer states that in PTG studies, literature concerned with the construction, deconstruction, and reconstruction of narratives "may be among the richest but also least utilized" (69). Proposing that narrative or "telling stories" may well be an apt description of how the human brain functions to make rational sense of the world around us, he establishes the basis of his research agenda by suggesting that

> demonstrably healthy profiles of postloss adaptation are consonant with the view that resilient survivors are able to assimilate loss into their existing self-narratives in a way that it does not radically undermine the central themes of their life stories, and indeed, may even affirm them. However, when such assimilation is not possible, survivors may find themselves struggling to accommodate their self-narratives to integrate the enormity of their loss. (Niemeyer 2006, 71)

If this is true, then a careful examination of historical texts in the aftermath of trauma may well be a rich source of reconstructing narratives of meaning as part of a strategy of survival and even continued social viability. Furthermore, since spirituality is often noted to be among the important contributors to one's "assumptive world" (Janoff-Bulman, 2006, 89) or "self-narrative" (Niemeyer 2006; cf. "spiritual crises" in Afuape 2011, 45–47, cf. Doka, 2002), analyzing religious narrative texts can be a fruitful line of inquiry for furthering the intersection of biblical studies and trauma studies.

Niemeyer's study of narrative resilience in trauma's aftermath is compatible with a variety of approaches that focus specifically on narratives as constitutive of the individual *and society*. For example, Afuape (2011) insists on the political elements of self-narratives, emphasizing the social and political realities contributing to one's self-identity. Such political contexts, inherently communal, must not be overshadowed by a distinctly Western clinical obsession with interiorized individualism (51–54). Volkan (1997, 36–49) writes of "chosen traumas," referring to historical events that can become inextricable parts of contemporary cultural identities—a "story" that is invariably a part of the contemporary self-narrative. Alexander (2012, 6) refers to "cultural trauma," which "occurs when members of a collectivity feel they have been subjected to a horrendous event that leaves indelible marks upon their group consciousness, marking their memories forever." These memories often appear in public life through literature (11). Through these and other storytelling means, "[c]ollective actors 'decide' to represent social pain as a fundamental threat to their sense of who they are, where they came from, and where they want to go" (15).

A further source of comparison for discussing this powerful sense of political, and thus communal, narrative is the literature regarding the testimonies of truth and reconciliation commissions (TRCs; see Haynor 2011, 11). Recent work on the TRC events suggests that these testimonies emerge as an exercise in developing a nation's new narrative contexts. Among the more controversial aspects of the TRCs is that they are thought to let people "off the hook" through the granting of amnesties (often required before some will even speak), short-circuiting judicial processes and thus not allowing new narratives to emerge in a context of social justice. Careful analysis of the TRC literature, however, suggests that such criticism radically overlooks the power of reconstructing narrative for communal healing. Haynor, for example, comments in relation to the South African cases, "Where justice was not possible, the minimal requirements for forgiveness, most insisted, was to be told the full, honest, and unvarnished truth" (2011, 3). Justice systems are often not up to the task in the immediate aftermath of the fall of an oppressive regime. Trials are difficult, and legal technicalities often squelch the voices of those who want to be heard. As Teresa Phelps observes:

> Rules of procedure, strictly observed, can impede open storytelling that might reveal some larger more inclusive truth. What a witness or victim may say is constrained. Most testimony about feelings, personal impact, or memories not entirely relevant to the matter at hand is impermissible, and thereby goes unsaid. Under diligent cross-examination, doubt may be cast on even a truthful witness's story. (2004, 67)

Thus, Haynor (2011, 92) reports, the "false duality" between justice and the TRCs is an obsolete debate—it is rather that one often serves the other: "[S]imply giving victims and witnesses a chance to tell their stories to an official commission—especially one that is respectful, non-confrontational, and genuinely interested in their stories—can help them regain their dignity and begin to recover"(146). Phelps develops this further with the idea of "recovery of language" (that is, the ability to actually speak about horrific events), arguing that *the retrieval of language puts the world back into some kind of order*" (2011, 55; my emphasis). The testimonies can then become the building blocks of new national identities and stories (60; cf. James and van de Vijver, 2000).

THE BIBLE AND NARRATIVE REPAIR

These theoretical contributions bolster arguments for the importance of narrative, suggesting that storytelling represents a clinically established and "field-tested" approach to

understanding personal and social responses to trauma. This provides a theoretical foundation for analyses of how biblical texts may evidence narrative repair following highly traumatic historical events (Carr 2014).

To illustrate this possibility, we turn to an obvious example of posttraumatic literature,
the book of Lamentations, as a narrative artifact of the Babylonian destruction of Jerusalem
and Judah in the early sixth century BCE. Fr. Daniel Berrigan (2002, 15), commenting on
Lamentations 1:7, writes, "Memories do not rebuild walls, nor restore a people destroyed."
But perhaps Fr. Berrigan is a bit hasty here. In fact, as we have seen, memories, especially
those that are constitutive of a national or communal narrative, are actually critical to the
rebuilding of a person, and a people. Could it be that the book of Lamentations' existence in
the canon suggests a profound willingness to give sacred space for a kind of truth and reconciliation commission between the Hebrews and God? Is the book attempting to heal the
cultural narrative of the Hebrew people?

LAMENTATIONS AS NARRATIVE REPAIR OF THE
HEBREW ASSUMPTIVE WORLD

The commentary literature on Lamentations is overwhelmingly interested in how a sor-
rowful book can still contribute to a healthy faith in God. For example, the older twentieth-
century commentaries on Lamentations are almost exclusively interested in the modern
religious and theological issues raised by lamenting itself, and are rarely concerned with the
historical, political, and social contexts in the sixth to fourth centuries BCE of lamenting in
Babylonian- and then Persian-occupied Palestine (see Parry 2010; Thomas 2013).

Religious interpretations primarily addressing modern personal and interiorized issues of
well-being can too easily ignore the realities of economic and political power in the ancient
Near East. Westermann (1994), in his important book on Lamentations, writes, "[T]there
is no other book in the Old Testament whose contents force the question of the life-setting
more strongly than Lamentations"(61). This is not to deny the texts' religiosity—but rather to
insist that part of the "religious work" of these texts is the critical task of rebuilding communal identity and worth in the wake of Nebuchadnezzar's devastation of Judah and deportation of thousands of prisoners of war.

To illustrate how an analysis of texts as narrative repair after trauma can highlight important aspects of Lamentations, we take up a question related to literary form. The specific
format of a lament has been thoroughly examined (for a helpful summary of the standard
lament form, see Lee 2002, 3–36); however, our concern here is not with the lament form
generally but with a particular characteristic of the book itself: five chapters are constructed
on the acrostic form. That is, chapters 1–3 contain twenty-two verses of three lines each,
and each verse begins with the next letter of the Hebrew alphabet. Chapter 3, however, is
notable because each letter of the alphabet has three verses each (that is, verses 1–3 begin
with "Aleph", etc.). Chapter 4 has two lines for each verse, again in the twenty-two letters,
but chapter 5 is famously "broken," and the acrostic is not complete. Although the acrostic form also occurs in Psalms 9–10, 25, 34, 37, 111, 112, 119, 145, as well as in Nahum 1:2–8
and Proverbs 31:10–31, nowhere else does it characterize a work as a whole as it does the
book of Lamentations. Westermann first proposed that the form was not an original but

"a secondary development" (1994, 63). But after summarizing various attempts to explain why the acrostic form was (allegedly) imposed at a later time, Westermann suggests, "A simple aesthetic explanation works best: shaping the poems in this fashion must have had a pleasing effect on early audiences" (99). Reading Lamentations with an interest in narrative repair of social identity resonates with this deceptively simple suggestion, but how can we move from Westermann's "pleasing effect" to the crucial work of narrative in recovery after trauma?

There are other notable features of the book relevant to our analysis. Consider, for example, calls to "remember" in the early verses of chapter 1:

> Jerusalem *remembers*, in the days of her affliction and wandering, all the precious things that were hers in days of old (Lam. 1:7a; emphasis mine)
>   Her uncleanness was in her skirts; she took no thought of [lit., *did not remember*] her future; her downfall was appalling, with none to comfort her. "O LORD, look at my affliction, for the enemy has triumphed!" (Lam. 1:9)

The specific imperative form of "remember" (*zakrah*) occurs outside these two occasions only in prayers directed to God and in late sources (e.g., in 2 Chron. 6:42, "O LORD God, do not reject your anointed one. Remember your steadfast love for your servant David"; cf. Nehemiah's requests to God to "remember" his actions: Neh. 5:19; 6:14; 13:14, 22, 29, 31). Hillers (1972, 2) renders the phrase in Lamentations 1:7 as "calls to mind," and Parry (2010, 36) suggests, simply, "Jerusalem remembered." Remembering, then, has a prominent place in Lamentations.

Another recurring theme can be found in the imperative form of requests for God to "see" (*r'eh YHWH*) Only in Ecclesiastes (where *r'eh* is often rendered as "consider") do we find more frequent occurrences of this specific form than in Lamentations. The term "affliction" (*'aniy*), though used heavily in Psalms, occurs most often in Lamentations. The request to "see" ones "affliction" is used only in requests to God, and only five times in the entire Bible (Gen. 31:42; Pss. 9:14; 25:18; 119:153; Lam. 1:9). Finally, it has been widely noted that Lamentations calls on God to take note of troubles no fewer than four times in the first two chapters:

> "O LORD, look at my affliction, for the enemy has triumphed!" (1:9)
> "Look, O LORD, and see how worthless I have become." (1:11)
> "See, O LORD, how distressed I am." (1:20)
> "Look, O LORD, and consider! To whom have you done this?" (2:20)

O'Conner (2002, 22) argues that this series establishes at the outset an important theme that continues to function centrally throughout the book. Even more notably, Lamentations is the only biblical book that features a *direct request* to God to take note in precisely this manner. But why would requests to God to "remember," "consider," and "see" be a significant way of thinking about the form of Lamentations as a work? Recent work is helpful on this question.

One of Westermann's (1994) concerns when he first wrote on Lamentations (the German edition was published in 1990) was what he saw as the neglect of the book of Lamentations in twentieth-century Christian theology (and worship). This virtual silence no longer exists. Linafelt's (2000) post-Holocaust reading of Lamentations, Lee's (2002, 2010) reflections on Lamentations in light of the violence in Sarajevo and other modern contexts, and O'Connor's (2002) personalized contemplation of Lamentations have all contributed to a revival of interest in contemporary theological reflections on Lamentations, as well as to renewed interest in its historical meaning.

To this mix, we would add Brueggemann's notion that lamentations are to be understood as expressions of protest as well as of sorrow:

> [T]his form of prayer . . . shifts the calculus and redresses the redistribution of power between the two parties, so that the petitionary party is taken seriously and the God who is addressed is newly engaged in the crisis in a way that puts God at risk (Brueggemann 1986, 59)
>
>   Lament occurs when the dysfunction reaches an unacceptable level, when the injustice is intolerable and change is insisted upon. (62)

Similarly, Westermann observed:

> These songs arose as an immediate reaction on the part of those affected by the collapse. Those so affected then expressed themselves in lamentations *the real significance of laments resides in the way they allow the suffering of the afflicted to find expression.* (1994, 81; my emphasis).

From the perspective of narrative repair and the healing of memories, the book of Lamentations insists on an "assumptive world," in which injustice and suffering are rejected. By protesting, Lamentations does not accept the new circumstances of leveled Jerusalem and devastated Judah as normal, acceptable, or permanent. In other words, Lamentations does not accept Nebuchadnezzar's narrative reality! Lamentations' demand that God see and hear is a demand to restore something of the previous narrative, the story that allowed the people of God to understand who they are. The crucial point is not that restoration will occur—it is the reaffirmation that it *should*. If God is God, then calling on God to see and hear is part of the "healing of the narrative" of the Hebrew people. Clearly, if there were a new, incontrovertible narrative—perhaps the Babylonian narrative about Nebuchadnezzar as representative of the all-powerful Marduk—then Hebrews would not bother to protest! If there were acceptance of the new reality of subordination to Babylon (and then Persia, Hellenistic rulers and Rome), then there might be other narratives conveying that acceptance, but they are surely not those expressed in Lamentations 3:

> But this I call to mind, and therefore I have hope: The steadfast love of the LORD never ceases, his mercies never come to an end; they are new every morning; great is your faithfulness. (Lam. 3:21–23 NRSV)

In short, the hope in chapter 3 is not merely a desperate attempt to feel comfort; nor is it, as many contemporary religious readers suppose, a theological overriding of the pain in the rest of the book. But it is, rather, a radical reaffirmation of the Hebrew narrative in the face of a pressing new narrative of defeat and devastation being forced on them by Babylon.

LAMENTATIONS AS PATTERNED
TESTIMONY—AND THE BLUES

One further issue is important to this analysis: if the poetry originating in the immediate aftermath of the destruction of Jerusalem in 587 BCE was clearly (and later) reworked, then why this particular acrostic pattern? One of the most common answers is the notion of a mnemonic device. Berlin, however, proposes that the acrostic pattern expresses a structure to suffering:

> The world of Lamentations has been disrupted; no order exists any longer in the real world. But as if to counteract this chaos, the poet has constructed his own linguistic order that he marks out graphically for us by the orderly progression of the letters of the alphabet. (2002, 5)

Gottwald's (1954) work is usually cited as the first to suggest the notion of a "totality" of suffering—that is, suffering from A to Z (so Parry 2010, 14; but see Berlin 2002, 4n6, for a midrashic anticipation of this notion). Shea suggests that the book of Lamentations represents the *qinah*, or "broken," meter of poetry that is unique to Lamentations—the acrostic form "breaks down" toward the end of the book, just as the *qinah* pattern omits an expected final beat in the poetic meter (Shea 1979; see Parry's affirmation and development of the concept 2010, 16–17).

O'Conner suggests that there is a "structure" to suffering, that it is not, therefore, considered outside "normality." The work on narrative repair following trauma supports O'Conner's instinct. In short, should the question perhaps be why there is *any intentional and carefully arranged structure at all*, rather than why there is specifically an acrostic structure? To put it another way—why did lamentations as a literary form *continue to be popular at all*?

One way to move forward is to ask about the role of laments more generally. In his fascinating work on modern traditions of lament across cultures, James Wilce echoes Brueggemann's insights when he writes that

> laments in nearly all of the world's traditions have a political edge to them—in the prototypical funeral setting, but perhaps even more clearly in other settings. This reflects the fact that laments were performances of grief but also grievance. . . . this political edge helps explain the widespread association of passion in general (not just lament) with danger. (Wilce, 2009, 49)

Wilce traces a long twentieth-century tradition of disdaining laments as indicators of "primitive and undeveloped" societies. Such a view, however, overlooks the political power of lament traditions to inspire change and protest as well as to express a debilitating sense of loss (2009, 150–160).

There was clearly a significant role for Lamentations in post-exilic Hebrew society; otherwise the book would not show the signs of being reworked, re-edited, and carefully constructed. "Ritual use" seems to be the inevitable suggestion for all proposed social uses of narrative in biblical analysis. But is liturgical ritual the only possibility for reusing texts? Is there another possibility?

Westermann's comment that the arrangement of acrostic laments is aesthetically "pleasing" prompts a comparison with another modern example of narratives of trauma. Westermann's suggestion that someone could actually "enjoy" a recitation of a set of poems with such devastating content begs a comparison with the famous African American musical form known as the blues. We have seen how the theorizing of narrative repair may suggest one viable way of reading Lamentations as healing, but was a reading of Lamentations also *pleasurable*?

LAMENTATIONS AS HEBREW BLUES?

Let us begin our concluding reflections on this question with the famous observation often attributed to the popular blues artist B. B. King, "Life sometimes gives you the blues, but the blues always gives you life!" The large amount of literature on the blues is telling (to begin: Davis 1995; Cohn 1993; Wyman 2001; Cone 1972 [2008]; Wald 2004; Oakley 1997; Spencer 1993; Lomax 1993; and Oliver 1990). Blues music is widely popular, and goes through occasional revivals of strikingly increased popularity (cf. Hamilton 2008). There are, of course, all kinds of interesting ambiguities about this popularity, such as whether certain racial and political realities of the origins of the blues is ignored by non-black audiences, who are less interested in the lyrics' inherent political criticism and more interested in the titillation (and reinforcement of prejudices) of the more sexualized lyrics (see, especially, Oliver [1990] and Spencer's [1993] important response).

In fact, it is the communal nature of blues music that provides a comparative key to Lamentations—suggesting both as forms of narrative repair. Blues music begins in a period of serious social disappointment after the failure of Reconstruction in the South and the rise of severe, legalized repression of African Americans that is normally referred to as "Jim Crow" (a term that has come to refer to an entire social ideology of repression but that is drawn from an old and quite racially offensive song from blackface Negro minstrel shows earlier in the nineteenth century).

We need not dwell at length on the social context of the Mississippi Delta in the relevant decades, which has been carefully chronicled (Schwartz 1976; Cobb 1992; Woodruff 2003). Such studies confirm the observation of blues historian Paul Oliver:

> In the blues were to be found the major catastrophes both personal and national, the triumphs and miseries that were shared by all, yet private to one. In the blues were reflected the family disputes, the violence and bitterness, the tears and upheavals caused by poverty and migration. In the blues an unsettled, unwanted people during these periods of social unrest found the security, the unity, and the strength it so desperately desired. (1990, 11)

James Cone's 1972 [2008] theological study, *The Spirituals and the Blues,* was the first major work to invite significant theological analysis of the blues. "The blues," writes Cone, "tell us how black people affirmed their existence and refused to be destroyed by the oppressive environment; how, despite white definitions to the contrary, they defined their own somebodiness and realized that America was not their true home" (105; cf. Spencer 1993). However, it is not my purpose to establish specific comparisons with the lyrics of selected blues songs and the themes of Lamentations. Rather, I explore what are actually more generally accessible questions, to wit: How does a musical form whose subjects are notoriously sad (broken relationships, broken lives, sad circumstances, poverty, death, and despair) end up becoming so strikingly popular? In other words—does the blues, and especially its consistent popularity, suggest some significant support for Westermann's observations about "enjoying" the book of Lamentations because of its' "aesthetic" qualities? Is it possible that one can enjoy a performance (e.g., a reading, or even a singing) of Lamentations as one enjoys a performance of the blues? And for the same reasons?

THE PLEASURES OF TELLING THE TRUTH

Westermann's suggestion that the acrostic form may render the reading (singing?) of Lamentations a more "pleasing" experience is actually more suggestive than he may have intended, especially when one makes the comparison to the work on narrative repair after trauma, and especially to the blues, as an aesthetically pleasing example of precisely the social significance of narrative repair. The comparison raises this possibility: the acrostic form, at the very least, suggests a reworking—a continued life—of Lamentations far beyond the initial cries from the events of 587 BCE. That prayer forms that are similar to Lamentations (namely, other calls on God) also date to late in the canon (e.g., Ezra 9; Neh. 9) further suggests a continued life of Lamentations as "Hebrew Blues"—perhaps suggesting a popular genre.

Comparisons between the biblical Lamentations and contemporary genres of lament and protest (blues, TRC testimonies, and other forms of social narrative repair) suggest that we must not minimize or reduce the social significance of the calls to see and remember in Lamentations and, especially, the insistence to hear—indeed, to sing—complaints and protest!

It surely is not insignificant to note that the use of the LXX Greek term from Lamentations, "look, consider" only occurs twice in Luke (among all the gospels): once when Mary thanks God for "seeing, noticing" a representative of poorer Israelites (Luke 1:48), and an imperative to Jesus to "look and notice" affliction and suffering ("Teacher, *I beg you to look* at my son," Luke 9:38 NRSV; my emphasis).

Like listening to the blues, anyone can be forgiven for actually appreciating, even enjoying, the recovered sense of agency that often accompanies protesting injustice—especially if those protests can be directed to the Creator! An analysis of Lamentations as worked and reworked poetry of sadness and protest should consider how and why laments and songs of sadness actually become popular cultural statements among the disenfranchised. Beginning with a reading of narrative as a recently theorized category for understanding resilience and recovery from trauma in the modern world, and considering the TRC testimony literature and the blues suggests the possibility that the ancient post-exilic Hebrews found memories of suffering to be important, and likely even healing, not because these memories were part of simply remembering defeat—but as part of continuing a story of survival and resilience—in short—a kind of narrative repair of identity.

The question of why there was an obvious continued life of Lamentations—established by evidence of careful reworking of the structure—may well be a question tentatively addressed by Westermann's suggestion about the pleasurable experience of reading acrostics, but is strongly supported in other ways by TRC testimonies and by the musical "testimonies" of B. B. King and Muddy Waters—voices that are related to modern postraumatic contexts. The Bible, too, sings the blues, and it contains a people's insistence on giving testimony, and thus protesting injustice. Liturgical settings may not be the only place for singing laments among ancient Judeans! Protesting injustice—and singing of injustice—is a healing act because it tells an important counterstory to an imperially sponsored narrative forced on a subject people.

This chapter, therefore, proposes a new level of dialogue among social theorists interested in narratives (socially shared as well as individually constructed) as a means of understanding processes of recovery and resilience in the aftermath of trauma, historians of the blues, historians of the TRC processes, and scholars interested in a contemporary analysis of the creative social, political, and theological role of lament in the Bible. Lament leads to a repaired social narrative because it refuses to accept that the communal narrative no longer exists (rather, God is still there to be appealed to), but also because it refuses to accept an imposed imperial narrative. The book of Lamentations creatively contributes to a revised narrative of Hebrew identity that will not accept subordination, oppression, and violence as the final "story."

Indeed, the book of Lamentations itself may be the answer to the despairing question asked in Psalm 137:4: "How can we sing the LORD's song in a foreign land?" Lamentations answers, "by making it the blues" and carrying on.

REFERENCES

Afuape, Taiwo. 2011. *Power, Resistance and Liberation in Therapy with Survivors of Trauma: To Have Our Hearts Broken*. London: Routledge.

Alexander, Jeffrey. 2012. *Trauma: A Social Theory*. London: Polity Press.

Berlin, Adele. 2002. *Lamentations*. Old Testament Library. Louisville, KY: Westminster/John Knox.

Berrigan, Daniel 2002. *Lamentations*. Chicago: Lanham.

Brueggemann, Walter. 1986. "The Costly Loss of Lament." *Journal for the Study of the Old Testament* 36: 57–71.

Calhoun, Lawrence G., and Richard Tedeschi, eds. 2006. *Handbook of Posttraumatic Growth: Research and Practice*. Mahwah, NJ: Lawrence Erlbaum Associates.

Carr, David. 2014. *Holy Resilience: The Bible's Traumatic Origins*. New Haven, CT: Yale University Press.

Caruth, Cathy. 1996. *Unclaimed Experience: Trauma, Narrative, and History*. Baltimore, MD: Johns Hopkins University Press.

Cobb, James C. 1992. *The Most Southern Place on Earth: The Mississippi Delta and the Roots of Regional Identity*. New York: Oxford University Press.

Cohn, Lawrence. 1993. *Nothin but the Blues*. New York: Abbeville.

Cone, James. 1972 [2008]. *The Spirituals and the Blues*. New York: Orbis.

Davis, Francis. 1995. *The History of the Blues: The Roots, the Music, the People from Charley Patton to Robert Cray*. New York: Hyperion.

Doka, Kenneth. 2002. "How Could God? Loss and the Spiritual Assumptive World." In *Loss of the Assumptive World: A Theory of Traumatic Loss*, edited by Jeffrey Kauffman, 49–54. New York: Brunner-Routledge.

Gottwald, Norman. 1954. *Studies in the Book of Lamentations*. London: SCM.

Hamilton, Marybeth. 2008. *In Search of the Blues*. New York: Basic Books.

Haynor, Priscilla. 2011. *Unspeakable Truths: Transitional Justice and the Challenge of Truth Commissions*. New York and London: Routledge.

Hillers, Delbert. 1972. *Lamentations*. Anchor Bible Commentary. New York: Doubleday.

James, Wilmot, and Linda van de Vijver, eds. 2000. *After the TRC: Reflections on Truth and Reconciliation in South Africa*. Athens: Ohio University Press.

Janoff-Bulman, Ronnie. 1992. *Shattered Assumptions: Towards a New Psychology of Trauma*. New York: Free Press.

Janoff-Bulman, Ronnie. 2006. "Schema-Change Perspectives on Posttraumatic Growth." In Calhoun and Tedeschi 2006, 81–99.

Janzen, David. 2012. *The Violent Gift: Trauma's Subversion of the Deuteronomistic History's Narrative*. Cambridge and New York: T&T Clark.

Lee, Nancy. 2002. *The Singers of Lamentations: Cities Under Siege, from Ur to Jerusalem to Sarajevo*. Leiden: E. J. Brill.

Linafelt, Tod. 2000. *Surviving Lamentations: Catastrophe, Lament*. Chicago: University of Chicago Press.

Lomax, Alan. 1993. *The Land Where the Blues Began*. New York: New Press.

Niemeyer, Robert A. 2006. "Re-Storying Loss: Fostering Growth in the Posttraumatic Narrative, In Calhoun and Tedeschi 2006, 68–80.

Oakley, Giles. 1997. *The Devil's Music: A History of the Blues*. London: Da Capo/BBC.

O'Conner, Kathleen. 2002. *Lamentations and the Tears of the World*. New York: Orbis.

Oliver, Paul. 1990. *Blues Fell This Morning: Meaning in the Blues*. New York: Cambridge University Press.

Parry, Robin. 2010. *Lamentations*. Two Horizons of Old Testament Commentary Series. Grand Rapids, MI: Eerdmans.

Phelps, Teresa Godwin. 2004. *Shattered Voices: Language, Violence, and the Work of Truth Commissions*. Philadelphia: University of Pennsylvania Press.

Sackheim, Eric, ed. 2003. *The Blues Line: Blues Lyrics from Leadbelly to Muddy Waters*. Boston: Da Capo Press.

Schwartz, Michael. 1976. *Radical Protest and Social Structure: The Southern Farmers' Alliance and Cotton Tenancy, 1880-1890*. Chicago: University of Chicago Press.

Shea, William. 1979. "The Qinah Structure of the Book of Lamentations" *Biblica* 60: 103–107.

Spencer, Jon Michael. 1993. *Blues and Evil*. Knoxville: University of Tennessee Press.

Tal, Kali. 1996. *Worlds of Hurt: Reading the Literatures of Trauma*. Cambridge Studies in American Literature and Culture 95. Cambridge: Cambridge University Press.

Tedeschi, Richard, and Lawrence G. Calhoun. 1995. *Trauma and Transformation: Growing in the Aftermath of Suffering*. Thousand Oaks, CA: Sage Publications.

Thomas, Heath A. 2013. "A Survey of Research on Lamentations (2002–2012)." *Currents in Biblical Research* 12: 8–38.

Volkan, Vamik. 1997. *Bloodlines: From Ethnic Pride to Ethnic Terrorism*. New York: Farrer, Straus, and Giroux.

Wald, Elijah. 2004. *Escaping the Delta: Robert Johnson and the Invention of the Blues*. New York: Amistad.

Westermann, Claus. 1994. *Lamentations: Issues and Interpretation*. Minneapolis, MN: Fortress Press.

Wilce, James M. 2009. *Crying Shame: Metaculture, Modernity, and the Exaggerated Death of Lament*. Oxford: Wiley-Blackwell.

Woodruff, Nan Elizabeth. 2003. *American Congo: The African American Freedom Struggle in the Delta*. Cambridge, MA: Harvard University Press.

Wyman, Bill. 2001. *Bill Wyman's Blues Odyssey: A Journey to Music's Heart and Soul*. London: DK Publishing.

PART V

ON READING

CHAPTER 49

CULTURE TRICKS IN BIBLICAL NARRATIVE

JIONE HAVEA AND MONICA JYOTSNA MELANCHTHON

BIBLICAL narratives establish, maintain, and cross boundaries (see also Fewell, "The Work of Biblical Narrative" in this volume); biblical narratives are inherently cross-cultural. So are readers. As individuals and as a writing team, we are unavoidably cross-cultural: Monica is Telugu and Dalit from India who has migrated to Melbourne, Australia, while Jione is a native of Tonga in the South Pacific (or Oceania) who has migrated to Sydney, Australia. With roots in the Asia-Pacific, we are openly cross-cultural and we engage in cross-cultural reading. We read the trickery of the Gibeonites in Joshua 9 as an invitation to cross cultures, to look for narrative and interpretive tricks, and to shift alliance from the invading Israelites toward the natives of the land and the out*castes*.

GIBEONITES

Joshua 9 narrates an incident in which Joshua, Israel's national hero, receives an enemy group into the Israelite camp. The narrative is in the form of a dialog between a party representing the Gibeonites—who "from the beginning of the episode, bear an essential resemblance to Israel" (Hawk 2000, 139)—and Joshua and the Israelite community in which each responds to the actions and words of the other. After a brief interrogation, Joshua and the Israelite leaders incorporate the Gibeonites into the structure of the Israelite community: Admission. Later, after discovering that the Gibeonites have tricked them, Joshua and the Israelite community inscribe for the Gibeonites roles that place them in servitude, first to the community, and then to its religious establishment as well: Castigation.

It is immaterial whether this incident happened or not (see Na'aman 2009, 101–102; van Seters 2011). What concerns us in this chapter is the power of narrative to realize an incident and then unroll it like a mat (which signifies welcome in our cultures). Narrative also has power to ignore and silence, so it is significant that the Gibeonites are not silenced or brushed off in Joshua 9. Equally significant are the points of disconnection (i.e., not connecting, talking past one another) in the exchange, something we expect in cross-cultural encounters.

The Gibeonites approach the Israelites out of fright due to the staggering victories of Israel, as far as the biblical narrative is concerned, over Jericho and Ai, and they come seeking to preempt something similar happening to them. They approach Joshua with worn-out clothing and sandals, dried food, wineskins, and sacks for their donkeys and present themselves as having come from a distant land. A narrative of trickery, the narrative itself is also tricky. It does not explain how the Gibeonites gained entry into the Israelite camp or how they were able to approach Joshua directly. It builds on the premise of an encounter of distant peoples, but it does not account for how distant lands mean different and foreign cultures and languages. How did the Gibeonites greet the Israelites? What language did they use? Their comprehensible speech, indistinguishable from that of Joshua, is a dead giveaway that they are not from distant land. In any case, the Gibeonites do not waste time in making their request known: "We have come from a far country; so now make a treaty with us."

The Gibeonites' request brings to mind the stipulation in Deuteronomy 20:10–15 (so Rosenberg 2014, 70–72), according to which Israel should first offer the opportunity to make a treaty to peoples whose land they enter, and Israel could also enter into treaties with towns "that are very far." Israel's initial response to the Gibeonites suggests that they are not listening. The narrator lets the Gibeonites speak, but does not let the Israelites hear. "Perhaps you live among us; then how can we make a treaty with you?" We expect this kind of disconnection when people from different language backgrounds converse, even when they converse in a common language. Having something "lost in translation" is common when crossing cultural borders. The more distant, the more lost.

For the sake of hearers (and readers), the request is repeated, and expanded, passing over Jericho and Ai into the wilderness and toward Egypt. Repetition and interruption are features of cross-cultural dialogues. The Gibeonites impress upon the Israelite hearers that they are there to be their "servants" because they had heard of Israel's God and all that this God had done in Egypt and across the Jordan, which had prompted their community to send them as emissaries to Joshua and to the Israelites to convince them to enter into a treaty. Moldy bread, worn wineskins, sandals, and garments are presented as proof of having come from a distant land. The Israelites are convinced after partaking of this moldy bread, so they make a treaty and the Gibeonites are assured life—all without any consultation with God. "[T]he encounter with the Gibeonites suggests that Yahweh is merely the legislative branch, and that the human judicial and executive branches have significant independence (at least at times)" (Rosenberg 2014, 81). Although often a point of critique for Joshua and the Israelite leaders, this is one example of a relationship made without bloodshed. Even the Israelites benefit from the lack of the loss of life.

Three days later the Israelites discover that the Gibeonites have lied and that they have come from nearby. Despite discovering the ruse, the Israelites honor the treaty; they allow the Gibeonites to live but consign them to being "hewers of wood and drawers of water for all the congregation."

The narrative offers an alternative to "the posture of total annihilation found in Joshua 1-12" (Dor and De-Malach 2013, 54) and counters the Deuteronomistic injunction of *herem* ("genocide"; Brett 2008, 86; see also Creangă, "The Conquest of Memory in the Book of Joshua" in this volume). Some critics suggest that the redeeming feature of the story lies in what they term "biblical humanism," which is manifested in the show of equality to the foreigner (Deut. 10:19; 25:17) and "the call to absorb foreigners into Israel and admit them to its society (e.g., Isa. 2:2–3; 56:6–7)" (Dor and De-Malach 2013, 46–47). But there is no show of equality here. The Gibeonites are admitted into society as the "other," made slaves but "not Israelites in the full sense of the term" (Blenkinsopp 1974, 1). They are relegated to the lowest rung of the temple ladder as "hewers of wood and drawers of water," enslaved to perform this task for generations. They have been shown mercy but not equality. Perhaps the Israelites realize that it would not benefit them to decimate the locals. The Israelites needed people to be their servants, and who better than the ones they could colonize? But do they really colonize the Gibeonites, the ones who come (to submit) with a trick up their sleeves?

Tricking

People play tricks on each other for different reasons: the itch to outwit, to control, to resist, to survive, and so forth. Some people trick their masters, such as when Shiphrah and Puah disregard Pharaoh's injunction to kill newborn boys but to let baby girls live (Exod. 1:15–17), and when the family heads of Gilead maneuver for the revision of the ruling established in favor of Zelophehad's daughters (Num. 27; 36). The midwives outwit Pharaoh, and the Gileadites win over the Josephites, Moses, and YHWH. Some people (counter)trick their rivals, such as when the Egyptian magicians match Aaron's plagues (Exod. 7: 19–24) thereby doubling the devastation on their own people. Proudly matching Aaron's magic, they only end up being the butt of the trick. Some people trick their own friends; Judah, for instance, sends Hirah the Adullamite to look for Tamar in Genesis 38. Imagine the look on the faces of the local people when this stranger comes asking, "Where is the cult prostitute, the one at Enaim, by the road?" (38:21), associating their town with cult prostitution. Tamar, of course, tricks Judah earlier on in the interest of economic security, but Judah sends his Adullamite friend to become an unsuspecting target of annoyance. Close to the top of the list of biblical tricksters would be Jacob, who tricks even his own blood kin. With the help of his mother Rebekah, Jacob dupes his father Isaac and brother Esau (Gen. 27:1–28:9). Isaac is made to think that Jacob is Esau, and Esau is cheated of his birthright and blessing. Trickery runs in Jacob's family, for his wife Rachel outsmarts her own father later on (Gen. 31:19–35).

Whoever the butt of the trick might be, and for whatever reason, trickery is in the fabric of—trickery is the stuff of—relationships. It is idealistic to expect relationships to build without frictions, slippages, and deflations. Relationships develop because of the energies of people who have interests and powers, driven by their desires and fears, and people in relationships are known to undermine and take advantage of, in other words, to trick, one another.

Trickery plays out differently according to the powers of the people in relationships. The more power one has, the less caring one tends to be about the consequences of one's tricks; the less power one has, the more desperate one is in one's tricks. Control and survival are critical in the playing out of tricks and in the weavings of relationships.

In the mission fields, the biting marks of trickery are passed off as the will of God and endorsed in the interest of religion. Tonga's Taufa'āhau, for instance, tricked his rival chiefs to submit their peoples and lands to the Christian mission in order that they might be "saved," and Ma'afu and his mob did the same in neighboring Fiji's Lau Group for the sake of their "conversion." In Tonga's national memory the "unification" of Tonga and "colonization" of the Lau Group are praised as missions of God and of the church. Thanks to a religious trick, natives are desensitized to the working of trickery to overpower and dispossess. Differences among people find expression on the religious plane. Control is achieved when the subordinated group regards its condition as a mark of distinction, such as the Gibeonite deception being validated because it led to temple service (Butler 2013, 31).

When people from different cultures, languages, and traditions relate, one expects some interweaving, as well as some ruffling and fraying, to occur. Trickery is one way to avoid strangulating in the reverberations of cross-cultural encounters. Pockets of resistance against Taufaʻāhau by communities that became known as *Kau Fakaongo* prevailed in Tonga, and the island of Laucala in Fiji used trickery to push back the invading Tongans. Inspired by the drive for survival, trickery can thus benefit people who need a tactic of resistance and people who are disadvantaged. As Fewell and Heard put it, trickery is "the underdog's most reliable tactic" (see "The Genesis of Identity in the Biblical World" in this volume).

Cross-Cultural Reading

Sometimes, some readers pretend that their readings are free of who they are and where they read, as if they are relation-free and context-free. That pretension is naïve because we are all rooted in cultural settings, traditional heritages, and more. We all are contexted.

As cultures give people features, tones, sways and scents, so do cultures seep into and flavor narratives. Narratives reflect the cultures that produced them, whether at the beginning or later on when the narratives transit between places, but those cultures do not fully control what the narratives say or do. Narratives are cultured, but they are not locked into those cultures. Narratives are also textured, but the dynamics of textuality do not limit what narratives say or do. On the flip side, narratives condition cultures and scriptures, but do not control those either. People, cultures, and narratives condition, (re)produce, and trick one another, tug and poke at one another, and they cross over borders and mediums. When people roam to and from the cultures that condition them, they carry their narratives and pose them to other narratives.

Our depiction of conditioning cultures is deceptively smooth, for we give the impression that a culture can be free from neighboring cultures. What culture is free of the narratives of other cultures? What narrative is free from the conditionings of other narratives? Behold, cultures are inherently cross-cultural. So are narratives. As products of crossing cultures, narratives are sites for trickery.

Sometime not too far back, contextual and intertextual critics set the stage by calling attention to the rootedness of readers, whether they read in the so-called third world or in the Western world (see Sugirtharajah 2006; Segovia and Tolbert 1995), and by normalizing the reading of narratives in juxtaposition because of shared sociopolitical settings, literary features, or thematic contents (see Boyarin 1990; Fewell 1992). The default tendency of intertextual critics, however, is to read narratives so that they establish and clarify each other. Intertextual critics bundle narratives together and read them so that they fit in each other's paths and arms (like the partnership of colonizers, explorers, and missionaries in the Asia-Pacific). We, on the other hand, prefer narratives to also ruffle each other. So we opt for another label, cross-cultural reading, which works for us because narratives and readers are already cross-cultural and because cross-cultural encounters are spiced with the possibility of trickery. There are other ways of doing cross-cultural reading (e.g., the political and cultural resistance reading by Miles 2013 and the cross-scriptural reading by Victor 2013), and narrative criticism has been used in different ways to read the book of Joshua (see Creangă in this volume), but in this essay we opt for the ruffling of narratives. Our preference for cross-cultural reading is also an objection to multicultural readers who favor the assimilation of cultures (e.g., Patten 2013, 198–203).

In our version of cross-cultural reading, trickery happens at several places. First, trickery happens in the plot of the narrative when characters "have a go" at each other. This is more evident in some narratives (e.g., the stories of Jacob and of the Gibeonites) than in others (e.g., the story of Ruth, the migrant worker who establishes herself in Bethlehem). Second, the reader tricks the narrative to say and do things that the narrative itself was not meant to say or do. But how might we know one way or the other? Third, cultural settings and traditional heritages trick critics to miss things that are in the narrative or to find things that are not there. Who is the reader that is not guilty in these ways? We miss some things (especially at the underside of the narrative), and we realize some things. And fourth, the reader is tricked by the narrative. This is where the matter of control (in canons and in readings) is critical (see Aichele 2001; Havea 2003), and the healthier response is to reread narratives and "poke" them so that they say/do more and more. We are therefore in agreement with Yonina Dor and Naomi De-Malach:

> We think that the advantage of a subversive reading is, first of all, that it highlights the fact that every text may say more than one thing. The goal is to extract the text's multiple aspects and full complexity. By this we do not mean arriving at a bottom line or unambiguous truth, but listening to the inner dialogue beneath the text and leaving room for submerged voices that do not represent the norm or the dominant view. (Dor and De-Malach 2013, 59)

To settle for one dominating reading is to give up on the possibilities that cross-cultural reading invites.

We have offered readings of Joshua 9 previously (Melanchthon 2014; Havea 2013), and we propose more readings here because cross-cultural reading is ongoing and because we are not satisfied with being tricked only once by this narrative. There is, however, a catch. Cross-cultural reading (with its bag of tricks) both *frees* and *freezes* the narrative. It *frees* biblical narratives to encounter other cultural narratives; one may, for instance, read the flood narrative in Genesis with the Epic of Gilgamesh because they come from similar backgrounds. In doing so, the cross-cultural reader *freezes* the narrative to a specific sociopolitical conditioning. Alternatively, the cross-cultural reader may read the Genesis flood narrative with stories from the 2009 Tsunami that affected Samoa and Tonga (see Young 2010). Cross-cultural reading thereby *frees* the biblical narrative from its imagined historical setting and *freezes* it in the mud of a contemporary natural disaster. In one way or the other, cross-cultural reading at once *sets free* and *freezes up* the narrative.

FIRST PEOPLES

The Gibeonites are among the First Peoples of Canaan, but they are not on the same page with the other First Nations. In response to the invasion by Joshua and the Israelites, whose interests are favored in the narrative, the kings of the lands west of the Jordan gather as one to fight against the invaders (Josh. 9:1–2). The Gibeonites, on the other hand, resort to trickery (9:4). They choose not to be in solidarity with their native neighbors. It is therefore naïve, in the first instance, to assume homogeneity among First Peoples (this applies to Second and Third Peoples also), something we tend to do when we call them "aboriginal" or "indigenous" because those two labels imply sameness (from a common origin).

First Peoples tricking one another is not foreign to the book of Joshua, which opens with Rahab tricking her king and his men (Josh. 2). "She betrays her people, slipping out of the city with her own family as Israelite warriors set about their work of butchering the men, women, and children among whom Rahab has lived" (Sharp 2012, 146). In the eyes of the narrative, there is nothing problematic with First Peoples tricking one another. This trickery shows that they are divided, and in the process (a narrative trick!) brushes over the division among invading Israelites. Israel does not become diverse and divided with the accommodation of non-Israelites. Israel is divided before that, as is evident in the grumbles of the people against Moses (Exod. 16) and disagreement with the spies (Num. 13).

The Gibeonites approach Joshua together with the "men of Israel" (9:6). The men of Israel are not convinced (9:7), and they question the Gibeonites. Instead of responding to the men of Israel, the Gibeonites direct their response to Joshua (9:8–13). This suggests that the Gibeonites have more respect for Joshua. But before Joshua states his decision on the Gibeonites' explanation, the men of Israel jump in to declare their approval (9:14). They do not ask for Joshua's opinion, nor do they consult YHWH. Joshua comes at the end to make a treaty that the men of Israel have already decided. The disconnection between Joshua and the men of Israel shows their division, and the Gibeonites expose this through their continuing to address Joshua even though the men of Israel are the ones raising doubts. It is unfair to expect First Peoples to be passive, homogenous, and welcoming, as when we call them "natives." First Peoples are diverse and dynamic, and they have the will to resist, to sidestep, to manipulate, and to differ from one another. This is true of the Gibeonites in Joshua 9 as well as of the Hivvites in the town of Shechem (cf. Gen. 34), which is not conquered by Joshua and Israel but which nevertheless provides the location for Joshua's institution of a covenant for Israel (Josh. 24; Dor and De-Malach 2013, 59).

There is no indication in the narrative of any communication between the Gibeonites and their First People neighbors, but we assume that the Gibeonites would have known that the other nations were gathering as one. In oral cultures, information can easily flow across cultural and linguistic borders. The fluidity of (information in) oral cultures is the grease in the wheels of trickery.

We cannot tell whether the Gibeonites have considered the consequences of their trickery, such as native neighbors feeling that they have been betrayed, but the Gibeonites clearly feel that they can fool the Israelites. The identity of the Gibeonites that the narrative constructs is not simply tied to space (i.e., the fact that they faked their land of origin) or subsequent social status (repeated, and in the process altered, in the two endings of the narrative, 9:18–21; 9:22–27; see Boer 2008, 127–132), but also on account of their courage, wisdom, and rhetorical abilities. They were daring, clever, and convincing. Not bad, we say, for native folks!

Perhaps something about the invading Israelite mob causes the Gibeonites to question Israelite intelligence and to see a weakness that might be exploited. The Gibeonites trick the Israelites so that they, the "indigenous Others" (Sharp 2012, 148), become "enemies within" (so Boer, Butler, and Miles). "Gibeon is the supreme example of how the land's

ancient inhabitants adapted themselves to the new situation of Israelite control. Its residents were enslaved and continued to live in Israel for generations; they were even among
those who returned from the Babylonian exile (Neh. 7:25)" (Dor and De-Malach 2013, 54).
The Gibeonites become "part of the inside Israel group but only as Rest or Other among the
Israelites, becoming slaves, not citizens" (Butler 2013, 33). And yet, they survive and infiltrate
the social and religious structures of Israel. "At this level, the text may become a postcolonial
celebration of the duping of dull colonial forces" (Boer 2008, 130). In the end, this narrative
subverts the assumptions of both natural domination and homogenous identity. Who are
the Israelites?

> [T]he Israelites may be no more than Gibeonites ... or the Gibeonites may be understood
> as Israelites; or, their story indicates a secondary narrative concerning the process by which
> "Israel" itself is gradually constituted in the text. The way the Gibeonites become part of
> "Israel" is one example of the way various groups constitute the textual construction of "Israel"
> in the first place, as do Rahab and her family in Joshua 2. (Boer 2008, 131)

In our cross-cultural eyes, there is nothing controversial about the mixing of ethnicities and
cultural identities. What is controversial is the assumption of purity.

The construction of identity is tied up with duty and labor. In the first ending of the narrative, the Gibeonite-Israelites (Gibeonites who have become part of the Israelite community)
were to hew wood and draw water for "all the congregation" (9:21), and in the second ending
they were also to serve "the altar of YHWH" (9:27). The "enemies within" have duties to the
community and to YHWH. They enter through trickery, and they become insiders by duty
and labor. This privilege, of being accepted and included because of duty and labor, is not
available to all peoples.

CASTEISM

Duty and labor are defined by one's caste or *jati* in Hindu/Indian societies (Kosambi 1970,
15). The primary mark and source of an Indian's identity is his or her caste. Society is divided
into groups based on birth, kinship, occupation, or order of settlement. These social divisions over time came to be viewed hierarchically resulting in "casteism" that enables some to
see themselves as superior to the rest, thereby justifying their privileged position and status
in society and structuring how one group relates to another.

Those who see themselves as superior base their sense of superiority on notions of
purity to seize control over and access to wealth, ownership, and power—social, religious,
and political. Those in the lower rungs of the caste ladder are deemed less pure, unclean or
"untouchable," and are reduced to function as servants and slaves to the dominant castes.
Modern India still sees people forced to work as scavengers, tanners, cobblers, weavers, and
manual laborers (occupations considered unclean). These people are drawn from communities that have rendered these services for centuries. These communities, now calling
themselves Dalits (having rejected the label "untouchables"), have endured centuries of
oppression and suffering, their dignity and their bodies assaulted, their culture eroded and
their humanity suppressed. Their identity is determined by birth, and the caste system does
not allow one to change one's occupation.

Of the various theories about the origin of the caste system, the most popular claims that it was a creation of the invading Aryans or "Vedic peoples" who migrated to South Asia about 2000 BCE. According to Basham (1988), "They migrated in bands westwards, southwards and eastwards, conquering local populations and inter-marrying with them to form a ruling class. They brought with them their patrilinear family system, their worship of sky gods and their horses and chariots" (30).

The invasion was an action of many tribes, and they were not a homogeneous lot but tribes that were allied for the purpose of invasion. These invading tribes were divided along class lines between the wealthy owners of herds of cattle and horses, and the poor who had none. The locals (Adivasi or Tribal people)—darker in skin tone, with a rich culture, which was also not necessarily egalitarian—were subdued and enslaved. A fourfold division of society was introduced with Brahmins (priests) at the top followed by the Kshatriyas (warriors), the Vaishyas (traders), and the Sudras (laborers). The Dalits were outside of this fourfold division and were reduced to a life of servitude and drudgery, having been rendered unclean and impure. Some people were locked into a position as owners of land and the means of production; others, as providers of labor creating the structure of the caste system. The system and the division were given religious sanction with a narrative that ascribed the origins of the various castes to parts of the divine body: the Brahmins emerged from the mouth of the Creator, the Kshatriyas from the shoulders, the Vaishyas from the thighs, and the Sudras from the feet. Using such a rationale, the upper castes ensured their dominance, privileges, and material interests.

Anyone familiar with the caste system will be able to find resonances in the narrative concerning the Gibeonite-Israelites. The framers of the caste system were aware that the service obligations could be jeopardized unless the structure of political power, occupational division, and command over labor services could be perpetuated in an orderly way through bounded social groups. Similarly, the subordination of the Gibeonite-Israelites had to be institutionalized, and their position in society had to be fixed, hence the new role thrust upon them, enforced by the power of the Israelite leadership.

The narrative provides an explanation for how the Gibeonites came to be the hewers of wood and carriers of water for the Israelite people. It also explains how they survived the Israelite onslaught on the Canaanites and the fact that the Gibeonites became so on account of their own ruse, positioning themselves as "insiders who choose to appear as outsiders . . . who seek to become colonized" (Butler 2013, 33). It was their deception that brought upon them this enslavement! Emphasizing their lie is not without an agenda: it absolves the Israelites from any guilt for having enslaved a people. In fact, the entire narrative lays the blame on the Gibeonites for their own enslavement. For, now, they have life! Not a small matter, and a better alternative than death. This is therefore not an adaptation to Israelite control but a means of survival.

The Gibeonite-Israelite perpetuation of Israelite power is achieved partly through their investment in a structure that has rewarded them even as it has subordinated them to stringent control. They probably were happy that they had not been killed and that their lives were safe; and yet they had succumbed to a life of slavery. The Israelites are able to achieve ultimate social control when the Gibeonites not only accept their condition but perhaps even come to regard it as a mark of distinction. After all, they have come into the service of a God whose power and acts precede the entry of the Israelites into Canaan. This is their *dharma* (the eternal law of the universe and, at the same time, the virtuous path of each individual) or duty from this point onward. Consigning them to work at the temple renders them less resistant. The difference between the Gibeonite-Israelites and the Israelites (proper) is expressed along religious lines. This hierarchy and its elaboration thus come to inform the local arrangements of the political, economic, and religious power of the Israelites.

Was every Gibeonite-Israelite willing to accept this unequal social and religious relation? Did they not contest the hegemonic ideology of the Israelites? We imagine that those who were at the bottom end of such a system would have wanted to find ways to escape or resist their degradation. Were they allowed to pursue other duties?

FREE(Z)ING NARRATIVE

The Gibeonite-Israelites free themselves from the death list of the Israelites and end up on their (religious) slave list. Joshua 9 explains that since the Gibeonite-Israelites had lied and deceived Israel, they bear ongoing judgment as Israel's servants/slaves. The Gibeonite-Israelites are thus set in contrast to other First Peoples who become slaves because the Israelites are not able to exterminate them (cf. 1 Kings 9:20–21; see also Brett 2008, 86).

We wind up this cross-cultural reading by calling attention to another narrative trick, the fact that in Joshua 10:2, Gibeon is identified as a large city, even larger than Ai, and that "all its men were warriors." This suggests that their decision to trick the Israelites was not made because they did not know how to fight or because they were not enough in number to war against Israel. Their trick in the end is a catalyst for the destruction of five neighboring kings—King Adoni-zedek of Jerusalem, King Hoham of Hebron, King Piram of Jarmuth, King Japhia of Lachish, and King Debir of Eglon (10:3)—and their cities.

The Gibeonite-Israelite trick brings Yhwh and Israel into war against five First Nations. The war narrative is spectacular. Yhwh hurls huge stones from the sky and kills more with hailstones than Israel does with weapons (10:11). And at Joshua's request, the sun stops (freezes) at midheaven so that Yhwh and Israel can defend the Gibeonite-Israelites (10:12–15). "Heaven and earth conspire to create an incomparable liminal moment in which all of Israel's fighting can be accomplished successfully, despite adverse odds and despite the normal physical laws of the universe" (Sharp 2012, 150). The narrator's observation is telling: "Neither before nor since has there ever been such a day, when Yhwh acted on words spoken by a man" (10,15). Yhwh is tricked into action by the words of Joshua, on behalf of the Gibeonite-Israelites, who live on into the stories of Saul and David (2 Sam. 21; cf. Blenkinsopp 1974; van Seters 2011). The Gibeonite-Israelites live on, free to survive and to be included. At the same time, the narrative freezes them under Israel's sovereignty (see Rosenberg 2014). How good is it to be insiders among the (invading) Israelites?

REFERENCES

Aichele, George. 2001. *The Control of Biblical Meaning: Canon as Semiotic Mechanism.* New York: T&T Clark.

Basham, A. L. 1988. *The Wonder That Was India.* Calcutta: Rupa.

Blenkinsopp, Joseph. 1974. "Did Saul Make Gibeon His Capital?" *Vetus Testamentum* 24: 1–7.

Boer, Roland. 2008. *Last Stop before Antarctica: The Bible and Postcolonialism in Australia*. 2nd ed. Atlanta, GA: Society of Biblical Literature.

Boyarin, Daniel. 1990. *Intertextuality and the Reading of Midrash*. Bloomington: Indiana University Press.

Brett, Mark G. 2008. *Decolonizing God: The Bible in the Tides of Empire*. Sheffield, Yorkshire: Phoenix.

Butler, Trent C. 2013. "Joshua-Judges and Postcolonial Criticism." In *Joshua and Judges*, edited by Athalya Brenner and Gale A. Yee, 27–38. Minneapolis, MN: Fortress.

Dor, Yonina, and Naomi De-Malach. 2013. "Teaching Bible Stories Critically: 'They Did Not Spare a Soul'; the Book of Joshua in an Israeli Secular Education Environment." In *Joshua and Judges*, edited by Athalya Brenner and Gale A. Yee, 39–68. Minneapolis, MN: Fortress.

Fewell, Danna Nolan, ed. 1992. *Reading between Texts: Intertextuality and the Hebrew Bible*. Louisville, KY: Westminster John Knox.

Havea, Jione. 2003. *Elusions of Control: Biblical Law on the Words of Women*. Atlanta, GA: Society of Biblical Literature.

Havea, Jione. 2013. "*Fekuki* of the Gibeonites (Joshua 9–10): Tricking Oceania Biblical Interpretation." *Pacific Journal of Theology* 50: 7–27.

Hawk, L. Daniel. 2000. *Joshua*. Berit Olam. Collegeville, MN: Liturgical.

Kosambi, D. D. 1970. *The Culture and Civilization of Ancient India in Historical Outline*. New Delhi: Vikas.

Melanchthon, Monica J. 2014. "Reading Rizpah across Borders, Cultures, Belongings … to India and Back." In *Bible, Borders, Belonging(s): Engaging Readings from Oceania*, edited by Jione Havea, David J. Neville and Elaine M. Wainwright, 171–190. Atlanta, GA: Society of Biblical Literature.

Miles, Johnny. 2013. "The 'Enemy Within': Refracting Colonizing Rhetoric in Narratives of Gibeonite and Japanese Identity." In *Postcolonialism and the Hebrew Bible: The Next Step*, edited by Roland Boer, 129–168. Atlanta, GA: Society of Biblical Literature.

Na'aman, Nadav. 2009. "The Sanctuary of the Gibeonites Revisited." *Journal of Ancient Near Easter Religions* 9: 101–124.

Patten, Malcolm. 2013. "Multicultural Dimensions of the Bible." *Evangelical Quarterly* 85: 195–210.

Rosenberg, Gil. 2014. "The Gibeonite Exception: Giorgio Agamben and Joshua 9." *Bible and Critical Theory* 10: 68–83.

Segovia, Fernando F., and Mary Ann Tolbert, eds. 1995. *Reading from This Place, Vol. 1: Social Location and Biblical Interpretation in the United States*. Minneapolis, MN: Fortress.

Sharp, Carolyn J. 2012. "'Are You for Us, or for Our Adversaries?' A Feminist and Postcolonial Interrogation of Joshua 2–12 for the Contemporary Church." *Interpretation* 66: 141–152.

Sugirtharajah, R. S. ed. 2006. *Voices from the Margin: Interpreting the Bible in the Third World*. 3rd ed. Maryknoll, NY: Orbis.

Van Seters, John. 2011. "David and the Gibeonites." *Zeitschrift für die alttestamentliche Wissenschaft* 123: 535–552.

Victor, Royce M. 2013. "Delilah—a Forgotten Hero (Judges 16:4–21): A Cross-Cultural Narrative Reading." In *Joshua and Judges*, edited by Athalya Brenner and Gale A. Yee, 235–255. Minneapolis, MN: Fortress.

Young, Lani Wendt. 2010. *The Pacific Tsunami "Galu Afi:" The Story of the Greatest Natural Disaster Samoa Has Ever Known*. Apia, Somoa: Hans Joachim Keil.

CHAPTER 50

GLOBAL THEFTS OF BIBLICAL NARRATIVE

GERALD WEST

BIBLICAL LEAKAGE

WHEN the Bible first settled in southern Africa in 1652, among the Dutch traders seeking to establish a refreshment station at the Cape for the Dutch trade route between Europe and Batavia, it was carefully constrained, restricted to formalized activities among the Dutch themselves. There was no attempt by these imperial traders to share the Bible's story with the indigenous peoples. But among the formalized activities that accommodated Bible reading were occasions in which designated "sick comforters" were required to read the Bible to the sick and to instruct the young to read. It is from such sites that there are indications that the Bible "leaked" from the confines imposed on it by the Dutch East India Company and into the lives of the indigenous peoples, with a young local girl, Krotoa (or "Eva," as the Dutch renamed her), as the initial agent (Landman 1996).

Quite what Krotoa took to her people from the Bible is not clear, though it appears to have been narratives of healing. What becomes evident in the years that follow is that it is the Bible as narrative that is appreciated and then appropriated by indigenous Africans.

FROM THE COAST TO THE INTERIOR

The southern coastal strip of the African continent, like its northern (Mediterranean) contour, was under imperial control more readily than the interior. Among the European settlers clinging, often precariously, to the southern rim, Christianity was controlled by the "established" churches in Europe. So nonconformist European missionaries, in search of African souls to civilize and save, quickly left the coastal zone and set off for the African interior (Comaroff and Comaroff 1991).

They, along with more adventurous traders and explorers, brought the Bible among the BaTlhaping people of the interior in the late 1700s. This carefully documented encounter enables us to catch glimpses of the Bible's arrival among an African indigenous people. The Bible as an artefact of trade was given as a gift by Jan Matthys Kok, a missionary-trader to chief Molehabangwe, the "king" of the BaTlhaping, in November 1802. What Molehabangwe makes of the Bible is not clear, for the missionary record emphasizes his primary interest in probing how missionaries fitted into the chain of trade between the coast and the interior. Christianity was, for all concerned, a matter of trade.

For the next ten years, during which time Mothibi would succeed his father Molehabangwe, the Bible would be considered just another of the "goods of strange power" associated with the arrival of whites in their land (Comaroff and Comaroff 1991, 182). But once the Bible was "opened," with the arrival, ten years later, of John Campbell, a director of the London Missionary Society, its power was revealed in a new way, as narrative.

CONNECTING NARRATIVES

On June 27, 1813, at "[a]bout eight o'clock in the morning" Campbell and his party witness "a procession of the women and girls, attended with much noisy singing and dancing, carrying poles mounted with ostrich feathers" (Campbell 1815, 191). Shortly after their midday worship at two o'clock, the missionaries are enveloped in "confusion," as,

> The women brought the girls, most fantastically dressed, and when a circle was formed, about four and twenty women, daubed with white spots of paint, in imitation leopards, entered and danced for some time. Next entered a woman dressed entirely in straw, so that nothing but her hands were visible . . . . Then entered the girls, who danced for a minute, when all of them suddenly dispersed, and our quiet was restored. (Campbell 1815, 191)

Included in, but confused by, this local ritual, the missionaries wait until evening to probe the ritual narrative more fully. Though an interpreter, Campbell asks the eldest brother of the late chief Molehabangwe a tangential question, "We enquired of him their reason for practising circumcision" (191). The missionaries add another component to the already layered discourse. Quite how the topic of circumcision emerges is not clear, for the ritual they have observed, in part, is a female ritual, having nothing to do with circumcision. Perhaps the ceremony witnessed was the female *bojale* initiation rite in which young girls of the same age set are inducted into adulthood (Schapera and Comaroff 1991, 32). If this is the case, then it demonstrates how layers of discourse are being laid down alongside each other in these early attempts at theological conversation. The missionaries invoke the topic of (male) circumcision because it is in the Bible.

Munaneets, chief Mothibi's uncle and a community elder, answers the missionaries, saying, "[I]t came to them from father to son." Having found an entry point to instruct the indigenous people about the Bible and Christianity, "We then asked, Do you not know why your fathers did it?" To which the BaTlhaping present "shook their heads, saying, No." The missionaries now push forward to their primary purpose in pursuing this conversation: "We told them that our book informed us how it [circumcision] began in the world, and gave them the names of Abraham, Ishmael, and Isaac, as the first persons who were circumcised" (Campbell 1815, 191–192). The missionaries are here making historical and theological claims about the priority of the Bible and its information. But the BaTlhaping receive this information differently. They receive it as a narrative with the potential to include their own narrative:

> This appeared to them very interesting information, and they all tried to repeat the names we had mentioned, over and over again, looking to us for correction, if they pronounced any of them wrong. Munaneets, and the others who joined the company, appeared anxious to have them fixed on their memories. (Campbell 1815, 192)

Their ancestors, the living dead, were the focus of BaTlhaping religious and cultural life. Though the BaTlhaping believed in a high God named *Modimo*, the dead elders of the clan, the *badimo*, were a significant part of their everyday life. Taking an active interest in the community of which they remained a part, they were regularly invoked, by name, during ceremonies such as the female *bojale* ceremony and the male *bogwêra* circumcision ceremony (Schapera and Comaroff 1991, 53). It appears that the BaTlhaping understood the missionaries to be offering a larger narrative from the Bible within which to locate their own local narrative.

The BaTlhaping would become incorporated, slowly, and initially on their own terms, in the colonial-missionary axis of the expanding Cape Colony. Among them, the first translation of the Bible into an indigenous language would take place (1830–1857), with them as the "local consultants" in the translation process. Robert Moffat, who came among the BaTlhaping in 1821, dedicated much of his time to the Bible's translation, believing that "the simple reading and study of the Bible alone will convert the world." The missionary was simply required "to gain for it [the Bible] admission and attention, and then let it speak for itself" (Moffat 1842, 618). Moffat recognized that the language spoken by the BaTlhaping was part of a language chain that "with slight variations, is spoken as far as the Equator," so that once the Bible was translated and the BaTlhaping were taught to read, they and then the chain of "scattered towns and hamlets" toward the interior would have "in their hands the means not only of recovering them from their natural darkness, but of keeping the lamp of life burning even amidst comparatively desert gloom" (Moffat 1842, 618).

Moffat had minimal theological education (Comaroff and Comaroff 1991, 82–83) and, like many missionaries, readily assumed that the Bible had a self-evident message. However, since being translated into the African vernacular, the Bible has shown a remarkable capacity to find other voices and to tell other stories, even when it was translated by missionaries like Moffat who had deliberate ideological agendas and an imprecise mastery of the language they were translating into. Not only does the Bible not have only one message, as modern biblical scholars know only too well, the very act of translating the Bible in the colonial encounter produced "a hybrid creation born of the colonial encounter itself" (Comaroff and Comaroff 1991, 218). Because, argues Lamin Sanneh, "language is the intimate, articulate expression of culture," the missionary adoption of African vernaculars "was tantamount to adopting indigenous cultural criteria for the message, a piece of radical indigenization far greater than the standard portrayal of mission as Western cultural imperialism" (Sanneh 1989, 2).

However, those African Christians who remained within missionary institutional control, for whatever reasons, had their forms of Christianity and their readings of the Bible distinctively shaped by the missionary metanarrative. For other Africans this kind of control was unacceptable.

STEALING THE BIBLE

In 1933, a hundred years after that first translation of the Bible into an African indigenous language, when colonialism had taken hold of southern Africa, Isaiah Shembe preached a sermon recounting how his people had stolen the Bible from the colonizer. What is clear here is that Bible is now itself being incorporated into another story, an African story. What is distinctive about Shembe is that he remains throughout his life independent of missionary-colonialists and wary of their *kholwa* (missionary "converted" and educated Africans)[1] offspring.

Born in the increasingly unstable southern African interior on a farm to a polygamous, tenant-farming, Zulu family, Shembe was baptized in July 1906 by Rev. William Leshega, a minister affiliated with the Baptist Union and the African Baptist Native Association. At this time Shembe was already healing and preaching in the interior without attachment to any church. Indeed, Leshega seems drawn to Shembe at least partially in order "to baptize those to whom Shembe had preached and in many cases healed" (Gunner 2002, 19–20), for Shembe showed no interest in establishing his own church.

Perhaps Shembe's wariness of institutionalized religion stemmed from what he witnessed happening to his mentor, Leshega. Although Leshega was a *kholwa* Christian, he was something of a dissident, regularly contending with both the British colonial establishment and the Baptist Union, primarily about access to land. As Elizabeth Gunner notes, though Leshega attempted to locate himself within the imperial British infrastructure, he was marginalized "by a social and religious order that blocked him many times in his efforts to gain legitimacy as an ordained minister and in his efforts to gain land for his church" (Gunner 2002, 20). Shembe may have learned from his association with Leshega the limits of *kholwa* Christianity in general and both the limits and potential of writing in contending with modernity, for Leshega was "a tireless writer of letters and user of print," across several languages (Gunner 2002, 20).

In her study of Shembe, Gunner emphasizes the role literacy plays "in negotiating various forms of modernity and in attempting to counter the power of the state's writing"; but she recognizes that Shembe would also have understood the limits of literacy and how "writing" must "also need to co-exist alongside and to intersect with others forms of experience, such as the visionary and the revelatory dream," key features of Shembe's "making of his church" (Gunner 2002, 22). For Shembe did go on to establish "a church" or, more precisely, a community, Ibandla lamaNazaretha (the Community/ Congregation of the Nazarites), upon return to his family's home region of KwaZulu-Natal, in the early 1900s, a time of considerable sociopolitical flux, affected by the Anglo-Zulu War, the Anglo-Boer War, the Bambatha Rebellion, and the formation of the Union of South Africa.

So while writing was a critical element in Shembe's construction of community, this writing "existed outside the ambit of the new [*kholwa*] African elite" (Gunner 2002, 26, 27). Indeed, Shembe both affirms the value of writing and reconfigures the very notion of "writing" and "text" (Cabrita 2010, 60). In a parable (recorded by Petros Dhlomo, the archivist of the Nazaretha church from the 1940s to the 1990s) Shembe draws on a biblical image from the apostle Paul, who writes to the Corinthian church:

[2] You yourselves are our letter, written on our hearts, to be known and read by all;

[3] and you show that you are a letter of Christ, prepared by us, written not with ink but with the Spirit of the living God, not on tablets of stone but on tablets of human hearts (2 Cor. 3:2–3 NRSV).[2]

Alluding to, but misciting, this text, Shembe rewrites Paul as he tells the following parable:

> The lord [Shembe] said these words in the village of Ekuphakameni [the sacred place of the amaNazaretha]. You are letter which is not written with ink but with diamonds which cannot be erased and is read by all people (II Cor. 5:1–3) [sic]. It is not written on flat stones. Rather it is written in your hearts. When the people of the system will come and take these letters of which the children here at Ekuphakameni are singing and when they will say: "You see all that Shembe was preaching has come to an end then even a child of Ekuphakameni could say: 'We greet you, Kuphakama; we greet you, Judia'" (No. 6 in the *Hymn Book of the amaNazaretha*). These things which were spoken at Ekuphakameni are written in the hearts of the people who love God (Malachi 4:2, 3). (Hexham and Oosthuizen 1996, 211, section 143)

Shembe rewrites, relocates, literally "incorporates," Paul and the Bible within the narrative of his emerging community. Shembe speaks here of the threat of the European state, the "people of the system," destroying the church's texts and in particular the body of hymns that were circulating in both oral and written form by the mid-1920s—"the books from which the children at Ekuphakameni are singing" (Cabrita 2010, 61). Shembe affirms, Joel Cabrita argues, "that if this were to happen, the true book of the church would be the Nazaretha community itself. The power of the written word can conjure up communities of people as enduring records; Isaiah tells the congregation at Ekuphakameni that a virtuous Nazaretha life is itself a written record for posterity"(Cabrita 2010, 61).

In another parable, Shembe tells of how he and his community obtained the Bible. Again, Dhlomo tells the story of Shembe's sermon, "the parable of the liberating Bible" (Hexham and Oosthuizen 1996, 224, sect. 152):

> In olden times there were two might[y] nations who were fighting over a certain issue. In their war the one conquered the other one and took all their cattle away. They took even their children captive and put them into the school of the victorious nation. (Hexham and Oosthuizen 1996, 224–225)

The story continues with a focus on three of these children, "sons of the same mother." Among the tasks given to these children was that they "had to sweep the houses of their teachers and the house of the Pope" (Hexham and Oosthuizen 1996, 225).

Shembe recounts, "All these children made good progress in school and passed their examinations well. Then they were trained as bishops." However, Shembe goes on to convey how there was a certain book that was locked away from them. The implication is clear. Children of the conquered nation had limited access to the texts of the victorious nation, thereby allowing them to rise to a level no higher than that of bishops. The Pope alone had access to one special text: the Bible. "In the house of the Pope there was a Bible which was kept under lock by him and only read by himself" (Hexham and Oosthuizen 1996, 225).[3] However, Shembe goes on to relate,

> On a certain day he [the Pope] had to go for a few weeks to another place and he forgot to lock the Bible up at home. When the boys were sweeping his home they found the Bible unlocked.

When they began to read it they discovered that their nation which had been demolished so badly by the war could never be restored unless they would get a book like this one and they considered what to do.

When they came back from school they bought a copybook and copied the whole Bible. When they had finished their work, they returned the Bible to its place. Thereafter the Pope came back and saw that he forgot to lock his Bible in. He called the boys who worked in his house and asked them whether they had opened this book. They denied it and said that they did not see that it had not been locked up. Then he forgot about it. The boys considered how they could bring this book to their parents at home.

At another day, they went and asked permission to visit their parents at home. They were permitted to go and they were given a time by which they must be back. When they came home, they did not stay there, rather they went from home to home and preached about this book until their time of leave was over and policeme were sent to look for these boys. Then they left this book there and returned to school. (Hexham and Oosthuizen 1996, 225)

Shembe's parable now shifts to what appears to be a catechetical exercise to which the boys are subjected on their return to school. "They were asked, 'Do you believe that Thixo [God] can only be found in the Roman Catholic Church?'" Shembe makes it clear that "[i]t was expected that all of them should say so" (Hexham and Oosthuizen 1996, 225–226). However, "the oldest boy did not. Rather he said: 'I believe that Thixo can be found in all beings on earth.'" The questioners were "greatly startled by these words," and he and the other boys, who answer similarly, are threatened with death by burning if they persist in "contradicting this our doctrine, in which you have been instructed" (Hexham and Oosthuizen 1996, 226). But the following day the first boy refuses again to follow what he has been taught, repeating "what he had said on the previous day." And when faced with "the fire," he sang a hymn and "went into the flames and was burned." The second boy met a similar fate, but when the third boy was questioned, his mother intervened, persuading him that it would not be so wrong "to say that Thixo belongs to the Roman Catholics, so that your life may be spared and that I may retain you on earth." He follows her advice. But the Pope demands not only oral but written assent as well, saying "that they should bring a book where he should write these words down and make an affidavit," which he did (Hexham and Oosthuizen 1996, 226–227).

That night, as the boy slept, "his spirit was taken up and brought to the joyful place of the elected ones. He heard a wonderful singing from a certain place and when he looked there he saw a large crowd of people who were clad in white gowns, on the other side of the river," where "he saw his two brothers." But when he "wanted to go to them," a voice said to him, "You cannot go to your brothers. Because they died for a promise while you did not die for it" (Hexham and Oosthuizen 1996, 227). Distraught, he weeps all night, then goes to the Pope to recant, and finally rekindles the fire in which his brothers died and "burned himself to death." But even then he has no peace, for even this does not unite him with his brothers. Breaking out of the parabolic form, "The lord of Ekuphakameni [Shembe] said: 'The death of the young man did not help him in any way. He did not go to the place where his brothers were because he did not die for the promise'" (Hexham and Oosthuizen 1996, 227). Shifting from narration to proclamation, Shembe then says:

Now I speak no longer of these people. Rather I speak today to you people of Ekuphakameni. . . . I ask you: what kind of a Bible do you write? Because you will suffer very much on the Last Day. And when you will then come to me and say: "Our father, I wish to enter the Kingdom." Then I shall be unable to do anything because you have broken the law of which you were told not to break it. (Hexham and Oosthuizen 1996, 227–228)

Shembe's parable narrates how the Bible became an African Nazarite book, a book that has to be continually written by his followers. The Bible is recognized by Shembe, as by the BaTlhaping before him, as a text of power. But now its power belongs to those who have stolen it, and its message is quite different from "the instruction" of missionary-*kholwa* Christianity. And yet Shembe requires of his followers a similar obedience to "the law" as that demanded by the Pope. Indeed, law is a key feature of Shembe's new community (West 2006), but a law constituted by an emerging African "Christian"[4] narrative.

SHAPING NARRATIVES

The hybrid narrative that constitutes Shembe's church includes elements from Nguni/Zulu traditional culture and religion, from the colonial context of the early 1900s, from missionary-*kholwa* Christianity, and from the stolen Bible. Shembe's sermons and hymns and testimonies from church members about Shembe's healing powers both take up and add new strands to the narrative weave that is an African Independent/Initiated Church in a changing southern African context.

Each of the biblical genres is appropriated and performed by Shembe's community. And although they assert that "the Bible interprets us; we do not interpret the Bible" (personal communication), their practice is similar to African slaves in America who, though they used the Bible extensively, "were not bound by the biblical text; rather they could critique it and modify it as they expressed their religious experience" (Bailey 1998, 71). Their own story predominates (Sithole 2009), providing shape to their appropriation and performance of the Bible.

While the shape provided by the missionary-colonial narrative is a powerful one, both in southern Africa and elsewhere (see Bailey 1998; Sugirtharajah 1998), the challenge of producing "a cogent account of religious change in any part of Africa over the last two centuries lies," argues J. D.Y. Peel, "in how to blend the three narrative themes which are pertinent to it: missionary endeavor, colonization, and the endogenous development of African societies." "Each of these offers," he continues, "a template by which certain key relationships are highlighted and (by the same token) others are pushed into the background (Peel 2000, 2).

In Peel's account of the "mutual engagement" of Christianity and the Yoruba people of southwestern Nigeria, he emphasizes the African narrative, assigning the other narratives a more minor, subservient role. Missionaries might serve as "catalysts" to the process of "conversion," and colonialism may produce an "increase in social scale" that results in "conversion," but from the African perspective, "conversion" is "conceived of less as the outcome of an encounter between two cultures or religions than as a matter of cognitive and practical adjustment to changes in social experience, within the terms of an existing [African] paradigm" (Peel 2000, 3).

However, this emphasis on the African narrative strand should not neglect the narrative power of "the world religions themselves, those great vehicles of trans-historical memory, ceaselessly re-activated in the consciousness of their adherents" (Peel 2000, 9). This mutual reconfiguration lies at the heart of Shembe's engagement with the Bible, and shows the capacity of this "stolen" story to shape contemporary African Christian communities and the nimbleness of postcolonial African communities to appropriate a range of resources, indigenous or not, for postcolonial reconstruction.

African Biblical Scholarship

Given how indigenous Africans (and other indigenous peoples from other parts of the post-colonial world) have transacted with the Bible, interleaving their own narrative layers with the Bible's, it is strange that African biblical scholars have been so reticent in taking up the "narrative turn" within biblical scholarship. Historical critical and sociological modes of reading the Bible have dominated African biblical scholarship since the 1960s (Holter 2000, 2002).

Bewitched in various ways by the "West," African biblical scholars have tended to work within the socio-historical domain. To some extent this is understandable, for historical and sociological methods offer the same kinds of analytical tools "to read" both biblical text and African context. Because African biblical scholarship has been committed to the postcolonial struggles of ordinary Africans (for whom the Bible is often a significant text), this multipurposed methodology has been particularly useful (Mosala 1989). But the cost of this choice has created a gap between African biblical scholars and ordinary African "readers" of the Bible. The entry point for African biblical scholars is the historical and sociological terrain "behind" the biblical text, while for ordinary Africans it is the narrative text itself.

But the liberation struggles of the 1970 and 1980s, in diverse contexts, have produced a range of collaborative "contextual" Bible reading practices, some of which start with the biblical narrative. In both Brazil and South Africa, for example, where socially engaged biblical scholars read "with" communities of the poor and marginalized, there has been a gradual shift away from the socio-historical domain as the starting point of collaborative modes of biblical interpretation (Schinelo 2009; West 2009). In the case of South Africa, the Ujamaa Centre works with a fourfold movement, beginning "in-front-of-the-text" with the generative themes of the local community, then moving to a close focus "on-the-text" itself (using narrative literary resources), before offering opportunities (via the narrative approach) to the world "behind-the-text," and finally concluding "in-front-of-the-text" with a more critical reappropriation of the text interpreted communally (West 2010). This method works with what ordinary readers already have: a deep grasp of narrative.

Significantly, Takatso Mofokeng, one of the pioneers of a socio-historical approach to biblical interpretation in the context of the South African struggle for liberation from apartheid, recognizes the dilemma of his starting point. While he wants the black masses to adopt the historical-materialist approach to the biblical text advocated by the second wave of Black Theology, he recognizes that the real resources for majority of black South Africans are those "passages and stories of the Bible" that resonate with "their Black experience, history and culture" (Mofokeng 1988, 38). Like the other advocate of the ideological significance of a socio-historical starting point to liberation hermeneutics, Itumeleng Mosala, Mofokeng grudgingly acknowledges that ordinary black South Africans have their own ways of discerning the ideological layers of the biblical text, by bringing their stories into dialogue with biblical stories.

Connecting Narratives

The Contextual Bible Study approach developed by the Ujamaa Centre provides a systematic structure for mutually engaging textual narrative and contextual narrative, facilitating an interface between African biblical scholarship and ordinary African readers of the Bible.

An example of the Ujamaa Centre's work, brought about by the ongoing struggle against gender violence in postapartheid South Africa, is a rereading of the rape of Tamar in 2 Samuel 13:1–22. The text was initially read around the central character, Tamar, with some attention to the plot. But space has now opened up to explore African masculinity using the same text (West 2013).

The Contextual Bible Study format is flexible, but a relatively stable version of it is as follows (see West 2013, 309-310):

> 2 Samuel 13:1–22 is read aloud, preferably dramatically. After the text has been read, a series of questions follow:
>
> 1. Have you heard this text (2 Sam 13:1–22) read publically, e.g., on a Sunday? Share with each other if, when, where you have heard this text read.
>
> 2. Who are the main characters in this story and what do we know about them?
>
> 3. What is the role of each male character in the rape of Tamar?
>
> 4. How would you characterize Amnon's masculinity in this text? Consider:
>> What prevents Amnon initially from acting on his love for Tamar (v2)?
>> What is it that changes Amnon's love (v1) to lust (v2)?
>> What is it then that enables him to act on his lust (v4–6)?
>> How does he react to Tamar's arguments (v14)?
>> How does he behave after he has raped Tamar (v15–17)?
>
> 5. What does Tamar's response to Amnon's assault tell us about her understanding of masculinity? Consider:
>> What does she say (v12–13,16), and what does each utterance tell us about her understanding of what it means to be "a man"?
>> What does she do (v19), and what does each of her actions tell us about her understanding of what it means to be "a man"?
>
> 6. What are the dominant forms of masculinity in our contexts (in various age groups), and what alternative forms of masculinity can we draw on from our cultural and religious traditions?
>
> 7. How can we raise the issue of masculinity in our various gender and age-groups?
>> The action plan is either reported to the plenary or presented on newsprint for other participants to study after the Bible study.

Question 1 begins with the reception history of the participants, recognizing the absence of this text in the male-dominated world of institutional religious life, whether Jewish, Christian, or Muslim (this Bible study has been done by participants from each of these faith traditions, in each case at their own initiative). Questions 2 and 3 focus on characterization, beginning generally in Question 2, then narrowing in Question 3 to focus on the role of masculinity in character construction, especially in the context of violence against women and children. Questions 4 and 5 deliberately slow the "reading" process, facilitating yet another rereading focusing on the kinds of textual detail familiar to biblical scholarship, including, for example, the kinds of rhetorical features Phyllis Trible identifies in her exegesis of the central chiasmus (Trible 1984, 44). Questions 2, 3, 4, and 5 all encourage rereadings, enabling initially overlooked details to emerge.

Question 6 provides space for participants' stories, already evoked by the earlier "textual" questions, to be brought alongside the biblical narrative. Question 7's request for a plan of action demonstrates how narrative connections are constructed for emancipatory ends.

BEYOND THE CONTRAPUNTAL

Long before postcolonial discourse was constructed by academics, ordinary Africans were interpreting the Bible from their various places in the postcolonial continuum. Central to their postcolonial appropriations was a contrapuntal movement between their own stories and biblical narrative. But unlike most academic appropriations of postcolonial discourse (Nelson 2012), ordinary Africans (and Asians, and Latin Americans, etc.) do not stop at contrapuntal proliferation. They connect their own "other" narratives with reconfigured biblical narratives for particular emancipatory projects. While African biblical scholarship can offer potential insight into this process, it should respect and not obstruct the ordinary African agenda of reading for social transformation. Indeed, ordinary African readers are calling upon African biblical scholars to work with them in placing local African narratives alongside biblical narratives (and some have heeded the call; see Dube 1996; Nadar 2001; Nzimande 2008), so that contrapuntal postcolonial readings might make a difference.

NOTES

1. I place "converted" in scare quotes to problematize the notion of what we might understand by African "conversion" to Christianity; see Peel (2000), 3–4.
2. Shembe would have been using the 1893 isiZulu translation.
3. There is no evidence that Shembe had a particular problem with the Roman Catholic Church, and so this church probably represents all of *kholwa* Christianity.
4. There is much scholarly and popular debate about whether Shembe's community, which has split into four factions since the death of its founder, is "Christian."

REFERENCES

Bailey, Randall C. 1998. "The Danger of Ignoring One's Own Cultural Bias in Interpreting the Text." In *The Postcolonial Bible*, edited by R. S. Sugirtharajah, 66–90. Sheffield, Yorkshire: Sheffield Academic Press.

Cabrita, Joel. 2010. "Texts, Authority, and Community in the South African 'Ibandla lamaNazaretha' (Church of the Nazaretha), 1910-1976." *Journal of Religion in Africa* 40: 60–95.

Campbell, John. 1815. *Travels in South Africa: Undertaken at the Request of the Missionary Society.* 3rd ed. Corrected ed. London: Black, Parry, & Co.

Comaroff, Jean, and John L. Comaroff. 1991. *Of Revelation and Revolution: Christianity, Colonialism and Consciousness in South Africa.* Vol. 1. Chicago: University of Chicago Press.

Dube, Musa W. 1996. "Readings of *Semoya*: Batswana Women's Interpretations of Matt. 15:21–28." In *Reading With: An Exploration of the Interface between Critical and Ordinary Readings of the Bible: African Overtures*, edited by Gerald West and Musa W. Dube. *Semeia* 73: 111–129.

Gunner, Elizabeth. 2002. *The Man of Heaven and the Beautiful Ones of God: Writings from Ibandla lamaNazaretha, a South African Church*. Leiden: Brill.

Hexham, Irving, and G. C. Oosthuizen, eds. 1996. *The Story of Isaiah Shembe: History and Traditions Centered on Ekuphakameni and Mount Nhlangakazi*. Vol. 1, *Sacred History and Traditions of the Amanazaretha*. Lewiston: Edwin Mellen Press.

Holter, Knut. 2000. "Old Testament Scholarship in Sub-Saharan African North of the Limpopo River." In *The Bible in Africa: Transactions, Trajectories, and Trends*, edited by Gerald O. West and Musa W. Dube, 54–71. Leiden: E. J. Brill.

Holter, Knut. 2002. *Old Testament Research for Africa: A Critical Analysis and Annotated Bibliography of African Old Testament Dissertations, 1967-2000*. New York: Peter Lang.

Landman, Christina. 1996. "The Religious Krotoa (c1642-1674)." *Kronos: Southern African Histories* 23: 22–35.

Moffat, Robert. 1842. *Missionary Labours and Scenes in Southern Africa*. London (Reprint, New York): John Snow (Reprint, Johnson Reprint Corporation).

Mofokeng, Takatso. 1988. "Black Christians, the Bible and Liberation." *Journal of Black Theology* 2: 34–42.

Mosala, Itumeleng J. 1989. *Biblical Hermeneutics and Black Theology in South Africa*. Grand Rapids, MI: Eerdmans.

Nadar, Sarojini. 2001. "A South African Indian Womanist Reading of the Character of Ruth." In *Other Ways of Reading: African Women and the Bible*, edited by Musa W. Dube, 159–175. Atlanta, GA: Society of Biblical Literature and WCC Publications.

Nelson, Alissa Jones. 2012. *Power and Responsibility in Biblical Interpretation: Reading the Book of Job with Edward Said*. Sheffield, Yorkshire: Equinox

Nzimande, Makhosazana K. 2008. "Reconfiguring Jezebel: A Postcolonial *Imbokodo* Reading of the Story of Naboth's Vineyard (1 Kings 21:1-16)." In *African and European Readers of the Bible in Dialogue: In Quest of a Shared Meaning*, edited by Hans de Wit and Gerald O. West, 223–258. Leiden: E. J. Brill.

Peel, J. D. Y. 2000. *Religious Encounter and the Making of the Yoruba*. Bloomington: Indiana University Press.

Sanneh, Lamin. 1989. *Translating the Message: The Missionary Impact on Culture*. Maryknoll, NY: Orbis.

Schapera, Isaac, and John L. Comaroff. 1991. *The Tswana*. Rev. ed. London and New York: Kegan Paul International. Original edition, 1953.

Schinelo, Edmilson, ed. 2009. *The Bible and Popular Education: Encounters of Solidarity and Dialogue*. São Leopoldo: CEBI.

Sithole, Nkosinathi. 2009. "The Mediation of Public and Private Selves in the Performance of Sermons and Narratives of Near-Death Experiences in the Nazarite Church." In *Religion and Spirituality in South Africa: New Perspectives*, edited by Duncan Brown, 249–265. Pietermaritzburg: University of KwaZulu-Natal Press.

Sugirtharajah, R. S. 1998. "A Postcolonial Exploration of Collusion and Construction in Biblical Interpretation." In *The Postcolonial Bible*, edited by R. S. Sugirtharajah, 91–116. Sheffield, Yorkshire: Sheffield Academic Press.

Trible, Phyllis. 1984. *Texts of Terror: Literary-Feminist Readings of Biblical Narratives*. Philadelphia, PA: Fortress.

West, Gerald O. 2006. "Reading Shembe 'Re-Membering' the Bible: Isaiah Shembe's Instructions on Adultery." *Neotestamentica* 40(1): 157–184.

West, Gerald O. 2009. "The Not So Silent Citizen: Hearing Embodied Theology in the Context of HIV and AIDS in South Africa." In *Heterotopic Citizen: New Research on Religious*

Work for the Disadvantaged, edited by Trygve Wyller, 23–42. Göttingen: Vandenhoeck & Ruprecht.

West, Gerald O. 2010. "The Contribution of Tamar's Story to the Construction of Alternative African Masculinities." In *Bodies, Embodiment, and Theology of the Hebrew Bible*, edited by S. Tamar Kamionkowski and Wonil Kim, 184–200. London: T&T Clark.

West, Gerald O. 2013. "Deploying the Literary Detail of a Biblical Text (2 Samuel 13:1-22) in Search of Redemptive Masculinities." In *Interested Readers: Essays on the Hebrew Bible in Honor of David J. A. Clines*, edited by James K. Aitken, Jeremy M. S. Clines, and Christl M. Maier, 297–312. Atlanta, GA: Society of Biblical Literature.

CHAPTER 51

....

THE COMMANDING FACES OF BIBLICAL STORIES

....

GARY A. PHILLIPS

In this volume's opening pages Danna Nolan Fewell cogently maps the "narrative turn" that now traverses the humanities, social sciences, and even natural sciences, inviting readers of the Bible to see the work of biblical narrative within a much wider field of vision. Concurrent with this narrative turn is an "ethical turn" with similar extension across the disciplines and professions (Altes 2006; Davis and Womack 2001; Schwartz 2001). From literary to biblical studies, philosophy to political theory, law to medicine, "ethics-talk" (Buell 2000, 1; Phillips and Fewell 1997, 10), like "narrative-talk," freely crosses disciplinary borders. Narrative's concern with the basic questions "Who am I?" and "What ought I to do?" and ethic's concern with the questions "Who is other to me?" and "How then shall we live responsibly?" are bound to no particular field of knowledge. Rather, narrativity and ethical responsibility are deeply rooted in our everyday lived experiences and in telling ways shape how we think and act, know and do. Thus philosopher/biblical interpreter Paul Ricoeur (1990) can speak of our precognitive, "prenarrative structure"; and philosopher/Talmudic exegete Emmanuel Levinas (1969, 1985), our ethical response to the commanding "face of the other" that precedes knowing. Complementary to one another, narrative and ethics together fashion our intersubjective identities as human beings and give shape to worlds, both real and imagined, that human beings inhabit. It is in this sense that the "narrative quality of experience" is intrinsically ethical (see Crites 1971).

ETHICAL TURN, NARRATIVE TURN, AND CULTURAL CRISIS

....

Ethical criticism is an umbrella term that names a wide and divergent set of readings concerned foremost with narrative and the ethical responsibility associated with reading. Other descriptive terms used include *ethics of reading* (Miller 1987; see Phillips and

Fewell 1997), *ethics of criticism* (Siebers 1988), *ethics of fiction* (Booth 1988), and *ethics of narrative/narrative ethics* (Newton 1995). While attention to narrative and ethical responsibility are certainly not new, literary and biblical studies have witnessed a recent upsurge in critical readings that expressly link the two. What accounts for the turn of narrative and ethics toward one another in biblical studies and the intensified interest in ethical criticism? What is the nature of the relationship between narrative and ethics (or other terms in these formulations) that "sit precariously on an ambiguous genitive" (Newton 1995, 10)?

The historical context of a century of war and unrestrained violence sheds some contextual light. Writing between two world wars, Walter Benjamin ([1936] 1969) anticipated the danger to narrative from a technological age of impersonal information that would bring the erosion of commonly shared experience, community, and historical memory (Kearney and William, 1996, 29). Storytelling was under threat by fragmentation of cultural and sensory experience and the loss of inherited wisdom. In his classic study of the role of realism in Western literature, fellow expatriate Eric Auerbach ([1953] 2003) famously characterized Hebrew narrative, in contrast to the Greek story form, as ethically "fraught with meaning." His reflection on the moral ambiguity of Abraham's actions in Genesis 22 was commentary on his experience as a Jew in exile and a response to the catastrophe overtaking European Jews. As with ancient biblical authors (see Fewell in this volume), the experience of displacement and trauma has shaped the response of modern writers and artists to cultural crises, inviting deep moral questioning about determining stories and normative ethical systems that would become the occasion, paradoxically, for creative narrative and artistic expression (see Fewell and Phillips 2008). Benjamin and Auerbach reflect a pervasive anxiety about the modern Enlightenment story of inevitable social and political progress and human moral improvement, raising doubts about the viability of any single master narrative or set of universal ethical norms. Disenchantment was one element in the response to sweeping sociocultural changes registered across the West. The change included an elevated importance of science and its signature technologies for disciplining and describing the modern self that displaced traditional, including religious, ways of defining what it meant to be self and community. W. B. Yeats's image from his 1919 poem "The Second Coming" captures this twentieth-century ethos of disintegration and loss of innocence: "Turning and turning in the widening gyre / The falcon cannot hear the falconer / Things fall apart / the centre cannot hold." In this cultural vortex Kant gives way to Nietzsche, Newton to Einstein, Milton to Eliot, Schleiermacher to Schweitzer. In Yeats's (1997) sobering words, "Mere anarchy is loosed upon the world / The blood-dimmed tide is loosed and everywhere / The ceremony of innocence is drowned; / The best lack all conviction, while the worst / Are full of passionate intensity."

In this decentered context twentieth-century ethics-talk has taken root. Jeffrey Stout characterizes this discourse as profoundly fragmented and anxiety-riven, reflecting the wider cultural currents. He concludes that the deep disagreements over what ethics is and what responsibility means makes ethics-talk all so much "Babel-talk." Neither the Bible nor its interpreters has been spared the discontent. In his midrash on the Babel Tower story, Auschwitz survivor Primo Levi characterized the Bible, too, as fragmented and anxiety-riven (Fewell and Phillips 2009). In the shadow cast by crematoria smoke stacks, biblical stories and their tellers are "incomprehensible." It is the age of a "new Bible," Levi (1993, 66) writes, one made up of equally incomprehensible stories of the hundreds of thousands of souls consigned to meaningless suffering and death in the camps. Exiled from human experience, modern self- and community-identity, the reading of biblical texts, indeed the Bible itself, is eclipsed (see Frei 1974).

In an era of continuing cultural uncertainty marked by unfathomable violence, the ethics of criticism has found a voice, or rather many voices. Readers of biblical narrative who "sit precariously on [the] ambiguous genitive" emphasize the character and centrality of narrative, the nature of ethical accountability, and the discursive role they can and ought to play as readers. The critical attention to narrative can be more or less theoretical; to ethics, more or less philosophical; and to discourse, more or less rhetorical. For some, ethical critical reading is theologically motivated, for others, not. Methodologically, readings are quite diverse. But for all their differences, ethical critical readers share an urgency to respond to text and context frequently issuing calls for interruptive action (Fewell 2003, 38–39; Patte 1995, 90–94; Phillips 2009; Schüssler Fiorenza 1988). Moreover, these readers are self-consciously transdisciplinary, hermeneutically suspicious, and concerned with moral identity questions related to those who read the Bible and those who are affected by its reading. (Concerning the impact on children, see Fewell 2003; Fewell and Phillips 2008). In contrast to prescriptive "ethics of the Bible" that catalog the Bible's moral content (see Burridge 2007), ethical criticism is a descriptive inquiry. Commenting on the explosion of ethical criticism in literary studies, Monica Johnstone (1995, 266) notes that the transformation in ethical philosophy away from prescription to description has created an opening for literary criticism—and for biblical criticism too—to reclaim, or perhaps claim for the first time, as its central critical question, what ought I to do as a reader when reading a text? (See MacIntyre 1981, 201)

While the historical event of the Holocaust is a significant factor for many ethical critics (Crossan 2009; Fewell and Phillips 2008, 2009; Linafelt 2000; Phillips 2002; 2009), other important influences can be singled out. The "tentacles" of influence, to recall Fewell's image, are many, and they interweave and overlay in surprisingly diverse ways, thereby contributing to an array of ethical readings of biblical narratives that defies neat categorizing. Not a fixed field of knowledge with prescribed methods and defined disciplinary lines, ethical criticism in important ways runs athwart disciplines and methods. Diverse philosophical, literary critical, rhetorical, psychoanalytic, sociological and semiological currents crisscross equally divergent feminist, narratological, structuralist, and poststructuralist/deconstructive reading approaches. The picture is messy. The particular character of the narrative and ethical work these readings rhetorically perform is a function then of the combination and weighting of multiple influencing factors and commitments. Many readers have overlapping affiliations and connections making classification a challenge. Nonetheless, we can identify two broad clusters of readers distinguished by common philosophical allegiances whose influences are mediated through rhetorical and literary third parties. The difficulty in drawing precise lines of demarcation suggests that ethical criticism, like narrative and ethics, does not adhere neatly to prescribed boundaries.

VIRTUE ETHICS, RHETORIC, AND WAYNE BOOTH

One cluster of biblical readers emphasizes in varying ways character ethics and/or communitarian ethos (Brown 2002; Carroll and Lapsley 2007; Lasine 2012; Young 1993). They draw philosophically upon the Aristotelian virtue ethics tradition (where wisdom or *phonēsis* is the practical outcome of reading in pursuit of the Good). Aristotle's influence may be directly bearing (Barton 1996) and/or mediated through prominent third-part rhetorical/literary critics like Wayne Booth (Young 1993) and Martha Nussbaum (Chun 2014). Booth (2001, 16) has been a leading voice for literary ethical criticism, which he argues "is relevant to all literature, no matter how broadly or narrowly we define that controversial term." Responding to twentieth century sterile aesthetic and formalist criticisms that isolate art from life and dismiss ethical criticism as "subjective," Booth writes, "We are at least partially constructed, in our most fundamental moral character, by the stories we have heard, or read, or viewed, or acted out in amateur theatricals: the stories we have really *listened* to" (18–19). Ethical development, namely the acquiring of wisdom in pursuit of the Good, happens through the concrete performance—the acting out and listening to—of narratives read over time by particular readers. From this perspective, biblical narratives develop moral character by summoning readers to grapple with ambiguous moral complexities presented by narrative characters and the choices they make. "Fraught with meaning," biblical narratives form and inform character. Equally fraught are critical readings of the Bible that wrestle practically with the question "What ought I to do as a critical reader?"

Schüssler Fiorenza (1988, 16) claims Booth as an ally in her call for an ethics of biblical interpretation, namely rhetorically informed criticism that interrogates and interrupts biblical scholarship's normative reading practices (Hurley 2006). She enlists him in support of feminist interpretation despite Booth's early ambivalence toward feministic criticism. In so doing Schüssler Fiorenza practices a "critical pluralism," Booth's term for the view that there is more than one valid way to read a text (compare Patte 1995). Critical pluralism promotes ethical clarification: "only a fully developed critical pluralism—of principle, of methods, of purposes, and of definitions of subject matter—can ever reduce the quantity of pointless quarreling over ethical matters. Different genres, different intentions, invite or reject different ethical judgments" all to the good (Booth 2001, 21; see Schüssler Fiorenza 1988, 13). Stuart Lasine's marshaling of character ethics, social psychology, and historical-critical methods to read the Elijah character in I Kings 19:1–14 offers a critical-pluralist approach (2012). His ethical-critical aim is to disrupt the tendency on the part of traditional critics to construct Hebrew Bible characters in their own psychological and moral self-image. In a related way Carol Newsom (2012) draws upon recent work in neuropsychology and the cross-cultural studies of agency to identify culturally distinctive forms of moral agency. She contends that the historical contextualizing of moral agency must always be a part of any study of the self. Hers is less a call for action and more a cautionary note about the rhetorical and strategic uses biblical critics make of the model of the self imputed to ancient texts.

PHENOMENOLOGY, HERMENEUTICS, AND PAUL RICOEUR

A second cluster of ethical critics draws broadly from the phenomenological tradition extending from Husserl through Heidegger and Derrida to Levinas either directly (Adam 2006; Fewell and Phillips 2009; Jennings 2006; Phillips 1994) and/or mediated through hermeneutical voices, notably Ricoeur (Gorospe 2007; Hettema 1996). While methodological

allegiances vary (from feminist, structuralist, poststructuralist, postcolonial to deconstructive), many readers voice suspicion about universalizing assumptions concerning subjectivity defined in Cartesian terms as the disembodied self; they are prone to reflect on the power
of discursive practices to construct and define subjective identity, hence the importance
of narrative. Advocate for the masters of suspicion (Marx, Nietzsche, and Freud), Ricoeur
mediates his commitments to Aristotle, Kant, Husserl, and Levinas with a focus on the
hermeneutics of narrative and historical subjectivity (compare Patte [1995] on multiplicity of
readings and the ordinary reader). "Selfhood is a cloth woven of stories told" (Ricoeur 2010,
246). "Tangled up in stories" and replete with "possible stories" (Ricoeur 1991, 31), human
identity, both individual and communal, is formed through narrative in practical ways. It is
an untidy process: "reading narrative is a moral laboratory," Ricoeur writes (1990, 139), a tan-
gle, where moral failures and successes are witnessed and real readers struggle; it is a messy,
testing place where the risks for readers can be enormous and the effects not limited to moral
development alone (see Magonet 2004; Kearney 2006).

Stories are not always "on the side of the angels" (Kearney and Williams 1996, 39), and certain story tellers and readers definitely not (see Newton 1995, 111–12). Narratives that damage
and bind their readers call for heightened scrutiny and accountability toward the subjects
of history that they affect—a point underappreciated by Booth, Nussbaum, and other neo-
humanists who overemphasize the constructive face of narrative. Ethical criticism employs
interruption as a strategy for dealing with such difficult texts (see Fewell's use of Levinas
in 2003, 34–35). For example, when we read about the blood curse attributed to the Jews in
Matthew's story (27:25) and link it to the carnage visited on Jews in history (Phillips 2002);
or Jesus's visit to Mary and Martha's home in Luke's story (10:38–42) and link it to the stereotyping and subordination of women in history, we come face-to-face with "possible stories" that can go terribly wrong (Crossan 2009; Phillips 2009). "Narrative understanding is
ethical because it is answerable to something beyond itself— to the other beyond the text"
(Kearney 2004, 112; Kearney 2006). Readers have a dual hermeneutical responsibility then to
the narratives they read and the subjects of history found outside those narratives. Schüssler
Fiorenza (1988, 14) proposes a similar double responsibility when she advocates for an "ethics of historical reading" and an "ethics of accountability."

Levinas's ethical philosophy is a critical resource for Ricoeur's view of hermeneutical responsibility. Levinas's ethics is not concerned with moral norms but rather with the
description of "the initiative of the other in the intersubjective relationship" (Ricoeur 1992,
188). Levinas describes this encounter with the other ("alterity of the Other") occurring in
the face-to-face relationship. By "alterity" Levinas refers to "an unbridgeable otherness, an
absolute alterity, that is not merely *other than me*" (Perpich 2008, 2). It is an alterity that binds
me to the other and to an, excessive, irrefusable ("infinite") obligation to and for the other.
This responsibility is so great it can traumatize when we realize we can never satisfy the
demand placed upon us, which leads Levinas (1981, 127) to say hyperbolically, "Subjectivity is
being a hostage." But the alterity that appears or is heard in the face, he cautions, can never be
adequately represented or reduced to an object of knowledge. It is not a datum of experience.
The face is not a "thing" grasped when I speak or read; it is that to which I am called upon to
respond. The face is a commanding paradoxical presence of alterity "whose first word is obligation" (Levinas 1969, 201). In biblical narrative terms, ethical responsiveness to the other is
expressed by the words *henini*, "*Here I am!*" Obligation means justice defined as excessive
care for "the stranger, the widow, the orphan, and the poor" (Levinas 1990, 24–26).

Athena Gorospe's (2007) reading of Exodus 4:18–26 illustrates the convergence of Levinasian themes filtered through Ricoeur's threefold mimetic structure of "prefiguration," "configuration," and "refiguration." She shows how an analysis of a problematic First Testament text responds to the plight of migrant Filipino workers who are the face of global economic migration. Her ethical performance reads "oneself as another" (Ricoeur 1992) through Moses's narrative face as a summons by the irreducible faces of specific, historical persons who demand an impossible accounting from me.

THE TURN TO LEVINAS, NARRATIVE ETHICS, AND MARY AND MARTHA

Literary ethical criticism has turned increasingly to Levinas to inform its work (Astell and Jackson 2009; Newton 1995; Wehrs 2013). *Narrative ethics* "implies simply narrative *as* ethics: the ethical consequences of narrating story and fictionalizing person, and the reciprocal claims binding teller, listener, witness, and reader in the process" (Newton 1995, 11). Levinas's philosophy supports description of the deep intersubjective entanglements in the face-to-face relationships within and with the text (between characters, between reader and characters). Narrative ethics views teller, listener, witness, and reader elements as simultaneously distinct *and* conjoined comparable to the way quantum physics sees the entanglement between atomic particles. In an entangled system particles, though physically separate, behave as if one object. By analogy, intersubjective life is an entangled system in which self and other are inseparably bound by responsibility. Narrative and ethics are to the construction of reader identity and world as the four fundamental quantum forces are to the creation of matter in the subatomic world. Narrative and ethics are the elementary forces responsible for binding and creating self with the other that make our world human and humane.

The goal of a narrative-ethical reading is not to solve a text's problems by disentangling the reader's self from the text or the text from its own snarl of issues, be they historical, compositional, or hermeneutical. Rather, as Lasine (2012), Gorospe (2007), Fewell (2015) and other ethical critics illustrate, narrative ethical readers engage a text's problems "in its concrete, formal, narrative particularity" (Newton 1995, 11; see Cosgrove 2004) as a summons to explore questions of identity and responsibility, self and community. Such readings seek to challenge readers to live obliged lives. For this reason, narrative ethics is concerned not with *finding resolution* to the search for meaning but *enacting response* to the immediacy of the commanding faces encountered in and through the narrative text. "One faces a text as one might face a person, having to confront the claims raised by that very immediacy, an immediacy of contact, not of meaning" (11). "Narrative situations create an immediacy and force, framing relationships of provocation, call, and response that bind narrator and listener, author and character, or reader and text" (13). Narrative thus emulates foundational ethical encounter in provocative and messy ways.

Luke's story of Jesus's visit to Mary and Martha's home (10:38–42) is one of those provocative, messy texts that tests readers and invites a narrative-ethical response. It is an enigmatic episode with perplexing characters, discourse, and actions that has long stymied interpreters. Traditional form-critical, linguistic-structural, and narrative analyses have forefronted the dualistic-oppositional features in which Mary plays the positive and Martha the negative role. The story is therefore read by many antagonistically to pit sister against sister in service of a point (Alexander 1992; Carter 2002; Schüssler Fiorenza 1992, 61–62). Readers have used the text rhetorically to construct women as ciphers for abstract theological purposes, allegorize them to suppress social action, polarize women's relationship with women, and debase their teaching and other leadership capacities (Schüssler Fiorenza, 57–59; Koperski 1999). The story has a history of caustic effects on the formation of both women's and men's identities.

The text is framed by two lengthy teaching stories: the lawyer/Jesus exchange about the identity of and care (*epemelēthē*) for the neighbor's needs illustrated through the good Samaritan story (10:25–37) and the disciples/Jesus exchange about prayer illustrated through discourse about meeting a friend's needs (*hosan chrēdzei*; 11:1–13). In contrast to the bracketing texts' excessively detailed actions and discourses, the Mary and Martha story is notably terse, with a dearth of detail, truncated speaking, silence, and nonresponse. It is a knot of text critical (Fee 1981), theological (Schüssler Fiorenza 1992), ethical (Schaberg 1992), and ideological (Phillips 1992) problems. Especially confounding is Jesus's concluding pronouncement to Martha about Mary that has especially vexed text critics and feminist readers alike (Reid 1996). Interpreters have tied themselves up in knots attempting to resolve the presentation of the sister-to-sister-to-Jesus relationships and the meaning of teaching and service (contrast Wall 1989).

The narrative begins simply enough. The narrator reports that Jesus enters a village. Martha has welcomed him into her home. Mary, her sister, is identified sitting at Jesus's feet listening to him (*ēkouen ton logon autou*), a posture connoting a teaching relationship. The narrator signals the first hint of trouble ahead with "but" (*de*), one of four adversative particles in the text: "*But* Martha was distracted (*periespato*) by her many tasks (*diakonian*)." Martha says, "Lord, do you not care (*ou melei soi*) that my sister has left me to do all the work by myself?" Quickly she follows with the command "Tell her then to help me." Jesus's response is adversative: "Martha, Martha, you are worried (*merimnas*) and distracted (*thorubadzē*) by many things; there is need of only one thing (*henos de estin chreia*). Mary has chosen the better part, which will not be taken away from her." In contrast to the story's clean opening, the end is an interpretive muddle.

Martha's commanding words are the first spoken in the story and the first by any woman directly to Jesus or the reader in the gospel (Schaberg 1992, 280). She is further distinguished as the only Lukan character, male or female, to interrupt Jesus as he teaches, a role the story itself plays in relation to the immediately surrounding teaching narratives. The negative form of Martha's question anticipates Jesus's positive response, which is not forthcoming. It stands in rhetorical contrast to Jesus's interrogatory and counterfactual conditional rhetoric found in the bracketing stories.

Martha's interruption of Jesus and the reader announces, "*Here I am!*" Her presence calls for a response. She insists on being heard and having her care be Jesus's concern (*ou melei soi*), the sort of care Jesus lavishly describes and prescribes to the lawyer (*epemēlēthē autou*, 10:34) and the disciples (11:5–13). Her words disrupt Jesus's established teaching pattern in the Lukan narrative as well as the discourse of readers whose response is frequently dismissive. Martha "interrupts male conversation; she argues with Jesus; she asserts the value of her own sphere of activity and demands help" (Alexander 1992, 199–200). Reading her interruption in negative terms, readers recoil from the abruptness of her words, which leads them to characterize Martha as patronizing and offensive, a nag, and to chide her for an unreasonable if not inappropriate request. Others subordinate Martha and story by reducing her to the female version of the lawyer out to test (*ekpeiradzōn*) Jesus. Often overlooked, however, is the thematic link with 11:5–8. Martha's home, where Jesus is welcomed as guest, connoting a setting of domestic care that contrasts with the nondescript place of the lawyer/Jesus conversation and the hazardous setting of the Jerusalem/Jericho road. The domestic scene in Jesus's imagined scenario in 11:5–8 ("the door has been locked and my children are in bed" [*he thurpa kekleistai kai ta paidia mou met'emou eis tēn koitēn eisin*]) and responding to the friend's needs (*dōsei autō hosōn chrēdzei*) accentuates Jesus's noncaring response to Martha in 10:38–42, inviting suspicion not about Martha's speaking and actions but instead about the consistency of Jesus's words and deeds as teacher.

Jesus's response is adversative: "Martha, Martha, you are worried [*merimnas*] and distracted [*thorubadzē*] by many things; there is need of only one thing (*henos de estin chreia*). Mary has chosen the better part, which will not be taken away from her." Both verbs are *hapax legomena*. The disputed *thorubadzē* is itself a source of worry as the manuscript variation attests (*turbadzē*). Either Jesus is not listening to Martha's question, or he has heard her all too clearly and his words betray him. In either case the response is ethically nonresponsive. His reply to the lawyer's and disciples' worries contrast markedly. With the men Jesus engages in extended conversation carefully making the point about care in response to their concerns. With Martha, however, the best he can do is stammer her name ("Martha, Martha") and attempt to turn the issue of his questionable care back upon her by contrasting her actions with Mary's. The textual stammering continues in verse 42 where narrator and commentators struggle to reduce the multiple variations to one and to exit the story making a clean apophthegmic point. However, easy resolution of the problem escapes all.

But the double vocative (*Martha, Martha*), taken often as an expression of negative judgment, is used elsewhere by Luke to signify respect and special status (e.g., Saul's conversion in Acts 9:4). Luke's disciples call out to Jesus, "Lord, Lord" (*kurie, kurie*) in 6:46, which Bultmann and others argue identifies Jesus as Teacher. Could Jesus be naming Martha *his* teacher even as fails to respond to her? Levinas (1969, 171) describes the relation to the other as a teaching relationship: "Alterity is manifested in *a mastery that does not conquer, but teaches.*" Teaching signals the event of ethics, the welcoming of the other, of obligation, teacher with student. As teacher, Jesus stands in a relationship with Mary, who sits at his feet. Martha stands, too, as teacher to Jesus otherwise. But does he respond? Welcome her? Care to be bothered? Does he do what he has taught the lawyer and disciples to do?

As for Mary, she is referred to only in the third person. Her passivity is mirrored in the verbal forms used by the narrator to speak about her ("called" [*kaloumenē*]; "was listening" [*parakathestheisa*]; "be taken away" [*aphairethēsetai*]). She is discursively nonpresent: Jesus speaks only to Martha, Martha speaks only to Jesus, and Mary says nothing at all. If as Levinas (1985, 12) describes, "ethics occurs across the hiatus of dialogue, not in the content of discourse . . . but in the demand for response"; ethics is not to be found among the characters: the discursive disconnect signals neither response nor excessive care for either Martha or Mary. It is a failed ethical moment on Jesus's part underscored by the contrast to the Samaritan's exceeding care for the wounded man and the extreme actions of the parent toward friend and child (11:5–13). Jesus seems able to teach *about the content* of ethical responsibility in the bracketing stories but in the face-to-face encounter with Martha and Mary responsibility is stillborn.

What does this reading suggest about Jesus's identity as teacher (*didaskolos*; 6:40; 22:11), a theme of major importance to Luke's narrator and later interpreters? What does it suggest about the identities of readers who read Luke's larger narrative and this troublesome story? The precocious twelve-year-old child who taught the teachers (*didaskolōn*) days on end listening and asking questions and astonishing (*existanto*) all who heard him (2:46–47), now, as an adult evades entanglement with a troublesome Martha in astonishing fashion. What is at stake if we were to imagine Martha teaching Jesus and the text its readers about who he is, who we are, and what worlds we create and inhabit? Could she be the astonishing teacher of the Lukan Messiah in the mold of John's Samaritan Woman who astonished (*ethaumadzon*; 4:27) the disciples and opened up Jesus's world to the Samaritans (4:42; Fewell and Phillips 1997; Moore 1993)?

Levinas says the ethical event occurs across the hiatus of discourse in the moment of teaching. Do we witness in Jesus's failure a teaching moment for readers nonetheless, whereby women do not serve as subordinate theological ciphers but are seen and heard instead as the provocative teachers of the teacher of Luke's disciples and the astonishing teachers of today's readers? Provocation, call, and response occur in the story by Martha not sitting at Jesus's feet but by *standing up* (*epistasa de eipen*) on her own and saying to Jesus and reader alike, "*Here I am!*" Notwithstanding—or maybe as a consequence of—Jesus's failure, are we readers prepared to respond by provocatively saying and doing as Martha does, thereby affirming that the ethical ties that bind Jesus to Martha bind us to her as well? Are we ready to embrace an ethical entanglement with Martha, Mary, and a knotted up text that enacts the ethical relationship through teaching, to take on an excessive responsibility that is beyond what is deemed reasonable?

Luke's abrupt story stages the messiness of ethics and the struggle to say and show how we come to find ourselves living with others with narrative. "Ethics is lived and understood ... as the demand for the ethics in the face of the failure of ethics" (Perpich 2008, xv). Failure is intrinsic to learning and living, as any good teacher will attest. This narrative of teaching/ethical failure, where entanglement is refused and obligation put off, runs athwart the teaching encountered in Luke's bracketing stories and elsewhere in the Gospel. The story of Jesus's failure to respond to the obligation to care teaches readers otherwise. But, as the history of interpretation of this story shows, not all readers care much for Martha, this text, or its negative effects upon others. Narrative ethics seeks to change that view.

Levinas (1985, 97) writes, "The tie with the other is knotted only as responsibility, this moreover, whether accepted or refused, whether knowing or not knowing how to assume it, whether able or unable to do something for the Other. To say: Here I am. To do something for the Other. To give. To be a human spirit, that's it." Biblical narratives, like Jesus's visit to Mary and Martha's home, are ethically significant not only because they stage moments of face-to-face encounter within the story world of a problematic text, but also because our engagement with a narrative replete with textual and hermeneutical knots replicates the messy ethical encounter readers have with faces encountered inside and outside the text. Narrative ethics sheds light on those encounters and the commanding faces with the "*Here am I!*" that signal our irrefutable ties to each other.

Biblical ethical criticism as currently performed in a host of rhetorically interruptive ways recognizes the intrinsic power of story and storytelling to fashion persons and worlds for the better but also, as Luke 10:38–42 shows, for the worse. Ricoeur reminds us, reading narrative is a moral laboratory where failed texts and readers are tested and taught. Narrative criticism—perhaps the commanding face of biblical criticism today—summons readers of the Bible *to do something*: to a heightened accountability for the ways the narratives they read, the ethical responsibilities they embrace, and the rhetorical strategies they deploy make the stories of the Bible more, not less, comprehensible and the worlds we make and inhabit as a result more, not less, just.

REFERENCES

Adam, A. K. M. 2006. *Faithful Interpretation: Reading the Bible in a Postmodern World.* Minneapolis, MN: Fortress Press.

Alexander, Loveday. 1992. "Sisters in Adversity: Retelling Martha's Story." In *Women in the Biblical Tradition*, edited by G. J. Brooke, 167–186. Studies in Women and Religion 31. Lewiston, NY: Mellen.

Altes, Liesbeth Korthals. 2006. "Some Dilemmas of an Ethics of Literature." In *Theology and Literature: Rethinking Reader Responsibility*, edited by Gaye Williams Ortiz and Clara A. B. Joseph, 15–31. New York: Palgrave.

Astell, Ann, and J. A. Jackson, eds. 2009. *Levinas and Medieval Literature: The 'Difficult Reading' of English and Rabbinic Texts.* Pittsburgh, PA: Duquesne University Press.

Auerbach, Erich. (1953) 2003. *Mimesis: The Representation of Reality in Western Literature.* Translated by Willard Trask. Princeton, NJ: Princeton University Press. First published 1953.

Barton, John Orient und Ok. 1996. "Reading for Life: The Use of the Bible in Ethics and the Work of Martha C. Nussbaum." In *The Bible in Ethics: The Second Sheffield Colloquium*, edited by John W. Rogerson, Margaret Davies, and M. Daniel Carroll R., 66–76. The Library of Hebrew Bible/Old Testament Studies 207. London: Bloomsbury T & T Clark.

Benjamin, Walter. 1969. "The Storyteller Reflections on the Works of Nikolai Leskov." *Illuminations.* Edited by Hannah Arendt. Translated by Harry Zohn. New York: Schocken Books. First published 1936 in Orient und Okzident.

Brown, William P. 2002. *Character and Scripture: Moral Formation, Community, and Biblical Interpretation.* Grand Rapids, MI: Eerdmans.

Buell, Lawrence. 2000. "What We Talk about When We Talk about Ethics." In *The Turn to Ethics*, edited by Marjorie Gerber, Beatrice Hanssen, and Rebecca L. Walkowitz, 1–14. London and New York: Routledge.

Burridge, Richard A. 2007. *Imitating Jesus: An Inclusive Approach to New Testament Ethics.* Grand Rapids, MI: Eerdmans.

Booth, Wayne. 1988. *The Company We Keep: An Ethics of Fiction.* Berkeley: University of California Press.

Booth, Wayne. 2001. "Why Ethical Criticism Can Never Be Simple." In *Levinas and Twentieth-Century Literature. Ethics and the Reconstitution of Subjectivity*, edited by Donald Wehrs, 16–29. Newark, NJ: University of Delaware Press.

Carroll R., M. Daniel, and Jacqueline Lapsley, eds. 2007. *Character Ethics and the Old Testament. Moral Dimensions of Scripture.* Louisville, KY: Westminster/John Knox Press.

Carter, Warren. 2002. "Getting Martha out of the Kitchen." In *A Feminist Companion to Luke*, edited by A. J. Levine, 215–231. Feminist Companion to the New Testament and Early Christian Writings 3. Sheffield, Yorkshire: Sheffield University Press.

Chun, S. Min. 2014. *Ethics and Biblical Narrative. A Literary and Discourse-Analytical Approach to the Story of Josiah*. Oxford: Oxford University Press.

Cosgrove, Charles H. 2004. *The Meanings We Choose: Hermeneutical Ethics, Indeterminacy and the Conflict of Interpretations*. London: T&T Clark International.

Crites, Stephen. 1971. "The Narrative Quality of Experience." *Journal of the American Academy of Religion* 39(3): 291–311.

Crossan, John Dominic. 2009. **Who Killed Jesus?**: *Exposing the Roots of Anti-Semitism in the Gospel Story of the Death of Jesus*. New York: Harper Collins.

Davis, Todd, and Kenneth Womack, eds. 2001. *Mapping the Ethical Turn. A Reader in Ethics, Culture, and Literary Theory*. Charlottesville: University Press of Virginia.

Fee, Gordon. 1981. "'One Thing Is Needful'? Luke 10:42." In *New Testament Textual Criticism: Its Significance for Exegesis*, edited by Eldon Jay Epp and Gordon Fee, 61–75. Oxford: Clarendon Press.

Fewell, Danna Nolan. 2003. *Children of Israel. Reading the Bible for the Sake of Our Children*. Nashville, TN: Abingdon Press.

Fewell, Danna Nolan. 2015. "Space for Moral Agency in the Book of Ruth." *Journal for the Study of the Old Testament* 40(1): 79–96.

Fewell, Danna Nolan, and Gary A. Phillips. 1997. "Drawn to Excess: Or Reading beyond Betrothal." In *Bible and Ethics of Reading*, edited by Danna Nolan Fewell and Gary A. Phillips. *Semeia* 77: 23–58.

Fewell, Danna Nolan, and Gary A. Phillips. 2008. "Genesis, Genocide and the Art of Samuel Bak: 'Unseamly' Reading after the Holocaust." In *Representing the Irreparable: The Shoah, the Bible and the Art of Samuel Bak*, edited by Danna Nolan Fewell, Gary A. Phillips, and Yvonne Sherwood, 75–92. Boston: Pucker Art Publication and Syracuse University Press.

Fewell, Danna Nolan, and Gary A. Phillips. 2009. "From Bak to the Bible: Imagination, Interpretation, and *Tikkun Olam*." *ARTS* 21(1): 21–30.

Frei, Hans W. 1974. *The Eclipse of Biblical Narrative. A Study in Eighteenth and Nineteenth Century Hermeneutics*. New Haven: Yale University Press.

Gorospe, Athena E. 2007. *Narrative and Identity: An Ethical Reading of Exodus 4*. Leiden: Brill.

Hettema, Theo L. 1996. *Reading for Good: Narrative Theology and Ethics in the Joseph Story from the Perspective of Ricoeur's Hermeneutics*. Kampen: Kok Pharos.

Hurley, Robert J. 2006. "The Ethics of Biblical Interpretations: Rhetorizing the Foundations." In *Theology and Literature: Rethinking Reader Responsibility*, edited by Gaye Williams Ortiz and Clara A. B. Joseph, 45–62. New York: Palgrave.

Jennings, Theodore W. 2006. *Reading Derrida/Thinking Paul: On Justice*. Redwood City, CA: Stanford University Press

Johnstone, Monica. 1995. "Wayne Booth and the Ethics of Fiction." In *Rhetoric and Pluralism: Legacies of Wayne Booth*, edited by Frederik Antczak, 59–70. Columbus: Ohio State University Press.

Kearney, Richard. 2004. *On Paul Ricoeur: The Owl of Minerva*. Transcending Boundaries in Philosophy. Burlington, VT: Ashgate.

Kearney, Richard. 2006. "Parsing Narrative—Story, History, Life." *Human Studies* 29(4): 477–490.

Kearney, Richard and James Williams. 1996. "Narrative and Ethics." *Proceedings of the Aristotelian Society, Supplementary Volumes*. Vol. 70: 29–45 + 47–61.

Koperski, Veronica. 1999. "Women and Discipleship in the Literary Context of Luke-Acts: Luke 10, 38-42 and Acts 6, 1-7." In *The Unity of Luke-Acts*, edited by J. Verheyden, 517–544. Leuven: Leuven University Press.

Lasine, Stuart. 2012. *Weighing Hearts: Character, Judgment, and the Ethics of Reading the Bible*. Library of Hebrew Bible/Old Testament Studies. New York: T&T Clark International.

Levi, Primo. 1993. *Survival in Auschwitz*. Translated by Stuart Woolf. New York: Macmillan.

Levinas, Emmanuel. 1985. *Ethics and Infinity. Conversations with Philippe Nemo*. Translated by Richard Cohen. Pittsburgh, PA: Duquesne University Press.

Levinas, Emmanuel. 1969. *Totality and Infinity. An Essay on Exteriority*. Translated by Alphonso Lingis. Pittsburgh, PA: Duquesne University Press.

Levinas, Emmanuel. 1981. *Otherwise than Being or Beyond Essence*. Translated by Alphonso Lingis. Boston: Martinus Nijhoff.

Levinas, Emmanuel. 1990. *Difficult Freedom*. Translated by Sean Hand. Baltimore, MD: Johns Hopkins University Press.

Linafelt, Tod, ed. 2000. *Strange Fire: Reading the Bible after the Holocaust*. New York: New York University Press.

MacIntyre, Alasdair. 1981. *After Virtue: A Study in Moral Theory*. Notre Dame, IN: University of Notre Dame Press.

Magonet, Jonathan. 2004. *A Rabbi Reads the Bible*. London: SCM Press.

Miller, J. Hillis. 1987. *The Ethics of Reading: Kant, de Man, Eliot, Trollope, James, and Benjamin*. New York: Columbia University Press.

Moore, Stephen D. 1993. "Are There Impurities in the Living Water That the Johannine Jesus Dispenses? Deconstruction, Feminism, and the Samaritan Woman." *Biblical Interpretation* 1(2): 207–227.

Newsom, Carol A. 2012. "Models of the Moral Self: Hebrew Bible and Second Temple Judaism." *Journal of Biblical Literature* 131(1): 5–25

Newton, Adam Zachary. 1995. *Narrative Ethics*. Cambridge, MA: Harvard University Press.

Nussbaum, Martha. 2001. *The Fragility of Goodness. Luck and Ethics in Greek Tragedy and Philosophy*. Cambridge: Cambridge University Press.

Patte, Daniel. 1995. *The Ethics of Biblical Interpretation: A Reevaluation*. Louisville, KY: Westminster/John Knox.

Perpich, Diane. 2008. *The Ethics of Emmanuel Levinas*. Cultural Memory in the Present. Redwood City, CA: Stanford University Press.

Phillips, Gary. 1992 "'What Is Written and How Do You Read?' The Gospel, Intertextuality and Doing Lukewise." In *Society of Biblical Literature Seminar Papers*, edited by Gene Lovering, 266–301. Atlanta, GA: Scholars Press.

Phillips, Gary. 1994. "The Ethics of Reading Deconstructively, or Speaking Face-to-Face: The Samaritan Woman meets Derrida at the Well." In *The New Literary Criticism and The New Testament*, edited by Elizabeth Struthers Malbon and Edgar McKnight, 283–326. Sheffield, Yorkshire: Sheffield Academic Press.

Phillips, Gary. 2002. "The Killing Fields of Matthew's Gospel." In *Reading the New Testament after the Holocaust. A Shadow of Glory*, edited by Tod Linafelt, 232–247. New York: Routledge.

Phillips, Gary. 2009. "More Than the Jews . . . . His Blood be upon *all* the Children: Biblical Violence, Bosnian Genocide, and Responsible Reading." In *Confronting Genocide: Judaism, Christianity, Islam*, edited by Steven Leonard Jacobs, 77–91. Lanham, MD: Lexington.

Phillips, Gary A., and Danna Nolan Fewell. 1997. "Ethics, Bible, Reading As If." In *Bible and Ethics of Reading*, edited by Danna Nolan Fewell and Gary A. Phillips. *Semeia* 77: 1–21.

Reid, Barbara. 1996. *Choosing the Better Part? Women in the Gospel of Luke*. Collegeville, MN: Liturgical Press.

Ricoeur, Paul. 1990. *Time and Narrative*. Vol. 2. Translated by Kathleen McLaughlin and David Pellauer. Chicago: University of Chicago Press.

Ricoeur, Paul. 1991. "Life in Quest of Narrative." In *On Paul Ricoeur: Narrative and Interpretation*, edited by David Wood, 20–33. London and New York: Routledge.

Ricoeur, Paul. 1992. *Oneself as Another*. Translated by Kathleen Blamey. Chicago: University of Chicago Press.

Ricoeur, Paul. 2010. *Time and Narrative*. Vol. 3. Translated by Kathleen Blamey and David Pellauer. Chicago: University of Chicago Press.

Schaberg, Jane. 1992. "The Gospel of Luke." In *The Women's Bible Commentary*, edited by Carol A. Newsom and Sharon H. Ringe, 275–292. Louisville, KY: Westminster/John Knox.

Schüssler Fiorenza, Elisabeth. 1988. "The Ethics of Biblical Interpretation: Decentering Biblical Scholarship." *Journal of Biblical Literature* 107: 3–17.

Schüssler Fiorenza, Elisabeth. 1992. *But She Said. Feminist Practices of Biblical Interpretation*. Boston: Beacon Press.

Schwartz, Daniel. 2001. "A Humanistic Ethics of Reading." In *Mapping the Ethical Turn. A Reader in Ethics, Culture, and Literary Theory*, edited by Todd Davis and Kenneth Womack, 3–15. Charlottesville: University Press of Virginia.

Siebers, Tobin. 1988. *The Ethics of Criticism*. Ithaca, NY: Cornell University Press.

Stout, Jeffrey. 1988. *Ethics after Babel: The Languages of Morals and Their Discontents*. Boston: Beacon.

Wall, Robert. 1989. "Martha and Mary (Luke 10:38-42) in the Context of a Christian Deuteronomy." *Journal for the Study of the New Testament* 35: 19–35.

Wehrs, Donald R., ed. 2013. *Levinas and Twentieth-Century Literature. Ethics and the Reconstitution of Subjectivity*. Newark, NJ: University of Delaware Press.

Yeats, W. B. 1997. *The Collected Works of W. B. Yeats. Volume 1: The Poems*. 2nd ed. Edited by Richard Finneran. New York: Scribners.

Young, Francis. 1993. "Allegory and the Ethics of Reading." In *The Open Text: New Directions for Biblical Studies?*, edited by Francis Watson, 103–120. London: SCM Press.

Index of Subjects and Names

Flint, P. 267, 495

Fludernik, M. 5, 9, 16, 29, 38–41

focalization 34, 37, 116, 118, 296–297,
   299–303, 354

Fokkelman, J. 28–29, 33, 113, 195, 201,
   482, 535

Foley, J. 73–74, 78–79

folklore 127, 267, 269, 401

food
   and animals 444, 446, 450–451,
   and Christology 495–496
   and empire 508, 512,
   in the book of Ruth 90, 493–495
   in Genesis 102, 458, 491–493
   in the wilderness 130–131, 149
   in Kings 209–211
   in Esther 261
   in Mark 429
   in trickery 564
   production and consumption 489–496,
   529, 531–532

form criticism 287, 518

formalism 29, 112, 115, 140–141

Forster, E. 40

Forti, T. L. 445

Foster, B. 14, 66, 358, 500, 532

Foucault, M. 36, 51, 206, 436

Fountain, A. K. 263

Fowler, R. 36, 297

Fox, E. 113

Fox, M. 257–259, 268–269

Francis, J. M. M. 424

Frank, A. 5, 7–9, 11–13, 18, 110–111, 116,
   119, 159

Freedman, A. D. 27

Freedman, D. N. 96, 98, 230

Frei, H. 125, 159, 587

Frerichs, E. S. 125

Fretheim, T. 126–127, 129, 132, 468

Freud, S. 12, 183, 246, 249–250, 472–473, 475

Frevel, C. 150

Frick, F. S. 519

Fried, L. 276, 545

Friedman, R. E. 159

Frolov, S. 197, 401

Frymer-Kensky, T. 18, 114, 162, 173

Fuchs, Ernst 353

Fuchs, Esther 115, 400, 406, 457, 459,
   461–462

Fuller, C. 18

Funk, R. 351, 353, 358

Gabriel 65

Gager, J. G. 520

Galatia(ns) 369, 510

Galilee 17, 297, 337

Gallagher, S. 416

Garber, D. 13

García-Treto, F. O. 437

Gardiner, J. K. 411–412

Gardner, J. 424

Garrett, S. R. 325

Garro, L. 10, 13, 15

Garroway, K. 423

Garsiel, M. 196

Gath 80, 176, 389, 391

Gaventa, B. R. 336–337

gay and lesbian studies 411, 415

Gaza 174, 176

Geller, S. 131, 208

gender. *See also* masculinity
   as critical lens in biblical studies 315,
   398–402, 412–414
   and ancient cultural values 518, 524
   and children 424, 429, 430
   and cultural history 415–419
   and food production 489, 492, 494,
   496
   and sexuality 456–460
   and sexual violence 460–462, 581
   as criterion of Otherness 436, 447, 448,
   450, 452
   in Genesis – Kings 102, 111, 116, 126,
   150–151, 173, 176, 180, 183, 186, 207,
   404–405, 451
   in Ruth 248, 252
   in Esther 259–260, 262–263
   in Chronicles 288, 292
   in the Gospels 36, 321, 326, 343,
   402–406, 429
   in Paul 369–371
   studies and theory 38, 41, 176, 183, 260,
   411–412

Genette, G. 28, 38, 300

INDEX OF REFERENCES